CROSSWORD
SOLVER

CROSSWORD SOLVER

EDITED BY ANNE STIBBS

BLOOMSBURY

www.bloomsbury.com/reference

First published 1988
Second edition published 1995
Third edition published 1997
Fourth edition published 2000
Reprinted 2004

Copyright © 1988, 1995, 1997, 2000
by Bloomsbury Publishing Plc

Bloomsbury Publishing Plc, 38 Soho Square, London W1D 3HB

A CIP record for this title is available from the British Library

ISBN 0 7475 7617 3

10 9 8 7 6 5 4 3 2 1

All papers used by Bloomsbury Publishing are natural, recyclable products made from wood grown in well-managed forests. The manufacturing processes conform to the environmental regulations of the country of origin.

Compiled and typeset by Market House Books Ltd, Aylesbury
Printed in Great Britain by Clays Ltd, St Ives plc

INTRODUCTION

This book consists of a set of lists of words specifically designed to help crossword-puzzle solvers. We have included over 100,000 English words organized into words with two letters, words with three letters, four letters, etc., up to fifteen letters. Within each section, the words are arranged alphabetically.

The words chosen include proper nouns, names of people and places, as well as common two- and three-word phrases. We have also given, in many cases, plurals of nouns, comparatives and superlatives of adjectives, and inflections of verbs. In general, '–ize' endings have been used for verbs. It should be noted that '–ise' endings are also possible for these.

We hope that the book will prove useful to all who enjoy doing crossword puzzles – and, in particular, to those who enjoy completing them.

AS
May, 2000

A	**D**	HI	**M**	PE	**U**
AA	DA	H'M	MA	PH	UK
AB	DJ	HO	ME	PI	UM
AC	DO	HQ	MI	PM	UN
AD			MO	PR	UP
AG	**E**	**I**	MP	PS	US
AH	EH	ID	MR	PT	UU
AI	ER	IF	MS	PX	
AM	EU	IN	MY		**V**
AN	EX	IQ		**Q**	VC
AS		IT	**N**	QC	VD
AT	**F**		NO	QT	VJ
AW	FA	**J**			VS
	FE	JP	**O**	**R**	
B	FM		OF	RE	**W**
BE		**K**	OH		WC
BO	**G**	KC	ON	**S**	WE
BY	GI	KO	OP	SH	
	GO		OR	SO	**X**
C	GP	**L**	OW		XU
CB	GS	LA	OX	**T**	
CD		LO		TA	**Y**
CO	**H**	LP	**P**	TI	YE
CV	HA	LR	PA	TO	YO
	HE		PC	TV	

A	BAG	CDS	DIG	ERR	GAP
ABC	BAH	CIA	DIM	ESP	GAS
ABH	BAN	CID	DIN	ESQ	GAY
ABO	BAR	CIS	DIP	EST	GCE
ACE	BAT	CJD	DIS	ETC	GDP
ACT	BAY	CND	DIY	EVE	GEC
ADD	BBC	CNS	DJS	EWE	GEE
ADJ	BBQ	COB	DNA	EYE	GEL
ADO	BED	COD	DOC		GEM
ADS	BEE	COG	DOE	**F**	GEN
ADV	BEG	COL	DOG	FAB	GET
AFT	BEN	CON	DOH	FAD	GIG
AGE	BET	COO	DON	FAG	GIN
AGM	BIB	COP	DOR	FAN	GI'S
AGO	BID	COS	DOS	FAR	GNP
AHA	BIG	COT	DOT	FAT	GNU
AID	BIN	COW	DRY	FAX	GOA
AIL	BIO-	COX	D T'S	FAY	GOB
AIM	BIT	COY	DUB	FBI	GOD
AIR	BOA	CPA	DUD	FED	GOO
A LA	BOB	CPS	DUE	FEE	GOP
ALE	BOD	CPU	DUG	FEN	GOT
ALL	BOG	CRC	DUN	FEW	GPS
AMP	BOO	CRY	DUO	FEY	GUM
AND	BOP	CSE	DYE	FEZ	GUN
ANT	BOW	CUB		FIB	GUT
ANY	BOX	CUD	**E**	FIE	GUV
AOC	BOY	CUE	EAR	FIG	GUY
APB	BPI	CUM	EAT	FIN	GYM
APE	BPS	CUP	EBB	FIR	GYP
APP	BRA	CUR	ECG	FIT	
APT	BUB	CUT	ECT	FIX	**H**
ARB	BUD	CVS	EEC	FLU	HAD
ARC	BUG	CWM	EEK	FLY	HAE
ARK	BUM		EEL	FOB	HAG
ARM	BUN	**D**	EFF	FOE	HAH
ART	BUR	DAB	EGG	FOG	HAM
ASH	BUS	DAD	EGO	FOP	HAN
ASK	BUT	DAM	EKG	FOR	HAP
ASP	BUY	DAY	ELF	FOX	HAS
ASS	BYE	DDI	ELK	FRO	HAT
ATE		DDR	ELM	FRY	HAW
ATM	**C**	DDT	ELT	FUG	HAY
AUK	CAB	DEB	EMU	FUN	HE'D
AWE	CAD	DEF	ENC	FUR	HEH
AWL	CAM	DEM	END		HEL
AXE	CAN	DEN	EON	**G**	HEM
AYE	CAP	DEP	EPS	GAB	HEN
B	CAR	DEW	ERA	GAD	HEP
BAA	CAT	DID	ERE	GAG	HER
BAD	CAW	DIE	ERG	GAL	HE'S

HET	IRE	LED	MOW	O'ER	PLY
HEW	IRK	LEE	MPS	OFF	PMS
HEX	ISM	LEG	MRI	OFT	POD
HEY	ITS	LEI	MRS	OHM	POP
HIB	ITV	LEO	MSC	OHO	POT
HIC	IUD	LET	MUD	OIK	POW
HID	IVY	LEV	MUG	OIL	POX
HIE		LIB	MUM	OLD	PPS
HIM	**J**	LID		ONE	PRE-
HIN	JAB	LIE	**N**	OOF	PRO
HIP	JAG	LIG	NAB	OPS	PRY
HIS	JAM	LIP	NAD	OPT	PTA
HIT	JAR	LIT	NAG	ORB	PTO
HOB	JAW	LOB	NAN	ORE	PUB
HOD	JAY	LOG	NAP	OTT	PUD
HOE	JET	LOO	NAV	OUR	PUG
HOG	JEW	LOP	NAY	OUT	PUN
HOM	JIB	LOT	NCO	OVA	PUP
HOO	JIG	LOW	NEC	OWE	PUS
HOP	JIT	LOX	NEE	OWL	PUT
HOT	JOB	LPS	NEG	OWN	PVC
HOW	JOG	LSD	NET		PYX
HOY	JOT	LUG	NEW	**P**	
HQS	JOY	LUV	NFL	PAD	**Q**
HRT	JPS		NHS	PAL	QCS
HSI	JUG	**M**	NIB	PAN	QUA
HUB	JUT	MAC	NIL	PAP	
HUE		MAD	NIP	PAR	**R**
HUG	**K**	MAG	NIT	PAS	RAD
HUH	KEG	MAM	NIX	PAT	RAF
HUM	KEN	MAN	NOB	PAW	RAG
HUN	KEY	MAP	NOD	PAY	RAI
HUT	KID	MAR	NON-	PCS	RAJ
	KIN	MAS	NOR	PEA	RAM
I	KIP	MAT	NOT	PEE	RAN
ICE	KIT	MAW	NOW	PEG	RAP
ICY	KOB	MAY	NRA	PEN	RAT
IDS	KOI	MEN	NSA	PEP	RAW
IFS		MET	NSU	PER	RAY
ILK	**L**	MEW	NTH	PET	REC
ILL	LAB	MIA	NUB	PEW	RED
IMP	LAD	MID	NUN	PHD	REF
INC	LAG	MIS	NUT	PHS	REP
INF	LAN	MIX		PIE	REV
INK	LAP	MOB	**O**	PIG	REX
INN	LAW	MOD	OAF	PIN	RIA
ION	LAX	MOM	OAK	PIP	RIB
IOU	LAY	MOO	OAP	PIS	RID
IPA	LCD	MOP	OAR	PIT	RIG
IQS	LCM	MOS	ODD	PIX	RIM
IRA	LEA	MOT	ODE	PLC	RIP

RNA	SEW	SUM	TOY	VET	WOO
ROB	SEX	SUN	TRY	VEX	WOP
ROC	SHE	SUP	TSK	VGA	WOT
ROD	SHY		TUB	VGC	WOW
ROE	SIC	**T**	TUC	VHF	WPC
ROM	SIN	TAB	TUG	VIA	WRY
ROT	SIP	TAG	TUT	VIE	
ROW	SIR	TAN	TVS	VIM	**Y**
RSE	SIS	TAP	TWO	VIP	YAK
RSI	SIT	TAR		VIZ	YAM
RUB	SIX	TAT	**U**	VLF	YAP
RUE	SKA	TAX	UFO	VOW	YAW
RUG	SKI	TEA	UGH	VTR	YEA
RUM	SKY	TEC	UHF		YEN
RUN	SLY	TEE	UMP	**W**	YES
RUT	SOB	TEN	UNI-	WAD	YET
RYE	SOD	THE	URN	WAG	YEW
	SOH	THY	USE	WAN	YID
S	SOL	TIA		WAR	YIN
SAC	SON	TIC	**V**	WAX	YOB
SAD	SOP	TIE	UTC	WAY	YOU
SAE	SOS	TIN	UTD	WEB	YTS
SAG	SOT	TIP	UVA	WED	
SAP	SOU	TIT	UVB	WEE	**Z**
SAT	SOW	TNT	UVC	WET	ZAP
SAW	SOX	TOD	UZI	WHO	ZED
SAY	SOY	TOE	VAC	WHY	ZEN
SDI	SPA	TOG	VAN	WIG	ZIG
SDP	SPY	TON	VAR	WIN	ZIP
SEA	STD	TOO	VAT	WIT	ZOO
SEC	STY	TOP	VCR	WOE	
SEE	SUB	TOR	VCS	WOG	
SEM	SUE	TOT	VDU	WOK	
SET	SUG	TOW	VEG	WON	

A

A	ALLY	AT IT	BARB	BILE	BORE
ABCS	ALMS	ATOM	BARD	BILK	BORN
ABED	ALOE	ATOP	BARE	BILL	BORT
ABET	ALPS	AUBE	BARI	BIND	BOSH
ABIA	ALSO	AUDE	BARK	BINS	BOSS
ABLE	ALTO	AUKS	BARN	BIRD	BOTH
ABLY	ALUM	AUNT	BARS	BIRL	BOUT
ABOS	AMBO	AURA	BASE	BIRO	BOWL
ABUT	AMEN	AUTO	BASH	BITE	BOWS
ACCT	AMEX	AVER	BASK	BITS	BOYS
AC/DC	AMID	AVID	BASS	BLAB	BOZO
ACER	AMIR	AVON	BAST	BLAG	BRAE
ACES	AMIS	AVOW	BATH	BLAH	BRAG
ACHE	AMOK	AWAY	BATS	BLED	BRAN
ACID	AMOY	AWED	BAUD	BLEW	BRAS
ACME	AMPS	AWLS	BAWD	BLIP	BRAT
ACNE	ANAL	AWOL	BAWL	BLOB	BRAY
ACRE	ANEW	AWRY	BAYS	BLOC	BREW
ACTS	ANKH	AXED	BEAD	BLOT	BRIM
ADAM	ANON	AXES	BEAK	BLOW	BRIT
ADEN	ANSI	AXIS	BEAM	BLUE	BRNO
ADZE	ANTE	AXLE	BEAN	BLUR	BROW
AEON	ANTI-	AYAH	BEAR	BOAR	BROZ
AERO-	ANTS	AYES	BEAT	BOAS	BUBO
AFAR	ANUS		BEAU	BOAT	BUBS
AFRO	APED	**B**	BECK	BOBS	BUCK
AGAL	APES	BAAS	BEDS	BODE	BUDS
AGED	APEX	BABE	BEEF	BODS	BUFF
AGES	APSE	BABU	BEER	BODY	BUGS
AGMS	AQUA	BABY	BEES	BOER	BULB
AGOG	ARAB	BACH	BEET	BOGS	BULK
AGRA	ARAN	BACK	BELL	BOIL	BULL
AGUE	ARCH	BADE	BELT	BOLD	BUMF
AHEM	ARCS	BAEZ	BEND	BOLE	BUMP
AHOY	ARDS	BAGS	BENS	BOLL	BUMS
AIDE	AREA	BAIL	BENT	BOLT	BUNA
AIDS	AREG	BAIT	BERK	BOMA	BUNG
AIMS	ARIA	BAJA	BERN	BOMB	BUNK
AIN'T	ARID	BAKE	BEST	BOND	BUNS
AINU	ARKS	BAKU	BETA	BONE	BUOY
AIRE	ARMS	BALD	BETS	BONN	BUPA
AIRS	ARMY	BALE	BEVY	BONY	BURB
AIRY	ARSE	BALI	BIAS	BOOB	BURK
AJAR	ARTS	BALK	BIBS	BOOK	BURN
AKIN	ARTY	BALL	BIDE	BOOM	BURP
ALAI	ASHY	BALM	BIDS	BOON	BURR
ALAR	ASIA	BAND	BIEL	BOOR	BURS
ALAS	AS IF	BANE	BIER	BOOS	BURY
ALBI	ASIR	BANG	BIFF	BOOT	BUSH
ALIT	ASPS	BANK	BIFU	BOPS	BUSK
ALKY	ASTI	BANS	BIKE	BORA	BUSS

BUST	CELL	COED	CROP	DAUB	DISS
BUSY	CENT	COGS	CROW	DAWN	DIVE
BUTE	CERT	COIF	CRUS	DAYS	DMSO
BUTS	CHAD	COIL	CRUX	DAZE	DOCK
BUTT	CHAP	COIN	CSES	D-DAY	DOCS
BUYS	CHAR	COIR	CUBA	DEAD	DODO
BUZZ	CHAT	COKE	CUBE	DEAF	DOER
BYES	CHEB	COLA	CUBS	DEAL	DOES
BYOB	CHEF	COLD	CUED	DEAN	DOFF
BYRE	CHER	COLS	CUES	DEAR	DOGE
BYTE	CHEW	COLT	CUFF	DEBS	DOGS
	CHIC	COMA	CULL	DEBT	DOHA
C	CHID	COMB	CULM	DECK	DO IT
CABS	CHIN	COME	CULT	DEED	DOLE
CADS	CHIP	COMO	CUNT	DEEM	DOLL
CAEN	CHIT	CONE	CUPS	DEEP	DOLT
CAFE	CHOP	CONK	CURB	DEER	DOME
CAGE	CHOU	CONS	CURD	DEFT	DONE
CAKE	CHOW	CONY	CURE	DEFY	DONS
CALF	CHUG	COOK	CURL	DELE	DON'T
CALI	CHUM	COOL	CURS	DELL	DOOM
CALK	CHUR	COON	CURT	DEMO	DOOR
CALL	C-IN-C	COOP	CUSP	DENS	DOPE
CALM	CINE-	COOS	CUSS	DENT	DORY
CALX	CITE	COOT	CUTE	DENY	DOSE
CAME	CITY	COPE	CUTS	DERV	DOSH
CAMP	CLAD	COPS	CYAN	DESK	DOSS
CAMS	CLAM	COPY	CYME	DEWY	DOTE
CANE	CLAN	CORD	CYST	DFEE	DOTS
CANS	CLAP	CORE	CZAR	DHAK	DOUR
CANT	CLAW	CORK		DHOW	DOVE
CAPE	CLAY	CORM	**D**	DIAL	DOWN
CAPO	CLEF	CORN	DABS	DICE	DOZE
CAPS	CLEW	COSH	DADO	DICK	DOZY
CARD	CLIP	COST	DADS	DIED	DRAB
CARE	CLOD	COSY	DAFT	DIET	DRAG
CARP	CLOG	COTS	DAGO	DIGS	DRAM
CARS	CLOP	COUP	DAIS	DIKE	DRAT
CART	CLOT	COVE	DALE	DILL	DRAW
CASE	CLOY	COWL	DAME	DIME	DRAY
CASH	CLUB	COWS	DAMN	DINE	DREW
CASK	CLUE	COXA	DAMP	DINK	DRIP
CAST	CLUJ	COZY	DAMS	DINS	DROP
CATS	COAL	CRAB	DANK	DINT	DRUB
CAUL	COAT	CRAG	DARE	DIPS	DRUG
CAVE	COAX	CRAM	DARK	DIRE	DRUM
CAVY	COBS	CRAP	DARN	DIRK	DUAL
CAWS	COCK	CRED	DART	DIRT	DUCK
CEDE	CODA	CREW	DASH	DISC	DUCT
CEDI	CODE	CRIB	DATA	DISH	DUDE
CELA	CODS	CROC	DATE	DISK	DUDS

DUEL	EGER	FAFF	FIRS	FOUL	GATE
DUES	EGGS	FAGS	FISH	FOUR	GAVE
DUET	EGOS	FAIL	FIST	FOWL	GAWD
DUFF	EIRE	FAIN	FITS	FOXY	GAWK
DUGS	ELAN	FAIR	FIVE	FRAP	GAWP
DUKE	ELBA	FAKE	FIZZ	FRAU	GAYA
DULL	ELBE	FALL	FLAB	FRAY	GAYS
DULY	ELIA	FAME	FLAG	FREE	GAZA
DUMA	ELKS	FANG	FLAK	FRET	GAZE
DUMB	ELMS	FANS	FLAN	FRIT	GCES
DUMP	ELSE	FARE	FLAP	FROE	GCSE
DUNE	EMIR	FARM	FLAT	FROG	G'DAY
DUNG	EMIT	FART	FLAW	FROM	GEAR
DUNK	EMUS	FAST	FLAX	FUCK	GEEK
DUNS	ENDS	FATE	FLAY	FUEL	GELD
DUOS	ENVY	FATS	FLEA	FUJI	GELS
DUPE	EONS	FAUN	FLED	FULL	GEMS
DUSK	EPEE	FAUX	FLEE	FUME	GENE
DUST	EPIC	FAWN	FLEW	FUMY	GENK
DUTY	ERAS	FAZE	FLEX	FUND	GENT
DWEM	ERGO	FEAR	FLIP	FUNK	GENU
DYAD	ERGS	FEAT	FLIT	FURL	GERA
DYED	ERIC	FEED	FLOE	FURS	GERM
DYER	ERNE	FEEL	FLOG	FURY	GERS
DYES	ERSE	FEES	FLOP	FUSE	GHAT
DYKE	ESPY	FEET	FLOW	FUSS	GHEE
DYNE	ET AL	FELL	FLUE	FUZZ	GIBE
	ETCH	FELT	FLUX		GIFT
E	ETON	FEND	FOAL	**G**	GIFU
EACH	EURE	FENS	FOAM	GAFF	GIGS
EARL	EURO	FERN	FOBS	GAGA	GILD
EARN	EVEN	FESS	FOCI	GAGE	GILL
EARS	EVER	FEST	FOES	GAGS	GILT
EASE	EVES	FETE	FOGS	GAIA	GIMP
EAST	EVIL	FEUD	FOGY	GAIN	GINS
EASY	EWER	FIAT	FOHN	GAIT	GIRD
EATS	EWES	FIBS	FOIL	GALA	GIRL
EBBS	EXAM	FIFE	FOLD	GALE	GIRO
ECGS	EXES	FIGS	FOLK	GALL	GIRT
ECHO	EXIT	FIJI	FOND	GALS	GISH
ECRU	EYED	FILE	FONT	GAME	GIST
EDAM	EYES	FILL	FOOD	GAMY	GIVE
EDDO	EYOT	FILM	FOOL	GANG	GIZA
EDDY	EYRE	FILO	FOOT	GAOL	GLAD
EDEN		FILS	FOPS	GAPE	GLEE
EDGE	**F**	FIND	FORA	GAPS	GLEN
EDGY	FACE	FINE	FORD	GARB	GLIB
EDIT	FACT	FINN	FORE	GARD	GLOW
EDTA	FADE	FINS	FORK	GARY	GLUE
EELS	FADO	FIRE	FORM	GASH	GLUM
EFIK	FADS	FIRM	FORT	GASP	GLUT

GNAT	GURU	HAST	HIND	HOVE	IDOL
GNAW	GUSH	HATE	HINT	HOWE	IFFY
GNUS	GUST	HATH	HIPS	HOWF	IGBO
GOAD	GUTS	HATS	HIRE	HOWL	IKBS
GOAL	GUVS	HAUL	HISS	HOYA	IKON
GOAT	GUYS	HAVE	HIST	HUBS	ILEX
GOBI	GYBE	HAWK	HITS	HUED	ILLS
GOBO	GYMS	HAZE	HIVE	HUES	IMAM
GOBS		HAZY	HOAD	HUFF	IMAX
GODS	**H**	HEAD	HOAR	HUGE	IMPI
GOER		HEAL	HOAX	HUGO	IMPS
GOES	HAAF	HEAP	HOBO	HUGS	INCA
GO-GO	HAAR	HEAR	HOBS	HULA	INCH
GOLD	HABU	HEAT	HOCK	HULK	INDO-
GOLF	HACK	HEBE	HODS	HULL	INDY
GONE	HADE	HECK	HOED	HUME	INFO
GONG	HADJ	HEED	HOER	HUMP	INKS
GOOD	HAEM	HEEL	HOES	HUMS	INKY
GOOF	HAFT	HEFT	HOGG	HUNG	INNS
GOON	HAGS	HEIR	HOGS	HUNK	INTI
GOOP	HA-HA	HELA	HOKE	HUNT	INTO
GORE	HAIG	HELD	HOKI	HUON	IONS
GORY	HAIK	HELL	HOLD	HURD	IOTA
GOSH	HAIL	HELM	HOLE	HURL	IOUS
GOUT	HAIR	HELP	HOLM	HURT	IOWA
GOWN	HAJJ	HEMP	HOLP	HUSH	IPOH
GRAB	HAKE	HEMS	HOLS	HUSK	IRAN
GRAF	HALE	HENS	HOLT	HUSS	IRAQ
GRAM	HALF	HENT	HOLY	HUTS	IRIS
GRAN	HALL	HERA	HOMA	HUTU	IRON
GRAY	HALM	HERB	HOME	HWAN	ISLE
GRAZ	HALO	HERD	HOMO	HWYL	ISMS
GREW	HALT	HERE	HOMS	HYDE	ITCH
GREY	HAMA	HERL	HOMY	HYMN	ITEM
GRID	HAME	HERM	HONE	HYPE	IUDS
GRIM	HAMM	HERN	HONG	HYPO	
GRIN	HAMS	HERO	HONK		**J**
GRIP	HAND	HERR	HOOD	**I**	JABS
GRIT	HANG	HERS	HOOF	IAMB	JACK
GROG	HANK	HESS	HOOK	IBEX	JADE
GROW	HARD	HEST	HOOP	IBID	JAGS
GRUB	HARE	HETH	HOOT	IBIS	JAIL
GUAM	HARK	HEWN	HOPE	ICBM	JAMB
GUFF	HARL	HICK	HOPI	ICED	JAMS
GULF	HARM	HIDE	HOPS	ICES	JAPE
GULL	HARP	HIED	HORA	ICON	JARS
GULP	HART	HI-FI	HORN	IDEA	JAWS
GUMS	HARZ	HIGH	HOSE	IDEM	JAYS
GUNN	HASA	HIKE	HOST	IDES	JAZZ
GUNS	HASH	HILL	HOTS	IDLE	JEEP
GURN	HASK	HILT	HOUR	IDLY	JEER
	HASP				

JELL	KEYS	LAID	LEWD	LOGO	MACH
JENA	KHAN	LAIN	LIAR	LOGS	MACS
JERK	KICK	LAIR	LIAS	LOGY	MADE
JEST	KIDS	LAKE	LICE	LOIN	MAFF
JETS	KIEL	LAKH	LICK	LOLL	MAGI
JEWS	KIEV	LAMA	LIDO	LONE	MAGS
JIBE	KIKE	LAMB	LIDS	LONG	MAID
JIBS	KILL	LAME	LIED	LOOK	MAIL
JIGS	KILN	LAMP	LIEF	LOOM	MAIM
JILT	KILO	LAND	LIEN	LOON	MAIN
JINN	KILT	LANE	LIES	LOOP	MAKE
JINX	KIND	LANK	LIEU	LOOS	MALE
JIVE	KINE	LAOS	LIFE	LOOT	MALI
JOBS	KING	LAPP	LIFT	LOPE	MALL
JOCK	KINK	LAPS	LIKE	LORD	MALM
JOGS	KIPS	LARD	LILO	LORE	MALT
JOHN	KIRK	LARK	LILT	LORN	MAMA
JOIN	KISS	LASH	LILY	LOSE	MAMS
JOKE	KITE	LASS	LIMA	LOSS	MANE
JOLT	KITS	LAST	LIMB	LOST	MANX
JOSH	KIVU	LATE	LIME	LOTH	MANY
JOVE	KIWI	LATH	LIMN	LOTS	MAPS
JOWL	KNAP	LAUD	LIMP	LOUD	MARE
JOYS	KNEE	LAUE	LIMY	LOUR	MARK
JUDO	KNEW	LAVA	LINE	LOUT	MARL
JUGS	KNIT	LAWN	LING	LOVE	MARS
JUJU	KNOB	LAWS	LINK	LOWS	MARY
JULY	KNOT	LAYS	LINT	LUCK	MASH
JUMP	KNOW	LAZE	LINZ	LUDO	MASK
JUNE	KOBE	LAZY	LION	LUFF	MASS
JUNK	KOFU	LEAD	LIPS	LUGO	MAST
JURA	KOGI	LEAF	LIRA	LUGS	MATE
JURY	KOHA	LEAK	LIRE	LULL	MATS
JUST	KOHL	LEAN	LISP	LUMP	MATT
JUTE	KOOK	LEAP	LIST	LUND	MAUI
	KOTA	LEAS	LITE	LUNG	MAUL
K	KRIS	LEEK	LIVE	LUNY	MAWS
KALE	KUDU	LEER	LOAD	LURE	MAYA
KANO	KURE	LEES	LOAF	LURK	MAYS
KCAL	KURU	LEFT	LOAM	LUSH	MAZE
KEEL	KYAT	LEGS	LOAN	LUST	MAZY
KEEN		LEIS	LOBE	LUTE	MEAD
KEEP	**L**	LENA	LOBS	LUVS	MEAL
KEGS		LEND	LOCH	LVIV	MEAN
KELP	LABS	LENS	LOCI	LYNX	MEAT
KENS	LACE	LENT	LOCK	LYON	MEEK
KENT	LACK	LEOS	LOCO	LYRE	MEET
KEOS	LACY	LESS	LODE		MEGA-
KEPT	LADE	LEST	LODI	**M**	MELK
KERB	LADS	LETS	LODZ	MA'AM	MELT
KERN	LADY	LEVY	LOFT	MACE	MEMO

MEND	MOOD	NATO	NUBS	ONYX	PALP
MENU	MOON	NAVE	NUDE	OOPS	PALS
MEOW	MOOR	NAVY	NUKE	OOZE	PANE
MERE	MOOS	NAYS	NULL	OOZY	PANG
MESH	MOOT	NAZI	NUMB	OPAL	PANS
MESS	MOPE	NCOS	NUNN	OPEC	PANT
METE	MOPS	NEAR	NUNS	OPEN	PAPA
METZ	MORE	NEAT	NUPE	OPUS	PAPS
MEWS	MORN	NECK	NURD	ORAL	PARA-
MICA	MOSS	NEED	NUTS	ORAN	PARE
MICE	MOST	NEEM	NUUK	ORBS	PARK
MICK	MOTE	NE'ER		OREL	PARS
MIDI	MOTH	NEJD	**O**	ORES	PART
MIEN	MOTS	NEON	OAFS	ORGY	PASS
MIKE	MOVE	NERD	OAHU	ORLY	PAST
MILD	MOWN	NEST	OAKS	ORNE	PATE
MILE	MOYA	NETS	OAPS	ORSK	PATH
MILK	MRIA	NETT	OARS	ORYX	PATS
MILL	MUCH	NEWS	OATH	OSLO	PAVE
MILT	MUCK	NEWT	OATS	OSUN	PAWL
MIME	MUFF	NEXT	OBAN	OUCH	PAWN
MIND	MUGS	NIBS	OBEY	OUDH	PAWS
MINE	MULE	NICE	OBOE	OULU	PAYE
MINI	MULL	NICK	ODDS	OURS	PEAK
MINK	MUMS	NIFF	ODES	OUST	PEAL
MINT	MUON	NIGH	OGLE	OUZO	PEAR
MINX	MURK	NINE	OGRE	OVAL	PEAS
MIPS	MUSE	NIPS	OGUN	OVEN	PEAT
MIRE	MUSH	NISI	OHIO	OVER	PECK
MIRY	MUSK	NITS	OHMS	OVUM	PEED
MISO	MUSS	NIUE	OH MY	OWED	PEEK
MISS	MUST	NOBS	OH NO	OWEN	PEEL
MIST	MUTE	NODE	OILS	OWLS	PEEP
MITE	MUTI	NODS	OILY	OXEN	PEER
MITT	MUTT	NOEL	OINK	OYEZ	PEGS
MOAN	MYNA	NOES	OISE		PEGU
MOAT	MYTH	NO GO	OITA	**P**	PELT
MOBS		NONE	OKAY	PACE	PENN
MOCK	**N**	NON-U	OKRA	PACK	PENS
MODE	NAFF	NOOK	OKTA	PACT	PERK
MODS	NAGS	NOON	OMAN	PACY	PERL
MOJO	NAHA	NOPE	OMEN	PADS	PERM
MOKE	NAIL	NORD	OMIT	PAGE	PERT
MOLD	NAME	NORM	OMNI-	PAID	PERU
MOLE	NANA	NOSE	OMSK	PAIL	PESO
MOLL	NAPE	NOSH	ONCE	PAIN	PEST
MOLT	NAPS	NOSY	ONDO	PAIR	PETS
MOMS	NARA	NOTE	ONES	PAKI	PEWS
MONK	NARC	NOUN	ONLY	PALE	PHEW
MONO	NARK	NOUS	ONTO	PALL	PHON
MONS	NASA	NOVA	ONUS	PALM	PHOT

PHUT	PONY	PUNK	RATE	RIPE	RULE
PICA	POOF	PUNS	RATS	RIPS	RUMP
PICK	POOH	PUNT	RAVE	RISE	RUMS
PIED	POOL	PUNY	RAYS	RISK	RUNE
PIER	POOP	PUPA	RAZE	RITE	RUNG
PIES	POOR	PUPS	READ	RIVE	RUNS
PIGS	POPE	PURE	REAL	ROAD	RUNT
PIKE	POPS	PURI	REAM	ROAM	RUSE
PILE	PORE	PURL	REAP	ROAN	RUSH
PILL	PORI	PURR	REAR	ROAR	RUSK
PIMP	PORK	PUSH	RECK	ROBE	RUST
PINE	PORN	PUSS	REDD	ROCK	RUTS
PING	PORT	PUTT	REDO	ROCS	RYES
PINK	POSE	PUTZ	REDS	RODE	
PINS	POSH	PYRE	REED	RODS	**S**
PINT	POST		REEF	ROEG	SABA
PINY	POSY	**Q**	REEK	ROES	SACK
PION	POTS	QUAD	REEL	ROLE	SACS
PIPE	POUF	QUAY	REFS	ROLL	SAFE
PIPS	POUR	QUID	REGO	ROME	SAFI
PISA	POUT	QUIN	REIN	ROMO	SAGA
PISH	POWS	QUIP	RELY	ROMP	SAGE
PISS	PRAM	QUIT	REND	ROMS	SAGO
PITH	PRAT	QUIZ	RENO	ROOD	SAGS
PITS	PRAY	QUOD	RENT	ROOF	SAID
PITY	PREP		REPO	ROOK	SAIL
PLAN	PREY	**R**	REPS	ROOM	SAKE
PLAY	PRIG	RACE	REST	ROOT	SALE
PLEA	PRIM	RACK	REUS	ROPE	SALK
PLEB	PROB	RACY	REVS	ROPY	SALT
PLED	PROD	RAFT	RHEA	RORT	SAME
PLOD	PROF	RAGA	RIAL	ROSE	SAMP
PLOP	PROG	RAGE	RIBS	ROSY	SAN'A
PLOT	PROM	RAGS	RICE	ROTA	SAND
PLOW	PROP	RAID	RICH	ROTE	SANE
PLOY	PROS	RAIL	RICK	ROTH	SANG
PLUG	PROW	RAIN	RIDE	ROTS	SANK
PLUM	PRUT	RAKE	RIFE	ROUE	SAPS
PLUS	PSST	RAMP	RIFF	ROUT	SARD
PODS	PUBS	RAMS	RIFT	ROUX	SARI
POEM	PUCE	RAND	RIGA	ROVE	SARK
POET	PUCK	RANG	RIGS	ROWS	SASH
POKE	PUDS	RANI	RILE	RUBS	SASS
POKY	PUFF	RANK	RILL	RUBY	SATE
POLE	PUGS	RANT	RIME	RUCK	SAVE
POLL	PUKE	RAPE	RIMS	RUDE	SAWN
POLO	PULA	RAPS	RIMY	RUED	SAWS
POLY	PULL	RAPT	RIND	RUFF	SAYS
POMP	PULP	RARE	RING	RUGS	SCAB
POND	PUMA	RASH	RINK	RUHR	SCAG
PONG	PUMP	RASP	RIOT	RUIN	SCAM

SCAN	SHOP	SLOB	SOUP	SUMP	TART
SCAR	SHOT	SLOE	SOUR	SUMS	TASH
SCAT	SHOW	SLOG	SOWN	SUMY	TASK
SCOT	SHUN	SLOP	SOWS	SUNG	TA-TA
SCUD	SHUT	SLOT	SPAM	SUNK	TATS
SCUM	SIAN	SLOW	SPAN	SUNS	TAUT
SEAL	SICK	SLUB	SPAR	SUPS	TAXI
SEAM	SIDE	SLUE	SPAS	SURD	TEAK
SEAR	SIFT	SLUG	SPAT	SURE	TEAL
SEAS	SIGH	SLUM	SPAY	SURF	TEAM
SEAT	SIGN	SLUR	SPEC	SUSS	TEAR
SECS	SIKH	SLUT	SPED	SUVA	TEAS
SECT	SILK	SMOG	SPEW	SWAB	TEAT
SEED	SILL	SMUG	SPIC	SWAG	TEED
SEEK	SILO	SMUT	SPIK	SWAM	TEEM
SEEM	SILT	SNAG	SPIN	SWAN	TEES
SEEN	SIND	SNAP	SPIT	SWAP	TELE-
SEEP	SINE	SNIP	SPIV	SWAT	TELL
SEER	SING	SNOB	SPOD	SWAY	TEMA
SEES	SINH	SNOG	SPOT	SWIG	TEMP
SELF	SINK	SNOT	SPRY	SWIM	TEND
SELL	SINO-	SNOW	SPUD	SWOP	TENS
SEME	SINS	SNUB	SPUN	SWOT	TENT
SEMI	SION	SNUG	SPUR	SWUM	TERM
SEND	SIPS	SOAK	STAB	SYNC	TERN
SENT	SIRE	SOAP	STAG		TEST
SERA	SIRS	SOAR	STAR	**T**	TEXT
SERE	SITE	SOBS	STAY	TABS	THAN
SERF	SIZE	SOCA	STEM	TACH	THAT
SETA	SKEW	SOCK	STEP	TACK	THAW
SETI	SKID	SODA	STET	TACO	THEE
SETS	SKIM	SODS	STEW	TACT	THEM
SEWN	SKIN	SOFA	STIR	TAGS	THEN
SEXY	SKIP	SOFT	STOL	TAIL	THEO-
SFAX	SKIS	SOIL	STOP	TAKE	THEY
SGML	SKIT	SOLD	STOW	TALC	THIN
SHAD	SKUA	SOLE	STUB	TALE	THIS
SHAG	SKYE	SOLO	STUD	TALK	THOU
SHAH	SLAB	SOMA	STUM	TALL	THRU
SHAM	SLAG	SOME	STUN	TAME	THUD
SHAT	SLAM	SONG	STYE	TAMP	THUG
SHED	SLAP	SONS	SUBS	TANG	THUN
SHEW	SLAT	SOON	SUCH	TANH	THUS
SHIM	SLAV	SOOT	SUCK	TANK	TICK
SHIN	SLAY	SOPS	SUDS	TANS	TICS
SHIP	SLED	SORE	SUED	TAPE	TIDE
SHIT	SLEW	SORT	SUER	TAPS	TIDY
SHOA	SLID	SO SO	SUET	TARE	TIED
SHOD	SLIM	SO-SO	SUEZ	TARN	TIER
SHOE	SLIP	SOTS	SUIT	TARO	TIES
SHOO	SLIT	SOUL	SULK	TARS	TIFF

TILE	TOWS	UH OH	VILE	WEED	WISH
TILL	TOYS	ULNA	VINE	WEEK	WISP
TILT	TRAD	UNDO	VINO	WEEP	WITH
TIME	TRAM	UNIT	VIOL	WEFT	WITS
TINE	TRAP	UNIX	VIPS	WEIR	WOAD
TING	TRAY	UNTO	VISA	WELD	WOES
TINS	TREE	UPON	VISE	WELL	WOGS
TINT	TREK	UP TO	VOID	WELS	WOKE
TINY	TRIM	UPVC	VOLE	WELT	WOKS
TIPS	TRIO	URDU	VOLT	WEND	WOLD
TIRE	TRIP	URFA	VOTE	WENT	WOLF
TIRO	TROD	URGE	VOWS	WEPT	WOMB
TITI	TROT	URIC	VTOL	WEST	WONT
TITS	TRST	URNS		WETA	WOOD
TOAD	TRUE	USED	**W**	WETS	WOOF
TO BE	TRUG	USER	WADE	WHAM	WOOL
TO DO	TSAR	USES	WADI	WHAP	WOPS
TO-DO	TUBA	UTAH	WADS	WHAT	WORD
TODS	TUBE	UVEA	WAFT	WHEN	WORE
TOED	TUBS		WAGE	WHET	WORK
TOES	TUCK	**V**	WAGS	WHEW	WORM
TOFF	TUFT	VACS	WAIF	WHEY	WORN
TOGA	TUGS	VAIN	WAIL	WHIG	WOVE
TOGO	TULA	VALE	WAIT	WHIM	WPCS
TOGS	TUNA	VAMP	WAKE	WHIP	WRAP
TOIL	TUNE	VANE	WALK	WHIR	WREN
TOLD	TURD	VANS	WALL	WHIT	WRIT
TOLL	TURF	VARY	WAND	WHIZ	WROT
TOMB	TURN	VASE	WANE	WHOA	WUHU
TOME	TUSH	VAST	WANK	WHOM	WUSS
TONE	TUSK	VATS	WANT	WHOP	
TONS	TUTU	VAUD	WARD	WHYS	**X**
TOOK	TVEI	VDUS	WARM	WICK	XMAS
TOOL	TVER	VEAL	WARN	WIDE	X-RAY
TOOT	TWAT	VEEP	WARP	WIFE	
TOPS	TWEE	VEER	WARS	WIGS	**Y**
TORE	TWIG	VEIL	WART	WILD	YAKS
TORN	TWIN	VEIN	WARY	WILL	YAMS
TORS	TWIT	VELD	WASH	WILT	YANG
TORT	TWOS	VEND	WASP	WILY	YANK
TORY	TYPE	VENT	WATT	WIMP	YAPS
TOSA	TYRE	VERB	WAUL	WIND	YARD
TOSH	TYRO	VERY	WAVE	WINE	YARN
TOSS	TZAR	VEST	WAVY	WING	YAWL
TOTE		VETO	WAXY	WINK	YAWN
TOTO	**U**	VETS	WAYS	WINS	YAWS
TOTS	UCAS	VIAL	WEAK	WINY	YAZD
TOUL	UCCA	VICE	WEAL	WIPE	YEAH
TOUR	UELE	VIED	WEAN	WIRE	YEAR
TOUT	UFOS	VIES	WEAR	WIRY	YEAS
TOWN	UGLY	VIEW	WEBS	WISE	YELL

13

YELP	YOBS	YOUR	**Z**	ZEST	ZIZZ
YENS	YOGA	YOWL	ZANY	ZIBO	ZOND
YETI	YOGI	YOYO	ZEAL	ZINC	ZONE
YEWS	YOKE	YUAN	ZEBU	ZINE	ZOOM
YIDS	YOLK	YUCK	ZEDS	ZION	ZOOS
YIPS	YORE	YULE	ZEIN	ZIPS	ZOUK
YLEM	YORK		ZERO	ZITS	ZULU

A

A	ADIEU	AILED	ALONG	ANNEX	ARIAN
AALII	ADIOS	AIMED	ALOOF	ANNOY	ARIAS
AARAU	AD LIB	AIOLI	ALOUD	ANNUL	ARICA
ABACA	AD-LIB	AIRED	ALPHA	ANODE	ARIEL
ABACK	ADMAN	AISLE	ALTAI	ANOLE	ARIEN
ABAFT	ADMEN	AISNE	ALTAR	ANOVA	ARIES
ABASE	ADMIT	AITCH	ALTER	ANTED	ARISE
ABASH	ADMIX	AJMER	ALTOS	ANTES	ARLES
ABATE	ADOBE	AKURE	AMASS	ANTIC	ARLON
ABBEY	ADOPT	ALACK	AMAZE	ANTSY	ARMCO
ABBOT	ADORE	ALAMO	AMBER	ANVIL	ARMED
ABEAM	ADORN	ALARM	AMBIT	ANZAC	AROID
ABELE	AD REM	ALARY	AMBLE	ANZIO	AROMA
ABHOR	ADUKI	ALATE	AMBRY	AORTA	AROSE
ABIDE	ADULT	ALBEE	AMEBA	AOSTA	ARRAN
ABLED	ADUWA	ALBUM	AMEND	APACE	ARRAS
ABODE	ADZES	ALCID	AMENT	APART	ARRAY
ABOHM	AEDES	ALDAN	AMICE	APEAK	ARRIS
A-BOMB	AEGIS	ALDER	AMIDE	APERY	ARROW
ABORT	AEONS	ALDOL	AMINE	APHID	ARSES
ABOUT	AESIR	ALECK	AMINO	APHIS	ARSIS
ABOVE	AFFIX	ALERT	AMIRS	APIAN	ARSON
ABUJA	AFIRE	ALGAE	AMISS	A PIED	ARTEL
ABUSE	AFOOT	ALGAL	AMITY	APING	ARTEX
ABYSS	AFOUL	ALGID	AMMAN	APISH	ARUBA
ACCRA	AFROS	ALGIN	AMNIO	APORT	ARYAN
ACHED	AFTER	ALGOL	AMONG	APPAL	ASCII
ACHES	AGAIN	ALGOR	AMOUR	APPEL	ASCOT
ACIDS	AGAMA	ALIAS	AMPLE	APPLE	ASCUS
ACKEE	AGAPE	ALIBI	AMPLY	APPLY	ASDIC
ACORN	AGATE	ALIEN	AMUCK	APRIL	ASHEN
ACRES	AGAVE	ALIGN	AMUSE	APRON	ASHES
ACRID	AGENT	ALIKE	ANCON	APSES	ASIAN
ACTED	AGGER	A LIST	ANDES	APSIS	ASIDE
ACTIN	AGGRO	ALIVE	ANGEL	APTLY	ASKED
ACTOR	AGILE	ALKYD	ANGER	AQABA	ASKER
ACT UP	AGING	ALKYL	ANGLE	ARABS	ASKEW
ACUTE	AGISM	ALLAH	ANGLO-	ARBER	ASPEN
ADAGE	AGIST	ALLAY	ANGRY	ARBOR	ASPER
ADAMS	AGLET	ALLEN	ANGST	ARDEN	ASPIC
ADANA	AGLOW	ALLEY	ANGUS	AREAL	ASSAI
ADAPT	AGNEW	ALL IN	ANHUI	AREAS	ASSAM
ADDAX	AGONY	ALLOA	ANILE	ARECA	ASSAY
ADDED	AGORA	ALLOT	ANIMA	ARENA	ASSEN
ADDER	AGREE	ALLOW	ANION	ARETE	ASSES
ADDLE	AGUES	ALLOY	ANISE	ARGIL	ASSET
ADD-ON	AHEAD	ALLYL	ANJOU	ARGOL	ASTER
ADD UP	AHERN	ALOFT	ANKLE	ARGON	ASTIR
ADEPT	AHWAZ	ALOHA	ANNAL	ARGOS	ASTRO-
A DEUX	AIDED	ALOIN	ANNAM	ARGOT	ASWAN
AD HOC	AIDES	ALONE	ANNAN	ARGUE	AT ALL

ATHOS	BABES	BARON	BEERS	BIFID	BLINI
ATLAS	BABUL	BARRA	BEERY	BIGHT	BLINK
ATOLL	BABUS	BARRE	BEETS	BIGOT	BLIPS
ATOMS	BACCY	BARRY	BEFIT	BIG UP	BLISS
ATONE	BACKS	BARTH	BEFOG	BIHAR	B LIST
ATONY	BACON	BARYE	BEGAN	BIJOU	BLITZ
ATRIA	BADGE	BASAL	BEGAT	BIKED	BLOAT
ATRIP	BADLY	BASED	BEGET	BIKES	BLOBS
AT SEA	BAGEL	BASEL	BEGIN	BILGE	BLOCH
ATTAR	BAGGY	BASER	BEGOT	BILLS	BLOCK
ATTIC	BAHAI	BASES	BEGUM	BILLY	BLOCS
AUDIO	BAHIA	BASHO	BEGUN	BINAL	BLOIS
AUDIT	BAILS	BASIC	BEIGE	BINGE	BLOKE
AUGER	BAIRN	BASIL	BEING	BINGO	BLOND
AUGHT	BAIZE	BASIN	BEIRA	BIOME	BLOOD
AUGUR	BAKED	BASIS	BELAY	BIOTA	BLOOM
AUNTS	BAKER	BASRA	BELCH	BIPED	BLOTS
AURAL	BALAS	BASSO	BELEM	BIPOD	BLOWN
AURAS	BALDY	BASTE	BELIE	BIRCH	BLOWS
AURIC	BALED	BATCH	BELLE	BIRDS	BLOWY
AUTOS	BALER	BATED	BELLS	BIROS	BLUER
AUXIN	BALES	BATHE	BELLY	BIRTH	BLUES
AVAIL	BALKH	BATHS	BELOW	BISON	BLUFF
AVENS	BALKS	BATIK	BELTS	BITCH	BLUNT
AVERT	BALLS	BATON	BEMBA	BITES	BLURB
AVIAN	BALLY	BATTY	BENCH	BITTY	BLURT
AVOID	BALMS	BATUM	BENDS	BIYSK	BLUSH
AWAIT	BALMY	BAULK	BENIN	BIZZY	BOARD
AWAKE	BALSA	BAWDS	BENTS	BLACK	BOARS
AWARD	BALTI	BAWDY	BENUE	BLADE	BOAST
AWARE	BALTI	BAYED	BENXI	BLAIN	BOATS
AWASH	BANAL	BAYOU	BERET	BLAIR	BOBBY
AWFUL	BANDA	BEACH	BERKS	BLAME	BOCHE
AWOKE	BANDS	BEADS	BERRY	BLANC	BODED
AXIAL	BANDY	BEADY	BERTH	BLAND	BODGE
AXILE	BANES	BEAKS	BERYL	BLANK	BOERS
AXING	BANFF	BEAKY	BESET	BLARE	BOGEY
AXIOM	BANGS	BEAMS	BESOM	BLASE	BOGGY
AYAHS	BANJO	BEANO	BETAS	BLAST	BOGIE
AZIDE	BANKS	BEANS	BETEL	BLAZE	BOGOR
AZINE	BANNS	BEARD	BEVEL	BLEAK	BOGUS
AZOIC	BANTU	BEARS	BEVVY	BLEAR	BOHEA
AZOLE	BARBS	BEAST	BEZEL	BLEAT	BOHOL
AZOTE	BARDS	BEATS	BHAJI	BLEED	BOILS
AZTEC	BARED	BEAUS	BHANG	BLEEP	BOISE
AZURE	BARER	BEAUT	BIBLE	BLEND	BOLES
	BARGE	BEAUX	BICKY	BLESS	BOLLS
	BARIC	BEBOP	BIDED	BLEST	BOLTS
B	BARKS	BECKS	BIDET	BLIDA	BOLUS
BAAED	BARMY	BEECH	BIERS	BLIMP	BOMBE
BABEL	BARNS	BEEFY	BIFFS	BLIND	BOMBS

BONDI	BOZOS	BROWN	BURST	CALVE	CAWED
BONDS	BRACE	BROWS	BUSBY	CALYX	CD-ROM
BONED	BRACT	BRUIN	BUSED	CAMEL	CEARA
BONES	BRAES	BRUIT	BUSES	CAMEO	CEASE
BONGO	BRAGA	BRUME	BUSHY	CAMPO	CEDAR
BONNY	BRAGG	BRUNO	BUSTS	CAMPS	CEDED
BONUS	BRAID	BRUNT	BUSTY	CANAL	CEDER
BONZE	BRAIL	BRUSH	BUTCH	CANDY	CEIBA
BOOBS	BRAIN	BRUTE	BUTTE	CANEA	CELEB
BOOBY	BRAKE	B-SIDE	BUTTS	CANED	CELLA
BOOED	BRAND	BUBAL	BUTTY	CANER	CELLE
BOOKS	BRASH	BUCHU	BUTYL	CANES	CELLO
BOOMS	BRASS	BUCKS	BUXOM	CANNA	CELLS
BOONS	BRATS	BUDDY	BUYER	CANNY	CENSE
BOORS	BRAVE	BUDGE	BWANA	CANOE	CENTO
BOOST	BRAVO	BUFFS	BYATT	CANON	CENTS
BOOTH	BRAWL	BUGGY	BYLAW	CANTO	CERES
BOOTS	BRAWN	BUGLE	BYRES	CANTS	CERIC
BOOTY	BRAXY	BUILD	BYTES	CAPER	CERTS
BOOZE	BRAYS	BUILT	BYTOM	CAPES	CETUS
BOOZY	BRAZE	BULBS	BYWAY	CAPON	CEUTA
BORAX	BREAD	BULGE		CAPRI	CHAFE
BORED	BREAK	BULGY	**C**	CAPUA	CHAFF
BORER	BREAM	BULKS	CABAL	CAPUT	CHAIN
BORES	BREDA	BULKY	CABBY	CARAT	CHAIR
BORIC	BREED	BULLA	CABER	CARDS	CHALK
BORNE	BRENT	BULLS	CABIN	CARED	CHAMP
BORNO	BREST	BULLY	CABLE	CARES	CHANT
BORNU	BREVE	BUMPH	CACAO	CARET	CHAOS
BORON	BRIAR	BUMPS	CACHE	CARGO	CHAPS
BOSKY	BRIBE	BUMPY	CACTI	CARNE	CHARD
BOSOM	BRICK	BUNCH	CADDY	CAROB	CHARM
BOSON	BRIDE	BUNDU	CADET	CAROL	CHARS
BOSSY	BRIEF	BUNGS	CADGE	CARPS	CHART
BOSUN	BRIER	BUNKS	CADIZ	CARRY	CHARY
BOTCH	BRILL	BUNNY	CADRE	CARTS	CHASE
BOUGH	BRINE	BUOYS	CAFES	CARVE	CHASM
BOULE	BRING	BURGH	CAFOD	CASED	CHATS
BOUND	BRINK	BURIN	CAGED	CASES	CHEAP
BOURN	BRINY	BURKE	CAGES	CASKS	CHEAT
BOUSE	BRISK	BURKS	CAGEY	CASTE	CHECK
BOUTS	BRITS	BURLY	CAINE	CASTS	CHEEK
BOVID	BROAD	BURMA	CAIRN	CATCH	CHEEP
BOWED	BROIL	BURNS	CAIRO	CATER	CHEER
BOWEL	BROKE	BURNT	CAJUN	CATTY	CHEFS
BOWER	BROME	BURPS	CAKED	CAULK	CHEJU
BOWIE	BRONX	BURRO	CAKES	CAUSE	CHELA
BOWLS	BROOD	BURRS	CALIX	CAVAN	CHERT
BOXED	BROOK	BURRY	CALLA	CAVED	CHESS
BOXER	BROOM	BURSA	CALLS	CAVES	CHEST
BOXES	BROTH	BURSE	CALOR	CAVIL	CHEWS

CHEWY	CIRCA	CLOUT	COMMA	COVES	CRIES
CHIBA	CISCO	CLOVE	COMPO	COVET	CRIME
CHICK	CISSY	CLOWN	CONCH	COVEY	CRIMP
CHIDE	CITED	CLUBS	CONES	COVIN	CRISP
CHIEF	CITES	CLUCK	CONEY	COWED	CROAK
CHILD	CIVET	CLUES	CONGA	COWER	CROAT
CHILE	CIVIC	CLUMP	CONGE	COWES	CROCK
CHILL	CIVIL	CLUNG	CONGO	COWLS	CROFT
CHIME	CLACK	CLUNK	CONIC	COWRY	CRONE
CHINA	CLADE	CLUNY	CONKS	COXAL	CRONY
CHINE	CLAIM	CLWYD	CONTE	COXED	CROOK
CHING	CLAMP	CLYDE	CONWY	COXES	CROON
CHINK	CLAMS	COACH	COOED	COYLY	CROPS
CHINS	CLANG	COALS	COOKS	COYPU	CRORE
CHIOS	CLANK	COALY	COOLS	COZEN	CROSS
CHIPS	CLANS	COAST	COONS	CRABS	CROUP
CHIRM	CLAPS	COATS	COOPS	CRACK	CROWD
CHIRP	CLARE	COBIA	CO-OPT	CRAFT	CROWN
CHIRR	CLARO	COBRA	COOTS	CRAGS	CROWS
CHITA	CLARY	COCKS	COPAL	CRAKE	CROZE
CHITS	CLASH	COCKY	COPED	CRAMP	CRUDE
CHIVY	CLASP	COCOA	COPES	CRANE	CRUEL
CHOCK	CLASS	CODAS	COPRA	CRANK	CRUET
CHOIR	CLAVE	CODED	COPSE	CRAPE	CRUMB
CHOKE	CLAWS	CODER	CORAL	CRAPS	CRUMP
CHOKO	CLEAN	CODES	CORDS	CRASH	CRURA
CHOKY	CLEAR	CODEX	CORED	CRASS	CRUSE
CHOMP	CLEAT	CODON	CORER	CRATE	CRUSH
CHOPS	CLEEK	COEDS	CORES	CRAVE	CRUST
CHORD	CLEFS	COGON	CORFU	CRAWL	CRYPT
CHORE	CLEFT	COHSE	CORGI	CRAZE	CUBAN
CHOSE	CLERK	COIFS	CORKS	CRAZY	CUBEB
CHOUX	CLEWS	COIGN	CORMS	CREAK	CUBED
CHOWS	CLICK	COILS	CORNS	CREAM	CUBES
CHRON-	CLIFF	COINS	CORNU	CREDO	CUBIC
CHUBB	CLIMB	COKES	CORNY	CREED	CUBIT
CHUCK	CLIME	COLDS	CORPS	CREEK	CUDDY
CHUFA	CLINE	COLEY	CORSE	CREEL	CUFFS
CHUFF	CLING	COLIC	COSTA	CREEP	CUING
CHUMP	CLINK	COLON	COSTS	CREME	CULCH
CHUMS	CLINT	COLTS	COTTA	CREPE	CULET
CHUNK	CLIPS	COLZA	COUCH	CREPT	CULEX
CHURL	CLOAK	COMAL	COUDE	CRESS	CULLS
CHURN	CLOCK	COMAS	COUGH	CREST	CULPA
CHUTE	CLODS	COMBI	COULD	CRETE	CULTS
CHYLE	CLOGS	COMBO	COUNT	CREWE	CUMIN
CHYME	CLONE	COMBS	COUPE	CREWS	CUNTS
CIDER	CLOSE	COMER	COUPS	CRIBS	CUPEL
CIGAR	CLOTH	COMET	COURT	CRICK	CUPID
CIMEX	CLOTS	COMFY	COVEN	CRIED	CUPPA
CINCH	CLOUD	COMIC	COVER	CRIER	CURBS

CURCH	DARED	DELOS	DINKY	DOORS	DRESS
CURDY	DARER	DELTA	DIODE	DOOZY	DRIBS
CURED	DARES	DELVE	DIRER	DOPED	DRIED
CURES	DARKS	DEMOB	DIRGE	DOPES	DRIER
CURET	DARKY	DEMON	DIRKS	DOPEY	DRIFT
CURIA	DARNS	DEMOS	DIRTY	DORIC	DRILL
CURIE	DARTS	DEMUR	DISCO	DOSED	DRILY
CURIO	DATED	DENAR	DISCS	DOSER	DRINK
CURLS	DATER	DENIM	DISHY	DOSES	DRIPS
CURLY	DATES	DENSE	DISKS	DOTED	DRIVE
CURRY	DATUM	DENTS	DITCH	DOTER	DROIT
CURSE	DAUBS	DEPOT	DITTO	DOTTY	DROLL
CURVE	DAUBY	DEPTH	DITTY	DOUAI	DROME
CUSEC	DAUNT	DERBY	DITZY	DOUBS	DRONE
CUSHY	DAVIT	DERMA	DIVAN	DOUBT	DROOL
CUSPS	DAVOS	DERRY	DIVED	DOUGH	DROOP
CUTER	DAWNS	DESKS	DIVER	DOURO	DROPS
CUTIN	DAZED	DETER	DIVES	DOUSE	DROSS
CUT IN	DAZES	DETOX	DIVOT	DOVER	DROVE
CUTIS	DEALS	DEUCE	DIVVY	DOVES	DROWN
CUT UP	DEALT	DEVIL	DIXIE	DOWDY	DRUGS
CUZCO	DEANS	DEVON	DIZZY	DOWEL	DRUID
CYBER	DEARS	DEWAR	DJINN	DOWER	DRUMS
CYCAD	DEARY	DHAKA	DOBBY	DOWNS	DRUNK
CYCLE	DEATH	DHOLE	DOBRO	DOWNY	DRUPE
CYDER	DEBAR	DHOTI	DOCKS	DOWRY	DRUSE
CYMAR	DEBIT	DHOWS	DODGE	DOWSE	DRYAD
CYMRY	DEBTS	DIALS	DODGY	DOYEN	DRYER
CYNIC	DEBUG	DIANA	DODOS	DOZED	DRYLY
CYSTS	DEBUT	DIARY	DOERS	DOZEN	DUALA
CYTON	DECAF	DIAZO	DO FOR	DOZER	DUBAI
CZARS	DECAL	DICED	DOGES	D PHIL	DUCAL
CZECH	DECAY	DICER	DOGGO	DRABS	DUCAT
	DECKS	DICEY	DOGGY	DRAFF	DUCHY
D	DECOR	DICKS	DOGIE	DRAFT	DUCKS
DACCA	DECOY	DICKY	DOGMA	DRAGS	DUCKY
DADDY	DECRY	DICTA	DOILY	DRAIL	DUCTS
DAGGA	DEEDS	DIETS	DOING	DRAIN	DUDES
DAGOS	DEFER	DIGIT	DOLBY	DRAKE	DUELS
DAILY	DEGAS	DIJON	DOLCE	DRAMA	DUETS
DAIRY	DE-ICE	DIKES	DOLED	DRAMS	DUFFS
DAISY	DEIFY	DILDO	DOLLS	DRANK	DUKES
DAKAR	DEIGN	DIMER	DOLLY	DRAPE	DULIA
DALES	DEISM	DIMES	DOLTS	DRAWL	DULLY
DALLY	DEIST	DIMLY	DOMED	DRAWN	DULSE
DAMAN	DEITY	DINAR	DOMES	DRAWS	DUMMY
DAMES	DEKKO	DINED	DONEE	DRAYS	DUMPS
DANCE	DELAY	DINER	DONNA	DREAD	DUMPY
DANDY	DELFT	DINGO	DONOR	DREAM	DUNCE
DANIO	DELHI	DINGY	DOOMS	DREAR	DUNES
DARAF	DELLS	DINKA	DOONA	DREGS	DUNGY

DUNKS	EDUCE	ENDED	ETUDE	FALUN	FERNY
DUPED	EDUCT	ENDER	EVADE	FAMED	FERRY
DUPER	EEJIT	END ON	EVENS	FANCY	FESSE
DUPES	EERIE	ENDOW	EVENT	FANGO	FETAL
DUPLE	EFFED	ENDUE	EVERT	FANGS	FETCH
DURAS	EGEST	ENEMA	EVERY	FANNY	FETED
DUREX	EGGER	ENEMY	EVICT	FANON	FETES
DUROC	EGHAM	ENJOY	EVILS	FANTI	FETID
DURRA	EGRET	ENNIS	EVOKE	FARAD	FETOR
DURUM	EGYPT	ENNUI	EWERS	FARCE	FETUS
DUSKY	EIDER	ENROL	EXACT	FARCI	FEUDS
DUSTY	EIFEL	ENSUE	EXALT	FARCY	FEVER
DUTCH	EIGER	ENTER	EXAMS	FARED	FEZES
DUVET	EIGHT	ENTRY	EXCEL	FARER	FIATS
DWARF	EIKON	ENUGU	EXERT	FARES	FIBRE
DWEEB	EILAT	ENURE	EXILE	FARLE	FICHU
DWELL	EJECT	ENVOY	EXIST	FARMS	FICUS
DWELT	EKMAN	EOSIN	EXITS	FARTS	FIELD
DYERS	ELAND	EPACT	EXPEL	FASTS	FIEND
DYFED	ELATE	EPEES	EXTOL	FATAL	FIERY
DYING	ELBOW	EPICS	EXTRA	FATED	FIFER
DYKES	ELCHE	EPOCH	EXUDE	FATES	FIFES
DYLAN	ELDER	EPODE	EXULT	FATTY	FIFTH
DYULA	ELECT	EPOXY	EYING	FAUGH	FIFTY
	ELEGY	EPROM	EYOTS	FAULT	FIGHT
E	ELEMI	EPSOM	EYRIE	FAUNA	FILAR
EAGER	ELFIN	EQUAL		FAUNS	FILCH
EAGLE	ELGIN	EQUIP	**F**	FAVUS	FILED
EAGRE	ELIDE	ERASE	FABLE	FAWNS	FILER
EARED	ELINT	ERBIL	FACED	FAXED	FILES
EARLS	ELITE	ERECT	FACER	FAZED	FILET
EARLY	ELOPE	ERGOT	FACES	FEARS	FILLY
EAROM	ELUDE	ERNIE	FACET	FEAST	FILMS
EARTH	ELUTE	ERODE	FACIA	FEATS	FILMY
EASED	ELVER	EROSE	FACTS	FEAZE	FILTH
EASEL	ELVES	ERRED	FADDY	FECAL	FILUM
EASER	EMBAY	ERROR	FADED	FECES	FINAL
EASTS	EMBED	ERUCT	FADER	FECIT	FINCH
EATEN	EMBER	ERUPT	FAERY	FED UP	FINDS
EATER	EMBOW	ESHER	FAILS	FEEDS	FINED
EAVES	EMCEE	ESKER	FAINT	FEIGN	FINER
EBBED	EMDEN	ESPOO	FAIRS	FEINT	FINES
E BOAT	EMEND	ESSAY	FAIRY	FELLS	FINGO
EBONY	EMERY	ESSEN	FAITH	FELON	FINIS
ECLAT	EMIRS	ESSEX	FAKED	FEMUR	FINNY
EDEMA	EMMEN	ESTER	FAKER	FENCE	FIORD
EDGED	EMMER	ESTOP	FAKES	FENNY	FIRED
EDGER	EMOTE	ETHER	FAKIR	FERAL	FIRER
EDGES	EMPTY	ETHIC	FALDO	FERIA	FIRES
EDICT	ENACT	ETHOS	FALLS	FERMI	FIRMS
EDIFY	ENATE	ETHYL	FALSE	FERNS	FIRRY

FIRST	FLOPS	FORTE	FUCUS	GALLS	GENUS
FIRTH	FLORA	FORTH	FUDGE	GAMED	GEODE
FISHY	FLORY	FORTS	FUELS	GAMER	GEOID
FISTS	FLOSS	FORTY	FUGAL	GAMES	GERMS
FITCH	FLOUR	FORUM	FUGGY	GAMEY	GESSO
FITLY	FLOUT	FOSSA	FUGUE	GAMIC	GET IT
FIVER	FLOWN	FOSSE	FULLY	GAMIN	GET ON
FIVES	FLUED	FOULS	FUMED	GAMMA	GET TO
FIXED	FLUES	FOUND	FUMER	GAMMY	GETUP
FIXER	FLUFF	FOUNT	FUMES	GAMUT	GET UP
FIXES	FLUID	FOURS	FUNDS	GANDA	GHANA
FIZZY	FLUKE	FOVEA	FUNEN	GANGS	GHATS
FJELD	FLUKY	FOWEY	FUNGI	GANJA	GHENT
FJORD	FLUME	FOWLS	FUNKS	GANSU	GHOST
FLACK	FLUNG	FOXED	FUNKY	GAOLS	GHOUL
FLAGS	FLUNK	FOXES	FUNNY	GAPED	GHYLL
FLAIL	FLUOR	FOYER	FURAN	GAPER	GIANT
FLAIR	FLUSH	FRAIL	FURRY	GAPES	GIBER
FLAKE	FLUTE	FRAME	FURZE	GARDA	GIBES
FLAKY	FLUTY	FRANC	FURZY	GASES	GIDDY
FLAME	FLYBY	FRANK	FUSED	GASPS	GIFTS
FLAMY	FLYER	FRAUD	FUSEE	GASSY	GIGOT
FLANK	FOALS	FREAK	FUSEL	GATED	GIGUE
FLANS	FOAMY	FREED	FUSES	GATES	GIJON
FLAPS	FOCAL	FREER	FUSIL	GAUDY	GILET
FLARE	FOCUS	FREON	FUSSY	GAUGE	GILLS
FLASH	FOGEY	FRESH	FUSTY	GAUNT	GILTS
FLASK	FOGGY	FRETS	FUTON	GAUSS	GIPSY
FLATS	FOILS	FRIAR	FUZZY	GAUZE	GIRLS
FLAWS	FOISM	FRIED	FYLDE	GAUZY	GIRON
FLAWY	FOIST	FRIER		GAVEL	GIRTH
FLEAM	FOLDS	FRIES	**G**	GAVLE	GIVEN
FLEAS	FOLIC	FRILL	GABBA	GAWKY	GIVER
FLECK	FOLIO	FRISE	GABBY	GAYER	GIZMO
FLEER	FOLKS	FRISK	GABES	GAZED	GLACE
FLEET	FOLLY	FRITT	GABLE	GAZER	GLADE
FLESH	FONTS	FRIZZ	GABON	GCSES	GLAIR
FLEWS	FOODS	FROCK	GADID	GEARS	GLAND
FLICK	FOOLS	FROGS	GAFFE	GECKO	GLANS
FLIER	FOOTS	FROND	GAFFS	GEESE	GLARE
FLIES	FOOTY	FRONS	GAGED	GEEST	GLARY
FLING	FORAY	FRONT	GAGES	GELID	GLASS
FLINT	FORCE	FROST	GAILY	GEMMA	GLAZE
FLIPS	FORDS	FROTH	GAINS	GENES	GLEAM
FLIRT	FORGE	FROWN	GAITS	GENET	GLEAN
FLOAT	FORGO	FROZE	GALAH	GENIC	GLEBE
FLOCK	FOR IT	FRUIT	GALAS	GENIE	GLEES
FLOES	FORKS	FRUMP	GALEA	GENII	GLEET
FLONG	FORLI	FRYER	GALES	GENOA	GLENN
FLOOD	FORME	FRY-UP	GALLA	GENRE	GLENS
FLOOR	FORMS	FUCKS	GALLE	GENTS	GLIDE

GLINT	GORKI	GRITS	GYPSY	HANOI	HEAVY
GLITZ	GORSE	GROAN	GYRAL	HANSA	HEBEI
GLOAT	GOTHA	GROAT		HANSE	HEDGE
GLOBE	GOT UP	GROIN	**H**	HANTS	HEDGY
GLOGG	GOUDA	GROOM	HABER	HAPLY	HEELS
GLOOM	GOUGE	GROPE	HABIT	HAPPY	HEFEI
GLOOP	GOURD	GROSS	HACEK	HARAR	HEFTY
GLORY	GOUTY	GROUP	HACKS	HARDS	HEGEL
GLOSS	GOWER	GROUT	HADAL	HARDY	HEIRS
GLOVE	GOWNS	GROVE	HADES	HARED	HEIST
GLUED	GRABS	GROWL	HADJI	HAREM	HEJAZ
GLUER	GRACE	GROWN	HADN'T	HARES	HEKLA
GLUEY	GRADE	GRUBS	HADST	HARPS	HELEN
GLUME	GRAFT	GRUEL	HAFIZ	HARPY	HELIX
GLUTS	GRAIL	GRUFF	HAFTS	HARRY	HELLE
GLYPH	GRAIN	GRUNT	HAGAR	HARSH	HELLO
GNARL	GRAMA	GUACO	HAGEN	HARTS	HELLS
GNASH	GRAMS	GUANO	HAGUE	HASN'T	HELMS
GNATS	GRAND	GUARD	HA-HAS	HASPS	HELOT
GNOME	GRANS	GUAVA	HAIDA	HASTE	HELPS
GOADS	GRANT	GUESS	HAIFA	HASTY	HELVE
GOALS	GRAPE	GUEST	HAIKU	HATCH	HE-MAN
GOATS	GRAPH	GUIDE	HAILS	HATED	HE-MEN
GODLY	GRASP	GUILD	HAIN'T	HATES	HENAN
GOERS	GRASS	GUILE	HAIRS	HAUGH	HENCE
GOFER	GRATE	GUILT	HAIRY	HAULM	HENGE
GOGGA	GRAVE	GUISE	HAITI	HAULS	HENIE
GOIAS	GRAVY	GULAG	HAJJI	HAUNT	HENNA
GOING	GRAYS	GULAR	HAKEA	HAUSA	HENRY
GOLDS	GRAZE	GULCH	HAKES	HAVEN	HENZE
GOLEM	GREAT	GULES	HAKIM	HAVER	HERAT
GOLLY	GREBE	GULFS	HALAL	HAVES	HERBS
GOMEL	GRECO-	GULLS	HALER	HAVOC	HERBY
GONAD	GREED	GULLY	HALIC	HAVRE	HERDS
GONDI	GREEK	GULPS	HALID	HAWES	HERES
GONER	GREEN	GUMBO	HALLE	HAWKS	HERNE
GONGS	GREER	GUMMA	HALLO	HAWSE	HEROD
GONNA	GREET	GUMMY	HALLS	HAYDN	HERON
GOODS	GREYS	GUNGE	HALMA	HAZED	HERTZ
GOODY	GRIDS	GUPPY	HALOS	HAZEL	HESSE
GOOEY	GRIEF	GURUS	HALTS	HAZER	HET UP
GOOFS	GRIFT	GUSSY	HALVE	HAZES	HEWED
GOOFY	GRIKE	GUSTO	HAMAL	H-BOMB	HEWER
GOOLE	GRILL	GUSTS	HAMMY	HEADS	HEXAD
GOONS	GRIME	GUSTY	HAMZA	HEADY	HEXED
GOOSE	GRIMY	GUTSY	HANAU	HEALY	HEXER
GOOSY	GRIND	GUTTA	HANCE	HEAPS	HEXES
GORAL	GRINS	GUYED	HANDS	HEARD	HEXYL
GORED	GRIPE	GUYOT	HANDY	HEART	HICKS
GORES	GRIPS	GWENT	HANKS	HEATH	HIDER
GORGE	GRIST	GWERU	HANKY	HEAVE	HIDES

HI-FIS	HOLLO	HOVEL	IBIZA	INKED	JAMBS
HIGHS	HOLLY	HOVER	ICIER	INK IN	JAMES
HIGHT	HOLST	HOWDY	ICILY	INKLE	JAMMU
HIJAZ	HOMER	HOWLS	ICING	IN-LAW	JAMMY
HIKED	HOMES	HOYLE	ICONS	INLAY	JAPAN
HIKER	HOMEY	HSIAN	ICTIC	INLET	JAPER
HIKES	HONAN	HUBBY	ICTUS	INNER	JAPES
HILAR	HONDO	HUBEI	IDAHO	INPUT	JAUNT
HILLA	HONED	HUBLI	IDEAL	INSET	JAWED
HILLS	HONEY	HUFFY	IDEAS	INTER	JAZZY
HILLY	HONKS	HUFUF	IDIOM	INTRO	JEANS
HILTS	HONKY	HUGER	IDIOT	INUIT	JEEPS
HILUM	HONOR	HULKS	IDLED	INURE	JEERS
HILUS	HOOCH	HULLO	IDLER	INURN	JEHOL
HINDI	HOODS	HULLS	IDOLS	INVAR	JELLO
HINDS	HOOEY	HULME	IDYLL	IODIC	JELLY
HINDU	HOO-HA	HUMAN	IGLOO	IONIC	JEMMY
HINES	HOOKE	HUMIC	IKEJA	IOTAS	JENNY
HINGE	HOOKS	HUMID	IKONS	IRAQI	JEREZ
HINNY	HOOKY	HUMPH	ILEAC	IRATE	JERKS
HI NRG	HOOPS	HUMPS	ILEUM	IRBID	JERKY
HINTS	HOOTS	HUMPY	ILEUS	IRISH	JESTS
HIPPO	HOPED	HUMUS	ILIAC	IRKED	JESUS
HIPPY	HOPEH	HUNAN	ILIAD	IRONS	JETTY
HIRAM	HOPER	HUNCH	ILIUM	IRONY	JEWEL
HIRED	HOPES	HUNKS	IMAGE	ISERE	JEWRY
HIRER	HORAE	HUNTS	IMAGO	ISLAM	JIBED
HIRST	HORAL	HUPEH	IMAMS	ISLAY	JIBES
HITCH	HORDE	HURDS	IMBED	ISLES	JIDDA
HIT ON	HOREB	HURON	IMBUE	ISLET	JIFFY
HIVED	HORME	HURRY	IMIDE	ISSUE	JIHAD
HIVES	HORNS	HURST	IMINE	ISTLE	JILIN
HOARD	HORNY	HURTS	IMPEL	ITALO-	JIMMY
HOARY	HORSA	HUSKS	IMPLY	ITALY	JINAN
HOBBS	HORSE	HUSKY	IN ALL	ITCHY	JINGO
HOBBY	HORST	HUSSY	INANE	ITEMS	JINJA
HOBOS	HORSY	HUTCH	INAPT	IVIED	JINKS
HOCKS	HORUS	HYADS	INCUR	IVIES	JINNI
HOCUS	HOSEA	HYDRA	INCUS	IVORY	JIVED
HOFEI	HOSED	HYDRO	INDEX	IZMIR	JOCKS
HOFUF	HOSES	HYENA	INDIA	IZMIT	JOINS
HOGAN	HOSTA	HYING	INDIC		JOINT
HO-HUM	HOSTS	HYMEN	INDRE	**J**	JOIST
HOICK	HOTAN	HYMNS	INDUS	JABOT	JOKED
HOIST	HOTEL	HYPED	INEPT	JACKS	JOKER
HOKKU	HOTLY	HYPER	INERT	JADED	JOKES
HOKUM	HOUGH	HYPOS	INFER	JADES	JOLLY
HOLDS	HOUND		INFIX	JAFFA	JOLTS
HOLES	HOURI	**I**	IN FOR	JAILS	JONAH
HOLEY	HOURS	IAMBS	INGOT	JALAP	JORUM
HOLLA	HOUSE	I-BEAM	INION	JAMBI	JOULE

JOUST	KEENS	KNOWS	LAMED	LEARN	LIFER
JOVES	KEEPS	KNURL	LAMER	LEASE	LIFTS
JOWLS	KELLS	KOALA	LAMPS	LEASH	LIGER
JOYED	KELLY	KOCHI	LANAI	LEAST	LIGHT
JUDAS	KENNY	KOINE	LANCE	LEAVE	LIKED
JUDGE	KENYA	KONGO	LANDS	LECCE	LIKEN
JUGAL	KERBS	KONYA	LANES	LEDGE	LIKES
JUGUM	KERCH	KOOKS	LANKY	LEDGY	LILAC
JUICE	KERRY	KOOKY	LAOAG	LED ON	LILLE
JUICY	KETCH	KORAN	LAOIS	LEECH	LILOS
JUJUS	KEVEL	KOREA	LA PAZ	LEEDS	LILTS
JULEP	KEYED	KORMA	LAPEL	LEEKS	LIMBO
JUMBO	KHAKI	KRAAL	LAPSE	LEERS	LIMBS
JUMPS	KHANS	KRAFT	LAP UP	LEERY	LIMED
JUMPY	KHMER	KRAIT	LARCH	LEFTY	LIMEN
JUNCO	KIANG	KREMS	LARGE	LEGAL	LIMES
JUNES	KICKS	KRILL	LARGO	LEGER	LIMEY
JUNKS	KIKES	KRONA	LARKS	LEGGY	LIMIT
JUNTA	KILIM	KRONE	LARNE	LEGIT	LINED
JUNTO	KILLS	KROON	LAROS	LEMMA	LINEN
JURAL	KILNS	KUDOS	LARVA	LEMON	LINER
JURAT	KILOS	KUDZU	LASER	LEMUR	LINES
JUREL	KILTS	KUFIC	LASSO	LENDL	LINGO
JUROR	KINDS	KUKRI	LASTS	LENIS	LININ
JURUA	KINGS	KULAK	LATCH	LENTO	LINKS
	KININ	KURIL	LATER	LEPER	LINTY
K	KINKS	KURSK	LATEX	LET ON	LIONS
KABUL	KINKY	KUTCH	LATHE	LETUP	LIPID
KALAT	KIOSK	KWARA	LATHS	LET UP	LIRAS
KANDY	KIRIN	KWELA	LATIN	LEVEE	LISLE
KANGA	KIRKS	KYOTO	LAUGH	LEVEL	LISTS
KANSU	KIROV		LAVAL	LEVER	LITER
KAPOK	KITES	**L**	LAVER	LEVIS	LITHE
KAPUT	KITTY	LABEL	LAWKS	LEWES	LITRE
KARAT	KITWE	LACED	LAWNS	LEWIS	LIT UP
KAREN	KIWIS	LACER	LAWNY	LEXIS	LIVED
KARMA	KLONG	LACES	LAXLY	LEYTE	LIVEN
KAROO	KNACK	LADEN	LAY-BY	LHASA	LIVER
KARST	KNAVE	LADER	LAYER	LIANA	LIVES
KASAI	KNEAD	LADLE	LAY UP	LIARS	LIVID
KASHI	KNEED	LAGAN	LAZED	LIBEL	LLAMA
KAUAI	KNEEL	LAGER	LAZIO	LIBRA	LLANO
KAURI	KNEES	LAGOS	LEACH	LIBYA	LLOYD
KAYAK	KNELL	LAHTI	LEADS	LICIT	LOACH
KAZAN	KNELT	LAIRD	LEADY	LICKS	LOADS
KAZOO	KNIFE	LAIRS	LEAFY	LIDOS	LOAMY
KBYTE	KNOBS	LAITY	LEAKS	LIEGE	LOANS
KEBAB	KNOCK	LAKER	LEAKY	LIE IN	LOATH
KEDAH	KNOLL	LAKES	LEANT	LIE-IN	LOBAR
KEDGE	KNOTS	LAMAS	LEAPS	LIENS	LOBBY
KEELS	KNOWN	LAMBS	LEAPT	LIEUS	LOBED

LOBES	LOWER	MACRO	MARRY	MERGE	MINSK
LOCAL	LOWLY	MADAM	MARSH	MERIT	MINTS
LOCHS	LOYAL	MADLY	MASAI	MERRY	MINUS
LOCKS	LUCCA	MAFIA	MASAN	MERSE	MIRED
LOCUM	LUCID	MAGIC	MASER	MESIC	MIRES
LOCUS	LUCKY	MAGMA	MASKS	MESNE	MIRID
LODEN	LUCRE	MAGUS	MASON	MESON	MIRTH
LODES	LUFFA	MAIDS	MASSA	MESSY	MISER
LODGE	LUGER	MAINE	MASTS	METAL	MISSY
LOESS	LUMEN	MAINS	MATCH	METED	MISTS
LOFTS	LUMME	MAINZ	MATED	METER	MISTY
LOFTY	LUMPS	MAIZE	MATER	METHS	MITES
LOGIC	LUMPY	MAJOR	MATES	METOL	MITIS
LOG IN	LUNAR	MAKER	MATEY	ME-TOO	MITRE
LOG ON	LUNCH	MAKES	MATIN	METRE	MITTS
LOGOS	LUNGE	MALAR	MATSU	METRO	MIXED
LOINS	LUNGS	MALAY	MATTE	MEUSE	MIXER
LOIRE	LUPIN	MALES	MAUVE	MEWED	MIXES
LOLLY	LUPUS	MALLE	MAXIM	MEZZO	MIX-UP
LONER	LURCH	MALLS	MAYAN	MIAMI	MIZAR
LOOKS	LURED	MALMO	MAYBE	MIAOW	MOANS
LOOMS	LURER	MALTA	MAYN'T	MICKS	MOATS
LOONS	LURES	MALTY	MAYOR	MICRO	MOCHA
LOONY	LUREX	MAMAS	MAYST	MIDDY	MOCKS
LOOPS	LURGY	MAMBA	MAZES	MIDGE	MODAL
LOOPY	LURID	MAMBO	MBEKI	MID-ON	MODEL
LOOSE	LUSTS	MAMET	MEADS	MIDST	MODEM
LOPED	LUSTY	MAMEY	MEALS	MIENS	MODES
LOPER	LUTES	MAMMA	MEALY	MIFFY	MOERS
LORAN	LUTON	MAMMY	MEANS	MIGHT	MOGGY
LORDS	LUXOR	MANDE	MEANT	MIKES	MOGUL
LOREN	LUZON	MANED	MEATH	MILAN	MOIRE
LORIS	LYCEE	MANES	MEATY	MILCH	MOIST
LORRY	LYING	MANGE	MECCA	MILER	MOKES
LOSER	LYMPH	MANGO	MEDAL	MILES	MOKPO
LOSSY	LYNCH	MANGY	MEDAN	MILKY	MOLAL
LOTIC	LYRES	MANIA	MEDIA	MILLS	MOLAR
LOTTA	LYRIC	MANIC	MEDIC	MIMED	MOLDS
LOTUS	LYSIN	MANLY	MEDOC	MIMER	MOLDY
LOUGH	LYSIS	MANNA	MEETS	MIMES	MOLES
LOUPE	LYSOL	MANOR	MELEE	MIMIC	MOLLS
LOUSE	LYTIC	MANSE	MELON	MINCE	MOLLY
LOUSY	LYTTA	MANTA	MELOS	MINDS	MOLTO
LOUTH		MANUS	MEMOS	MINED	MOLTS
LOUTS	**M**	MAORI	MENAI	MINER	MOMMA
LOVAT	MACAO	MAPLE	MENDS	MINES	MOMMY
LOVED	MACAW	MARAE	MENUS	MINGY	MONAD
LOVER	MACES	MARCH	MEOWS	MINIM	MONAL
LOVES	MACHO	MARES	MERCA	MINIS	MONCK
LOVEY	MACLE	MARKS	MERCY	MINNA	MONEY
LOWED	MACON	MARNE	MERES	MINOR	MONKS

MONTH	MUCIN	NAILS	NEVER	NOPAL	ODIUM
MONZA	MUCKY	NAIVE	NEVIS	NO-PAR	ODOUR
MOOCH	MUCRO	NAKED	NEWEL	NORMS	OFFAL
MOODS	MUCUS	NALGO	NEWER	NORSE	OFFER
MOODY	MUDDY	NAMED	NEWLY	NORTH	OFGAS
MOOED	MUFFS	NAMES	NEWRY	NOSED	OFTEL
MOOLI	MUFTI	NAMUR	NEWSY	NOSES	OFTEN
MOONS	MUGGY	NANCY	NEWTS	NOTCH	OFWAT
MOONY	MULCH	NANNY	NEXUS	NOTED	OGIVE
MOORS	MULCT	NAPES	NICAD	NOTES	OGLED
MOOSE	MULES	NAPPA	NICAM	NOTUM	OGLER
MOPED	MULEY	NAPPE	NICER	NOUNS	OGRES
MOPER	MULGA	NAPPY	NICHE	NOVAE	OILED
MOP UP	MULLS	NARES	NICKS	NOVAS	OILER
MOP-UP	MULTI-	NARKS	NIDAL	NOVEL	OINKS
MORAL	MUMMY	NARKY	NIDUS	NO WAY	OKAPI
MORAY	MUMPS	NARVA	NIECE	NO-WIN	OKAYS
MOREL	MUMSY	NASAL	NIFFY	NOYON	OLDEN
MORES	MUNCH	NASIK	NIFTY	NUCHA	OLDER
MORNS	MUNGO	NASTY	NIGER	NUDDY	OLEUM
MORON	MURAL	NATAL	NIGHT	NUDES	OLIVE
MORPH	MUREX	NATES	NIHIL	NUDGE	OLMEC
MOSEY	MURKY	NATTY	NIKKO	NUKED	OMAGH
MOSSI	MURRE	NAURU	NIMBI	NUKUS	OMAHA
MOSSO	MUSED	NAVAL	NIMBY	NURSE	OMEGA
MOSSY	MUSER	NAVAR	NIMES	NUTTY	OMENS
MOSUL	MUSES	NAVEL	NINES	NYALA	OMUTA
MOTEL	MUSHY	NAVES	NINNY	NYLON	ON AIR
MOTES	MUSIC	NAVVY	NINON	NYMPH	ON-AIR
MOTET	MUSKY	NAXOS	NINTH		ON CUE
MOTHS	MUSTH	NAZIS	NIPPY	**O**	ONEGA
MOTHY	MUSTY	NDOLA	NISEI		ON ICE
MOTIF	MUTED	'NEATH	NISUS	OAKEN	ONION
MOTOR	MUTES	NECKS	NITRE	OAKUM	ONSET
MOTTO	MUTTS	NEEDS	NITTY	OARED	ON TAP
MOULD	MUZAK	NEEDY	NIVAL	OASES	ON TOW
MOULT	MUZZY	NEGEV	NIXED	OASIS	OOMPH
MOUND	MWERU	NEGRO	NOBLE	OATEN	OOTID
MOUNT	MYALL	NEGUS	NOBLY	OATHS	OOZED
MOURN	MYNAH	NEIGH	NODAL	OBEAH	OPALS
MOUSE	MYOMA	NELLY	NODDY	OBESE	OP ART
MOUSY	MYOPE	NEMAN	NODES	OBOES	OPERA
MOUTH	MYRRH	NEMEA	NODUS	OCCUR	OPINE
MOVED	MYTHS	NEPAL	NOHOW	OCEAN	OPIUM
MOVER		NEPER	NOISE	OCHRE	OPTED
MOVES	**N**	NERDS	NOISY	OCREA	OPTIC
MOVIE		NERVE	NOMAD	OCTAD	ORACH
MOWED	NAAFI	NERVY	NONCE	OCTAL	ORATE
MOWER	NABOB	NESTS	NOOKS	OCTET	ORBIT
MOXIE	NACRE	NEURO-	NO ONE	ODDER	ORDER
MOYLE	NADIR	NEUSS	NOOSE	ODDLY	ORGAN
	NAIAD			ODEUM	

ORIBI	PACES	PARRY	PENNY	PIMPS	PLICA
ORIEL	PACKS	PARSE	PENZA	PINCH	PLIED
ORION	PACTS	PARTS	PEONY	PINED	PLIER
ORIYA	PADDY	PARTY	PERAK	PINES	PLONK
ORLON	PADRE	PASAY	PERCH	PINEY	PLOTS
ORLOP	PADUA	PASHA	PERES	PINGO	PLOWS
ORMER	PAEAN	PASSE	PERIL	PINKO	PLOYS
ORRIS	PAEON	PASTA	PERKS	PINKS	PLUCK
ORURO	PAGAN	PASTE	PERKY	PINNA	PLUGS
OSAKA	PAGED	PASTO	PERRY	PINNY	PLUMB
OSCAR	PAGER	PASTS	PERSE	PINSK	PLUME
OSIER	PAGES	PASTY	PER SE	PINTA	PLUMP
OSMIC	PAILS	PATCH	PERTH	PINTO	PLUMS
OTAGO	PAINS	PATEN	PESKY	PINTS	PLUMY
OTHER	PAINT	PATER	PESOS	PINUP	PLUNK
OTTER	PAIRS	PATES	PESTO	PIOUS	PLUSH
OUGHT	PALEA	PATHS	PESTS	PIPAL	PLUTO
OUIJA	PALED	PATIO	PETAL	PIPED	PLZEN
OUJDA	PALER	PATNA	PETER	PIPER	POACH
OUNCE	PALES	PATSY	PETIT	PIPES	PO BOX
OUTDO	PALLS	PATTY	PETTY	PIPIT	PODGY
OUTER	PALLY	PAUSE	PEWFF	PIQUE	PODIA
OUTGO	PALMA	PAVED	PEWIT	PISTE	POEMS
OUTRE	PALMS	PAVIA	PHASE	PITCH	POESY
OUTRO	PALMY	PAWED	PHIAL	PITHY	POETS
OUZEL	PALSY	PAWKY	PHLOX	PITON	POGGE
OVALS	PANDA	PAWNS	PHONE	PITTA	POILU
OVARY	PANEL	PAYEE	PHONO	PIURA	POINT
OVATE	PANES	PEACE	PHOTO	PIVOT	POISE
OVENS	PANGS	PEACH	PHUTS	PIXEL	POKED
OVERS	PANIC	PEAKS	PHYLA	PIXIE	POKER
OVERT	PANNE	PEAKY	PHYLE	PIZZA	POKES
OVINE	PANSY	PEALS	PIANO	PLACE	POLAR
OVOID	PANTS	PEARL	PIAUI	PLAGE	POLED
OVOLO	PANTY	PEARS	PICKS	PLAID	POLES
OVULE	PAPAL	PEATS	PICKY	PLAIN	POLIO
OWING	PAPAS	PEATY	PICOT	PLAIT	POLJE
OWLET	PAPAW	PECAN	PIECE	PLANE	POLKA
OWNED	PAPER	PECKS	PIERS	PLANK	POLLS
OWNER	PAPPY	PEDAL	PIETA	PLANS	POLYP
OXBOW	PAPUA	PEEPS	PIETY	PLANT	POLYS
OXEYE	PARAS	PEERS	PIGGY	PLASH	POMMY
OXFAM	PARCH	PEEVE	PIGMY	PLASM	PONCE
OXIDE	PARED	PEKOE	PIING	PLATE	PONCY
OXIME	PARER	PELTS	PIKER	PLATY	PONDS
OXLIP	PARIS	PEMBA	PIKES	PLAYS	PONGS
OZONE	PARKA	PENAL	PILAF	PLAZA	PONGY
	PARKS	PENCE	PILED	PLEAD	POOCH
P	PARKY	PENIS	PILES	PLEAS	POOFS
	PARMA	PENNA	PILLS	PLEAT	POOFY
PACED	PAROL	PENNE	PILOT	PLEBS	POOLE
PACER					

27

POOLS	PRILL	PULPS	QUASH	RAGED	READY
POONA	PRIME	PULPY	QUASI-	RAGES	REALM
POOPS	PRIMO	PULSE	QUAYS	RAGGA	REAMS
POPES	PRIMP	PUMAS	QUEEN	RAIDS	REARM
POPPA	PRINK	PUMPS	QUEER	RAILS	REARS
POPPY	PRINT	PUNCH	QUELL	RAINS	REBEL
POPSY	PRION	PUNKA	QUERN	RAINY	REBUS
POP-UP	PRIOR	PUNKS	QUERY	RAISE	REBUT
PORCH	PRISE	PUNTS	QUEST	RAITA	RECAP
PORED	PRISM	PUNTY	QUEUE	RAJAH	RECON
PORES	PRIVY	PUPAE	QUICK	RAKED	RECTO
PORGY	PRIZE	PUPAL	QUIET	RAKER	RECUR
PORKY	PRO-AM	PUPAS	QUIFF	RAKES	REDAN
PORNO	PROBE	PUPIL	QUILL	RALLY	REDIA
PORTS	PRODS	PUPPY	QUILT	RAMIE	REDID
POSED	PROEM	PUREE	QUINE	RAMPS	REEDS
POSER	PROFS	PURER	QUINS	RAMUS	REEDY
POSES	PROLE	PURGE	QUINT	RANCE	REEFS
POSEY	PROMO	PURRS	QUIPS	RANCH	REEKY
POSIT	PROMS	PURSE	QUIRE	R AND B	REELS
POSSE	PRONE	PUSAN	QUIRK	R AND D	REEVE
POSTS	PRONG	PUSHY	QUIRT	RANDY	REFER
POTTO	PROOF	PUSSY	QUITE	RANEE	REFIT
POTTY	PROPS	PUT ON	QUITO	RANGE	REGAL
POUCH	PROSE	PUT-ON	QUITS	RANGY	REICH
POUFS	PROST	PUTTO	QUOIN	RANKS	REIFY
POULT	PROSY	PUTTS	QUOIT	RAPED	REIGN
POUND	PROTO-	PUTTY	QUORN	RAPES	REIKI
POUTS	PROUD	PYGMY	QUOTA	RAPHE	REIMS
POWAN	PROVE	PYLON	QUOTE	RAPID	REINS
POWER	PROWL	PYOID	QUOTH	RARER	REJIG
POWYS	PROWS	PYRAN	QUR'AN	RASHT	REKEY
POXES	PROXY	PYRES		RASPS	RELAX
PRAMS	PRUDE	PYREX	**R**	RATAL	RELAY
PRANK	PRUNE	PYXES	RABAT	RATED	RELIC
PRASE	PSALM	PYXIE	RABBI	RATEL	REMEX
PRATE	PSEUD	PYXIS	RABIC	RATES	REMIT
PRATO	PSKOV		RABID	RATIO	RENAL
PRATS	PSOAS	**Q**	RABIN	RATTY	RENEW
PRAWN	PSYCH	QATAR	RACED	RAVED	RENIN
PREEN	PUBES	QUACK	RACER	RAVEL	RENTE
PREPS	PUBIC	QUADS	RACES	RAVEN	RENTS
PRESA	PUBIS	QUAFF	RACKS	RAVER	REPAY
PRESS	PUCKS	QUAIL	RADAR	RAWER	REPEL
PRICE	PUDGY	QUAKE	RADII	RAWLY	REPLY
PRICK	PUFFS	QUAKY	RADIO	RAYON	RERAN
PRICY	PUFFY	QUALE	RADIX	RAZED	RERUN
PRIDE	PUKED	QUALM	RADOM	RAZER	RESAT
PRIED	PUKKA	QUANT	RADON	RAZOR	RESET
PRIER	PULER	QUARK	RAFTS	REACH	RESIN
PRIGS	PULLS	QUART	RAGAS	REACT	RESIT

RESTS	RIVER	ROWAN	SADLY	SAUCE	SCOUT
RETCH	RIVET	ROWDY	SAFER	SAUCY	SCOWL
RETRO	RIYAL	ROWED	SAFES	SAUNA	SCRAG
RETRO-	ROACH	ROWEL	SAGAS	SAURY	SCRAM
RETRY	ROADS	ROWER	SAGES	SAUTE	SCRAP
REUSE	ROANS	ROYAL	SAGGY	SAVED	SCREE
REVEL	ROARS	RUBLE	SAHIB	SAVER	SCREW
REVET	ROAST	RUCHE	SAIDA	SAVES	SCRIM
REVUE	ROBED	RUCKS	SAIGA	SAVIN	SCRIP
REXES	ROBES	RUDDY	SAILS	SAVOY	SCRUB
RHEAS	ROBIN	RUDER	SAINT	SAVVY	SCRUM
RHEUM	ROBLE	RUFFE	SAKAI	SAWED	SCUBA
RHINE	ROBOT	RUFFS	SAKER	SAWER	SCUFF
RHINO	ROCKS	RUGBY	SAKES	SAXON	SCULL
RHONE	ROCKY	RUING	SALAD	SAYER	SCURF
RHUMB	RODEO	RUINS	SALEM	SAY SO	SCUTE
RHYME	ROGER	RULED	SALEP	SAY-SO	SEALS
RIALS	ROGUE	RULER	SALES	SCABS	SEAMS
RICIN	ROLES	RULES	SALIC	SCADS	SEAMY
RICKS	ROLLS	RUMBA	SALLY	SCALD	SEATS
RIDER	ROMAN	RUMEN	SALOL	SCALE	SEBUM
RIDES	ROMEO	RUMMY	SALON	SCALL	SECCO
RIDGE	ROMER	RUMPS	SALOP	SCALP	SECTS
RIDGY	ROMPS	RUNES	SALPA	SCALY	SEDAN
RIFFS	RONDO	RUNGS	SALTA	SCAMP	SEDGE
RIFLE	ROODS	RUNIC	SALTS	SCAMS	SEDGY
RIFTS	ROOFS	RUN IN	SALTY	SCANS	SEDUM
RIGHT	ROOKS	RUN-IN	SALVE	SCANT	SEEDS
RIGID	ROOMS	RUNNY	SALVO	SCAPE	SEEDY
RIGOR	ROOMY	RUNTS	SAMAR	SCARE	SEERS
RILED	ROOST	RUNTY	SAMBA	SCARF	SEGNO
RILEY	ROOTS	RUN-UP	SAMEY	SCARP	SEINE
RILLS	ROPED	RUPEE	SAMOA	SCARS	SEISE
RINDS	ROPES	RURAL	SAMOS	SCART	SEISM
RINGS	ROPEY	RUSES	SANDS	SCARY	SEIZE
RINKS	ROSES	RUSHY	SANDY	SCAUP	SELBY
RINSE	ROSIN	RUSKS	SANER	SCEND	SELES
RIOJA	ROTAS	RUSSO-	SAPID	SCENE	SELVA
RIOTS	ROTOR	RUSTY	SAPPY	SCENT	SEMEN
RIPEN	ROUEN	RUTTY	SARAN	SCHWA	SEMIS
RIPER	ROUES		SARGE	SCION	SENNA
RIPON	ROUGE	**S**	SARIN	SCOFF	SENOR
RISEN	ROUGH	SABAH	SARIS	SCOLD	SENSE
RISER	ROUND	SABER	SARKY	SCONE	SENZA
RISES	ROUPY	SABIN	SAROS	SCOOP	SEOUL
RISKS	ROUSE	SABLE	SASSY	SCOOT	SEPAL
RISKY	ROUST	SABOT	SATAN	SCOPE	SEPIA
RITES	ROUTE	SABRA	SATED	SCORE	SEPOY
RITZY	ROUTS	SABRE	SATEM	SCORN	SERAC
RIVAL	ROVED	SACKS	SATIN	SCOTS	SERFS
RIVEN	ROVER	SADHU	SATYR	SCOUR	SERGE

29

SERIF	SHELF	SHYER	SIXTE	SLICE	SNACK
SERIN	SHELL	SHYLY	SIXTH	SLICK	SNAFU
SEROW	SHERD	SIBIU	SIXTY	SLIDE	SNAGS
SERUM	SHEWN	SIBYL	SIZAR	SLIGO	SNAIL
SERVE	SHIAH	SICKO	SIZED	SLILY	SNAKE
SERVO	SHIED	SIDED	SIZES	SLIME	SNAKY
SETAL	SHIER	SIDES	SKATE	SLIMY	SNAPS
SET ON	SHIES	SIDLE	SKEET	SLING	SNARE
SET TO	SHIFT	SIEGE	SKEIN	SLINK	SNARL
SET-TO	SHILY	SIENA	SKELP	SLIPS	SNATH
SET UP	SHINE	SIEVE	SKEWS	SLITS	SNEAK
SET-UP	SHINS	SIGHS	SKIDS	SLOBS	SNECK
SEVEN	SHINY	SIGHT	SKIED	SLOES	SNEER
SEVER	SHIPS	SIGLA	SKIEN	SLOGS	SNICK
SEWED	SHIRE	SIGMA	SKIER	SLOOP	SNIDE
SEWER	SHIRK	SIGNS	SKIES	SLOPE	SNIFF
SEXED	SHIRR	SIKHS	SKIFF	SLOPS	SNIPE
SEXES	SHIRT	SILEX	SKILL	SLOSH	SNIPS
SHABA	SHITE	SILKS	SKIMP	SLOTH	SNOBS
SHACK	SHITS	SILKY	SKINK	SLOTS	SNOEK
SHADE	SHIVE	SILLS	SKINS	SLUED	SNOGS
SHADY	SHLUH	SILLY	SKINT	SLUGS	SNOOD
SHAFT	SHOAL	SILOS	SKIPS	SLUMP	SNOOK
SHAGS	SHOAT	SILTY	SKIRL	SLUMS	SNOOP
SHAHS	SHOCK	SIMLA	SKIRT	SLUNG	SNORE
SHAKE	SHOED	SIMON	SKITS	SLUNK	SNORT
SHAKO	SHOER	SINAI	SKIVE	SLURP	SNOUT
SHAKY	SHOES	SINCE	SKUAS	SLURS	SNOWS
SHALE	SHONA	SINES	SKULK	SLUSH	SNOWY
SHALL	SHONE	SINEW	SKULL	SLUTS	SNUBS
SHALT	SHOOK	SINGE	SKUNK	SLYER	SNUFF
SHALY	SHOOT	SINKS	SLABS	SLYPE	SNUGS
SHAME	SHOPS	SINUS	SLACK	SMACK	SOAKS
SHAMS	SHORE	SIOUX	SLAGS	SMALL	SOAPS
SHANK	SHORN	SIRED	SLAIN	SMALT	SOAPY
SHAN'T	SHORT	SIREN	SLAKE	SMARM	SOBER
SHAPE	SHOTS	SIRES	SLANG	SMART	SOCHE
SHARD	SHOTT	SISAL	SLANT	SMASH	SOCHI
SHARE	SHOUT	SISSY	SLAPS	SMEAR	SOCIO-
SHARK	SHOVE	SITAR	SLASH	SMELL	SOCKS
SHARP	SHOWN	SITED	SLATE	SMELT	SOCLE
SHAVE	SHOWS	SITES	SLATS	SMILE	SODAS
SHAWL	SHOWY	SIT-IN	SLATY	SMIRK	SOFAR
SHEAF	SHRED	SITKA	SLAVE	SMITE	SOFAS
SHEAR	SHREW	SIT ON	SLAVS	SMITH	SOFIA
SHEDS	SHRUB	SIT UP	SLEDS	SMOCK	SOFTA
SHEEN	SHRUG	SIT-UP	SLEEK	SMOKE	SOFTY
SHEEP	SHUCK	SITUS	SLEEP	SMOKY	SOGGY
SHEER	SHUNT	SIVAS	SLEET	SMOLT	SOILS
SHEET	SHUSH	SIXES	SLEPT	SMOTE	SOLAR
SHEIK	SHYED	SIXMO	SLEWS	SMUTS	SOLED

SOLES	SPEND	SPUNK	STICH	STUFF	SWASH
SOL-FA	SPENT	SPURN	STICK	STULL	SWATH
SOLID	SPERM	SPURS	STIES	STUMP	SWATS
SOLOS	SPICA	SPURT	STIFF	STUNG	SWAZI
SOLTI	SPICE	SQUAB	STILE	STUNK	SWEAR
SOLUM	SPICS	SQUAD	STILL	STUNT	SWEAT
SOLVE	SPICY	SQUAT	STILT	STUPE	SWEDE
SOMME	SPIED	SQUAW	STING	STYLE	SWEEP
SONAR	SPIEL	SQUIB	STINK	SUAVE	SWEET
SONDE	SPIES	SQUID	STINT	SUCRE	SWELL
SONGS	SPIFF	STABS	STIPE	SUDAN	SWEPT
SONIC	SPIKE	STACK	STIRK	SUDOR	SWIFT
SONNY	SPIKS	STAFF	STIRS	SUDSY	SWIGS
SOOTY	SPIKY	STAGE	STOAT	SUEDE	SWILL
SOPOR	SPILE	STAGS	STOCK	SUETY	SWIMS
SOPPY	SPILL	STAGY	STOEP	SUGAR	SWINE
SORES	SPILT	STAID	STOIC	SUING	SWING
SORGO	SPINE	STAIN	STOKE	SUINT	SWIPE
SORRY	SPINS	STAIR	STOLE	SUITE	SWIRL
SORTS	SPINY	STAKE	STOMA	SUITS	SWISH
SORUS	SPIRE	STALE	STOMP	SULKS	SWISS
SOTHO	SPIRY	STALK	STONE	SULKY	SWOON
SOUGH	SPITE	STALL	STONY	SULLY	SWOOP
SOULS	SPITS	STAMP	STOOD	SUMBA	SWOPS
SOUND	SPITZ	STAND	STOOK	SUMPS	SWORD
SOUPS	SPIVS	STANK	STOOL	SUNNI	SWORE
SOUPY	SPLAT	STANS	STOOP	SUNNY	SWORN
SOUSE	SPLAY	STARE	STOPE	SUN-UP	SWOTS
SOUTH	SPLIT	STARK	STOPS	SUPER	SWUNG
SOWED	SPOCK	STARS	STORE	SUPRA	SYLPH
SOWER	SPODE	START	STORK	SURAH	SYLVA
SOYUZ	SPOIL	STASH	STORM	SURAL	SYNOD
SPACE	SPOKE	STATE	STORY	SURAT	SYRIA
SPADE	SPOOF	STAVE	STOSS	SURDS	SYRUP
SPAIN	SPOOK	STAYS	STOUP	SURER	SYSOP
SPALL	SPOOL	STEAD	STOUR	SURFY	
SPANK	SPOON	STEAK	STOUT	SURGE	**T**
SPARE	SPOOR	STEAL	STOVE	SURLY	TABBY
SPARK	SPORE	STEAM	STRAP	SUSHI	TABES
SPARS	SPORT	STEED	STRAW	SWABS	TABLE
SPASM	SPOTS	STEEL	STRAY	SWAGE	TABOO
SPATE	SPOUT	STEEP	STREW	SWAIN	TABOR
SPATS	SPRAG	STEER	STRIA	SWALE	TACET
SPAWN	SPRAT	STEIN	STRIP	SWAMI	TACIT
SPEAK	SPRAY	STELE	STROP	SWAMP	TACKS
SPEAR	SPREE	STEMS	STRUM	SWANK	TACKY
SPECK	SPRIG	STEPS	STRUT	SWANS	TACOS
SPECS	SPRIT	STERE	STUBS	SWAPS	TAEGU
SPEED	SPRUE	STERN	STUCK	SWARD	TAFFY
SPELL	SPUDS	STEWS	STUDS	SWARF	TAFIA
SPELT	SPUME	STEYR	STUDY	SWARM	TAIGA

TAILS	TAWNY	TEXTS	TIE-UP	TOLLS	TOYED
TAINO	TAXED	THANE	TIFFS	TOLYL	TOYER
TAINT	TAXER	THANK	TIGER	TOMBS	TRACE
TA'IZZ	TAXES	THAWS	TIGHT	TOMES	TRACK
TAJIK	TAXIS	THECA	TIGON	TOMMY	TRACT
TAKEN	TAXON	THEFT	TIGRE	TOMSK	TRADE
TAKER	TAYRA	THEGN	TIKKA	TONAL	TRAIL
TAKES	TAZZA	THEIR	TILDE	TONDO	TRAIN
TAKIN	T-BONE	THEME	TILED	TONED	TRAIT
TALCA	TEACH	THERA	TILER	TONER	TRAMP
TALES	TEAKS	THERE	TILES	TONES	TRAMS
TALKS	TEAMS	THERM	TILLS	TONGA	TRANS-
TALLY	TEARS	THESE	TILTH	TONGS	TRAPS
TALON	TEASE	THETA	TILTS	TONIC	TRASH
TALUS	TEATS	THEWS	TIMED	TONNE	TRASS
TAMED	TECHY	THICK	TIMER	TON UP	TRAVE
TAMER	TEENS	THIEF	TIMES	TON-UP	TRAWL
TAMMY	TEENY	THIGH	TIMID	TONUS	TRAYS
TAMPA	TEETH	THINE	TINEA	TOOLS	TREAD
TANGA	TELEX	THING	TINES	TOOTH	TREAT
TANGO	TELIC	THINK	TINGE	TOOTS	TREEN
TANGY	TELLY	THIOL	TINGS	TOPAZ	TREES
TANKS	TEMPI	THIRD	TINNY	TOPEE	TREKS
TANSY	TEMPO	THOLE	TINTS	TOPER	TREND
TANTA	TEMPS	THONG	TIPSY	TOPIC	TRESS
TANTO	TEMPT	THORN	TIP UP	TOPOS	TREWS
TAPAS	TENCH	THOSE	TIRED	TOP UP	TRIAD
TAPED	TENET	THREE	TIREE	TOQUE	TRIAL
TAPER	TENON	THREW	TIRES	TORAH	TRIBE
TAPES	TENOR	THROB	TIROS	TORCH	TRICE
TAPIR	TENSE	THROW	TITAN	TORIC	TRICK
TAPIS	TENTH	THRUM	TITHE	TORSK	TRIED
TARDY	TENTS	THUDS	TITLE	TORSO	TRIER
TARES	TEPAL	THUGS	TITRE	TORTS	TRIES
TARGA	TEPEE	THUJA	TITTY	TORUN	TRIKE
TARNS	TEPIC	THUMB	TIZZY	TORUS	TRILL
TAROS	TEPID	THUMP	TOADS	TOTAL	TRIMS
TAROT	TERMS	THUNK	TOADY	TOTED	TRINE
TARRY	TERNE	THYME	TOAST	TOTEM	TRIOL
TARSI	TERNI	TIARA	TODAY	TOTER	TRIOS
TARTS	TERNS	TIBET	TODDY	TOTES	TRIPE
TARTU	TERRA	TIBIA	TO-DOS	TOUCH	TRIPS
TASKS	TERRY	TICAL	TOE-IN	TOUGH	TRITE
TASTE	TERSE	TICKS	TOFFS	TOURS	TROLL
TASTY	TESLA	TIDAL	TOGAS	TOUTS	TRONA
TATAR	TESOL	TIDED	TOILE	TOWED	TRONK
TATRA	TESTA	TIDES	TOILS	TOWEL	TROOP
TATTY	TESTS	TIE-IN	TOKAY	TOWER	TROPE
TAUNT	TESTY	TIE-ON	TOKEN	TOWNS	TROTH
TAUPE	TETRA	TIERS	TOKYO	TOXIC	TROTS
TAWER	TEXAS	TIE UP	TOLAN	TOXIN	TROUT

TROVE	TUTOR	UNARY	UTTER	VERVE	VOIDS
TRUCE	TUTSI	UNBAR	U-TURN	VESTA	VOILE
TRUCK	TUTTI	UNCAP	UVEAL	VESTS	VOLAR
TRUER	TUTTY	UNCLE	UVULA	VETCH	VOLES
TRUES	TUTUS	UNCUS	UZBEK	VEXED	VOLTA
TRUGO	TWAIN	UNCUT		VEXER	VOLTS
TRUGS	TWANG	UNDER	**V**	VIALS	VOLVA
TRULY	TWATS	UNDID		VIAND	VOMER
TRUMP	TWEAK	UNDUE	VAASA	VIBES	VOMIT
TRUNK	TWEED	UNFIT	VADUZ	VICAR	VOTED
TRURO	'TWEEN	UNFIX	VAGAL	VICES	VOTER
TRUSS	TWEET	UNIAT	VAGUE	VICHY	VOTES
TRUST	TWERP	UNIFY	VAGUS	VIDAL	VOUCH
TRUTH	TWICE	UNION	VALES	VIDEO	VOWED
TRYMA	TWIGS	UNITE	VALET	VIEWS	VOWEL
TRY ON	TWILL	UNITS	VALID	VIGIA	VOWER
TRY-ON	TWINE	UNITY	VALSE	VIGIL	V-SIGN
TRYST	TWINS	UNLAY	VALUE	VILER	VULVA
TSARS	TWIRL	UNMAN	VALVE	VILLA	VYING
TUBAL	TWIRP	UNPEG	VAMPS	VIMEN	
TUBAS	TWIST	UNPIN	VANDA	VINCA	**W**
TUBBY	TWITE	UNRIG	VANES	VINES	WACKY
TUBER	TWITS	UNRIP	VAPID	VINIC	WADDY
TUBES	TWIXT	UNSAY	VARIA	VINYL	WADED
TUCKS	TYING	UNSET	VARIX	VIOLA	WADER
TUDOR	TYPED	UNSEX	VARNA	VIOLS	WADGE
TUFTS	TYPES	UNTIE	VARUS	VIPER	WADIS
TUFTY	TYRES	UNTIL	VARVE	VIRAL	WAFER
TULIP	TYROL	UNZIP	VASES	VIREO	WAGED
TULLE	TYROS	UP-BOW	VAULT	VIRGA	WAGER
TULSA	TYSON	UPEND	VAUNT	VIRGO	WAGES
TUMID	TZARS	UPOLU	VEDDA	VIRTU	WAGON
TUMMY	TZU-PO	UPPER	VEDIC	VIRUS	WAHOO
TUNAS		UPSET	VEERY	VISAS	WAIFS
TUNED	**U**	URALS	VEGAN	VISBY	WAIST
TUNER	U-BOAT	URATE	VEILS	VISES	WAIVE
TUNES	UDDER	URBAN	VEINS	VISEU	WAJDA
TUNIC	UDINE	UREAL	VEINY	VISIT	WAKED
TUNIS	UGRIC	UREDO	VELAR	VISOR	WAKEN
TUNNY	UHURU	URGED	VELUM	VISTA	WAKER
TUQUE	UIGUR	URGER	VENAL	VITAL	WAKES
TURDS	ULCER	URGES	VENDA	VITTA	WALES
TURFS	ULNAR	URINE	VENIN	VIVID	WALKS
TURFY	ULNAS	USAGE	VENOM	VIXEN	WALLS
TURIN	ULTRA-	USERS	VENTS	V-NECK	WALLY
TURKI	ULURU	USHER	VENUE	VOCAB	WALTZ
TURKU	UMBEL	USING	VENUS	VOCAL	WANDS
TURNS	UMBER	USUAL	VERBS	VODKA	WANED
TURPS	UMBRA	USURP	VERGE	VOGUE	WANES
TUSKS	UMIAK	USURY	VERSE	VOGUL	WANEY
TUTEE	UNAPT	UTERI	VERSO	VOICE	WANLY

WANTS	WHACK	WILDS	WOOFS	XENON	YOKES
WARDS	WHALE	WILES	WOOZY	XERIC	YOLKS
WARES	WHAMS	WILLS	WORDS	XEROX	YOLKY
WARPS	WHANG	WILLY	WORDY	XHOSA	YONKS
WARTS	WHARF	WIMPS	WORKS	X-RAYS	YONNE
WARTY	WHEAL	WIMPY	WORLD	X-UNIT	YOUNG
WASHY	WHEAT	WINCE	WORMS	XYLAN	YOURS
WASPS	WHEEL	WINCH	WORMY	XYLEM	YOUSE
WASTE	WHELK	WINDS	WORRY	XYLOL	YOUTH
WATCH	WHELP	WINDY	WORSE	XYLYL	YOWLS
WATER	WHERE	WINED	WORST		YOYOS
WATTS	WHICH	WINES	WORTH	**Y**	YPRES
WAVED	WHIFF	WINEY	WOULD		YUCCA
WAVER	WHIGS	WINGE	WOUND	YACHT	YUCKY
WAVES	WHILE	WINGS	WOVEN	YAHOO	YUKON
WAXED	WHIMS	WINKS	WOWED	YAKUT	YULAN
WAXEN	WHINE	WINZE	WRACK	YALTA	YUMAN
WAXER	WHINY	WIPED	WRAPS	YANAN	
WEALD	WHIPS	WIPER	WRATH	YANKS	
WEALS	WHIRL	WIPES	WREAK	YAPOK	**Z**
WEARY	WHIRR	WIRED	WRECK	YAPPY	
WEAVE	WHIRS	WIRER	WRENS	YARDS	ZAIRE
WEBBY	WHISK	WIRES	WREST	YARNS	ZAMIA
WEBER	WHIST	WISER	WRIED	YAWED	ZANTE
WEDGE	WHITE	WISPS	WRIER	YAWLS	ZAPPY
WEDGY	WHITS	WISPY	WRING	YAWNS	ZARGA
WEEDS	WHIZZ	WITCH	WRIST	Y-AXIS	ZARIA
WEEDY	WHOLE	WITHE	WRITE	YEARN	ZARQA
WEEKS	WHOOP	WITHY	WRITS	YEARS	Z-AXIS
WEENY	WHORE	WITTY	WRONG	YEAST	ZEBRA
WEEPY	WHORL	WIVES	WROTE	YELLS	ZEIST
WEIGH	WHOSE	WIZEN	WROTH	YELPS	ZENIC
WEIRD	WICCA	WOKEN	WRUNG	YEMEN	ZEROS
WEIRS	WICKS	WOLDS	WRYER	YERBA	ZESTY
WELCH	WIDEN	WOLOF	WRYLY	YETIS	ZIBET
WELDS	WIDER	WOMAN	WUHAN	YIBIN	ZILCH
WELLS	WIDES	WOMBS	WURST	YIELD	ZINGY
WELLY	WIDOW	WOMEN	WUSIH	YIKES	ZIPPY
WELSH	WIDTH	WONKY		YODEL	ZLOTY
WELTS	WIELD	WOODS		YOGIC	ZOMBA
WENCH	WIGAN	WOODY	**X**	YOGIS	ZONAL
WESER	WIGHT	WOOED	X-AXIS	YOKED	ZONED
WETLY	WILCO	WOOER	XENIA	YOKEL	ZONES
					ZOOID

A	ACCORD	ADVENT	AILING	ALL OUT	AMRITA
AACHEN	ACCOST	ADVERB	AIMING	ALLOYS	AMULET
AARGAU	ACCRUE	ADVERT	AIRBED	ALLUDE	AMUSED
AARHUS	ACCUSE	ADVICE	AIRBUS	ALLURE	AMYLUM
ABACUS	ACETAL	ADVISE	AIR-DRY	ALMADA	AMYTAL
ABADAN	ACETIC	ADYGEI	AIRGUN	AL MARJ	ANABAS
ABAKAN	ACETUM	ADZHAR	AIRIER	ALMATY	ANADYR
ABASED	ACETYL	AECIUM	AIRILY	ALMOND	ANALOG
ABATED	ACHAEA	AEDILE	AIRING	ALMOST	ANCHOR
ABATIS	ACHENE	AEGEAN	AIRMAN	ALMUCE	ANCONA
ABATOR	ACHING	AERATE	AIRMEN	ALNICO	ANDEAN
ABBACY	ACIDIC	AERIAL	AIRWAY	ALPACA	ANDONG
ABBESS	ACINIC	AERIFY	AISLES	ALPHAS	ANDROS
ABBEYS	ACINUS	AEROBE	AKIMBO	ALPINE	ANEMIA
ABBOTS	ACNODE	AERUGO	AKMOLA	ALSACE	ANEMIC
ABDUCT	ACORNS	AETHER	AL-ANON	ALSIKE	ANERGY
ABELIA	ACQUIT	AFFAIR	ALARMS	ALTAIC	ANGARY
ABIDED	ACROSS	AFFECT	ALASKA	ALTAIR	ANGELS
ABIDER	ACTING	AFFINE	ALBANY	ALTARS	ANGERS
ABJECT	ACTION	AFFIRM	ALBEDO	ALTONA	ANGINA
ABJURE	ACTIVE	AFFLUX	ALBEIT	ALUDEL	ANGKOR
ABKHAZ	ACTORS	AFFORD	ALBINO	ALUMNA	ANGLED
ABLAUT	ACTS UP	AFFRAY	ALBION	ALUMNI	ANGLER
ABLAZE	ACTUAL	AFGHAN	ALBITE	ALVINE	ANGLES
ABOARD	ACUITY	AFIELD	ALBUMS	ALWAYS	ANGOLA
ABODES	ACUMEN	AFLAME	ALCOVE	AMADOU	ANGORA
ABORAL	ADAGES	AFL-CIO	ALDISS	AMATOL	ANHALT
ABOUND	ADAGIO	AFLOAT	ALDOSE	AMAZED	ANHWEI
ABRADE	ADDEND	AFRAID	ALDRIN	AMAZON	ANIMAL
ABROAD	ADDERS	AFRESH	ALECKS	AMBALA	ANIMUS
ABRUPT	ADDICT	AFRICA	ALEGAR	AMBARY	ANKARA
ABSEIL	ADDING	AFTERS	ALEPPO	AMBITS	ANKING
ABSENT	ADDLED	AGADIR	ALERTS	AMBLED	ANKLES
ABSORB	ADD-ONS	AGAMIC	A LEVEL	AMBLER	ANKLET
ABSURD	ADDUCE	AGARIC	ALGOID	AMBUSH	ANLAGE
ABULIA	ADDUCT	AGATES	AL HASA	AMEBAS	ANNABA
ABULIC	ADEPTS	AGEING	ALIBIS	AMEBIC	ANNALS
ABUSED	ADHERE	AGEISM	ALIENS	AMENDS	ANNEAL
ABUSER	ADIEUS	AGEIST	ALIGHT	AMHARA	ANNECY
ABUSES	ADIEUX	AGENCY	ALIPED	AMIDIC	ANNEXE
ABVOLT	ADJOIN	AGENDA	ALKALI	AMIDOL	ANNUAL
ABWATT	ADJURE	AGENTS	ALKANE	AMIDST	ANODES
ACACIA	ADJUST	AGE OLD	ALKENE	AMIENS	ANODIC
ACADIA	ADMIRE	AGHAST	ALKYNE	AMMINE	ANOINT
ACAJOU	ADNATE	AGNATE	ALLEGE	AMNION	ANOMIC
ACARID	ADNOUN	AGOGIC	ALLELE	AMOEBA	ANOMIE
ACARUS	ADORED	AGONIC	ALLEYS	AMORAL	ANORAK
ACCEDE	ADRIFT	AGOUTI	ALLIED	AMOUNT	ANOXIA
ACCENT	ADROIT	AGREED	ALLIER	AMOURS	ANOXIC
ACCEPT	ADSORB	AIDING	ALLIES	AMPERE	ANQING
ACCESS	ADULTS	AIKIDO	ALLIUM	AMPULE	ANSATE

ANSHAN	ARABIC	ARRIVE	ATHENS	AVENGE	BAKERS
ANSWER	ARABLE	ARROBA	AT HOME	AVENUE	BAKERY
ANTEED	ARAGON	ARROWS	AT-HOME	AVERSE	BAKING
ANTHEM	ARARAT	ARSINE	AT LAST	AVIARY	BALATA
ANTHER	ARBOUR	ARTERY	ATOLLS	AVIATE	BALBOA
ANTICS	ARCADE	ARTFUL	ATOMIC	AVIDIN	BALDLY
ANTLER	ARCANA	ARTIER	ATONAL	AVIDLY	BALEEN
ANTRIM	ARCANE	ARTIST	ATONED	AVOCET	BALING
ANTRUM	ARCHED	ARTOIS	ATONER	AVOWAL	BALKAN
ANTUNG	ARCHER	ARUNTA	ATONIC	AVOWED	BALKED
ANURAN	ARCHES	ASARUM	AT REST	AVOWER	BALKER
ANURIA	ARCHLY	ASCEND	ATRIUM	AWAKED	BALLAD
ANUSES	ARCTIC	ASCENT	ATTACH	AWAKEN	BALLET
ANVILS	ARDENT	ASCOTS	ATTACK	AWARDS	BALLOT
ANYANG	ARDOUR	ASHDOD	ATTAIN	AWEIGH	BALSAM
ANYHOW	ARENAS	ASHIER	ATTEND	AWHILE	BALSAS
ANYONE	AREOLA	ASHLAR	ATTEST	AWNING	BALTIC
ANYWAY	ARETES	ASHORE	ATTICA	AWOKEN	BAMAKO
AORIST	AREZZO	ASIANS	ATTICS	AXENIC	BAMBOO
AORTAS	ARGALI	ASIDES	ATTIRE	AXILLA	BANABA
AORTIC	ARGENT	ASKING	ATTORN	AXIOMS	BANANA
AOUDAD	ARGOSY	ASLANT	ATTRIT	AYE AYE	BANDED
AOUITA	ARGOTS	ASLEEP	ATTUNE	AYMARA	BANDIT
APACHE	ARGUED	ASMARA	ATWOOD	AZALEA	BANDOG
APATHY	ARGUER	ASPECT	AUBADE	AZORES	BANGED
APEMAN	ARGYLE	ASPIRE	AUBURN	AZOTIC	BANGER
APERCU	ARGYLL	ASSAIL	AUDILE		BANGLE
APEXES	ARIEGE	ASSAYS	AUDITS	**B**	BANGOR
APHIDS	ARIGHT	ASSENT	AU FAIT	BAAING	BANGUI
APHTHA	ARIOSO	ASSERT	AU FOND	BABBLE	BANISH
APIARY	ARISEN	ASSESS	AUGEND	BABIED	BANJOS
APICAL	ARISTA	ASSETS	AUGERS	BABIES	BANJUL
APICES	ARKOSE	ASSIGN	AUGITE	BABOON	BANKED
APIECE	ARMADA	ASSISI	AUGURY	BACKED	BANKER
APLITE	ARMAGH	ASSIST	AUGUST	BACKER	BANNED
APLOMB	ARMFUL	ASSIZE	AUKLET	BACK UP	BANNER
APNOEA	ARMIES	ASSORT	AU LAIT	BACKUP	BANTAM
APODAL	ARMING	ASSUME	AUMBRY	BADGER	BANTER
APOGEE	ARMLET	ASSURE	AU PAIR	BADGES	BANYAN
APOLLO	ARMOUR	ASTANA	AUREUS	BAFFLE	BAOBAB
APPEAL	ARMPIT	ASSUAN	AURORA	BAGELS	BAOTOU
APPEAR	ARMURE	ASTERN	AUROUS	BAGGED	BARBED
APPEND	ARNHEM	ASTHMA	AUSSIE	BAGUIO	BARBEL
APPLES	ARNICA	ASTRAL	AUSTIN	BAILED	BARBER
APPLET	AROMAS	ASTRAY	AUSTRO-	BAILEE	BARBET
APPOSE	AROUND	ASTUTE	AUTEUR	BAILER	BARBIE
APRILS	AROUSE	ASWARM	AUTHOR	BAILEY	BARDIC
APRONS	ARRACK	ASYLUM	AUTISM	BAILOR	BARELY
APULIA	ARRANT	ATAXIA	AUTUMN	BAIL UP	BAREST
AQUILA	ARRAYS	ATAXIC	AVATAR	BAIRNS	BARGED
ARABIA	ARREST	ATBARA	AVEIRO	BAITED	BARGEE

BARGES	BATTLE	BEHEAD	BETTED	BINGOS	BLINKS
BARING	BATTUE	BEHELD	BETTER	BINMAN	BLINTZ
BARIUM	BAUBLE	BEHEST	BEVELS	BINNED	BLITHE
BARKED	BAUCHI	BEHIND	BEVIES	BIOGAS	BLOCKS
BARKER	BAULKS	BEHOLD	BEWAIL	BIOGEN	BLOKES
BARLEY	BAWLED	BEHOVE	BEWARE	BIONIC	BLONDE
BARMAN	BAWLER	BEINGS	BEXLEY	BIOPIC	BLOODS
BARMEN	BAYEUX	BEIRUT	BEYOND	BIOPSY	BLOODY
BARNET	BAYING	BELFRY	BEZIER	BIOTIC	BLOOMS
BARNEY	BAYOUS	BELIED	BEZOAR	BIOTIN	BLOTCH
BARODA	BAZAAR	BELIEF	BHOPAL	BIPEDS	BLOTTO
BARONS	BEACON	BELIER	BHUTAN	BIRDIE	BLOUSE
BARONY	BEADED	BELIZE	BHUTTO	BIRTHS	BLOWER
BARQUE	BEADLE	BELLES	BIAFRA	BISCAY	BLOWSY
BARRED	BEAGLE	BELLOW	BIASED	BISECT	BLOW-UP
BARREL	BEAKER	BELONG	BIASES	BISHOP	BLOWZY
BARREN	BEAMED	BELSEN	BIBLES	BISKRA	BLUEST
BARROW	BEARDS	BELTED	BICEPS	BISONS	BLUFFS
BARTER	BEARER	BELTER	BICKER	BISQUE	BLUISH
BARTON	BEASTS	BELUGA	BICORN	BISSAU	BLUNGE
BARYON	BEATEN	BEMOAN	BIDDEN	BISTRE	BLURBS
BARYTE	BEATER	BEMUSE	BIDETS	BISTRO	BLURRY
BASALT	BEAUNE	BENDER	BIDING	BITCHY	B-MOVIE
BASELY	BEAUTS	BENGAL	BIFFED	BITING	BOARDS
BASEST	BEAUTY	BENGBU	BIFFIN	BITMAP	BOASTS
BASHED	BEAVER	BENIGN	BIGAMY	BITOLJ	BOATED
BASHES	BECAME	BENONI	BIG CAT	BITTEN	BOATER
BASICS	BECKET	BENUMB	BIG END	BITTER	BOATIE
BASIFY	BECKON	BENZOL	BIGGER	BLACKS	BOBBED
BASING	BECOME	BENZYL	BIGGIE	BLADES	BOBBER
BASINS	BEDAUB	BERATE	BIGHTS	BLAMED	BOBBIN
BASION	BEDBUG	BEREFT	BIGOTS	BLANCH	BOBBLE
BASKED	BEDDED	BERETS	BIG TOP	BLANKS	BOBCAT
BASKET	BEDDER	BERGEN	BIGWIG	BLARED	BOCHUM
BASQUE	BEDECK	BERING	BIHARI	BLASTS	BODEGA
BASRAH	BEDLAM	BERLEY	BIKING	BLAZED	BODICE
BASSES	BEDPAN	BERLIN	BIKINI	BLAZER	BODIES
BASSET	BEDSIT	BERTHS	BILBAO	BLAZES	BODILY
BASTED	BEEFED	BERYLS	BILGES	BLAZON	BODING
BASTIA	BEETLE	BESEEM	BILKED	BLEACH	BODKIN
BASUCO	BEFALL	BESIDE	BILKER	BLEARY	BODMIN
BATHED	BEFELL	BESOMS	BILLED	BLEATS	BOFFIN
BATHER	BEFOOL	BESTED	BILLET	BLEEPS	BOGEYS
BATHOS	BEFORE	BESTIR	BILLON	BLENCH	BOGGED
BATLEY	BEFOUL	BESTOW	BILLOW	BLENDE	BOGGLE
BATMAN	BEGGAR	BETAKE	BILLY-O	BLENDS	BOGIES
BATMEN	BEGGED	BETHEL	BINARY	BLENNY	BOGOTA
BATONS	BEGONE	BETIDE	BINATE	BLIGHT	BOILED
BATTED	BEGUMS	BETONY	BINDER	BLIMEY	BOILER
BATTEN	BEHALF	BETOOK	BINGEN	BLIMPS	BOLAND
BATTER	BEHAVE	BETRAY	BINGES	BLINDS	BOLDER

BOLDLY	BOSOMY	BRAKED	BRONZY	BUNGED	BUSSED
BOLERO	BOSSED	BRAKES	BROOCH	BUNGEE	BUSTED
BOLIDE	BOSSES	BRANCH	BROODS	BUNGLE	BUSTER
BOLSHY	BOSTON	BRANDO	BROODY	BUNION	BUSTLE
BOLSON	BOSUNS	BRANDS	BROOKS	BUNKED	BUST-UP
BOLTED	BOTANY	BRANDT	BROOMS	BUNKER	BUTANE
BOLTER	BOTCHY	BRANDY	BROWNS	BUNKUM	BUTENE
BOLTON	BOTFLY	BRASHY	BROWSE	BUNK-UP	BUTLER
BOMBAY	BOTHER	BRASOV	BRUGES	BUOYED	BUTTED
BOMBED	BOTTLE	BRASSY	BRUISE	BURBLE	BUTTER
BOMBER	BOTTOM	BRAVED	BRUMAL	BURBOT	BUTTES
BONBON	BOUAKE	BRAVER	BRUMBY	BURDEN	BUTTIE
BONDED	BOUCLE	BRAVES	BRUNCH	BUREAU	BUTTON
BONGOS	BOUGHS	BRAVOS	BRUNEI	BURGAS	BUXTON
BONIER	BOUGHT	BRAWLS	BRUTAL	BURGEE	BUYERS
BONILY	BOUGIE	BRAWNY	BRUTES	BURGER	BUYING
BONING	BOULES	BRAYED	BRUTON	BURGHS	BUYOUT
BONITO	BOULLE	BRAYER	BRYONY	BURGLE	BUZZED
BON MOT	BOUNCE	BRAZEN	BUBBLE	BURGOS	BUZZER
BONNET	BOUNCY	BRAZER	BUBBLY	BURIAL	BUZZES
BONSAI	BOUNDS	BRAZIL	BUCCAL	BURIED	BY-BLOW
BONZER	BOUNTY	BREACH	BUCKED	BURIER	BYGONE
BOOBED	BOURNS	BREAKS	BUCKET	BURLAP	BYLAWS
BOOGIE	BOURSE	BREAST	BUCKLE	BURLER	BY-LINE
BOOHOO	BOVINE	BRECON	BUDDED	BURLEY	BYPASS
BOOING	BOVVER	BREECH	BUDDHA	BURLEY	BYPLAY
BOOKED	BOWELS	BREEZE	BUDDLE	BURNED	BYROAD
BOOKIE	BOWERS	BREEZY	BUDGED	BURNER	BYSSUS
BOOMED	BOWERY	BREGMA	BUDGET	BURNET	BYWAYS
BOOSTS	BOWFIN	BREMEN	BUFFED	BURPED	BYWORD
BOOTED	BOWING	BRETON	BUFFER	BURPEE	
BOOTEE	BOWLED	BREVET	BUFFET	BURRED	
BOOTHS	BOWLER	BREWER	BUGGED	BURROS	C
BOOTLE	BOWMAN	BRIBER	BUGGER	BURROW	CABALS
BOOZED	BOWMEN	BRIDAL	BUGLER	BURSAL	CABANA
BOOZER	BOWSAW	BRIDGE	BUGLES	BURSAR	CABBIE
BOPPED	BOWSER	BRIDLE	BUILDS	BURSTS	CABERS
BORAGE	BOW TIE	BRIERY	BUKAVU	BURTON	CABINS
BORANE	BOWWOW	BRIGHT	BULBAR	BURYAT	CABLED
BORATE	BOWYER	BRITON	BULBIL	BUSBAR	CABLES
BORDER	BOXCAR	BROACH	BULBUL	BUS BOY	CABLET
BOREAL	BOXERS	BROADS	BULGED	BUSBOY	CABMAN
BORERS	BOXING	BROCHE	BULGES	BUSHED	CACHES
BORIDE	BOYISH	BROGUE	BULKED	BUSHEL	CACHET
BORING	BRACED	BROKEN	BULLET	BUSHES	CACHOU
BORNEO	BRACER	BROKER	BUMBLE	BUSIED	CACKLE
BORROW	BRACES	BROLLY	BUMMED	BUSIER	CACTUS
BORZOI	BRAIDS	BROMAL	BUMPED	BUSILY	CAD/CAM
BOSKET	BRAINS	BROMIC	BUMPER	BUSING	CADDIE
BOSNIA	BRAINY	BRONCO	BUNCHY	BUSKED	CADDIS
BOSOMS	BRAISE	BRONZE	BUNDLE	BUSKER	CADENT
				BUSKIN	CADETS

CADGED	CAMPER	CARESS	CATION	CEROUS	CHEESY
CADGER	CAMPOS	CARETS	CATKIN	CERUSE	CHEQUE
CADRES	CAMPUS	CARGOS	CATNAP	CERVID	CHERRY
CAECUM	CANADA	CARHOP	CATNIP	CERVIX	CHERTY
CAELUM	CANALS	CARIES	CATSUP	CETANE	CHERUB
CAEOMA	CANAPE	CARINA	CATTLE	CETNIK	CHESTS
CAESAR	CANARD	CARING	CAUCUS	CEYLON	CHESTY
CAFTAN	CANARY	CARLOW	CAUDAD	CHA CHA	CHEWED
CAGIER	CANCAN	CARMAN	CAUDAL	CHA-CHA	CHEWER
CAGILY	CANCEL	CARMEL	CAUDEX	CHACMA	CHICHI
CAGING	CANCER	CARNAL	CAUDLE	CHAETA	CHICKS
CAHIER	CANDID	CARNES	CAUGHT	CHAFED	CHICLE
CAICOS	CANDLE	CARNET	CAUSAL	CHAFER	CHICLY
CAIQUE	CANINE	CAROBS	CAUSED	CHAFFY	CHIDED
CAIRNS	CANING	CAROLS	CAUSES	CHAINS	CHIDER
CAJOLE	CANKER	CARPAL	CAVEAT	CHAIRS	CHIEFS
CAKING	CANNED	CARPED	CAVE-IN	CHAISE	CHIGOE
CALAIS	CANNEL	CARPEL	CAVERN	CHAKRA	CHILES
CALASH	CANNES	CARPET	CAVIAR	CHALET	CHILLI
CALCAR	CANNON	CARPUS	CAVING	CHALKS	CHILLS
CALCES	CANNOT	CARREL	CAVITY	CHALKY	CHILLY
CALCIC	CANOED	CARROT	CAVORT	CHAMPS	CHIMED
CALICO	CANOES	CARSON	CAWING	CHANCE	CHIMES
CALIPH	CANONS	CARTED	CAXTON	CHANCY	CHINES
CALKED	CANOPY	CARTEL	CAYMAN	CHANGE	CHINKS
CALKIN	CANTAL	CARTER	CD-ROMS	CHANIA	CHINTZ
CALLAO	CANTED	CARTON	CEASED	CHANTS	CHIPPY
CALLED	CANTER	CARVED	CEDARS	CHANTY	CHIRAC
CALLER	CANTIC	CARVER	CEDING	CHAOAN	CHIRPS
CALL-IN	CANTLE	CASABA	CELAYA	CHAPEL	CHIRPY
CALLOW	CANTON	CASEFY	CELERY	CHARDS	CHISEL
CALL-UP	CANTOR	CASEIN	CELLAR	CHARGE	CHITIN
CALLUS	CANTOS	CASERN	CELLOS	CHARMS	CHITON
CALMED	CANTUS	CASHED	CELTIC	CHARTS	CHITTY
CALMER	CANVAS	CASHEW	CEMENT	CHASED	CHIVES
CALMLY	CANYON	CASING	CENSER	CHASER	CHOCKA
CALPAC	CAPERS	CASINO	CENSOR	CHASES	CHOCKS
CALQUE	CAPIAS	CASKET	CENSUS	CHASMS	CHOICE
CALVED	CAPONS	CASLON	CENTAL	CHASSE	CHOIRS
CALVES	CAPOTE	CASQUE	CENTER	CHASTE	CHOKED
CALVIN	CAPPED	CASSIA	CENTRE	CHATTY	CHOKER
CAMASS	CAPPER	CASSIS	CENTUM	CHAT UP	CHOKES
CAMBER	CAPSID	CASTER	CERATE	CHEATS	CHOLER
CAMDEN	CAPTOR	CASTES	CERCAL	CHECKS	CHOLLA
CAMELS	CARAFE	CASTLE	CERCIS	CHECKY	CHONJU
CAMEOS	CARATS	CASTOR	CERCUS	CHEEKS	CHOOSE
CAMERA	CARBON	CASTRO	CEREAL	CHEEKY	CHOOSY
CAMION	CARBOY	CASUAL	CEREUS	CHEEPS	CHOPPY
CAMISE	CARDED	CATCHY	CERISE	CHEERS	CHORAL
CAMLET	CAREEN	CATENA	CERIUM	CHEERY	CHORDS
CAMPED	CAREER	CATGUT	CERMET	CHEESE	CHOREA

CHORES	CLAMPS	CLOTHS	COGNAC	COMPER	CORBAN
CHORIC	CLAQUE	CLOUDS	COHEIR	COMPLY	CORBEL
CHORUS	CLARET	CLOUDY	COHERE	CONCHA	CORDED
CHOSEN	CLARKE	CLOUTS	COHORT	CONCHY	CORDON
CHOUGH	CLASPS	CLOVEN	COHOSH	CONCUR	CORERS
CHRISM	CLASSY	CLOVER	COHUNE	CONDOM	CORFAM
CHRIST	CLAUSE	CLOVES	COILED	CONDOR	CORGIS
CHROMA	CLAWED	CLOWNS	COILER	CONEYS	CORING
CHROME	CLAWER	CLOYED	COINED	CONFER	CORIUM
CHUBBY	CLAYEY	CLUBBY	COINER	CONGAS	CORKED
CHUCKS	CLEATS	CLUCKS	COIN-OP	CONGER	CORKER
CHUKAR	CLEAVE	CLUCKY	COITAL	CONGES	CORMEL
CHUKKA	CLEESE	CLUMPS	COITUS	CONGOU	CORNEA
CHUMMY	CLEFTS	CLUMPY	COLDER	CONICS	CORNEL
CHUMPS	CLENCH	CLUMSY	COLDLY	CONIES	CORNER
CHUNKS	CLEOME	CLUNKY	COLEUS	CONIUM	CORNET
CHUNKY	CLERGY	CLUTCH	COLEYS	CONKED	CORONA
CHURCH	CLERIC	COALED	COLIMA	CONKER	CORPSE
CHURLS	CLERKS	COALER	COLLAR	CONMAN	CORPUS
CHURNS	CLEVER	COARSE	COLLET	CONMEN	CORRAL
CHUTES	CLEVIS	COASTS	COLLIE	CONNED	CORSES
CICADA	CLICHE	COATED	COLMAR	CONOID	CORSET
CICERO	CLICKS	COAXED	COLONS	CONSUL	CORTEX
CIDERS	CLIENT	COAXER	COLONY	CONTRA-	CORVID
CIGARS	CLIFFS	COBALT	COLOUR	CONVEX	CORYMB
CILICE	CLIMAX	COBBER	COLUGO	CONVEY	CORYZA
CILIUM	CLIMBS	COBBLE	COLUMN	CONVOY	COSECH
CINDER	CLIMES	COBNUT	COLURE	COOING	COSHED
CINEMA	CLINAL	COBRAS	COMATE	COOKED	COSHES
CINEOL	CLINCH	COBURG	COMBAT	COOKER	COSIER
CINQUE	CLINES	COBWEB	COMBED	COOKIE	COSIES
CIPHER	CLINGY	COCCID	COMBER	COOLED	COSILY
CIRCLE	CLINIC	COCCUS	COMBOS	COOLER	COSINE
CIRCUM-	CLIP-ON	COCCYX	COMEDO	COOLIE	COSMIC
CIRCUS	CLIQUE	COCHIN	COMEDY	COOLLY	COSMOS
CIRQUE	CLITIC	COCKED	COMELY	COOLTH	COSSET
CIRRUS	CLOACA	COCKLE	COME ON	COOPED	COSTAL
CISKEI	CLOAKS	COCK-UP	COME-ON	COOPER	CO-STAR
CITIES	CLOCHE	COCOON	COMERS	COPALM	COSTLY
CITIFY	CLOCKS	CODDLE	COMETS	COPIED	COTTER
CITING	CLODDY	CODGER	COMFIT	COPIER	COTTON
CITRAL	CLOGGY	CODIFY	COMICS	COPIES	COUCAL
CITRIC	CLONAL	CODING	COMING	COPING	COUGAR
CITRIN	CLONES	COELOM	COMITY	COP-OUT	COUGHS
CITRON	CLONIC	COERCE	COMMAS	COPPED	COULEE
CITRUS	CLONUS	COEVAL	COMMIS	COPPER	COULIS
CIVETS	CLOSED	COFFEE	COMMIT	COPSES	COUNTS
CIVICS	CLOSER	COFFER	COMMON	COPTIC	COUNTY
CIVIES	CLOSES	COFFIN	COMORO	COPULA	COUPES
CLAIMS	CLOSET	COGENT	COMOSE	COQUET	COUPLE
CLAMMY	CLOTHE	COGGED	COMPEL	CORALS	COUPON

COURSE	CREAKY	CROWER	CURDLE	**D**	DAPPER
COURTS	CREAMS	CROWNS	CURFEW	DABBED	DAPPLE
COUSIN	CREAMY	CRUDER	CURIAE	DABBER	DARDIC
COVENS	CREASE	CRUETS	CURING	DABBLE	DARFUR
COVERS	CREATE	CRUISE	CURIOS	DACHAU	DARING
COVERT	CRECHE	CRUMBS	CURIUM	DACITE	DARKEN
COVEYS	CREDIT	CRUMBY	CURLED	DACOIT	DARKER
COWAGE	CREDOS	CRUMMY	CURLER	DACRON	DARKLY
COWARD	CREEDS	CRUNCH	CURLEW	DACTYL	DARNED
COWBOY	CREEKS	CRURAL	CURL UP	DADOES	DARNEL
COWING	CREELS	CRUSES	CURSED	DAEMON	DARNER
COWMAN	CREEPS	CRUSTS	CURSES	DAFTER	DARTED
COWMEN	CREEPY	CRUSTY	CURSOR	DAFTLY	DARTER
COWPAT	CRENEL	CRUTCH	CURTLY	DAGGER	DARWIN
COWPEA	CREOLE	CRUXES	CURTSY	DAGOES	DASHED
COWPOX	CRESOL	CRYING	CURVED	DAHLIA	DASHER
COWRIE	CRESTS	CRYPTS	CURVES	DAINTY	DASHES
COXING	CRETAN	CUBANE	CURVET	DAISES	DATARY
COYOTE	CRETIC	CUBBED	CUSCUS	DAKOTA	DATING
COYPUS	CRETIN	CUBING	CUSPID	DALASI	DATIVE
COZIER	CREUSE	CUBISM	CUSSED	DALIAN	DATURA
COZILY	CREWED	CUBIST	CUSSES	DALLAS	DAUBED
CRABBY	CREWEL	CUBITS	CUSTOM	DALLES	DAUBER
CRACKS	CRICKS	CUBOID	CUTELY	DALTON	DAVIES
CRACOW	CRIERS	CUCKOO	CUTEST	DAMAGE	DAVITS
CRADLE	CRIKEY	CUCUTA	CUTESY	DAMARA	DAWDLE
CRAFTS	CRIMEA	CUDDLE	CUTLER	DAMASK	DAWNED
CRAFTY	CRIMES	CUDDLY	CUTLET	DAMMAR	DAYBOY
CRAGGY	CRINGE	CUDGEL	CUTOFF	DAMMED	DAYGLO
CRAMBO	CRINUM	CUESTA	CUT OFF	DAMNED	DAYTON
CRAMPS	CRIPES	CUFFED	CUTOUT	DAMPED	DAZING
CRANED	CRISES	CUIABA	CUTTER	DAMPEN	DAZZLE
CRANES	CRISIS	CULLED	CUTUPS	DAMPER	DEACON
CRANIA	CRISPS	CULLER	CYANIC	DAMPLY	DEADEN
CRANKS	CRISPY	CULLET	CYBORG	DAMSEL	DEADLY
CRANKY	CRISTA	CULLIS	CYCLED	DAMSON	DEAFEN
CRANNY	CRITIC	CULTIC	CYCLES	DA NANG	DEALER
CRAPPY	CROAKS	CUMANA	CYCLIC	DANCED	DEARER
CRASIS	CROCKS	CUMBER	CYDERS	DANCER	DEARLY
CRATED	CROCUS	CUNEAL	CYGNET	DANCES	DEARTH
CRATER	CROFTS	CUPIDS	CYGNUS	DANDER	DEATHS
CRATES	CRONES	CUPOLA	CYMBAL	DANDLE	DEBARK
CRATON	CROOKS	CUPPAS	CYMENE	DANGER	DEBASE
CRAVAT	CRORES	CUPPED	CYMOID	DANGLE	DEBATE
CRAVED	CROSSE	CUPRIC	CYMOSE	DANIEL	DEBITS
CRAVEN	CROTCH	CUP TIE	CYMRIC	DANISH	DEBRIS
CRAWLS	CROTON	CUPULE	CYNICS	DANKER	DEBTOR
CRAYON	CROUCH	CURACY	CYPHER	DANUBE	DEBUNK
CRAZED	CROUPS	CURARE	CYPRUS	DANZIG	DEBUTS
CRAZES	CROWDS	CURATE	CYSTIC	DAPHNE	DECADE
CREAKS	CROWED	CURBED		DAPPED	DECALS

DECAMP	DELPHI	DERRIS	DIDDLE	DISEUR	DOLLAR
DECANE	DELTAS	DESCRY	DIEPPE	DISHED	DOLLED
DECANT	DELUDE	DESERT	DIESEL	DISHES	DOLLOP
DECARE	DELUGE	DESIGN	DIESIS	DISMAL	DOLMAN
DECCAN	DE LUXE	DESIRE	DIETED	DISMAY	DOLMAS
DECEIT	DELVED	DESIST	DIETER	DISOWN	DOLMEN
DECENT	DELVER	DESMAN	DIFFER	DISPEL	DOLOUR
DECIDE	DEMAND	DESMID	DIGAMY	DISTAL	DOMAIN
DECILE	DEMEAN	DESORB	DIGEST	DISTIL	DOMINO
DECKED	DEMISE	DESPOT	DIGGER	DISUSE	DONATE
DECKLE	DEMIST	DESSAU	DIGITS	DITHER	DONDER
DECOCT	DEMODE	DETACH	DIGLOT	DITTOS	DONJON
DECODE	DEMONS	DETAIL	DIK-DIK	DIVANS	DONKEY
DECOKE	DEMOTE	DETAIN	DIKTAT	DIVERS	DONNED
DECORS	DEMURE	DETECT	DILATE	DIVERT	DONORS
DECOYS	DEMURS	DETENT	DILDOS	DIVEST	DOODLE
DECREE	DENARY	DETEST	DILUTE	DIVIDE	DOO-DOO
DEDUCE	DENEST	DETOUR	DIMITY	DIVINE	DOOMED
DEDUCT	DENGUE	DE TROP	DIMMED	DIVING	DOPANT
DEEMED	DENIAL	DETTOL	DIMMER	DIWALI	DOPIER
DEEPEN	DENIED	DETUNE	DIMPLE	DJAMBI	DOPING
DEEPER	DENIER	DEUCED	DIMPLY	DJINNS	DORIAN
DEEPLY	DENIMS	DEVEIN	DIM SUM	DOABLE	DORIES
DEFACE	DE NIRO	DEVICE	DIMWIT	DOBBIN	DORMER
DEFAME	DENNED	DEVILS	DINARS	DOCENT	DORMIE
DEFEAT	DENOTE	DEVISE	DINERO	DOCILE	DORSAD
DEFECT	DENSER	DEVOID	DINERS	DOCKED	DORSAL
DEFEND	DENTAL	DEVOTE	DINGHY	DOCKER	DORSET
DEFIED	DENTED	DEVOUR	DINGLE	DOCKET	DORSUM
DEFIER	DENTEX	DEVOUT	DINING	DOCTOR	DOSAGE
DEFILE	DENTIL	DEWIER	DINKUM	DODDER	DO-SI-DO
DEFINE	DENTIN	DEWILY	DINNED	DODDLE	DOSING
DEFORM	DENUDE	DEWLAP	DINNER	DODGED	DOSSAL
DEFRAY	DENVER	DEWORM	DIOXAN	DODGEM	DOSSED
DEFTLY	DEODAR	DEXTER	DIOXIN	DODGER	DOSSER
DEFUSE	DEPART	DHARUK	DIPLEX	DODGES	DOTAGE
DEGAGE	DEPEND	DHOTIS	DIPLOE	DODOES	DOTARD
DEGREE	DEPICT	DIACID	DIPODY	DODOMA	DOTING
DEHORN	DEPLOY	DIADEM	DIPOLE	DO DUTY	DOTTED
DE-ICED	DEPORT	DIALED	DIPPED	DOFFED	DOTTER
DE-ICER	DEPOSE	DIAPER	DIPPER	DOFFER	DOTTLE
DEIFIC	DEPOTS	DIAPIR	DIRECT	DOG-EAR	DOUALA
DEISTS	DEPTHS	DIARCH	DIREST	DOGGED	DOUBLE
DEIXIS	DEPUTE	DIATOM	DIRGES	DOGGER	DOUBLY
DEJA VU	DEPUTY	DIBBED	DIRHAM	DOGIES	DOUBTS
DEJECT	DERAIL	DIBBER	DIRNDL	DOGLEG	DOUCHE
DE JURE	DERIDE	DIBBLE	DISARM	DOGMAS	DOUGHY
DELAYS	DERIVE	DICIER	DISBAR	DOG TAG	DOURLY
DELETE	DERMAL	DICING	DISBUD	DOINGS	DOUSED
DELIAN	DERMIC	DICKER	DISCOS	DOLINE	DOUSER
DELICT	DERMIS	DICTUM	DISCUS	DOLING	DOVISH

DOWNED	DRONES	DUPERY	ECLAIR	ELIDED	ENLACE
DOWNER	DRONGO	DUPING	ECTYPE	ELIXIR	ENLIST
DOWSED	DROOPY	DUPLET	ECURIE	ELOPED	ENMESH
DOWSER	DROPSY	DUPLEX	ECZEMA	ELOPER	ENMITY
DOYENS	DROSSY	DURBAN	EDDIED	EL PASO	ENNAGE
DOYLEY	DROVER	DURBAR	EDDIES	ELUDED	ENNEAD
DOZENS	DROVES	DURESS	EDGIER	ELUDER	ENOSIS
DOZIER	DROWSE	DURHAM	EDGILY	ELYSEE	ENOUGH
DOZILY	DROWSY	DURIAN	EDGING	EMBALM	ENRAGE
DOZING	DRUDGE	DURING	EDIBLE	EMBANK	ENRICH
DRABLY	DRUIDS	DUSTED	EDICTS	EMBARK	ENROBE
DRACHM	DRUNKS	DUSTER	EDIRNE	EMBERS	ENROOT
DRAFFY	DRYADS	DUSTUP	EDITED	EMBLEM	ENSIGN
DRAFTS	DRYERS	DUTIES	EDITOR	EMBODY	ENSILE
DRAFTY	DRY ICE	DUVETS	EDWARD	EMBOLY	ENSOUL
DRAGEE	DRYING	DWARFS	EERILY	EMBOSS	ENSUED
DRAGGY	DRY ROT	DYABLE	EFFACE	EMBRYO	ENSURE
DRAGON	DUBBED	DYADIC	EFFECT	EMERGE	ENTAIL
DRAINS	DUBBIN	DYEING	EFFETE	EMESIS	ENTICE
DRAKES	DUBLIN	DYNAMO	EFFIGY	EMETIC	ENTIRE
DRAMAS	DUCATS	DYNAST	EFFING	EMIGRE	ENTITY
DRAPED	DUCKED	DYNODE	EFFLUX	EMOTER	ENTOMB
DRAPER	DUCKER		EFFORT	EMPALE	ENTRAP
DRAPES	DUDEEN	**E**	EFFUSE	EMPIRE	ENTREE
DRAWEE	DUDLEY	EAGLES	EFTPOS	EMPLOY	ENVIED
DRAWER	DUELED	EAGLET	EGESTA	ENABLE	ENVIER
DRAWLS	DUELLO	EALING	EGGCUP	ENAMEL	ENVIES
DRAWLY	DUENNA	EARFUL	EGGNOG	ENATIC	ENVOYS
DREADS	DUFFEL	EARING	EGOISM	EN BLOC	ENWIND
DREAMS	DUFFER	EARNED	EGOIST	ENCAGE	ENWOMB
DREAMT	DUGONG	EARNER	EGRESS	ENCAMP	ENWRAP
DREAMY	DUGOUT	EARTHS	EGRETS	ENCASE	ENZYME
DREARY	DUIKER	EARTHY	EIGHTH	ENCASH	EOCENE
DREDGE	DULCET	EARWAX	EIGHTS	ENCODE	EOGENE
DREGGY	DULLED	EARWIG	EIGHTY	ENCORE	EOLITH
DRENCH	DULLER	EASELS	EITHER	ENCYST	EONISM
DRESSY	DULUTH	EASIER	EJECTA	ENDEAR	EOZOIC
DRIERS	DUMBER	EASILY	ELANDS	ENDING	EPARCH
DRIEST	DUMBLY	EASING	ELAPID	ENDIVE	EPIRUS
DRIFTS	DUMDUM	EASTER	ELAPSE	ENDUED	EPONYM
DRIFTY	DUMPED	EATERS	ELATED	ENDURE	EPOPEE
DRILLS	DUMPER	EATING	ELATER	ENEMAS	EPPING
DRINKS	DUNBAR	EBBING	ELBOWS	ENERGY	EQUALS
DRIPPY	DUNCES	ECARTE	ELDERS	ENFACE	EQUATE
DRIVEL	DUNDEE	ECESIS	ELDEST	ENFOLD	EQUINE
DRIVEN	DUNITE	ECHARD	ELEGIT	ENGAGE	EQUITY
DRIVER	DUNKED	ECHOED	ELEVEN	ENGINE	ERASED
DRIVES	DUNKER	ECHOES	ELEVON	ENGRAM	ERASER
DROGUE	DUNLIN	ECHOEY	ELFISH	ENGULF	ERBIUM
DROLLY	DUNNED	ECHOIC	EL GIZA	ENIGMA	ERFURT
DRONED	DUNNER	ECKERT	ELICIT	ENJOIN	ERLANG

ERMINE	EVOLVE	FABLES	FARMED	FENCED	FIJIAN
ERODED	EVZONE	FABRIC	FARMER	FENCER	FILETS
EROTIC	EXAMEN	FACADE	FAR-OFF	FENCES	FILIAL
ERRAND	EXARCH	FACETS	FAR-OUT	FENDED	FILING
ERRANT	EXCEED	FACIAL	FARROW	FENDER	FILLED
ERRATA	EXCEPT	FACIES	FARTED	FENIAN	FILLER
ERRING	EXCESS	FACILE	FASCIA	FENNEC	FILLET
ERRORS	EXCISE	FACING	FASTED	FENNEL	FILL-IN
ERSATZ	EXCITE	FACTOR	FASTEN	FENTON	FILLIP
ERYNGO	EXCUSE	FACULA	FASTER	FERBAM	FILMED
ESCAPE	EXEDRA	FADE-IN	FAT CAT	FERIAL	FILMIC
ESCARP	EXEMPT	FADING	FATHER	FERMAT	FILOSE
ESCHAR	EXETER	FAECAL	FATHOM	FERRET	FILTER
ESCHEW	EXEUNT	FAECES	FATTEN	FERRIC	FILTHY
ESCORT	EXHALE	FAENZA	FATTER	FERULA	FIMBLE
ESCROW	EXHORT	FAERIE	FAUCAL	FERULE	FINALE
ESCUDO	EXHUME	FAG END	FAUCES	FERVID	FINALS
ESKIMO	EXILED	FAGGED	FAUCET	FESCUE	FINDER
ESPIAL	EXILES	FAGGOT	FAULTS	FESTAL	FINELY
ESPIED	EXILIC	FAILED	FAULTY	FESTER	FINERY
ESPIER	EXITED	FAILLE	FAUNAL	FETIAL	FINEST
ESPRIT	EXODUS	FAINTS	FAUNAS	FETING	FINGAL
ESSAYS	EXONYM	FAIRER	FAVOUR	FETISH	FINGER
ESTATE	EXOTIC	FAIRLY	FAWNED	FETTER	FINIAL
ESTEEM	EXPAND	FAITHS	FAWNER	FETTLE	FINING
ESTRAY	EXPECT	FAJITA	FAXING	FEUDAL	FINISH
ETALON	EXPEND	FAKERS	FAZING	FEUDED	FINITE
ETCHED	EXPERT	FAKING	FEALTY	FEZZAN	FINNED
ETCHER	EXPIRE	FAKIRS	FEARED	FEZZED	FINNIC
ETHANE	EXPIRY	FALCON	FEARER	FEZZES	FIORDS
ETHENE	EXPORT	FALLAL	FEASTS	FIACRE	FIORIN
ETHICS	EXPOSE	FALLEN	FECULA	FIANCE	FIPPLE
ETHNIC	EXSERT	FALLER	FECUND	FIASCO	FIRING
ETHYNE	EXTANT	FALLOW	FEDORA	FIBBED	FIRKIN
ETYMON	EXTEND	FALSER	FEEBLE	FIBBER	FIRMED
EUBOEA	EXTENT	FALTER	FEEBLY	FIBRED	FIRMER
EUCHRE	EXTERN	FAMILY	FEEDER	FIBRES	FIRMLY
EULOGY	EXTINE	FAMINE	FEELER	FIBRIL	FIRSTS
EUNUCH	EXTORT	FAMISH	FEIJOA	FIBRIN	FIRTHS
EUREKA	EXTRAS	FAMOUS	FEINTS	FIBULA	FISCAL
EURO MP	EXUDED	FANDOM	FEISTY	FICKLE	FISHED
EUROPE	EYEFUL	FANGED	FELINE	FIDDLE	FISHER
EVADED	EYEING	FANGIO	FELLED	FIDDLY	FISHES
EVADER	EYELET	FANION	FELLER	FIDGET	FISTIC
EVENLY	EYELID	FANJET	FELLOE	FIELDS	FITFUL
EVENTS	EYRIES	FANNED	FELLOW	FIENDS	FITTED
EVILER		FANNER	FELONS	FIERCE	FITTER
EVILLY	**F**	FAN-TAN	FELONY	FIESTA	FIVERS
EVINCE	FABIAN	FARCES	FEMALE	FIFTHS	FIXATE
EVOKED	FABLED	FARINA	FEMORA	FIGHTS	FIXERS
EVOKER	FABLER	FARING	FEMURS	FIGURE	FIXING

FIXITY	FLIRTS	FOLIOS	FOULLY	FROCKS	FUNKER
FIZGIG	FLITCH	FOLIUM	FOUL-UP	FROGGY	FUNNEL
FIZZED	FLOATS	FOLKIE	FOUNTS	FROLIC	FUN RUN
FIZZER	FLOATY	FOLKSY	FOURTH	FRONDS	FURFUR
FIZZLE	FLOCKS	FOLLOW	FOVEAL	FRONTS	FURIES
FJORDS	FLOCKY	FOLSOM	FOWLER	FROSTS	FURLED
FLABBY	FLOODS	FOMENT	FOWLES	FROSTY	FURLER
FLACON	FLOORS	FONDER	FOXIER	FROTHS	FURORE
FLAGGY	FLOOZY	FONDLE	FOXILY	FROTHY	FURRED
FLAGON	FLOPPY	FONDLY	FOXING	FROWNS	FURROW
FLAILS	FLORAL	FONDUE	FOYERS	FROWZY	FUSAIN
FLAKED	FLORET	FONTAL	FRACAS	FROZEN	FUSHUN
FLAKER	FLORID	FOODIE	FRAMED	FRUGAL	FUSILE
FLAKES	FLORIN	FOOLED	FRAMER	FRUITS	FUSING
FLAMBE	FLOSSY	FOOTER	FRAMES	FRUITY	FUSION
FLAMED	FLOURY	FOOTLE	FRANCE	FRUMPS	FUSSED
FLAMER	FLOWED	FOOZLE	FRANCS	FRUMPY	FUSSER
FLAMES	FLOWER	FORAGE	FRAPPE	FRUNZE	FUSSES
FLANGE	FLUENT	FORAYS	FRATER	FRYERS	FUSTIC
FLANKS	FLUFFY	FORBAD	FRAUDS	FRYING	FUTILE
FLARED	FLUIDS	FORBID	FRAUEN	FRY-UPS	FUTONS
FLARES	FLUKES	FORCED	FRAYED	FU-CHOU	FUTURE
FLASHY	FLUKEY	FORCER	FRAZIL	FUCKED	FUZHOU
FLASKS	FLUNKY	FORCES	FREAKS	FUCKER	FUZZED
FLATLY	FLURRY	FORDED	FREAKY	FUCK-UP	
FLATUS	FLUTED	FOREGO	FREELY	FUCOID	**G**
FLAUNT	FLUTER	FOREST	FREEST	FUDDLE	GABBED
FLAVIN	FLUTES	FORFAR	FREEZE	FUDGED	GABBER
FLAWED	FLYBYS	FORGED	FRENCH	FUELED	GABBLE
FLAXEN	FLYERS	FORGER	FRENZY	FUGARD	GABBRO
FLAYED	FLYING	FORGES	FRESCO	FUGATO	GABION
FLAYER	FLYSCH	FORGET	FRESNO	FUGING	GABLED
FLECHE	FOALED	FORGOT	FRIARS	FUGUES	GABLES
FLECKS	FOAMED	FORKED	FRIARY	FUHRER	GADDED
FLEDGE	FOBBED	FORMAL	FRIDAY	FUJIAN	GADDER
FLEECE	FO'C'SLE	FORMAN	FRIDGE	FUKIEN	GADFLY
FLEECY	FODDER	FORMAT	FRIEND	FULANI	GADGET
FLEETS	FOETAL	FORMED	FRIERS	FULCRA	GADOID
FLENSE	FOCTID	FORMER	FRIEZE	FULFIL	GAFLIC
FLESHY	FOETOR	FORMIC	FRIGHT	FULLER	GAFFER
FLETCH	FOETUS	FORMYL	FRIGID	FULL-ON	GAFFES
FLEXED	FOGBOW	FORNIX	FRIJOL	FULMAR	GAGGED
FLEXES	FOGDOG	FORTES	FRILLS	FUMBLE	GAGGER
FLEXOR	FOGGED	FORTIS	FRILLY	FUMING	GAGGLE
FLICKS	FOGGIA	FORUMS	FRINGE	FUNDED	GAGING
FLIERS	FOGIES	FOSHAN	FRINGY	FUNDIC	GAIETY
FLIGHT	FOIBLE	FOSSIL	FRISKS	FUNDUS	GAIJIN
FLIMSY	FOILED	FOSTER	FRISKY	FUNGAL	GAINED
FLINCH	FOLDED	FOUGHT	FRIULI	FUNGIC	GAINER
FLINTS	FOLDER	FOULED	FRIVOL	FUNGUS	GAINLY
FLINTY	FOLIAR	FOULER	FRIZZY	FUNKED	GAITER

GALATA	GARRET	GENIES	GLACIS	GOBBLE	GRAECO-
GALATI	GARTER	GENIUS	GLADES	GOBIAN	GRAFTS
GALAXY	GASBAG	GENOME	GLADLY	GOBLET	GRAINS
GALENA	GASCON	GENRES	GLAIRY	GOBLIN	GRAINY
GALERE	GASHED	GENTLE	GLANCE	GODARD	GRAMME
GALIBI	GASHES	GENTLY	GLANDS	GODSON	GRANDS
GALIOT	GASIFY	GENTRY	GLARED	GODWIT	GRANGE
GALLED	GASKET	GEODIC	GLARES	GOFERS	GRANNY
GALLEY	GASKIN	GERBIL	GLARUS	GOFFER	GRANTS
GALLIC	GASMAN	GERMAN	GLASSY	GOGGLE	GRAPES
GALLON	GASMEN	GERMEN	GLAZED	GOITRE	GRAPHS
GALLOP	GASPED	GERUND	GLAZER	GO-KART	GRASSY
GALORE	GASPER	GETTER	GLAZES	GOLDEN	GRATED
GALOSH	GASSED	GETUPS	GLEAMS	GOLFER	GRATER
GALWAY	GASSER	GEYSER	GLEBES	GOLLOP	GRATES
GALYAK	GASSES	GEZIRA	GLEETY	GOMUTI	GRATIS
GAMBIA	GATEAU	GHETTO	GLIBLY	GONADS	GRAVEL
GAMBIT	GATHER	GHIBLI	GLIDED	GONDAR	GRAVEN
GAMBLE	GAUCHE	GHOSTS	GLIDER	GONERS	GRAVER
GAMBOL	GAUCHO	GHOULS	GLIDES	GONION	GRAVES
GAMELY	GAUGED	GHYLLS	GLINTS	GOODLY	GRAVID
GAMETE	GAUGER	GIANTS	GLIOMA	GOOFED	GRAYED
GAMIER	GAUGES	GIAOUR	GLITCH	GOOGLY	GRAYER
GAMINE	GAVAGE	GIBBED	GLITZY	GOOGOL	GRAZED
GAMING	GAVELS	GIBBER	GLOATS	GOOIER	GRAZER
GAMMAS	GAVIAL	GIBBET	GLOBAL	GOPHER	GRAZES
GAMMED	GAWKED	GIBBON	GLOBES	GORGED	GREASE
GAMMON	GAWKER	GIBE AT	GLOBIN	GORGER	GREASY
GANDER	GAWPED	GIBEON	GLOOMY	GORGES	GREATS
GANGED	GAYEST	GIBSON	GLORIA	GORGON	GREBES
GANGER	GAZEBO	GIDDAY	GLOSSA	GORICA	GREECE
GANGES	GAZING	GIFTED	GLOSSY	GORIER	GREEDY
GANGUE	GAZUMP	GIGGLE	GLOVED	GORILY	GREENS
GANNET	GDANSK	GIGGLY	GLOVER	GORING	GREYED
GANOID	GDYNIA	GIGOLO	GLOVES	GO-SLOW	GREYER
GANTRY	GEARED	GILDED	GLOWED	GOSPEL	GRIEVE
GAOLED	GECKOS	GILDER	GLOWER	GOSSIP	GRIFFE
GAOLER	GEDACT	GILLED	GLUING	GOTHIC	GRIGRI
GAPING	GEE-GEE	GILLIE	GLUMLY	GOUGED	GRILLE
GAPPED	GEEZER	GIMLET	GLUTEN	GOUGER	GRILLS
GARAGE	GEISHA	GIMMAL	GLYCOL	GOUGES	GRILSE
GARBED	GELADA	GINGER	GNAWED	GOURDS	GRIMLY
GARBLE	GELDED	GINKGO	GNAWER	GOVERN	GRINDS
GARCON	GELDOF	GIRDED	GNEISS	GRABEN	GRINGO
GARDEN	GELLED	GIRDER	GNOMES	GRACED	GRIPED
GARGET	GEMINI	GIRDLE	GNOMIC	GRACES	GRIPER
GARGLE	GEMMED	GIRLIE	GNOMON	GRADED	GRIPES
GARISH	GENDER	GIRTHS	GNOSIS	GRADER	GRISLY
GARLIC	GENERA	GIUSTO	GOADED	GRADES	GRISON
GARNER	GENEVA	GIVE IN	GOATEE	GRADIN	GRISTS
GARNET	GENIAL	GIVING	GOBBET	GRADUS	GRITTY

GRIVET	GUITAR	HAEMAL	HANKER	HATRED	HEBRON
GROANS	GULDEN	HAEMIC	HANKIE	HATTER	HECATE
GROATS	GULLAH	HAEMIN	HANKOW	HAULED	HECKLE
GROCER	GULLED	HAERES	HANNAH	HAULER	HECTIC
GRODNO	GULLET	HAFTER	HANSEL	HAUNCH	HECTOR
GROGGY	GULLEY	HAGBUT	HANSEN	HAUNTS	HECUBA
GROINS	GULPED	HAGGAI	HANSOM	HAVANA	HEDDLE
GROOMS	GULPER	HAGGIS	HAPPEN	HAVANT	HEDGED
GROOVE	GUMBOS	HAGGLE	HAPTEN	HAVENS	HEDGER
GROOVY	GUMMED	HAIDAN	HAPTIC	HAVEN'T	HEDGES
GROPED	GUNDOG	HAIDUK	HARALD	HAVING	HEDJAZ
GROPER	GUNG-HO	HAILED	HARARE	HAWAII	HEEDED
GROPES	GUNMAN	HAILER	HARASS	HAWHAW	HEEDER
GROTTO	GUNMEN	HAINAN	HARBIN	HAWICK	HEE-HAW
GROTTY	GUNNED	HAIRDO	HARD BY	HAWKED	HEELED
GROUCH	GUNNEL	HAIRIF	HARDEN	HAWKER	HEELER
GROUND	GUNNER	HAJJES	HARDER	HAWSER	HEENAN
GROUPS	GUNSHY	HAJJIS	HARDIE	HAYBOX	HEFTER
GROUSE	GUNTUR	HAKIMS	HARDLY	HAYMOW	HEGIRA
GROUTS	GUNYAH	HALEST	HARD-ON	HAZARD	HEIDUC
GROVEL	GURGLE	HALIDE	HARD UP	HAZELS	HEIFER
GROVFS	GURJUN	HALITE	HAREEM	HAZIER	HEIGHT
GROWER	GURKHA	HALLAH	HAREMS	HAZILY	HEJIRA
GROWLS	GUSHED	HALLEL	HARING	HAZING	HEKATE
GROWTH	GUSHER	HALLEY	HARKED	H-BOMBS	HELENA
GROYNE	GUSSET	HALLOO	HARKEN	HEADED	HELIOS
GROZNY	GUSTED	HALLOS	HARLEM	HEADER	HELIUM
GRUBBY	GUTTED	HALLOW	HARLEY	HEAD-ON	HELLAS
GRUDGE	GUTTER	HALLUX	HARLOT	HEALED	HELLEN
GRUGRU	GUVNOR	HALOES	HARLOW	HEALER	HELLER
GRUMPY	GUYANA	HALOID	HARMED	HEALEY	HELLES
GRUNGE	GUYING	HALTED	HARMER	HEALTH	HELLOS
GRUNGY	GUZZLE	HALTER	HARNEY	HEANEY	HELMET
GRUNTS	GYPPED	HALTON	HAROLD	HEAPED	HELPED
GUARDS	GYPSUM	HALVAH	HARPED	HEAPER	HELPER
GUAVAS	GYRATE	HALVED	HARPER	HEARER	HELVES
GUELPH	GYROSE	HALVES	HARRAR	HEARSE	HEMMED
GUENON		HAMATE	HARRIS	HEARST	HEMMER
GUESTS	**H**	HAMELN	HARROW	HEARTH	HEMPEN
GUFFAW	HAAKON	HAMITE	HARTAL	HEARTS	HENBIT
GUIANA	HABANA	HAMLET	HARVEY	HEARTY	HENDRY
GUIDED	HABILE	HAMLYN	HASHED	HEATED	HENLEY
GUIDER	HABITS	HAMMED	HASHES	HEATER	HEPCAT
GUIDES	HACKED	HAMMER	HASLET	HEATHS	HEPTAD
GUIDON	HACKER	HAMPER	HASSAN	HEATHY	HERALD
GUILDS	HACKLE	HANDED	HASSLE	HEAUME	HERBAL
GUILIN	HADEAN	HANDEL	HASTEN	HEAVED	HERDED
GUILTY	HADITH	HANDLE	HATBOX	HEAVEN	HERDER
GUIMPE	HADJES	HANGAR	HATHOR	HEAVER	HERDIC
GUINEA	HADJIS	HANGER	HATING	HEAVES	HEREAT
GUISES	HADRON	HANG-UP	HATPIN	HEBREW	HEREBY

HEREIN	HINGER	HOLISM	HORSEY	HULLER	HYPHEN
HEREOF	HINGES	HOLLER	HOSIER	HULLOS	HYPING
HEREON	HINTED	HOLLOW	HOSING	HUMANE	
HERERO	HINTER	HOLMES	HOSTED	HUMANS	**I**
HERESY	HIPPED	HOLMIC	HOSTEL	HUMBER	IAMBIC
HERETO	HIPPER	HOLPEN	HOSTIE	HUMBLE	IAMBUS
HERIOT	HIPPIE	HOMAGE	HOT AIR	HUMBLY	IBADAN
HERMES	HIRING	HOMBRE	HOTBED	HUMBUG	IBAGUE
HERMIT	HISPID	HOMELY	HOT DOG	HUMISM	IBERIA
HERMON	HISSED	HOMIER	HOTELS	HUMMED	IBEXES
HERNIA	HISSER	HOMILY	HOTIEN	HUMMEL	IBIBIO
HEROES	HISSES	HOMING	HOT KEY	HUMMER	IBISES
HEROIC	HI-TECH	HOMINY	HOTPOT	HUMMUS	ICE AGE
HEROIN	HITHER	HONEST	HOT ROD	HUMOUR	ICEBOX
HERONS	HITLER	HONIED	HOTTER	HUMPED	ICE CAP
HERPES	HIT MAN	HONING	HOTTIE	HUMPTY	ICEMAN
HERREN	HIT MEN	HONKED	HOUDAN	HUNGER	ICEMEN
HERZOG	HITTER	HONKER	HOUNDS	HUNGRY	ICHANG
HESIOD	HIVING	HONOUR	HOURIS	HUNKER	I CHING
HESTIA	HOARDS	HONSHU	HOURLY	HUNTED	ICICLE
HETMAN	HOARSE	HOODED	HOUSED	HUNTER	ICIEST
HEWERS	HOAXED	HOODOO	HOUSEL	HUPPAH	ICONIC
HEWING	HOAXER	HOOFED	HOUSES	HURDLE	ID CARD
HEXANE	HOAXES	HOOKAH	HOVELS	HURLED	IDEALS
HEXING	HOBART	HOOKED	HOWARD	HURLER	IDEATE
HEXONE	HOBBES	HOOKER	HOWDAH	HURLEY	IDIOCY
HEXOSE	HOBBLE	HOOKUP	HOWE'ER	HURRAH	IDIOMS
HEYDAY	HOBNOB	HOOPED	HOWLED	HURRAY	IDIOTS
HIATAL	HOBOES	HOOPER	HOWLER	HURTER	IDLEST
HIATUS	HOCKED	HOOP-LA	HOWLET	HURTLE	IDLING
HICCUP	HOCKER	HOOPOE	HOWRAH	HUSAIN	IDYLLS
HICKEY	HOCKEY	HOORAH	HOYDEN	HUSHED	IGLOOS
HICKOK	HODDEN	HOORAY	HSIANG	HUSH-UP	IGNITE
HIDDEN	HODDIN	HOOTED	HUAMBO	HUSKER	IGNORE
HIDING	HODMAN	HOOTER	HUBBLE	HUSSAR	IGUACU
HIEING	HOEING	HOOVER	HUBBUB	HUSTLE	IGUANA
HIEMAL	HOGGED	HOOVES	HUBCAP	HUSTON	ILESHA
HIGGLE	HOGGER	HOPING	HUBRIS	HUXLEY	ILEXES
HIGHER	HOGGET	HOPPED	HUCKLE	HUZZAH	ILIGAN
HIGHLY	HOGNUT	HOPPER	HUDDLE	HYADES	ILKLEY
HIJACK	HOGTIE	HOPPLE	HUDSON	HYAENA	ILL-USE
HIKERS	HOHHOT	HOPPUS	HUELVA	HYALIN	ILOILO
HIKING	HOICKS	HORACE	HUESCA	HYBRID	ILORIN
HILARY	HOIDEN	HORARY	HUFFED	HYBRIS	IMAGES
HILLEL	HOISTS	HORDES	HUGELY	HYDRAS	IMBIBE
HILLER	HOLDEN	HORMIC	HUGEST	HYDRIA	IMBRUE
HIMEJI	HOLDER	HORMUZ	HUGGED	HYDRIC	IMBUED
HINDER	HOLDUP	HORNED	HUGGER	HYENAS	IMIDIC
HINDOO	HOLD UP	HORNET	HUGHES	HYMENS	IMMUNE
HINDUS	HOLIER	HORRID	HUGHIE	HYMNAL	IMMURE
HINGED	HOLILY	HORROR	HULLED	HYMNED	IMPACT

IMPAIR	INFUSE	INTROS	ITCHED	JETSAM	JOULES
IMPALA	INGEST	INTUIT	ITCHES	JET SET	JOUNCE
IMPALE	INGOTS	INUITS	ITHACA	JETTED	JOURNO
IMPART	INHALE	INULIN	ITSELF	JETTON	JOVIAL
IMPEDE	INHAUL	INURED		JEWELS	JOYFUL
IMPEND	INHERE	INVADE	**J**	JEWESS	JOYING
IMPHAL	INHUME	INVENT	JABBED	JEWISH	JOYOUS
IMPISH	INJECT	INVERT	JABBER	JHANSI	JUDAEA
IMPORT	INJURE	INVEST	JABIRU	JIBBED	JUDAIC
IMPOSE	INJURY	INVITE	JACANA	JIBBER	JUDDER
IMPOST	INK-CAP	INVOKE	JACKAL	JIBING	JUDGED
IMPROV	INKIER	INWARD	JACKED	JIGAWA	JUDGER
IMPUGN	INKING	IODATE	JACKET	JIGGED	JUDGES
IMPURE	INKPAD	IODIDE	JACKIE	JIGGER	JUDOGI
IMPUTE	INLAID	IODINE	JAFFNA	JIGGLE	JUDOKA
INARCH	INLAND	IODISM	JAGGED	JIGGLY	JUGATE
INBORN	IN-LAWS	IODIZE	JAGUAR	JIGSAW	JUGGED
INBRED	INLAYS	IODOUS	JAILED	JIHADS	JUGGLE
INCEPT	INLETS	IONIAN	JAILER	JILTED	JUICED
INCEST	INLIER	IONIZE	JAIPUR	JILTER	JUICES
INCHED	INMATE	IPECAC	JALAPA	JINGLE	JUJUBE
INCHES	INMOST	IREFUL	JALOPY	JINGLY	JULEPS
INCHON	INNATE	IRENIC	JAMMED	JINXED	JULIES
INCISE	INNING	IRIDIC	JAMMER	JINXES	JUMBLE
INCITE	INNUIT	IRISES	JANGLE	JITTER	JUMP AT
INCOME	INROAD	IRITIC	JAPERY	JIVING	JUMPED
INCUBI	INRUSH	IRITIS	JAPURA	JOBBED	JUMPER
INCUSE	INSANE	IRKING	JARGON	JOBBER	JUNEAU
INDEED	INSECT	IRONED	JARRAH	JOBBIE	JUNGLE
INDENE	INSERT	IRONER	JARRED	JOB LOT	JUNGLY
INDENT	INSETS	IRONIC	JARROW	JOCKEY	JUNIOR
INDIAN	INSIDE	IRRUPT	JASPER	JOCOSE	JUNKED
INDICT	INSIST	IRTYSH	JAUNTS	JOCUND	JUNKET
INDIGO	IN SITU	IRVINE	JAUNTY	JOGGED	JUNKIE
INDITE	INSOLE	ISATIN	JAWARA	JOGGER	JUNTAS
INDIUM	INSTAR	ISCHIA	JAWING	JOGGLE	JURIED
INDOLE	INSTEP	ISLAND	JAZZED	JOHNNY	JURIES
INDOOR	INSTIL	ISLETS	JEERED	JOHORE	JURIST
INDORE	INSULA	ISOBAR	JEERER	JOINED	JURORS
INDRIS	INSULT	ISOGON	JEJUNE	JOINER	JUSTLY
INDUCE	INSURE	ISOHEL	JELLED	JOINTS	JUTTED
INDUCT	INTACT	ISOLEX	JENNET	JOISTS	JUTTER
INDULT	INTAKE	ISOMER	JERBOA	JOKERS	
INFAMY	INTEND	ISOPOD	JERKED	JOKING	**K**
INFANT	INTENT	ISRAEL	JERKER	JOLTED	KABILA
INFECT	INTERN	INTIMA	JERKIN	JORDAN	KABYLE
INFEST	INTIMA	ISSUED	JERSEY	JOSHED	KADUNA
INFIRM	INTINE	ISSUER	JESTED	JOSHES	KAFFIR
INFLOW	INTONE	ISSUES	JESTER	JOSTLE	KAFTAN
INFLUX	IN TOTO	ISTRIA	JESUIT	JOTTED	KAISER
INFORM	IN TRIM	ITALIC	JET LAG	JOTTER	KAIZEN

49

KAKAPO	KEYING	KNIVES	LACKED	LAPPER	LATVIA
KALISZ	KEYWAY	KNOCKS	LACKEY	LAPPET	LAUDED
KALMAR	KHALIF	KNOLLS	LACTAM	LAPSED	LAUDER
KALMIA	KHULNA	KNOTTY	LACTIC	LAPSER	LAUGHS
KALONG	KHYBER	KNOWER	LACUNA	LAPSES	LAUNCH
KALUGA	KIBOSH	KOALAS	LADDER	LAPSUS	LAUREL
KAMALA	KICKED	KODIAK	LADDIE	LAPTOP	LAVABO
KANARA	KICKER	KOHIMA	LA-DI-DA	LAP-TOP	LAVAGE
KANBAN	KICK IN	KOKAND	LADIES	LARDED	LAVISH
KANGAS	KIDDED	KOLYMA	LADING	LARDER	LAWFUL
KANPUR	KIDDER	KOPECK	LADINO	LARDON	LAWYER
KANSAS	KIDDIE	KOPPIE	LADLED	LAREDO	LAXITY
KAOLIN	KIDNAP	KOREAN	LADLER	LARGER	LAY-BYS
KARATE	KIDNEY	KORUNA	LADLES	LARGOS	LAYERS
KARATS	KIELCE	KOSHER	LADOGA	LARIAM	LAYING
KARIBA	KIGALI	KOSICE	LAGENA	LARIAT	LAYMAN
KARMIC	KIKUYU	KOVROV	LAGERS	LARINE	LAYMEN
KARPOV	KILLED	KOWTOW	LAGGED	LARISA	LAY-OFF
KASBAH	KILLER	KRAALS	LAGOON	LARKED	LAY OUT
KASSEL	KILTED	KRISES	LAHORE	LARKER	LAYOUT
KAUNAS	KILTER	KRONER	LAICAL	LARNAX	LAZIER
KAYAKS	KIMONO	KRONOR	LAID UP	LARVAE	LAZILY
KAZAKH	KINASE	KRUGER	LAIRDS	LARVAL	LAZING
KEBABS	KINDER	KUKRIS	LALANG	LARYNX	LEADEN
KEDIRI	KINDLE	KUMASI	LAMBDA	LASCAR	LEADER
KEEGAN	KINDLY	KUMISS	LAMBED	LASERS	LEAD-IN
KEELED	KINGLY	KUMMEL	LAMELY	LASHED	LEAGUE
KEENED	KIOSKS	KUNG FU	LAMENT	LASHER	LEAKED
KEENER	KIPPED	KUNLUN	LAMEST	LASHES	LEAKER
KEENLY	KIPPER	KUOPIO	LAMINA	LASHIO	LEANED
KEEPER	KIRKBY	KURGAN	LAMING	LASH-UP	LEANER
KEEP ON	KIRKUK	KUWAIT	LAMMAS	LASKET	LEAN TO
KELLER	KIRMAN	KWACHA	LAMPAS	LASSES	LEAN-TO
KELOID	KIRSCH	KWANZA	LANATE	LASSOS	LEAPED
KELPIE	KIRUNA	KYRGYZ	LANCED	LASTED	LEAPER
KELTIC	KISMET	KYUSHU	LANCER	LASTER	LEARNT
KELVIN	KISSED		LANCES	LASTLY	LEASED
KENDAL	KISSER	**L**	LANCET	LATEEN	LEASER
KENNED	KISSES		LANDAU	LATELY	LEASES
KENNEL	KISUMU	LAAGER	LANDED	LATENT	LEAVED
KENYAN	KIT BAG	LABELS	LANDES	LATEST	LEAVEN
KERALA	KITSCH	LABIAL	LANGER	LATHER	LEAVER
KERMAN	KITTED	LABILE	LANGUE	LATHES	LEAVES
KERMES	KITTEN	LABIUM	LANGUR	LATINA	LECHER
KERNEL	KLAXON	LABLAB	LANKER	LATINO	LECTIN
KERSEY	KNAVES	LABOUR	LANKLY	LATINS	LECTOR
KETENE	KNAWEL	LABRET	LANNER	LATISH	LEDGER
KETONE	KNELLS	LABRUM	LANUGO	LATIUM	LEDGES
KETOSE	KNIFED	LACHES	LAPDOG	LATRIA	LEERED
KETTLE	KNIFER	LACIER	LAPELS	LATTEN	LEEWAY
KEVLAR	KNIGHT	LACING	LAPPED	LATTER	LEGACY

LEGATE	LIBIDO	LINKED	LOCHIA	LOPPER	LUNGER
LEGATO	LIBRAN	LINKUP	LOCKED	LOQUAT	LUNGES
LEGEND	LIBYAN	LINNET	LOCKER	LORDED	LUNULA
LEGERS	LICHEN	LINTEL	LOCKET	LORDLY	LUPINE
LEGGED	LICKED	LINTER	LOCKUP	LORICA	LUPINS
LEGION	LICKER	LIPASE	LOCULE	LOSERS	LURING
LEGIST	LIDDED	LI PENG	LOCUMS	LOSING	LURKED
LEGUAN	LIEGES	LIPIDS	LOCUST	LOSSES	LURKER
LEGUME	LIE-INS	LIPOID	LODGED	LOTION	LUSAKA
LEIDEN	LIENAL	LIPOMA	LODGER	LOTTED	LUSHES
LEKKER	LIERNE	LIQUID	LODGES	LOUDEN	LU-SHUN
LE MANS	LIFERS	LIQUOR	LOFTED	LOUDER	LUSTED
LEMNOS	LIFFEY	LISBON	LOFTER	LOUDLY	LUSTRE
LEMONS	LIFTED	LISPED	LOGGED	LOUGHS	LUTEAL
LEMONY	LIFTER	LISPER	LOGGER	LOUISE	LUVVIE
LEMURS	LIGAND	LISSOM	LOGGIA	LOUNGE	LUXATE
LENDER	LIGATE	LISTED	LOGIER	LOURED	LUXURY
LENGTH	LIGHTS	LISTEN	LOGION	LOURIE	LYCEES
LENITY	LIGNIN	LITANY	LOGJAM	LOUSED	LYCEUM
LENSES	LIGULA	LITCHI	LOGLOG	LOUVAR	LYCHEE
LENTEN	LIGULE	LITERS	LOG OUT	LOUVRE	LYNXES
LENTIC	LIKASI	LITHIA	LOIRET	LOVAGE	LYRATE
LENTIL	LIKELY	LITHIC	LOITER	LOVELY	LYRICS
LEOBEN	LIKING	LITMUS	LOLLED	LOVERS	LYRIST
LEONID	LILACS	LITRES	LOLLER	LOVEYS	LYSINE
LEPERS	LILIES	LITTER	LOLLOP	LOVING	
LEPTON	LILLEE	LITTLE	LOMBOK	LOWEST	**M**
LESBOS	LIMBER	LIVE-IN	LOMENT	LOWING	MACACO
LESION	LIMBIC	LIVELY	LONDON	LOW-KEY	MACAWS
LESSEE	LIMBOS	LIVENS	LONELY	LOYANG	MACEIO
LESSEN	LIMBUS	LIVERS	LONERS	LOZERE	MACKAY
LESSER	LIMEYS	LIVERY	LONGAN	L-PLATE	MACKLE
LESSON	LIMIER	LIVING	LONGED	LUANDA	MACRON
LESSOR	LIMING	LIZARD	LONGER	LUBBER	MACULA
LETHAL	LIMITS	LLAMAS	LOOFAH	LUBECK	MADAME
LETTER	LIMNED	LOADED	LOOKED	LUBLIN	MADAMS
LETUPS	LIMNER	LOADER	LOOKER	LUCENT	MADCAP
LEVANT	LIMPED	LOAFED	LOOK-IN	LUDLOW	MADDEN
LEVEES	LIMPER	LOAFER	LOOK UP	LUFFED	MADDER
LEVELS	LIMPET	LOANED	LOOMED	LUGANO	MADE-UP
LEVERS	LIMPID	LOANER	LOONEY	LUGGED	MADMAN
LEVIED	LIMPLY	LOATHE	LOOPED	LUGGER	MADMEN
LEVIER	LINAGE	LOAVES	LOOPER	LULLED	MADRAS
LEVIES	LINDEN	LOBATE	LOOSED	LUMBAR	MADRID
LEVITY	LINEAL	LOBBED	LOOSEN	LUMBER	MADURO
LEWDLY	LINEAR	LOBITO	LOOSER	LUMMOX	MAENAD
LIABLE	LINERS	LOBOLA	LOOSES	LUMPED	MAGGOT
LIAISE	LINEUP	LOBULE	LOOTED	LUMPEN	MAGIAN
LIBBER	LINGER	LOCALE	LOOTER	LUNACY	MAGNET
LIBELS	LINGUA	LOCALS	LOPING	LUNATE	MAGNUM
LIBERO	LINING	LOCATE	LOPPED	LUNGED	MAGPIE

MAGUEY	MANILA	MASCOT	MEDICK	MESCAL	MILKED
MAGYAR	MANISA	MASERS	MEDICO	MESHED	MILKER
MAHOUT	MANLEY	MASERU	MEDICS	MESHES	MILLED
MAIDEN	MANNED	MASHED	MEDINA	MESSED	MILLER
MAIKOP	MANNER	MASHER	MEDIUM	MESSES	MILLET
MAILED	MANORS	MASHES	MEDLAR	MESS-UP	MILORD
MAILER	MANQUE	MASHIE	MEDLEY	METAGE	MILTER
MAI MAI	MANTEL	MASJID	MEEKER	METALS	MIMICS
MAIMED	MANTIC	MASKED	MEEKLY	METEOR	MIMING
MAIMER	MANTIS	MASKER	MEERUT	METERS	MIMOSA
MAINLY	MANTLE	MASONS	MEETER	METHOD	MINCED
MAJORS	MANTUA	MASQUE	MEGARA	METHYL	MINCER
MAKALU	MANUAL	MASSED	MEGILP	METIER	MINDED
MAKE DO	MANURE	MASSES	MEGOHM	METING	MINDEL
MAKE IT	MAOISM	MASSIF	MEKNES	METOPE	MINDER
MAKERS	MAOIST	MASTER	MEKONG	METRES	MINERS
MAKE UP	MAPLES	MASTIC	MELEES	METRIC	MINGLE
MAKE-UP	MAPPED	MATADI	MELLOW	METROS	MINIFY
MAKING	MAPUTO	MATING	MELODY	METTLE	MINIMA
MALABO	MAQUIS	MATINS	MELOID	MEWING	MINIMS
MALADY	MARACA	MATRIX	MELONS	MEWLER	MINING
MALAGA	MARAUD	MATRON	MELTED	MEXICO	MINION
MALANG	MARBLE	MATTED	MELTER	MEZZOS	MINIUM
MALATE	MARBLY	MATTER	MELTON	MIAOWS	MINNOW
MALAWI	MARCHE	MATURE	MEMBER	MIASMA	MINOAN
MALAYA	MARGAY	MAULED	MEMOIR	MICKEY	MINORS
MALDON	MARGIN	MAULER	MEMORY	MICMAC	MINTED
MALEIC	MARIAN	MAUNDY	MENACE	MICRON	MINTER
MALICE	MARINA	MAUSER	MENADO	MICROS	MINUET
MALIGN	MARINE	MAXIMA	MENAGE	MIDAIR	MINUTE
MALLEE	MARKED	MAXIMS	MENDED	MIDDAY	MINXES
MALLET	MARKER	MAY BUG	MENDER	MIDDEN	MIOSIS
MALLOW	MARKET	MAY DAY	MENHIR	MIDDLE	MIOTIC
MALTED	MARKKA	MAYFLY	MENIAL	MIDGES	MIRAGE
MALTHA	MARKUP	MAYHEM	MENSES	MIDGET	MIRING
MAMBAS	MARLIN	MAYORS	MENTAL	MIDGUT	MIRROR
MAMMAL	MARMOT	MAZILY	MENTON	MID-OFF	MISCUE
MAMMON	MAROON	MAZUMA	MENTOR	MIDRIB	MISERE
MANAGE	MARQUE	MCEWAN	MEOWED	MIDSTS	MISERS
MANAMA	MARRED	MEADOW	MERANO	MIDWAY	MISERY
MANANA	MARRER	MEAGRE	MERCER	MIERES	MISFIT
MANAUS	MARRON	MEALIE	MERELY	MIFFED	MISHAP
MANCHE	MARROW	MEANER	MERGED	MIGHTY	MISHIT
MANCHU	MARSHY	MEANLY	MERGER	MIKADO	MISLAY
MANEGE	MARTEN	MEASLY	MERINO	MILADY	MISLED
MANFUL	MARTIN	MEATUS	MERITS	MILDER	MISSAL
MANGER	MARTYR	MECCAS	MERLIN	MILDEW	MISSED
MANGLE	MARVEL	MEDALS	MERLON	MILDLY	MISSES
MANGOS	MARY II	MEDDLE	MERMAN	MILERS	MISSIS
MANIAC	MASCLE	MEDIAL	MERSIN	MILIEU	MISSUS
MANIAS	MASCON	MEDIAN	MERTON	MILIUM	MISTED

MISTER	MONISM	MOTTLE	MUSCID	NAGANA	NECTAR
MISUSE	MONIST	MOTTOS	MUSCLE	NAGANO	NEEDED
MITRAL	MONKEY	MOULDS	MUSCLY	NAGGED	NEEDLE
MITRES	MONTHS	MOULDY	MUSEUM	NAGGER	NEEDN'T
MITTEN	MOOING	MOULIN	MUSHES	NAGOYA	NEGATE
MIXERS	MOONED	MOULTS	MUSING	NAGPUR	NEGROS
MIXING	MOORED	MOUNDS	MUSKET	NAIADS	NEIGHS
MIX-UPS	MOOTED	MOUNTS	MUSKIE	NAILED	NEKTON
MIZZEN	MOOTER	MOUSER	MUSLIM	NAILER	NELSON
MOANED	MOPANI	MOUSEY	MUSLIN	NAKURU	NEM CON
MOANER	MOPEDS	MOUSSE	MUSSED	NAMELY	NEPALI
MOATED	MOPING	MOUTHS	MUSSEL	NAMING	NEPHEW
MOBBED	MOPOKE	MOUTON	MUSTEE	NANTES	NEREID
MOBBER	MOPPED	MOVERS	MUSTER	NAPALM	NEREIS
MOBILE	MOPPET	MOVIES	MUSTN'T	NAPIER	NERVED
MOCKED	MORALE	MOVING	MUTANT	NAPKIN	NERVES
MOCKER	MORALS	MOWERS	MUTARE	NAPLES	NESTED
MOCK UP	MORASS	MOWING	MUTATE	NAPPED	NESTER
MOCK-UP	MORBID	MOWLAM	MUTELY	NAPPER	NESTLE
MOD CON	MOREEN	MUCKED	MUTING	NARIAL	NETHER
MODELS	MORGUE	MUCKER	MUTINY	NARKED	NETTED
MODEMS	MORION	MUCOID	MUTISM	NARROW	NETTLE
MODENA	MORLEY	MUCOUS	MUTTER	NARVIK	NETTLY
MODERN	MORMON	MUDCAT	MUTTON	NASALS	NEURAL
MODEST	MORNAY	MUDDED	MUTUAL	NASIAL	NEURON
MODIFY	MORONI	MUDDLE	MUTULE	NASION	NEUTER
MODISH	MORONS	MUD PIE	MUZZLE	NASSAU	NEVADA
MODULE	MOROSE	MUESLI	MYELIN	NATANT	NEVERS
MOGULS	MORROW	MUFFED	MYNAHS	NATION	NEW AGE
MOHAIR	MORSEL	MUFFIN	MYOPIA	NATIVE	NEWARK
MOHAWK	MORTAL	MUFFLE	MYOPIC	NATRON	NEWEST
MOHOLE	MORTAR	MUFTIS	MYOSIN	NATTER	NEWHAM
MOIETY	MORULA	MUGABE	MYRIAD	NATURE	NEWISH
MOLARS	MORYAH	MUGGED	MYRICA	NAUGHT	NEWMAN
MOLDED	MOSAIC	MUGGER	MYRTLE	NAUSEA	NEWTON
MOLDER	MOSCOW	MUKLUK	MYSELF	NAUTCH	NIAMEY
MOLEST	MOSLEM	MULISH	MYSORE	NAVAHO	NIBBLE
MOLISE	MOSQUE	MULLAH	MYSTIC	NAVELS	NIBLET
MOLOCH	MOSSIE	MULLED	MYTHOS	NAVIES	NICELY
MOLOPO	MOSTLY	MULLER	MY WORD	NAZISM	NICEST
MOLTED	MOTELS	MULLET	MYXOMA	NEARBY	NICETY
MOLTEN	MOTETS	MULTAN		NEARED	NICHES
MOMENT	MOTHER	MUMBLE	**N**	NEARER	NICKED
MOMISM	MOTIFS	MUMMER	NAAFIS	NEARLY	NICKEL
MOMMAS	MOTILE	MUNICH	NABBED	NEATEN	NICKER
MONACO	MOTION	MURALS	NABLUS	NEATER	NIDIFY
MONDAY	MOTIVE	MURCIA	NABOBS	NEATLY	NIECES
MONEYS	MOTLEY	MURDER	NACHOS	NEBULA	NIELLO
MONGER	MOTMOT	MURINE	NACRED	NECKAR	NIEVRE
MONGOL	MOTORS	MURMUR	NADIRS	NECKED	NIGGER
MONIES	MOTOWN	MUSCAT	NAEVUS	NECKER	NIGGLE

NIGHTS	NOSIER	**O**	OGDOAD	OPENER	OSHAWA
NILGAI	NOSILY	OAFISH	OGIVAL	OPENLY	OSIERS
NIMBLE	NOSING	OAKHAM	OGLING	OPERAS	OSIJEK
NIMBLY	NOSTOC	OAXACA	OGRESS	OPERON	OSMIUM
NIMBUS	NOTARY	OBELUS	OHMAGE	OPHITE	OSMOSE
NINETY	NOTICE	OBEYED	OIDIUM	OPIATE	OSMOUS
NINGBO	NOTIFY	OBEYER	OILCAN	OPINED	OSPREY
NINGPO	NOTING	OBJECT	OILCUP	OPIOID	OSSEIN
NINTHS	NOTION	OBLAST	OILIER	OPORTO	OSSIFY
NIOBIC	NOUGAT	OBLATE	OILILY	OPPOSE	OSTEAL
NIP OUT	NOUGHT	OBLIGE	OILING	OPPUGN	OSTEND
NIPPED	NOUNAL	OBLONG	OILMAN	OPTICS	OSTIUM
NIPPER	NOVARA	OBOIST	OILMEN	OPTING	OSTLER
NIPPLE	NOVELS	O'BRIEN	OILRIG	OPTION	OTHERS
NIPPON	NOVENA	OBSESS	OIL RIG	OPUSES	OTIOSE
NITRIC	NOVICE	OBTAIN	OINKED	ORACLE	OIIIIS
NITWIT	NOWISE	OBTECT	OKAYED	ORADEA	O'TOOLE
NIXING	NOZZLE	OBTUSE	OLD AGE	ORALLY	OTTAVA
NO BALL	NUANCE	OBVERT	OLD BOY	ORANGE	OTTAWA
NO-BALL	NUBBLE	OCCULT	OLDEST	ORATOR	OTTERS
NOBBLE	NUBBLY	OCCUPY	OLDHAM	ORBITS	OUNCES
NOBLER	NUBILE	OCEANS	OLD HAT	ORCEIN	OUSTED
NOBLES	NUCHAL	OCELOT	OLDISH	ORCHID	OUSTER
NOBODY	NUCLEI	O'CLOCK	OLD LAG	ORCHIL	OUTAGE
NODDED	NUDGED	OCTANE	OLD MAN	ORCHIS	OUTBID
NODDLE	NUDGER	OCTANT	OLEATE	ORDAIN	OUTCRY
NOD OFF	NUDGES	OCTAVE	O LEVEL	ORDEAL	OUTDID
NODOSE	NUDISM	OCTAVO	OLIVES	ORDERS	OUTFIT
NODULE	NUDIST	OCTETS	OMASUM	ORDURE	OUTFOX
NOESIS	NUDITY	OCTOPI	OMEGAS	OREBRO	OUTGAS
NOETIC	NUGGET	OCTROI	ONAGER	OREGON	OUTING
NOGGIN	NUKING	OCULAR	ONCOST	ORENSE	OUTLAW
NOISES	NUMBAT	ODDEST	ON EDGE	ORGANS	OUTLAY
NOMADS	NUMBED	ODDITY	ONE-OFF	ORGASM	OUTLET
NOMISM	NUMBER	ODD JOB	ONE-WAY	ORGEAT	OUTMAN
NONAGE	NUMBLY	ODDS ON	ONIONS	ORGIES	OUTPUT
NONCES	NUNCIO	ODDS-ON	ONLINE	ORIENT	OUTRAN
NONEGO	NURSED	ODENSE	ONRUSH	ORIGAN	OUTRUN
NOODLE	NURSES	ODESSA	ONSIDE	ORIGIN	OUTSET
NOOSES	NUTANT	ODIOUS	ONWARD	ORIOLE	OUTWIT
NOOTKA	NUTLET	ODOURS	OOCYTE	ORISON	OVERDO
NORDIC	NUTMEG	OEDEMA	OODLES	ORISSA	OVERLY
NORITE	NUTRIA	OEUVRE	OOGAMY	ORMOLU	OVIEDO
NORMAL	NUTTED	OFFALY	OOLITE	ORNATE	OVISAC
NORMAN	NUTTER	OFFEND	OOLOGY	ORNERY	OVOIDS
NORTHS	NUZZLE	OFFERS	OOLONG	OROIDE	OVULAR
NORWAY	NYLONS	OFFICE	OOZIER	ORPHAN	OWELTY
NOSHED	NYMPHA	OFFING	OOZILY	ORPINE	OWERRI
NOSH-UP	NYMPHS	OFFSET	OOZING	ORRERY	OWLETS
NO SIDE		OFSTED	OPAQUE	OSCARS	OWLISH
NO-SIDE		OGADEN	OPENED	OSCINE	OWNERS

OWNING	PAMPAS	PARSEE	PEACES	PENMAN	PHASIC
OXALIS	PAMPER	PARSER	PEACHY	PENNED	PHENOL
OXCART	PANADA	PARSON	PEAHEN	PENNEY	PHENOM
OXFORD	PANAMA	PARTED	PEAKED	PENNON	PHENYL
OXIDES	PANDAS	PARTLY	PEALED	PEN PAL	PHIALS
OXTAIL	PANDER	PARTON	PEANUT	PENTAD	PHILAE
OXYGEN	PANDIT	PARURE	PEARLS	PENT UP	PHIZOG
OYSTER	PANELS	PASHTO	PEARLY	PENTYL	PHLEGM
OZALID	PANICS	PASSED	PEBBLE	PENULT	PHLOEM
	PANJIM	PASSES	PEBBLY	PENURY	PHOBIA
P	PANNED	PASSIM	PECANS	PEOPLE	PHOBIC
PACIFY	PANTED	PASTED	PECKED	PEORIA	PHOBOS
PACING	PANTRY	PASTEL	PECKER	PEPLUM	PHOEBE
PACINO	PANZER	PASTES	PECTEN	PEPPED	PHONED
PACKED	PAOTOW	PASTOR	PECTIC	PEPPER	PHONES
PACKER	PAPACY	PASTRY	PECTIN	PEPSIN	PHONEY
PACKET	PAPAIN	PATCHY	PEDALS	PEPTIC	PHONIC
PADANG	PAPAYA	PATENT	PEDANT	PERFIN	PHONON
PADAUK	PAPERS	PATERS	PEDATE	PERILS	PHOOEY
PADDED	PAPERY	PATHAN	PEDDLE	PERIOD	PHOTIC
PADDLE	PAPHOS	PATHOS	PEDLAR	PERISH	PHOTON
PADRES	PAPIST	PATINA	PEDWAY	PERKED	PHOTOS
PAEANS	PAPPUS	PATIOS	PEEING	PERLIS	PHRASE
PAELLA	PAPUAN	PATMOS	PEEKED	PERMED	PHUKET
PAEONY	PAPULE	PATOIS	PEELED	PERMIT	PHYLUM
PAGANS	PAPYRI	PATRAS	PEELER	PERNIK	PHYSIC
PAGING	PARADE	PATROL	PEEPBO	PERNOD	PHYSIO
PAGODA	PARAMO	PATRON	PEEPED	PER PRO	PHYTON
PAHANG	PARANA	PATTED	PEEPER	PERRON	PIAFFE
PAID-UP	PARANG	PATTEN	PEEPUL	PERSIA	PIANOS
PAINED	PARAPH	PATTER	PEERED	PERSON	PIAZZA
PAINTS	PARCEL	PAUCAL	PEEVED	PERTLY	PICKED
PAIRED	PARDON	PAUNCH	PEEWIT	PERUKE	PICKER
PAJAMA	PARENT	PAUPER	PEGGED	PERUSE	PICKET
PALACE	PARGET	PAUSED	PEG LEG	PESADE	PICKLE
PALAIS	PARIAH	PAUSER	PEKING	PESARO	PICK-UP
PALATE	PARIAN	PAUSES	PELAGE	PESETA	PICNIC
PALELY	PARIES	PAVANE	PELITE	PESTER	PIDDLE
PALEST	PARING	PAVING	PELLET	PESTLE	PIDGIN
PALING	PARISH	PAWING	PELMET	PETALS	PIECED
PALISH	PARITY	PAWNED	PELOTA	PETARD	PIECER
PALLAS	PARKAS	PAWPAW	PELTED	PETERS	PIECES
PALLED	PARKED	PAXWAX	PELTER	PETITE	PIERCE
PALLET	PARKIN	PAYBED	PELTRY	PETREL	PIERRE
PALLID	PARLEY	PAYDAY	PELVES	PETROL	PIFFLE
PALLOR	PARODY	PAYEES	PELVIC	PETTED	PIGEON
PALMAR	PAROLE	PAYING	PELVIS	PETTER	PIGGED
PALMED	PARREL	PAYOFF	PENANG	PEWITS	PIGGIN
PALTER	PARROT	PAYOLA	PENCHI	PEWTER	PIGLET
PALTRY	PARSEC	PAYOUT	PENCIL	PHASED	PIGNUS
PAMIRS	PARSED	PCMCIA	PENGPU	PHASES	PIGNUT

PIGSTY	PISS-UP	PLEBBY	POLISH	PORTED	PREFAB
PILAFS	PISTIL	PLEDGE	POLITE	PORTER	PREFER
PILEUM	PISTOL	PLEIAD	POLITY	PORTLY	PREFIX
PILEUP	PISTON	PLENTY	POLKAS	POSERS	PREPAY
PILEUS	PITCHY	PLENUM	POLLAN	POSEUR	PREPPY
PILFER	PITHOS	PLEURA	POLLED	POSHER	PRESET
PILING	PITIED	PLEVEN	POLLEN	POSIES	PRESTO
PILLAR	PITIES	PLEXOR	POLLEX	POSING	PRETTY
PILLOW	PITMAN	PLEXUS	POLLUX	POSSES	PREWAR
PILOSE	PITMEN	PLIANT	POLONY	POSSET	PREYED
PILOTS	PITSAW	PLICAL	POL POT	POSSUM	PREYER
PILULE	PITTED	PLIERS	POLYPS	POSTAL	PRICED
PIMPED	PIVOTS	PLIGHT	POMACE	POSTED	PRICES
PIMPLE	PIXELS	PLINTH	POMADE	POSTER	PRICEY
PIMPLY	PIXIES	PLISSE	POMMEL	POSTIE	PRICKS
PINCER	PIZZAS	PLOUGH	POMPOM	POSTIL	PRIDED
PINEAL	PLACED	PLOVER	POMPON	POTAGE	PRIDES
PINENE	PLACER	PLOWED	PONCES	POTASH	PRIEST
PINERY	PLACES	PLUCKS	PONCEY	POTATO	PRIMAL
PINGED	PLACET	PLUCKY	PONCHO	POTBOY	PRIMED
PINIER	PLACID	PLUMED	PONDER	POTEEN	PRIMER
PINING	PLAGAL	PLUMES	PONDOK	POTENT	PRIMES
PINION	PLAGUE	PLUMMY	PONGED	POTFUL	PRIMLY
PINITE	PLAGUY	PLUNGE	PONGEE	POTHER	PRIMUS
PINKED	PLAICE	PLURAL	PONGID	POTION	PRINCE
PINKER	PLAIDS	PLUSES	PONIES	POTTED	PRINTS
PINKIE	PLAINS	PLUTON	PONTIC	POTTER	PRIORS
PINKOS	PLAINT	PLYING	PONTIL	POUCHY	PRIORY
PINNED	PLAITS	PNEUMA	POODLE	POUNCE	PRIPET
PINNER	PLANAR	POCKED	POOLED	POUNDS	PRISED
PINTAS	PLANED	POCKET	POOPED	POURED	PRISMS
PINTER	PLANER	PODDED	POOPER	POURER	PRISON
PINTLE	PLANES	PODIUM	POORER	POUTED	PRISSY
PINUPS	PLANET	PODZOL	POORLY	POUTER	PRIVET
PINXIT	PLANKS	POETIC	POOTLE	POWDER	PRIZED
PIPAGE	PLANTS	POETRY	POP ART	POWELL	PRIZES
PIPALS	PLAQUE	POGROM	POPERY	POWERS	PRO-AMS
PIPERS	PLASHY	POINTE	POPGUN	POWWOW	PROBED
PIPING	PLASMA	POINTS	POPISH	POZNAN	PROBER
PIPITS	PLATAN	POISED	POPLAR	PRAGUE	PROBES
PIPKIN	PLATED	POISON	POPLIN	PRAISE	PROFIT
PIPPED	PLATEN	POKERS	POPPAS	PRANCE	PROJET
PIPPIN	PLATER	POKIER	POPPED	PRANKS	PROLEG
PIQUED	PLATES	POKILY	POPPER	PRATED	PROLES
PIQUES	PLAUEN	POKING	POPPET	PRATER	PROLIX
PIQUET	PLAYED	POLAND	POPPLE	PRAWNS	PROLOG
PIRACY	PLAYER	POLDER	PORING	PRAXIS	PROMOS
PIRATE	PLAZAS	POLEYN	PORISM	PRAYED	PROMPT
PISCES	PLEACH	POLICE	PORKER	PRAYER	PRONGS
PISSED	PLEASE	POLICY	POROUS	PREACH	PRONTO
PISSES	PLEATS	POLING	PORTAL	PRECIS	PROOFS

PROPEL	PUNDIT	PUTTEE	QUINSY	RAGTAG	RARELY
PROPER	PUNIER	PUTTER	QUIRES	RAGUSA	RAREST
PROPYL	PUNISH	PUZZLE	QUIRKS	RAIDED	RARING
PROSES	PUNJAB	PYKNIC	QUIRKY	RAIDER	RARITY
PROTEA	PUNKAH	PYLONS	QUIVER	RAILED	RASCAL
PRO TEM	PUNNED	PYOSIS	QUOITS	RAILER	RASHER
PROTON	PUNNET	PYRENE	QUORUM	RAILEX	RASHES
PROVED	PUNTED	PYRITE	QUOTAS	RAINED	RASHLY
PROVEN	PUNTER	PYRONE	QUOTED	RAISED	RASPED
PROVIE	PUPATE	PYROPE	QUOTES	RAISER	RASPER
PROWLS	PUPILS	PYTHON	QWERTY	RAISES	RASTER
PROZAC	PUPPED	PYURIA		RAISIN	RATBAG
PRUDES	PUPPET		**R**	RAJAHS	RATHER
PRUNED	PUPPIS	**Q**	RABATO	RAJKOT	RATIFY
PRUNER	PURDAH	QATARI	RABAUL	RAJPUT	RATINE
PRUNES	PUREED	QINTAR	RABBIS	RAKING	RATING
PRYING	PUREES	QUACKS	RABBIT	RAKISH	RATION
PSALMS	PURELY	QUAGGA	RABBLE	RAMBLE	RATIOS
PSEUDO-	PUREST	QUAGGY	RABIES	RAMIFY	RATITE
PSEUDS	PURFLE	QUAHOG	RACEME	RAMJET	RATLAM
PSEUDY	PURGED	QUAILS	RACERS	RAMMED	RATOON
PSYCHE	PURGER	QUAINT	RACHIS	RAMMER	RATTAN
PSYCHO-	PURGES	QUAKED	RACIAL	RAMOSE	RAT-TAT
PTISAN	PURIFY	QUAKER	RACIER	RAMPUR	RATTED
PTOSIS	PURINE	QUAKES	RACILY	RAMROD	RATTER
PUBLIC	PURISM	QUALMS	RACING	RAMTIL	RATTLE
PUCKER	PURIST	QUANGO	RACISM	RANCHI	RATTLY
PUDDLE	PURITY	QUANTA	RACIST	RANCID	RAVAGE
PUDDLY	PURLED	QUARKS	RACKED	RANDAN	RAVENS
PUDSEY	PURLER	QUARRY	RACKER	RANDOM	RAVERS
PUEBLA	PURLIN	QUARTO	RACKET	RANEES	RAVE-UP
PUEBLO	PURPLE	QUARTS	RACOON	RANGED	RAVINE
PUFFED	PURRED	QUARTZ	RADDLE	RANGER	RAVING
PUFFER	PURSED	QUASAR	RADIAL	RANGES	RAVISH
PUFFIN	PURSER	QUAVER	RADIAN	RANKED	RAWEST
PUGGED	PURSES	QUAYLE	RADIOS	RANKER	RAZING
PUKING	PURSUE	QUEASY	RADISH	RANKLE	RAZORS
PULLED	PURVEY	QUEBEC	RADIUM	RANKLY	RAZZLE
PULLET	PUSHED	QUEENS	RADIUS	RANSOM	READER
PULLEY	PUSHER	QUEERS	RADOME	RANTED	REALLY
PULL-IN	PUSHES	QUEMOY	RADULA	RANTER	REALMS
PULL-ON	PUSH-UP	QUENCH	RAFFIA	RAPIDS	REAMED
PULPED	PUSSES	QUESTS	RAFFLE	RAPIER	REAMER
PULPIT	PUTLOG	QUEUED	RAFTED	RAPINE	REAPED
PULSAR	PUT OFF	QUEUES	RAFTER	RAPING	REAPER
PULSED	PUT-OFF	QUICHE	RAGBAG	RAPIST	REARED
PULSES	PUT-ONS	QUIFFS	RAGGED	RAPPED	REARER
PUMICE	PUT OUT	QUILLS	RAGING	RAPPEL	REASON
PUMMEL	PUTRID	QUILTS	RAGLAN	RAPPER	REBASE
PUMPED	PUTSCH	QUINCE	RAGMAN	RAPTOR	REBATE
PUNCHY	PUTTED	QUINOL	RAGOUT	RAREFY	REBELS

REBIND	REFLET	REMOTE	RESUME	RIBBED	RISKED
REBOOT	REFLEX	REMOVE	RETAIL	RIBBON	RISKER
REBORN	REFLUX	RENAME	RETAIN	RIBERA	RISQUE
REBUFF	REFORM	RENDER	RETAKE	RIBOSE	RITUAL
REBUKE	REFUEL	RENEGE	RETARD	RICHER	RIVALS
RECALL	REFUGE	RENNES	RETELL	RICHES	RIVERS
RECANT	REFUND	RENNET	RETENE	RICHLY	RIVETS
RECAPS	REFUSE	RENNIN	RETIAL	RICKED	RIYADH
RECAST	REFUTE	RENOWN	RETINA	RICTAL	RIYALS
RECEDE	REGAIN	RENTAL	RETIRE	RICTUS	ROAMED
RECENT	REGALE	RENTED	RETOLD	RIDDED	ROAMER
RECEPT	REGARD	RENTER	RETOOK	RIDDEN	ROARED
RECESS	REGENT	RENVOI	RETOOL	RIDDER	ROARER
RECIFE	REGGAE	REOPEN	RETORT	RIDDLE	ROASTS
RECIPE	REGIME	REPAID	RETUNE	RIDERS	ROBALO
RECITE	REGINA	REPAIR	RETURN	RIDGED	ROBAND
RECKED	REGION	REPAND	RETUSE	RIDGES	ROBBED
RECKON	REGLET	REPAST	REUSED	RIDING	ROBBER
RECODE	REGRET	REPEAL	REVAMP	RIFFLE	ROBBIN
RECOIL	REGULO	REPEAT	REVEAL	RIFLED	ROBING
RECORD	REHASH	REPENT	REVERE	RIFLER	ROBINS
RECOUP	REHEAR	REPINE	REVERS	RIFLES	ROBOTS
RECTAL	REHEAT	REPLAN	REVERT	RIGGED	ROBSON
RECTOR	REHOME	REPLAY	REVEST	RIGGER	ROBUST
RECTOS	REIGNS	REPONE	REVIEW	RIGHTS	ROCHET
RECTUM	REINED	REPORT	REVILE	RIGOUR	ROCKED
RECTUS	REJECT	REPOSE	REVISE	RIG-OUT	ROCKER
REDACT	REJIGS	REPUTE	REVIVE	RIJEKA	ROCKET
REDBUD	REJOIN	REREAD	REVOKE	RILEYS	ROCOCO
REDCAP	RELAID	RERUNS	REVOLT	RILING	RODENT
REDDEN	RELATE	RESALE	REVUES	RILLET	RODEOS
REDDER	RELAYS	RESCUE	REVVED	RIMINI	ROGERS
REDEEM	RELENT	RESEAT	REWARD	RIMMED	ROGUES
RED EYE	RELICS	RESEAU	REWIND	RIMOSE	ROLLED
REDFIN	RELICT	RESECT	REWIRE	RINGED	ROLLER
RED-HOT	RELIED	RESEDA	REWORD	RINGER	ROLL ON
REDONE	RELIEF	RESEED	REWORK	RING IN	ROLL-ON
REDOWA	RELINE	RESENT	RHEBOK	RINSED	ROMAIC
RED SEA	RELISH	RESHIP	RHESUS	RINSER	ROMANO
REDUCE	RELIVE	RESIDE	RHEUMY	RINSES	ROMANS
REECHO	RELOAD	RESIGN	RHEYDT	RIOTED	ROMANY
REEFED	REMADE	RESILE	RHINAL	RIOTER	ROMEOS
REEFER	REMAIN	RESINS	RHODES	RIPEST	ROMPED
REEKED	REMAKE	RESIST	RHODIC	RIP-OFF	RONDEL
REELED	REMAND	RESITS	RHOTIC	RIPPED	RONDOS
REELER	REMARK	RESIZE	RHYMED	RIPPER	ROOFED
REEVES	REMEDY	RESORB	RHYMES	RIPPLE	ROOKED
REFACE	REMIND	RESORT	RHYTHM	RIPPLY	ROOKIE
REFILL	REMISE	RESTED	RHYTON	RIPSAW	ROOMED
REFINE	REMISS	RESTER	RIALTO	RISERS	ROOMER
REFITS	REMORA	RESULT	RIBALD	RISING	ROOSTS

ROOTED	RUEFUL	SACRUM	SAMITE	SAWFLY	SCORES
ROOTER	RUFFLE	SADDEN	SAMOAN	SAWING	SCORIA
ROOTSY	RUFFLY	SADDER	SAMOSA	SAWYER	SCORNS
ROPIER	RUFOUS	SADDLE	SAMPAN	SAXONS	SCOTCH
ROPILY	RUGGED	SADHUS	SAMPLE	SAXONY	SCOTER
ROPING	RUGOSA	SADISM	SAMSUN	SAYING	SCOTIA
ROQUET	RUGOSE	SADIST	SANDAL	SCABBY	SCOUSE
ROSARY	RUINED	SAFARI	SANDED	SCALAR	SCOUTS
ROSIER	RUINER	SAFELY	SANDER	SCALDS	SCOWLS
ROSILY	RULERS	SAFEST	SANDHI	SCALED	SCRAPE
ROSINY	RULING	SAFETY	SANELY	SCALER	SCRAPS
ROSTER	RUMBAS	SAGELY	SANEST	SCALES	SCRAWL
ROSTOV	RUMBLE	SAGGAR	SANIES	SCALPS	SCREAM
ROSTRA	RUMBLY	SAGGED	SANITY	SCAMPI	SCREED
ROTARY	RUMMER	SAHARA	SANTER	SCAMPS	SCREEN
ROTATE	RUMOUR	SAHIBS	SANTOS	SCANTY	SCREWS
ROTGUT	RUMPLE	SAIGON	SAPELE	SCARAB	SCREWY
ROTORS	RUMPLY	SAILED	SAPOTA	SCARCE	SCRIBE
ROTTED	RUMPUS	SAILER	SAPPED	SCARED	SCRIMP
ROTTEN	RUNDLE	SAILOR	SAPPER	SCARER	SCRIPT
ROTTER	RUNNEL	SAINTS	SARGES	SCARES	SCROLL
ROTUND	RUNNER	SAIPAN	SARNIA	SCAREY	SCROOP
ROUBLE	RUN-OFF	SAITHE	SARNIE	SCARFS	SCROTA
ROUGED	RUN-UPS	SALAAM	SARONG	SCARPS	SCRUBS
ROUNDS	RUNWAY	SALADS	SARTHE	SCATTY	SCRUFF
ROUSED	RUPEES	SALAMI	SASEBO	SCENES	SCRUMP
ROUSER	RUPIAH	SALARY	SASHAY	SCENIC	SCRUMS
ROUTED	RUSHED	SALIFY	SASHES	SCENTS	SCUBAS
ROUTER	RUSHER	SALINE	SASSED	SCHEMA	SCUFFS
ROUTES	RUSHES	SALIVA	SASSES	SCHEME	SCULPT
ROVERS	RUSSET	SALLEE	SATEEN	SCHISM	SCUMMY
ROVING	RUSSIA	SALLOW	SATING	SCHIST	SCUNGY
ROWANS	RUSTED	SALMON	SATINY	SCHLEP	SCURFY
ROWERS	RUSTIC	SALONS	SATIRE	SCHOOL	SCURRY
ROWING	RUSTLE	SALOON	SATURN	SCHORL	SCURVY
ROYALS	RUTILE	SALOOP	SATYRS	SCHUSS	SCUTCH
ROZZER	RUTTED	SALTED	SAUCED	SCHWAS	SCUTUM
RUBATO	RWANDA	SALTER	SAUCER	SCHWYZ	SCUZZY
RUBBED	RYAZAN	SALTUS	SAUCES	SCILLA	SCYLLA
RUBBER		SALUKI	SAUGER	SCIONS	SCYTHE
RUBBLE	**S**	SALUTE	SAUNAS	SCLAFF	SEABED
RUBBLY	SABBAT	SALVED	SAVAGE	SCLERA	SEA DOG
RUBIES	SABERS	SALVER	SAVAII	SCOFFS	SEALED
RUBLES	SABLES	SALVES	SAVANT	SCOLDS	SEALER
RUBRIC	SABRAS	SALVIA	SAVERS	SCOLEX	SEAMAN
RUCKED	SABRES	SALVOR	SAVING	SCONCE	SEAMEN
RUCKUS	SACHET	SALVOS	SAVOIE	SCONES	SEAMER
RUDDER	SACKED	SALYUT	SAVONA	SCOOPS	SEANCE
RUDDLE	SACKER	SAMARA	SAVORY	SCORCH	SEARCH
RUDELY	SACRAL	SAMBAR	SAVOUR	SCORED	SEARED
RUDEST	SACRED	SAMBAS	SAVOYS	SCORER	SEASON

SEATED	SENNIT	SEXPOT	SHERRY	SHROUD	SILVAN
SEATER	SENORA	SEXTET	SHEWED	SHRUBS	SILVER
SEAWAY	SENORS	SEXTON	SHIELD	SHRUGS	SIMIAN
SECANT	SENSED	SEXUAL	SHIEST	SHRUNK	SIMILE
SECEDE	SENSES	SHABBY	SHIFTS	SHTOOK	SIMMER
SECOND	SENSOR	SHACKS	SHIFTY	SHUCKS	SIMNEL
SECRET	SENTRY	SHADED	SHIITE	SHUFTI	SIMONY
SECTOR	SEPALS	SHADES	SHINER	SHUFTY	SIMOOM
SECUND	SEPSIS	SHADOW	SHINNY	SHUNTS	SIMPER
SECURE	SEPTAL	SHAFTS	SHINTO	SHYEST	SIMPLE
SEDANS	SEPTET	SHAGGY	SHINTY	SHYING	SIMPLY
SEDATE	SEPTIC	SHAKEN	SHIRAZ	SIALIC	SINDHI
SEDILE	SEPTUM	SHAKER	SHIRES	SIBYLS	SINEWS
SEDUCE	SEQUEL	SHAKES	SHIRTS	SICILY	SINEWY
SEEDED	SEQUIN	SHALOM	SHIRTY	SICKED	SINFUL
SEEDER	SERAPH	SHAMAN	SHITTY	SICKEN	SINGED
SEEING	SERBIA	SHAMED	SHIVER	SICKER	SINGER
SEEKER	SEREIN	SHAMMY	SHOALS	SICKIE	SINGES
SEEMED	SERENE	SHANDY	SHOALY	SICKLE	SINGLE
SEEMER	SERIAL	SHANKS	SHOCKS	SICKLY	SINGLY
SEEMLY	SERIES	SHANNY	SHODDY	SIDE-ON	SINING
SEEPED	SERIFS	SHANSI	SHOGUN	SIDING	SINKER
SEESAW	SERINE	SHANTY	SHOOED	SIDLED	SINNED
SEETHE	SERMON	SHANXI	SHOO-IN	SIDLER	SINNER
SEFTON	SEROSA	SHAPED	SHOOTS	SIECLE	SINTER
SEICHE	SEROUS	SHAPES	SHORAN	SIEGEN	SIOUAN
SEINES	SERUMS	SHARDS	SHORED	SIEGES	SIPHON
SEISER	SERVAL	SHARED	SHORES	SIENNA	SIPPED
SEISIN	SERVED	SHARER	SHORTS	SIERRA	SIPPER
SEIZED	SERVER	SHARES	SHORTY	SIESTA	SIPPET
SEIZER	SERVES	SHARIA	SHOULD	SIEVED	SIRENS
SEJANT	SERVOS	SHARKS	SHOUTS	SIEVES	SIRING
SELDOM	SESAME	SHARPS	SHOVED	SIFAKA	SIRIUS
SELECT	SESTET	SHAVED	SHOVEL	SIFTED	SIRRAH
SELLER	SET-OFF	SHAVEN	SHOVER	SIFTER	SISERA
SELVES	SETOSE	SHAVER	SHOVES	SIGHED	SISKIN
SEMEME	SETTEE	SHAVES	SHOWED	SIGHER	SISTER
SEMITE	SETTER	SHAWLS	SHOWER	SIGHTS	SITARS
SEMPRE	SETTLE	SHEARS	SHOW UP	SIGNAL	SITCOM
SEMTEX	SET-UPS	SHEATH	SHRANK	SIGNED	SITING
SENARY	SEVENS	SHEAVE	SHREDS	SIGNEE	SIT-INS
SENATE	SEVERE	SHEETS	SHREWD	SIGNER	SITTER
SENDAI	SEVRES	SHEIKH	SHREWS	SIGNET	SIT-UPS
SENDER	SEWAGE	SHEILA	SHRIEK	SIGN ON	SIXTHS
SEND UP	SEWERS	SHEKEL	SHRIFT	SIGNOR	SIZING
SEND-UP	SEWING	SHELLS	SHRIKE	SIKKIM	SIZZLE
SENECA	SEXIER	SHELVE	SHRILL	SILAGE	SKATED
SENEGA	SEXILY	SHENSI	SHRIMP	SILENT	SKATER
SENILE	SEXING	SHERDS	SHRINE	SILICA	SKATES
SENIOR	SEXISM	SHERIA	SHRINK	SILKEN	SKEINS
SENNAR	SEXIST	SHERPA	SHRIVE	SILTED	SKELLY

SKETCH	SLICKS	SMITER	SNORER	SOMBRE	SPEARS
SKEWED	SLIDES	SMITHS	SNORES	SOMITE	SPECIE
SKEWER	SLIGHT	SMITHY	SNORTS	SONANT	SPECKS
SKIBOB	SLIMLY	SMOCKS	SNOTTY	SONATA	SPEECH
SKIDOO	SLINGS	SMOGGY	SNOUTS	SONNET	SPEEDS
SKIERS	SLINKY	SMOKED	SNOWED	SONORA	SPEEDY
SKIFFS	SLIP-ON	SMOKER	SNUBBY	SONTAG	SPEISS
SKIING	SLIPPY	SMOKES	SNUFFY	SOONER	SPELLS
SKIKDA	SLIP-UP	SMOOCH	SNUGLY	SOOTHE	SPERMS
SKILLS	SLIVER	SMOOTH	SOAKED	SOPPED	SPEWED
SKIMPY	SLOGAN	SMUDGE	SOAKER	SORBET	SPEWER
SKINNY	SLOOPS	SMUDGY	SOAPED	SORBIC	SPEYER
SKIRTS	SLOPED	SMUGLY	SOARED	SORDID	SPHENE
SKIVED	SLOPER	SMUTCH	SOARER	SORELY	SPHERE
SKIVER	SLOPES	SMUTTY	SOARES	SORREL	SPHINX
SKIVVY	SLOPPY	SNACKS	SOBBED	SORROW	SPICED
SKOPJE	SLOSHY	SNAFUS	SOBBER	SORTED	SPICER
SKULLS	SLOTHS	SNAGGY	SO BE IT	SORTER	SPICES
SKUNKS	SLOUCH	SNAILS	SOCAGE	SORTIE	SPIDER
SKYCAP	SLOUGH	SNAKED	SOCCER	SOTHIC	SPIELS
SKYLAB	SLOVAK	SNAKES	SOCIAL	SOUGHS	SPIGOT
SKYROS	SLOVEN	SNAPPY	SOCKED	SOUGHT	SPIKED
SLACKS	SLOWED	SNARED	SOCKET	SOUNDS	SPIKES
SLAGGY	SLOWER	SNARER	SOCMAN	SOURCE	SPILLS
SLAKED	SLOWLY	SNARES	SODDED	SOURED	SPINAL
SLAKER	SLUDGE	SNARLS	SODDEN	SOURER	SPINEL
SLALOM	SLUDGY	SNARLY	SODIUM	SOURLY	SPINES
SLANGY	SLUICE	SNATCH	SODOMY	SOUSED	SPINET
SLANTS	SLUING	SNAZZY	SOEVER	SOUSSE	SPIRAL
SLAP-UP	SLUMMY	SNEAKS	SOFFIT	SOVIET	SPIRES
SLATED	SLUMPS	SNEAKY	SOFTEN	SOWERS	SPIRIT
SLATER	SLURRY	SNEERS	SOFTER	SOWETO	SPITAL
SLATES	SLUSHY	SNEEZE	SOFTIE	SOWING	SPITED
SLAVED	SLYEST	SNEEZY	SOFTLY	SPACED	SPLAKE
SLAVER	SMACKS	SNICKS	SOIGNE	SPACER	SPLASH
SLAVES	SMALLS	SNIDER	SOILED	SPACES	SPLEEN
SLAVIC	SMALTO	SNIFFS	SOIREE	SPADER	SPLICE
SLAYER	SMARMY	SNIFFY	SOKOTO	SPADES	SPLINE
SLEAVE	SMEARS	SNIPED	SOLACE	SPADIX	SPLINT
SLEAZE	SMEARY	SNIPER	SOLDER	SPANKS	SPLITS
SLEAZY	SMEGMA	SNIPES	SOLELY	SPARED	SPLOSH
SLEDGE	SMELLS	SNIPPY	SOLEMN	SPARER	SPOILS
SLEEPY	SMELLY	SNITCH	SOLENT	SPARES	SPOILT
SLEETY	SMELTS	SNIVEL	SOLIDI	SPARID	SPOKEN
SLEEVE	SMILAX	SNOBOL	SOLIDS	SPARKS	SPOKES
SLEIGH	SMILED	SNOOPS	SOLING	SPARRY	SPONGE
SLEUTH	SMILER	SNOOPY	SO LONG	SPARSE	SPONGY
SLEWED	SMILES	SNOOTY	SOLUTE	SPASMS	SPOOFS
SLICED	SMILEY	SNOOZE	SOLVED	SPATHE	SPOOKS
SLICER	SMIRCH	SNOOZY	SOLVER	SPAVIN	SPOOKY
SLICES	SMIRKS	SNORED	SOMALI	SPAYED	SPOOLS

SPOONS	STABLE	STEEDS	STOOLS	STRUNG	SULTAN
SPOORS	STABLY	STEELS	STOP-GO	STRUTS	SULTRY
SPORES	STACKS	STEELY	STOP IN	STUBBY	SUMACH
SPORTS	STADIA	STEERS	STORAX	STUCCO	SUMMAT
SPORTY	STAFFS	STEEVE	STORED	STUDIO	SUMMED
SPOT-ON	STAGED	STEINS	STORES	STUFFY	SUMMER
SPOTTY	STAGER	STELAR	STOREY	STUMER	SUMMIT
SPOUSE	STAGES	STENCH	STORKS	STUMPS	SUMMON
SPOUTS	STAGEY	STEPPE	STORMS	STUMPY	SUNBED
SPRAIN	STAINS	STEP UP	STORMY	STUNTS	SUNBOW
SPRANG	STAIRS	STEREO	STOUPS	STUPID	SUNDAE
SPRATS	STAKED	STERIC	STOVER	STUPOR	SUNDAY
SPRAWL	STAKES	STERNA	STOVES	STURDY	SUNDER
SPRAYS	STALAG	STERNS	STOWED	STYLAR	SUNDEW
SPREAD	STALED	STEROL	STRAFE	STYLED	SUNDRY
SPREES	STALER	STEWED	STRAIN	STYLER	SUN GOD
SPRIER	STALKS	STICKS	STRAIT	STYLES	SUNKEN
SPRIGS	STALKY	STICKY	STRAKE	STYLET	SUNLIT
SPRING	STALLS	STIFFS	STRAND	STYLUS	SUNNED
SPRINT	STAMEN	STIFLE	STRAPS	STYMIE	SUNNIS
SPRITE	STAMPS	STIGMA	STRATA	STYRAX	SUNRAY
SPROUT	STANCE	STILES	STRAWS	STYRIA	SUNSET
SPRUCE	STANCH	STILLS	STRAWY	SUABLE	SUNTAN
SPRUIT	STANDS	STILLY	STRAYS	SUAKIN	SUPERB
SPRUNG	STANZA	STILTS	STREAK	SUBBED	SUPER-G
SPRYLY	STAPES	STINGS	STREAM	SUBDUE	SUPINE
SPUNKY	STAPLE	STINGY	STREEP	SUBITO	SUPPED
SPURGE	STARCH	STINKS	STREET	SUBLET	SUPPER
SPURRY	STARED	STINTS	STRESS	SUBMIT	SUPPLE
SPURTS	STARER	STIPEL	STREWN	SUBORN	SUPPLY
SPUTUM	STARES	STIPES	STRICK	SUBSET	SURELY
SPYING	STARRY	STIRPS	STRICT	SUBTLE	SUREST
SQUABS	STARTS	STIR UP	STRIDE	SUBTLY	SURETY
SQUADS	STARVE	STITCH	STRIFE	SUBURB	SURFED
SQUALL	STASIS	STOATS	STRIKE	SUBWAY	SURFER
SQUAMA	STATED	STOCKS	STRING	SUCHOU	SURFIE
SQUARE	STATER	STOCKY	STRIPE	SUCKED	SURGED
SQUASH	STATES	STODGE	STRIPS	SUCKER	SURGER
SQUATS	STATIC	STODGY	STRIPY	SUCKLE	SURGES
SQUAWK	STATOR	STOICS	STRIVE	SUDDEN	SURREY
SQUAWS	STATUE	STOKED	STROBE	SUFFER	SURTAX
SQUEAK	STATUS	STOKER	STRODE	SUFFIX	SURVEY
SQUEAL	STAVED	STOKES	STROKE	SUGARS	SUSLIK
SQUIBS	STAVES	STOLEN	STROLL	SUGARY	SUSSED
SQUIDS	STAYED	STOLES	STROMA	SUITED	SUTTEE
SQUILL	STAYER	STOLID	STRONG	SUITES	SUTTON
SQUINT	STAY IN	STOLON	STROPS	SUITOR	SUTURE
SQUIRE	STEADS	STONED	STROUD	SULCUS	SUU KYI
SQUIRM	STEADY	STONER	STROVE	SULKED	SUZHOU
SQUIRT	STEAKS	STONES	STRUCK	SULKER	SVELTE
SQUISH	STEAMY	STOOGE	STRUMA	SULLEN	SWABIA

SWAGER	SYRUPY	TAMPON	TAUTLY	TENNIS	THEISM
SWAINS	SYSTEM	TANDEM	TAUTOG	TENONS	THEIST
SWAMIS	SYZRAN	TANGLE	TAVERN	TENORS	THEMES
SWAMPS	SYZYGY	TANGLY	TAWDRY	TENPIN	THEMIS
SWAMPY	SZEGED	TANGOS	TAXEME	TENREC	THENAR
SWANKS		TANKER	TAXIED	TENSED	THENCE
SWANKY	**T**	TANNED	TAXING	TENSER	THEORY
SWARDS	TABARD	TANNER	TAXMAN	TENSES	THERMS
SWARMS	TABBED	TANNIC	TAXMEN	TENSOR	THESES
SWATCH	TABLED	TANNIN	TAYLOR	TENTER	THESIS
SWATHE	TABLES	TANNOY	T-BONES	TENTHS	THETIC
SWATHS	TABLET	TAOISM	TEABAG	TENURE	THICKO
SWATOW	TABOOS	TAOIST	TEACUP	TENUTO	THIEVE
SWAYED	TABRIZ	TAPERS	TEAMED	TEPEES	THIGHS
SWAYER	TACKED	TAPING	TEAPOT	TEPEFY	THIMBU
SWEATS	TACKER	TAPIRS	TEAPOY	TERBIC	THINGS
SWEATY	TACKLE	TAPPED	TEARER	TERCEL	THINLY
SWEDEN	TACOMA	TAPPER	TEASED	TERCET	THIRDS
SWEDES	TACTIC	TAPPET	TEASEL	TEREDO	THIRST
SWEENY	TADJIK	TARAWA	TEASER	TERESA	THIRTY
SWEEPS	TAEJON	TARBES	TEASES	TERETE	THOLOS
SWEETS	TAG END	TARGET	TECHIE	TERGAL	THONGS
SWELLS	TAGGED	TARIFF	TECHNO	TERGUM	THORAX
SWERVE	TAHITI	TARMAC	TEDDER	TERMED	THORIC
SWIFTS	TAIHOA	TAROTS	TEDIUM	TERMLY	THORNS
SWILLS	TAILED	TARPAN	TEEING	TERMOR	THORNY
SWINES	TAILOR	TARPON	TEEMED	TERRET	THORON
SWINGE	TAINAN	TARRED	TEEPEE	TERROR	THOUGH
SWINGS	TAIPAN	TARSAL	TEETER	TERUEL	THRALL
SWIPED	TAIPEI	TARSUS	TEETHE	TESTED	THRASH
SWIPES	TAIWAN	TARTAN	TEFLON	TESTER	THREAD
SWIRLS	TAKERS	TARTAR	TEGMEN	TESTES	THREAT
SWIRLY	TAKEUP	TARTLY	TEHRAN	TESTIS	THREES
SWITCH	TAKING	TASKER	TELEDU	TETCHY	THRESH
SWIVEL	TALCUM	TASMAN	TELIAL	TETHER	THRICE
SWIVET	TALENT	TASSEL	TELIUM	TETRAD	THRIFT
SWOONS	TALION	TASTED	TELLER	TETRYL	THRILL
SWOOPS	TALKED	TASTER	TELPAL	TETTER	THRIPS
SWOOSH	TALKER	TASTES	TELSON	TETUAN	THRIVE
SWORDS	TALKIE	TATAMI	TEMPED	TEUTON	THROAT
SYDNEY	TALLER	TATARY	TEMPER	THAMES	THROBS
SYLVAN	TALLOW	TATTED	TEMPLE	THANES	THROES
SYMBOL	TALMUD	TATTER	TEMPOS	THANKS	THRONE
SYNCOM	TALONS	TATTIE	TEMUCO	THATCH	THRONG
SYNDIC	TAMBOV	TATTLE	TENACE	THAWED	THROVE
SYNODS	TAMELY	TATTOO	TENANT	THAWER	THROWN
SYNTAX	TAMERS	TAUGHT	TENDED	THECAL	THROWS
SYPHER	TAMEST	TAUNTS	TENDER	THEFTS	THRUSH
SYPHON	TAMING	TAURUS	TENDON	THEGNS	THRUST
SYRIAN	TAMPED	TAUTEN	TENETS	THEINE	THUMBS
SYRINX	TAMPER	TAUTER	TENNER	THEIRS	THUMPS

THWACK	TINGLY	TOLEDO	TOUCAN	TRENDY	TROVES
THWART	TIN GOD	TOLLED	TOUCHE	TRENTO	TROWEL
THYMIC	TIN HAT	TOLUCA	TOUCHY	TREPAN	TROYES
THYMOL	TINIER	TOLUYL	TOULON	TRESSY	TRUANT
THYMUS	TINKER	TOMATO	TOUPEE	TRIADS	TRUCES
THYRSE	TINKLE	TOMBAC	TOURED	TRIAGE	TRUCKS
TIARAS	TINKLY	TOMBOY	TOURER	TRIALS	TRUDGE
TIBIAE	TINNED	TOMCAT	TOUSLE	TRIBAL	TRUEST
TIBIAS	TIN-POT	TOM-TOM	TOUTED	TRIBES	TRUISM
TICINO	TINSEL	TONGAN	TOWAGE	TRICES	TRUMAN
TICKED	TINTED	TONGUE	TOWBAR	TRICKS	TRUMPS
TICKER	TIP-OFF	TONICS	TOWELS	TRICKY	TRUNKS
TICKET	TIPPED	TONING	TOWEES	TRICOT	TRUSTS
TICKLE	TIPPER	TONKIN	TOWHEE	TRIERS	TRUSTY
TIC TAC	TIPPET	TONNES	TOWING	TRIFID	TRUTHS
TIDBIT	TIPPLE	TONSIL	TOWNEE	TRIFLE	TRYING
TIDDLY	TIPTOE	TOOLED	TOWNIE	TRIGER	TRY-OUT
TIDIER	TIP-TOP	TOOLER	TOXINS	TRIKES	TRYSTS
TIDILY	TIRADE	TOOTED	TOXOID	TRILBY	T-SHIRT
TIDING	TIRANA	TOOTER	TOYAMA	TRILLS	TSINAN
TIDYED	TIRING	TOOTHY	TOYING	TRIMER	TSONGA
TIE-DYE	TISANE	TOOTLE	TRACED	TRIMLY	TSOTSI
TIE-INS	TISSUE	TOP DOG	TRACER	TRINAL	TSWANA
TIEPIN	TITANS	TOPEES	TRACES	TRIODE	TUAREG
TIERCE	TITBIT	TOPEKA	TRACKS	TRIOSE	TUBBED
TIE-UPS	TITCHY	TOP HAT	TRACTS	TRIPLE	TUBERS
TIFFIN	TITFER	TOPHUS	TRADED	TRIPOD	TUBING
TIFLIS	TITHER	TOPICS	TRADER	TRIPOS	TUBULE
TIGERS	TITHES	TOPPED	TRADES	TRIPPY	TUCKED
TIGHTS	TITLED	TOPPER	TRAGAL	TRITON	TUCKER
TIGRIS	TITLES	TOPPLE	TRAGIC	TRIUNE	TUCK-IN
TILDES	TITTER	TORBAY	TRAGUS	TRIVET	TUCSON
TILERS	TITTLE	TORERO	TRAILS	TRIVIA	TUFFET
TILING	TITTUP	TORIES	TRAINS	TROCAR	TUFTED
TILLED	TIVOLI	TOROID	TRAITS	TROCHE	TUFTER
TILLER	TMESIS	TOROSE	TRALEE	TROGON	TUGGED
TILTED	TOASTS	TORPID	TRAMPS	TROIKA	TUGGER
TILTER	TOBAGO	TORPOR	TRANCE	TROJAN	TULIPS
TIMARU	TOBRUK	TORQUE	TRANNY	TROLLS	TUMBLE
TIMBAL	TOCSIN	TORRID	TRASHY	TROMPE	TUMEFY
TIMBER	TO DATE	TORSOS	TRAUMA	TROOPS	TUMOUR
TIMBRE	TODDLE	TOSSED	TRAVEL	TROPES	TUMULI
TIMELY	TOE CAP	TOSSER	TRAWLS	TROPHY	TUMULT
TIMERS	TOEING	TOSSES	TREADS	TROPIC	TUNDRA
TIMING	TOFFEE	TOSS UP	TREATS	TROPPO	TUNERS
TINCAL	TOGGED	TOSS-UP	TREATY	TROTHS	TUNE-UP
TINDER	TOGGLE	TOTALS	TREBLE	TROTYL	TUNGUS
TINEAL	TOILED	TOTEMS	TREBLY	TROUGH	TUNICA
TINEID	TOILER	TOTING	TREMOR	TROUPE	TUNICS
TINGED	TOILET	TOTTED	TRENCH	TROUTS	TUNING
TINGLE	TOKENS	TOTTER	TRENDS	TROVER	TUNNEL

TUPELO	TWIRLS	UNCORK	UNPLUG	UPRISE	VACUUM
TUPPED	TWIRLY	UNCURL	UNREAD	UPROAR	VADOSE
TURBAN	TWIRPS	UNDEAD	UNREAL	UPROOT	VAGARY
TURBID	TWISTS	UNDIES	UNREST	UPSETS	VAGINA
TURBIT	TWISTY	UNDOER	UNRIPE	UPSHOT	VAINER
TURBOT	TWITCH	UNDONE	UNROLL	UPSIDE	VAINLY
TUREEN	TWO-BIT	UNDULY	UNRULY	UPTAKE	VALAIS
TURFED	TWO-PLY	UNEASE	UNSAFE	UPTICK	VALETA
TURGID	TWO-WAY	UNEASY	UNSAID	UPTILT	VALETS
TURGOR	TYCOON	UNESCO	UNSEAL	UPTIME	VALGUS
TURION	TYMPAN	UNEVEN	UNSEAM	UPTOWN	VALINE
TURKEY	TYPHUS	UNFAIR	UNSEAT	UPTURN	VALISE
TURKIC	TYPIFY	UNFOLD	UNSEEN	UPWARD	VALIUM
TURNED	TYPING	UNFREE	UNSEXY	UPWIND	VALLEY
TURNER	TYPIST	UNFURL	UNSHIP	URACIL	VALOUR
TURN IN	TYRANT	UNGUAL	UNSNAP	URALIC	VALUED
TURNIP	TYRONE	UNGUIS	UNSTEP	URANIC	VALUER
TURN ON	TYUMEN	UNGULA	UNSTOP	URANUS	VALUES
TURN-ON		UNHAIR	UNSUNG	URANYL	VALVES
TURN UP	**U**	UNHAND	UNSURE	URATIC	VANDAL
TURN-UP	UBANGI	UNHOLY	UNTIDY	URBANE	VANISH
TURRET	U-BOATS	UNHOOD	UNTIED	URCHIN	VANITY
TURTLE	UDDERS	UNHOOK	UNTOLD	UREASE	VAPOUR
TURVES	UDMURT	UNICEF	UNTRUE	UREIDE	VARDAR
TUSCAN	UGANDA	UNIONS	UNTUCK	URETER	VARESE
TUSCHE	UGLIER	UNIPOD	UNUSED	URETIC	VARIED
TUSHES	UGLIFY	UNIQUE	UNVEIL	URGENT	VARLET
TUSKER	UGRIAN	UNISEX	UNWARY	URGING	VASSAL
TUSSAH	UJJAIN	UNISON	UNWELL	URINAL	VASTLY
TUSSIS	ULCERS	UNISON	UNWEPT	UROPOD	VAULTS
TUSSLE	ULLAGE	UNITED	UNWIND	URSINE	VAUNTS
TUTORS	ULSTER	UNITER	UNWISE	URTEXT	VECTOR
TUTSAN	ULTIMA	UNJUST	UNWRAP	USABLE	VEERED
TUT-TUT	UMBRAL	UNKIND	UNYOKE	USAGES	VEGANS
TUVALU	UMBRIA	UNKNIT	UPBEAT	USANCE	VEILED
TUXEDO	UMLAUT	UNLACE	UPCAST	USED TO	VEILER
TUYERE	UMPIRE	UNLAID	UPDATE	USEFUL	VEINAL
TWANGS	UMTATA	UNLASH	UPDIKE	USHERS	VEINED
TWANGY	UNABLE	UNLEAD	UPHELD	USURER	VELARS
TWEAKS	UNAWED	UNLESS	UPHILL	UTAHAN	VELATE
TWEEDS	UNBELT	UNLIKE	UPHOLD	UTERUS	VELCRO
TWEEDY	UNBEND	UNLIVE	UPHROE	UTMOST	VELETA
TWEETS	UNBENT	UNLOAD	UPKEEP	UTOPIA	VELLUM
TWELVE	UNBIND	UNLOCK	UPLAND	U-TURNS	VELOCE
TWENTY	UNBOLT	UNMADE	UPLIFT	UVULAE	VELOUR
TWERPS	UNBORN	UNMAKE	UPLINK	UVULAR	VELSEN
TWIGGY	UNCIAL	UNMASK	UPLOAD	UVULAS	VELURE
TWILIT	UNCLAD	UNMOOR	UPPERS		VELVET
TWINED	UNCLES	UNPACK	UPPISH	**V**	VENDED
TWINER	UNCLOG	UNPAID	UPPITY	VACANT	VENDEE
TWINGE	UNCOIL	UNPICK	UPREAR	VACATE	VENDOR

VENEER	VIBORG	VOICES	WAKING	WASHIN	WESKER
VENERY	VIBRIO	VOIDED	WALKED	WASTED	WESTER
VENETO	VICARS	VOIDER	WALKER	WASTER	WETHER
VENIAL	VICTIM	VOLANT	WALK-IN	WASTES	WETTED
VENICE	VICTOR	VOLLEY	WALK-ON	WATERS	WETTER
VENIRE	VICUNA	VOLUME	WALK-UP	WATERY	WHACKS
VENOSE	VIDEOS	VOLUTE	WALLAH	WATTLE	WHALER
VENOUS	VIENNA	VOLVOX	WALLED	WATUSI	WHALES
VENTED	VIENNE	VOODOO	WALLET	WAVIER	WHAMMY
VENTER	VIEWED	VORTEX	WALLOP	WAVILY	WHARFS
VENUES	VIEWER	VOSGES	WALLOW	WAVING	WHARVE
VENULE	VIGILS	VOSTOK	WALNUT	WAXIER	WHEELS
VERBAL	VIGOUR	VOTARY	WALRUS	WAXILY	WHEEZE
VERBID	VIKING	VOTERS	WALTON	WAXING	WHEEZY
VERDIN	VILELY	VOTING	WAMPUM	WAYLAY	WHELKS
VERDUN	VILEST	VOTIVE	WANDER	WAY-OUT	WHELPS
VERGED	VILIFY	VOTYAK	WANGLE	WEAKEN	WHENCE
VERGER	VILLAS	VOWELS	WANING	WEAKER	WHERRY
VERGES	VILLUS	VOWING	WANKED	WEAKLY	WHEYEY
VERIFY	VINERY	VOX POP	WANKER	WEALTH	WHIFFS
VERILY	VINOUS	VOYAGE	WANNED	WEANED	WHIFFY
VERISM	VINYLS	VOYEUR	WANNER	WEAPON	WHILED
VERIST	VIOLAS	V-SIGNS	WANT AD	WEARER	WHILST
VERITY	VIOLET	VULGAR	WANTED	WEASEL	WHIMSY
VERMIN	VIOLIN	VULVAE	WANTER	WEAVER	WHINED
VERMIS	VIPERS	VULVAL	WANTON	WEAVES	WHINER
VERNAL	VIRAGO	VULVAS	WAPITI	WEBBED	WHINES
VERONA	VIRGIN	VYBORG	WARBLE	WEDDED	WHINGE
VERSED	VIRGOS		WAR CRY	WEDELN	WHINNY
VERSES	VIRILE	**W**	WARDED	WEDGED	WHIPPY
VERSOS	VIRTUE	WADDLE	WARDEN	WEDGES	WHIRLS
VERSUS	VISAED	WADERS	WARDER	WEEDED	WHISKS
VERTEX	VISAGE	WADGES	WARIER	WEEDER	WHISKY
VERVET	VISCID	WADING	WARILY	WEEING	WHITBY
VESICA	VISION	WAFERS	WARLEY	WEEKLY	WHITEN
VESPER	VISITS	WAFFLE	WARMED	WEEPER	WHITER
VESPID	VISORS	WAFTED	WARMER	WEEVER	WHITES
VESSEL	VISTAS	WAFTER	WARMLY	WEEVIL	WHIZZY
VESTAL	VISUAL	WAGERS	WARMTH	WEE-WEE	WHOLLY
VESTED	VITALS	WAGGED	WARM-UP	WEIGHT	WHOOPS
VESTRY	VITRIC	WAGGLE	WARNED	WEIHAI	WHOOSH
VETOED	VIVACE	WAGGLY	WARNER	WEIMAR	WHORES
VETOER	VIVIFY	WAGING	WARPED	WEIRDO	WHORLS
VETOES	VIXENS	WAGONS	WARPER	WELDED	WHYDAH
VETTED	VIZIER	WAILED	WARRED	WELDER	WICKED
VEXING	V-NECKS	WAILER	WARREN	WELDON	WICKER
VIABLE	VOCABS	WAISTS	WARSAW	WELKIN	WICKET
VIABLY	VOCALS	WAITED	WARTED	WELKOM	WIDELY
VIAGRA	VOGUES	WAITER	WASHED	WELLED	WIDEST
VIANDS	VOICED	WAIVED	WASHER	WELTER	WIDGET
VIBIST	VOICER	WAIVER	WASHES	WENDED	WIDISH

WIDNES	WINKED	WOODEN	XIAMEN	YEMENI	ZEALOT
WIDOWS	WINKER	WOOERS	XMASES	YENTAI	ZEBRAS
WIDTHS	WINKLE	WOOFER	X-RAYED	YEOMAN	ZENIST
WIELDY	WINNER	WOOING	XUZHOU	YEOMEN	ZENITH
WIFELY	WINNOW	WOOLLY	XYLENE	YES-MAN	ZEPHYR
WIGEON	WINTER	WORDED	XYLOID	YES-MEN	ZEROED
WIGGED	WINTRY	WORKED	XYLOSE	YIELDS	ZEROES
WIGGLE	WIPING	WORKER	XYSTER	YIPPEE	ZESTER
WIGGLY	WIRIER	WORLDS		YODELS	ZEUGMA
WIGHTS	WIRILY	WORMED	**Y**	YOGISM	ZIGONG
WIGWAG	WIRING	WORMER	YACHTS	YOGURT	ZIGZAG
WIGWAM	WIRRAL	WORSEN	YAGARA	YOKELS	ZIMMER
WILDER	WISDOM	WORTHY	YAKKED	YOKING	ZINCIC
WILDLY	WISELY	WOUNDS	YAMMER	YONDER	ZINCKY
WILFUL	WISEST	WOWING	YANGON	YORKER	ZINNIA
WILIER	WISHED	WRAITH	YANKED	YORUBA	ZIPPED
WILLED	WISHER	WRASSE	YANKEE	YOUTHS	ZIPPER
WILLER	WISHES	WREATH	YANTAI	YOWLED	ZIRCON
WILLET	WISMAR	WRECKS	YAPPED	YOWLER	ZITHER
WILLOW	WITHAL	WRENCH	YAPPER	YTTRIA	ZODIAC
WILSON	WITHER	WRETCH	YARDIE	YTTRIC	ZOMBIE
WILTED	WITHIN	WRIEST	YARNED	YUCCAS	ZONATE
WIMBLE	WIZARD	WRIGHT	YARROW	YUNNAN	ZONING
WIMPLE	WOBBLE	WRISTS	YATTER	YUPPIE	ZONKED
WINCED	WOBBLY	WRISTY	YAUPON		ZONULE
WINCER	WOEFUL	WRITER	YAUTIA	**Z**	ZOOMED
WINCES	WOKING	WRITHE	YAWING	ZABRZE	ZOSTER
WINCEY	WOLFED	WRONGS	YAWNED	ZAFFER	ZOYSIA
WINDED	WOLVER	WRYEST	YAWNER	ZAGREB	ZURICH
WINDER	WOLVES	WRYING	YEARLY	ZAMBIA	ZWOLLE
WINDOW	WOMBAT	WYVERN	YEASTY	ZANDER	ZYDECO
WIND UP	WONDER		YELLED	ZANIER	ZYGOMA
WINGED	WONSAN	**X**	YELLER	ZANILY	ZYGOSE
WINGER	WONTED	XENIAL	YELLOW	ZAPPED	ZYGOTE
WINGES	WONTON	XEROMA	YELPED	ZAPPER	ZYMASE
WINING	WOODED	XHOSAN	YELPER	ZAREBA	ZYRIAN

A	ACADIAN	ACYCLIC	AFFAIRE	AIRPORT	ALKANET
AALBORG	ACAROID	ADAGIOS	AFFAIRS	AIR RAID	ALKMAAR
ABALONE	ACAUDAL	ADAMANT	AFFIANT	AIRSHIP	ALLAYED
ABANDON	ACAUSAL	ADAMAWA	AFFIXED	AIRSICK	ALLEGED
ABASHED	ACCEDED	ADAPTED	AFFIXES	AIRWAYS	ALLEGRO
ABASING	ACCEDER	ADAPTER	AFFLICT	AITCHES	ALLELIC
ABATING	ACCENTS	ADAPTOR	AFFRAYS	AJACCIO	ALLERGY
ABAXIAL	ACCLAIM	ADAXIAL	AFFRONT	ALABAMA	ALLHEAL
ABDOMEN	ACCORDS	ADDENDA	AFGHANS	ALAGOAS	ALLONYM
ABELARD	ACCOUNT	ADDICTS	AFRICAN	A LA	ALL OVER
ABELIAN	ACCRETE	ADDRESS	AGAINST	MODE	ALLOWAY
ABERFAN	ACCRUAL	ADDUCED	AGAMETE	ALANINE	ALLOWED
ABETTED	ACCRUED	ADENINE	AGEISTS	ALARMED	ALLOYED
ABETTOR	ACCUSED	ADENOID	AGELESS	ALASKAN	ALLSEED
ABEYANT	ACCUSER	ADENOMA	AGENDAS	ALBANIA	ALL-STAR
ABFARAD	ACERATE	ADEPTLY	AGENDUM	ALBERTA	ALL-TIME
ABHENRY	ACERBIC	ADHERED	AGGRADE	ALBINIC	ALLUDED
ABIDING	ACEROSE	ADIPOSE	AGGRESS	ALBINOS	ALLURED
ABIDJAN	ACETATE	ADIVASI	AGILELY	ALBITIC	ALLURER
ABILITY	ACETIFY	ADJOINT	AGILITY	ALBUMEN	ALLUVIA
ABIOSIS	ACETONE	ADJOURN	AGITATE	ALBUMIN	ALLYING
ABJURED	ACETOUS	ADJUDGE	AGITATO	ALCAZAR	ALMA-ATA
ABJURER	ACHAEAN	ADJUNCT	AGNOMEN	ALCHEMY	ALMANAC
ABLATOR	ACHIEVE	ADJURED	AGONIES	ALCOHOL	ALMERIA
ABLEISM	ACICULA	ADJURER	AGONIST	ALCOPOP	ALMONDS
ABOLISH	ACIDIFY	ADMIRAL	AGONIZE	ALCOVES	ALMONER
ABORTED	ACIDITY	ADMIRED	AGRAFFE	AL DENTE	ALMS MAN
ABRADED	ACNODAL	ADMIRER	AGRAPHA	ALEMBIC	ALOETIC
ABRADER	ACOLYTE	ADOPTED	AGROUND	ALERTED	ALOOFLY
ABREACT	ACONITE	ADORING	AILERON	ALERTLY	ALPACAS
ABREAST	ACOUCHI	ADORNED	AILMENT	A LEVELS	ALPHORN
ABRIDGE	ACQUIRE	ADRENAL	AIMLESS	ALFALFA	ALREADY
ABRUZZI	ACREAGE	ADULATE	AIRBASE	ALGARVE	ALRIGHT
ABSCESS	ACRILAN	ADVANCE	AIRBEDS	ALGEBRA	ALSO RAN
ABSCISE	ACROBAT	ADVENTS	AIR-COOL	ALGERIA	ALSO-RAN
ABSCOND	ACROGEN	ADVERBS	AIRCREW	ALGIERS	ALTDORF
ABSENCE	ACRONYM	ADVERSE	AIRDRIE	AL HUFUF	ALTERED
ABSINTH	ACROTER	ADVICES	AIRDROP	ALIASES	ALTHAEA
ABSOLVE	ACRYLIC	ADVISED	AIRFLOW	ALI BABA	ALTHING
ABSTAIN	ACRYLYL	ADVISER	AIRGLOW	ALIDADE	ALTHORN
ABUSING	ACTABLE	AEGISES	AIRGUNS	ALIENEE	ALUMNAE
ABUSIVE	ACTINAL	AEONIAN	AIRIEST	ALIENOR	ALUMNUS
ABUTTAL	ACTINIA	AERATED	AIRINGS	ALIFORM	ALUNDUM
ABUTTED	ACTINIC	AERATOR	AIRLANE	ALIGARH	ALUNITE
ABUTTER	ACTINON	AERIALS	AIRLESS	ALIGNED	ALYSSUM
ABYSMAL	ACTIONS	AEROBIC	AIRLIFT	ALIMENT	AMADODA
ABYSSAL	ACTRESS	AEROGEL	AIRLINE	ALIMONY	AMALGAM
ABYSSES	ACTUARY	AEROSOL	AIRLOCK	ALIQUOT	AMANITA
ACACIAS	ACTUATE	AETOLIA	AIRMAIL	ALIUNDE	AMASSED
ACADEME	ACULEUS	AFFABLE	AIRMILE	ALKALIC	AMASSER
ACADEMY	ACUTELY	AFFABLY	AIRPLAY	ALKALIS	AMATEUR

AMATORY	ANATOMY	ANNUITY	APLITIC	ARCHINE	ARTISTS
AMAZING	ANCHORS	ANNULAR	APOCARP	ARCHING	ARTLESS
AMAZONS	ANCHOVY	ANNULET	APOCOPE	ARCHIVE	ARTWORK
AMBIENT	ANCHUSA	ANNULUS	APOGAMY	ARCHWAY	ARUGULA
AMBLING	ANCIENT	ANODIZE	APOGEES	ARCUATE	ARUNDEL
AMBOYNA	ANCONAL	ANODYNE	APOLOGY	ARDECHE	ASCARID
AMENDED	ANDANTE	ANOMALY	APOLUNE	ARDENCY	ASCENTS
AMENDER	ANDIRON	ANORAKS	APOMICT	ARDUOUS	ASCETIC
AMENITY	ANDORRA	ANOSMIA	APOSTIL	AREAWAY	ASCITES
AMENTIA	ANDROID	ANOTHER	APOSTLE	ARENITE	ASCITIC
AMERICA	ANEMONE	ANSWERS	APOTHEM	AREOLAR	ASCRIBE
AMHARIC	ANERGIC	ANTACID	APPAREL	ARGOLIS	ASEPSIS
AMIABLE	ANEROID	ANTEFIX	APPEALS	ARGONNE	ASEPTIC
AMIABLY	ANEURIN	ANTEING	APPEASE	ARGOTIC	ASEXUAL
AMMETER	ANGARSK	ANTENNA	APPLAUD	ARGUING	ASHAMED
AMMONAL	ANGELIC	ANTHEMS	APPLIED	ARIDITY	ASHANTI
AMMONIA	ANGELOU	ANTHERS	APPLIER	ARIETTA	ASHDOWN
AMMONIC	ANGELUS	ANT HILL	APPOINT	ARISING	ASHFORD
AMNESIA	ANGERED	ANTHILL	APPRISE	ARIZONA	ASHIEST
AMNESTY	ANGEVIN	ANT HILL	APPROVE	ARMADAS	ASHTRAY
AMNIOTE	ANGINAL	ANTHRAX	APPULSE	ARMBAND	ASIATIC
AMOEBAE	ANGIOMA	ANTIBES	APRAXIA	ARMENIA	ASININE
AMOEBAS	ANGLIAN	ANTIGEN	APRAXIC	ARMFULS	ASKANCE
AMOEBIC	ANGLIFY	ANTIGUA	APRICOT	ARMHOLE	ASOCIAL
AMORIST	ANGLING	ANTIOCH	A PRIORI	ARMIGER	ASPECTS
AMOROSO	ANGOLAN	ANTIQUE	APROPOS	ARMLESS	ASPERSE
AMOROUS	ANGORAS	ANTLERS	APSIDAL	ARMLOCK	ASPHALT
AMOUNTS	ANGRIER	ANTLION	APTERAL	ARMOIRE	ASPIRED
AMPHORA	ANGRILY	ANTONYM	APTNESS	ARMOURY	ASPIRER
AMPLIFY	ANGUINE	ANTWERP	AQUARIA	ARMPITS	ASPIRIN
AMPOULE	ANGUISH	ANUROUS	AQUATIC	ARMREST	ASSAULT
AMPULLA	ANGULAR	ANXIETY	AQUAVIT	AROUSAL	ASSAYED
AMPUTEE	ANHINGA	ANXIOUS	AQUEOUS	AROUSED	ASSAYER
AMULETS	ANILINE	ANYBODY	AQUIFER	AROUSER	ASSEGAI
AMUSING	ANILITY	ANYMORE	ARABIAN	ARRAIGN	ASSHOLE
AMYLASE	ANIMALS	ANYWAYS	ARABIST	ARRANGE	ASSIZES
AMYLENE	ANIMATE	ANYWISE	ARACAJU	ARRAYAL	ASSUAGE
AMYLOID	ANIMATO	APAGOGE	ARAL SEA	ARRAYED	ASSUMED
AMYLOSE	ANIMISM	APATITE	ARAMAIC	ARREARS	ASSUMER
ANAEMIA	ANIMIST	APELIKE	ARANEID	ARRESTS	ASSURED
ANAEMIC	ANIONIC	APETALY	ARAPAHO	ARRIVAL	ASSURER
ANAGOGE	ANISEED	APHAGIA	ARAROBA	ARRIVED	ASSYRIA
ANAGRAM	ANISOLE	APHASIA	ARBITER	ARRIVER	ASTATIC
ANAHEIM	ANKLETS	APHESIS	ARBOURS	ARROWED	ASTOUND
ANALOGY	ANNATES	APHONIA	ARBUTUS	ARSENAL	ASTRIDE
ANALYSE	ANNATTO	APHONIC	ARCADES	ARSENIC	ASTROID
ANALYST	ANNELID	APHOTIC	ARCADIA	ART DECO	ASTYLAR
ANAMBRA	ANNEXED	APHYLLY	ARCANUM	ARTICLE	ASUNDER
ANAPEST	ANNEXES	APIEZON	ARCHAIC	ARTIEST	ASYLUMS
ANARCHY	ANNOYED	APLASIA	ARCHERS	ARTISAN	ATACTIC
ANATASE	ANNUALS	APLENTY	ARCHERY	ARTISTE	ATAVISM

69

ATAVIST	AUXERRE	BACKERS	BALLS-UP	BARENTS	BATTENS
ATELIER	AUXESIS	BACKING	BALMIER	BARGAIN	BATTERS
AT HEART	AVAILED	BACKLOG	BALMILY	BARGEES	BATTERY
ATHEISM	AVARICE	BACK OFF	BALNEAL	BARGING	BATTIER
ATHEIST	AVATARS	BACKSAW	BALONEY	BARILLA	BATTING
ATHLETE	AVENGED	BACKUPS	BALSAMS	BARKERS	BATTLED
ATHWART	AVENGER	BACOLOD	BALTICS	BARKING	BATTLES
ATLANTA	AVENUES	BACTRIA	BALUCHI	BARMAID	BATWING
ATLASES	AVERAGE	BACULUM	BAMBARA	BARMIER	BAUBLES
ATOMISM	AVERRED	BADAJOZ	BAMBERG	BARNAUL	BAUHAUS
ATOMIST	AVERTED	BAD DEBT	BAMBINO	BARNEYS	BAULKED
ATOMIZE	AVESTAN	BAD FORM	BAMBOOS	BARONET	BAUTZEN
ATONING	AVEYRON	BADGERS	BANANAS	BAROQUE	BAUXITE
ATROPHY	AVIATOR	BADNESS	BANBURY	BAROTSE	BAVARIA
ATTACHE	AVIDITY	BAFFLED	BANDAGE	BARQUES	BAWDIER
ATTACKS	AVIGNON	BAFFLER	BANDBOX	BARRACK	BAWDILY
ATTAINT	AVIONIC	BAFFLES	BANDEAU	BARRAGE	BAWLING
ATTEMPT	AVOCADO	BAGANDA	BANDIED	BARRELS	BAYAMON
ATTIRED	AVOIDED	BAGASSE	BANDIER	BARRIER	BAYONET
ATTRACT	AVOIDER	BAGGAGE	BANDING	BARRING	BAYONNE
ATTUNED	AVOWALS	BAGGIER	BANDITS	BARROWS	BAYWOOD
AUBERGE	AVOWING	BAGGILY	BANDUNG	BARYTES	BAZAARS
AUCTION	AWAITED	BAGGING	BANEFUL	BASCULE	BAZOOKA
AUDIBLE	AWAKING	BAGHDAD	BANGERS	BASENJI	BEACHED
AUDIBLY	AWARDED	BAG LADY	BANGING	BASHFUL	BEACHES
AUDITED	AWARDEE	BAGPIPE	BANGKOK	BASHING	BEACONS
AUDITOR	AWARDER	BAGWORM	BANGLES	BASHKIR	BEADIER
AUGITIC	AWESOME	BAHAISM	BANKERS	BASILAN	BEADILY
AUGMENT	AWFULLY	BAHAIST	BANKING	BASILAR	BEADING
AUGURAL	AWKWARD	BAHAMAS	BANKSIA	BASILIC	BEADLES
AUGURED	AWLWORT	BAHRAIN	BANNERS	BASKETS	BEAGLES
AUGUSTA	AWNINGS	BAILEYS	BANNING	BASKING	BEAKERS
AU PAIRS	AXOLOTL	BAILIFF	BANNOCK	BASOTHO	BEAMING
AURALLY	AZIMUTH	BAILING	BANQUET	BAS-RHIN	BEARDED
AUREATE	AZURITE	BAIL OUT	BANSHEE	BASSEIN	BEARERS
AUREOLE	AZYGOUS	BAILOUT	BANTAMS	BASSETS	BEAR HUG
AURICLE		BAINITE	BANTOID	BASSIST	BEARING
AURORAE	**B**	BAITING	BANYANS	BASSOON	BEARISH
AURORAL	BAALBEK	BALANCE	BAODING	BASTARD	BEASTLY
AURORAS	BABASSU	BALATON	BAPTISM	BASTING	BEATERS
AUSPICE	BABBITT	BALCONY	BAPTIST	BASTION	BEATIFY
AUSSIES	BABBLED	BALDING	BAPTIZE	BATCHES	BEATING
AUSTERE	BABBLER	BALEFUL	BARBARY	BATFISH	BEATNIK
AUSTRAL	BABOONS	BALKING	BARBATE	BATHERS	BEAVERS
AUSTRIA	BABYING	BALLADE	BARBELL	BATHING	BECAUSE
AUTARKY	BABYISH	BALLADS	BARBERS	BATH MAT	BECKETT
AUTHORS	BABY-SAT	BALLARD	BARBOUR	BATHTUB	BEDBUGS
AUTOCUE	BABY-SIT	BALLAST	BARBUDA	BATHYAL	BEDDING
AUTOMAT	BACCATE	BALLETS	BARBULE	BATISTE	BEDEVIL
AUTOPSY	BACILLI	BALLOON	BARCHAN	BATSMAN	BEDEWED
AUTUMNS	BACKBAR	BALLOTS	BAR CODE	BATSMEN	BEDFORD

BEDHEAD	BEMUSED	BETTING	BILTONG	BLADDER	BLOUSES
BEDLAMS	BENARES	BETWEEN	BIMODAL	BLAMING	BLOW-DRY
BEDOUIN	BENCHER	BETWIXT	BIMORPH	BLANDER	BLOWERS
BEDPANS	BENCHES	BEVELED	BEWITCH	BLANDLY	BLOWFLY
BEDPOST	BENDIGO	BEWITCH	BINDERS	BLANKET	BLOWIER
BEDRAIL	BENDING	BEXHILL	BINDERY	BLANKLY	BLOWING
BEDROCK	BENEATH	BEYOGLU	BINDING	BLARING	BLOWOUT
BEDROOM	BENEFIT	BEZIQUE	BINNING	BLARNEY	BLOW OUT
BEDSIDE	BENELUX	BHANGRA	BIOCIDE	BLASTED	BLOW-UPS
BEDSORE	BENGALI	BIASING	BIODATA	BLATANT	BLUBBER
BEDTIME	BENNETT	BIASSED	BIOFUEL	BLATHER	BLUE GUM
BEECHES	BENTHOS	BIAXIAL	BIOHERM	BLAUBOK	BLUEING
BEEFIER	BENZENE	BIBCOCK	BIOLOGY	BLAYDON	BLUE JAY
BEEFING	BENZINE	BIBELOT	BIOMASS	BLAZERS	BLUE LAW
BEEF TEA	BENZOIC	BICYCLE	BIONICS	BLAZING	BLUE-SKY
BEEHIVE	BENZOIN	BIDDING	BIOPICS	BLAZONS	BLUETIT
BEELINE	BENZOYL	BIEN HOA	BIOPTIC	BLEAKER	BLUFFED
BEESWAX	BEOGRAD	BIFFING	BIOTECH	BLEAKLY	BLUFFER
BEETFLY	BEQUEST	BIFILAR	BIOTITE	BLEATED	BLUFFLY
BEETLED	BERATED	BIFOCAL	BIOTOPE	BLEATER	BLUNDER
BEETLES	BERBERA	BIG CATS	BIOTYPE	BLEEDER	BLUNGER
BEGGARS	BEREAVE	BIG DEAL	BIPLANE	BLEEPED	BLUNTED
BEGGARY	BERGAMO	BIG ENDS	BIPOLAR	BLEEPER	BLUNTLY
BEGGING	BERMUDA	BIGENER	BIRCHED	BLEMISH	BLURRED
BEGONIA	BERNESE	BIGFOOT	BIRCHES	BLENDED	BLURTED
BEGUILE	BERRIES	BIG GAME	BIRD DOG	BLENDER	BLUSHED
BEHAVED	BERSEEM	BIGGEST	BIRDIFS	BLESBOK	BLUSHER
BEHINDS	BERSERK	BIGGIES	BIRETTA	BLESSED	BLUSHES
BEIJING	BERTHED	BIGHEAD	BISCUIT	BLETHER	BLUSTER
BEJEWEL	BESEECH	BIGHORN	BISHKEK	BLEWITS	B-MOVIES
BELARUS	BESIDES	BIG NAME	BISHOPS	BLIGHTS	BOARDED
BELATED	BESIEGE	BIGNESS	BISMUTH	BLINDED	BOARDER
BELAYED	BESMEAR	BIGOTED	BISTORT	BLINDLY	BOARISH
BELCHED	BESPEAK	BIGOTRY	BISTROS	BLINKED	BOASTED
BELCHES	BESPOKE	BIG SHOT	BITCHED	BLINKER	BOASTER
BELFAST	BESTIAL	BIG TIME	BITCHES	BLISTER	BOATERS
BELFORT	BESTING	BIG TOPS	BITCHIN'	BLITZED	BOATING
BELGAUM	BEST MAN	BIGWIGS	BIT PART	BLITZES	BOATMAN
BELGIAN	BEST-OFF	BIJAPUR	BITTERN	BLOATED	BOATMEN
BELGIUM	BESTREW	BIKANER	BITTERS	BLOATER	BOBBERY
BELIEFS	BESTRID	BIKINIS	BITTIER	BLOCKED	BOBBIES
BELIEVE	BETAINE	BILBOES	BITUMEN	BLONDER	BOBBING
BELLBOY	BETAKEN	BILIARY	BIVALVE	BLONDES	BOBBINS
BELLEEK	BETHANY	BILIOUS	BIVOUAC	BLOODED	BOBBLES
BELLIES	BETHELS	BILKING	BIZARRE	BLOOMED	BOBSLED
BELLOWS	BETHINK	BILLETS	BIZERTE	BLOOMER	BOBSTAY
BELOVED	BETIDED	BILLIES	BLABBED	BLOOPER	BOBTAIL
BELTING	BETIMES	BILLING	BLABBER	BLOSSOM	BODICES
BELT MAN	BETOKEN	BILLION	BLACKED	BLOTCHY	BODKINS
BELTWAY	BETROTH	BILLOWS	BLACKEN	BLOTTED	BOFFINS
BELYING	BETTERS	BILLOWY	BLACKER	BLOTTER	BOGARDE

BOGGIER	BOOTLEG	BOWSHOT	BRECCIA	BROODED	BUGGERY
BOGGING	BOOZERS	BOW TIES	BREEDER	BROODER	BUGGIES
BOGGLED	BOOZE UP	BOXCARS	BRENDEL	BROOKED	BUGGING
BOHEMIA	BOOZE-UP	BOXROOM	BRENNER	BROTHEL	BUGLERS
BOHRIUM	BOOZIER	BOX SEAT	BRENTON	BROTHER	BUGLOSS
BOILERS	BOOZILY	BOXWOOD	BRESCIA	BROWNED	BUILDER
BOILING	BOOZING	BOYCOTT	BREVIER	BROWNER	BUILDUP
BOK CHOY	BOPPING	BOYHOOD	BREVITY	BROWNIE	BUILD UP
BOLDEST	BORACIC	BRABANT	BREWAGE	BROWSED	BUILT-IN
BOLEROS	BORAZON	BRABHAM	BREWERY	BROWSER	BUILT-UP
BOLETUS	BORDERS	BRACING	BREWING	BRUCINE	BUKHARA
BOLIVAR	BORDURE	BRACKEN	BRIBERY	BRUISED	BULBOUS
BOLIVIA	BOREDOM	BRACKET	BRICOLE	BRUISER	BULGIER
BOLLARD	BORNEEL	BRADAWL	BRIDGET	BRUISES	BULGING
BOLOGNA	BORNITE	BRAEMAR	BRIDOON	BRUITED	BULIMIA
BOLONEY	BOROUGH	BRAGGED	BRIGADE	BRUMOUS	BULKIER
BOLSHIE	BORSCHT	BRAGGER	BRIGAND	BRUSHED	BULKILY
BOLSTER	BORSTAL	BRAHMAN	BRIMFUL	BRUSHER	BULKING
BOLTING	BORZOIS	BRAIDED	BRIMMER	BRUSHES	BULLACE
BOLZANO	BOSCAGE	BRAIDER	BRINDLE	BRUSH-UP	BULLATE
BOMBARD	BOSNIAN	BRAILLE	BRING UP	BRUSQUE	BULLDOG
BOMBAST	BOSSIER	BRAINED	BRIOCHE	BRUTISH	BULLETS
BOMBERS	BOSSILY	BRAISED	BRISKER	BRYANSK	BULLIED
BOMBING	BOSSING	BRAKING	BRISKET	BUBBLED	BULLIES
BONAIRE	BOTCHED	BRAKPAN	BRISKLY	BUBBLER	BULLION
BONANZA	BOTCHER	BRAMBLE	BRISTLE	BUBBLES	BULLISH
BONBONS	BOTCH-UP	BRAMLEY	BRISTLY	BUBONIC	BULLOCK
BONDAGE	BOTTLED	BRANAGH	BRISTOL	BUCKETS	BULRUSH
BONDING	BOTTLES	BRANDED	BRITISH	BUCKEYE	BULWARK
BONE-DRY	BOTTOMS	BRANSON	BRITONS	BUCKING	BUMBLED
BONESET	BOTTROP	BRAN TUB	BRITPOP	BUCKLED	BUMBLER
BONFIRE	BOTULIN	BRASHER	BRITTLE	BUCKLER	BUMBOAT
BONGOES	BOUCHEE	BRASHLY	BROADEN	BUCKLES	BUMMING
BONIEST	BOUDOIR	BRASSES	BROADER	BUCKRAM	BUMPERS
BONJOUR	BOULDER	BRASSIE	BROADLY	BUCKSAW	BUMPIER
BONKERS	BOUNCED	BRAVADO	BROCADE	BUCOLIC	BUMPILY
BONNETS	BOUNCER	BRAVAIS	BROCKET	BUDDIES	BUMPING
BONNIER	BOUNCES	BRAVELY	BROGLIE	BUDDING	BUMPKIN
BONUSES	BOUNDED	BRAVERY	BROGUES	BUDGETS	BUNCHED
BOOBIES	BOUNDEN	BRAVEST	BROILED	BUDGING	BUNCHES
BOOBING	BOUNDER	BRAVING	BROILER	BUFFALO	BUNDLED
BOOKEND	BOUQUET	BRAVURA	BROKERS	BUFFERS	BUNDLER
BOOKING	BOURBON	BRAWLED	BROMATE	BUFFETS	BUNDLES
BOOKISH	BOURDON	BRAWLER	BROMIDE	BUFFING	BUNGING
BOOKLET	BOURGES	BRAYING	BROMINE	BUFFOON	BUNGLED
BOOMING	BOUYANT	BRAZIER	BROMISM	BUGABOO	BUNGLER
BOORISH	BOWHEAD	BREADTH	BROMLEY	BUGANDA	BUNGLES
BOOSTED	BOWKNOT	BREAKER	BRONCHI	BUGBANE	BUNIONS
BOOSTER	BOWLERS	BREAK-IN	BRONCOS	BUGBEAR	BUNKERS
BOOTEES	BOWLINE	BREATHE	BRONZED	BUG-EYED	BUNKING
BOOTING	BOWLING	BREATHY	BRONZES	BUGGERS	BUNK OFF

BUNK-UPS	BUSKING	CADAVER	CALOTTE	CANTERS	CAREERS
BUNNIES	BUSSING	CADDIED	CALTROP	CANTHUS	CAREFUL
BUNTING	BUS STOP	CADDIES	CALUMNY	CANTING	CARFARE
BUOYAGE	BUSTARD	CADDISH	CALVARY	CANTONS	CARGOES
BUOYANT	BUSTERS	CADELLE	CALVING	CANTORS	CARHOPS
BUOYING	BUSTIER	CADENCE	CALYCES	CANVASS	CARIBOU
BURBLED	BUSTING	CADENCY	CALYCLE	CANYONS	CARIOCA
BURBLER	BUSTLED	CADENZA	CALYPSO	CANZONA	CARIOLE
BURDENS	BUSTLER	CADGERS	CALYXES	CANZONE	CARIOUS
BURDOCK	BUSTLES	CADGING	CAMBERS	CAPABLE	CARJACK
BUREAUX	BUST-UPS	CADMIUM	CAMBIAL	CAPABLY	CARLINE
BURETTE	BUSYING	CAESIUM	CAMBIST	CAP-A-	CARLING
BURGEON	BUTANOL	CAESURA	CAMBIUM	PIE	CARMINE
BURGERS	BUTCHER	CAFTANS	CAMBRAI	CAPE COD	CARNAGE
BURGESS	BUTLERS	CAGIEST	CAMBRIC	CAPELIN	CARNIFY
BURGHAL	BUTLERY	CAGOULE	CAMELOT	CAPELLA	CAROLED
BURGHER	BUTTERY	CAHOOTS	CAMERAL	CAPERED	CAROLUS
BURGLAR	BUTTIES	CAIQUES	CAMERAS	CAPITAL	CAROTID
BURGLED	BUTTING	CAISSON	CAMP BED	CAPITOL	CAROUSE
BURIALS	BUTTOCK	CAJOLED	CAMPERS	CAPORAL	CARPALE
BURLIER	BUTTONS	CAJUPUT	CAMPHOR	CAPPING	CAR PARK
BURMESE	BUTYRIC	CALABAR	CAMPING	CAPRICE	CARPETS
BURNERS	BUTYRIN	CALAMUS	CAMPION	CAPSIZE	CARPING
BURNING	BUY INTO	CALCIFY	CAM RANH	CAPSTAN	CAR POOL
BURNISH	BUYOUTS	CALCINE	CAMWOOD	CAPSULE	CARPORT
BURNLEY	BUZZARD	CALCITE	CANAPES	CAPTAIN	CARRARA
BURNOUS	BUZZERS	CALCIUM	CANARDS	CAPTION	CARRICK
BURNOUT	BUZZING	CALCULI	CANASTA	CAPTIVE	CARRIED
BURPING	BYE-BYES	CALDERA	CANCANS	CAPTORS	CARRIER
BURRING	BYELOVO	CALDRON	CANCERS	CAPTURE	CARRIES
BURRITO	BYGONES	CALENDS	CANDELA	CARABAO	CARRION
BURROWS	BY-LINES	CALGARY	CANDIED	CARABID	CARROTS
BURSARS	BYRONIC	CALIBRE	CANDIES	CARACAL	CARROTY
BURSARY	BYWORDS	CALICHE	CANDLER	CARACAS	CARRY ON
BURSTER		CALICOS	CANDLES	CARACUL	CARRY-ON
BURTHEN	**C**	CALIPEE	CANDOUR	CARAFES	CARSICK
BURTONS	CABARET	CALIPHS	CANELLA	CARAMBA	CARTAGE
BURUNDI	CABBAGE	CALKING	CANINES	CARAMEL	CARTELS
BURWEED	CABBALA	CALLAIS	CANKERS	CARAVAN	CARTERS
BURYING	CABBIES	CALLANT	CANNERY	CARAVEL	CARTING
BUSBIES	CABEZON	CALL BOX	CANNIER	CARAWAY	CARTONS
BUS BOYS	CABIMAS	CALLBOY	CANNILY	CARBENE	CARTOON
BUSHELS	CABINDA	CALLERS	CANNING	CARBIDE	CARVERS
BUSHIER	CABINET	CALLING	CANNOCK	CARBINE	CARVING
BUSHING	CABLING	CALL-INS	CANNONS	CARBONS	CASCADE
BUSHIRE	CABOOSE	CALLOUS	CANNULA	CARBOYS	CASCARA
BUSHMAN	CAB RANK	CALMEST	CANONRY	CARCASS	CASEASE
BUSHPIG	CACHETS	CALMING	CANOPUS	CARDIAC	CASEATE
BUSHTIT	CACKLED	CALOMEL	CANTALA	CARDIFF	CASEOSE
BUSIEST	CACKLER	CALORIC	CANTATA	CARDING	CASEOUS
BUSKERS	CACKLES	CALORIE	CANTEEN	CARDOON	CASERTA

CASHEWS	CATTERY	CENTURY	CHANTED	CHECK ON	CHIMNEY
CASHIER	CATTIER	CEPHEUS	CHANTER	CHECKUP	CHINESE
CASHING	CATTILY	CERAMIC	CHANTRY	CHEDDAR	CHINKED
CASINGS	CATTISH	CERATED	CHAOTIC	CHEEKED	CHINOOK
CASINOS	CATWALK	CEREALS	CHAPATI	CHEEPED	CHINTZY
CASKETS	CAUDATE	CEREBRA	CHAPEAU	CHEEPER	CHINWAG
CASPIAN	CAULINE	CERTAIN	CHAPELS	CHEERED	CHIPPED
CASQUED	CAULKED	CERTIFY	CHAPLET	CHEERIO	CHIPPER
CASQUES	CAULKER	CERUMEN	CHAPPAL	CHEESES	CHIRPED
CASSATA	CAUSING	CERVINE	CHAPPED	CHEETAH	CHIRPER
CASSAVA	CAUSTIC	CESSION	CHAPTER	CHELATE	CHIRRUP
CASSINO	CAUTERY	CESSPIT	CHARADE	CHEMISE	CHISELS
CASSOCK	CAUTION	CESTODE	CHARGED	CHEMIST	CHIVIED
CASTERS	CAVALLA	CESTOID	CHARGER	CHENGTU	CHLORAL
CASTILE	CAVALRY	CETINJE	CHARGES	CHENNAI	CHLORIC
CASTING	CAVEATS	CETOOGY	CHARIER	CHEQUER	CHOC-ICE
CASTLED	CAVE-INS	CHABLIS	CHARILY	CHEQUES	CHOCKED
CASTLES	CAVEMAN	CHABROL	CHARIOT	CHERISH	CHOCTAW
CAST OFF	CAVEMEN	CHA-CHAS	CHARITY	CHEROOT	CHOICER
CAST-OFF	CAVERNS	CHAFFED	CHARKHA	CHERUBS	CHOICES
CASTORS	CAVES IN	CHAFFER	CHARLES	CHERVIL	CHOKERS
CASUIST	CAVETTO	CHAFING	CHARLIE	CHESTED	CHOKING
CATALAN	CAVILED	CHAGRIN	CHARMED	CHESTER	CHOLERA
CATALPA	CAYENNE	CHAINED	CHARMER	CHEVIOT	CHOLINE
CATANIA	CEASING	CHAIRED	CHARNEL	CHEVRON	CHOLULA
CATARRH	CEDILLA	CHAISES	CHARPOY	CHEWIER	CHOMPED
CATBIRD	CEILING	CHALAZA	CHARQUI	CHEWING	CHOOSER
CATBOAT	CELADON	CHALCID	CHARRED	CHIANTI	CHOPPED
CATCALL	CELEBES	CHALCIS	CHARTED	CHIAPAS	CHOPPER
CATCHER	CELESTA	CHALDEA	CHARTER	CHIASMA	CHORALE
CATCHES	CELLARS	CHALETS	CHASERS	CHIBOUK	CHORDAL
CATCH IT	CELLIST	CHALICE	CHASING	CHICAGO	CHOREAL
CATCH UP	CELLNET	CHALKED	CHASMAL	CHICANE	CHORION
CATECHU	CELLULE	CHALLAH	CHASSIS	CHICANO	CHORLEY
CATERED	CELSIUS	CHALLIS	CHASTEN	CHICKEN	CHOROID
CATERER	CEMBALO	CHALONE	CHASTER	CHICORY	CHORTLE
CATFISH	CENACLE	CHAMBER	CHATEAU	CHIDDEN	CHORZOW
CATHEAD	CENSORS	CHAMFER	CHATHAM	CHIDING	CHOWDER
CATHODE	CENSUAL	CHAMOIS	CHATTED	CHIEFLY	CHROMIC
CATKINS	CENSURE	CHAMPAC	CHATTEL	CHIFFON	CHROMYL
CATLING	CENTAUR	CHAMPED	CHATTER	CHIGGER	CHRONIC
CATMINT	CENTAVO	CHANCED	CHAYOTE	CHIGNON	CHRONON
CATNAPS	CENTERS	CHANCEL	CHEAPEN	CHILEAN	CHUCKED
CAT'S-EAR	CENTIME	CHANCES	CHEAPER	CHILIAD	CHUCK IN
CAT'S EYE	CENTIMO	CHANCRE	CHEAPIE	CHILIES	CHUCKLE
CAT'S PAW	CENTNER	CHANGDE	CHEAPLY	CHILLED	CHUFFED
	CENTRAL	CHANGED	CHEATED	CHILLUM	CHUGGED
CATSUIT	CENTRED	CHANGER	CHEATER	CHILUNG	CHUKCHI
CATTALO	CENTRES	CHANGES	CHECHEN	CHIMERA	CHUKKER
	CENTRIC	CHANNEL	CHECKED	CHIMERE	CHUMMED
	CENTRUM	CHANSON	CHECK-IN	CHIMING	CHURNED

CHUTNEY	CLAPPER	CLINKER	COAXIAL	COLDISH	COMPARE
CHUVASH	CLAQUES	CLINTON	COAXING	COLDITZ	COMPASS
CHYMOUS	CLARIFY	CLIPPED	COBBERS	COLD WAR	COMPEER
CICADAS	CLARINO	CLIPPER	COBBLED	COLICKY	COMPERE
CICHLID	CLARION	CLIPPIE	COBBLER	COLITIC	COMPETE
CILIARY	CLARITY	CLIQUES	COBWEBS	COLITIS	COMPILE
CILIATE	CLARKIA	CLIQUEY	COCAINE	COLLAGE	COMPING
CIMBRIC	CLASHED	CLOACAL	COCCOID	COLLARD	COMPLEX
CINDERS	CLASHER	CLOAKED	COCCOUS	COLLARS	COMPLIN
CINDERY	CLASHES	CLOBBER	COCHLEA	COLLATE	COMPONY
CINEMAS	CLASPED	CLOCHES	COCKADE	COLLECT	COMPORT
CINERIN	CLASPER	CLOCKED	COCKIER	COLLEEN	COMPOSE
CIPHERS	CLASSED	CLOGGED	COCKING	COLLEGE	COMPOST
CIPOLIN	CLASSES	CLONMEL	COCKLES	COLLIDE	COMPOTE
CIRCLED	CLASSIC	CLOPPED	COCKNEY	COLLIER	COMPTON
CIRCLER	CLASSIS	CLOSELY	COCKPIT	COLLIES	COMPUTE
CIRCLES	CLASTIC	CLOSEST	COCK-UPS	COLLOID	COMRADE
CIRCLET	CLATTER	CLOSETS	COCONUT	COLLUDE	CONAKRY
CIRCLIP	CLAUSAL	CLOSE-UP	COCOONS	COLOBUS	CONATUS
CIRCUIT	CLAUSES	CLOSING	COCOTTE	COLOGNE	CONCAVE
CIRQUES	CLAVATE	CLOSURE	COCOYAM	COLOMBO	CONCEDE
CIRRATE	CLAVIER	CLOTHED	CODDLED	COLONEL	CONCEIT
CIRSOID	CLAVIUS	CLOTHES	CODEINE	COLONIC	CONCEPT
CISSIES	CLAWING	CLOTTED	CODFISH	COLOSSI	CONCERN
CISSOID	CLAYPAN	CLOTURE	CODGERS	COLOURS	CONCERI
CISTERN	CLEANED	CLOUDED	CODICES	COLTISH	CONCHAL
CISTRON	CLEANER	CLOUTED	CODICIL	COLUMNS	CONCHES
CITABLE	CLEANLY	CLOWNED	CODLING	COMBATS	CONCISE
CITADEL	CLEANSE	CLOYING	COELIAC	COMBERS	CONCOCT
CITHARA	CLEANUP	CLUBBED	COEQUAL	COMBINE	CONCORD
CITIZEN	CLEAN UP	CLUBMAN	COERCED	COMBING	CONCUSS
CITRATE	CLEARED	CLUCKED	COETZEE	COMB-OUT	CONDEMN
CITRINE	CLEARER	CLUMPED	COEVALS	COMBUST	CONDIGN
CITRONS	CLEARLY	CLUNIAC	COEXIST	COMECON	CONDOLE
CIVILLY	CLEAR UP	CLUPEID	COFFERS	COMEDIC	CONDOMS
CIVVIES	CLEAVED	CLUSTER	COFFINS	COMFIER	CONDONE
CLACKED	CLEAVER	CLUTTER	COGENCY	COMFITS	CONDORS
CLADODE	CLEMENT	CLYPEAL	COGGING	COMFORT	CONDUCE
CLAIMED	CLERICS	CLYPEUS	COGNACS	COMFREY	CONDUCT
CLAIMER	CLERKED	COACHED	COGNATE	COMICAL	CONDUIT
CLAMANT	CLICHED	COACHES	COGNIZE	COMINGS	CONDYLE
CLAMBER	CLICHES	COAL GAS	COHABIT	COMMAND	CONFECT
CLAMMED	CLICKED	COALING	COHERED	COMMEND	CONFESS
CLAMOUR	CLICKER	COAL TAR	COHORTS	COMMENT	CONFIDE
CLAMPED	CLIENTS	COAMING	COILING	COMMODE	CONFINE
CLAMPER	CLIMATE	COARSEN	COIMBRA	COMMONS	CONFIRM
CLANGED	CLIMBED	COARSER	COINAGE	COMMUNE	CONFORM
CLANGER	CLIMBER	COASTAL	COINERS	COMMUTE	CONFUSE
CLANGOR	CLINGER	COASTED	COINING	COMOROS	CONFUTE
CLANKED	CLINICS	COASTER	COLBERT	COMPACT	CONGEAL
CLAPPED	CLINKED	COATING	COLDEST	COMPANY	

CONGEST	COOLIES	CORONER	COUNTED	CRABBED	CRESSET
CONGIUS	COOLING	CORONET	COUNTER	CRACKED	CRESTED
CONICAL	COOLISH	CORPORA	COUNTRY	CRACKER	CRETINS
CONIFER	COONTIE	CORPSES	COUPLED	CRACKLE	CREVICE
CONIINE	COOPERS	CORRADE	COUPLER	CRACK UP	CREW CUT
CONJOIN	CO-OPTED	CORRALS	COUPLES	CRACKUP	CREWING
CONJURE	COPAIBA	CORRECT	COUPLET	CRADLED	CRIBBED
CONKERS	COPEPOD	CORREZE	COUPONS	CRADLES	CRICKED
CONKING	COPIERS	CORRIDA	COURAGE	CRAFTED	CRICKET
CONNATE	COPILOT	CORRODE	COURIER	CRAIOVA	CRICOID
CONNECT	COPINGS	CORRUPT	COURSED	CRAMMED	CRIMEAN
CONNERY	COPIOUS	CORSAGE	COURSER	CRAMMER	CRIMPED
CONNING	COP-OUTS	CORSAIR	COURSES	CRAMPED	CRIMPER
CONNIVE	COPPERS	CORSETS	COURTED	CRAMPON	CRIMPLE
CONNOTE	COPPERY	CORSICA	COURTLY	CRANIAL	CRIMSON
CONQUER	COPPICE	CORTEGE	COUSINS	CRANING	CRINGED
CONSENT	COPPING	CORTONA	COUTURE	CRANIUM	CRINGLE
CONSIGN	COPULAR	CORVINE	COUVADE	CRANKED	CRINITE
CONSIST	COPYCAT	COSENZA	COVERED	CRANK UP	CRINKLE
CONSOLE	COPYING	COSHING	COVERER	CRAPPED	CRINKLY
CONSOLS	COPYIST	COSIEST	COVERTS	CRAPPIE	CRINOID
CONSORT	COQUINA	COSINES	COVER-UP	CRASHED	CRIOLLO
CONSULS	COQUITO	COSMINE	COVETED	CRASHES	CRIPPLE
CONSULT	CORACLE	COSMOID	COVETER	CRASSLY	CRISPED
CONSUME	CORBEIL	COSTARD	COWARDS	CRATERS	CRISPLY
CONTACT	CORBELS	CO-STARS	COWARDY	CRATING	CRISSAL
CONTAIN	CORDAGE	COSTATE	COWBANE	CRAVATS	CRISSUM
CONTEMN	CORDATE	COSTING	COWBELL	CRAVING	CRITICS
CONTEND	CORDIAL	COSTIVE	COWBIND	CRAWLED	CRITTER
CONTENT	CORDING	COSTNER	COWBIRD	CRAWLER	CROAKED
CONTEST	CORDITE	COSTUME	COWBOYS	CRAWLEY	CROAKER
CONTEXT	CORDOBA	COTE-	COWDREY	CRAYONS	CROATIA
CONTORT	CORDONS	D'OR	COWERED	CRAZIER	CROCEIN
CONTOUR	CORINTH	COTERIE	COWFISH	CRAZILY	CROCHET
CONTROL	CORKAGE	COTIDAL	COWGIRL	CREAKED	CROCKET
CONTUSE	CORKERS	COTINGA	COWHAND	CREAMED	CROFTER
CONVENE	CORKING	COTONOU	COWHERB	CREAMER	CRONIES
CONVENT	CORMOUS	COTTAGE	COWHERD	CREASED	CROOKED
CONVERT	CORNCOB	COTTONY	COWHIDE	CREASES	CROONED
CONVICT	CORNEAL	COUCHED	COWLICK	CREATED	CROONER
CONVOKE	CORNERS	COUCHER	COWLING	CREATOR	CROPPED
CONVOYS	CORNETS	COUCHES	COWPATS	CRECHES	CROPPER
COOKERS	CORNICE	COUGARS	COWRIES	CREDENT	CROQUET
COOKERY	CORNIER	COUGHED	COWSHED	CREDITS	CROSIER
COOKIES	CORNISH	COULDN'T	COWSLIP	CREEDAL	CROSSED
COOKING	CORNUAL	COULDST	COXCOMB	CREEPER	CROSSER
COOKOUT	CORNUTE	COULOIR	COYNESS	CREMATE	CROSSES
COOKSON	COROLLA	COULOMB	COYOTES	CREMONA	CROSSLY
COOLANT	CORONAE	COULTER	COZENED	CRENATE	CROUTON
COOLERS	CORONAL	COUNCIL	COZENER	CREOLES	CROWBAR
COOLEST	CORONAS	COUNSEL	COZIEST	CREOSOL	CROWDED

CROWING	CULPRIT	CUSPATE	DADAIST	DASHEEN	DECADAL
CROWNED	CULTISH	CUSSING	DADDIES	DASHIKI	DECADES
CROYDON	CULTISM	CUSTARD	DADROCK	DASHING	DECAGON
CROZIER	CULTIST	CUSTODY	DAEMONS	DASYURE	DECANAL
CRUCIAL	CULTURE	CUSTOMS	DAFTEST	DATABLE	DECAPOD
CRUCIFY	CULVERT	CUTAWAY	DAGGERS	DATA BUS	DECAYED
CRUDELY	CUMBRIA	CUTBACK	DAGLOCK	DATIVAL	DECEASE
CRUDEST	CUMQUAT	CUT DOWN	DAHLIAS	DATIVES	DECEIVE
CRUDITY	CUMULET	CUTICLE	DAHOMAN	DAUBERY	DECENCY
CRUELLY	CUMULUS	CUTLASS	DAHOMEY	DAUBING	DECIARE
CRUELTY	CUNEATE	CUTLERS	DAILIES	DAUNTED	DECIBEL
CRUISED	CUNNING	CUTLERY	DAIRIES	DAUNTER	DECIDED
CRUISER	CUP CAKE	CUTLETS	DAISIES	DAUPHIN	DECIDER
CRUISES	CUPOLAS	CUTOFFS	DAKOTAN	DAWDLED	DECIDUA
CRUMBLE	CUPPING	CUTOUTS	DALLIED	DAWDLER	DECIMAL
CRUMBLY	CUPRITE	CUTTACK	DAMAGED	DAWKINS	DECKING
CRUMPET	CUPROUS	CUTTERS	DAMAGER	DAWNING	DECLAIM
CRUMPLE	CUP TIES	CUTTING	DAMAGES	DAYBOOK	DECLARE
CRUMPLY	CURABLE	CUTWORK	DAMMING	DAYBOYS	DECLASS
CRUNCHY	CURABLY	CUTWORM	DAMNIFY	DAY CARE	DECLINE
CRUNODE	CURACAO	CWMBRAN	DAMNING	DAY-CARE	DECODED
CRUPPER	CURATES	CYANATE	DAMPERS	DAYLONG	DECORUM
CRUSADE	CURAIOR	CYANIDE	DAMPEST	DAYROOM	DECOYED
CRUSHED	CURBING	CYANINE	DAMPING	DAYTIME	DECOYER
CRUSHES	CURCUMA	CYANITE	DAMPISH	DAZEDLY	DECREED
CRUSTAL	CURDLED	CYBALER	DAMSELS	DAZZLED	DECREER
CRUZADO	CURE-ALL	CYCLING	DAMSONS	DEACONS	DECREES
CRYBABY	CURETTE	CYCLIST	DANCERS	DEAD END	DECRIAL
CRYOGEN	CURFEWS	CYCLOID	DANCING	DEADEYE	DECRIED
CRYPTAL	CURIOSA	CYCLONE	DANDERS	DEADPAN	DECRIER
CRYPTIC	CURIOUS	CYCLOPS	DANDIER	DEAD SET	DECUPLE
CRYSTAL	CURLERS	CYGNETS	DANDIES	DEAF-AID	DEDUCED
CTENOID	CURLEWS	CYMBALS	DANDIFY	DEALATE	DEEMING
CUBBING	CURLIER	CYNICAL	DANDLED	DEALERS	DEEPEST
CUBICAL	CURLING	CYPHERS	DANDLER	DEALING	DEEP FRY
CUBICLE	CURRANT	CYPRESS	DANGERS	DEANERY	DEFACED
CUBITAL	CURRENT	CYPRIOT	DANGLED	DEAREST	DEFACER
CUCKOLD	CURRIED	CYPSELA	DANGLER	DEARIES	DE FACTO
CUCKOOS	CURRIER	CYSTINE	DANKEST	DEATHLY	DEFAMED
CUDBEAR	CURRIES	CYSTOID	DANSEUR	DEBACLE	DEFAMER
CUDDLED	CURRISH	CYTHERA	DAPHNIA	DEBASED	DEFAULT
CUDGELS	CURSING	CZARDAS	DAPPING	DEBASER	DEFEATS
CUDLIPP	CURSIVE	CZARINA	DAPPLED	DEBATED	DEFECTS
CUDWEED	CURSORS		DAPSONE	DEBATER	DEFENCE
CUE BALL	CURSORY	**D**	DARESAY	DEBATES	DEFIANT
CUFFING	CURTAIL		DARIOLE	DEBAUCH	DEFICIT
CUIRASS	CURTAIN	DABBING	DARKEST	DEBITED	DEFILED
CUISINE	CURTESY	DABBLED	DARKIES	DEBORAH	DEFILER
CULCHIE	CURVING	DABBLER	DARLING	DEBOUCH	DEFILES
CULICID	CUSHIER	DAB HAND	DARNING	DEBRIEF	DEFINED
CULLING	CUSHION	DACTYLS	DARTING	DEBTORS	DEFINER
		DADAISM			

DEFLATE	DENEUVE	DESIRES	DHAHRAN	DILATED	DISCORD
DEFLECT	DENIALS	DESKTOP	DIABASE	DILATOR	DISCUSS
DEFORCE	DENIERS	DESMOID	DIABOLO	DILDOES	DISDAIN
DEFRAUD	DENIZEN	DESPAIR	DIADEMS	DILEMMA	DISEASE
DEFROCK	DENMARK	DESPISE	DIAGRAM	DILUENT	DISEUSE
DEFROST	DENNING	DESPITE	DIALECT	DILUTED	DISGUST
DEFUNCT	DENOTED	DESPOIL	DIALING	DILUTEE	DISHFUL
DEFUSED	DENSELY	DESPOND	DIALLED	DILUTER	DISHIER
DEFYING	DENSEST	DESPOTS	DIALLER	DIMETER	DISHING
DEGAUSS	DENSITY	DESSERT	DIALYSE	DIMMERS	DISJECT
DEGRADE	DENTATE	DESTINE	DIAMINE	DIMMEST	DISJOIN
DEGREES	DENTINE	DESTINY	DIAMOND	DIMMING	DISLIKE
DEHISCE	DENTING	DESTOCK	DIANOIA	DIMNESS	DISMAST
DEICIDE	DENTIST	DESTROY	DIAPERS	DIMORPH	DISMISS
DE-ICING	DENTOID	DETAILS	DIARCHY	DIMPLES	DISOBEY
DEICTIC	DENTURE	DETENTE	DIARIES	DIMWITS	DISPLAY
DEIFIED	DENUDED	DETERGE	DIARIST	DINERIC	DISPORT
DEIFIER	DENUDER	DETINUE	DIASTER	DINETTE	DISPOSE
DEIFORM	DENYING	DETOURS	DIAZINE	DINGIER	DISPUTE
DEIGNED	DEONTIC	DETRACT	DIAZOLE	DINGILY	DISRATE
DEISTIC	DEPISER	DETRAIN	DIBASIC	DINGLES	DISROBE
DEITIES	DEPLETE	DETROIT	DIBBING	DINGOES	DISRUPT
DEJECTA	DEPLORE	DETRUDE	DIBBLED	DINKIER	DISSECT
DE KLERK	DEPLUME	DEUTZIA	DIBBLER	DINNERS	DISSENT
DELAINE	DEPOSAL	DEVALUE	DIBBLES	DINNING	DISTAFF
DELAYED	DEPOSED	DEVELOP	DICIEST	DIOCESE	DISTANT
DELAYER	DEPOSER	DEVIANT	DICKENS	DIOPTRE	DISTEND
DELETED	DEPOSIT	DEVIATE	DICKIER	DIORAMA	DISTICH
DELIGHT	DEPRAVE	DEVICES	DICKIES	DIORITE	DISTORT
DELIMIT	DEPRESS	DEVILED	DICLINY	DIOXIDE	DISTURB
DELIVER	DEPRIVE	DEVILRY	DICTATE	DIPHASE	DISUSED
DELOUSE	DEPSIDE	DEVIOUS	DICTION	DIPLOID	DITCHED
DELPHIC	DEPUTED	DEVISAL	DICTUMS	DIPLOMA	DITCHER
DELTAIC	DERANGE	DEVISED	DIDDLED	DIPLONT	DITCHES
DELTOID	DERBIES	DEVISEE	DIDICOY	DIPNOAN	DITTANY
DELUDED	DERIDED	DEVISER	DIEBACK	DIPOLAR	DITTIES
DELUDER	DERIDER	DEVISOR	DIE-CAST	DIPPERS	DIURNAL
DELUGED	DERIVED	DEVIZES	DIEHARD	DIPPING	DIVERGE
DELUGES	DERIVER	DEVOICE	DIESELS	DIPSHIT	DIVERSE
DELVING	DERMOID	DEVOIRS	DIETARY	DIPTYCH	DIVIDED
DEMANDS	DERRICK	DEVOLVE	DIETING	DIREFUL	DIVIDER
DEMERGE	DERVISH	DEVOTED	DIFFUSE	DIRNDLS	DIVIDES
DEMERIT	DESCALE	DEVOTEE	DIGAMMA	DIRTIED	DIVINED
DEMESNE	DESCANT	DEWATER	DIGESTS	DIRTIER	DIVINER
DEMIGOD	DESCEND	DEWCLAW	DIGGERS	DIRTILY	DIVISOR
DEMIVEG	DESCENT	DEWDROP	DIGGING	DISABLE	DIVORCE
DEMONIC	DESERTS	DEWIEST	DIGITAL	DISAVOW	DIVULGE
DEMOTED	DESERVE	DEWLAPS	DIGNIFY	DISBAND	DIZZIER
DEMOTIC	DESIGNS	DEXTRAL	DIGNITY	DISCARD	DIZZILY
DEMOUNT	DESIRED	DEXTRAN	DIGRAPH	DISCERN	DNIEPER
DEMURER	DESIRER	DEXTRIN	DIGRESS	DISCOID	D-NOTICE

DOBRUJA	DOODLED	DRAFTED	DRONING	DUELLED	DYNAMIC
DOCKAGE	DOODLER	DRAFTEE	DRONISH	DUELLER	DYNAMOS
DOCKERS	DOODLES	DRAFTER	DROOLED	DUENNAS	DYNASTY
DOCKETS	DOOMING	DRAGGED	DROOPED	DUFFERS	DYSURIA
DOCKING	DO-OR-	DRAGGLE	DROPLET	DUGOUTS	DYSURIC
DOCTORS	DIE	DRAGNET	DROP OFF	DUKEDOM	DZONGKA
DODDERY	DOORMAN	DRAGONS	DROPOUT	DULLARD	
DODDLES	DOORMAT	DRAGOON	DROPPED	DULLEST	**E**
DODGEMS	DOORMEN	DRAINED	DROPPER	DULLING	EACH WAY
DODGERS	DOORWAY	DRAINER	DROSHKY	DULOSIS	EAGERLY
DODGIER	DOPIEST	DRAPERS	DROUGHT	DUMBEST	EAGLETS
DODGING	DORMANT	DRAPERY	DROVERS	DUMMIES	EARACHE
DODOISM	DORMERS	DRAPING	DROWNED	DUMPERS	EARDRUM
DOESKIN	DORMICE	DRASTIC	DROWNER	DUMPIER	EARFLAP
DOFFING	DORNICK	DRATTED	DROWSED	DUMPING	EARHOLE
DOGBANE	DOSAGES	DRAUGHT	DRUBBER	DUNDALK	EARLDOM
DOGCART	DOSSERS	DRAWBAR	DRUDGED	DUNEDIN	EARLIER
DOG DAYS	DOSSIER	DRAWERS	DRUDGER	DUNGEON	EARLOBE
DOGFISH	DOSSING	DRAWING	DRUDGES	DUNKING	EARMARK
DOGGERY	DOTAGES	DRAWLED	DRUGGED	DUNKIRK	EARMUFF
DOGGIES	DOTTIER	DRAWLER	DRUGGET	DUNNAGE	EARNERS
DOGGING	DOTTING	DRAWS IN	DRUIDIC	DUNNEST	EARNEST
DOGGONE	DOUBLED	DRAWS UP	DRUMLIN	DUNNING	EARNING
DOGLEGS	DOUBLER	DREADED	DRUMMED	DUNNITE	EARPLUG
DOG ROSE	DOUBLES	DREAMED	DRUMMER	DUODENA	EARRING
DOG TAGS	DOUBLET	DREAMER	DRUNKEN	DUOTONE	EARSHOT
DOGTROT	DOUBTED	DREDGED	DRUNKER	DUPABLE	EARTHED
DOGVANE	DOUBTER	DREDGER	DRUTHER	DURABLE	EARTHEN
DOGWOOD	DOUCHES	DRENTHE	DRYABLE	DURABLY	EARTHLY
DOILIES	DOUGHTY	DRESDEN	DRYADIC	DURANGO	EARWIGS
DOLEFUL	DOUGLAS	DRESSED	DRY DOCK	DURMAST	EASEFUL
DOLLARS	DOURINE	DRESSER	DRY-EYED	DUSKIER	EASIEST
DOLLIES	DOUSING	DRESSES	DRY LAND	DUSTBIN	EAST END
DOLLING	DOWABLE	DRESS UP	DRYNESS	DUSTERS	EASTERN
DOLLISH	DOWAGER	DRIBBLE	DRY-SALT	DUSTIER	EASTERS
DOLLOPS	DOWDIER	DRIBLET	DRY-SHOD	DUSTING	EASTING
DOLMENS	DOWDILY	DRIED UP	DRYWALL	DUSTMAN	EATABLE
DOLPHIN	DOWN-BOW	DRIFTED	DUALISM	DUSTMEN	EBB TIDE
DOLTISH	DOWNERS	DRIFTER	DUALIST	DUSTPAN	EBONITE
DOMAINS	DOWNIER	DRILLED	DUALITY	DUSTUPS	EBONIZE
DOMICAL	DOWNING	DRILLER	DUBBING	DUTIFUL	ECBOLIC
DOMINEE	DOWRIES	DRINKER	DUBIETY	DUVETYN	ECCRINE
DONATED	DOWSERS	DRIP-DRY	DUBIOUS	DVANDVA	ECDYSIS
DONATOR	DOWSING	DRIPPED	DUBNIUM	DWARFED	ECHELON
DONBASS	DOYLEYS	DRIVE IN	DUCHESS	DWARVES	ECHIDNA
DONEGAL	DOZENTH	DRIVE-IN	DUCHIES	DWELLED	ECHINUS
DONETSK	DOZIEST	DRIVERS	DUCKIES	DWELLER	ECHOING
DON JUAN	DRABBER	DRIVING	DUCKING	DWINDLE	ECHOISM
DONKEYS	DRABBLE	DRIZZLE	DUCTILE	DYARCHY	ECLAIRS
DONNING	DRACHMA	DRIZZLY	DUDGEON	DYELINE	ECLIPSE
DONNISH	DRACHMS	DROLLER	DUELING	DYEWOOD	ECLOGUE

ECOCIDE	ELATIVE	EMITTER	ENERGID	ENTRAIN	EQUATOR
ECOLOGY	ELBOWED	EMOTION	ENFEOFF	ENTRANT	EQUERRY
ECONOMY	ELDERLY	EMOTIVE	ENFIELD	ENTREAT	EQUINOX
ECORCHE	ELEATIC	EMPALER	ENFORCE	ENTREES	ERASERS
ECOTONE	ELECTED	EMPANEL	ENGAGED	ENTRIES	ERASING
ECOTYPE	ELECTOR	EMPATHY	ENGAGER	ENTROPY	ERASION
ECSTASY	ELEGANT	EMPEROR	EN GARDE	ENTRUST	ERASURE
ECTHYMA	ELEGIAC	EMPIRES	ENGINES	ENTWINE	ERECTED
ECTOPIA	ELEGIES	EMPIRIC	ENGLAND	E NUMBER	ERECTER
ECTOPIC	ELEGIST	EMPLACE	ENGLISH	ENVELOP	ERECTLY
ECTYPAL	ELEGIZE	EMPORIA	ENGORGE	ENVENOM	ERECTOR
ECUADOR	ELEMENT	EMPOWER	ENGRAFT	ENVIOUS	EREMITE
EDACITY	ELEUSIS	EMPRESS	ENGRAIL	ENVIRON	EREPSIN
EDAPHIC	ELEVATE	EMPTIED	ENGRAIN	ENVYING	ERISTIC
EDDYING	ELEVENS	EMPTIER	ENGRAVE	ENZYMES	ERITREA
EDGIEST	ELIDING	EMPTIES	ENGROSS	EOBIONT	ERMINES
EDGINGS	ELISION	EMPTILY	ENHANCE	EOSINIC	ERODENT
EDICTAL	ELITISM	EMPYEMA	ENIGMAS	EPARCHY	ERODING
EDIFICE	ELITIST	EMULATE	ENJOYED	EPAULET	EROSION
EDIFIED	ELIXIRS	EMULOUS	ENJOYER	EPEEIST	EROSIVE
EDIFIER	ELLIPSE	ENABLED	ENLARGE	EPEIRIC	EROTEMA
EDITING	EL MINYA	ENABLER	ENLIVEN	EPERGNE	EROTICA
EDITION	EL OBEID	ENACTED	EN MASSE	EPIBOLY	ERRANCY
EDITORS	ELOPING	ENACTOR	ENNOBLE	EPICARP	ERRANDS
EDUCATE	ELUDING	ENAMOUR	ENOUNCE	EPICENE	ERRATIC
EEL-LIKE	ELUSION	ENCASED	ENPLANE	EPICURE	ERRATUM
EELPOUT	ELUSIVE	ENCHAIN	ENQUIRE	EPIDOTE	ERRHINE
EELWORM	ELUVIAL	ENCHANT	ENQUIRY	EPIGEAL	ERUDITE
EFFACED	ELUVIUM	EN CLAIR	ENRAGED	EPIGENE	ERUPTED
EFFACER	ELYSIAN	ENCLAVE	ENROBER	EPIGONE	ERZURUM
EFFECTS	ELYSIUM	ENCLOSE	EN ROUTE	EPIGRAM	ESBJERG
EFFORTS	ELYTRON	ENCODED	ENSIGNS	EPIGYNY	ESCAPED
EGGCUPS	EMANATE	ENCODER	ENSLAVE	EPIMERE	ESCAPEE
EGGHEAD	EMBARGO	ENCOMIA	ENSNARE	EPISODE	ESCAPER
EGG ROLL	EMBASSY	ENCORES	ENSUING	EPISOME	ESCAPES
EGOISTS	EMBLEMS	ENCRUST	ENSURED	EPISTLE	ESCOLAR
EGOTISM	EMBOLIC	ENDARCH	ENSURER	EPITAPH	ESCORTS
EGOTIST	EMBOLUS	ENDEMIC	ENTASIA	EPITAXY	ESERINE
EGO TRIP	EMBRACE	END GAME	ENTASIS	EPITHET	ESKIMOS
EIDETIC	EMBROIL	ENDINGS	ENTEBBE	EPITOME	ESPARTO
EIDOLON	EMBRYOS	ENDIVES	ENTENTE	EPIZOIC	ESPOUSE
EIGHTHS	EMENDED	ENDLESS	ENTERED	EPIZOON	ESPYING
EIGHTVO	EMERALD	ENDMOST	ENTERER	EPOCHAL	ESQUIRE
EINKORN	EMERGED	ENDORSE	ENTERIC	EPOCHES	ESSAYED
EJECTED	EMERSED	ENDOWED	ENTERON	EPONYMY	ESSENCE
EJECTOR	EMETICS	ENDOWER	ENTHRAL	EPSILON	ESSONNE
ELAMITE	EMETINE	ENDUING	ENTHUSE	EQUABLE	ESTATES
ELAPSED	EMIGRES	ENDURED	ENTICED	EQUABLY	ESTHETE
ELASTIC	EMINENT	END USER	ENTICER	EQUALED	ESTONIA
ELASTIN	EMIRATE	ENDWAYS	ENTITLE	EQUALLY	ESTORIL
ELATION	EMITTED	ENEMIES	ENTOPIC	EQUATED	ESTREAT

ESTUARY	EXACTOR	EXPOSAL	FADEOUT	FARADAY	FEASTED
ETAGERE	EXALTED	EXPOSED	FAEROES	FARADIC	FEASTER
ETAMINE	EXALTER	EXPOSER	FAG ENDS	FARAWAY	FEATHER
ETCHERS	EXAMINE	EXPOSES	FAGGING	FARCEUR	FEATURE
ETCHING	EXAMPLE	EXPOUND	FAGGOTS	FAR EAST	FEBRILE
ETERNAL	EXARATE	EXPRESS	FAIENCE	FAR-GONE	FEDERAL
ETESIAN	EXCERPT	EXPUNGE	FAILING	FARMERS	FEDORAS
ETHANOL	EXCIMER	EXSCIND	FAILURE	FARMING	FEEBLER
ETHERIC	EXCISED	EXTENTS	FAINTED	FARNESS	FEEDBAG
ETHICAL	EXCITED	EXTINCT	FAINTER	FARRAGO	FEEDERS
ETHMOID	EXCITER	EXTRACT	FAINTLY	FARRIER	FEEDING
ETHYLIC	EXCITON	EXTREME	FAIREST	FARTHER	FEEDLOT
ETRURIA	EXCITOR	EXTRUDE	FAIRIES	FARTING	FEELERS
EUBOEAN	EXCLAIM	EXUDING	FAIRING	FARTLEK	FEELING
EUCAINE	EXCLAVE	EXULTED	FAIRISH	FASCIAL	FEIGNED
EUGENIC	EXCLUDE	EXURBIA	FAIR SEX	FASCIAS	FEIGNER
EUGENOL	EXCRETA	EXUVIAE	FAIRWAY	FASCINE	FEINTED
EUGLENA	EXCRETE	EXUVIAL	FAJITAS	FASCISM	FELAFEL
EULOGIA	EXCUSAL	EX-WORKS	FALAFEL	FASCIST	FELINES
EUNUCHS	EXCUSED	EYEBALL	FALANGE	FASHION	FELLERS
EUPHONY	EXCUSES	EYEBATH	FALASHA	FASTEST	FELLING
EUPHROE	EXECUTE	EYEBOLT	FALBALA	FASTING	FELLOWS
EUPLOID	EXEGETE	EYEBROW	FALCATE	FATALLY	FELONRY
EUPNOEA	EXERGUE	EYELASH	FALCONS	FATBACK	FELSITE
EURASIA	EXERTED	EYELESS	FALKIRK	FAT CATS	FELSPAR
EURATOM	EXHALED	EYELETS	FALLACY	FATEFUL	FELTING
EURIPUS	EXHAUST	EYELIDS	FALL GUY	FATHEAD	FELUCCA
EUSTASY	EXHIBIT	EYESHOT	FALLING	FATHERS	FELWORT
EVACUEE	EXHUMED	EYESORE	FALLOUT	FATHOMS	FEMALES
EVADING	EXHUMER	EYESPOT	FALSELY	FATIGUE	FEMORAL
EVANGEL	EXIGENT	EYEWASH	FALSEST	FATLING	FENCERS
EVASION	EXILING		FALSIES	FATNESS	FENCING
EVASIVE	EXISTED	**F**	FALSIFY	FATSHAN	FENDERS
EVENING	EXITING	FABIANS	FALSITY	FATTEST	FENDING
EVEREST	EXMOUTH	FABRICS	FALSTER	FATTIER	FENLAND
EVERTOR	EXODERM	FACADES	FAMILLE	FATTIES	FERGANA
EVESHAM	EXOGAMY	FACEBAR	FAMINES	FATTILY	FERMATA
EVICTED	EXOTICA	FACE-OFF	FANATIC	FATTISH	FERMENT
EVICTOR	EXPANSE	FACIALS	FAN BELT	FATTISM	FERMION
EVIDENT	EX PARTE	FACINGS	FANCIED	FATUITY	FERMIUM
EVILEST	EXPENSE	FACTFUL	FANCIER	FATUOUS	FERNERY
EVIL EYE	EXPERTS	FACTION	FANCIES	FAUCETS	FERRARA
EVILLER	EXPIATE	FACTORS	FANCILY	FAULTED	FERRATE
EVINCED	EXPIRED	FACTORY	FAN CLUB	FAUVISM	FERRETS
EVOKING	EXPIRER	FACTUAL	FANFARE	FAUVIST	FERRETY
EVOLUTE	EXPLAIN	FACULAR	FANNIES	FAUX PAS	FERRIED
EVOLVED	EXPLANT	FACULTY	FANNING	FAVRILE	FERRIES
EVOLVER	EXPLODE	FADABLE	FANTAIL	FAVOURS	FERRITE
EWE-NECK	EXPLOIT	FADDISH	FANTAST	FAWNING	FERROUS
EXACTED	EXPLORE	FADDISM	FANTASY	FEARFUL	FERRULE
EXACTLY	EXPORTS	FADDIST	FANZINE	FEARING	FERTILE

FERVENT	FILBERT	FISH-EYE	FLAWING	FLOUNCE	FOGYISH
FERVOUR	FILCHED	FISHGIG	FLAYING	FLOURED	FOIBLES
FESTIVE	FILCHER	FISHIER	FLEABAG	FLOUTED	FOILING
FESTOON	FILETED	FISHING	FLEAPIT	FLOUTER	FOISTED
FETCHED	FILIATE	FISHNET	FLECKED	FLOWAGE	FOLACIN
FETCHER	FILIBEG	FISSILE	FLEECED	FLOWERS	FOLDERS
FETLOCK	FILINGS	FISSION	FLEECES	FLOWERY	FOLDING
FETTERS	FILLETS	FISSURE	FLEEING	FLOWING	FOLDOUT
FETUSES	FILLIES	FISTULA	FLEETER	FLUENCY	FOLIAGE
FEUDING	FILLING	FITMENT	FLEMING	FLUFFED	FOLIATE
FEVERED	FILL-INS	FITNESS	FLEMISH	FLUIDAL	FOLIOSE
FEWNESS	FILLIPS	FITTERS	FLENSER	FLUIDIC	FOLKISH
FEYNESS	FILMIER	FITTEST	FLESHED	FLUMMOX	FOLLIES
FIANCES	FILMILY	FITTING	FLESHER	FLUNKED	FONDANT
FIASCOS	FILMING	FIXABLE	FLESHES	FLUNKEY	FONDEST
FIBBERS	FILMSET	FIXATED	FLESHLY	FLUORIC	FONDLED
FIBBING	FILTERS	FIXEDLY	FLEURON	FLUSHED	FONDLER
FIBROID	FIMBRIA	FIXTURE	FLEXILE	FLUSHER	FONDUES
FIBROIN	FINABLE	FIZZIER	FLEXING	FLUSHES	FOOCHOW
FIBROMA	FINAGLE	FIZZING	FLEXION	FLUSTER	FOODIES
FIBROUS	FINALES	FLACCID	FLEXURE	FLUTING	FOOLERY
FIBULAE	FINALLY	FLAG DAY	FLICKED	FLUTIST	FOOLING
FIBULAR	FINANCE	FLAGGED	FLICKER	FLUTTER	FOOLISH
FIBULAS	FINBACK	FLAGGER	FLIGHTS	FLUVIAL	FOOTAGE
FICTILE	FINCHES	FLAGMAN	FLIGHTY	FLUXION	FOOTBOY
FICTION	FINDING	FLAGONS	FLINGER	FLYABLE	FOOTING
FIDDLED	FINE ART	FLAILED	FLIPPED	FLYAWAY	FOOTMAN
FIDDLER	FINE-CUT	FLAKIER	FLIPPER	FLYBACK	FOOTMEN
FIDDLES	FINESSE	FLAKING	FLIRTED	FLYBLOW	FOOTPAD
FIDEISM	FINFOOT	FLAMING	FLIRTER	FLYBOAT	FOOTSIE
FIDEIST	FINGERS	FLANEUR	FLITTED	FLYBOOK	FOOT-TON
FIDGETS	FINICKY	FLANGER	FLITTER	FLY-FISH	FOOTWAY
FIDGETY	FININGS	FLANGES	FLIVVER	FLY HALF	FOOZLER
FIELDED	FINLAND	FLANKED	FLOATED	FLYLEAF	FOPPERY
FIELDER	FINNING	FLANKER	FLOATEL	FLYOVER	FOPPISH
FIERCER	FINNISH	FLANNEL	FLOATER	FLYPAST	FORAGED
FIERIER	FIREARM	FLAPPED	FLOCCUS	FLYTRAP	FORAGER
FIESOLE	FIREBOX	FLAPPER	FLOCKED	FOALING	FORAGES
FIESTAS	FIREBUG	FLARE-UP	FLOGGED	FOAMIER	FORAMEN
FIFTEEN	FIREDOG	FLARING	FLOGGER	FOAMING	FORAYED
FIFTIES	FIREFLY	FLASHED	FLOODED	FOBBING	FORAYER
FIGHTER	FIREMAN	FLASHER	FLOODER	FO'C'SLE	FORBADE
FIG LEAF	FIREMEN	FLASHES	FLOORED	S	FORBEAR
FIGMENT	FIREPAN	FLASKET	FLOPPED	FOCUSED	FORBORE
FIG TREE	FIRMEST	FLAT-BED	FLORIDA	FOCUSER	FORCEPS
FIGURAL	FIRMING	FLATLET	FLORINS	FOCUSES	FORCING
FIGURED	FIRSTLY	FLATTEN	FLORIST	FOGGIER	FORDING
FIGURER	FIRTREE	FLATTER	FLORUIT	FOGGILY	FOREARM
FIGURES	FISCALS	FLAUNCH	FLOSSED	FOGGING	FOREGUT
FIGWORT	FISCHER	FLAVONE	FLOTAGE	FOGHORN	FOREIGN
FILARIA	FISHERY	FLAVOUR	FLOTSAM	FOG LAMP	FORELEG

FOREMAN	FOXHOLE	FRIEDAN	FUKUOKA	FUTTOCK	GAMBLER
FOREMEN	FOXHUNT	FRIENDS	FULCRUM	FUTURES	GAMBOGE
FOREPAW	FOXIEST	FRIEZES	FULGENT	FUZZIER	GAMBOLS
FORERUN	FOXLIKE	FRIGATE	FULLEST	FUZZILY	GAMBREL
FORESAW	FOXTAIL	FRIGHTS	FULMARS	FUZZING	GAMELAN
FORESEE	FOXTROT	FRILLED	FULNESS	FYZABAD	GAMETAL
FORESTS	FRACTAL	FRINGED	FULSOME		GAMIEST
FORETOP	FRACTUS	FRINGES	FULVOUS	**G**	GANDERS
FOREVER	FRAENUM	FRISBEE	FUMARIC	GABBING	GANDZHA
FORFEIT	FRAGILE	FRISEUR	FUMBLED	GABBLED	GANGERS
FORGAVE	FRAILER	FRISIAN	FUMBLER	GABBLER	GANGING
FORGERS	FRAILTY	FRISKED	FUMBLES	GABFEST	GANGTOK
FORGERY	FRAKTUR	FRISKER	FUNCHAL	GADDING	GANGWAY
FORGING	FRAME UP	FRISKET	FUNDING	GADGETS	GANNETS
FORGIVE	FRAME-UP	FRISSON	FUNERAL	GADGETY	GANTLET
FORGOER	FRAMING	FRITTER	FUNFAIR	GADROON	GAOLERS
FORGONE	FRANCIS	FRIZZED	FUNGOID	GADWALL	GAOLING
FORKFUL	FRANKED	FRIZZER	FUNGOUS	GAFFERS	GAPPING
FORKING	FRANKER	FRIZZLE	FUNICLE	GAGAUZI	GAP YEAR
FORLORN	FRANKLY	FROEBEL	FUNKIER	GAGGING	GARAGED
FORMANT	FRANTIC	FROG-BIT	FUNKING	GAHNITE	GARAGES
FORMATE	FRAPPES	FROGMAN	FUNNELS	GAINERS	GARBAGE
FORMATS	FRAUGHT	FROGMEN	FUNNIER	GAINFUL	GARBING
FORMICA	FRAYING	FROLICS	FUNNILY	GAINING	GARBLED
FORMING	FRAZIER	FRONDED	FUN RUNS	GAINSAY	GARBLER
FORMOSA	FRAZZLE	FRONTAL	FUNSTER	GAITERS	GARCONS
FORMULA	FREAKED	FRONTED	FURBISH	GALATEA	GARDENS
FORSAKE	FRECKLE	FROSTED	FURCATE	GALEATE	GARFISH
FORSOOK	FREEBIE	FROTHED	FURCULA	GALENIC	GARGETY
FORSYTH	FREEDOM	FROWARD	FURIOSO	GALICIA	GARGLED
FORTIES	FREEING	FROWNED	FURIOUS	GALILEE	GARGLER
FORTIFY	FREEMAN	FROWNER	FURLING	GALIPOT	GARGLES
FORTUNE	FREEMEN	FROWSTY	FURLONG	GALLANT	GARLAND
FORWARD	FREESIA	FRUITED	FURNACE	GALLEON	GARMENT
FORWENT	FREEWAY	FRUITER	FURNESS	GALLERY	GARNETS
FOSSILS	FREEZER	FRUSTUM	FURNISH	GALLEYS	GARNISH
FOUETTE	FREIGHT	FUCHSIA	FURRIER	GALLFLY	GARONNE
FOULARD	FREMONT	FUCHSIN	FURRING	GALLING	GARPIKE
FOULEST	FRESCOS	FUCK ALL	FURROWS	GALLIUM	GARRETS
FOULING	FRESHEN	FUCKERS	FURROWY	GALLNUT	GARTERS
FOUL-UPS	FRESHER	FUCKING	FURTHER	GALLONS	GASBAGS
FOUNDED	FRESHET	FUCK-UPS	FURTIVE	GALLOON	GASCONY
FOUNDER	FRESHLY	FUDDLED	FUSCOUS	GALLOPS	GASEOUS
FOUNDRY	FRESNEL	FUDDLES	FUSIBLE	GALLOUS	GASHING
FOURIER	FRETFUL	FUDGING	FUSILLI	GALLOWS	GASKETS
FOURTHS	FRETSAW	FUEGIAN	FUSSIER	GALUMPH	GAS MAIN
FOUR-WAY	FRETTED	FUELING	FUSSILY	GAMBADO	GAS MASK
FOVEATE	FRIABLE	FUELLED	FUSSING	GAMBIAN	GASOHOL
FOVEOLA	FRIBBLE	FUELLER	FUSSPOT	GAMBIER	GASPING
FOWLING	FRIDAYS	FUENTES	FUSTIAN	GAMBITS	GAS PIPE
FOXFIRE	FRIDGES	FUGGIER	FUSTIER	GAMBLED	GASSIER

GASSING	GENTILE	GINSENG	GLOBOID	GODSEND	GRAINER
GASTRIC	GENUINE	GIN TRAP	GLOBOSE	GOGGLED	GRAMMAR
GASTRIN	GEODESY	GIPSIES	GLOBULE	GOGGLES	GRAMMES
GATEAUX	GEOLOGY	GIRAFFE	GLORIED	GOIANIA	GRAMPUS
GATE-LEG	GEORDIE	GIRASOL	GLORIES	GO-KARTS	GRANADA
GATEWAY	GEORGIA	GIRDERS	GLORIFY	GOLDEYE	GRANARY
GATHERS	GEORGIC	GIRDING	GLOSSAL	GOLFERS	GRANDAD
GAUCHOS	GERBILS	GIRDLED	GLOSSED	GOLFING	GRANDEE
GAUDERY	GERENUK	GIRDLER	GLOSSER	GOLIATH	GRANDER
GAUDIER	GERMANE	GIRDLES	GLOTTAL	GONADAL	GRANDLY
GAUDILY	GERMANS	GIRLISH	GLOTTIC	GONDOLA	GRANDMA
GAUGING	GERMANY	GIRONDE	GLOTTIS	GOODBYE	GRANDPA
GAUHATI	GERUNDS	GIRONNY	GLOWING	GOOD DAY	GRANGES
GAUTENG	GESTALT	GISARME	GLUCOSE	GOODIES	GRANITE
GAUZIER	GESTAPO	GITTERN	GLUE EAR	GOODISH	GRANOLA
GAVOTTE	GESTATE	GIVABLE	GLUEING	GOOFIER	GRANTED
GAWKERS	GESTURE	GIZZARD	GLUMMER	GOOFILY	GRANTEE
GAWKIER	GETABLE	GLACIAL	GLUTEAL	GOOFING	GRANTER
GAWKING	GETAWAY	GLACIER	GLUTEUS	GOOIEST	GRANTOR
GAWPING	GETTING	GLADDEN	GLUTTED	GOPHERS	GRANULE
GAYNESS	GEYSERS	GLADDER	GLUTTON	GORGING	GRAPHIC
GAZEBOS	GHASTLY	GLADDON	GLYCINE	GORGONS	GRAPNEL
GAZELLE	GHAZALI	GLAD EYE	GLYPHIC	GORIEST	GRAPPLE
GAZETTE	GHERKIN	GLAMOUR	GLYPTIC	GORILLA	GRASPED
GEARBOX	GHETTOS	GLANCED	GNARLED	GORIZIA	GRASPER
GEARING	GHILLIE	GLANCES	GNASHED	GOSHAWK	GRASSED
GECKOES	GHOSTED	GLARING	GNASHES	GOSLING	GRASSES
GEE-GEES	GHOSTLY	GLASGOW	GNATHIC	GO-SLOWS	GRASS UP
GEELONG	GIBBETS	GLASSED	GNAWING	GOSPELS	GRATERS
GEEZERS	GIBBING	GLASSES	GNOCCHI	GOSPLAN	GRATIFY
GEISHAS	GIBBONS	GLAZIER	GNOMISH	GOSPORT	GRATING
GELATIN	GIBBOUS	GLAZING	GNOSTIC	GOSSIPS	GRAUPEL
GELDING	GIBLETS	GLEAMED	GOADING	GOSSIPY	GRAVELY
GELLING	GIDDIER	GLEANED	GO-AHEAD	GOTLAND	GRAVEST
GEMMATE	GIDDILY	GLEANER	GOATEED	GOUACHE	GRAVITY
GEMMING	GIESSEN	GLEEFUL	GOATEES	GOUGING	GRAVLAX
GEMMULE	GIGGLED	GLENCOE	GOBBETS	GOULASH	GRAVURE
GEMSBOK	GIGGLER	GLENOID	GOBBLED	GOURAMI	GRAYEST
GENAPPE	GIGGLES	GLIADIN	GOBBLER	GOURMET	GRAYING
GENDERS	GIG LAMP	GLIBBER	GOBBLES	GRAB BAG	GRAZIER
GENERAL	GIGOLOS	GLIDERS	GOBELIN	GRABBED	GRAZING
GENERIC	GILBERT	GLIDING	GOBIOID	GRABBER	GREASED
GENESIS	GILDING	GLIMMER	GOBLETS	GRABBLE	GREASER
GENETIC	GILLIES	GLIMPSE	GOBLINS	GRACILE	GREATER
GENEVAN	GIMBALS	GLINTED	GODDAMN	GRACING	GREATLY
GENIPAP	GIMLETS	GLISTEN	GODDESS	GRACKLE	GREAVES
GENITAL	GIMMICK	GLITTER	GODHEAD	GRADATE	GRECIAN
GENITOR	GINGERY	GLIWICE	GODHOOD	GRADING	GREENED
GENOESE	GINGHAM	GLOATED	GODLESS	GRADUAL	GREENER
GENTEEL	GINGILI	GLOATER	GODLIER	GRAFTED	GREENIE
GENTIAN	GINGIVA	GLOBATE	GODLIKE	GRAFTER	GREETED

GREETER	GROSSES	GUISING	GYPSIES	HALIBUT	HANKIES
GREISEN	GROSSLY	GUITARS	GYRATED	HALIDOM	HANOVER
GREMIAL	GROTTOS	GUIYANG	GYRATOR	HALIFAX	HANSARD
GREMLIN	GROUCHY	GUIZHOU		HALLWAY	HANSOMS
GRENADA	GROUNDS	GUJARAT	**H**	HALOGEN	HANUMAN
GRENADE	GROUPED	GULCHES	HAARLEM	HALTERE	HANYANG
GREYEST	GROUPER	GULDENS	HABDABS	HALTERS	HA'PENNY
GREYHEN	GROUPIE	GULLETS	HABITAT	HALTING	HAPLESS
GREYING	GROUSED	GULLIES	HABITED	HALVING	HAPLITE
GREYISH	GROUSER	GULLING	HABITUE	HALYARD	HAPLOID
GREYLAG	GROUSES	GULPING	HABITUS	HAMADAN	HAP'ORTH
GRIBBLE	GROUTER	GUMBOIL	HACHURE	HAMBURG	HAPPIER
GRIDDLE	GROWERS	GUMBOOT	HACKBUT	HAMELIN	HAPPILY
GRIEVED	GROWING	GUMDROP	HACKERS	HAMHUNG	HAPTENE
GRIEVER	GROWLED	GUMMIER	HACKING	HAMITIC	HARAPPA
GRIFFIN	GROWLER	GUMMING	HACKLER	HAMLETS	HARBOUR
GRIFFON	GROWN-UP	GUMMITE	HACKLES	HAMMERS	HARDEST
GRILLED	GROWTHS	GUMSHOE	HACKNEY	HAMMING	HARDIER
GRILLER	GROYNES	GUM TREE	HACKSAW	HAMMOCK	HARDILY
GRILLES	GRUBBED	GUNBOAT	HADAWAY	HAMMOND	HARDING
GRIMACE	GRUBBER	GUNDOGS	HADDOCK	HAMPDEN	HARD NUT
GRIMIER	GRUDGED	GUNFIRE	HADRIAN	HAMPERS	HARD-ONS
GRIMMER	GRUDGER	GUNLOCK	HAEMOID	HAMPTON	HARD PAD
GRIMSBY	GRUDGES	GUNNELS	HAFNIUM	HAMSTER	HARDPAN
GRINDER	GRUFFER	GUNNERS	HAGFISH	HAMULAR	HARDTOP
GRINGOS	GRUFFLY	GUNNERY	HAGGARD	HAMULUS	HARELIP
GRINNED	GRUMBLE	GUNNING	HAGGISH	HANAPER	HARICOT
GRINNER	GRUMOUS	GUNSHOT	HAGGLED	HANCOCK	HARIJAN
GRIPERS	GRUNTED	GUNWALE	HAGGLER	HANDBAG	HARKING
GRIPING	GRUNTER	GURGLED	HAGLIKE	HANDFUL	HARLECH
GRIPPED	GRUYERE	GURNARD	HAHNIUM	HANDGUN	HARLOTS
GRIPPER	GRYPHON	GUSHERS	HAILING	HANDIER	HARMFUL
GRISTLE	G-STRING	GUSHING	HAINAUT	HANDILY	HARMING
GRISTLY	GUANACO	GUSSETS	HAIRCUT	HANDING	HARMONY
GRITTED	GUANASE	GUSTIER	HAIRDOS	HANDLED	HARNESS
GRIZZLE	GUANINE	GUSTILY	HAIRIER	HANDLER	HARPIES
GRIZZLY	GUARANI	GUSTING	HAIRNET	HANDLES	HARPING
GROANED	GUARDED	GUTLESS	HAIRPIN	HANDOUT	HARPINS
GROANER	GUARDER	GUTSIER	HAITIAN	HANDSAW	HARPIST
GROCERS	GUAYULE	GUTTATE	HAITINK	HANDSEL	HARPOON
GROCERY	GUDGEON	GUTTERS	HAKLUYT	HANDSET	HARRIED
GROGRAM	GUESSED	GUTTING	HALAKAH	HANDS-ON	HARRIER
GROLIER	GUESSER	GUVNORS	HALAKIC	HANDS UP	HARROWS
GROMMET	GUESSES	GUZZLED	HALAVAH	HANGARS	HARSHER
GROOMED	GUESTED	GUZZLER	HALBERD	HANGDOG	HARSHLY
GROOMER	GUFFAWS	GWALIOR	HALCYON	HANGERS	HARSLET
GROOVED	GUIDING	GWYNEDD	HALDANE	HANGING	HARTLEY
GROOVES	GUILDER	GWYNIAD	HALF-CUT	HANGMAN	HARVARD
GROPING	GUINEAN	GYMNAST	HALFWAY	HANGMEN	HARVEST
GROSSED	GUINEAS	GYMSLIP	HALF WIT	HANGOUT	HARWICH
GROSSER	GUIPURE	GYPPING	HALF-WIT	HANG-UPS	HARYANA

HAS BEEN	HAZIEST	HEINOUS	HERNIAS	HIPLIKE	HOGLIKE
HAS-BEEN	HAZLITT	HEIRDOM	HEROICS	HIPPEST	HOGNOSE
HASHING	HEADERS	HEIRESS	HEROINE	HIPPIES	HOGWASH
HASHISH	HEADIER	HEISTER	HEROISM	HIPSTER	HOGWEED
HASIDIC	HEADILY	HEITIKI	HERONRY	HIRABLE	HOISTED
HASIDIM	HEADING	HELICAL	HERRICK	HIRCINE	HOISTER
HASSELT	HEADMAN	HELICES	HERRING	HIRSUTE	HOKONUI
HASSIUM	HEADMEN	HELICON	HERSELF	HIRUDIN	HOKUSAI
HASSLED	HEADPIN	HELIPAD	HERTZOG	HIS NIBS	HOLDALL
HASSLES	HEADSET	HELLBOX	HESIONE	HISSING	HOLDERS
HASSOCK	HEADWAY	HELLCAT	HESSIAN	HISTOID	HOLDING
HASTATE	HEALERS	HELLENE	HESSITE	HISTONE	HOLD OUT
HASTIER	HEALING	HELLERY	HETAERA	HISTORY	HOLDUPS
HASTILY	HEALTHS	HELLION	HETAIRA	HITACHI	HOLIBUT
HATBAND	HEALTHY	HELLISH	HEXADIC	HITCHED	HOLIDAY
HATCHED	HEAPING	HELLUVA	HEXAGON	HITCHER	HOLIEST
HATCHEL	HEARING	HELMAND	HEXAPLA	HITCHES	HOLLAND
HATCHER	HEARKEN	HELMETS	HEXAPOD	HIT LIST	HOLLERS
HATCHES	HEARSAY	HELOISE	HEXOSAN	HITTING	HOLLOWS
HATCHET	HEARSES	HELOTRY	HEYDUCK	HITTITE	HOLMIUM
HATEFUL	HEARTEN	HELPFUL	HEYSHAM	HOARDED	HOLSTER
HATLESS	HEARTHS	HELPING	HEYWOOD	HOARDER	HOLY SEE
HATLIKE	HEATERS	HEMIOLA	HIALEAH	HOARIER	HOMBURG
HATPINS	HEATHEN	HEMIPOD	HIBACHI	HOARILY	HOMERIC
HATTERS	HEATHER	HEMLINE	HICCUPS	HOARSEN	HOME RUN
HAUBERK	HEATING	HEMLOCK	HICKORY	HOARSER	HOMIEST
HAUGHTY	HEAVENS	HEMMING	HIDABLE	HOATZIN	HOMINID
HAULAGE	HEAVIER	HENBANE	HIDALGO	HOAXERS	HOMOLOG
HAULIER	HEAVIES	HENCOOP	HIDEOUS	HOAXING	HOMONYM
HAULING	HEAVILY	HEN COOP	HIDINGS	HOBBEMA	HONESTY
HAUNTED	HEAVING	HENDRIX	HIELAND	HOBBIES	HONEYED
HAUNTER	HEBETIC	HENGELO	HIGHBOY	HOBBISM	HONIARA
HAURAKI	HEBRAIC	HENGIST	HIGHEST	HOBBIST	HONITON
HAUTBOY	HEBREWS	HENNERY	HIGH HAT	HOBBLED	HONKIES
HAUTEUR	HECKLED	HENPECK	HIGH TEA	HOBBLER	HONKING
HAVE-A-	HECKLER	HEPARIN	HIGHWAY	HOBLIKE	HONOURS
GO	HECTARE	HEPATIC	HIJACKS	HOBNAIL	HOODLUM
HAWKBIT	HEDGING	HEPBURN	HILBERT	HOBOISM	HOODOOS
HAWKERS	HEDONIC	HEPTANE	HILLARY	HOBOKEN	HOOGHLY
HAWKING	HEEDFUL	HEPTOSE	HILLERY	HOCKING	HOOKAHS
HAWKINS	HEEDING	HERALDS	HILLIER	HOCKNEY	HOOKERS
HAWKISH	HEELING	HERBAGE	HILLMAN	HODEIDA	HOOKIES
HAWORTH	HEELTAP	HERBALS	HILLOCK	HODGKIN	HOOKING
HAWSERS	HEERLEN	HERBERT	HIMSELF	HOEDOWN	HOOKUPS
HAYCOCK	HEFTIER	HERDING	HINDGUT	HOELIKE	HOORAYS
HAYFORK	HEFTILY	HEREDES	HINGING	HOFFMAN	HOOTERS
HAYRACK	HEGUMEN	HERETIC	HINTING	HOGARTH	HOOTING
HAYSEED	HEIFERS	HERISAU	HIONATE	HOGBACK	HOOVERS
HAYWARD	HEIFETZ	HERITOR	HIPBATH	HOGFISH	HOPEFUL
HAYWIRE	HEIGH-HO	HERMITS	HIPBONE	HOGGING	HOPHEAD
HAZARDS	HEIGHTS	HERNIAL	HIPLESS	HOGGISH	HOPKINS

HOPLITE	HOVERER	HURDLED	ICEBALL	IMPACTS	INCOMES
HOPPERS	HOWBEIT	HURDLER	ICEBERG	IMPALAS	INCROSS
HOPPING	HOWDAHS	HURDLES	ICE CAPS	IMPALED	INCUBUS
HOPPLER	HOWEVER	HURLING	ICE-COLD	IMPALER	INCURVE
HOPSACK	HOWLAND	HURRAYS	ICEFALL	IMPANEL	INDENTS
HORDEIN	HOWLERS	HURRIED	ICELAND	IMPASSE	IN DEPTH
HORDERN	HOWLING	HURTFUL	ICE PACK	IMPASTE	IN-DEPTH
HORIZON	HOYDENS	HURTING	ICE PICK	IMPASTO	INDEXED
HORMONE	HOYLAKE	HURTLED	ICE RINK	IMPEACH	INDEXER
HORNETS	HSIA-MEN	HUSBAND	ICHNITE	IMPEDED	INDEXES
HORNIER	HSINING	HUSHABY	ICICLED	IMPEDER	INDIANA
HORNILY	HSU-CHOU	HUSHING	ICICLES	IMPERIL	INDIANS
HORRIFY	HUAINAN	HUSKIER	ICINESS	IMPETUS	INDICAN
HORRORS	HUAI-NAN	HUSKIES	ICTERIC	IMPIETY	INDICIA
HORSENS	HUBBIES	HUSKILY	ICTERUS	IMPINGE	INDOORS
HORSIER	HUBCAPS	HUSSARS	ID CARDS	IMPIOUS	INDORSE
HORSILY	HUDDLED	HUSSEIN	IDEALLY	IMPLANT	INDOXYL
HOSANNA	HUDDLER	HUSSIES	IDEATUM	IMPLEAD	INDRAWN
HOSIERS	HUDDLES	HUSSISM	IDENTIC	IMPLIED	INDUCED
HOSIERY	HUFFIER	HUSSITE	IDIOTIC	IMPLODE	INDUCER
HOSPICE	HUFFILY	HUSTLED	IDOLIZE	IMPLORE	INDULGE
HOSTAGE	HUFFING	HUSTLER	IDYLLIC	IMPORTS	INEPTLY
HOSTELS	HUFFISH	HUTCHES	IGNEOUS	IMPOSED	INERTIA
HOSTESS	HUGGING	HUTCHIE	IGNITED	IMPOSER	INERTLY
HOSTILE	HUHEHOT	HUTLIKE	IGNITER	IMPOUND	INEXACT
HOSTING	HULKING	HUTMENT	IGNOBLE	IMPRESA	INFANCY
HOSTLER	HULLING	HUYGENS	IGNOBLY	IMPRESS	INFANTA
HOTBEDS	HUMANLY	HWANG HO	IGNORED	IMPREST	INFANTE
HOT DOGS	HUMBLED	HYAENAS	IGNORER	IMPRINT	INFANTS
HOTFOOT	HUMBLER	HYAENIC	IGUANAS	IMPROVE	INFARCT
HOTHEAD	HUMBUGS	HYALINE	IKEBANA	IMPULSE	INFERNO
HOTLINE	HUMDRUM	HYALITE	ILEITIS	IMPUTED	INFIDEL
HOT LINE	HUMERAL	HYALOID	ILL-BRED	IMPUTER	INFIELD
HOT LINK	HUMERUS	HYBRIDS	ILLEGAL	INANELY	INFLAME
HOTNESS	HUMIDLY	HYDATID	ILLICIT	INANITY	INFLATE
HOTPOTS	HUMIDOR	HYDRANT	ILLNESS	INAPTLY	INFLECT
HOT RODS	HUMMING	HYDRATE	ILL WILL	IN A	INFLICT
HOT SEAT	HUMMOCK	HYDRIDE	IMAGERY	WORD	INFLOWS
HOT SPOT	HUMORAL	HYDROID	IMAGINE	INBOARD	INFRACT
HOTSPUR	HUMOURS	HYGIENE	IMAGISM	INBOUND	INFUSED
HOTTEST	HUMPING	HYMNALS	IMAGIST	INBREED	INFUSER
HOTTING	HUNCHED	HYMNING	IMAMATE	INCENSE	INGENUE
HOUDINI	HUNCHES	HYPED UP	IMBIBED	INCHING	INGESTA
HOUMOUS	HUNDRED	HYPHENS	IMBIBER	INCIPIT	INGOING
HOUNDED	HUNGARY	HYPONYM	IMBRUTE	INCISED	INGRAIN
HOUNDER	HUNGNAM		IMBUING	INCISOR	INGRATE
HOUSING	HUNKERS	**I**	IMITATE	INCITED	INGRESS
HOUSMAN	HUNLIKE		IMMENSE	INCITER	IN-GROUP
HOUSTON	HUNNISH	IAMBICS	IMMERSE	INCLINE	INGROWN
HOUTING	HUNTERS	IAPETUS	IMMORAL	INCLOSE	INHABIT
HOVERED	HUNTING	IBERIAN	IMMURED	INCLUDE	INHALED

INHALER	INTERNS	ISOCHOR	JAMAICA	JIBBING	JOTTERS
INHERIT	INTIMAL	ISOGAMY	JAMES II	JIGGERS	JOTTING
INHIBIT	INTONED	ISOGENY	JAMMIER	JIGGING	JOURNAL
IN-HOUSE	INTONER	ISOHYET	JAMMING	JIGGLED	JOURNEY
INHUMAN	INTROIT	ISOLATE	JANGLED	JIGGLES	JOURNOS
INHUMER	INTRUDE	ISOLINE	JANGLER	JIGSAWS	JOUSTED
INITIAL	INTRUST	ISONOMY	JANITOR	JILTING	JOUSTER
INJURED	INURING	ISOTONE	JANUARY	JIM CROW	JOYLESS
INJURER	INUTILE	ISOTOPE	JARGONS	JIMJAMS	JOYRIDE
INKATHA	IN VACUO	ISOTOPY	JARRING	JIMMIES	JUBILEE
INKIEST	INVADED	ISOTRON	JASMINE	JINGLED	JUDAEAN
INKLING	INVADER	ISRAELI	JAUNTED	JINGLER	JUDAICA
INKPADS	INVALID	ISSUING	JAVELIN	JINGLES	JUDAISM
INKWELL	INVEIGH	ISTHMUS	JAWBONE	JINXING	JUDAIST
INLAYER	INVERSE	ISTRIAN	JAYWALK	JINZHOU	JUDAIZE
INMATES	INVITED	ITALIAN	JAZZIER	JITTERS	JUDASES
INNARDS	INVITER	ITALICS	JAZZILY	JITTERY	JUDGING
INNERVE	IN VITRO	ITCHIER	JAZZING	JOBBERS	JUDOIST
INNINGS	INVOICE	ITCHING	JEALOUS	JOBBERY	JUGGING
IN ORDER	INVOKED	ITEMIZE	JEERING	JOBBING	JUGGLED
INQUEST	INVOKER	ITERANT	JEHOVAH	JOBCLUB	JUGGLER
INQUIET	INVOLVE	ITERATE	JEJUNAL	JOBLESS	JUGULAR
INQUIRE	INWARDS	ITHACAN	JEJUNUM	JOB LOTS	JUICIER
INQUIRY	INWEAVE	IVANOVO	JELLABA	JOCKEYS	JUICILY
INROADS	IODIZER	IVORIAN	JELLIED	JOCULAR	JUICING
INSECTS	IONIZED	IVORIES	JELLIES	JODHPUR	JUJITSU
INSERTS	IONIZER	IZHEVSK	JELLIFY	JOGGING	JUJUBES
INSHORE	IPOMOEA		JELLING	JOGGLED	JUKEBOX
INSIDER	IPSWICH	**J**	JEMMIED	JOGGLER	JUMBLED
INSIDES	IQUIQUE	JABBING	JEMMIES	JOGGLES	JUMBLER
INSIGHT	IQUITOS	JACAMAR	JENNIES	JOG TROT	JUMBLES
INSIPID	IRANIAN	JACKALS	JERICHO	JOHN DOE	JUMPERS
INSOFAR	IRATELY	JACKASS	JERKIER	JOHNSON	JUMPIER
INSOLES	IRELAND	JACKDAW	JERKILY	JOINDER	JUMPILY
INSPECT	IRENICS	JACKETS	JERKING	JOINERS	JUMPING
INSPIRE	IRIDIUM	JACKING	JERKINS	JOINERY	JUMP-OFF
INSTALL	IRKSOME	JACKPOT	JERK OFF	JOINING	JUNDIAI
INSTANT	IRKUTSK	JACKSON	JERSEYS	JOINTED	JUNGIAN
INSTATE	IRON AGE	JACK TAR	JESTERS	JOINTER	JUNGLES
INSTEAD	IRONIES	JACOBIN	JESTING	JOINTLY	JUNIORS
INSTEPS	IRONING	JACONET	JESUITS	JOLLIED	JUNIPER
INSULAR	IRONIST	JACUZZI	JETFOIL	JOLLIER	JUNKETS
INSULIN	IRON ORE	JADEITE	JETPORT	JOLLIFY	JUNKIES
INSULTS	ISAGOGE	JAGGERY	JETTIES	JOLLILY	JUNKING
INSURED	ISCHIAL	JAGGING	JETTING	JOLLITY	JUPITER
INSURER	ISCHIUM	JAGUARS	JEWFISH	JOLTING	JURISTS
INSWING	ISFAHAN	JAILERS	JEW'S-	JONESES	JURY BOX
INTAKES	ISLAMIC	JAILING	EAR	JONQUIL	JURYMAN
INTEGER	ISLANDS	JAKARTA	JEZEBEL	JOSHING	JUSSIVE
INTENSE	ISOBARS	JALAPIC	JIANGSU	JOSTLED	JUSTICE
INTERIM	ISOBATH	JALISCO	JIANGXI	JOSTLER	JUSTIFY

JUTLAND
JUTTING

K

KABADDI
KAFFIRS
KAFTANS
KAIFENG
KAINITE
KAISERS
KALENDS
KALININ
KALMUCK
KAMPALA
KANANGA
KANNADA
KANTIAN
KAOLACK
KAPITZA
KARACHI
KARAKUL
KARBALA
KARELIA
KAROSHI
KARSTIC
KASHGAR
KASHMIR
KASSALA
KATANGA
KATSINA
KATYDID
KAYAKER
KAYSERI
KEATING
KEELING
KEELSON
KEENEST
KEENING
KEEPERS
KEEPING
KEEPNET
KEITLOA
KELVINS
KENDREW
KENNEDY
KENNELS
KENNING
KENOSIS
KENOTIC
KENTISH
KERATIN

KERBING
KERNELS
KERNITE
KESTREL
KESWICK
KETCHES
KETCHUP
KETONIC
KETOSIS
KETTLES
KEYED UP
KEYHOLE
KEYNOTE
KEY RING
KHADDAR
KHAKASS
KHALIFS
KHALKHA
KHAMSIN
KHANATE
KHARKOV
KHERSON
KHINGAN
KHOISAN
KIANGSI
KIANGSU
KIBBUTZ
KICKING
KICKOFF
KICK OFF
KIDDERS
KIDDIES
KIDDING
KIDNEYS
KIDSKIN
KILDARE
KILLERS
KILLICK
KILLING
KILLJOY
KILOTON
KILTERS
KIMONOS
KINDEST
KINDLED
KINDLER
KINDRED
KINETIC
KINFOLK
KINGCUP
KINGDOM

KINGPIN
KINKIER
KINKILY
KINNOCK
KINSHIP
KINSMAN
KINSMEN
KIPPERS
KIPPING
KIRGHIZ
KIRUNDI
KISSERS
KISSING
KIT BAGS
KITCHEN
KITSCHY
KITTENS
KITTIES
KITTING
KLAXONS
KNAPPER
KNAVERY
KNAVISH
KNEADED
KNEADER
KNEECAP
KNEEING
KNEELED
KNEEPAD
KNEES UP
KNIFING
KNIGHTS
KNITTED
KNITTER
KNOBBLY
KNOCKED
KNOCKER
KNOCK-ON
KNOCK-UP
KNOSSOS
KNOTTED
KNOTTER
KNOW-ALL
KNOW-HOW
KNOWING
KNUCKLE
KNUCKLY
KOBARID
KOBLENZ
KOFTGAR

KOKANEE
KOKOBEH
KOLDING
KOLKHOZ
KOLOMNA
KONGONI
KOOKIER
KOONING
KOPECKS
KOPEISK
KOUPREY
KOWLOON
KREFELD
KREMLIN
KRISHNA
KRYPTON
KUBELIK
KUBRICK
KUCHING
KUMAYRI
KUMQUAT
KUNDERA
KUNMING
KUNZITE
KURDISH
KUTAISI
KUWAITI
KWANGJU
KWAZULU
KWEILIN
KYANIZE

L

LABELED
LABIALS
LABIATE
LABOURS
LABROID
LACIEST
LACKEYS
LACKING
LACONIC
LACQUER
LACTASE
LACTATE
LACTEAL
LACTONE
LACTOSE
LACUNAE
LACUNAR
LACUNAS

LADDERS
LADDIES
LADDISH
LADINGS
LADLING
LAGGARD
LAGGING
LAGOONS
LAICISM
LAICIZE
LALLANS
LAMAISM
LAMAIST
LAMBADA
LAMBAST
LAMBENT
LAMBERT
LAMBETH
LAMBING
LAMELLA
LAMENTS
LAMINAR
LAMPERN
LAMPOON
LAMPREY
LANCERS
LANCETS
LANCHOW
LANCING
LANDAUS
LANDING
LANDTAG
LANGRES
LANGUID
LANGUOR
LANIARY
LANKEST
LANKIER
LANKILY
LANOLIN
LANSING
LANTANA
LANTERN
LANYARD
LAOTIAN
LA PALMA
LAPDOGS
LAPLACE
LAPLAND
LA PLATA
LAPPING

LAPSING
LAPWING
LARCENY
LARCHES
LARDERS
LARDING
LARGELY
LARGESS
LARGEST
LARGISH
LARIATS
LARKING
LARWOOD
LASAGNA
LASAGNE
LA SALLE
LA SCALA
LASCAUX
LASHING
LASH OUT
LASH-UPS
LASSOED
LASSOER
LAST END
LASTING
LATAKIA
LATCHED
LATCHES
LATCHET
LATENCY
LATERAL
LATHERY
LATIMER
LATRINE
LATTICE
LATVIAN
LAUDING
LAUGHED
LAUGHER
LAUNDER
LAUNDRY
LAURELS
LAWLESS
LAW LORD
LAWSUIT
LAWYERS
LAXNESS
LAYERED
LAYETTE
LAY-OFFS
LAYOUTS

LAZIEST	LEGIBLE	LEVERED	LIMPING	LIVENED	LOLLAND
L-DRIVER	LEGIBLY	LEVERET	LIMPKIN	LIVENER	LOLLARD
LEACHED	LEGIONS	LEVYING	LIMPOPO	LIVIDLY	LOLLIES
LEACHER	LEGLESS	LEXICAL	LIMULUS	LIVINGS	LOLLING
LEADERS	LEGNICA	LEXICON	LINABLE	LIVONIA	LOMBARD
LEADING	LEG-PULL	LIAISED	LINARES	LIVORNO	LONG AGO
LEAD-INS	LEGROOM	LIAISON	LINCOLN	LIZARDS	LONGBOW
LEAD OFF	LEG ROOM	LIANOID	LINCTUS	LOADING	LONGEST
LEAFAGE	LEG SIDE	LIASSIC	LINDANE	LOAFERS	LONGING
LEAFIER	LEGUMES	LIBBERS	LINDENS	LOAFING	LONGISH
LEAFLET	LEGUMIN	LIBELED	LINEAGE	LOANING	LONG TON
LEAGUED	LEGWORK	LIBERAL	LINEATE	LOATHED	LOOFAHS
LEAGUES	LE HAVRE	LIBEREC	LINEMAN	LOATHER	LOOKERS
LEAKAGE	LEIPZIG	LIBERIA	LINEMEN	LOATHLY	LOOKING
LEAKIER	LEISTER	LIBERTY	LINE-OUT	LOBBIED	LOOKOUT
LEAKING	LEISURE	LIBIDOS	LINEUPS	LOBBIES	LOOK OUT
LEANEST	LEITRIM	LIBRARY	LINGCOD	LOBBING	LOOMING
LEANING	LEMBERG	LIBRATE	LINGOES	LOBBYER	LOONIER
LEAN-TOS	LEMMING	LICENCE	LINGUAL	LOBELIA	LOONIES
LEAPING	LEMPIRA	LICENSE	LININGS	LOBSTER	LOOPING
LEARNED	LENDERS	LICKING	LINKAGE	LOBULAR	LOOSELY
LEARNER	LENDING	LIE-DOWN	LINKING	LOCALES	LOOSEST
LEASHES	LENGTHS	LIESTAL	LINKMAN	LOCALLY	LOOSING
LEASING	LENGTHY	LIFTING	LINKUPS	LOCARNO	LOOTERS
LEATHER	LENIENT	LIFTOFF	LINNETS	LOCATED	LOOTING
LEAVENS	LENTIGO	LIFT-OFF	LINOCUT	LOCATER	LOPPING
LEAVING	LENTILS	LIGHTED	LINSANG	LOCHIAL	LOQUATS
LEBANON	LEONINE	LIGHTEN	LINSEED	LOCKAGE	LORDING
LECHERS	LEOPARD	LIGHTER	LINTELS	LOCKERS	LORELEI
LECHERY	LEOTARD	LIGHTLY	LIONESS	LOCKETS	LORGNON
LECTERN	LEPANTO	LIGNIFY	LIONIZE	LOCKING	LORIENT
LECTION	LEPORID	LIGNITE	LIPETSK	LOCKJAW	LORRIES
LECTURE	LEPROSE	LIGROIN	LIP-READ	LOCKNUT	LOSABLE
LEDGERS	LEPROSY	LIGULAR	LIQUATE	LOCKOUT	LOSINGS
LEECHES	LEPROUS	LIGURIA	LIQUEFY	LOCKUPS	LOTIONS
LEERIER	LERWICK	LIKABLE	LIQUEUR	LOCOISM	LOTTERY
LEERING	LESBIAN	LIKENED	LIQUIDS	LOCULAR	LOTTING
LEE TIDE	LESIONS	LIKINGS	LISBURN	LOCUSTS	LOTUSES
LEEWARD	LESOTHO	LILTING	LISIEUX	LODGERS	LOUDEST
LEFTIES	LESSEES	LIMACON	LISPING	LODGING	LOUNGED
LEFTISM	LESSONS	LIMBATE	LISTING	LOFTIER	LOUNGER
LEFTIST	LESSORS	LIMBURG	LITCHIS	LOFTILY	LOUNGES
LEGALLY	LETDOWN	LIMEADE	LITERAL	LOFTING	LOURDES
LEGASPI	LETTERS	LIMIEST	LITHELY	LOGBOOK	LOURING
LEGATEE	LETTING	LIMINAL	LITHEST	LOGGERS	LOUSIER
LEGATES	LETTUCE	LIMITED	LITHIUM	LOGGIAS	LOUSILY
LEGATOR	LEUCINE	LIMITER	LITHOID	LOGGING	LOUSING
LEGENDS	LEUCITE	LIMNING	LITOTES	LOGICAL	LOUTISH
LEGGIER	LEUCOMA	LIMOGES	LITTERS	LOGIEST	LOUVAIN
LEGGING	LEVATOR	LIMPEST	LITURGY	LOGJAMS	LOUVRES
LEGHORN	LEVELED	LIMPETS	LIVABLE	LOGWOOD	LOVABLE

LOWBORN
LOWBROW
LOW BROW
LOW DOWN
LOW-DOWN
LOWERED
LOWLAND
LOWLIER
LOW LIFE
LOWNESS
LOW-RISE
LOW TIDE
LOYALLY
LOYALTY
LOZENGE
L-PLATES
LUALABA
LUBBOCK
LUCERNE
LUCIDLY
LUCIFER
LUCKIER
LUCKILY
LUCKNOW
LUDDITE
LUFFING
LUGANDA
LUGANSK
LUGGAGE
LUGGERS
LUGGING
LUGHOLE
LUGSAIL
LUGWORM
LULLABY
LULLING
LUMBAGO
LUMENAL
LUMPIER
LUMPILY
LUMPING
LUMPISH
LUMP SUM
LUMUMBA
LUNATIC
LUNCHED
LUNCHER
LUNCHES
LUNETTE
LUNGING
LUOYANG

LUPULIN
LURCHED
LURCHER
LURCHES
LURGIES
LURIDLY
LURKING
LUSATIA
LUSTFUL
LUSTILY
LUSTING
LUSTRAL
LUSTRES
LUTEOUS
LUTHIER
LYCHEES
LYCHNIS
LYCOPOD
LYDDITE
LYING-IN
LYNCEAN
LYNCHED
LYNCHER
LYRICAL

M

MACABRE
MACADAM
MACAQUE
MACEDON
MACHETE
MACHINE
MACLEAN
MACRAME
MACULAR
MADDEST
MADEIRA
MADE OUT
MADISON
MADNESS
MADONNA
MADRONA
MADURAI
MADWORT
MAENADS
MAESTRI
MAESTRO
MAFIOSO
MAGENTA
MAGGOTS
MAGGOTY

MAGHREB
MAGICAL
MAGNATE
MAGNETO
MAGNETS
MAGNIFY
MAGNUMS
MAGPIES
MAHATMA
MAHFOUZ
MAHICAN
MAH JONG
MAH-JONG
MAHONIA
MAHOUTS
MAIDENS
MAILBAG
MAILBOX
MAILING
MAILMAN
MAILMEN
MAIMING
MAINTOP
MAJESTY
MAJORCA
MAJORED
MAJORLY
MAKASAR
MAKE OUT
MAKES DO
MAKINGS
MAKURDI
MALABAR
MALACCA
MALAISE
MALARIA
MALATYA
MALAYAN
MALEATE
MALEFIC
MALINES
MALINKE
MALLARD
MALLETS
MALLEUS
MALLOWS
MALMSEY
MALTASE
MALTESE
MALTING
MALTOSE

MALVERN
MAMILLA
MAMMALS
MAMMARY
MAMMIES
MAMMOTH
MANACLE
MANAGED
MANAGER
MANAGUA
MANAKIN
MANATEE
MANDATE
MANDELA
MANDREL
MANGERS
MANGIER
MANGILY
MANGLED
MANGLER
MANGLES
MANGOES
MANHOLE
MANHOOD
MANHOUR
MANHUNT
MANIACS
MANIKIN
MANIPUR
MAN JACK
MANKIND
MANLIER
MANLIKE
MAN-MADE
MANNERS
MANNING
MANNISH
MANNITE
MANNOSE
MANRESA
MANROPE
MANSARD
MANSELL
MANSION
MANTLED
MANTLES
MANUALS
MANUKAU
MANURED
MANURER
MANX CAT

MANXMAN
MAOISTS
MAPPING
MARABOU
MARACAS
MARACAY
MARASCA
MARATHA
MARATHI
MARBLED
MARBLER
MARBLES
MARBURG
MARCHED
MARCHER
MARCHES
MAREMMA
MARGATE
MARGAUX
MARGINS
MARIBOR
MARIMBA
MARINAS
MARINER
MARINES
MARITAL
MARKERS
MARKETS
MARKHOR
MARKING
MARKUPS
MARLINE
MARLINS
MARLITE
MARMITE
MARMOTS
MAROONS
MARQUEE
MARQUIS
MARRIED
MARRIER
MARRING
MARROWS
MARSALA
MARSHAL
MARSHES
MARTENS
MARTIAL
MARTIAN
MARTINI
MARTINS

MARTYRS
MARTYRY
MARVELS
MARXIAN
MARXISM
MARXIST
MASBATE
MASCARA
MASCOTS
MASHHAD
MASHING
MASKING
MASONIC
MASONRY
MASQUES
MASSAGE
MASSAWA
MASSEUR
MASSIFS
MASSING
MASSIVE
MASTERS
MASTERY
MASTIFF
MASTOID
MASURIA
MATADOR
MATCHED
MATCHES
MATHURA
MATINEE
MATLOCK
MATRONS
MATTERS
MATTING
MATTINS
MATTOCK
MATURED
MAUDLIN
MAULING
MAUNDER
MAWKISH
MAXILLA
MAXIMAL
MAXIMIN
MAXIMUM
MAXIMUS
MAXWELL
MAY DAYS
MAYENNE
MAYFAIR

MAYORAL	MENACES	MICRONS	MINGIER	MISTERS	MOLLUSC
MAYOTTE	MENAGES	MIDDENS	MINGLED	MISTILY	MOLOKAI
MAYPOLE	MENDERS	MIDDLE C	MINIBAR	MISTIME	MOLTING
MAYWEED	MENDING	MIDGETS	MINIBUS	MISTING	MOMBASA
MAZURKA	MENDIPS	MIDIRON	MINICAB	MISTOOK	MOMENTA
MAZZARD	MENDOZA	MIDLAND	MINIMAL	MISTRAL	MOMENTS
MBABANE	MENFOLK	MIDMOST	MINIMAX	MISUSED	MOMMIES
MCENROE	MENIALS	MIDRIFF	MINIMUM	MISUSER	MONACAN
MEADOWS	MENTHOL	MIDTERM	MINIMUS	MISUSES	MONADIC
MEALIER	MENTION	MIDWEEK	MINIONS	MITCHUM	MONARCH
MEANDER	MENTORS	MIDWEST	MINIVER	MITHRAS	MONARDA
MEANEST	MEOWING	MIDWIFE	MINIVET	MITOSIS	MONCTON
MEANING	MERCIES	MIDYEAR	MINNOWS	MITOTIC	MONDAYS
MEASLES	MERCURY	MIGHTN'T	MINORCA	MITTENS	MONEYED
MEASURE	MERGERS	MIGRANT	MINSTER	MITZVAH	MONGOLS
MEATIER	MERGING	MIGRATE	MINTAGE	MIXABLE	MONGREL
MEATILY	MERITED	MIKADOS	MINTING	MIXED UP	MONITOR
MEDDLED	MERMAID	MILAZZO	MINUETS	MIXTURE	MONKEYS
MEDDLER	MERRIER	MILDEST	MINUSES	MIZORAM	MONKISH
MEDIACY	MERRILY	MILDEWY	MINUTED	MOANERS	MONOCLE
MEDIANS	MESARCH	MILEAGE	MINUTES	MOANING	MONOMER
MEDIANT	MESHING	MILIARY	MINXISH	MOBBING	MONSOON
MEDIATE	MESSAGE	MILIEUS	MIOCENE	MOBILES	MONSTER
MEDICAL	MESSIAH	MILIEUX	MIRACLE	MOBSTER	MONTAGE
MEDICOS	MESSIER	MILITIA	MIRADOR	MOCKERS	MONTANA
MEDIUMS	MESSILY	MILKERS	MIRAGES	MOCKERY	MONTANE
MEDLARS	MESSINA	MILKIER	MIRRORS	MOCKING	MONTHLY
MEDLEYS	MESSING	MILKILY	MISCALL	MOCK-UPS	MOOCHED
MEDULLA	MESS-UPS	MILKING	MISCAST	MODALLY	MOOCHER
MEEKEST	MESTIZA	MILKMAN	MISDEAL	MOD CONS	MOODIER
MEERKAT	MESTIZO	MILKMEN	MISDEED	MODELED	MOODILY
MEETING	METALED	MILK RUN	MISERLY	MODERAS	MOONEYE
MEGATON	METAMER	MILKSOP	MISFILE	MODERNS	MOONILY
MEIOSIS	METEORS	MILLDAM	MISFIRE	MODESTY	MOONING
MEIOTIC	METERED	MILLERS	MISFITS	MODICUM	MOONLIT
MEISSEN	METHANE	MILLINE	MISHAPS	MODISTE	MOONSET
MELANGE	METHODS	MILLING	MISHEAR	MODULAR	MOORAGE
MELANIC	METIERS	MILLION	MISKOLC	MODULES	MOORHEN
MELANIN	METONYM	MILLRUN	MISLAID	MODULUS	MOORING
MELILLA	METOPIC	MIMESIS	MISLEAD	MOFETTE	MOORISH
MELILOT	METRICS	MIMETIC	MISNAME	MOGADOR	MOOTING
MELISMA	METRIFY	MIMICRY	MISPLAY	MOGGIES	MOPPETS
MELODIC	METRIST	MINABLE	MISREAD	MOGILEV	MOPPING
MELTAGE	MEXICAN	MINARET	MISRULE	MOHICAN	MORAINE
MELTING	MIAOWED	MINCERS	MISSALS	MOIDORE	MORALLY
MEMBERS	MIASMAL	MINCING	MISSIES	MOISTEN	MORAVIA
MEMENTO	MIASMAS	MINDERS	MISSILE	MOISTLY	MORCEAU
MEMOIRS	MICELLE	MINDFUL	MISSING	MOLDIER	MORDANT
MEMPHIS	MICHAEL	MINDING	MISSION	MOLDING	MORDENT
MENACED	MICKEYS	MINDORO	MISSIVE	MOLDOVA	MORDVIN
MENACER	MICROBE	MINERAL	MISTAKE	MOLLIFY	MOREISH

MORELIA	MUCKILY	MURKIER	**N**	NEAREST	NEST EGG
MORELLO	MUCKING	MURKILY	NABBING	NEARING	NESTING
MORELOS	MUD BATH	MURMURS	NACELLE	NEATEST	NESTLED
MORGUES	MUDDIED	MURRAIN	NAEVOID	NEBULAE	NESTLER
MORMONS	MUDDIER	MUSCLED	NAGGERS	NEBULAR	NETBALL
MORNING	MUDDILY	MUSCLES	NAGGING	NEBULAS	NETSUKE
MOROCCO	MUDDING	MUSEFUL	NAHUATL	NECKING	NETTING
MORONIC	MUDDLED	MUSEUMS	NAIADES	NECKLET	NETTLED
MORROWS	MUDDLER	MUSHIER	NAILING	NECKTIE	NETTLES
MORSELS	MUDDLES	MUSHILY	NAIPAUL	NECROSE	NETWORK
MORTALS	MUDFISH	MUSICAL	NAIROBI	NECTARY	NEUROMA
MORTARS	MUDFLAP	MUSKETS	NAIVELY	NEEDFUL	NEURONE
MORTIFY	MUDFLAT	MUSKIER	NAIVETE	NEEDIER	NEUTRAL
MORTISE	MUDPACK	MUSKRAT	NAIVETY	NEEDING	NEUTRON
MORULAR	MUD PIES	MUSLIMS	NAKEDLY	NEEDLED	NEWBORN
MOSAICS	MUEZZIN	MUSSELS	NALCHIK	NEEDLES	NEW BORN
MOSELEY	MUFFING	MUSSING	NAMABLE	NEGATED	NEWBURY
MOSELLE	MUFFINS	MUSTANG	NAME DAY	NEGATOR	NEW CHUM
MOSEYED	MUFFLED	MUSTARD	NAMIBIA	NEGLECT	NEW DEAL
MOSLEMS	MUFFLER	MUSTERS	NANJING	NEGRESS	NEW MOON
MOSOTHO	MUGGERS	MUSTIER	NANKEEN	NEGRITO	NEWNESS
MOSQUES	MUGGIER	MUSTILY	NANKING	NEGROES	NEWPORT
MOSSIER	MUGGILY	MUTABLE	NANNIES	NEGROID	NEWTOWN
MOTHERS	MUGGING	MUTABLY	NANNING	NEIGHED	NEW TOWN
MOTIONS	MUGGINS	MUTAGEN	NANTONG	NEITHER	NEW WAVE
MOTIVES	MUGSHOT	MUTANTS	NANTUNG	NELLIES	NEW YEAR
MOTORED	MUGWORT	MUTTONY	NAPHTHA	NELUMBO	NEW YORK
MOTTLED	MUGWUMP	MUZZIER	NAPKINS	NEMATIC	NEXUSES
MOTTOES	MULATTO	MUZZILY	NAPPIES	NEMESES	NIAGARA
MOUFLON	MULCHED	MUZZLED	NAPPING	NEMESIS	NIBBLED
MOUILLE	MULCTED	MUZZLER	NARKIER	NEOCENE	NIBBLER
MOULDED	MULLAHS	MUZZLES	NARKING	NEOGAEA	NIBBLES
MOULDER	MULLEIN	MYALGIA	NARRATE	NEOGENE	NICKELS
MOULTED	MULLETS	MYALGIC	NARROWS	NEOLITH	NICKING
MOULTER	MULLING	MYALISM	NARTHEX	NEONATE	NICOBAR
MOUNTED	MULLION	MYANMAR	NARWHAL	NEOTENY	NICOSIA
MOUNTER	MULLITE	MYCENAE	NASALLY	NEOTYPE	NIFTIER
MOUNTIE	MUMBLED	MYCOSIS	NASCENT	NEOZOIC	NIFTILY
MOURNED	MUMBLER	MYCOTIC	NASTIER	NEPHEWS	NIGELLA
MOURNER	MUMMERS	MYELOID	NASTILY	NEPHRON	NIGERIA
MOUSERS	MUMMERY	MYELOMA	NATIONS	NEPOTIC	NIGGARD
MOUSIER	MUMMIES	MYIASIS	NATIVES	NEPTUNE	NIGGERS
MOUSING	MUMMIFY	MYKONOS	NATTIER	NEREIDS	NIGGLED
MOUSSES	MUMMING	MYNHEER	NATTILY	NERITIC	NIGGLER
MOUTHED	MUNCHED	MYOLOGY	NATURAL	NERVATE	NIGHTIE
MOUTHER	MUNCHER	MYOTOME	NATURES	NERVIER	NIGHTLY
MOVABLE	MUNDANE	MYRIADS	NAUGHTY	NERVILY	NIIGATA
MOVABLY	MUNSTER	MYRTLES	NAURUAN	NERVINE	NILOTIC
MOVIOLA	MUNTJAC	MYSTERY	NAVARRE	NERVING	NIMBLER
MUBARAK	MURDERS	MYSTICS	NAVVIES	NERVOUS	NINEPIN
MUCKIER	MURDOCH	MYSTIFY	NAYARIT	NERVURE	NINNIES

NIOBITE	NOONDAY	NUMERAL	OBTRUDE	OINKING	OOSPORE
NIOBIUM	NO-PLACE	NUMMARY	OBVERSE	OKAYAMA	OOTHECA
NIOBOUS	NORFOLK	NUNATAK	OBVIATE	OKAYING	OOZIEST
NIPPERS	NORMANS	NUNAVUT	OBVIOUS	OKINAWA	OPACITY
NIPPIER	NORWICH	NUN BUOY	OCARINA	OLD BOYS	OPALINE
NIPPILY	NOSEBAG	NUNCIOS	OCCIPUT	OLD HAND	OPEN-AIR
NIPPING	NOSEGAY	NUNNERY	OCCLUDE	OLD LADY	OPEN DAY
NIPPLES	NOSHING	NUPTIAL	OCEANIA	OLD LAGS	OPENERS
NIRVANA	NOSIEST	NURSERY	OCEANIC	OLD MAID	OPENING
NITEROI	NOSTRIL	NURSING	OCELLAR	OLD NICK	OPERAND
NITRATE	NOSTRUM	NURTURE	OCELLUS	OLDSTER	OPERANT
NITRIDE	NOTABLE	NUTCASE	OCELOTS	OLDTIME	OPERATE
NITRIFY	NOTABLY	NUTGALL	OCHROID	OLDUVAI	OPHITIC
NITRILE	NOTCHED	NUTMEGS	OCREATE	OLEFINE	OPIATES
NITRITE	NOTCHES	NUTRIAS	OCTADIC	O LEVELS	OPINING
NITROSO	NOTELET	NUTTIER	OCTAGON	OLIVARY	OPINION
NITROUS	NOTEPAD	NUTTILY	OCTANES	OLIVINE	OPOSSUM
NITWITS	NOTHING	NUTTING	OCTAVES	OLOMOUC	OPPOSED
NIVEOUS	NOTICED	NUTWOOD	OCTOBER	OLSZTYN	OPPOSER
NO BALLS	NOTICES	NUZZLED	OCTOPOD	OLYMPIA	OPPRESS
NOBBLED	NOTIONS	NYMPHAL	OCTOPUS	OLYMPIC	OPSONIC
NOBBLER	NO TRUMP	NYMPHET	OCTUPLE	OLYMPUS	OPSONIN
NOBLEST	NO-TRUMP	NYUNGAR	OCULIST	OMENTUM	OPTICAL
NOCTUID	NOUGATS		ODDBALL	OMICRON	OPTIMAL
NOCTULE	NOUGHTS	**O**	ODDMENT	OMINOUS	OPTIMUM
NOCTURN	NOURISH		ODDNESS	OMITTED	OPTIONS
NODDING	NOUVEAU	OAKLAND	ODOROUS	OMITTER	OPULENT
NODDLES	NOVALIS	OARFISH	ODYSSEY	OMNIBUS	OPUNTIA
NODICAL	NOVELLA	OARLOCK	OEDIPAL	ON A	OQUASSA
NO DOUBT	NOVELLE	OARSMAN	OERSTED	WHIM	ORACLES
NODULAR	NOVELTY	OARSMEN	OESTRUS	ONE EYED	ORALISM
NODULES	NOVICES	OATCAKE	OFFBEAT	ONENESS	ORANGES
NO ENTRY	NOVI SAD	OATMEAL	OFFENCE	ONE-OFFS	ORATION
NOGGING	NOWHERE	OBCONIC	OFFERED	ONEROUS	ORATORS
NOGGINS	NOXIOUS	OBELISK	OFFERER	ONESELF	ORATORY
NOISIER	NOZZLES	OBELIZE	OFFHAND	ONE-STAR	ORBITAL
NOISILY	NUANCES	OBESITY	OFFICER	ONE STEP	ORBITED
NOISOME	NUCLEAR	OBEYING	OFFICES	ONE-STEP	ORCHARD
NOMADIC	NUCLEIN	OBJECTS	OFFINGS	ONETIME	ORCHIDS
NOMBRIL	NUCLEON	OBLIGED	OFF-LOAD	ON-GLIDE	ORCINOL
NOMINAL	NUCLEUS	OBLIGEE	OFF-PEAK	ONGOING	ORDEALS
NOMINEE	NUCLIDE	OBLIGER	OFFSIDE	ONITSHA	ORDERED
NONAGON	NUDGING	OBLIGOR	OGREISH	ON LEAVE	ORDERER
NON-IRON	NUDISTS	OBLIQUE	OHM'S	ONSHORE	ORDERLY
NONPLUS	NUGGETS	OBLONGS	LAW	ON SIGHT	ORDINAL
NON-PROS	NUGGETY	OBLOQUY	OILBIRD	ON STAGE	ORECTIC
NONSTOP	NULLIFY	OBOISTS	OILCANS	ONTARIO	OREGANO
NON STOP	NULLITY	OBOVATE	OILIEST	ONWARDS	ORGANIC
NONSUIT	NULL SET	OBOVOID	OILRIGS	OOLITIC	ORGANON
NON USER	NUMBERS	OBSCENE	OILSKIN	OOPHYTE	ORGANUM
NOODLES	NUMBING	OBSCURE	OIL WELL	OOSPERM	ORGANZA

ORGASMS	OUTBACK	OVATION	PACKERS	PANAMAS	PARESIS
ORIENTE	OUTCAST	OVERACT	PACKETS	PAN-ARAB	PARETIC
ORIFICE	OUTCOME	OVERAGE	PACK ICE	PANCAKE	PARFAIT
ORIGAMI	OUTCROP	OVERALL	PACKING	PANCHAX	PARIAHS
ORIGINS	OUTDATE	OVERARM	PADDIES	PANDECT	PARINGS
ORINOCO	OUTDONE	OVERAWE	PADDING	PANDITS	PARKIER
ORISONS	OUTDOOR	OVERBID	PADDLED	PANDORE	PARKING
ORIZABA	OUTFACE	OVERDID	PADDLER	PANELED	PARKWAY
ORKNEYS	OUTFALL	OVERDUE	PADDLES	PANGAEA	PARLEYS
ORLANDO	OUTFITS	OVERFLY	PADDOCK	PANICKY	PARLOUR
ORLEANS	OUTFLOW	OVERJOY	PADLOCK	PANICLE	PARLOUS
OROGENY	OUTGREW	OVERLAP	PADRONE	PANNIER	PARODIC
OROLOGY	OUTGROW	OVERLAY	PAGEANT	PANNING	PAROLED
OROTUND	OUTHAUL	OVERLIE	PAGEBOY	PANOCHA	PAROLES
ORPHANS	OUTINGS	OVERMAN	PAGINAL	PANOPLY	PARONYM
ORPHREY	OUTLAST	OVERPAY	PAGODAS	PANSIES	PAROTIC
ORTOLAN	OUTLAWS	OVERRAN	PAHSIEN	PANTHER	PAROTID
ORVIETO	OUTLAYS	OVERRUN	PAINFUL	PANTIES	PARQUET
OSCULAR	OUTLETS	OVERSAW	PAINING	PANTILE	PARRIED
OSCULUM	OUTLIER	OVERSEE	PAINTED	PANTING	PARRIES
OSHOGBO	OUTLINE	OVERSET	PAINTER	PANTOUM	PARROTS
OSMIOUS	OUTLIVE	OVERSEW	PAIRING	PANZERS	PARSEES
OSMOSIS	OUTLOOK	OVERTAX	PAIR-OAR	PAOTING	PARSERS
OSMOTIC	OUTMOST	OVERTLY	PAISLEY	PAPAYAS	PARSING
OSMUNDA	OUTPACE	OVERTOP	PAJAMAS	PAPEETE	PARSLEY
OSPREYS	OUTPLAY	OVERUSE	PALACES	PAPERED	PARSNIP
OSSEOUS	OUTPORT	OVIDUCT	PALADIN	PAPERER	PARSONS
OSSETIA	OUTPOST	OVIFORM	PALATAL	PAPILLA	PARTAKE
OSSETIC	OUTPOUR	OVULATE	PALATES	PAPISTS	PARTIAL
OSSICLE	OUTPUTS	OWN GOAL	PALAVER	PAPOOSE	PARTIED
OSSUARY	OUTRAGE	OXALATE	PALE ALE	PAPPIES	PARTIES
OSTEOID	OUTRANK	OXAZINE	PALERMO	PAPPOSE	PARTING
OSTEOMA	OUTRIDE	OXBLOOD	PALETTE	PAPRIKA	PARTITA
OSTIOLE	OUTRODE	OXCARTS	PALFREY	PAPYRUS	PARTITE
OSTLERS	OUTSELL	OXHEART	PALINGS	PARABLE	PARTNER
OSTMARK	OUTSIDE	OXIDANT	PALLETS	PARADED	PARTOOK
OSTOSIS	OUTSIZE	OXIDASE	PALLIER	PARADER	PARVENU
OSTRAVA	OUTSOLD	OXIDATE	PALLING	PARADES	PASCHAL
OSTRICH	OUTSOLE	OXIDIZE	PALLIUM	PARADOR	PASMORE
OTOCYST	OUTSTAY	OXONIAN	PALMATE	PARADOX	PASSADE
OTOLITH	OUT-TAKE	OXYACID	PALMIER	PARAGON	PASSAGE
OTOLOGY	OUTTALK	OXYSALT	PALMING	PARAIBA	PASSANT
OTRANTO	OUT-TRAY	OXYTONE	PALMIRA	PARAPET	PAS SEUL
OTTOMAN	OUTVOTE	OYSTERS	PALMIST	PARASOL	PASS FOR
OUABAIN	OUTWARD	OZONIZE	PALM OIL	PARATHA	PASSING
OUGHTN'T	OUTWASH		PALMYRA	PARBOIL	PASSION
OUR LADY	OUTWEAR	**P**	PALPATE	PARCELS	PASSIVE
OUR LORD	OUTWORK	PABULUM	PALSIED	PARCHED	PASSKEY
OURSELF	OUTWORN	PACHUCA	PAMPEAN	PARDONS	PASS OFF
OUSTERS	OVARIAN	PACIFIC	PANACEA	PAREIRA	PASS OUT
OUSTING	OVARIES	PACKAGE	PANACHE	PARENTS	PASTELS

PASTERN	PAYSLIP	PELTING	PERFUSE	PETTISH	PICKLES
PASTE UP	PEACHES	PENALLY	PERGOLA	PETUNIA	PICK-UPS
PASTE-UP	PEACOCK	PENALTY	PERHAPS	PFENNIG	PICNICS
PASTIER	PEAFOWL	PENANCE	PERIDOT	PHAETON	PICOTEE
PASTIES	PEAHENS	PENDANT	PERIGEE	PHALANX	PICRATE
PASTILY	PEAKIER	PENDENT	PERIGON	PHALLIC	PICRITE
PASTIME	PEAKING	PENDING	PERIODS	PHALLUS	PICTISH
PASTING	PEALING	PENGUIN	PERIQUE	PHANTOM	PICTURE
PASTORS	PEANUTS	PENISES	PERIWIG	PHARAOH	PIDDLED
PASTURE	PEARLER	PEN NAME	PERJURE	PHARYNX	PIDDOCK
PATCHED	PEASANT	PENNANT	PERJURY	PHASING	PIDGINS
PATCHER	PEBBLES	PENNATE	PERKIER	PHASMID	PIEBALD
PATCHES	PECCANT	PENNIES	PERKILY	PHELLEM	PIECING
PATELLA	PECCARY	PENNING	PERKING	PHILTRE	PIE-EYED
PATENCY	PECCAVI	PENNONS	PERLITE	PHIZOGS	PIERCED
PATENTS	PECKERS	PEN PALS	PERMIAN	PHLOXES	PIERCER
PATHANS	PECKING	PENRITH	PERMING	PHOBIAS	PIETIES
PATHWAY	PECKISH	PENROSE	PERMITS	PHOBICS	PIGEONS
PATIALA	PECTASE	PENSILE	PERMUTE	PHOCINE	PIGFISH
PATIENT	PECTATE	PENSION	PERPEND	PHOENIX	PIGGERY
PATRIAL	PECTIZE	PENSIVE	PERPLEX	PHONATE	PIGGIER
PATRICK	PEDALED	PENTANE	PERSEID	PHONE-IN	PIGGIES
PATRIOT	PEDANTS	PENTENE	PERSIAN	PHONEME	PIGGING
PATROLS	PEDDLED	PENTODE	PERSIST	PHONEYS	PIGGISH
PATRONS	PEDDLER	PENTOSE	PERSONA	PHONICS	PIG IRON
PATTENS	PEDICEL	PEONIES	PERSONS	PHONIER	PIG LEAD
PATTERN	PEDICLE	PEOPLED	PERSPEX	PHONING	PIGLETS
PATTERS	PEDLARS	PEOPLES	PERTAIN	PHRASAL	PIGMENT
PATTIES	PEDOCAL	PEPPERS	PERTURB	PHRASED	PIGMIES
PATTING	PEEBLES	PEPPERY	PERUGIA	PHRASES	PIGSKIN
PAUCITY	PEEKING	PEP PILL	PERUSAL	PHRATRY	PIGTAIL
PAULINE	PEELING	PEPPING	PERUSED	PHRENIC	PIGWEED
PAULIST	PEEPERS	PEP TALK	PERUSER	PHYSICS	PIKEMAN
PAUNCHY	PEEPING	PEPTIDE	PERVADE	PHYSIOS	PIKEMEN
PAUPERS	PEERAGE	PEPTIZE	PERVERT	PIANISM	PILEATE
PAUSING	PEERESS	PEPTONE	PESCARA	PIANIST	PILEOUS
PAVANES	PEERING	PERACID	PESETAS	PIANOLA	PILEUPS
PAVINGS	PEEVING	PERCALE	PESKIER	PIASTRE	PILGRIM
PAVIOUR	PEEVISH	PER CENT	PESSARY	PIAZZAS	PILLAGE
PAWKIER	PEEWITS	PERCEPT	PESTLES	PIBROCH	PILLARS
PAWKILY	PEGGING	PERCHED	PETARDS	PICADOR	PILLBOX
PAWNAGE	PEG LEGS	PERCHER	PETCOCK	PICARDY	PILLION
PAWNING	PELAGIC	PERCHES	PETIOLE	PICCOLO	PILLOCK
PAWPAWS	PELICAN	PERCOID	PET NAME	PICEOUS	PILLORY
PAYABLE	PELITIC	PERCUSS	PETRELS	PICKAXE	PILLOWS
PAYBEDS	PELLETS	PER DIEM	PETRIFY	PICKERS	PILOTED
PAY DIRT	PELMETS	PEREIRA	PETROUS	PICKETS	PILSNER
PAYLOAD	PELORIA	PERFECT	PETSAMO	PICKIER	PILULAR
PAYMENT	PELORUS	PERFIDY	PETTIER	PICKING	PIMENTO
PAYOUTS	PELOTAS	PERFORM	PETTILY	PICKLED	PIMPING
PAYROLL	PELTATE	PERFUME	PETTING	PICKLER	PIMPLED

PIMPLES	PISTOLS	PLASTID	PLUMAGE	POLYGON	PORTICO
PINBALL	PISTONS	PLATEAU	PLUMATE	POLYMER	PORTING
PINCERS	PIT A	PLATINA	PLUMBED	POLYNYA	PORTION
PINCHED	PAT	PLATING	PLUMBER	POLYPOD	PORTRAY
PINCHES	PIT-A-	PLATOON	PLUMBIC	POLYPUS	POSEURS
PINE NUT	PAT	PLATTER	PLUMING	POMMELS	POSHEST
PINETUM	PITCHED	PLAUDIT	PLUMMET	POMMIES	POSITED
PINFISH	PITCHER	PLAY-ACT	PLUMPED	POMPANO	POSITIF
PINFOLD	PITCHES	PLAYBOY	PLUMPER	POMPEII	POSSESS
PINGING	PITEOUS	PLAYERS	PLUMULE	POMPOMS	POSSETS
PINGUID	PITFALL	PLAYFUL	PLUNDER	POMPOUS	POSSUMS
PINHEAD	PITHEAD	PLAYING	PLUNGED	PONCHOS	POSTAGE
PINHOLE	PITHIER	PLAYLET	PLUNGER	PONGIER	POSTBAG
PINIEST	PITHILY	PLAY OFF	PLURALS	PONGING	POSTBOX
PINIONS	PITIFUL	PLAY-OFF	PLUSHER	PONIARD	POSTERN
PINKEST	PIT PONY	PLAYPEN	PLUVIAL	PONTIFF	POSTERS
PINKEYE	PIT PROP	PLEADED	PLYWOOD	PONTINE	POSTFIX
PINK GIN	PITTING	PLEADER	POACHED	PONTOON	POSTIES
PINKIES	PITYING	PLEASED	POACHER	POOCHES	POSTING
PINKING	PIVOTAL	PLEASER	PO BOXES	POODLES	POSTMAN
PINKISH	PIVOTED	PLEATED	POCHARD	POOFIER	POSTMEN
PINKOES	PIZZAZZ	PLEATER	POCKETS	POOH-BAH	POSTURE
PINNACE	PLACARD	PLEDGED	PODAGRA	POOLING	POSTWAR
PINNATE	PLACATE	PLEDGER	PODDING	POOPERS	POTABLE
PINNIES	PLACEBO	PLEDGES	PODESTA	POOR BOX	POTAGER
PINNING	PLACING	PLEDGET	PODGIER	POOREST	POTENCY
PINNULE	PLACKET	PLEDGOR	PODGILY	POOR LAW	POTFULS
PINTAIL	PLACOID	PLENARY	PODIUMS	POPADUM	POTHEEN
PINWORK	PLAFOND	PLEURAL	PODOLSK	POPCORN	POTHERB
PINWORM	PLAGUED	PLEURON	POETESS	POPEDOM	POTHOLE
PIONEER	PLAGUER	PLIABLE	POETICS	POP-EYED	POTHOOK
PIOUSLY	PLAGUES	PLIANCY	PO-FACED	POPGUNS	POTICHE
PIPETTE	PLAINER	PLICATE	POGONIA	POPLARS	POTIONS
PIPPING	PLAINLY	PLIGHTS	POGROMS	POPOVER	POT LUCK
PIPPINS	PLAINTS	PLINTHS	POINTED	POPPERS	POTLUCK
PIQUANT	PLAITED	PLODDED	POINTER	POPPETS	POTOMAC
PIQUING	PLANETS	PLODDER	POISING	POPPIES	POTSDAM
PIRAEUS	PLANING	PLOESTI	POISONS	POPPING	POTSHOT
PIRANHA	PLANISH	PLONKED	POKIEST	POP STAR	POTTAGE
PIRATED	PLANNED	PLOPPED	POLARIS	POPULAR	POTTERS
PIRATES	PLANNER	PLOSION	POLEAXE	PORCHES	POTTERY
PIRATIC	PLANTAR	PLOSIVE	POLECAT	PORCINE	POTTIER
PISCARY	PLANTED	PLOTTED	POLEMIC	PORIRUA	POTTIES
PISCINA	PLANTER	PLOTTER	POLICED	PORKERS	POTTING
PISCINE	PLANULA	PLOUGHS	POLITIC	PORKIER	POUCHED
PISHPEK	PLAQUES	PLOVDIV	POLLACK	PORK PIE	POUCHES
PISSING	PLASMID	PLOVERS	POLLARD	PORTAGE	POULARD
PISS-UPS	PLASMIN	PLOWING	POLLING	PORTALS	POULTRY
PISTEUR	PLASMON	PLUCKED	POLL TAX	PORTEND	POUNCED
PISTILS	PLASTER	PLUCKER	POLLUTE	PORTENT	POUNCES
PISTOIA	PLASTIC	PLUGGED	POLTAVA	PORTERS	POUNDAL

POUNDED	PRESAGE	PRIZING	PROTEGE	PUFFINS	PURSUIT
POUNDER	PRESENT	PROBANG	PROTEIN	PUGGING	PURVIEW
POURING	PRESIDE	PROBATE	PROTEST	PULLETS	PUSHERS
POUTING	PRESSED	PROBING	PROTIST	PULLEYS	PUSHIER
POVERTY	PRESSES	PROBITY	PROTIUM	PULLING	PUSHILY
POWDERS	PRESSOR	PROBLEM	PROTONS	PULL-INS	PUSHING
POWDERY	PRESS UP	PROCARP	PROTYLE	PULLMAN	PUSHKIN
POWERED	PRESS-UP	PROCEED	PROUDER	PULLOUT	PUSHROD
POWWOWS	PRESTON	PROCESS	PROUDLY	PULPIER	PUSH-UPS
PRAIRIE	PRESTOS	PROCTOR	PROVERB	PULPING	PUSSIES
PRAISED	PRESUME	PROCURE	PROVIDE	PULPITS	PUSTULE
PRAISER	PRETEEN	PRODDED	PROVING	PULSARS	PUTAMEN
PRAISES	PRETEND	PRODDER	PROVISO	PULSATE	PUT DOWN
PRALINE	PRETEST	PRODIGY	PROVOKE	PULSING	PUT-DOWN
PRANCED	PRETEXT	PRODUCE	PROVOST	PUMPING	PUT-OFFS
PRANCER	PRETZEL	PRODUCT	PROWESS	PUMPKIN	PUTREFY
PRATING	PREVAIL	PROFANE	PROWLED	PUNCHED	PUTTERS
PRATTLE	PREVENT	PROFESS	PROWLER	PUNCHER	PUTTING
PRAWNER	PREVIEW	PROFFER	PROXIES	PUNCHES	PUTTNAM
PRAYERS	PREYING	PROFILE	PROXIMA	PUNCH UP	PUT-UPON
PRAYING	PREZZIE	PROFITS	PRUDENT	PUNCH-UP	PUZZLED
PREBEND	PRICIER	PRO-FORM	PRUDERY	PUNDITS	PUZZLER
PRECAST	PRICING	PROFUSE	PRUDISH	PUNGENT	PUZZLES
PRECEDE	PRICKED	PROGENY	PRUNING	PUNIEST	PYAEMIA
PRECEPT	PRICKER	PROGRAM	PRURIGO	PUNJABI	PYAEMIC
PRECESS	PRICKET	PROJECT	PRUSSIA	PUNKAHS	PYGMIES
PRECISE	PRICKLE	PROLATE	PSALMIC	PUNNETS	PYJAMAS
PRECOOK	PRICKLY	PRO-LIFE	PSALTER	PUNNING	PYLORUS
PREDATE	PRIDING	PROLINE	PSYCHED	PUNSTER	PYNCHON
PREDICT	PRIESTS	PROLONG	PSYCHES	PUNTERS	PYRALID
PREEMPT	PRIMACY	PROMISE	PSYCHIC	PUNTING	PYRAMID
PREENED	PRIMARY	PROMMER	PSYLLID	PUPPETS	PYRETIC
PREENER	PRIMATE	PROMOTE	PTERYLA	PUPPIES	PYREXIA
PREFABS	PRIMERS	PROMPTS	PTYALIN	PUPPING	PYRITES
PREFACE	PRIMINE	PRONATE	PUBERTY	PURCELL	PYRITIC
PREFECT	PRIMING	PRONOUN	PUBLISH	PURGING	PYROGEN
PREHEAT	PRIMMER	PROOFED	PUCCOON	PURISTS	PYROSIS
PRELACY	PRIMULA	PROPANE	PUCKERS	PURITAN	PYRRHIC
PRELATE	PRINCES	PROPEND	PUCKISH	PURLIEU	PYRROLE
PRELIMS	PRINKER	PROPENE	PUDDING	PURLING	PYTHONS
PRELUDE	PRINTED	PROPHET	PUDDLED	PURLOIN	
PREMIER	PRINTER	PROPOSE	PUDDLER	PURPLES	**Q**
PREMISE	PRISING	PROPPED	PUDDLES	PURPORT	Q-FACTOR
PREMISS	PRISONS	PRO RATA	PUDENDA	PURPOSE	QINGDAO
PREMIUM	PRITHEE	PROSAIC	PUDGIER	PURPURA	QUACKED
PREPACK	PRIVACY	PROSIER	PUDGILY	PURPURE	QUADRAT
PREPAID	PRIVATE	PROSILY	PUERILE	PURRING	QUADRIC
PREPARE	PRIVIER	PROSODY	PUFFERY	PURSERS	QUAFFER
PREPONE	PRIVIES	PROSPER	PUFFIER	PURSING	QUAILED
PREPOSE	PRIVILY	PROTEAN	PUFFILY	PURSUED	QUAKERS
PREPUCE	PRIVITY	PROTECT	PUFFING	PURSUER	QUAKILY

QUAKING	QUININE	RAGBAGS	RANGING	RAVENNA	RECEDED
QUALIFY	QUINONE	RAGGING	RANGOON	RAVE-UPS	RECEIPT
QUALITY	QUINTAL	RAGOUTS	RANKERS	RAVINES	RECEIVE
QUANGOS	QUINTAN	RAGTAIL	RANKING	RAVINGS	RECIPES
QUANTAL	QUINTET	RAGTIME	RANKLED	RAVIOLI	RECITAL
QUANTIC	QUINTIC	RAGWEED	RANSACK	RAW DEAL	RECITED
QUANTUM	QUIPPED	RAG WEEK	RANSOMS	RAWHIDE	RECITER
QUARREL	QUITTED	RAGWORM	RANTERS	RAWNESS	RECKING
QUARTAN	QUITTER	RAGWORT	RANTING	RAZZLES	RECLAIM
QUARTER	QUITTOR	RAIDERS	RAPHIDE	REACHED	RECLINE
QUARTET	QUIVERS	RAIDING	RAPIDLY	REACHER	RECLUSE
QUARTIC	QUIVERY	RAILING	RAPIERS	REACHES	RECORDS
QUARTOS	QUI VIVE	RAILWAY	RAPISTS	REACTED	RECOUNT
QUASARS	QUIZZED	RAIMENT	RAPPING	REACTOR	RECOVER
QUASHED	QUIZZER	RAINBOW	RAPPORT	READERS	RECRUIT
QUASSIA	QUIZZES	RAINIER	RAPTURE	READIED	RECTIFY
QUAVERS	QUONDAM	RAINILY	RAREBIT	READIER	RECTORS
QUAVERY	QUORATE	RAINING	RASBORA	READIES	RECTORY
QUAYAGE	QUORUMS	RAINOUT	RASCALS	READILY	RECTRIX
QUECHUA	QUOTHED	RAISERS	RASHERS	READING	RECTUMS
QUEENED	QUOTING	RAISING	RASHEST	READOUT	RECURVE
QUEENLY		RAISINS	RASPING	REAGENT	RECYCLE
QUEERED	**R**	RAISINY	RATABLE	REALGAR	RED BOOK
QUEERER	RABBITS	RAKE-OFF	RATABLY	REALIGN	RED CARD
QUEERLY	RABBLER	RALEIGH	RATAFIA	REALISM	REDCOAT
QUELLED	RABBLES	RALLIED	RAT-A-	REALIST	RED DEER
QUELLER	RACCOON	RALLIER	TAT	REALITY	REDDEST
QUERIED	RACEMIC	RALLIES	RATBAGS	REALIZE	REDDISH
QUERIES	RACHIAL	RALLINE	RATCHET	REALTOR	REDFISH
QUERIST	RACIEST	RAMADAN	RATE-CAP	REAMERS	RED FLAG
QUESTED	RACISTS	RAMBLED	RATINGS	REAMING	REDFORD
QUESTER	RACKETS	RAMBLER	RATIONS	REAPERS	REDHEAD
QUETZAL	RACKETY	RAMBLES	RATLINE	REAPING	RED MEAT
QUEUING	RACKING	RAMEKIN	RATPACK	REARING	REDNECK
QUIBBLE	RACOONS	RAMMING	RAT RACE	REARMED	REDNESS
QUICHES	RACQUET	RAMMISH	RATTIER	REASONS	REDOING
QUICKEN	RADIALS	RAMPAGE	RATTILY	REBADGE	REDOUBT
QUICKER	RADIANT	RAMPANT	RATTING	REBATER	REDOUND
QUICKIE	RADIATE	RAMPART	RATTISH	REBATES	REDPOLL
QUICKLY	RADICAL	RAMPION	RATTLED	REBIRTH	REDRAFT
QUIETEN	RADICEL	RAM RAID	RATTLES	REBOUND	REDRESS
QUIETER	RADICES	RAMRODS	RAT TRAP	REBRAND	REDROOT
QUIETLY	RADICLE	RAMSONS	RAUCOUS	REBUFFS	REDSKIN
QUIETUS	RADIOED	RANCHER	RAUNCHY	REBUILD	RED SPOT
QUILMES	RADULAR	RANCHES	RAVAGED	REBUILT	RED TAPE
QUILTED	RAFFISH	RANCOUR	RAVAGER	REBUKED	REDUCED
QUILTER	RAFFLED	RANDERS	RAVAGES	REBUKER	REDUCER
QUIMPER	RAFFLER	RANDIER	RAVELED	REBUKES	REDWING
QUINARY	RAFFLES	RANDOMS	RAVELIN	REBUSES	REDWOOD
QUINATE	RAFTERS	RANGERS	RAVELLY	RECALLS	REEDIER
QUINCES	RAFTING	RANGILY	RAVENER	RECAPED	REEDING

REEFERS	REISSUE	REPASTS	RESTING	REVIVAL	RIGHTER
REEFING	REJECTS	REPEATS	RESTIVE	REVIVED	RIGHTLY
REEKING	REJOICE	REPINED	RESTOCK	REVIVER	RIGHT-ON
RE-ELECT	RELAPSE	REPLACE	RESTORE	REVOICE	RIGIDLY
REELING	RELATED	REPLAYS	RESTYLE	REVOKED	RIG-OUTS
REELMAN	RELATER	REPLETE	RESULTS	REVOKER	RIM-FIRE
RE-ENTER	RELATOR	REPLEVY	RESUMED	REVOLTS	RIMLESS
RE-ENTRY	RELATUM	REPLICA	RESUMES	REVOLVE	RIMMING
REFACED	RELAXED	REPLIED	RETABLE	REVVING	RIMROCK
REFEREE	RELAXER	REPLIER	RETAKEN	REWARDS	RINGENT
REFILLS	RELAXIN	REPLIES	RETAKER	REWIRED	RINGERS
REFINED	RELAYED	REPORTS	RETAKES	REWRITE	RINGING
REFINER	RELEASE	REPOSAL	RETCHED	REWROTE	RINGLET
REFLATE	RELIANT	REPOSED	RETHINK	REYNOSA	RINSING
REFLECT	RELIEFS	REPOSER	RETICLE	RHAETIC	RIOT ACT
REFORMS	RELIEVE	REPOSIT	RETINAE	RHATANY	RIOTERS
REFRACT	RELINED	REPRESS	RETINAL	RHENIUM	RIOTING
REFRAIN	RELIVED	REPRINT	RETINAS	RHEUMIC	RIOTOUS
REFRESH	RELYING	REPRISE	RETINOL	RHIZOID	RIPCORD
REFUGEE	REMAINS	REPROOF	RETINUE	RHIZOME	RIPENED
REFUGES	REMAKES	REPROVE	RETIRED	RHODIUM	RIPENER
REFUNDS	REMANDS	REPTANT	RETIRER	RHOMBIC	RIP-OFFS
REFUSAL	REMARKS	REPTILE	RETITLE	RHOMBUS	RIPOSTE
REFUSED	REMARRY	REPULSE	RETORTS	RHONDDA	RIPPING
REFUSER	REMATCH	REPUTED	RETOUCH	RHUBARB	RIPPLED
REFUTED	REMNANT	REQUEST	RETRACE	RHYMING	RIPPLER
REFUTER	REMODEL	REQUIEM	RETRACT	RHYTHMS	RIPPLES
REGALIA	REMORSE	REQUIRE	RETREAD	RIBBAND	RIPPLET
REGALLY	REMOTER	REQUITE	RETREAT	RIBBING	RIPSAWS
REGARDS	REMOULD	REREDOS	RETRIAL	RIBBONS	RIPTIDE
REGATTA	REMOUNT	RESCIND	RETSINA	RIB CAGE	RISIBLE
REGENCY	REMOVAL	RESCUED	RETURNS	RIBWORT	RISIBLY
REGENTS	REMOVED	RESCUER	REUNIFY	RICHARD	RISINGS
REGIMEN	REMOVER	RESCUES	REUNION	RICHEST	RISKIER
REGIMES	REMOVES	RESERVE	REUNITE	RICHLER	RISKILY
REGINAS	RENAMED	RESHAPE	REUSING	RICHTER	RISKING
REGIONS	RENDELL	RESIDED	REVALUE	RICKETS	RISOTTO
REGNANT	RENDING	RESIDER	REVELED	RICKETY	RISSOLE
REGOSOL	RENEGED	RESIDUE	REVELRY	RICKING	RITUALS
REGRATE	RENEGER	RESKILL	REVENGE	RIDDING	RIVALED
REGRESS	RENEWAL	RESNAIS	REVENUE	RIDDLED	RIVALRY
REGRETS	RENEWED	RESOLVE	REVERED	RIDDLER	RIVETED
REGROUP	RENEWER	RESORTS	REVERER	RIDDLES	RIVETER
REGULAR	RENFREW	RESOUND	REVERIE	RIDGING	RIVIERA
REGULOS	RENTALS	RESPECT	REVERSE	RIDOTTO	RIVIERE
REGULUS	RENT BOY	RESPIRE	REVIEWS	RIFFLED	RIVULET
REHOUSE	RENTERS	RESPITE	REVILED	RIFFLER	ROACHES
REIFIER	RENTIER	RESPOND	REVILER	RIFLERY	ROADBED
REIGATE	RENTING	RESTAGE	REVISAL	RIFLING	ROAD HOG
REIGNED	REORDER	RESTATE	REVISED	RIGGING	ROADMAN
REINING	REPAIRS	RESTFUL	REVISER	RIGHTED	ROAD MAP

ROADMEN	ROOMIER	ROWLOCK	RUPTURE	SALLIES	SAO LUIS
ROAD TAX	ROOMILY	ROYALLY	RUSHDIE	SALLOWS	SAPHENA
ROADWAY	ROOMING	ROYALTY	RUSHING	SALMONS	SAPIENT
ROAMERS	ROOSTED	ROZZERS	RUSSIAN	SALOONS	SAPLESS
ROAMING	ROOSTER	RUBBERS	RUSTICS	SALPINX	SAPLING
ROARING	ROOTAGE	RUBBERY	RUSTIER	SALSIFY	SAPONIN
ROASTED	ROOTING	RUBBING	RUSTILY	SALTANT	SAPPERS
ROASTER	ROOTLET	RUBBISH	RUSTING	SALTBOX	SAPPIER
ROBBERS	ROPIEST	RUBDOWN	RUSTLED	SALTERN	SAPPILY
ROBBERY	RORAIMA	RUBELLA	RUSTLER	SALTIER	SAPPING
ROBBING	RORQUAL	RUBEOLA	RUTLAND	SALTILY	SAPPORO
ROBUSTA	ROSARIO	RUBICON	RUTTILY	SALTING	SAPROBE
ROCK BUN	ROSEATE	RUBIDIC	RUTTING	SALTIRE	SAPSAGO
ROCKERS	ROSEBUD	RUBIOUS	RUTTISH	SALTPAN	SAPWOOD
ROCKERY	ROSE HIP	RUBRICS	RYBINSK	SALTPOT	SARACEN
ROCKETS	ROSELLA	RUCHING		SALUTED	SARANSK
ROCKIER	ROSEOLA	RUCKING	**s**	SALUTER	SARATOV
ROCKIES	ROSETTA	RUCTION	SABBATH	SALUTES	SARAWAK
ROCKING	ROSETTE	RUDDERS	SACATON	SALVAGE	SARCASM
ROCKOON	ROSIEST	RUDDIER	SACCATE	SALVERS	SARCOID
RODENTS	ROSINED	RUDDILY	SACCULE	SALVING	SARCOMA
RODLIKE	ROSTERS	RUDERAL	SACHETS	SALVOES	SARCOUS
ROEBUCK	ROSTOCK	RUFFIAN	SACKING	SALWEEN	SARDINE
ROE DEER	ROSTRAL	RUFFLED	SADDEST	SAMISEN	SARDIUS
ROGUERY	ROSTRUM	RUFFLER	SADDLED	SAMNIUM	SARKIER
ROGUISH	ROTATED	RUFFLES	SADDLER	SAMOSAS	SARNIES
ROISTER	ROTATOR	RUINING	SADDLES	SAMOVAR	SARONGS
ROLL BAR	ROTIFER	RUINOUS	SADIRON	SAMOYED	SARONIC
ROLLERS	ROTORUA	RULABLE	SADISTS	SAMPANS	SASSABY
ROLLICK	ROTTERS	RULINGS	SADNESS	SAMPLED	SASSARI
ROLLING	ROTTING	RUMANIA	SAFARIS	SAMPLER	SASSIER
ROLLMOP	ROTUNDA	RUMBLED	SAFFIAN	SAMPLES	SASSING
ROLL-ONS	ROUBAIX	RUMBLER	SAFFRON	SAMPRAS	SATANIC
ROLL-TOP	ROUBLES	RUMBLES	SAFROLE	SAMURAI	SATCHEL
ROLLWAY	ROUGHEN	RUMMAGE	SAGGIER	SANCTUM	SATIATE
ROMAGNA	ROUGHER	RUMMEST	SAGGING	SANCTUS	SATIETY
ROMANCE	ROUGHLY.	RUMOURS	SAGUARO	SANDALS	SATINET
ROMANIA	ROUGING	RUMPLED	SAHARAN	SANDBAG	SATIRES
ROMPERS	ROULEAU	RUNAWAY	SAILING	SANDBAR	SATISFY
ROMPING	ROULERS	RUNCORN	SAILORS	SANDBOX	SATSUMA
RONDEAU	ROUNDED	RUN DOWN	SAINTED	SANDERS	SATYRIC
RONDURE	ROUNDEL	RUN-DOWN	SAINTLY	SAND FLY	SATYRID
RONTGEN	ROUNDER	RUN INTO	SALAAMS	SANDIER	SAUCERS
ROOFING	ROUNDLY	RUNNELS	SALABLE	SANDING	SAUCIER
ROOFTOP	ROUNDUP	RUNNERS	SALAMIS	SANDPIT	SAUCILY
ROOINEK	ROUND UP	RUNNIER	SALERNO	SANGRIA	SAUCING
ROOKERY	ROUSING	RUNNING	SALFORD	SANICLE	SAUNTER
ROOKIES	ROUTINE	RUN-OFFS	SALICIN	SAN JOSE	SAURIAN
ROOKING	ROUTING	RUN OVER	SALIENT	SAN JUAN	SAUSAGE
ROOMERS	ROWDIER	RUNTISH	SALLIED	SAN REMO	SAUTEED
ROOMFUL	ROWDILY	RUNWAYS	SALLIER	SANTA FE	SAVABLE

SAVAGED	SCHEMES	SCREWER	SEASIDE	SELL-OUT	SESOTHO
SAVAGES	SCHERZO	SCREW UP	SEASONS	SELTZER	SESSILE
SAVANNA	SCHISMS	SCRIBAL	SEATING	SELVAGE	SESSION
SAVANTS	SCHLUMP	SCRIBER	SEATTLE	SEMATIC	SESTINA
SAVE-ALL	SCHMUCK	SCRIBES	SEAWALL	SEMINAL	SETBACK
SAVINGS	SCHOLAR	SCRIMPY	SEAWARE	SEMINAR	SET FREE
SAVIOUR	SCHOOLS	SCRIPTS	SEAWAYS	SEMITIC	SETLINE
SAVOURY	SCIATIC	SCROLLS	SEAWEED	SENATES	SETTEES
SAWBILL	SCIENCE	SCROOGE	SECEDED	SENATOR	SETTERS
SAWDUST	SCISSOR	SCROTUM	SECEDER	SENDERS	SETTING
SAWFISH	SCOFFED	SCRUBBY	SECLUDE	SENDING	SETTLED
SAWMILL	SCOFFER	SCRUFFS	SECONDO	SEND-OFF	SETTLER
SAWN-OFF	SCOLDED	SCRUFFY	SECONDS	SEND-UPS	SETTLES
SAXHORN	SCOLDER	SCRUMPY	SECRECY	SENEGAL	SEVENTH
SAXTUBA	SCOLLOP	SCRUNCH	SECRETE	SENIORS	SEVENTY
SAYINGS	SCONCES	SCRUPLE	SECRETS	SENORAS	SEVERAL
SCABBLE	SCOOPED	SCUDDED	SECTARY	SENSATE	SEVERED
SCABIES	SCOOPER	SCUFFED	SECTILE	SENSING	SEVILLE
SCALARS	SCOOTED	SCUFFLE	SECTION	SENSORS	SEXIEST
SCALDED	SCOOTER	SCULLED	SECTORS	SENSORY	SEXISTS
SCALENE	SCOPULA	SCULLER	SECULAR	SENSUAL	SEXLESS
SCALIER	SCORERS	SCULPIN	SECURED	SEPTATE	SEXPOTS
SCALING	SCORIFY	SCUMBLE	SECURER	SEPTETS	SEXTANT
SCALLOP	SCORING	SCUMMER	SEDATED	SEPTIME	SEXTETS
SCALPED	SCORNED	SCUPPER	SEDILIA	SEQUELA	SEXTILE
SCALPEL	SCORNER	SCUTATE	SEDUCED	SEQUELS	SEXTONS
SCALPER	SCORPER	SCUTTLE	SEDUCER	SEQUENT	SFUMATO
SCAMPER	SCORPIO	SCYTHED	SEEDBED	SEQUINS	SHAANXI
SCANDAL	SCOTOMA	SCYTHES	SEED BED	SEQUOIA	SHACKED
SCANDIC	SCOURED	SEABIRD	SEEDIER	SERAPHS	SHACKLE
SCANNED	SCOURER	SEACOCK	SEEDILY	SERBIAN	SHADIER
SCANNER	SCOURGE	SEA DOGS	SEEDING	SERFDOM	SHADILY
SCAPOSE	SCOUSES	SEAFOOD	SEEKERS	SERGIPE	SHADING
SCAPULA	SCOUTED	SEAGIRT	SEEKING	SERIALS	SHADOOF
SCARABS	SCOUTER	SEA GULL	SEEMING	SERIATE	SHADOWS
SCARCER	SCOWLED	SEAGULL	SEEPAGE	SERICIN	SHADOWY
SCARIER	SCOWLER	SEA-LANE	SEEPING	SERIEMA	SHAFTED
SCARIFY	SCRAGGY	SEALANT	SEESAWS	SERINGA	SHAGGED
SCARING	SCRAPED	SEA LEGS	SEETHED	SERIOUS	SHAHDOM
SCARLET	SCRAPER	SEALERS	SEGMENT	SERMONS	SHAKERS
SCARPER	SCRAPES	SEALERY	SEGOVIA	SERPENT	SHAKE UP
SCARRED	SCRAPPY	SEALING	SEISMIC	SERPIGO	SHAKE-UP
SCARVES	SCRATCH	SEA LION	SEIZING	SERRATE	SHAKHTY
SCATTED	SCRAWLS	SEAMARK	SEIZURE	SERRIED	SHAKIER
SCATTER	SCRAWLY	SEAMIER	SEKONDI	SERUMAL	SHAKILY
SCENERY	SCRAWNY	SEA MILE	SELENIC	SERVANT	SHAKING
SCENTED	SCREAMS	SEA MIST	SELFISH	SERVERS	SHALLOP
SCEPTIC	SCREECH	SEANCES	SELLERS	SERVERY	SHALLOT
SCEPTRE	SCREEDS	SEAPORT	SELLING	SERVICE	SHALLOW
SCHEMED	SCREENS	SEARING	SELL OFF	SERVILE	SHAMANS
SCHEMER	SCREWED	SEASICK	SELL OUT	SERVING	SHAMBLE

SHAMING	SHINGLE	SHRINKS	SIGHTLY	SIPHONS	SKITTER
SHAMMED	SHINGLY	SHRIVEL	SIGMATE	SIPPING	SKITTLE
SHAMMER	SHINIER	SHRIVER	SIGMOID	SIRLOIN	SKIVERS
SHAMPOO	SHINING	SHROUDS	SIGNALS	SIROCCO	SKIVING
SHANKLY	SHINNED	SHRUBBY	SIGNETS	SIRRAHS	SKULKED
SHANNON	SHIPPED	SHUCKED	SIGNIFY	SISSIER	SKULKER
SHANTOU	SHIPPER	SHUCKER	SIGNING	SISSIES	SKY BLUE
SHAPELY	SHIPWAY	SHUDDER	SIGN OFF	SISTERS	SKY-BLUE
SHAPING	SHIRKED	SHUFFLE	SIGNORA	SITCOMS	SKYCAPS
SHARERS	SHIRKER	SHUNNED	SIGNORE	SIT-DOWN	SKYDIVE
SHARING	SHITBAG	SHUNNER	SIGNORS	SITTERS	SKY-HIGH
SHARPEN	SHITTED	SHUNTED	SILENCE	SITTING	SKYJACK
SHARPER	SHIVERS	SHUNTER	SILENTS	SITUATE	SKYLARK
SHARPLY	SHIVERY	SHUSHED	SILESIA	SIXFOLD	SKYLINE
SHATTER	SHOCKED	SHUT-EYE	SILICIC	SIX-PACK	SKYSAIL
SHAVERS	SHOCKER	SHUT-OFF	SILICLE	SIXTEEN	SKYWALK
SHAVING	SHOEING	SHUTOUT	SILICON	SIXTIES	SLACKED
SHAWNEE	SHOGUNS	SHUTTER	SILIQUA	SIZABLE	SLACKEN
SHEARED	SHOOING	SHUTTLE	SILKIER	SIZZLED	SLACKER
SHEARER	SHOOTER	SHYLOCK	SILKILY	SIZZLER	SLACKLY
SHEATHE	SHOPPED	SHYNESS	SILLIER	SKATING	SLAGGED
SHEATHS	SHOPPER	SHYSTER	SILLIES	SKATOLE	SLAKING
SHEAVES	SHORING	SIALKOT	SILTING	SKEPTIC	SLALOMS
SHEBANG	SHORTED	SIALOID	SILURID	SKETCHY	SLAMMED
SHE BEAR	SHORTEN	SIAMANG	SILVERS	SKEWERS	SLANDER
SHEBEEN	SHORTER	SIAMESE	SILVERY	SKEWING	SLANGED
SHEDDER	SHORTIE	SIBERIA	SIMIANS	SKIABLE	SLANTED
SHEERED	SHORTLY	SIBLING	SIMILAR	SKIBOBS	SLAPPED
SHEERER	SHOTGUN	SICHUAN	SIMILES	SKIDDED	SLAPPER
SHEIKHS	SHOT PUT	SICKBAY	SIMIOUS	SKIDPAN	SLASHED
SHEILAS	SHOTTEN	SICKBED	SIMPERS	SKID ROW	SLASHER
SHEKELS	SHOUTED	SICKEST	SIMPLER	SKIFFLE	SLASHES
SHELLAC	SHOUTER	SICKING	SIMPLEX	SKI JUMP	SLATING
SHELLED	SHOVELS	SICKLES	SIMULAR	SKILFUL	SLATTED
SHELTER	SHOVING	SICK PAY	SINALOA	SKI LIFT	SLAVERS
SHELVED	SHOWERS	SIDEARM	SINCERE	SKILLED	SLAVERY
SHELVER	SHOWERY	SIDECAR	SINE DIE	SKILLET	SLAVING
SHELVES	SHOWIER	SIDE CAR	SINGING	SKIMMED	SLAVISH
SHEPARD	SHOWILY	SIDINGS	SINGLED	SKIMMER	SLAYERS
SHEPPEY	SHOWING	SIDLING	SINGLES	SKIMMIA	SLAYING
SHERBET	SHOWMAN	SIEMENS	SINGLET	SKIMPED	SLEDDED
SHERIFF	SHOWMEN	SIERRAN	SINITIC	SKINFUL	SLEDDER
SHERPAS	SHOWN UP	SIERRAS	SINKERS	SKINNED	SLEDGED
SHEWING	SHOW OFF	SIESTAS	SINKING	SKINNER	SLEDGES
SHIELDS	SHOW-OFF	SIEVERT	SINLESS	SKI POLE	SLEEKED
SHIFTED	SHRIEKS	SIEVING	SINNERS	SKIPPED	SLEEKER
SHIFTER	SHRIFTS	SIFTERS	SINNING	SKIPPER	SLEEKLY
SHIITES	SHRIKES	SIFTING	SINUATE	SKIPPET	SLEEPER
SHIKOKU	SHRILLY	SIGHING	SINUIJU	SKIPTON	SLEETED
SHIMMER	SHRIMPS	SIGHTED	SINUOUS	SKIRRET	SLEEVES
SHINDIG	SHRINES	SIGHTER	SINUSES	SKIRTED	SLEIGHS

SLEIGHT	SMALL AD	SNEEZED	SOBBING	SOOTHER	SPANKED
SLENDER	SMALLER	SNEEZER	SOBERED	SOOTIER	SPANKER
SLEUTHS	SMARTED	SNEEZES	SOBERLY	SOOTILY	SPANNED
SLEWING	SMARTEN	SNICKED	SOCAGER	SOPHISM	SPANNER
SLICING	SMARTER	SNICKER	SOCIALS	SOPHIST	SPARING
SLICKED	SMARTLY	SNIDELY	SOCIETY	SOPPIER	SPARKED
SLICKER	SMASHED	SNIDEST	SOCKETS	SOPPILY	SPARKLE
SLICKLY	SMASHER	SNIFFED	SOCKEYE	SOPPING	SPARRED
SLIDING	SMASHES	SNIFFER	SOCKING	SOPRANO	SPARROW
SLIGHTS	SMASH-UP	SNIFFLE	SODDING	SORBETS	SPARSER
SLIMIER	SMATTER	SNIFTER	SOD'S	SORBOSE	SPARTAN
SLIMILY	SMEARED	SNIGGER	LAW	SORCERY	SPASTIC
SLIMMED	SMEARER	SNIGGLE	SOFA BED	SORDINO	SPATHIC
SLIMMER	SMECTIC	SNIPERS	SOFTEST	SORGHUM	SPATIAL
SINGER	SMELLED	SNIPING	SOFTIES	SORITES	SPATTER
SLIP-ONS	SMELTED	SNIPPED	SOGGIFR	SOROSIS	SPATULA
SLIPPED	SMELTER	SNIPPET	SOGGILY	SORRIER	SPAWNED
SLIPPER	SMIDGIN	SNOGGED	SOILAGE	SORRILY	SPAWNER
SLIP-UPS	SMILING	SNOOKER	SOILING	SORROWS	SPAYING
SLIPWAY	SMIRKED	SNOOPED	SOIREES	SORTIES	SPEAKER
SLITHER	SMIRKER	SNOOPER	SOJOURN	SORTING	SPEARED
SLITTED	SMITING	SNOOZED	SOLACED	SORT-OUT	SPEARER
SLITTER	SMITTEN	SNOOZER	SOLACER	SO THERE	SPECIAL
SLIVERS	SMOKERS	SNOOZES	SOLACES	SOTTISH	SPECIES
SLOBBER	SMOKIER	SNORERS	SOLANUM	SOUFFLE	SPECIFY
SLOGANS	SMOKILY	SNORING	SOLARIA	SOUGHED	SPECKLE
SLOGGED	SMOKING	SNORKEL	SOLDIER	SOUKOUS	SPECTRA
SLOGGER	SMOLDER	SNORTED	SOLICIT	SOULFUL	SPECTRE
SLOPING	SMOTHER	SNORTER	SOLIDLY	SOUNDED	SPEEDED
SLOPPED	SMUDGED	SNOWCAP	SOLIDUS	SOUNDER	SPEEDER
SLOSHED	SMUDGES	SNOWIER	SOLOIST	SOUNDLY	SPELLED
SLOTTED	SMUGGER	SNOWILY	SOLOMON	SOUPCON	SPELLER
SLOTTER	SMUGGLE	SNOWING	SOLUBLE	SOUPFIN	SPELTER
SLOUCHY	SMUTCHY	SNOWMAN	SOLVATE	SOURCES	SPENCER
SLOUGHS	SNACKED	SNOWMEN	SOLVENT	SOUREST	SPENDER
SLOUGHY	SNAFFLE	SNUBBED	SOLVERS	SOURING	SPEWING
SLOVENE	SNAGGED	SNUBBER	SOLVING	SOURSOP	SPHENIC
SLOWEST	SNAKILY	SNUFFED	SOMALIA	SOUSING	SPHERAL
SLOWING	SNAKING	SNUFFER	SOMATIC	SOUTANE	SPHERES
SLUGGED	SNAPPED	SNUFFLE	SOMEDAY	SOUTHER	SPICATE
SLUICED	SNAPPER	SNUFFLY	SOMEHOW	SOVIETS	SPICERY
SLUICES	SNARING	SNUGGLE	SOMEONE	SOVKHOZ	SPICIER
SLUMBER	SNARLED	SOAKAGE	SOMEWAY	SOWETAN	SPICILY
SLUMMED	SNARLER	SOAKING	SOMITAL	SOZZLED	SPICING
SLUMMER	SNARL UP	SO-AND-	SONANCE	SPACING	SPICULE
SLUMPED	SNARL-UP	SO	SONATAS	SPANCEL	SPIDERS
SLURPED	SNATCHY	SOAPBOX	SONDAGE	SPANDEX	SPIDERY
SLURRED	SNEAKED	SOAPIER	SONGFUL	SPANGLE	SPIELER
SLYNESS	SNEAKER	SOAPILY	SONNETS	SPANGLY	SPIGNEL
SMACKED	SNEERED	SOAPING	SOOCHOW	SPANIEL	SPIGOTS
SMACKER	SNEERER	SOARING	SOOTHED	SPANISH	SPIKIER

SPIKILY	SPORRAN	SQUELCH	STANNIC	STEERER	STIPEND
SPIKING	SPORTED	SQUIDGY	STANZAS	STELLAR	STIPPLE
SPILLED	SPORTER	SQUIFFY	STAPLED	STEMMED	STIPULE
SPILLER	SPORULE	SQUILLA	STAPLER	STEMMER	STIR-FRY
SPINACH	SPOTLIT	SQUINCH	STAPLES	STEMSON	STIRRED
SPINDLE	SPOTTED	SQUINTS	STARCHY	STENCIL	STIRRER
SPINDLY	SPOTTER	SQUINTY	STARDOM	STEN GUN	STIRRUP
SPIN-DRY	SPOUSAL	SQUIRES	STARING	STENTOR	STOCKED
SPINETS	SPOUSES	SQUIRMS	STARKER	STEPDAD	STOCKER
SPINNER	SPOUTED	SQUIRMY	STARKLY	STEPMUM	STOICAL
SPINNEY	SPOUTER	SQUIRTS	STARLET	STEPPED	STOKERS
SPIN-OFF	SPRAINS	SQUISHY	STARLIT	STEPPER	STOKING
SPINOSE	SPRAINT	STABBED	STARRED	STEPPES	STOMACH
SPINOUS	SPRAWLS	STABBER	STARTED	STEPSON	STOMPED
SPIN OUT	SPRAWLY	STABILE	STARTER	STEPS UP	STOMPER
SPINULE	SPRAYED	STABLED	STARTLE	STEREOS	STONIER
SPIRAEA	SPRAYER	STABLES	START UP	STERILE	STONILY
SPIRALS	SPREADS	STACKED	STARVED	STERLET	STONING
SPIRANT	SPRIEST	STACKER	STARVER	STERNAL	STOOD UP
SPIREME	SPRIGGY	STADDLE	STASHED	STERNER	STOOGES
SPIRITS	SPRINGE	STADIUM	STASHES	STERNLY	STOOKER
SPIROID	SPRINGS	STAFFED	STATANT	STERNUM	STOOPED
SPIRULA	SPRINGY	STAFFER	STATELY	STEROID	STOOPER
SPITING	SPRINTS	STAGGER	STATICS	STERTOR	STOPGAP
SPITTER	SPRITES	STAGILY	STATING	STETSON	STOPING
SPITTLE	SPROUTS	STAGING	STATION	STEWARD	STOPPED
SPLASHY	SPRUCED	STAIDLY	STATISM	STEWART	STOPPER
SPLAYED	SPRUCES	STAINED	STATIST	STEWING	STORAGE
SPLEENS	SPUMONE	STAINER	STATIVE	STHENIC	STOREYS
SPLENIC	SPUMOUS	STAINES	STATUED	STIBINE	STORIED
SPLICED	SPURNED	STAKING	STATUES	STICHIC	STORIES
SPLICER	SPURNER	STALEST	STATURE	STICKER	STORING
SPLICES	SPURRED	STALING	STATUTE	STICKLE	STORMED
SPLINTS	SPURTED	STALKED	STAUNCH	STICK-ON	STOUTER
SPLODGE	SPUTNIK	STALKER	STAVING	STICK UP	STOUTLY
SPLODGY	SPUTTER	STALLED	STAYERS	STICK-UP	STOWAGE
SPLURGE	SQUABBY	STAMBUL	STAYING	STIFFEN	STOWING
SPOILED	SQUACCO	STAMENS	STEALER	STIFFER	STRAFED
SPOILER	SQUALID	STAMINA	STEALTH	STIFFLY	STRAFER
SPOKANE	SQUALLS	STAMMEL	STEAMED	STIFLED	STRAINS
SPONDEE	SQUALLY	STAMMER	STEAMER	STIFLER	STRAITS
SPONGED	SQUALOR	STAMPED	STEAM UP	STIGMAS	STRANDS
SPONGER	SQUARED	STAMPER	STEARIC	STILLED	STRANGE
SPONGES	SQUARER	STANCES	STEARIN	STILLER	STRATAL
SPONGIN	SQUARES	STANDBY	STEELED	STILTED	STRATAS
SPONSON	SQUASHY	STAND BY	STEEPED	STILTON	STRATUM
SPONSOR	SQUAWKS	STANDER	STEEPEN	STIMULI	STRATUS
SPOOFER	SQUEAKS	STAND-IN	STEEPER	STINGER	STRAYED
SPOOKED	SQUEAKY	STAND UP	STEEPLE	STINKER	STRAYER
SPOONED	SQUEALS	STAND-UP	STEEPLY	STINTED	STREAKS
SPOORER	SQUEEZE	STANLEY	STEERED	STINTER	STREAKY

STREAMS	STYLIST	SUCRASE	SUNROOF	SWANSEA	SYLPHIC
STREETS	STYLIZE	SUCROSE	SUNSETS	SWAPPED	SYLPHID
STRETCH	STYLOID	SUCTION	SUNSPOT	SWAPPER	SYLVITE
STRETTA	STYLOPS	SUDANIC	SUNSTAR	SWARMED	SYMBOLS
STRETTO	STYMIED	SUDBURY	SUNTANS	SWARTHY	SYMPTOM
STREWED	STYPSIS	SUDETES	SUNTRAP	SWATHED	SYNAPSE
STREWER	STYPTIC	SUFFICE	SUNWISE	SWATTED	SYNCARP
STREWTH	STYRENE	SUFFOLK	SUPPERS	SWATTER	SYNCHRO
STRIATE	SUAVELY	SUFFUSE	SUPPING	SWAYING	SYNCOPE
STRIDES	SUAVITY	SUGARED	SUPPLER	SWEARER	SYNERGY
STRIDOR	SUBACID	SUGGEST	SUPPORT	SWEATED	SYNESIS
STRIKER	SUB-AQUA	SUICIDE	SUPPOSE	SWEATER	SYNGAMY
STRIKES	SUBARID	SUITING	SUPREME	SWEDISH	SYNODAL
STRINGS	SUBBASE	SUITORS	SUPREMO	SWEEPER	SYNODIC
STRINGY	SUBBASS	SUKHUMI	SURBASE	SWEETEN	SYNONYM
STRIPED	SUBBING	SULCATE	SURCOAT	SWEETER	SYNOVIA
STRIPER	SUBDUAL	SULKIER	SURFACE	SWEETIE	SYPHONS
STRIPES	SUBDUCT	SULKILY	SURFEIT	SWEETLY	SYRINGA
STRIPEY	SUBDUED	SULKING	SURFERS	SWELLED	SYRINGE
STRIVEN	SUBEDIT	SULLAGE	SURFING	SWELTER	SYRPHID
STRIVER	SUBERIN	SULLIED	SURGEON	SWERVED	SYSTEMS
STROBIC	SUBFUSC	SULPHUR	SURGERY	SWERVER	SYSTOLE
STROKED	SUBJECT	SULTANA	SURGING	SWERVES	SZILARD
STROKES	SUBJOIN	SULTANS	SURINAM	SWIFTER	
STROLLS	SUBLIME	SUMATRA	SURLIER	SWIFTLY	**T**
STROPHE	SUBPLOT	SUMBAWA	SURLILY	SWIGGED	
STROPPY	SUB ROSA	SUMMAND	SURMISE	SWIGGER	TABANID
STRUDEL	SUBSETS	SUMMARY	SURNAME	SWILLED	TABASCO
STUBBED	SUBSIDE	SUMMERS	SURPASS	SWILLER	TABBIES
STUBBLE	SUBSIDY	SUMMERY	SURPLUS	SWIMMER	TABBING
STUBBLY	SUBSIST	SUMMING	SURREAL	SWINDLE	TABLEAU
STUCK-UP	SUBSOIL	SUMMITS	SURREYS	SWINDON	TABLING
STUDDED	SUBSUME	SUMMONS	SURVEYS	SWINGER	TABLOID
STUDENT	SUBTEND	SUNBEAM	SURVIVE	SWINGLE	TABORET
STUDIED	SUBTEXT	SUNBEDS	SUSPECT	SWINISH	TABORIN
STUDIES	SUBTLER	SUNBELT	SUSPEND	SWIPING	TABULAR
STUDIOS	SUBTYPE	SUNBIRD	SUSSING	SWIPPLE	TACHYON
STUFFED	SUBUNIT	SUNBURN	SUSTAIN	SWIRLED	TACITLY
STUFFER	SUBURBS	SUNDAES	SUTURAL	SWISHED	TACKIER
STUMBLE	SUBVERT	SUNDAYS	SUTURED	SWISHER	TACKIES
STUMPED	SUBWAYS	SUNDIAL	SUTURES	SWISHES	TACKILY
STUMPER	SUCCEED	SUNDOWN	SWABBED	SWIVELS	TACKING
STUNNED	SUCCESS	SUNFISH	SWABBER	SWIZZLE	TACKLED
STUNNER	SUCCOUR	SUNGLOW	SWABIAN	SWOLLEN	TACKLER
STUNTED	SUCCUBI	SUN GODS	SWADDLE	SWOONED	TACKLES
STUPEFY	SUCCUMB	SUNLAMP	SWAGGER	SWOOPED	TACNODE
STUPORS	SUCCUSS	SUNLESS	SWAHILI	SWOPPED	TACTFUL
STUTTER	SUCKERS	SUNNIER	SWALLOW	SWOTTED	TACTICS
STYGIAN	SUCKING	SUNNILY	SWAMPED	SYCOSIS	TACTILE
STYLING	SUCKLED	SUNNING	SWANKED	SYENITE	TACTUAL
STYLISH	SUCKLER	SUNRISE	SWANNED	SYLLABI	TADPOLE
					TADZHIK

TAFFETA	TANGLER	TAUNTED	TELEXES	TERRORS	THIMBLE
TAFFIES	TANGLES	TAUNTER	TELFORD	TERSELY	THIN AIR
TAGGERS	TANGOED	TAUNTON	TELLERS	TERTIAL	THINNED
TAGGING	TANGRAM	TAUREAN	TELLIES	TERTIAN	THINNER
TAG LINE	TANKAGE	TAURINE	TELLING	TESSERA	THIONIC
TAGMEME	TANKARD	TAUTEST	TELPHER	TESTACY	THIONYL
TAIL END	TANKERS	TAVENER	TELSTAR	TESTATE	THIRSTS
TAILING	TANNAGE	TAVERNS	TEMPERA	TEST BAN	THIRSTY
TAILORS	TANNATE	TAXABLE	TEMPERS	TESTERS	THISTLE
TAINTED	TANNERS	TAX-FREE	TEMPEST	TESTIER	THISTLY
TAIYUAN	TANNERY	TAXICAB	TEMPING	TESTIFY	THITHER
TAKABLE	TANNING	TAXIING	TEMPLES	TESTILY	THORITE
TAKEOFF	TANTRUM	TAXIWAY	TEMPTED	TESTING	THORIUM
TAKE OFF	TAN-TUNG	TBILISI	TEMPTER	TETANIC	THOUGHT
TAKEOUT	TAOISTS	TBILIZI	TENABLE	TETANUS	THRALLS
TAKE OUT	TAPERED	TEABAGS	TENANCY	TETHERS	THREADS
TAKEUPS	TAPERER	TEACAKE	TENANTS	TETRODE	THREADY
TAKINGS	TAPETAL	TEA CAKE	TENCHES	TEXTILE	THREATS
TALCOSE	TAPETUM	TEACHER	TENDERS	TEXTUAL	THREE
TALENTS	TAPHOLE	TEACH-IN	TENDING	TEXTURE	R'S
TALIBAN	TAPIOCA	TEA COSY	TENDONS	THALLIC	THRIFTS
TALIPED	TAPPETS	TEACUPS	TENDRIL	THALLUS	THRIFTY
TALIPES	TAPPING	TEA GOWN	TENFOLD	THANKED	THRILLS
TALIPOT	TAPROOM	TEALEAF	TENNERS	THAWING	THRIVED
TALKERS	TAPROOT	TEAMING	TENONER	THE ARTS	THROATS
TALKIES	TARANTO	TEAPOTS	TENPINS	THEATRE	THROATY
TALKING	TARDIER	TEARFUL	TENSELY	THE BARD	THRONES
TALLAGE	TARDILY	TEAR GAS	TENSEST	THEISTS	THRONGS
TALLBOY	TARGETS	TEARING	TENSILE	THEOREM	THROUGH
TALLEST	TARIFFS	TEAROOM	TENSING	THERAPY	THROWER
TALLIED	TARMACS	TEASELS	TENSION	THEREAT	THROW IN
TALLIER	TARNISH	TEASERS	TENSIVE	THEREBY	THROW-IN
TALLIES	TARRASA	TEASHOP	TENTAGE	THEREIN	THRUSTS
TALLINN	TARRIED	TEASING	TENUITY	THEREOF	THRUWAY
TALLISH	TARRING	TEA TREE	TENUOUS	THEREON	THUDDED
TALLYHO	TARSIER	TECHILY	TEPIDLY	THERETO	THULIUM
TAMABLE	TARTANS	TECHNIC	TEQUILA	THERMAL	THUMBED
TAMARAU	TARTARS	TECTRIX	TERBIUM	THERMIC	THUMPED
TAMARIN	TASSELS	TEDIOUS	TERMING	THERMIT	THUMPER
TAMBOUR	TASTERS	TEEMING	TERMINI	THERMOS	THUNDER
TAMPERE	TASTIER	TEENAGE	TERMITE	THEROID	THURGAU
TAMPICO	TASTILY	TEEPEES	TERNARY	THEROUX	THWACKS
TAMPING	TASTING	TEGULAR	TERNATE	THEURGY	THYMINE
TAMPONS	TATOUAY	TEHERAN	TERPENE	THE WASH	THYROID
TANAGER	TATTERS	TEKTITE	TERRACE	THICKEN	THYRSUS
TANBARK	TATTIER	TELAMON	TERRAIN	THICKER	THYSELF
TANDEMS	TATTILY	TEL AVIV	TERRANE	THICKET	TIANJIN
TANGELO	TATTING	TELEOST	TERRENE	THICKIE	TIBETAN
TANGENT	TATTLED	TELERAN	TERRIER	THICKLY	TICKERS
TANGIER	TATTLER	TELESIS	TERRIFY	THIEVED	TICKETS
TANGLED	TATTOOS	TELEXED	TERRINE	THIEVES	TICKING

TICKLED	TIPPERS	TOLLING	TORREFY	TRADE IN	TRELLIS
TICKLER	TIPPETT	TOLUATE	TORRENT	TRADE-IN	TREMBLE
TICKLES	TIPPING	TOLUENE	TORREON	TRADERS	TREMBLY
TIDBITS	TIPPLER	TOMBOLA	TORSADE	TRADING	TREMOLO
TIDDLER	TIPPLES	TOMBOLO	TORSION	TRADUCE	TREMORS
TIDEWAY	TIPSIER	TOMBOYS	TORTOLA	TRAFFIC	TRENTON
TIDIEST	TIPSILY	TOMCATS	TORTONI	TRAGEDY	TREPANG
TIDINGS	TIPSTER	TOMFOOL	TORTUGA	TRAILED	TRESSES
TIDYING	TIPTOED	TOM-TOMS	TORTURE	TRAILER	TRESTLE
TIE-DIED	TIPTOES	TONEPAD	TORYISM	TRAINED	TREVISO
TIEPINS	TIRADES	TONETIC	TOSSING	TRAINEE	TRIABLE
TIFFANY	TIREDLY	TONGUES	TOSS-UPS	TRAINER	TRIACID
TIGHTEN	TISSUES	TONIGHT	TOTALED	TRAIPSE	TRIADIC
TIGHTER	TITANIA	TONNAGE	TOTALLY	TRAITOR	TRIBADE
TIGHTLY	TITANIC	TONNEAU	TOTE BAG	TRAJECT	TRIBUNE
TIGRESS	TITBITS	TONSILS	TOTEMIC	TRAMCAR	TRIBUTE
TIJUANA	TITFERS	TONSURE	TOTTERY	TRAMMEL	TRICEPS
TILAPIA	TITHING	TONTINE	TOTTING	TRAMPED	TRICKED
TILBURG	TITMICE	TOOLING	TOUCANS	TRAMPER	TRICKER
TILLAGE	TITOISM	TOOTING	TOUCHED	TRAMPLE	TRICKLE
TILLERS	TITOIST	TOOTLED	TOUCHER	TRAMWAY	TRICKLY
TILLING	TITRANT	TOOTLER	TOUCHES	TRANCES	TRICKSY
TILTING	TITRATE	TOOTLES	TOUGHEN	TRANCHE	TRICORN
TIMBALE	TITTERS	TOOTSIE	TOUGHER	TRANSIT	TRIDENT
TIMBERS	TITTIES	TOPARCH	TOUGHLY	TRANSOM	TRIDUUM
TIMBREL	TITULAR	TOPAZES	TOUPEES	TRAPANI	TRIED ON
TIMBRES	TIZZIES	TOPCOAT	TOURACO	TRAPEZE	TRIESTE
TIME LAG	TLEMCEN	TOP DOGS	TOURING	TRAPPED	TRIFLED
TIME-OUT	TOADIED	TOP HATS	TOURISM	TRAPPER	TRIFLER
TIMIDLY	TOADIES	TOPIARY	TOURIST	TRASHED	TRIFLES
TIMPANI	TOADLET	TOPICAL	TOURNAI	TRAUMAS	TRIGGER
TINAMOU	TOASTED	TOPKNOT	TOURNEY	TRAVAIL	TRILLED
TINFOIL	TOASTER	TOPLESS	TOUSLED	TRAVELS	TRILOGY
TINGING	TOASTIE	TOPMAST	TOUTING	TRAVOIS	TRIMBLE
TINGLED	TOBACCO	TOPMOST	TOWARDS	TRAWLED	TRIMMED
TINGLER	TOBOLSK	TOPONYM	TOWBOAT	TRAWLER	TRIMMER
TIN GODS	TOBY JUG	TOPPERS	TOWELED	TREACLE	TRINARY
TIN HATS	TOCCATA	TOPPING	TOWERED	TREACLY	TRINITY
TINIEST	TOCSINS	TOPPLED	TOWHEAD	TREADER	TRINKET
TINKERS	TODDIES	TOPSAIL	TOWLINE	TREADLE	TRIOLET
TINKLED	TODDLED	TOPSIDE	TOWPATH	TREAD ON	TRIPLED
TINKLES	TODDLER	TOPSOIL	TOWROPE	TREASON	TRIPLET
TINNIER	TOE CAPS	TOPSPIN	TOW ROPE	TREATED	TRIPLEX
TINNILY	TOEHOLD	TORCHES	TRABZON	TREATER	TRIPODS
TINNING	TOENAIL	TORFAEN	TRACERS	TREBLED	TRIPODY
TINTACK	TOFFEES	TORMENT	TRACERY	TREBLES	TRIPOLI
TINTING	TOGGING	TORNADO	TRACHEA	TREFOIL	TRIPPED
TINTYPE	TOGGLES	TORONTO	TRACING	TREHALA	TRIPPER
TINWARE	TOHEROA	TORPEDO	TRACKED	TREKKED	TRIPPET
TINWORK	TOILETS	TORQUAY	TRACKER	TREKKER	TRIPURA
TIP-OFFS	TOILING	TORQUES	TRACTOR	TREKKIE	TRIREME

TRISECT	TRUSTED	TURNERS	TWOSOME	UNCHAIN	UNPAGED
TRISMIC	TRUSTEE	TURNERY	TWO-STAR	UNCINUS	UNPOSED
TRISMUS	TRUSTER	TURNING	TWO-STEP	UNCIVIL	UNQUIET
TRISOME	TRYPSIN	TURNIPS	TWO-TIME	UNCLASP	UNQUOTE
TRISOMY	TRYPTIC	TURNKEY	TWO-TONE	UNCLEAN	UNRAVEL
TRITELY	TRYSAIL	TURN OFF	TYCHISM	UNCLEAR	UNREADY
TRITIUM	TRYSTER	TURN-OFF	TYCOONS	UNCLOAK	UNREEVE
TRITONE	TSARDOM	TURN-ONS	TYLOSIS	UNCLOSE	UNSCREW
TRIUMPH	TSARINA	TURN OUT	TYMPANA	UNCOUTH	UNSLING
TRIVETS	TSARIST	TURNOUT	TYMPANY	UNCOVER	UNSNARL
TRIVIAL	T-SHIRTS	TURNS UP	TYNWALD	UNCROSS	UNSOUND
TROCHAL	T-SQUARE	TURN-UPS	TYPEBAR	UNCTION	UNSTICK
TROCHEE	TSUNAMI	TURPETH	TYPESET	UNDERDO	UNSTRAP
TRODDEN	TUATARA	TURRETS	TYPHOID	UNDERGO	UNSTUCK
TROIKAS	TUBBIER	TURTLER	TYPHOON	UNDOING	UNSWEAR
TROJANS	TUBBING	TURTLES	TYPHOUS	UNDRESS	UNTHINK
TROLLED	TUBIFEX	TUSCANY	TYPICAL	UNDYING	UNTRIED
TROLLEY	TUBULAR	TUSKERS	TYPISTS	UNEARTH	UNTRUSS
TROLLOP	TUCKING	TUSSIVE	TYRANNY	UNEQUAL	UNTRUTH
TROMMEL	TUCUMAN	TUSSLED	TYRANTS	UNFROCK	UNTYING
TROOPED	TUESDAY	TUSSLES	TYRONIC	UNFUSSY	UNUSUAL
TROOPER	TUGGING	TUSSOCK	TZARINA	UNGODLY	UNVOICE
TROPHIC	TUITION	TUTORED		UNGUENT	UNWAGED
TROPICS	TUMBLED	TUTUILA	**U**	UNGULAR	UNWOUND
TROPISM	TUMBLER	TUTUOLA	UDAIPUR	UNHAPPY	UP-AND-
TROTTED	TUMBLES	TUXEDOS	UGANDAN	UNHEARD	UP
TROTTER	TUMBREL	TWADDLE	UGLIEST	UNHINGE	UPBRAID
TROUBLE	TUMMIES	TWANGED	UKRAINE	UNHORSE	UPBUILD
TROUGHS	TUMOURS	TWEAKED	UKULELE	UNICORN	UPCHUCK
TROUNCE	TUMULAR	TWEETED	ULANOVA	UNIFIED	UPDATED
TROUPER	TUMULTS	TWEETER	ULAN-UDE	UNIFIER	UPDATER
TROUPES	TUMULUS	TWELFTH	ULLAGED	UNIFORM	UPDATES
TROUSER	TUNABLE	TWELVES	ULULANT	UNITARY	UPDRAFT
TROWELS	TUNEFUL	TWIDDLE	ULULATE	UNITIES	UPENDED
TRUANCY	TUNICLE	TWIDDLY	UMBRAGE	UNITING	UPFRONT
TRUANTS	TUNISIA	TWIGGED	UMBRIAN	UNITIVE	UP FRONT
TRUCKED	TUNNELS	TWIN BED	UMBRIEL	UNKEMPT	UPGRADE
TRUCKER	TUNNIES	TWINGES	UMLAUTS	UNKNOWN	UPHEAVE
TRUCKLE	TUPPING	TWINING	UMPIRED	UNLATCH	UPLANDS
TRUDGED	TURBANS	TWINKLE	UMPIRES	UNLEARN	UPPSALA
TRUDGEN	TURBARY	TWINNED	UMPTEEN	UNLEASH	UPRAISE
TRUDGER	TURBINE	TWIN SET	UNAIDED	UNLOOSE	UPRIGHT
TRUDGES	TURBOTS	TWIRLED	UNARMED	UNLUCKY	UPRISER
TRUFFLE	TURDINE	TWIRLER	UNAWARE	UNMAKER	UPRIVER
TRUISMS	TUREENS	TWISTED	UNBONED	UNMANLY	UPSCALE
TRUMPED	TURFING	TWISTER	UNBOSOM	UNMEANT	UPSILON
TRUMPET	TURGITE	TWITTED	UNBOUND	UNMORAL	UPSKILL
TRUNDLE	TURKEYS	TWITTER	UNBOWED	UNMOVED	UPSTAGE
TRUSSED	TURKISH	TWIZZLE	UNBRACE	UNNAMED	UPSTART
TRUSSER	TURKMEN	TWOFOLD	UNCAGED	UNNERVE	UPSURGE
TRUSSES	TURMOIL	TWONESS	UNCANNY	UNOWNED	UPSWEEP

UPSWING	UTTERED	VARMINT	VERMONT	VILNIUS	VOCALLY
UPTAKES	UTTERER	VARNISH	VERNIER	VINASSE	VOCODER
UPTHROW	UTTERLY	VARSITY	VERONAL	VINEGAR	VOETSEK
UPTIGHT	UVEITIC	VARYING	VERRUCA	VINTAGE	VOICING
UP TO	UVEITIS	VASSALS	VERSACE	VINTNER	VOIDING
YOU	UVULARS	VASTITY	VERSANT	VIOLATE	VOIOTIA
UPTURNS	UXORIAL	VATICAN	VERSIFY	VIOLENT	VOLAPUK
UPWARDS		VAUDOIS	VERSION	VIOLETS	VOLCANO
URAEMIA	**V**	VAULTED	VERTIGO	VIOLINS	VOLLEYS
URAEMIC		VAULTER	VERVAIN	VIOLIST	VOLOGDA
URALITE	VACANCY	VAUNTED	VESICAL	VIRAGOS	VOLTAGE
URANIAN	VACATED	VAUNTER	VESICLE	VIRELAY	VOLTAIC
URANIDE	VACCINE	VECTORS	VESPERS	VIRGATE	VOLUBLE
URANITE	VACUITY	VEDALIA	VESPINE	VIRGINS	VOLUBLY
URANIUM	VACUOLE	VEDDOID	VESSELS	VIRGOAN	VOLUMED
URANOUS	VACUOUS	VEDETTE	VESTIGE	VIRGULE	VOLUMES
URCHINS	VACUUMS	VEERING	VESTING	VIRTUAL	VOLVATE
UREDIAL	VAGINAL	VEGETAL	VESTRAL	VIRTUES	VOMITED
UREDIUM	VAGINAS	VEHICLE	VESTURE	VIRUSES	VOMITER
URETHRA	VAGRANT	VEILING	VETCHES	VISAGES	VOMITUS
URGENCY	VAGUELY	VEINING	VETERAN	VISAING	VORLAGE
URIDINE	VAINEST	VEINLET	VETIVER	VIS-A-	VOTABLE
URINALS	VALANCE	VELAMEN	VETOING	VIS	VOUCHED
URINANT	VALENCE	VELIGER	VETTING	VISAYAN	VOUCHER
URINARY	VALENCY	VELLORE	VEXEDLY	VISCERA	VOX POPS
URINATE	VALERIC	VELOURS	VIADUCT	VISCOID	VOYAGED
URINOUS	VALIANT	VELVETY	VIBRANT	VISCOSE	VOYAGER
URMSTON	VALIDLY	VENALLY	VIBRATE	VISCOUS	VOYAGES
URNLIKE	VALISES	VENATIC	VIBRATO	VISIBLE	VOYEURS
URODELE	VALLEYS	VENDACE	VICENZA	VISIBLY	VULGATE
UROLITH	VALONIA	VENDING	VICEROY	VISIONS	VULPINE
UROLOGY	VALUERS	VENDORS	VICINAL	VISITED	VULTURE
URUAPAN	VALUING	VENEERS	VICIOUS	VISITOR	
URUGUAY	VALVATE	VENISON	VICOMTE	VISTAED	**W**
URUMCHI	VALVULE	VENTAGE	VICTIMS	VISTULA	WADABLE
USELESS	VAMOOSE	VENTING	VICTORS	VITALLY	WADDING
USHERED	VAMPIRE	VENTRAL	VICTORY	VITAMIN	WADDLED
USUALLY	VANADIC	VENTURE	VICTRIX	VITEBSK	WADDLER
USURERS	VANDALS	VENULAR	VICTUAL	VITIATE	WADDLES
USURPED	VANILLA	VERANDA	VICUNAS	VITORIA	WAFFLED
USURPER	VANTAGE	VERBENA	VIDEOED	VITRAIN	WAFFLES
UTENSIL	VANUATU	VERBIFY	VIDICON	VITRIFY	WAFTAGE
UTERINE	VANWARD	VERBOSE	VIETNAM	VITRINE	WAFTING
UTILITY	VAPIDLY	VERDANT	VIEWERS	VITRIOL	WAGERED
UTILIZE	VAPOURS	VERDICT	VIEWING	VITTATE	WAGERER
UT INFRA	VARIANT	VERDURE	VIKINGS	VIVIDLY	WAGGING
UTOPIAN	VARIATE	VERGERS	VILLACH	VIYELLA	WAGGISH
UTOPIAS	VARIETY	VERGING	VILLAGE	VIZIERS	WAGGLED
UTRECHT	VARIOLA	VERGLAS	VILLAIN	V-NECKED	WAGGLES
UTRICLE	VARIOLE	VERISMO	VILLEIN	VOCABLE	WAGONER
UT SUPRA	VARIOUS	VERMEIL	VILLOUS	VOCALIC	WAGTAIL

WAILFUL	WAR GAME	WAXWING	WELLING	WHIFFLE	WIGWAMS
WAILING	WARHEAD	WAXWORK	WELL-OFF	WHILING	WILDCAT
WAISTED	WARIEST	WAYBILL	WELL-SET	WHIMPER	WILD DOG
WAITERS	WARLIKE	WAYLAID	WELSHED	WHINERS	WILDEST
WAITING	WARLOCK	WAYLAIN	WELSHER	WHINGED	WILDING
WAIVERS	WARLORD	WAYSIDE	WEMBLEY	WHINGER	WILIEST
WAIVING	WARMEST	WAYWARD	WENCHED	WHINING	WILLIES
WAKEFUL	WARMING	WEAKEST	WENCHER	WHIPPED	WILLING
WAKENED	WARM-UPS	WEALTHY	WENCHES	WHIPPER	WILLOWS
WAKENER	WARNING	WEANING	WENDING	WHIPPET	WILLOWY
WALCOTT	WARPAGE	WEAPONS	WENDISH	WHIPSAW	WILTING
WALKERS	WARPATH	WEARIED	WEST END	WHIRLED	WIMPIES
WALKIES	WARPING	WEARIER	WESTERN	WHIRLER	WIMPISH
WALKING	WARRANT	WEARILY	WESTING	WHIRRED	WIMPLES
WALKMAN	WARRENS	WEARING	WET-LOOK	WHISKED	WINCHED
WALK OFF	WARRING	WEASELS	WETNESS	WHISKER	WINCHER
WALK-ONS	WARRIOR	WEATHER	WET SUIT	WHISKEY	WINCHES
WALKOUT	WARSHIP	WEAVERS	WETTEST	WHISPER	WINCING
WALK-UPS	WARTHOG	WEAVING	WETTING	WHISTLE	WINDAGE
WALLABY	WARTIME	WEBBING	WETTISH	WHITEST	WINDBAG
WALLAHS	WARWICK	WEBFOOT	WEXFORD	WHITHER	WINDIER
WALLETS	WASHDAY	WEBSITE	WHACKED	WHITING	WINDILY
WALLEYE	WASHERS	WEB-TOED	WHACKER	WHITLOW	WINDING
WALLIES	WASHERY	WEDDING	WHALERS	WHITSUN	WINDOWS
WALLING	WASHING	WEDGING	WHALING	WHITTLE	WINDROW
WALLOON	WASHOUT	WEDLOCK	WHANGEE	WHIZZED	WINDSOR
WALLOPS	WASHTUB	WEEDIER	WHARVES	WHIZZES	WINE BAR
WALLOWS	WASPILY	WEEDILY	WHAT FOR	WHOEVER	WINGERS
WALNUTS	WASPISH	WEEDING	WHATNOT	WHOOPED	WINGING
WALSALL	WASSAIL	WEEKDAY	WHATSIT	WHOOPEE	WINGLET
WALTZED	WASTAGE	WEEKEND	WHEATEN	WHOOPER	WING NUT
WALTZER	WASTERS	WEENIER	WHEEDLE	WHOPPED	WINKERS
WALTZES	WASTING	WEEPING	WHEELED	WHOPPER	WINKING
WANGLED	WASTREL	WEEVILS	WHEELER	WHORISH	WINKLED
WANGLER	WATCHED	WEEVILY	WHEELIE	WHORLED	WINKLES
WANGLES	WATCHER	WEIGELA	WHEEZED	WHYALLA	WINLESS
WANKERS	WATCHES	WEIGHED	WHEEZER	WICHITA	WINNERS
WANKING	WATERED	WEIGHER	WHEEZES	WICKETS	WINNING
WANNABE	WATERER	WEIGHTS	WHEREAS	WICKING	WINSOME
WANNESS	WATFORD	WEIGHTY	WHEREAT	WICKLOW	WINTERS
WANNEST	WATTAGE	WEIRDER	WHEREBY	WIDE BOY	WIRETAP
WANNING	WATTEAU	WEIRDIE	WHEREIN	WIDENED	WIRIEST
WANT ADS	WATTLES	WEIRDLY	WHEREOF	WIDENER	WISBECH
WANTING	WAVELET	WEIRDOS	WHEREON	WIDGEON	WISE GUY
WAPITIS	WAVEOFF	WELCHED	WHERETO	WIDOWED	WISHFUL
WARBLED	WAVERED	WELCOME	WHERRIT	WIDOWER	WISHING
WARBLER	WAVERER	WELDERS	WHETHER	WIELDED	WISPIER
WARDENS	WAVIEST	WELDING	WHETTED	WIELDER	WISPILY
WARDERS	WAXBILL	WELFARE	WHETTER	WIGGING	WISTFUL
WARDING	WAXIEST	WELL-FED	WHICKER	WIGGLED	WITCHES
WARFARE	WAXLIKE	WELLIES	WHIFFER	WIGGLER	WITHERS

WITHOUT	WORKERS	WRESTER	XEROXES	YIELDER	ZENITHS
WITLESS	WORKING	WRESTLE	XIPHOID	YINGKOU	ZEOLITE
WITNESS	WORKMAN	WREXHAM	X-RAYING	YINGKOW	ZEPHYRS
WITTIER	WORKMEN	WRIGGLE		YODELED	ZERMATT
WITTILY	WORKOUT	WRIGGLY	**Y**	YOGHURT	ZEROING
WIZARDS	WORKSHY	WRINGER	YACHTIE	YONKERS	ZESTFUL
WIZENED	WORKSOP	WRINKLE	YAKKING	YORKIST	ZHDANOV
WOBBLED	WORKTOP	WRINKLY	YAKUTSK	YORUBAN	ZIGZAGS
WOBBLER	WORLDLY	WRITE-IN	YANGTZE	YOUNGER	ZILLION
WOBBLES	WORMIER	WRITERS	YANKEES	YOWLING	ZINCATE
WOLFING	WORMING	WRITE-UP	YANKING	YTTRIUM	ZINCITE
WOLFISH	WORN-OUT	WRITHED	YAOUNDE	YUCATAN	ZIONISM
WOLFRAM	WORRIED	WRITHER	YAPPING	YUCKIER	ZIONIST
WOMANLY	WORRIER	WRITING	YARDAGE	YUKONER	ZIP CODE
WOMBATS	WORRIES	WRITTEN	YARDARM	YULE LOG	ZIPPERS
WONDERS	WORSHIP	WROCLAW	YARD ARM	YUPPIES	ZIPPIER
WONKIER	WORSTED	WRONGED	YARNING	YUPPIFY	ZIPPING
WOODCUT	WOTCHER	WRONGER	YASHMAK		ZITHERS
WOODIER	WOULD-BE	WRONGLY	YATHRIB	**Z**	ZODIACS
WOODMAN	WOULDN'T	WROUGHT	YAWNING	ZAGAZIG	ZOISITE
WOODSIA	WOUNDED	WRYBILL	YEAR DOT	ZAIREAN	ZOMBIES
WOOFERS	WOUNDER	WRYNECK	YEARNED	ZAIRESE	ZONALLY
WOOFTER	WOUND-UP	WRYNESS	YEARNER	ZAMBEZI	ZONULAR
WOOLLEN	WRAITHS	WYCH-ELM	YELLING	ZAMBIAN	ZOOLOGY
WOOMERA	WRANGLE	WYOMING	YELLOWS	ZANIEST	ZOOMING
WOOZIER	WRAPPED	WYVERNS	YELPING	ZAPOTEC	ZOOTOMY
WOOZILY	WRAPPER		YENISEI	ZAPPIER	ZORILLA
WORDAGE	WREAKED	**X**	YEREVAN	ZAPPING	ZWICKAU
WORDIER	WREAKER	XANTHIC	YESHIVA	ZEALAND	ZYGOSIS
WORDILY	WREATHE	XANTHIN	YEW TREE	ZEALOTS	ZYGOTIC
WORDING	WREATHS	XERARCH	Y-FRONTS	ZEALOUS	ZYMOGEN
WORKBAG	WRECKED	XEROSIS	YICHANG	ZEBRINE	ZYMOSIS
WORKBOX	WRECKER	XEROTIC	YIDDISH	ZEDOARY	ZYMOTIC
WORKDAY	WRESTED	XEROXED	YIELDED	ZEELAND	ZYMURGY

A
AARDVARK
AARDWOLF
ABACUSES
ABAMPERE
ABATTOIR
ABBATIAL
ABBESSES
ABDICATE
ABDOMENS
ABDUCENT
ABDUCTED
ABELMOSK
ABEOKUTA
ABERDARE
ABERDEEN
ABERRANT
ABETTING
ABETTORS
ABEYANCE
ABHORRED
ABHORRER
ABIDANCE
ABINGDON
AB
  INITIO
ABJECTLY
ABJURING
ABKHAZIA
ABLATION
ABLATIVE
ABLUTION
ABNEGATE
ABNORMAL
ABOMASUM
ABORTING
ABORTION
ABORTIVE
ABOUNDED
ABRADANT
ABRADING
ABRASION
ABRASIVE
ABRIDGED
ABRIDGER
ABROGATE
ABRUPTLY
ABSCISSA
ABSEILED
ABSENCES
ABSENTED

ABSENTEE
ABSENTER
ABSENTLY
ABSINTHE
ABSOLUTE
ABSOLVED
ABSOLVER
ABSORBED
ABSORBER
ABSTRACT
ABSTRUSE
ABSURDLY
ABU
  DHABI
ABUNDANT
ABUTILON
ABUTMENT
ABUTTALS
ABUTTING
ACADEMIA
ACADEMIC
ACANTHUS
ACAPULCO
ACARPOUS
ACCEDING
ACCENTED
ACCENTOR
ACCEPTED
ACCEPTOR
ACCESSED
ACCESSES
ACCIDENT
ACCOLADE
ACCORDED
ACCORDER
ACCOSTED
ACCOUNTS
ACCREDIT
ACCRUING
ACCURACY
ACCURATE
ACCURSED
ACCUSERS
ACCUSING
ACCUSTOM
ACCUTRON
ACENTRIC
ACERBATE
ACERBITY
ACERVATE
ACESCENT

ACHENIAL
ACHIEVED
ACHIEVER
ACHILLES
ACHROMAT
ACHROMIC
ACICULAR
ACICULUM
ACID
  DROP
ACID-
  FAST
ACIDNESS
ACIDOSIS
ACIDOTIC
ACID
  RAIN
ACID
  TEST
ACIERATE
ACOLYTES
ACONITIC
ACOUSTIC
ACQUAINT
ACQUIRED
ACQUIRER
ACRE-
  FOOT
ACRE-
  INCH
ACRIDINE
ACRIDITY
ACRIMONY
ACROBATS
ACRODONT
ACROLEIN
ACROLITH
ACROMION
ACRONYMS
ACROSTIC
ACRYLICS
ACTINIDE
ACTINISM
ACTINIUM
ACTINOID
ACTIVATE
ACTIVELY
ACTIVISM
ACTIVIST
ACTIVITY
ACT OF
  GOD

ACTUALLY
ACTUATED
ACTUATOR
ACULEATE
ACUTANCE
ADAMS
  ALE
ADAMSITE
ADAPTERS
ADAPTING
ADAPTIVE
ADDENDUM
ADDICTED
ADDITION
ADDITIVE
ADDUCENT
ADDUCING
ADDUCTOR
ADELAIDE
ADENITIS
ADENOIDS
ADEQUACY
ADEQUATE
ADHERENT
ADHERING
ADHESION
ADHESIVE
ADJACENT
ADJOINED
ADJUDGED
ADJUNCTS
ADJURING
ADJUSTED
ADJUTANT
ADJUVANT
AD-
  LIBBED
AD-
  LIBBER
ADMIRALS
ADMIRERS
ADMIRING
ADMITTED
ADMONISH
ADOPTING
ADOPTION
ADOPTIVE
ADORABLE
ADORNING
ADRIATIC
ADROITLY

ADULARIA
ADULATOR
ADULTERY
ADUMBRAL
ADVANCED
ADVANCER
ADVANCES
ADVERTED
ADVISERS
ADVISING
ADVISORY
ADVOCAAT
ADVOCACY
ADVOCATE
ADYNAMIA
ADYNAMIC
AEGROTAT
AERATING
AERATION
AERIALLY
AEROBICS
AERODYNE
AEROFOIL
AEROGRAM
AEROLITE
AEROLOGY
AERONAUT
AEROSOLS
AEROSTAT
AESTHETE
AFEBRILE
AFFECTED
AFFERENT
AFFIANCE
AFFINITY
AFFIRMED
AFFIRMER
AFFIXING
AFFLATUS
AFFLUENT
AFFORDED
AFFOREST
AFFRONTS
AFFUSION
AFLUTTER
AFRICANS
AGARTALA
AGE
  GROUP
AGENCIES
AGENESIS

AGENETIC
AGENTIAL
AGENTIVE
AGERATUM
AGGRIEVE
AGIOTAGE
AGITATED
AGITATOR
AGITPROP
AGMINATE
AGNOSTIC
AGONIZED
AGRAPHIA
AGRARIAN
AGRESTAL
AGRIMONY
AGROLOGY
AGRONOMY
AGUEWEED
AIGRETTE
AIGUILLE
AILERONS
AILMENTS
AIRBASES
AIRBORNE
AIRBRAKE
AIRBRICK
AIRBRUSH
AIRBURST
AIRBUSES
AIRCRAFT
AIRCREWS
AIREDALE
AIRFIELD
AIRFORCE
AIR
  FORCE
AIRFRAME
AIRINESS
AIRLANES
AIRLIFTS
AIRLINER
AIRLINES
AIRLOCKS
AIR
  MILES
AIRPLANE
AIRPORTS
AIR
  RAIDS
AIRSCREW

AIRSHIPS	ALKALINE	ALTER	AMPUTATE	ANFINSEN	ANTIBODY
AIRSPACE	ALKALIZE	EGO	AMPUTEES	ANGELENO	ANTIDOTE
AIRSPEED	ALKALOID	ALTERING	AMRAVATI	ANGELICA	ANTIGENS
AIRSTRIP	ALLANITE	ALTHOUGH	AMRITSAR	ANGERING	ANTIHERO
AIRTIGHT	ALLAYING	ALTITUDE	AMYGDALA	ANGINOSE	ANTI
AIR-TO-	ALL	ALTRUISM	AMYGDALE	ANGLESEY	HERO
AIR	CLEAR	ALTRUIST	ANABAENA	ANGLICAN	ANTI-
AIRWAVES	ALLEGING	ALUMROOT	ANABASIS	ANGRIEST	ICER
AIRWOMAN	ALLEGORY	ALVEOLAR	ANABATIC	ANGSTROM	ANTILLES
AIRWOMEN	ALLELISM	ALVEOLUS	ANABLEPS	ANGUILLA	ANTIMERE
A LA	ALLELUIA	AMALGAMS	ANABOLIC	ANGULATE	ANTIMONY
CARTE	ALLEPPEY	AMARANTH	ANACONDA	ANHEDRAL	ANTI-
ALACRITY	ALLERGEN	AMARELLE	ANAEROBE	ANIMATED	NAZI
ALARMING	ALLERGIC	AMARILLO	ANAGLYPH	ANIMATOR	ANTINODE
ALARMISM	ALLEYWAY	AMASSING	ANAGOGIC	ANIMISTS	ANTINOMY
ALARMIST	ALLIANCE	AMATEURS	ANAGRAMS	ANISETTE	ANTIPHON
ALBACORE	ALLOCATE	AMAZONAS	ANALCITE	ANKERITE	ANTIQUES
ALBANIAN	ALLODIAL	AMBEROID	ANALECTS	ANKYLOSE	ANTI-
ALBINISM	ALLODIUM	AMBIENCE	ANALEMMA	ANNALIST	RIOT
ALCATRAZ	ALLOGAMY	AMBITION	ANALOGUE	ANN	ANTITANK
ALCHEMIC	ALLOPATH	AMBIVERT	ANALYSED	ARBOR	ANTONINE
ALCHEVSK	ALLOTTED	AMBROSIA	ANALYSER	ANNEALED	ANTONYMS
ALCIDINE	ALLOTTEE	AMBULANT	ANALYSES	ANNEALER	ANTRORSE
ALCOHOLS	ALLOWING	AMBULATE	ANALYSIS	ANNEXING	ANURESIS
ALDEHYDE	ALLOYING	AMBUSHED	ANALYSTS	ANNOTATE	ANYPLACE
ALDERMAN	ALL	AMBUSHES	ANALYTIC	ANNOUNCE	ANYTHING
ALDERMEN	RIGHT	AMENABLE	ANAPAEST	ANNOYING	ANYWHERE
ALDERNEY	ALL	AMENDING	ANAPHASE	ANNUALLY	AORISTIC
ALDOXIME	ROUND	AMERICAN	ANAPHORA	ANNULATE	APAGOGIC
ALEATORY	ALL-	AMETHYST	ANARCHIC	ANNULLED	APATETIC
ALEHOUSE	ROUND	AMICABLE	ANASARCA	ANNULOSE	APERIENT
ALERTING	ALLSPICE	AMICABLY	ANATHEMA	ANODYNES	APERITIF
ALFRESCO	ALL	AMITOSIS	ANATOLIA	ANOINTED	APERTURE
ALGERIAN	THERE	AMITOTIC	ANCESTOR	ANOINTER	APHANITE
ALGERINE	ALLUDING	AMMETERS	ANCESTRY	ANOREXIA	APHELIAN
ALGINATE	ALLURING	AMMONIAC	ANCHORED	ANSERINE	APHELION
ALGOLOGY	ALLUSION	AMMONIFY	ANCIENTS	ANSWERED	APHORISM
ALGORISM	ALLUSIVE	AMMONITE	ANDANTES	ANTABUSE	APHORIST
ALHAMBRA	ALLUVIAL	AMMONIUM	ANDERSON	ANTEATER	APHORIZE
ALICANTE	ALLUVIUM	AMNESIAC	ANDESINE	ANTECEDE	APIARIAN
ALIENAGE	ALMANACS	AMNIOTIC	ANDESITE	ANTEDATE	APIARIES
ALIENATE	ALMIGHTY	AMOEBOID	ANDIRONS	ANTELOPE	APIARIST
ALIENISM	ALMONERS	AMORETTO	ANDIZHAN	ANTENNAS	APIOLOGY
ALIENIST	ALOPECIA	AMORTIZE	ANDORRAN	ANTE-	APLASTIC
ALIGHTED	ALPHABET	AMOUNTED	ANDROGEN	POST	APOCRINE
ALIGNING	ALPHOSIS	AMPERAGE	ANDROIDS	ANTERIOR	APODOSIS
ALIQUANT	ALPINISM	AMPHIPOD	ANECDOTE	ANTEROOM	APOGAMIC
ALIZARIN	ALPINIST	AMPHORAE	ANECHOIC	ANTEVERT	APOLOGIA
ALKAHEST	ALSATIAN	AMPHORAS	ANEMONES	ANTHELIX	APOLOGUE
ALKALIES	ALSO-	AMPOULES	ANETHOLE	ANTHESIS	APOMIXIS
ALKALIFY	RANS	AMPULLAR	ANEURYSM	ANTHILLS	APOPHYGE
					APOPLEXY

APOSPORY	ARCHAEAN	ARRIVALS	ASSAYING	ATOM	AUTOGAMY
APOSTASY	ARCHAISM	ARRIVING	ASSEGAIS	BOMB	AUTOGIRO
APOSTATE	ARCHAIST	ARROGANT	ASSEMBLE	ATOMIZER	AUTOLYSE
APOSTLES	ARCHAIZE	ARROGATE	ASSEMBLY	ATONABLE	AUTOMATA
APPALLED	ARCHDUKE	ARROWING	ASSENTED	ATONALLY	AUTOMATE
APPANAGE	ARCHIVAL	ARSENALS	ASSENTOR	ATROCITY	AUTOMATS
APPARENT	ARCHIVES	ARSENATE	ASSERTED	ATROPHIC	AUTONOMY
APPEALED	ARCHNESS	ARSENIDE	ASSERTER	ATROPINE	AUTOSOME
APPEALER	ARCHWAYS	ARSENITE	ASSESSED	ATTACHED	AUTOTOMY
APPEARED	ARC	ARSONIST	ASSESSOR	ATTACHER	AUTOTYPE
APPEASED	LIGHT	ARTEFACT	ASSHOLES	ATTACHES	AUTOTYPY
APPELLEE	ARCTURUS	ARTERIAL	ASSIGNAT	ATTACKED	AUTUMNAL
APPENDED	ARDENNES	ARTERIES	ASSIGNED	ATTACKER	AUTUNITE
APPENDIX	ARDENTLY	ARTESIAN	ASSIGNEE	ATTAINED	AUVERGNE
APPESTAT	AREA	ARTFULLY	ASSIGNER	ATTEMPTS	AVADAVAT
APPETITE	CODE	ART	ASSIGNOR	ATTENDED	AVAILING
APPLAUSE	ARENITIC	HOUSE	ASSISTED	ATTENDEE	AVE
APPLE	AREQUIPA	ARTICLED	ASSISTER	ATTESTED	MARIA
PIE	ARETHUSA	ARTICLES	ASSONANT	ATTIRING	AVENGERS
APPLIQUE	ARGENTIC	ARTIFACT	ASSORTED	ATTITUDE	AVENGING
APPLYING	ARGININE	ARTIFICE	ASSORTER	ATTORNEY	AVERAGED
APPOSITE	ARGUABLE	ARTINESS	ASSUAGED	ATTUNING	AVERAGES
APPRAISE	ARGUABLY	ARTISANS	ASSUAGER	ATYPICAL	AVERMENT
APPRISED	ARGUMENT	ARTISTES	ASSUMING	AUBUSSON	AVERRING
APPROACH	ARIANISM	ARTISTIC	ASSURING	AUCKLAND	AVERSION
APPROVAL	ARILLATE	ARTISTRY	ASSYRIAN	AUCTIONS	AVERSIVE
APPROVED	ARILLODE	ARYANIZE	ASTATINE	AUDACITY	AVERTING
APRES-	ARISTATE	ASBESTOS	ASTERISK	AUDIENCE	AVIARIES
SKI	ARKANSAS	ASCENDED	ASTERISM	AUDITING	AVIATION
APRICOTS	ARMAGNAC	ASCENDER	ASTERNAL	AUDITION	AVIATORS
APTEROUS	ARMALITE	ASCETICS	ASTEROID	AUDITORS	AVIATRIX
APTITUDE	ARMAMENT	ASCIDIAN	ASTHENIA	AUDITORY	AVIDNESS
APYRETIC	ARMATURE	ASCIDIUM	ASTHENIC	AUGSBURG	AVIEMORE
AQUALUNG	ARMBANDS	ASCOCARP	ASTONISH	AUGURIES	AVIFAUNA
AQUANAUT	ARMCHAIR	ASCORBIC	ASTRAGAL	AUGURING	AVIONICS
AQUARIST	ARMENIAN	ASCRIBED	ASTURIAS	AUGUSTLY	AVOCADOS
AQUARIUM	ARMHOLES	ASHTRAYS	ASTUTELY	AUREOLES	AVOIDING
AQUARIUS	ARMIDALE	ASNIERES	ASSYRIAN	AU	AVOWABLE
AQUATICS	ARMORIAL	ASPERITY	ASUNCION	REVOIR	AVULSION
AQUATINT	ARMOURED	ASPERSER	ATARAXIA	AURICLES	AWAITING
AQUEDUCT	ARMOURER	ASPHODEL	AT	AURICULA	AWAKENED
AQUILINE	ARMS	ASPHYXIA	BOTTOM	AUSPICES	AWARDING
ARACHNID	RACE	ASPIRANT	ATHEISTS	AUSTRIAN	AWEATHER
ARAPAIMA	AROMATIC	ASPIRATE	ATHENIAN	AUTACOID	AXILLARY
ARAWAKAN	AROUSING	ASPIRING	ATHEROMA	AUTARCHY	AXIOLOGY
ARBITERS	ARPEGGIO	ASPIRINS	ATHLETES	AUTARKIC	AXLETREE
ARBITRAL	ARRANGED	ASSAILED	ATHLETIC	AUTHORED	AYRSHIRE
ARBOREAL	ARRANGER	ASSAILER	ATLANTIC	AUTISTIC	AYURVEDA
ARBROATH	ARRAYING	ASSAMESE	ATLANTIS	AUTOBAHN	AZIMUTHS
ARCADIAN	ARRESTED	ASSASSIN	AT	AUTOCRAT	AZOTEMIA
ARCATURE	ARRESTER	ASSAULTS	LENGTH	AUTOCUES	AZOTEMIC

B

BABBLERS
BABBLING
BABIRUSA
BABYHOOD
BABY
  TALK
BACCARAT
BACCHIUS
BACHELOR
BACILLUS
BACKACHE
BACKBEAT
BACKBITE
BACKBONE
BACKCHAT
BACKCOMB
BACKDATE
BACK
  DOOR
BACKDROP
BACKFILL
BACKFIRE
BACKHAND
BACKINGS
BACKLASH
BACKLESS
BACKLIST
BACKLOGS
BACKPACK
BACK
  SEAT
BACKSIDE
BACKSLID
BACKSPIN
BACKSTAY
BACKSTOP
BACK
  TALK
BACKWARD
BACKWASH
BACKYARD
BACTERIA
BACTERIN
BACTRIAN
BADALONA
BAD
  BLOOD
BAD
  DEBTS
BADGERED
BADINAGE

BADLANDS
BADLY-
  OFF
BAD-
  MOUTH
BAEDEKER
BAFFLING
BAGGAGES
BAGGIEST
BAGPIPES
BAGUETTE
BAHAMIAN
BAHRAINI
BAILABLE
BAILIFFS
BAILMENT
BAILSMAN
BAKELITE
BAKERIES
BALANCED
BALANCER
BALANCES
BALDNESS
BALEARIC
BALINESE
BALLADES
BALLADRY
BALLARAT
BALLCOCK
BALL
  GAME
BALLONET
BALLOONS
BALLOTED
BALL
  PARK
BALLROOM
BALLS-
  UPS
BALLYHOO
BALMIEST
BALMORAL
BALSAMIC
BALUSTER
BANALITY
BANDAGED
BANDAGES
BANDANNA
BANDIEST
BANDITRY
BANDPASS
BANDSMAN

BANDSMEN
BANDYING
BANISHED
BANISTER
BANKABLE
BANKBOOK
BANK
  NOTE
BANK
  RATE
BANKROLL
BANKRUPT
BANNOCKS
BANQUETS
BANSHEES
BANSTEAD
BANTERED
BANTERER
BAPTISMS
BAPTISTS
BAPTIZED
BARATHEA
BARBADOS
BARBARIC
BARBECUE
BARBERRY
BARBICAN
BARBICEL
BAR
  CHART
BAR
  CODES
BAREBACK
BAREFOOT
BAREILLY
BARENESS
BARGAINS
BAR
  GRAPH
BARITONE
BARLETTA
BARMAIDS
BARMIEST
BARNACLE
BARNSLEY
BARNYARD
BAROGRAM
BARONAGE
BARONESS
BARONETS
BARONIAL
BARONIES

BAROSTAT
BAROUCHE
BARRACKS
BARRAGES
BARRATOR
BARRATRY
BARRETTE
BARRIERS
BARTERED
BARTERER
BARTIZAN
BASEBALL
BASEHEAD
BASELESS
BASELINE
BASEMENT
BASENESS
BASE
  RATE
BASICITY
BASIDIAL
BASIDIUM
BASILARY
BASILDON
BASILICA
BASILISK
BASKETRY
BASOPHIL
BASS
  CLEF
BASS
  DRUM
BASSINET
BASSISTS
BASSOONS
BASSWOOD
BASTARDS
BASTARDY
BASTILLE
BASTIONS
BASTOGNE
BATANGAS
BATHETIC
BATH
  MATS
BATHROBE
BATHROOM
BATHTUBS
BATHURST
BATSWANA
BATTENED
BATTERED

BATTERER
BATTIEST
BATTLING
BAUHINIA
BAULKING
BAVARIAN
BAWDIEST
BAYBERRY
BAYONETS
BAYREUTH
BAZOOKAS
BDELLIUM
BEACHING
BEADIEST
BEADINGS
BEAGLING
BEAM-
  ENDS
BEANPOLE
BEARABLE
BEARABLY
BEARDING
BEAR
  HUGS
BEARINGS
BEARSKIN
BEATABLE
BEATIFIC
BEATINGS
BEATNIKS
BEAT
  TIME
BEAULIEU
BEAUMONT
BEAUTIES
BEAUTIFY
BEAUVAIS
BEAVERED
BECALMED
BECHAMEL
BECKONED
BECKONER
BECOMING
BEDAUBED
BEDAZZLE
BEDECKED
BEDIMMED
BED
  LINEN
BEDOUINS
BEDPLATE
BEDPOSTS

BEDROOMS
BEDSIDES
BEDSORES
BEDSTEAD
BEDSTRAW
BEDTIMES
BEDWORTH
BEEBREAD
BEECHNUT
BEE-
  EATER
BEEFCAKE
BEEFIEST
BEEFWOOD
BEEHIVES
BEELINES
BEESWING
BEETLING
BEETROOT
BEFALLEN
BEFITTED
BEFOULER
BEFRIEND
BEGETTER
BEGGARED
BEGGARLY
BEGINING
BEGINNER
BEGOTTEN
BEGRUDGE
BEGUILED
BEGUILER
BEHAVING
BEHEADED
BEHOLDEN
BEHOLDER
BELABOUR
BELAYING
BELCHING
BELFRIES
BELGRADE
BELIEVED
BELIEVER
BELITTLE
BELLBIRD
BELLBOYS
BELLOWED
BELLOWER
BELLPULL
BELLWORT
BELLYFUL

BELMOPAN	BEVELING	BILLIONS	BISMARCK	BLAZONRY	BLOWHOLE
BELONGED	BEVELLED	BILLOWED	BISTOURY	BLEACHED	BLOWIEST
BELOVEDS	BEVERAGE	BILOBATE	BITCHIER	BLEACHER	BLOWLAMP
BELTWAYS	BEVERLEY	BIMANOUS	BITCHILY	BLEAKEST	BLOWOUTS
BEMOANED	BEWAILED	BINAURAL	BITCHING	BLEARIER	BLOWPIPE
BENADRYL	BEWAILER	BINDINGS	BITINGLY	BLEARILY	BLOW-
BEN	BEWARING	BINDWEED	BIT	BLEATING	WAVE
BELLA	BEWIGGED	BIN-	PARTS	BLEEDERS	BLOWZIER
BENEFICE	BEWILDER	LINER	BITSTOCK	BLEEDING	BLOWZILY
BENEFITS	BHATPARA	BINNACLE	BITTERLY	BLEEPERS	BLUDGEON
BENFLEET	BIANNUAL	BINOMIAL	BITTERNS	BLEEPING	BLUE
BENGHAZI	BIARRITZ	BIOASSAY	BITTIEST	BLENCHED	BABY
BENGUELA	BIASSING	BIO-	BIVALENT	BLENCHER	BLUEBELL
BENIGNLY	BIATHLON	ASSAY	BIVALVES	BLENDERS	BLUEBIRD
BENTINCK	BIBLICAL	BIOCIDAL	BIVOUACS	BLENDING	BLUE
BENTWOOD	BIBULOUS	BIOCYCLE	BIWEEKLY	BLENHEIM	BOOK
BENUMBED	BICKERED	BIODATAS	BIYEARLY	BLESSING	BLUE
BENZOATE	BICKERER	BIOLYSIS	BLABBING	BLIGHTED	CHIP
BEQUEATH	BICOLOUR	BIOLYTIC	BLACK	BLIGHTER	BLUE
BEQUESTS	BICONVEX	BIOMETRY	ART	BLIMPISH	FILM
BERATING	BICUSPID	BIONOMIC	BLACK	BLINDAGE	BLUEFISH
BERCEUSE	BICYCLED	BIOPLASM	BOX	BLINDERS	BLUE
BERFAVED	BICYCLES	BIOPSIES	BLACKCAP	BLINDING	FLAG
BEREZINA	BICYCLIC	BIOSCOPE	BLACKEST	BLINKERS	BLUEGILL
BERGAMET	BIDDABLE	BIOSCOPY	BLACK	BLINKING	BLUE
BERIBERI	BIENNIAL	BIOTITIC	EYE	BLISSFUL	GUMS
BERKELEY	BIFACIAL	BIOTYPIC	BLACKFLY	BLISTERS	BLUE
BERTHING	BIFIDITY	BIPAROUS	BLACK	BLITHELY	JAYS
BERYLINE	BIFOCALS	BIPHENYL	ICE	BLITZING	BLUE
BESANCON	BIGAMIST	BIPLANES	BLACKING	BLIZZARD	LAWS
BESIEGED	BIGAMOUS	BIRACIAL	BLACKISH	BLOATERS	BLUE
BESIEGER	BIGHEADS	BIRADIAL	BLACKLEG	BLOCKADE	MOON
BESMIRCH	BIG	BIRAMOUS	BLACKOUT	BLOCKAGE	BLUENESS
BESOTTED	NAMES	BIRCHING	BLACK	BLOCKING	BLUFFING
BESOUGHT	BIGNONIA	BIRDBATH	TIE	BLOKEISH	BLUNDERS
BESPOKEN	BIG	BIRDCAGE	BLACK-	BLONDEST	BLUNKETT
BESTIARY	SHOTS	BIRD	TIE	BLOODFIN	BLUNTING
BESTOWAL	BIG	DOGS	BLACKTOP	BLOODILY	BLURRING
BESTOWED	STICK	BIRDLIKE	BLADDERS	BLOODING	BLURTING
BESTOWER	BIG-	BIRDLIME	BLAMABLE	BLOOD	BLUSHERS
BESTREWN	TIMER	BIRDSEED	BLAMEFUL	RED	BLUSHING
BESTRIDE	BIG	BIRDS	BLANCHED	BLOOMERS	BLUSTERY
BESTRODE	WHEEL	EYE	BLANDEST	BLOOMERY	BOARDERS
BETAKING	BIJUGATE	BIRD'S-	BLANDISH	BLOOMING	BOARDING
BETATRON	BILABIAL	EYE	BLANKETS	BLOOPERS	BOARFISH
BETIDING	BILBERRY	BIRETTAS	BLASTEMA	BLOSSOMS	BOASTERS
BETRAYAL	BILINEAR	BIRTHDAY	BLASTING	BLOTCHES	BOASTFUL
BETRAYED	BILLETED	BIRTHING	BLAST-	BLOTTERS	BOASTING
BETRAYER	BILLFISH	BISCUITS	OFF	BLOTTING	BOAT
BETTERED	BILLFOLD	BISECTED	BLASTULA	BLOWFISH	HOOK
BEVATRON	BILLHOOK	BISECTOR	BLATANCY	BLOWHARD	BOATLOAD
	BILLIARD	BISEXUAL	BLAZONED		

BOA
VISTA
BOBBINET
BOBBY
PIN
BOBOLINK
BOBRUISK
BOBTAILS
BOBWHITE
BODILESS
BODLEIAN
BODY
BLOW
BODYWORK
BOEHMITE
BOGEYMAN
BOGGIEST
BOGGLING
BOHEMIAN
BOILABLE
BOLDFACE
BOLDNESS
BOLIVIAN
BOLLARDS
BOLLOCKS
BOLLWORM
BOLSHIER
BOLSTERS
BOLTHOLE
BOLT
HOLE
BOLTONIA
BOLTROPE
BOMBARDE
BOMBSITE
BOMBYCID
BONA
FIDE
BONANZAS
BONEFISH
BONEHEAD
BONE-
IDLE
BONELESS
BONE
MEAL
BONFIRES
BONHOMIE
BONINESS
BONNIEST
BONS
MOTS

BONTEBOK
BOOHOOED
BOOKABLE
BOOKCASE
BOOK
CLUB
BOOKENDS
BOOKINGS
BOOKLETS
BOOKMARK
BOOKRACK
BOOKSHOP
BOOKWORM
BOOSTERS
BOOSTING
BOOT
CAMP
BOOTLACE
BOOTLESS
BOOZE-
UPS
BOOZIEST
BORA
BORA
BORACITE
BORDEAUX
BORDELLO
BORDERED
BORDERER
BOREHOLE
BORINGLY
BORNHOLM
BOROUGHS
BORROWED
BORROWER
BORSTALS
BOSPORUS
BOSS-
EYED
BOSSIEST
BOTANIST
BOTANIZE
BOTCHERS
BOTCHIER
BOTCHILY
BOTCHING
BOTCH-
UPS
BOTHERED
BOTRYTIS
BOTSWANA
BOTTLING

BOTTOMRY
BOTULISM
BOUDOIRS
BOUFFANT
BOUILLON
BOULDERS
BOULLION
BOULOGNE
BOUNCERS
BOUNCIER
BOUNCILY
BOUNCING
BOUNDARY
BOUNDERS
BOUNDING
BOUNTIES
BOUQUETS
BOUTIQUE
BOUZOUKI
BOW
BELLS
BOWSHOTS
BOWSPRIT
BOXBERRY
BOXBOARD
BOXROOMS
BOYCOTTS
BOYISHLY
BOY
SCOUT
BRACELET
BRACHIAL
BRACHIUM
BRACKETS
BRACKISH
BRACTEAL
BRADAWLS
BRADBURY
BRADFORD
BRAGGART
BRAGGING
BRAHMANI
BRAHMANS
BRAIDING
BRAINBOX
BRAINIER
BRAINING
BRAINPAN
BRAISING
BRAMBLES
BRANCHED

BRANCHES
BRANCHIA
BRANDIES
BRANDING
BRANDISH
BRAND-
NEW
BRASHEST
BRASILIA
BRASSARD
BRASS
HAT
BRASSICA
BRASSIER
BRASSILY
BRATTICE
BRAUNITE
BRAWLERS
BRAWLING
BRAWNIER
BRAWNILY
BRAZENED
BRAZENLY
BRAZIERS
BRAZILIN
BREACHED
BREACHES
BREAD
BIN
BREADNUT
BREADTHS
BREAKAGE
BREAKERS
BREAKING
BREAK-
INS
BREATHER
BREECHES
BREEDING
BREEZILY
BRETHREN
BREVETCY
BREVIARY
BRIBABLE
BRICKBAT
BRIDGEND
BRIDGING
BRIEFING
BRIGHTEN
BRIGHTON
BRINDISI
BRIOCHES

BRISANCE
BRISBANE
BRISKEST
BRISLING
BRISTLED
BRISTLES
BRITCHES
BRITTANY
BROACHED
BROACHER
BROADEST
BROADWAY
BROCADED
BROCCOLI
BROCHURE
BROILERS
BROILING
BROKENLY
BROLLIES
BROMIDES
BRONCHIA
BRONCHOS
BRONCHUS
BRONZING
BROOCHES
BROODERS
BROODIER
BROODILY
BROODING
BROOKING
BROOKITE
BROOKLYN
BROOKNER
BROTHELS
BROTHERS
BROUGHAM
BROUHAHA
BROWBEAT
BROWNEST
BROWNIES
BROWNING
BROWNISH
BROWSING
BRUISERS
BRUISING
BRUITING
BRUNCHES
BRUNETTE
BRUSHING
BRUSH
OFF

BRUSH-
OFF
BRUSH-
UPS
BRUSSELS
BRUTALLY
BRYOLOGY
BRYOZOAN
BUBALINE
BUBBLIER
BUBBLING
BUCHSHEE
BUCKAROO
BUCKBEAN
BUCKETED
BUCKHORN
BUCKLERS
BUCKLING
BUCKSHEE
BUCKSHOT
BUCKSKIN
BUDAPEST
BUDDHISM
BUDDHIST
BUDDLEIA
BUDGETED
BUFFALOS
BUFFERED
BUFFETED
BUFFETER
BUFFOONS
BUGABOOS
BUGBEARS
BUGGERED
BUILDERS
BUILDING
BUILDUPS
BUKOVINI
BULAWAYO
BULGARIA
BULGIEST
BULKHEAD
BULKIEST
BULL
BARS
BULLDOGS
BULLDOZE
BULLETIN
BULLFROG
BULLHEAD
BULLHORN

BULLNECK
BULLOCKS
BULLRING
BULLS
  EYE
BULL'S-
  EYE
BULLSHIT
BULLYBOY
BULLYING
BULLY-
  OFF
BULWARKS
BUMBLING
BUMPIEST
BUMPKINS
BUNCHING
BUNDLING
BUNGALOW
BUNGHOLE
BUNGLERS
BUNGLING
BUNTLINE
BUOYANCY
BURAYDAH
BURBERRY
BURBLING
BURDENED
BURGHERS
BURGLARS
BURGLARY
BURGLING
BURGUNDY
BURLIEST
BURNOOSE
BURNOUTS
BURRITOS
BURROWED
BURROWER
BURSITIS
BURSTING
BURTHENS
BUSHBABY
BUSHBUCK
BUSHIEST
BUSHVELD
BUSINESS
BUS
  STOPS
BUSTIEST
BUSTLING
BUSYBODY

BUSYNESS
BUTANONE
BUTCHERS
BUTCHERY
BUTTERED
BUTTOCKS
BUTTONED
BUTTRESS
BUTYRATE
BUZZARDS
BUZZWORD
BY-
  BIDDER
BYPASSED
BYPASSES
BYRONISM

C

CABARETS
CABBAGES
CABIN
  BOY
CABINETS
CABLE
  CAR
CABLEWAY
CABOCHON
CABOODLE
CABOOSES
CABOTAGE
CAB
  RANKS
CABRILLA
CABRIOLE
CACHALOT
CACHEPOT
CACHEXIA
CACHUCHA
CACKLERS
CACKLING
CACTUSES
CADASTER
CADAVERS
CADDYING
CADENCES
CADENZAS
CADUCEUS
CADUCITY
CADUCOUS
CAERLEON
CAESURAS

CAFFEINE
CAGELING
CAGINESS
CAGLIARI
CAGOULES
CAISSONS
CAJOLERY
CAJOLING
CAKEWALK
CALABASH
CALABRIA
CALADIUM
CALAMINE
CALAMINT
CALAMITE
CALAMITY
CALATHUS
CALCIFIC
CALCITIC
CALCULUS
CALCUTTA
CALDRONS
CALENDAR
CALENDER
CALF
  LOVE
CALFSKIN
CALIBRED
CALIBRES
CALIPASH
CALIPERS
CALISAYA
CALLABLE
CALL
  GIRL
CALLINGS
CALLIOPE
CALLIPER
CALLISTO
CALLUSES
CALMNESS
CALOR
  GAS
CALORIES
CALUTRON
CALVADOS
CALVARIA
CALYCATE
CALYCINE
CALYPSOS
CALYPTRA

CAMAGUEY
CAMBODIA
CAMBOGIA
CAMBRIAN
CAMELEER
CAMELLIA
CAMEROON
CAMISOLE
CAMOMILE
CAMPAGNA
CAMPAIGN
CAMPANIA
CAMP
  BEDS
CAMPECHE
CAMPFIRE
CAMPHENE
CAMPINAS
CAMPSITE
CAMPUSES
CAMSHAFT
CANADIAN
CANAIGRE
CANAILLE
CANALIZE
CANARIES
CANBERRA
CANCELED
CANCROID
CANDIDLY
CANFIELD
CANISTER
CANNABIC
CANNABIN
CANNABIS
CANNIBAL
CANNIEST
CANNIKIN
CANNONED
CANNONRY
CANOEING
CANOEIST
CANONESS
CANONIST
CANONIZE
CANON
  LAW
CANOODLE
CANOPIES
CANTATAS
CANTEENS

CANTERED
CANT
  HOOK
CANTICLE
CANTONAL
CANVASES
CANZONET
CAPACITY
CAPERING
CAPESKIN
CAPE
  TOWN
CAPITALS
CAPITATE
CAPONIZE
CAPRICES
CAPRIFIG
CAPRIOLE
CAPSICUM
CAPSIZED
CAPSTANS
CAPSTONE
CAPSULAR
CAPSULES
CAPTAINS
CAPTIONS
CAPTIOUS
CAPTIVES
CAPTURED
CAPTURES
CAPUCHIN
CAPYBARA
CARACARA
CARACOLE
CARAMELS
CARANGID
CARAPACE
CARAVANS
CARAWAYS
CARBINES
CARBOLIC
CARBONIC
CARBONYL
CARBURET
CARDAMOM
CARDENAL
CARDIGAN
CARDINAL
CARDIOID
CARDITIS
CAREENED

CAREERED
CAREFREE
CARELESS
CARESSED
CARESSER
CARESSES
CAREWORN
CARIBOUS
CARILLON
CARINATE
CARLISLE
CARNAUBA
CARNIVAL
CAROLINA
CAROLINE
CAROLING
CAROLLED
CAROTENE
CAROUSAL
CAROUSED
CAROUSEL
CAR
  PARKS
CARPETED
CAR
  POOLS
CARPORTS
CARRERAS
CARRIAGE
CARRIERS
CARRYALL
CARRYCOT
CARRYING
CARRY
  OFF
CARRYOUT
CARRY
  OUT
CARTOONS
CARUNCLE
CARVINGS
CARYATID
CASANOVA
CASCADED
CASCADES
CASEMATE
CASEMENT
CASEWORK
CASHABLE
CASHBACK
CASH
  BACK

CASH-BOOK	CATHETER	CEMENTER	CHAIRMAN	CHARTING	CHESSMAN
CASH CARD	CATHEXIS	CEMENTUM	CHAIRMEN	CHARTISM	CHESTIER
CASH CROP	CATHODES	CEMETERY	CHALAZAL	CHARTIST	CHESTILY
CASH DESK	CATHODIC	CENOTAPH	CHALDRON	CHARTRES	CHESTNUT
CASH FLOW	CATHOLIC	CENOZOIC	CHALICES	CHASSEUR	CHEVRONS
CASHIERS	CATIONIC	CENSORED	CHALKIER	CHASTELY	CHEWABLE
CASHLESS	CAT'S EYES	CENSURED	CHALKING	CHASTEST	CHEWIEST
CASHMERE	CAT'S-FOOT	CENSURES	CHAMBERS	CHASTISE	CHEYENNE
CASSETTE	CAT'S PAWS	CENSUSES	CHAMBRAY	CHASTITY	CHIASMAL
CASSOCKS	CATSUITS	CENTAURS	CHAMONIX	CHASUBLE	CHIASMIC
CASTAWAY	CATTIEST	CENTAURY	CHAMPING	CHAT SHOW	CHIASMUS
CASTINGS	CATTLEYA	CENTAVOS	CHAMPION	CHATTELS	CHIASTIC
CAST IRON	CATWALKS	CENTERED	CHANCELS	CHATTIER	CHICANER
CAST-IRON	CAUCASIA	CENTIARE	CHANCERY	CHATTILY	CHICANOS
CASTRATE	CAUCASUS	CENTIMES	CHANCIER	CHATTING	CHICKENS
CASTRATO	CAUCUSES	CENTRING	CHANCILY	CHAUFFER	CHICKPEA
CASTRIES	CAUDALLY	CENTRIST	CHANCING	CHEAPEST	CHICLAYO
CASUALLY	CAULDRON	CENTROID	CHANDLER	CHEATING	CHIGETAI
CASUALTY	CAULICLE	CEPHALAD	CHANGING	CHECKERS	CHIGGERS
CASUISTS	CAULKING	CEPHALIC	CHANGSHA	CHECKING	CHIGNONS
CATACOMB	CAUSABLE	CEPHALIN	CHANGTEH	CHECK-INS	CHIGWELL
CATALASE	CAUSALLY	CERAMICS	CHANNELS	CHECKOUT	CHILDISH
CATALYSE	CAUSERIE	CERAMIST	CHANTIES	CHECKUPS	CHILDREN
CATALYST	CAUSEWAY	CERASTES	CHANTING	CHEDDITE	CHILIASM
CATAMITE	CAUTIONS	CERATOID	CHANUKAH	CHEEKIER	CHILIAST
CATAPULT	CAUTIOUS	CERCARIA	CHAOCHOW	CHEEKILY	CHILLIER
CATARACT	CAVALIER	CEREBRAL	CHAPATTI	CHEEKING	CHILLIES
CATCALLS	CAVATINA	CEREBRIC	CHAPBOOK	CHEEPING	CHILLING
CATCH ALL	CAVEATOR	CEREBRUM	CHAPERON	CHEERFUL	CHILL OUT
CATCH-ALL	CAVEFISH	CEREMENT	CHAPLAIN	CHEERIER	CHILOPOD
CATCHFLY	CAVICORN	CEREMONY	CHAPLETS	CHEERILY	CHIMAERA
CATCHIER	CAVILING	CERNUOUS	CHAPPING	CHEERING	CHIMBOTE
CATCHILY	CAVILLED	CEROTYPE	CHAPTERS	CHEETAHS	CHIMERAS
CATCHING	CAVILLER	CERULEAN	CHARACIN	CHEKIANG	CHIMKENT
CATECHIN	CAVITIES	CERVELAT	CHARADES	CHEMICAL	CHIMNEYS
CATECHOL	CAVORTED	CERVICAL	CHARCOAL	CHEMISES	CHINAMAN
CATEGORY	CEDILLAS	CERVICES	CHARENTE	CHEMISTS	CHIN-CHOU
CATENANE	CEILINGS	CERVIXES	CHARGERS	CHEMNITZ	CHINDWIN
CATENARY	CELERIAC	CESAREAN	CHARGING	CHEMURGY	CHINKING
CATENATE	CELERITY	CESSIONS	CHARIEST	CHENILLE	CHINLESS
CATENOID	CELIBACY	CESSPITS	CHARIOTS	CHENOPOD	CHIPMUNK
CATERING	CELIBATE	CESSPOOL	CHARISMA	CHEPSTOW	CHIPPIES
CATHEDRA	CELLARER	CETACEAN	CHARLADY	CHEQUERS	CHIPPING
	CELLARET	CEVENNES	CHARLIES	CHEROKEE	CHIP SHOP
	CELLISTS	CHACONNE	CHARLOCK	CHEROOTS	CHIRPIER
	CELLULAR	CHAFFING	CHARLTON	CHERRIES	CHIRPILY
	CELULOID	CHAINING	CHARMERS	CHERTSEY	CHIRPING
	CEMENTED	CHAINMAN	CHARMING	CHERUBIC	CHIRRUPY
		CHAIN SAW	CHARQUID	CHESHIRE	
		CHAIRING	CHARRING		
			CHARTERS		

CHISELED	CHUBBIER	CITY	CLEAR-	CLOSURES	COBBLING
CHITCHAT	CHUCKING	HALL	CUT	CLOTHIER	COBWEBBY
CHIT	CHUCKLED	CIVILIAN	CLEAREST	CLOTHING	COCA-
CHAT	CHUCKLER	CIVILITY	CLEARING	CLOTTING	COLA
CHIVALRY	CHUCKLES	CIVILIZE	CLEAROUT	CLOUDIER	COCCYGES
CHIVVYING	CHUCK	CIVIL	CLEARWAY	CLOUDILY	COCHLEAE
CHLORATE	OFF	LAW	CLEAVAGE	CLOUDING	COCHLEAR
CHLORIDE	CHUGGING	CIVIL	CLEAVERS	CLOUDLET	COCKADES
CHLORINE	CHUKKERS	WAR	CLEAVING	CLOUTING	COCKATOO
CHLORITE	CHUMMIER	CLACKING	CLEMATIS	CLOWNERY	COCKCROW
CHLOROUS	CHUMMILY	CLAIMANT	CLEMENCY	CLOWNING	COCK
CHOC-	CHUMMING	CLAIMING	CLENCHED	CLOWNISH	CROW
ICES	CHUNKIER	CLAMBAKE	CLENCHES	CLUBBING	COCKEREL
CHOCKING	CHURCHES	CLAMMIER	CLERICAL	CLUBFEET	COCKEYED
CHOICELY	CHURINGA	CLAMMILY	CLERIHEW	CLUBFOOT	COCKIEST
CHOICEST	CHURLISH	CLAMMING	CLERKDOM	CLUBHAUL	COCKNEYS
CHOIRBOY	CHURNING	CLAMOURS	CLERKING	CLUCKING	COCKPITS
CHOIRMAN	CHUTZPAH	CLAMPING	CLEVEITE	CLUELESS	COCKSPUR
CHOISEUL	CHYMOSIN	CLANGERS	CLEVERLY	CLUMPING	COCKSURE
CHOLERIC	CIABATTA	CLANGING	CLICKING	CLUMPISH	COCKTAIL
CHOMPING	CIBORIUM	CLANKING	CLIENTAL	CLUMSIER	COCONUTS
CHONGJIN	CICATRIX	CLANNISH	CLIMATES	CLUMSILY	COCOONED
CHOOSIER	CICERONE	CLANSMAN	CLIMATIC	CLUPEOID	CUDDLING
CHOP	CICHLOID	CLANSMEN	CLIMAXED	CLUSTERS	CODICILS
CHOP	CIMBRIAN	CLAPPERS	CLIMAXES	CLUSTERY	CODIFIED
CHOP-	CINCHONA	CLAPPING	CLIMBERS	CLUTCHED	CODIFIER
CHOP	CINCTURE	CLAPTRAP	CLIMBING	CLUTCHES	CODOMAIN
CHOPPERS	CINEASTE	CLARINET	CLINCHED	COACHING	CODPIECE
CHOPPIER	CINERAMA	CLARIONS	CLINCHER	COACHMAN	CO
CHOPPILY	CINERARY	CLASHING	CLINCHES	COACHMEN	DRIVER
CHOPPING	CINGULUM	CLASPING	CLINGING	COACTION	COENURUS
CHOP	CINNABAR	CLASSICS	CLINICAL	COACTIVE	COENZYME
SUEY	CINNAMON	CLASSIER	CLINKERS	COAGULUM	COEQUALS
CHORALES	CINQUAIN	CLASSIFY	CLINKING	COAHUILA	COERCING
CHORDATE	CIPHERED	CLASSING	CLIPPERS	COALESCE	COERCION
CHORDING	CIRCLETS	CLASSISM	CLIPPIES	COALFACE	COERCIVE
CHORIAMB	CIRCLING	CLASSIST	CLIPPING	COALFISH	COEXTEND
CHORTLED	CIRCUITS	CLATTERS	CLIQUISH	COALHOLE	COGENTLY
CHORTLES	CIRCUITY	CLATTERY	CLITORAL	COALMINE	COGITATE
CHORUSED	CIRCULAR	CLAVICLE	CLITORIS	COALPORT	COGNATES
CHORUSES	CIRCUSES	CLAYLIKE	CLOAKING	COARSELY	COGNOMEN
CHOW-	CISLUNAR	CLAYMORE	CLOCKING	COARSEST	COGWHEEL
CHOW	CISTERNA	CLEAN	CLODDISH	COASTERS	COHERENT
CHOW	CISTERNS	CUT	CLOGGING	COASTING	COHERING
MEIN	CITADELS	CLEAN-	CLOISTER	COATINGS	COHESION
CHRESARD	CITATION	CUT	CLOPPING	COATROOM	COHESIVE
CHRISMAL	CITIFIED	CLEANERS	CLOSE-	COAT-	COHOBATE
CHRISTEN	CITIZENS	CLEANEST	SET	TAIL	COIFFEUR
CHROMATE	CITREOUS	CLEANING	CLOSETED	COAUTHOR	COIFFURE
CHROMITE	CITRUSES	CLEANSED	CLOSE-	COBALTIC	COINAGES
CHROMIUM		CLEANSER	UPS	COBBLERS	COINCIDE
CHROMOUS					

121

COINSURE
COLANDER
COLD
  CUTS
COLD
  FEET
COLD
  FISH
COLDNESS
COLD
  SNAP
COLD
  SORE
COLD-
  WELD
COLESLAW
COLISEUM
COLLAGEN
COLLAGES
COLLAPSE
COLLARED
COLLATED
COLLATOR
COLLECTS
COLLEENS
COLLEGES
COLLIDED
COLLIDER
COLLIERS
COLLIERY
COLLOGUE
COLLOQUY
COLLUDED
COLOMBES
COLOMBIA
COLONELS
COLONIAL
COLONIES
COLONIST
COLONIZE
COLOPHON
COLORADO
COLORANT
COLOSSAL
COLOSSUS
COLOTOMY
COLOURED
COLPITIS
COLUBRID
COLUMBIA
COLUMBIC
COLUMBUS

COLUMNAR
COLUMNED
COMANCHE
COMATOSE
COMBATED
COMBATER
COMBINED
COMBINER
COMBINES
COMEBACK
COMEDIAN
COMEDIES
COMEDOWN
COMELIER
COMFIEST
COMFORTS
COMITIES
COMMANDO
COMMANDS
COMMENCE
COMMENTS
COMMERCE
COMMODES
COMMONER
COMMONLY
COMMUNAL
COMMUNED
COMMUNES
COMMUTED
COMMUTER
COMPACTS
COMPADRE
COMPARED
COMPARER
COMPARES
COMPERED
COMPERES
COMPETED
COMPILED
COMPILER
COMPLAIN
COMPLETE
COMPLIED
COMPLIER
COMPLINE
COMPOSED
COMPOSER
COMPOTES
COMPOUND
COMPRESS

COMPRISE
COMPUTED
COMPUTER
COMRADES
CONATION
CONATIVE
CONCEDED
CONCEITS
CONCEIVE
CONCEPTS
CONCERNS
CONCERTO
CONCERTS
CONCHOID
CONCLAVE
CONCLUDE
CONCRETE
CONDENSE
CONDOLED
CONDOLER
CONDONED
CONDONER
CONDUCED
CONDUCER
CONDUITS
CONDYLAR
CONFEREE
CONFERVA
CONFETTI
CONFIDED
CONFIDER
CONFINED
CONFINES
CONFLATE
CONFLICT
CONFOCAL
CONFOUND
CONFRERE
CONFRONT
CONFUSED
CONFUTED
CONFUTER
CONGENER
CONGRATS
CONGRESS
CONIDIAL
CONIDIUM
CONIFERS
CONJOINT
CONJUGAL
CONJUNCT

CONJURED
CONJURER
CONJUROR
CONNACHT
CONNIVED
CONNIVER
CONNOTED
CONOIDAL
CONQUEST
CONSERVE
CONSIDER
CONSOLED
CONSOLER
CONSOLES
CONSOMME
CONSORTS
CONSPIRE
CONSTANT
CONSTRUE
CONSULAR
CONSUMED
CONSUMER
CONTACTS
CONTANGO
CONTEMPT
CONTENTS
CONTESTS
CONTEXTS
CONTINUA
CONTINUE
CONTINUO
CONTOURS
CONTRACT
CONTRAIL
CONTRARY
CONTRAST
CONTRITE
CONTRIVE
CONTROLS
CONTUSED
CONVENED
CONVENER
CONVENTS
CONVERGE
CONVERSE
CONVERTS
CONVEXLY
CONVEYED
CONVEYER
CONVEYOR

CONVICTS
CONVINCE
CONVOKED
CONVOKER
CONVOYED
CONVULSE
COOKABLE
COOKBOOK
COOKOUTS
COOLABAR
COOLANTS
COOLIBAH
COOLNESS
COONSKIN
COOPTING
COOPTION
COPILOTS
COPLANAR
COPPERAS
COPULATE
COPYBOOK
COPYCATS
COPY-
  EDIT
COPYHOLD
COPYISTS
COQUETRY
COQUETTE
COQUILLE
CORACLES
CORACOID
CORDIALS
CORDLESS
CORDONED
CORDOVAN
CORDUROY
CORDWOOD
CORE
  TIME
CORKWOOD
CORNCOBS
CORNEOUS
CORNERED
CORNETTE
CORNICES
CORNICHE
CORNIEST
CORN
  PONE
CORNWALL
CORONARY

CORONERS
CORONETS
CORPORAL
CORRIDOR
CORRODED
CORRODER
CORSAGES
CORSAIRS
CORSELET
CORSETED
CORSETRY
CORTEGES
CORTICAL
CORTICES
CORTISOL
CORUNDUM
CORVETTE
CORYPHEE
COSECANT
COSINESS
COSMETIC
COSTLIER
COSTMARY
COST-
  PLUS
COSTUMES
COT
  DEATH
COTENANT
COTERIES
COTOPAXI
COTSWOLD
COTTAGER
COTTAGES
COTYLOID
COUCHANT
COUCHING
COUGHING
COULISSE
COUMARIC
COUMARIN
COUNCILS
COUNTERS
COUNTESS
COUNTIES
COUNTING
COUPLETS
COUPLING
COURANTE
COURLAND
COURSING

COURTESY	CRAM-	CREEPING	CROSSBOW	CRYOTRON	CURE-
COURTIER	FULL	CREMATED	CROSSCUT	CRYSTALS	ALLS
COURTING	CRAMMERS	CREMATOR	CROSS	CUBATURE	CURITIBA
COUSCOUS	CRAMMING	CREODONT	CUT	CUBE	CURLICUE
COUSTEAU	CRAMPING	CREOSOTE	CROSSEST	ROOT	CURLIEST
COVALENT	CRAMPONS	CRESCENT	CROSS-	CUBICLES	CURRANTS
COVENANT	CRANE	CRESTING	EYE	CUBIFORM	CURRENCY
COVENTRY	FLY	CRESYLIC	CROSSING	CUBISIST	CURRENTS
COVERAGE	CRANIATE	CRETONNE	CROSSLET	CUBISTIC	CURRICLE
COVERING	CRANIUMS	CREVASSE	CROSSPLY	CUCKOLDS	CURRIERY
COVERLET	CRANKIER	CREVICES	CROSTINI	CUCUMBER	CURRYING
COVERTLY	CRANKING	CREW	CROTCHES	CUCURBIT	CURSEDLY
COVER-	CRANKPIN	CUTS	CROTCHET	CUDDLIER	CURTAINS
UPS	CRANNIED	CREW	CROUCHED	CUDDLING	CURTNESS
COVETING	CRANNIES	NECK	CROUPIER	CUDGELED	CURTSIED
COVETOUS	CRAPPIER	CRIBBAGE	CROUPOUS	CUFF	CURTSIES
COWARDLY	CRAPPING	CRIBBING	CROUTONS	LINK	CUSHIEST
COWBELLS	CRASHING	CRICKETS	CROWBARS	CUL-DE-	CUSHIONS
COWBERRY	CRASH	CRICKING	CROWBOOT	SAC	CUSHIONY
COWERING	PAD	CRIMINAL	CROWDING	CULIACAN	CUSPIDOR
COWHANDS	CRAVENLY	CRIMPING	CROWFOOT	CULINARY	CUSSEDLY
COWHERDS	CRAVINGS	CRIMSONS	CROWNING	CULOTTES	CUSTARDS
COWHIDES	CRAWFISH	CRINGING	CROZIERS	CULOUSLY	CUSTOMER
COWLICKS	CRAWLERS	CRINKLED	CRUCIATE	CULPABLE	CUSTUMAL
COWLINGS	CRAWLING	CRINKLES	CRUCIBLE	CULPABLY	CUT A
CO-	CRAYFISH	CRIPPLED	CRUCIFER	CULPRITS	DASH
WORKER	CRAYONED	CRIPPLES	CRUCIFIX	CULTIGEN	CUTAWAYS
COWSHEDS	CRAZIEST	CRISPATE	CRUDITES	CULTIVAR	CUTBACKS
COWSLIPS	CREAKIER	CRISPIER	CRUISERS	CULTRATE	CUTENESS
COXALGIA	CREAKILY	CRISPING	CRUISING	CULTURAL	CUT
COXALGIC	CREAKING	CRISTATE	CRUMBLED	CULTURED	GLASS
COXCOMBS	CREAMERS	CRITERIA	CRUMBLES	CULTURES	CUTICLES
COXSWAIN	CREAMERY	CRITICAL	CRUMHORN	CULVERIN	CUTICULA
COZENAGE	CREAMIER	CRITIQUE	CRUMMIER	CULVERTS	CUTINIZE
COZENING	CREAMING	CRITTERS	CRUMPETS	CUMBERED	CUT-
COZINESS	CREASING	CROAKILY	CRUMPLED	CUMBRIAN	PRICE
CRABBIER	CREATINE	CROAKING	CRUNCHED	CUMQUATS	CUTPURSE
CRABBING	CREATING	CROATIAN	CRUSADED	CUMULOUS	CUTTINGS
CRABWISE	CREATION	CROCKERY	CRUSADER	CUPBOARD	CUTWATER
CRACKERS	CREATIVE	CROCOITE	CRUSADES	CUP	CUXHAVEN
CRACKING	CREATORS	CROCUSES	CRUSHING	CAKES	CYANITIC
CRACKLED	CREATURE	CROFTERS	CRUSTIER	CUP	CYANOGEN
CRACKNEL	CREDENCE	CROMLECH	CRUSTILY	FINAL	CYANOSIS
CRACKPOT	CREDENZA	CRONYISM	CRUSTOSE	CUPIDITY	CYANOTIC
CRACKUPS	CREDIBLE	CROOKING	CRUTCHES	CUPREOUS	CYBERPET
CRADLING	CREDIBLY	CROONERS	CRUZEIRO	CUPULATE	CYCLADES
CRAFTIER	CREDITED	CROONING	CRY	CURARIZE	CYCLAMEN
CRAFTILY	CREDITOR	CROPPERS	HAVOC	CURASSOW	CYCLISTS
CRAFTING	CREEPERS	CROPPING	CRYOLITE	CURATIVE	CYCLONES
CRAGGIER	CREEPIER	CROSIERS	CRYONICS	CURATORS	CYCLONIC
	CREEPILY	CROSSBAR	CRYOSTAT	CURCULIO	CYCLOSIS
				CURDLING	CYLINDER

CYMATIUM
CYMOGENE
CYNICISM
CYNOSURE
CYPHERED
CYPRINID
CYRILLIC
CYSTEINE
CYSTITIS
CYTASTER
CYTIDINE
CYTOLOGY
CYTOSINE
CZARINAS

D

DABBLERS
DABBLING
DABCHICK
DAB
  HANDS
DACTYLIC
DAEMONIC
DAFFODIL
DAFTNESS
DAGESTAN
DAINTIER
DAINTIES
DAINTILY
DAIQUIRI
DAIRYMAN
DAIRYMEN
DALESMAN
DALLYING
DALMATIA
DALMATIC
DALTONIC
DAMAGING
DAMANHUR
DAMASCUS
DAMNABLE
DAMNABLY
DAMOCLES
DAMPENED
DAMPENER
DAMPNESS
DANDIEST
DANDLING
DANDRUFF
DANDYISH
DANDYISM

DANEWORT
DANGLING
DANKNESS
DANUBIAN
DARINGLY
DARK
  AGES
DARKENED
DARKENER
DARKNESS
DARKROOM
DARK
  ROOM
DARLINGS
DARTFORD
DATABASE
DATEABLE
DATELINE
DATE
  RAPE
DATOLITE
DAUGHTER
DAUNTING
DAUPHINE
DAUPHINS
DAVENTRY
DAWDLERS
DAWDLING
DAYBREAK
DAYDREAM
DAYLIGHT
DAYROOMS
DAYTIMES
DAY-TO-
  DAY
DAZZLING
DEACONRY
DEADBEAT
DEAD
  BEAT
DEAD
  DUCK
DEAD
  ENDS
DEADENED
DEADENER
DEADFALL
DEADHEAD
DEAD
  HEAT
DEADLIER
DEADLINE

DEADLOCK
DEADNESS
DEAD
  WOOD
DEAF-
  AIDS
DEAFENED
DEAF-
  MUTE
DEAFNESS
DEALFISH
DEALINGS
DEANSHIP
DEARESTS
DEARNESS
DEATHBED
DEATH
  ROW
DEBACLES
DEBARKED
DEBARRED
DEBASING
DEBATERS
DEBATING
DEBILITY
DEBITING
DEBONAIR
DEBRECEN
DEBUGGED
DEBUGGER
DEBUNKED
DEBUNKER
DEBUTANT
DECADENT
DECAMPED
DECANOIC
DECANTED
DECANTER
DECAYING
DECEASED
DECEIVED
DECEIVER
DECEMBER
DECENTLY
DECENTRE
DECIBELS
DECIDING
DECIDUAL
DECIMALS
DECIMATE
DECIPHER
DECISION

DECISIVE
DECKHAND
DECK
  HAND
DECLARED
DECLARER
DECLASSE
DECLINED
DECLINER
DECLINES
DECODING
DECOLOUR
DECOROUS
DECOYING
DECREASE
DECREPIT
DECRETAL
DECRYING
DECURVED
DEDICATE
DEDUCING
DEDUCTED
DEED
  POLL
DEEMSTER
DEEPENED
DEEPENER
DEEPNESS
DEERSKIN
DEFACING
DEFAMING
DEFAULTS
DEFEATED
DEFEATER
DEFECATE
DEFECTED
DEFECTOR
DEFENCES
DEFENDED
DEFENDER
DEFERENT
DEFERRED
DEFERRER
DEFIANCE
DEFICITS
DEFILERS
DEFILING
DEFINING

DEFINITE
DEFLATED
DEFLATOR
DEFLEXED
DEFLOWER
DEFOREST
DEFORMED
DEFORMER
DEFRAYAL
DEFRAYED
DEFRAYER
DEFTNESS
DEFUSING
DEGASSER
DEGRADED
DEGRADER
DEICIDAL
DEIFYING
DEIGNING
DEJECTED
DELAWARE
DELAYING
DELEGACY
DELEGATE
DELETING
DELETION
DELICACY
DELICATE
DELIGHTS
DELIRIUM
DELIVERY
DELOUSED
DELPHIAN
DELUDING
DELUGING
DELUSION
DELUSIVE
DELUSORY
DEMAGOGY
DEMANDED
DEMANDER
DEMARCHE
DEMEANED
DEMENTED
DEMENTIA
DEMERARA
DEMERGER
DEMERITS
DEMERSAL
DEMESNES
DEMIGODS

DEMIJOHN
DEMILUNE
DEMISTED
DEMISTER
DEMIVOLT
DEMOBBED
DEMOCRAT
DEMOLISH
DEMONIAC
DEMONISM
DEMONIST
DEMONIZE
DEMOTING
DEMOTION
DEMOTIST
DEMPSTER
DEMURELY
DEMUREST
DEMURRAL
DEMURRED
DEMURRER
DENATURE
DENDRITE
DENDROID
DENIABLE
DENIZENS
DENOTING
DENOUNCE
DENTICLE
DENTINAL
DENTURES
DENUDATE
DENUDING
DEPARTED
DEPENDED
DEPICTED
DEPICTER
DEPILATE
DEPLETED
DEPLORED
DEPLORER
DEPLOYED
DEPONENT
DEPORTED
DEPORTEE
DEPOSING
DEPOSITS
DEPRAVED
DEPRAVER
DEPRIVED
DEPRIVER

DEPURATE	DETESTER	DIANTHUS	DIGITATE	DIRIMENT	DISPENSE
DEPUTIES	DETHRONE	DIAPASON	DIGITIZE	DIRT	DISPERSE
DEPUTING	DETONATE	DIAPAUSE	DIGITRON	BIKE	DISPIRIT
DEPUTIZE	DETRITAL	DIAPHONE	DIGRAPHS	DIRTIEST	DISPLACE
DERAILED	DETRITUS	DIAPHONY	DIHEDRAL	DIRT	DISPLAYS
DERANGED	DEUCEDLY	DIARCHIC	DIHEDRON	ROAD	DISPOSAL
DERELICT	DEUTERON	DIARISTS	DIHYBRID	DIRTYING	DISPOSED
DERIDING	DEVALUED	DIASCOPE	DILATANT	DISABLED	DISPOSER
DERISION	DEVIANCE	DIASPORA	DILATING	DISABUSE	DISPROOF
DERISIVE	DEVIANTS	DIASPORE	DILATION	DISAGREE	DISPROVE
DERISORY	DEVIATED	DIASTASE	DILATIVE	DISALLOW	DISPUTED
DERIVING	DEVIATOR	DIASTEMA	DILATORY	DISANNUL	DISPUTER
DEROGATE	DEVILING	DIASTOLE	DILEMMAS	DISARMED	DISPUTES
DERRICKS	DEVILISH	DIASTRAL	DILIGENT	DISARMER	DISQUIET
DESCALED	DEVILLED	DIASTYLE	DILUTING	DISARRAY	DISROBED
DESCANTS	DEVISING	DIATOMIC	DILUTION	DISASTER	DISROBER
DESCENTS	DEVOLVED	DIATONIC	DILUVIAL	DISBURSE	DISSEISE
DESCRIBE	DEVONIAN	DIATRIBE	DIMERISM	DISCARDS	DISSENTS
DESCRIED	DEVOTEES	DIAZEPAM	DIMERIZE	DISCIPLE	DISSEVER
DESCRIER	DEVOTING	DICENTRA	DIMEROUS	DISCLAIM	DISSOLVE
DESEEDER	DEVOTION	DICHROIC	DIMETRIC	DISCLOSE	DISSUADE
DESERTED	DEVOURED	DICKERED	DIMINISH	DISCORDS	DISTAFFS
DESERTER	DEVOURER	DICKIEST	DINGDONG	DISCOUNT	DISTANCE
DESERVED	DEVOUTER	DICROTIC	DINGHIES	DISCOVER	DISTASTE
DESERVER	DEVOUTLY	DICTATED	DINGIEST	DISCREET	DISTINCT
DESIGNED	DEWBERRY	DICTATES	DINKIEST	DISCRETE	DISTRACT
DESIGNER	DEWDROPS	DICTATOR	DINOSAUR	DISCUSES	DISTRAIN
DESINENT	DEWINESS	DIDACTIC	DIOCESAN	DISEASED	DISTRAIT
DESIRING	DEWY-	DIDDLING	DIOCESES	DISEASES	DISTRESS
DESIROUS	EYED	DIDYMIUM	DIOPSIDE	DISENDOW	DISTRICT
DESISTED	DEXTROSE	DIDYMOUS	DIOPTASE	DISGORGE	DISTRUST
DESKWORK	DIABASIC	DIEHARDS	DIOPTRAL	DISGRACE	DISUNION
DESOLATE	DIABETES	DIELDRIN	DIOPTRIC	DISGUISE	DISUNITE
DESPATCH	DIABETIC	DIERESES	DIORAMIC	DISHEVEL	DISUNITY
DESPISED	DIABOLIC	DIERESIS	DIORITIC	DISHFULS	DITCHING
DESPOTIC	DIACIDIC	DIERETIC	DIOXIDES	DISHIEST	DITHEISM
DESSERTS	DIACONAL	DIES	DIPHENYL	DISINTER	DITHEIST
DESTINED	DIAGNOSE	IRAE	DIPLEGIA	DISJOINT	DITHERED
DESTRUCT	DIAGONAL	DIESTOCK	DIPLEXER	DISJUNCT	DITHERER
DETACHED	DIAGRAMS	DIETETIC	DIPLOMAS	DISKETTE	DIURESIS
DETACHER	DIAGRAPH	DIFFERED	DIPLOMAT	DISLIKED	DIURETIC
DETAILED	DIALECTS	DIFFRACT	DIPLOPIA	DISLIKES	DIVALENT
DETAINED	DIALLAGE	DIFFUSED	DIPLOPIC	DISLODGE	DIVE-
DETAINEE	DIALLING	DIFFUSER	DIPLOPOD	DISLOYAL	BOMB
DETAINER	DIALOGUE	DIGAMIST	DIPLOSIS	DISMALLY	DIVERGED
DETECTED	DIALYSER	DIGAMOUS	DIPSTICK	DISMAYED	DIVERTED
DETECTER	DIALYSIS	DIGESTED	DIPTERAL	DISMOUNT	DIVERTER
DETECTOR	DIALYTIC	DIGESTER	DIPTERAN	DISORDER	DIVESTED
DETENTES	DIAMANTE	DIGESTIF	DIRECTED	DISOWNED	DIVIDEND
DETERRED	DIAMETER	DIGGINGS	DIRECTLY	DISOWNER	DIVIDERS
DETESTED	DIAMONDS		DIRECTOR	DISPATCH	DIVIDING

DIVI-DIVI	DOG'S-TAIL	DORTMUND	DRAFTING	DRIPPING	DRY-STONE
DIVINELY	DOG TIRED	DOSSIERS	DRAGGIER	DRIVABLE	DUBONNET
DIVINERS	DOG-TIRED	DOTATION	DRAGGING	DRIVE-INS	DUCKLING
DIVINING	DOGTOOTH	DOTINGLY	DRAGGLED	DRIVELED	DUCKWEED
DIVINITY	DOGTROTS	DOTTEREL	DRAGLINE	DRIVEWAY	DUCTILES
DIVINIZE	DOGWATCH	DOTTIEST	DRAGNETS	DRIZZLED	DUELLING
DIVISION	DOG WATCH	DOUBLETS	DRAGOMAN	DROGHEDA	DUELLIST
DIVISIVE	DOGWOODS	DOUBLE UP	DRAGONET	DROLLERY	DUE NORTH
DIVISORS	DOLDRUMS	DOUBLING	DRAGOONS	DROLLEST	DUE SOUTH
DIVORCED	DOLERITE	DOUBLOON	DRAGROPE	DROOLING	DUETTIST
DIVORCEE	DOLOMITE	DOUBLURE	DRAINAGE	DROOPILY	DUISBURG
DIVORCER	DOLOROSO	DOUBTERS	DRAINING	DROOPING	DUKEDOMS
DIVORCES	DOLOROUS	DOUBTFUL	DRAMATIC	DROP-DEAD	DULCIANA
DIVULGED	DOLPHINS	DOUBTING	DRAPABLE	DROPLETS	DULCIMER
DIVULGER	DOMELIKE	DOUGHNUT	DRATTING	DROPOUTS	DULLARDS
DIZZIEST	DOMESTIC	DOUNREAY	DRAUGHTS	DROPPERS	DULLNESS
DJAKARTA	DOMICILE	DOURNESS	DRAUGHTY	DROPPING	DUMBBELL
DJIBOUTI	DOMINANT	DOVECOTE	DRAWABLE	DROP SHOT	DUMB-CANE
DNIESTER	DOMINATE	DOVETAIL	DRAWBACK	DROPSIED	DUMB DOWN
D-NOTICES	DOMINEER	DOWAGERS	DRAWBORE	DROPS OFF	DUMBNESS
DOCILITY	DOMINICA	DOWDIEST	DRAWCORD	DROPWORT	DUMB SHOW
DOCKETED	DOMINION	DOWNBEAT	DRAWDOWN	DROUGHTS	DUMFRIES
DOCKLAND	DOMINIUM	DOWNCAST	DRAWINGS	DROUGHTY	DUMMY RUN
DOCKSIDE	DOMINOES	DOWNFALL	DRAWLING	DROWNING	DUMPIEST
DOCKYARD	DONATING	DOWNHAUL	DRAWTUBE	DROWSILY	DUMPLING
DOCTORAL	DONATION	DOWNHILL	DREADFUL	DROWSING	DUNGAREE
DOCTORED	DONATIVE	DOWNIEST	DREADING	DRUBBING	DUNGEONS
DOCTRINE	DON JUANS	DOWNLOAD	DREAMERS	DRUDGERY	DUNGHILL
DOCUMENT	DONLEAVY	DOWNPIPE	DREAMILY	DRUDGING	DUODENAL
DOCU-SOAP	DOODLING	DOWNPLAY	DREAMING	DRUGGETS	DUODENUM
DODDERED	DOOMSDAY	DOWNPOUR	DREARIER	DRUGGING	DUOLOGUE
DODDERER	DOOMSTER	DOWNSIZE	DREARILY	DRUGGIST	DUPLEXES
DODGIEST	DOORBELL	DOWNSIZE	DREDGERS	DRUIDISM	DURATION
DOGBERRY	DOORJAMB	DOWNTIME	DREDGING	DRUMBEAT	DURATIVE
DOGCARTS	DOORKNOB	DOWNTOWN	DRENCHED	DRUMFIRE	DUSHANBE
DOG-EARED	DOORMATS	DOWNTURN	DRENCHER	DRUMFISH	DUSKIEST
DOGFIGHT	DOORNAIL	DOWNWARD	DRESSAGE	DRUMHEAD	DUSTBINS
DOGGEDLY	DOORPOST	DOWNWASH	DRESSERS	DRUMMERS	DUSTBOWL
DOGGEREL	DOORSILL	DOWNWIND	DRESSIER	DRUMMING	DUSTCART
DOGGONED	DOORSTEP	DOXASTIC	DRESSILY	DRUNKARD	DUSTIEST
DOGGY BAG	DOORSTOP	DOXOLOGY	DRESSING	DRUNKEST	DUSTPANS
DOGHOUSE	DOORWAYS	DOZINESS	DRIBBLED	DRUPELET	DUTCH CAP
DOGMATIC	DOPAMINE	DRABBEST	DRIBBLER	DRY-CLEAN	DUTCHMAN
DO-GOODER	DOPINESS	DRABNESS	DRIBBLES	DRY DOCKS	DUTIABLE
DOGSBODY	DORDOGNE	DRACAENA	DRIBLETS	DRY GOODS	
	DORMANCY	DRACHMAE	DRIFTAGE		
	DORMOUSE	DRACHMAS	DRIFTERS		
		DRACONIC	DRIFTING		
		DRAFTEES	DRILLING		
		DRAFTIER	DRINKERS		
			DRINKING		

DUTY-
 FREE
DWARFING
DWARFISH
DWARFISM
DWELLING
DWINDLED
DYARCHIC
DYESTUFF
DYNAMICS
DYNAMISM
DYNAMIST
DYNAMITE
DYNASTIC
DYNATRON
DYSGENIC
DYSLEXIA
DYSLEXIC
DYSPNOEA
DYTISCID

E
EALING
EARDROPS
EARDRUMS
EARLDOMS
EARLIEST
EARLOBES
EARMUFFS
EARNINGS
EARPHONE
EARPIECE
EARPLUGS
EARRINGS
EARSHOTS
EARTHIER
EARTHILY
EARTHING
EARTHNUT
EASEMENT
EASINESS
EASTERLY
EAST
 SIDE
EASTWARD
EASTWOOD
EASY
 CARE
EASY
 MARK
EBB
 TIDES

EBBW
 VALE
ECCLESIA
ECDYSIAL
ECDYSONE
ECHELONS
ECHINATE
ECHINOID
ECLECTIC
ECLIPSED
ECLIPSER
ECLIPSES
ECLIPSIS
ECLIPTIC
ECLOGITE
ECLOSION
ECONOMIC
ECOTONAL
ECOTYPIC
ECRASEUR
ECSTATIC
ECTODERM
ECTOMERE
ECTOSARC
ECUMENIC
EDACIOUS
EDENTATE
EDGEWAYS
EDGINESS
EDIFICES
EDIFYING
EDITIONS
EDMONTON
EDUCABLE
EDUCATED
EDUCATOR
EDUCIBLE
EDUCTION
EDUCTIVE
EELGRASS
EERINESS
EFFACING
EFFECTED
EFFECTER
EFFECTOR
EFFERENT
EFFICACY
EFFIGIAL
EFFIGIES
EFFLUENT
EFFUSION

EFFUSIVE
EGESTION
EGESTIVE
EGGHEADS
EGGPLANT
EGG
 ROLLS
EGGSHELL
EGG
 TIMER
EGOISTIC
EGOMANIA
EGOTISTS
EGO
 TRIPS
EGYPTIAN
EIGHTEEN
EIGHTIES
EISENACH
EITHER-
 OR
EJECTING
EJECTION
EJECTIVE
EKISTICS
ELAPSING
ELASTANE
ELATERID
ELATERIN
ELBOWING
EL
 DORADO
ELDRITCH
ELECTING
ELECTION
ELECTIVE
ELECTORS
ELECTRET
ELECTRIC
ELECTRON
ELECTRUM
ELEGANCE
ELEMENTS
ELENCHUS
ELENCTIC
ELEPHANT
ELEVATED
ELEVATOR
ELEVENTH
EL
 FAIYUM

EL
 FERROL
ELF
 LOCKS
ELICITED
ELICITOR
ELIDIBLE
ELIGIBLE
ELISIONS
ELITISTS
ELKHOUND
ELLIPSES
ELLIPSIS
ELONGATE
ELOQUENT
ELYTROID
EMACIATE
EMANATED
EMANATOR
EMBALMED
EMBALMER
EMBARKED
EMBATTLE
EMBEDDED
EMBEZZLE
EMBITTER
EMBLAZON
EMBODIED
EMBOLDEN
EMBOLISM
EMBOSSED
EMBOSSER
EMBRACED
EMBRACER
EMBRACES
EMBRYOID
EMENDING
EMERALDS
EMERGENT
EMERGING
EMERITUS
EMERSION
EMIGRANT
EMIGRATE
EMINENCE
EMIRATES
EMISSARY
EMISSION
EMISSIVE
EMITTING
EMOTIONS

EMPATHIC
EMPERORS
EMPHASES
EMPHASIS
EMPHATIC
EMPLOYED
EMPLOYEE
EMPLOYER
EMPORIUM
EMPTIEST
EMPTYING
EMPYEMIC
EMPYREAL
EMPYREAN
EMULATED
EMULATOR
EMULSIFY
EMULSION
EMULSIVE
EMULSOID
ENABLING
ENACTING
ENACTIVE
ENACTORY
ENAMELED
ENCAENIA
ENCAMPED
ENCASING
ENCIPHER
ENCIRCLE
ENCLAVES
ENCLITIC
ENCLOSED
ENCLOSER
ENCODING
ENCOMIUM
ENCROACH
ENCUMBER
ENCYCLIC
ENDAMAGE
ENDANGER
END-
 BLOWN
ENDBRAIN
ENDEARED
ENDEMIAL
ENDEMISM
ENDERMIC
END
 GAMES
ENDOCARP

ENDODERM
ENDOGAMY
ENDOGENY
ENDORSED
ENDORSEE
ENDORSER
ENDORSOR
ENDOSOME
ENDOWING
ENDPAPER
ENDPLATE
ENDURING
END
 USERS
ENERGIZE
ENERVATE
ENFEEBLE
ENFILADE
ENFOLDED
ENFOLDER
ENFORCED
ENFORCER
ENGADINE
ENGAGING
ENGENDER
ENGINEER
ENGINERY
ENGRAVED
ENGRAVER
ENGULFED
ENHANCED
ENHANCER
ENIWETOK
ENJOINED
ENJOINER
ENJOYING
ENKINDLE
ENLARGED
ENLARGER
ENLISTED
ENLISTER
ENMESHED
ENNEADIC
ENNEAGON
ENNOBLED
ENNOBLER
ENORMITY
ENORMOUS
ENQUIRED
ENQUIRER
ENRAGING

ENRICHED
ENRICHER
ENROLLED
ENROLLEE
ENROLLER
ENSCHEDE
ENSCONCE
ENSEMBLE
ENSHRINE
ENSHROUD
ENSIFORM
ENSILAGE
ENSLAVED
ENSLAVER
ENSNARED
ENSNARER
ENSPHERE
ENSURING
ENSWATHE
ENTAILED
ENTAILER
ENTANGLE
ENTELLUS
ENTENDRE
ENTENTES
ENTERING
ENTHALPY
ENTHETIC
ENTHRONE
ENTHUSED
ENTICING
ENTIRELY
ENTIRETY
ENTITIES
ENTITLED
ENTODERM
ENTOMBED
ENTOZOIC
ENTOZOON
ENTR'ACT
E
ENTRAILS
ENTRANCE
ENTRANTS
ENTREATY
ENTRENCH
ENTREPOT
ENTRESOL
ENTRYISM
ENTRYWAY
ENTWINED

E
NUMBER
S
ENURESIS
ENURETIC
ENVELOPE
ENVIABLE
ENVIABLY
ENVIRONS
ENVISAGE
ENVISION
ENWREATH
ENZOOTIC
EOLITHIC
EPAULETS
EPHEMERA
EPIBLAST
EPIBOLIC
EPICALYX
EPICOTYL
EPICURES
EPICYCLE
EPIDEMIC
EPIDOTIC
EPIDURAL
EPIFOCAL
EPIGRAMS
EPIGRAPH
EPILEPSY
EPILOGUE
EPINASTY
EPIPHANY
EPIPHYTE
EPISCOPE
EPISODES
EPISODIC
EPISTLER
EPISTLES
EPISTYLE
EPITAPHS
EPITASIS
EPITHETS
EPITOMIC
EPIZOISM
EPIZOITE
EPONYMIC
EQUALING
EQUALITY
EQUALIZE
EQUALLED
EQUATING

EQUATION
EQUINITY
EQUIPAGE
EQUIPPED
EQUIPPER
EQUITANT
EQUITIES
ERADIATE
ERASABLE
ERASTIAN
ERASURES
ERECTILE
ERECTING
ERECTION
EREMITIC
ERETHISM
ERGOTISM
ERIGERON
ERITREAN
ERLANGEN
ERRANTRY
ERUMPENT
ERUPTING
ERUPTION
ERUPTIVE
ERYTHEMA
ESCALADE
ESCALATE
ESCALOPE
ESCAPADE
ESCAPEES
ESCAPING
ESCAPISM
ESCAPIST
ESCHEWAL
ESCHEWED
ESCHEWER
ESCORTED
ESCULENT
ESKIMOAN
ESKIMOID
ESOTERIC
ESPALIER
ESPECIAL
ESPOUSAL
ESPOUSED
ESPOUSER
ESPRESSO
ESSAYING
ESSAYIST
ESSENCES

ESTANCIA
ESTEEMED
ESTERASE
ESTERIFY
ESTHETES
ESTIMATE
ESTONIAN
ESTOPPEL
ESTOVERS
ESTRAGON
ESTRANGE
ESURIENT
ET
CETERA
ETCHINGS
ETERNITY
ETERNIZE
ETHEREAL
ETHERIFY
ETHERIZE
ETHERNET
ETHICIST
ETHICIZE
ETHIOPIA
ETHIOPIC
ETHNARCH
ETHOLOGY
ETHONONE
ETHOXIDE
ETHYLATE
ETHYLENE
ETIOLATE
ETIOLOGY
ETON
CROP
ETRUSCAN
EUCHARIS
EUGENICS
EULACHON
EULOGIES
EULOGIST
EULOGIZE
EUONYMUS
EUPEPSIA
EUPEPTIC
EUPHONIC
EUPHORIA
EUPHORIC
EUPHOTIC
EUPHRASY
EUPHUISM

EUPHUIST
EUPNOEIC
EURASIAN
EUROCRAT
EURONOTE
EUROPEAN
EUROPIUM
EUSTATIC
EUTECTIC
EUXENITE
EVACUANT
EVACUATE
EVACUEES
EVADABLE
EVALUATE
EVANESCE
EVANSTON
EVASIONS
EVECTION
EVENINGS
EVENNESS
EVENSONG
EVENTFUL
EVENTIDE
EVENTUAL
EVERMORE
EVERSION
EVERYDAY
EVERYMAN
EVERYONE
EVICTING
EVICTION
EVIDENCE
EVILDOER
EVILLEST
EVILNESS
EVINCING
EVINCIVE
EVOCABLE
EVOCATOR
EVOLVING
EVONYMUS
EXACTING
EXACTION
EXALTING
EXAMINED
EXAMINEE
EXAMINER
EXAMPLES
EXARCHAL
EXCAVATE

EXCEEDED
EXCEEDER
EXCELLED
EXCEPTED
EXCERPTS
EXCESSES
EXCHANGE
EXCISING
EXCISION
EXCITANT
EXCITING
EXCLUDED
EXCLUDER
EXCRETAL
EXCRETED
EXCRETER
EXCURSUS
EXCUSING
EXECRATE
EXECUTED
EXECUTER
EXECUTOR
EXEGESES
EXEGESIS
EXEGETIC
EXEMPLAR
EXEMPLUM
EXEMPTED
EXEQUIES
EXERCISE
EXERGUAL
EXERTING
EXERTION
EXERTIVE
EX
GRATIA
EXHALANT
EXHALING
EXHAUSTS
EXHIBITS
EXHORTED
EXHORTER
EXHUMING
EXIGENCY
EXIGIBLE
EXIGUITY
EXIGUOUS
EXISTENT
EXISTING
EXITANCE

EX LIBRIS	EXTORTER	FAINTING	FANFARES	FAUTEUIL	FERVIDLY
EXOCRINE	EXTRACTS	FAINTISH	FANLIGHT	FAVONIAN	FESTERED
EXOERGIC	EXTRADOS	FAIR COPY	FANTASIA	FAVOURED	FESTIVAL
EXORABLE	EXTREMES	FAIR GAME	FANZINES	FAVOURER	FESTOONS
EXORCISE	EXTRORSE	FAIRINGS	FARADISM	FAYALITE	FETATION
EXORCISM	EXTRUDED	FAIRLEAD	FARADIZE	FEARLESS	FETCHING
EXORCIST	EXULTANT	FAIRNESS	FARCEUSE	FEARSOME	FETIALES
EXORCIZE	EXULTING	FAIRWAYS	FARCICAL	FEASIBLE	FETICIDE
EXORDIAL	EXUVIATE	FAITHFUL	FAREWELL	FEASIBLY	FETISHES
EXORDIUM	EYEBALLS	FAIZABAD	FAR-FLUNG	FEASTING	FETLOCKS
EXOSPORE	EYEBROWS	FALCHION	FARINOSE	FEATHERS	FETTERED
EXOTERIC	EYEGLASS	FALCONER	FARMABLE	FEATHERY	FETTERER
EXOTOXIC	EYELINER	FALCONET	FARMHAND	FEATURED	FETTLING
EXOTOXIN	EYEPATCH	FALCONRY	FARMLAND	FEATURES	FEVERFEW
EXPANDED	EYEPIECE	FALDERAL	FARMYARD	FEBRIFIC	FEVERISH
EXPANDER	EYESHADE	FALKLAND	FARNESOL	FEBRUARY	FIASCOES
EXPECTED	EYESIGHT	FALL BACK	FAROUCHE	FECKLESS	FIBRILAR
EXPEDITE	EYESORES	FALLFISH	FARRIERS	FECULENT	FIBROSIS
EXPELLED	EYESTALK	FALL GUYS	FARRIERY	FEDERATE	FIBROTIC
EXPELLEE	EYETEETH	FALLIBLE	FARROWED	FEEBLEST	FICTIONS
EXPELLER	EYETOOTH	FALLOUTS	FARTHEST	FEEDABLE	FIDDLING
EXPENDED		FALL OVER	FARTHING	FEEDBACK	FIDELITY
EXPENDER	**F**	FALMOUTH	FASCIATE	FEEDBAGS	FIDGETED
EXPENSES	FABULIST	FALSETTO	FASCICLE	FEELINGS	FIDUCIAL
EXPERTLY	FABULOUS	FALTBOAT	FASCISTS	FEIGNING	FIELD DAY
EXPIABLE	FACEABLE	FALTERED	FASHIONS	FEINTING	FIELDERS
EXPIATED	FACE CARD	FALTERER	FASTBACK	FELDSPAR	FIELDING
EXPIATOR	FACE DOWN	FAMILIAL	FASTENED	FELICITY	FIENDISH
EXPIRING	FACELESS	FAMILIAR	FASTENER	FELINITY	FIERCELY
EXPLICIT	FACE-LIFT	FAMILIES	FAST FOOD	FELLABLE	FIERCEST
EXPLODED	FACE PACK	FAMISHED	FASTNESS	FELLATIO	FIERIEST
EXPLODER	FACETIAE	FAMOUSLY	FATALISM	FELONIES	FIFTIETH
EXPLOITS	FACIALLY	FANAGALO	FATALIST	FELSITIC	FIGHTERS
EXPLORED	FACILELY	FANATICS	FATALITY	FEMININE	FIGHTING
EXPLORER	FACILITY	FAN BELTS	FATHEADS	FEMINISM	FIG LEAFS
EXPONENT	FACTIONS	FANCIERS	FATHERED	FEMINIST	FIGMENTS
EXPORTED	FACTIOUS	FANCIEST	FATHERLY	FEMINIZE	FIGURANT
EXPORTER	FACTOTUM	FANCIFUL	FATHOMED	FENDERED	FIGURATE
EXPOSING	FADELESS	FANCYING	FATHOMER	FENESTRA	FIGURINE
EXPOSURE	FADEOUTS	FANCY MAN	FATIGUED	FERETORY	FIGURING
EXPUNGED	FAEROESE	FANCY MEN	FATIGUES	FEROCITY	FILAGREE
EXPUNGER	FAHLBAND	FAN DANCE	FATTENED	FERREOUS	FILAMENT
EXTENDED	FAILINGS	FANDANGO	FATTENER	FERRETED	FILARIAL
EXTENDER	FAIL-SAFE		FATTIEST	FERRETER	FILATURE
EXTENSOR	FAILURES		FAUBOURG	FERRIAGE	FILCHING
EXTERIOR	FAINEANT		FAULTIER	FERRITIN	FILECARD
EXTERNAL	FAINTEST		FAULTILY	FERRULES	FILEFISH
EXTOLLED			FAULTING	FERRYING	FILENAME
EXTOLLER			FAUSTIAN	FERRYMAN	FILETING
EXTORTED				FERRYMEN	FERVENCY

FILICIDE
FILIFORM
FILIGREE
FILIPINO
FILLETED
FILLINGS
FILMIEST
FILM STAR
FILTERED
FILTHIER
FILTHILY
FILTRATE
FIMBRIAL
FINAGLER
FINALISM
FINALIST
FINALITY
FINALIZE
FINANCED
FINANCES
FINDABLE
FINDINGS
FINEABLE
FINE ARTS
FINE-DRAW
FINE GAEL
FINENESS
FINESPUN
FINE SPUN
FINE-TUNE
FINGERED
FINGERER
FINIALED
FINISHED
FINISHER
FINISHES
FINITELY
FINNMARK
FINOCHIO
FIREABLE
FIREARMS
FIREBACK
FIREBALL
FIREBOAT
FIREBRAT
FIREBUGS

FIRE-CURE
FIREDAMP
FIREDOGS
FIRE-PLUG
FIRESIDE
FIRETRAP
FIREWALL
FIREWEED
FIREWOOD
FIREWORK
FIRMNESS
FIRMWARE
FIRST AID
FIRST-DAY
FIRTREES
FISCALLY
FISHABLE
FISHBOLT
FISHBOWL
FISHCAKE
FISH FARM
FISH-HOOK
FISHIEST
FISHMEAL
FISHNETS
FISHSKIN
FISHTAIL
FISHWIFE
FISSIPED
FISSURES
FISTMELE
FITFULLY
FITMENTS
FITTABLE
FITTINGS
FIVEFOLD
FIVEPINS
FIVE-STAR
FIXATION
FIXATIVE
FIXTURES
FIZZIEST
FLABBIER
FLABBILY

FLAG DAYS
FLAG FALL
FLAGGING
FLAGPOLE
FLAGRANT
FLAGSHIP
FLAILING
FLAKIEST
FLAMBEAU
FLAMENCO
FLAMEOUT
FLAMINGO
FLANDERS
FLANERIE
FLANKING
FLANNELS
FLAPJACK
FLAPPING
FLARE-UPS
FLASHERS
FLASHEST
FLASHGUN
FLASH GUN
FLASHIER
FLASHILY
FLASHING
FLATBOAT
FLATETTE
FLAT FEET
FLATFISH
FLATFOOT
FLATHEAD
FLATLETS
FLATMATE
FLATNESS
FLAT RACE
FLAT SPIN
FLATTERY
FLATTEST
FLATTING
FLATTISH
FLATWARE
FLATWAYS
FLATWORM
FLAUNTED

FLAUNTER
FLAUTIST
FLAVOURS
FLAWLESS
FLAXSEED
FLEABAGS
FLEABANE
FLEABITE
FLEA BITE
FLEAPITS
FLEAWORT
FLECKING
FLECTION
FLEECING
FLEETEST
FLEETING
FLESHIER
FLESHING
FLESHPOT
FLETCHER
FLEXIBLE
FLEXIBLY
FLEXUOUS
FLEXURAL
FLICKERY
FLICKING
FLIMFLAM
FLIMSIER
FLIMSILY
FLINCHED
FLINCHER
FLINGING
FLINTIER
FLIP-FLOP
FLIPPANT
FLIPPERS
FLIPPEST
FLIPPING
FLIP SIDE
FLIRTING
FLITTING
FLOATAGE
FLOATERS
FLOATING
FLOCCOSE
FLOCCULE
FLOCKING
FLOGGING

FLOODING
FLOODLIT
FLOORAGE
FLOORING
FLOOZIES
FLOPPIER
FLOPPILY
FLOPPING
FLORALLY
FLORENCE
FLORIDLY
FLORIGEN
FLORISTS
FLOSSING
FLOTILLA
FLOUNCED
FLOUNCES
FLOUNDER
FLOURING
FLOURISH
FLOUTING
FLOWERED
FLOWERER
FLUE-CURE
FLUENTLY
FLUFFIER
FLUFFING
FLUIDICS
FLUIDITY
FLUIDIZE
FLUMMERY
FLUNKEYS
FLUNKING
FLUORENE
FLUORIDE
FLUORINE
FLURRIED
FLURRIES
FLUSHING
FLUTISTS
FLUTTERS
FLUTTERY
FLYBLOWN
FLYOVERS
FLYPAPER
FLYPASTS
FLYSHEET
FLYSPECK
FLYWHEEL
FLYWHISK

FOAMIEST
FOAMLIKE
FOB WATCH
FOCALIZE
FOCUSING
FOCUSSED
FOETUSES
FOGBOUND
FOGGIEST
FOGHORNS
FOG LAMPS
FOGLIGHT
FOIE GRAS
FOILABLE
FOILSMAN
FOISTING
FOLDABLE
FOLDAWAY
FOLDBOAT
FOLIATED
FOLKLORE
FOLK-ROCK
FOLKTALE
FOLKWAYS
FOLLICLE
FOLLOWED
FOLLOWER
FOLLOW-ON
FOLLOW-UP
FOMENTED
FOMENTER
FONDANTS
FONDLING
FONDNESS
FOOLSCAP
FOOTBALL
FOOTFALL
FOOTGEAR
FOOTHILL
FOOTHOLD
FOOTLING
FOOTMARK
FOOTNOTE
FOOTPACE
FOOTPADS
FOOTPATH

FOOTRACE	FORESEER	FOULNESS	FREEBIES	FRIENDLY	FRUITIER
FOOTREST	FORESIDE	FOUL	FREEBOOT	FRIESIAN	FRUITING
FOOTROPE	FORESKIN	PLAY	FREEBORN	FRIGATES	FRUITION
FOOTSIES	FORESTAL	FOUNDERS	FREEDMAN	FRIGGING	FRUMENTY
FOOTSLOG	FORESTAY	FOUNDING	FREE-	FRIGHTEN	FRUMPIER
FOOTSORE	FORESTED	FOUNTAIN	FALL	FRIGIDLY	FRUMPISH
FOOTSTEP	FORESTER	FOUR-	FREEFONE	FRILLIER	FRUSTULE
FOOTWALL	FORESTRY	BALL	FREEHAND	FRINGING	FUCHSIAS
FOOTWEAR	FORETELL	FOUR-	FREEHOLD	FRIPPERY	FUCOIDAL
FOOTWELL	FORETIME	DEAL	FREE	FRISBEES	FUDDLING
FOOTWORK	FORETOLD	FOUR-	KICK	FRISETTE	FUELLING
FOOTWORN	FOREWARN	EYED	FREELOAD	FRISKIER	FUGACITY
FORAGING	FOREWENT	FOUREYES	FREE	FRISKILY	FUGGIEST
FOR A	FOREWIND	FOURFOLD	PASS	FRISKING	FUGITIVE
SONG	FOREWING	FOUR-	FREE	FRISSONS	FUGLEMAN
FORAYING	FOREWORD	LEAF	PORT	FRITTATA	FULCRUMS
FORBEARS	FOREYARD	FOURSOME	FREEPOST	FRITTERS	FULLBACK
FORBORNE	FORFEITS	FOUR-	FREE	FRIULIAN	FULL
FORCE-	FORGINGS	STAR	REIN	FRIZZIER	MOON
FED	FORGIVEN	FOURTEEN	FREESIAS	FRIZZING	FULLNESS
FORCEFUL	FORGIVER	FOVEOLAR	FREE	FRIZZLED	FULL-
FORCIBLE	FORGOING	FOWLIANG	TIME	FRIZZLER	PAGE
FORCIBLY	FORJUDGE	FOWL	FREETOWN	FROCKING	FULL
FORDABLE	FORK-	PEST	FREEWARE	FROGFISH	STOP
FOREARMS	LIFT	FOXGLOVE	FREEWAYS	FROMENTY	FULL-
FOREBEAR	FORMABLE	FOXHOLES	FREE	FRONDEUR	TIME
FOREBODE	FORMALIN	FOXHOUND	WILL	FRONTAGE	FULL
FORECAST	FORMALLY	FOXHUNTS	FREEZERS	FRONTIER	TOSS
FOREDECK	FORMERLY	FOXINESS	FREEZE	FRONTING	FULMINIC
FOREDOOM	FORMLESS	FOXTROTS	UP	FRONTLET	FUMAROLE
FOREFEET	FORMULAE	FRACTION	FREEZE-	FRONT	FUMATORY
FOREFOOT	FORMULAS	FRACTURE	UP	MAN	FUMBLING
FOREGOER	FORMWORK	FRAGMENT	FREEZING	FRONT	FUMELESS
FOREGONE	FORNICAL	FRAGRANT	FREIBURG	MEN	FUMIGANT
FOREHAND	FORSAKEN	FRAILEST	FREMITUS	FROSTIER	FUMIGATE
FOREHEAD	FORSAKER	FRAMABLE	FRENETIC	FROSTILY	FUMINGLY
FOREKNOW	FORSOOTH	FRAME-	FRENULUM	FROSTING	FUMITORY
FORELAND	FORSWEAR	UPS	FRENZIED	FROTHIER	FUNCTION
FORELEGS	FORSWORE	FRANCIUM	FREQUENT	FROTHILY	FUNERALS
FORELIMB	FORSWORN	FRANKEST	FRESCOES	FROTHING	FUNERARY
FORELOCK	FORTIETH	FRANKING	FRESHEST	FROUFROU	FUNEREAL
FOREMAST	FORT	FRANKISH	FRESHMAN	FROWNING	FUNFAIRS
FOREMOST	KNOX	FRANKLIN	FRESHMEN	FROWZIER	FUNGIBLE
FORENAME	FORTRESS	FRASCATI	FRETLESS	FRUCTIFY	FUNGUSES
FORENOON	FORTUNES	FRAULEIN	FRETSAWS	FRUCTOSE	FUNKIEST
FORENSIC	FORWARDS	FRAZZLED	FRETTING	FRUGALLY	FUNNELED
FOREPART	FORZANDO	FREAKING	FRETWORK	FRUITAGE	FUNNIEST
FOREPEAK	FOSSETTE	FREAKISH	FREUDIAN	FRUIT	FURBELOW
FOREPLAY	FOSTERED	FRECKLED	FRIARIES	BAT	FURCATED
FORESAIL	FOSTERER	FRECKLES	FRIBBLER	FRUIT	FURFURAN
FORESEEN		FREE-	FRIBOURG	FLY	FURLABLE
		BASE	FRICTION	FRUITFUL	FURLONGS

FURLOUGH
FURNACES
FURRIERS
FURRIERY
FURRIEST
FURROWED
FURROWER
FURTHEST
FURUNCLE
FUSELAGE
FUSIFORM
FUSILIER
FUSSIEST
FUSSPOTS
FUSTIEST
FUTILITY
FUTURISM
FUTURIST
FUTURITY
FUZZIEST

G

GABBLING
GABBROIC
GABONESE
GABORONE
GADABOUT
GADFLIES
GADGETRY
GAFFSAIL
GAINABLE
GAINSAID
GALACTIC
GALANGAL
GALAXIES
GALBANUM
GALENISM
GALENIST
GALICIAN
GALILEAN
GALLANTS
GALLEASS
GALLEONS
GALLERIA
GALLIARD
GALLIPOT
GALLOPED
GALLOPER
GALLOWAY
GALOSHES
GALVANIC

GAMBLERS
GAMBLING
GAMBOLED
GAMECOCK
GAME
  FOWL
GAMENESS
GAMESTER
GAMINESS
GAMMA
  RAY
GAMMONER
GANDHIAN
GANG-
  BANG
GANGLAND
GANGLIAL
GANGLING
GANGLION
GANGRENE
GANGSTER
GANGWAYS
GANISTER
GANTLINE
GANTRIES
GANYMEDE
GAOLBIRD
GAOXIONG
GAPEWORM
GAPINGLY
GARAGING
GARAMOND
GARBLESS
GARBLING
GARBOARD
GARDENED
GARDENER
GARDENIA
GARGANEY
GARGLING
GARGOYLE
GARISHLY
GARLANDS
GARLICKY
GARMENTS
GARNERED
GARRISON
GARROTTE
GASIFIER
GASIFORM
GASLIGHT

GAS
  MASKS
GASOLIER
GASOLINE
GASSIEST
GASTIGHT
GASTRULA
GASWORKS
GATEFOLD
GATEPOST
GATEWAYS
GATHERED
GATHERER
GAUDIEST
GAULLISM
GAULLIST
GAUNTLET
GAUZIEST
GAVOTTES
GAWKIEST
GAZELLES
GAZETTES
GAZPACHO
GAZUMPED
GAZUMPER
GELATINE
GELATION
GELDINGS
GELIDITY
GEMINATE
GEMOLOGY
GEMSTONE
GENDARME
GENDERED
GENERALS
GENERATE
GENEROUS
GENETICS
GENIALLY
GENITALS
GENITIVE
GENIUSES
GENOCIDE
GENOTYPE
GENTIANS
GENTILES
GENTRIFY
GEODESIC
GEODETIC
GEOGNOSY
GEOMANCY

GEOMETER
GEOMETRY
GEOPHAGY
GEOPHYTE
GEOPONIC
GEORDIES
GEORGIAN
GEOTAXIS
GERANIAL
GERANIOL
GERANIUM
GERMANIC
GERM
  CELL
GERMINAL
GESTALTS
GESTAPOS
GESTURAL
GESTURED
GESTURER
GESTURES
GET
  THERE
GHANAIAN
GHERKINS
GHETTOES
GHOSTING
GHOULISH
GIANTESS
GIBBERED
GIBBSITE
GIBINGLY
GIDDIEST
GIFT-
  WRAP
GIGAFLOP
GIGANTIC
GIGGLING
GILTHEAD
GILTWOOD
GIMCRACK
GIMMICKS
GIMMICKY
GINGERED
GINGERLY
GINGIVAL
GIN
  RUMMY
GINSBERG
GIN
  SLING

GIN
  TRAPS
GIRAFFES
GIRDLING
GIRLHOOD
GISBORNE
GIVEAWAY
GIZZARDS
GLABELLA
GLABROUS
GLACIATE
GLACIERS
GLADBECK
GLADDEST
GLAD
  HAND
GLADIATE
GLADIOLI
GLADNESS
GLAD
  RAGS
GLANCING
GLANDERS
GLANDULE
GLASSIER
GLASSINE
GLASSING
GLASSMAN
GLAUCOMA
GLAUCOUS
GLAZIERS
GLAZIERY
GLEAMING
GLEANING
GLENDALE
GLIBBEST
GLIBNESS
GLIMMERS
GLIMPSED
GLIMPSER
GLIMPSES
GLINTING
GLISSADE
GLITCHES
GLITTERS
GLITTERY
GLITZIER
GLOAMING
GLOATING
GLOBALLY
GLOBULAR

GLOBULES
GLOBULIN
GLOOMFUL
GLOOMIER
GLOOMILY
GLORIOUS
GLORYING
GLOSSARY
GLOSSIER
GLOSSILY
GLOSSING
GLOWERED
GLOW-
  WORM
GLOXINIA
GLUCAGON
GLUCINUM
GLUCOSIC
GLUMMEST
GLUMNESS
GLUTELIN
GLUTTING
GLUTTONS
GLUTTONY
GLYCERIC
GLYCERIN
GLYCEROL
GLYCERYL
GLYCOGEN
GLYCOLIC
GLYPTICS
GNASHERS
GNASHING
GNATHION
GNATHITE
GNAWABLE
GNEISSIC
GNOMONIC
GOAL
  LINE
GOALPOST
GOATHERD
GOATSKIN
GOAT'S-
  RUE
GOBBLING
GOBSHITE
GOD-
  AWFUL
GODCHILD
GODLIEST
GODSENDS

GODSPEED
GODTHAAB
GOETHITE
GO-
  GETTER
GOGGLING
GOIDELIC
GOINGS
  ON
GOINGS-
  ON
GOITROUS
GOLD
  COAT
GOLD
  DUST
GOLDFISH
GOLD
  LEAF
GOLDMINE
GOLD
  RUSH
GOLF
  BALL
GOLF
  CLUB
GOLIATHS
GOLLIWOG
GOLLOPER
GOMBROON
GONDOLAS
GONIDIAL
GONIDIUM
GONOCYTE
GONOPORE
GOOD
  BOOK
GOODBYES
GOODLIER
GOODNESS
GOOD
  TURN
GOODWILL
GOODWOOD
GOOD
  WORD
GOOFIEST
GOOGLIES
GO
  PLACES
GORDIMER
GORGEDLY

GORGEOUS
GORGERIN
GORILLAS
GORINESS
GORLOVKA
GORMLESS
GOSLINGS
GOSPODIN
GOSSAMER
GOSSIPED
GOSSIPER
GOSSYPOL
GOTEBORG
GO TO
  TOWN
GOUACHES
GOURMAND
GOURMETS
GOUTWEED
GOVERNED
GOVERNOR
GRAB
  BAGS
GRABBING
GRABBLER
GRACEFUL
GRACIOUS
GRADABLE
GRADIENT
GRADUATE
GRAECISM
GRAFFITI
GRAFFITO
GRAFTERS
GRAFTING
GRAINING
GRAMPIAN
GRANDADS
GRANDEES
GRANDEST
GRANDEUR
GRAND
  MAL
GRANDMAS
GRANDPAS
GRANDSON
GRANITIC
GRANNIES
GRANTHAM
GRANTING
GRANULAR

GRANULES
GRAPHEME
GRAPHICS
GRAPHITE
GRAPNELS
GRAPPLED
GRAPPLER
GRASPING
GRASSIER
GRASSING
GRATEFUL
GRATINGS
GRATUITY
GRAVAMEN
GRAVELED
GRAVELLY
GRAVITAS
GRAVITON
GRAYLING
GREASERS
GREASIER
GREASILY
GREASING
GREATEST
GREEDIER
GREEDILY
GREENERY
GREENEST
GREENFLY
GREENING
GREENISH
GREENLET
GREENOCK
GREEN
  TEA
GREETING
GREMLINS
GRENADES
GRENOBLE
GREY
  AREA
GREYBACK
GREYNESS
GRIDDLES
GRIDIRON
GRIDLOCK
GRIEVING
GRIEVOUS
GRIFFINS
GRILLAGE
GRILLING

GRIMACED
GRIMACER
GRIMACES
GRIMIEST
GRIMMEST
GRIMNESS
GRINDERS
GRINDERY
GRINDING
GRINNING
GRIPPING
GRISEOUS
GRISETTE
GRISLIER
GRITTIER
GRITTILY
GRITTING
GRIZZLED
GRIZZLER
GROANING
GROGGIER
GROGGILY
GROMWELL
GROOMING
GROOVIER
GROSBEAK
GROSCHEN
GROSSEST
GROSSING
GROTTIER
GROTTOES
GROUCHED
GROUCHES
GROUNDED
GROUPIES
GROUPING
GROUSING
GROVELED
GROWABLE
GROWLERS
GROWLING
GROWMORE
GROWN-
  UPS
GRUBBIER
GRUBBILY
GRUBBING
GRUDGING
GRUESOME
GRUFFEST
GRUFFISH

GRUMBLED
GRUMBLER
GRUMBLES
GRUMPIER
GRUMPILY
GRUNTING
GRYPHONS
G-
  STRING
  S
GUAIACOL
GUAIACUM
GUARANTY
GUARDANT
GUARDIAN
GUARDING
GUERNSEY
GUERRERO
GUESSING
GUESTING
GUFFAWED
GUIANESE
GUIDABLE
GUIDANCE
GUILDERS
GUILEFUL
GUILTIER
GUILTILY
GUJARATI
GULFWEED
GULLIBLE
GULLIBLY
GUMBOILS
GUMBOOTS
GUMBOTIL
GUMDROPS
GUMMIEST
GUMMOSIS
GUMPTION
GUMSHOES
GUM
  TREES
GUNBOATS
GUNFLINT
GUNMETAL
GUNPAPER
GUNPOINT
GUNSHOTS
GUNSMITH
GUNSTOCK
GUNWALES

GURGLING
GURKHALI
GUSTIEST
GUTSIEST
GUTTERED
GUTTURAL
GUYANESE
GUZZLERS
GUZZLING
GYMKHANA
GYMNASTS
GYMSLIPS
GYNANDRY
GYNARCHY
GYPSEOUS
GYRATING
GYRATION
GYRATORY

H

HABAKKUK
HABANFRA
HABITANT
HABITATS
HABITUAL
HABITUDE
HABITUES
HABSBURG
HACIENDA
HACKETTE
HACKNEYS
HACKSAWS
HACKWORK
HADRONIC
HAEMATIC
HAEMATIN
HAEREMAI
HA-ERH-
  PIN
HAFTARAH
HAGGADAH
HAGGADIC
HAGGLING
HAILWOOD
HAIPHONG
HAIRBALL
HAIRCUTS
HAIRGRIP
HAIRIEST
HAIRLESS
HAIRLIKE

HAIRLINE	HANDBELL	HARAMBEE	HARKENER	HAVELOCK	HEADWORK
HAIRNETS	HANDBILL	HARANGUE	HARLOTRY	HAVE-	HEALABLE
HAIRPINS	HANDBOOK	HARAPPAN	HARMLESS	NOTS	HEARABLE
HAIRTAIL	HANDCART	HARASSED	HARMONIC	HAVERING	HEAR
HAIRWORM	HANDCLAP	HARASSER	HARPINGS	HAVILDAR	HEAR
HAKODATE	HANDCUFF	HARBOURS	HARPISTS	HAVOCKER	HEARINGS
HALAFIAN	HANDFAST	HARD AT	HARPOONS	HAWAIIAN	HEARTIER
HALATION	HANDFEED	IT	HARRIDAN	HAWFINCH	HEARTILY
HALBERDS	HANDFULS	HARDBACK	HARRIERS	HAWKBILL	HEATEDLY
HALCYONE	HANDGRIP	HARDBAKE	HARRIMAN	HAWK-	HEATHENS
HALENESS	HANDGUNS	HARDBALL	HARRISON	EYED	HEATHERY
HALFBACK	HANDHOLD	HARD	HARROWED	HAWKLIKE	HEATLESS
HALFBEAK	HANDICAP	CASH	HARROWER	HAWKWEED	HEAT
HALF	HANDIEST	HARD	HARRUMPH	HAWTHORN	PUMP
COCK	HANDLERS	COPY	HARRYING	HAYCOCKS	HEAT
HALF-	HANDLESS	HARDCORE	HARSHEST	HAY	RASH
LIFE	HANDLIKE	HARD	HARTFORD	FEVER	HEAT
HALF-	HANDLING	CORE	HARTNELL	HAYFORKS	WAVE
MAST	HANDLOOM	HARDCORE	HARUSPEX	HAYMAKER	HEAVENLY
HALF	HANDMADE	HARD-	HARVESTS	HAYSTACK	HEAVIEST
MOON	HANDOUTS	CORE	HAS-	HAZARDED	HEAVY-
HALF	HANDOVER	HARD	BEENS	HAZELHEN	SET
NOTE	HANDRAIL	DISK	HASIDISM	HAZELNUT	HEBDOMAD
HALF	HANDS-	HARDENED	HASSLING	HAZINESS	HEBETATE
TERM	OFF	HARDENER	HASSOCKS	HEADACHE	HEBETUDE
HALF	HANDSOME	HARDHACK	HASTEFUL	HEADACHY	HEBRAISM
TIME	HANDYMAN	HARDIEST	HASTENED	HEADBAND	HEBRAIST
HALFTONE	HANDYMEN	HARD	HASTENER	HEADFAST	HEBRAIZE
HALF-	HANGBIRD	LINE	HASTIEST	HEADGEAR	HEBRIDES
WITS	HANGCHOW	HARD	HASTINGS	HEADHUNT	HECATOMB
HALF-	HANGER-	LUCK	HATBANDS	HEADIEST	HECKLERS
YEAR	ON	HARDNESS	HATCHERY	HEADINGS	HECKLING
HALIBUTS	HANGINGS	HARD	HATCHETS	HEADLAND	HECTARES
HALLIARD	HANGNAIL	NUTS	HATCHING	HEADLESS	HECTORED
HALLMARK	HANGOUTS	HARD	HATCHWAY	HEADLIKE	HEDGEHOG
HALLOWED	HANGOVER	SELL	HATEABLE	HEADLINE	HEDGEHOP
HALLOWER	HANGZHOU	HARDSHIP	HATFIELD	HEADLOCK	HEDGEROW
HALLWAYS	HANKERED	HARD	HATHAWAY	HEADLONG	HEDONICS
HALMSTAD	HANKERER	TACK	HATHORIC	HEADMOST	HEDONISM
HALO-	HANNIBAL	HARDTOPS	HATTERAS	HEADRACE	HEDONIST
LIKE	HANNOVER	HARD	HAT	HEADRAIL	HEEDLESS
HALYARDS	HANRATTY	UPON	TRICK	HEADREST	HEELBALL
HAMARTIA	HANUKKAH	HARDWARE	HAULIERS	HEADROOM	HEELLESS
HAMILTON	HAPLITIC	HARDWOOD	HAUNCHED	HEADSAIL	HEELPOST
HAMMERED	HAPLOSIS	HAREBELL	HAUNCHES	HEADSETS	HEFTIEST
HAMMERER	HAPPENED	HARELIKE	HAUNTING	HEADSHIP	HEGELIAN
HAMMOCKS	HAPPIEST	HARFLEUR	HAUSFRAU	HEADSMAN	HEGEMONY
HAMPERED	HAPSBURG	HARGEISA	HAUTBOIS	HEADWARD	HEIGHTEN
HAMPERER	HAPTERON	HARICOTS	HAUTBOYS	HEADWAYS	HEIMDALL
HAMSTERS	HARA-	HARIKARI	HAUT-	HEADWIND	HEIRLESS
HANDBAGS	KIRI	HARINGEY	RHIN	HEADWORD	HEIRLOOM
HANDBALL		HARKENED			HEIRSHIP

HELIACAL	HERALDRY	HIGHBORN	HIPPARCH	HOLSTERS	HONIEDLY
HELICOID	HERBLIKE	HIGHBOYS	HIPSTERS	HOLYHEAD	HONOLULU
HELIPORT	HERCULES	HIGHBROW	HIRAGANA	HOLYOAKE	HONORARY
HELLADIC	HERDSMAN	HIGHER-	HIRELING	HOLYTIDE	HONOURED
HELL-	HERDSMEN	UP	HIRI	HOLY	HONOURER
BENT	HERDWICK	HIGHJACK	MOTU	WEEK	HOODLESS
HELLCATS	HEREDITY	HIGH	HIROHITO	HOLY	HOODLIKE
HELLENES	HEREFORD	JUMP	HISPANIA	WRIT	HOODLUMS
HELLENIC	HEREINTO	HIGHLAND	HISPANIC	HOMBURGS	HOODWINK
HELLFIRE	HERESIES	HIGH	HISTOGEN	HOMEBODY	HOOFLESS
HELLHOLE	HERETICS	LIFE	HISTORIC	HOMEBRED	HOOFLIKE
HELMETED	HEREUNTO	HIGH	HITCHING	HOME	HOOKLESS
HELMINTH	HEREUPON	MASS	HITHERTO	BREW	HOOKLIKE
HELMLESS	HEREWARD	HIGHNESS	HIT	HOME	HOOKNOSE
HELMSMAN	HEREWITH	HIGH	LISTS	HELP	HOOKWORM
HELMSMEN	HERITAGE	RISE	HIVELIKE	HOMELAND	HOOLIGAN
HELOTISM	HERMETIC	HIGH-	HOACTZIN	HOMELESS	HOOPLIKE
HELPABLE	HERMITIC	RISE	HOARDING	HOMELIER	HOOSEGOW
HELPINGS	HERODIAS	HIGH	HOARIEST	HOMELIKE	HOOVERED
HELPLESS	HERPETIC	ROAD	HOARSELY	HOMEMADE	HOPEFULS
HELPMANN	HERRINGS	HIGH	HOARSEST	HOME	HOPELESS
HELPMATE	HERSCHEL	SEAS	HOBBLING	PAGE	HOPLITIC
HELPMEET	HERTFORD	HIGH	HOBBYIST	HOMERIAN	HORATIAN
HELSINKI	HERTZIAN	SPOT	HOBNAILS	HOME	HORIZONS
HELVETIA	HESIODIC	HIGHTAIL	HOCHHUTH	RULE	HORMONAL
HELVETIC	HESITANT	HIGH	HOCKTIDE	HOME	HORMONES
HELVETII	HESITATE	TECH	HOGMANAY	RUNS	HORNBEAM
HEMIOLIC	HESPERIA	HIGH	HOGSHEAD	HOMESICK	HORNBILL
HEMIPODE	HESPERUS	TIDE	HOISTING	HOMESPUN	HORNBOOK
HEMLINES	HESSIANS	HIGH	HOKKAIDO	HOMETOWN	HORNFELS
HEMLOCKS	HETAERIC	TIME	HOLDABLE	HOMEWARD	HORNIEST
HENBANES	HEXAGONS	HIGHVELD	HOLDALLS	HOMEWORK	HORNLESS
HENCHMAN	HEXAGRAM	HIGHWAYS	HOLD	HOMICIDE	HORNLIKE
HENCHMEN	HEXANOIC	HIJACKED	DEAR	HOMILIES	HORNPIPE
HENEQUEN	HEXAPLAR	HIJACKER	HOLDFAST	HOMILIST	HORNTAIL
HENGYANG	HEXAPODY	HILARITY	HOLDINGS	HOMINESS	HORNWORT
HENG-	HEZEKIAH	HILLFORT	HOLDOVER	HOMINOID	HOROLOGE
YANG	HIATUSES	HILL	HOLIDAYS	HOMODONT	HOROLOGY
HEN	HIAWATHA	FORT	HOLINESS	HOMOGAMY	HOROWITZ
HOUSE	HIBERNAL	HILLIARD	HOLISTIC	HOMOGENY	HORRIBLE
HEN	HIBERNIA	HILLIEST	HOLLANDS	HOMOGONY	HORRIBLY
PARTY	HIBISCUS	HILLOCKS	HOLLERED	HOMOLOGY	HORRIDLY
HENRYSON	HICCUPED	HILLSIDE	HOLLIDAY	HOMONYMS	HORRIFIC
HENSLOWE	HIDDENLY	HIMATION	HOLLOWED	HONDURAN	HORSEBOX
HEPATICA	HIDEAWAY	HINAYANA	HOLLOWER	HONDURAS	HORSEFLY
HEPTAGON	HIDELESS	HINCKLEY	HOLLOWLY	HONEGGER	HORSEMAN
HEPTARCH	HIDROSIS	HINDERED	HOLOCENE	HONESTLY	HORSEMEN
HEPWORTH	HIDROTIC	HINDERER	HOLOGRAM	HONEWORT	HORSIEST
HERACLEA	HIERARCH	HINDMOST	HOLOTYPE	HONEYBEE	HOSANNAS
HERACLES	HIERATIC	HINDUISM	HOLOZOIC	HONEYDEW	HOSEPIPE
HERALDED	HIGHBALL	HIPBATHS	HOLSTEIN	HONG	HOSPICES
HERALDIC		HIP		KONG	
		FLASK			

HOSPITAL	HUMBLEST	HYMENEAL	IGNITRON	IMPERIUM	INCREASE
HOSPODAR	HUMBLING	HYPERNYM	IGNOMINY	IMPETIGO	INCUBATE
HOSTAGES	HUMBOLDT	HYPNOSIS	IGNORANT	IMPINGED	INCUDATE
HOSTELRY	HUMIDIFY	HYPNOTIC	IGNORING	IMPINGER	INCURRED
HOSTLERS	HUMIDITY	HYSTERIA	IGUANIAN	IMPISHLY	INDAMINE
HOTCHPOT	HUMILITY	HYSTERIC	ILKESTON	IMPLANTS	INDEBTED
HOTELIER	HUMMOCKS		ILLATIVE	IMPLICIT	INDECENT
HOT	HUMMOCKY	**I**	ILL-	IMPLODED	INDENTED
FLUSH	HUMORIST	IAMBUSES	FATED	IMPLORED	INDENTER
HOTHEADS	HUMOROUS	ICEBERGS	ILLINOIS	IMPLORER	INDEXERS
HOTHOUSE	HUMOURED	ICEBLINK	ILLIQUID	IMPLYING	INDEXING
HOT	HUMPBACK	ICEBOUND	ILL-	IMPOLICY	INDICANT
LINES	HUMPHREY	ICEBOXES	TIMED	IMPOLITE	INDICATE
HOTPLATE	HUMPLIKE	ICE	ILL-	IMPORTED	INDICIAL
HOT	HUNCHING	CREAM	TREAT	IMPORTER	INDICTED
SPOTS	HUNDREDS	ICE	ILLUSION	IMPOSING	INDICTEE
HOT	HUNGERED	LOLLY	ILLUSORY	IMPOSTOR	INDIGENE
STUFF	HUNG	ICE	ILMENITE	IMPOTENT	INDIGENT
HOT	JURY	PACKS	IMAGINAL	IMPRINTS	INDIGOID
WATER	HUNGRIER	ICE	IMAGINED	IMPRISON	INDIRECT
HOUNDING	HUNGRILY	PICKS	IMAGINER	IMPROPER	INDOCILE
HOUNSLOW	HUNTEDLY	ICE	IMBECILE	IMPROVED	INDOLENT
HOUSEBOY	HUNTRESS	RINKS	IMBEDDED	IMPROVER	INDOLOGY
HOUSEFLY	HUNTSMAN	ICE	IMBIBING	IMPUDENT	INDORSED
HOUSEFUL	HUNTSMEN	SHEET	IMITABLE	IMPUGNED	INDUCING
HOUSEMAN	HURDLERS	ICE	IMITATED	IMPUGNER	INDUCTED
HOUSEMEN	HURDLING	SKATE	IMITATOR	IMPULSES	INDUCTOR
HOUSETOP	HURRYING	ICE	IMMANENT	IMPUNITY	INDULGED
HOUSINGS	HURTLING	WATER	IMMATURE	IMPURITY	INDULGER
HOVERERS	HUSBANDS	ICHTHYIC	IMMERSED	IMPUTING	INDULINE
HOVERING	HUSH-	IDEALISM	IMMINENT	INACTION	INDUSIAL
HOWITZER	HUSH	IDEALIST	IMMOBILE	INACTIVE	INDUSIUM
HRVATSKA	HUSKIEST	IDEALITY	IMMODEST	INASMUCH	INDUSTRY
HSINKING	HUSKLIKE	IDEALIZE	IMMOLATE	IN	INEDIBLE
HUANG	HUSTINGS	IDEATION	IMMORTAL	CAMERA	INEDIBLY
HUA	HUSTLERS	IDEATIVE	IMMOTILE	INCENSED	INEDITED
HUCKSTER	HUSTLING	IDEE	IMMUNITY	INCEPTOR	INEQUITY
HUDDLING	HWANG	FIXE	IMMUNIZE	INCHOATE	INERTIAL
HUFFIEST	HAI	IDENTIFY	IMMURING	INCIDENT	INESSIVE
HUGENESS	HYACINTH	IDENTITY	IMPACTED	INCISING	INEXPERT
HUGGABLE	HYDER	IDEOGRAM	IMPAIRED	INCISION	INFAMIES
HUGUENOT	ALI	IDEOLOGY	IMPAIRER	INCISIVE	INFAMOUS
HULA	HYDRACID	IDIOCIES	IMPALING	INCISORS	INFANTAS
HOOP	HYDRANTH	IDIOLECT	IMPARITY	INCISURE	INFANTRY
HULL-	HYDRANTS	IDLENESS	IMPARTED	INCITING	INFECTED
LESS	HYDRATED	IDOLATER	IMPARTER	INCLINED	INFECTOR
HUMANELY	HYDRATES	IDOLATRY	IMPASSES	INCLINER	INFERIOR
HUMANISM	HYDRATOR	IDOLIZED	IMPEDING	INCLINES	INFERNAL
HUMANIST	HYDROGEL	IDOLIZER	IMPELLED	INCLOSED	INFERNOS
HUMANITY	HYDROGEN	IDYLLIST	IMPELLER	INCLUDED	INFERRED
HUMANIZE	HYDROMEL	IGNITING	IMPERIAL	INCOMING	INFERRER
HUMANOID	HYGIENIC	IGNITION			

INFESTED	INLANDER	INTENTLY	INVESTOR	ISOPHONE	JAPANNED
INFESTER	INNATELY	INTERACT	INVIABLE	ISOPLETH	JAPINGLY
INFIDELS	INNER	INTERCOM	INVITING	ISOPODAN	JAPONICA
INFINITE	MAN	INTEREST	INVOICED	ISOPRENE	JAROSITE
INFINITY	INNOCENT	INTERIMS	INVOICES	ISOSTASY	JASMINES
INFIXION	IN NO	INTERIOR	INVOKING	ISOTHERE	JAUNDICE
INFLAMED	TIME	INTERLAY	INVOLUTE	ISOTHERM	JAUNTIER
INFLAMER	INNOVATE	INTERMIT	INVOLVED	ISOTONIC	JAUNTILY
INFLATED	INNUENDO	INTERMIX	INVOLVER	ISOTOPES	JAUNTING
INFLATER	INOCULUM	INTERNAL	INWARDLY	ISOTOPIC	JAVANESE
INFLEXED	INOSITOL	INTERNED	IODATION	ISOTROPY	JAVELINS
IN	INPUTTED	INTERNEE	IODOFORM	ISRAELIS	JAWBONES
FLIGHT	INQUESTS	INTERNET	IODOPSIN	ISSUABLE	JAYAPURA
IN-	INQUIRED	INTERNET	IONIZERS	ISSUANCE	JAZZIEST
FLIGHT	INQUIRER	INTERPOL	IONIZING	ISSYK-	JEALOUSY
INFLUENT	INSANELY	INTERRED	IOTACISM	KUL	JEHOVIAN
INFLUXES	INSANITY	INTERREX	IRAKLION	ISTANBUL	JEMAPPES
INFORMAL	INSCRIBE	INTERSEX	IRISHMAN	ISTHMIAN	JEMMYING
INFORMED	INSECURE	INTERVAL	IRISHMEN	ISTHMOID	JEOPARDY
INFORMER	INSERTED	INTERWAR	IRONBARK	ITALIANS	JEREMIAD
INFRA	INSERTER	IN THE	IRONCLAD	ITCHIEST	JERKIEST
DIG	INSETTED	BAG	IRON-	ITEMIZED	JEROBOAM
INFRARED	INSETTER	IN THE	GREY		JESUITIC
INFRINGE	INSIDERS	END	IRON	**J**	JET-
INFUSING	INSIGHTS	INTIMACY	HAND	JABALPUR	BLACK
INFUSION	INSIGNIA	INTIMATE	IRONWARE	JABBERED	JETFOILS
INFUSIVE	INSISTED	INTONATE	IRONWOOD	JABBERER	JETLINER
INGATHER	INSISTER	INTONING	IRONWORK	JACKBOOT	JETTISON
INGENUES	INSOLATE	INTRADOS	IROQUOIS	JACKDAWS	JEWELLED
INGESTED	INSOLENT	INTRANET	IRRIGATE	JACKFISH	JEWELLER
INGRATES	INSOMNIA	INTRENCH	IRRITANT	JACKPOTS	JEW'S
IN-	INSOMUCH	INTREPID	IRRITATE	JACKSTAY	HARP
GROUPS	INSPIRED	INTRIGUE	ISAGOGIC	JACK	JEZEBELS
INGROWTH	INSPIRER	INTRORSE	ISATINIC	TARS	JIGGERED
INGUINAL	INSPIRIT	INTRUDED	ISCHEMIC	JACOBEAN	JIGGLING
INHALANT	INSTANCE	INTRUDER	ISLAMIST	JACOBIAN	JINGLING
INHALERS	INSTANTS	INTUBATE	ISLANDER	JACOBITE	JINGOISM
INHALING	INSTINCT	INTUITED	ISMAILIA	JACQUARD	JINGOIST
INHERENT	INSTRUCT	INUNDANT	ISOBARIC	JACUZZIS	JINJIANG
INHUMANE	INSULANT	INUNDATE	ISOCHEIM	JAGGEDLY	JIPIJAPA
INIMICAL	INSULATE	INVADERS	ISOCLINE	JAILBAIT	JIUJITSU
INIQUITY	INSULTED	INVADING	ISOCRACY	JAILBIRD	JOCKEYED
INITIALS	INSULTER	INVALIDS	ISOGLOSS	JALOPIES	JOCOSELY
INITIATE	INSURERS	INVASION	ISOGONIC	JALOUSIE	JOCOSITY
INJECTED	INSURING	INVASIVE	ISOLABLE	JAMAICAN	JODHPURI
INJECTOR	INTAGLIO	INVEIGLE	ISOLATED	JAMBOREE	JODHPURS
INJURIES	INTARSIA	INVENTED	ISOLATOR	JAMMIEST	JOGGLING
INJURING	INTEGERS	INVENTOR	ISOLOGUE	JAMNAGAR	JOHN
INKBERRY	INTEGRAL	INVERTED	ISOMERIC	JANGLING	BULL
INKINESS	INTENDED	INVERTER	ISOMETRY	JANITORS	JOHNNIES
INKSTAND	INTENDER	INVESTED	ISOMORPH	JAPANESE	JOINTING

JOINTURE
JOKINGLY
JOLLIEST
JOLLYING
JOSTLING
JOTTINGS
JOURNALS
JOURNEYS
JOUSTING
JOVIALLY
JOYFULLY
JOYOUSLY
JOYRIDER
JOYRIDES
JOYSTICK
JUBILANT
JUBILATE
JUBILEES
JUDAIZER
JUDDERED
JUDGMENT
JUDICIAL
JUGGLERS
JUGGLERY
JUGGLING
JUGULARS
JUICIEST
JULIENNE
JUMBLING
JUMBO
JET
JUMPABLE
JUMPED-
UP
JUMPIEST
JUMPSUIT
JUNAGADH
JUNCTION
JUNCTURE
JUNGFRAU
JUNIPERS
JUNKETER
JUNK
FOOD
JUNK
MAIL
JUNKYARD
JURASSIC
JURATORY
JURISTIC
JUSTICES
JUSTNESS

JUVENILE

K

KAI
MOANA
KAIROUAN
KAKEMONO
KALAHARI
KAMACITE
KAMAKURA
KAMIKAZE
KANARESE
KANAZAWA
KANDAHAR
KANGAROO
KAOLIANG
KAOLINIC
KARELIAN
KASHMIRI
KATAKANA
KATMANDU
KATOWICE
KATTEGAT
KAUMATUA
KAWASAKI
KAYAKERS
KEDGEREE
KEENNESS
KEEPSAKE
KEESHOND
KEEWATIN
KEIGHLEY
KELANTAN
KELOIDAL
KEMEROVO
KENNELED
KENTUCKY
KERATOID
KERATOSE
KERCHIEF
KERKRADE
KEROSENE
KESTEVEN
KESTRELS
KETAMINE
KETOXIME
KEYBOARD
KEYHOLES
KEY
MONEY
KEYNOTES

KEYPUNCH
KEY
RINGS
KEYSTONE
KHARTOUM
KHMERIAN
KHOIKHOI
KHUSKHUS
KIAOCHOW
KIBOSHES
KICKABLE
KICKBACK
KICKOFFS
KICKSHAW
KID-
GLOVE
KIDNAPED
KILKENNY
KILLDEER
KILLINGS
KILLJOYS
KILOBYTE
KILOGRAM
KILOVOLT
KILOWATT
KIMONOED
KINABALU
KINDLIER
KINDLING
KINDNESS
KINDREDS
KINETICS
KINGBIRD
KINGBOLT
KINGDOMS
KINGFISH
KINGLIER
KINGPINS
KINGSHIP
KING-
SIZE
KINGSTON
KINGWANA
KINGWOOD
KINKAJOU
KINKIEST
KINSFOLK
KINSHASA
KIRIBATI
KIRIGAMI
KIRKLEES

KIRKWALL
KISHINEV
KISSABLE
KITCHENS
KLAIPEDA
KLANSMAN
KLONDIKE
KLYSTRON
KNAPSACK
KNAPWEED
KNEADING
KNEECAPS
KNEE
DEEP
KNEE-
DEEP
KNEE-
HIGH
KNEE-
JERK
KNEELING
KNICKERS
KNIGHTED
KNIGHTLY
KNITTERS
KNITTING
KNITWEAR
KNOCKERS
KNOCKING
KNOCKOUT
KNOCK-
UPS
KNOTHOLE
KNOTTIER
KNOTTILY
KNOTTING
KNOTWEED
KNOWABLE
KNOW-
ALLS
KNOWSLEY
KNUCKLED
KNUCKLES
KOHINOOR
KOHLRABI
KOLHAPUR
KOLINSKY
KOMSOMOL
KOOKIEST
KOOTENAY
KORDOFAN
KOSTROMA

KOWTOWED
KOWTOWER
KRAKATOA
KUMAMOTO
KUMQUATS
KUROSAWA
KURTOSIS
KUZNETSK
KWEICHOW
KWEIYANG
KYPHOSIS
KYPHOTIC

L

LABDANUM
LABELING
LABELLED
LABELLER
LABELLUM
LABILITY
LABOURED
LABOURER
LABRADOR
LABURNUM
LACANIAN
LACERANT
LACERATE
LACEWING
LACEWORK
LACINESS
LA
CORUNA
LACRIMAL
LACROSSE
LACTONIC
LACUNOSE
LADDERED
LADYBIRD
LADYLIKE
LADYSHIP
LAEVULIN
LAGGARDS
LA
GUAIRA
LAH-DI-
DAH
LAID-
BACK
LAMASERY
LAMBASTE
LAMBDOID

LAMBENCY
LAMBSKIN
LAME
DUCK
LAMELLAR
LAMENESS
LAMENTED
LAMENTER
LAMINATE
LAMPOONS
LAMPPOST
LAMPREYS
LANCELET
LANDFALL
LANDFORM
LANDINGS
LANDLADY
LANDLORD
LANDMARK
LANDMASS
LANDMINE
LANDRACE
LANDSHUT
LANDSIDE
LANDSLIP
LANDWARD
LANGLAUF
LANGUAGE
LANGUISH
LANKIEST
LANKNESS
LANNERET
LANTERNS
LANYARDS
LAPBOARD
LAP-
CHART
LAPELLED
LAPIDARY
LAPILLUS
LAPPETED
LAPSABLE
LAPWINGS
LARBOARD
LARGESSE
LARKSOME
LARKSPUR
LARRIGAN
LARRIKIN
LARYNGES
LARYNXES

LASHINGS	LAZINESS	LEGALESE	LEVIABLE	LIFE	LINGERIE
LA	LAZULITE	LEGALISM	LEVIGATE	WORK	LINGUINE
SPEZIA	LAZURITE	LEGALIST	LEVITATE	LIFTABLE	LINGUIST
LASSOING	L-	LEGALITY	LEVKOSIA	LIFT-	LINIMENT
LAST	DRIVER	LEGALIZE	LEWDNESS	OFFS	LINKABLE
POST	S	LEGATEES	LEWISHAM	LIGAMENT	LINKAGES
LAST	LEACHING	LEGATINE	LEWISITE	LIGATION	LINKWORK
WORD	LEADSMAN	LEGATION	LEXICONS	LIGATIVE	LINOCUTS
LAS	LEAD	LEGENDRY	LIAISING	LIGATURE	LINOLEUM
VEGAS	TIME	LEGGIEST	LIAISONS	LIGHT	LINOTYPE
LATCHING	LEADWORT	LEGGINGS	LIAONING	ALE	LINSTOCK
LATCHKEY	LEAFIEST	LEG-	LIAOTUNG	LIGHT	LIONFISH
LATENESS	LEAF-	PULLS	LIAOYANG	BOX	LIONIZED
LATERALS	LARD	LEG	LIBATION	LIGHTERS	LIONIZER
LATERITE	LEAFLETS	SIDES	LIBECCIO	LIGHTEST	LIPOGRAM
LATHERED	LEAGUING	LEINSTER	LIBELING	LIGHTING	LIPOIDAL
LATINATE	LEAKAGES	LEISURED	LIBELLED	LIGNEOUS	LIPSTICK
LATINISM	LEAKIEST	LEMMINGS	LIBELLEE	LIGNITIC	LIQUESCE
LATINIST	LEANINGS	LEMONADE	LIBELLER	LIGULATE	LIQUEURS
LATINITY	LEANNESS	LEMUROID	LIBERALS	LIGULOID	LISSOMLY
LATINIZE	LEAPFROG	LENGTHEN	LIBERATE	LIGURIAN	LISTABLE
LATITUDE	LEAP	LENIENCY	LIBERIAN	LIKELIER	LISTENED
LATRINES	YEAR	LENINISM	LIBRETTI	LIKENESS	LISTENER
LATTERLY	LEARNERS	LENINIST	LIBRETTO	LIKENING	LISTEN
LATTICES	LEARNING	LENITIVE	LICENCES	LIKEWISE	IN
LAUDABLE	LEASABLE	LENTICEL	LICENSED	LILONGWE	LISTLESS
LAUDABLY	LEATHERY	LEOPARDS	LICENSEE	LIMA	LITANIES
LAUDANUM	LEAVENED	LEOTARDS	LICENSER	BEAN	LITERACY
LAUGHING	LEAVINGS	LEPIDOTE	LICHENIN	LIMACINE	LITERALS
LAUGHTER	LECITHIN	LEPORINE	LICH	LIMASSOL	LITERARY
LAUNCHED	LECTERNS	LESBIANS	GATE	LIMAVADY	LITERATE
LAUNCHER	LECTURED	LES	LICKINGS	LIMBLESS	LITERATI
LAUNCHES	LECTURER	CAYES	LICORICE	LIMEKILN	LITHARGE
LAUREATE	LECTURES	LESSENED	LIE-	LIMERICK	LITIGANT
LAUSANNE	LEEBOARD	LETDOWNS	DOWNS	LIMINESS	LITIGATE
LAVATION	LEERIEST	LETHALLY	LIENTERY	LIMITARY	LITTERED
LAVATORY	LEE	LETHARGY	LIFE	LIMITING	LITTORAL
LAVENDER	SHORE	LETRASET	BELT	LIMNETIC	LIVE
LAVISHED	LEE	LETTERED	LIFEBOAT	LIMONENE	BAIT
LAVISHER	TIDES	LETTERER	LIFE	LIMONITE	LIVELIER
LAVISHLY	LEFT-	LETTINGS	BUOY	LIMOUSIN	LIVELONG
LAWFULLY	HAND	LETTUCES	LIFELESS	LIMPIDLY	LIVENING
LAWGIVER	LEFTISTS	LEUCITIC	LIFELIKE	LIMPNESS	LIVERIED
LAWSUITS	LEFTOVER	LEUKEMIA	LIFELINE	LINALOOL	LIVERIES
LAXATION	LEFT	LEVANTER	LIFELONG	LINCHPIN	LIVERISH
LAXATIVE	OVER	LEVELING	LIFE	LINDWALL	LIVETRAP
LAYABOUT	LEFTWARD	LEVELLED	PEER	LINEAGES	LIVEWARE
LAYERING	LEFT	LEVELLER	LIFE-	LINEALLY	LIVE
LAYETTES	WING	LEVERAGE	SIZE	LINESMAN	WIRE
LAYSHAFT	LEGACIES	LEVERETS	LIFESPAN	LINESMEN	LIVONIAN
LAYWOMAN	LEGAL	LEVERING	LIFETIME	LINGERED	LIXIVIUM
LAYWOMEN	AID			LINGERER	

LLANDAFF
LLANELLI
LOADINGS
LOADSTAR
LOANABLE
LOANWORD
LOATHING
LOBBYING
LOBBYISM
LOBBYIST
LOBELINE
LOBLOLLY
LOBOTOMY
LOBSTERS
LOCALISM
LOCALIST
LOCALITY
LOCALIZE
LOCATING
LOCATION
LOCATIVE
LOCKABLE
LOCKOUTS
LOCOWEED
LOCUTION
LODESTAR
LODGINGS
LODGMENT
LODICULE
LOESSIAL
LOFTIEST
LOGBOOKS
LOG
CABIN
LOGICIAN
LOGICISM
LOGISTIC
LOGOGRAM
LOGOTYPE
LOGOTYPY
LOITERED
LOITERER
LOLLARDY
LOLLIPOP
LOLLOPED
LOMBARDY
LONDONER
LONDRINA
LONELIER
LONESOME

LONE
WOLF
LONGBOAT
LONGBOWS
LONGERON
LONG
FACE
LONGFORD
LONGHAND
LONG-
HAUL
LONGHORN
LONGINGS
LONG
JUMP
LONG-
LIFE
LONGSHIP
LONG
SHOT
LONGSPUR
LONG
SUIT
LONG-
TERM
LONG
TONS
LONGUEUR
LONG
WAVE
LONGWAYS
LOOKER-
ON
LOOKOUTS
LOONIEST
LOONY
BIN
LOOPHOLE
LOOSEBOX
LOOSE
END
LOOSENED
LOOSENER
LOP-
EARED
LOP-
SIDED
LOQUITUR
LORDLIER
LORDOSIS
LORDOTIC
LORDSHIP
LORICATE

LORIKEET
LORRAINE
LOTHARIO
LOTHIANS
LOUDNESS
LOUNGERS
LOUNGING
LOUSIEST
LOVEBIRD
LOVELESS
LOVELIER
LOVELIES
LOVELORN
LOVESICK
LOVINGLY
LOWBROWS
LOWERING
LOWLANDS
LOWLIEST
LOW-
LYING
LOW
TIDES
LOW
WATER
LOYALISM
LOYALIST
LOZENGES
LUCIDITY
LUCKIEST
LUCKLESS
LUCKY
DIP
LUDDITES
LUDHIANA
LUGHOLES
LUGSAILS
LUGWORMS
LUKEWARM
LUMBERED
LUMBERER
LUMINARY
LUMINOUS
LUMPFISH
LUMPIEST
LUMP
SUMS
LUNATICS
LUNATION
LUNCHEON
LUNCHING
LUNEBURG

LUNGFISH
LUNGWORM
LUNGWORT
LUNULATE
LURCHING
LURINGLY
LUSATIAN
LUSCIOUS
LUSHNESS
LUSTRATE
LUSTROUS
LUTANIST
LUTENIST
LUTEOLIN
LUTETIUM
LUTHERAN
LUXATION
LUXURIES
LYALLPUR
LYCH
GATE
LYCHGATE
LYCH
GATE
LYINGS-
IN
LYMPHOID
LYMPHOMA
LYNCHING
LYNCH
LAW
LYNCHPIN
LYONNAIS
LYREBIRD
LYRICISM
LYRICIST
LYSOSOME
LYSOZYME

M

MACADMIA
MACARONI
MACAROON
MACERATE
MACHETES
MACHINED
MACHINES
MACHISMO
MACKEREL
MACRURAL
MACRURAN

MADDENED
MADHOUSE
MADONNAS
MADRIGAL
MADURESE
MAEBASHI
MAENADIC
MAESTOSO
MAESTROS
MAFIKENG
MAGAZINE
MAGELLAN
MAGHREBI
MAGIC
EYE
MAGICIAN
MAGNATES
MAGNESIA
MAGNETIC
MAGNETON
MAGNETOS
MAGNOLIA
MAHARAJA
MAHARANI
MAHATMAS
MAHOGANY
MAIDENLY
MAIEUTIC
MAILABLE
MAILBAGS
MAILSHOT
MAINLAND
MAIN
LINE
MAINMAST
MAINSAIL
MAINSTAY
MAINTAIN
MAJESTIC
MAJOLICA
MAJORCAN
MAJORING
MAJORITY
MAKE
GOOD
MAKING
DO
MALADIES
MALAGASY
MALAISES
MALARIAL
MALARKEY

MALAYSIA
MAL DE
MER
MALDIVES
MALENESS
MALIGNED
MALIGNER
MALIGNLY
MALINGER
MALLARDS
MALPOSED
MALTREAT
MALTSTER
MALVASIA
MAMA'S
BOY
MAMMOTHS
MANACLED
MANACLES
MANAGERS
MANAGING
MANASSAS
MANATOID
MANCIPLE
MANDALAY
MANDAMUS
MANDARIN
MANDATED
MANDATES
MANDIBLE
MANDOLIN
MANDORLA
MANDRAKE
MANDRILL
MAN-
EATER
MANEUVER
MANFULLY
MANGABEY
MANGANIC
MANGANIN
MANGIEST
MANGLING
MANGONEL
MANGROVE
MANHOLES
MANHOURS
MANHUNTS
MANIACAL
MANICURE
MANIFEST

MANIFOLD	MARINERS	MATADORS	MEDICALS	MENSWEAR	MEZEREON
MANIKINS	MARIPOSA	MATANZAS	MEDICARE	MENTALLY	MEZEREUM
MANITOBA	MARITIME	MATCHBOX	MEDICATE	MENTIONS	MEZIERES
MANLIEST	MARJORAM	MATCHING	MEDICINE	MEPHITIC	MIAOWING
MANNERED	MARKDOWN	MATERIAL	MEDIEVAL	MEPHITIS	MICELLAR
MANNERLY	MARKEDLY	MATERIEL	MEDIOCRE	MERCHANT	MICHIGAN
MANNHEIM	MARKETED	MATERNAL	MEDITATE	MERCIFUL	MICROBES
MANNITIC	MARKETER	MATINEES	MEDUSOID	MERCURIC	MICRODOT
MANNITOL	MARKINGS	MATRICES	MEEKNESS	MERGENCE	MIDBRAIN
MAN OF	MARKSMAN	MATRIXES	MEETINGS	MERIDIAN	MIDDLE
WAR	MARKSMEN	MATRONAL	MEGALITH	MERINGUE	CS
MAN-OF-	MARMOSET	MATRONLY	MEGATONS	MERISTEM	MIDDLING
WAR	MAROONED	MATTERED	MEGAVOLT	MERISTIC	MIDFIELD
MANORIAL	MAROQUIN	MATTRESS	MEGAWATT	MERITING	MIDLANDS
MANPOWER	MARQUEES	MATURATE	MELAMINE	MERMAIDS	MIDNIGHT
MANSARDS	MARQUESS	MATURELY	MELANGES	MERRIEST	MIDPOINT
MANSHOLT	MARQUISE	MATURING	MELANISM	MERRY	MIDRIFFS
MANSIONS	MARRIAGE	MATURITY	MELANIST	MEN	MIDWIVES
MAN-	MARRIEDS	MAUBEUGE	MELANITE	MESCALIN	MIGHTIER
SIZED	MARRYING	MAVERICK	MELANOID	MESDAMES	MIGHTILY
MANTILLA	MARSHALS	MAXILLAR	MELANOMA	MESMERIC	MIGRAINE
MANTISES	MARSH	MAXIMIZE	MELANOUS	MESOCARP	MIGRANTS
MANTISSA	GAS	MAXIMUMS	MELINITE	MESODERM	MIGRATED
MANTLING	MARTABAN	MAYORESS	MELLOWED	MESOGLEA	MIGRATOR
MAN-TO-	MARTAGON	MAYPOLES	MELLOWER	MESOZOIC	MILANESE
MAN	MARTELLO	MAZATLAN	MELLOWLY	MESQUITE	MILCH
MANUALLY	MARTIANS	MAZURKAS	MELODEON	MESSAGES	COW
MANURING	MARTINET	MEA	MELODIES	MESSENIA	MILDEWED
MANX	MARTINIS	CULPA	MELODIST	MESSIAHS	MILDNESS
CATS	MARTYRED	MEAGRELY	MELODIZE	MESSIEST	MILEAGES
MANYFOLD	MARVELED	MEALIEST	MELTABLE	MESSMATE	MILEPOST
MAPPABLE	MARXISTS	MEALWORM	MELTDOWN	MESSUAGE	MILIARIA
MAPPINGS	MARYLAND	MEANINGS	MEMBRANE	MESTIZOS	MILITANT
MAQUETTE	MARZIPAN	MEANNESS	MEMENTOS	METALING	MILITARY
MARABOUS	MASSACRE	MEANTIME	MEMORIAL	METALLED	MILITATE
MARANHAO	MASSAGED	MEASURED	MEMORIES	METALLIC	MILITIAS
MARASMIC	MASSAGER	MEASURER	MEMORIZE	METAMALE	MILKFISH
MARASMUS	MASSAGES	MEASURES	MEMSAHIB	METAMERE	MILKIEST
MARATHON	MASSEDLY	MEATBALL	MENACING	METAPHOR	MILKMAID
MARAUDER	MASSETER	MEATIEST	MENARCHE	METAZOAN	MILK
MARBLING	MASSEURS	MECHANIC	MENDABLE	METAZOIC	RUNS
MARCHERS	MASSICOT	MECHELEN	MENHADEN	METEORIC	MILKSOPS
MARCHESA	MASTERED	MECONIUM	MENIALLY	METERING	MILKWEED
MARCHESE	MASTERLY	MEDALLIC	MENINGES	METHANOL	MILKWORT
MARCHING	MASTHEAD	MEDDLERS	MENISCUS	METHYLAL	MILKY
MARGARIC	MASTIFFS	MEDDLING	MEN-OF-	METHYLIC	WAY
MARGINAL	MASTITIS	MEDELLIN	WAR	METONYMY	MILLABLE
MARIANAO	MASTODON	MEDIALLY	MENOLOGY	METRICAL	MILLIAMP
MARIGOLD	MASTOIDS	MEDIATED	MEN'S	METRITIS	MILLIARD
MARIMBAS	MASURIAN	MEDIATOR	ROOM	MEUNIERE	MILLIARY
MARINADE	MATABELE	MEDICAID	MENSURAL	MEXICALI	MILLIBAR
MARINATE					MILLIGAN

MILLINER	MISLAYER	MODIFIER	MONOCRAT	MORALISM	MOULDIER
MILLIONS	MISMATCH	MODIOLUS	MONOCYTE	MORALIST	MOULDING
MILLPOND	MISNOMER	MODISHLY	MONOGAMY	MORALITY	MOULMEIN
MILLRACE	MISOGAMY	MODULATE	MONOGENY	MORALIZE	MOULTING
MILTONIC	MISOGYNY	MOHAMMED	MONOGRAM	MORASSES	MOUNTAIN
MIMETITE	MISOLOGY	MOIETIES	MONOGYNY	MORATORY	MOUNTIES
MIMICKED	MISPLACE	MOISTURE	MONOHULL	MORAVIAN	MOUNTING
MIMICKER	MISPLEAD	MOLALITY	MONOLITH	MORBIDLY	MOURNERS
MINARETS	MISPRINT	MOLASSES	MONOLOGY	MORBIFIC	MOURNFUL
MINATORY	MISQUOTE	MOLDAVIA	MONOMIAL	MORBIHAN	MOURNING
MINCE	MISSHAPE	MOLDERED	MONOPOLE	MORDANCY	MOUSIEST
PIE	MISSILES	MOLDIEST	MONOPOLY	MOREOVER	MOUSSAKA
MINDANAO	MISSIONS	MOLDINGS	MONORAIL	MORESQUE	MOUTHFUL
MINDLESS	MISSIVES	MOLECULE	MONOSEMY	MORIBUND	MOUTHING
MIND'S	MISSOURI	MOLEHILL	MONOSOME	MORNINGS	MOVABLES
EYE	MISSPELL	MOLESKIN	MONOTONE	MOROCCAN	MOVEMENT
MINERALS	MISSPELT	MOLESTED	MONOTONY	MORONISM	MOVINGLY
MINGIEST	MISSPEND	MOLESTER	MONOTYPE	MOROSELY	MOZZETTA
MINGLING	MISSPENT	MOLLUSCS	MONOXIDE	MORPHEME	MUCHNESS
MINICABS	MISSTATE	MOLUCCAS	MONROVIA	MORPHEUS	MUCILAGE
MINIMIZE	MISTAKEN	MOLYBDIC	MONSIEUR	MORPHINE	MUCINOUS
MINIMUMS	MISTAKES	MOMENTUM	MONSOONS	MORPHING	MUCKHEAP
MINISTER	MISTIMED	MONACHAL	MONSTERS	MORRISON	MUCKIEST
MINISTRY	MISTREAT	MONADISM	MONTAGES	MORTALLY	MUCKRAKE
MINORCAN	MISTRESS	MONAGHAN	MONTEITH	MORTGAGE	MUCKWORM
MINORITY	MISTRIAL	MONANDRY	MONTEREY	MORTIMER	MUCOSITY
MINOTAUR	MISTRUST	MONARCHS	MONTREAL	MORTISER	MUD
MINSTERS	MISUSAGE	MONARCHY	MONTREUX	MORTISES	BATHS
MINSTREL	MISUSING	MONASTIC	MONUMENT	MORTMAIN	MUDDIEST
MINUTELY	MITCHELL	MONAURAL	MOOCHING	MORTUARY	MUDDLING
MINUTIAE	MITICIDE	MONAZITE	MOODIEST	MOSEYING	MUDDYING
MINUTING	MITIGATE	MONETARY	MOONBEAM	MOSQUITO	MUDFLATS
MIRACLES	MITTIMUS	MONETIZE	MOONCALF	MOSSIEST	MUDGUARD
MIREPOIX	MIXED	MONEYBOX	MOONFISH	MOTHBALL	MUDPACKS
MIRRORED	BAG	MONGOLIA	MOONLESS	MOTHERED	MUDSTONE
MIRTHFUL	MIXTURES	MONGOLIC	MOONRISE	MOTHERLY	MUENSTER
MISANDRY	MNEMONIC	MONGOOSE	MOONSEED	MOTILITY	MUEZZINS
MISAPPLY	MOBILITY	MONGRELS	MOON	MOTIONED	MUFFLERS
MISCARRY	MOBILIZE	MONISTIC	SHOT	MOTIONER	MUFFLING
MISCHIEF	MOBOCRAT	MONITION	MOONWORT	MOTIVATE	MUFULIRA
MISCIBLE	MOBSTERS	MONITORS	MOORCOCK	MOTIVITY	MUGGIEST
MISCOUNT	MOCCASIN	MONITORY	MOORHENS	MOT	MUGGINGS
MISDEEDS	MOCKABLE	MONKEYED	MOORINGS	JUSTE	MUG'S
MISERERE	MODALITY	MONKFISH	MOORLAND	MOTORBUS	GAME
MISERIES	MODELING	MON-	MOORWORT	MOTORCAR	MUGSHOTS
MISFIRED	MODELLED	KHMER	MOOSE	MOTORING	MUGWUMPS
MISFIRES	MODELLER	MONKHOOD	JAW	MOTORIST	MULATTOS
MISGUIDE	MODERATE	MONMOUTH	MOPINGLY	MOTORIZE	MULBERRY
MISHEARD	MODERATO	MONOACID	MOQUETTE	MOTORMAN	MULCHING
MISHMASH	MODESTLY	MONOCARP	MORAINAL	MOTORMEN	MULCTING
MISJUDGE	MODIFIED	MONOCLES	MORAINES	MOTORWAY	MULETEER

MULHOUSE	MUZZIEST	NARKIEST	NEEDLESS	NEW	NITRATES
MULISHLY	MUZZLING	NARRATED	NEEDLING	HAVEN	NITROGEN
MULLIONS	MYCELIAL	NARRATOR	NEGATING	NEWLYWED	NITROSYL
MULTIFID	MYCELIUM	NARROWED	NEGATION	NEW	NIVATION
MULTIPED	MYCELOID	NARROWLY	NEGATIVE	MOONS	NOBBLING
MULTIPLE	MYCETOMA	NASALITY	NEGLIGEE	NEWSCAST	NOBELIUM
MULTIPLY	MYCOLOGY	NASALIZE	NEGRILLO	NEWSPEAK	NOBILITY
MUMBLING	MYELINIC	NASCENCE	NEGRITIC	NEWSREEL	NOBLEMAN
MUNCHING	MYELITIS	NASTIEST	NEGROISM	NEWSROOM	NOBLEMEN
MUNIMENT	MYLONITE	NATATION	NEIGHING	NEW	NOBODIES
MUNITION	MYOGENIC	NATIONAL	NEKTONIC	TOWNS	NOCTURNE
MURALIST	MYOGRAPH	NATIVISM	NEMATODE	NEW	NODALITY
MURDERED	MYOLOGIC	NATIVIST	NEMBUTAL	WAVES	NODOSITY
MURDERER	MYOSOTIS	NATIVITY	NEOGAEAN	NEW	NO-GO
MURICATE	MYOTONIA	NATTERED	NEOMYCIN	WORLD	AREA
MURKIEST	MYOTONIC	NATTIEST	NEONATAL	NEXT-	NOISIEST
MURMANSK	MYRIAPOD	NATURALS	NEOPHYTE	DOOR	NOMADISM
MURMURED	MYSTICAL	NATURISM	NEOPLASM	NHA	NOMINATE
MURMURER	MYSTIQUE	NATURIST	NEOPRENE	TRANG	NOMINEES
MURRAINS	MYTHICAL	NAUPLIUS	NEOTERIC	NIARCHOS	NOMISTIC
MURRELET	MYTILENE	NAUSEATE	NEPALESE	NIBBLING	NOMOLOGY
MURRHINE		NAUSEOUS	NEPENTHE	NICENESS	NONESUCH
MUSCATEL	**N**	NAUTICAL	NEPHRITE	NICETIES	NON-
MUSCLING	NABOBERY	NAUTILUS	NEPOTISM	NICHROME	EVENT
MUSCULAR	NACELLES	NAVICERT	NEPOTIST	NICKELED	NONJUROR
MUSHIEST	NACREOUS	NAVIGATE	NERVIEST	NICKELIC	NON
MUSHROOM	NAGALAND	NAVY	NESCIENT	NICKNACK	LICET
MUSICALE	NAGASAKI	BLUE	NEST	NICKNAME	NONMETAL
MUSICALS	NAIL	NAZARENE	EGGS	NICOTINE	NON
MUSICIAN	FILE	NAZARETH	NESTLING	NIELLIST	RIGID
MUSINGLY	NAILHEAD	NDJAMENA	NETTLING	NIFTIEST	NONSENSE
MUSKETRY	NAINSOOK	NEAP	NETWORKS	NIGERIAN	NONSTICK
MUSKIEST	NAISSANT	TIDE	NEURITIC	NIGGARDS	NONTOXIC
MUSQUASH	NAMANGAN	NEARCTIC	NEURITIS	NIGGLERS	NONUNION
MUSTACHE	NAME	NEAR	NEURONIC	NIGGLING	NONVOTER
MUSTANGS	DAYS	EAST	NEUROSES	NIGHTCAP	NONWHITE
MUSTELID	NAMEDROP	NEAR	NEUROSIS	NIGHTJAR	NOONTIME
MUSTERED	NAMELESS	MISS	NEUROTIC	NIGHT	NORMALLY
MUSTIEST	NAMESAKE	NEARNESS	NEUTERED	OWL	NORMANDY
MUTATION	NAMETAPE	NEARSIDE	NEUTRALS	NIHILISM	NORSEMAN
MUTENESS	NAMIBIAN	NEATNESS	NEUTRINO	NIHILIST	NORSEMEN
MUTICOUS	NANCHANG	NEBRASKA	NEUTRONS	NIHILITY	NORTHERN
MUTILATE	NANTERRE	NEBULIZE	NEW	NIJMEGEN	NORTHING
MUTINEER	NAPHTHOL	NEBULOUS	BLOOD	NIMBLEST	NOSEBAGS
MUTINIED	NAPHTHYL	NECKBAND	NEW	NIMBUSES	NOSEBAND
MUTINIES	NAPIFORM	NECKLACE	BROOM	NINEFOLD	NOSE
MUTINOUS	NARBONNE	NECKLETS	NEWCOMER	NINEPINS	BAND
MUTTERED	NARCEINE	NECKLINE	NEW	NINETEEN	NOSECONE
MUTTERER	NARCISSI	NECKTIES	DEALS	NINETIES	NOSEDIVE
MUTUALLY	NARCOSIS	NECROSIS	NEW-	NIPPIEST	NOSEGAYS
MUZOREWA	NARCOTIC	NECROTIC	FOUND	NIRVANAS	NOSINESS
		NEEDIEST	NEWHAVEN	NIRVANIC	NOSOLOGY

NOSTRILS	NURISTAN	OBVOLUTE	OILFIELD	ONCOMING	OPINICUS
NOSTRUMS	NURSLING	OCARINAS	OIL-	ONDAATJE	OPINIONS
NOTA	NURTURED	OCCASION	FIRED	ONDOGRAM	OPIUMISM
BENE	NURTURER	OCCIDENT	OILINESS	ONE-	OPOSSUMS
NOTABLES	NUTATION	OCCLUSAL	OIL	HORSE	OPPILATE
NOTARIAL	NUT-	OCCUPANT	PAINT	ONE-ON-	OPPONENT
NOTARIES	BROWN	OCCUPIED	OILSKINS	ONE	OPPOSING
NOTARIZE	NUTCASES	OCCUPIER	OIL	ONE-	OPPOSITE
NOTATION	NUTHATCH	OCCURRED	SLICK	PIECE	OPPUGNER
NOTCHING	NUTHOUSE	OCEANIAN	OILSTONE	ONE-	OPSONIZE
NOTEBOOK	NUTRIENT	OCHREOUS	OIL	SIDED	OPTATIVE
NOTECASE	NUTSHELL	OCOTILLO	WELLS	ONE-TO-	OPTICIAN
NOTELETS	NUTTIEST	OCTAGONS	OINTMENT	ONE	OPTIMISM
NOTEPADS	NUZZLING	OCTARCHY	OKAVANGO	ONE-	OPTIMIST
NOTICING	NYMPHETS	OCTOBERS	OKLAHOMA	TRACK	OPTIMIZE
NOTIFIED	NYSTATIN	OCTOROON	OLD	ONLOOKER	OPTIONAL
NOTIFIER		OCULISTS	FLAME	ONRUSHES	OPULENCE
NOTIONAL	**O**	ODDBALLS	OLD	ON-	ORACULAR
NOTOGAEA	OAFISHLY	ODDITIES	GUARD	SCREEN	ORANGERY
NOTORNIS	OAKVILLE	ODDMENTS	OLD	ONSTREAM	ORATIONS
NOVATION	OARLOCKS	ODIOUSLY	HANDS	ONTOGENY	ORATORIO
NOVELIST	OATCAKES	ODOMETER	OLD	ONTOLOGY	ORBITING
NOVELLAS	OBDURACY	ODONTOID	MAIDS	OOGAMOUS	ORCHARDS
NOVEMBER	OBDURATE	ODYSSEYS	OLDSTERS	OOGONIAL	ORCHITIC
NOVGOROD	OBEDIENT	OENOLOGY	OLD-	OOGONIUM	ORCHITIS
NOWADAYS	OBEISANT	OESTRIOL	TIMER	OOLOGIST	ORDAINED
NUBECULA	OBELISKS	OESTRONE	OLD	OOPHYTIC	ORDAINER
NUBILITY	OBERLAND	OESTROUS	WOMAN	OOSPHERE	ORDERING
NUCELLAR	OBITUARY	OFF AND	OLD	OOSPORIC	ORDINALS
NUCELLUS	OBJECTED	ON	WOMEN	OOTHECAL	ORDINAND
NUCLEASE	OBJECTOR	OFF	OLD	OOZINESS	ORDINARY
NUCLEATE	OBLATION	BREAK	WORLD	OPALESCE	ORDINATE
NUDENESS	OBLATORY	OFFENCES	OLEANDER	OPAQUELY	ORDNANCE
NUDICAUL	OBLIGATE	OFFENDED	OLEASTER	OPENCAST	ORENBURG
NUGATORY	OBLIGING	OFFENDER	OLEFINIC	OPEN-	ORGANDIE
NUISANCE	OBLIQUES	OFFERING	OLIBANUM	EYED	ORGANISM
NULL	OBLIVION	OFF-	OLIGARCH	OPEN	ORGANIST
SETS	OBSCURED	GLIDE	OLIGURIA	FIRE	ORGANIZE
NUMBERED	OBSERVED	OFFICERS	OLIVE	OPENINGS	ORGASMIC
NUMBFISH	OBSERVER	OFFICIAL	OIL	OPENNESS	ORIENTAL
NUMBNESS	OBSESSED	OFFPRINT	OLYMPIAD	OPEN-	ORIFICES
NUMERACY	OBSIDIAN	OFFSHOOT	OLYMPIAN	PLAN	ORIGINAL
NUMERALS	OBSOLETE	OFFSHORE	OMDURMAN	OPEN	ORINASAL
NUMERARY	OBSTACLE	OFFSTAGE	OMELETTE	SHOP	ORNAMENT
NUMERATE	OBSTRUCT	OFF	OMISSION	OPENWORK	ORNATELY
NUMEROUS	OBTAINED	STAGE	OMITTING	OPERABLE	ORNITHIC
NUMINOUS	OBTAINER	OFF-	OMNIVORE	OPERABLY	OROGENIC
NUMMULAR	OBTRUDED	WHITE	OMPHALOS	OPERATED	OROMETER
NUMSKULL	OBTRUDER	OFT	ON AND	OPERATIC	ORPHANED
NUNEATON	OBTUSELY	TIMES	OFF	OPERATOR	ORPIMENT
NUPTIALS	OBVIATED	OHMMETER	ONCE-	OPERETTA	ORRERIES
		OILCLOTH	OVER	OPHIDIAN	
			ONCOLOGY		

ORTHODOX	OUTLINES	OVERDREW	OVERWORK	PALENCIA	PANPIPES
ORTHOEPY	OUTLIVED	OVERFLEW	OVIDUCAL	PALENESS	PANSOPHY
OSCITANT	OUTLOOKS	OVERFLOW	OVIPOSIT	PALETTES	PANTHEON
OSCULANT	OUTLYING	OVERGROW	OVULATED	PALFREYS	PANTHERS
OSCULATE	OUTMODED	OVERHAND	OWLISHLY	PALINODE	PANTILES
OSNABURG	OUTPOINT	OVERHANG	OWN	PALISADE	PANTRIES
OSSIFIED	OUTPOSTS	OVERHAUL	GOALS	PALLADIC	PAPACIES
OSSIFIER	OUTRAGED	OVERHEAD	OXBRIDGE	PALLIATE	PAPERBOY
OSTEITIC	OUTRAGES	OVERHEAR	OXIDASIC	PALLIDLY	PAPERING
OSTEITIS	OUTREACH	OVERHEAT	OXIDIZED	PALLIEST	PAPILLON
OSTINATO	OUTRIDER	OVERHUNG	OXIDIZER	PALL	PAPISTRY
OSTIOLAR	OUTRIGHT	OVERKILL	OXPECKER	MALL	PAPOOSES
OSTRACOD	OUTRIVAL	OVERLAID	OXTONGUE	PALMETTE	PARABLES
OTIOSITY	OUTSHINE	OVERLAIN	OXYGENIC	PALMETTO	PARABOLA
OTOSCOPE	OUTSHONE	OVERLAND	OXYMORON	PALMIEST	PARADIGM
OTTOMANS	OUTSHOOT	OVERLAPS	OXYTOCIC	PALMISTS	PARADING
OUTBLUFF	OUTSIDER	OVERLAYS	OXYTOCIN	PALMITIN	PARADISE
OUTBOARD	OUTSIDES	OVERLEAF	OZONIZER	PALO	PARADROP
OUTBOUND	OUTSMART	OVERLOAD		ALTO	PARAFFIN
OUTBRAVE	OUTSTAND	OVERLONG	**P**	PALOMINO	PARAGOGE
OUTBREAK	OUTSTARE	OVERLOOK		PALPABLE	PARAGONS
OUTBREED	OUTSTRIP	OVERLORD	PACIFIED	PALPABLY	PARAGUAY
OUTBURST	OUTSWING	OVERMUCH	PACIFIER	PALPATED	PARAKEET
OUTCASTE	OUT-	OVERPAID	PACIFISM	PALTERER	PARALLAX
OUTCASTS	TAKES	OVERPASS	PACIFIST	PALTRIER	PARALLEL
OUTCLASS	OUTVOTED	OVERPLAY	PACKABLE	PALTRILY	PARALYSE
OUTCOMES	OUTWARDS	OVERRATE	PACKAGED	PAMPERED	PARAMENT
OUTCRIES	OUTWEIGH	OVERRIDE	PACKAGER	PAMPERER	PARAMOUR
OUTCROPS	OUTWORKS	OVERRIPE	PACKAGES	PAMPHLET	PARANOIA
OUTCROSS	OVALNESS	OVERRODE	PADDLING	PAMPLONA	PARANOID
OUTDATED	OVARITIS	OVERRULE	PADDOCKS	PANACEAN	PARAPETS
OUTDOING	OVATIONS	OVERSEAS	PADLOCKS	PANACEAS	PARAQUAT
OUTDOORS	OVENBIRD	OVERSEEN	PAEONIES	PANATELA	PARASITE
OUTFACED	OVENWARE	OVERSEER	PAGANISM	PANCAKES	PARASOLS
OUTFALLS	OVERALLS	OVERSELL	PAGANIST	PANCREAS	PARAVANE
OUTFIELD	OVERARCH	OVERSHOE	PAGANIZE	PANDA	PAR
OUTFIGHT	OVERAWED	OVERSHOT	PAGEANTS	CAR	AVION
OUTFLANK	OVERBEAR	OVERSIDE	PAGINATE	PANDANUS	PARAZOAN
OUTFLOWS	OVERBIDS	OVERSIZE	PAGO	PANDEMIC	PARCELED
OUTFLUNG	OVERBOOK	OVERSOLD	PAGO	PANDERED	PARCENER
OUTFOXED	OVERBORE	OVERSTAY	PAGURIAN	PANDERER	PARCHING
OUTGOING	OVERCALL	OVERSTEP	PAHOEHOE	PANELING	PARDONED
OUT-	OVERCAME	OVERTAKE	PAINLESS	PANELLED	PARDONER
GROUP	OVERCAST	OVERTIME	PAINTERS	PANGOLIN	PARENTAL
OUTGROWN	OVERCOAT	OVERTIRE	PAINTING	PANICKED	PARHELIC
OUT-	OVERCOME	OVERTONE	PAKISTAN	PANICLED	PARIETAL
HEROD	OVERCOOK	OVERTOOK	PALADINS	PANMIXIA	PARISHES
OUTHOUSE	OVERCROP	OVERTURE	PALATALS	PANNIERS	PARISIAN
OUTLAWED	OVERDONE	OVERTURN	PALATIAL	PANNIKIN	PARKIEST
OUTLAWRY	OVERDOSE	OVERVIEW	PALATINE	PANOPTIC	PARKLAND
OUTLINED	OVERDRAW	OVERWIND	PALAVERS	PANORAMA	PARKWAYS

PARLANCE	PASTE-	PEACOCKS	PENANCES	PERISARC	PHAETONS
PARLANDO	UPS	PEAFOWLS	PENCHANT	PERISHED	PHALANGE
PARLEYED	PASTICHE	PEA	PENCILED	PERISHER	PHANTASM
PARLEYER	PASTIEST	GREEN	PENDANTS	PERIWIGS	PHANTASY
PARLOURS	PASTILLE	PEAKIEST	PENDULUM	PERJURED	PHANTOMS
PARMESAN	PASTIMES	PEARLIER	PENGUINS	PERJURER	PHARAOHS
PARODIED	PASTINGS	PEARLITE	PENITENT	PERKIEST	PHARISEE
PARODIES	PASTORAL	PEARMAIN	PENKNIFE	PERLITIC	PHARMACY
PARODIST	PASTRAMI	PEASANTS	PEN	PERMEANT	PHASE-
PAROLING	PASTRIES	PEBBLING	NAMES	PERMEATE	OUT
PAROTOID	PASTURED	PECCABLE	PENNANTS	PERMUTED	PHEASANT
PAROXYSM	PASTURES	PECCANCY	PENNINES	PERONEAL	PHENETIC
PARROTED	PATAGIUM	PECTORAL	PENN'ORT	PERORATE	PHENOLIC
PARRYING	PATCHIER	PECULATE	H	PEROXIDE	PHILLIPS
PARSABLE	PATCHILY	PECULIAR	PENOLOGY	PERSONAL	PHILTRES
PARSIFAL	PATCHING	PEDAGOGY	PENSIONS	PERSONAS	PHIMOSIS
PARSNIPS	PATELLAR	PEDALFER	PENSTOCK	PERSPIRE	PHONE
PARTAKEN	PATELLAS	PEDALING	PENTACLE	PERSUADE	BOX
PARTAKER	PATENTED	PEDALLED	PENTAGON	PERTNESS	PHONE-
PARTERRE	PATENTEE	PEDANTIC	PENTOMIC	PERUSALS	INS
PARTHIAN	PATENTLY	PEDANTRY	PENTOSAN	PERUSING	PHONEMES
PARTIBLE	PATENTOR	PEDDLERS	PENUMBRA	PERUVIAN	PHONEMIC
PARTICLE	PATERNAL	PEDDLING	PENZANCE	PERVADED	PHONETIC
PARTINGS	PATERSON	PEDERAST	PEOPLING	PERVADER	PHONIEST
PARTISAN	PATHETIC	PEDESTAL	PEPPERED	PERVERSE	PHOSGENE
PARTNERS	PATHLESS	PEDICURE	PEP	PERVERTS	PHOSPHOR
PART-	PATHOGEN	PEDIFORM	PILLS	PERVIOUS	PHOTOFIT
SONG	PATHWAYS	PEDIGREE	PEP	PESHAWAR	PHOTOMAP
PART-	PATIENCE	PEDIMENT	TALKS	PESKIEST	PHOTOPIA
TIME	PATIENTS	PEDIPALP	PEPTIZER	PESTERED	PHOTOPIC
PART	PATRIALS	PEDOLOGY	PER	PESTERER	PHOTOSET
WORK	PATRIOTS	PEDUNCLE	ANNUM	PESTHOLE	PHRASING
PARTYING	PATRONAL	PEEKABOO	PERCEIVE	PETALINE	PHRATRIC
PAR	PATTERED	PEELINGS	PERCHING	PETALODY	PHREATIC
VALUE	PATTERNS	PEEPHOLE	PERFORCE	PETALOID	PHTHALIC
PARVENUS	PATULOUS	PEEPSHOW	PERFUMED	PETECHIA	PHTHISIC
PARZIVAL	PAUNCHES	PEERAGES	PERFUMER	PETITION	PHTHISIS
PASADENA	PAVEMENT	PEERLESS	PERFUMES	PETIT	PHYLETIC
PASSABLE	PAVILION	PEGBOARD	PERGOLAS	MAL	PHYLLITE
PASSABLY	PAVLODAR	PEIGNOIR	PERIANTH	PET	PHYLLODE
PASSAGES	PAVONINE	PEKINESE	PERIBLEM	NAMES	PHYLLOID
PASSBOOK	PAWKIEST	PELICANS	PERICARP	PETRARCH	PHYLLOME
PASS	PAWNSHOP	PELLAGRA	PERIDERM	PETROLIC	PHYSICAL
BOOK	PAYCHECK	PELLICLE	PERIDIUM	PETROSAL	PHYSIQUE
PASSERBY	PAYLOADS	PELL-	PERIGEAN	PETTIEST	PIACENZA
PASSIBLE	PAYMENTS	MELL	PERIGEES	PETTIFOG	PIACULAR
PASSIONS	PAY	PELLUCID	PERIGYNY	PETULANT	PIANISTS
PASSKEYS	PHONE	PELVISES	PERILOUS	PETUNIAS	PIANOLAS
PASSOVER	PAYROLLS	PEMBROKE	PERILUNE	PETUNTSE	PIASSAVA
PASSPORT	PAYSLIPS	PEMMICAN	PERINEUM	PEWTERER	PIASTRES
PASSWORD	PEACEFUL	PENALIZE	PERIODIC	PFENNIGS	PICADORS
PASTERNS			PERIOTIC		

PICCANIN	PINCE-	PITILESS	PLAYBOYS	PLUMPEST	POLLUTER
PICCOLOS	NEZ	PIT	PLAYGOER	PLUMPING	POLO
PICKABLE	PINCHING	PROPS	PLAYLIST	PLUNGERS	NECK
PICKAXES	PINETREE	PITTANCE	PLAYMATE	PLUNGING	POLONIUM
PICKEREL	PINEWOOD	PIVOTING	PLAY-	PLUSHEST	POLTROON
PICKETED	PING-	PIXELATE	OFFS	PLUTONIC	POLYGALA
PICKETER	PONG	PIZZERIA	PLAYPENS	PLUVIOUS	POLYGAMY
PICKIEST	PINHEADS	PLACABLE	PLAYROOM	PLYMOUTH	POLYGENE
PICKINGS	PINIONED	PLACARDS	PLAYSUIT	POACEOUS	POLYGLOT
PICKLING	PINK	PLACATED	PLAYTIME	POACHERS	POLYGONS
PICKLOCK	GINS	PLACEBOS	PLEADING	POACHING	POLYGYNY
PICK ME	PINKROOT	PLACE	PLEASANT	POCKETED	POLYMATH
UP	PIN	MAT	PLEASING	POCKMARK	POLYMERS
PICK-ME-	MONEY	PLACENTA	PLEASURE	PODAGRAL	POLYPARY
UP	PINNACES	PLACIDLY	PLEATING	PODGIEST	POLYPODY
PICOLINE	PINNACLE	PLAGUILY	PLEBBIER	PODIATRY	POLYPOID
PICTURED	PINNIPED	PLAGUING	PLEBEIAN	PODZOLIC	POLYPOUS
PICTURES	PINOCHLE	PLAINEST	PLECTRUM	POETICAL	POLYSEMY
PIDDLING	PINPOINT	PLAITING	PLEDGING	POIGNANT	POLYURIA
PIEBALDS	PINPRICK	PLANCHET	PLEIADES	POINTERS	POLYURIC
PIE	PINTABLE	PLANFORM	PLEIN-	POINTING	POLYZOAN
CHART	PINT-	PLANGENT	AIR	POISONED	POLYZOIC
PIECRUST	SIZE	PLANKING	PLEONASM	POISONER	POMANDER
PIEDMONT	PINWHEEL	PLANKTON	PLETHORA	POITIERS	POMOLOGY
PIERCING	PIONEERS	PLANNERS	PLEURISY	POKEWEED	PONDERED
PIFFLING	PIPE	PLANNING	PLEUSTON	POKINESS	PONDERER
PIGGIEST	BOMB	PLANOSOL	PLIANTLY	POLANSKI	PONDWEED
PIGMENTS	PIPECLAY	PLANTAIN	PLIGHTED	POLARITY	PONGIEST
PIGSKINS	PIPEFISH	PLANTERS	PLIGHTER	POLARIZE	PONIARDS
PIGSTICK	PIPELINE	PLANTING	PLIMSOLL	POLAROID	PONTIFEX
PIGSTIES	PIPE	PLANULAR	PLIOCENE	POLEAXED	PONTIFFS
PIGSWILL	RACK	PLASTEEL	PLODDERS	POLECATS	PONTOONS
PIGTAILS	PIPERINE	PLASTERS	PLODDING	POLEMICS	PONYTAIL
PILASTER	PIPETTES	PLASTICS	PLONKING	POLE	POOFIEST
PILCHARD	PIPEWORT	PLASTRAL	PLOPPING	STAR	POOH-
PILEWORT	PIQUANCY	PLASTRON	PLOSIVES	POLICIES	POOH
PILFERED	PIRACIES	PLATELET	PLOTTING	POLICING	POOLSIDE
PILFERER	PIRANHAS	PLATFORM	PLOUGHED	POLISHED	POOR
PILGRIMS	PIRATING	PLATINIC	PLOUGHER	POLISHER	LAWS
PILIFORM	PIS	PLATINUM	PLUCKIER	POLISHES	POORLIER
PILLAGED	ALLER	PLATONIC	PLUCKILY	POLITELY	POORNESS
PILLAGER	PISIFORM	PLATOONS	PLUCKING	POLITICO	POPADUMS
PILLIONS	PISOLITE	PLATTERS	PLUGGING	POLITICS	POPINJAY
PILLOCKS	PISS-	PLATYPUS	PLUGHOLE	POLITIES	POPOVERS
PILLOWED	TAKE	PLAUDITS	PLUMBAGO	POLKA	POPPADOM
PILOTAGE	PITCHERS	PLAUSIVE	PLUMBERS	DOT	POPSICLE
PILOTING	PITCHING	PLAYABLE	PLUMBERY	POLLARDS	POPULACE
PIMENTOS	PITFALLS	PLAYBACK	PLUMBING	POLLICAL	POPULATE
PIMIENTO	PITHEADS	PLAY	PLUMBISM	POLLINIC	POPULISM
PINAFORE	PITHIEST	BALL	PLUMBOUS	POLLSTER	POPULIST
PINASTER	PITIABLE	PLAYBILL	PLUMMIER	POLLUTED	POPULOUS

PORKIEST	POTATOES	PREDATOR	PRETEXTS	PROBABLY	PROPHETS
PORK	POT-AU-	PREDELLA	PRETORIA	PROBATED	PROPOLIS
PIES	FEU	PREENING	PRETREAT	PROBATES	PROPOSAL
POROSITY	POTBELLY	PREEXIST	PRETTIER	PROBLEMS	PROPOSED
PORPHYRY	POTBOUND	PRE-	PRETTIFY	PROCAINE	PROPOSER
PORPOISE	POTENTLY	EXIST	PRETTILY	PROCEEDS	PROPOUND
PORRIDGE	POTHOLER	PREFACED	PRETZELS	PROCLAIM	PROPPING
PORTABLE	POTHOLES	PREFACER	PREVIEWS	PROCTORS	PROROGUE
PORTENTS	POTLUCKS	PREFACES	PREVIOUS	PROCURED	PROSAISM
PORTHOLE	POT	PREFECTS	PREZZIES	PROCURER	PROSIEST
PORTICOS	PLANT	PREFIXAL	PRIAPISM	PRODDING	PROSODIC
PORTIERE	POTSHERD	PREFIXED	PRICE	PRODIGAL	PROSPECT
PORTIONS	POTSHOTS	PREFIXES	TAG	PRODROME	PROSTATE
PORTLAND	POTSTONE	PREGNANT	PRICIEST	PRODUCED	PROSTYLE
PORTLIER	POTTERED	PREJUDGE	PRICKING	PRODUCER	PROTASIS
PORTRAIT	POTTERER	PRELATES	PRICKLED	PRODUCTS	PROTEGEE
PORT	POTTIEST	PRELATIC	PRICKLES	PROEMIAL	PROTEGES
SAID	POULTICE	PRELUDER	PRIDEFUL	PROFANED	PROTEINS
PORT	POUNCING	PRELUDES	PRIE-	PROFANER	PROTEOSE
SIDE	POUNDAGE	PREMIERE	DIEU	PROFILED	PROTESTS
PORTUGAL	POUNDING	PREMIERS	PRIESTLY	PROFILES	PROTOCOL
POSITING	POWDERED	PREMISES	PRIGGERY	PROFITED	PROTOZOA
POSITION	POWDERER	PREMIUMS	PRIGGISH	PROFITER	PROTRACT
POSITIVE	POWERFUL	PREMOLAR	PRIGGISM	PRO	PROTRUDE
POSITRON	POWERING	PREMORSE	PRIMATES	FORMA	PROUDEST
POSOLOGY	POZIDRIV	PRENATAL	PRIMEVAL	PROFOUND	PROVABLE
POSSIBLE	POZZUOLI	PREPARED	PRIMMEST	PROGRAMS	PROVABLY
POSSIBLY	PRACTICE	PREPENSE	PRIMNESS	PROGRESS	PROVENCE
POSTBAGS	PRACTISE	PRESAGED	PRIMROSE	PROHIBIT	PROVENLY
POSTCARD	PRAEDIAL	PRESAGER	PRIMULAS	PROJECTS	PROVERBS
POSTCAVA	PRAESEPE	PRESAGES	PRIMUSES	PROLAPSE	PROVIDED
POSTCODE	PRAIRIES	PRESCOTT	PRINCELY	PROLIFIC	PROVIDER
POSTDATE	PRAISING	PRESENCE	PRINCESS	PROLOGUE	PROVINCE
POST-	PRALINES	PRESENTS	PRINCIPE	PROMISED	PROVISOS
FREE	PRANCING	PRESERVE	PRINTERS	PROMISER	PROVOKED
POSTGRAD	PRANDIAL	PRESIDED	PRINTING	PROMISES	PROVOSTS
POST	PRANKISH	PRESIDER	PRINTOUT	PROMISOR	PROWL
HORN	PRATIQUE	PRESIDIA	PRIORATE	PROMOTED	CAR
POSTICHE	PRATTLED	PRESIDIO	PRIORESS	PROMOTER	PROWLERS
POSTINGS	PRATTLER	PRESS	PRIORIES	PROMPTED	PROWLING
POSTLUDE	PREACHED	BOX	PRIORITY	PROMPTER	PROXIMAL
POSTMARK	PREACHER	PRESSING	PRISMOID	PROMPTLY	PRUDENCE
POST-	PREAMBLE	PRESSMAN	PRISONER	PRONATOR	PRUINOSE
OBIT	PREAXIAL	PRESSMEN	PRISSIER	PRONOUNS	PRUNABLE
POSTPAID	PREBENDS	PRESS-	PRISSILY	PROOFING	PRUNELLA
POSTPONE	PRECEDED	UPS	PRISTINE	PROPERLY	PRUNELLE
POSTURAL	PRECEPTS	PRESSURE	PRIVATES	PROPERTY	PRURIENT
POSTURED	PRECINCT	PRESTIGE	PRIVIEST	PROPHAGE	PRURITIC
POSTURER	PRECIOUS	PRESUMED	PRIZE	PROPHASE	PRURITUS
POSTURES	PRECLUDE	PRESUMER	DAY	PROPHECY	PRUSSIAN
POTASSIC	PREDATED	PRETENCE	PROBABLE	PROPHESY	PSALMIST
POTATION					

148

PSALMODY	PUNISHED	PUT-UP	QUASHING	QUOTHING	RAMBUTAN
PSALTERS	PUNISHER	JOB	QUATRAIN	QUOTIENT	RAMEKINS
PSALTERY	PUNITIVE	PUZZLERS	QUAVERED		RAMENTUM
PSEPHITE	PUNSTERS	PUZZLING	QUAVERER	**R**	RAMIFIED
PSORALEA	PUPARIAL	PYELITIC	QUEASIER	RABBITED	RAMOSITY
PSYCHICS	PUPARIUM	PYELITIS	QUEASILY	RABBITER	RAMPAGED
PSYCHING	PUPATION	PYGIDIAL	QUECHUAN	RABBITRY	RAMPAGER
PTEROPOD	PUPPETRY	PYGIDIUM	QUEENDOM	RABIDITY	RAMPANCY
PTOMAINE	PUPPY	PYINKADO	QUEENING	RACCOONS	RAMPARTS
PTYALISM	FAT	PYODERMA	QUEEREST	RACEMISM	RAMSGATE
PUB-	PUPPYISH	PYOGENIC	QUEERING	RACEMOSE	RAMULOSE
CRAWL	PURBLIND	PYRAMIDS	QUELLING	RACIALLY	RANCAGUA
PUBLICAN	PURCHASE	PYRAZOLE	QUENCHED	RACINESS	RANCHERS
PUBLICLY	PUREBRED	PYRENEAN	QUENCHER	RACK-	RANDIEST
PUCKERED	PUREEING	PYRENEES	QUERCINE	RENT	RANDOMLY
PUDDINGS	PURENESS	PYRENOID	QUERYING	RACLETTE	RANKLING
PUDDLING	PURFLING	PYREXIAL	QUESTING	RACQUETS	RANKNESS
PUDENDUM	PURIFIED	PYRIDINE	QUESTION	RADIALLY	RANSOMED
PUDGIEST	PURIFIER	PYRIFORM	QUIBBLED	RADIANCE	RANSOMER
PUFFBALL	PURISTIC	PYROSTAT	QUIBBLER	RADIATED	RAPACITY
PUFFBIRD	PURITANS	PYROXENE	QUIBBLES	RADIATOR	RAPESEED
PUFFIEST	PURLIEUS	PYRROLIC	QUIBERON	RADICALS	RAPIDITY
PUGILISM	PURPLISH	PYRRUVIC	QUICKEST	RADICAND	RAPTNESS
PUGILIST	PURPOSED	PYTHONIC	QUICKIES	RADIOING	RAPTURES
PUISSANT	PURPOSES	PYXIDIUM	QUICKSET	RADISHES	RARA
PULLMANS	PURPURIN		QUIDDITY	RAFFLING	AVIS
PULLOUTS	PURSLANE	**Q**	QUIDNUNC	RAGGEDLY	RAREFIED
PULLOVER	PURSUANT		QUIETEST	RAG	RAREFIER
PULMONIC	PURSUERS	QUACKERY	QUIETISM	TRADE	RARENESS
PULMOTOR	PURSUING	QUACKING	QUIETIST	RAILHEAD	RARITIES
PULPIEST	PURSUITS	QUAD	QUIETUDE	RAILINGS	RASCALLY
PULPWOOD	PURULENT	BIKE	QUILL	RAILLERY	RASHNESS
PULSATED	PURVEYED	QUADRANT	PEN	RAILROAD	RASORIAL
PULSATOR	PURVEYOR	QUADRATE	QUILTING	RAILWAYS	RASPINGS
PULSEJET	PUSHBIKE	QUADROON	QUINCUNX	RAINBAND	RAT-
PULVINUS	PUSHCART	QUAGMIRE	QUI	RAINBOWS	ARSED
PUMMELED	PUSHIEST	QUAILING	NHONG	RAINCOAT	RATCHETS
PUMPKINS	PUSHOVER	QUAINTLY	QUINTETS	RAINDROP	RATIFIED
PUMP	PUSH-	QUALMISH	QUINTILE	RAINFALL	RATIFIER
ROOM	PULL	QUANDARY	QUIPPING	RAINIEST	RATIONAL
PUNCHBAG	PUSSYCAT	QUANDONG	QUIPSTER	RAINLESS	RATIONED
PUNCHEON	PUSTULAR	QUANTIFY	QUIRKIER	RAINY	RATSBANE
PUNCHIER	PUSTULES	QUANTITY	QUIRKILY	DAY	RATTIEST
PUNCHING	PUT	QUANTIZE	QUISLING	RAISABLE	RATTLING
PUNCH-	ABOUT	QUARRELS	QUITTERS	RAKE-	RAT
UPS	PUTATIVE	QUARRIED	QUITTING	OFFS	TRAPS
PUNCTATE	PUT-	QUARRIER	QUIVERED	RAKISHLY	RAVAGING
PUNCTUAL	DOWNS	QUARRIES	QUIVERER	RALLYING	RAVELING
PUNCTURE	PUTSCHES	QUARTERN	QUIXOTIC	RAMAT	RAVELLED
PUNGENCY	PUTTERED	QUARTERS	QUIZZING	GAN	RAVELLER
PUNINESS	PUT TO	QUARTETS	QUOTABLE	RAMBLERS	RAVENING
	SEA	QUARTILE		RAMBLING	

RAVENOUS	RECANTER	RED	REFORMED	REKINDLE	REMOVING
RAVISHED	RECAPPED	FACED	REFORMER	RELAPSED	RENAMING
RAVISHER	RECEDING	RED-	REFRAINS	RELAPSER	RENDERED
RAW-	RECEIPTS	FACED	REFUELED	RELAPSES	RENDERER
BONED	RECEIVED	RED	REFUGEES	RELATING	RENDIBLE
RAW	RECEIVER	FLAGS	REFUGIUM	RELATION	RENDZINA
DEALS	RECENTLY	RED	REFUNDED	RELATIVE	RENEGADE
RAWHIDES	RECEPTOR	GIANT	REFUNDER	RELAUNCH	RENEGING
RAZOR-	RECESSED	REDGRAVE	REFUSALS	RELAXANT	RENEWALS
CUT	RECESSES	REDHEADS	REFUSING	RELAXING	RENEWING
REACHING	RECHARGE	REDIRECT	REFUTING	RELAYING	RENIFORM
REACTANT	RECISION	RED	REGAINED	RELEASED	RENOUNCE
REACTING	RECITALS	LIGHT	REGAINER	RELEASER	RENOVATE
REACTION	RECITERS	REDNECKS	REGALITY	RELEASES	RENOWNED
REACTIVE	RECITING	REDOLENT	REGARDED	RELEGATE	RENTABLE
REACTORS	RECKLESS	REDOUBLE	REGATTAS	RELENTED	RENT
READABLE	RECKONED	REDOUBTS	REGELATE	RELEVANT	BOYS
READABLY	RECKONER	REDSHANK	REGENTAL	RELIABLE	RENT-
READIEST	RECLINED	RED	REGICIDE	RELIABLY	FREE
READINGS	RECLINER	SHIFT	REGIMENS	RELIANCE	RENTIERS
READJUST	RECLUSES	REDSKINS	REGIMENT	RELIEVED	RENT-
READOUTS	RECOILED	REDSTART	REGIONAL	RELIEVER	ROLL
READYING	RECOILER	REDUCING	REGISTER	RELIGION	REOFFEND
READY-	RECOMMIT	REDUVIID	REGISTRY	RELINING	REOPENED
MIX	RECORDED	REDWOODS	REGRATER	RELISHED	REPAIRED
REAFFIRM	RECORDER	REECHOED	REGROWTH	RELISHES	REPAIRER
REAGENTS	RECOUNTS	REDBUCK	REGULARS	RELIVING	REPARTEE
REALISTS	RECOUPED	REEDIEST	REGULATE	RELOADED	REPAYING
REALIZED	RECOURSE	REEDLING	REGULINE	RELOCATE	REPEALED
REALIZER	RECOVERY	REEF	REHASHED	REMAINED	REPEALER
REALNESS	RECREANT	KNOT	REHASHES	REMAKING	REPEATED
REAL-	RECREATE	REELABLE	REHEARSE	REMANDED	REPEATER
TIME	RECRUITS	REELABLY	REHEATER	REMARKED	REPELLED
REALTORS	RECTALLY	RE-	REHOBOAM	REMARKER	REPELLER
REAPABLE	RECURRED	EMPLOY	REHOUSED	REMARQUE	REPENTED
REAPPEAR	RECUSANT	RE-	REIGNING	REMEDIAL	REPENTER
REARMING	RECYCLED	EXPORT	REIMPORT	REMEDIED	REPEOPLE
REARMOST	REDACTOR	REFACING	REIMPOSE	REMEDIES	REPETEND
REARWARD	RED	REFEREED	REINDEER	REMEMBER	REPHRASE
REASONED	ALERT	REFEREES	REINSURE	REMIGIAL	REPINING
REASONER	REDBRICK	REFERENT	REINVENT	REMINDED	REPLACED
REASSURE	REDCOATS	REFERRAL	REINVEST	REMINDER	REPLACER
REAWAKEN	RED	REFERRED	REISSUED	REMITTED	REPLAYED
REBELLED	CROSS	REFERRER	REISSUER	REMITTER	REPLEVIN
REBOUNDS	REDDENED	REFILLED	REISSUES	REMNANTS	REPLICAS
REBUFFED	REDDITCH	REFINERY	REJECTED	REMOTELY	REPLYING
REBUKING	REDEEMED	REFINING	REJECTER	REMOTEST	REPORTED
REBUTTAL	REDEEMER	REFINISH	REJIGGED	REMOULDS	REPORTER
REBUTTED	REDEMAND	REFITTED	REJOICED	REMOUNTS	REPOSING
REBUTTER	REDEPLOY	REFLATED	REJOICER	REMOVALS	REPOUSSE
RECALLED	REDESIGN	REFLEXES	REJOINED	REMOVERS	REPRIEVE
RECANTED		REFOREST			

REPRINTS	RESORTED	REUNITED	REYNOLDS	RIJSWIJK	ROASTERS
REPRISAL	RESORTER	REUNITER	RHAETIAN	RIMOSITY	ROASTING
REPRISES	RESOURCE	REUSABLE	RHAPSODY	RINGBOLT	ROBINSON
REPROACH	RESPECTS	REVALUED	RHEOBASE	RINGBONE	ROBOTICS
REPROOFS	RESPIRED	REVAMPED	RHEOLOGY	RINGDOVE	ROBOTISM
REPROVAL	RESPITES	REVAMPER	RHEOSTAT	RING-	ROBUSTLY
REPROVED	RESPONSE	REVEALED	RHETORIC	DYKE	ROCAILLE
REPROVER	RESTATED	REVEALER	RH	RINGETTE	ROCHDALE
REPTILES	REST	REVEILLE	FACTOR	RINGHALS	ROCK
REPUBLIC	CURE	REVELING	RHINITIS	RINGLETS	BAND
REPULSED	REST	REVELLED	RHIZOMES	RING	ROCK
REPULSER	HOME	REVELLER	RHIZOPOD	ROAD	CAKE
REPULSES	RESTLESS	REVENANT	RHIZOPUS	RINGSIDE	ROCK
REQUESTS	RESTORED	REVENGED	RHODESIA	RINGWORM	DASH
REQUIEMS	RESTORER	REVENGER	RHODINAL	RINKHALS	ROCKETED
REQUIRED	RESTRAIN	REVENUED	RHOMBOID	RINSABLE	ROCKETRY
REQUIRER	RESTRICT	REVEREND	RHONCHAL	RIOT	ROCKFALL
REQUITAL	REST	REVERENT	RHONCHUS	ACTS	ROCKFISH
REQUITED	ROOM	REVERIES	RHUBARBS	RIPARIAN	ROCKFORD
REQUITER	RESUBMIT	REVERING	RHYOLITE	RIPCORDS	ROCKIEST
RESCRIPT	RESULTED	REVERSAL	RHYTHMIC	RIPENESS	ROCKLING
RESCUERS	RESUMING	REVERSED	RIBALDRY	RIPENING	ROCKROSE
RESCUING	RETAILED	REVERSER	RIB	RIPOSTED	ROCK
RESEARCH	RETAILER	REVERSES	CAGES	RIPOSTES	SALT
RESEMBLE	RETAINED	REVERTED	RIBOSOME	RIPPABLE	ROCKWEED
RESENTED	RETAINER	REVERTER	RICEBIRD	RIPPLING	ROEBUCKS
RESERVED	RETAKING	REVIEWAL	RICHMOND	RIPTIDES	ROENTGEN
RESERVER	RETARDED	REVIEWED	RICHNESS	RISKIEST	ROGATION
RESERVES	RETARDER	REVIEWER	RICKRACK	RISOTTOS	ROGATORY
RESETTER	RETCHING	REVILERS	RICKSHAW	RISSOLES	ROLE
RESETTLE	RETICENT	REVILING	RICOCHET	RITENUTO	PLAY
RESIDENT	RETICULE	REVISERS	RIDDANCE	RITUALLY	ROLLAWAY
RESIDING	RETINENE	REVISING	RIDDLING	RIVALING	ROLL
RESIDUAL	RETINITE	REVISION	RIDICULE	RIVALLED	BARS
RESIDUES	RETINUED	REVISORY	RIESLING	RIVERBED	ROLL
RESIDUUM	RETINUES	REVIVALS	RIFENESS	RIVERINE	CALL
RESIGNAL	RETIRING	REVIVIFY	RIFFLING	RIVETERS	ROLLMOPS
RESIGNED	RETORTED	REVIVING	RIFFRAFF	RIVETING	ROLL
RESIGNER	RETORTER	REVOKING	RIFLEMAN	RIVIERAS	OVER
RESINATE	RETRACED	REVOLTED	RIGADOON	RIVULETS	ROLLOVER
RESINOID	RETREADS	REVOLTER	RIGATONI	ROAD	ROLY-
RESINOUS	RETREATS	REVOLUTE	RIGHTFUL	HOGS	POLY
RESISTED	RETRENCH	REVOLVED	RIGHTING	ROAD	ROMANCED
RESISTER	RETRIALS	REVOLVER	RIGHTISM	RAGE	ROMANCES
RESISTOR	RETRIEVE	REWARDED	RIGHTIST	ROADSHOW	ROMANIES
RESOLUTE	RETROACT	REWARDER	RIGHT	ROADSIDE	ROMAN
RESOLVED	RETROFIT	REWINDER	OFF	ROAD	LAW
RESOLVER	RETRORSE	REWIRING	RIGIDITY	SIGN	ROMANSCH
RESOLVES	RETURNED	REWORDED	RIGORISM	ROADSTER	ROMANTIC
RESONANT	RETURNER	REWORKED	RIGORIST	ROAD	RONDAVEL
RESONATE	REUNIONS	REWRITES	RIGOROUS	TEST	RONDELET
				ROADWORK	RONTGENS

ROOFLESS
ROOF
  RACK
ROOFTOPS
ROOFTREE
ROOMIEST
ROOMMATE
ROOM
  MATE
ROOSTERS
ROOSTING
ROOT
  BEER
ROOT
  CROP
ROOTLESS
ROOTLIKE
ROPEWALK
ROPINESS
ROSARIAN
ROSARIES
ROSEBUSH
ROSEFISH
ROSE
  HIPS
ROSEMARY
ROSEOLAR
ROSE-
  ROOT
ROSETTES
ROSEWOOD
ROSINESS
ROSINING
ROSKILDE
ROSTRUMS
ROTARIAN
ROTATING
ROTATION
ROTATIVE
ROTATORY
ROTENONE
ROTHESAY
ROTOTILL
ROTTENLY
ROTUNDAS
ROUGHAGE
ROUGH-
  DRY
ROUGHEST
ROUGH-
  HEW
ROUGHING

ROULETTE
ROUND-
  ARM
ROUNDELS
ROUNDERS
ROUNDEST
ROUNDING
ROUNDISH
ROUNDUPS
ROUTINES
ROVE-
  OVER
ROWDIEST
ROWDYISM
ROW
  HOUSE
ROWLOCKS
ROYALISM
ROYALIST
RUBBINGS
RUBBISHY
RUBDOWNS
RUBELITE
RUBEOLAR
RUBICONS
RUBICUND
RUBIDIUM
RUBRICAL
RUCKSACK
RUCKUSES
RUDDIEST
RUDENESS
RUDIMENT
RUEFULLY
RUFFIANS
RUFFLING
RUGGEDLY
RUGOSITY
RUINABLE
RULEBOOK
RUMANIAN
RUMBLING
RUMINANT
RUMINATE
RUMMAGED
RUMMAGER
RUMMAGES
RUMOURED
RUMPLING
RUN-
  ABOUT
RUNAWAYS

RUNDOWNS
RUNNER
  UP
RUNNER-
  UP
RUNNIEST
RUPTURED
RUPTURES
RURALISM
RURALIST
RURALITY
RURALIZE
RUSH
  HOUR
RUST
  BELT
RUSTICAL
RUSTIEST
RUSTLERS
RUSTLING
RUTABAGA
RUTHENIC
RUTHLESS
RYDER
  CUP
RYE-
  BROME
RYEGRASS

S

SAARLAND
SABADELL
SABBATIC
SABOTAGE
SABOTEUR
SABULOUS
SACKLIKE
SACK
  RACE
SACREDLY
SACRISTY
SADDENED
SADDLERS
SADDLERY
SADDLING
SADISTIC
SAFENESS
SAFE
  SEAT
SAFETIES
SAGACITY
SAGGIEST

SAGITTAL
SAILABLE
SAILFISH
SAILINGS
SAILORLY
SAINFOIN
SAKHALIN
SALAAMED
SALACITY
SALARIED
SALARIES
SALEABLE
SALEABLY
SALEROOM
SALESMAN
SALESMEN
SALES
  TAX
SALIENCE
SALIENTS
SALINGER
SALINITY
SALIVARY
SALIVATE
SALLYING
SALPICON
SALTBUSH
SALTIEST
SALTILLO
SALTLICK
SALTNESS
SALTPANS
SALTWORT
SALUTARY
SALUTING
SALVABLE
SALVABLY
SALVADOR
SALVAGED
SALVAGER
SALZBURG
SAMARIUM
SAMENESS
SAMIZDAT
SAMOVARS
SAMPHIRE
SAMPLERS
SAMPLING
SAMURAIS
SANCTIFY
SANCTION

SANCTITY
SANCTUMS
SANDAKAN
SANDARAC
SANDBAGS
SANDBANK
SANDBARS
SAND-
  CAST
SAND
  DUNE
SAN
  DIEGO
SANDIEST
SANDPITS
SANDSHOE
SANDSOAP
SAND
  TRAP
SANDWELL
SANDWICH
SANDWORM
SANDWORT
SANENESS
SANGAREE
SANGUINE
SANITARY
SANITIZE
SANSKRIT
SANTA
  ANA
SANTAREM
SANTIAGO
SANTONIN
SAO
  PAULO
SAPIDITY
SAPIENCE
SAPLINGS
SAPONIFY
SAPONITE
SAPPHIRE
SAPPIEST
SAPROBIC
SAPROPEL
SARABAND
SARACENS
SARAJEVO
SARDINES
SARDINIA
SARDONIC
SARDONYX

SARGASSO
SARGODHA
SARKIEST
SARMATIA
SARRAUTE
SASHAYED
SASH
  CORD
SASSIEST
SASTRUGA
SATANISM
SATANIST
SATCHELS
SATIABLE
SATIABLY
SATIATED
SATIRIST
SATIRIZE
SATSUMAS
SATURANT
SATURATE
SATURDAY
SAUCEPAN
SAUCIEST
SAUNTERS
SAUROPOD
SAUSAGES
SAUTEING
SAVAGELY
SAVAGERY
SAVAGING
SAVANNAH
SAVANNAS
SAVIOURS
SAVORIES
SAVOROUS
SAVOURED
SAVOYARD
SAWBONES
SAWGRASS
SAWHORSE
SAWMILLS
SAWTOOTH
SCABBARD
SCABBIER
SCABBILY
SCABIOUS
SCABROUS
SCAFFOLD
SCALABLE
SCALABLY

SCALAWAG	SCHOOLIE	SCOWLING	SCURVILY	SECEDING	SELF-MADE
SCALDING	SCHOONER	SCRABBLE	SCUTTLED	SECLUDED	SELF-PITY
SCALENUS	SCHWERIN	SCRAGGED	SCUTTLES	SECONDED	SELF-RULE
SCALIEST	SCIAENID	SCRAGGLY	SCYTHING	SECONDER	SELFSAME
SCALLION	SCIATICA	SCRAMBLE	SEABIRDS	SECONDLY	SELF-WILL
SCALLOPS	SCIENCES	SCRAMMED	SEABOARD	SECRETED	SELL-OUTS
SCALPELS	SCILICET	SCRANTON	SEABORNE	SECRETIN	SELVAGES
SCALPERS	SCIMITAR	SCRAPERS	SEACOAST	SECRETLY	SEMANTIC
SCALPING	SCINCOID	SCRAPING	SEAFARER	SECTIONS	SEMARANG
SCAMMONY	SCIRRHUS	SCRAP MAN	SEAFRONT	SECTORAL	SEMESTER
SCAMPISH	SCISSILE	SCRAPPED	SEAGIRTS	SECURELY	SEMIARID
SCANDALS	SCISSION	SCRATCHY	SEAGOING	SECUREST	SEMIDOME
SCANDIUM	SCISSORS	SCRAWLED	SEA GREEN	SECURING	SEMINARS
SCANNERS	SCIURINE	SCRAWLER	SEAGULLS	SECURITY	SEMINARY
SCANNING	SCIUROID	SCREAMED	SEAHORSE	SEDATELY	SEMIOTIC
SCANSION	SCLAFFER	SCREAMER	SEALABLE	SEDATING	SEMITICS
SCANTIER	SCLERITE	SCREECHY	SEA LEVEL	SEDATION	SEMITIST
SCANTILY	SCLEROID	SCREENED	SEA LIONS	SEDATIVE	SEMITONE
SCAPULAR	SCLEROMA	SCREENER	SEALSKIN	SEDIMENT	SEMOLINA
SCAPULAS	SCLEROUS	SCREWIER	SEALYHAM	SEDITION	SEMPLICE
SCARCELY	SCOFFING	SCREWING	SEAMIEST	SEDUCERS	SENATORS
SCARCEST	SCOLDING	SCREW TOP	SEA MILES	SEDUCING	SENDABLE
SCARCITY	SCOLLOPS	SCRIBBLE	SEA MISTS	SEDULITY	SEND-OFFS
SCARGILL	SCOOPING	SCRIMPED	SEAMLESS	SEDULOUS	SENILITY
SCARIEST	SCOOTERS	SCRIPTED	SEAMOUNT	SEEDBEDS	SENORITA
SCARIOUS	SCOOTING	SCROFULA	SEAPLANE	SEEDCASE	SENSIBLE
SCARRING	SCORCHED	SCROLLED	SEAPORTS	SEEDCORN	SENSIBLY
SCATHING	SCORCHER	SCROOGES	SEA POWER	SEEDIEST	SENSUOUS
SCATTIER	SCORCHES	SCROTUMS	SEAQUAKE	SEEDLESS	SENTENCE
SCATTILY	SCORNFUL	SCROUNGE	SEARCHED	SEEDLING	SENTIENT
SCATTING	SCORNING	SCRUBBED	SEARCHER	SEEDSMAN	SENTINEL
SCAVENGE	SCORPION	SCRUBBER	SEARCHES	SEEDSMEN	SENTRIES
SCENARIO	SCORPIOS	SCRUMPED	SEASCAPE	SEESAWED	SEPALLED
SCENTING	SCORPIUS	SCRUNCHY	SEASHELL	SEETHING	SEPALOID
SCEPTICS	SCORSESE	SCRUPLED	SEASHORE	SEGMENTS	SEPARATE
SCEPTRES	SCOTCHED	SCRUPLES	SEA SNAKE	SEIGNEUR	SEPHARDI
SCHEDULE	SCOT FREE	SCRUTINY	SEASONAL	SEISABLE	SEPTUPLE
SCHEMATA	SCOT-FREE	SCUDDING	SEASONED	SEISMISM	SEQUENCE
SCHEMERS	SCOTLAND	SCUFFING	SEASONER	SEIZABLE	SEQUINED
SCHEMING	SCOTOPIA	SCUFFLED	SEAT BELT	SEIZURES	SEQUOIAS
SCHERZOS	SCOTOPIC	SCUFFLES	SEA SNAKE	SELANGOR	SERAGLIO
SCHIEDAM	SCOTSMAN	SCULLERS	SEASONAL	SELECTED	SERAJEVO
SCHILLER	SCOTTISH	SCULLERY	SEASONED	SELECTOR	SERAPHIC
SCHIZOID	SCOURERS	SCULLING	SEASONER	SELENATE	SERAPHIM
SCHIZONT	SCOURGED	SCULLION	SEAT BELT	SELENITE	SEREMBAN
SCHMALTZ	SCOURGER	SCULPSIT	SEA TROUT	SELENIUM	SERENADE
SCHMUCKS	SCOURGES	SCULPTOR	SEAWALLS	SELFHEAL	
SCHNAPPS	SCOURING	SCUPPERS	SEAWARDS	SELF-HELP	
SCHOLARS	SCOUTING	SCURRIED		SELFHOOD	
SCHOLIUM				SELFLESS	
SCHOOLED					

153

SERENATA	SHABBILY	SHEBEENS	SHIRTING	SHRAPNEL	SIDE
SERENELY	SHACKING	SHEDABLE	SHITLESS	SHREDDED	DISH
SERENITY	SHACKLED	SHEDDING	SHITTIER	SHREDDER	SIDE-
SERGEANT	SHACKLER	SHEEPDIP	SHITTING	SHREWDER	FOOT
SERIALLY	SHACKLES	SHEEPDOG	SHIVERED	SHREWDLY	SIDEKICK
SERIATIM	SHADDOCK	SHEEPISH	SHIVERER	SHREWISH	SIDELINE
SERMONIC	SHADIEST	SHEEREST	SHIZUOKA	SHRIEKED	SIDELONG
SEROLOGY	SHADINGS	SHEERING	SHOCKERS	SHRIEKER	SIDEREAL
SEROSITY	SHADOWED	SHEETING	SHOCKING	SHRIEVAL	SIDERITE
SEROTINE	SHADOWER	SHEIKDOM	SHODDIER	SHRILLER	SIDE
SERPENTS	SHAFTING	SHELDUCK	SHODDILY	SHRIMPER	ROAD
SERPULID	SHAGBARK	SHELLING	SHOEBILL	SHRINKER	SIDESHOW
SERRANID	SHAGGIER	SHELTERS	SHOEHORN	SHROUDED	SIDESLIP
SERRATED	SHAGGILY	SHELVING	SHOELACE	SHRUGGED	SIDESMAN
SERVABLE	SHAGGING	SHENYANG	SHOETREE	SHRUNKEN	SIDESTEP
SERVANTS	SHAGREEN	SHEPHERD	SHOLAPUR	SHUCKING	SIDEWALK
SERVICED	SHAKABLE	SHERATON	SHOOTERS	SHUDDERS	SIDEWALL
SERVICES	SHAKEOUT	SHERBETS	SHOOTING	SHUDDERY	SIDEWAYS
SERVINGS	SHAKE-	SHERIFFS	SHOOT-	SHUFFLED	SIEGBAHN
SERVITOR	UPS	SHETLAND	OUT	SHUFFLER	SIFTINGS
SERVQUAL	SHAKIEST	SHIELDED	SHOOT-	SHUFFLES	SIGHTING
SESAMOID	SHALLOON	SHIELDER	OUT	SHUNNING	SIGHTSEE
SESSIONS	SHALLOTS	SHIELING	SHOPGIRL	SHUNTERS	SIGNALED
SET	SHALLOWS	SHIFTIER	SHOPLIFT	SHUNTING	SIGNALLY
ASIDE	SHAMABLE	SHIFTILY	SHOPPERS	SHUSHING	SIGNINGS
SETBACKS	SHAMBLED	SHIFTING	SHOPPING	SHUTDOWN	SIGNORAS
SETIFORM	SHAMBLES	SHIFT	SHOPTALK	SHUTTERS	SIGNPOST
SET	SHAMEFUL	KEY	SHORTAGE	SHUTTING	SILASTIC
PIECE	SHAMMIES	SHIITAKE	SHORT	SHUTTLED	SILENCED
SET	SHAMMING	SHILLING	CUT	SHUTTLES	SILENCER
POINT	SHAMPOOS	SHILLONG	SHORT-	SHYSTERS	SILENCES
SET	SHAMROCK	SHIMMERY	DAY	SIANGTAN	SILENTLY
RIGHT	SHANDIES	SHINBONE	SHORTEST	SIBERIAN	SILICATE
SETSCREW	SHANDONG	SHINDIGS	SHORTIES	SIBILANT	SILICIDE
SETTINGS	SHANGHAI	SHINGLER	SHORTING	SIBILATE	SILICIFY
SETTLERS	SHANTIES	SHINGLES	SHOTGUNS	SIBLINGS	SILICONE
SETTLE	SHANTUNG	SHINIEST	SHOULDER	SICILIAN	SILKIEST
UP	SHAPABLE	SHINNIED	SHOULDN'	SICKBAYS	SILKWORM
SETTLING	SHARABLE	SHINNING	T	SICKBEDS	SILLABUB
SEVENTHS	SHARE-	SHIPABLE	SHOUTING	SICK	SILLIEST
SEVERELY	OUT	SHIPLOAD	SHOVELED	CALL	SILOXANE
SEVERING	SHARP	SHIPMATE	SHOVELER	SICKENED	SILURIAN
SEVERITY	END	SHIPMENT	SHOWBOAT	SICKENER	SILVERED
SEWERAGE	SHARPEST	SHIPPERS	SHOWCASE	SICKLIER	SILVERER
SEXINESS	SHARPISH	SHIPPING	SHOWDOWN	SICKNESS	SIMBIRSK
SEXOLOGY	SHARP-	SHIPWORM	SHOWERED	SICKROOM	SIMMERED
SEX	SET	SHIPYARD	SHOWGIRL	SIDEARMS	SIMONIAC
ORGAN	SHAVABLE	SHIRKERS	SHOWIEST	SIDE	SIMONIST
SEXTANTS	SHAVINGS	SHIRKING	SHOWINGS	ARMS	SIMPERED
SEXTUPLE	SHEADING	SHIRRING	SHOW-	SIDEBAND	SIMPERER
SEXUALLY	SHEARING	SHIRTIER	OFFS	SIDEBAND	SIMPLEST
SHABBIER	SHEATHED	SHIRTING	SHOWROOM	SIDECARS	SIMPLEST

SIMPLIFY	SKEPTISM	SLACKEST	SLINKIER	SLURRING	SNACKING
SIMPLISM	SKERRICK	SLACKING	SLINKILY	SLUSHIER	SNAFFLED
SIMULANT	SKETCHED	SLAGGING	SLINKING	SLUTTISH	SNAFFLES
SIMULATE	SKETCHER	SLAGHEAP	SLIPCASE	SMACKERS	SNAGGING
SINAITIC	SKETCHES	SLAG	SLIPKNOT	SMACKING	SNAPBACK
SINAPISM	SKEWBACK	HEAP	SLIP	SMALL	SNAPPERS
SINCIPUT	SKEWBALD	SLAKABLE	KNOT	ADS	SNAPPIER
SINECURE	SKEWERED	SLAMMING	SLIP	SMALLEST	SNAPPILY
SINFONIA	SKIDDING	SLANDERS	OVER	SMALL	SNAPPING
SINFULLY	SKIDPANS	SLANGILY	SLIPPAGE	FRY	SNAPPISH
SINGABLE	SKIJORER	SLANGING	SLIPPERS	SMALLISH	SNAP
SINGEING	SKI	SLANTING	SLIPPERY	SMALLPOX	SHOT
SINGLETS	JUMPS	SLAP-	SLIPPIER	SMALTITE	SNAPSHOT
SINGLING	SKI	BANG	SLIPPING	SMARMIER	SNARLING
SINGSONG	LIFTS	SLAPDASH	SLIP	SMARTEST	SNARL-
SINGULAR	SKILLETS	SLAPHEAD	ROAD	SMARTING	UPS
SINISTER	SKIMMERS	SLAPPING	SLIPSHOD	SMASHERS	SNATCHED
SINKABLE	SKIMMING	SLASHING	SLIPWAYS	SMASHING	SNATCHER
SINKHOLE	SKIMPIER	SLATTERN	SLITHERY	SMASH-	SNATCHES
SINN	SKIMPILY	SLAVERED	SLITTING	UPS	SNAZZIER
FEIN	SKIMPING	SLAVERER	SLIVERER	SMEARING	SNAZZILY
SINOLOGY	SKINCARE	SLAVONIA	SLOBBERY	SMELLIER	SNEAKERS
SINUSOID	SKIN	SLAVONIC	SLOE-	SMELLING	SNEAKIER
SIPHONAL	DEEP	SLEAZIER	EYED	SMELTERY	SNEAKILY
SIPHONED	SKIN-	SLEAZILY	SLOGGERS	SMELTING	SNEAKING
SIRENIAN	DEEP	SLEDDING	SLOGGING	SMIRCHED	SNEERING
SIRLOINS	SKIN-	SLEDGING	SLOPPIER	SMIRCHER	SNEEZING
SIROCCOS	DIVE	SLEEKEST	SLOPPILY	SMIRKING	SNICKERS
SISSIEST	SKINHEAD	SLEEKING	SLOPPING	SMITHERY	SNICKING
SISSYISH	SKINLESS	SLEEPERS	SLOPWORK	SMITHIES	SNIFFING
SISTERLY	SKINNIER	SLEEPIER	SLOSHING	SMOCKING	SNIFFLED
SISTROID	SKINNING	SLEEPILY	SLOTHFUL	SMOKABLE	SNIFFLER
SITARIST	SKIPJACK	SLEEPING	SLOTTING	SMOKIEST	SNIFFLES
SIT-	SKI	SLEETING	SLOUCHED	SMOLENSK	SNIFTERS
DOWNS	PLANE	SLEEVING	SLOUCHER	SMOOCHED	SNIGGERS
SITOLOGY	SKI	SLEIGHER	SLOUGHED	SMOOTHED	SNIGGERY
SITTINGS	POLES	SLICKERS	SLOVAKIA	SMOOTHEN	SNIGGLER
SITUATED	SKIPPERS	SLICKEST	SLOVENIA	SMOOTHER	SNIPPETS
SITZMARK	SKIPPING	SLICKING	SLOVENLY	SMOOTHIE	SNIPPILY
SIX-	SKIRMISH	SLIDABLE	SLOWDOWN	SMOOTHLY	SNIPPING
PACKS	SKIRTING	SLIGHTED	SLOW	SMOTHERY	SNITCHED
SIXPENCE	SKITTISH	SLIGHTER	DOWN	SMOULDER	SNITCHES
SIXPENNY	SKITTLES	SLIGHTLY	SLOWNESS	SMUDGILY	SNIVELED
SIXTEENS	SKIVVIED	SLIM	SLOWWORM	SMUDGING	SNIVELLY
SIXTIETH	SKIVVIES	DOWN	SLUDGIER	SMUGGEST	SNOBBERY
SIZEABLE	SKULKING	SLIMIEST	SLUGGARD	SMUGGLED	SNOBBISH
SIZZLERS	SKULLCAP	SLIMMERS	SLUGGING	SMUGGLER	SNOGGING
SIZZLING	SKYDIVER	SLIMMEST	SLUGGISH	SMUGNESS	SNOOPERS
SKELETAL	SKYLARKS	SLIMMING	SLUICING	SMUTTIER	SNOOPING
SKELETON	SKYLIGHT	SLIMNESS	SLUMMING	SMUTTILY	SNOOTIER
SKEPTICS	SKYLINES	SLINGING	SLUMPING	SNACK	SNOOTILY
	SKYWARDS		SLURPING	BAR	

SNOOZING
SNORKELS
SNORTERS
SNORTING
SNOTTIER
SNOTTILY
SNOWBALL
SNOWBIRD
SNOWDROP
SNOWFALL
SNOWIEST
SNOWLINE
SNOWSHED
SNOWSHOE
SNUBBING
SNUFFBOX
SNUFFERS
SNUFFING
SNUFFLED
SNUFFLER
SNUFFLES
SNUGGERY
SNUGGLED
SNUGNESS
SO-AND-
   SOS
SOAPBARK
SOAPIEST
SOAPLESS
SOAPSUDS
SOAPWORT
SOBERING
SOBRIETY
SOB
   STORY
SO-
   CALLED
SOCIABLE
SOCIABLY
SOCIALLY
SOCIETAL
SOCRATIC
SODALITE
SODAMIDE
SODOMITE
SODOMIZE
SOFTBALL
SOFT
   COPY
SOFTENED
SOFTENER
SOFTNESS

SOFT
   SELL
SOFT
   SOAP
SOFT
   SPOT
SOFTWARE
SOFTWOOD
SOGGIEST
SOISSONS
SOJOURNS
SOLACING
SOLANDER
SOLARIUM
SOLARIZE
SOLATIUM
SOLDERED
SOLDERER
SOLDIERS
SOLDIERY
SOLECISM
SOLECIST
SOLEMNLY
SOLENOID
SOLIDAGO
SOLIDARY
SOLIDIFY
SOLIDITY
SOLIHULL
SOLINGEN
SOLITARY
SOLITUDE
SOLOISTS
SOLONETZ
SOLSTICE
SOLUTION
SOLVABLE
SOLVENCY
SOLVENTS
SOMALIAN
SOMBRELY
SOMBRERO
SOMBROUS
SOMEBODY
SOME
   HOPE
SOMERSET
SOMETIME
SOMEWHAT
SONANTAL
SONATINA
SONGBIRD

SONGBOOK
SONGSTER
SON-IN-
   LAW
SONOBUOY
SONORANT
SONORITY
SONOROUS
SOOTHING
SOOTHSAY
SOOTIEST
SOPHISMS
SOPHISTS
SOPPIEST
SOPRANOS
SORBITOL
SORBONNE
SORCERER
SORDIDLY
SOREDIUM
SORENESS
SORICINE
SOROCABA
SORORATE
SORORITY
SORPTION
SORRENTO
SORRIEST
SORROWED
SORROWER
SORTABLE
SOUCHONG
SOUFFLES
SOUGHING
SOUL
   FOOD
SOULLESS
SOUNDBOX
SOUNDING
SOUND
   OFF
SOURDINE
SOURNESS
SOURPUSS
SOUTACHE
SOUTHERN
SOUTHING
SOUTHPAW
SOUVENIR
SOWBREAD
SOYA
   BEAN

SOY
   SAUCE
SPACE
   AGE
SPACE-
   AGE
SPACE
   BAR
SPACE-
   BAR
SPACEMAN
SPACEMEN
SPACIOUS
SPANDREL
SPANGLED
SPANGLES
SPANIARD
SPANIELS
SPANKING
SPANNERS
SPANNING
SPANSPEK
SPARABLE
SPAR
   DECK
SPARERIB
SPARE
   RIB
SPARKING
SPARKLED
SPARKLER
SPARKLES
SPARLING
SPARRING
SPARROWS
SPARSELY
SPARSEST
SPASTICS
SPATTERS
SPATULAR
SPATULAS
SPAWNING
SPEAKERS
SPEAKING
SPEARING
SPECIALS
SPECIFIC
SPECIMEN
SPECIOUS
SPECKLED
SPECKLES
SPECTATE

SPECTRAL
SPECTRES
SPECTRUM
SPECULAR
SPECULUM
SPEECHES
SPEEDIER
SPEEDILY
SPEEDING
SPEEDWAY
SPELAEAN
SPELLING
SPENDERS
SPENDING
SPERMARY
SPERMINE
SPERMOUS
SPHAGNUM
SPHENOID
SPHERICS
SPHEROID
SPHERULE
SPHINXES
SPHYGMIC
SPICCATO
SPICIEST
SPICULUM
SPIKELET
SPIKIEST
SPILLAGE
SPILLING
SPILLWAY
SPINDLES
SPINIFEX
SPINNERS
SPINNEYS
SPINNING
SPIN-
   OFFS
SPINSTER
SPIRACLE
SPIRALED
SPIRITED
SPITEFUL
SPITFIRE
SPITTING
SPITTOON
SPLASHED
SPLASHER
SPLATTED
SPLATTER

SPLAYING
SPLENDID
SPLENIAL
SPLENIUS
SPLICERS
SPLICING
SPLINTER
SPLIT
   END
SPLIT
   PEA
SPLITTER
SPLODGES
SPLOSHED
SPLOSHES
SPLURGED
SPLURGES
SPLUTTER
SPOILAGE
SPOILERS
SPOILING
SPOLIATE
SPONDAIC
SPONDEES
SPONGERS
SPONGIER
SPONGILY
SPONGING
SPONSION
SPONSORS
SPOOKIER
SPOOKILY
SPOOKING
SPOOKISH
SPOON-
   FED
SPOONFUL
SPOONING
SPORADIC
SPORRANS
SPORTFUL
SPORTIER
SPORTILY
SPORTING
SPORTIVE
SPOTLAMP
SPOTLESS
SPOTTERS
SPOTTIER
SPOTTILY
SPOTTING

SPOT- WELD	SQUAWKED	STAMPEDE	STATURES	STICKIER	STODGIER
SPOUTERS	SQUAWKER	STAMPING	STATUSES	STICKILY	STODGILY
SPOUTING	SQUEAKED	STANCHED	STATUTES	STICKING	STOICISM
SPRADDLE	SQUEAKER	STANCHER	STAYSAIL	STICKLER	STOLIDLY
SPRAINED	SQUEALED	STANDARD	STEADIED	STICKPIN	STOMACHS
SPRAWLED	SQUEALER	STANDBYS	STEADIER	STICK- UPS	STOMACHY
SPRAWLER	SQUEEGEE	STANDING	STEADILY	STIFFEST	STOMATAL
SPRAYERS	SQUEEZED	STAND- INS	STEALING	STIFLING	STOMATIC
SPRAY GUN	SQUEEZER	STANDISH	STEALTHY	STIGMATA	STOMPING
SPRAYING	SQUEEZES	STANDOFF	STEAMERS	STILBENE	STONABLE
SPREADER	SQUELCHY	STAND OUT	STEAMIER	STILBITE	STONE AGE
SPRIGGER	SQUIGGLE	STANNARY	STEAMILY	STILETTO	STONEFLY
SPRINGER	SQUIGGLY	STANNITE	STEAMING	STILLEST	STONIEST
SPRINKLE	SQUINTED	STANNOUS	STEAPSIN	STILLING	STONKING
SPRINTED	SQUINTER	STANZAIC	STEARATE	STIMULUS	STOOD OUT
SPRINTER	SQUIRMED	STAPELIA	STEATITE	STINGERS	STOOPING
SPRITELY	SQUIRMER	STAPLERS	STEELIER	STINGIER	STOPCOCK
SPROCKET	SQUIRREL	STAPLING	STEELING	STINGILY	STOPGAPS
SPROUTED	SQUIRTED	STARCHED	STEEPEST	STINGING	STOPPING
SPRUCELY	SQUIRTER	STARCHER	STEEPING	STINGRAY	STOPOVER
SPRUCING	SQUISHED	STARCHES	STEEPLES	STING RAY	STOPPAGE
SPRYNESS	SRI LANKA	STARDUST	STEERAGE	STINKERS	STOPPARD
SPUNKIER	SRINAGAR	STARFISH	STEERING	STINKING	STOPPERS
SPUNKILY	STABBERS	STARGAZE	STEINBOK	STINTING	STOPPING
SPURIOUS	STABBING	STARKERS	STELLATE	STIPENDS	STORABLE
SPURNING	STABLING	STARKEST	STELLIFY	STIPPLED	STOREYED
SPURRING	STACCATO	STARLESS	STELLITE	STIPPLER	STORMIER
SPURTING	STACKING	STARLETS	STEMHEAD	STIPULAR	STORMILY
SPUTTERS	STADIUMS	STARLIKE	STEMMING	STIRLING	STORMING
SPYGLASS	STAFFING	STARLING	STENCHES	STIRRERS	STORMONT
SQUABBLE	STAFFMAN	STARRIER	STENCILS	STIRRING	STOUTEST
SQUAD CAR	STAFFORD	STARRILY	STEN GUNS	STIRRUPS	STOWAWAY
SQUADRON	STAGGARD	STARRING	STENOSIS	STITCHED	STRABANE
SQUALENE	STAGGERS	STARSHIP	STENOTIC	STITCHER	STRADDLE
SQUALLED	STAGINGS	STAR SIGN	STEP DOWN	STITCHES	STRAFING
SQUALLER	STAGNANT	STARTERS	STEPPING	STITCH UP	STRAGGLE
SQUAMATE	STAGNATE	STARTING	STEPWISE	STOCKADE	STRAGGLY
SQUAMOUS	STAINING	STARTLED	STERIGMA	STOCKCAR	STRAIGHT
SQUANDER	STAIRWAY	STARTLER	STERLING	STOCK CAR	STRAINED
SQUARELY	STAKE OUT	STARVING	STERNEST	STOCKIER	STRAINER
SQUAREST	STALKERS	STAR WARS	STERNSON	STOCKILY	STRAITEN
SQUARING	STALKILY	STARWORT	STERNUMS	STOCKING	STRANDED
SQUARISH	STALKING	STASHING	STERNWAY	STOCKIST	STRANGER
SQUASHED	STALLING	STATABLE	STEROIDS	STOCKMAN	STRANGLE
SQUASHER	STALLION	STATELET	STETSONS	STOCKMEN	STRAPPED
SQUASHES	STALWART	STATICAL	STEWARDS	STOCKOUT	STRAPPER
SQUATTED	STAMFORD	STATIONS	STIBNITE	STOCKPOT	STRATEGY
SQUATTER	STAMINAL	STATUARY	STICKERS	STOCKTON	STRATIFY
	STAMMERS		STICKFUL		STRAW MAN

STRAW	STUDBOOK	SUBORDER	SULPHATE	SUPPLIED	SWANKILY
MEN	STUDDING	SUBORNED	SULPHIDE	SUPPLIER	SWANKING
STRAYING	STUDENTS	SUBORNER	SULPHITE	SUPPLIES	SWANNERY
STREAKED	STUD	SUBOTICA	SULPHONE	SUPPORTS	SWANNING
STREAKER	FARM	SUBOXIDE	SULTANAS	SUPPOSED	SWANSKIN
STREAMED	STUDIOUS	SUBPLOTS	SULTANIC	SUPPOSER	SWANSONG
STREAMER	STUDWORK	SUBPOENA	SULTRIER	SUPPRESS	SWAN
STRENGTH	STUDYING	SUBSERVE	SULTRILY	SUPREMOS	SONG
STRESSED	STUFFIER	SUBSHRUB	SUMATRAN	SURABAYA	SWAP
STRESSES	STUFFILY	SUBSIDED	SUMMERED	SURCOATS	MEET
STRETCHY	STUFFING	SUBSIDER	SUMMITAL	SUREFIRE	SWAPPING
STREUSEL	STULTIFY	SUBSOLAR	SUMMONED	SURE	SWARMING
STREWING	STUMBLED	SUBSONIC	SUM	FIRE	SWASTIKA
STRIATED	STUMBLER	SUBSTAGE	TOTAL	SURENESS	SWATCHES
STRICKEN	STUMBLES	SUBSUMED	SUNBAKED	SURETIES	SWATHING
STRICKLE	STUMPIER	SUBTITLE	SUNBATHE	SURFABLE	SWATTERS
STRICTER	STUMPING	SUBTLEST	SUNBEAMS	SURFACED	SWATTING
STRICTLY	STUNNERS	SUBTLETY	SUNBELTS	SURFACER	SWAYABLE
STRIDDEN	STUNNING	SUBTONIC	SUNBURNT	SURFACES	SWAY-
STRIDENT	STUNTING	SUBTOTAL	SUNBURST	SURFBIRD	BACK
STRIGOSE	STUNT	SUBTRACT	SUNDERED	SURFBOAT	SWEARING
STRIKERS	MAN	SUBULATE	SUNDIALS	SURFLIKE	SWEATBOX
STRIKING	STUNT	SUBURBAN	SUNDRIES	SURGEONS	SWEATERS
STRIMMER	MEN	SUBURBIA	SUNGLASS	SURGICAL	SWEATIER
STRINGER	STUPIDER	SUCCINCT	SUNLAMPS	SURICATE	SWEATILY
STRIPIER	STUPIDLY	SUCCINIC	SUNLIGHT	SURLIEST	SWEATING
STRIPPED	STURDIER	SUCCUBUS	SUNNIEST	SURMISED	SWEEPERS
STRIPPER	STURDILY	SUCHLIKE	SUNRISES	SURMISER	SWEEPING
STROBILA	STURGEON	SUCKLING	SUNROOFS	SURMISES	SWEETEST
STROKING	STUTTERS	SUDANESE	SUNSHADE	SURMOUNT	SWEETIES
STROLLED	STYLISTS	SUDATORY	SUNSHINE	SURNAMES	SWEET
STROLLER	STYLIZED	SUDDENLY	SUNSHINY	SURPLICE	PEA
STRONGER	STYLIZER	SUFFERED	SUNSPOTS	SURPRINT	SWEETSOP
STRONGLY	STYLUSES	SUFFERER	SUNTRAPS	SURPRISE	SWELLING
STROPHES	STYMYING	SUFFICED	SUN	SURROUND	SWERVING
STROPHIC	STYPTICS	SUFFICER	VISOR	SURVEYED	SWIFTEST
STRUDELS	SUBACUTE	SUFFIXAL	SUNWARDS	SURVEYOR	SWIGGING
STRUGGLE	SUBADULT	SUFFIXES	SUPADRIV	SURVIVAL	SWILLING
STRUMMED	SUBAGENT	SUFFRAGE	SUPERBLY	SURVIVED	SWIMMERS
STRUMMER	SUBCLASS	SUFFUSED	SUPEREGO	SURVIVOR	SWIMMING
STRUMPET	SUBDUING	SUGARING	SUPERFIX	SUSPECTS	SWIMSUIT
STRUNG-	SUBERIZE	SUICIDAL	SUPERIOR	SUSPENSE	SWINDLED
UP	SUBEROSE	SUICIDES	SUPERMAN	SUTURING	SWINDLER
STRUTTED	SUBFLOOR	SUITABLE	SUPERMEN	SUZERAIN	SWINDLES
STRUTTER	SUBGENUS	SUITABLY	SUPERNAL	SVALBARD	SWINEPOX
STUBBIER	SUBGROUP	SUITCASE	SUPERSEX	SVENGALI	SWINGBIN
STUBBILY	SUBHUMAN	SULAWESI	SUPERTAX	SWABBING	SWINGERS
STUBBING	SUBJECTS	SULKIEST	SUPINATE	SWADDLED	SWINGING
STUBBLED	SUBLEASE	SULLENER	SUPINELY	SWALLOWS	SWIRLING
STUBBORN	SUBMERGE	SULLENLY	SUPPLANT	SWAMPING	SWISHEST
STUCCOED	SUBMERSE	SULLYING	SUPPLEST	SWANKIER	SWISHING
					SWITCHED

SWITCHER	SYSTOLIC	TAKES	TAPPABLE	TEACAKES	TELLURIC
SWITCHES	SYZYGIAL	OFF	TAPROOTS	TEACHERS	TELSONIC
SWIVELED	SZCZECIN	TAKORADI	TARAKIHI	TEA	TEMERITY
SWOONING	SZECHWAN	TALAPOIN	TARBOOSH	CHEST	TEMPERED
SWOOPING		TALENTED	TARDIEST	TEACHING	TEMPERER
SWOPPING	**T**	TALESMAN	TARGETED	TEACH-	TEMPESTS
SWOTTING	TABLEAUS	TALISMAN	TARLATAN	INS	TEMPLATE
SYBARITE	TABLEAUX	TALKABLE	TARRAGON	TEA	TEMPORAL
SYCAMINE	TABLEMAT	TALK	TARRYING	CLOTH	TEMPTERS
SYCAMORE	TABLOIDS	SHOW	TARTARIC	TEAHOUSE	TEMPTING
SYCONIUM	TABULATE	TALLBOYS	TARTNESS	TEA-	TENACITY
SYENITIC	TACITURN	TALLNESS	TARTRATE	MAKER	TENANTRY
SYLLABIC	TACKIEST	TALLYING	TASHKENT	TEAM-	TENDENCY
SYLLABLE	TACKLING	TALLYMAN	TASKWORK	MATE	TENDERED
SYLLABUB	TACONITE	TALMUDIC	TASK	TEAMSTER	TENDERER
SYLLABUS	TACTICAL	TAMANDUA	WORK	TEAMWORK	TENDERLY
SYLVATIC	TACTLESS	TAMARACK	TASMANIA	TEA	TENDRILS
SYMBIONT	TADPOLES	TAMARIND	TASSELED	PARTY	TENEFIFE
SYMBOLIC	TAFFRAIL	TAMARISK	TASSELLY	TEARABLE	TENEMENT
SYMMETRY	TAGANROG	TAMBOURS	TASTABLE	TEARAWAY	TENERIFE
SYMPATHY	TAGMEMIC	TAMEABLE	TASTE	TEARDROP	TENESMIC
SYMPHILE	TAHITIAN	TAMENESS	BUD	TEAROOMS	TENESMUS
SYMPHONY	TAICHUNG	TAMESIDE	TASTEFUL	TEASE	TEN
SYMPOSIA	TAILBACK	TAMPERED	TASTIEST	OUT	GURUS
SYMPTOMS	TAILCOAT	TAMPERER	TATARIAN	TEASPOON	TENON
SYNAPSIS	TAIL	TAMWORTH	TATTERED	TEA	SAW
SYNAPTIC	ENDS	TANDOORI	TATTIEST	TOWEL	TENORIST
SYNARCHY	TAILGATE	TANGENCY	TATTLERS	TECHNICS	TENORITE
SYNCARPY	TAILINGS	TANGENTS	TATTLING	TECTONIC	TENOTOMY
SYNCLINE	TAILLESS	TANGIBLE	TATTOOED	TEDDY	TENSED
SYNCOPIC	TAILORED	TANGIBLY	TATTOOER	BOY	UP
SYNDESIS	TAIL	TANGIEST	TAUNTING	TEENAGER	TENSIBLE
SYNDETIC	PIPE	TANGLING	TAURANGA	TEE	TENSIONS
SYNDETON	TAILRACE	TANGOING	TAUTENED	SHIRT	TENTACLE
SYNDICAL	TAILSKID	TANGOIST	TAUTNESS	TEESSIDE	TENURIAL
SYNDROME	TAILSPIN	TANGSHAN	TAUTOMER	TEETERED	TEOCALLI
SYNERGIC	TAIL	TANKARDS	TAUTONYM	TEETHING	TEOSINTE
SYNGAMIC	SPIN	TANKED	TAVERNER	TEETOTAL	TEPHRITE
SYNONYMS	TAILWIND	UP	TAWDRILY	TEGMINAL	TEPIDITY
SYNONYMY	TAIL	TANTALIC	TAXATION	TELECAST	TERAFLOP
SYNOPSES	WIND	TANTALUM	TAX	TELECOMS	TERATISM
SYNOPSIS	TAINTING	TANTALUS	HAVEN	TELEGONY	TERATOID
SYNOPTIC	TAJ	TANTRUMS	TAXINGLY	TELEGRAM	TERATOMA
SYNOVIAL	MAHAL	TANZANIA	TAXI	TELEMARK	TERAWATT
SYNTONIC	TAKE A	TAP	RANK	TELEPLAY	TERCEIRA
SYPHILIS	BOW	DANCE	TAXONOMY	TELETEXT	TEREBENE
SYPHONED	TAKEAWAY	TAPE	TAXPAYER	TELETYPE	TERESINA
SYRACUSE	TAKE	DECK	TEABERRY	TELEVISE	TERMINAL
SYRINGED	CARE	TAPENADE	TEA	TELEWORK	TERMINUS
SYRINGES	TAKEOFFS	TAPERING	BREAK	TELEXING	TERMITES
SYSTEMIC	TAKEOUTS	TAPESTRY	TEA	TELLABLE	TERMITIC
	TAKEOVER	TAPEWORM	CADDY	TELLTALE	

TERMLESS	THATCHER	THORACES	THWARTER	TINNITUS	TOILSOME
TERNOPOL	THATCHES	THORACIC	THYROIDS	TINPLATE	TOKENISM
TERPENIC	THEARCHY	THORAXES	THYRSOID	TINSELLY	TOLERANT
TERRACES	THEATRES	THORNIER	TIAN	TINSMITH	TOLERATE
TERRAINS	THEBAINE	THORNILY	SHAN	TINTACKS	TOLIDINE
TERRAPIN	THE	THOROUGH	TIBERIAS	TIPPABLE	TOLL
TERRAZZO	BIBLE	THOUGHTS	TICKETED	TIPPLERS	CALL
TERRIBLE	THE	THOUSAND	TICKLING	TIPSIEST	TOLL-
TERRIBLY	BLUES	THRALDOM	TICKLISH	TIPSTAFF	FREE
TERRIERS	THE	THRASHED	TICK	TIPSTERS	TOLLGATE
TERRIFIC	BRINY	THRASHER	OVER	TIRELESS	TOMAHAWK
TERTIARY	THEISTIC	THREADED	TICKTACK	TIRESIAS	TOMATOES
TERYLENE	THEMATIC	THREADER	TICKTOCK	TIRESOME	TOMBAUGH
TERZETTO	THEOCRAT	THREATEN	TIDDLERS	TITANATE	TOMBLIKE
TESSERAL	THEOLOGY	THREE-D	TIDEMARK	TITANISM	TOM
TESTABLE	THEOREMS	THREE-	TIDEWAYS	TITANITE	BROWN
TESTATOR	THEORIES	PLY	TIDINESS	TITANIUM	TOMENTUM
TEST	THEORIST	THRENODY	TIE	TITANOUS	TOMMY
BANS	THEORIZE	THRESHED	BREAK	TITCHIER	GUN
TEST	THEREMIN	THRESHER	TIE-	TITHABLE	TOMMYROT
CARD	THERMALS	THRESHES	BREAK	TITIVATE	TOMMY
TEST	THERMION	THRILLED	TIE-	TITOGRAD	ROT
CASE	THERMITE	THRILLER	DYING	TITTERED	TOMORROW
TEST-	THEROPOD	THRIVING	TIENTSIN	TITTERER	TONALITY
CASE	THESIGER	THROBBED	TIGHTEST	TJIREBON	TONE-
TESTICLE	THESPIAN	THROMBIN	TIGHTWAD	TLAXCALA	DEAF
TESTIEST	THESSALY	THROMBUS	TIGRAYAN	TOADFISH	TONELESS
TEST	THEURGIC	THRONGED	TILEFISH	TOADFLAX	TONE
TUBE	THE	THROTTLE	TILLABLE	TOADYING	POEM
TETANIZE	WEALD	THROWING	TILLICUM	TOADYISM	TONICITY
TETCHIER	THIAMINE	THROW-	TIMBRELS	TO AND	TONLE
TETCHILY	THIAZINE	INS	TIMBUKTU	FRO	SAP
TETHERED	THIAZOLE	THRUMMED	TIME	TO-AND-	TONNAGES
TETRACID	THICKEST	THRUMMER	BOMB	FRO	TONSURES
TETRAPOD	THICKETS	THRUSHES	TIMECARD	TOASTERS	TOOTHIER
TETRARCH	THICKSET	THRUSTER	TIME	TOASTING	TOOTHILY
TEUTONIC	THIEVERY	THRUWAYS	LAGS	TOBACCOS	TOOTLING
TEXTBOOK	THIEVING	THUDDING	TIMELESS	TOBOGGAN	TOOTSIES
TEXTILES	THIEVISH	THUGGERY	TIMELIER	TOBY	TOPARCHY
TEXTUARY	THIMBLES	THUMBING	TIMEWORK	JUGS	TOP
TEXTURAL	THIN-	THUMBNUT	TIMEWORN	TOCCATAS	BRASS
TEXTURES	FILM	THUMPING	TIME	TOCOLOGY	TOPCOATS
THAILAND	THINKING	THUNDERS	ZONE	TODDLERS	TOP-
THALAMIC	THINNESS	THUNDERY	TIMIDITY	TODDLING	DRESS
THALAMUS	THINNEST	THURIBLE	TIMORESE	TOEHOLDS	TOP-
THALLIUM	THINNING	THURIFER	TIMOROUS	TOENAILS	HEAVY
THALLOID	THIONINE	THURROCK	TINCTURE	TOGETHER	TOPKNOTS
THALLOUS	THIOUREA	THURSDAY	TINGLING	TOGOLESE	TOP-
THANKFUL	THIRTEEN	THWACKED	TINKERED	TOILETRY	LEVEL
THANKING	THIRTIES	THWACKER	TINKERER	TOILETTE	TOP-
THANKYOU	THISTLES	THWARTED	TINKLING		NOTCH
THATCHED	THONBURI		TINNIEST		TOPOLOGY

TOPONYMY	TOWERING	TRANNIES	TRENDIER	TRIMNESS	TRUE-
TOPOTYPE	TOWN	TRANQUIL	TRENDIES	TRIMORPH	LIFE
TOPPINGS	HALL	TRANSACT	TRENDIFY	TRINIDAD	TRUELOVE
TOPPLING	TOWNSHIP	TRANSECT	TRENDILY	TRINKETS	TRUE
TOP-	TOWNSMAN	TRANSEPT	TREPHINE	TRIOXIDE	LOVE
SHELL	TOWNSMEN	TRANSFER	TRESPASS	TRIPLANE	TRUENESS
TORCHERE	TOWPATHS	TRANSFIX	TRESSURE	TRIPLETS	TRUFFLES
TORCHIER	TOWPLANE	TRANSITS	TRESTLES	TRIPLING	TRUISTIC
TOREADOR	TOWROPES	TRANSKEI	TRIADISM	TRIPLOID	TRUJILLO
TORE	TOXAEMIA	TRANSMIT	TRIAL	TRIPODAL	TRUMPERY
DOWN	TOXAEMIC	TRANSOMS	RUN	TRIPOSES	TRUMPETS
TOREUTIC	TOXICANT	TRANSUDE	TRIANGLE	TRIPPERS	TRUMPING
TORMENTS	TOXICITY	TRAPDOOR	TRIARCHY	TRIPPING	TRUNCATE
TORNADIC	TRACHEAL	TRAPEZES	TRIASSIC	TRIPTANE	TRUNDLED
TORNADOS	TRACHEAS	TRAPEZIA	TRIAXIAL	TRIPTYCH	TRUNNION
TOROIDAL	TRACHEID	TRAPPERS	TRIAZINE	TRIPWIRE	TRUSSING
TORPIDLY	TRACHOMA	TRAPPING	TRIAZOLE	TRIREMES	TRUSTEES
TORQUATE	TRACHYTE	TRAPPIST	TRIBADIC	TRISOMIC	TRUSTFUL
TORRANCE	TRACINGS	TRAPUNTO	TRIBASIC	TRISTICH	TRUSTIER
TORRENTS	TRACKING	TRASHCAN	TRIBRACH	TRITICUM	TRUSTIES
TORRIDLY	TRACTATE	TRASHIER	TRIBUNAL	TRIUMPHS	TRUSTILY
TORTELLI	TRACTILE	TRASHILY	TRIBUNES	TRIUNITY	TRUSTING
TORTILLA	TRACTION	TRASHING	TRIBUTES	TROCHAIC	TRUTHFUL
TORTIOUS	TRACTIVE	TRAVELED	TRICHINA	TROCHEES	TSARINAS
TORTOISE	TRACTORS	TRAVERSE	TRICHITE	TROCHLEA	TSESSEBI
TORTUOUS	TRADABLE	TRAVESTY	TRICHOID	TROCHOID	TSINGHAI
TORTURED	TRADE	TRAWLERS	TRICHOME	TROLLEYS	TSINGTAO
TORTURER	GAP	TRAWLING	TRICKERY	TROLLING	T-
TORTURES	TRADE	TREADING	TRICKIER	TROLLOPS	SQUARE
TOTALING	OFF	TREADLER	TRICKILY	TROMBONE	S
TOTALITY	TRADE-	TREADLES	TRICKING	TROOPERS	TSUSHIMA
TOTALIZE	OFF	TREASURE	TRICKLED	TROOPING	TUBBIEST
TOTALLED	TRAD	TREASURY	TRICTRAC	TROPHIES	TUBELESS
TOTE	JAZZ	TREATIES	TRICYCLE	TROPICAL	TUBERCLE
BAGS	TRADUCED	TREATING	TRIDENTS	TROTLINE	TUBEROSE
TOTEMISM	TRADUCER	TREATISE	TRIFLING	TROTTERS	TUBEROUS
TOTEMIST	TRAFFORD	TREATIZE	TRIFOCAL	TROTTING	TUBIFORM
TOTTERED	TRAGOPAN	TREBLING	TRIGGERS	TROUBLED	TUBULATE
TOTTERER	TRAILERS	TREE	TRIGLYPH	TROUBLER	TUBULOUS
TOUCHIER	TRAILING	FERN	TRIGONAL	TROUBLES	TUCKERED
TOUCHILY	TRAINEES	TREELESS	TRIGRAPH	TROUNCED	TUCOTUCO
TOUCHING	TRAINERS	TREELINE	TRILBIES	TROUPERS	TUESDAYS
TOUGHEST	TRAINING	TREENAIL	TRILEMMA	TROUPIAL	TUG OF
TOULOUSE	TRAIN	TREFOILS	TRILLING	TROUSERS	WAR
TOURAINE	SET	TREKKING	TRILLION	TRUCKERS	TUG-OF-
TOURISTS	TRAIPSED	TREMBLED	TRILLIUM	TRUCKING	WAR
TOURISTY	TRAITORS	TREMBLER	TRIMARAN	TRUCKLED	TUMBLERS
TOURNEYS	TRAMLINE	TREMBLES	TRIMETER	TRUDGING	TUMBLING
TOUSLING	TRAMMELS	TREMOLOS	TRIMMERS	TRUE-	TUMBRELS
TOWELING	TRAMPING	TRENCHER	TRIMMEST	BLUE	TUMIDITY
TOWELLED	TRAMPLED	TRENCHES	TRIMMING	TRUEBORN	TUMOROUS
	TRAMPLER				TUMULOSE

TUNELESS	TWENTIES	TYPE	UNBUTTON	UNFORCED	UNPLACED
TUNGSTEN	TWIDDLED	CAST	UNCAPPED	UNFORMED	UNPOLLED
TUNGSTIC	TWIDDLER	TYPEFACE	UNCHASTE	UNFREEZE	UNPRICED
TUNGUSIC	TWIDDLES	TYPE	UNCHURCH	UNFURLED	UNPROFOR
TUNICATE	TWIGGING	FACE	UNCIFORM	UNGAINLY	UNPROVEN
TUNISIAN	TWILIGHT	TYPE-	UNCINATE	UNGUENTS	UNREASON
TUNNELED	TWIN	HIGH	UNCLENCH	UNGULATE	UNRIDDLE
TUNNELER	BEDS	TYPHONIC	UNCLE	UNHANDED	UNRIFLED
TUPPENCE	TWINKLED	TYPHOONS	SAM	UNHEALED	UNROLLED
TUPPENNY	TWINKLER	TYPIFIED	UNCLE	UNHINGED	UNSADDLE
TURBANED	TWINNING	TYPIFIER	TOM	UNHORSED	UNSEATED
TURBINES	TWIN	TYPOLOGY	UNCLOTHE	UNIATISM	UNSEEDED
TURBOCAR	SETS	TYRAMINE	UNCOINED	UNIAXIAL	UNSEEING
TURBOFAN	TWIRLERS	TYROLESE	UNCOMMON	UNICORNS	UNSEEMLY
TURBOJET	TWIRLING	TYROSINE	UNCORKED	UNICYCLE	UNSETTLE
TURGIDLY	TWISTERS	TZARINAS	UNCOUPLE	UNIFORMS	UNSHAPEN
TURKOMAN	TWISTIER	TZATZIKI	UNCTUOUS	UNIFYING	UNSHAVEN
TURMERIC	TWISTING		UNDAMPED	UNIONISM	UNSOCIAL
TURNABLE	TWITCHED	**U**	UNDERACT	UNIONIST	UNSPOKEN
TURNCOAT	TWITCHER		UNDERAGE	UNIONIZE	UNSTABLE
TURNCOCK	TWITCHES	UBIQUITY	UNDERARM	UNIPOLAR	UNSTEADY
TURN	TWITTERS	UBI	UNDERBID	UNIQUELY	UNSTRING
DOWN	TWITTERY	SUPRA	UNDERBUY	UNITEDLY	UNSUBTLE
TURNINGS	TWITTING	UGLIFIER	UNDERCUT	UNIVALVE	UNSUITED
TURNKEYS	TWOCCING	UGLINESS	UNDERDOG	UNIVERSE	UNSWATHE
TURN-	TWO-	UIGURIAN	UNDERFUR	UNIVOCAL	UNTANGLE
OFFS	EDGED	UKULELES	UNDERLAY	UNKENNEL	UNTAPPED
TURNOUTS	TWOFACED	ULCERATE	UNDERLET	UNKINDER	UNTAUGHT
TURNOVER	TWO	ULCEROUS	UNDERLIE	UNKINDLY	UNTHREAD
TURNPIKE	FACED	ULTERIOR	UNDERLIP	UNKNOWNS	UNTIDILY
TURNSOLE	TWOPENCE	ULTIMATA	UNDERPAY	UNLAWFUL	UNTIMELY
TURRETED	TWO	ULTIMATE	UNDERPIN	UNLIKELY	UNTIRING
TUSKLIKE	PENCE	ULTRAISM	UNDERSEA	UNLIMBER	UNTITLED
TUSSLING	TWOPENNY	ULTRAIST	UNDERSET	UNLISTED	UNTOWARD
TUSSOCKS	TWO-	UMBONATE	UNDERTOW	UNLOADED	UNTRENDY
TUSSOCKY	PHASE	UMBRAGES	UNDERUSE	UNLOADER	UNTRUTHS
TUTELAGE	TWO-	UMBRELLA	UNDULANT	UNLOCKED	UNUSABLE
TUTELARY	PIECE	UMPIRING	UNDULATE	UNLOOSED	UNVALUED
TUTORAGE	TWO-	UNABATED	UNEARNED	UNLOOSEN	UNVEILED
TUTORIAL	SIDED	UNAWARES	UNEASIER	UNLOVELY	UNVERSED
TUTORING	TWOSOMES	UNBACKED	UNEASILY	UNMANNED	UNVOICED
TV	TWO-	UNBARRED	UNENDING	UNMARKED	UNWALLED
DINNER	STEPS	UNBEATEN	UNERRING	UNMASKED	UNWASHED
TWADDLER	TWO-	UNBELIEF	UNEVENLY	UNMASKER	UNWEIGHT
TWANGING	TIMED	UNBIASED	UNFAIRER	UNMUZZLE	UNWIELDY
TWEAKING	TWO-	UNBIDDEN	UNFAIRLY	UNNERVED	UNWINDER
TWEETERS	TIMER	UNBODIED	UNFASTEN	UNOPENED	UNWISHED
TWEETING	TYMPANIC	UNBOLTED	UNFETTER	UNPACKED	UNWONTED
TWEEZERS	TYMPANUM	UNBRIDLE	UNFILIAL	UNPACKER	UNWORTHY
TWELFTHS	TYNESIDE	UNBROKEN	UNFOLDED	UNPEOPLE	UNZIPPED
TWELVEMO	TYPECAST	UNBUCKLE	UNFOLDER	UNPICKED	

UP-	UROSCOPY	VALVULAR	VENEERED	VESUVIAN	VINOSITY
ANCHOR	UROSTYLE	VAMBRACE	VENEERER	VESUVIUS	VINTAGER
UP-AND-	URSULINE	VAMOOSED	VENERATE	VETERANS	VINTAGES
UPS	URTICATE	VAMPIRES	VENEREAL	VEXATION	VINTNERS
UPCOMING	URUSHIOL	VAMPIRIC	VENETIAN	VEXILLUM	VIOLABLE
UPDATING	USEFULLY	VANADATE	VENGEFUL	VEXINGLY	VIOLATED
UPENDING	USHERING	VANADIUM	VENOMOUS	VIADUCTS	VIOLATOR
UPGRADED	USUFRUCT	VANADOUS	VENOSITY	VIA	VIOLENCE
UPGRADER	USURIOUS	VANGUARD	VENTOLIN	MEDIA	VIPERINE
UPGROWTH	USURPERS	VANILLIC	VENTOUSE	VIATICAL	VIPEROUS
UPHEAVAL	USURPING	VANILLIN	VENTURED	VIATICUM	VIRAGOES
UPHOLDER	UTENSILS	VANISHED	VENTURER	VIBRANCY	VIRGINAL
UPLIFTED	UTERUSES	VANISHER	VENTURES	VIBRATED	VIRGINIA
UPLIFTER	UTILIZED	VANQUISH	VENUSIAN	VIBRATOR	VIRIDIAN
UP-	UTILIZER	VAPIDITY	VERACITY	VIBRATOS	VIRIDITY
MARKET	UTTERING	VAPORIZE	VERACRUZ	VIBRIOID	VIRILISM
UPPERCUT	UVULITIS	VAPOROUS	VERANDAS	VIBRISSA	VIRILITY
UPRAISER	UXORIOUS	VAPOURER	VERBALLY	VIBRONIC	VIROLOGY
UPRISING		VARACTOR	VERBATIM	VIBURNUM	VIRTUOSI
UPROOTED	**V**	VARANASI	VERBIAGE	VICARAGE	VIRTUOSO
UPROOTER		VARIABLE	VERBOTEN	VICARIAL	VIRTUOUS
UPSETTER	VACANTLY	VARIABLY	VERCELLI	VICELIKE	VIRULENT
UPSTAGED	VACATING	VARIANCE	VERDANCY	VICENARY	VISCACHA
UPSTAIRS	VACATION	VARIANTS	VERDICTS	VICEROYS	VISCERAL
UPSTARTS	VACCINAL	VARICOSE	VERIFIED	VICINITY	VISCOUNT
UPSTREAM	VACCINES	VARIETAL	VERIFIER	VICTORIA	VISIONAL
UPSTROKE	VACCINIA	VARIFORM	VERISTIC	VICTUALS	VISITANT
UPSURGES	VACUOLAR	VARIOLAR	VERITIES	VIDEOFIT	VISITING
UPSWINGS	VACUUMED	VARIORUM	VERJUICE	VIDEOING	VISITORS
UPTHRUST	VADODARA	VARISTOR	VERLIGTE	VIENNESE	VISUALLY
UP TO	VAGABOND	VARITYPE	VERMOUTH	VIETCONG	VITALISM
DATE	VAGARIES	VARMINTS	VERONESE	VIETMINH	VITALIST
UP-TO	VAGINATE	VASCULAR	VERONICA	VIEWLESS	VITALITY
DATE	VAGOTOMY	VASCULUM	VERRUCAE	VIGILANT	VITALIZE
UPTURNED	VAGRANCY	VASELINE	VERRUCAS	VIGNETTE	VITAMINS
URALITIC	VAGRANTS	VASTERAS	VERSICLE	VIGOROSO	VITELLIN
URANITIC	VAINNESS	VASTNESS	VERSIONS	VIGOROUS	VITIABLE
URANYLIC	VALANCED	VAUCLUSE	VERTEBRA	VILENESS	VITIATED
URBANELY	VALANCES	VAULTERS	VERTEXES	VILIFIED	VITIATOR
URBANITY	VALDIVIA	VAULTING	VERTICAL	VILIFIER	VITII
URBANIZE	VAL-	VAUNTING	VERTICES	VILLAGER	LEVU
URCTERAL	D'OISE	VEGETATE	VERTICIL	VILLAGES	VITILIGO
URETHANE	VALENCIA	VEHEMENT	VESICANT	VILLAINS	VITREOUS
URETHRAL	VALERIAN	VEHICLES	VESICATE	VILLAINY	VITULINE
URETHRAS	VALIANCE	VEILEDLY	VESICLES	VILLATIC	VIVACITY
URGENTLY	VALIDATE	VELARIZE	VESPERAL	VILLEINS	VIVARIUM
URGINGLY	VALIDITY	VELOCITY	VESPIARY	VINCULUM	VIVA
URINATED	VALLETTA	VENALITY	VESTIGES	VINDALOO	VOCE
URNFIELD	VALORIZE	VENATION	VESTMENT	VINEGARY	VIVIFIER
UROCHORD	VALOROUS	VENDETTA	VESTRIES	VINEYARD	VIVISECT
UROLOGIC	VALUABLE	VENDIBLE	VESTURAL	VINNITSA	VIXENISH
UROPODAL	VALUATOR				

VLADIMIR	W	WARFARIN	WATT-	WELL	WHICKERS
VOCALESE	WADDLING	WAR	HOUR	HEAD	WHIFFIER
VOCALISE	WAFFLING	GAMES	WAVE	WELL-	WHIGGERY
VOCALISM	WAGERING	WARHEADS	BAND	HUNG	WHIGGISH
VOCALIST	WAGGLING	WARHORSE	WAVEFORM	WELL-	WHIMBREL
VOCALITY	WAGON-	WARINESS	WAVELIKE	KNIT	WHIMPERS
VOCALIZE	LIT	WARLOCKS	WAVERERS	WELL-	WHIMSIES
VOCATION	WAGTAILS	WARLORDS	WAVERING	NIGH	WHINCHAT
VOCATIVE	WAINSCOT	WARMNESS	WAVINESS	WELL	WHINGING
VOICE	WAITRESS	WARNINGS	WAXBERRY	READ	WHINNIED
BOX	WAKASHAN	WAR	WAXINESS	WELL-	WHINNIES
VOICEFUL	WAKAYAMA	PAINT	WAXPLANT	READ	WHIPCORD
VOIDABLE	WAKELESS	WARPATHS	WAXWORKS	WELL-TO-	WHIP
VOIDANCE	WAKENING	WARPLANE	WAYBILLS	DO	HAND
VOLATILE	WALKABLE	WARRANTS	WAYFARER	WELL-	WHIPLASH
VOLCANIC	WALKAWAY	WARRANTY	WAYLAYER	WORN	WHIPLIKE
VOLCANOS	WALKMANS	WARRIGAL	WEAKENED	WELSHERS	WHIPPETS
VOLITION	WALKOUTS	WARRIORS	WEAKENER	WELSHING	WHIPPING
VOLITIVE	WALKOVER	WARSHIPS	WEAKFISH	WENCHING	WHIPWORM
VOLLEYED	WALLAROO	WARTBURG	WEAKLING	WEREWOLF	WHIRLING
VOLLEYER	WALLASEY	WARTHOGS	WEAKNESS	WESLEYAN	WHIRRING
VOLPLANE	WALLEYED	WASHABLE	WEANLING	WEST	WHISKERS
VOLTAGES	WALL-	WASHBOWL	WEAPONED	BANK	WHISKERY
VOLTAISM	LIKE	WASHDAYS	WEAPONRY	WESTERLY	WHISKIES
VOLUTION	WALLOPED	WASHED-	WEARABLE	WESTERNS	WHISKING
VOLVULUS	WALLOPER	UP	WEARIEST	WESTWARD	WHISPERS
VOMERINE	WALLOWED	WASHOUTS	WEARYING	WESTWOOD	WHISTLED
VOMITING	WALLOWER	WASHROOM	WEASELED	WET	WHISTLER
VOMITIVE	WALLSEND	WASTABLE	WEASELLY	DREAM	WHISTLES
VOMITORY	WALRUSES	WASTEFUL	WEDDINGS	WET	WHITE
VONNEGUT	WALTZING	WASTRELS	WEDGWOOD	NURSE	ANT
VOORSKOT	WANDERED	WATCHDOG	WEEDIEST	WET	WHITECAP
VORACITY	WANDERER	WATCHFUL	WEEKDAYS	SUITS	WHITE-
VORONEZH	WANDEROO	WATCHING	WEEKENDS	WETTABLE	EYE
VORTEXES	WANGANUI	WATCHMAN	WEEKLIES	WETTINGS	WHITEFLY
VORTICAL	WANGLING	WATCHMEN	WEENIEST	WEYMOUTH	WHITE-
VORTICES	WANTONLY	WATERAGE	WEIGHING	WHACKING	HOT
VOTARESS	WARANGAL	WATER	WEIGHTED	WHARFAGE	WHITE
VOTARIES	WARBLERS	BAG	WEIGHTER	WHATEVER	LIE
VOTARIST	WARBLING	WATERBED	WEIRDEST	WHATNOTS	WHITENED
VOUCHERS	WAR	WATER	WELCHING	WHATSITS	WHITENER
VOUCHING	CRIES	ICE	WELCOMED	WHEATEAR	WHITEOUT
VOUSSOIR	WAR	WATERING	WELCOMER	WHEEDLED	WHITE-
VOWELIZE	CRIME	WATERLOO	WELCOMES	WHEEDLER	TIE
VOYAGERS	WAR	WATERMAN	WELDABLE	WHEELIES	WHITINGS
VOYAGING	DANCE	WATER	WELL-	WHEELING	WHITLOWS
VULGARLY	WARDENRY	RAT	BRED	WHEEZILY	WHITTLED
VULTURES	WARDRESS	WATER	WELL	WHEEZING	WHITTLER
VULVITIS	WARDROBE	SKI	DONE	WHENEVER	WHIZ-
	WARDROOM	WATER-	WELL-	WHEREVER	BANG
	WARDSHIP	SKI	DONE	WHETTING	WHIZZING
		WATERWAY	WELLHEAD	WHEYFACE	

WHIZZ	WINDHOEK	WITHHELD	WORKABLE	WRESTING	YARN-
KID	WINDIEST	WITHHOLD	WORKADAY	WRESTLED	DYED
WHODUNIT	WINDLASS	WITTIEST	WORKBAGS	WRESTLER	YASHMAKS
WHOMEVER	WINDMILL	WIZARDRY	WORKBOOK	WRETCHED	YEANLING
WHOOPEES	WINDPIPE	WOBBLIER	WORKDAYS	WRETCHES	YEARBOOK
WHOOPING	WINDSAIL	WOBBLING	WORKED	WRIGGLED	YEARLING
WHOOSHES	WINDSOCK	WOEFULLY	UP	WRIGGLER	YEARLONG
WHOPPERS	WINDWARD	WOLFFISH	WORKINGS	WRIGGLES	YEARNING
WHOPPING	WINE	WOLFLIKE	WORKLOAD	WRINGERS	YEASTILY
WHOREDOM	BARS	WOMANISH	WORKOUTS	WRINGING	YELLOWED
WICKEDLY	WINESKIN	WOMANIST	WORKROOM	WRINKLED	YEOMANLY
WIDE	WINGLESS	WOMANIZE	WORKSHOP	WRINKLES	YEOMANRY
BOYS	WINGLIKE	WOMBLIKE	WORKTOPS	WRISTLET	YIELDING
WIDE-	WING	WONDERED	WORLD	WRITE-	YODELING
EYED	NUTS	WONDERER	CUP	INS	YODELLED
WIDENESS	WINGOVER	WONDROUS	WORM	WRITE	YODELLER
WIDENING	WINGSPAN	WONKIEST	CAST	OFF	YOKELISH
WIDE	WINKLING	WOODBINE	WORM	WRITE-	YOKOHAMA
OPEN	WINNABLE	WOODCHAT	GEAR	OFF	YOKOSUKA
WIDE-	WINNINGS	WOODCOCK	WORMHOLE	WRITE-	YOUNGEST
OPEN	WINNIPEG	WOODCUTS	WORMIEST	UPS	YOUNGISH
WIDGEONS	WINNOWED	WOODENLY	WORMLIKE	WRITHING	YOURSELF
WIDOWERS	WINNOWER	WOODIEST	WORMSEED	WRITINGS	YOUTHFUL
WIELDERS	WINTERED	WOODLAND	WORMWOOD	WRONGFUL	YTTERBIA
WIELDING	WINTERER	WOODLARK	WORRIERS	WRONGING	YUCKIEST
WIGGINGS	WINTRIER	WOODLICE	WORRYING	WURZBURG	YUGOSLAV
WIGGLING	WINTRILY	WOODNOTE	WORSENED		YULE
WILD	WIPED	WOODPILE	WORSE-	**X**	LOGS
BOAR	OUT	WOOD	OFF	XANTHATE	YULETIDE
WILD	WIREDRAW	PULP	WORSHIPS	XANTHEIN	YVELINES
CARD	WIRELESS	WOODRUFF	WORSTING	XANTHENE	
WILDCATS	WIRETAPS	WOODRUSH	WORST-	XANTHINE	**Z**
WILD-	WIRE	WOODSHED	OFF	XANTHOMA	ZAANSTAD
EYED	WOOL	WOODSMAN	WORTHIER	XANTHOUS	ZAIBATSU
WILDFIRE	WIREWORK	WOODSMEN	WORTHIES	XENOGAMY	ZANINESS
WILDFOWL	WIREWORM	WOODWIND	WORTHILY	XENOLITH	ZANZIBAR
WILDLIFE	WIRE-	WOODWORK	WORTHING	XEROSERE	ZAPPIEST
WILDNESS	WOVE	WOODWORM	WOUNDING	XEROXING	ZARAGOZA
WILD	WIRINESS	WOOLLENS	WRANGLED	XIANGTAN	ZARATITE
OATS	WISEACRE	WOOLLIER	WRANGLER	X-RAY	ZEALOTRY
WILD	WISE	WOOLLIES	WRANGLES	TUBE	ZECCHINO
WEST	GUYS	WOOLLILY	WRAPOVER	XYLIDINE	ZENITHAL
WILFULLY	WISENESS	WOOLPACK	WRAPPERS	XYLOCARP	ZEOLITIC
WILINESS	WISHBONE	WOOLSACK	WRAPPING	XYLOTOMY	ZEPPELIN
WILLABLE	WISPIEST	WOOZIEST	WRATHFUL		ZERO
WILLIWAW	WISTERIA	WORDBOOK	WREAKING	**Y**	HOUR
WINCHING	WITCHERY	WORD-	WREATHED	YACHTING	ZHEJIANG
WINDABLE	WITCHING	DEAF	WRECKAGE	YAHOOISM	ZHITOMIR
WINDBAGS	WITHDRAW	WORDIEST	WRECKERS	YAKITORI	ZIBELINE
WINDBURN	WITHDREW	WORDLESS	WRECKING	YAMMERED	ZILLIONS
WINDFALL	WITHERED	WORDPLAY	WRENCHED	YAMMERER	ZIMBABWE
WINDGALL	WITHERER		WRENCHES	YARDARMS	

ZIONISTS	ZLATOUST	ZOOGLOEA	ZOONOSIS	ZOOTOXIC	ZYGOTENE
ZIP	ZODIACAL	ZOOLATER	ZOOPHILE	ZOOTOXIN	ZYMOLOGY
CODES	ZOMBIISM	ZOOLATRY	ZOOPHYTE	ZUCCHINI	
ZIPPIEST	ZONATION	ZOOMETRY	ZOOSPERM	ZUGZWANG	
ZIRCONIA	ZONETIME	ZOOM	ZOOSPORE	ZULULAND	
ZIRCONIC	ZOOCHORE	LENS	ZOOTOMIC	ZWIEBACK	

A
AARONS ROD
ABACTINAL
ABANDONED
ABASEMENT
ABASHEDLY
ABATEMENT
ABATTOIRS
ABCOULOMB
ABDICABLE
ABDICATED
ABDICATOR
ABDOMINAL
ABDUCTING
ABDUCTION
ABERRANCE
ABHORRENT
ABHORRING
ABIDINGLY
ABILITIES
A BIT
  THICK
ABJECTION
ABLUTIONS
ABNEGATOR
ABOLISHED
ABOLISHER
ABOLITION
ABOMINATE
ABORIGINE
ABORTIONS
ABOUNDING
ABOUT TURN
ABOUT-TURN
ABRASIONS
ABRASIVES
ABRIDGING
ABROGATED
ABROGATOR
ABSCESSES
ABSCONDED
ABSCONDER
ABSEILING
ABSENTEES
ABSENTING
ABSOLVING
ABSORBENT
ABSORBING
ABSTAINED
ABSTAINER
ABSTINENT

ABSTRACTS
ABSURDISM
ABSURDITY
ABUNDANCE
ABU SIMBEL
ABUSIVELY
ABUTMENTS
ABYSSINIA
ACADEMICS
ACANTHINE
ACANTHOID
ACANTHOUS
ACARIASIS
ACAROLOGY
ACCEDENCE
ACCENTING
ACCENTUAL
ACCEPTANT
ACCEPTING
ACCESSING
ACCESSION
ACCESSORY
ACCIDENCE
ACCIDENTS
ACCIPITER
ACCLAIMED
ACCLIVITY
ACCOLADES
ACCOMPANY
ACCORDANT
ACCORDING
ACCORDION
ACCOSTING
ACCOUNTED
ACCRETION
ACCRETIVE
ACCRUMENT
ACCUMBENT
ACELLULAR
ACESCENCE
ACETAMIDE
ACETIFIER
ACETYLATE
ACETYLENE
ACETYLIDE
ACHEULIAN
ACHIEVING
ACICULATE
ACID HOUSE
ACIDIFIED
ACIDIFIER

ACIDOPHIL
ACID TESTS
ACIDULATE
ACIDULOUS
ACINIFORM
ACOUSTICS
ACQUIESCE
ACQUIRING
ACQUITTAL
ACQUITTED
ACQUITTER
ACROBATIC
ACRODROME
ACROGENIC
ACRONYMIC
ACROPETAL
ACROPOLIS
ACROSPIRE
ACROSTICS
ACTINOPOD
ACTIVATED
ACTIVATOR
ACTIVISTS
ACTRESSES
ACTS OF
  GOD
ACTUALITY
ACTUALIZE
ACTUARIAL
ACTUARIES
ACTUATING
ACTUATION
ACUMINATE
ACUMINOUS
ACUTENESS
ACYCLOVIR
ADAMANTLY
ADAPTABLE
ADDICTION
ADDICTIVE
ADDITIONS
ADDITIVES
ADDRESSED
ADDRESSEE
ADDRESSER
ADDRESSES
ADDUCTION
ADEMPTION
ADENOIDAL
ADENOSINE
ADHERENCE

ADHERENTS
ADHESIONS
ADHESIVES
ADIABATIC
AD INTERIM
ADIPOCERE
ADJACENCY
ADJECTIVE
ADJOINING
ADJOURNED
ADJUDGING
ADJUSTING
ADJUTANCY
ADJUTANTS
AD-LIBBING
ADMEASURE
ADMINICLE
ADMIRABLE
ADMIRABLY
ADMIRALTY
ADMISSION
ADMISSIVE
ADMITTING
ADMIXTURE
AD NAUSEAM
ADNOMINAL
ADOPTIONS
ADORATION
ADORNMENT
ADRENALIN
ADSORBATE
ADSORBENT
ADULATION
ADULATORY
ADULTERER
ADUMBRATE
AD VALOREM
ADVANCING
ADVANTAGE
ADVECTION
ADVENTIVE
ADVENTURE
ADVERBIAL
ADVERSARY
ADVERSELY
ADVERSITY
ADVERTING
ADVERTISE
ADVISABLE
ADVISEDLY
ADVOCATED

ADVOCATES
AEOLIPILE
AEPYORNIS
AEROBATIC
AERODROME
AEROLOGIC
AEROMETER
AEROMETRY
AEROPAUSE
AEROPHONE
AEROPLANE
AEROSPACE
AESTHESIA
AESTHETES
AESTHETIC
AESTIVATE
AETHEREAL
AETIOLOGY
AFFECTING
AFFECTION
AFFECTIVE
AFFIANCED
AFFIDAVIT
AFFILIATE
AFFIRMING
AFFIXTURE
AFFLICTED
AFFLUENCE
AFFORDING
AFFRICATE
AFFRONTED
AFLATOXIN
AFORESAID
A FORTIORI
AFRIKAANS
AFRIKANER
AFRO-ASIAN
AFTERBODY
AFTERCARE
AFTERDAMP
AFTERDECK
AFTERGLOW
AFTERHEAT
AFTERLIFE
AFTERMATH
AFTERNOON
AFTERWORD
AGE GROUPS
AGGRAVATE
AGGREGATE
AGGRESSOR

AGGRIEVED
AGITATING
AGITATION
AGITATORS
AGNOLOTTI
AGNOMINAL
AGNOSTICS
AGONISTIC
AGONIZING
AGREEABLE
AGREEABLY
AGREEMENT
AGRIGENTO
AGRONOMIC
AGTERSKOT
AHMEDABAD
AILANTHUS
AIMLESSLY
AIRBRAKES
AIRFIELDS
AIRFORCES
AIR GUITAR
AIR-INTAKE
AIRLETTER
AIRLIFTED
AIRLINERS
AIRPLANES
AIRPOCKET
AIRSTREAM
AIRSTRIPS
AIRWORTHY
AITCHBONE
ALABAMIAN
ALABASTER
ALARM BELL
ALARMISTS
ALBATROSS
ALBERTITE
ALBESCENT
ALCHEMIST
ALCHEMIZE
ALCOHOLIC
ALDEBARAN
ALDEBURGH
ALDERSHOT
ALEHOUSES
ALEMANNIC
ALEPH-NULL
ALERTNESS
ALFILARIA
ALGARROBA

ALGEBRAIC
ALGECIRAS
ALGOMETER
ALGOMETRY
ALGONQUIN
ALGORITHM
ALICE BAND
ALICYCLIC
ALIENABLE
ALIENATED
ALIENATOR
ALIGHTING
ALIGNMENT
ALIPHATIC
ALKALOSIS
ALLA BREVE
ALLAHABAD
ALLANTOIC
ALLANTOID
ALLANTOIS
ALL-AROUND
ALL AT
  ONCE
ALLEGEDLY
ALLELUIAS
ALL ENDS
  UP
ALLENTOWN
ALLERGIES
ALLERGIST
ALLETHRIN
ALLEVIATE
ALLEYWAYS
ALLIANCES
ALLIGATOR
ALLOCATED
ALLOGRAFT
ALLOGRAPH
ALLOMETRY
ALLOMORPH
ALLOPATHY
ALLOPHANE
ALLOPHONE
ALLOPLASM
ALLOTMENT
ALLOTROPE
ALLOTROPY
ALLOTTING
ALLOWABLE
ALLOWABLY
ALLOWANCE

ALLOWEDLY
ALLUSIONS
ALLUVIUMS
ALMA MATER
ALMANDINE
ALMSHOUSE
ALMS-HOUSE
ALONGSIDE
ALOOFNESS
ALPENGLOW
ALPHABETS
ALSATIANS
ALTERABLE
ALTERCATE
ALTER EGOS
ALTERNATE
ALTIMETER
ALTIMETRY
ALTIPLANO
ALTISSIMO
ALTITUDES
ALTRICIAL
ALTRUISTS
ALUMINATE
ALUMINIUM
ALUMINIZE
ALUMINOUS
ALVEOLARS
ALVEOLATE
AMAGASAKI
AMARYLLIS
AMAUROSIS
AMAUROTIC
AMAZEMENT
AMAZINGLY
AMAZONIAN
AMAZONITE
AMBERGRIS
AMBERJACK
AMBIENCES
AMBIGUITY
AMBIGUOUS
AMBITIONS
AMBITIOUS
AMBLESIDE
AMBLYOPIA
AMBLYOPIC
AMBROSIAL
AMBROTYPE
AMBULANCE
AMBUSHING

AMENDABLE
AMENDMENT
AMENITIES
AMERASIAN
AMERICANA
AMERICANS
AMERICIUM
AMERINDIC
AMETHYSTS
AMETROPIA
AMIANTHUS
AMIDSHIPS
AMINO ACID
AMMOCOETE
AMMONIATE
AMMONICAL
AMMONITIC
AMNESIACS
AMNESTIES
AMOEBAEAN
AMORALITY
AMOROUSLY
AMORPHISM
AMORPHOUS
AMORTIZED
AMOUNTING
AMPERSAND
AMPHIBIAN
AMPHIBOLE
AMPHIGORY
AMPHIOXUS
AMPLIFIED
AMPLIFIER
AMPLITUDE
AMPUTATED
AMSTERDAM
AMUSEMENT
AMUSINGLY
AMYGDALIN
AMYLOPSIN
ANABANTID
ANABIOSIS
ANABOLISM
ANABOLITE
ANACLINAL
ANACLISIS
ANACLITIC
ANACONDAS
ANACRUSIS
ANAEROBIC
ANALECTIC

ANALEPTIC
ANALGESIA
ANALGESIC
ANALOGIES
ANALOGIST
ANALOGIZE
ANALOGOUS
ANALOGUES
ANALYSAND
ANALYSING
ANALYTICS
ANAMNESIS
ANANDROUS
ANANTHOUS
ANAPAESTS
ANAPESTIC
ANAPHORAL
ANAPLASIA
ANAPLASTY
ANAPTYXIS
ANARCHISM
ANARCHIST
ANARTHRIA
ANATHEMAS
ANATOLIAN
ANATOMIES
ANATOMIST
ANATOMIZE
ANCESTORS
ANCESTRAL
ANCHORAGE
ANCHORESS
ANCHORING
ANCHORITE
ANCHOVIES
ANCILLARY
ANCIPITAL
ANDALUSIA
ANDANTINO
ANDRADITE
ANDROLOGY
ANDROMEDA
ANECDOTAL
ANECDOTES
ANECDOTIC
ANEMOLOGY
ANEUPLOID
ANGEL CAKE
ANGELFISH
ANGELICAL
ANGIOGRAM

ANGIOLOGY	ANSWERING	APERITIFS	APPOINTER	ARCTOGAEA
ANGLE IRON	ANTALKALI	APERTURES	APPOINTOR	ARCTURIAN
ANGLESITE	ANTARCTIC	APETALOUS	APPORTION	ARCUATION
ANGLEWORM	ANTEATERS	APHERESIS	APPRAISAL	ARDUOUSLY
ANGLICANS	ANTECHOIR	APHIDIOUS	APPRAISED	AREA CODES
ANGLICISM	ANTEDATED	APHORISMS	APPRAISER	ARGENTINA
ANGLICIZE	ANTEFIXAL	APHYLLOUS	APPREHEND	ARGENTINE
ANGOSTURA	ANTELOPES	APICULATE	APPRESSED	ARGENTITE
ANGUISHED	ANTENATAL	APISHNESS	APPRISING	ARGENTOUS
ANHYDRIDE	ANTENNULE	APIVOROUS	APPROBATE	ARGILLITE
ANHYDRITE	ANTEROOMS	APLANATIC	APPROVING	ARGUMENTS
ANHYDROUS	ANTHELION	APOCOPATE	APPULSIVE	ARMADILLO
ANIMALISM	ANTHEMION	APOCRYPHA	APRIL FOOL	ARMAMENTS
ANIMALIST	ANTHODIUM	APODICTIC	APRIORITY	ARMATURES
ANIMALITY	ANTHOLOGY	APOENZYME	APTITUDES	ARMCHAIRS
ANIMALIZE	ANTHOTAXY	APOGAMOUS	AQUALUNGS	ARMISTICE
ANIMATEUR	ANTHOZOAN	APOLOGIAS	AQUAPLANE	ARMOURERS
ANIMATING	ANTHURIUM	APOLOGIES	AQUARELLE	ARMOURIES
ANIMATION	ANTICHLOR	APOLOGIST	AQUARIUMS	ARMS RACES
ANIMATISM	ANTICLINE	APOLOGIZE	AQUATINTS	AROMATIZE
ANIMISTIC	ANTIDOTES	APOPHASIS	AQUEDUCTS	ARPEGGIOS
ANIMOSITY	ANTIGENIC	APOPHYSIS	AQUILEGIA	ARRAIGNED
ANISOGAMY	ANTIKNOCK	APOPTOSIS	AQUITAINE	ARRAIGNER
ANKLEBONE	ANTIMERIC	APOSTATES	ARABESQUE	ARRANGING
ANKLE BONE	ANTIMONIC	APOSTOLIC	ARABINOSE	ARRESTING
ANKYLOSIS	ANTIMONYL	APPALLING	ARACHNOID	ARRIVISTE
ANNALISTS	ANTINODAL	APPALOOSA	ARAGONESE	ARROGANCE
ANNAPOLIS	ANTINOMIC	APPARATUS	ARAGONITE	ARROGATED
ANNAPURNA	ANTIPATHY	APPARITOR	ARAUCANIA	ARROGATOR
ANNEALING	ANTIPHONY	APPEALING	ARAUCARIA	ARROWHEAD
ANNELIDAN	ANTIPODAL	APPEARING	ARBITRAGE	ARROWROOT
ANNOTATED	ANTIPODES	APPEASING	ARBITRARY	ARROWWOOD
ANNOTATOR	ANTIQUARY	APPELLANT	ARBITRATE	ARROWWORM
ANNOUNCED	ANTIQUATE	APPELLATE	ARBITRESS	ARSENICAL
ANNOUNCER	ANTIQUITY	APPENDAGE	ARBOREOUS	ARSENIOUS
ANNOYANCE	ANTISERUM	APPENDANT	ARBORETUM	ARSONISTS
ANNUITANT	ANTITOXIC	APPENDING	ARBOVIRUS	ARTEFACTS
ANNUITIES	ANTITOXIN	APPENZELL	ARCHAISMS	ARTEMISIA
ANNULLING	ANTIVENIN	APPERTAIN	ARCHAIZER	ARTERIOLE
ANNULMENT	ANTIVIRAL	APPETENCE	ARCHANGEL	ARTERITIS
ANOESTRUS	ANTIWORLD	APPETITES	ARCHDUCAL	ARTHRITIC
ANOINTING	ANTONIONI	APPETIZER	ARCHDUCHY	ARTHRITIS
ANOMALIES	ANXIETIES	APPLAUDED	ARCHDUKES	ARTHROPOD
ANOMALOUS	ANXIOUSLY	APPLAUDER	ARCHENEMY	ARTICHOKE
ANONYMITY	ANY AMOUNT	APPLE CART	ARCHETYPE	ARTICLING
ANONYMOUS	APARTHEID	APPLEJACK	ARCHFIEND	ARTICULAR
ANOPHELES	APARTMENT	APPLE PIES	ARCHICARP	ARTIFACTS
ANORTHITE	APATHETIC	APPLIANCE	ARCHITECT	ARTIFICER
ANOSMATIC	APELDOORN	APPLICANT	ARCHIVIST	ARTIFICES
ANOXAEMIA	APENNINES	APPOINTED	ARCHIVOLT	ARTILLERY
ANOXAEMIC	APERIODIC	APPOINTEE	ARCOGRAPH	ARTLESSLY

ARYTENOID	ASSUREDLY	ATTENDING	AUTOGRAPH	BACILLARY
ASCENDANT	ASSURGENT	ATTENTION	AUTOICOUS	BACKACHES
ASCENDING	ASTERISKS	ATTENTIVE	AUTOLYSIN	BACKBENCH
ASCENSION	ASTEROIDS	ATTENUANT	AUTOLYSIS	BACKBITER
ASCERTAIN	ASTHMATIC	ATTENUATE	AUTOLYTIC	BACKBOARD
ASCOSPORE	ASTOUNDED	ATTESTANT	AUTOMATED	BACKBONES
ASCRIBING	ASTRADDLE	ATTESTING	AUTOMATIC	BACKCLOTH
ASEPALOUS	ASTRAKHAN	AT THE	AUTOMATON	BACKCROSS
ASEXUALLY	ASTROCYTE	TIME	AUTONOMIC	BACKDATED
ASHAMEDLY	ASTRODOME	ATTITUDES	AUTOPHYTE	BACK DOORS
ASHKENAZI	ASTROLABE	ATTORNEYS	AUTOPSIES	BACKDROPS
ASHKHABAD	ASTROLOGY	ATTRACTED	AUTOSOMAL	BACKFIRED
ASININITY	ASTRONAUT	ATTRACTOR	AUTOTIMER	BACKHANDS
ASPARAGUS	ASTRONOMY	ATTRIBUTE	AUTOTOMIC	BACKPACKS
ASPERSION	ASYLLABIC	ATTRITION	AUTOTOXIC	BACKPEDAL
ASPERSIVE	ASYMMETRY	ATTRITIVE	AUTOTOXIN	BACK PEDAL
ASPHALTED	ASYMPTOTE	AUBERGINE	AUTOTYPIC	BACK SEATS
ASPHALTIC	ASYNDETIC	AUBRIETIA	AUXILIARY	BACK SHIFT
ASPHALTUM	ASYNDETON	AU COURANT	AVAILABLE	BACKSIDES
ASPHYXIAL	AT A	AUCTIONED	AVAILABLY	BACKSIGHT
ASPIRANTS	GLANCE	AUCTORIAL	AVALANCHE	BACKSLIDE
ASPIRATED	ATARACTIC	AUDACIOUS	AVERAGING	BACKSPACE
ASPIRATES	ATAVISTIC	AUDIENCES	AVERSIONS	BACKSTAGE
ASPIRATOR	ATHEISTIC	AUDIO BOOK	AVERTIBLE	BACKSWEPT
ASSAILANT	ATHENAEUM	AUDIOLOGY	AVIFAUNAL	BACKTRACK
ASSAILING	ATHLETICS	AUDIPHONE	AVIRULENT	BACKWARDS
ASSASSINS	ATLANTEAN	AUDITIONS	AVOCATION	BACKWATER
ASSAULTED	ATMOLYSIS	AUGMENTED	AVOIDABLE	BACKWOODS
ASSAULTER	ATMOMETER	AUGMENTOR	AVOIDANCE	BACKYARDS
ASSAYABLE	ATMOMETRY	AU NATUREL	AVUNCULAR	BACTERIAL
ASSEMBLED	ATOM BOMBS	AUNT SALLY	AWAKENING	BACTERIUM
ASSEMBLER	ATOMICITY	AURICULAR	AWARDABLE	BACTEROID
ASSENTING	ATOMISTIC	AUSCHWITZ	AWARENESS	BADGERING
ASSERTING	ATOMIZERS	AUSTENITE	AWESTRUCK	BADMINTON
ASSERTION	ATONALISM	AUSTERELY	AWFULNESS	BAGATELLE
ASSERTIVE	ATONALITY	AUSTERITY	AWKWARDLY	BAGGINESS
ASSESSING	ATONEMENT	AUSTRALIA	AXIOMATIC	BAG LADIES
ASSESSORS	AT ONE	AUTARCHIC	AYAHUASCA	BAHUVRIHI
ASSIDUITY	TIME	AUTARKIES	AYATOLLAH	BAILIWICK
ASSIDUOUS	ATONICITY	AUTHENTIC	AYUTTHAYA	BAIN-MARIE
ASSIGNING	AT PRESENT	AUTHORESS	AZEDARACH	BAKHTARAN
ASSISTANT	ATROCIOUS	AUTHORIAL	AZEOTROPE	BALACLAVA
ASSISTING	ATROPHIED	AUTHORITY	AZIMUTHAL	BALAKLAVA
ASSOCIATE	ATTACHING	AUTHORIZE		BALALAIKA
ASSONANCE	ATTACKERS	AUTOCLAVE	**B**	BALANCING
ASSORTING	ATTACKING	AUTOCRACY		BALCONIES
ASSUAGING	ATTAINDER	AUTOCRATS	BAAGANDJI	BALEFULLY
ASSUASIVE	ATTAINING	AUTOCROSS	BABY TEETH	BALKANIZE
ASSUMABLE	ATTEMPTED	AUTOECISM	BABY TOOTH	BALLASTED
ASSURABLE	ATTEMPTER	AUTOFOCUS	BACCHANAL	BALLCOCKS
ASSURANCE	ATTENDANT	AUTOGRAFT	BACCIFORM	BALLERINA
			BACHELORS	

BALL GAMES	BARCELONA	BATTENING	BEERSHEBA	BERYLLIUM
BALLISTIC	BAR CHARTS	BATTERIES	BEESTINGS	BESEECHED
BALLOONED	BARE BONES	BATTERING	BEETLE OFF	BESETTING
BALLOTING	BAREFACED	BATTINESS	BEETROOTS	BESIEGING
BALLOTINI	BARE-FACED	BATTLEAXE	BEFALLING	BESMEARED
BALLPOINT	BARGAINED	BATTLE CRY	BEFITTING	BESPATTER
BALLROOMS	BARGAINER	BAWDINESS	BEGETTING	BESTIALLY
BALLYMENA	BARGE POLE	BAYONETED	BEGGARING	BESTIRRED
BALMINESS	BAR GRAPHS	BAY WINDOW	BEGINNERS	BESTOWING
BALTHAZAR	BARITONES	BEACH BALL	BEGINNING	BESTREWED
BALTIMORE	BAR KOCHBA	BEACHHEAD	BEGRUDGED	BETE NOIRE
BAMBOOZLE	BARNACLES	BEACHSIDE	BEGUILING	BETE-NOIRE
BANBRIDGE	BARN DANCE	BEACHWEAR	BEHAVIOUR	BETHLEHEM
BANDAGING	BARNSTORM	BEADINESS	BEHEADING	BETHOUGHT
BANDANNAS	BARNYARDS	BEAN FEAST	BEHOLDERS	BETOKENED
BANDEROLE	BAROGRAPH	BEARBERRY	BEHOLDING	BETRAYALS
BANDICOOT	BAROMETER	BEARDLESS	BELATEDLY	BETRAYERS
BANDOLEER	BARONETCY	BEARISHLY	BELEAGUER	BETRAYING
BANDOLIER	BAROSCOPE	BEARNAISE	BELEMNITE	BETROTHAL
BANDSTAND	BARRACKED	BEAR'S-	BELGRAVIA	BETROTHED
BANDWAGON	BARRACUDA	FOOT	BELIEVERS	BETTERING
BANDWIDTH	BARRETTES	BEARSKINS	BELIEVING	BETTER-OFF
BANEBERRY	BARRICADE	BEASTLIER	BELITTLED	BEVELLING
BANEFULLY	BARRISTER	BEATIFIED	BELITTLER	BEVERAGES
BANGALORE	BARROW BOY	BEATITUDE	BELLATRIX	BEWAILING
BANISHING	BARTENDER	BEAUMARIS	BELLICOSE	BEWITCHED
BANISTERS	BARTERING	BEAU MONDE	BELLOWING	BHAGALPUR
BANJA LUKA	BASEBALLS	BEAUTEOUS	BELLYACHE	BHARATIYA
BANKBOOKS	BASEBOARD	BEAUTIFUL	BELLY FLOP	BHAVNAGAR
BANK DRAFT	BASELINES	BEAUX-ARTS	BELONGING	BHUTANESE
BANK NOTES	BASEMENTS	BEAVERING	BELVEDERE	BIALYSTOK
BANKROLLS	BASE METAL	BEBEERINE	BEMOANING	BIBLIOTIC
BANKRUPTS	BASE RATES	BEBINGTON	BENCHMARK	BICIPITAL
BANNISTER	BASHFULLY	BECCAFICO	BENCH MARK	BICKERING
BANQUETED	BASICALLY	BECKONING	BENEFICES	BICONCAVE
BANQUETTE	BASIFIXED	BECQUEREL	BENEFITED	BICYCLING
BANTERING	BASILICAN	BEDAUBING	BENEVENTO	BICYCLIST
BANTUSTAN	BASILICAS	BEDECKING	BENGALESE	BIDENTATE
BAPTISMAL	BASILISKS	BEDEVILED	BENGALINE	BIELEFELD
BAPTIZING	BASIPETAL	BEDFELLOW	BENIGHTED	BIFARIOUS
BARBADIAN	BAS RELIEF	BEDRAGGLE	BENIGNANT	BIFOLIATE
BARBARIAN	BAS-RELIEF	BEDRIDDEN	BENIGNITY	BIFURCATE
BARBARISM	BASS CLEFS	BED-SITTER	BENIN CITY	BIGAMISTS
BARBARITY	BASSINETS	BEDSPREAD	BENTONITE	BIGARREAU
BARBARIZE	BASTINADO	BEDSTEADS	BENZIDINE	BIG DIPPER
BARBAROUS	BATH CHAIR	BEEFEATER	BERBERINE	BIGENERIC
BARBECUED	BATHOLITH	BEEFINESS	BEREAVING	BIG-TIMERS
BARBECUES	BATHROBES	BEEFSTEAK	BEREZNIKI	BIGUANIDE
BARBICANS	BATHROOMS	BEEKEEPER	BERIOSOVA	BIG WHEELS
BARBITONE	BATHWATER	BEELZEBUB	BERKELIUM	BIJECTION
BARCAROLE	BATTALION	BEERINESS	BERKSHIRE	BIJECTIVE

BILABIALS	BITTERNUT	BLENNIOID	BLUE BLOOD	BOMBPROOF
BILABIATE	BITTINESS	BLESSEDLY	BLUE BOOKS	BOMBSHELL
BILATERAL	BIVALENCY	BLESSINGS	BLUE CHIPS	BOMBSIGHT
BILHARZIA	BIZARRELY	BLETHERED	BLUE FILMS	BOMBSITES
BILINGUAL	BLABBERED	BLIGHTERS	BLUEGRASS	BONA FIDES
BILIRUBIN	BLACKBALL	BLIGHTING	BLUE JEANS	BONEBLACK
BILLBOARD	BLACK BELT	BLIND DATE	BLUE PETER	BONE CHINA
BILLETING	BLACKBIRD	BLINDFISH	BLUEPRINT	BONEHEADS
BILLFOLDS	BLACKBUCK	BLINDFOLD	BLUESTONE	BONINGTON
BILLHOOKS	BLACKBURN	BLINDNESS	BLUFFNESS	BON VIVANT
BILLIARDS	BLACKCOCK	BLIND SPOT	BLUNDERED	BOOBY TRAP
BILLIONTH	BLACKDAMP	BLINKERED	BLUNDERER	BOOHOOING
BILLOWING	BLACKENED	BLISTERED	BLUNTNESS	BOOKCASES
BILLY GOAT	BLACK EYES	BLIZZARDS	BLURREDLY	BOOK CLUBS
BILOCULAR	BLACKFACE	BLOCKADED	BLUSTERED	BOOKMAKER
BIMONTHLY	BLACKFISH	BLOCKADER	BLUSTERER	BOOKMARKS
BIN-LINERS	BLACKHEAD	BLOCKADES	BOARDROOM	BOOKPLATE
BINOCULAR	BLACK HOLE	BLOCKAGES	BOARDWALK	BOOKSHELF
BINOMIALS	BLACK ISLE	BLOCKHEAD	BOARHOUND	BOOKSHOPS
BINTURONG	BLACKJACK	BLOCK VOTE	BOAT HOOKS	BOOKSTALL
BINUCLEAR	BLACK LEAD	BLONDNESS	BOATHOUSE	BOOKSTAND
BIOGRAPHY	BLACKLEGS	BLOOD BANK	BOATSWAIN	BOOK TOKEN
BIOHAZARD	BLACKLIST	BLOODBATH	BOAT TRAIN	BOOKWORMS
BIOLOGIST	BLACKMAIL	BLOOD FEUD	BOBBEJAAN	BOOMERANG
BIOMETRIC	BLACK MASS	BLOOD HEAT	BOBBY PINS	BOOMSLANG
BIONOMICS	BLACKNESS	BLOODLESS	BOBSLEIGH	BOONDOCKS
BIONOMIST	BLACKOUTS	BLOOD LUST	BOBTAILED	BOORISHLY
BIOSPHERE	BLACKPOLL	BLOODROOT	BOCCACCIO	BOOTBLACK
BIOSTATIC	BLACKPOOL	BLOODSHED	BODACIOUS	BOOTHROYD
BIOSTROME	BLACK SPOT	BLOODSHOT	BODY BLOWS	BOOTLACES
BIPARTITE	BLACKTAIL	BLOOD TYPE	BODYCHECK	BOOTMAKER
BIPINNATE	BLAMELESS	BLOODWORM	BODYGUARD	BOOTSTRAP
BIRDHOUSE	BLANCHING	BLOSSOMED	BOGGINESS	BOOZINESS
BIRD HOUSE	BLANDNESS	BLOTCHIER	BOHEMIANS	BORDELLOS
BIRD'S-	BLANKETED	BLOTCHILY	BOILINGLY	BORDERING
FOOT	BLANKNESS	BLOW-DRIED	BOLDFACED	BOREHOLES
BIRTHDAYS	BLASPHEME	BLOW-DRIES	BOLECTION	BORN-AGAIN
BIRTHMARK	BLASPHEMY	BLOWFLIES	BOLEGNESE	BORROWERS
BIRTHRATE	BLASTEMIC	BLOWHARDS	BOLIVIANO	BORROWING
BIRTHROOT	BLASTULAR	BLOWHOLES	BOLLINGER	BOSSA NOVA
BIRTHWORT	BLATANTLY	BLOWLAMPS	BOLLYWOOD	BOSSINESS
BISECTING	BLATHERED	BLOWPIPES	BOLOMETER	BOTANICAL
BISECTION	BLAZONING	BLOWTORCH	BOLSHEVIK	BOTANISTS
BISECTRIX	BLEACHERS	BLOWZIEST	BOLSHIEST	BOTANIZED
BISERRATE	BLEACHING	BLUBBERED	BOLSTERED	BOTCHIEST
BISEXUALS	BLEAKNESS	BLUDGEONS	BOLSTERER	BOTHERING
BISHOPRIC	BLEARIEST	BLUEBEARD	BOLTHOLES	BOTTLE-FED
BISMUTHAL	BLEMISHED	BLUEBELLS	BOMBARDED	BOTULINUS
BISMUTHIC	BLEMISHER	BLUEBERRY	BOMBARDON	BOUILLONS
BISULCATE	BLEMISHES	BLUEBIRDS	BOMBASTIC	BOULEVARD
BITCHIEST	BLENCHING	BLUE-BLACK	BOMBAZINE	BOUNCIEST

BOUNDLESS
BOUNTEOUS
BOUNTIFUL
BOURGEOIS
BOUTIQUES
BOWERBIRD
BOW LEGGED
BOW-LEGGED
BOWSPRITS
BOWSTRING
BOW WINDOW
BOX AND
    COX
BOXING DAY
BOX NUMBER
BOX OFFICE
BOYCOTTED
BOYFRIEND
BOYLES LAW
BOYLE'S
    LAW
BOY SCOUTS
BRACELETS
BRACHIATE
BRACINGLY
BRACKETED
BRACKNELL
BRACTEATE
BRACTEOLE
BRAGGARTS
BRAINIEST
BRAINLESS
BRAINSICK
BRAINWASH
BRAINWAVE
BRAIN WAVE
BRAINWAVE
BRAKE SHOE
BRAKESMAN
BRAMBLING
BRANCHIAL
BRANCHING
BRANDLING
BRAND NAME
BRANTFORD
BRASHNESS
BRASS BAND
BRASSERIE
BRASS HATS
BRASSIERE
BRASSIEST

BRAVENESS
BRAWNIEST
BRAZENING
BRAZILEIN
BRAZILIAN
BREACHING
BREAD BINS
BREADLINE
BREADROOT
BREAKABLE
BREAKAGES
BREAKAWAY
BREAKBEAT
BREAKDOWN
BREAKEVEN
BREAKFAST
BREAKNECK
BREATHILY
BREATHING
BREECHING
BRENTWOOD
BRIARROOT
BRIC A
    BRAC
BRIC-A-
    BRAC
BRICKWORK
BRICKYARD
BRICOLAGE
BRIEFCASE
BRIGADIER
BRIGHOUSE
BRILLIANT
BRIMSTONE
BRININESS
BRIOLETTE
BRIQUETTE
BRISKNESS
BRISTLING
BRITANNIA
BRITANNIC
BRITICISM
BRITISHER
BRITTONIC
BROACHING
BROADBAND
BROAD BEAN
BROADBILL
BROADCAST
BROADENED
BROAD JUMP

BROADLEAF
BROADLOOM
BROADNESS
BROADSIDE
BROADTAIL
BROCADING
BROCHETTE
BROCHURES
BROKERAGE
BROMELIAD
BROMEOSIN
BROMINATE
BROMOFORM
BRONCHIAL
BRONZE AGE
BROODIEST
BROOKABLE
BROOKLIME
BROOKWEED
BROOMCORN
BROOMRAPE
BROSCOPIC
BROTHERLY
BROUGHAMS
BROWN RICE
BRUNETTES
BRUNSWICK
BRUSH-OFFS
BRUSHWOOD
BRUSHWORK
BRUSQUELY
BRUTALITY
BRUTALIZE
BRUTISHLY
BRYLCREEM
BRYOPHYTE
BRYTHONIC
BUBBLE GUM
BUBBLIEST
BUCCANEER
BUCHAREST
BUCKBOARD
BUCKETING
BUCKHOUND
BUCKTEETH
BUCKTHORN
BUCKTOOTH
BUCKWHEAT
BUCKYBALL
BUCKYTUBE
BUDDH GAYA

BUDDHISTS
BUDGETARY
BUDGETING
BUFFALOES
BUFFERING
BUFFETING
BUGGER ALL
BUGGERING
BUGLE CALL
BUGLEWEED
BUHRSTONE
BUILDINGS
BUJUMBURA
BULGARIAN
BULGINESS
BULGINGLY
BULKHEADS
BULKINESS
BULLDOZED
BULLDOZER
BULLETINS
BULLFIGHT
BULLFINCH
BULLFROGS
BULLHORNS
BULLISHLY
BULLRINGS
BULL'S-
    EYES
BULLY BEEF
BULLYBOYS
BULLY-OFFS
BULRUSHES
BUMBLEBEE
BUMIPUTRA
BUMPINESS
BUMPTIOUS
BUNDABERG
BUNDESRAT
BUNDESTAG
BUNGALOWS
BUNGHOLES
BUNKHOUSE
BUOYANTLY
BUPRESTID
BURDENING
BURGEONED
BURGESSES
BURLESQUE
BURLINESS
BURMA ROAD

BURNINGLY
BURNISHED
BURNISHER
BURNOUSES
BURROUGHS
BURROWING
BURSARIAL
BURSARIES
BURSIFORM
BURTHENED
BUSHELLER
BUSHINESS
BUSHWHACK
BUTADIENE
BUTCHERED
BUTENANDT
BUTESHIRE
BUTHELEZI
BUTTERBUR
BUTTERCUP
BUTTERFAT
BUTTERFLY
BUTTERINE
BUTTERING
BUTTERNUT
BUTTONING
BUXOMNESS
BUZZWORDS
BYDGOSZCZ
BYPASSING
BY-PRODUCT
BYSTANDER
BY THE
    BOOK
BYZANTINE
BYZANTIUM

C

CABALLERO
CABIN BOYS
CABINETRY
CABLE CARS
CABLEGRAM
CABLE-LAID
CABOODLES
CABRIOLET
CACHECTIC
CACODEMON
CACOETHES
CACOETHIC
CACOPHONY

CACUMINAL	CANAANITE	CAPSULATE	CAROLLING	CASTILIAN
CAECILIAN	CANAL BOAT	CAPTAINCY	CAROTIDAL	CASTOR OIL
CAESAREAN	CANALIZED	CAPTAINED	CAROUSALS	CASTRATED
CAFETERIA	CANAVERAL	CAPTIVATE	CAROUSELS	CASTRATOR
CAIRNGORM	CANCELING	CAPTIVITY	CAROUSING	CASUARINA
CAITHNESS	CANCELLED	CAPTURING	CARPACCIO	CASUISTIC
CALABOOSE	CANCELLER	CARAPACES	CARPENTER	CASUISTRY
CALAMANCO	CANCEROUS	CARBAMATE	CARPENTRY	CATABASIS
CALCANEAL	CANDIDACY	CARBANION	CARPETBAG	CATABATIC
CALCANEUS	CANDIDATE	CARBAZOLE	CARPETING	CATABOLIC
CALCICOLE	CANDLEMAS	CARBINEER	CARPOLOGY	CATACLYSM
CALCIFIED	CANDLENUT	CARBOLIZE	CARRAGEEN	CATACOMBS
CALCIFUGE	CANDYTUFT	CARBONADO	CARREFOUR	CATALEPSY
CALCIMINE	CANESCENT	CARBONATE	CARRIAGES	CATALOGUE
CALCULATE	CANICULAR	CARBONIZE	CARRYALLS	CATALONIA
CALCULOUS	CANISTERS	CARBONOUS	CARRYCOTS	CATALYSER
CALENDARS	CANKEROUS	CARBON TAX	CARRY-OVER	CATALYSIS
CALENDERS	CANNELURE	CARBUNCLE	CARTAGENA	CATALYSTS
CALENDULA	CANNERIES	CARBURIZE	CARTESIAN	CATALYTIC
CALENTURE	CANNIBALS	CARCASSES	CARTHORSE	CATAMARAN
CALIBRATE	CANNINESS	CARCINOMA	CARTILAGE	CATAMENIA
CALIPHATE	CANNONADE	CARDBOARD	CARTOGRAM	CATAMOUNT
CALL A	CANNONING	CARDIGANS	CARTOUCHE	CAT-AND-
HALT	CANNULATE	CARDINALS	CARTRIDGE	DOG
CALL BOXES	CANOEISTS	CARD INDEX	CART TRACK	CATAPHYLL
CALL GIRLS	CANONICAL	CARDPHONE	CARTULARY	CATAPLASM
CALLOSITY	CANONIZED	CARD PUNCH	CARTWHEEL	CATAPLEXY
CALLOUSLY	CANOODLED	CARDPUNCH	CARYATIDS	CATAPULTS
CALMATIVE	CAN OPENER	CARDSHARP	CARYOPSIS	CATARACTS
CALORIFIC	CANTABILE	CARD SHARP	CASANOVAS	CATARRHAL
CALUMNIES	CANTALOUP	CARD TABLE	CASCADING	CATATONIA
CALVARIES	CANTERING	CAREENING	CASEATION	CATATONIC
CALVINISM	CANTICLES	CAREERING	CASEBOUND	CATCALLED
CALVINIST	CANTONESE	CAREERISM	CASE STUDY	CATCH CROP
CALVITIES	CANVASSED	CAREERIST	CASH CARDS	CATCHIEST
CAMBISTRY	CANVASSER	CAREFULLY	CASH CROPS	CATCHMENT
CAMBRIDGE	CANVASSES	CARESSING	CASH DESKS	CATCHWORD
CAMELHAIR	CAPACIOUS	CARETAKER	CASHIERED	CATECHISM
CAMELLIAS	CAPACITOR	CARIBBEAN	CASSAREEP	CATECHIST
CAMEMBERT	CAPARISON	CARIBBEES	CASSATION	CATECHIZE
CAMERAMAN	CAPE VERDE	CARILLONS	CASSEROLE	CATERWAUL
CAMERAMEN	CAPILLARY	CARINTHIA	CASSETTES	CATHARSES
CAMERA SHY	CAP IN	CARIOSITY	CASSIMERE	CATHARSIS
CAMISOLES	HAND	CARMELITE	CASSINGLE	CATHARTIC
CAMPAIGNS	CAPITULAR	CARNALIST	CASSOCKED	CATHEDRAL
CAMPANILE	CAPITULUM	CARNALITY	CASSOULET	CATHEPSIN
CAMPANULA	CAPRICCIO	CARNATION	CASSOWARY	CATHETERS
CAMPFIRES	CAPRICORN	CARNELIAN	CAST ABOUT	CATHOLICS
CAMPHORIC	CAPSAICIN	CARNIVALS	CASTANETS	CATOPTRIC
CAMPSITES	CAPSICUMS	CARNIVORE	CASTAWAYS	CATTERIES
CAMSHAFTS	CAPSIZING	CARNOTITE	CASTIGATE	CATTINESS

CATTLEMAN	CENTRISTS	CHAPERONS	CHEMPADUK	CHLORIDIC
CAUCASOID	CENTURIAL	CHAPLAINS	CHEMURGIC	CHLORITIC
CAUDATION	CENTURIES	CHAPLETED	CHENGCHOW	CHLOROSIS
CAUGHT OUT	CENTURION	CHARABANC	CHEONGSAM	CHLOROTIC
CAULDRONS	CERACEOUS	CHARACTER	CHEQUERED	CHOCK-FULL
CAUSALGIA	CERATODUS	CHARBROIL	CHERBOURG	CHOCOLATE
CAUSALITY	CERCARIAL	CHARCOALS	CHERISHED	CHOCOLATY
CAUSATION	CEREBROID	CHARINESS	CHERISHER	CHOIRBOYS
CAUSATIVE	CEREBRUMS	CHARITIES	CHERNOZEM	CHOKEABLE
CAUSEWAYS	CERECLOTH	CHARIVARI	CHERRY PIE	CHOLEROID
CAUTERANT	CERTAINLY	CHARLATAN	CHESTIEST	CHOMSKIAN
CAUTERIZE	CERTAINTY	CHARLOTTE	CHESTNUTS	CHONDRIFY
CAUTIONED	CERTIFIED	CHARMEUSE	CHEVALIER	CHONDRITE
CAVALCADE	CERTITUDE	CHARTABLE	CHEVRETTE	CHONDROMA
CAVALIERS	CERUSSITE	CHARTERED	CHICALOTE	CHONDRULE
CAVENDISH	CESAREANS	CHARWOMAN	CHICANERY	CHONGQING
CAVERNOUS	CESSATION	CHARWOMEN	CHICKADEE	CHOOSIEST
CAVILLERS	CETACEANS	CHASTENED	CHICKPEAS	CHOPHOUSE
CAVILLING	CHABAZITE	CHASTENER	CHICKWEED	CHOPLOGIC
CAVORTING	CHA-CHA-	CHASTISED	CHIEFTAIN	CHOPPIEST
CEASEFIRE	CHA	CHASUBLES	CHIHUAHUA	CHOPSTICK
CEASE-FIRE	CHAETOPOD	CHATELAIN	CHILBLAIN	CHORIONIC
CEASELESS	CHAFFINCH	CHATOYANT	CHILDHOOD	CHORISTER
CELANDINE	CHAGRINED	CHAT SHOWS	CHILDLESS	CHOROLOGY
CELEBRANT	CHAIN GANG	CHATTERED	CHILDLIKE	CHORTLING
CELEBRATE	CHAIN MAIL	CHATTERER	CHILIADAL	CHORUSING
CELEBRITY	CHAIN SAWS	CHATTIEST	CHILLIEST	CHOWKIDAR
CELESTIAL	CHAIRLIFT	CHAUFFEUR	CHINATOWN	CHRISTIAN
CELESTITE	CHAIR LIFT	CHEAPENED	CHINAWARE	CHRISTMAS
CELIBATES	CHALCOGEN	CHEAP-JACK	CHINKIANG	CHROMATIC
CELLARAGE	CHALKIEST	CHEAPNESS	CHINSTRAP	CHROMATID
CELLARMAN	CHALLENGE	CHECHENIA	CHINTZIER	CHROMATIN
CELLOIDIN	CHAMELEON	CHECKABLE	CHIPBOARD	CHROMOGEN
CELLULASE	CHAMFERER	CHECKERED	CHIPMUNKS	CHRONAXIE
CELLULOID	CHAMOMILE	CHECKLIST	CHIPOLATA	CHRONICLE
CELLULOSE	CHAMPAGNE	CHECKMATE	CHIPPINGS	CHRYSALID
CELTICIST	CHAMPAIGN	CHECKOUTS	CHIROPODY	CHRYSALIS
CEMENTING	CHAMPERTY	CHECKROOM	CHIROPTER	CHTHONIAN
CEMENTITE	CHAMPIONS	CHEEKBONE	CHIRPIEST	CHUBBIEST
CENOTAPHS	CHAMPLEVE	CHEEKIEST	CHIRRUPER	CHUCKLING
CENSORIAL	CHANCIEST	CHEERIEST	CHISELING	CHUMMIEST
CENSORING	CHANCROID	CHEERLESS	CHISELLED	CHUNGKING
CENSURING	CHANCROUS	CHELASHIP	CHISELLER	CHUNKIEST
CENTAURUS	CHANDELLE	CHELATION	CHISIMAIO	CHURCHMAN
CENTENARY	CHANDLERS	CHELICERA	CHITINOID	CHURRASCO
CENTERING	CHANDLERY	CHELIFORM	CHITINOUS	CICATRICE
CENTESIMO	CHANGCHOW	CHELONIAN	CHIVALRIC	CICATRIZE
CENTIGRAM	CHANGCHUN	CHEMICALS	CHLORACNE	CICERONES
CENTIPEDE	CHANNELED	CHEMISORB	CHLORDANE	CIGARETTE
CENTRALLY	CHANTEUSE	CHEMISTRY	CHLORELLA	CIGARILLO
CENTRIOLE	CHANTILLY	CHEMOSTAT	CHLORIDES	CILIATION

CILIOLATE
CIMMERIAN
CINCTURES
CINEMATIC
CINEPHILE
CINERARIA
CINEREOUS
CINGULATE
CIPHERING
CIRALPINE
CIRCADIAN
CIRCASSIA
CIRCINATE
CIRCUITAL
CIRCUITRY
CIRCULARS
CIRCULATE
CIRRHOSED
CIRRHOSIS
CIRRHOTIC
CIRRIPEDE
CITATIONS
CITIZENRY
CITY HALLS
CITY-STATE
CIVICALLY
CIVILIANS
CIVILIZED
CIVILIZER
CIVIL LIST
CIVIL WARS
CLADOGRAM
CLAIMABLE
CLAIMANTS
CLAMBAKES
CLAMBERED
CLAMMIEST
CLAMOROUS
CLAMOURED
CLAMPDOWN
CLAMP DOWN
CLAPBOARD
CLARENDON
CLARIFIED
CLARIFIER
CLARINETS
CLASSICAL
CLASSIEST
CLASSLESS
CLASSMATE
CLASSROOM

CLATHRATE
CLATTERED
CLAVICLES
CLAVICORN
CLAYMORES
CLAYSTONE
CLAYTONIA
CLEANABLE
CLEANNESS
CLEANSERS
CLEANSING
CLEARANCE
CLEAR-EYED
CLEARINGS
CLEARNESS
CLEARWAYS
CLEARWING
CLEAVAGES
CLEMENTLY
CLENCHING
CLERGYMAN
CLERGYMEN
CLERIHEWS
CLERKSHIP
CLEVELAND
CLIENTELE
CLIMACTIC
CLIMAXING
CLIMB DOWN
CLIMB-DOWN
CLINCHERS
CLINCHING
CLINGFILM
CLINGFISH
CLINICIAN
CLINOSTAT
CLINQUANT
CLINTONIA
CLIPBOARD
CLIP JOINT
CLIPPINGS
CLITELLUM
CLOAKROOM
CLOBBERED
CLOCKWISE
CLOCKWORK
CLOG DANCE
CLOISONNE
CLOISTERS
CLOISTRAL
CLONICITY

CLOSE CALL
CLOSEDOWN
CLOSE KNIT
CLOSE-KNIT
CLOSENESS
CLOSETING
CLOTHIERS
CLOUDBANK
CLOUDIEST
CLOUDLESS
CLOUD NINE
CLOYINGLY
CLUBBABLE
CLUBHOUSE
CLUMSIEST
CLUSTERED
CLUTCH BAG
CLUTCHING
CLUTTERED
CLYDEBANK
CNIDARIAN
COACHWORK
COADJUTOR
COADUNATE
COAGULANT
COAGULASE
COAGULATE
COALESCED
COALFACES
COALFIELD
COALHOLES
COALHOUSE
COALITION
COALMINES
COARCTATE
COARSENED
COASTLINE
COAT TAILS
COAXINGLY
COBALTITE
COBALTOUS
COCA-COLAS
COCAINISM
COCAINIZE
COCCOLITH
COCCYGEAL
COCHINEAL
COCHLEATE
COCK A
HOOP

COCK-A-
HOOP
COCKATIEL
COCKATOOS
COCKED HAT
COCKERELS
COCKFIGHT
COCKHORSE
COCKINESS
COCKLEBUR
COCKNEYFY
COCKROACH
COCKSCOMB
COCKSFOOT
COCKTAILS
COCOONING
CODIFYING
CODPIECES
COELOSTAT
COENOBITE
COENOCYTE
COENOSARC
COEQUALLY
COERCIBLE
COEVALITY
COEXISTED
COFFEE BAR
COFFEEPOT
COFFERDAM
COGITATED
COGITATOR
COGNATION
COGNITION
COGNITIVE
COGNIZANT
COGNOMENS
COGWHEELS
COHABITED
COHERENCE
COIFFEURS
COIFFURED
COIFFURES
COINCIDED
COINTREAU
COKULORIS
COLANDERS
COLCHICUM
COLCOTHAR
COLD CREAM
COLD-DRAWN
COLD FRAME

COLD FRONT
COLD SNAPS
COLD SORES
COLD STEEL
COLD SWEAT
COLECTOMY
COLERAINE
COLICROOT
COLICWEED
COLLAGIST
COLLAPSAR
COLLAPSED
COLLAPSES
COLLARING
COLLATING
COLLATION
COLLATIVE
COLLEAGUE
COLLECTED
COLLECTOR
COLLEGIAL
COLLEGIAN
COLLEGIUM
COLLIDING
COLLIGATE
COLLIMATE
COLLINEAR
COLLINSIA
COLLISION
COLLOCATE
COLLODION
COLLOIDAL
COLLOTYPE
COLLUDING
COLLUSION
COLLUSIVE
COLLUVIAL
COLLUVIUM
COLLYRIUM
COLOCYNTH
COLOMBIAN
COLONELCY
COLONIALS
COLONISTS
COLONIZED
COLONIZER
COLONNADE
COLORIFIC
COLOR LINE
COLOSTOMY
COLOSTRAL

COLOSTRUM	COMMODORE	CONCEALED	CONFLUENT	CONSONANT
COLOUR BAR	COMMONAGE	CONCEDING	CONFORMAL	CONSORTED
COLOUREDS	COMMONERS	CONCEITED	CONFORMED	CONSORTER
COLOURFUL	COMMON LAW	CONCEIVED	CONFORMER	CONSORTIA
COLOURING	COMMON-LAW	CONCENTRE	CONFRERES	CONSPIRED
COLOURIST	COMMOTION	CONCEPTUS	CONFUCIAN	CONSTABLE
COLOURWAY	COMMUNING	CONCERNED	CONFUSING	CONSTANCE
COLTISHLY	COMMUNION	CONCERTED	CONFUSION	CONSTANCY
COLTSFOOT	COMMUNISM	CONCERTOS	CONFUTING	CONSTANTA
COLUBRINE	COMMUNIST	CONCIERGE	CONGEALED	CONSTANTS
COLUMBIAN	COMMUNITY	CONCILIAR	CONGENIAL	CONSTRAIN
COLUMBINE	COMMUNIZE	CONCISELY	CONGER EEL	CONSTRICT
COLUMBITE	COMMUTATE	CONCISION	CONGERIES	CONSTRUCT
COLUMBIUM	COMMUTERS	CONCLAVES	CONGESTED	CONSTRUED
COLUMELLA	COMMUTING	CONCLUDED	CONGOLESE	CONSTRUER
COLUMNIST	COMPACTED	CONCOCTED	CONGRUENT	CONSULATE
COLWYN BAY	COMPACTER	CONCOCTER	CONGRUITY	CONSULTED
COMATULID	COMPACTLY	CONCORDAT	CONGRUOUS	CONSULTEE
COMBATANT	COMPANDER	CONCOURSE	CONHOIDAL	CONSULTER
COMBATING	COMPANIES	CONCRETED	CONICALLY	CONSUMERS
COMBATIVE	COMPANION	CONCUBINE	CONJOINED	CONSUMING
COMBATTED	COMPARING	CONCURRED	CONJOINER	CONTACTED
COMBINING	COMPASSES	CONCUSSED	CONJUGANT	CONTACTOR
COMBUSTOR	COMPELLED	CONDEMNED	CONJUGATE	CONTAGION
COME ABOUT	COMPELLER	CONDEMNER	CONJURERS	CONTAGIUM
COMEBACKS	COMPENDIA	CONDENSED	CONJURING	CONTAINED
COMEDIANS	COMPERING	CONDENSER	CONNECTED	CONTAINER
COMEDOWNS	COMPETENT	CONDIGNLY	CONNECTOR	CONTEMNER
COMELIEST	COMPETING	CONDIMENT	CONNEMARA	CONTENDED
COME OFF	COMPILERS	CONDITION	CONNIVENT	CONTENDER
IT	COMPILING	CONDOLING	CONNIVING	CONTENTED
COMFORTED	COMPLAINT	CONDONING	CONNOTING	CONTESTED
COMFORTER	COMPLETED	CONDUCING	CONNUBIAL	CONTESTER
COMICALLY	COMPLETER	CONDUCIVE	CONQUERED	CONTINENT
COMMANDED	COMPLEXES	CONDUCTED	CONQUEROR	CONTINUAL
COMMANDER	COMPLIANT	CONDUCTOR	CONQUESTS	CONTINUED
COMMANDOS	COMPLYING	CONDYLOID	CONSCIOUS	CONTINUER
COMMENCED	COMPONENT	CONDYLOMA	CONSCRIPT	CONTINUOS
COMMENDAM	COMPORTED	CONFERRED	CONSENSUS	CONTINUUM
COMMENDED	COMPOSERS	CONFERRER	CONSENTED	CONTORTED
COMMENSAL	COMPOSING	CONFERVAL	CONSENTER	CONTOURED
COMMENTED	COMPOSITE	CONFESSED	CONSERVED	CONTRACTS
COMMENTER	COMPOSTED	CONFESSOR	CONSERVER	CONTRAILS
COMMINGLE	COMPOSURE	CONFIDANT	CONSERVES	CONTRALTO
COMMINUTE	COMPOUNDS	CONFIDENT	CONSIGNED	CONTRASTS
COMMISSAR	COMPRISAL	CONFIDING	CONSIGNEE	CONTRASTY
COMMITTAL	COMPRISED	CONFINING	CONSIGNOR	CONTRIVED
COMMITTED	COMPUTERS	CONFIRMED	CONSISTED	CONTUMACY
COMMITTEE	COMPUTING	CONFITURE	CONSOCIES	CONTUMELY
COMMITTER	COMRADELY	CONFLATED	CONSOLING	CONTUSING
COMMODITY	CONCAVITY	CONFLICTS	CONSOLUTE	CONTUSION

CONTUSIVE	CORNELIAN	COTANGENT	CRACKLING	CREVASSES
CONUNDRUM	CORNERING	COT DEATHS	CRACKPOTS	CREWELIST
CONVECTOR	CORNETIST	COTE	CRACKSMAN	CREW NECKS
CONVENERS	CORNFIELD	D'AZUR	CRACKSMEN	CRIBELLUM
CONVENING	CORNFLOUR	COTENANCY	CRAFTIEST	CRICKETER
CONVERGED	CORNSTALK	COTILLION	CRAFTSMAN	CRIME WAVE
CONVERSED	COROLLARY	COTTAGERS	CRAFTSMEN	CRIMINALS
CONVERSER	CORPORALE	COTTONADE	CRAFTWORK	CRIMPLENE
CONVERTED	CORPORALS	COTTON GIN	CRAGGIEST	CRIMSONED
CONVERTER	CORPORATE	COTYLEDON	CRAIGAVON	CRINKLIER
CONVEXITY	CORPOREAL	COUCHETTE	CRANBERRY	CRINKLING
CONVEYERS	CORPOSANT	COUNSELED	CRANKCASE	CRINOLINE
CONVEYING	CORPULENT	COUNTABLE	CRANKIEST	CRIPPLING
CONVICTED	CORPUSCLE	COUNTDOWN	CRAPPIEST	CRISPIEST
CONVINCED	CORRALLED	COUNTERED	CRAPULOUS	CRISPNESS
CONVINCER	CORRASION	COUNTLESS	CRASH-DIVE	CRITERION
CONVIVIAL	CORRASIVE	COUNT NOUN	CRASH-LAND	CRITICISM
CONVOKING	CORRECTED	COUNTRIES	CRASH TEAM	CRITICIZE
CONVOLUTE	CORRECTLY	COUP	CRASSNESS	CRITIQUES
CONVOYING	CORRECTOR	D'ETAT	CRATEROUS	CROCHETED
CONVULSED	CORRELATE	COUPLINGS	CRAYONING	CROCHETER
COOKHOUSE	CORRIDORS	COURGETTE	CRAYONIST	CROCODILE
COOKSTOWN	CORRODANT	COURT CARD	CRAZINESS	CROISSANT
COOPERAGE	CORRODING	COURTELLE	CREAKIEST	CROMLECHS
COOPERATE	CORROSION	COURTEOUS	CREAMCUPS	CROOKEDLY
COORDINAL	CORROSIVE	COURTESAN	CREAMIEST	CROP-EARED
COPARTNER	CORRUGATE	COURTIERS	CREATIONS	CROQUETTE
COPESTONE	CORRUPTED	COURTLIER	CREATURAL	CROSSBARS
COPIOUSLY	CORRUPTER	COURTROOM	CREATURES	CROSSBEAM
COPOLYMER	CORRUPTLY	COURTSHIP	CREDENDUM	CROSSBILL
COPROLITE	CORSELETS	COURT SHOE	CREDITING	CROSSBOWS
COPULATED	CORTICATE	COURTYARD	CREDITORS	CROSSBRED
COPYBOOKS	CORTISONE	COUTURIER	CREDULITY	CROSS-EYED
COPYRIGHT	CORUSCATE	COVALENCY	CREDULOUS	CROSSFIRE
COQUETTES	CORVETTES	COVENANTS	CREEPIEST	CROSSHEAD
CORALLINE	CORYDALIS	COVERALLS	CREMATING	CROSSINGS
CORALLOID	CORYMBOSE	COVERINGS	CREMATION	CROSS-LINK
CORALROOT	COSEISMAL	COVERLESS	CREMATORY	CROSSNESS
CORBICULA	COSMETICS	COVERLETS	CRENATION	CROSSOVER
COR BLIMEY	COSMIC RAY	COVER NOTE	CRENULATE	CROSS TALK
CORDIALLY	COSMOGONY	COVERTURE	CREOLIZED	CROSSTREE
CORDIFORM	COSMOLOGY	COWABUNGA	CREOPHAGY	CROSSWALK
CORDONING	COSMONAUT	COWARDICE	CREOSOTED	CROSSWIND
COREOPSIS	COSMOTRON	CO-WORKERS	CREOSOTIC	CROSSWISE
CORIANDER	COSSETTED	COXCOMBRY	CREPITANT	CROSSWORD
CORKBOARD	COSTA RICA	COYOTILLO	CREPITATE	CROSSWORT
CORKSCREW	CO-STARRED	CRAB APPLE	CRESCENDO	CROTCHETS
CORMORANT	COSTLIEST	CRABBEDLY	CRESCENTS	CROTCHETY
CORN BREAD	COSTOTOMY	CRABBIEST	CRETINISM	CROUCHING
CORNBREAD	COST PRICE	CRABSTICK	CRETINOID	CROUPIERS
CORNCRAKE	COSTUMIER	CRACKDOWN	CRETINOUS	CROWBERRY

CROWN LAND
CROWNWORK
CROW'S FEET
CROW'S FOOT
CROW'S NEST
CRUCIALLY
CRUCIBLES
CRUCIFIED
CRUCIFIER
CRUCIFORM
CRUDITIES
CRUELTIES
CRUMBLIER
CRUMBLING
CRUMMIEST
CRUMPLING
CRUNCHIER
CRUNCHILY
CRUNCHING
CRUSADERS
CRUSADING
CRUSTIEST
CRYBABIES
CRYOMETER
CRYOMETRY
CRYOPHYTE
CRYOSCOPE
CRYOSCOPY
CRYPTOGAM
CTENIDIUM
CUBBYHOLE
CUBBY HOLE
CUBE ROOTS
CUBISISTS
CUB SCOUTS
CUCKOLDED
CUCULLATE
CUCUMBERS
CUDDLIEST
CUDGELING
CUDGELLED
CUDGELLER
CUFF LINKS
CUIRASSES
CUL-DE-SACS
CULLENDER
CULMINANT
CULMINATE

CULTIVATE
CULTURIST
CUMBERING
CUMBRANCE
CUNEIFORM
CUNNINGLY
CUPBEARER
CUPBOARDS
CUP FINALS
CUPOLATED
CURATIVES
CURDINESS
CURETTAGE
CURIOSITY
CURIOUSLY
CURLICUES
CURLINESS
CURLPAPER
CURRENTLY
CURRICULA
CURRYCOMB
CURSIVELY
CURSORIAL
CURSORILY
CURTAILED
CURTAINED
CURTILAGE
CURTSYING
CURVATURE
CUSHINESS
CUSHIONED
CUSPIDATE
CUSPIDORS
CUSTODIAL
CUSTODIAN
CUSTOMARY
CUSTOMERS
CUSTOMIZE
CUT A CAPER
CUT AND RUN
CUTANEOUS
CUTICULAR
CUTLASSES
CUTPURSES
CUTTHROAT
CUT-THROAT
CUTTINGLY
CYANAMIDE
CYANOTYPE

CYBERCAFE
CYBERNATE
CYBERPUNK
CYBERPUNT
CYCLAMATE
CYCLOIDAL
CYCLONITE
CYCLOPSES
CYCLORAMA
CYCLOTRON
CYLINDERS
CYMBALIST
CYMOGRAPH
CYMOPHANE
CYNICALLY
CYNOSURES
CYPHERING
CYPRESSES
CYPRINOID
CYRENAICA
CYSTEINIC
CYSTOCARP
CYSTOCELE
CYSTOLITH
CYSTOTOMY
CYTOLYSIN
CYTOLYSIS
CYTOPLASM
CYTOPLAST

D

DACHSHUND
DACTYLICS
DADAISTIC
DAFFODILS
DAILY HELP
DAINTIEST
DAIQUIRIS
DAIRY FARM
DAIRYMAID
DALAI LAMA
DALLIANCE
DALMATIAN
DALTONISM
DAMASCENE
DAMNATION
DAMNATORY
DAMNEDEST
DAMPENING
DAMP SQUIB
DAMSELFLY

DANDELION
DANDIFIED
DANGEROUS
DAREDEVIL
DARKENING
DARK HORSE
DARKROOMS
DARMSTADT
DARTBOARD
DARTMOUTH
DASHBOARD
DASHINGLY
DASTARDLY
DATABASES
DATA BUSES
DATEDNESS
DATELINES
DATE STAMP
DAUGHTERS
DAUNTLESS
DAVENPORT
DAYDREAMS
DAYDREAMY
DAYFLOWER
DAYLIGHTS
DAY SCHOOL
DEACONESS
DEADBEATS
DEAD DUCKS
DEADENING
DEAD HEART
DEAD HEATS
DEADLIEST
DEADLIGHT
DEADLINES
DEADLOCKS
DEADLY SIN
DEAD MARCH
DEAFBLIND
DEAFENING
DEAF-MUTES
DEALATION
DEAMINATE
DEANERIES
DEATHBEDS
DEATHBLOW
DEATH DUTY
DEATHLESS
DEATHLIKE
DEATH MASK
DEATH RATE

DEATH TOLL
DEATH TRAP
DEATH WISH
DEAUVILLE
DEBARKING
DEBARMENT
DEBARRING
DEBATABLE
DEBAUCHED
DEBAUCHEE
DEBAUCHER
DEBAUCHES
DEBENTURE
DEBOUCHED
DEBRIEFED
DEBUGGING
DEBUNKERS
DEBUNKING
DEBUTANTE
DECADENCE
DECAGONAL
DECALCIFY
DECALOGUE
DECAMPING
DECANTERS
DECANTING
DECAPODAL
DECASTYLE
DECATHLON
DECEITFUL
DECEIVERS
DECEIVING
DECEMBERS
DECENCIES
DECENNIAL
DECEPTION
DECEPTIVE
DECIDABLE
DECIDEDLY
DECIDUOUS
DECILLION
DECIMALLY
DECIMATED
DECIMATOR
DECIMETRE
DECISIONS
DECK CARGO
DECKCHAIR
DECKHANDS
DECKHOUSE
DECLAIMED

DECLAIMER	DEFENDING	DEMEANOUR	DEPORTING	DESPERATE
DECLARANT	DEFENSIVE	DEMIJOHNS	DEPOSABLE	DESPISING
DECLARING	DEFERENCE	DEMIMONDE	DEPOSITED	DESPOILED
DECLINATE	DEFERMENT	DEMISABLE	DEPOSITOR	DESPOILER
DECLINING	DEFERRING	DEMISTING	DEPRAVING	DESPOTISM
DECLIVITY	DEFIANTLY	DEMITASSE	DEPRAVITY	DESPUMATE
DECOCTION	DEFICIENT	DEMOBBING	DEPRECATE	DESTINIES
DECOLLATE	DEFINABLE	DEMOCRACY	DEPRESSED	DESTITUTE
DECOLLETE	DEFINIENS	DEMOCRATS	DEPRESSOR	DESTROYED
DECOMPOSE	DEFLATING	DEMOTIONS	DEPRIVING	DESTROYER
DECONTROL	DEFLATION	DEMULCENT	DEPURATOR	DESUETUDE
DECORATED	DEFLECTED	DEMULSIFY	DEPUTIZED	DESULTORY
DECORATOR	DEFLECTOR	DEMURRAGE	DERAILING	DETACHING
DECOUPAGE	DEFOLIANT	DEMURRING	DERELICTS	DETAILING
DECREASED	DEFOLIATE	DEMYSTIFY	DE RIGUEUR	DETAINEES
DECREASES	DEFORMING	DENDRITIC	DERISIBLE	DETAINING
DECREEING	DEFORMITY	DENIGRATE	DERIVABLE	DETECTING
DECREMENT	DEFRAUDED	DENITRATE	DERMATOID	DETECTION
DECRETIVE	DEFRAUDER	DENITRIFY	DERMATOME	DETECTIVE
DECRETORY	DEFRAYING	DENOTABLE	DEROGATED	DETECTORS
DECUMBENT	DEFROCKED	DENOUNCED	DERRING DO	DETENTION
DECURRENT	DEFROSTED	DENOUNCER	DERRING-DO	DETERGENT
DECUSSATE	DEFROSTER	DENSENESS	DERRINGER	DETERMENT
DEDICATED	DEGRADING	DENSITIES	DERVISHES	DETERMINE
DEDICATEE	DEGREE-DAY	DENTALIUM	DESCALING	DETERRENT
DEDICATOR	DEHISCENT	DENTATION	DESCANTER	DETERRING
DEDUCIBLE	DEHYDRATE	DENTIFORM	DESCENDED	DETERSIVE
DEDUCTING	DEJECTION	DENTISTRY	DESCENDER	DETESTING
DEDUCTION	DELEGABLE	DENTITION	DESCRIBED	DETHRONED
DEDUCTIVE	DELEGATED	DENTURIST	DESCRIBER	DETHRONER
DEED POLLS	DELEGATES	DEODORANT	DESCRYING	DETONATED
DEEDS POLL	DELETIONS	DEODORIZE	DESECRATE	DETONATOR
DEEPENING	DELICIOUS	DEOXIDIZE	DESERTERS	DETRACTED
DEEP FRIED	DELIGHTED	DEPARDIEU	DESERTING	DETRACTOR
DEEP SOUTH	DELIGHTER	DEPARTING	DESERTION	DETRAINED
DEERGRASS	DELIMITED	DEPARTURE	DESERVING	DETRIMENT
DEERHOUND	DELINEATE	DEPASTURE	DESICCANT	DETRITION
DEFALCATE	DELIRIANT	DEPENDANT	DESICCATE	DETRUSION
DEFAULTED	DELIRIOUS	DEPENDENT	DESIGNATE	DEUTERIDE
DEFAULTER	DELIRIUMS	DEPENDING	DESIGNERS	DEUTERIUM
DEFEATING	DELIVERED	DEPICTING	DESIGNING	DEVALUATE
DEFEATISM	DELIVERER	DEPICTION	DESINENCE	DEVALUING
DEFEATIST	DELOUSING	DEPICTIVE	DESIRABLE	DEVASTATE
DEFECATED	DELUSIONS	DEPICTURE	DESIRABLY	DEVELOPED
DEFECATOR	DEMAGOGIC	DEPILATOR	DESISTING	DEVELOPER
DEFECTING	DEMAGOGUE	DEPLETING	DESMIDIAN	DEVIATING
DEFECTION	DEMANDANT	DEPLETION	DES MOINES	DEVIATION
DEFECTIVE	DEMANDING	DEPLETIVE	DESOLATED	DEVIATORY
DEFECTORS	DEMANTOID	DEPLORING	DESOLATER	DEVILFISH
DEFENDANT	DEMARCATE	DEPLOYING	DESPAIRED	DEVILLING
DEFENDERS	DEMEANING	DEPORTEES	DESPERADO	DEVILMENT

DEVIOUSLY	DIATRIBES	DILATABLE	DISAVOWAL	DISH TOWEL
DEVISABLE	DIATROPIC	DILATANCY	DISAVOWED	DISHWATER
DEVITRIFY	DIAZONIUM	DILIGENCE	DISAVOWER	DISINFECT
DEVOLVING	DIAZOTIZE	DILUTIONS	DISBANDED	DISINFEST
DEVOTEDLY	DIBROMIDE	DIMENSION	DISBANDED	DISK DRIVE
DEVOTIONS	DICHASIAL	DIMIDIATE	DISBARRED	DISKETTES
DEVOURING	DICHASIUM	DIMISSORY	DISBELIEF	DISLIKING
DEVOUTEST	DICHOGAMY	DIM-WITTED	DISBRANCH	DISLOCATE
DEXEDRINE	DICHOTOMY	DINGDONGS	DISBURDEN	DISLODGED
DEXTERITY	DICHROISM	DINGINESS	DISBURSED	DISMANTLE
DEXTEROUS	DICHROITE	DINING CAR	DISBURSER	DISMASTED
DEXTRORSE	DICHROMIC	DINOCERAS	DISCALCED	DISMAYING
DIABETICS	DICKERING	DINOSAURS	DISCARDED	DISMEMBER
DIABLERIE	DICKYBIRD	DINOTHERE	DISCARDER	DISMISSAL
DIABOLISM	DICLINISM	DIOECIOUS	DISCERNED	DISMISSED
DIABOLIST	DICLINOUS	DIOESTRUS	DISCERNER	DISOBEYED
DIABOLIZE	DICROTISM	DIPHTHONG	DISCHARGE	DISOBEYER
DIACONATE	DICTATING	DIPLOIDIC	DISCIPLES	DISOBLIGE
DIACRITIC	DICTATION	DIPLOMACY	DISCLIMAX	DISORDERS
DIACTINIC	DICTATORS	DIPLOMATE	DISCLOSED	DISOWNING
DIAERESES	DIDACTICS	DIPLOMATS	DISCLOSER	DISPARAGE
DIAERESIS	DIETETICS	DIPLOTENE	DISCOIDAL	DISPARATE
DIAGNOSED	DIETICIAN	DIPSTICKS	DISCOLOUR	DISPARITY
DIAGNOSES	DIETITIAN	DIPSWITCH	DISCOMFIT	DISPELLED
DIAGNOSIS	DIFFERENT	DIPTEROUS	DISCOMMON	DISPELLER
DIAGONALS	DIFFERING	DIRECTING	DISCOUNTS	DISPENSED
DIALECTAL	DIFFICULT	DIRECTION	DISCOURSE	DISPENSER
DIALECTIC	DIFFIDENT	DIRECTIVE	DISCOVERT	DISPERSAL
DIALOGISM	DIFFUSELY	DIRECTORS	DISCOVERY	DISPERSED
DIALOGIST	DIFFUSING	DIRECTORY	DISCREDIT	DISPERSER
DIALOGIZE	DIFFUSION	DIRECTRIX	DISCUSSED	DISPLACED
DIALOGUER	DIFFUSIVE	DIRECT TAX	DISDAINED	DISPLACER
DIALOGUES	DIGASTRIC	DIREFULLY	DISEMBARK	DISPLAYED
DIAMAGNET	DIGENESIS	DIRIGIBLE	DISEMBODY	DISPLAYER
DIAMETERS	DIGENETIC	DIRT BIKES	DISENABLE	DISPLEASE
DIAMETRAL	DIGESTANT	DIRT CHEAP	DISENGAGE	DISPORTED
DIAMETRIC	DIGESTING	DIRTINESS	DISENTAIL	DISPOSING
DIANDROUS	DIGESTION	DIRT ROADS	DISESTEEM	DISPRAISE
DIANOETIC	DIGESTIVE	DIRT TRACK	DISFAVOUR	DISPROVAL
DIAPHONIC	DIGITALIN	DIRTY WORK	DISFIGURE	DISPROVED
DIAPHRAGM	DIGITALIS	DISABLING	DISFOREST	DISPUTANT
DIAPHYSIS	DIGITIZED	DISABLIST	DISGORGED	DISPUTING
DIARRHOEA	DIGITIZER	DISABUSAL	DISGORGER	DISREGARD
DIASTASIC	DIGITOXIN	DISABUSED	DISGRACED	DISRELISH
DIASTASIS	DIGLOTTIC	DISACCORD	DISGRACER	DISREPAIR
DIASTATIC	DIGNIFIED	DISAFFECT	DISGUISED	DISREPUTE
DIASTOLIC	DIGNITARY	DISAFFIRM	DISGUISER	DISROBING
DIATHERMY	DIGNITIES	DISAGREED	DISGUISES	DISRUPTED
DIATHESIS	DIGRAPHIC	DISAPPEAR	DISGUSTED	DISRUPTER
DIATHETIC	DIGRESSED	DISARMING	DISHCLOTH	DISSECTED
DIATOMITE	DIGRESSER	DISASTERS	DISHONEST	DISSECTOR
			DISHONOUR	

DISSEISIN	DIVORCING	DONATIONS	DRAGGIEST	DRUGGISTS
DISSEISOR	DIVORCIVE	DONCASTER	DRAGHOUND	DRUGSTORE
DISSEMBLE	DIVULGING	DONNISHLY	DRAGOMANS	DRUMBEATS
DISSENTED	DIVULSION	DONORSHIP	DRAGONESS	DRUM MAJOR
DISSENTER	DIVULSIVE	DOODLEBUG	DRAGONFLY	DRUMSTICK
DISSIDENT	DIXIELAND	DOOHICKEY	DRAGONISH	DRUNKARDS
DISSIPATE	DIZZINESS	DOOJIGGER	DRAGOONED	DRUNKENLY
DISSOLUTE	DJAJAPURA	DOOMSAYER	DRAINABLE	DUALISTIC
DISSOLVED	DOBSONFLY	DOORBELLS	DRAINPIPE	DUBIOUSLY
DISSOLVER	DOCK BRIEF	DOORFRAME	DRAMAMINE	DUBITABLE
DISSONANT	DOCKETING	DOORKNOBS	DRAMATICS	DUBROVNIK
DISSUADED	DOCKYARDS	DOORNAILS	DRAMATIST	DUCHESSES
DISSUADER	DOCTORATE	DOORPLATE	DRAMATIZE	DUCKBOARD
DISTANCED	DOCTORING	DOORSTEPS	DRAPERIED	DUCKLINGS
DISTANCES	DOCTRINAL	DORDRECHT	DRAPERIES	DUCTILITY
DISTANTLY	DOCTRINES	DORMITORY	DRAUGHTER	DUDE RANCH
DISTEMPER	DOCUMENTS	DORMOBILE	DRAVIDIAN	DUELLISTS
DISTENDED	DODDERERS	DORONICUM	DRAWBACKS	DUFFEL BAG
DISTENDER	DODDERING	DORYPHORE	DRAWKNIFE	DULCIMERS
DISTICHAL	DODECAGON	DOSIMETER	DRAWPLATE	DUMBARTON
DISTILLED	DODGE CITY	DOSIMETRY	DREAMBOAT	DUMBBELLS
DISTILLER	DOG COLLAR	DOSSHOUSE	DREAMLAND	DUMBFOUND
DISTINGUE	DOG-EAT-	DOTTINESS	DREAMLESS	DUMB SHOWS
DISTORTED	DOG	DOUBLE BED	DREAMLIKE	DUMMY RUNS
DISTORTER	DOGFIGHTS	DOUBLED UP	DREAMTIME	DUMPINESS
DISTRAINT	DOGFISHES	DOUBLETON	DREARIEST	DUMPLINGS
DISTRICTS	DOGGY BAGS	DOUBLOONS	DRENCHING	DUNCES CAP
DISTURBED	DOGHOUSES	DOUBTABLE	DRESS CODE	DUNCE'S
DISTURBER	DOGLEGGED	DOUBTLESS	DRESS DOWN	CAP
DISUNITED	DOGMATICS	DOUGHNUTS	DRESSIEST	DUNE BUGGY
DITHERING	DOGMATISM	DOUGHTIER	DRESSINGS	DUNGANNON
DITHYRAMB	DOGMATIST	DOVECOTES	DRIBBLING	DUNGAREES
DITTANDER	DOGMATIZE	DOVETAILS	DRIFTWOOD	DUNGENESS
DIURETICS	DO-GOODERS	DOWDINESS	DRILLABLE	DUNKERQUE
DIURNALLY	DOG PADDLE	DOWITCHER	DRINKABLE	DUNSINANE
DIVALENCY	DOLEFULLY	DOWNCOMER	DRIP-DRIED	DUNSTABLE
DIVERGENT	DOLERITIC	DOWNFALLS	DRIPSTONE	DUODECIMO
DIVERGING	DOLGELLAU	DOWNGRADE	DRIVE HOME	DUODENARY
DIVERSELY	DOLLY BIRD	DOWNPOURS	DRIVELING	DUODENUMS
DIVERSIFY	DOLOMITES	DOWNRANGE	DRIVELLED	DUOLOGUES
DIVERSION	DOLOMITIC	DOWNRIGHT	DRIVELLER	DUPLEXITY
DIVERSITY	DOLTISHLY	DOWNSPOUT	DRIVE-TIME	DUPLICATE
DIVERTING	DOMESTICS	DOWNSTAGE	DRIVEWAYS	DUPLICITY
DIVERTIVE	DOMICILED	DOWNSWING	DRIZZLING	DURALUMIN
DIVESTING	DOMICILES	DOWNTHROW	DROLLNESS	DURICRUST
DIVIDABLE	DOMINANCE	DOWNTURNS	DROMEDARY	DUSKINESS
DIVIDENDS	DOMINATED	DOWNWARDS	DROPLIGHT	DUSTBOWLS
DIVINABLE	DOMINATOR	DRACONIAN	DROPPINGS	DUSTCARTS
DIVISIBLE	DOMINICAL	DRAFTIEST	DROPSICAL	DUSTSHEET
DIVISIONS	DOMINICAN	DRAFTSMAN	DROPSONDE	DUST STORM
DIVORCEES	DOMINIONS	DRAFTSMEN	DRUBBINGS	DUTCH BARN

DUTCH CAPS	EARTHWARD	EFFECTIVE	ELEVATION	EMBRYONIC
DUTCH OVEN	EARTHWORK	EFFECTUAL	ELEVATORS	EMENDABLE
DUTIFULLY	EARTHWORM	EFFERENCE	ELEVENSES	EMENDATOR
DUTY-FREES	EASTBOUND	EFFICIENT	ELEVENTHS	EMERGENCE
DWARF STAR	EAST ENDER	EFFLUENCE	ELICITING	EMERGENCY
DWELLINGS	EASTER EGG	EFFLUENTS	ELIMINANT	EMIGRANTS
DWINDLING	EASTERNER	EFFLUVIAL	ELIMINATE	EMIGRATED
DYER'S-	EASTLEIGH	EFFLUVIUM	ELIZABETH	EMINENCES
WEED	EASTWARDS	EFFORTFUL	ELLESMERE	EMINENTLY
DYNAMETER	EASY CHAIR	EFFULGENT	ELLIPSOID	EMISSIONS
DYNAMITED	EASYGOING	EFFUSIONS	EL MANSURA	EMMENTHAL
DYNAMITER	EASY GOING	EGG BEATER	ELOCUTION	EMOLLIENT
DYNAMITIC	EASY TERMS	EGGPLANTS	ELONGATED	EMOLUMENT
DYNAMOTOR	EAVESDROP	EGGSHELLS	ELOPEMENT	EMOTIONAL
DYNASTIES	EBULLIENT	EGG TIMERS	ELOQUENCE	EMOTIVELY
DYSENTERY	ECCENTRIC	EGLANTINE	ELSEWHERE	EMOTIVISM
DYSGENICS	ECHOLALIA	EGOMANIAC	ELUCIDATE	EMPANELED
DYSLECTIC	ECHOLALIC	EGOTISTIC	ELUSIVELY	EMPATHIZE
DYSPEPSIA	ECLAMPSIA	EGREGIOUS	ELUTRIATE	EMPENNAGE
DYSPEPTIC	ECLAMPTIC	EGYPTIANS	EMACIATED	EMPHASIZE
DYSPHAGIA	ECLIPSING	EIDERDOWN	EMANATING	EMPHYSEMA
DYSPHAGIC	ECOLOGIST	EIGHTFOLD	EMANATION	EMPIRICAL
DYSPHASIA	ECONOMICS	EIGHTIETH	EMANATIVE	EMPLOYEES
DYSPHASIC	ECONOMIES	EINDHOVEN	EMANATORY	EMPLOYERS
DYSPHONIA	ECONOMIST	EIRENICON	EMBALMERS	EMPLOYING
DYSPHONIC	ECONOMIZE	EISEGESIS	EMBALMING	EMPORIUMS
DYSPHORIA	ECOSPHERE	EJACULATE	EMBARGOED	EMPOWERED
DYSPHORIC	ECOSYSTEM	EKISTICAL	EMBARGOES	EMPRESSES
DYSPLASIA	ECSTASIES	ELABORATE	EMBARKING	EMPTIABLE
DYSPNOEAL	ECSTATICS	EL ALAMEIN	EMBARRASS	EMPTINESS
DYSTHYMIA	ECTOBLAST	ELAN VITAL	EMBASSIES	EMPYREUMA
DYSTHYMIC	ECTOMERIC	ELASTANCE	EMBATTLED	EMULATING
DYSTROPHY	ECTOMORPH	ELASTOMER	EMBAYMENT	EMULATION
DZUNGARIA	ECTOPHYTE	ELATERITE	EMBEDDING	EMULATIVE
	ECTOPLASM	ELATERIUM	EMBEDMENT	EMULSIONS
E	ECTOPROCT	ELBOWROOM	EMBELLISH	EMUNCTORY
EACH OTHER	ECUMENISM	ELBOW ROOM	EMBEZZLED	ENACTMENT
EAGERNESS	EDDYSTONE	ELDERSHIP	EMBEZZLER	ENAMELING
EAGLE-EYED	EDELWEISS	ELECTIONS	EMBODYING	ENAMELLED
EAGLEWOOD	EDEMATOUS	ELECTORAL	EMBOLISMS	ENAMELLER
EARLINESS	EDIBILITY	ELECTRESS	EMBOSOMED	ENAMOURED
EARLY BIRD	EDIFICIAL	ELECTRICS	EMBOSSING	ENCAMPING
EARMARKED	EDINBURGH	ELECTRIFY	EMBOWMENT	ENCAUSTIC
EARNESTLY	EDITORIAL	ELECTRODE	EMBRACEOR	ENCHAINED
EARPHONES	EDUCATING	ELECTRONS	EMBRACERY	ENCHANTED
EARPIECES	EDUCATION	ELECTUARY	EMBRACING	ENCHANTER
EARTHIEST	EDUCATIVE	ELEGANTLY	EMBRASURE	ENCHILADA
EARTHLIER	EDUCATORS	ELEMENTAL	EMBROCATE	ENCHORIAL
EARTHLING	EDUCATORY	ELEOPTENE	EMBROIDER	ENCIRCLED
EARTHRISE	EDWARDIAN	ELEPHANTS	EMBROILED	ENCLOSING
EARTHSTAR	EFFECTING	ELEVATING	EMBROILER	ENCLOSURE

183

ENCOMIAST	ENHANCING	ENTRANCES	EPISTASIS	ESCALATOR
ENCOMIUMS	ENHANCIVE	ENTRAPPED	EPISTATIC	ESCALOPES
ENCOMPASS	ENIGMATIC	ENTRAPPER	EPISTAXIS	ESCAPABLE
ENCOUNTER	ENJOINING	ENTREATED	EPISTEMIC	ESCAPADES
ENCOURAGE	ENJOYABLE	ENTRECHAT	EPITAPHIC	ESCAPISTS
ENCRINITE	ENJOYABLY	ENTRECOTE	EPITAXIAL	ESCHEWING
ENCRUSTED	ENJOYMENT	ENTREMETS	EPITHETIC	ESCORTING
ENDAMOEBA	ENKINDLER	ENTRE NOUS	EPITOMIST	ESKISEHIR
ENDEARING	ENLARGING	ENTRUSTED	EPITOMIZE	ESOPHAGUS
ENDEAVOUR	ENLIGHTEN	ENTRYWAYS	EPIZOOTIC	ESPERANTO
ENDLESSLY	ENLISTING	ENTWINING	EPONYMOUS	ESPIONAGE
ENDOBLAST	ENLIVENED	ENUCLEATE	EQUAL-AREA	ESPLANADE
ENDOCRINE	ENLIVENER	ENUMERATE	EQUALIZED	ESPOUSALS
ENDOERGIC	ENMESHING	ENUNCIATE	EQUALIZER	ESPOUSING
ENDOLYMPH	ENNOBLING	ENVELOPED	EQUALLING	ESPRESSOS
ENDOMORPH	EN PASSANT	ENVELOPES	EQUATABLE	ESSAOUIRA
ENDOPHYTE	ENQUIRIES	ENVIOUSLY	EQUATIONS	ESSAYISTS
ENDOPLASM	ENQUIRING	ENVISAGED	EQUERRIES	ESSENTIAL
ENDORSING	ENRAGEDLY	ENVYINGLY	EQUINOXES	ESSLINGEN
ENDOSCOPE	EN RAPPORT	ENZYMATIC	EQUIPMENT	ESTABLISH
ENDOSCOPY	ENRAPTURE	EPARCHIAL	EQUIPOISE	ESTAMINET
ENDOSPERM	ENRICHING	EPHEDRINE	EQUIPPING	ESTATE CAR
ENDOSPORE	ENROLLING	EPHEMERAL	EQUISETUM	ESTEEMING
ENDOSTEAL	ENROLMENT	EPHEMERID	EQUITABLE	ESTHETICS
ENDOSTEUM	ENSCONCED	EPHEMERIS	EQUITABLY	ESTIMABLE
ENDOTOXIC	ENSEMBLES	EPHEMERON	EQUIVOCAL	ESTIMATED
ENDOTOXIN	ENSHRINED	EPICENISM	EQUIVOQUE	ESTIMATES
ENDOWMENT	ENSLAVING	EPICENTRE	ERADICANT	ESTIMATOR
ENDURABLE	ENSNARING	EPICRISIS	ERADICATE	ESTOPPAGE
ENDURANCE	ENSTATITE	EPICRITIC	ERECTABLE	ESTRANGED
ENERGETIC	ENSUINGLY	EPICUREAN	ERECTIONS	ESTRANGER
ENERGIZED	ENTAILING	EPICURISM	ERECTNESS	ESTUARIAL
ENERGIZER	ENTAMOEBA	EPICYCLIC	EREMITISM	ESTUARIES
ENERGUMEN	ENTANGLED	EPIDEMICS	ERGOGRAPH	ESTUARINE
ENERVATED	ENTANGLER	EPIDERMAL	ERGOMETER	ESURIENCE
ENERVATOR	ENTELECHY	EPIDERMIS	ERGONOMIC	ETCETERAS
EN FAMILLE	ENTENDRES	EPIDURALS	ERISTICAL	ETERNALLY
ENFEEBLED	ENTERABLE	EPIGENOUS	EROGENOUS	ETHERIZER
ENFEEBLER	ENTERALLY	EPIGRAPHY	EROSIONAL	ETHICALLY
ENFILADED	ENTERITIS	EPIGYNOUS	EROTICISM	ETHIOPIAN
ENFILADES	ENTERTAIN	EPILEPTIC	EROTICIZE	ETHMOIDAL
ENFOLDING	ENTHRONED	EPILOGIST	ERRONEOUS	ETHNARCHY
ENFORCING	ENTHUSING	EPILOGUES	ERSTWHILE	ETHNOGENY
ENGINEERS	ENTHYMEME	EPIMYSIUM	ERUDITELY	ETHNOLOGY
ENGLACIAL	ENTITLING	EPINASTIC	ERUDITION	ETHOLOGIC
ENGRAMMIC	ENTOBLAST	EPIPHANIC	ERUPTIBLE	ETHYLENIC
ENGRAVERS	ENTOMBING	EPIPHRAGM	ERUPTIONS	ETIOLATED
ENGRAVING	ENTOPHYTE	EPIPHYSIS	ERYTHRISM	ETIQUETTE
ENGROSSED	ENTOURAGE	EPIPHYTIC	ERYTHRITE	ETRAMETER
ENGROSSER	ENTRAINED	EPIROGENY	ESCALADER	ETYMOLOGY
ENGULFING	ENTRANCED	EPISCOPAL	ESCALATED	EUCHARIST

EUCLIDEAN	EXCALIBUR	EXEMPLARY	EXPLAINER	EXTRAVERT
EUDEMONIA	EXCAUDATE	EXEMPLIFY	EXPLETIVE	EXTREMELY
EUDEMONIC	EXCAVATED	EXEMPTING	EXPLICATE	EXTREMISM
EUKARYOTE	EXCAVATOR	EXEMPTION	EXPLODING	EXTREMIST
EULOGISTS	EXCEEDING	EXEQUATUR	EXPLOITED	EXTREMITY
EULOGIZED	EXCELLENT	EXERCISED	EXPLOITER	EXTRICATE
EUPHEMISM	EXCELLING	EXERCISER	EXPLORERS	EXTRINSIC
EUPHEMIST	EXCELSIOR	EXERCISES	EXPLORING	EXTROVERT
EUPHEMIZE	EXCEPTING	EXERTIONS	EXPLOSION	EXTRUDING
EUPHONIUM	EXCEPTION	EXFOLIATE	EXPLOSIVE	EXTRUSION
EUPHONIZE	EXCEPTIVE	EXHALABLE	EXPONENTS	EXTRUSIVE
EUPHORBIA	EXCERPTER	EXHAUSTED	EXPONIBLE	EXUBERANT
EUPHRATES	EXCESSIVE	EXHAUSTER	EXPORTERS	EXUBERATE
EUPLASTIC	EXCHANGED	EXHIBITED	EXPORTING	EXUDATION
EURHYTHMY	EXCHANGER	EXHIBITOR	EXPOSABLE	EXUDATIVE
EUROCRATS	EXCHANGES	EXHORTING	EXPOSITOR	EYEBALLED
EUROPHILE	EXCHEQUER	EXISTENCE	EXPOSURES	EYEBRIGHT
EUROPOORT	EXCIPIENT	EXODONTIA	EXPOUNDED	EYELASHES
EUTHENICS	EXCISABLE	EXOENZYME	EXPOUNDER	EYELETEER
EUTHENIST	EXCISEMAN	EX OFFICIO	EXPRESSED	EYE OPENER
EUTHERIAN	EXCISIONS	EXOGAMOUS	EXPRESSER	EYE-OPENER
EUTROPHIC	EXCITABLE	EXOGENOUS	EXPRESSES	EYEPIECES
EVACUATED	EXCITEDLY	EXONERATE	EXPRESSLY	EYE SHADOW
EVACUATOR	EXCLAIMED	EXORCISER	EXPULSION	EYES RIGHT
EVADINGLY	EXCLAIMER	EXORCISMS	EXPULSIVE	EYESTRAIN
EVAGINATE	EXCLUDING	EXORCISTS	EXPUNGING	EYE STRAIN
EVALUATED	EXCLUSION	EXORCIZED	EXPURGATE	
EVALUATOR	EXCLUSIVE	EXOSMOSIS	EXQUISITE	**F**
EVAPORATE	EXCORIATE	EXOSMOTIC	EXSECTION	FABACEOUS
EVAPORITE	EXCREMENT	EXOSPHERE	EXSERTILE	FABIANISM
EVASIVELY	EXCRETING	EXOSTOSIS	EXSERTION	FABRICATE
EVENTUATE	EXCRETION	EXOTICISM	EXSICCATE	FABRIKOID
EVERGREEN	EXCRETIVE	EXPANDING	EXSTROPHY	FACE CARDS
EVERSIBLE	EXCRETORY	EXPANSILE	EXTEMPORE	FACECLOTH
EVERYBODY	EXCULPATE	EXPANSION	EXTENDING	FACE-LIFTS
EVICTIONS	EXCURRENT	EXPANSIVE	EXTENSION	FACE PACKS
EVIDENTLY	EXCURSION	EXPATIATE	EXTENSITY	FACEPLATE
EVILDOERS	EXCURSIVE	EXPECTANT	EXTENSIVE	FACE SAVER
EVILDOING	EXCUSABLE	EXPECTING	EXTENUATE	FACE-SAVER
EVINCIBLE	EXCUSABLY	EXPEDIENT	EXTERIORS	FACETIOUS
EVOCATION	EXECRABLE	EXPEDITED	EXTERNALS	FACE VALUE
EVOCATIVE	EXECRABLY	EXPEDITER	EXTIRPATE	FACSIMILE
EVOLUTION	EXECRATED	EXPELLANT	EXTOLLING	FACTIONAL
EVOLVABLE	EXECUTANT	EXPELLING	EXTOLMENT	FACTITIVE
EXACTABLE	EXECUTING	EXPENDING	EXTORTING	FACTORAGE
EXACTNESS	EXECUTION	EXPENSIVE	EXTORTION	FACTORIAL
EXALTEDLY	EXECUTIVE	EXPERTISE	EXTORTIVE	FACTORIES
EXAMINERS	EXECUTORS	EXPIATING	EXTRABOLD	FACTORING
EXAMINING	EXECUTORY	EXPIATION	EXTRACTED	FACTORIZE
EXANIMATE	EXECUTRIX	EXPIATORY	EXTRACTOR	FACTUALLY
EXANTHEMA	EXEGETICS	EXPLAINED	EXTRADITE	FACULTIES

FADDINESS	FARRAGOES	FERMENTER	FILMINESS	FIRST FOOT
FADDISHLY	FARROWING	FEROCIOUS	FILM SPEED	FIRSTHAND
FADEDNESS	FAR-SEEING	FERRETING	FILM STARS	FIRST LADY
FAGACEOUS	FARTHINGS	FERROCENE	FILM STOCK	FIRSTLING
FAGGOTING	FASCICLED	FERROTYPE	FILMSTRIP	FIRST NAME
FAINEANCE	FASCICULE	FERTILITY	FILOPLUME	FIRST-RATE
FAINTNESS	FASCIITIS	FERTILIZE	FILOSELLE	FISHCAKES
FAIRBANKS	FASCINATE	FERVENTLY	FILTERING	FISHERIES
FAIRYLAND	FASCISTIC	FESTERING	FILTER TIP	FISHERMAN
FAIRY-LIKE	FASHIONED	FESTIVALS	FILTHIEST	FISHERMEN
FAIRY RING	FASHIONER	FESTIVITY	FIMBRIATE	FISH FARMS
FAIRY-TALE	FASTENERS	FESTOONED	FINALISTS	FISHGUARD
FAITHFULS	FASTENING	FETICIDAL	FINALIZED	FISHINESS
FAITHLESS	FATALISTS	FETISHISM	FINANCIAL	FISH KNIFE
FALANGISM	FATEFULLY	FETISHIST	FINANCIER	FISHPLATE
FALANGIST	FATHEADED	FETISHIZE	FINANCING	FISH SLICE
FALCONERS	FATHERING	FETTERING	FINE-GRAIN	FISH STICK
FALCONINE	FATHOMING	FETTUCINE	FINE PRINT	FISSILITY
FALDSTOOL	FATIGABLE	FEUDALISM	FINE-TOOTH	FISTULOUS
FALLACIES	FATIGUING	FEUDALIST	FINE-TUNED	FIXATIONS
FALLALERY	FATTENING	FEUDALITY	FINGERING	FIXATIVES
FALL APART	FATTINESS	FEUDALIZE	FINGERTIP	FIXED-HEAD
FALLOPIAN	FATUITOUS	FEUDATORY	FINISHING	FIXED STAR
FALSEHOOD	FATUOUSLY	FEVERWORT	FINISTERE	FIZZINESS
FALSENESS	FAULTIEST	FIBONACCI	FIRE ALARM	FLABBIEST
FALSIFIED	FAULTLESS	FIBREFILL	FIREBALLS	FLABELLUM
FALSIFIER	FAVEOLATE	FIBRIFORM	FIREBOXES	FLACCIDLY
FALSITIES	FAVOURING	FIBRINOUS	FIREBRAND	FLAGELLAR
FALTERING	FAVOURITE	FICTIONAL	FIREBREAK	FLAGELLUM
FAMAGUSTA	FAWNINGLY	FIDEISTIC	FIREBRICK	FLAGEOLET
FAMILIARS	FEARFULLY	FIDGETING	FIRECREST	FLAGPOLES
FAMILY MAN	FEATHERED	FIDUCIARY	FIRE DRILL	FLAGRANCE
FAMILY MEN	FEATURING	FIELD ARMY	FIRE-EATER	FLAGRANCY
FANATICAL	FEBRICITY	FIELD DAYS	FIREFIGHT	FLAGSHIPS
FANCINESS	FEBRIFUGE	FIELDFARE	FIREFLIES	FLAGSTAFF
FANCY-FREE	FEBRILITY	FIELD GOAL	FIREGUARD	FLAGSTONE
FANCYWORK	FECULENCE	FIELDSMAN	FIRE IRONS	FLAG-WAVER
FANDANGLE	FECUNDATE	FIELDSMEN	FIRELIGHT	FLAKINESS
FANDANGOS	FECUNDITY	FIELD-TEST	FIREPLACE	FLAMELIKE
FANLIGHTS	FEDERATED	FIELD TRIP	FIRE-PLUGS	FLAMINGOS
FAN-TAILED	FEEDSTOCK	FIELDWORK	FIREPOWER	FLAMMABLE
FANTASIES	FEEDSTUFF	FIFTEENTH	FIREPROOF	FLANNELED
FANTASIZE	FEELINGLY	FIFTIETHS	FIRESIDES	FLAPJACKS
FANTASTIC	FEE-PAYING	FIG LEAVES	FIRESTONE	FLARE PATH
FARADIZER	FELICIFIC	FIGURE OUT	FIRESTORM	FLASHBACK
FARANDOLE	FELONIOUS	FIGURINES	FIRETHORN	FLASHBULB
FAREWELLS	FEMINISTS	FILAMENTS	FIRETRAPS	FLASHCUBE
FARMHANDS	FENESTRAL	FILIATION	FIREWATER	FLASHGUNS
FARMHOUSE	FENUGREEK	FILICIDAL	FIREWORKS	FLASHIEST
FARMSTEAD	FERMANAGH	FILLETING	FIRMAMENT	FLASHOVER
FARMYARDS	FERMENTED	FILLISTER	FIRSTBORN	FLATMATES

FLAT SPINS	FLOWCHART	FOOLHARDY	FORESHORE	FORWARDLY
FLATTENED	FLOWERAGE	FOOLISHLY	FORESIGHT	FOSSILIZE
FLATTENER	FLOWERBED	FOOLPROOF	FORESKINS	FOSSORIAL
FLATTERED	FLOWERING	FOOTBALLS	FORESTALL	FOSTERAGE
FLATTERER	FLOWERPOT	FOOTBOARD	FORESTERS	FOSTERING
FLATULENT	FLOWINGLY	FOOTFALLS	FORETASTE	FOUNDERED
FLAUNTING	FLOWMETER	FOOT FAULT	FORETOKEN	FOUNDLING
FLAUTISTS	FLUCTUANT	FOOTHILLS	FORETOOTH	FOUNDRIES
FLAVOROUS	FLUCTUATE	FOOTHOLDS	FOREWOMAN	FOUNTAINS
FLAVOURED	FLUFFIEST	FOOTLOOSE	FOREWOMEN	FOURSOMES
FLAVOURER	FLUIDIZER	FOOTNOTES	FOREWORDS	FOUR-WHEEL
FLEABITES	FLUKINESS	FOOTPATHS	FORFEITED	FOVEOLATE
FLEDGLING	FLUMMOXED	FOOTPLATE	FORFEITER	FOXGLOVES
FLEETNESS	FLUORESCE	FOOT-POUND	FORFICATE	FOXHOUNDS
FLEETWOOD	FLUOROSIS	FOOTPRINT	FORGATHER	FOXHUNTER
FLENSBURG	FLUORSPAR	FOOTRACES	FORGEABLE	FRACTIONS
FLESHIEST	FLURRYING	FOOTSTALK	FORGERIES	FRACTIOUS
FLESHINGS	FLUSTERED	FOOTSTALL	FORGETFUL	FRACTURAL
FLESHPOTS	FLUTTERED	FOOTSTEPS	FORGETTER	FRACTURED
FLEURETTE	FLUTTERER	FOOTSTOOL	FORGIVING	FRACTURES
FLEXIONAL	FLUXIONAL	FORAMINAL	FORGOTTEN	FRAGILITY
FLEXITIME	FLUXMETER	FORBEARER	FORLORNIY	FRAGMENTS
FLICKERED	FLY-FISHER	FORBIDDEN	FORMALISM	FRAGONARD
FLIGHTIER	FLY HALVES	FORBIDDER	FORMALIST	FRAGRANCE
FLIGHTILY	FLYING FOX	FORCEABLE	FORMALITY	FRAILTIES
FLIMSIEST	FLYLEAVES	FORCE FEED	FORMALIZE	FRAMBOISE
FLINCHING	FLYSHEETS	FORCE-FEED	FORMATION	FRAMEWORK
FLINTIEST	FLYWEIGHT	FORCEMEAT	FORMATIVE	FRANCHISE
FLINTLOCK	FLYWHEELS	FORCINGLY	FORMATTED	FRANCOLIN
FLIP-FLOPS	FLYWHISKS	FOREARMED	FORMICARY	FRANGIBLE
FLIPPANCY	FOAMINESS	FOREBEARS	FORMULAIC	FRANGLAIS
FLOATABLE	FOCUSABLE	FOREBODED	FORMULARY	FRANKABLE
FLOAT-FEED	FOCUSSING	FOREBODER	FORMULATE	FRANKFORT
FLOCCULUS	FOETATION	FOREBRAIN	FORMULISM	FRANKNESS
FLOGGINGS	FOETICIDE	FORECASTS	FORMULIST	FRATERNAL
FLOODABLE	FOGGINESS	FORECLOSE	FORNICATE	FRAUDSTER
FLOODGATE	FOLIATION	FORECOURT	FORSAKING	FREE AGENT
FLOOD TIDE	FOLIOLATE	FOREFRONT	FORSYTHIA	FREE-BASED
FLOOR SHOW	FOLK DANCE	FOREGOING	FORTALEZA	FREEBOARD
FLOPHOUSE	FOLKLORIC	FOREHANDS	FORTALICE	FREEHOLDS
FLOPPIEST	FOLK MUSIC	FOREHEADS	FORTHWITH	FREE HOUSE
FLOPTICAL	FOLKTALES	FOREIGNER	FORTIETHS	FREE KICKS
FLORIATED	FOLLICLES	FOREJUDGE	FORTIFIED	FREELANCE
FLORIDITY	FOLLOWERS	FORELOCKS	FORTIFIER	FREE-LIVER
FLORISTIC	FOLLOWING	FORENAMED	FORTITUDE	FREEMASON
FLOS FERRI	FOLLOW-UPS	FORENAMES	FORTNIGHT	FREEPHONE
FLOTATION	FOMENTING	FORENSICS	FORTUNATE	FREE PORTS
FLOTILLAS	FOOD CHAIN	FOREREACH	FORT WORTH	FREE-RANGE
FLOUNCING	FOOD STAMP	FORESHANK	FORTY-FIVE	FREESHEET
FLOUNDERS	FOODSTUFF	FORESHEET	FORWARDED	FREE STATE
FLOURMILL	FOOLERIES	FORESHOCK	FORWARDER	FREESTONE

FREESTYLE	FROSTIEST	FUNNY BONE	GALLSTONE	GATEPOSTS
FREE TRADE	FROSTWORK	FUNNY FARM	GALUMPHED	GATESHEAD
FREE VERSE	FROTHIEST	FURBISHED	GALVANISM	GATHERING
FREEWHEEL	FROWSTIER	FURBISHER	GALVANIZE	GAUCHERIE
FREE WORLD	FROWZIEST	FURCATION	GALWEGIAN	GAUDINESS
FREEZABLE	FRUCTUOUS	FURIOUSLY	GAMBOGIAN	GAUGEABLE
FREEZE-DRY	FRUGALITY	FURLOUGHS	GAMBOLING	GAUGEABLY
FREIGHTED	FRUIT BATS	FURNISHED	GAMECOCKS	GAULEITER
FREIGHTER	FRUITCAKE	FURNISHER	GAMMADION	GAUNTLETS
FREMANTLE	FRUITERER	FURNITURE	GAMMA RAYS	GAUNTNESS
FRENCHIFY	FRUITIEST	FURRINESS	GANDHIISM	GAUZINESS
FRENCHMAN	FRUITLESS	FURROWING	GANG-BANGS	GAWKINESS
FRENCHMEN	FRUMPIEST	FURTHERED	GANGLIONS	GAZA STRIP
FREQUENCE	FRUSTRATE	FURTHERER	GANGPLANK	GAZEHOUND
FREQUENCY	FRYING PAN	FURTIVELY	GANGSTERS	GAZETTEER
FRESHENED	FUGACIOUS	FUSELAGES	GAOLBIRDS	GAZIANTEP
FRESHENER	FUGITIVES	FUSILLADE	GARBOLOGY	GAZUMPING
FRESHNESS	FUKUSHIMA	FUSIONISM	GARDENERS	GEARBOXES
FRETBOARD	FULFILLED	FUSIONIST	GARDENIAS	GEAR LEVER
FRETFULLY	FULFILLER	FUSSINESS	GARDENING	GEAR STICK
FRETWORKS	FULGURITE	FUSTINESS	GARGOYLED	GEARWHEEL
FRIARBIRD	FULGUROUS	FUTURISTS	GARGOYLES	GEHLENITE
FRICASSEE	FULLBACKS	FUZZINESS	GARIBALDI	GELIGNITE
FRICATIVE	FULL-BLOWN		GARLANDED	GELLIGAER
FRIESIANS	FULL BOARD	**G**	GARNERING	GELSEMIUM
FRIESLAND	FULLERENE	GABARDINE	GARNISHED	GEMMATION
FRIGHTFUL	FULL-FACED	GABERDINE	GARNISHER	GEMUTLICH
FRIGIDITY	FULL-GROWN	GABIONADE	GARNISHES	GENDARMES
FRILLIEST	FULL HOUSE	GADABOUTS	GARNITURE	GENEALOGY
FRISKIEST	FULL MARKS	GADOLINIC	GARRISONS	GENE CLONE
FRITTERED	FULL MONTY	GADROONED	GARROTTED	GENERABLE
FRITTERER	FULL MOONS	GAINFULLY	GARROTTER	GENERALLY
FRIVOLITY	FULL-SCALE	GAINSAYER	GARROTTES	GENERATED
FRIVOLLER	FULL STOPS	GALACTOSE	GARRULITY	GENERATOR
FRIVOLOUS	FULMINANT	GALANTINE	GARRULOUS	GENIALITY
FRIZZIEST	FULMINATE	GALAPAGOS	GAS FITTER	GENITALIC
FRIZZLING	FULSOMELY	GALEIFORM	GAS HEATER	GENITALLY
FROCK COAT	FUMAROLIC	GALENICAL	GASHOLDER	GENITIVAL
FROGMARCH	FUMIGATED	GALINGALE	GASLIGHTS	GENITIVES
FROGMOUTH	FUMIGATOR	GALLANTLY	GAS MANTLE	GENOCIDAL
FROGSPAWN	FUNCTIONS	GALLANTRY	GASOLINIC	GENOTYPIC
FROLICKED	FUNDAMENT	GALLERIED	GASOMETER	GENTEELLY
FROLICKER	FUNGICIDE	GALLERIES	GASOMETRY	GENTILITY
FRONTAGES	FUNGIFORM	GALLICISM	GASPINGLY	GENTLEMAN
FRONTALLY	FUNGISTAT	GALLICIZE	GASSINESS	GENTLEMEN
FRONT DOOR	FUNICULAR	GALLINULE	GASTRITIC	GENTLE SEX
FRONTIERS	FUNICULUS	GALLIPOLI	GASTRITIS	GENUFLECT
FRONT LINE	FUNNELING	GALLIVANT	GASTROPOD	GENUINELY
FRONT-PAGE	FUNNELLED	GALLIWASP	GASTRULAR	GEODESIST
FRONT ROOM	FUNNINESS	GALLONAGE	GATECRASH	GEOGRAPHY
FROSTBITE		GALLOPING	GATEHOUSE	GEOLOGIST

GEOLOGIZE	GIRANDOLE	GLOWERING	GOOD TIMES	GRAPHITIC
GEOMANCER	GIRL GUIDE	GLOWINGLY	GOOD WORDS	GRAPPELLI
GEOMANTIC	GIRLISHLY	GLOW-WORMS	GOOFINESS	GRAPPLING
GEOMETRIC	GIRONDISM	GLUCOSIDE	GOOSANDER	GRASPABLE
GEOMETRID	GIRONDIST	GLUTAMINE	GOOSEFOOT	GRASSIEST
GEOPHYTIC	GIVEAWAYS	GLUTENOUS	GOOSENECK	GRASSLAND
GEOPONICS	GIVEN NAME	GLUTINOUS	GOOSESTEP	GRASSQUIT
GEORGETTE	GLABELLAR	GLYCERIDE	GOOSINESS	GRATICULE
GEOSTATIC	GLADDENED	GLYCERINE	GORAKHPUR	GRATIFIED
GEOTACTIC	GLADDENER	GLYCOSIDE	GORGEABLE	GRATIFIER
GEOTROPIC	GLADIATOR	GOAL LINES	GORGONIAN	GRATINGLY
GERANIUMS	GLADIOLUS	GOALMOUTH	GORILLIAN	GRATITUDE
GERIATRIC	GLAIREOUS	GOALPOSTS	GORILLOID	GRAVELING
GERMANDER	GLAMORGAN	GOATHERDS	GOSPELLER	GRAVELISH
GERMANISM	GLAMORIZE	GOATSKINS	GOSSIPING	GRAVELLED
GERMANITE	GLAMOROUS	GO BETWEEN	GOTHICISM	GRAVENESS
GERMANIUM	GLANDERED	GO-BETWEEN	GO THROUGH	GRAVESEND
GERMANIZE	GLANDULAR	GODESBERG	GO TO	GRAVESIDE
GERMANOUS	GLARINGLY	GODFATHER	EARTH	GRAVEYARD
GERM CELLS	GLASSIEST	GODLESSLY	GOTTINGEN	GRAVIDITY
GERMICIDE	GLASSWARE	GODLINESS	GOURMANDS	GRAVITATE
GERMINANT	GLASSWORK	GODMOTHER	GOUTINESS	GRAVY BOAT
GERMINATE	GLASSWORT	GODPARENT	GOVERNESS	GREASE GUN
GERMISTON	GLEANABLE	GO-GETTERS	GOVERNING	GREASIEST
GERUNDIAL	GLEANINGS	GOGGLE BOX	GOVERNORS	GREAT-AUNT
GERUNDIVE	GLEEFULLY	GOING-OVER	GRACELESS	GREAT BEAR
GESTATION	GLENGARRY	GOLDCREST	GRADATION	GREAT BELT
GESTATORY	GLIDINGLY	GOLDEN AGE	GRADIENTS	GREATCOAT
GESTURING	GLIMMERED	GOLDENEYE	GRADUALLY	GREAT DANE
GETTING ON	GLIMPSING	GOLDEN EYE	GRADUATED	GREATNESS
GEYSERITE	GLISSADER	GOLDENROD	GRADUATES	GREEDIEST
GHASTLIER	GLISSANDO	GOLDFIELD	GRADUATOR	GREENAWAY
GHETTOIZE	GLISTENED	GOLDFINCH	GRAMPUSES	GREENBACK
GHOSTLIER	GLITTERED	GOLD MEDAL	GRANARIES	GREEN BEAN
GHOST TOWN	GLITZIEST	GOLD-MINER	GRANDADDY	GREEN BELT
GIANT STAR	GLOBALISM	GOLDMINES	GRANDIOSE	GREEN EYED
GIBBERING	GLOBALIST	GOLD PLATE	GRANDIOSO	GREENGAGE
GIBBERISH	GLOBALIZE	GOLDSMITH	GRAND JURY	GREENHEAD
GIBRALTAR	GLOBE FISH	GOLF BALLS	GRANDNESS	GREENHORN
GIDDINESS	GLOBOSITY	GOLF CLUBS	GRAND PRIX	GREENLAND
GIFT HORSE	GLOMERATE	GOLF LINKS	GRAND SLAM	GREENLING
GIGAHERTZ	GLOMERULE	GOLLIWOGS	GRANDSONS	GREENNESS
GIGANTISM	GLOOMIEST	GOMPHOSIS	GRANITITE	GREENROOM
GILSONITE	GLORIFIED	GONDOLIER	GRANIVORE	GREEN ROOM
GILT-EDGED	GLORIFIER	GONIATITE	GRANOLITH	GREENSAND
GIMMICKRY	GLORY HOLE	GONOPHORE	GRANTABLE	GREENWICH
GINGER ALE	GLOSSIEST	GONORRHEA	GRANULATE	GREENWOOD
GINGERING	GLOSSITIC	GOODLIEST	GRANULITE	GREETINGS
GINGER NUT	GLOSSITIS	GOOD LOOKS	GRANULOMA	GREGARINE
GIN SLINGS	GLOTTIDES	GOODNIGHT	GRAPESHOT	GREGORIAN
GIPSYWORT	GLOTTISES	GOOD-SIZED	GRAPEVINE	GRENADIER

GRENADINE
GREY AREAS
GREYBEARD
GREYHOUND
GREY-STATE
GREYWACKE
GREY WATER
GRIDIRONS
GRIEVANCE
GRILLROOM
GRIMACING
GRIMALKIN
GRIMINESS
GRINDELIA
GRIPINGLY
GRISAILLE
GRISLIEST
GRISTLIER
GRISTMILL
GRITTIEST
GRIZZLING
GROCERIES
GROGGIEST
GRONINGEN
GROOMSMAN
GROOVIEST
GROPINGLY
GROSGRAIN
GROSSNESS
GROTESQUE
GROTTIEST
GROUCHIER
GROUCHILY
GROUCHING
GROUNDAGE
GROUNDING
GROUNDNUT
GROUNDSEL
GROUPINGS
GROUPWARE
GROVELING
GROVELLED
GROVELLER
GRUBBIEST
GRUBSTAKE
GRUELLING
GRUFFNESS
GRUMBLERS
GRUMBLING
GRUMPIEST
GUANABARA
190

GUANGDONG
GUANIDINE
GUANOSINE
GUARANTEE
GUARANTOR
GUARDABLE
GUARDEDLY
GUARDIANS
GUARDRAIL
GUARDROOM
GUARDSMAN
GUARDSMEN
GUARD'S
 VAN
GUATEMALA
GUAYAQUIL
GUERRILLA
GUESSABLE
GUESSWORK
GUESTROOM
GUFFAWING
GUIDELINE
GUIDEPOST
GUIDINGLY
GUILDFORD
GUILDHALL
GUILDSMAN
GUILELESS
GUILLEMOT
GUILLOCHE
GUILTIEST
GUILTLESS
GUINEA PIG
GUITARIST
GULPINGLY
GUMMATOUS
GUMMINESS
GUMSHIELD
GUN COTTON
GUNPOWDER
GUNRUNNER
GUNSMITHS
GUSHINGLY
GUSTATORY
GUSTINESS
GUTTERING
GYMKHANAS
GYMNASIUM
GYMNASTIC
GYNAECOID
GYNARCHIC

GYNOECIUM
GYNOPHORE
GYRATIONS
GYRFALCON
GYROSCOPE

H

HABERGEON
HABITABLE
HABITABLY
HABITUATE
HACIENDAS
HACKAMORE
HACKBERRY
HACKNEYED
HADROSAUR
HAECCEITY
HAEMATEIN
HAEMATITE
HAEMATOID
HAEMATOMA
HAEMOCOEL
HAEMOCYTE
HAEMOSTAT
HAGBUTEER
HAGGADIST
HAGGARDLY
HAGGISHLY
HAGIARCHY
HAGIOLOGY
HAG-RIDDEN
HAIDAR ALI
HAILSTONE
HAILSTORM
HAIRBRUSH
HAIRCLOTH
HAIRGRIPS
HAIRINESS
HAIRLINES
HAIRPIECE
HAIR SHIRT
HAIR SLIDE
HAIRSTYLE
HALEAKALA
HALESOWEN
HALFBACKS
HALF-BAKED
HALF BOARD
HALF-BREED
HALF-CASTE
HALF CROWN

HALF DOZEN
HALF-DOZEN
HALF-HITCH
HALF LIGHT
HALF-LIGHT
HALF-LIVES
HALF MOONS
HALF NOTES
HALFPENCE
HALFPENNY
HALF-PLATE
HALFTONES
HALF-TRUTH
HALITOSIS
HALLELUJA
HALLIARDS
HALL-JONES
HALLMARKS
HALLOWEEN
HALLOWE'EN
HALLOWING
HALLOWMAS
HALLSTATT
HALMAHERA
HALOBIONT
HALOPHYTE
HALOTHANE
HALTINGLY
HAMADRYAD
HAMADRYAS
HAMAMATSU
HAMBURGER
HAMERSLEY
HAM-FISTED
HAMMERING
HAMMERTOE
HAMMER TOE
HAMMURABI
HAMPERING
HAMPSHIRE
HAMPSTEAD
HAMSTRING
HAMSTRUNG
HANDBASIN
HANDBILLS
HANDBOOKS
HANDBRAKE
HANDCARTS
HANDCLAPS
HANDCLASP
HANDCRAFT

HANDCUFFS
HANDICAPS
HANDINESS
HANDIWORK
HANDLEBAR
HANDLOOMS
HANDOVERS
HANDRAILS
HANDS DOWN
HANDSHAKE
HANDSPIKE
HANDSTAND
HANGERS ON
HANGERS-ON
HANGNAILS
HANGOVERS
HANKERING
HANSEATIC
HAPHAZARD
HAPHTARAH
HAPLESSLY
HAPLOLOGY
HAPPENING
HAPPINESS
HAPPY HOUR
HARANGUED
HARANGUER
HARANGUES
HARASSING
HARBINGER
HARBOURED
HARBOURER
HARDBACKS
HARDBOARD
HARDBOUND
HARD CIDER
HARD CORES
HARD COURT
HARDCOVER
HARD DISKS
HARD DRINK
HARDENING
HARDHEADS
HARDHOUSE
HARDIHOOD
HARDINESS
HARD-LINER
HARD LINES
HARD-NOSED
HARDSHIPS
HARD TIMES

HARDWOODS	HAWTHORNE	HEATHFOWL	HEMSTITCH	HEY PRESTO
HAREBELLS	HAWTHORNS	HEATHLAND	HENDIADYS	HIBERNATE
HARKENING	HAYMAKING	HEATHLIKE	HEN HOUSES	HIBERNIAN
HARLEQUIN	HAYSTACKS	HEAT PUMPS	HENPECKED	HICCUPING
HARMATTAN	HAZARDING	HEAT WAVES	HEOMANIAC	HICKORIES
HARMFULLY	HAZARDOUS	HEAVINESS	HEPATITIS	HIDDENITE
HARMONICA	HEADACHES	HEAVISIDE	HEPTAGONS	HIDEAWAYS
HARMONICS	HEADBANDS	HEAVY-DUTY	HEPTARCHY	HIDEBOUND
HARMONIES	HEADBOARD	HEBRAIZER	HERACLEAN	HIDEOUSLY
HARMONIST	HEADDRESS	HEBRIDEAN	HERALDING	HIERARCHY
HARMONIUM	HEADFIRST	HECTOGRAM	HERALDIST	HIERODULE
HARMONIZE	HEAD FIRST	HECTORING	HERBALIST	HIEROGRAM
HARMOTOME	HEADINESS	HEDGE FUND	HERBARIAL	HIEROLOGY
HARNESSED	HEADLANDS	HEDGEHOGS	HERBARIUM	HIFALUTIN
HARNESSER	HEADLIGHT	HEDGEROWS	HERBICIDE	HIGHBALLS
HARNESSES	HEADLINED	HEDONISTS	HERBIVORE	HIGHBROWS
HARPOONED	HEADLINER	HEEDFULLY	HERCULEAN	HIGH CHAIR
HARPOONER	HEADLINES	HEELPIECE	HERCYNIAN	HIGH-CLASS
HARQUEBUS	HEADPIECE	HEFTINESS	HEREAFTER	HIGH COURT
HARRIDANS	HEADREACH	HEGEMONIC	HERETICAL	HIGHER-UPS
HARROGATE	HEADRESTS	HEGUMENOS	HEREUNDER	HIGH-FLIER
HARROVIAN	HEADSCARF	HEILBRONN	HERITABLE	HIGH-FLOWN
HARROWING	HEADSHIPS	HEIMDALLR	HERITABLY	HIGH-FLYER
HARSHNESS	HEADSTALL	HEINOUSLY	HERITRESS	HIGH-GRADE
HARTBEEST	HEADSTAND	HEIRESSES	HERMITAGE	HIGH HOPES
HARTSHORN	HEAD START	HEIRLOOMS	HERMITIAN	HIGH HORSE
HARUSPICY	HEADSTOCK	HELGOLAND	HERNIATED	HIGH JINKS
HARVESTED	HEADSTONE	HELICALLY	HERODOTUS	HIGH JUMPS
HARVESTER	HEADWARDS	HELICLINE	HESELTINE	HIGHLANDS
HASDRUBAL	HEADWINDS	HELIOSTAT	HESITANCY	HIGH-LEVEL
HASHEMITE	HEADWORDS	HELIOTYPE	HESITATED	HIGHLIGHT
HASTENING	HEALINGLY	HELIOZOAN	HESITATER	HIGH POINT
HASTINESS	HEALTHFUL	HELIPORTS	HESPERIAN	HIGH-RISES
HATCHABLE	HEALTHIER	HELLDIVER	HESSONITE	HIGH ROADS
HATCHBACK	HEALTHILY	HELLEBORE	HESYCHAST	HIGH-SPEED
HATCHLING	HEARKENED	HELLENIAN	HETAERISM	HIGH SPOTS
HATCHMENT	HEARKENER	HELLENISM	HETAERIST	HIGH TABLE
HATCHWAYS	HEARTACHE	HELLENIST	HETAIRISM	HIGH TIDES
HATEFULLY	HEARTBEAT	HELLENIZE	HETERODOX	HIGH-TONED
HAT TRICKS	HEARTBURN	HELLHOUND	HETERONYM	HIGH WATER
HAUGHTIER	HEARTENED	HELLISHLY	HETEROSIS	HIJACKERS
HAUGHTILY	HEARTFELT	HELPFULLY	HEURISTIC	HIJACKING
HAVE A	HEARTHRUG	HELPMATES	HEXACHORD	HILARIOUS
BASH	HEARTIEST	HELVELLYN	HEXAGONAL	HILLBILLY
HAVENLESS	HEARTLAND	HELVETIAN	HEXAGRAMS	HILLOCKED
HAVERSACK	HEARTLESS	HELVETIUS	HEXAMETER	HILLSIDES
HAVERSIAN	HEARTSICK	HEMIALGIA	HEXAPODIC	HILVERSUM
HAVERSINE	HEARTSOME	HEMICYCLE	HEXASTICH	HIMALAYAS
HAWKSBILL	HEARTWOOD	HEMINGWAY	HEXASTYLE	HIMYARITE
HAWSEHOLE	HEARTWORM	HEMISTICH	HEXATEUCH	HINDBRAIN
HAWSEPIPE	HEATHERED	HEMITROPE	HEYERDAHL	HINDERING

HINDOOISM
HINDRANCE
HINDSIGHT
HINDU KUSH
HINDUSTAN
HINGELESS
HINGELIKE
HIP FLASKS
HIP POCKET
HIPPOCRAS
HIPPOLYTA
HIPPOLYTE
HIRELINGS
HIROSHIGE
HIROSHIMA
HIRUNDINE
HISPIDITY
HISTAMINE
HISTIDINE
HISTOGENY
HISTOGRAM
HISTOLOGY
HISTORIAN
HISTORIES
HIT AND
  RUN
HIT-AND-
  RUN
HITCHCOCK
HITCHHIKE
HITLERISM
HIT-OR-
  MISS
HIT PARADE
HIT WICKET
HOARDINGS
HOARFROST
HOARHOUND
HOARINESS
HOATCHING
HOBBESIAN
HOBGOBLIN
HOBNAILED
HOBNOBBED
HO CHI
  MINH
HODOMETER
HODOMETRY
HODOSCOPE
HOGGISHLY
HOGSHEADS
HOHENLOHE

HOIDENISH
HOI POLLOI
HOLARCTIC
HOLDOVERS
HOLD WATER
HOLE IN
  ONE
HOLIDAYED
HOLINSHED
HOLLANDER
HOLLANDIA
HOLLERING
HOLLOWEST
HOLLOWING
HOLLYHOCK
HOLLYWOOD
HOLOCAINE
HOLOCAUST
HOLOCRINE
HOLOGRAMS
HOLOGRAPH
HOLOPHYTE
HOLOTYPIC
HOLSTEINS
HOLSTERED
HOLY GHOST
HOLY GRAIL
HOLYSTONE
HOME ALONE
HOME FRONT
HOMEGROWN
HOME GUARD
HOME HELPS
HOMELANDS
HOMELIEST
HOMEMAKER
HOME MOVIE
HOMEOPATH
HOMEOWNER
HOMESTEAD
HOMETOWNS
HOME TRUTH
HOMEWARDS
HOMEYNESS
HOMICIDAL
HOMICIDES
HOMILETIC
HOMOGRAFT
HOMOGRAPH
HOMOLYSIS
HOMOLYTIC

HOMONYMIC
HOMOPHILE
HOMOPHONE
HOMOPHONY
HOMOPHYLY
HOMOPLASY
HOMOPOLAR
HOMOSPORY
HOMOTAXIC
HOMOTAXIS
HONEYBEES
HONEYCOMB
HONEYEDLY
HONEY-LIKE
HONEYMOON
HONEYTRAP
HONKY-TONK
HONORARIA
HONORIFIC
HONOR ROLL
HONOURING
HOODOOISM
HOOFBOUND
HOOK NOSED
HOOK-NOSED
HOOKWORMS
HOOLIGANS
HOOTNANNY
HOOVERING
HOPE CHEST
HOPEFULLY
HOP GARDEN
HOPLOLOGY
HOPSCOTCH
HOREHOUND
HORNBILLS
HORNINESS
HORNPIPES
HORNSTONE
HOROLOGIC
HOROSCOPE
HOROSCOPY
HORRIFIED
HORSEBACK
HORSE FAIR
HORSEHAIR
HORSEHIDE
HORSELESS
HORSELIKE
HORSEMINT
HORSEPLAY

HORSESHIT
HORSESHOE
HORSETAIL
HORSEWEED
HORSEWHIP
HORSINESS
HORTATIVE
HORTATORY
HOSPITALS
HOSPITIUM
HOSTELLER
HOSTESSES
HOSTILELY
HOSTILITY
HOTELIERS
HOTFOOTED
HOTHEADED
HOTHOUSES
HOTPLATES
HOT POTATO
HOTTENTOT
HOT WATERS
HOURGLASS
HOUSEBOAT
HOUSEBOYS
HOUSECARL
HOUSECOAT
HOUSEHOLD
HOUSELEEK
HOUSELESS
HOUSELINE
HOUSEMAID
HOUSEROOM
HOUSETOPS
HOUSEWIFE
HOUSEWORK
HOUSTONIA
HOVERPORT
HOW ARE
  YOU
HOWITZERS
HOWLINGLY
HOWSOEVER
HOWTOWDIE
HOYDENISH
HSUAN
  T'UNG
HUBRISTIC
HUCKABACK
HUCKSTERS

HUE AND
  CRY
HUFFINESS
HUGH CAPET
HU-HO-HAO-
  T'E
HUMANISTS
HUMANIZED
HUMANIZER
HUMANKIND
HUMAN-LIKE
HUMANNESS
HUMANOIDS
HUMAN RACE
HUMBLEBEE
HUMBUGGER
HUMDINGER
HUMECTANT
HUMERUSES
HUMIDNESS
HUMILIATE
HUMONGOUS
HUMORISTS
HUMOURFUL
HUMOURING
HUMPBACKS
HUMPINESS
HUNCHBACK
HUNDREDJH
HUNGARIAN
HUNGERING
HUNGRIEST
HUNKY DORY
HUNKY-DORY
HUNNISHLY
HURRICANE
HURRIEDLY
HURTFULLY
HUSBANDED
HUSBANDER
HUSBANDRY
HUSH MONEY
HUSKINESS
HYACINTHS
HYBRIDISM
HYBRIDITY
HYBRIDIZE
HYBRISTIC
HYDANTOIN
HYDATHODE
HYDERABAD

HYDRANGEA	IDIOPATHY	IMMOLATED	IMPOTENCE	INCLUSION
HYDRASTIS	IDIOPHONE	IMMOLATOR	IMPOUNDED	INCLUSIVE
HYDRATION	IDOLATERS	IMMORALLY	IMPOUNDER	INCOGNITO
HYDRAULIC	IDOLIZING	IMMORTALS	IMPRECATE	INCOME TAX
HYDRAZINE	IGNESCENT	IMMOVABLE	IMPRECISE	INCOMMODE
HYDRAZOIC	IGNITABLE	IMMOVABLY	IMPRESSED	INCORRECT
HYDRIODIC	IGNORAMUS	IMMUNIZED	IMPRESSER	INCORRUPT
HYDROCELE	IGNORANCE	IMMUNIZER	IMPRESSES	INCREASED
HYDROFOIL	IGNORATIO	IMMUTABLE	IMPRINTED	INCREASER
HYDROLOGY	IGUANODON	IMMUTABLY	IMPRINTER	INCREASES
HYDROLYSE	ILEOSTOMY	IMPACTING	IMPROBITY	INCREMENT
HYDROLYTE	ILL AT	IMPACTION	IMPROMPTU	INCRETION
HYGIENIST	EASE	IMPAIRING	IMPROVING	INCUBATED
HYPERBOLA	ILLAWARRA	IMPARTIAL	IMPROVISE	INCUBATOR
HYPERBOLE	ILLEGALLY	IMPARTING	IMPRUDENT	INCUBUSES
HYPERCUBE	ILLEGIBLE	IMPASSION	IMPUDENCE	INCULCATE
HYPERTEXT	ILLEGIBLY	IMPASSIVE	IMPUGNING	INCULPATE
HYPHENATE	ILL GOTTEN	IMPATIENS	IMPULSION	INCUMBENT
HYPNOTISM	ILL-GOTTEN	IMPATIENT	IMPULSIVE	INCURABLE
HYPNOTIST	ILLIBERAL	IMPEACHED	IMPUTABLE	INCURABLY
HYPNOTIZE	ILLICITLY	IMPEACHER	IN A BAD	INCURIOUS
HYPOCRISY	ILLNESSES	IMPEDANCE	WAY	INCURRENT
HYPOCRITE	ILLOGICAL	IMPELLENT	INABILITY	INCURRING
HYSTERICS	ILL-OMENED	IMPELLING	INAMORATA	INCURSION
	ILLUSIONS	IMPENDING	INANIMATE	INCURSIVE
I	IMAGINARY	IMPERFECT	INANITIES	INCURVATE
IBUPROFEN	IMAGINING	IMPERILED	INANITION	INDECENCY
ICE CREAMS	IMAGISTIC	IMPERIOUS	INAPTNESS	INDECORUM
ICE HOCKEY	IMBALANCE	IMPETRATE	INAUDIBLE	INDELIBLE
ICELANDER	IMBECILES	IMPETUOUS	INAUDIBLY	INDELIBLY
ICELANDIC	IMBEDDING	IMPETUSES	INAUGURAL	INDEMNIFY
ICE SHEETS	IMBRICATE	IMPIETIES	IN BETWEEN	INDEMNITY
ICE SKATED	IMBROGLIO	IMPINGING	INCAPABLE	INDENTING
ICE-SKATED	IMIDAZOLE	IMPIOUSLY	INCAPABLY	INDENTION
ICE-SKATER	IMITATING	IMPLANTED	INCARNATE	INDENTURE
ICE-SKATES	IMITATION	IMPLANTER	INCAUTION	INDEXICAL
ICHNEUMON	IMITATIVE	IMPLEADER	INCENSING	INDIAN INK
ICHNOLOGY	IMITATORS	IMPLEMENT	INCENTIVE	INDICATED
ICHTHYOID	IMMANENCE	IMPLICATE	INCEPTION	INDICATOR
ICONOLOGY	IMMANENCY	IMPLODING	INCEPTIVE	INDICTING
IDEALISTS	IMMEDIACY	IMPLORING	INCESSANT	INDIGENCE
IDEALIZED	IMMEDIATE	IMPLOSION	INCIDENCE	INDIGNANT
IDEALIZER	IMMENSELY	IMPLOSIVE	INCIDENTS	INDIGNITY
IDENTICAL	IMMENSITY	IMPOLITIC	INCIPIENT	INDIGOTIC
IDENTIKIT	IMMERSING	IMPORTANT	INCISIONS	INDISPOSE
IDEOGRAMS	IMMERSION	IMPORTERS	INCISURAL	INDOCHINA
IDEOLOGUE	IMMIGRANT	IMPORTING	INCLEMENT	INDOLENCE
IDEOMOTOR	IMMIGRATE	IMPORTUNE	INCLINING	INDONESIA
IDIOBLAST	IMMINENCE	IMPOSABLE	INCLOSING	INDORSING
IDIOLECTS	IMMINGHAM	IMPOSTORS	INCLOSURE	INDRAUGHT
IDIOMATIC	IMMODESTY	IMPOSTURE	INCLUDING	INDUCIBLE

INDUCTILE	INFUSORIA	INOTROPIC	INSWINGER	INTERVENE
INDUCTING	IN GENERAL	IN PATIENT	INTAGLIOS	INTERVIEW
INDUCTION	INGENIOUS	IN-PATIENT	INTEGRAND	INTERWOVE
INDUCTIVE	INGENUITY	INPUTTING	INTEGRANT	INTESTACY
INDULGENT	INGENUOUS	INQUILINE	INTEGRATE	INTESTATE
INDULGING	INGESTING	INQUIRIES	INTEGRITY	INTESTINE
INEBRIANT	INGESTION	INQUIRING	INTELLECT	IN THE
INEBRIATE	INGESTIVE	INQUORATE	INTENDANT	CLUB
INEBRIETY	INGLENOOK	INSCRIBED	INTENDEDS	IN THE
INEFFABLE	INGRAINED	INSCRIBER	INTENDING	DARK
INEFFABLY	INGROWING	INSECTEAN	INTENSELY	IN THE
INELASTIC	INHABITED	INSELBERG	INTENSIFY	LINE
INELEGANT	INHALANTS	INSENSATE	INTENSION	IN THE
INEPTNESS	INHALATOR	INSERTING	INTENSITY	SOUP
INERTNESS	INHAMBANE	INSERTION	INTENSIVE	IN THE
INFANTILE	INHARMONY	IN-SERVICE	INTENTION	SWIM
INFARCTED	IN HARNESS	INSETTING	INTER ALIA	INTIMATED
INFATUATE	INHERENCE	INSIDE JOB	INTERBRED	INTIMATES
INFECTING	INHERITED	INSIDE OUT	INTERCEDE	INTORSION
INFECTION	INHERITOR	INSIDIOUS	INTERCEPT	IN TRANSIT
INFECTIVE	INHIBITED	INSINCERE	INTERCITY	INTRICACY
INFERABLE	INHIBITER	INSINUATE	INTERCOMS	INTRICATE
INFERENCE	INHIBITOR	INSIPIDLY	INTERCROP	INTRIGUED
INFERIORS	INITIALED	INSISTENT	INTERDICT	INTRIGUER
INFERRING	INITIALER	INSISTING	INTERESTS	INTRIGUES
INFERTILE	INITIALLY	IN SO FAR	INTERFACE	INTRINSIC
INFESTING	INITIATED	AS	INTERFERE	INTRODUCE
INFIELDER	INITIATES	INSOLENCE	INTERFILE	INTROITAL
INFIGHTER	INITIATOR	INSOLUBLE	INTERFUSE	INTROJECT
INFIRMARY	INJECTING	INSOLVENT	INTERIORS	INTROVERT
INFIRMITY	INJECTION	INSOMNIAC	INTERJECT	INTRUDERS
INFLAMING	INJECTIVE	INSPECTED	INTERLACE	INTRUDING
INFLATING	INJURABLE	INSPECTOR	INTERLARD	INTRUSION
INFLATION	INJURIOUS	INSPIRING	INTERLEAF	INTRUSIVE
INFLECTED	INJUSTICE	INSTALLED	INTERLINE	INTRUSTED
INFLECTOR	INKSTANDS	INSTALLER	INTERLINK	INTUITING
INFLICTED	INMIGRANT	INSTANCED	INTERLOCK	INTUITION
INFLICTER	INNER CITY	INSTANCES	INTERLOPE	INTUITIVE
INFLUENCE	INNERMOST	INSTANTER	INTERLUDE	INTUMESCE
INFLUENZA	INNER TUBE	INSTANTLY	INTERMENT	INUNCTION
INFORMANT	INNERVATE	INSTIGATE	INTERNEES	INUNDATED
INFORMERS	INNKEEPER	INSTILLED	INTERNING	INUNDATOR
INFORMING	INN KEEPER	INSTILLER	INTERNIST	INUTILITY
INFRACTOR	INNOCENCE	INSTINCTS	INTERNODE	INVADABLE
INFRADIAN	INNOCUOUS	INSTITUTE	INTERPLAY	INVALIDED
INFRINGED	INNOVATED	INSULATED	INTERPOSE	INVALIDLY
INFRINGER	INNOVATOR	INSULATOR	INTERPRET	INVARIANT
INFURIATE	INNSBRUCK	INSULTING	INTERRING	INVASIONS
INFUSCATE	INNUENDOS	INSURABLE	INTERRUPT	INVECTIVE
INFUSIBLE	INOCULATE	INSURANCE	INTERSECT	INVEIGHED
INFUSIONS	INORGANIC	INSURGENT	INTERVALS	INVEIGHER
				INVEIGLED

INVEIGLER	IRRITATOR	ITSY BITSY	JEWELLERS	JUNOESQUE
INVENTING	IRRUPTION	ITSY-BITSY	JEWELLERY	JURIDICAL
INVENTION	IRRUPTIVE	IVY LEAGUE	JEWELLING	JURY BOXES
INVENTIVE	ISAGOGICS		JEW'S	JUSTICIAR
INVENTORS	ISALLOBAR	**J**	HARPS	JUSTIFIED
INVENTORY	ISCHAEMIA	JABBERERS	JIB-HEADED	JUSTIFIER
INVERARAY	ISINGLASS	JABBERING	JITTERBUG	JUTLANDER
INVERNESS	ISLAMABAD	JABORANDI	JOBCENTRE	JUVENILES
INVERSELY	ISLANDERS	JACARANDA	JOB CENTRE	JUVENILIA
INVERSION	ISLE OF	JACKASSES	JOBSWORTH	JUXTAPOSE
INVERSIVE	MAN	JACKBOOTS	JOCKEYING	
INVERTASE	ISLINGTON	JACK FROST	JOCKSTRAP	**K**
INVERTING	ISOBARISM	JACKFRUIT	JOCULARLY	KADAITCHA
INVESTING	ISOBATHIC	JACK KNIFE	JOCUNDITY	KADIYEVKA
INVIDIOUS	ISOCHORIC	JACKSHAFT	JOE PUBLIC	KAGOSHIMA
INVIOLACY	ISOCLINAL	JACKSMELT	JOINTRESS	KAISERDOM
INVIOLATE	ISOCRATIC	JACKSNIPE	JOINTWORM	KALAMAZOO
INVISIBLE	ISOGAMETE	JACOBITES	JOLLINESS	KALANCHOE
INVISIBLY	ISOGAMOUS	JAILBIRDS	JONKOPING	KAMA SUTRA
INVOCABLE	ISOGENOUS	JAILBREAK	JORDANIAN	KAMCHATKA
INVOICING	ISOLATING	JAILHOUSE	JOSS STICK	KAMILAROI
INVOLUCEL	ISOLATION	JALANDHAR	JOURNEYED	KAMPUCHEA
INVOLUCRE	ISOLATIVE	JAMBOREES	JOURNEYER	KANAMYCIN
INVOLVING	ISOLOGOUS	JAM-PACKED	JOVIALITY	KANGAROOS
IODOMETRY	ISOMERISM	JANISSARY	JOYLESSLY	KAOHSIUNG
IONOPAUSE	ISOMERIZE	JANSENISM	JOYRIDERS	KAOLINITE
IPSO FACTO	ISOMEROUS	JANSENIST	JOYRIDING	KARABINER
IRASCIBLE	ISOMETRIC	JANUARIES	JOYSTICKS	KARAGANDA
IRASCIBLY	ISONIAZID	JAPANNING	JUBILANCE	KARAKORAM
IRIAN JAYA	ISOOCTANE	JAPONICAS	JUDDERING	KARAKORUM
IRIDOTOMY	ISOPROPYL	JARGONIZE	JUDGEABLE	KARLSRUHE
IRISH BULL	ISOSCELES	JAUNDICED	JUDGEMENT	KARNATAKA
IRISH STEW	ISOSMOTIC	JAUNTIEST	JUDGESHIP	KARYOGAMY
IRONBOUND	ISOSTATIC	JAYWALKED	JUDGINGLY	KARYOSOME
IRON CROSS	ISOSTERIC	JAYWALKER	JUDGMENTS	KARYOTYPE
IRON HORSE	ISOTACTIC	JEALOUSLY	JUDICABLE	KATABATIC
IRONSIDES	ISOTHERAL	JEERINGLY	JUDICATOR	KATANGESE
IRONSTONE	ISOTHERMS	JELLY BEAN	JUDICIARY	KATHIAWAR
IRONWORKS	ISOTROPIC	JELLYFISH	JUDICIOUS	KAWAGUCHI
IROQUOIAN	ISRAELITE	JELLY ROLL	JUICINESS	KEEP ORDER
IRRADIANT	ISTHMUSES	JEREMIADS	JUKEBOXES	KEEPSAKES
IRRADIATE	ITALICIZE	JERKINESS	JULLUNDUR	KEEP STATE
IRRAWADDY	ITCHINESS	JERKINGLY	JUMBO JETS	KELTICISM
IRREGULAR	ITCHY FEET	JEROBOAMS	JUMPINESS	KELTICIST
IRRIGABLE	ITCHY PALM	JERUSALEM	JUMP START	KENNELING
IRRIGATED	ITEMIZING	JESTINGLY	JUMP-START	KENNELLED
IRRIGATOR	ITERATION	JESUITISM	JUMPSUITS	KENTLEDGE
IRRITABLE	ITERATIVE	JET ENGINE	JUNCTIONS	KEPT WOMAN
IRRITABLY	ITINERANT	JET-SETTER	JUNCTURES	KEPT WOMEN
IRRITANTS	ITINERARY	JET STREAM	JUNGLE GYM	KERATITIS
IRRITATED	ITINERATE	JEWELFISH	JUNKETING	KERATOSIS

KERBSTONE	KNACKERED	LACERABLE	LANDWARDS	LAW SCHOOL
KERCHIEFS	KNAPSACKS	LACERATED	LANGOUSTE	LAXATIVES
KERFUFFLE	KNAVERIES	LACERTIAN	LANGUAGES	LAYABOUTS
KETONURIA	KNAVISHLY	LACHRYMAL	LANGUEDOC	LAY FIGURE
KETTERING	KNIFE EDGE	LACINIATE	LANGUIDLY	LAYPERSON
KEYBOARDS	KNIFE-EDGE	LACQUERED	LANKINESS	LAY READER
KEYHOLDER	KNIGHTING	LACQUERER	LANOLATED	LAY SISTER
KEYSTONES	KNIPHOFIA	LACTATION	LANTHANUM	LAZARETTO
KEYSTROKE	KNITTABLE	LADDERING	LAODICEAN	LAZYBONES
KIBBUTZES	KNOBBLIER	LADIES MAN	LAPLANDER	LEADERENE
KIBBUTZIM	KNOCKDOWN	LADIES'	LARCENIES	LEAD TIMES
KICKBACKS	KNOCKOUTS	MAN	LARCENIST	LEAFINESS
KICK-START	KNOTGRASS	LADIES'	LARCENOUS	LEAFLETED
KID GLOVES	KNOTTIEST	MEN	LARGENESS	LEAF MOULD
KIDNAPING	KNOWINGLY	LADYBIRDS	LARGHETTO	LEAFSTALK
KIDNAPPED	KNOWLEDGE	LADYSHIPS	LARKSPURS	LEAKINESS
KIDNAPPER	KNOXVILLE	LAEVULOSE	LARVICIDE	LEAP YEARS
KIDSTAKES	KNUCKLING	LAGOMORPH	LARYNGEAL	LEARNABLE
KIESERITE	KONIOLOGY	LALLATION	LASHINGLY	LEARNEDLY
KILLARNEY	KOOKINESS	LAMAISTIC	LAS PALMAS	LEASEBACK
KILLIFISH	KOSCIUSKO	LAMBASTED	LASSITUDE	LEASEHOLD
KILLINGLY	KOTA BHARU	LAMBSKINS	LAST-DITCH	LEASTWAYS
KILOBYTES	KOWTOWING	LAME DUCKS	LASTINGLY	LEAVENING
KILOCYCLE	KOZHIKODE	LAMENTING	LAST RITES	LECHEROUS
KILOGRAMS	KRASNODAR	LAMINABLE	LAST STRAW	LECTORATE
KILOHERTZ	KRAUTROCK	LAMINARIA	LAST THING	LECTURERS
KILOLITRE	KRIVOY ROG	LAMINATED	LATCHKEYS	LECTURING
KILOMETRE	KRONSTADT	LAMINATES	LATECOMER	LEERINGLY
KILOWATTS	KUIBYSHEV	LAMINATOR	LATERALLY	LEE SHORES
KIMBERLEY	KURDISTAN	LAMINITIS	LATERITIC	LEFTOVERS
KINDLIEST	KURRAJONG	LAMP-BLACK	LATHERING	LEFTWARDS
KINEMATIC	KWANGTUNG	LAMPOONED	LATIMERIA	LEGALIZED
KINGLIEST	KYMOGRAPH	LAMPOONER	LATINIZER	LEGATIONS
KINGMAKER		LAMPPOSTS	LATITUDES	LEGENDARY
KING'S		LAMPSHADE	LATTER-DAY	LEGGINESS
EVIL	**L**	LANCASTER	LAUDATION	LEGGINGED
KINGS HEAD	LABELLING	LANCEWOOD	LAUDATORY	LEGIONARY
KING'S	LABELLOID	LANCINATE	LAUGHABLE	LEGISLATE
LYNN	LABIALISM	LAND AGENT	LAUGHABLY	LEG-WARMER
KINGSTOWN	LABIALITY	LANDAULET	LAUNCHING	LEICESTER
KINKINESS	LABIALIZE	LANDFALLS	LAUNCH PAD	LEISURELY
KINSWOMAN	LABORIOUS	LANDLORDS	LAUNDERED	LEITMOTIF
KIRGHIZIA	LABOUR DAY	LANDMARKS	LAUNDERER	LEITMOTIV
KIRKCALDY	LABOURERS	LANDMINES	LAUNDRESS	LEMNISCUS
KIROVABAD	LABOURING	LAND OF	LAUNDRIES	LEMON CURD
KISANGANI	LABOURISM	NOD	LAUREATES	LEMON SOLE
KISSINGER	LABOURIST	LANDOWNER	LAVISHING	LEND-LEASE
KITCHENER	LABOURITE	LAND ROVER	LAWGIVING	LENGTHIER
KITTENISH	LABRADORS	LANDSCAPE	LAWLESSLY	LENGTHILY
KITTIWAKE	LABURNUMS	LANDSLIDE	LAWNMOWER	LENIENTLY
KLEENEXES	LABYRINTH	LANDSLIPS	LAWN PARTY	LENINABAD
	LACCOLITH			

LENINAKAN	LIFE CYCLE	LIP READER	LOBECTOMY	LOOK AFTER
LENINGRAD	LIFEGUARD	LIP-READER	LOCAL CALL	LOOK-ALIKE
LENIN PEAK	LIFELINES	LIPSTICKS	LOCALIZED	LOOK ALIVE
LEPONTINE	LIFE PEERS	LIQUATION	LOCALIZER	LOOKING UP
LEPTOSOME	LIFE-SAVER	LIQUEFIED	LOCAL TIME	LOOM-STATE
LEPTOTENE	LIFESPANS	LIQUEFIER	LOCATABLE	LOONINESS
LESSENING	LIFE STORY	LIQUIDATE	LOCATIONS	LOONY BINS
LETHALITY	LIFESTYLE	LIQUIDITY	LOCKERBIE	LOOPHOLES
LETHARGIC	LIFETIMES	LIQUIDIZE	LOCKSMITH	LOOSE ENDS
LETTERBOX	LIGAMENTS	LIQUORICE	LOCOMOTOR	LOOSE-LEAF
LETTERING	LIGATURES	LISPINGLY	LOCUTIONS	LOOSENESS
LEUCOCYTE	LIGHT BULB	LISTENERS	LODESTARS	LOOSENING
LEUCOTOMY	LIGHTENED	LISTENING	LODESTONE	LOQUACITY
LEUKAEMIA	LIGHT-FAST	LISTERISM	LODGEABLE	LORDLIEST
LEVANTINE	LIGHTNESS	LIST PRICE	LOFTINESS	LORDSHIPS
LEVELLERS	LIGHTNING	LITERALLY	LOGAOEDIC	LORGNETTE
LEVELLING	LIGHT RAIL	LITERATIM	LOGARITHM	LORRY PARK
LEVIATHAN	LIGHTSHIP	LITHENESS	LOG CABINS	LOS ALAMOS
LEVIGATOR	LIGHTS OUT	LITHIASIS	LOGICALLY	LOST CAUSE
LEVITATED	LIGHTS-OUT	LITHOPONE	LOGICIANS	LOTTERIES
LEVITATOR	LIGHT YEAR	LITHOLOGY	LOGISTICS	LOUDMOUTH
LEXICALLY	LIGNIFORM	LITHOTOMY	LOGOGRIPH	LOUISBURG
LEXINGTON	LIKELIEST	LITHUANIA	LOGOMACHY	LOUISIANA
LIABILITY	LILY-WHITE	LITIGABLE	LOINCLOTH	LOUNGE BAR
LIBATIONS	LIMA BEANS	LITIGANTS	LOITERERS	LOUSEWORT
LIBELLANT	LIME GREEN	LITIGATED	LOITERING	LOUSINESS
LIBELLING	LIMELIGHT	LITIGATOR	LOLLINGLY	LOVEBIRDS
LIBELLOUS	LIMERICKS	LITIGIOUS	LOLLIPOPS	LOVECHILD
LIBERALLY	LIMESTONE	LITTERBIN	LOLLOPING	LOVE FEAST
LIBERATED	LIMEWATER	LITTERING	LOMBARDIC	LOVELIEST
LIBERATOR	LIMITABLE	LITTORALS	LONELIEST	LOVE MATCH
LIBERTIES	LIMITLESS	LITURGICS	LONE WOLFS	LOVING CUP
LIBERTINE	LIMNOLOGY	LITURGIES	LONG BEACH	LOW COMEDY
LIBIDINAL	LIMOUSINE	LITURGISM	LONGBOATS	LOWERABLE
LIBRARIAN	LIMPIDITY	LITURGIST	LONGCLOTH	LOWER CASE
LIBRARIES	LIMPINGLY	LIVELIEST	LONG EATON	LOWERMOST
LIBRATION	LINCHPINS	LIVERPOOL	LONGEVITY	LOWESTOFT
LIBRATORY	LINEAMENT	LIVERWORT	LONGEVOUS	LOWLANDER
LIBRETTOS	LINEARITY	LIVERYMAN	LONG FACES	LOWLINESS
LIBRIFORM	LINEATION	LIVERYMEN	LONGICORN	LOW-MINDED
LICENSEES	LINEOLATE	LIVESTOCK	LONGINGLY	LOW-NECKED
LICENSING	LINGERERS	LIVE WIRES	LONGITUDE	LOW SEASON
LICHENOID	LINGERING	LIVIDNESS	LONG JOHNS	LOYALISTS
LICHENOUS	LINGUISTS	LJUBLJANA	LONG-LIVED	LOYALTIES
LIDOCAINE	LINGULATE	LLANDUDNO	LONG-RANGE	LUBRICANT
LIEGE LORD	LINKOPING	LOADSTARS	LONGSHIPS	LUBRICATE
LIENTERIC	LINOLEATE	LOADSTONE	LONGSHORE	LUBRICITY
LIFE BELTS	LINOTYPER	LOAMINESS	LONG SHOTS	LUBRICOUS
LIFEBLOOD	LIONIZING	LOAN SHARK	LONG SINCE	LUCIFERIN
LIFEBOATS	LIPOLYSIS	LOANWORDS	LONGUEUIL	LUCKINESS
LIFE BUOYS	LIPOLYTIC	LOATHSOME	LONGUEURS	LUCKY DIPS

LUCRATIVE
LUCUBRATE
LUDICROUS
LUFTWAFFE
LULLABIES
LULLINGLY
LUMBERING
LUMBERMAN
LUMBERMEN
LUMBRICAL
LUMINAIRE
LUMINANCE
LUMINESCE
LUMPINESS
LUNATICAL
LUNISOLAR
LUNITIDAL
LURIDNESS
LURKINGLY
LUSTFULLY
LUSTINESS
LUTANISTS
LUTHERISM
LUXEMBURG
LUXURIANT
LUXURIATE
LUXURIOUS
LYCHGATES
LYME REGIS
LYMINGTON
LYMPHATIC
LYONNAISE
LYOPHILIC
LYOPHOBIC
LYREBIRDS
LYRICALLY
LYRICISMS
LYRICISTS
LYSIMETER
LYSOSOMAL

M

MACARONIC
MACAROONS
MACEDOINE
MACEDONIA
MACERATED
MACERATER
MACHINATE
MACHINERY
MACHINING

MACHINIST
MACHMETER
MACKENZIE
MACKERELS
MACROCOSM
MACROCYST
MACROCYTE
MACRUROID
MACRUROUS
MADDENING
MADELEINE
MAD HATTER
MADHOUSES
MADREPORE
MADRIGALS
MAELSTROM
MAGAZINES
MAGDEBURG
MAGICALLY
MAGIC EYES
MAGICIANS
MAGIC WAND
MAGISTERY
MAGISTRAL
MAGMATISM
MAGNESIAN
MAGNESITE
MAGNESIUM
MAGNETICS
MAGNETISM
MAGNETITE
MAGNETIZE
MAGNETRON
MAGNIFICO
MAGNIFIED
MAGNIFIER
MAGNITUDE
MAGNOLIAS
MAHAJANGA
MAHARAJAH
MAHARAJAS
MAHARANIS
MAIDSTONE
MAIDUGURI
MAILBOXES
MAILCOACH
MAIL ORDER
MAILSHOTS
MAINFRAME
MAINLINED
MAIN LINES

MAINMASTS
MAINSAILS
MAINSHEET
MAINSTAYS
MAJESTICS
MAJESTIES
MAJORDOMO
MAJOR DOMO
MAJORETTE
MAJOR SUIT
MAJUSCULE
MAKE A
MOVE
MAKE MERRY
MAKE PEACE
MAKE READY
MAKESHIFT
MAKEYEVKA
MALACHITE
MALADROIT
MALAGUENA
MALANDERS
MALATHION
MALAYALAM
MALAYSIAN
MALDIVIAN
MALFORMED
MALGRE LUI
MALIC ACID
MALICIOUS
MALIGNANT
MALIGNING
MALIGNITY
MALLEABLE
MALLEMUCK
MALLEOLAR
MALLEOLUS
MALTINESS
MALTSTERS
MALVOISIE
MAMA'S
BOYS
MAMILLARY
MAMILLATE
MAMMALIAN
MAMMALOGY
MAMMOGRAM
MAMMONISM
MAMMONIST
MANACLING

MAN-AT-
ARMS
MANCHURIA
MANCUNIAN
MANDARINS
MANDATARY
MANDATING
MANDATORY
MANDIBLES
MANDOLINS
MANDRAKES
MANDRILLS
MAN-EATERS
MAN-EATING
MANEUVERS
MAN FRIDAY
MANGALORE
MANGANATE
MANGANESE
MANGANITE
MANGANOUS
MANGETOUT
MANGINESS
MANGROVES
MANHANDLE
MANHATTAN
MANHUNTER
MANICURED
MANICURES
MANIFESTO
MANIFESTS
MANIFOLDS
MANIZALES
MANLINESS
MANNEQUIN
MANNERISM
MANNERIST
MANNISHLY
MANOEUVRE
MANOMETER
MANOMETRY
MANSFIELD
MANTILLAS
MANUBRIAL
MANUBRIUM
MANY-SIDED
MAPLE LEAF
MARACAIBO
MARATHONS
MARAUDERS
MARAUDING

MARCASITE
MARCH HARE
MARCH-PAST
MARCO POLO
MARDI GRAS
MARE'S
NEST
MARGARINE
MARGARITA
MARGARITE
MARGINATE
MARIEHAMN
MARIENBAD
MARIGOLDS
MARIJUANA
MARINADES
MARINATED
MARITALLY
MARKDOWNS
MARKETEER
MARKETERS
MARKETING
MARK TWAIN
MARMALADE
MARMOREAL
MARMOSETS
MAROONING
MARQUETRY
MARQUISES
MARRAKECH
MARRIAGES
MARROWFAT
MARSEILLE
MARSHALCY
MARSHALED
MARSUPIAL
MARSUPIUM
MARTINETS
MARTINMAS
MARTYRDOM
MARTYRING
MARVELING
MARVELLED
MARZIPANS
MASCULINE
MASOCHISM
MASOCHIST
MASSACRED
MASSACRER
MASSACRES
MASSAGING

MASSIVELY	MEATBALLS	MEMORIALS	MESOPAUSE	MICROTOME
MASS MEDIA	MEATINESS	MEMORIZED	MESOPHYLL	MICROTOMY
MASTERDOM	MECHANICS	MEMORIZER	MESOPHYTE	MICROTONE
MASTERFUL	MECHANISM	MEMSAHIBS	MESSALINE	MICROWAVE
MASTERING	MECHANIST	MENADIONE	MESSENGER	MIDDLE AGE
MASTER KEY	MECHANIZE	MENAGERIE	MESSIANIC	MIDDLEMAN
MASTHEADS	MEDALLION	MEN-AT-	MESSIEURS	MIDDLEMEN
MASTICATE	MEDALLIST	ARMS	MESSINESS	MIDDLESEX
MASTODONS	MEDIAEVAL	MENDACITY	MESTRANOL	MIDDLETON
MATAMOROS	MEDIATING	MENDELIAN	METABOLIC	MIDHEAVEN
MATCHLESS	MEDIATION	MENDELISM	METALLINE	MIDNIGHTS
MATCHMARK	MEDIATIVE	MENDICANT	METALLING	MIDPOINTS
MATCH PLAY	MEDIATIZE	MENISCOID	METALLIST	MIDSTREAM
MATCHWOOD	MEDIATORS	MENOPAUSE	METALLIZE	MIDSUMMER
MATELASSE	MEDICABLE	MEN'S	METALLOID	MID-WICKET
MATERIALS	MEDICABLY	ROOMS	METALWORK	MIDWIFERY
MATERNITY	MEDICALLY	MENSTRUAL	METAMERAL	MIDWINTER
MATEYNESS	MEDICATED	MENSTRUUM	METAMERIC	MIFFINESS
MATRIARCH	MEDICINAL	MENTAL AGE	METAPHASE	MIGHTIEST
MATRICIDE	MEDICINES	MENTALISM	METAPHORS	MIGRAINES
MATRIMONY	MEDITATED	MENTALITY	METAPLASM	MIGRATING
MATRONAGE	MEDITATOR	MENTIONED	METAXYLEM	MIGRATION
MATSUMOTO	MEDULLARY	MENTIONER	METEORITE	MIGRATORY
MATSUYAMA	MEGACYCLE	MENTORIAL	METEOROID	MILCH COWS
MATTERING	MEGADEATH	MEPACRINE	METHADONE	MILESTONE
MATUTINAL	MEGAHERTZ	MERBROMIN	METHODISM	MILITANCY
MAULSTICK	MEGALITHS	MERCAPTAN	METHODIST	MILITANTS
MAUNDERED	MEGAPHONE	MERCENARY	METHODIZE	MILITARIA
MAUNDERER	MEGASPORE	MERCERIZE	METHOXIDE	MILITATED
MAURITIAN	MEGASTORE	MERCHANTS	METHYLATE	MILK FLOAT
MAURITIUS	MEGHALAYA	MERCILESS	METHYLENE	MILKINESS
MAUSOLEAN	MELANESIA	MERCURATE	METRALGIA	MILKMAIDS
MAUSOLEUM	MELANOSIS	MERCURIAL	METRICIZE	MILK SHAKE
MAVERICKS	MELATONIN	MERCUROUS	METRIC TON	MILK TOOTH
MAWKISHLY	MELBOURNE	MERGANSER	METRIFIER	MILLBOARD
MAXILLARY	MELIORATE	MERIDIANS	METROLOGY	MILLENARY
MAXIMALLY	MELIORISM	MERINGUES	METRONOME	MILLENNIA
MAXIMIZED	MELITOPOL	MERITEDLY	MEZZANINE	MILLEPEDE
MAXIMIZER	MELLOWEST	MERITLESS	MEZZOTINT	MILLEPORE
MAYFLOWER	MELLOWING	MEROCRINE	MICACEOUS	MILLERITE
MAYORALTY	MELODIOUS	MEROZOITE	MICHOACAN	MILLIBARS
MAYORSHIP	MELODIZER	MERRIMENT	MICROBIAL	MILLIGRAM
MBUJIMAYI	MELODRAMA	MERRINESS	MICROCHIP	MILLINERS
MCCARTNEY	MELTDOWNS	MERSEBURG	MICROCOPY	MILLINERY
MEANDERED	MELTINGLY	MESCALINE	MICROCOSM	MILLIONTH
MEANDERER	MELTWATER	MESENTERY	MICROCYTE	MILLIPEDE
MEANDROUS	MELUNGEON	MESICALLY	MICRODONT	MILLIVOLT
MEANS TEST	MEMBRANES	MESMERISM	MICROFILM	MILLPONDS
MEANTIMES	MEMORABLE	MESMERIST	MICROMESH	MILLSTONE
MEANWHILE	MEMORABLY	MESMERIZE	MICROPYLE	MILLWHEEL
MEASURING	MEMORANDA	MESOMORPH	MICROSOME	MILOMETER

MILWAUKEE	MISMANAGE	MOLECULAR	MONOMETER	MORTALITY
MIMICKING	MISNOMERS	MOLECULES	MONOPHAGY	MORTAL SIN
MINARETED	MISONEISM	MOLEHILLS	MONOPHONY	MORTGAGED
MINCEMEAT	MISONEIST	MOLESKINS	MONOPLANE	MORTGAGEE
MINCE PIES	MISPLACED	MOLESTERS	MONOPSONY	MORTGAGES
MINCINGLY	MISPRINTS	MOLESTING	MONORAILS	MORTGAGOR
MINEFIELD	MISQUOTED	MOLLIFIED	MONOSOMIC	MORTICIAN
MINELAYER	MISREPORT	MOLLIFIER	MONOSTICH	MORTIFIED
MINIATURE	MISSHAPEN	MOLLUSCAN	MONOSTOME	MORTIFIER
MINIBUSES	MISSILERY	MOLYBDATE	MONOTONIC	MOSAICIST
MINIDRESS	MISSIONER	MOLYBDOUS	MONOTREME	MOSCHATEL
MINIMALLY	MISSTATED	MOMENTARY	MONOTYPER	MOSQUITOS
MINIMIZED	MISTAKING	MOMENTOUS	MONOTYPIC	MOSS-GROWN
MINIMIZER	MISTIMING	MOMENTUMS	MONOXIDES	MOSSINESS
MINISCULE	MISTINESS	MONACHISM	MONSIGNOR	MOTHBALLS
MINISKIRT	MISTLETOE	MONADNOCK	MONSTROUS	MOTH EATEN
MINISTERS	MISTRIALS	MONARCHAL	MONTAUBAN	MOTH-EATEN
MINITRACK	MITICIDAL	MONASTERY	MONT BLANC	MOTHERING
MINNESOTA	MITIGABLE	MONATOMIC	MONTERREY	MOTHPROOF
MINOR SUIT	MITIGATED	MONEYBAGS	MONTHLIES	MOTIONING
MINSTRELS	MITIGATOR	MONEYLESS	MONTICULE	MOTIVATED
MINT JULEP	MITREWORT	MONEYWORT	MONTREUIL	MOTOCROSS
MINUSCULE	MNEMONICS	MONGERING	MONUMENTS	MOTORBIKE
MINUTE GUN	MOANINGLY	MONGOLIAN	MONZONITE	MOTORBOAT
MINUTE MAN	MOBILIZED	MONGOLISM	MOODINESS	MOTORCADE
MIRRORING	MOBOCRACY	MONGOLOID	MOONBEAMS	MOTORCARS
MIRTHLESS	MOCCASINS	MONGOOSES	MOON-FACED	MOTORHOME
MISADVISE	MOCKERIES	MONITORED	MOONINESS	MOTORISTS
MISBEHAVE	MOCKINGLY	MONITRESS	MOONLIGHT	MOTORIZED
MISBELIEF	MODELLING	MONKEYING	MOONRAKER	MOTORWAYS
MISCALLED	MODERATED	MONKEY NUT	MOONSCAPE	MOULDABLE
MISCHANCE	MODERATES	MONKSHOOD	MOONSHINE	MOULDERED
MISCHIEFS	MODERATOR	MONOBASIC	MOON SHOTS	MOULDIEST
MISCOUNTS	MODERATOS	MONOCHORD	MOONSTONE	MOULDINGS
MISCREANT	MODERNISM	MONOCLINE	MOOT POINT	MOUNTABLE
MISCREATE	MODERNIST	MONOCOQUE	MORACEOUS	MOUNTAINS
MISDEALER	MODERNITY	MONOCRACY	MORADABAD	MOUSETAIL
MISDIRECT	MODERNIZE	MONOCULAR	MORALISTS	MOUSETRAP
MISERABLE	MODIFIERS	MONOCYTIC	MORALIZED	MOUSINESS
MISERABLY	MODIFYING	MONODRAMA	MORALIZER	MOUSTACHE
MISFIRING	MODILLION	MONOGENIC	MORATORIA	MOUTHFULS
MISGIVING	MODULATED	MONOGRAMS	MORBIDITY	MOUTHPART
MISGOVERN	MODULATOR	MONOGRAPH	MORDACITY	MOUTHWASH
MISGUIDED	MOGADISHU	MONOLATER	MORDANTLY	MOVEABLES
MISGUIDER	MOISTENED	MONOLATRY	MORECAMBE	MOVEMENTS
MISHANDLE	MOISTENER	MONOLAYER	MORGANITE	MOVIE STAR
MISINFORM	MOISTNESS	MONOLITHS	MORMONISM	MOVIETONE
MISJUDGED	MOLDAVIAN	MONOLOGIC	MORPHEMES	MOVING VAN
MISJUDGER	MOLDAVITE	MONOLOGUE	MORPHEMIC	MUCIC ACID
MISLAYING	MOLDERING	MONOMANIA	MORPHOSIS	MUCKHEAPS
MISLEADER	MOLDINESS	MONOMERIC	MORSE CODE	MUCKINESS

MUCKRAKER	MUSTELINE	NARCOTIZE	NEMERTEAN	NEW MEXICO
MUCRONATE	MUSTERING	NARRATING	NEODYMIUM	NEW ROMNEY
MUDDINESS	MUSTINESS	NARRATION	NEOLITHIC	NEWSAGENT
MUDGUARDS	MUTAGENIC	NARRATIVE	NEOLOGISM	NEWSGROUP
MUGGINESS	MUTATIONS	NARRATORS	NEOLOGIST	NEWSHOUND
MUGGINSES	MUTILATED	NARROWING	NEOLOGIZE	NEWSINESS
MULATTOES	MUTILATOR	NASHVILLE	NEON LIGHT	NEWSPAPER
MULETEERS	MUTINEERS	NASTINESS	NEOPHYTES	NEWSPRINT
MULLINGAR	MUTINYING	NATIONALS	NEOPHYTIC	NEWSREELS
MULLIONED	MUTTERERS	NATROLITE	NEOPLASTY	NEWSROOMS
MULTICIDE	MUTTERING	NATTERING	NEOTENOUS	NEWSSHEET
MULTIFOIL	MUTUALITY	NATTINESS	NEPHELINE	NEWSSTAND
MULTIFOLD	MUTUALIZE	NATURALLY	NEPHOGRAM	NEWTONIAN
MULTIFORM	MUZZINESS	NATURISTS	NEPHOLOGY	NEW YORKER
MULTIHULL	MYCENAEAN	NAUGHTIER	NEPHRITIC	NICARAGUA
MULTIPARA	MYDRIASIS	NAUGHTILY	NEPHRITIS	NICCOLITE
MULTIPLES	MYDRIATIC	NAUSEATED	NEPHROSIS	NICHOLSON
MULTIPLET	MYOGLOBIN	NAUTILOID	NEPHROTIC	NICKELING
MULTIPLEX	MYOGRAPHY	NAVICULAR	NEPTUNIAN	NICKELLED
MULTITUDE	MYOLOGIST	NAVIGABLE	NEPTUNIUM	NICKELOUS
MUMMIFIED	MYROBALAN	NAVIGABLY	NERVE CELL	NICKNACKS
MUNDANELY	MYSTAGOGY	NAVIGATED	NERVELESS	NICKNAMED
MUNICIPAL	MYSTERIES	NAVIGATOR	NERVINESS	NICKNAMES
MUNIMENTS	MYSTICISM	NEAP TIDES	NERVOUSLY	NICOTIANA
MUNITIONS	MYSTIFIED	NEAR THING	NESCIENCE	NICOTINIC
MURDERERS	MYSTIFIER	NEBULIZER	NESTLINGS	NICTITATE
MURDERESS	MYSTIQUES	NECESSARY	NESTORIAN	NIFTINESS
MURDERING	MYTHICIZE	NECESSITY	NETANYAHU	NIGGARDLY
MURDEROUS	MYTHOLOGY	NECKBANDS	NETWORKED	NIGHTCAPS
MURKINESS	MYXOEDEMA	NECKCLOTH	NEUCHATEL	NIGHTCLUB
MURMURING	MYXOVIRUS	NECKLACES	NEURALGIA	NIGHTFALL
MUSACEOUS		NECKLINES	NEURALGIC	NIGHTGOWN
MUSCADINE	**N**	NECKPIECE	NEUROGLIA	NIGHTHAWK
MUSCARINE	NAHUATLAN	NECROLOGY	NEUROLOGY	NIGHTLIFE
MUSCATELS	NAILBRUSH	NECROTOMY	NEUROPATH	NIGHTLONG
MUSCLEMAN	NAIL FILES	NECTARIAL	NEUROTICS	NIGHTMARE
MUSCLEMEN	NAIVENESS	NECTARINE	NEUROTOMY	NIGHT OWLS
MUSCOVADO	NAIVETIES	NEEDFULLY	NEUTERING	NIGHT SOIL
MUSCOVITE	NAKEDNESS	NEEDINESS	NEUTRALLY	NIGHTTIME
MUSEOLOGY	NAMECHECK	NEFARIOUS	NEUTRETTO	NIGHTWEAR
MUSHINESS	NAMEPLATE	NEGATIONS	NEVER MIND	NIGROSINE
MUSHROOMS	NAME PLATE	NEGATIVED	NEVERMORE	NIHILISTS
MUSICALLY	NAMESAKES	NEGATIVES	NEW BROOMS	NIKOLAYEV
MUSIC HALL	NANNY GOAT	NEGLECTED	NEWCASTLE	NINETEENS
MUSICIANS	NANOMETER	NEGLECTER	NEWCOMERS	NINETIETH
MUSKETEER	NANTUCKET	NEGLIGEES	NEW FOREST	NIPPINESS
MUSKINESS	NAPHTHENE	NEGLIGENT	NEW GUINEA	NIPPONESE
MUSKMELON	NAPPINESS	NEGOTIANT	NEW JERSEY	NISI PRIUS
MUSLIMISM	NARCISSUS	NEGOTIATE	NEWLYWEDS	NISSEN HUT
MUSTACHES	NARCOTICS	NEGRITUDE	NEWLY WEDS	NITPICKER
MUSTACHIO	NARCOTISM	NEIGHBOUR	NEWMARKET	NITRAMINE

NITRATION
NITRIDING
NIVERNAIS
NO ACCOUNT
NO-ACCOUNT
NOBILIARY
NOBLENESS
NOCTILUCA
NOCTURNAL
NOCTURNES
NO-GO
  AREAS
NOISELESS
NOISINESS
NOMINALLY
NOMINATED
NOMINATOR
NOMOCRACY
NOMOGRAPH
NONAGONAL
NONEDIBLE
NONENTITY
NON-EVENTS
NON-FINITE
NONILLION
NONLINEAR
NONPAREIL
NONPAROUS
NONRACIAL
NONSMOKER
NONVERBAL
NONWHITES
NORMALITY
NORMALIZE
NORMATIVE
NORTH DOWN
NORTHEAST
NORTHERLY
NORTH POLE
NORTHWARD
NORTHWEST
NORTHWICH
NORWEGIAN
NOSEBLEED
NOSECONES
NOSEDIVED
NOSEDIVES
NOSE PIECE
NOSTALGIA
NOSTALGIC
NOSTOLOGY

NOTARIZED
NOT AT
  HOME
NOTATIONS
NOTEBOOKS
NOTEPAPER
NOTHING ON
NOTIFYING
NO-TILLAGE
NOTOCHORD
NOTOGAEAN
NOTORIETY
NOTORIOUS
NOT PROVEN
NOTRE DAME
NOURISHED
NOURISHER
NOVELETTE
NOVELISTS
NOVELTIES
NOVEMBERS
NOVITIATE
NOVOCAINE
NOXIOUSLY
NUCLEATOR
NUCLEOLAR
NUCLEOLUS
NUCLEONIC
NUEVO LEON
NUISANCES
NUKU'ALOFA
NULLIFIED
NULLIFIER
NULLIPARA
NULLIPORE
NULLITIES
NUMBERING
NUMBER ONE
NUMBER TEN
NUMBSKULL
NUMERABLE
NUMERABLY
NUMERATOR
NUMERICAL
NUMMULITE
NUMSKULLS
NUNNERIES
NUREMBERG
NURSELING
NURSEMAID
NURSERIES

NURSLINGS
NURTURING
NUTHOUSES
NUTRIENTS
NUTRIMENT
NUTRITION
NUTRITIVE
NUTSHELLS
NUTTINESS
NYASALAND
NYMPHALID
NYSTAGMIC
NYSTAGMUS

O

OAST HOUSE
OBBLIGATO
OBCORDATE
OBEDIENCE
OBEISANCE
OBELISCAL
OBFUSCATE
OBJECTIFY
OBJECTING
OBJECTION
OBJECTIVE
OBJECTORS
OBJET
  D'ART
OBJURGATE
OBLATIONS
OBLIGABLE
OBLIGATED
OBLIGATOR
OBLIQUITY
OBLIVIOUS
OBNOXIOUS
OBREPTION
OBSCENELY
OBSCENITY
OBSCURANT
OBSCURELY
OBSCURING
OBSCURITY
OBSEQUENT
OBSEQUIES
OBSERVANT
OBSERVERS
OBSERVING
OBSESSING
OBSESSION

OBSESSIVE
OBSOLESCE
OBSTACLES
OBSTETRIC
OBSTINACY
OBSTINATE
OBSTRUENT
OBTAINING
OBTRUDING
OBTRUSION
OBTRUSIVE
OBVERSION
OBVIATING
OBVIATION
OBVIOUSLY
OCCASIONS
OCCIPITAL
OCCLUDENT
OCCLUSION
OCCLUSIVE
OCCULTISM
OCCULTIST
OCCUPANCY
OCCUPANTS
OCCUPIERS
OCCUPYING
OCCURRENT
OCCURRING
OCELLATED
OCHLOCRAT
OCTAGONAL
OCTAMETER
OCTENNIAL
OCTILLION
OCTOPUSES
ODALISQUE
ODD JOBMAN
ODD-JOB
  MAN
ODD MAN
  OUT
ODD MEN
  OUT
ODOMETERS
ODOURLESS
OESTROGEN
OFF CHANCE
OFF COLOUR
OFFENBACH
OFFENDERS
OFFENDING

OFFENSIVE
OFFERINGS
OFFERTORY
OFFHANDED
OFFICE BOY
OFFICIALS
OFFICIANT
OFFICIARY
OFFICIATE
OFFICIOUS
OFF-LOADED
OFF-ROADER
OFF SEASON
OFFSHOOTS
OFFSPRING
OFF-STREET
OFF THE
  PEG
OGBOMOSHO
OILFIELDS
OIL PAINTS
OIL SLICKS
OIL TANKER
OINTMENTS
OKLAHOMAN
OLDENBURG
OLD FLAMES
OLD MASTER
OLD SCHOOL
OLD STAGER
OLD-TIMERS
OLEACEOUS
OLEANDERS
OLECRANAL
OLECRANON
OLEOGRAPH
OLEORESIN
OLFACTION
OLFACTORY
OLIGARCHY
OLIGOCENE
OLIGOPOLY
OLIVE DRAB
OLIVENITE
OLYMPIADS
OLYMPIANS
OMBUDSMAN
OMBUDSMEN
OMELETTES
OMINOUSLY
OMISSIBLE

OMISSIONS	OPPORTUNE	OSMOMETER	OUTRANKED	OVERLORDS
OMNIBUSES	OPPOSABLE	OSMOMETRY	OUTRIDDEN	OVERLYING
OMNIRANGE	OPPOSABLY	OSNABRUCK	OUTRIDERS	OVERNIGHT
OMOPHAGIA	OPPOSITES	OSSICULAR	OUTRIDING	OVERPAINT
OMOPHAGIC	OPPRESSED	OSSIFRAGE	OUTRIGGER	OVERPOWER
ON ACCOUNT	OPPRESSOR	OSSIFYING	OUTRUNNER	OVERPRICE
ON A	OPTICALLY	OSTENSIVE	OUTSIDERS	OVERPRINT
STRING	OPTICIANS	OSTEOLOGY	OUTSKIRTS	OVERPROOF
ONCE A	OPTIMISTS	OSTEOPATH	OUTSOURCE	OVERRATED
WEEK	OPTIMIZED	OSTEOTOME	OUTSPOKEN	OVERREACH
ONCE-OVERS	OPTOMETER	OSTEOTOMY	OUTSPREAD	OVERREACT
ONCOGENIC	OPTOMETRY	OSTRACISM	OUTSTARED	OVERRIDER
ONDOGRAPH	OPULENTLY	OSTRACIZE	OUTSTAYED	OVERRULED
ONDOMETER	ORANGEADE	OSTRICHES	OUTTALKED	OVERSCORE
ONEROUSLY	ORANGEISM	OTHERNESS	OUTVOTING	OVERSEERS
ONION DOME	ORANGEMAN	OTHERWISE	OUTWARDLY	OVERSEXED
ONIONSKIN	ORANGE TIP	OTOCYSTIC	OUT WITH	OVERSHOES
ONLOOKERS	ORANG-UTAN	OTOLITHIC	IT	OVERSHOOT
ONLOOKING	ORATORIES	OTOLOGIST	OUTWITTED	OVERSIGHT
ONOMASTIC	ORATORIOS	OTOSCOPIC	OUTWORKER	OVERSIZED
ONRUSHING	ORBICULAR	OUBLIETTE	OVATIONAL	OVERSKIRT
ONSLAUGHT	ORCHESTRA	OUR FATHER	OVEN-READY	OVERSLEEP
ON THE	ORDAINING	OURSELVES	OVERACTED	OVERSLEPT
BEAM	ORDER ARMS	OUT AND	OVERAWING	OVERSPEND
ON THE	ORDERLIES	OUT	OVERBLOWN	OVERSPILL
MEND	ORDINANCE	OUT-AND-	OVERBOARD	OVERSTATE
ON THE	ORGANELLE	OUT	OVERBORNE	OVERSTOCK
NAIL	ORGANISMS	OUTBRAVED	OVERBUILD	OVERTAKEN
ON THE	ORGANISTS	OUTBREAKS	OVERCHECK	OVERTAXED
SPOT	ORGANIZED	OUTBURSTS	OVERCLOUD	OVERTHREW
ON THE	ORGANIZER	OUTCASTES	OVERCOATS	OVERTHROW
TROT	ORGANZINE	OUTERMOST	OVERCROWD	OVERTONES
ONTOGENIC	ORGIASTIC	OUTFACING	OVERDOING	OVERTRADE
OOGENESIS	ORIENTALS	OUTFITTED	OVERDOSED	OVERTRICK
OOGENETIC	ORIENTATE	OUTFITTER	OVERDOSES	OVERTRUMP
OOLOGICAL	ORIGINALS	OUTFOUGHT	OVERDRAFT	OVERTURES
OPEN-ENDED	ORIGINATE	OUTFOXING	OVERDRAWN	OVERVIEWS
OPEN-FACED	ORNAMENTS	OUTGOINGS	OVERDRESS	OVERWEIGH
OPEN HOUSE	ORNITHINE	OUTGROWTH	OVERDRIVE	OVERWHELM
OPENING UP	OROGRAPHY	OUTHOUSES	OVERFLOWN	OVERWRITE
OPEN ORDER	OROLOGIST	OUTLASTED	OVERFLOWS	OVIFEROUS
OPEN SHOPS	ORPHANAGE	OUTLAWING	OVERGLAZE	OVIPAROUS
OPERATING	ORPHANING	OUTLAYING	OVERGROWN	OVOTESTIS
OPERATION	ORRIS ROOT	OUTLINING	OVERHANGS	OVULATING
OPERATIVE	ORTANIQUE	OUTLIVING	OVERHAULS	OVULATION
OPERATORS	ORTHODOXY	OUTNUMBER	OVERHEADS	OWNERSHIP
OPERCULAR	ORTHOEPIC	OUT-OF-	OVERHEARD	OXIDATION
OPERCULUM	ORTHOPTER	DATE	OVERISSUE	OXIDATIVE
OPERETTAS	ORTHOPTIC	OUT OF	OVERJOYED	OXIDIZING
OPHIOLOGY	OSCILLATE	STEP	OVERLADEN	OXYGENATE
OPPONENCY	OSCITANCY	OUTPLAYED	OVERLOADS	OXYGENIZE
OPPONENTS		OUTRAGING		

OYSTER BED	PALTRIEST	PARALYSIS	PARTI PRIS	PATROL CAR
OZOCERITE	PAMPERING	PARALYTIC	PARTISANS	PATROLLED
	PAMPHLETS	PARAMATTA	PARTITION	PATROLLER
P	PANATELAS	PARTITIVE	PATROLMAN
PACEMAKER	PANDA CARS	PARAMEDIC	PARAMETER	PARTNERED	PATROLMEN
PACHYDERM	PANDEMICS	PARAMORPH	PARTRIDGE	PATRONAGE
PACHYTENE	PANDERING	PARAMOUNT	'PART-SONGS	PATRONESS
PACIFIERS	PANDURATE	PARAMOURS	PART WORKS	PATRONIZE
PACIFISTS	PANEGYRIC	PARANOIAC	PARTY LINE	PATTERING
PACIFYING	PANELLING	PARAPLASM	PARTY WALL	PATTERNED
PACKAGERS	PANELLIST	PARASITES	PAS DE	PAULOWNIA
PACKAGING	PANHANDLE	PARASITIC	DEUX	PAUPERISM
PACKED-OUT	PANICKING	PARATAXIS	PASO DOBLE	PAUPERIZE
PACKHORSE	PANMUNJOM	PARATHION	PASSBOOKS	PAUSINGLY
PADERBORN	PANNIKINS	PARBOILED	PASSED OUT	PAVEMENTS
PADLOCKED	PANOPLIED	PARBUCKLE	PASSENGER	PAVILIONS
PAEDERAST	PANORAMAS	PARCELING	PASSERINE	PAWKINESS
PAEDOLOGY	PANORAMIC	PARCELLED	PASSERSBY	PAWNSHOPS
PAGANIZER	PANSOPHIC	PARCENARY	PASSIONAL	PAYCHECKS
PAGEANTRY	PANTHEISM	PARCHMENT	PASSIVELY	PAYMASTER
PAILLASSE	PANTHEIST	PARDONERS	PASSIVISM	PAY PACKET
PAILLETTE	PANTHEONS	PARDONING	PASSIVIST	PAY PHONES
PAINFULLY	PANTOMIME	PARDUBICE	PASSIVITY	PEACEABLE
PAINTBALL	PANTY HOSE	PAREGORIC	PASSOVERS	PEACEABLY
PAINTERLY	PAPARAZZI	PARENTAGE	PASSPORTS	PEACE PIPE
PAINTINGS	PAPARAZZO	PARENTING	PASSWORDS	PEACETIME
PAINTWORK	PAPERBACK	PARGETING	PASTICHES	PEARLIEST
PAKISTANI	PAPERBOYS	PARHELION	PASTILLES	PEARLITIC
PALANQUIN	PAPER CLIP	PARI PASSU	PASTINESS	PEARLIZED
PALATABLE	PAPER TAPE	PARISIANS	PASTORALE	PEARMAINS
PALATABLY	PAPERWORK	PARLEYING	PASTORALS	PEASANTRY
PALEFACES	PAPETERIE	PARLOR CAR	PASTORATE	PEA SOUPER
PALEMBANG	PAPILLARY	PARNASSUS	PASTURAGE	PECCARIES
PALESTINE	PAPILLOMA	PAROCHIAL	PASTURING	PECTINATE
PALISADES	PAPILLOTE	PARODISTS	PATAGONIA	PECULATED
PALLADIAN	PAPYRUSES	PARODYING	PATCHABLE	PECULATOR
PALLADIUM	PARABLAST	PAROICOUS	PATCHIEST	PECUNIARY
PALLADOUS	PARABOLAS	PAROLABLE	PATCHOULI	PEDAGOGIC
PALLIASSE	PARABOLIC	PARONYMIC	PATCHWORK	PEDAGOGUE
PALLIATED	PARACHUTE	PAROTITIS	PATELLATE	PEDALLING
PALLIATOR	PARADIGMS	PAROXYSMS	PATENTEES	PEDATIFID
PALMATION	PARADISAL	PARQUETRY	PATENTING	PEDERASTS
PALM BEACH	PARADISES	PARRICIDE	PATERNITY	PEDERASTY
PALMETTOS	PARADOXES	PARROTING	PATHOLOGY	PEDESTALS
PALMISTRY	PARAGOGIC	PARSIMONY	PATIENTLY	PEDICULAR
PALMITATE	PARAGRAPH	PARSONAGE	PATRIARCH	PEDICURES
PALOMINOS	PARAKEETS	PARTAKING	PATRICIAN	PEDIGREED
PALPATING	PARALLELS	PARTERRES	PATRICIDE	PEDIGREES
PALPATION	PARALYSED	PARTHENON	PATRIMONY	PEDIMENTS
PALPEBRAL	PARALYSER	PARTIALLY	PATRIOTIC	PEDUNCLED
PALPITATE	PARALYSES	PARTICLES	PATRISTIC	PEEPHOLES

PEERESSES	PEPTIDASE	PERMEANCE	PETTINESS	PHOSPHENE
PEEVISHLY	PEPTONIZE	PERMEATED	PETTISHLY	PHOSPHIDE
PEGGED OUT	PERBORATE	PERMEATOR	PETTY CASH	PHOSPHINE
PEGMATITE	PERCALINE	PER MENSEM	PETULANCE	PHOSPHITE
PEKINESES	PER CAPITA	PERMITTED	PFORZHEIM	PHOTOCELL
PEKINGESE	PERCEIVED	PERMITTER	PHAGOCYTE	PHOTOCOPY
PEKING MAN	PERCEIVER	PERMUTING	PHALANGER	PHOTOGRAM
PELLITORY	PERCHANCE	PERPETUAL	PHALANGES	PHOTONICS
PELMANISM	PERCHERON	PERPIGNAN	PHALANXES	PHOTOSTAT
PELTATION	PERCOLATE	PERPLEXED	PHALAROPE	PHOTOTUBE
PEMPHIGUS	PERCUSSOR	PERSECUTE	PHALLUSES	PHOTOTYPE
PENALIZED	PERDITION	PERSEVERE	PHANTASMS	PHRENITIC
PENALTIES	PEREGRINE	PERSIMMON	PHARISAIC	PHRENITIS
PENCHANTS	PERENNATE	PERSISTED	PHARISEES	PHTHALEIN
PENCILING	PERENNIAL	PERSISTER	PHARYNXES	PHYCOLOGY
PENCILLED	PERFECTED	PERSONAGE	PHASE-OUTS	PHYLLITIC
PENCILLER	PERFECTER	PERSONALS	PHEASANTS	PHYLLOMIC
PENDRAGON	PERFECTLY	PERSONATE	PHELLOGEN	PHYLOGENY
PENDULOUS	PERFIDIES	PERSONIFY	PHENACITE	PHYSICALS
PENDULUMS	PERFORATE	PERSONNEL	PHENAZINE	PHYSICIAN
PENEPLAIN	PERFORMED	PERSPIRED	PHENETOLE	PHYSICIST
PENETRANT	PERFORMER	PERSUADED	PHENOCOPY	PHYSIQUES
PENETRATE	PERFUMERY	PERSUADER	PHENOLATE	PHYTOTRON
PEN FRIEND	PERFUMING	PERTAINED	PHENOLOGY	PIANISTIC
PENINSULA	PERFUSION	PERTINENT	PHENOMENA	PICKETING
PENITENCE	PERFUSIVE	PERTURBED	PHENOTYPE	PICKINESS
PENITENTS	PERICLASE	PERTUSSIS	PHENOXIDE	PICK-ME-
PENKNIVES	PERICLINE	PERVADING	PHEROMONE	UPS
PENNILESS	PERICYCLE	PERVASIVE	PHILANDER	PICK PURSE
PENNINITE	PERILYMPH	PERVERTED	PHILATELY	PICNICKED
PENN'ORTHS	PERIMETER	PERVERTER	PHILIPPIC	PICNICKER
PENNY-WISE	PERIMETRY	PESSARIES	PHILOLOGY	PICOLINIC
PENNYWORT	PERIMORPH	PESSIMISM	PHLEBITIC	PICTORIAL
PEN PUSHER	PERINATAL	PESSIMIST	PHLEBITIS	PICTURING
PENSILITY	PERIODATE	PESTERING	PHLYCTENA	PIECE-DYED
PENSIONED	PERIPHERY	PESTICIDE	PHNOM PENH	PIECEMEAL
PENSIONER	PERISCOPE	PESTILENT	PHOENICIA	PIECEWORK
PENSIVELY	PERISHERS	PETAL-LIKE	PHOENIXES	PIE CHARTS
PENTAGONS	PERISHING	PETALODIC	PHONATION	PIECRUSTS
PENTAGRAM	PERISPERM	PETECHIAL	PHONATORY	PIERCABLE
PENTARCHY	PERISTOME	PETERSHAM	PHONE BOOK	PIERIDINE
PENTECOST	PERISTYLE	PETIOLATE	PHONEMICS	PIGGERIES
PENTHOUSE	PERITONEA	PETIOLULE	PHONETICS	PIGGISHLY
PENTOTHAL	PERITRACK	PETIT FOUR	PHONEY WAR	PIGGYBACK
PENTOXIDE	PERJURERS	PETITIONS	PHONINESS	PIGGYBANK
PENUMBRAL	PERJURIES	PETRI DISH	PHONOGRAM	PIGHEADED
PENUMBRAS	PERJURING	PETRIFIED	PHONOLITE	PIG-HEADED
PENURIOUS	PERKINESS	PETRIFIER	PHONOLOGY	PIGTAILED
PEPPERING	PERMALLOY	PETROLEUM	PHONOTYPE	PIKEPERCH
PEPPER POT	PERMANENT	PETROLOGY	PHONOTYPY	PIKESTAFF
PEPSINATE	PERMEABLE	PETTICOAT	PHOSPHATE	PILASTERS

PILCHARDS	PLACARDED	PLAYROOMS	PODGINESS	POLYBASIC
PILFERAGE	PLACATING	PLAYTHING	POETASTER	POLYCARPY
PILFERERS	PLACATION	PLEADABLE	POETESSES	POLYESTER
PILFERING	PLACATORY	PLEADINGS	POETICIZE	POLYGLOTS
PILLAGERS	PLACEBOES	PLEASABLE	POGO STICK	POLYGONAL
PILLAGING	PLACE CARD	PLEASANCE	POIGNANCY	POLYGONUM
PILLAR BOX	PLACE MATS	PLEASEDLY	POINCIANA	POLYGRAPH
PILLBOXES	PLACEMENT	PLEASURES	POINT DUTY	POLYMATHS
PILLORIED	PLACENTAE	PLEBBIEST	POINTEDLY	POLYMERIC
PILLORIES	PLACENTAL	PLEBEIANS	POINTLESS	POLYMORPH
PILLOWING	PLACENTAS	PLECTRUMS	POINTSMAN	POLYMYXIN
PIMPERNEL	PLACIDITY	PLENARILY	POISONERS	POLYNESIA
PINACEOUS	PLACODERM	PLENITUDE	POISON GAS	POLYPHASE
PINAFORES	PLAIN-LAID	PLENTEOUS	POISONING	POLYPHONE
PINCHBECK	PLAINNESS	PLENTIFUL	POISON IVY	POLYPHONY
PINCHCOCK	PLAINSMAN	PLEONASMS	POISONOUS	POLYPLOID
PINEAPPLE	PLAINSONG	PLEURITIC	POKEBERRY	POLYPTYCH
PINETREES	PLAINTIFF	PLEXIFORM	POKER FACE	POLYSOMIC
PINEWOODS	PLAINTIVE	PLICATION	POKERWORK	POLYTHENE
PINIONING	PLANARIAN	PLIGHTING	POLAR BEAR	POLYTONAL
PINNACLES	PLANATION	PLIMSOLLS	POLARIZED	POLYTYPIC
PINNATION	PLANETARY	PLOUGHBOY	POLARIZER	POLYVINYL
PINPOINTS	PLANETOID	PLOUGHING	POLAROIDS	POMACEOUS
PINPRICKS	PLANE TREE	PLOUGHMAN	POLEAXING	POMANDERS
PINSTRIPE	PLANGENCY	PLOUGHMEN	POLEMICAL	POMERANIA
PINTABLES	PLANISHER	PLUCKIEST	POLE VAULT	POMPADOUR
PINTADERA	PLANTABLE	PLUGBOARD	POLICE DOG	POMPOSITY
PINWHEELS	PLANTAINS	PLUGHOLES	POLICEMAN	POMPOUSLY
PIONEERED	PLASMAGEL	PLUMBABLE	POLICEMEN	PONDERING
PIOUSNESS	PLASMASOL	PLUMBEOUS	POLISHING	PONDEROUS
PIPE DREAM	PLASTERED	PLUMBICON	POLITBURO	PONDOLAND
PIPELINES	PLASTERER	PLUMB LINE	POLITESSE	PONTIANAK
PIPE RACKS	PLATELETS	PLUMMETED	POLITICAL	PONTYPOOL
PIPERONAL	PLATE RACK	PLUMMIEST	POLITICOS	PONYTAILS
PIPESTONE	PLATFORMS	PLUMPNESS	POLKA DOTS	POORHOUSE
PIPSQUEAK	PLATINIZE	PLUNDERED	POLLARDED	POORLIEST
PIQUANTLY	PLATINOID	PLUNDERER	POLLINATE	POORLY OFF
PIRATICAL	PLATINOUS	PLURALISM	POLLINIUM	POOR WHITE
PIROUETTE	PLATITUDE	PLURALIST	POLLSTERS	POPE'S
PISS-TAKES	PLAUSIBLE	PLURALITY	POLL TAXES	NOSE
PISTACHIO	PLAUSIBLY	PLURALIZE	POLLUCITE	POPINJAYS
PITCH-DARK	PLAY-ACTED	PLUS FOURS	POLLUTANT	POPLITEAL
PITCHFORK	PLAYBACKS	PLUSHNESS	POLLUTING	POPPYCOCK
PITEOUSLY	PLAY DOUGH	PLUTOCRAT	POLLUTION	POPPYHEAD
PITHINESS	PLAYED-OUT	PLUTONIUM	POLLYANNA	POPSICLES
PITOT TUBE	PLAYFULLY	PNEUMATIC	POLONAISE	POPULARLY
PIT PONIES	PLAYGOERS	PNEUMONIA	POLO NECKS	POPULATED
PITTANCES	PLAYGROUP	PNEUMONIC	POLO SHIRT	POPULISTS
PITUITARY	PLAYHOUSE	POCKETFUL	POLTROONS	PORBEAGLE
PITYINGLY	PLAYMAKER	POCKETING	POLYAMIDE	PORCELAIN
PIZZICATO	PLAYMATES	POCKMARKS	POLYANDRY	PORCUPINE

PORIFERAN	POT-BOILER	PRECISION	PRESCRIBE	PRIME COST
PORKINESS	POTENTATE	PRECLUDED	PRESCRIPT	PRIMENESS
POROMERIC	POTENTIAL	PRECOCIAL	PRESENCES	PRIME RATE
PORPHYRIN	POTHOLERS	PRECOCITY	PRESENTED	PRIME TIME
PORPOISES	POTHOLING	PRECONIZE	PRESENTEE	PRIMIPARA
PORRINGER	POTHUNTER	PRECOOKED	PRESENTER	PRIMITIVE
PORTACRIB	POT PLANTS	PRECURSOR	PRESENTLY	PRIMROSES
PORTADOWN	POTPOURRI	PREDATING	PRESERVED	PRINCEDOM
PORTATIVE	POT POURRI	PREDATION	PRESERVER	PRINCETON
PORT BLAIR	POTSHERDS	PREDATORS	PRESERVES	PRINCIPAL
PORTENDED	POTTERIES	PREDATORY	PRESETTER	PRINCIPLE
PORTERAGE	POTTERING	PREDICANT	PRESHRUNK	PRINTABLE
PORTFOLIO	POTTINESS	PREDICATE	PRESIDENT	PRINTINGS
PORTHOLES	POULTERER	PREDICTED	PRESIDING	PRINTOUTS
PORTICOES	POULTICES	PREDICTOR	PRESIDIUM	PRISMATIC
PORTIONED	POULTRIES	PREDIGEST	PRESSGANG	PRISONERS
PORTLIEST	POUNDINGS	PRE-EMPTED	PRESS GANG	PRISSIEST
PORT LOUIS	POURBOIRE	PRE-EMPTOR	PRESSINGS	PRITCHETT
PORTO NOVO	POUTINGLY	PREFACING	PRESSMARK	PRIVATEER
PORTRAITS	POVERTIES	PREFATORY	PRESSROOM	PRIVATELY
PORTRAYAL	POWDERING	PREFERRED	PRESS-STUD	PRIVATION
PORTRAYED	POWDER KEG	PREFIGURE	PRESSURED	PRIVATIVE
PORTRAYER	POWER BASE	PREFIXING	PRESSURES	PRIVATIZE
PORT SUDAN	POWERBOAT	PREFLIGHT	PRESSWORK	PRIVILEGE
PORTULACA	POWER DIVE	PREGNABLE	PRESTIGES	PRIZE DAYS
POSITIONS	POWERLESS	PREGNANCY	PRESTRESS	PROACTIVE
POSITIVES	PRACTICAL	PREHEATED	PRESTWICH	PROBABLES
POSITRONS	PRACTICES	PREJUDGED	PRESTWICK	PROBATING
POSSESSED	PRACTISED	PREJUDGER	PRESUMING	PROBATION
POSSESSOR	PRAESIDIA	PREJUDICE	PRETENCES	PROBATIVE
POSSIBLES	PRAGMATIC	PRELATISM	PRETENDED	PROBEABLE
POSTAXIAL	PRANKSTER	PRELATIST	PRETENDER	PROBINGLY
POSTCARDS	PRATINGLY	PRELATURE	PRETERITE	PROBOSCIS
POSTCODES	PRATTLERS	PRELUDIAL	PRETTIEST	PROCEDURE
POSTDATED	PRATTLING	PRELUSION	PREVAILED	PROCEEDED
POSTERIOR	PRAYERFUL	PRELUSIVE	PREVAILER	PROCEEDER
POSTERITY	PRAYER RUG	PREMATURE	PREVALENT	PROCESSED
POSTHASTE	PREACHERS	PREMIERED	PREVENTED	PROCESSES
POST HORNS	PREACHIFY	PREMIERES	PREVENTER	PROCESSOR
POSTICOUS	PREACHING	PREOCCUPY	PREVIEWED	PROCLITIC
POSTILION	PREAMBLES	PREORDAIN	PREVISION	PROCONSUL
POSTMARKS	PREBENDAL	PREPACKED	PRICELESS	PROCREANT
POSTNATAL	PRECANCEL	PREPARING	PRICE TAGS	PROCREATE
POSTPONED	PRECEDENT	PREPAYING	PRICINESS	PROCTORED
POSTPONER	PRECEDING	PREPOTENT	PRICKLIER	PROCURERS
POSTULANT	PRECENTOR	PREPUTIAL	PRICKLING	PROCURING
POSTULATE	PRECEPTOR	PRERECORD	PRIESTESS	PRODIGALS
POSTURING	PRECINCTS	PRESAGING	PRIMAEVAL	PRODIGIES
POTASSIUM	PRECIPICE	PRESBYTER	PRIMARIES	PRODROMAL
POTATIONS	PRECISELY	PRESCHOOL	PRIMARILY	PRODUCERS
POTBOILER	PRECISIAN	PRESCIENT	PRIMATIAL	PRODUCING

PROFANELY	PROPHETIC	PROXIMATE	PULVILLUS	PUTREFIED
PROFANING	PROPONENT	PROXIMITY	PULVINATE	PUTREFIER
PROFANITY	PROPOSALS	PRUDENTLY	PUMICEOUS	PUTRIDITY
PROFESSED	PROPOSERS	PRUDISHLY	PUMMELING	PUTTERING
PROFESSOR	PROPOSING	PRURIENCE	PUMMELLED	PUTTYROOT
PROFFERED	PROPRIETY	PRUSSIATE	PUMP ROOMS	PUT-UP
PROFFERER	PROPTOSIS	PRYTANEUM	PUNCHBALL	JOBS
PROFILING	PROPYLITE	PSALMISTS	PUNCH BALL	PUY DE
PROFITEER	PROROGUED	PSALMODIC	PUNCH BOWL	DOME
PROFITING	PROSCRIBE	PSEUDONYM	PUNCHIEST	PYCNIDIUM
PROFLUENT	PROSECTOR	PSORIASIS	PUNCH LINE	PYONGYANG
PROFUSELY	PROSECUTE	PSORIATIC	PUNCTILIO	PYORRHOEA
PROFUSION	PROSELYTE	PSYCHICAL	PUNCTUATE	PYRAMIDAL
PROGESTIN	PROSIMIAN	PSYCHOSES	PUNCTURED	PYRETHRIN
PROGNOSES	PROSINESS	PSYCHOSIS	PUNCTURER	PYRETHRUM
PROGNOSIS	PROSODIST	PSYCHOTIC	PUNCTURES	PYRIDOXAL
PROGRAMED	PROSPECTS	PTARMIGAN	PUNGENTLY	PYROGENIC
PROGRAMER	PROSPERED	PTERYGOID	PUNISHING	PYROLITIC
PROGRAMME	PROSTATES	PTOLEMAIC	PUPILLAGE	PYROLYSIS
PROJECTED	PROSTATIC	PUB-CRAWLS	PUPILLARY	PYROMANCY
PROJECTOR	PROSTRATE	PUBESCENT	PUPPETEER	PYROMANIA
PROLACTIN	PROTAMINE	PUBLICANS	PUPPYHOOD	PYROMETER
PROLAMINE	PROTANDRY	PUBLIC BAR	PUPPY LOVE	PYROMETRY
PROLAPSED	PROTECTED	PUBLICIST	PURCHASED	PYROXENIC
PROLAPSES	PROTECTOR	PUBLICITY	PURCHASER	PYROXYLIN
PROLEPSIS	PROTESTER	PUBLICIZE	PURCHASES	
PROLEPTIC	PROTHESIS	PUBLISHED	PUREBREDS	**Q**
PROLIXITY	PROTHETIC	PUBLISHER	PURGATION	QUADRANTS
PROLOGUES	PROTHORAX	PUCKERING	PURGATIVE	QUADRATIC
PROLONGED	PROTOCOLS	PUCKISHLY	PURGATORY	QUADRIFID
PROLONGER	PROTOGYNY	PUDGINESS	PURIFIERS	QUADRILLE
PROLUSION	PROTONEMA	PUERILISM	PURIFYING	QUADRUPED
PROLUSORY	PROTOSTAR	PUERILITY	PURLOINED	QUADRUPLE
PROMENADE	PROTOTYPE	PUERPERAL	PURLOINER	QUADRUPLY
PROMINENT	PROTOXIDE	PUFF ADDER	PURPORTED	QUAGMIRES
PROMISING	PROTOZOAN	PUFFINESS	PURPOSELY	QUAKERISM
PROMOTERS	PROTRUDED	PUGILISTS	PURPOSING	QUAKINESS
PROMOTING	PROUDNESS	PUGNACITY	PURPOSIVE	QUALIFIED
PROMOTION	PROUSTITE	PUISSANCE	PURSUANCE	QUALIFIER
PROMOTIVE	PROVENCAL	PULLOVERS	PURULENCE	QUALITIES
PROMPTING	PROVENDER	PULL ROUND	PURVEYING	QUARRELED
PRONATION	PROVIDENT	PULLULATE	PURVEYORS	QUARRYING
PRONENESS	PROVIDERS	PULMONARY	PUSHBIKES	QUARTERED
PRONGHORN	PROVIDING	PULMONATE	PUSHCARTS	QUARTERLY
PRONOUNCE	PROVINCES	PULPINESS	PUSHCHAIR	QUARTZITE
PROOFREAD	PROVISION	PULSATILE	PUSH CHAIR	QUATRAINS
PROPAGATE	PROVISORY	PULSATING	PUSHINESS	QUAVERING
PROPAGULE	PROVOKING	PULSATION	PUSHINGLY	QUEASIEST
PRO PATRIA	PROVOLONE	PULSATIVE	PUSSYFOOT	QUEBECKER
PROPELLED	PROWESSES	PULSATORY	PUSTULANT	QUEBECOIS
PROPELLER	PROWL CARS	PULVERIZE	PUSTULATE	QUEBRACHO

QUEEN-SIZE	RADIATING	RATIONING	RECEPTIVE	REDACTION
QUEERNESS	RADIATION	RATTINESS	RECESSING	RED ALERTS
QUENCHING	RADIATIVE	RATTLEBOX	RECESSION	REDBREAST
QUERCETIN	RADIATORS	RAUCOUSLY	RECESSIVE	REDBRICKS
QUERETARO	RADICALLY	RAUNCHIER	RECHARGED	REDBRIDGE
QUERULOUS	RADIOGRAM	RAUNCHILY	RECHARGER	RED CARPET
QUESTIONS	RADIOLOGY	RAUWOLFIA	RECHAUFFE	REDDENING
QUEUE-JUMP	RADIO STAR	RAVELLING	RECHERCHE	REDEEMERS
QUIBBLERS	RAFFINOSE	RAVISHING	RECIPIENT	REDEEMING
QUIBBLING	RAFFISHLY	RAZORBACK	RECITABLE	REDELIVER
QUICKENED	RAFFLESIA	RAZORBILL	RECKONING	REDEVELOP
QUICKLIME	RAIL GAUGE	RAZOR EDGE	RECLAIMED	RED GIANTS
QUICKNESS	RAILHEADS	REACHABLE	RECLINATE	RED-HANDED
QUICKSAND	RAILROADS	REACTANCE	RECLINING	RED-HEADED
QUICKSTEP	RAIN CHECK	REACTIONS	RECLUSION	RED INDIAN
QUIESCENT	RAINCOATS	READDRESS	RECLUSIVE	RED LIGHTS
QUIETENED	RAINDROPS	READINESS	RECOGNIZE	REDOLENCE
QUIETISTS	RAINFALLS	READY-MADE	RECOILING	REDOUBLED
QUIETNESS	RAIN GAUGE	REALIGNED	RECOLLECT	REDOUNDED
QUIETUSES	RAININESS	REALISTIC	RECOMMEND	RED-PENCIL
QUILLWORT	RAINMAKER	REALITIES	RECOMPOSE	RED PEPPER
QUINIDINE	RAINPROOF	REALIZING	RECONCILE	REDRESSED
QUINOLINE	RAINSTORM	REANIMATE	RECONDITE	REDRESSER
QUINONOID	RAINWATER	REAPPOINT	RECONVERT	REDUCIBLE
QUINTUPLE	RAJASTHAN	REARGUARD	RECORDERS	REDUCTASE
QUIRKIEST	RAMIFYING	REAR LIGHT	RECORDING	REDUCTION
QUISLINGS	RAMPAGING	REARRANGE	RECOUNTAL	REDUNDANT
QUITCLAIM	RAMPANTLY	REARWARDS	RECOUNTED	RE-ECHOING
QUITTANCE	RANCIDITY	REASONING	RECOUPING	REEDINESS
QUIVERFUL	RANCOROUS	REASSURED	RE-COVERED	RE-EDUCATE
QUIVERING	RANDINESS	REASSURER	RECOVERER	REEF KNOTS
QUIXOTISM	RANDOMIZE	REBATABLE	RECREANTS	REEKINGLY
QUIZZICAL	RANGINESS	REBELLING	RECREATED	RE-ELECTED
QUODLIBET	RANSACKED	REBELLION	RE-CREATOR	RE-ENFORCE
QUOTATION	RANSACKER	REBINDING	RECREMENT	RE-ENTRANT
QUOTIDIAN	RANSOMERS	REBOUNDED	RECRUITED	RE-ENTRIES
QUOTIENTS	RANSOMING	REBOUNDER	RECRUITER	RE-EXAMINE
	RANTINGLY	REBUFFING	RECTANGLE	REFECTION
R	RAPACIOUS	REBUKABLE	RECTIFIED	REFECTORY
RABBINATE	RAPID-FIRE	REBUTTALS	RECTIFIER	REFERABLE
RABBITING	RAPIDNESS	REBUTTING	RECTITUDE	REFERENCE
RABBITTED	RAPTORIAL	RECALLING	RECTOCELE	REFERENDA
RACEHORSE	RAPTUROUS	RECANTING	RECTORATE	REFERRALS
RACETRACK	RARE EARTH	RECAPPING	RECTORIAL	REFERRING
RACIALISM	RASCALITY	RECAPTION	RECTORIES	REFILLING
RACIALIST	RASPBERRY	RECAPTURE	RECUMBENT	REFINABLE
RACKETEER	RASPINGLY	RECASTING	RECURRENT	REFINANCE
RACONTEUR	RASTERIZE	RECEIVERS	RECURRING	REFITTING
RADIAL-PLY	RATEPAYER	RECEIVING	RECUSANCY	REFLATING
RADIANCES	RATIFYING	RECENSION	RECUSANTS	REFLATION
RADIANTLY	RATIONALE	RECEPTION	RECYCLING	REFLECTED

REFLECTOR	REINSURER	REMOULDED	REPRESSOR	RESIDUARY
REFLEXIVE	REISSUING	REMOUNTED	REPRIEVED	RESIGNING
REFORMERS	REITERANT	REMOVABLE	REPRIEVER	RESILIENT
REFORMING	REITERATE	REMOVABLY	REPRIEVES	RESINATED
REFORMISM	REJECTING	REMSCHEID	REPRIMAND	RESISTANT
REFORMIST	REJECTION	RENASCENT	REPRINTED	RESISTERS
REFRACTED	REJECTIVE	RENDERING	REPRINTER	RESISTING
REFRACTOR	REJIGGING	RENDITION	REPRISALS	RESISTORS
REFRAINED	REJOICING	RENEGADES	REPROBACY	RESITTING
REFRAINER	REJOINDER	RENEWABLE	REPROBATE	RESNATRON
REFRESHED	REJOINING	RENEWEDLY	REPROCESS	RESOLUBLE
REFRESHER	REKINDLED	RENOUNCED	REPRODUCE	RESOLVENT
REFUELING	RELAPSING	RENOUNCER	REPROVING	RESOLVING
REFUELLED	RELATABLE	RENOVATED	REPTILIAN	RESONANCE
REFULGENT	RELATIONS	RENOVATOR	REPTILOID	RESONATED
REFUNDING	RELATIVES	REOPENING	REPUBLICS	RESONATOR
REFURBISH	RELAXABLE	REPAIRING	REPUBLISH	RESORBENT
REFUSABLE	RELAXEDLY	REPAIRMAN	REPUDIATE	RESORTING
REFUSE BIN	RELEASING	REPARABLE	REPUGNANT	RESOUNDED
REFUSE TIP	RELEGATED	REPARABLY	REPULSING	RESOURCES
REFUTABLE	RELENTING	REPARTEES	REPULSION	RESPECTED
REGAINING	RELEVANCE	REPAYABLE	REPULSIVE	RESPECTER
REGARDANT	RELEVANCY	REPAYMENT	REPUTABLE	RESPIRING
REGARDFUL	RELIEF MAP	REPEALING	REPUTABLY	RESPONDED
REGARDING	RELIEVING	REPEATERS	REPUTEDLY	RESPONDER
REGENCIES	RELIGIONS	REPEATING	REQUESTED	RESPONSER
REGICIDAL	RELIGIOSE	REPECHAGE	REQUESTER	RESPONSES
REGICIDES	RELIGIOUS	REPELLENT	REQUIRING	RESTATING
REGIMENTS	RELIQUARY	REPELLING	REQUISITE	REST CURES
REGISTERS	RELISHING	REPENTANT	REQUITING	RESTFULLY
REGISTRAR	RELIVABLE	REPENTING	REREDOSES	REST HOMES
REGRESSED	RELOADING	REPERTORY	RERUNNING	RESTIFORM
REGRESSOR	RELOCATED	REPHRASED	RESALABLE	RESTIVELY
REGRETFUL	RELUCTANT	REPLACING	RESCINDED	RESTOCKED
REGRETTED	REMAINDER	REPLAYING	RESCINDER	RESTORERS
REGRETTER	REMAINING	REPLEADER	RESCUABLE	RESTORING
REGROUPED	REMANDING	REPLENISH	RESECTION	RESTRAINT
REGULABLE	REMANENCE	REPLETION	RESEMBLED	REST ROOMS
REGULARLY	REMARKING	REPLETIVE	RESEMBLER	RESULTANT
REGULATED	REMARRIED	REPLICATE	RESENTFUL	RESULTING
REGULATOR	REMEDYING	REPLY-PAID	RESENTING	RESUMABLE
REHASHING	REMINDERS	REPORTAGE	RESERPINE	RESURFACE
REHEARSAL	REMINDFUL	REPORTERS	RESERVING	RESURGENT
REHEARSED	REMINDING	REPORTING	RESERVIST	RESURRECT
REHEARSER	REMINISCE	REPOSEDLY	RESERVOIR	RETAILERS
REHOUSING	REMISSION	REPOSEFUL	RESETTING	RETAILING
REIMBURSE	REMISSIVE	REPOSSESS	RESETTLED	RETAINERS
REINFORCE	REMITTING	REPREHEND	RESHUFFLE	RETAINING
REINSTALL	REMODELED	REPRESENT	RESIDENCE	RETALIATE
REINSTATE	REMONTANT	REPRESSED	RESIDENCY	RETARDANT
REINSURED	REMONTOIR	REPRESSER	RESIDENTS	RETARDATE

RETARDING	REVISIONS	RIDGEPOLE	ROCKINESS	ROUNDSMAN
RETELLING	REVIVABLE	RIDICULED	ROCK 'N'	ROUNDSMEN
RETENTION	REVIVABLY	RIDICULER	ROLL	ROUND TRIP
RETENTIVE	REVOCABLE	RIFLEBIRD	ROCK PLANT	ROUND-TRIP
RETHOUGHT	REVOCABLY	RIGHTEOUS	ROCKSHAFT	ROUNDWORM
RETICENCE	REVOKABLE	RIGHT-HAND	ROENTGENS	ROUTINELY
RETICULES	REVOKABLY	RIGHTISTS	ROGUERIES	ROUTINISM
RETICULUM	REVOLTING	RIGHTNESS	ROGUISHLY	ROUTINIST
RETINITIS	REVOLVERS	RIGHTSIZE	ROISTERER	ROVING EYE
RETORSION	REVOLVING	RIGHTWARD	ROLE MODEL	ROWAN TREE
RETORTING	REVULSION	RIGHT WING	ROLE PLAYS	ROWDINESS
RETORTION	REVULSIVE	RIGMAROLE	ROLL CALLS	ROW HOUSES
RETOUCHED	REWARDING	RING A	ROLLINGLY	ROYAL BLUE
RETOUCHER	REWIRABLE	BELL	ROMANCING	ROYALISTS
RETRACING	REWORDING	RING ROADS	ROMAN NOSE	ROYALTIES
RETRACTED	REWORKING	RIO BRANCO	ROMANTICS	RUBBERIZE
RETRACTOR	REWRITING	RIO GRANDE	ROMPINGLY	RUBBISHED
RETREADED	REYKJAVIK	RIOTOUSLY	ROOF RACKS	RUBESCENT
RETREATAL	RHAPSODIC	RIPOSTING	ROOKERIES	RUBRICATE
RETREATED	RHEOMETER	RISE ABOVE	ROOMINESS	RUBRICIAN
RETRIEVAL	RHEOMETRY	RISKINESS	ROOMMATES	RUCKSACKS
RETRIEVED	RHEOSTATS	RITUALISM	ROOT CROPS	RUDACEOUS
RETRIEVER	RHEOTAXIS	RITUALIST	ROOTINESS	RUDBECKIA
RETROCEDE	RHEUMATIC	RITUALIZE	ROOTSTOCK	RUDDINESS
RETROFIRE	RH FACTORS	RIVALLING	ROPE TRICK	RUDIMENTS
RETROFLEX	RHIGOLENE	RIVALRIES	ROQUEFORT	RUFESCENT
RETROPACK	RHINELAND	RIVALROUS	ROSACEOUS	RUFFIANLY
RETROUSSE	RHINOLOGY	RIVERBEDS	ROSCOMMON	RUINATION
RETURNING	RHIZOBIUM	RIVERBOAT	ROSEWATER	RUINOUSLY
REUNITING	RHIZOIDAL	RIVERHEAD	ROSINWEED	RULEBOOKS
REUTILIZE	RHIZOTOMY	RIVERSIDE	ROSTELLUM	RUMBLINGS
REVALUING	RHODAMINE	ROADBLOCK	ROTAMETER	RUMINANTS
REVAMPING	RHODESIAN	ROADHOUSE	ROTARIANS	RUMINATED
REVEALING	RHODOLITE	ROADSHOWS	ROTATABLE	RUMINATOR
REVELATOR	RHODONITE	ROADSTEAD	ROTATIONS	RUMMAGING
REVELLING	RHODOPSIN	ROADSTERS	ROTAVATOR	RUMP STEAK
REVELMENT	RHOMBOIDS	ROAD TAXES	ROTHERHAM	RUN-ABOUTS
REVELROUS	RHOMBUSES	ROAD TESTS	ROTIFERAL	RUN ACROSS
REVENGING	RHOTACISM	ROADWORKS	ROTOVATOR	RUN-AROUND
REVERABLE	RHOTACIST	ROAD WORKS	ROTTERDAM	RUNCINATE
REVERENCE	RHYMESTER	ROAST BEEF	ROTUNDITY	RUNNERS-UP
REVERENDS	RHYOLITIC	ROASTINGS	ROUGHCAST	RUNNER-UPS
REVERSALS	RHYTHMICS	ROBBERIES	ROUGH DEAL	RUNNYMEDE
REVERSING	RIBOSOMAL	ROBOT-LIKE	ROUGHENED	RUNTINESS
REVERSION	RICE PADDY	ROCHESTER	ROUGH-HEWN	RUN TO
REVERTING	RICE PAPER	ROCKBOUND	ROUGHNECK	SEED
REVERTIVE	RICKSHAWS	ROCK CAKES	ROUGHNESS	RUPTURING
REVETMENT	RICOCHETS	ROCKERIES	ROUGHSHOD	RUSH HOURS
REVIEWERS	RIDDANCES	ROCKETEER	ROUNDELAY	RUSHINESS
REVIEWING	RIDERLESS	ROCKETING	ROUNDHEAD	RUSHINGLY
REVISABLE	RIDGELING	ROCKFALLS	ROUNDNESS	RUSHLIGHT

RUSH LIGHT	SAINTLILY	SAND TRAPS	SAUCEPANS	SCHILLING
RUSSETISH	SAINT-OUEN	SANFORIZE	SAUCINESS	SCHISTOSE
RUSTICATE	SAINT PAUL	SANGFROID	SAUNTERED	SCHIZOPOD
RUSTICITY	SAINT'S	SANITARIA	SAUNTERER	SCHLEPPED
RUSTINESS	DAY	SANITIZED	SAUTERNES	SCHLIEREN
RUSTPROOF	SALAAMING	SAN MARINO	SAVOURING	SCHLIERIC
RUTABAGAS	SALACIOUS	SANS SERIF	SAXIFRAGE	SCHMALTZY
RUTACEOUS	SALAD DAYS	SANTA CRUZ	SAXOPHONE	SCHNAUZER
RUTHENIAN	SALAMANCA	SANTANDER	SCABBARDS	SCHNITZEL
RUTHENIUM	SALARYMAN	SANTONICA	SCABBIEST	SCHNORKEL
RUTILATED	SALERATUS	SAPHENOUS	SCABIETIC	SCHOLARLY
RUTTINESS	SALEROOMS	SAPIENTLY	SCAFFOLDS	SCHOLIAST
RUWENZORI	SALESGIRL	SAPODILLA	SCAGLIOLA	SCHOOLBOY
	SALESROOM	SAPPHIRES	SCALAWAGS	SCHOOLING
S	SALES SLIP	SAPPINESS	SCALDFISH	SCHOONERS
SABADILLA	SALES TALK	SAPRAEMIA	SCALINESS	SCIENTIAL
SABOTAGED	SALIMETER	SAPRAEMIC	SCALLIONS	SCIENTISM
SABOTEURS	SALIMETRY	SAPROLITE	SCALLOPED	SCIENTIST
SACCHARIN	SALISBURY	SAPROZOIC	SCALLOPER	SCIMITARS
SACCULATE	SALIVATED	SAPSUCKER	SCALLYWAG	SCINTILLA
SACKCLOTH	SALMONOID	SARABANDE	SCAMPERED	SCIOMANCY
SACK RACES	SALOON BAR	SARABANDS	SCAMPERER	SCIRRHOID
SACRAMENT	SALPIFORM	SARACENIC	SCANTIEST	SCIRRHOUS
SACRARIUM	SALTATION	SARCASTIC	SCANTLING	SCLERITIC
SACRED COW	SALTINESS	SARCOCARP	SCANTNESS	SCLERITIS
SACRIFICE	SALTLICKS	SARDINIAN	SCAPA FLOW	SCLEROSAL
SACRILEGE	SALTPETRE	SARGASSUM	SCAPEGOAT	SCLEROSED
SACRISTAN	SALT SPOON	SARTORIAL	SCAPHOPOD	SCLEROSES
SADDENING	SALTWATER	SARTORIUS	SCAPOLITE	SCLEROSIS
SADDLEBAG	SALTWORKS	SASHAYING	SCARABOID	SCLEROTIC
SADDLEBOW	SALVAGING	SASKATOON	SCARECROW	SCOLDABLE
SAFEGUARD	SALVATION	SASSAFRAS	SCARFSKIN	SCOLDINGS
SAFE HOUSE	SAMARITAN	SASSENACH	SCARIFIED	SCOLECITE
SAFELIGHT	SAMARKAND	SATANISTS	SCARIFIER	SCOLIOSIS
SAFETY NET	SANATORIA	SATELLITE	SCARINGLY	SCOLIOTIC
SAFETY PIN	SANCTIONS	SATIATING	SCARPERED	SCOLLOPED
SAFFLOWER	SANCTUARY	SATIATION	SCATOLOGY	SCOMBROID
SAFRANINE	SANDALLED	SATINWOOD	SCATTERED	SCOPOLINE
SAGACIOUS	SANDBANKS	SATIRICAL	SCATTERER	SCOPULATE
SAGEBRUSH	SANDBLAST	SATIRIZED	SCATTIEST	SCORBUTIC
SAGE DERBY	SAND-BLIND	SATIRIZER	SCAVENGED	SCORCHERS
SAGE GREEN	SANDBOXES	SATISFIED	SCAVENGER	SCORCHING
SAGITTATE	SAND DUNES	SATISFIER	SCENARIOS	SCORECARD
SAILBOARD	SAND FLIES	SATURABLE	SCENARIST	SCORIFIER
SAILCLOTH	SANDHURST	SATURATED	SCENTLESS	SCORPIOID
SAILOR HAT	SANDINESS	SATURATER	SCEPTICAL	SCORPIONS
SAILPLANE	SANDPAPER	SATURDAYS	SCHEDULAR	SCOTCH EGG
SAINTE FOY	SANDPIPER	SATURNIAN	SCHEDULED	SCOTCHING
SAINT GALL	SANDSHOES	SATURNIID	SCHEDULES	SCOUNDREL
SAINTHOOD	SANDSTONE	SATURNINE	SCHEELITE	SCOURGING
SAINT JOHN	SANDSTORM	SATURNISM	SCHEMATIC	SCOURINGS

SCRABBLED	SCRUMPING	SECTIONAL	SENESCENT	SERRIFORM
SCRABBLER	SCRUNCHED	SECTIONED	SENESCHAL	SERRULATE
SCRAGGIER	SCRUNCHIE	SECTORIAL	SENIORITY	SERVERIES
SCRAGGILY	SCRUPLING	SECUNDINE	SENORITAS	SERVICING
SCRAGGING	SCUFFLING	SECURABLE	SENSATION	SERVIETTE
SCRAMBLED	SCULLIONS	SEDATIVES	SENSELESS	SERVILELY
SCRAMBLER	SCULPTORS	SEDENTARY	SENSILLUM	SERVILITY
SCRAMBLES	SCULPTURE	SEDIMENTS	SENSITIVE	SERVITORS
SCRAMMING	SCUPPERED	SEDITIOUS	SENSITIZE	SERVITUDE
SCRAPABLE	SCURRYING	SEDUCIBLE	SENSORIUM	SESSILITY
SCRAPBOOK	SCUTATION	SEDUCTION	SENTENCED	SESSIONAL
SCRAP HEAP	SCUTCHEON	SEDUCTIVE	SENTENCES	SETACEOUS
SCRAPINGS	SCUTELLAR	SEEDINESS	SENTIENCE	SET FIRE
SCRAP IRON	SCUTELLUM	SEEDLINGS	SENTIMENT	TO
SCRAPPIER	SCUTIFORM	SEEMINGLY	SENTINELS	SET PIECES
SCRAPPILY	SCUTTLING	SEESAWING	SENTRY BOX	SET SPEECH
SCRAPPING	SEABOARDS	SEGMENTAL	SEPARABLE	SETSQUARE
SCRATCHED	SEA BREEZE	SEGMENTED	SEPARABLY	SET SQUARE
SCRATCHER	SEA CHANGE	SEGREGATE	SEPARATED	SET THEORY
SCRATCHES	SEAFARING	SEIGNEURS	SEPARATES	SETTLED IN
SCRAWLING	SEAFRONTS	SELACHIAN	SEPARATOR	SETTLINGS
SCRAWNIER	SEAHORSES	SELECTING	SEPHARDIC	SET-TOP
SCRAWNILY	SEAL-POINT	SELECTION	SEPIOLITE	BOX
SCREAMING	SEALYHAMS	SELECTIVE	SEPTARIAN	SEVENFOLD
SCREECHED	SEAMINESS	SELECTORS	SEPTARIUM	SEVENTEEN
SCREECHER	SEAPLANES	SELENIOUS	SEPTEMBER	SEVENTIES
SCREECHES	SEA POWERS	SELF-ABUSE	SEPTENARY	SEVERABLE
SCREENING	SEARCHING	SELF-DOUBT	SEPTICITY	SEVERALLY
SCREWBALL	SEASCAPES	SELF-DRIVE	SEPTUPLET	SEVERALTY
SCREWIEST	SEA SHANTY	SELFISHLY	SEPULCHRE	SEVERANCE
SCREW TOPS	SEASHELLS	SELLOTAPE	SEPULTURE	SEX APPEAL
SCREWWORM	SEASONING	SELL SHORT	SEQUACITY	SEXENNIAL
SCRIBBLED	SEAT BELTS	SEMANTICS	SEQUENCER	SEX OBJECT
SCRIBBLER	SEA URCHIN	SEMAPHORE	SEQUENCES	SEX ORGANS
SCRIBBLES	SEAWORTHY	SEMBLANCE	SEQUESTER	SEXTUPLET
SCRIMMAGE	SEBACEOUS	SEMESTERS	SERAGLIOS	SEXUALITY
SCRIMPILY	SECATEURS	SEMESTRAL	SERENADED	SFORZANDO
SCRIMPING	SECESSION	SEMI-BANTU	SERENADER	SGRAFFITO
SCRIMSHAW	SECLUDING	SEMIBREVE	SERENADES	SHABBIEST
SCRIPTURE	SECLUSION	SEMICOLON	SERGEANCY	SHACKLING
SCROLLING	SECLUSIVE	SEMIFINAL	SERGEANTS	SHADINESS
SCROUNGED	SECONDARY	SEMIFLUID	SERIALISM	SHADOW-BOX
SCROUNGER	SECONDERS	SEMILUNAR	SERIALIZE	SHADOWIER
SCRUBBERS	SECONDING	SEMIOTICS	SERICEOUS	SHADOWING
SCRUBBIER	SECRETARY	SEMIRIGID	SERIGRAPH	SHAGGIEST
SCRUBBING	SECRETING	SEMISOLID	SERIOUSLY	SHAKE A
SCRUBLAND	SECRETION	SEMISWEET	SERMONIZE	LEG
SCRUFFIER	SECRETIVE	SEMITONES	SEROLOGIC	SHAKEDOWN
SCRUMHALF	SECRETORY	SEMITONIC	SEROTINAL	SHAKEOUTS
SCRUM HALF	SECTARIAN	SEMIVOCAL	SEROTONIN	SHAKINESS
SCRUMMAGE	SECTILITY	SEMIVOWEL	SERRATION	SHALLOWED

213

SHALLOWER	SHININESS	SHOWPIECE	SIDEWARDS	SINGULARS
SHALLOWLY	SHINNYING	SHOW PIECE	SIGHTABLE	SINGULTUS
SHAMANISM	SHIPBOARD	SHOWPLACE	SIGHTINGS	SINHALESE
SHAMANIST	SHIPMATES	SHOWROOMS	SIGHTLESS	SINISTRAL
SHAMATEUR	SHIPMENTS	SHOW TRIAL	SIGHT-READ	SINOLOGUE
SHAMBLING	SHIPOWNER	SHREDDERS	SIGHTSEER	SINUOSITY
SHAMBOLIC	SHIPSHAPE	SHREDDING	SIGMATION	SINUOUSLY
SHAMELESS	SHIPWRECK	SHREWDEST	SIGNAL BOX	SINUSITIS
SHAMPOOED	SHIPYARDS	SHRIEKING	SIGNALING	SIPHONAGE
SHAMPOOER	SHIRTIEST	SHRILLEST	SIGNALIZE	SIPHONING
SHANGRI-LA	SHIRTTAIL	SHRINKAGE	SIGNALLED	SISYPHEAN
SHAN STATE	SHITTIEST	SHRINKING	SIGNALLER	SIT AT
SHAPELESS	SHIVERING	SHRIVELED	SIGNALMAN	HOME
SHAPELIER	SHOCKABLE	SHROUDING	SIGNALMEN	SITATUNGA
SHARECROP	SHODDIEST	SHRUBBERY	SIGNATORY	SITUATING
SHARE SHOP	SHOEHORNS	SHRUGGING	SIGNATURE	SITUATION
SHAREWARE	SHOELACES	SHUBUNKIN	SIGNBOARD	SITZKREIG
SHARKSKIN	SHOEMAKER	SHUDDERED	SIGNIFIED	SIX-FOOTER
SHARPENED	SHOESHINE	SHUFBOARD	SIGNIFIER	SIXPENCES
SHARPENER	SHOETREES	SHUFFLERS	SIGNORINA	SIXTEENMO
SHARP-EYED	SHOOT-'EM-	SHUFFLING	SIGNPOSTS	SIXTEENTH
SHARPNESS	UP	SHUNNABLE	SIKKIMESE	SIXTH FORM
SHATTERED	SHOOTINGS	SHUTDOWNS	SILENCERS	SIXTIETHS
SHATTERER	SHOOT-OUTS	SHUTTERED	SILENCING	SIZARSHIP
SHEARLING	SHOP FLOOR	SHUTTLING	SILICATES	SKAGERRAK
SHEATFISH	SHORELESS	SIBILANCE	SILICEOUS	SKEDADDLE
SHEATHING	SHORELINE	SIBILANTS	SILICOSIS	SKELETONS
SHEEPDIPS	SHORTAGES	SIBYLLINE	SILIQUOSE	SKEPTICAL
SHEEPDOGS	SHORTCAKE	SICCATIVE	SILKALINE	SKETCHERS
SHEEPFOLD	SHORT CUTS	SICKENING	SILKINESS	SKETCHIER
SHEEPSKIN	SHORTENED	SICK LEAVE	SILKWORMS	SKETCHILY
SHEEPWALK	SHORTENER	SICKLIEST	SILLABUBS	SKETCHING
SHEERLEGS	SHORTFALL	SICKROOMS	SILLINESS	SKETCHPAD
SHEERNESS	SHORTHAND	SIC PASSIM	SILTATION	SKEWBALDS
SHEFFIELD	SHORT-HAUL	SIDEBOARD	SILVERING	SKEWERING
SHEIKHDOM	SHORTHORN	SIDEBURNS	SIMAROUBA	SKEW-WHIFF
SHELDUCKS	SHORT LIST	SIDE-DRESS	SIMILARLY	SKIASCOPE
SHELF LIFE	SHORTNESS	SIDE ISSUE	SIMMERING	SKIASCOPY
SHELLFIRE	SHORT SLIP	SIDEKICKS	SIMPATICO	SKIDPROOF
SHELLFISH	SHORT-TERM	SIDELIGHT	SIMPERING	SKIJORING
SHELTERED	SHORT TIME	SIDELINED	SIMPLETON	SKILFULLY
SHELTERER	SHORT WAVE	SIDELINES	SIMULACRA	SKIMMINGS
SHEPHERDS	SHOT TOWER	SIDE ORDER	SIMULATED	SKIMPIEST
SHERBORNE	SHOULDERS	SIDERITIC	SIMULATOR	SKIN-DIVED
SHIELDING	SHOVELING	SIDEROSIS	SINCERELY	SKIN DIVER
SHIFTIEST	SHOVELLED	SIDEROTIC	SINCERITY	SKIN FLICK
SHIFT KEYS	SHOWCASES	SIDESHOWS	SINECURES	SKINFLINT
SHIFTLESS	SHOWDOWNS	SIDESLIPS	SINGAPORE	SKIN GRAFT
SHILLINGS	SHOWERING	SIDESTEPS	SINGINGLY	SKINHEADS
SHIMMERED	SHOWGIRLS	SIDESWIPE	SINGLETON	SKINNIEST
SHINBONES	SHOWINESS	SIDETRACK	SINGSONGS	SKIN-TIGHT

SKI PLANES	SLOBBERER	SNAKESKIN	SOARINGLY	SOLSTICES
SKIPPERED	SLOPINGLY	SNAKINESS	SOBBINGLY	SOLUTIONS
SKITTERED	SLOPPIEST	SNAPPABLE	SOBERNESS	SOLUTREAN
SKIVVYING	SLOUCH HAT	SNAPPIEST	SOBRIQUET	SOLVATION
SKULLCAPS	SLOUCHILY	SNAPSHOTS	SOB SISTER	SOMBREROS
SKYDIVERS	SLOUCHING	SNARE DRUM	SOCIALISM	SOMEPLACE
SKYDIVING	SLOUGHING	SNARINGLY	SOCIALIST	SOMETHING
SKYJACKED	SLOVAKIAN	SNATCHILY	SOCIALITE	SOMETIMES
SKYJACKER	SLOVENIAN	SNATCHING	SOCIALITY	SOMEWHERE
SKYLARKED	SLOWCOACH	SNAZZIEST	SOCIALIZE	SOMMELIER
SKYLARKER	SLOWDOWNS	SNEAKIEST	SOCIETIES	SOMNOLENT
SKYLIGHTS	SLOW MATCH	SNICKERED	SOCIOLOGY	SONGBIRDS
SKYROCKET	SLOWWORMS	SNIDENESS	SOCIOPATH	SONGBOOKS
SKYWRITER	SLUDGIEST	SNIFFLERS	SODA WATER	SONG CYCLE
SLACKENED	SLUGGARDS	SNIFFLING	SODOMITES	SONGOLOLO
SLACKNESS	SLUMBERED	SNIGGERED	SOFTENING	SONGSTERS
SLAGHEAPS	SLUMBERER	SNIPEFISH	SOFT FRUIT	SONIC BOOM
SLANDERED	SLUSH FUND	SNITCHING	SOFT GOODS	SONNETEER
SLANDERER	SLUSHIEST	SNIVELING	SOFT METAL	SON-OF-A-
SLANTWISE	SMALL ARMS	SNIVELLED	SOFT-PEDAL	GUN
SLAPHAPPY	SMALL BEER	SNIVELLER	SOFT SPOTS	SONS-IN-
SLAPSTICK	SMALLNESS	SNOOKERED	SOFT TOUCH	LAW
SLATINESS	SMALL TALK	SNOOTIEST	SOFTWOODS	SOOTINESS
SLATTERNS	SMALL-TIME	SNOTTIEST	SOGGINESS	SOPHISTER
SLAUGHTER	SMARMIEST	SNOWBALLS	SOI-DISANT	SOPHISTIC
SLAVERING	SMART ALEC	SNOWBERRY	SOJOURNED	SOPHISTRY
SLAVISHLY	SMART CARD	SNOW-BLIND	SOJOURNER	SOPHOMORE
SLAVONIAN	SMARTENED	SNOWBLINK	SOLAR CELL	SOPORIFIC
SLEAZIEST	SMARTNESS	SNOWBOUND	SOLARIUMS	SOPPINESS
SLEEKNESS	SMASHABLE	SNOWDONIA	SOLAR YEAR	SOPRANINO
SLEEPIEST	SMATTERER	SNOWDRIFT	SOLDERING	SORCERERS
SLEEPLESS	SMEAR TEST	SNOWDROPS	SOLDIERED	SORCERESS
SLEEPWALK	SMELLIEST	SNOWFALLS	SOLDIERLY	SORCEROUS
SLICEABLE	SMILINGLY	SNOWFIELD	SOLDIER ON	SORE POINT
SLICKNESS	SMIRCHING	SNOWFLAKE	SOLECISMS	SORITICAL
SLIDE RULE	SMOKELESS	SNOW GOOSE	SOLEMNELY	SORRINESS
SLIGHTEST	SMOKINESS	SNOWINESS	SOLEMNITY	SORROWFUL
SLIGHTING	SMOLDERED	SNOWSHOER	SOLEMNIZE	SORROWING
SLIMINESS	SMOOCHING	SNOWSHOES	SOLENODON	SORTILEGE
SLINGSHOT	SMOOTHEST	SNOWSTORM	SOLFATARA	SORTITION
SLINKIEST	SMOOTHIES	SNOW-WHITE	SOLFEGGIO	SOSNOWIEC
SLIPCASES	SMOOTHING	SNUB-NOSED	SOLFERINO	SOSTENUTO
SLIPKNOTS	SMOTHERED	SNUFFLING	SOLICITED	SOTTO VOCE
SLIPNOOSE	SMUGGLERS	SNUGGLING	SOLICITOR	SOUBRETTE
SLIPPAGES	SMUGGLING	SOAKINGLY	SOLIDNESS	SOULFULLY
SLIPPIEST	SMUTTIEST	SOAPBERRY	SOLILOQUY	SOUL MUSIC
SLIP ROADS	SNACK BARS	SOAPBOXES	SOLIPSISM	SOUNDABLE
SLIPSHEET	SNAFFLING	SOAPINESS	SOLIPSIST	SOUNDINGS
SLITHERED	SNAIL MAIL	SOAP OPERA	SOLITAIRE	SOUNDLESS
SLIVOVITZ	SNAKEBITE	SOAPSTONE	SOLONCHAK	SOUNDNESS
SLOBBERED	SNAKEROOT	SOAPSUDSY	SOLOTHURN	SOUNDPOST

SOUND POST	SPEARWORT	SPINNERET	SPOROZOAN	SQUEAKERS
SOUP SPOON	SPECIALLY	SPINOSITY	SPORTIEST	SQUEAKIER
SOUR CREAM	SPECIALTY	SPINSTERS	SPORTS CAR	SQUEAKING
SOUTH BEND	SPECIFICS	SPINULOSE	SPORTSMAN	SQUEALERS
SOUTHDOWN	SPECIFIED	SPIRALING	SPORTSMEN	SQUEALING
SOUTHEAST	SPECIFIER	SPIRALLED	SPORULATE	SQUEAMISH
SOUTHERLY	SPECIMENS	SPIRILLAR	SPOT CHECK	SQUEEGEES
SOUTHPAWS	SPECTACLE	SPIRILLUM	SPOTLIGHT	SQUEEZERS
SOUTH POLE	SPECTATED	SPIRITING	SPOTTABLE	SQUEEZING
SOUTHPORT	SPECTATOR	SPIRITOSO	SPOTTIEST	SQUELCHED
SOUTHWARD	SPECULATE	SPIRITOUS	SPRAINING	SQUELCHER
SOUTHWARK	SPEECH DAY	SPIRITUAL	SPRAWLING	SQUIDGIER
SOUTHWEST	SPEECHIFY	SPIROGYRA	SPRAY GUNS	SQUIFFIER
SOUVENIRS	SPEEDBOAT	SPITFIRES	SPREADING	SQUIGGLER
SOU'WESTER	SPEEDIEST	SPIT IT	SPRIGHTLY	SQUIGGLES
SOVEREIGN	SPEEDSTER	OUT	SPRINGBOK	SQUINTING
SOVIETISM	SPEED TRAP	SPITTOONS	SPRINGIER	SQUIRMING
SOVIETIST	SPEEDWAYS	SPLASHIER	SPRINGILY	SQUIRRELS
SOVIETIZE	SPEEDWELL	SPLASHILY	SPRINGING	SQUIRTERS
SOYA BEANS	SPELLABLE	SPLASHING	SPRINKLED	SQUIRTING
SPACEBAND	SPELLBIND	SPLATTING	SPRINKLER	SQUISHIER
SPACED OUT	SPELLINGS	SPLAYFOOT	SPRINKLES	SQUISHING
SPACELESS	SPELUNKER	SPLEENFUL	SPRINTERS	SQUITTERS
SPACEPORT	SPENDABLE	SPLEENISH	SPRINTING	STABILITY
SPACESHIP	SPERMATIC	SPLENDOUR	SPRITSAIL	STABILIZE
SPACESUIT	SPERMATID	SPLENETIC	SPROCKETS	STABLE BOY
SPACE-TIME	SPHAGNOUS	SPLENITIS	SPROUTING	STAGE DOOR
SPACEWALK	SPHAGNUMS	SPLINTERS	SPUNKIEST	STAGEHAND
SPADEFISH	SPHENODON	SPLINTERY	SPUTTERED	STAGE HAND
SPADEWORK	SPHERICAL	SPLIT ENDS	SPUTTERER	STAGE NAME
SPAGHETTI	SPHEROIDS	SPLIT PEAS	SQUABBLED	STAGGERED
SPANGLING	SPHERULAR	SPLIT RING	SQUABBLER	STAGGERER
SPANIARDS	SPHINCTER	SPLITTING	SQUABBLES	STAGHOUND
SPANKINGS	SPHYGMOID	SPLOSHING	SQUAD CARS	STAGINESS
SPARENESS	SPICINESS	SPLURGING	SQUADRONS	STAGNANCY
SPARE PART	SPICULATE	SPLUTTERS	SQUALIDLY	STAGNATED
SPARERIBS	SPIDERMAN	SPODUMENE	SQUALLIER	STAG PARTY
SPARE TYRE	SPIDERWEB	SPOKEN FOR	SQUALLING	STAIDNESS
SPARINGLY	SPIELBERG	SPOKESMAN	SQUAMOSAL	STAINABLE
SPARKLERS	SPIKENARD	SPONGE BAG	SQUARE LEG	STAINLESS
SPARKLING	SPIKE-RUSH	SPONGIEST	SQUARE ONE	STAIRCASE
SPARK PLUG	SPIKINESS	SPONSORED	SQUARROSE	STAIRHEAD
SPARTEINE	SPILLIKIN	SPOOKIEST	SQUASHIER	STAIRWELL
SPASMODIC	SPILLWAYS	SPOONBILL	SQUASHILY	STALEMATE
SPATIALLY	SPINDLIER	SPOON-FEED	SQUASHING	STALENESS
SPATTERED	SPIN-DRIED	SPOONFULS	SQUATNESS	STALINISM
SPATULATE	SPINDRIFT	SPOONSFUL	SQUATTERS	STALINIST
SPEAKABLE	SPIN-DRYER	SPOROCARP	SQUATTEST	STALL-FEED
SPEAKEASY	SPINELESS	SPOROCYST	SQUATTING	STALLIONS
SPEARHEAD	SPININESS	SPOROCYTE	SQUAWKERS	STALWARTS
SPEARMINT	SPINNAKER	SPOROGONY	SQUAWKING	STAMINATE

STAMINODE	STEADFAST	STILLNESS	STONEWORK	STRESSFUL
STAMINODY	STEADIEST	STILL ROOM	STONEWORT	STRESSING
STAMMERED	STEADYING	STILTEDLY	STONINESS	STRETCHED
STAMMERER	STEAMBOAT	STIMULANT	STOPCOCKS	STRETCHER
STAMPEDED	STEAMED-UP	STIMULATE	STOPLIGHT	STRETCHES
STAMPEDER	STEAMIEST	STINGIEST	STOPOVERS	STRETFORD
STAMPEDES	STEAM IRON	STINGRAYS	STOPPABLE	STRIATION
STAMP MILL	STEAMROLL	STINK-BOMB	STOPPAGES	STRICTEST
STANCHING	STEAMSHIP	STINKHORN	STOPPERED	STRICTURE
STANCHION	STEATITIC	STINKWEED	STOP PRESS	STRIDENCE
STANDARDS	STEEL BAND	STINKWOOD	STOPWATCH	STRIDENCY
STAND FIRM	STEELHEAD	STIPIFORM	STOREROOM	STRIKE PAY
STAND OVER	STEELIEST	STIPITATE	STORMIEST	STRINGENT
STANDPIPE	STEEL WOOL	STIPPLING	STORNOWAY	STRINGIER
STAPEDIAL	STEELWORK	STIPULATE	STORYBOOK	STRINGILY
STAR-APPLE	STEELYARD	STIR-FRIED	STORY LINE	STRINGING
STARBOARD	STEEPENED	STIRRABLE	STORYLINE	STRIP CLUB
STARBURST	STEEPNESS	STITCHING	STOUTNESS	STRIPIEST
STARCHIER	STEERABLE	STOCKADED	STOVEPIPE	STRIPLING
STARCHILY	STEERSMAN	STOCKADES	STOWAWAYS	STRIPPERS
STARCHING	STEERSMEN	STOCKCARS	STRADDLED	STRIPPING
STARE DOWN	STELLULAR	STOCK CUBE	STRADDLER	STROBILUS
STARGAZER	STENCILED	STOCKFISH	STRAGGLED	STROLLERS
STARKNESS	STENOTYPE	STOCKHOLM	STRAGGLER	STROLLING
STARLIGHT	STENOTYPY	STOCKIEST	STRAIGHTS	STROMATIC
STARLINGS	STEPCHILD	STOCKINET	STRAINERS	STRONGARM
STARRIEST	STERADIAN	STOCKINGS	STRAINING	STRONGBOX
STAR SIGNS	STERILANT	STOCKISTS	STRALSUND	STRONGEST
STARTLING	STERILITY	STOCKPILE	STRANGELY	STRONGYLE
STATE DUMA	STERILIZE	STOCKPORT	STRANGERS	STRONTIAN
STATEHOOD	STERNMOST	STOCKPOTS	STRANGEST	STRONTIUM
STATELESS	STERNNESS	STOCKROOM	STRANGLED	STROPPIER
STATEMENT	STERNPOST	STOCK TAKE	STRANGLER	STRUCTURE
STATEROOM	STEVEDORE	STOCKYARD	STRANGLES	STRUGGLED
STATESIDE	STEVENAGE	STODGIEST	STRANGURY	STRUGGLER
STATESMAN	STICK AT	STOICALLY	STRANRAER	STRUGGLES
STATESMEN	IT	STOKEHOLD	STRAPLESS	STRUMATIC
STATIONED	STICKIEST	STOKEHOLE	STRAPPING	STRUMMING
STATIONER	STICKLERS	STOLIDITY	STRATAGEM	STRUMPETS
STATISTIC	STICKPINS	STOMACHED	STRATEGIC	STRUNG-OUT
STATOCYST	STICKSEED	STOMACHIC	STRAW POLL	STRUTTING
STATOLITH	STICKWEED	STONECHAT	STREAKERS	STRYCHNIC
STATUETTE	STICKY BUN	STONE-COLD	STREAKIER	STUBBIEST
STATUS QUO	STICKY END	STONECROP	STREAKILY	STUDBOOKS
STATUTORY	STIFFENED	STONE-DEAD	STREAKING	STUDHORSE
STAUNCHED	STIFFENER	STONE-DEAF	STREAMERS	STUFFIEST
STAUNCHER	STIFFNESS	STONEFISH	STREAMING	STUMBLING
STAUNCHLY	STIGMATIC	STONELESS	STREETCAR	STUMPIEST
STAVANGER	STILETTOS	STONE-LILY	STREISAND	STUPEFIED
STAVROPOL	STILLBORN	STONEWALL	STRENGTHS	STUPEFIER
ST BERNARD	STILL LIFE	STONEWARE	STRENUOUS	STUPIDEST

STUPIDITY	SUBMITTER	SUFFOCATE	SUPERHEAT	SUSPECTED
STUPOROUS	SUBMUCOSA	SUFFRAGAN	SUPERHERO	SUSPECTER
STURDIEST	SUBNORMAL	SUFFRAGES	SUPERIORS	SUSPENDED
STURGEONS	SUBORNING	SUFFUSING	SUPERNOVA	SUSPENDER
STUTTERED	SUBPHYLAR	SUFFUSION	SUPERPOSE	SUSPENSOR
STUTTERER	SUBPHYLUM	SUFFUSIVE	SUPERSEDE	SUSPICION
STUTTGART	SUBPOENAS	SUGAR BEET	SUPERSTAR	SUSTAINED
STYLEBOOK	SUBREGION	SUGAR CANE	SUPERVENE	SUSTAINER
STYLELESS	SUBROGATE	SUGARCANE	SUPERVISE	SUSURRANT
STYLIFORM	SUBSCRIBE	SUGGESTED	SUPINATOR	SUSURRATE
STYLISHLY	SUBSCRIPT	SUGGESTER	SUPPERADD	SUZERAINS
STYLISTIC	SUBSIDIES	SUITCASES	SUPPLIANT	SWADDLING
STYLIZING	SUBSIDING	SULCATION	SUPPLIERS	SWAGGERED
STYLOBATE	SUBSIDIZE	SULKINESS	SUPPLYING	SWAGGERER
STYLOLITE	SUBSISTED	SULLENEST	SUPPORTED	SWAHILIAN
STYLOPIZE	SUBSISTER	SULLIABLE	SUPPORTER	SWALLOWED
STYPTICAL	SUBSOCIAL	SULPHATES	SUPPOSING	SWALLOWER
STYROFOAM	SUBSOILER	SULPHIDES	SUPPURATE	SWAMPLAND
SUABILITY	SUBSTANCE	SULPHITIC	SUPREMACY	SWANKIEST
SUAVENESS	SUBSTRATA	SULPHURET	SUPREMELY	SWANS DOWN
SUBALPINE	SUBSTRATE	SULPHURYL	SUPREMITY	SWAN'S-
SUBALTERN	SUBSUMING	SULTANATE	SURAKARTA	DOWN
SUBARCTIC	SUBSYSTEM	SULTRIEST	SURCHARGE	SWANSONGS
SUBATOMIC	SUBTENANT	SUMMARIES	SURCINGLE	SWAP MEETS
SUBCLIMAX	SUBTENDED	SUMMARILY	SURCULOSE	SWARTHIER
SUBCORTEX	SUBTILIZE	SUMMARIZE	SURE THING	SWARTHILY
SUBDEACON	SUBTITLED	SUMMATION	SURFACING	SWASTIKAS
SUBDIVIDE	SUBTITLES	SUMMERING	SURFBOARD	SWATHABLE
SUBDUABLE	SUBTOTALS	SUMMING-UP	SURFEITED	SWAYINGLY
SUBDUEDLY	SUBVERTED	SUMMONING	SURFEITER	SWAZILAND
SUBEDITED	SUBVERTER	SUMMONSED	SURFPERCH	SWEARWORD
SUBEDITOR	SUBWOOFER	SUMMONSES	SURGEONCY	SWEATBAND
SUBFAMILY	SUCCEEDED	SUMPTUARY	SURGERIES	SWEATIEST
SUBJACENT	SUCCEEDER	SUMPTUOUS	SURLINESS	SWEATSHOP
SUBJECTED	SUCCENTOR	SUNBATHED	SURMISING	SWEEPBACK
SUBJOINED	SUCCESSES	SUNBATHER	SURPASSED	SWEEPINGS
SUB JUDICE	SUCCESSOR	SUNBURNED	SURPLICES	SWEET CORN
SUBJUGATE	SUCCINATE	SUNDERING	SURPLUSES	SWEETENER
SUBLEASED	SUCCOURED	SUNDOWNER	SURPRISED	SWEETMEAT
SUBLEASES	SUCCOURER	SUNDSVALL	SURPRISER	SWEETNESS
SUBLESSEE	SUCCULENT	SUNFLOWER	SURPRISES	SWEET PEAS
SUBLESSOR	SUCCUMBED	SUN LOUNGE	SURRENDER	SWEET TALK
SUBLIMATE	SUCCUMBER	SUNNINESS	SURROGACY	SWELLFISH
SUBLIMELY	SUCKLINGS	SUNSHADES	SURROGATE	SWELLINGS
SUBLIMITY	SUCTIONAL	SUNSTROKE	SURROUNDS	SWELTERED
SUBLUNARY	SUCTORIAL	SUNTANNED	SURTITLES	SWEPT-BACK
SUBMARINE	SUDORIFIC	SUN VISORS	SURVEYING	SWEPTWING
SUBMENTAL	SUFFERERS	SUPERABLE	SURVEYORS	SWERVABLE
SUBMERGED	SUFFERING	SUPERCOOL	SURVIVALS	SWIFTNESS
SUBMITTAL	SUFFICING	SUPEREGOS	SURVIVING	SWIMMABLE
SUBMITTED	SUFFIXION	SUPERFINE	SURVIVORS	SWIMMERET

SWINDLERS	SYNCOPATE	TAILGATED	TARGETING	TEDDY BEAR
SWINDLING	SYNCRETIC	TAILGATES	TARMACKED	TEDDY BOYS
SWINEHERD	SYNCYTIUM	TAILLIGHT	TARNISHED	TEDIOUSLY
SWINGEING	SYNDACTYL	TAIL-LIGHT	TARNISHER	TEENAGERS
SWING-WING	SYNDICATE	TAILORING	TARPAULIN	TEE SHIRTS
SWINISHLY	SYNDROMES	TAILPIECE	TARRAGONA	TEETERING
SWISS ROLL	SYNDROMIC	TAIL PIPES	TARTARIZE	TELECASTS
SWITCHING	SYNECTICS	TAILPLANE	TARTAROUS	TELEGENIC
SWITCH OFF	SYNERESIS	TAILSPINS	TASIMETER	TELEGONIC
SWIVELING	SYNERGISM	TAILSTOCK	TASIMETRY	TELEGRAMS
SWIVELLED	SYNERGIST	TAILWHEEL	TASK FORCE	TELEGRAPH
SWORDBILL	SYNIZESIS	TAILWINDS	TASMANIAN	TELEMETER
SWORDFISH	SYNKARYON	TAIWANESE	TASMAN SEA	TELEMETRY
SWORDPLAY	SYNOEKETE	TAKAMATSU	TASTE BUDS	TELEOLOGY
SWORDSMAN	SYNONYMIC	TAKEAWAYS	TASTELESS	TELEPATHY
SWORDSMEN	SYNOVITIC	TAKE LEAVE	TASTINESS	TELEPHONE
SWORDTAIL	SYNOVITIS	TAKE NOTES	TATTINESS	TELEPHONY
SYBARITES	SYNTACTIC	TAKEOVERS	TATTOOING	TELESCOPE
SYBARITIC	SYNTHESES	TAKE STEPS	TATTOOIST	TELESCOPY
SYCAMORES	SYNTHESIS	TAKE STOCK	TAUTENING	TELESTICH
SYCOPHANT	SYNTHETIC	TAKING OFF	TAUTOLOGY	TELEVISED
SYKTYVKAR	SYPHERING	TALIGRADE	TAUTONYMY	TELLINGLY
SYLLABARY	SYPHILOID	TALISMANS	TAXACEOUS	TELLIALES
SYLLABIFY	SYPHILOMA	TALKATIVE	TAX HAVENS	TELLURATE
SYLLABISM	SYPHONING	TALKING-TO	TAXIDERMY	TELLURIAN
SYLLABLES	SYRINGEAL	TALK SHOWS	TAXIMETER	TELLURIDE
SYLLABUBS	SYRINGING	TALL ORDER	TAXI RANKS	TELLURION
SYLLEPSIS	SYSTALTIC	TALL STORY	TAXONOMIC	TELLURITE
SYLLEPTIC		TALMUDISM	TAXPAYERS	TELLURIUM
SYLLOGISM	**T**	TALMUDIST	TEA BREAKS	TELLURIZE
SYLLOGIZE	TABESCENT	TAMARINDS	TEACHABLE	TELLUROUS
SYLPHLIKE	TABLATURE	TAMIL NADU	TEA CHESTS	TELOPHASE
SYLVANITE	TABLELAND	TAMOXIFEN	TEA CLOTHS	TELPHERIC
SYMBIOSIS	TABLEMATS	TAMPERING	TEA COSIES	TEMAZEPAM
SYMBIOTIC	TABLEWARE	TANDOORIS	TEAGARDEN	TEMPERATE
SYMBOLISM	TABLE WINE	TANGERINE	TEAHOUSES	TEMPERING
SYMBOLIST	TABULABLE	TANNERIES	TEAKETTLE	TEMPLATES
SYMBOLIZE	TABULATED	TANTALATE	TEALEAVES	TEMPORARY
SYMBOLOGY	TABULATOR	TANTALITE	TEAMSTERS	TEMPORIZE
SYMPATHIN	TACAMAHAC	TANTALIZE	TEARAWAYS	TEMPTABLE
SYMPATRIC	TACHYLYTE	TANTALOUS	TEARDROPS	TEMPTRESS
SYMPHONIC	TACITNESS	TANZANIAN	TEARFULLY	TENACIOUS
SYMPHYSIS	TACKINESS	TAP DANCER	TEARINGLY	TENACULUM
SYMPODIAL	TACTFULLY	TAP DANCES	TEASINGLY	TENANCIES
SYMPODIUM	TACTICIAN	TAPE DECKS	TEASPOONS	TENDEREST
SYMPOSIAC	TACTILITY	TAPEWORMS	TEA TASTER	TENDERING
SYMPOSIUM	TAENIASIS	TAPHONOMY	TEA TOWELS	TENDERIZE
SYNAGOGUE	TAGMEMICS	TARANTISM	TECHINESS	TENDINOUS
SYNALEPHA	TAILBACKS	TARANTULA	TECHNICAL	TENEBRISM
SYNCHRONY	TAILBOARD	TARAXACUM	TECHNIQUE	TENEBRIST
SYNCLINAL	TAILCOATS	TARDINESS	TECTONICS	TENEBROUS

TENEMENTS	TETRAPODY	THIRTIETH	TIDAL WAVE	TOADSTOOL
TENNESSEE	TETRARCHY	THITHERTO	TIDEMARKS	TOAMASINA
TENOR CLEF	TETROXIDE	THONINESS	TIDEWATER	TOAST RACK
TENSENESS	TEXTBOOKS	THORNBACK	TIED HOUSE	TOBOGGANS
TENSILITY	THALASSIC	THORNBILL	TIE-DYEING	TOCANTINS
TENSIONAL	THANJAVUR	THORNIEST	TIGER LILY	TOGLIATTI
TENSORIAL	THANKLESS	THOUSANDS	TIGHTENED	TOLERABLE
TENTACLES	THANKYOUS	THRALLDOM	TIGHTENER	TOLERABLY
TENTATION	THATCHERS	THRASHING	TIGHTEN UP	TOLERANCE
TENTATIVE	THATCHING	THREADFIN	TIGHTKNIT	TOLERATED
TENUOUSLY	THEACEOUS	THREADING	TIGHTNESS	TOLERATOR
TEPHRITIC	THEARCHIC	THREEFOLD	TIGHTROPE	TOLLBOOTH
TEREBINTH	THEATRICS	THREESOME	TIGHT SPOT	TOLLGATES
TERMAGANT	THE BROADS	THREE-STAR	TIGRESSES	TOLLHOUSE
TERMINALS	THECODONT	THREONINE	TIME BOMBS	TOLL HOUSE
TERMINATE	THE CREEPS	THRESHERS	TIME LAPSE	TOMAHAWKS
TERPINEOL	THEME PARK	THRESHING	TIME-LAPSE	TOMBOYISH
TERRAFORM	THEME SONG	THRESHOLD	TIMELIEST	TOMBSTONE
TERRAPINS	THEOCRACY	THRIFTIER	TIME LIMIT	TOMMY GUNS
TERRARIUM	THEOCRASY	THRIFTILY	TIMEPIECE	TOMORROWS
TERRIFIED	THEOMANIA	THRILLERS	TIMESAVER	TONBRIDGE
TERRIFIER	THEORISTS	THRILLING	TIME SHEET	TONE POEMS
TERRITORY	THEORIZED	THROATIER	TIMETABLE	TONKA BEAN
TERRORFUL	THEORIZER	THROATILY	TIME ZONES	TONOMETER
TERRORISM	THEOSOPHY	THROBBING	TIMISOARA	TONOMETRY
TERRORIST	THERAPIES	THRONGING	TIMOCRACY	TONSILLAR
TERRORIZE	THERAPIST	THROTTLED	TIMPANIST	TONSORIAL
TERSENESS	THERAPSID	THROTTLER	TINCTURES	TOOL-MAKER
TERVALENT	THEREFORE	THROTTLES	TINDERBOX	TOOTHACHE
TESSERACT	THEREINTO	THROWAWAY	TINGALING	TOOTHCOMB
TESSITURA	THEREUPON	THROWBACK	TINKERING	TOOTHIEST
TESTAMENT	THEREWITH	THROWSTER	TINNINESS	TOOTHLESS
TESTATORS	THERMOSES	THRUMMING	TIN OPENER	TOOTHPICK
TESTATRIX	THESAURUS	THRUSTERS	TIP AND	TOOTHSOME
TEST CARDS	THESPIANS	THRUSTING	RUN	TOOTHWORT
TEST CASES	THE STATES	THUMBNAIL	TIPPERARY	TOOWOOMBA
TESTICLES	THEURGIST	THUMBTACK	TIPSINESS	TOP DOLLAR
TESTIFIED	THICKENED	THUNDERED	TIREDNESS	TOP DRAWER
TESTIFIRE	THICKENER	THUNDERER	TITCHIEST	TOP FLIGHT
TESTIMONY	THICKHEAD	THURINGIA	TIT FOR	TOP-FLIGHT
TESTINESS	THICKLEAF	THURSDAYS	TAT	TOPIARIAN
TESTINGLY	THICKNESS	THWACKING	TITILLATE	TOPIARIST
TEST MATCH	THIGHBONE	THWARTING	TITIVATED	TOPICALLY
TEST PILOT	THINKABLE	THYLACINE	TITIVATOR	TOPMINNOW
TEST TUBES	THINK TANK	THYMIDINE	TITLE DEED	TOPOLOGIC
TETCHIEST	THINNINGS	THYRATRON	TITLE PAGE	TOPONYMIC
TETE-A-	THIO-ETHER	THYRISTOR	TITLE ROLE	TOP SECRET
TETE	THIOPHENE	THYROXINE	TITRATION	TOP-SECRET
TETHERING	THIRD-RATE	TICKETING	TITTERING	TORCHWOOD
TETRAGRAM	THIRSTIER	TIC TAC	T-JUNCTION	TOREADORS
TETRALOGY	THIRSTILY	MAN	TOADSTONE	TOREUTICS

TORMENTED	TRACEABLE	TRASHIEST	TRIBUNALS	TRIUMPHAL
TORMENTIL	TRACHYTIC	TRATTORIA	TRIBUNARY	TRIUMPHED
TORMENTOR	TRACKABLE	TRAUMATIC	TRIBUNATE	TRIUMPHER
TORNADOES	TRACKLESS	TRAVAILED	TRIBUTARY	TRIVALENT
TORPEDOED	TRACKSUIT	TRAVELING	TRICEPSES	TRIVIALLY
TORPEDOES	TRACK SUIT	TRAVELLED	TRICHITIC	TRIWEEKLY
TORPIDITY	TRACTABLE	TRAVELLER	TRICHOMIC	TROCHLEAR
TORRIDITY	TRADE GAPS	TRAVERSAL	TRICHOSIS	TROMBONES
TORSIONAL	TRADEMARK	TRAVERSED	TRICHROIC	TRONDHEIM
TORTILLAS	TRADE NAME	TRAVERSER	TRICKIEST	TROOPSHIP
TORTOISES	TRADE-OFFS	TRAVERSES	TRICKLING	TROOSTITE
TORTRICID	TRADESMAN	TREACHERY	TRICKSTER	TROPISTIC
TORTURERS	TRADESMEN	TREADMILL	TRICLINIC	TROPOLOGY
TORTURING	TRADE WIND	TREASURED	TRICOLOUR	TROSSACHS
TOTALIZER	TRADITION	TREASURER	TRICOTINE	TROUBLING
TOTALLING	TRADUCERS	TREASURES	TRICROTIC	TROUBLOUS
TOTAQUINE	TRADUCING	TREATABLE	TRICUSPID	TROUNCING
TOTEM POLE	TRAFALGAR	TREATISES	TRICYCLES	TROUSSEAU
TO THE	TRAGEDIAN	TREATMENT	TRICYCLIC	TROWELLER
FORE	TRAGEDIES	TREE FERNS	TRIDACTYL	TRPORIFIC
TOTTERING	TRAINABLE	TREENWARE	TRIENNIAL	TRUCK FARM
TOTTING UP	TRAININGS	TREE SHREW	TRIENNIUM	TRUCKLING
TOUCHABLE	TRAIN SETS	TREHALOSE	TRIFOLIUM	TRUCKLOAD
TOUCHDOWN	TRAIPSING	TREILLAGE	TRIFORIAL	TRUCK STOP
TOUCH DOWN	TRAMLINES	TRELLISES	TRIFORIUM	TRUCULENT
TOUCHIEST	TRAMMELER	TREMATODE	TRIGGERED	TRUELOVES
TOUCHLINE	TRAMPLING	TREMBLING	TRIGONOUS	TRUE NORTH
TOUCHMARK	TRANSCEND	TREMOLITE	TRIHEDRAL	TRUMP CARD
TOUCH-TYPE	TRANSEPTS	TREMOROUS	TRIHEDRON	TRUMPETED
TOUCHWOOD	TRANSEUNT	TREMULANT	TRIHYDRIC	TRUMPETER
TOUGHENED	TRANSFERS	TREMULOUS	TRILINEAR	TRUNCATED
TOUGHENER	TRANSFORM	TRENCHANT	TRILLIONS	TRUNCHEON
TOUGH LUCK	TRANSFUER	TRENCHERS	TRILOBATE	TRUNDLING
TOUGHNESS	TRANSFUSE	TRENDIEST	TRILOBITE	TRUNK CALL
TOURCOING	TRANSIENT	TRENGGANU	TRILOGIES	TRUNKFISH
TOURISTIC	TRANSLATE	TREPANNED	TRIMARANS	TRUNK ROAD
TOUT A	TRANSMUTE	TREPHINED	TRIMEROUS	TRUSTABLE
FAIT	TRANSONIC	TREPHINES	TRIMESTER	TRUST FUND
TOWELLING	TRANSPIRE	TREPONEMA	TRIMETRIC	TRUSTIEST
TOWN CLERK	TRANSPORT	TRIALLIST	TRIMMINGS	TRYING OUT
TOWN CRIER	TRANSPOSE	TRIAL RUNS	TRINITIES	TRY SQUARE
TOWN HALLS	TRANSSHIP	TRIANGLES	TRINOMIAL	TSETSE FLY
TOWN HOUSE	TRANSVAAL	TRIATHLON	TRIOELEIN	TSITSIHAR
TOWNSCAPE	TRAPDOORS	TRIATOMIC	TRIPLEXES	TUBBINESS
TOWNSHIPS	TRAPEZIAL	TRIAZOLIC	TRIPTYCHS	TUBULATOR
TOXAPHENE	TRAPEZIUM	TRIBADISM	TRIPWIRES	TUCKER BAG
TOXICALLY	TRAPEZIUS	TRIBALISM	TRISECTED	TUCKER-BAG
TOXICOSIS	TRAPEZOID	TRIBALIST	TRISECTOR	TUCKERING
TOXOPHILY	TRAPPINGS	TRIBESMAN	TRISERIAL	TUG-OF-
TRABEATED	TRAPPISTS	TRIBESMEN	TRITENESS	LOVE
TRABECULA	TRASHCANS	TRIBOLOGY	TRITURATE	

TUGS-OF-WAR	TWINKLING	UNADOPTED	UNDERGIRD	UNFLEDGED
TUILERIES	TWISTABLE	UNADVISED	UNDERGOER	UNFOLDING
TUITIONAL	TWISTEDLY	UNALLOYED	UNDERGONE	UNFOUNDED
TULIP TREE	TWISTIEST	UNANIMITY	UNDERHAND	UNFROCKED
TULIPWOOD	TWITCHING	UNANIMOUS	UNDERHUNG	UNFURLING
TULLAMORE	TWITTERED	UNAPTNESS	UNDERLAIN	UNGUARDED
TUMBLE-DRY	TWITTERER	UNASHAMED	UNDERLAYS	UNGUINOUS
TUMESCENT	TWO-BY-	UNASSUMED	UNDERLIER	UNHANDING
TUMULUSES	FOUR	UNAUDITED	UNDERLINE	UNHAPPILY
TUNEFULLY	TWO-HANDED	UNBALANCE	UNDERLING	UNHARNESS
TUNGSTITE	TWOPENCES	UNBARRING	UNDERMINE	UNHEALTHY
TUNGUSIAN	TWO-SEATER	UNBEKNOWN	UNDERMOST	UNHEARD OF
TUNING PEG	TWO-STROKE	UNBENDING	UNDERPAID	UNHEARD-OF
TUNNELLERS	TWO-TIMERS	UNBINDING	UNDERPASS	UNHINGING
TUNNELING	TWO-TIMING	UNBLESSED	UNDERPLAY	UNHORSING
TUNNELLED	TYMPANIST	UNBOSOMED	UNDERPLOT	UNHURRIED
TUNNELLER	TYMPANUMS	UNBOUNDED	UNDERPROP	UNICOLOUR
TUPPENCES	TYNEMOUTH	UNBRIDLED	UNDERRATE	UNIFIABLE
TURBIDITY	TYNESIDER	UNBUCKLED	UNDERSEAL	UNIFORMED
TURBINATE	TYPEFACES	UNCANNIER	UNDERSELL	UNIFORMLY
TURBOJETS	TYPEWRITE	UNCANNILY	UNDERSHOT	UNIJUGATE
TURBOPROP	TYPHLITIC	UNCEASING	UNDERSIDE	UNINSURED
TURBULENT	TYPHLITIS	UNCERTAIN	UNDERSOIL	UNION FLAG
TURFINESS	TYPHOIDAL	UNCHARGED	UNDERSOLD	UNIONISTS
TURGIDITY	TYPHOIDIN	UNCHARTED	UNDERTAKE	UNIONIZED
TURKESTAN	TYPICALLY	UNCHECKED	UNDERTINT	UNION JACK
TURNABOUT	TYPIFYING	UNCLIMBED	UNDERTONE	UNION SHOP
TURN ABOUT	TYRANNIES	UNCONCERN	UNDERTOOK	UNIPAROUS
TURNCOATS	TYRANNIZE	UNCORKING	UNDERWEAR	UNIPLANAR
TURNCOCKS	TYRANNOUS	UNCOUNTED	UNDERWENT	UNIRAMOUS
TURNOVERS	TZETZE FLY	UNCOUPLED	UNDERWING	UNISEXUAL
TURNPIKES		UNCOUTHLY	UNDESIRED	UNISONOUS
TURNROUND	**U**	UNCOVERED	UNDIVIDED	UNITARIAN
TURN ROUND	UITLANDER	UNCREATED	UNDOUBTED	UNIT TRUST
TURNSTILE	UKRAINIAN	UNCROWDED	UNDRESSED	UNIVALENT
TURNSTONE	ULAN BATOR	UNCROWNED	UNDULANCE	UNIVERSAL
TURNTABLE	ULCERATED	UNDAUNTED	UNDULATED	UNIVERSES
TURPITUDE	ULMACEOUS	UNDECAGON	UNDULATOR	UNKINDEST
TURQUOISE	ULOTRICHY	UNDECEIVE	UNEARTHED	UNKNOWING
TUSCARORA	ULTIMATUM	UNDECIDED	UNEARTHLY	UNLEARNED
TUTIORISM	ULTRADIAN	UNDERBODY	UNEASIEST	UNIFASHED
TUTIORIST	ULTRA HIGH	UNDERBRED	UNEATABLE	UNLIMITED
TUTORIALS	ULULATION	UNDERCLAY	UNELECTED	UNLOADERS
TUT-TUTTED	ULYANOVSK	UNDERCOAT	UNEQUALLY	UNLOADING
TV DINNERS	UMBELLATE	UNDERCOOK	UNETHICAL	UNLOCKING
TWAYBLADE	UMBELLULE	UNDERDOGS	UNFAILING	UNLOOSING
TWENTIETH	UMBILICAL	UNDERDONE	UNFAIREST	UNLUCKILY
TWICE-LAID	UMBILICUS	UNDERFEED	UNFANCIED	UNMARRIED
TWICE-TOLD	UMBRELLAS	UNDERFELT	UNFEELING	UNMASKING
TWIDDLING	UMPTEENTH	UNDERFOOT	UNFEIGNED	UNMATCHED
	UNABASHED	UNDERFUND	UNFITNESS	UNMEANING

UNMINDFUL	UNUSUALLY	UROPYGIAL	VANDALIZE	VENIALITY
UNMUSICAL	UNVEILING	UROPYGIUM	VANGUARDS	VENTILATE
UNNATURAL	UNWATCHED	UROSCOPIC	VANISHING	VENTRICLE
UNNERVING	UNWEARIED	URSA MAJOR	VAPIDNESS	VENTURERS
UNNOTICED	UNWEIGHED	URTICARIA	VAPORETTO	VENTURING
UNOPPOSED	UNWELCOME	URUGUAYAN	VAPORIFIC	VENUSBERG
UNPACKING	UNWILLING	USABILITY	VAPORIZED	VERACIOUS
UNPICKING	UNWINDING	USELESSLY	VAPORIZER	VERANDAED
UNPLUGGED	UNWITTING	USHERETTE	VAPOURISH	VERATRINE
UNPLUMBED	UNWORLDLY	USUALNESS	VARANGIAN	VERBALISM
UNPOLITIC	UNWRITTEN	UTILITIES	VARIABLES	VERBALIST
UNPOPULAR	UNZIPPING	UTILIZING	VARIANCES	VERBALIZE
UNPOWERED	UP AND	UTRICULAR	VARIATION	VERBASCUM
UNRAVELED	DOWN	UTTERABLE	VARICELLA	VERBOSELY
UNREALISM	UP-AND-	UTTERANCE	VARICOSIS	VERBOSITY
UNREALITY	DOWN	UTTERLESS	VARIEGATE	VERDIGRIS
UNREFINED	UPBRAIDED	UVAROVITE	VARIETIES	VERDUROUS
UNRELATED	UPBRAIDER	UXORICIDE	VARIFOCAL	VERIDICAL
UNRESERVE	UPBUILDER		VARIOLATE	VERIFYING
UNRIDDLER	UP-COUNTRY	**V**	VARIOLITE	VERITABLE
UNROLLING	UPGRADING	VACANCIES	VARIOLOID	VERITABLY
UNROUNDED	UPHEAVALS	VACATABLE	VARIOLOUS	VERMICIDE
UNRUFFLED	UPHOLDERS	VACATIONS	VARIOUSLY	VERMIFORM
UNSADDLED	UPHOLDING	VACCINATE	VARISCITE	VERMIFUGE
UNSAVOURY	UPHOLSTER	VACCINIAL	VARITYPER	VERMILION
UNSCATHED	UPLIFTING	VACILLANT	VARNISHED	VERMINOUS
UNSCREWED	UPLIGHTER	VACILLATE	VARNISHER	VERMONTER
UNSEATING	UPPER CASE	VACUOLATE	VARNISHES	VERNALIZE
UNSECURED	UPPERCUTS	VACUOUSLY	VARSITIES	VERNATION
UNSELFISH	UPPER HAND	VACUUMING	VARYINGLY	VERRUCOSE
UNSERIOUS	UPPERMOST	VAGABONDS	VASECTOMY	VERSATILE
UNSETTLED	UPRIGHTLY	VAGINITIS	VASOMOTOR	VERSIFIER
UNSHACKLE	UPRISINGS	VAGOTONIA	VASSALAGE	VERSIONAL
UNSHEATHE	UPROOTING	VAGUENESS	VASSALIZE	VERS LIBRE
UNSIGHTED	UPSETTING	VAINGLORY	VECTORIAL	VERTEBRAE
UNSIGHTLY	UPSTAGING	VALENCIES	VEERINGLY	VERTEBRAL
UNSKILFUL	UP THE	VALENTINE	VEGETABLE	VERY LIGHT
UNSKILLED	ANTE	VALIANTLY	VEGETATED	VESICULAR
UNSPARING	UP THE	VALIDATED	VEHEMENCE	VESTIBULE
UNSPOTTED	DUFF	VALIDNESS	VEHICULAR	VESTIGIAL
UNSPRAYED	UP THE	VALLATION	VEINSTONE	VESTMENTS
UNSTOPPED	POLE	VALLECULA	VELODROME	VESTRYMAN
UNSTRIPED	URANINITE	VALUABLES	VELVETEEN	VETCHLING
UNSTUDIED	URBAN MYTH	VALUATION	VENDETTAS	VEXATIONS
UNTANGLED	URCEOLATE	VALUELESS	VENDITION	VEXATIOUS
UNTENABLE	URINATING	VALVELESS	VENEERING	VEXEDNESS
UNTENURED	URINATION	VAMOOSING	VENERABLE	VEXILLARY
UNTOUCHED	URINATIVE	VAMPIRISM	VENERATED	VEXILLATE
UNTREATED	UROCHROME	VANASPATI	VENERATOR	VIABILITY
UNTUTORED	UROGENOUS	VANCOUVER	VENEZUELA	VIAREGGIO
UNTYPICAL	UROLITHIC	VANDALISM	VENGEANCE	VIBRANTLY

VIBRATILE
VIBRATING
VIBRATION
VIBRATIVE
VIBRATORS
VIBRISSAL
VICARAGES
VICARIATE
VICARIOUS
VICARSHIP
VICEGERAL
VICENNIAL
VICEREGAL
VICEREINE
VICE VERSA
VICIOUSLY
VICKSBURG
VICTIMIZE
VICTORIAN
VICTORIES
VICTUALED
VIDELICET
VIDEODISC
VIDEO GAME
VIDEO TAPE
VIDEOTAPE
VIENTIANE
VIEWPOINT
VIGESIMAL
VIGILANCE
VIGILANTE
VIGNETTES
VILIFYING
VILLAGERS
VILLIFORM
VILLOSITY
VIMINEOUS
VINACEOUS
VINCENNES
VINDICATE
VINEYARDS
VIOLATING
VIOLATION
VIOLATIVE
VIOLATORS
VIOLENTLY
VIOLINIST
VIRESCENT
VIRGINALS
VIRGINIAN
VIRGINITY

VIRGULATE
VIRTUALLY
VIRTUOSIC
VIRTUOSOS
VIRULENCE
VIRULENCY
VISCIDITY
VISCOSITY
VISCOUNTS
VISIONARY
VISITABLE
VISUAL AID
VISUALIZE
VITACEOUS
VITALIZER
VITAMINIC
VITELLINE
VITIATING
VITIATION
VITRIFIED
VITRIFORM
VITRIOLIC
VIVACIOUS
VIVARIUMS
VIVA VOCES
VIVERRINE
VIVIDNESS
VOCALISTS
VOCALIZER
VOCATIONS
VOCATIVES
VOICELESS
VOICE MAIL
VOICE-OVER
VOJVODINA
VOL-AU-
VENT
VOLCANISM
VOLCANIZE
VOLCANOES
VOLGOGRAD
VOLLEYING
VOLTE-FACE
VOLTMETER
VOLUMETER
VOLUMETRY
VOLUNTARY
VOLUNTEER
VOODOOISM
VOODOOIST
VORACIOUS

VORTICISM
VORTICIST
VOUCHSAFE
VOYEURISM
VULCANIAN
VULCANITE
VULCANIZE
VULGARIAN
VULGARISM
VULGARITY
VULGARIZE
VULNERARY
VULTURINE
VULTUROUS
VULVIFORM

W

WACKINESS
WAD MEDANI
WAFER-THIN
WAGE SLAVE
WAGGISHLY
WAGONETTE
WAGONLOAD
WAILINGLY
WAINSCOTS
WAISTBAND
WAISTCOAT
WAISTLINE
WAIT FOR
IT
WAKEFIELD
WAKEFULLY
WAKE ROBIN
WAKE-ROBIN
WALBRZYCH
WALCHEREN
WALKABOUT
WALKAWAYS
WALK ON
AIR
WALKOVERS
WALLABIES
WALLBOARD
WALLCHART
WALLOPING
WALLOWING
WALLPAPER
WALVIS BAY
WANDERERS
WANDERING

WAR CLOUDS
WAR CRIMES
WAR DANCES
WARDROBES
WARDROOMS
WAREHOUSE
WARHORSES
WARM FRONT
WARMONGER
WARRANTED
WARRANTEE
WARRANTER
WARRANTOR
WASHBASIN
WASHBOARD
WASHCLOTH
WASHED-OUT
WASHINESS
WASHING-UP
WASHROOMS
WASHSTAND
WASPINESS
WASPISHLY
WASSAILER
WASTELAND
WATCHDOGS
WATCHWORD
WATER BIRD
WATERBUCK
WATER BUTT
WATER-COOL
WATERFALL
WATERFORD
WATERFOWL
WATERHOLE
WATER ICES
WATER JUMP
WATERLESS
WATER LILY
WATERLINE
WATER MAIN
WATERMARK
WATERMILL
WATER PIPE
WATER POLO
WATER RATE
WATER RATS
WATERSHED
WATER-SICK
WATERSIDE
WATER VOLE

WATERWAYS
WATERWEED
WATERWORN
WATTMETER
WAVE BANDS
WAVEGUIDE
WAVELLITE
WAVEMETER
WAXWORKER
WAYFARERS
WAYFARING
WAYLAYING
WEAKENING
WEAKER SEX
WEAK-KNEED
WEAKLINGS
WEALTHIER
WEALTHILY
WEAPONEER
WEARINESS
WEARINGLY
WEARISOME
WEARPROOF
WEASELING
WEATHERED
WEATHERER
WEB-FOOTED
WEB OFFSET
WEDNESDAY
WEEDINESS
WEEKENDED
WEEKENDER
WEEKNIGHT
WEEPINESS
WEEPINGLY
WEIGHABLE
WEIGH DOWN
WEIGHTILY
WEIGHTING
WEIRDNESS
WELCOMING
WELL-ACTED
WELL-AWARE
WELLBEING
WELL-FOUND
WELL-KNOWN
WELL-LINED
WELL-MEANT
WELL OILED
WELL-OILED
WELL-TIMED

WELL-TRIED
WERNERITE
WESLEYANS
WESTBOUND
WESTERING
WESTERNER
WESTMEATH
WESTWARDS
WET DREAMS
WET-NURSED
WET NURSES
WHACKINGS
WHALEBOAT
WHALEBONE
WHANGAREI
WHEAT GERM
WHEATWORM
WHEEDLING
WHEELBASE
WHEELWORK
WHEREFORE
WHEREUPON
WHEREWITH
WHERRYMAN
WHETSTONE
WHICHEVER
WHICKERED
WHIFFIEST
WHIMPERED
WHIMPERER
WHIMSICAL
WHININGLY
WHINNYING
WHINSTONE
WHIPPER-IN
WHIPPINGS
WHIP ROUND
WHIP-ROUND
WHIPSTALL
WHIPSTOCK
WHIRLIGIG
WHIRLPOOL
WHIRLWIND
WHISKERED
WHISPERED
WHISPERER
WHISTLING
WHITE ANTS
WHITEBAIT
WHITECAPS
WHITEDAMP

WHITEFISH
WHITE FLAG
WHITEHALL
WHITE HEAT
WHITE HOPE
WHITE LEAD
WHITE LIES
WHITE MEAT
WHITENESS
WHITENING
WHITE ROSE
WHITEWALL
WHITEWASH
WHITEWOOD
WHITTLERS
WHITTLING
WHIZZ-BANG
WHIZZ KIDS
WHODUNITS
WHODUNNIT
WHOLEFOOD
WHOLEMEAL
WHOLENESS
WHOLE NOTE
WHOLESALE
WHOLESOME
WHOSOEVER
WIDE-ANGLE
WIDE-AWAKE
WIDOWHOOD
WIDTHWISE
WIELDABLE
WIESBADEN
WIGWAGGER
WILD BOARS
WILDFIRES
WILLEMITE
WILLINGLY
WILLPOWER
WILTSHIRE
WINCINGLY
WINDBLOWN
WIND-BORNE
WINDBOUND
WINDBREAK
WINDBURNT
WINDFALLS
WIND GAUGE
WINDINESS
WINDINGLY
WINDMILLS

WINDOW BOX
WINDPIPES
WINDROWER
WINDSOCKS
WINDSTORM
WINDSWEPT
WINEGLASS
WINEMAKER
WINEPRESS
WINGSPANS
WINNEBAGO
WINNOWING
WINSOMELY
WINTERING
WINTRIEST
WIRADHURI
WIRE-GAUGE
WIREWORKS
WIREWORMS
WISCONSIN
WISECRACK
WISHBONES
WISPINESS
WISTFULLY
WITCH-HUNT
WITCHLIKE
WITH A
  WILL
WITHDRAWN
WITHERING
WITHERITE
WITHSTAND
WITHSTOOD
WITLESSLY
WITNESSED
WITNESSER
WITNESSES
WITTICISM
WITTINESS
WOBBLIEST
WOEBEGONE
WOKINGHAM
WOLFHOUND
WOLFSBANE
WOLFSBURG
WOLVERINE
WOMANHOOD
WOMANIZED
WOMANIZER
WOMANKIND
WOMAN-LIKE

WOMENFOLK
WOMEN'S
  LIB
WONDERFUL
WONDERING
WOODBLOCK
WOODBORER
WOODCHUCK
WOODCOCKS
WOODCRAFT
WOODINESS
WOODLOUSE
WOODPRINT
WOODSCREW
WOOD SCREW
WOODSHEDS
WOODSMOKE
WOODSTOCK
WOOLLIEST
WOOZINESS
WORCESTER
WORDBREAK
WORDINESS
WORKBENCH
WORKBOOKS
WORKFORCE
WORKHORSE
WORKHOUSE
WORKLOADS
WORK OF
  ART
WORKPIECE
WORKPLACE
WORKROOMS
WORKSHEET
WORKSHOPS
WORK-STUDY
WORKTABLE
WORLD BANK
WORLDLIER
WORLDLING
WORLDWIDE
WORM CASTS
WORM-EATEN
WORM GEARS
WORMHOLES
WORRIEDLY
WORRISOME
WORRYWART
WORSENING
WORSHIPED

WORTHIEST
WORTHLESS
WOUNDABLE
WOUNDWORT
WRANGLERS
WRANGLING
WRAPPINGS
WREATHING
WRECKFISH
WRENCHING
WRESTLERS
WRESTLING
WRIGGLING
WRINKLING
WRISTBAND
WRISTLETS
WRISTLOCK
WRITE-OFFS
WRONGDOER
WRONGNESS
WROUGHT-UP
WULFENITE
WUPPERTAL
WYANDOTTE
WYCH-HAZEL

X

XENOCRYST
XENOGRAFT
XENOPHILE
XENOPHOBE
XERICALLY
XERODERMA
XEROPHILY
XEROPHYTE
XYLOGRAPH
XYLOPHONE

Y

YACHTINGS
YACHTSMAN
YACHTSMEN
YAMMERING
YANKEEISM
YARDSTICK
YAROSLAVL
YAWNINGLY
YEA AND
  NAY
YEARBOOKS
YEARLINGS

YEARNINGS	**Z**	ZEPPELINS	ZOOGLOEAL	ZUCCHINIS
YELLOWFIN	ZACATECAS	ZESTFULLY	ZOOGRAPHY	ZUGSPITZE
YELLOWING	ZAMBEZIAN	ZEUGMATIC	ZOOLOGIST	ZUIDER ZEE
YELLOWISH	ZAMBOANGA	ZHANGZHOU	ZOOMETRIC	ZYGOMATIC
YESTERDAY	ZANZIBARI	ZHENGZHOU	ZOOPHILIA	ZYGOPHYTE
YIELDABLE	ZAPOTECAN	ZIGZAGGED	ZOOPHILIC	ZYGOSPORE
YODELLING	ZEALOUSLY	ZIGZAGGER	ZOOPHOBIA	ZYMOGENIC
YOHIMBINE	ZEBRA-LIKE	ZINKENITE	ZOOPHYTIC	ZYMOLOGIC
YORKSHIRE	ZEBRAWOOD	ZIONISTIC	ZOOPLASTY	ZYMOLYSIS
YOUNGSTER	ZEEBRUGGE	ZIRCALLOY	ZOOSPORIC	ZYMOLYTIC
YTTERBITE	ZEELANDER	ZIRCONIUM	ZOOSTEROL	ZYMOMETER
YTTERBIUM	ZEITGEIST	ZITHERIST	ZOOTOMIST	

A
ABANDONING
ABBREVIATE
ABDICATING
ABDICATION
ABDICATIVE
ABERRATION
ABHORRENCE
ABIOGENIST
ABIRRITANT
ABIRRITATE
ABJURATION
ABLE-
  BODIED
ABLE
  SEAMAN
ABLE
  SEAMEN
ABNEGATION
ABNEY
  LEVEL
ABNORMALLY
ABOLISHING
ABOMINABLE
ABOMINABLY
ABOMINATED
ABOMINATOR
ABORIGINAL
ABORIGINES
ABORTICIDE
ABORTIONAL
ABORTIVELY
ABOUT-
  TURNS
ABOVEBOARD
ABOVE
  BOARD
ABRASIVELY
ABREACTION
ABRIDGABLE
ABRIDGMENT
ABROGATING
ABROGATION
ABRUPTNESS
ABSCISSION
ABSCONDING
ABSOLUTELY
ABSOLUTION
ABSOLUTISM
ABSOLUTORY
ABSOLVABLE
ABSORBABLE

ABSORBANCE
ABSORBEDLY
ABSORBENCY
ABSORBENTS
ABSORPTION
ABSORPTIVE
ABSTAINERS
ABSTAINING
ABSTEMIOUS
ABSTENTION
ABSTERGENT
ABSTINENCE
ABSTRACTED
ABUNDANTLY
ABYSSINIAN
ACCELERANT
ACCELERATE
ACCENTUATE
ACCEPTABLE
ACCEPTABLY
ACCEPTANCE
ACCEPTEDLY
ACCESSIBLE
ACCESSIONS
ACCESS
  ROAD
ACCESS
  TIME
ACCIDENTAL
ACCIPITRAL
ACCLAIMING
ACCOMPLICE
ACCOMPLISH
ACCORDABLE
ACCORDANCE
ACCORDIONS
ACCOSTABLE
ACCOUNTANT
ACCOUNTING
ACCREDITED
ACCRESCENT
ACCRETIONS
ACCUMBENCY
ACCUMULATE
ACCURATELY
ACCUSATION
ACCUSATIVE
ACCUSINGLY
ACCUSTOMED
ACEPHALOUS
ACETABULUM

ACETIC
  ACID
ACETOMETER
ACETYLENIC
ACHIEVABLE
ACHONDRITE
ACHROMATIC
ACHROMATIN
ACIDIFYING
ACIDIMETER
ACIDOMETER
ACIERATION
ACOTYLEDON
ACQUAINTED
ACQUIESCED
ACQUIRABLE
ACQUITTALS
ACQUITTING
ACROBATICS
ACROMEGALY
ACRONYCHAL
ACROPHOBIA
ACROPHOBIC
ACTABILITY
ACTINIFORM
ACTINOLITE
ACTINOMERE
ACTINOZOAN
ACTIONABLE
ACTIVATING
ACTIVATION
ACTIVENESS
ACTIVITIES
ACTOMYOSIN
ACT THE
  GOAT
ADACTYLOUS
ADAMANTINE
ADAMS
  APPLE
ADAM'S
  APPLE
ADAPTATION
ADDICTIONS
ADDIS
  ABABA
ADDITIONAL
ADDRESSEES
ADDRESSING
ADDUCEABLE
ADENECTOMY
ADENOVIRUS

ADEQUATELY
ADIRONDACK
ADJECTIVAL
ADJECTIVES
ADJOURNING
ADJUDICATE
ADJUNCTIVE
ADJURATION
ADJURATORY
ADJUSTABLE
ADJUSTMENT
ADMINISTER
ADMIRATION
ADMIRINGLY
ADMISSIBLE
ADMISSIONS
ADMITTANCE
ADMITTEDLY
ADMIXTURES
ADMONISHED
ADMONISHER
ADMONITION
ADMONITORY
ADOLESCENT
ADORNMENTS
ADRENALINE
ADRENERGIC
ADROITNESS
ADSORBABLE
ADSORPTION
ADULTERANT
ADULTERATE
ADULTERERS
ADULTERESS
ADULTERINE
ADULTEROUS
ADUMBRATED
ADVANTAGES
ADVENTITIA
ADVENTURER
ADVENTURES
ADVERBIALS
ADVERTENCE
ADVERTISED
ADVERTISER
ADVOCATING
ADVOCATION
ADVOCATORY
ADZUKI
  BEAN
AECIOSPORE

AERENCHYMA
AEROBATICS
AEROBIOSIS
AEROBIOTIC
AERODROMES
AERO-
  ENGINE
AEROGRAMME
AEROGRAPHY
AEROLOGIST
AEROMETRIC
AERONAUTIC
AEROPHAGIA
AEROPHOBIA
AEROPHOBIC
AEROPLANES
AEROSPHERE
AEROSTATIC
AEROTOWING
AESTHETICS
AESTIVATOR
AFFABILITY
AFFECTEDLY
AFFECTIONS
AFFECTLESS
AFFETTUOSO
AFFIDAVITS
AFFILIATED
AFFILIATES
AFFINITIES
AFFINITIVE
AFFLICTING
AFFLICTION
AFFLICTIVE
AFFORDABLE
AFFORESTED
AFFRICATES
AFFRONTING
AFICIONADO
AFRIKANDER
AFRIKANERS
AFTERBIRTH
AFTERBRAIN
AFTERGLOWS
AFTERIMAGE
AFTERLIVES
AFTERMATHS
AFTERNOONS
AFTERPAINS
AFTERPIECE
AFTERSHAFT

AFTERSHAVE
AFTERSHOCK
AFTERTASTE
AFTERWARDS
AGAMICALLY
AGAPANTHUS
AGGLUTININ
AGGRANDIZE
AGGRAVATED
AGGREGATED
AGGREGATES
AGGRESSION
AGGRESSIVE
AGGRESSORS
AGITATIONS
AGREEMENTS
AGRONOMICS
AGRONOMIST
AGRYPNOTIC
AHMEDNAGAR
AIDE-DE-
CAMP
AIR-
HOSTESS
AIR-
LETTERS
AIR-
LIFTING
AIR
MARSHAL
AIRPOCKETS
AIR
WAYBILL
AKTYUBINSK
ALACRITOUS
ALARM
CLOCK
ALARMINGLY
ALBESCENCE
ALBUMENIZE
ALBUMINATE
ALBUMINOID
ALBUMINOUS
ALCHEMISTS
ALCHERINGA
ALCOHOLICS
ALCOHOLISM
ALCOHOLIZE
ALDERMANIC
ALEXANDRIA
ALGEBRAIST
ALGOLAGNIA

ALGOLAGNIC
ALGONQUIAN
ALGOPHOBIA
ALGORISMIC
ALGORITHMS
ALIENATING
ALIENATION
ALIGNMENTS
ALIMENTARY
ALKALINITY
ALKYLATION
ALLARGANDO
ALLEGATION
ALLEGIANCE
ALLEGORIES
ALLEGORIST
ALLEGORIZE
ALLEGRETTO
ALLERGENIC
ALLEVIATED
ALLEVIATOR
ALLIACEOUS
ALLIGATORS
ALLITERATE
ALLOCATING
ALLOCATION
ALLOCUTION
ALLOGAMOUS
ALLOMERISM
ALLOMEROUS
ALLOMETRIC
ALLOPATHIC
ALLOPATRIC
ALLOPHONIC
ALLOTMENTS
ALLOTROPIC
ALLOWANCES
ALL-
PURPOSE
ALL-
ROUNDER
ALL THE
TIME
ALLUREMENT
ALLUSIVELY
ALMA
MATERS
ALMIGHTIER
ALMIGHTILY
ALMS-
HOUSES
ALONGSHORE

ALPENSTOCK
ALPESTRINE
ALTARPIECE
ALTAZIMUTH
ALTERATION
ALTERATIVE
ALTERNATED
ALTERNATOR
ALTIMETERS
ALTOGETHER
ALTRINCHAM
ALTRUISTIC
AMALGAMATE
AMANUENSES
AMANUENSIS
AMATEURISH
AMATEURISM
AMBASSADOR
AMBIVALENT
AMBOCEPTOR
AMBULACRAL
AMBULACRUM
AMBULANCES
AMBULATION
AMBULATORY
AMELIORANT
AMELIORATE
AMENDMENTS
AMERINDIAN
AMIABILITY
AMIANTHINE
AMINO
ACIDS
AMMONIACAL
AMMUNITION
AMOEBIASIS
AMOEBOCYTE
AMORTIZING
AMPELOPSIS
AMPERE-
HOUR
AMPERE-
TURN
AMPERSANDS
AMPHEATRIC
AMPHIASTER
AMPHIBIANS
AMPHIBIOUS
AMPHIBOLIC
AMPHIBRACH
AMPHICTYON

AMPHIGORIC
AMPHIMACER
AMPHIMIXIS
AMPHOTERIC
AMPLIFIERS
AMPLIFYING
AMPUTATING
AMPUTATION
AMUSEMENTS
AMYGDALATE
AMYGDALINE
AMYGDALOID
AMYLACEOUS
AMYLOLYSIS
ANABOLITIC
ANACHORISM
ANACOUSTIC
ANACRUSTIC
ANADROMOUS
ANAGLYPHIC
ANALGESICS
ANALOGICAL
ANALYSABLE
ANAMNESTIC
ANAMORPHIC
ANAPAESTIC
ANAPLASTIC
ANAPTYCTIC
ANARCHISTS
ANARTHROUS
ANASARCOUS
ANASTIGMAT
ANASTOMOSE
ANATOMICAL
ANATOMISTS
ANATOMIZER
ANATROPOUS
ANCESTRESS
ANCESTRIES
ANCHORAGES
ANCHORITES
ANDALUSITE
ANDERLECHT
ANDROECIAL
ANDROECIUM
ANDROGENIC
ANECDOTAGE
ANECDOTIST
ANEMICALLY
ANEMOCHORE
ANEMOGRAPH

ANEMOMETER
ANEMOMETRY
ANEMOPHILY
ANEMOSCOPE
ANESTHESIA
ANESTHETIC
ANEURYSMAL
ANGELOLOGY
ANGIOSPERM
ANGLEPOISE
ANGLICISMS
ANGLICIZED
ANGLOPHILE
ANGLOPHOBE
ANGLOPHONE
ANGLO-
SAXON
ANGULARITY
ANGULATION
ANGWANTIBO
ANIMADVERT
ANIMALCULE
ANIMAL
FARM
ANIMATEDLY
ANISOTROPY
ANKYLOSAUR
ANNALISTIC
ANNEXATION
ANNIHILATE
ANNO
DOMINI
ANNOTATING
ANNOTATION
ANNOTATIVE
ANNOUNCERS
ANNOUNCING
ANNOYANCES
ANNULATION
ANNULLABLE
ANNULMENTS
ANNUNCIATE
ANOINTMENT
ANORTHITIC
ANSWERABLE
ANSWERABLY
ANTAGONISM
ANTAGONIST
ANTAGONIZE
ANTARCTICA
ANTEBELLUM

ANTECEDENT
ANTEDATING
ANTE-
  MORTEM
ANTEPENULT
ANTHOPHORE
ANTHRACENE
ANTHRACITE
ANTHRACOID
ANTHROPOID
ANTIBARYON
ANTIBIOSIS
ANTIBIOTIC
ANTIBODIES
ANTICHRIST
ANTICIPANT
ANTICIPATE
ANTICLIMAX
ANTICLINAL
ANTIDROMIC
ANTIFREEZE
ANTIFUNGAL
ANTIHEROES
ANTILEPTON
ANTILOGISM
ANTIMATTER
ANTIMERISM
ANTIMONIAL
ANTIMONOUS
ANTIPHONAL
ANTIPODEAN
ANTIPROTON
ANTIPYRINE
ANTIQUATED
ANTI-
  SEMITE
ANTISEPSIS
ANTISEPTIC
ANTISOCIAL
ANTISTATIC
ANTITHESIS
ANTITRADES
ANTITRAGUS
ANXIOLYTIC
APARTMENTS
APGAR
  SCORE
APHORISTIC
APHRODISIA
APICULTURE
APIOLOGIST

APLACENTAL
APOCALYPSE
APOCARPOUS
APOCHROMAT
APOCRYPHAL
APOLITICAL
APOLOGETIC
APOLOGISTS
APOLOGIZED
APOLOGIZER
APOPHTHEGM
APOPHYSATE
APOPHYSIAL
APOPLECTIC
APOSEMATIC
APOSTASIES
APOSTATIZE
APOSTOLATE
APOSTROPHE
APOTHECARY
APOTHECIAL
APOTHECIUM
APOTHEOSES
APOTHEOSIS
APOTROPAIC
APPALACHIA
APPARELLED
APPARENTLY
APPARITION
APPEALABLE
APPEARANCE
APPEASABLE
APPENDAGES
APPENDICES
APPENDICLE
APPENDIXES
APPERCEIVE
APPETIZERS
APPETIZING
APPLAUDING
APPLE
  CARTS
APPLIANCES
APPLICABLE
APPLICANTS
APPLICATOR
APPOINTEES
APPOINTING
APPOSITION
APPOSITIVE
APPRAISALS

APPRAISING
APPRAISIVE
APPRECIATE
APPRENTICE
APPROACHED
APPROACHES
APPROXIMAL
APRIL
  FOOLS
APTERYGIAL
AQUAMARINE
AQUAPHOBIA
AQUAPLANED
AQUAPLANES
ARABESQUES
ARACHNIDAN
ARAKAN
  YOMA
ARAUCANIAN
ARBITRABLE
ARBITRATED
ARBITRATOR
ARCHAISTIC
ARCHANGELS
ARCHBISHOP
ARCHDEACON
ARCHERFISH
ARCHESPORE
ARCHETYPAL
ARCHETYPES
ARCHIMEDES
ARCHITECTS
ARCHITRAVE
ARCHIVISTS
ARCHOPLASM
ARCTOGAEAN
ARC
  WELDING
ARENACEOUS
AREOGRAPHY
AREOLATION
ARGENTEUIL
ARGILLITIC
ARGUMENTUM
ARISTOCRAT
ARITHMETIC
ARMADILLOS
ARMAGEDDON
ARMIPOTENT
ARMISTICES
ARNHEM
  LAND

ARRAIGNING
ARRHYTHMIA
ARROGANTLY
ARROGATING
ARROGATION
ARROGATIVE
ARROWHEADS
ARTFULNESS
ARTHRALGIA
ARTHRALGIC
ARTHRITICS
ARTHROMERE
ARTICHOKES
ARTICULATE
ARTIFICERS
ARTIFICIAL
ART
  NOUVEAU
ARTY-
  CRAFTY
ASAFOETIDA
ASARABACCA
ASBESTOSIS
ASCARIASIS
ASCENDANCY
ASCENDANTS
ASCETICISM
ASCOGONIUM
ASCOMYCETE
ASCRIBABLE
ASCRIPTION
ASEXUALITY
ASPARAGINE
ASPERITIES
ASPERSIONS
AS PER
  USUAL
ASPHALTING
ASPHALTITE
ASPHYXIANT
ASPHYXIATE
ASPIDISTRA
ASPIRATING
ASPIRATION
ASPIRATORY
ASSAILABLE
ASSAILANTS
ASSAILMENT
ASSAULTING
ASSEMBLAGE
ASSEMBLIES

ASSEMBLING
ASSERTIBLE
ASSERTIONS
ASSESSABLE
ASSESSMENT
ASSET
  VALUE
ASSEVERATE
ASSIBILATE
ASSIGNABLE
ASSIGNMENT
ASSIMILATE
ASSISTANCE
ASSISTANTS
ASSOCIABLE
ASSOCIATED
ASSOCIATES
ASSONANTAL
ASSORTMENT
ASSUMPTION
ASSUMPTIVE
ASSURANCES
ASTATICISM
ASTERIATED
ASTERISKED
ASTEROIDAL
ASTHENOPIA
ASTHENOPIC
ASTHMATICS
ASTIGMATIC
ASTOMATOUS
ASTONISHED
ASTOUNDING
ASTRAGALUS
ASTRINGENT
ASTROLOGER
ASTROMETRY
ASTRONAUTS
ASTRONOMER
ASTUTENESS
ASYMMETRIC
ASYMPTOTIC
AT ALL
  TIMES
AT A
  STRETCH
ATHERMANCY
ATMOSPHERE
ATOMICALLY
ATOMIC
  BOMB

ATOMIC
PILE
ATROCITIES
ATROPHYING
ATTACHABLE
ATTACHMENT
ATTAINABLE
ATTAINMENT
ATTEMPTING
ATTENDANCE
ATTENDANTS
ATTENTIONS
ATTENUATED
ATTENUATOR
ATTESTABLE
AT THE
READY
ATTORNMENT
ATTRACTING
ATTRACTION
ATTRACTIVE
ATTRIBUTED
ATTRIBUTER
ATTRIBUTES
ATYPICALLY
AUBERGINES
AUCTIONEER
AUCTIONING
AUDIBILITY
AUDIOGENIC
AUDIOMETER
AUDIOMETRY
AUDITIONED
AUDITORIUM
AUGMENTING
AUREOMYCIN
AURICULATE
AURIFEROUS
AUSCULTATE
AUSFORMING
AUSPICIOUS
AUSTENITIC
AUSTERLITZ
AUSTRALIAN
AUSTRALOID
AUSTRALORP
AUTARCHIES
AUTECOLOGY
AUTHORIZED
AUTHORIZER
AUTHORSHIP

AUTOCHTHON
AUTOCRATIC
AUTOECIOUS
AUTOGAMOUS
AUTOGENOUS
AUTOGRAPHS
AUTOGRAPHY
AUTOMATICS
AUTOMATING
AUTOMATION
AUTOMATISM
AUTOMATIST
AUTOMATONS
AUTOMATOUS
AUTOMOBILE
AUTOMOTIVE
AUTONOMIST
AUTONOMOUS
AUTOPHYTIC
AUTOPLASTY
AUTOSTRADA
AUTOTOMIZE
AUTUMNALLY
AUXOCHROME
AVALANCHES
AVANT
GARDE
AVANT-
GARDE
AVARICIOUS
AVELLANEDA
AVENTURINE
AVICULTURE
AVOCATIONS
AVUNCULATE
AWAKENINGS
AXIOLOGIST
AYATOLLAHS
AZEOTROPIC
AZERBAIJAN
AZOBENZENE

B
BABY-
MINDER
BABY
SITTER
BABY-
SITTER
BACCHANALS
BACITRACIN
BACKBITERS

BACKBITING
BACKCLOTHS
BACKCOMBED
BACKDATING
BACKFIRING
BACKGAMMON
BACKGROUND
BACKHANDED
BACKHANDER
BACKLASHES
BACK
MATTER
BACK
NUMBER
BACKPACKER
BACKSLIDER
BACKSPACES
BACKSTAIRS
BACKSTITCH
BACK
STREET
BACKSTROKE
BACKWARDLY
BACKWATERS
BACULIFORM
BADEN-
BADEN
BAD HAIR
DAY
BAD-
MOUTHED
BAFFLEMENT
BAGGAGE
CAR
BAHAWALPUR
BAINBRIDGE
BALACLAVAS
BALALAIKAS
BALDERDASH
BALDHEADED
BALIKPAPAN
BALLASTING
BALLERINAS
BALLFLOWER
BALLISTICS
BALLOONING
BALLOONIST
BALLPOINTS
BALLYMONEY
BALNEOLOGY
BALUSTRADE
BAMBOOZLED

BAMBOOZLER
BANALITIES
BANANA
SKIN
BANDERILLA
BANDLEADER
BANDMASTER
BANDOLEERS
BANDSTANDS
BANDWAGONS
BANFFSHIRE
BANGLADESH
BANISHMENT
BANK
DRAFTS
BANKROLLED
BANKRUPTCY
BANKRUPTED
BANNERETTE
BANQUETING
BAPTISTERY
BARBARIANS
BARBARISMS
BARBARIZED
BARBECUING
BARBED
WIRE
BARBELLATE
BAREHEADED
BARELEGGED
BARGAINING
BARGE
POLES
BARIUM
MEAL
BARLEYCORN
BARLEY
WINE
BAR
MITZVAH
BARN
DANCES
BARNSTAPLE
BAROMETERS
BAROMETRIC
BARONESSES
BARONETAGE
BARRACKING
BARRACUDAS
BARRAMUNDA
BARRAMUNDI
BARRATROUS

BARRENNESS
BARRENWORT
BARRICADED
BARRICADER
BARRICADES
BARRISTERS
BARROW
BOYS
BARTENDERS
BARYCENTRE
BARYSPHERE
BASALTWARE
BASE
METALS
BASILICATA
BASKETBALL
BASKET-
STAR
BASKETWORK
BAS-
RELIEFS
BASSE-
TERRE
BASSETERRE
BASS
GUITAR
BASSOONIST
BASTARDIZE
BASUTOLAND
BATH
CHAIRS
BATHOMETER
BATHOMETRY
BATHYMETRY
BATHYSCAPH
BATON
ROUGE
BATTALIONS
BATTLEAXES
BATTLEDORE
BATTLEMENT
BATTLESHIP
BAYONETING
BAY
WINDOWS
BEACH
BALLS
BEACH
BUGGY
BEACHCHAIR
BEACHFRONT
BEACHHEADS

BEANSPROUT
BEAR
 GARDEN
BEASTLIEST
BEATIFYING
BEATITUDES
BEAUJOLAIS
BEAUTICIAN
BEAUTIFIED
BEAUTY
 SPOT
BECOMINGLY
BECQUERELS
BEDCLOTHES
BEDEVILING
BEDEVILLED
BEDFELLOWS
BED OF
 NAILS
BED OF
 ROSES
BEDRAGGLED
BED-
 SITTERS
BEDSPREADS
BEEFEATERS
BEEF
 TOMATO
BEER
 GARDEN
BEFOREHAND
BEFOULMENT
BEFRIENDED
BEGGARWEED
BEGINNINGS
BEGRUDGING
BEHIND
 BARS
BEHINDHAND
BEHIND
 TIME
BELABOURED
BELIEVABLE
BELIEVABLY
BELITTLING
BELIZE
 CITY
BELLADONNA
BELLARMINE
BELLETRIST
BELLINZONA

BELL-
 RINGER
BELL THE
 CAT
BELLWETHER
BELL
 WETHER
BELLYACHED
BELLYACHES
BELLY
 DANCE
BELLY
 FLOPS
BELLY
 LAUGH
BELONGINGS
BELORUSSIA
BENCH
 MARKS
BENCH
 PRESS
BENEDICITE
BENEFACTOR
BENEFICENT
BENEFICIAL
BENEFITING
BENEVOLENT
BENIGNANCY
BENNINGTON
BENZOCAINE
BENZODRINE
BENZOFURAN
BEQUEATHED
BEQUEATHER
BERIBBONED
BERLIN
 WALL
BERTOLUCCI
BESEECHING
BESMEARING
BESMIRCHED
BESPEAKING
BESSARABIA
BESTIALITY
BESTIALIZE
BESTIARIES
BESTIRRING
BESTREWING
BESTRIDDEN
BESTRIDING
BEST-
 SELLER

BETELGEUSE
BETHINKING
BETOKENING
BETROTHALS
BETROTHING
BETTERMENT
BETWS-Y-
 COED
BEWILDERED
BEWITCHING
BIANNULATE
BIBLIOPOLE
BIBLIOTICS
BIBLIOIIST
BICHLORIDE
BICYCLISTS
BIENNIALLY
BIFURCATED
BIGAMOUSLY
BIG
 BROTHER
BIG
 DIPPERS
BIJOUTERIE
BILBERRIES
BILINGUALS
BILIVERDIN
BILL AND
 COO
BILLBOARDS
BILLET-
 DOUX
BILLIONTHS
BILL OF
 FARE
BILL OF
 SALE
BILLY
 GOATS
BIMESTRIAL
BIMETALLIC
BINOCULARS
BINUCLEATE
BIOCELLATE
BIODYNAMIC
BIOECOLOGY
BIOGENESIS
BIOGENETIC
BIOGRAPHER
BIOGRAPHIC
BIOLOGICAL
BIOLOGISTS

BIOMEDICAL
BIOPHYSICS
BIOPLASMIC
BIOPOIESIS
BIORHYTHMS
BIOSTATICS
BIPARIETAL
BIPARTISAN
BIPETALOUS
BIQUADRATE
BIRD OF
 PREY
BIRKENHEAD
BIRMINGHAM
BIRTHMARKS
BIRTHPLACE
BIRTH-
 RATES
BIRTHRIGHT
BIRTHSTONE
BIRTWISTLE
BISEXUALLY
BISHOPBIRD
BISHOPRICS
BISMUTHOUS
BISSEXTILE
BISULPHATE
BISULPHIDE
BISULPHITE
BISYMMETRY
BITARTRATE
BITCHINESS
BIT OF
 FLUFF
BITTERLING
BITTERNESS
BITTERWEED
BITTERWOOD
BITUMINIZE
BITUMINOUS
BIVALVULAR
BIVOUACKED
BLABBERING
BLACKAMOOR
BLACK
 BELTS
BLACKBERRY
BLACKBIRDS
BLACKBOARD
BLACK
 BOXES

BLACK
 DEATH
BLACKENING
BLACKGUARD
BLACKHEADS
BLACKHEART
BLACK
 HOLES
BLACKJACKS
BLACKLISTS
BLACK
 MAGIC
BLACK
 MARIA
BLACK
 POWER
BLACK
 SHEEP
BLACKSHIRT
BLACKSMITH
BLACKSNAKE
BLACK
 SPOTS
BLACKTHORN
BLACK
 WATCH
BLACK
 WIDOW
BLADDERNUT
BLANCMANGE
BLANKETING
BLANK
 VERSE
BLASPHEMED
BLASPHEMER
BLASTOCOEL
BLASTOCYST
BLASTODERM
BLASTOMERE
BLASTOPORE
BLATHERING
BLEACHABLE
BLEARINESS
BLEATINGLY
BLEMISHING
BLETHERING
BLIND
 ALLEY
BLIND
 DATES
BLIND
 DRUNK

BLINDFOLDS
BLIND
  SPOTS
BLISSFULLY
BLISTERING
BLITHENESS
BLITHERING
BLITHESOME
BLOCKADING
BLOCKHEADS
BLOCKHOUSE
BLOCK
  VOTES
BLONDENESS
BLOOD
  BANKS
BLOODBATHS
BLOOD
  COUNT
BLOOD
  DONOR
BLOOD
  FEUDS
BLOOD
  GROUP
BLOODHOUND
BLOODINESS
BLOOD
  LUSTS
BLOOD
  MONEY
BLOOD
  SPORT
BLOODSTAIN
BLOODSTOCK
BLOODSTONE
BLOOD
  TYPES
BLOODY
  MARY
BLOOMSBURY
BLOSSOMING
BLOTCHIEST
BLOW-BY-
  BLOW
BLOW-
  DRYING
BLOWZINESS
BLUBBERING
BLUDGEONED
BLUDGEONER
BLUE
  BABIES

BLUEBEARDS
BLUEBOTTLE
BLUE
  CHEESE
BLUE-
  COLLAR
BLUE
  DEVILS
BLUE
  MURDER
BLUE-
  PENCIL
BLUEPRINTS
BLUETHROAT
BLUE
  TONGUE
BLUNDERERS
BLUNDERING
BLUSHINGLY
BLUSTERERS
BLUSTERING
BOARDROOMS
BOARDWALKS
BOASTFULLY
BOASTINGLY
BOATHOUSES
BOATSWAINS
BOAT
  TRAINS
BOBBY
  SOCKS,
BOBSLEIGHS
BODY
  DOUBLE
BODYGUARDS
BODY
  SEARCH
BOILER
  SUIT
BOISTEROUS
BOLLOCKS-
  UP
BOLL
  WEEVIL
BOLOMETRIC
BOLSHEVIKS
BOLSHEVISM
BOLSTERING
BOMBARDIER
BOMBARDING
BOMBAY
  DUCK
BOMBSHELLS

BONDHOLDER
BONEHEADED
BONE
  MARROW
BONESHAKER
BONKBUSTER
BON
  VIVANTS
BOOBY
  PRIZE
BOOBY
  TRAPS
BOOKBINDER
BOOKKEEPER
BOOKMAKERS
BOOKMOBILE
BOOKPLATES
BOOKSELLER
BOOKSTALLS
BOOK
  TOKENS
BOOMERANGS
BOOTBLACKS
BOOTLEGGED
BOOTLEGGER
BOOTLOADER
BOOTSTRAPS
BORDERLAND
BORDERLINE
BORGERHOUT
BORROWINGS
BOTANIZING
BOTCHINESS
BOTHERSOME
BOTRYOIDAL
BOTTLE
  BANK
BOTTLE-
  FEED
BOTTLENECK
BOTTLE
  SHOP
BOTTOMLESS
BOTTOM
  LINE
BOTTOMMOST
BOULEVARDS
BOUNCINESS
BOUNDARIES
BOWDLERISM
BOWDLERIZE

BOW
  WINDOWS
BOX
  NUMBERS
BOX
  OFFICES
BOYCOTTING
BOYFRIENDS
BOYISHNESS
BRACHIOPOD
BRACHYLOGY
BRACHYURAN
BRACKETING
BRADYKININ
BRAGGINGLY
BRAHMANISM
BRAINCHILD
BRAIN
  DRAIN
BRAININESS
BRAINSTORM
BRAINWAVES
BRAKE
  SHOES
BRANCHIATE
BRANDISHED
BRANDISHER
BRAND
  NAMES
BRANDY
  SNAP
BRASHINESS
BRASS
  BANDS
BRASSBOUND
BRASSED
  OFF
BRASSERIES
BRASSIERES
BRASSINESS
BRASS
  TACKS
BRATISLAVA
BRAVISSIMO
BRAWNINESS
BRAZENNESS
BREADBOARD
BREADCRUMB
BREADFRUIT
BREADLINES
BREAKAWAYS
BREAKDOWNS

BREAKFASTS
BREAKFRONT
BREAKWATER
BREASTBONE
BREASTWORK
BREATHABLE
BRECCIATED
BREEZINESS
BRICKLAYER
BRIDEGROOM
BRIDESMAID
BRIDGEABLE
BRIDGEHEAD
BRIDGEPORT
BRIDGETOWN
BRIDGEWORK
BRIDGWATER
BRIGANTINE
BRIGHTENER
BRIGHTNESS
BRIGHTWORK
BRILLIANCE
BRILLIANCY
BRIQUETTES
BRITISHERS
BROAD
  BEANS
BROADCASTS
BROADCLOTH
BROADENING
BROAD
  GAUGE
BROADSHEET
BROADSIDES
BROADSWORD
BROCATELLE
BROKEN
  DOWN
BROKEN-
  DOWN
BROKENNESS
BROMSGROVE
BRONCHIOLE
BRONCHITIC
BRONCHITIS
BRONX
  CHEER
BROODINESS
BROOMSTICK
BROWBEATEN
BROWNED-
  OFF

BROWNFIELD
BROWNSTONE
BRUTALIZED
BRYOLOGIST
BRYOPHYTIC
BUBBLE
  WRAP
BUBONOCELE
BUCCANEERS
BUCCINATOR
BUCHENWALD
BUCKBOARDS
BUCKET
  SEAT
BUCKET
  SHOP
BUCKINGHAM
BUDGERIGAR
BUFFER
  ZONE
BUFFLEHEAD
BUFFOONERY
BULLDOZERS
BULLDOZING
BULLFIGHTS
BULLHEADED
BULLNECKED
BULLROARER
BULLY
  COURT
BUMBLEBEES
BUNCHINESS
BUNKHOUSES
BUNYA-
  BUNYA
BUON
  GIORNO
BURBERRIES
BURDENSOME
BUREAUCRAT
BURGENLAND
BURGEONING
BURGLARIES
BURGUNDIAN
BURLESQUED
BURLESQUER
BURLESQUES
BURLINGTON
BURNISHING
BURTHENING
BUSHBABIES
BUSHHAMMER

BUSHMASTER
BUSHRANGER
BUSINESSES
BUS
  STATION
BUSYBODIES
BUTCHERING
BUTTER
  BEAN
BUTTERCUPS
BUTTERFISH
BUTTERMILK
BUTTERWORT
BUTTON-
  DOWN
BUTTONHOLE
BUTTONHOOK
BUTTONWOOD
BUTTRESSED
BUTTRESSES
BY-
  ELECTION
BY-
  PRODUCTS
BYSTANDERS

C

CABANATUAN
CABIN
  CLASS
CACCIATORE
CACHINNATE
CACK-
  HANDED
CACOGENICS
CACOGRAPHY
CACOMISTLE
CACOPHONIC
CACTACEOUS
CADAVERINE
CADAVEROUS
CADET
  CORPS
CAERPHILLY
CAESAREANS
CAESPITOSE
CAFETERIAS
CALABASHES
CALABOOSES
CALAMANDER
CALAMITIES
CALAMITOUS

CALAMONDIN
CALAVERITE
CALCAREOUS
CALCEIFORM
CALCIFEROL
CALCIFUGAL
CALCIFYING
CALCITONIN
CALCSINTER
CALCULABLE
CALCULATED
CALCULATOR
CALCULUSES
CALDERDALE
CALEDONIAN
CALIBRATED
CALIBRATOR
CALIFORNIA
CALIPHATES
CALL
  CENTRE
CALL IT A
  DAY
CALLOWNESS
CALORICITY
CALUMNIATE
CALUMNIOUS
CALVINISTS
CALYPTRATE
CAMEMBERTS
CAMERAWORK
CAMERLENGO
CAMOUFLAGE
CAMPAIGNED
CAMPAIGNER
CAMPANILES
CAMPESTRAL
CAMPGROUND
CAMPHORATE
CAMPOBELLO
CANAL
  BOATS
CANALIZING
CANCELLATE
CANCELLING
CANDELABRA
CANDIDATES
CANDLEFISH
CANDLEPINS
CANDLEWICK
CANDLEWOOD

CANDYFLOSS
CANKERWORM
CANNABINOL
CANNELLONI
CANNONADES
CANNONBALL
CANONICATE
CANONICITY
CANONIZING
CANOODLING
CAN
  OPENERS
CANTABRIAN
CANTALOUPE
CANTALOUPS
CANTATRICE
CANTERBURY
CANTILEVER
CANTILLATE
CANTONMENT
CANVASBACK
CANVASSERS
CANVASSING
CAOUTCHOUC
CAPABILITY
CAPACITATE
CAPACITIES
CAPACITIVE
CAPACITORS
CAPARISONS
CAPE
  COLONY
CAP-
  HAITIEN
CAPITALISM
CAPITALIST
CAPITALIZE
CAPITATION
CAPITATIVE
CAPITULATE
CAPPUCCINO
CAPREOLATE
CAPRICIOUS
CAPRICORNS
CAPTAINING
CAPTIOUSLY
CAPTIVATED
CAPTIVATOR
CARAMELIZE
CARAVAGGIO
CARBOLATED

CARBONATED
CARBON
  COPY
CARBONIZED
CARBUNCLES
CARCINOGEN
CARDIALGIA
CARDIALGIC
CARDIOGRAM
CARDIOLOGY
CARD
  READER
CARDSHARPS
CAREERISTS
CARELESSLY
CARETAKERS
CARICATURE
CARJACKING
CARMARTHEN
CARNALLITE
CARNASSIAL
CARNATIONS
CARNELIANS
CARNIVORES
CAROLINIAN
CAROTENOID
CARPATHIAN
CARPELLARY
CARPELLATE
CARPENTERS
CARPOPHORE
CARPOSPORE
CARRIER
  BAG
CARRYING-
  ON
CARRY-
  OVERS
CARSON
  CITY
CARTHORSES
CARTHUSIAN
CARTILAGES
CARTOMANCY
CARTOONIST
CARTRIDGES
CART
  TRACKS
CARTWHEELS
CARUNCULAR
CARYATIDAL
CASABLANCA

CASCARILLA
CASE-
HARDEN
CASEINOGEN
CASEWORKER
CASHIERING
CASSEROLES
CASSIOPEIA
CASTIGATED
CASTIGATOR
CASTING
OFF
CASTRATING
CASTRATION
CASUALNESS
CASUALTIES
CASUS
BELLI
CATABOLISM
CATABOLITE
CATACLINAL
CATACLYSMS
CATAFALQUE
CATALECTIC
CATALEPTIC
CATALOGUED
CATALOGUER
CATALOGUES
CATAMARANS
CATAMENIAL
CATAPLASIA
CATAPULTED
CATARRHINE
CATASTASIS
CAT
BURGLAR
CATCALLING
CATCH A
CRAB
CATCH
CROPS
CATCHINESS
CATCHPENNY
CATCHWORDS
CATECHESIS
CATECHISMS
CATECHISTS
CATECHIZED
CATEGORIES
CATEGORIZE
CATENARIAN
CATENATION

CATENULATE
CATHEDRALS
CATHOLICON
CATOPTRICS
CAT'S
CRADLE
CATTLE
GRID
CAULESCENT
CAUTERIZED
CAUTIONARY
CAUTIONING
CAUTIOUSLY
CAVALCADES
CAVALRYMAN
CAVALRYMEN
CAVITATION
CAVITY
WALL
CEASE-
FIRES
CEILOMETER
CELEBRATED
CELEBRATOR
CELLOBIOSE
CELLOPHANE
CELLULITIS
CELLULOSIC
CEMETERIES
CENOTAPHIC
CENSORABLE
CENSORIOUS
CENSORSHIP
CENSURABLE
CENTENNIAL
CENTESIMAL
CENTIGRADE
CENTIGRAMS
CENTILITRE
CENTILLION
CENTIMETRE
CENTIPEDES
CENTIPOISE
CENTRALISM
CENTRALITY
CENTRALIZE
CENTRE-
FIRE
CENTRE-
FOLD
CENTRE
HALF

CENTRE
PASS
CENTRICITY
CENTRIFUGE
CENTROMERE
CENTROSOME
CENTURIONS
CEPHALONIA
CEPHALOPOD
CEREBELLAR
CEREBELLUM
CEREBRALLY
CEREDIGION
CEREMONIAL
CEREMONIES
CEROGRAPHY
CERTIFYING
CERTIORARI
CERUMINOUS
CERVICITIS
CESSATIONS
CESSIONARY
CETOLOGIST
CHAGRINING
CHAIN
GANGS
CHAINPLATE
CHAIN-
REACT
CHAIN
SMOKE
CHAIN-
SMOKE
CHAIN
STORE
CHAIR
LIFTS
CHAIRWOMAN
CHAIRWOMEN
CHALCEDONY
CHALCIDICE
CHALCOCITE
CHALKBOARD
CHALKINESS
CHALLENGED
CHALLENGER
CHALLENGES
CHALYBEATE
CHAMBER
POT
CHAMELEONS
CHAMOMILES

CHAMPIGNON
CHAMPIONED
CHANCELLOR
CHANCERIES
CHANCINESS
CHANDELIER
CHANDIGARH
CHANGEABLE
CHANGEABLY
CHANGELESS
CHANGELING
CHANGEOVER
CHANGE
OVER
CHANNEL-
HOP
CHANNELLED
CHANNELLER
CHAPERONED
CHAPFALLEN
CHAPLAINCY
CHARABANCS
CHARACTERS
CHARDONNAY
CHARGEABLE
CHARGE
CARD
CHARGE
HAND
CHARIOTEER
CHARITABLE
CHARITABLY
CHARLADIES
CHARLATANS
CHARLESTON
CHARMINGLY
CHARTERING
CHARTREUSE
CHASTENING
CHASTISING
CHATELAINE
CHATOYANCY
CHATTERBOX
CHATTERERS
CHATTERING
CHAUDFROID
CHAUFFEURS
CHAUVINISM
CHAUVINIST
CHEAPENING
CHEAPSKATE
CHEBOKSARY

CHECKLISTS
CHECKMATED
CHECKMATES
CHECKPOINT
CHECKROOMS
CHEEKBONES
CHEEKINESS
CHEEKPIECE
CHEERFULLY
CHEERINESS
CHEESECAKE
CHEESED
OFF
CHEESINESS
CHEKHOVIAN
CHELICERAL
CHELMSFORD
CHELTENHAM
CHEMICALLY
CHEMISETTE
CHEMOTAXIS
CHEQUEBOOK
CHEQUE
CARD
CHERISHING
CHERNOVTSY
CHERRYWOOD
CHERUBICAL
CHESAPEAKE
CHESSBOARD
CHESTINESS
CHEVALIERS
CHEVROTAIN
CHEWING
GUM
CHEW THE
CUD
CHEW THE
FAT
CHEW THE
RAG
CHICHESTER
CHICKEN
POX
CHIEFTAINS
CHIFFCHAFF
CHIFFONIER
CHIHUAHUAS
CHILBLAINS
CHILDBIRTH
CHILDISHLY

CHILD'S
PLAY
CHILIASTIC
CHILLINESS
CHIMERICAL
CHIMNEYPOT
CHIMPANZEE
CHINABERRY
CHINATOWNS
CHINCHILLA
CHINQUAPIN
CHINSTRAPS
CHINTZIEST
CHIPOLATAS
CHIROMANCY
CHIRPINESS
CHISELLERS
CHISELLING
CHITARRONE
CHITTAGONG
CHIVALROUS
CHLAMYDATE
CHLORAMINE
CHLORINATE
CHLOROFORM
CHOANOCYTE
CHOCKSTONE
CHOCOHOLIC
CHOCOLATES
CHOICENESS
CHOKEBERRY
CHONDRITIC
CHOPHOUSES
CHOPPINESS
CHOPSTICKS
CHORIAMBIC
CHORISTERS
CHRISTENED
CHRISTENER
CHRISTIANS
CHROMATICS
CHROMATIST
CHROMOMERE
CHROMONEMA
CHROMOSOME
CHRONICITY
CHRONICLED
CHRONICLER
CHRONICLES
CHRONOGRAM
CHRONOLOGY

CHRYSOLITE
CHRYSOTILE
CHUBBINESS
CHUCKER-
OUT
CHUCKWALLA
CHUKKA
BOOT
CHUMMINESS
CHUNKINESS
CHURCHGOER
CHURCHYARD
CHURLISHLY
CHYLACEOUS
CICATRICES
CICATRICLE
CICATRIZER
CIGARETTES
CINCHONINE
CINCHONISM
CINCHONIZE
CINCINNATI
CINDERELLA
CINERARIUM
CINNAMONIC
CINQUEFOIL
CIRCUITOUS
CIRCULATED
CIRCULATOR
CIRCUMCISE
CIRCUMFLEX
CIRCUMFUSE
CIRCUMVENT
CISMONTANE
CISTACEOUS
CISTERCIAN
CITRIC
ACID
CITRONELLA
CITRULLINE
CITY
FATHER
CITY-
STATES
CIVILITIES
CIVILIZING
CLACTONIAN
CLADISTICS
CLADOCERAN
CLAMBERING
CLAMMINESS
CLAMOURING

CLAMPDOWNS
CLANGOROUS
CLANNISHLY
CLANSWOMAN
CLAPPED-
OUT
CLARABELLA
CLARIFYING
CLASP
KNIFE
CLASSIC
CAR
CLASSICISM
CLASSICIST
CLASSIFIED
CLASSIFIER
CLASSMATES
CLASSROOMS
CLATTERING
CLAVICHORD
CLAVICULAR
CLAY
PIGEON
CLEANSABLE
CLEAN
SHEET
CLEAN
SWEEP
CLEARANCES
CLEFT
STICK
CLEMENTINE
CLERESTORY
CLERICALLY
CLEVER
DICK
CLEVERNESS
CLIENTELES
CLINGINESS
CLINGSTONE
CLINICALLY
CLINKSTONE
CLINOMETER
CLINOMETRY
CLIPBOARDS
CLIP
JOINTS
CLOAKROOMS
CLOBBERING
CLOCKMAKER
CLOCK
TOWER

CLODDISHLY
CLODHOPPER
CLOGGINESS
CLOISTERED
CLOSE
CALLS
CLOSED
BOOK
CLOSEDOWNS
CLOSED
SHOP
CLOSE
SHAVE
CLOSE
THING
CLOTHBOUND
CLOTHES
PEG
CLOUDBANKS
CLOUDBERRY
CLOUDBURST
CLOUDINESS
CLOVE
HITCH
CLOVERLEAF
CLOWNISHLY
CLOYEDNESS
CLUBFOOTED
CLUBHOUSES
CLUMSINESS
CLUSTERING
CLUTCH
BAGS
CLUTTERING
CLYDESDALE
CNIDOBLAST
COACERVATE
COACTIVITY
COADJUTANT
COADJUTORS
COAGULABLE
COAGULATED
COALBUNKER
COALESCENT
COALESCING
COALFIELDS
COALHOUSES
COALITIONS
COAPTATION
COARSENESS
COARSENING
COASTGUARD

COASTLINES
COAT
HANGER
COAT OF
ARMS
COCHABAMBA
COCHINEALS
COCKABULLY
COCKALORUM
COCKCHAFER
COCKED
HATS
COCKFIGHTS
COCKHORSES
COCKNEYISM
COCKSCOMBS
COCONUT
SHY
CODSWALLOP
COELACANTH
COENOCYTIC
COEQUALITY
COERCIVELY
COERCIVITY
COEXISTENT
COEXISTING
COFFEE
BARS
COFFEEPOTS
COFFEE
SHOP
COFFERDAMS
COGITATING
COGITATION
COGITATIVE
COGNIZABLE
COGNIZANCE
COHABITANT
COHABITING
COHERENTLY
COHESIVELY
COIMBATORE
COINCIDENT
COINCIDING
COLATITUDE
COLCHESTER
COLCHICINE
COLD
CHISEL
COLD
FISHES

COLD	COMANCHEAN	COMMUNIQUE	COMPULSORY	CONDUCTING
FRAMES	COMBATABLE	COMMUNISTS	COMPUTABLE	CONDUCTION
COLD	COMBATANTS	COMMUTABLE	CONCEALING	CONDUCTIVE
FRONTS	COMBATTING	COMMUTATOR	CONCEDEDLY	CONDUCTORS
COLDSTREAM	COMBINABLE	COMPACTING	CONCEIVING	CONEFLOWER
COLD	COMBUSTION	COMPANIONS	CONCENTRIC	CONFECTION
TURKEY	COMEDIENNE	COMPARABLE	CONCEPCION	CONFERENCE
COLEMANITE	COME-	COMPARABLY	CONCEPTION	CONFERMENT
COLEOPTILE	HITHER	COMPARATOR	CONCEPTIVE	CONFERRING
COLEORHIZA	COMELINESS	COMPARISON	CONCEPTUAL	CONFERVOID
COLLAGENIC	COMESTIBLE	COMPASSION	CONCERNING	CONFESSING
COLLAPSING	COME TO	COMPATIBLE	CONCERTINA	CONFESSION
COLLARBONE	HAND	COMPATIBLY	CONCERTINO	CONFESSORS
COLLAR	COME TO	COMPATRIOT	CONCESSION	CONFIDANTS
STUD	MIND	COMPELLING	CONCESSIVE	CONFIDENCE
COLLATERAL	COMFORTERS	COMPENDIUM	CONCHIOLIN	CONFIRMING
COLLATIONS	COMFORTING	COMPENSATE	CONCHOLOGY	CONFISCATE
COLLEAGUES	COMIC	COMPETENCE	CONCIERGES	CONFLATING
COLLECTING	OPERA	COMPETENCY	CONCILIATE	CONFLATION
COLLECTION	COMIC	COMPETITOR	CONCINNITY	CONFLICTED
COLLECTIVE	STRIP	COMPLACENT	CONCINNOUS	CONFLUENCE
COLLECTORS	COMMANDANT	COMPLAINED	CONCLAVIST	CONFORMERS
COLLEGIATE	COMMANDEER	COMPLAINER	CONCLUDING	CONFORMING
COLLIERIES	COMMANDERS	COMPLAINTS	CONCLUSION	CONFORMIST
COLLIMATOR	COMMANDING	COMPLEMENT	CONCLUSIVE	CONFORMITY
COLLISIONS	COMMEASURE	COMPLETELY	CONCOCTING	CONFOUNDED
COLLOCATED	COMMENCING	COMPLETING	CONCOCTION	CONFOUNDER
COLLOQUIAL	COMMENDING	COMPLETION	CONCOCTIVE	CONFRONTED
COLLOQUIES	COMMENTARY	COMPLETIST	CONCORDANT	CONFRONTER
COLLOQUIUM	COMMENTATE	COMPLETIVE	CONCORDATS	CONFUSABLE
COLLOTYPIC	COMMENTING	COMPLEXION	CONCOURSES	CONFUSEDLY
COLONIZERS	COMMERCIAL	COMPLEXITY	CONCRETELY	CONGEALING
COLONIZING	COMMISSARS	COMPLIANCE	CONCRETING	CONGENERIC
COLONNADED	COMMISSARY	COMPLICATE	CONCRETION	CONGENITAL
COLONNADES	COMMISSION	COMPLICITY	CONCRETIVE	CONGER
COLORATION	COMMISSURE	COMPLIMENT	CONCRETIZE	EELS
COLORATURA	COMMITMENT	COMPONENTS	CONCUBINES	CONGESTION
COLOR	COMMITTALS	COMPORTING	CONCURRENT	CONGESTIVE
LINES	COMMITTEES	COMPOSITES	CONCURRING	CONGLOBATE
COLOSSALLY	COMMITTING	COMPOSITOR	CONCUSSING	CONGREGATE
COLOSSUSES	COMMODIOUS	COMPOSTING	CONCUSSION	CONGRESSES
COLOURABLE	COMMODORES	COMPOUNDED	CONCUSSIVE	CONGRUENCE
COLOUR	COMMONABLE	COMPOUNDER	CONDEMNING	CONIFEROUS
BARS	COMMONALTY	COMPREHEND	CONDENSATE	CONJECTURE
COLOURFAST	COMMONNESS	COMPRESSED	CONDENSERS	CONJOINING
COLOUR	COMMON	COMPRESSES	CONDENSING	CONJOINTLY
FAST	NOUN	COMPRESSOR	CONDESCEND	CONJUGABLE
COLOURINGS	COMMON	COMPRISING	CONDIMENTS	CONJUGATED
COLOURLESS	ROOM	COMPROMISE	CONDITIONS	CONJUGATOR
COLUMBINES	COMMONWEAL	COMPULSION	CONDOLENCE	CONNECTING
COLUMELLAR	COMMOTIONS	COMPULSIVE	CONDUCIBLE	CONNECTION
COLUMNISTS	COMMUNIONS			

CONNECTIVE
CONNIVANCE
CONQUERING
CONQUERORS
CONSCIENCE
CONSCRIPTS
CONSECRATE
CONSENSUAL
CONSENTING
CONSEQUENT
CONSERVING
CONSIDERED
CONSIDERER
CONSIGNEES
CONSIGNING
CONSIGNORS
CONSISTENT
CONSISTING
CONSISTORY
CONSOCIATE
CONSOLABLE
CONSONANCE
CONSONANTS
CONSORTIAL
CONSORTING
CONSORTIUM
CONSPECTUS
CONSPIRACY
CONSPIRING
CONSTABLES
CONSTANTAN
CONSTANTIA
CONSTANTLY
CONSTIPATE
CONSTITUTE
CONSTRAINT
CONSTRUCTS
CONSTRUING
CONSUETUDE
CONSULATES
CONSULSHIP
CONSULTANT
CONSULTING
CONSUMMATE
CONTACTING
CONTACTUAL
CONTAGIONS
CONTAGIOUS
CONTAINERS
CONTAINING
CONTENDERS

CONTENDING
CONTENTING
CONTENTION
CONTESTANT
CONTESTING
CONTEXTUAL
CONTEXTURE
CONTIGUITY
CONTIGUOUS
CONTINENCE
CONTINENTS
CONTINGENT
CONTINUANT
CONTINUING
CONTINUITY
CONTINUOUS
CONTINUUMS
CONTORTING
CONTORTION
CONTOURING
CONTRABAND
CONTRABASS
CONTRACTED
CONTRACTOR
CONTRADICT
CONTRAFLOW
CONTRALTOS
CONTRARIES
CONTRARILY
CONTRASTED
CONTRAVENE
CONTRIBUTE
CONTRITELY
CONTRITION
CONTRIVING
CONTROLLED
CONTROLLER
CONTROVERT
CONTUSIONS
CONUNDRUMS
CONVALESCE
CONVECTION
CONVECTIVE
CONVECTORS
CONVENABLE
CONVENANCE
CONVENIENT
CONVENTION
CONVENTUAL
CONVERGENT
CONVERGING

CONVERSANT
CONVERSELY
CONVERSING
CONVERSION
CONVERTERS
CONVERTING
CONVEYABLE
CONVEYANCE
CONVICTING
CONVICTION
CONVICTIVE
CONVINCING
CONVOCATOR
CONVOLUTED
CONVULSING
CONVULSION
CONVULSIVE
COOCH
  BEHAR
COOKHOUSES
COOL-
  HEADED
COOPERATED
COOPERATOR
COOPTATION
COOPTATIVE
COORDINATE
COPARCENER
COPENHAGEN
COPPER
  BELT
COPPERHEAD
COPROLALIA
COPROLITIC
COPROPHAGY
COPULATING
COPULATION
COPULATIVE
COPY
  EDITOR
COPYHOLDER
COPYRIGHTS
COPYWRITER
COQUELICOT
COQUETRIES
COQUETTISH
COR
  ANGLAIS
CORDIALITY
CORDIERITE
CORDILLERA

CORDON
  BLEU
CORIACEOUS
CORINTHIAN
CORKSCREWS
CORMOPHYTE
CORMORANTS
CORNACEOUS
CORNCOCKLE
CORNCRAKES
CORNED
  BEEF
CORNELIANS
CORNFLAKES
CORNFLOWER
CORNSTARCH
CORNUCOPIA
CORNWALLIS
CORONATION
CORPORATOR
CORPOREITY
CORPULENCE
CORPUSCLES
CORRALLING
CORRECTING
CORRECTION
CORRECTIVE
CORRELATED
CORRELATES
CORRESPOND
CORRIENTES
CORRIGENDA
CORRIGIBLE
CORROBOREE
CORRODIBLE
CORRUGATED
CORRUPTING
CORRUPTION
CORRUPTIVE
CORSETIERE
CORUSCATED
COS
  LETTUCE
COSMICALLY
COSMIC
  RAYS
COSMODROME
COSMOGONAL
COSMOGONIC
COSMONAUTS
COSSETTING

COSTA
  RICAN
CO-
  STARRING
COSTLINESS
COST
  PRICES
COSTUMIERS
COTANGENTS
COTILLIONS
COTTAGE
  PIE
COTTON
  GINS
COTTONSEED
COTTONTAIL
COTTONWOOD
COTTON
  WOOL
COUCHETTES
COUCH
  GRASS
COULOMETER
COUNCILLOR
COUNCILMAN
COUNCILMEN
COUNCIL
  TAX
COUNSELLED
COUNSELLOR
COUNTDOWNS
COUNTERACT
COUNTERING
COUNTERSPY
COUNTESSES
COUNT
  NOUNS
COUNTRYMAN
COUNTRYMEN
COUNTY
  TOWN
COUPS
  D'ETAT
COURAGEOUS
COURGETTES
COURSEBOOK
COURT
  CARDS
COURTESANS
COURTESIES
COURTHOUSE
COURTLIEST

COURTSHIPS
COURTYARDS
COUTURIERS
COVARIANCE
COVENANTAL
COVENANTED
COVENANTEE
COVENANTER
COVENANTOR
COVER
  NOTES
COVER
  POINT
COVETOUSLY
COWCATCHER
CRAB
  APPLES
CRACKBRAIN
CRACKDOWNS
CRADLE
  SONG
CRAFTINESS
CRANE
  FLIES
CRANESBILL
CRANIOLOGY
CRANIOTOMY
CRANKSHAFT
CRAPULENCE
CRAQUELURE
CRASH-
  DIVED
CRASH-
  DIVES
CRAVENNESS
CRAYFISHES
CREAKINESS
CREAMERIES
CREAMINESS
CREATININE
CREATIONAL
CREATIVELY
CREATIVITY
CREDITABLE
CREDITABLY
CREDIT
  CARD
CREDIT
  NOTE
CREEPINESS
CREMATIONS
CREMATORIA

CRENELLATE
CREOSOTING
CREPE
  PAPER
CRESCENDOS
CRESCENTIC
CRETACEOUS
CREWELWORK
CRIBRIFORM
CRICKETERS
CRIMINALLY
CRIMSONING
CRINKLIEST
CRINOLINES
CRISPATION
CRISPINESS
CRISSCROSS
CRITERIONS
CRITICALLY
CRITICISMS
CRITICIZED
CRITICIZER
CROAKINESS
CROCHETING
CROCODILES
CROISSANTS
CROQUETTES
CROSSBONES
CROSSBREED
CROSSCHECK
CROSSHATCH
CROSS-
  INDEX
CROSSPATCH
CROSSPIECE
CROSS-
  REFER
CROSSROADS
CROSS-
  SLIDE
CROSSTREES
CROSSWALKS
CROSSWINDS
CROSSWORDS
CROWDED
  OUT
CROWN
  COURT
CROWN
  DERBY
CROWNPIECE

CROW'S
  NESTS
CRUCIFIXES
CRUCIFYING
CRUMBLIEST
CRUNCHIEST
CRUSTACEAN
CRUSTINESS
CRYOGENICS
CRYOPHILIC
CRYOSCOPIC
CRYPTOLOGY
CRYPTOZOIC
CRYSTAL
  SET
CTENOPHORE
CUBBYHOLES
CUCKOLDING
CUCKOOPINT
CUCKOO
  PINT
CUCULIFORM
CUDDLESOME
CUDGELLING
CUERNAVACA
CULLENDERS
CULTIVABLE
CULTIVATED
CULTIVATOR
CULTURALLY
CUMBERSOME
CUMMERBUND
CUMULATION
CUMULATIVE
CUMULIFORM
CUPBEARERS
CURABILITY
CURATE'S
  EGG
CURATORIAL
CURMUDGEON
CURRENCIES
CURRICULAR
CURRICULUM
CURTAILING
CURTAINING
CURVACEOUS
CURVATURES
CUSHIONING
CUSSEDNESS
CUSTARD
  PIE

CUSTODIANS
CUSTOMIZED
CUSTOM
  MADE
CUSTOM-
  MADE
CUTTHROATS
CUTTLEBONE
CUTTLEFISH
CUT UP
  ROUGH
CYANOGENIC
CYBERNETIC
CYBERSPACE
CYCLAMATES
CYCLICALLY
CYCLOMETER
CYCLOMETRY
CYCLORAMIC
CYCLOSTOME
CYCLOSTYLE
CYLINDROID
CYMBALISTS
CYMIFEROUS
CYSTECTOMY
CYSTOSCOPE
CYSTOSCOPY
CYTOCHROME
CYTOLOGIST

D
DACHSHUNDS
DAIL
  EIRANN
DAILY
  BREAD
DAIMYO
  BOND
DAINTINESS
DAIRY
  FARMS
DAIRYMAIDS
DAISY
  WHEEL
DALAI
  LAMAS
DALMATIANS
DAMAGEABLE
DAMP
  COURSE
DAMP
  SQUIBS

DAMSELFISH
DANDELIONS
DAPPLE-
  GREY
DAREDEVILS
DARJEELING
DARK
  HORSES
DARLINGTON
DARTBOARDS
DASHBOARDS
DAUGAVPILS
DAUGHTERLY
DAYDREAMED
DAYDREAMER
DAY-
  NEUTRAL
DAY
  NURSERY
DAY
  SCHOOLS
DAY-
  TRIPPER
DEACONSHIP
DEACTIVATE
DEAD
  CENTRE
DEAD
  LETTER
DEADLINESS
DEADLY
  SINS
DEAD-
  NETTLE
DEAD
  RINGER
DEALERSHIP
DEATHBLOWS
DEATH
  MASKS
DEATH
  RATES
DEATH'S-
  HEAD
DEATH
  SQUAD
DEATH
  TOLLS
DEATH
  TRAPS
DEATHWATCH
DEBASEMENT
DEBAUCHEES

DEBAUCHERY
DEBAUCHING
DEBENTURES
DEBILITATE
DEBOUCHING
DEBRIEFING
DEBUTANTES
DECADENTLY
DECAHEDRAL
DECAHEDRON
DECAMPMENT
DECAPITATE
DECATHLONS
DECEIVABLE
DECELERATE
DECEPTIONS
DECIMALIZE
DECIMATING
DECIMATION
DECIPHERED
DECIPHERER
DECISIONAL
DECISIVELY
DECKCHAIRS
DECLAIMING
DECLARABLE
DECLASSIFY
DECLENSION
DECLINABLE
DECOCTIONS
DECOLLATOR
DECOLONIZE
DECOLORANT
DECOLORIZE
DECOMPOSED
DECOMPOSER
DECOMPOUND
DECOMPRESS
DECORATING
DECORATION
DECORATIVE
DECORATORS
DECOROUSLY
DECOUPLING
DECREASING
DECREEABLE
DECREE
    NISI
DECRESCENT
DECUMBENCE
DEDICATING

DEDICATION
DEDICATORY
DEDUCTIBLE
DEDUCTIONS
DEEP
    FREEZE
DEEP
    FRYING
DEEP-
    ROOTED
DEEP-
    SEATED
DE-
    ESCALATE
DEFACEABLE
DEFACEMENT
DEFALCATOR
DEFAMATION
DEFAMATORY
DEFAULTERS
DEFAULTING
DEFEASANCE
DEFEASIBLE
DEFEATISTS
DEFECATING
DEFECATION
DEFECTIONS
DEFENDABLE
DEFENDANTS
DEFENSIBLE
DEFENSIBLY
DEFENSIVES
DEFERMENTS
DEFERRABLE
DEFICIENCY
DEFILEMENT
DEFINITELY
DEFINITION
DEFINITIVE
DEFINITUDE
DEFLAGRATE
DEFLECTING
DEFLECTION
DEFLECTIVE
DEFLOWERED
DEFLOWERER
DEFOLIANTS
DEFOLIATED
DEFOLIATOR
DEFORESTED
DEFORESTER
DEFORMABLE

DEFRAUDING
DEFRAYABLE
DEFROCKING
DEFROSTERS
DEFROSTING
DEFUNCTIVE
DEGENERACY
DEGENERATE
DEGRADABLE
DEGRESSION
DEHISCENCE
DEHUMANIZE
DEHUMIDIFY
DEHYDRATED
DEHYDRATOR
DEJECTEDLY
DELAMINATE
DELAWAREAN
DELECTABLE
DELECTABLY
DELEGATING
DELEGATION
DELIBERATE
DELICACIES
DELICATELY
DELIGHTFUL
DELIGHTING
DELIMITING
DELINEATED
DELINEATOR
DELINQUENT
DELIQUESCE
DELIVERIES
DELIVERING
DELOCALIZE
DELPHINIUM
DELTIOLOGY
DELUSIONAL
DELUSIVELY
DEMAGOGUES
DEMANDABLE
DEMARCATED
DEMARCATOR
DEMEANOURS
DEMENTEDLY
DEMICANTON
DEMIVIERGE
DEMOBILIZE
DEMOCRATIC
DEMODULATE
DEMOGRAPHY

DEMOISELLE
DEMOLISHED
DEMOLISHER
DEMOLITION
DEMONETIZE
DEMONIACAL
DEMONOLOGY
DEMORALIZE
DEMOTIVATE
DEMURENESS
DEMURRABLE
DENATURANT
DENDRIFORM
DENDROGRAM
DENDROLOGY
DENEGATION
DENIGRATED
DENIGRATOR
DENOMINATE
DENOTATION
DENOTATIVE
DENOTEMENT
DENOUEMENT
DENOUNCING
DENSIMETER
DENSIMETRY
DENTIFRICE
DENUDATION
DENUNCIATE
DENVER
    BOOT
DEODORANTS
DEODORIZED
DEODORIZER
DEONTOLOGY
DEOXIDIZER
DEPARTMENT
DEPARTURES
DEPENDABLE
DEPENDABLY
DEPENDANTS
DEPENDENCE
DEPENDENCY
DEPICTIONS
DEPILATION
DEPILATORY
DEPLETABLE
DEPLORABLE
DEPLORABLY
DEPLOYMENT
DEPOLARIZE

DEPOPULATE
DEPORTABLE
DEPORTMENT
DEPOSITARY
DEPOSITING
DEPOSITION
DEPOSITORS
DEPOSITORY
DEPRECATED
DEPRECATOR
DEPRECIATE
DEPRESSANT
DEPRESSING
DEPRESSION
DEPRESSIVE
DEPRIVABLE
DEPURATION
DEPURATIVE
DEPUTATION
DEPUTIZING
DERACINATE
DERAILLEUR
DERAILMENT
DERBYSHIRE
DEREGULATE
DERISIVELY
DERISORILY
DERIVATION
DERIVATIVE
DERMATITIS
DERMATOGEN
DERMATOMIC
DERMATOSIS
DEROGATING
DEROGATION
DEROGATIVE
DEROGATORY
DESALINATE
DESALINIZE
DESCENDANT
DESCENDENT
DESCENDING
DESCRIBING
DESECRATED
DESECRATOR
DESERTIONS
DESERVEDLY
DESHABILLE
DESICCANTS
DESICCATED
DESICCATOR

DESIDERATA	DETRUNCATE	DICTIONARY	DIPHTHERIA	DISCOMMODE
DESIDERATE	DEUTOPLASM	DICTOGRAPH	DIPHTHONGS	DISCOMPOSE
DESIGNABLE	DEUX-	DICYNODONT	DIPHYLETIC	DISCONCERT
DESIGNATED	SEVRES	DIDYNAMOUS	DIPHYLLOUS	DISCONNECT
DESIGNATOR	DEVASTATED	DIE-	DIPHYODONT	DISCONTENT
DESIGNEDLY	DEVASTATOR	CASTING	DIPLODOCUS	DISCOPHILE
DESISTANCE	DEVELOPERS	DIE-	DIPLOMATIC	DISCORDANT
DESOLATELY	DEVELOPING	HARDISM	DIPSOMANIA	DISCOUNTED
DESOLATING	DEVIATIONS	DIELECTRIC	DIRECTIONS	DISCOUNTER
DESOLATION	DEVILISHLY	DIETICIANS	DIRECTIVES	DISCOURAGE
DESPAIRING	DEVITALIZE	DIFFERENCE	DIRECTNESS	DISCOURSED
DESPATCHED	DEVOCALIZE	DIFFICULTY	DIRECTOIRE	DISCOURSER
DESPATCHER	DEVOLUTION	DIFFIDENCE	DIRECTRESS	DISCOURSES
DESPATCHES	DEVOTEMENT	DIFFRACTED	DIRIGIBLES	DISCOVERED
DESPERADOS	DEVOTIONAL	DIFFUSIBLE	DIRT	DISCOVERER
DESPICABLE	DEVOUTNESS	DIGESTIBLE	FARMER	DISCREETLY
DESPICABLY	DEXTRALITY	DIGESTIONS	DIRT	DISCREPANT
DESPOILING	DIABOLICAL	DIGESTIVES	TRACKS	DISCRETELY
DESPONDENT	DIACAUSTIC	DIGITALISM	DIRTY	DISCRETION
DESQUAMATE	DIACHRONIC	DIGITALIZE	TRICK	DISCURSIVE
DESSIATINE	DIACRITICS	DIGITATION	DISABILITY	DISCUSSANT
DESTROYERS	DIACTINISM	DIGITIFORM	DISABUSING	DISCUSSING
DESTROYING	DIADROMOUS	DIGITIZERS	DISALLOWED	DISCUSSION
DESTRUCTOR	DIAGENESIS	DIGITIZING	DISAPPOINT	DISDAINFUL
DETACHABLE	DIAGNOSING	DIGNIFYING	DISAPPROVE	DISDAINING
DETACHMENT	DIAGNOSTIC	DIGRESSING	DISARRANGE	DISEMBOGUE
DETAINABLE	DIAGONALLY	DIGRESSION	DISASTROUS	DISEMBOWEL
DETAINMENT	DIAKINESIS	DIGRESSIVE	DISAVOWALS	DISEMBROIL
DETECTABLE	DIALECTICS	DILAPIDATE	DISAVOWING	DISEMPOWER
DETECTIVES	DIALYSABLE	DILATATION	DISBANDING	DISENCHANT
DETERGENCY	DIAPASONAL	DILEMMATIC	DISBARMENT	DISENDOWER
DETERGENTS	DIAPEDESIS	DILETTANTE	DISBARRING	DISENGAGED
DETERMINED	DIAPEDETIC	DILETTANTI	DISBELIEVE	DISENTHRAL
DETERMINER	DIAPHANOUS	DILIGENTLY	DISBENEFIT	DISENTITLE
DETERRENCE	DIAPHRAGMS	DILLYDALLY	DISBURSING	DISENTWINE
DETERRENTS	DIAPHYSIAL	DIMENSIONS	DISCARDING	DISEPALOUS
DETESTABLE	DIARRHOEAL	DIMINISHED	DISC	DISFEATURE
DETESTABLY	DIASTALSIS	DIMINUENDO	BRAKES	DISFIGURED
DETHRONING	DIASTALTIC	DIMINUTION	DISCERNING	DISFIGURER
DETONATING	DIATHERMIC	DIMINUTIVE	DISCHARGED	DISGORGING
DETONATION	DIATROPISM	DIMORPHISM	DISCHARGER	DISGRACING
DETONATIVE	DIBASICITY	DIMORPHOUS	DISCHARGES	DISGRUNTLE
DETONATORS	DICHLORIDE	DINERS	DISC	DISGUISING
DETOXICANT	DICHROMATE	CLUB	HARROW	DISGUSTING
DETOXICATE	DICKENSIAN	DINING	DISCIPLINE	DISHABILLE
DETRACTING	DICKEY	CARS	DISC	DISHARMONY
DETRACTION	BIRD	DINING	JOCKEY	DISHCLOTHS
DETRACTIVE	DICKYBIRDS	ROOM	DISCLAIMED	DISHEARTEN
DETRACTORS	DICTAPHONE	DINNER	DISCLAIMER	DISHONESTY
DETRAINING	DICTATIONS	BELL	DISCLOSING	DISH
DETRIMENTS	DICTATRESS	DIPETALOUS	DISCLOSURE	TOWELS
		DIPHOSGENE	DISCOMFORT	

DISHWASHER
DISINCLINE
DISINHERIT
DISJOINTED
DISK
DRIVES
DISLIKABLE
DISLOCATED
DISLODGING
DISLOYALLY
DISLOYALTY
DISMALNESS
DISMANTLED
DISMANTLER
DISMASTING
DISMISSALS
DISMISSING
DISMISSIVE
DISMOUNTED
DISOBEYING
DISOBLIGED
DISORDERED
DISORDERLY
DISOWNMENT
DISPARAGED
DISPARAGER
DISPASSION
DISPATCHED
DISPATCHES
DISPELLING
DISPENSARY
DISPENSERS
DISPENSING
DISPERMOUS
DISPERSING
DISPERSION
DISPERSIVE
DISPERSOID
DISPIRITED
DISPLACING
DISPLAYING
DISPLEASED
DISPORTING
DISPOSABLE
DISPOSSESS
DISPRAISER
DISPROVING
DISPUTABLE
DISPUTABLY
DISQUALIFY
DISQUIETED

DISRESPECT
DISRUPTING
DISRUPTION
DISRUPTIVE
DISSATISFY
DISSECTING
DISSECTION
DISSEMBLED
DISSEMBLER
DISSENSION
DISSENTERS
DISSENTING
DISSERVICE
DISSIDENCE
DISSIDENTS
DISSIMILAR
DISSIPATED
DISSIPATER
DISSOCIATE
DISSOLUBLE
DISSOLVING
DISSONANCE
DISSUADING
DISSUASION
DISSUASIVE
DISTANCING
DISTENDING
DISTENSION
DISTICHOUS
DISTILLATE
DISTILLERS
DISTILLERY
DISTILLING
DISTINCTLY
DISTORTING
DISTORTION
DISTORTIVE
DISTRACTED
DISTRACTER
DISTRAINED
DISTRAINEE
DISTRAINOR
DISTRAUGHT
DISTRESSED
DISTRIBUTE
DISTRUSTED
DISTRUSTER
DISTURBING
DISULFIRAM
DISULPHATE
DISULPHIDE

DISUNITING
DISUTILITY
DISYLLABIC
DITHEISTIC
DITHIONITE
DIVARICATE
DIVE-
BOMBED
DIVE-
BOMBER
DIVERGENCE
DIVERGENCY
DIVERSIONS
DIVERTEDLY
DIVERTIBLE
DIVESTIBLE
DIVESTMENT
DIVINATION
DIVINATORY
DIVING
BELL
DIVINITIES
DIVISIONAL
DIVISIVELY
DIVULGENCE
DIYARBAKIR
DOCENTSHIP
DOC
MARTENS
DOCTORATES
DOCTRINISM
DOCUMENTED
DODECANESE
DOG
BISCUIT
DOGCATCHER
DOG
COLLARS
DOGGEDNESS
DOGMATISTS
DOGMATIZER
DOGSBODIES
DOLCELATTE
DOLLARFISH
DOLL'S
HOUSE
DOLLY
BIRDS
DOLOROUSLY
DOMINATING
DOMINATION
DOMINATIVE

DOMINATRIX
DOMINEERED
DOMINICANS
DONER
KEBAB
DONKEYWORK
DONNYBROOK
DOORKEEPER
DOORPLATES
DORCHESTER
DORSIGRADE
DOSIMETRIC
DOSSHOUSES
DO THE
TRICK
DOTTED
LINE
DOUBLE
BASS
DOUBLE
BEDS
DOUBLE
BIND
DOUBLE
CHIN
DOUBLE
DATE
DOUBLE-
HUNG
DOUBLE-
PARK
DOUBLE-
REED
DOUBLE-
STOP
DOUBLE
TAKE
DOUBLE-
TALK
DOUBLE
TIME
DOUBLETREE
DOUBTFULLY
DOUGHTIEST
DOVETAILED
DOWN-AND-
OUT
DOWN AT
HEEL
DOWN-AT-
HEEL
DOWNGRADED
DOWNLOADED

DOWN-
MARKET
DOWNPLAYED
DOWNSIZING
DOWNSPOUTS
DOWNSTAIRS
DOWNSTREAM
DRAGONHEAD
DRAGONROOT
DRAGOONAGE
DRAGOONING
DRAINPIPES
DRAMATISTS
DRAMATIZED
DRAMATIZER
DRAMATURGE
DRAMATURGY
DRAWBRIDGE
DRAWING
PIN
DRAWSTRING
DREADFULLY
DREADLOCKS
DREAMBOATS
DREAMINESS
DREAMINGLY
DREAMLANDS
DREAM
WORLD
DREARINESS
DRESSINESS
DRESSMAKER
DRILLSTOCK
DRIP-
DRYING
DRIVELLERS
DRIVELLING
DROLLERIES
DROOPINESS
DROSOPHILA
DROSSINESS
DROWSINESS
DRUGSTORES
DRUM
MAJORS
DRUMSTICKS
DRUPACEOUS
DRY
BATTERY
DRY-
CLEANED

DRY
  CLEANER
DUBITATION
DUCKBOARDS
DUFFEL
  BAGS
DUFFEL
  COAT
DUMBSTRUCK
DUMBWAITER
DUNCE'S
  CAPS
DUNDERHEAD
DUODECIMAL
DUODENITIS
DUPABILITY
DUPLICABLE
DUPLICATED
DUPLICATES
DUPLICATOR
DURABILITY
DURATIONAL
DUSSELDORF
DUST
  JACKET
DUSTSHEETS
DUST
  STORMS
DUTCH
  BARNS
DUTCH
  OVENS
DUTCH
  TREAT
DUTCH
  UNCLE
DYNAMISTIC
DYNAMITING
DYSENTERIC
DYSPLASTIC
DYSPROSIUM
DYSTROPHIC
DZERZHINSK

E

EAGLESTONE
EARLY
  BIRDS
EARMARKING
EARTHBOUND
EARTHINESS
EARTHLIEST

EARTHLIGHT
EARTHLINGS
EARTHQUAKE
EARTHSHINE
EARTHWARDS
EARTHWORKS
EARTHWORMS
EAR
  TRUMPET
EAST
  ANGLIA
EAST
  BERLIN
EAST
  ENDERS
EASTER
  EGGS
EASTERNERS
EASTERTIDE
EAST
  GERMAN
EAST
  INDIAN
EAST
  INDIES
EASTWARDLY
EASY
  CHAIRS
EASY DOES
  IT
EASY
  STREET
EASY
  VIRTUE
EBRACTEATE
EBULLIENCE
EBULLITION
EBURNATION
ECCENTRICS
ECCHYMOSIS
ECHINODERM
ECHOPRAXIA
ECOCENTRIC
ECOLOGICAL
ECOLOGISTS
ECONOMICAL
ECONOMISTS
ECONOMIZED
ECONOMIZER
ECOSPECIES
ECOSYSTEMS
ECOTOURISM

ECTODERMAL
ECTOENZYME
ECTOGENOUS
ECTOMORPHY
ECUADORIAN
ECUMENICAL
ECZEMATOUS
EDENTULOUS
EDIFYINGLY
EDITORIALS
EDITORSHIP
EDULCORATE
EDWARDIANS
EFFACEABLE
EFFACEMENT
EFFECTIBLE
EFFECTUATE
EFFEMINACY
EFFEMINATE
EFFERVESCE
EFFETENESS
EFFICIENCY
EFFLORESCE
EFFORTLESS
EFFRONTERY
EFFULGENCE
EFFUSIVELY
EGOCENTRIC
EGYPTOLOGY
EIDERDOWNS
EIGHTEENMO
EIGHTEENTH
EIGHTH
  NOTE
EIGHTIETHS
EISENSTADT
EISTEDDFOD
EJACULATED
EJACULATOR
ELABORATED
ELABORATOR
ELAEOPTENE
ELASTICITY
ELASTICIZE
ELATEDNESS
ELDERBERRY
ELEATICISM
ELECAMPANE
ELECTIVITY
ELECTORATE
ELECTRICAL

ELECTRODES
ELECTROJET
ELECTRONIC
ELEMENTARY
ELEVATIONS
ELEVEN-
  PLUS
ELICITABLE
ELIMINABLE
ELIMINATED
ELIMINATOR
ELLIPTICAL
ELONGATING
ELONGATION
ELONGATIVE
ELOPEMENTS
ELOQUENTLY
EL
  SALVADOR
ELUCIDATED
ELUCIDATOR
ELUTRIATOR
ELUVIATION
EMACIATION
EMANATIONS
EMANCIPATE
EMARGINATE
EMASCULATE
EMBALMMENT
EMBANKMENT
EMBARGOING
EMBARKMENT
EMBEZZLERS
EMBEZZLING
EMBITTERED
EMBITTERER
EMBLAZONED
EMBLAZONRY
EMBLEMATIC
EMBLEMENTS
EMBODIMENT
EMBOLDENED
EMBOLISMIC
EMBONPOINT
EMBOSSMENT
EMBOUCHURE
EMBRASURED
EMBRASURES
EMBRECTOMY
EMBROIDERY
EMBROILING

EMBRYOGENY
EMBRYOLOGY
EMENDATION
EMENDATORY
EMETICALLY
EMIGRATING
EMIGRATION
EMIGRATIVE
EMISSARIES
EMISSIVITY
EMMENTALER
EMMETROPIA
EMMETROPIC
EMOLLIENCE
EMOLLIENTS
EMOLUMENTS
EMPALEMENT
EMPANELING
EMPANELLED
EMPHASIZED
EMPIRICISM
EMPIRICIST
EMPLOYABLE
EMPLOYMENT
EMPOWERING
EMULSIFIED
EMULSIFIER
EMULSIONED
ENACTMENTS
ENAMELLING
ENAMELLIST
ENAMELWARE
ENAMELWORK
ENCAMPMENT
ENCASEMENT
ENCASHABLE
ENCASHMENT
ENCEPHALIC
ENCEPHALON
ENCHAINING
ENCHANTERS
ENCHANTING
ENCHILADAS
ENCIPHERER
ENCIRCLING
ENCLOSABLE
ENCLOSURES
ENCODEMENT
ENCOUNTERS
ENCOURAGED
ENCOURAGER

ENCROACHED
ENCROACHER
ENCRUSTANT
ENCUMBERED
ENCYCLICAL
ENCYSTMENT
ENDANGERED
ENDEARMENT
ENDEAVOURS
ENDOCARPAL
ENDOCRINAL
ENDOCRINIC
ENDODERMAL
ENDODERMIC
ENDODERMIS
ENDODONTIA
ENDODONTIC
ENDOENZYME
ENDOGAMOUS
ENDOGENOUS
ENDOMORPHY
ENDOPHYTIC
ENDORSABLE
ENDOSCOPIC
ENDOSMOSIS
ENDOSMOTIC
ENDOSTOSIS
ENDOWMENTS
END
    PRODUCT
ENDURINGLY
ENERGETICS
ENERGIZING
ENERVATING
ENERVATION
ENERVATIVE
ENFACEMENT
ENFEEBLING
ENFILADING
ENFLEURAGE
ENFOLDMENT
ENFORCEDLY
ENGAGEMENT
ENGAGINGLY
ENGENDERED
ENGENDERER
ENGINEERED
ENGINE
    ROOM
ENGLISHMAN
ENGLISHMEN

ENGRAVINGS
ENGROSSING
ENGULFMENT
ENHARMONIC
ENJAMBMENT
ENJOINMENT
ENJOYMENTS
ENLACEMENT
ENLISTMENT
ENLIVENING
ENORMITIES
ENORMOUSLY
ENPHYTOTIC
ENRAGEMENT
ENRAPTURED
ENRICHMENT
ENROLMENTS
ENSANGUINE
ENSCONCING
ENSHRINING
ENSHROUDED
ENSIGNSHIP
ENTAILMENT
ENTANGLING
ENTEROTOMY
ENTERPRISE
ENTHRALLED
ENTHRALLER
ENTHRONING
ENTHUSIASM
ENTHUSIAST
ENTICEMENT
ENTICINGLY
ENTIRENESS
ENTODERMAL
ENTOMBMENT
ENTOMOLOGY
ENTOPHYTIC
ENTOURAGES
ENTRAINING
ENTRANCING
ENTRAPMENT
ENTRAPPING
ENTREATIES
ENTREATING
ENTRENCHED
ENTRENCHER
ENTRUSTING
ENTRY-
    LEVEL
ENUCLEATOR

ENUMERATED
ENUMERATOR
ENUNCIABLE
ENUNCIATED
ENUNCIATOR
ENVELOPING
ENVISAGING
ENZYMOLOGY
EOSINOPHIL
EPEIROGENY
EPENTHESIS
EPENTHETIC
EPEXEGESIS
EPEXEGETIC
EPIBLASTIC
EPICANTHUS
EPICARDIAC
EPICARDIUM
EPICENTRAL
EPICENTRES
EPICUREANS
EPICYCLOID
EPIDEICTIC
EPIDEMICAL
EPIDIDYMAL
EPIDIDYMIS
EPIGASTRIC
EPIGENESIS
EPIGENETIC
EPIGLOTTAL
EPIGLOTTIS
EPIGRAPHER
EPIGRAPHIC
EPILEPTICS
EPILEPTOID
EPIMORPHIC
EPINEURIAL
EPINEURIUM
EPIPHONEMA
EPIPHYSEAL
EPIROGENIC
EPISCOPACY
EPISCOPATE
EPISIOTOMY
EPISPASTIC
EPISTERNUM
EPISTOLARY
EPITAPHIST
EPITHELIAL
EPITHELIUM
EPITOMIZED

EPITOMIZER
EPOXY
    RESIN
EPSOM
    SALTS
EQUABILITY
EQUALIZERS
EQUALIZING
EQUANIMITY
EQUANIMOUS
EQUATIONAL
EQUATORIAL
EQUESTRIAN
EQUIPOTENT
EQUITATION
EQUIVALENT
EQUIVOCATE
ERADIATION
ERADICABLE
ERADICATED
ERADICATOR
ERECTILITY
ERETHISMIC
ERGONOMICS
ERGOSTEROL
ERICACEOUS
ERINACEOUS
EROGENEITY
EROTEMATIC
EROTICALLY
EROTOGENIC
EROTOMANIA
ERRATICISM
ERUBESCENT
ERUCTATION
ERUCTATIVE
ERUPTIONAL
ERUPTIVITY
ERYSIPELAS
ERYTHRITOL
ESCADRILLE
ESCALATING
ESCALATION
ESCALATORS
ESCAPEMENT
ESCAPOLOGY
ESCARPMENT
ESCHAROTIC
ESCRITOIRE
ESCUTCHEON
ESKILSTUNA

ESPADRILLE
ESPECIALLY
ESPLANADES
ESSENTIALS
ESTATE
    CARS
ESTHETICAL
ESTIMATING
ESTIMATION
ESTIMATIVE
ESTIMATORS
ESTIPULATE
ESTRANGING
ETERNALITY
ETERNALIZE
ETERNITIES
ETHANEDIOL
ETHEREALLY
ETHNICALLY
ETHNOGENIC
ETHNOLOGIC
ETHOLOGIST
ETHYLATION
ETIOLATION
EUBACTERIA
EUCALYPTOL
EUCALYPTUS
EUCHLORINE
EUDEMONICS
EUDEMONISM
EUDIOMETER
EUDIOMETRY
EUGENICIST
EUHEMERISM
EUHEMERIST
EUHEMERIZE
EULOGISTIC
EULOGIZING
EUPATORIUM
EUPHAUSIID
EUPHEMISMS
EUPHEMIZER
EUPHONIOUS
EUPHONIUMS
EUPHORIANT
EUPHUISTIC
EURE-ET-
    LOIR
EURHYTHMIC
EUROCHEQUE
EUROCLYDON

FURODOLLAR	EXCAVATION	EXOCENTRIC	EXPUNCTION	FACE-HARDEN
EUROMARKET	EXCAVATORS	EXODONTIST	EXPURGATED	FACE POWDER
EURYPTERID	EXCEEDABLE	EXONERATED	EXPURGATOR	FACE-SAVERS
EURYTHMICS	EXCELLENCE	EXONERATOR	EXSANGUINE	FACE-SAVING
EURYTROPIC	EXCELLENCY	EXORBITANT	EXSICCATOR	FACE TO FACE
EUSTACHIAN	EXCEPTABLE	EXORCIZING	EXTENDIBLE	FACE-TO-FACE
EUTHANASIA	EXCEPTIONS	EXOSPOROUS	EXTENSIBLE	FACE VALUES
EVACUATING	EXCHANGING	EXOTHERMIC	EXTENSIONS	FACILENESS
EVACUATION	EXCITATION	EXOTICALLY	EXTENUATED	FACILITATE
EVACUATIVE	EXCITATIVE	EXOTICNESS	EXTENUATOR	FACILITIES
EVALUATING	EXCITEMENT	EXPANDABLE	EXTERNALLY	FACSIMILES
EVALUATION	EXCITINGLY	EXPANSIBLE	EXTINCTION	FACTITIOUS
EVALUATIVE	EXCLAIMING	EXPANSIONS	EXTINCTIVE	FACT OF LIFE
EVANESCENT	EXCLUDABLE	EXPATIATED	EXTINGUISH	FACTORABLE
EVANGELISM	EXCLUSIVES	EXPATIATOR	EXTIRPATED	FACTORIZED
EVANGELIST	EXCOGITATE	EXPATRIATE	EXTIRPAIOR	FACTORSHIP
EVANGELIZE	EXCORIATED	EXPECTABLE	EXTORTIONS	FACTUALISM
EVANSVILLE	EXCRESCENT	EXPECTANCY	EXTRACTING	FACTUALIST
EVAPORABLE	EXCRETIONS	EXPEDIENCE	EXTRACTION	FAHRENHEIT
EVAPORATED	EXCRUCIATE	EXPEDIENCY	EXTRACTIVE	FAINTINGLY
EVAPORATOR	EXCULPABLE	EXPEDIENTS	EXTRACTORS	FAIR COPIES
EVECTIONAL	EXCULPATED	EXPEDITING	EXTRADITED	FAIR DINKUM
EVEN-HANDED	EXCURSIONS	EXPEDITION	EXTRAMURAL	FAIRGROUND
EVENING ALL	EXCUSATORY	EXPELLABLE	EXTRANEOUS	FAIR-MINDED
EVENING OUT	EXECRATING	EXPENDABLE	EXTRAVERTS	FAIR-SPOKEN
EVENTFULLY	EXECRATION	EXPERIENCE	EXTRICABLE	FAIRYLANDS
EVENTUALLY	EXECRATIVE	EXPERIMENT	EXTRICATED	FAIRY LIGHT
EVERGLADES	EXECUTABLE	EXPERTNESS	EXTROVERTS	FAIRY TALES
EVERGREENS	EXECUTANTS	EXPIRATION	EXTRUSIONS	FAISALABAD
EVERY OTHER	EXECUTIONS	EXPIRATORY	EXUBERANCE	FAITHFULLY
EVERYTHING	EXECUTIVES	EXPLAINING	EXULTANTLY	FALLACIOUS
EVERYWHERE	EXEMPTIBLE	EXPLETIVES	EXULTATION	FALLOW DEER
EVIDENTIAL	EXEMPTIONS	EXPLICABLE	EXULTINGLY	FALLOWNESS
EVIL-MINDED	EXENTERATE	EXPLICABLY	EXUVIATION	FALSE ALARM
EVISCERATE	EXERCISING	EXPLICATED	EYEBALLING	FALSEHOODS
EVOCATIONS	EXHALATION	EXPLICATOR	EYE-CATCHER	FALSE SCENT
EVOLVEMENT	EXHAUSTING	EXPLICITLY	EYEDROPPER	
EXACERBATE	EXHAUSTION	EXPLOITERS	EYEGLASSES	
EXACTINGLY	EXHAUSTIVE	EXPLOITING	EYE-OPENERS	
EXACTITUDE	EXHIBITING	EXPLOSIONS	EYE SHADOWS	
EXAGGERATE	EXHIBITION	EXPLOSIVES	EYEWITNESS	
EXALTATION	EXHIBITIVE	EXPORTABLE		
EXAMINABLE	EXHIBITORS	EXPOSITION	**F**	
EXASPERATE	EXHIBITORY	EXPOSITORY	FABRICATED	
EX CATHEDRA	EXHILARANT	EXPOUNDING	FABRICATOR	
EXCAVATING	EXHILARATE	EXPRESSAGE	FABULOUSLY	
	EXHUMATION	EXPRESSING	FACECLOTHS	
	EXIGENCIES	EXPRESSION		
	EXIGUOUSLY	EXPRESSIVE		
	EXISTENCES	EXPRESSWAY		
	EXOBIOLOGY	EXPULSIONS		

FALSE
  START
FALSE
  TEETH
FALSIFYING
FAMILIARLY
FAMILY
  NAME
FAMILY
  TREE
FAMISHMENT
FAMOUSNESS
FANATICISM
FANATICIZE
FANCIFULLY
FANCY
  DRESS
FANCY
  WOMAN
FANCY
  WOMEN
FANTASIZED
FANTOCCINI
FARCICALLY
FAR
  EASTERN
FARFETCHED
FARMHOUSES
FARMSTEADS
FARSIGHTED
FASCIATION
FASCICULAR
FASCICULUS
FASCINATED
FASHIONING
FASTENINGS
FASTIDIOUS
FASTIGIATE
FASTNESSES
FATALISTIC
FATALITIES
FATHERHOOD
FATHERLAND
FATHERLESS
FATHER-
  LIKE
FATHOMABLE
FATHOMETER
FATHOMLESS
FAT-
  SOLUBLE
FATTENABLE

FAULTINESS
FAVOURABLE
FAVOURABLY
FAVOURITES
FEARLESSLY
FEARNOUGHT
FEATHER
  BED
FEATHER
  BOA
FEATHERING
FEBRIFUGAL
FEBRUARIES
FECKLESSLY
FECUNDATOR
FEDERALISM
FEDERALIST
FEDERALIZE
FEDERATING
FEDERATION
FEDERATIVE
FEEBLENESS
FEET OF
  CLAY
FEIGNINGLY
FELICITATE
FELICITIES
FELICITOUS
FELIXSTOWE
FELLMONGER
FELLOWSHIP
FELT-TIP
  PEN
FEMALENESS
FEMININITY
FENESTELLA
FER-DE-
  LANCE
FERMENTING
FEROCITIES
FERRITE-
  ROD
FERTILIZED
FERTILIZER
FESTOONERY
FESTOONING
FETCHINGLY
FETIPAROUS
FETISHISTS
FETTUCCINE
FEUILLETON
FEVERISHLY

FFESTINIOG
FIANNA
  FAIL
FIBREBOARD
FIBREGLASS
FIBRINOGEN
FIBROBLAST
FIBROSITIS
FICKLENESS
FICTIONIST
FICTITIOUS
FIDDLEHEAD
FIDDLEWOOD
FIELD
  EVENT
FIELDMOUSE
FIELDSTONE
FIELD-
  TESTS
FIELD
  TRIPS
FIENDISHLY
FIERCENESS
FIFTEENTHS
FIFTY
  FIFTY
FIFTY-
  FIFTY
FIGURATION
FIGURATIVE
FIGUREHEAD
FILARIASIS
FILE
  SERVER
FILIALNESS
FILIBUSTER
FILMSETTER
FILMSTRIPS
FILTERABLE
FILTER
  TIPS
FILTHINESS
FILTRATION
FINALIZING
FINANCIERS
FINE-
  TUNING
FINGER
  BOWL
FINGERLING
FINGERNAIL
FINGERTIPS

FINISTERRE
FINNO-
  UGRIC
FIRE
  ALARMS
FIREBRANDS
FIREBREAKS
FIREBRICKS
FIRE
  DRILLS
FIRE-
  EATERS
FIRE-
  EATING
FIRE
  ENGINE
FIRE
  ESCAPE
FIREGUARDS
FIREPLACES
FIRE-
  RAISER
FIRESTORMS
FIRING
  LINE
FIRST
  CLASS
FIRST-
  CLASS
FIRST
  FLOOR
FIRST
  NAMES
FIRST
  NIGHT
FISH
  FINGER
FISH
  KNIVES
FISHMONGER
FISH
  SLICES
FISH
  STICKS
FISSIPEDAL
FISTICUFFS
FIT OF
  ANGER
FIT OF
  PIQUE
FIT THE
  BILL
FITZGERALD

FIVE-
  FINGER
FIXED-
  POINT
FIXED
  STARS
FLABBINESS
FLABELLATE
FLACCIDITY
FLAGELLANT
FLAGELLATE
FLAGITIOUS
FLAGRANTLY
FLAGSTAFFS
FLAGSTONES
FLAG-
  WAVING
FLAMBOYANT
FLAMEPROOF
FLAMINGOES
FLANNELING
FLANNELLED
FLARE
  PATHS
FLASHBACKS
FLASHBOARD
FLASHBULBS
FLASHCUBES
FLASHINESS
FLASHLIGHT
FLASH
  POINT
FLATFISHES
FLAT-
  FOOTED
FLAT
  RACING
FLATTENING
FLATTERERS
FLATTERING
FLATULENCE
FLAVESCENT
FLAVOURFUL
FLAVOURING
FLAWLESSLY
FLEA-
  BITTEN
FLEA
  MARKET
FLECTIONAL
FLEDGLINGS
FLEECINESS

FLEETINGLY
FLESHINESS
FLESH WOUND
FLETCHINGS
FLEUR-DE-LIS
FLEUR-DE-LYS
FLICKERING
FLICK KNIFE
FLIGHT DECK
FLIGHTIEST
FLIGHTLESS
FLIGHT PATH
FLIMSINESS
FLINTINESS
FLINTLOCKS
FLINTSHIRE
FLIPPANTLY
FLIRTATION
FLIRTINGLY
FLOATATION
FLOCCULANT
FLOCCULATE
FLOCCULENT
FLOODGATES
FLOODLIGHT
FLOOD TIDES
FLOORBOARD
FLOOR CLOTH
FLOOR SHOWS
FLOPHOUSES
FLOPPINESS
FLOPPY DISK
FLORENTINE
FLORIBUNDA
FLORISTICS
FLOTATIONS
FLOUNDERED
FLOURISHED
FLOURISHER
FLOURISHES
FLOURMILLS
FLOUTINGLY

FLOWCHARTS
FLOWERBEDS
FLOWER GIRL
FLOWERLESS
FLOWER-LIKE
FLOWERPOTS
FLUCTUATED
FLUFFINESS
FLUGELHORN
FLUID OUNCE
FLUMMOXING
FLUORIDATE
FLUORINATE
FLUSTERING
FLUTTERING
FLY-BY-NIGHT
FLYCATCHER
FLY-FISHING
FLYING BOAT
FLYING FISH
FLYSPECKED
FLYSWATTER
FLYWEIGHTS
FOAMFLOWER
FOAM RUBBER
FOB WATCHES
FOCAL POINT
FOCUS GROUP
FOLIACEOUS
FOLK DANCER
FOLK DANCES
FOLKESTONE
FOLKLORIST
FOLKSINESS
FOLLICULAR
FOLLICULIN
FOLLOWABLE
FOLLOWINGS
FONDLINGLY

FONTANELLE
FOOD STAMPS
FOODSTUFFS
FOOTBALLER
FOOTBRIDGE
FOOT-CANDLE
FOOT FAULTS
FOOTLIGHTS
FOOTPLATES
FOOTPRINTS
FOOTSTOOLS
FORBEARING
FORBIDDING
FORCEDNESS
FORCEFULLY
FORE AND AFT
FOREARMING
FOREBODING
FORECASTED
FORECASTER
FORECASTLE
FORECLOSED
FORECOURSE
FORECOURTS
FOREDOOMED
FOREFATHER
FOREFINGER
FOREGATHER
FOREGOINGS
FOREGROUND
FOREIGN AID
FOREIGNERS
FOREIGNISM
FOREMOTHER
FOREORDAIN
FORERUNNER
FORESEEING
FORESHADOW
FOREST-LIKE
FORETELLER
FOREWARNED
FOREWARNER
FORFEITERS
FORFEITING
FORFEITURE
FORGETTING

FORGIVABLE
FORGIVABLY
FORKEDNESS
FORMALISTS
FORMALIZED
FORMALIZER
FORMATIONS
FORMATTING
FORMIC ACID
FORMIDABLE
FORMIDABLY
FORMLESSLY
FORMULATED
FORMULATOR
FOR MY MONEY
FORNICATED
FORNICATOR
FORSTERITE
FORSWEARER
FORTE-PIANO
FORTHRIGHT
FORTIFIERS
FORTIFYING
FORTISSIMO
FORTNIGHTS
FORTRESSES
FORT SUMTER
FORTUITISM
FORTUITIST
FORTUITOUS
FORTY-NINER
FORTY WINKS
FORWARDING
FOSSILIZED
FOSTERLING
FOUDROYANT
FOUNDATION
FOUNDERING
FOUNDLINGS
FOURCHETTE
FOUR-COLOUR
FOUR-HANDED
FOURIERISM
FOURIERIST

FOUR-IN-HAND
FOUR-POSTER
FOURRAGERE
FOURSQUARE
FOUR-STROKE
FOURTEENTH
FOXHUNTERS
FOXHUNTING
FOX TERRIER
FRACTIONAL
FRACTURING
FRAGMENTAL
FRAGMENTED
FRAGRANCES
FRAGRANTLY
FRAMEWORKS
FRANCHISED
FRANCHISES
FRANCISCAN
FRANCONIAN
FRANGIPANI
FRATERNITY
FRATERNIZE
FRATRICIDE
FRAUDULENT
FRAUENFELD
FRAXINELLA
FRAY BENTOS
FREAKINESS
FREAKISHLY
FREDERICIA
FREE AGENTS
FREE-BASING
FREEBOARDS
FREEBOOTER
FREE CHURCH
FREEDWOMAN
FREE FOR ALL
FREE-FOR-ALL
FREE-HANDED
FREEHOLDER

FREE
HOUSES
FREELANCED
FREELANCER
FREELANCES
FREE-
LIVING
FREELOADED
FREELOADER
FREEMARTIN
FREEMASONS
FREE
PARDON
FREE
PASSES
FREE-
SPOKEN
FREE-
TRADER
FREIGHTAGE
FREIGHTERS
FREIGHTING
FRENCH
BEAN
FRENCH
HORN
FRENCH
KISS
FRENCH
LOAF
FRENZIEDLY
FREQUENTED
FREQUENTER
FREQUENTLY
FRESHENING
FRESHWATER
FRIABILITY
FRICANDEAU
FRICASSEES
FRICATIVES
FRICTIONAL
FRIENDLESS
FRIENDLIER
FRIENDLIES
FRIENDLILY
FRIENDSHIP
FRIGHTENED
FRIGHTENER
FRILLINESS
FRISKINESS
FRITILLARY
FRITTERING

FRIZZINESS
FROCK
COATS
FROGHOPPER
FROLICKING
FROLICSOME
FRONTALITY
FRONTBENCH
FRONT
DOORS
FRONT
ROOMS
FRONTWARDS
FROSTBOUND
FROSTINESS
FROTHINESS
FROWNINGLY
FROWZINESS
FROZENNESS
FRUCTIFIED
FRUCTIFIER
FRUITCAKES
FRUITERERS
FRUIT
FLIES
FRUITFULLY
FRUITINESS
FRUIT
SALAD
FRUSTRATED
FRUSTRATER
FRUTESCENT
FRYING
PANS
FUDDY-
DUDDY
FULFILLING
FULFILMENT
FULIGINOUS
FULL-
BODIED
FULL
HOUSES
FULL-
LENGTH
FULL-
RIGGED
FULL-
SAILED
FULLY-
GROWN
FULMINATED

FULMINATOR
FUMATORIUM
FUMBLINGLY
FUMIGATING
FUMIGATION
FUNCTIONAL
FUNCTIONED
FUNDHOLDER
FUNEREALLY
FUNGICIDAL
FUNGICIDES
FUNICULARS
FUNICULATE
FUNNELLING
FUNNY
BONES
FUNNY
FARMS
FURBISHING
FURNISHING
FURTHERING
FURUNCULAR
FUSIBILITY
FUSILLADES
FUSTANELLA
FUTURISTIC
FUTUROLOGY
FUZZY
LOGIC

G
GABARDINES
GADOLINITE
GADOLINIUM
GAFF-
RIGGED
GAILLARDIA
GAINLINESS
GAINSAYING
GALASHIELS
GALLICIZER
GALLOGLASS
GALLSTONES
GALLUP
POLL
GALUMPHING
GALVANIZED
GALVANIZER
GAMEKEEPER
GAMETOCYTE
GAME
WARDEN

GANG-
BANGED
GANG-
BANGER
GANGLIONIC
GANGPLANKS
GANGRENOUS
GANGSTA
RAP
GANTT
CHART
GARAGE
SALE
GARBAGE
CAN
GARDEN
CITY
GARGANTUAN
GARISHNESS
GARLANDING
GARNIERITE
GARNISHING
GARRISONED
GARROTTING
GAS
FITTERS
GASHOLDERS
GASIFIABLE
GASOMETERS
GASOMETRIC
GAS
STATION
GASTRALGIA
GASTRALGIC
GASTROLITH
GASTRONOME
GASTRONOMY
GASTROTOMY
GAS
TURBINE
GATEHOUSES
GATEKEEPER
GATHERABLE
GATHERINGS
GAUCHENESS
GAULTHERIA
GAUSSMETER
GAZETTEERS
GEAR
LEVERS
GELATINIZE
GELATINOID

GELATINOUS
GELDERLAND
GEMINATION
GEMMACEOUS
GEMOLOGIST
GENERALIST
GENERALITY
GENERALIZE
GENERATING
GENERATION
GENERATIVE
GENERATORS
GENERATRIX
GENEROSITY
GENEROUSLY
GENETICIST
GENICULATE
GENIUS
LOCI
GENTLEFOLK
GENTLENESS
GENTRIFYED
GEOCENTRIC
GEOCHEMIST
GEODYNAMIC
GEOGNOSTIC
GEOGRAPHER
GEOLOGICAL
GEOLOGISTS
GEOMETRIZE
GEOMORPHIC
GEOPHAGIST
GEOPHAGOUS
GEOPHYSICS
GEORGETOWN
GEORGE
TOWN
GEOSCIENCE
GEOSTATICS
GEOTHERMAL
GEOTROPISM
GERATOLOGY
GERIATRICS
GERMANIZER
GERMICIDAL
GERMICIDES
GERMINABLE
GERMINATED
GERMINATOR
GERUNDIVAL
GESTATIONS

GESUNDHEIT
GET
  HITCHED
GET-UP-
  AND-GO
GHASTLIEST
GHOSTLIEST
GHOST
  TOWNS
GHOSTWRITE
GIANT
  PANDA
GIARDIASIS
GIFTEDNESS
GIFT
  HORSES
GILLINGHAM
GINGER
  ALES
GINGER
  BEER
GINGER
  NUTS
GINGIVITIS
GIPPY
  TUMMY
GIRL
  FRIDAY
GIRLFRIEND
GIRL
  GUIDES
GIVEN
  NAMES
GIVE RISE
  TO
GLACIALIST
GLACIATION
GLACIOLOGY
GLADDENING
GLADIATORS
GLAGOLITIC
GLAIRINESS
GLAMORIZED
GLAMORIZER
GLANCINGLY
GLANDEROUS
GLASS
  FIBRE
GLASSHOUSE
GLASSINESS
GLASS-
  MAKER
GLASSWORKS

GLASWEGIAN
GLAUCONITE
GLAZING-
  BAR
GLEAMINGLY
GLENROTHES
GLIMMERING
GLIOMATOUS
GLISTENING
GLITTERATI
GLITTERING
GLOATINGLY
GLOBALISTS
GLOCHIDIUM
GLOMERULAR
GLOMERULUS
GLOOMINESS
GLORIFYING
GLORIOUSLY
GLORY
  HOLES
GLOSSARIAL
GLOSSARIES
GLOSSARIST
GLOSSINESS
GLOTTIDEAN
GLOUCESTER
GLUCOSIDAL
GLUMACEOUS
GLUTTINGLY
GLUTTONOUS
GLYCOGENIC
GLYCOLYSIS
GLYCOSIDIC
GLYCOSURIA
GLYCOSURIC
GNASHINGLY
GOALKEEPER
GOALMOUTHS
GOALSCORER
GOATSBEARD
GO-
  BETWEENS
GODFATHERS
GOD-
  FEARING
GODMOTHERS
GODPARENTS
GOGGLE-
  EYED
GOINGS-
  OVER

GOLD-
  BEATER
GOLD
  DIGGER
GOLDEN
  AGES
GOLDEN
  HOUR
GOLDEN
  MEAN
GOLDEN
  RULE
GOLDENSEAL
GOLDFIELDS
GOLDILOCKS
GOLD
  MEDALS
GOLD-
  MINING
GOLD-
  PLATED
GOLD
  RUSHES
GOLDSMITHS
GOLDTHREAD
GOLF
  COURSE
GONDOLIERS
GONGOOZLER
GONIOMETER
GONIOMETRY
GONOCOCCAL
GONOCOCCUS
GONOPHORIC
GONORRHOEA
GOOD
  FRIDAY
GOOD
  HUMOUR
GOODLINESS
GOOD
  LOOKER
GOOD
  NATURE
GOODS
  TRAIN
GOODY-
  GOODY
GOOGOLPLEX
GOOSEBERRY
GOOSEFLESH
GOOSESTEPS
GORGEOUSLY

GORGONZOLA
GORMANDIZE
GORMLESSLY
GORNO-
  ALTAI
GOTHICALLY
GO
  TOGETHER
GO TO
  GROUND
GO TO
  PIECES
GOVERNABLE
GOVERNANCE
GOVERNMENT
GRACEFULLY
GRACIOUSLY
GRADATIONS
GRADUALISM
GRADUALIST
GRADUATING
GRADUATION
GRAININESS
GRAMICIDIN
GRAMINEOUS
GRAMMARIAN
GRAMOPHONE
GRANADILLA
GRANDCHILD
GRAND
  OPERA
GRANDPAPPY
GRAND
  PIANO
GRAND
  SLAMS
GRANDS
  PRIX
GRANDSTAND
GRANGERISM
GRANGERIZE
GRANNY
  KNOT
GRANOPHYRE
GRANT-IN-
  AID
GRANULATED
GRANULATOR
GRANULITIC
GRAPEFRUIT
GRAPEVINES
GRAPHITIZE

GRAPHOLOGY
GRAPH
  PAPER
GRAPTOLITE
GRASSFINCH
GRASSINESS
GRASS
  ROOTS
GRASS
  WIDOW
GRATEFULLY
GRATIFYING
GRATUITIES
GRATUITOUS
GRAUBUNDEN
GRAVELLING
GRAVESTONE
GRAVETTIAN
GRAVEYARDS
GRAVIMETER
GRAVIMETRY
GRAVITATED
GRAVITATER
GRAVY
  BOATS
GRAVY
  TRAIN
GREASE
  GUNS
GREASEWOOD
GREASINESS
GREATCOATS
GREAT
  DANES
GREAT-
  NIECE
GREAT
  STOUR
GREAT-
  UNCLE
GREEDINESS
GREEDY-
  GUTS
GREEK
  CROSS
GREENBACKS
GREEN
  BEANS
GREEN
  BELTS
GREENBRIER
GREENFINCH
GREENFLIES

GREENGAGES
GREENHEART
GREENHORNS
GREENHOUSE
GREEN
  LIGHT
GREEN
  PAPER
GREEN
  POUND
GREENSBORO
GREENSHANK
GREENSTONE
GREEN
  THUMB
GREGARIOUS
GRENADIERS
GRENADINES
GRESSORIAL
GREYHOUNDS
GREY
  MARKET
GREY
  MATTER
GRIEVANCES
GRIEVINGLY
GRIEVOUSLY
GRIM
  REAPER
GRINDSTONE
GRIPPINGLY
GRISLINESS
GRISTLIEST
GRITTINESS
GROANINGLY
GROGGINESS
GROTESQUES
GROTTINESS
GROUCHIEST
GROUND
  BAIT
GROUND
  CREW
GROUNDLESS
GROUNDLING
GROUNDMASS
GROUNDNUTS
GROUND
  PLAN
GROUND
  RENT

GROUND
  RULE
GROUNDSMAN
GROUNDSMEN
GROUNDWORK
GROUPTHINK
GROVELLERS
GROVELLING
GRUBBINESS
GRUBSTAKES
GRUDGINGLY
GRUESOMELY
GRUMPINESS
GRUNTINGLY
GUADELOUPE
GUANAJUATO
GUANTANAMO
GUARANTEED
GUARANTEES
GUARANTIES
GUARANTORS
GUARDHOUSE
GUARDRAILS
GUARDROOMS
GUARD'S
  VANS
GUERRILLAS
GUESSINGLY
GUESTHOUSE
GUESTROOMS
GUIDELINES
GUILDHALLS
GUILEFULLY
GUILLEMOTS
GUILLOTINE
GUILTINESS
GUINEA
  FOWL
GUINEA
  PIGS
GUITARFISH
GUITARISTS
GUJRANWALA
GULF
  STREAM
GUNRUNNERS
GUNRUNNING
GURGLINGLY
GYMNASIAST
GYMNASIUMS
GYMNASTICS
GYMNOSPERM

GYNANDROUS
GYNOPHORIC
GYPSOPHILA
GYROSCOPES
GYROSCOPIC
GYROSTATIC

H

HABILIMENT
HABILITATE
HABITATION
HABITUALLY
HABITUATED
HACKBUTEER
HACKNEYISM
HADHRAMAUT
HAECKELIAN
HAEMAGOGUE
HAEMATINIC
HAEMATITIC
HAEMATOSIS
HAEMATURIA
HAEMATURIC
HAEMOLYMPH
HAEMOLYSIN
HAEMOLYSIS
HAEMOLYTIC
HAEMOPHILE
HAGIOCRACY
HAGIOLATER
HAGIOLATRY
HAGIOLOGIC
HAGIOSCOPE
HAILSTONES
HAILSTORMS
HAIRPIECES
HAIR
  SHIRTS
HAIR
  SLIDES
HAIRSPRING
HAIRSTREAK
HAIRSTYLES
HALBERDIER
HALF A
  CROWN
HALF-
  BOTTLE
HALF-
  BREEDS
HALF-
  CASTES

HALF
  CROWNS
HALF-
  LENGTH
HALF-
  ROTTEN
HALF-
  SISTER
HALF-
  TRUTHS
HALF
  VOLLEY
HALF-
  WITTED
HALLELUJAH
HALLMARKED
HALOGENATE
HALOGENOID
HALOGENOUS
HALOPHYTIC
HALTER-
  LIKE
HALTERNECK
HAMBURGERS
HAMMERFEST
HAMMERHEAD
HAMMERLESS
HAMMER-
  LIKE
HAMSHACKLE
HAMSTRINGS
HANDBALLER
HANDBARROW
HANDBRAKES
HANDCUFFED
HANDICRAFT
HAND IN
  HAND
HANDLEABLE
HANDLEBARS
HANDLELESS
HANDMAIDEN
HAND-ME-
  DOWN
HANDPICKED
HANDSHAKES
HANDSOMELY
HANDSPRING
HANDSTANDS
HANDSTROKE
HANKERINGS

HANKY-
  PANKY
HANOVERIAN
HAPLOLOGIC
HAPPENINGS
HAPPY
  EVENT
HAPPY
  HOURS
HARANGUING
HARASSMENT
HARBINGERS
HARBOURAGE
HARBOURING
HARD-
  BITTEN
HARD-
  BOILED
HARD
  CIDERS
HARDHEADED
HARD
  LABOUR
HARD-
  LINERS
HARD
  LIQUOR
HARD
  PALATE
HARELIPPED
HARGREAVES
HARLEQUINS
HARMLESSLY
HARMONICAS
HARMONIOUS
HARMONIUMS
HARMONIZED
HARMONIZER
HARMSWORTH
HARNESSING
HARPOONING
HARRISBURG
HARROWMENT
HARTEBEEST
HARTLEPOOL
HARUSPICAL
HARVESTERS
HARVESTING
HARVESTMAN
HASH
  BROWNS
HASTEFULLY

HATCHBACKS
HATCHELLER
HATCHERIES
HATCHET JOB
HATCHET MAN
HATCHET MEN
HATSHEPSUT
HATTERSLEY
HAUBERGEON
HAUGHTIEST
HAUNTINGLY
HAUSTELLUM
HAUSTORIAL
HAUSTORIUM
HAUTE-LOIRE
HAUTE-MARNE
HAVE A HEART
HAVE A POINT
HAVERSACKS
HAZARDABLE
HAZARD-FREE
HEADBOARDS
HEADCHEESE
HEADHUNTED
HEADHUNTER
HEADLIGHTS
HEADLINING
HEADMASTER
HEAD OF HAIR
HEADPHONES
HEADPIECES
HEADSPRING
HEADSQUARE
HEADSTONES
HEADSTREAM
HEADSTRONG
HEADWATERS
HEADWORKER
HEALTH FOOD
HEALTHIEST
HEARING AID

HEARKENING
HEARTBEATS
HEARTBREAK
HEARTENING
HEARTHRUGS
HEARTINESS
HEARTSEASE
HEARTTHROB
HEATEDNESS
HEATHBERRY
HEATHENDOM
HEATHENISH
HEATHENISM
HEATHENIZE
HEAT RASHES
HEAT SHIELD
HEATSTROKE
HEAT STROKE
HEAVEN-SENT
HEAVENWARD
HEAVY-LADEN
HEAVY METAL
HEAVY WATER
HEBDOMADAL
HEBETATION
HEBETATIVE
HEBRAISTIC
HECTICALLY
HECTOGRAPH
HEDONISTIC
HEEDLESSLY
HEIDELBERG
HEIGHTENED
HEIGHTENER
HEISENBERG
HELIANTHUS
HELICOPTER
HELIGOLAND
HELIOGRAPH
HELIOLATER
HELIOLATRY
HELIOMETER
HELIOMETRY
HELIOPOLIS
HELIOTAXIS

HELIOTROPE
HELIOTYPIC
HELLACIOUS
HELLBENDER
HELLENIZER
HELLESPONT
HELLRAISER
HELMET-LIKE
HELMINTHIC
HELPLESSLY
HEMELYTRAL
HEMELYTRON
HEMICYCLIC
HEMIHEDRAL
HEMIPLEGIA
HEMIPLEGIC
HEMIPTERAN
HEMIPTERON
HEMISPHERE
HEMITROPIC
HEMOGLOBIN
HEMOPHILIA
HEMORRHAGE
HEMORRHOID
HENCEFORTH
HENDECAGON
HENOTHEISM
HENOTHEIST
HEN PARTIES
HEPARINOID
HEPHAESTUS
HEPHAISTOS
HEPTAGONAL
HEPTAMETER
HEPTARCHIC
HEPTASTICH
HEPTATEUCH
HEPTATHLON
HERACLIDAN
HERACLITUS
HERBACEOUS
HERBALISTS
HERBICIDAL
HERBIVORES
HEREABOUTS
HEREDITARY
HEREDITIST
HERESIARCH
HERETOFORE

HERMITAGES
HERMOSILLO
HEROICALLY
HEROPHILUS
HESITANTLY
HESITATING
HESITATION
HESITATIVE
HESPERIDES
HESPERIDIN
HETERODONT
HETERODOXY
HETERODYNE
HETEROGAMY
HETEROGONY
HETEROLOGY
HETERONOMY
HETEROTOPY
HEULANDITE
HEURISTICS
HEXADECANE
HEXAEMERIC
HEXAEMERON
HEXAHEDRAL
HEXAHEDRON
HEXAMERISM
HEXAMEROUS
HEXAMETERS
HEXAMETRIC
HEXANGULAR
HEXAVALENT
HIBERNACLE
HIBERNATED
HIBERNATOR
HIBISCUSES
HIDDENNESS
HIERARCHAL
HIEROCRACY
HIERODULIC
HIEROGLYPH
HIEROLOGIC
HIERONYMIC
HIERONYMUS
HIEROPHANT
HIGHBINDER
HIGH CHAIRS
HIGH CHURCH
HIGH COURTS

HIGH-FLIERS
HIGH-FLYING
HIGH-HANDED
HIGH HORSES
HIGHJACKER
HIGH JUMPER
HIGHLANDER
HIGHLIGHTS
HIGH MASSES
HIGH-MINDED
HIGHNESSES
HIGH-OCTANE
HIGH POINTS
HIGH PRIEST
HIGH RELIEF
HIGH SCHOOL
HIGH SEASON
HIGH STREET
HIGH-STRUNG
HIGHWAYMAN
HIGHWAYMEN
HIJACKINGS
HILDEBRAND
HILDESHEIM
HILLINGDON
HIMYARITIC
HINAYANIST
HINDENBURG
HINDERMOST
HINDRANCES
HINDUSTANI
HINTERLAND
HIPHUGGERS
HIPPARCHUS
HIP POCKETS
HIPPOCRENE
HIPPODROME

HIPPOGRIFF
HIPPOLYTAN
HIPPOLYTUS
HIPPOMENES
HISPANIOLA
HISTAMINIC
HISTIOCYTE
HISTOGRAMS
HISTOLYSIS
HISTOLYTIC
HISTORIANS
HISTORICAL
HISTRIONIC
HIT-AND-
  MISS
HITCHHIKED
HITCHHIKER
HITHERMOST
HIT
  PARADES
HIT THE
  SACK
HOARSENESS
HOBBYHORSE
HOBGOBLINS
HOBNOBBING
HOCHHEIMER
HOCUS-
  POCUS
HODGEPODGE
HOGARTHIAN
HOITY-
  TOITY
HOKEY
  COKEY
HOKEY-
  POKEY
HOLDERSHIP
HOLES IN
  ONE
HOLIDAYING
HOLINESSES
HOLLOWNESS
HOLLYHOCKS
HOLOCAUSTS
HOLOENZYME
HOLOFERNES
HOLOGRAPHY
HOLOHEDRAL
HOLOPHYTIC
HOLUS-
  BOLUS

HOLY
  ISLAND
HOLY
  SPIRIT
HOMEBODIES
HOME-
  BREWED
HOMECOMING
HOME
  GUARDS
HOMELINESS
HOMEMAKERS
HOMEMAKING
HOME
  MOVIES
HOME
  OFFICE
HOMEOPATHS
HOMEOPATHY
HOMEOTYPIC
HOMESTEADS
HOME
  TRUTHS
HOMFWORKER
HOMILETICS
HOMOCERCAL
HOMOCYCLIC
HOMOEOPATH
HOMOEROTIC
HOMOGAMOUS
HOMOGENATE
HOMOGENIZE
HOMOGENOUS
HOMOGONOUS
HOMOGRAPHS
HOMOLOGATE
HOMOLOGIZE
HOMOLOGOUS
HOMOLOSINE
HOMONYMITY
HOMOOUSIAN
HOMOPHONES
HOMOPHONIC
HOMOPLASTY
HOMORGANIC
HOMOSEXUAL
HOMOZYGOTE
HOMOZYGOUS
HOMUNCULAR
HOMUNCULUS
HONESTNESS
HONEYBUNCH

HONEYCOMBS
HONEYDEWED
HONEY-
  EATER
HONEYMOONS
HONORARIUM
HONORIFICS
HONOURABLE
HONOURABLY
HONOURLESS
HOODLUMISM
HOODWINKED
HOODWINKER
HOOKEDNESS
HOOTENANNY
HOPE
  CHESTS
HOPELESSLY
HOPPING
  MAD
HORIZONTAL
HORNBLENDE
HORNEDNESS
HORN-
  RIMMED
HOROLOGIST
HOROLOGIUM
HOROSCOPES
HOROSCOPIC
HORRENDOUS
HORRIDNESS
HORRIFYING
HORROR
  FILM
HORSEBOXES
HORSEFLESH
HORSEFLIES
HORSELAUGH
HORSELEECH
HORSE
  OPERA
HORSEPOWER
HORSE
  SENSE
HORSESHOES
HORSEWOMAN
HORSEWOMEN
HOSPITABLE
HOSPITABLY
HOSPITALET
HOSTELLERS
HOSTELLING

HOSTELRIES
HOT-
  BLOODED
HOTCHPOTCH
HOT
  DESKING
HOT
  FLUSHES
HOTFOOTING
HOUSEBOATS
HOUSEBOUND
HOUSECOATS
HOUSECRAFT
HOUSEFLIES
HOUSE
  GUEST
HOUSEHOLDS
HOUSEMAIDS
HOUSE OF
  GOD
HOUSE
  PARTY
HOUSEPLANT
HOUSE-
  PROUD
HOUSE-
  TRAIN
HOUSEWIVES
HOVERCRAFT
HOVERINGLY
HOVERTRAIN
HOW DO YOU
  DO
HUA KUO-
  FENG
HUCKLEBONE
HUDDLESTON
HUGUENOTIC
HULLABALOO
HUMANENESS
HUMANISTIC
HUMANITIES
HUMANIZING
HUMBERSIDE
HUMBLENESS
HUMBLINGLY
HUMBUGGERY
HUMDINGERS
HUMIDIFIED
HUMIDIFIER
HUMIDISTAT
HUMILIATED

HUMILIATOR
HUMORESQUE
HUMORISTIC
HUMOROUSLY
HUMOURLESS
HUMOURSOME
HUMPBACKED
HUNCHBACKS
HUNDREDTHS
HUNGRINESS
HUNTINGDON
HUNTRESSES
HUNTSVILLE
HURDY-
  GURDY
HURLY-
  BURLY
HURRICANES
HURRYINGLY
HUSBANDING
HUSBANDMAN
HUSBANDMEN
HYACINTHUS
HYALOPLASM
HYALURONIC
HYBRIDIZER
HYDRANGEAS
HYDRASTINE
HYDRAULICS
HYDROCORAL
HYDROFOILS
HYDROGRAPH
HYDROLOGIC
HYDROLYSER
HYDROLYSIS
HYDROLYTIC
HYDROMANCY
HYDROPONIC
HYGIENISTS
HYPERBOLAS
HYPERBOLES
HYPERBOLIC
HYPERMEDIA
HYPERSPACE
HYPHENATED
HYPNOTISTS
HYPNOTIZED
HYPOCRITES
HYPODERMIC
HYPOTENUSE
HYPOTHESES

HYPOTHESIS
HYSTERICAL

I
IAMBICALLY
IATROGENIC
ICEBREAKER
ICE
  BREAKER
ICE
  LOLLIES
ICE-
  SKATERS
ICE-
  SKATING
ICHINOMIYA
ICHTHYOSIS
ICHTHYOTIC
ICONOCLASM
ICONOCLAST
ICONOLATER
ICONOLATRY
ICONOMATIC
ICONOSCOPE
IDEALISTIC
IDEALIZING
IDEATIONAL
IDEMPOTENT
IDENTIFIED
IDENTIFIER
IDENTIKITS
IDENTITIES
IDEOGRAPHY
IDEOLOGIES
IDEOLOGIST
IDEOLOGUES
IDIOLECTAL
IDIOPATHIC
IDIOPHONIC
IDOLATRIZE
IDOLATROUS
IGNES
  FATUI
IGNOBILITY
IGNOMINIES
IJSSELMEER
ILL-
  ADVISED
ILLEGALITY
ILLEGALIZE
ILLITERACY
ILLITERATE

ILL-
  NATURED
ILLOCUTION
ILL-
  STARRED
ILL-
  TREATED
ILLUMINANT
ILLUMINATE
ILLUMINATI
ILLUMINISM
ILLUMINIST
ILLUSORILY
ILLUSTRATE
IMAGINABLE
IMBALANCES
IMBECILITY
IMBIBITION
IMBRICATED
IMBROGLIOS
IMITATIONS
IMMACULACY
IMMACULATE
IMMATERIAL
IMMATURELY
IMMATURITY
IMMEMORIAL
IMMERSIBLE
IMMIGRANTS
IMMIGRATED
IMMIGRATOR
IMMINENTLY
IMMISCIBLE
IMMOBILITY
IMMOBILIZE
IMMODERACY
IMMODERATE
IMMODESTLY
IMMOLATING
IMMOLATION
IMMORALIST
IMMORALITY
IMMORTELLE
IMMOTILITY
IMMUNIZING
IMMUNOLOGY
IMPAIRMENT
IMPALEMENT
IMPALPABLE
IMPANATION
IMPANELLED

IMPARTIBLE
IMPASSABLE
IMPATIENCE
IMPEACHING
IMPECCABLE
IMPECCABLY
IMPEDANCES
IMPEDIMENT
IMPEDINGLY
IMPENDENCE
IMPENITENT
IMPERATIVE
IMPERIALLY
IMPERILLED
IMPERSONAL
IMPERVIOUS
IMPETRATOR
IMPISHNESS
IMPLACABLE
IMPLANTING
IMPLEMENTS
IMPLICATED
IMPLICITLY
IMPLOSIONS
IMPOLITELY
IMPORTANCE
IMPORTUNED
IMPORTUNER
IMPOSINGLY
IMPOSITION
IMPOSSIBLE
IMPOSSIBLY
IMPOSTROUS
IMPOSTURES
IMPOTENTLY
IMPOUNDAGE
IMPOUNDING
IMPOVERISH
IMPREGNATE
IMPRESARIO
IMPRESSING
IMPRESSION
IMPRESSIVE
IMPRIMATUR
IMPRINTING
IMPRISONED
IMPRISONER
IMPROBABLE
IMPROBABLY
IMPROPERLY
IMPROVABLE

IMPROVISED
IMPROVISER
IMPRUDENCE
IMPUDENTLY
IMPUISSANT
IMPULSIONS
IMPUNITIES
IMPURITIES
IMPUTATION
IMPUTATIVE
IN
  ABSENTIA
INACCURACY
INACCURATE
INACTIVATE
INACTIVELY
INACTIVITY
IN
  ADDITION
INADEQUACY
INADEQUATE
INAMORATAS
IN ANY
  EVENT
INAPPOSITE
INAPTITUDE
INARTISTIC
INAUGURATE
INBREEDING
INCANDESCE
INCAPACITY
INCAPARINA
INCARNATED
INCAUTIOUS
INCENDIARY
INCENTIVES
INCEPTIONS
INCESSANCY
INCESTUOUS
INCHOATION
INCHOATIVE
INCIDENTAL
INCINERATE
INCIPIENCE
INCIPIENCY
INCISIVELY
INCITATION
INCITEMENT
INCITINGLY
INCIVILITY
INCLEMENCY

INCLINABLE
INCLOSURES
INCLUDABLE
INCLUSIONS
INCOHERENT
INCOMMODED
INCOMPLETE
INCONSTANT
INCRASSATE
INCREASING
INCREDIBLE
INCREDIBLY
INCREMENTS
INCRESCENT
INCUBATING
INCUBATION
INCUBATIVE
INCUBATORS
INCULCATED
INCULCATOR
INCULPABLE
INCULPATED
INCUMBENCY
INCUMBENTS
INCUNABULA
INCURRABLE
INCURRENCE
INCURSIONS
INDECENTLY
INDECISION
INDECISIVE
INDECOROUS
INDEFINITE
INDELICACY
INDELICATE
INDENTURED
INDENTURES
INDEXATION
INDIAN
  CORN
INDICATING
INDICATION
INDICATIVE
INDICATORS
INDICATORY
INDICTABLE
INDICTMENT
INDIGENOUS
INDIRECTLY
INDISCREET
INDISCRETE

INDISPOSED
INDISTINCT
INDIVIDUAL
INDOCILITY
INDOLENTLY
INDOLOGIST
INDONESIAN
INDOPHENOL
INDUCEMENT
INDUCTANCE
INDUCTIONS
INDULGENCE
INDUSTRIAL
INDUSTRIES
INEBRIATED
INEBRIATES
INEDUCABLE
INEDUCABLY
INEFFICACY
INELEGANCE
INELIGIBLE
INELOQUENT
INEPTITUDE
INEQUALITY
INEQUITIES
INEVITABLE
INEVITABLY
INEXISTENT
INEXORABLE
INEXORABLY
INEXPERTLY
INEXPIABLE
INEXPLICIT
IN
  EXTREMIS
INFALLIBLE
INFALLIBLY
INFARCTION
INFATUATED
INFECTIONS
INFECTIOUS
INFELICITY
INFERENCES
INFERNALLY
INFIBULATE
INFIDELITY
INFIELDERS
INFIGHTING
INFILTRATE
INFINITELY
INFINITIVE

INFINITUDE
INFLATABLE
INFLATEDLY
INFLECTING
INFLECTION
INFLECTIVE
INFLEXIBLE
INFLEXIBLY
INFLICTING
INFLICTION
INFLICTIVE
INFLUENCED
INFLUENCER
INFLUENCES
INFLUENZAL
INFORMALLY
INFORMANTS
INFORMEDLY
INFRACLASS
INFRACTION
INFRASONIC
INFREQUENT
INFRINGING
INFURIATED
INFUSORIAL
INGESTIBLE
INGLENOOKS
INGLORIOUS
INGOLSTADT
INGRATIATE
INGREDIENT
INGRESSION
INGRESSIVE
INGUSHETIA
INHABITANT
INHABITING
INHALATION
INHARMONIC
INHERENTLY
INHERITING
INHIBITING
INHIBITION
INHIBITIVE
IN HOT
  WATER
INHUMANELY
INHUMANITY
INHUMATION
INIMITABLE
INIMITABLY
INIQUITIES

INIQUITOUS
INITIALING
INITIALIZE
INITIALLED
INITIATING
INITIATION
INITIATIVE
INITIATORY
INJECTABLE
INJECTIONS
INJUNCTION
INJUNCTIVE
INJURY
  TIME
INJUSTICES
IN
  MEMORIAM
INNER
  CHILD
INNER
  TUBES
INNKEEPERS
INNOCENTLY
INNOMINATE
INNOVATING
INNOVATION
INNOVATIVE
INNOVATORS
INNUENDOES
INNUMERACY
INNUMERATE
INOCULABLE
INOCULATED
INOCULATOR
IN ONE
  PIECE
IN ONES
  CUPS
INOPERABLE
INORDINACY
INORDINATE
INOSCULATE
IN-
  PATIENTS
INQUIETUDE
INQUISITOR
INSALIVATE
INS AND
  OUTS
INSANITARY
INSATIABLE
INSATIABLY

INSCRIBING
INSECURELY
INSECURITY
INSEMINATE
INSENSIBLE
INSENSIBLY
INSENTIENT
INSERTABLE
INSERTIONS
INSIDE
  JOBS
INSIDE
  LANE
INSIGHTFUL
INSINUATED
INSINUATOR
INSIPIDITY
INSISTENCE
INSOBRIETY
INSOLATION
INSOLENTLY
INSOLVABLE
INSOLVENCY
INSOLVENTS
INSOMNIACS
INSOMNIOUS
INSOUCIANT
INSPECTING
INSPECTION
INSPECTIVE
INSPECTORS
INSPIRABLE
INSPIRITER
INSTALLING
INSTALMENT
INSTANCING
INSTIGATED
INSTIGATOR
INSTILLING
INSTILMENT
INSTITUTED
INSTITUTES
INSTITUTOR
INSTRUCTED
INSTRUCTOR
INSTRUMENT
INSUFFLATE
INSULARISM
INSULARITY
INSULATING
INSULATION

INSULATORS
INSURANCES
INSURGENCE
INSURGENCY
INSURGENTS
INTANGIBLE
INTANGIBLY
INTEGRABLE
INTEGRATED
INTEGRATOR
INTEGUMENT
INTELLECTS
INTENDANCE
INTENDANCY
INTENDMENT
INTENTIONS
INTENTNESS
INTERACTED
INTER
  ALIOS
INTERBRAIN
INTERBREED
INTERCEDED
INTERCEDER
INTERDICTS
INTERESTED
INTERFACED
INTERFACES
INTERFERED
INTERFERER
INTERFERON
INTERFLUVE
INTERGRADE
INTERGROUP
INTERLACED
INTERLAKEN
INTERLEAVE
INTERLINER
INTERLOPER
INTERLUDES
INTERLUNAR
INTERMARRY
INTERMENTS
INTERMEZZI
INTERMEZZO
INTERMODAL
INTERNALLY
INTERNMENT
INTERNODAL
INTERNSHIP
INTERPHASE

INTERPHONE	INVALIDATE	IRREGULARS	JAILBREAKS	JOYOUSNESS
INTERPLEAD	INVALID	IRRELATIVE	JAM	JUBILANTLY
INTERPOSAL	CAR	IRRELEVANT	SESSION	JUBILATION
INTERPOSED	INVALIDING	IRRELIGION	JAMSHEDPUR	JUDGMENTAL
INTERPOSER	INVALIDISM	IRRESOLUTE	JANITORIAL	JUDICATIVE
INTERREGNA	INVALIDITY	IRREVERENT	JARDINIERE	JUDICATORY
INTERSPACE	INVALUABLE	IRRIGATING	JAUNTINESS	JUDICATURE
INTERSTATE	INVARIABLE	IRRIGATION	JAWBREAKER	JUDICIALLY
INTERSTICE	INVARIABLY	IRRIGATIVE	JAYWALKERS	JUGGERNAUT
INTERTIDAL	INVARIANCE	IRRITATING	JAYWALKING	JUIZ DE
INTERTWINE	INVEIGHING	IRRITATION	JEALOUSIES	FORA
INTERVENED	INVEIGLING	IRRITATIVE	JELLY	JUMBLE
INTERVENER	INVENTIBLE	IRRUPTIONS	BEANS	SALE
INTERVIEWS	INVENTIONS	ISENTROPIC	JELLY	JUMBLINGLY
INTERWEAVE	INVERACITY	ISKENDERUN	ROLLS	JUNCACEOUS
INTERWOVEN	INVERCLYDE	ISOANTIGEN	JEOPARDIZE	JUNCTIONAL
INTESTINAL	INVERSIONS	ISOCHEIMAL	JERRY-	JUNKETINGS
INTESTINES	INVERTIBLE	ISOCHRONAL	BUILD	JURY-
IN THE	INVESTABLE	ISOCHROOUS	JERRY-	RIGGED
EVENT	INVESTMENT	ISOCYANIDE	BUILT	JUST AS
IN THE	INVETERACY	ISODYNAMIC	JERSEY	WELL
MONEY	INVETERATE	ISOGAMETIC	CITY	JUSTICIARY
INTIMACIES	INVIGILATE	ISOGLOSSAL	JESUITICAL	JUSTIFYING
INTIMATELY	INVIGORATE	ISOGLOTTIC	JET	JUST IN
INTIMATING	INVINCIBLE	ISOLEUCINE	ENGINES	CASE
INTIMATION	INVINCIBLY	ISOMETRICS	JET-	JUST-IN-
INTIMIDATE	INVIOLABLE	ISOMORPHIC	SETTERS	TIME
INTINCTION	INVITATION	ISOPIESTIC	JETTISONED	JUVENILITY
INTOLERANT	INVITATORY	ISOSEISMAL	JIANG	JUXTAPOSED
INTONATION	INVITINGLY	ISOTHERMAL	ZEMIN	
INTOXICANT	INVOCATION	ISOTROPOUS	JIGGERMAST	**K**
INTOXICATE	INVOCATORY	ISRAELITES	JINGDEZHEN	KABARAGOYA
IN	INVOLUCRAL	ITALIANATE	JINGOISTIC	KALGOORLIE
TRAINING	INVOLUTION	ITALICIZED	JITTERBUGS	KANSAS
INTRAMURAL	IODIZATION	ITCHY	JOB	CITY
INTRENCHED	IODOMETRIC	PALMS	CENTRES	KANTIANISM
INTREPIDLY	IONIZATION	ITINERANCY	JOBSHARING	KAPFENBERG
INTRIGUING	IONOSPHERE	IVORY	JOCKSTRAPS	KARA-
INTRODUCED	IRENICALLY	TOWER	JOCULARITY	KALPAK
INTRODUCER	IRIDACEOUS		JOGJAKARTA	KARAMANLIS
INTROSPECT	IRIDECTOMY	**J**	JOLLY	KARLSKRONA
INTROVERTS	IRIDESCENT	JACKANAPES	ROGER	KARYOGAMIC
INTRUSIONS	IRISH	JACKHAMMER	JOSS	KARYOLYMPH
INTRUSTING	STEWS	JACK-	STICKS	KARYOLYSIS
INTUBATION	IRISHWOMAN	KNIFED	JOURNALESE	KARYOLYTIC
INTUITABLE	IRONICALLY	JACK	JOURNALISM	KARYOPLASM
INTUITIONS	IRONMONGER	KNIVES	JOURNALIST	KARYOTYPIC
INUNDATING	IRRADIANCE	JACKRABBIT	JOURNALIZE	KASHMIRIAN
INUNDATION	IRRADIATED	JACK THE	JOURNEYING	KAZAKHSTAN
INUREDNESS	IRRADIATOR	LAD	JOURNEYMAN	KEEP TABS
INVAGINATE	IRRATIONAL	JACOBITISM	JOURNEYMEN	ON
		JAGUARONDI	JOYFULNESS	KENILWORTH

KENNELLING
KENTUCKIAN
KERATINIZE
KERATOTOMY
KERCHIEFED
KERFUFFLES
KERMANSHAH
KERSEYMERE
KETTLEDRUM
KEYBOARDED
KEYBOARDER
KEYPUNCHED
KEYPUNCHER
KEYPUNCHES
KHABAROVSK
KIDNAPPERS
KIDNAPPING
KIDNEY
  BEAN
KIESELGUHR
KILMARNOCK
KILOLITRES
KTIOMETRES
KILOMETRIC
KIMBERLITE
KINCARDINE
KINDLINESS
KINDNESSES
KINEMATICS
KINGFISHER
KINGLINESS
KINGMAKERS
KING-OF-
  ARMS
KING'S
  BENCH
KIRITIMATI
KIROVOGRAD
KISS OF
  LIFE
KITAKYUSHU
KITH AND
  KIN
KITTIWAKES
KLAGENFURT
KLANGFARBE
KNEECAPPED
KNEE-
  LENGTH
KNICK-
  KNACK

KNIFE-
  EDGES
KNIGHTHEAD
KNIGHTHOOD
KNOBBLIEST
KNOBKERRIE
KNOCKABOUT
KNOCK-
  KNEED
KOEKSISTER
KOMMUNARSK
KOMSOMOLSK
KOOKABURRA
KRAGUJEVAC
KRAMATORSK
KREMENCHUG
KRIEGSPIEL
KRISHNAISM
KRUGERRAND
KU KLUX
  KLAN
KUOMINTANG

L
LABIONASAL
LABIOVELAR
LABORATORY
LABOR
  UNION
LABOUR
  CAMP
LABOUR
  DAYS
LABOUREDLY
LABYRINTHS
LACERATING
LACERATION
LACERATIVE
LACHRYMOSE
LACKLUSTRE
LACQUERING
LACRIMATOR
LACTESCENT
LACTIC
  ACID
LACTOGENIC
LACTOMETER
LACTOSCOPE
LACUNOSITY
LACUSTRINE
LADY-
  KILLER

LADY'S-
  SMOCK
LAMARCKIAN
LAMARCKISM
LAMASERIES
LAMBASTING
LAMBDACISM
LAMBREQUIN
LAMBS
  TAILS
LAMELLATED
LAMENTABLE
LAMENTABLY
LAMINATING
LAMINATION
LAMPOONERY
LAMPOONING
LAMPSHADES
LANCASHIRE
LANCEOLATE
LAND
  AGENTS
LAND
  FORCES
LANDING
  NET
LANDLADIES
LANDLOCKED
LANDLUBBER
LANDMASSES
LAND
  ROVERS
LANDSCAPED
LANDSCAPES
LANDSLIDES
LANGLAUFER
LANGUISHED
LANGUISHER
LANGUOROUS
LANIFEROUS
LANTHANIDE
LAPAROTOMY
LAP
  DANCING
LAPIDARIAN
LAPIDARIES
LARGE-
  SCALE
LA
  ROCHELLE
LARVICIDAL
LARYNGITIC

LARYNGITIS
LASCIVIOUS
LAST
  MINUTE
LATECOMERS
LATENT
  HEAT
LATTERMOST
LAUGHINGLY
LAUNCESTON
LAUNCH
  PADS
LAUNDERING
LAUNDROMAT
LAUNDRYMAN
LAURACEOUS
LAUREATION
LAURENTIAN
LAVATIONAL
LAVATORIAL
LAVATORIES
LAVISHNESS
LAW-
  ABIDING
LAW-
  BREAKER
LAWFULNESS
LAWNMOWERS
LAWN
  TENNIS
LAWRENCIUM
LAY
  BROTHER
LAY
  FIGURES
LAYPERSONS
LAY
  READERS
LAY
  SISTERS
LEADERSHIP
LEAF-
  HOPPER
LEAFLETING
LEASEBACKS
LEAVENINGS
LEBENSRAUM
LECTIONARY
LECTORSHIP
LEEUWARDEN
LEFT-
  HANDED

LEFT-
  HANDER
LEFT-
  WINGER
LEGAL
  EAGLE
LEGALISTIC
LEGALIZING
LEGATESHIP
LEGATORIAL
LEGIBILITY
LEGISLATED
LEGISLATOR
LEGITIMACY
LEGITIMATE
LEGITIMISM
LEGITIMIST
LEGITIMIZE
LEGUMINOUS
LEG-
  WARMERS
LEISHMANIA
LEITMOTIVS
LEMNISCATE
LEMON
  GRASS
LEMON
  SOLES
LENGTHENED
LENGTHENER
LENGTHIEST
LENGTHWAYS
LENTAMENTE
LENTICULAR
LENTISSIMO
LEOPARDESS
LEPIDOLITE
LEPRECHAUN
LEPTOSOMIC
LESBIANISM
LESSEESHIP
LETCHWORTH
LETHBRIDGE
LETS FACE
  IT
LETTER
  BOMB
LETTERHEAD
LEUCOCYTES
LEUCOCYTIC
LEUCODERMA
LEUCOMAINE

LEUCOPENIA
LEUCOPENIC
LEUCOPLAST
LEVERKUSEN
LEVIATHANS
LEVIGATION
LEVITATING
LEVITATION
LEXICALITY
LEXICOLOGY
LIBATIONAL
LIBERALISM
LIBERALIST
LIBERALITY
LIBERALIZE
LIBERATING
LIBERATION
LIBERATORS
LIBERTINES
LIBIDINOUS
LIBRARIANS
LIBRETTIST
LIBREVILLE
LICENSABLE
LICENTIATE
LICENTIOUS
LIE IN
STATE
LIEUTENANT
LIFE
CYCLES
LIFEGUARDS
LIFE
JACKET
LIFELESSLY
LIFE-
SAVING
LIFESTYLES
LIGHT
BULBS
LIGHTENING
LIGHTERAGE
LIGHTHOUSE
LIGHTNINGS
LIGHTSHIPS
LIGHT
YEARS
LIGNOCAINE
LIKELIHOOD
LIKE-
MINDED
LIKENESSES

LILIACEOUS
LIMICOLINE
LIMICOLOUS
LIMITARIAN
LIMITATION
LIMOUSINES
LINEAMENTS
LINECASTER
LINGUIFORM
LINGUISTIC
LINLITHGOW
LINSEED
OIL
LIPOMATOUS
LIPOPHILIC
LIP-
READING
LIP
SERVICE
LIQUEFYING
LIQUESCENT
LIQUIDATED
LIQUIDATOR
LIQUIDIZED
LIQUIDIZER
LIQUORICES
LISSOMNESS
LISTENABLE
LISTLESSLY
LIST
PRICES
LITERALISM
LITERALIST
LITERARILY
LITERATELY
LITERATION
LITERATURE
LITHOGRAPH
LITHOLOGIC
LITHOMARGE
LITHOPHYTE
LITHOTOMIC
LITHOTRITY
LITHUANIAN
LITIGATING
LITIGATION
LITTERBINS
LITTERLOUT
LITTLE
BELT
LITTLE
ROCK

LITURGICAL
LIVABILITY
LIVELIHOOD
LIVELINESS
LIVING
ROOM
LIVINGSTON
LIVING
WAGE
LIVING
WILL
LLANGOLLEN
LOADSTONES
LOBOTOMIES
LOBSTERPOT
LOBULATION
LOCAL
DERBY
LOCALISTIC
LOCALITIES
LOCALIZING
LOCKER
ROOM
LOCK
KEEPER
LOCKSMITHS
LOCKSTITCH
LOCOMOTION
LOCOMOTIVE
LOCULATION
LODESTONES
LOGANBERRY
LOGARITHMS
LOGGERHEAD
LOGICALITY
LOGISTICAL
LOGOGRAPHY
LOGOPAEDIC
LOGORRHOEA
LOGROLLING
LOINCLOTHS
LOIR-ET-
CHER
LONELINESS
LONGBENTON
LONGHAIRED
LONG-
HEADED
LONG
ISLAND
LONGITUDES

LONG-
JUMPER
LONGWINDED
LOOK-
ALIKES
LOPHOPHORE
LOQUACIOUS
LORDLINESS
LORGNETTES
LORRY
PARKS
LOS
ANGELES
LOSS
LEADER
LOST
CAUSES
LOTUS-
EATER
LOUDHAILER
LOUDMOUTHS
LOUISVILLE
LOUNGE
BARS
LOUNGE
SUIT
LOVABILITY
LOVE
AFFAIR
LOVELINESS
LOVEMAKING
LOVING
CUPS
LOW-
ALCOHOL
LOWBROWISM
LOWER
CLASS
LOWER
HOUSE
LOWERINGLY
LOWLANDERS
LOW-
PITCHED
LOW
PROFILE
LOW-
TENSION
LOXODROMIC
LUBRICANTS
LUBRICATED
LUBRICATOR
LUBRICIOUS

LUBUMBASHI
LUCUBRATOR
LUGGAGE
VAN
LUGUBRIOUS
LULUABOURG
LUMBERJACK
LUMBER-
ROOM
LUMBERYARD
LUMBRICOID
LUMINARIES
LUMINOSITY
LUMINOUSLY
LUMISTEROL
LUNAR
MONTH
LURCHINGLY
LUSCIOUSLY
LUSTRATION
LUSTRATIVE
LUSTREWARE
LUSTROUSLY
LUTINE
BELL
LUXEMBOURG
LUXURIANCE
LUXURIATED
LYCOPODIUM
LYMPHOCYTE
LYOPHILIZE

M
MAASTRICHT
MAASTRICHT
MACADAMIZE
MACEBEARER
MACEDONIAN
MACERATING
MACERATION
MACERATIVE
MACHINABLE
MACHINATOR
MACHINE
GUN
MACHINISTS
MACH
NUMBER
MACKINTOSH
MACROCOSMS
MACROCYTIC
MACROGRAPH

MACROPHAGE
MACROSPORE
MACULATION
MADAGASCAN
MADAGASCAR
MADCHESTER
MADREPORAL
MAELSTROMS
MAGIC
WANDS
MAGISTRACY
MAGISTRATE
MAGNA
CARTA
MAGNETITIC
MAGNETIZED
MAGNETIZER
MAGNIFIERS
MAGNIFYING
MAGNITUDES
MAGNUM
OPUS
MAIDENHAIR
MAIDENHEAD
MAIDENHOOD
MAIDEN
NAME
MAIN
CHANCE
MAIN
CLAUSE
MAINFRAMES
MAINLINING
MAINSPRING
MAINSTREAM
MAINTAINED
MAINTAINER
MAISONETTE
MAJOR-
DOMOS
MAJORETTES
MAJORITIES
MAJOR
SUITS
MAJUSCULAR
MAKE A
POINT
MAKESHIFTS
MAKEWEIGHT
MALACOLOGY
MALADDRESS
MALAPROPOS

MALCONTENT
MALEFACTOR
MALEFICENT
MALEVOLENT
MALFEASANT
MALIGNANCY
MALINGERED
MALINGERER
MALODOROUS
MALPIGHIAN
MALTED
MILK
MALTHUSIAN
MALTREATED
MALTREATER
MALVACEOUS
MANAGEABLE
MANAGEABLY
MANAGEMENT
MANAGERESS
MANAGERIAL
MANCHESTER
MANCHINEEL
MANCHURIAN
MANCUNIANS
MANEUVERED
MAN
FRIDAYS
MANFULNESS
MANGOSTEEN
MANHANDLED
MANIACALLY
MANICURING
MANICURIST
MANIFESTED
MANIFESTLY
MANIFESTOS
MANIFOLDER
MANIPULATE
MANNEQUINS
MANNERISMS
MANOEUVRED
MANOEUVRER
MANOEUVRES
MAN OF
STRAW
MANOMETERS
MANOMETRIC
MANOR
HOUSE
MANSERVANT
MANTELTREE

MANTICALLY
MANUSCRIPT
MANZANILLA
MARASCHINO
MARCESCENT
MARCH-
PASTS
MARCONI
RIG
MARE'S
NESTS
MARGARITAS
MARGINALIA
MARGINALLY
MARGUERITE
MARINATING
MARINATION
MARIONETTE
MARKEDNESS
MARKETABLE
MARKETABLY
MARKETEERS
MARKET
TOWN
MARKSWOMAN
MARLACIOUS
MARQUISATE
MARROWBONE
MARSHALING
MARSHALLED
MARSHALLER
MARSHINESS
MARSUPIALS
MARTELLATO
MARTENSITE
MARTIAL
ART
MARTIALISM
MARTIALIST
MARTIAL
LAW
MARTINGALE
MARTINICAN
MARTINIQUE
MARVELLING
MARVELLOUS
MARVELMENT
MARXIANISM
MASCARPONE
MASOCHISTS
MASQUERADE
MASSACRING

MASSASAUGA
MASSETERIC
MASTECTOMY
MASTER
CARD
MASTERHOOD
MASTER
KEYS
MASTERMIND
MASTERSHIP
MASTERWORK
MASTICABLE
MASTICATED
MASTICATOR
MASTURBATE
MATCHBOARD
MATCHBOXES
MATCHMAKER
MATCH
POINT
MATCHSTICK
MATERIALLY
MATERNALLY
MATO
GROSSO
MATOZINHOS
MATRIARCHS
MATRIARCHY
MATRICIDAL
MATRICIDES
MATRILOCAL
MATTERHORN
MATTRESSES
MATURATION
MATURATIVE
MAUDLINISM
MAUNDERING
MAURITANIA
MAUSOLEUMS
MAXILLIPED
MAXIMALIST
MAXIMIZING
MAXISINGLE
MAYONNAISE
MAYORESSES
MEADOWLARK
MEAGRENESS
MEANDERING
MEANINGFUL
MEANS
TESTS
MEASLINESS

MEASURABLE
MEASURABLY
MEASUREDLY
MECHANICAL
MECHANISMS
MECHANIZED
MECHANIZER
MECONOPSIS
MEDALLIONS
MEDALLISTS
MEDDLESOME
MEDDLINGLY
MEDICAMENT
MEDICATION
MEDICATIVE
MEDIOCRITY
MEDITATING
MEDITATION
MEDITATIVE
MEDIUM
WAVE
MEDULLATED
MEERSCHAUM
MEFLOQUINE
MEGAGAMETE
MEGALITHIC
MEGAPHONES
MEGAPHONIC
MEGASPORIC
MEITNERIUM
MELANCHOLY
MELANESIAN
MELANISTIC
MELANOCYTE
MELANOSITY
MELBURNIAN
MELIACEOUS
MELIORABLE
MELIORATOR
MELISMATIC
MELLOPHONE
MELLOWNESS
MELODRAMAS
MELTING
POT
MEMBERSHIP
MEMBRANOUS
MEMORANDUM
MEMORIZING
MENACINGLY
MENAGERIES

MENARCHEAL	METAPHRASE	MICROPRINT	MILLESIMAL	MISCH
MENDACIOUS	METAPHRAST	MICROPYLAR	MILLIGRAMS	METAL
MENDICANCY	METAPHYSIC	MICROSCOPE	MILLILITRE	MISCONDUCT
MENDICANTS	METAPLASIA	MICROSCOPY	MILLIMETRE	MISCOUNTED
MENINGITIC	METASTABLE	MICROSEISM	MILLIONTHS	MISCREANTS
MENINGITIS	METASTASIS	MICROSOMAL	MILLIPEDES	MISERICORD
MEN OF	METASTATIC	MICROSPORE	MILLSTONES	MISFORTUNE
STRAW	METATARSUS	MICROTOMIC	MILLSTREAM	MISGIVINGS
MENOPAUSAL	METATHEORY	MICROTONAL	MILLWHEELS	MISHANDLED
MENOPAUSIC	METATHESIS	MICROWAVES	MILLWORKER	MISHEARING
MENSTRUATE	METATHETIC	MIDAS	MILLWRIGHT	MISJOINDER
MENSTRUOUS	METATHORAX	TOUCH	MILOMETERS	MISJUDGING
MENSURABLE	METEORITES	MIDDELBURG	MIMEOGRAPH	MISLEADING
MENTAL	METEORITIC	MIDDLE-	MINATORILY	MISMANAGED
AGES	METHIONINE	AGED	MINDLESSLY	MISMANAGER
MENTAL.	METHODICAL	MIDDLE	MIND	MISMATCHED
NOTE	METHODISTS	AGES	READER	MISMATCHES
MENTIONING	METHODIZER	MIDDLEBROW	MINEFIELDS	MISOGAMIST
MERCANTILE	METHUSELAH	MIDDLE	MINERALIZE	MISOGYNIST
MERCAPTIDE	METHYLATOR	EAST	MINERALOGY	MISOGYNOUS
MERCIFULLY	METHYLDOPA	MIDDLE	MINERAL	MISOLOGIST
MERIDIONAL	METICULOUS	NAME	OIL	MISPLACING
MERRYMAKER	METOESTRUS	MIDDLE	MINESTRONE	MISPRINTED
MERSEY	METRICALLY	WEST	MINIATURES	MISPRISION
BEAT	METRICIZED	MIDLOTHIAN	MINIMALIST	MISQUOTING
MERSEYSIDE	METRIC	MIDSECTION	MINIMIZING	MISREADING
MESENCHYME	TONS	MIDSHIPMAN	MINISTERED	MISSIONARY
MESENTERIC	METRONOMES	MIDSHIPMEN	MINISTRANT	MISSOURIAN
MESENTERON	METRONOMIC	MIDWESTERN	MINISTRIES	MISSPELLED
MESITYLENE	METRONYMIC	MIGHTINESS	MINNESOTAN	MISSTATING
MESMERISTS	METROPOLIS	MIGNONETTE	MINORITIES	MISSUPPOSE
MESMERIZED	METTLESOME	MIGRAINOID	MINOR	MISTAKABLE
MESMERIZER	MEXICO	MIGRATIONS	SUITS	MISTAKABLY
MESOCRATIC	CITY	MILEOMETER	MINSTRELSY	MISTAKENLY
MESODERMAL	MEZZANINES	MILESTONES	MINT	MISTRESSES
MESOLITHIC	MEZZOTINTS	MILITANTLY	JULEPS	MISTRUSTED
MESOMORPHY	MIAMI	MILITARILY	MINUSCULAR	MISTRUSTER
MESOPHYTIC	BEACH	MILITARISM	MINUTE	MITIGATING
MESOSPHERE	MICHAELMAS	MILITARIST	HAND	MITIGATION
MESOTHORAX	MICROCHIPS	MILITARIZE	MINUTENESS	MITIGATIVE
MESSENGERS	MICROCLINE	MILITATING	MIRACIDIAL	MITTERRAND
METABOLISM	MICROCOSMS	MILITATION	MIRACIDIUM	MIXABILITY
METABOLITE	MICROCYTIC	MILITIAMAN	MIRACULOUS	MIXED
METABOLIZE	MICROFICHE	MILK	MIRTHFULLY	GRILL
METACARPAL	MICROFILMS	FLOATS	MISAPPLIED	MIXOLYDIAN
METACARPUS	MICROGRAPH	MILK	MISBEHAVED	MIZZENMAST
METACENTRE	MICROMETER	SHAKES	MISBEHAVER	MOBILE
METAFEMALE	MICROMETRY	MILK	MISCALLING	HOME
METAGALAXY	MICRONESIA	TOOTHS	MISCARRIED	MOBILIZING
METALLURGY	MICROPHONE	MILLENNIAL	MISCASTING	MOBOCRATIC
METAMERISM	MICROPHYTE	MILLENNIUM	MISCELLANY	MOCK-
METAPHORIC		MILLEPEDES	MISCHANCES	HEROIC

MODERATELY
MODERATING
MODERATION
MODERATORS
MODERNISMS
MODERNISTS
MODERNIZED
MODERNIZER
MODERNNESS
MODIFIABLE
MODISHNESS
MODULATING
MODULATION
MODULATIVE
MOGADISCIO
MOHAMMEDAN
MOISTENING
MOISTURIZE
MOLLIFYING
MOLLUSCOID
MOLYBDENUM
MONADISTIC
MONADOLOGY
MONANDROUS
MONANTHOUS
MONARCHIES
MONARCHISM
MONARCHIST
MONEGASQUE
MONETARISM
MONETARIST
MONEYBOXES
MONEYMAKER
MONEY
ORDER
MONGRELISM
MONGRELIZE
MONILIFORM
MONITORIAL
MONITORING
MONKEY
NUTS
MONOCARPIC
MONOCHROME
MONOCLINAL
MONOCLINIC
MONOCRATIC
MONOCYCLIC
MONOCYTOID
MONOECIOUS
MONOGAMIST

MONOGAMOUS
MONOGENOUS
MONOGRAPHS
MONOGYNIST
MONOGYNOUS
MONOHYBRID
MONOLITHIC
MONOLOGIST
MONOLOGUES
MONOMANIAC
MONOMEROUS
MONOPHOBIA
MONOPHOBIC
MONOPHONIC
MONOPLANES
MONOPLEGIA
MONOPLEGIC
MONOPODIAL
MONOPODIUM
MONOPOLIES
MONOPOLISM
MONOPOLIST
MONOPOLIZE
MONOPTEROS
MONOTHEISM
MONOTHEIST
MONOTONOUS
MONOVALENT
MONSIGNORS
MONSTRANCE
MONTE
CARLO
MONTEGO
BAY
MONTENEGRO
MONTEVIDEO
MONTGOMERY
MONTMARTRE
MONTPELIER
MONTSERRAT
MONUMENTAL
MONZONITIC
MOONFLOWER
MOONSCAPES
MOONSTONES
MOONSTRUCK
MOOT
POINTS
MORALISTIC
MORALITIES
MORALIZERS

MORALIZING
MORATORIUM
MORAYSHIRE
MORBIDNESS
MORDACIOUS
MORDVINIAN
MORGANATIC
MOROSENESS
MORPHEUSES
MORPHINISM
MORPHOLOGY
MORTAL
SINS
MORTGAGEES
MORTGAGING
MORTGAGORS
MORTICIANS
MORTIFYING
MORTUARIES
MOSQUITOES
MOSTAGANEM
MOTHERHOOD
MOTHERLESS
MOTHER'S
BOY
MOTHER'S
DAY
MOTHER-TO-
BE
MOTHERWELL
MOTHERWORT
MOTIONLESS
MOTIVATING
MOTIVATION
MOTIVATIVE
MOTIVELESS
MOTONEURON
MOTORBIKES
MOTORBOATS
MOTORCADES
MOTORCYCLE
MOTORIZING
MOTOR
LODGE
MOTS
JUSTES
MOULDBOARD
MOULDERING
MOULDINESS
MOUNTEBANK
MOURNFULLY
MOUSETRAPS

MOUSSELINE
MOUSTACHES
MOUTH
ORGAN
MOUTHPIECE
MOVABILITY
MOVIE
STARS
MOVING
VANS
MOZAMBIQUE
MOZZARELLA
MPUMALANGA
MUCKRAKERS
MUCKRAKING
MUDDLINGLY
MUDSKIPPER
MUDSLINGER
MUHAMMADAN
MUJAHEDDIN
MULBERRIES
MULIEBRITY
MULISHNESS
MULTIBIRTH
MULTIMEDIA
MULTIPLANE
MULTIPLIED
MULTIPLIER
MULTISTAGE
MULTITUDES
MUMBLINGLY
MUMBO
JUMBO
MUMMIFYING
MUNIFICENT
MURPHY'S
LAW
MUSCOVITES
MUSCULARLY
MUSHROOMED
MUSICAL
BOX
MUSIC
HALLS
MUSICOLOGY
MUSKETEERS
MUSKETRIES
MUSTACHIOS
MUSTARD
GAS
MUTABILITY
MUTATIONAL

MUTILATING
MUTILATION
MUTILATIVE
MUTINOUSLY
MUTUAL
FUND
MYASTHENIA
MYASTHENIC
MYCETOZOAN
MYCOLOGIST
MYCOPLASMA
MYCORRHIZA
MYCOSTATIN
MYOCARDIAL
MYOCARDIUM
MYOGRAPHIC
MYOPICALLY
MYRIAPODAN
MYRTACEOUS
MYSTAGOGIC
MYSTAGOGUE
MYSTERIOUS
MYSTICALLY
MYSTIFYING
MYTHICIZER
MYTHOMANIA
MYTHOPOEIA
MYTHOPOEIC
MYXOEDEMIC
MYXOMATOUS
MYXOMYCETE

N
NAIL-
BITING
NAIRNSHIRE
NAMBY-
PAMBY
NAMEPLATES
NANNY
GOATS
NANOSECOND
NAPKIN
RING
NAPOLEONIC
NARCISSISM
NARCISSIST
NARCOLEPSY
NARRATABLE
NARRATIONS
NARRATIVES

NARROW
  BOAT
NARROWNESS
NASTURTIUM
NATATIONAL
NATIONALLY
NATIONHOOD
NATIONWIDE
NATIVISTIC
NATIVITIES
NATTERJACK
NATURAL
  GAS
NATURALISM
NATURALIST
NATURALIZE
NATUROPATH
NAUGHTIEST
NAUSEATING
NAUSEATION
NAUSEOUSLY
NAUTICALLY
NAVIGATING
NAVIGATION
NAVIGATORS
NEAPOLITAN
NEAR
  MISSES
NEAR
  THINGS
NEBULOSITY
NEBULOUSLY
NECROLATRY
NECROMANCY
NECROPHOBE
NECROPOLIS
NEEDLEFISH
NEEDLESSLY
NEEDLEWORK
NE'ER-DO-
  WELL
NEGATIVELY
NEGATIVING
NEGATIVISM
NEGATIVIST
NEGLECTFUL
NEGLECTING
NEGLIGENCE
NEGLIGIBLE
NEGLIGIBLY
NEGOTIABLE
NEGOTIATED

NEGOTIATOR
NEIGHBOURS
NEMATOCYST
NEOLOGICAL
NEOLOGISMS
NEON
  LIGHTS
NEOPLASTIC
NEPENTHEAN
NEPHOGRAPH
NEPHOSCOPE
NEPHRALGIA
NEPHRALGIC
NEPHRIDIAL
NEPHRIDIUM
NEPHROTOMY
NEPOTISTIC
NETHERMOST
NETIQUETTE
NETTLE
  RASH
NETTLESOME
NETWORKING
NEURECTOMY
NEUROBLAST
NEUROCOELE
NEUROGENIC
NEUROLEMMA
NEUROPATHY
NEUROTOXIN
NEUTRALISM
NEUTRALIST
NEUTRALITY
NEUTRALIZE
NEUTROPHIL
NEVER-
  NEVER
NEW
  BEDFORD
NEW
  BRITAIN
NEW
  ENGLAND
NEWFANGLED
NEW
  IRELAND
NEW
  ORLEANS
NEWS
  AGENCY
NEWSAGENTS
NEWSCASTER

NEWSHOUNDS
NEWSLETTER
NEWSPAPERS
NEWSREADER
NEWSSHEETS
NEWSSTANDS
NEWSVENDOR
NEWSWORTHY
NEWTON'S
  LAW
NEW
  ZEALAND
NICARAGUAN
NICKELLING
NICKNAMING
NICOTINISM
NIDICOLOUS
NIDIFUGOUS
NIGHTCLUBS
NIGHTDRESS
NIGHTLIGHT
NIGHTMARES
NIGHTSHADE
NIGHT
  SHIFT
NIGHTSHIRT
NIGHTSTICK
NIGRESCENT
NIHILISTIC
NIMBLENESS
NINCOMPOOP
NINETEENTH
NINETIETHS
NINETY-
  NINE
NINGSIA
  HUI
NIPPLEWORT
NISSEN
  HUTS
NITPICKERS
NITPICKING
NITRIC
  ACID
NITROMETER
NO-
  ACCOUNTS
NOBEL
  PRIZE
NOBILITIES
NO-MAN'S-
  LAND

NOM DE
  PLUME
NOMINALISM
NOMINALIST
NOMINATING
NOMINATION
NOMINATIVE
NOMOGRAPHY
NOMOLOGIST
NOMOTHETIC
NONALIGNED
NONCHALANT
NONDRINKER
NONESUCHES
NONETHICAL
NONFACTUAL
NONFERROUS
NONFICTION
NONJOINDER
NONMEDICAL
NO-
  NONSENSE
NONPAREILS
NONPAYMENT
NONPLUSSED
NONSMOKERS
NONSMOKING
NONSTARTER
NONSTATIVE
NON-
  STRIKER
NONTYPICAL
NONVIOLENT
NORMALIZED
NORRKOPING
NORTHBOUND
NORTHERNER
NORTH
  POLES
NORTHWARDS
NOSEBLEEDS
NOSEDIVING
NOSOGRAPHY
NOSOLOGIST
NOSTOLOGIC
NOSY
  PARKER
NOTABILITY
NOTARIZING
NOTATIONAL
NOTEWORTHY
NOTICEABLE

NOTICEABLY
NOTIFIABLE
NOTTINGHAM
NOUAKCHOTT
NOURISHING
NOVACULITE
NOVA
  SCOTIA
NOVELETTES
NOVELISTIC
NOVITIATES
NUCLEATION
NUCLEONICS
NUCLEOSIDE
NUCLEOTIDE
NUDIBRANCH
NULLIFYING
NUMBERLESS
NUMBSKULLS
NUMERATION
NUMERATIVE
NUMERATORS
NUMEROLOGY
NUMEROUSLY
NUMISMATIC
NUMMULITIC
NUNCIATURE
NURSELINGS
NURSEMAIDS
NURSERYMAN
NURSERYMEN
NURTURABLE
NUTATIONAL
NUTCRACKER
NUTRITIOUS
NYCTALOPIA
NYCTINASTY
NYMPHOLEPT

O

OAFISHNESS
OAST
  HOUSES
OBDURATELY
OBEDIENTLY
OBEISANCES
OBELISKOID
OBERHAUSEN
OBFUSCATED
OBITUARIES
OBITUARIST

OBJECTIONS
OBJECTIVES
OBJETS DART
OBJETS D'ART
OBJURGATOR
OBLIGATING
OBLIGATION
OBLIGATIVE
OBLIGATORY
OBLIGINGLY
OBLITERATE
OBSEQUIOUS
OBSERVABLE
OBSERVABLY
OBSERVANCE
OBSESSIONS
OBSESSIVES
OBSTETRICS
OBSTRUCTED
OBSTRUCTER
OBTAINABLE
OBTAINMENT
OBTUSENESS
OBVOLUTION
OBVOLUTIVE
OCCASIONAL
OCCASIONED
OCCIDENTAL
OCCUPATION
OCCURRENCE
OCEANARIUM
OCEANGOING
OCEANOLOGY
OCELLATION
OCHLOCRACY
OCTAHEDRAL
OCTAHEDRON
OCTAMEROUS
OCTANGULAR
OCTAVALENT
OCTODECIMO
OCULOMOTOR
ODALISQUES
ODD-PINNATE
ODIOUSNESS
ODONTALGIA
ODONTALGIC
ODONTOLOGY

OEDEMATOUS
OENOLOGIST
OESOPHAGUS
OESTRADIOL
OFFENSIVES
OFFICE BOYS
OFFICIALLY
OFFICIATED
OFFICIATOR
OFF-LICENCE
OFF-LOADING
OFF-PUTTING
OFFSETTING
OFF THE CUFF
OFF THE HOOK
OFF-THE-WALL
OIL-BEARING
OIL TANKERS
OLDE WORLDE
OLD MAIDISH
OLD MASTERS
OLD SCHOOLS
OLD SCRATCH
OLEAGINOUS
OLEOGRAPHY
OLIGARCHIC
OLIGOCLASE
OLIGOPSONY
OLIGURETIC
OLIVACEOUS
OLIVE GREEN
OMMATIDIAL
OMMATIDIUM
OMNIPOTENT
OMNISCIENT
OMNIVOROUS
ONCOLOGIST

ONE ANOTHER
ONE-MAN BAND
ONE-SIDEDLY
ONOMASTICS
ONSLAUGHTS
ON THE ALERT
ON THE CARDS
ON THE ROCKS
ON THE ROPES
ON THE SPREE
OOPHORITIC
OOPHORITIS
OOPS-A-DAISY
OPALESCENT
OPAQUENESS
OPEN-HANDED
OPEN LETTER
OPEN MARKET
OPEN-MINDED
OPEN SEASON
OPEN SECRET
OPEN SESAME
OPERA BUFFA
OPERA HOUSE
OPERATIONS
OPERATIVES
OPERETTIST
OPHICLEIDE
OPHTHALMIA
OPHTHALMIC
OPPILATION
OPPOSINGLY
OPPOSITION
OPPRESSING
OPPRESSION

OPPRESSIVE
OPPRESSORS
OPPROBRIUM
OPTICAL ART
OPTIMISTIC
OPTIMIZING
OPTIONALLY
OPTOMETRIC
ORANGEWOOD
ORANGUTANG
ORATORICAL
ORCHESTRAL
ORCHESTRAS
ORDER PAPER
ORDINANCES
ORDINARILY
ORDINATION
ORDONNANCE
ORDOVICIAN
ORGANICISM
ORGANICIST
ORGANISMAL
ORGANIZERS
ORGANIZING
ORGANOLOGY
ORIENTATED
ORIGINALLY
ORIGINATED
ORIGINATOR
ORIMULSION
ORNAMENTAL
ORNAMENTED
ORNATENESS
ORNITHOPOD
ORNITHOSIS
OROGRAPHER
OROGRAPHIC
OROLOGICAL
ORPHANAGES
ORTHOCLASE
ORTHOGENIC
ORTHOGONAL
OSCILLATED
OSCILLATOR
OSCULATION
OSCULATORY
OSMIRIDIUM
OSMOMETRIC
OSSIFEROUS

OSTENSIBLE
OSTENSIBLY
OSTEOBLAST
OSTEOCLAST
OSTEOPATHS
OSTEOPATHY
OSTEOPHYTE
OSTRACIZED
OSTRACIZER
OSTRACODAN
OTOLOGICAL
OUANANICHE
OUBLIETTES
OUIJA BOARD
OUTBALANCE
OUTBIDDING
OUTBRAVING
OUTCLASSED
OUTFIELDER
OUTFITTERS
OUTFITTING
OUTFLANKED
OUTGENERAL
OUTGROWING
OUTGROWTHS
OUT-HERODED
OUTLANDISH
OUTLASTING
OUT OF COURT
OUT OF DOORS
OUT OF ORDER
OUT OF PLACE
OUT OF SIGHT
OUTPATIENT
OUTPERFORM
OUTPLAYING
OUTPOINTED
OUTPOURING
OUTRAGEOUS
OUTRANKING
OUTRIGGERS
OUTRIVALED
OUTRUNNING
OUTSELLING
OUTSHINING

OUTSMARTED
OUTSTARING
OUTSTATION
OUTSTAYING
OUTSTRETCH
OUTSWINGER
OUTTALKING
OUTWEIGHED
OUTWITTING
OUTWORKERS
OVARIOTOMY
OVERACTING
OVERACTIVE
OVERARCHED
OVERBOOKED
OVERBURDEN
OVERCHARGE
OVERCOMING
OVERDOSAGE
OVERDOSING
OVERDRAFTS
OVEREXPOSE
OVERFLIGHT
OVERFLOWED
OVERFLYING
OVERHAULED
OVERIJSSEL
OVERLAPPED
OVERLAYING
OVERLOADED
OVERLOOKED
OVERMANNED
OVERMASTER
OVERMATTER
OVERPASSES
OVERPLAYED
OVERRATING
OVERRIDDEN
OVERRIDING
OVERRULING
OVERSEEING
OVERSHADOW
OVERSIGHTS
OVERSPILLS
OVERSPREAD
OVERSTATED
OVERSTAYED
OVERSTRUNG
OVERTAXING
OVER THE
 TOP

OVERTHROWN
OVERTHROWS
OVERTHRUST
OVERTOPPED
OVERTURNED
OVERWEIGHT
OVERWORKED
OVIPOSITOR
OVULATIONS
OXIDIMETRY
OXYCEPHALY
OXYGENATED
OXYGENIZER
OXYGEN
 MASK
OXYGEN
 TENT
OYSTER
 BEDS
OZONOLYSIS

P

PACE
 BOWLER
PACEMAKERS
PACHYDERMS
PACIFIC
 RIM
PACK
 ANIMAL
PACKSADDLE
PACKTHREAD
PADDLEFISH
PADLOCKING
PAEDERASTS
PAEDERASTY
PAEDIATRIC
PAGANISTIC
PAGINATION
PAILLASSES
PAINKILLER
PAINLESSLY
PAINTBRUSH
PAKISTANIS
PALAEOCENE
PALAEOGENE
PALAEOLITH
PALAEOZOIC
PALANQUINS
PALATALIZE
PALATIALLY
PALATINATE

PALEACEOUS
PALIMPSEST
PALINDROME
PALLBEARER
PALLIASSES
PALLIATING
PALLIATION
PALLIATIVE
PALLIDNESS
PALMACEOUS
PALMETTOES
PALM
 SUNDAY
PALPATIONS
PALPEBRATE
PALPITATED
PALSY-
 WALSY
PALTRINESS
PALYNOLOGY
PANAMA
 CITY
PANAMANIAN
PAN-
 ARABISM
PANCAKE
 DAY
PANCREASES
PANCREATIC
PANCREATIN
PANEGYRICS
PANEGYRIST
PANEGYRIZE
PANELLISTS
PANGENESIS
PANGENETIC
PANHANDLED
PANHANDLER
PANHANDLES
PANICULATE
PANJANDRUM
PANTALOONS
PANTHEISTS
PANTOGRAPH
PANTOMIMES
PANTOMIMIC
PAPANDREOU
PAPAVERINE
PAPERBACKS
PAPERBOARD
PAPER
 CHASE

PAPER
 CLIPS
PAPERINESS
PAPER
 KNIFE
PAPER
 MONEY
PAPER
 TIGER
PAPISTICAL
PARABIOSIS
PARABIOTIC
PARABOLIST
PARABOLIZE
PARABOLOID
PARACHUTED
PARACHUTES
PARADIDDLE
PARAGRAPHS
PARAGUAYAN
PARALLELED
PARALOGISM
PARALOGIST
PARALYSING
PARALYTICS
PARAMARIBO
PARAMECIUM
PARAMEDICS
PARAMETERS
PARAMETRIC
PARAMNESIA
PARANOIACS
PARANORMAL
PARAPHRASE
PARAPHYSIS
PARAPLEGIA
PARAPLEGIC
PARAPODIUM
PARAPRAXIS
PARASELENE
PARASITISM
PARASITIZE
PARASITOID
PARASTICHY
PARATACTIC
PARATROOPS
PARBOILING
PARCELLING
PARCEL
 POST
PARCHMENTS
PARDONABLE

PARDONABLY
PARENCHYMA
PARENTERAL
PARENTHOOD
PARI-
 MUTUEL
PARISH-
 PUMP
PARKING
 LOT
PARK
 KEEPER
PARLIAMENT
PARLOR
 CARS
PARONYMOUS
PAROXYSMAL
PARRICIDAL
PARRICIDES
PARROTFISH
PARSONAGES
PARTIALITY
PARTICIPLE
PARTICULAR
PARTITIONS
PARTITIVES
PARTNERING
PARTRIDGES
PARTURIENT
PARTY
 LINES
PARTY
 PIECE
PARTY
 WALLS
PARVOVIRUS
PASQUINADE
PASSAGEWAY
PASSENGERS
PASSIONATE
PASTEBOARD
PASTELLIST
PASTEURISM
PASTEURIZE
PAST
 MASTER
PASTY-
 FACED
PATCHINESS
PATCHWORKS
PATENTABLE
PATERNALLY

PATHFINDER
PATHOGENIC
PATISSERIE
PATRIARCHS
PATRIARCHY
PATRICIANS
PATRICIATE
PATRICIDAL
PATRICIDES
PATRILOCAL
PATRIOTISM
PATROL
CARS
PATROLLING
PATRONIZED
PATRONIZER
PATRONYMIC
PATTERNING
PAWNBROKER
PAYMASTERS
PAY
PACKETS
PAY PER
VIEW
PAY
STATION
PEACE
CORPS
PEACEFULLY
PEACEMAKER
PEACE
PIPES
PEACHINESS
PEACH
MELBA
PEARL
DIVER
PEARLINESS
PEAR-
SHAPED
PEASHOOTER
PEA
SHOOTER
PEA
SOUPERS
PEBBLEDASH
PECCADILLO
PECTIZABLE
PECULATING
PECULATION
PECULIARLY
PEDAGOGISM

PEDAGOGUES
PEDANTRIES
PEDERASTIC
PEDESTRIAN
PEDIATRICS
PEDICULATE
PEDICULOUS
PEDICURIST
PEDIMENTAL
PEDOLOGIST
PEEPING
TOM
PEGMATITIC
PEJORATION
PEJORATIVE
PELLAGROUS
PELLICULAR
PELLUCIDLY
PENALIZING
PENCILLING
PENDENTIVE
PENDERECKI
PENETRABLE
PENETRALIA
PENETRANCE
PENETRATED
PENETRATOR
PEN
FRIENDS
PENICILLIN
PENINSULAR
PENINSULAS
PENITENTLY
PENMANSHIP
PENNINE
WAY
PENNY
BLACK
PENNYCRESS
PENNYROYAL
PENNYWORTH
PENOLOGIST
PEN
PUSHERS
PENSIONARY
PENSIONERS
PENSIONING
PENTAGONAL
PENTAGRAMS
PENTAMETER
PENTAQUINE
PENTASTICH

PENTATEUCH
PENTATHLON
PENTHOUSES
PENTIMENTO
PENTSTEMON
PEPPERCORN
PEPPER
MILL
PEPPERMINT
PEPPER
POTS
PEPPERWORT
PEPSINOGEN
PEPTIZABLE
PEPTONIZER
PERACIDITY
PERCEIVING
PERCENTAGE
PERCENTILE
PERCEPTION
PERCEPTIVE
PERCEPTUAL
PERCIPIENT
PERCOLATED
PERCOLATOR
PERCUSSION
PERCUSSIVE
PEREMPTORY
PERENNIALS
PERFECTING
PERFECTION
PERFECTIVE
PERFIDIOUS
PERFOLIATE
PERFORABLE
PERFORATED
PERFORATOR
PERFORMERS
PERFORMING
PERICLINAL
PERICYCLIC
PERIDERMAL
PERIDOTITE
PERIGYNOUS
PERIHELION
PERILOUSLY
PERIMETERS
PERIMETRIC
PERIMYSIUM
PERIODICAL
PERIOSTEUM

PERIPETEIA
PERIPHERAL
PERIPHYTON
PERIPTERAL
PERISARCAL
PERISCOPES
PERISCOPIC
PERISHABLE
PERISTOMAL
PERISTYLAR
PERISTYLES
PERITONEAL
PERITONEUM
PERITRICHA
PERIWINKLE
PERMAFROST
PERMANENCE
PERMANENCY
PERMANENTS
PERMEATING
PERMEATION
PERMEATIVE
PERMETHRIN
PERMISSION
PERMISSIVE
PERMITTING
PERNAMBUCO
PERNICIOUS
PERNICKETY
PERORATION
PEROXIDASE
PERPETRATE
PERPETUATE
PERPETUITY
PERPLEXING
PERPLEXITY
PERQUISITE
PERSECUTED
PERSECUTOR
PERSEVERED
PERSIAN
CAT
PERSIENNES
PERSIFLAGE
PERSIMMONS
PERSISTENT
PERSISTING
PERSONABLE
PERSONABLY
PERSONAGES
PERSONALLY

PERSONALTY
PERSONATOR
PERSPIRING
PERSUADING
PERSUASION
PERSUASIVE
PERTAINING
PERTHSHIRE
PERTINENCE
PERTURBING
PERVERSELY
PERVERSION
PERVERSITY
PERVERTING
PESCADORES
PESSIMISTS
PESTICIDAL
PESTICIDES
PESTILENCE
PETERSBURG
PETIT
FOURS
PETITIONED
PETITIONER
PETIT
POINT
PETITS
POIS
PETRIFYING
PETROGLYPH
PETROLATUM
PETROPOLIS
PETTICOATS
PETULANTLY
PHAGOCYTES
PHAGOCYTIC
PHAGOMANIA
PHALANGEAL
PHALANGIST
PHALLICISM
PHALLICIST
PHANEROGAM
PHANTASIES
PHANTASMAL
PHARISAISM
PHARMACIES
PHARMACIST
PHARYNGEAL
PHELLODERM
PHENACAINE
PHENACETIN

PHENFORMIN
PHENOCRYST
PHENOMENAL
PHENOMENON
PHENOTYPIC
PHILATELIC
PHILIPPICS
PHILIPPINE
PHILISTINE
PHILOSOPHY
PHLEBOTOMY
PHLEGMATIC
PHLOGISTIC
PHLOGISTON
PHLOGOPITE
PHOCOMELIA
PHOENICIAN
PHONE
  BOOKS
PHONE
  BOXES
PHONEYNESS
PHONEY
  WARS
PHONICALLY
PHONOGRAPH
PHONOLITIC
PHONOMETER
PHONOSCOPE
PHONOTYPIC
PHOSGENITE
PHOSPHATES
PHOSPHATIC
PHOSPHORIC
PHOSPHORUS
PHOTOFLOOD
PHOTOGENIC
PHOTOGRAPH
PHOTOLYSIS
PHOTOLYTIC
PHOTOMETER
PHOTOMETRY
PHOTOMURAL
PHOTONASTY
PHOTONOVEL
PHOTOPHILY
PHOTOPHORE
PHOTOSTATS
PHOTOTAXIS
PHOTOTONIC
PHOTOTONUS

PHOTOTYPIC
PHRASEBOOK
PHRENOLOGY
PHTHISICAL
PHYLACTERY
PHYLLODIAL
PHYLLOXERA
PHYLOGENIC
PHYSIATRIC
PHYSICALLY
PHYSICIANS
PHYSICISTS
PHYSIOCRAT
PHYSIOLOGY
PHYTOGENIC
PHYTOPHAGY
PHYTOTOXIN
PIANISSIMO
PIANOFORTE
PICARESQUE
PICCADILLY
PICCALILLI
PICCANINNY
PICHICIEGO
PICKPOCKET
PICNICKERS
PICNICKING
PICRIC
  ACID
PICROTOXIC
PICROTOXIN
PICTOGRAPH
PIED-A-
  TERRE
PIERCINGLY
PIGEONHOLE
PIGEON-
  TOED
PIGGYBACKS
PIGGYBANKS
PIGMENTARY
PIGSTICKER
PIKESTAFFS
PILE
  DRIVER
PILGRIMAGE
PILIFEROUS
PILLORYING
PILLOWCASE
PILLOW
  TALK

PILOT
  LIGHT
PIMPERNELS
PIMPLINESS
PINA
  COLADA
PINCERLIKE
PINCHPENNY
PINCUSHION
PINEAPPLES
PINE
  MARTEN
PINFEATHER
PINGUIDITY
PINNATIFID
PINNATIPED
PINPOINTED
PINSTRIPED
PINSTRIPES
PIONEERING
PIPED
  MUSIC
PIPE
  DREAMS
PIPERAZINE
PIPERIDINE
PIPSISSEWA
PIPSQUEAKS
PIROUETTED
PIROUETTES
PISTACHIOS
PISTILLATE
PISTON
  RING
PITCH-
  BLACK
PITCHFORKS
PITCHINESS
PITCHSTONE
PITH
  HELMET
PITILESSLY
PITOT
  TUBES
PITTSBURGH
PITYRIASIS
PLACARDING
PLACE
  CARDS
PLACEMENTS
PLAGIARISM
PLAGIARIST

PLAGIARIZE
PLAINCHANT
PLAIN
  FLOUR
PLAINTIFFS
PLANCHETTE
PLANETARIA
PLANE
  TREES
PLANGENTLY
PLANIMETER
PLANIMETRY
PLANK-
  SHEER
PLANKTONIC
PLANOMETER
PLANOMETRY
PLANTATION
PLASMAGENE
PLASMODIUM
PLASMOLYSE
PLASMOSOME
PLASTERERS
PLASTERING
PLASTIC
  ART
PLASTICINE
PLASTICITY
PLASTICIZE
PLAT DU
  JOUR
PLATE
  GLASS
PLATELAYER
PLATE
  RACKS
PLATITUDES
PLATTELAND
PLATYPUSES
PLAY-
  ACTING
PLAYFELLOW
PLAYGROUND
PLAYGROUPS
PLAYHOUSES
PLAYSCHOOL
PLAYTHINGS
PLAYWRIGHT
PLEASANTER
PLEASANTLY
PLEASANTRY
PLEASINGLY

PLEBISCITE
PLEIOTROPY
PLEONASTIC
PLESIOSAUR
PLEURODONT
PLEUROTOMY
PLEXIGLASS
PLIABILITY
PLODDINGLY
PLOUGHBOYS
PLOUGHLAND
PLUCKINESS
PLUMB
  LINES
PLUMMETING
PLUNDERERS
PLUNDERING
PLUNDEROUS
PLUPERFECT
PLURALISTS
PLURALIZER
PLUTOCRACY
PLUTOCRATS
PNEUMATICS
POCKETABLE
POCKETBOOK
POCKETFULS
POCKMARKED
PODIATRIST
POETASTERS
POETICALLY
POGO
  STICKS
POIGNANTLY
POINSETTIA
POINT-
  BLANK
POKER-
  FACED
POLAR
  BEARS
POLARITIES
POLARIZING
POLEMICIST
POLES
  APART
POLE
  VAULTS
POLITBUROS
POLITENESS
POLITICIAN
POLITICIZE

POLLARDING
POLLINATED
POLLINATOR
POLLINOSIS
POLLUTANTS
POLONAISES
POLYANTHUS
POLYATOMIC
POLYBASITE
POLYCARPIC
POLYCHAETE
POLYCHROME
POLYCHROMY
POLYCLINIC
POLYCOTTON
POLYCYCLIC
POLYDACTYL
POLYDIPSIA
POLYDIPSIC
POLYGAMIST
POLYGAMOUS
POLYGRAPHS
POLYGYNIST
POLYGYNOUS
POLYHEDRAL
POLYHEDRON
POLYMATHIC
POLYMERASE
POLYMERISM
POLYMERIZE
POLYMEROUS
POLYNESIAN
POLYNOMIAL
POLYPHAGIA
POLYPHONIC
POLYPLOIDY
POLYPODOUS
POLYRHYTHM
POLYSEMOUS
POLYTHEISM
POLYTHEIST
POLYVALENT
POMERANIAN
POMIFEROUS
POMOLOGIST
PONDERABLE
POND-
  SKATER
PONTEFRACT
PONTEVEDRA
PONTIFICAL

PONTYPRIDD
POOH-
  POOHED
POOL
  MALEBO
POORHOUSES
POOR
  WHITES
POPE'S
  NOSES
POPISHNESS
POPULARITY
POPULARIZE
POPULATING
POPULATION
PORCUPINES
PORIFEROUS
PORK
  BARREL
PORNOCRACY
POROUSNESS
PORPHYROID
PORTAMENTO
PORTCULLIS
PORTENDING
PORTENTOUS
PORTFOLIOS
PORT-
  GENTIL
PORTIONING
PORTLAOISE
PORTLINESS
PORTOBELLO
PORT OF
  CALL
PORTRAYALS
PORTRAYING
PORTSMOUTH
PORT
  TALBOT
PORTUGUESE
POSITIONAL
POSITIONED
POSITIVELY
POSITIVISM
POSITIVIST
POSSESSING
POSSESSION
POSSESSIVE
POSSESSORS
POSSESSORY

POST-
  BELLUM
POST-
  CYCLIC
POSTDATING
POSTERIORS
POSTHUMOUS
POSTILIONS
POSTLIMINY
POSTMARKED
POSTMASTER
POSTMORTEM
POST
  OFFICE
POSTPARTUM
POSTPONING
POSTSCRIPT
POSTULANCY
POSTULANTS
POSTULATED
POSTULATES
POSTULATOR
POTABILITY
POTATO
  CHIP
POTBELLIED
POTBELLIES
POTBOILERS
POTENTATES
POTENTIATE
POTENTILLA
POTENTNESS
POTHUNTERS
POTPOURRIS
POULTERERS
POULTRYMAN
POURPARLER
POWDER
  KEGS
POWDER
  PUFF
POWDER
  ROOM
POWER
  BASES
POWERBOATS
POWER
  DIVES
POWERFULLY
POWERHOUSE
POWER
  PLANT

POWER
  POINT
POZZUOLANA
PRACTICALS
PRACTISING
PRAESIDIUM
PRAGMATICS
PRAGMATISM
PRAGMATIST
PRAIRIE
  DOG
PRANCINGLY
PRANKSTERS
PRASELENIC
PRATINCOLE
PRAYER
  RUGS
PREACHMENT
PREADAMITE
PREAMBULAR
PREARRANGE
PREBENDARY
PRECARIOUS
PRECAUTION
PRECEDENCE
PRECEDENTS
PRECENTORS
PRECEPTIVE
PRECESSION
PRECIOSITY
PRECIOUSLY
PRECIPICED
PRECIPICES
PRECIPITIN
PRECISIONS
PRECLUDING
PRECLUSION
PRECLUSIVE
PRECOCIOUS
PRECONCERT
PRECOOKING
PRECURSORS
PRECURSORY
PREDACIOUS
PREDECEASE
PREDESTINE
PREDICABLE
PREDICATED
PREDICATES
PREDICTING
PREDICTION

PREDICTIVE
PREDISPOSE
PRE-
  EMINENT
PRE-
  EMPTING
PRE-
  EMPTION
PRE-
  EMPTIVE
PRE-
  EMPTORY
PREEXISTED
PREFECTURE
PREFERABLE
PREFERABLY
PREFERENCE
PREFERMENT
PREFERRING
PREFIGURED
PREFRONTAL
PREGLACIAL
PREGNANTLY
PREHEATING
PREHENSILE
PREHENSION
PREHISTORY
PREHOMINID
PREJUDGING
PREJUDICED
PREJUDICES
PRELEXICAL
PREMARITAL
PREMAXILLA
PREMEDICAL
PRENATALLY
PRENOMINAL
PREPACKAGE
PREPACKING
PREPAREDLY
PREPAYABLE
PREPAYMENT
PREPOSSESS
PREPOTENCY
PREP
  SCHOOL
PRESAGEFUL
PRESBYOPIA
PRESBYOPIC
PRESBYTERY
PRESCHOOLS
PRESCIENCE

PRESCRIBED
PRESCRIBER
PRESCRIPTS
PRESENT DAY
PRESENT-DAY
PRESENTERS
PRESENTING
PRESERVERS
PRESERVING
PRESETTING
PRESIDENCY
PRESIDENTS
PRESIDIUMS
PRESIGNIFY
PRESS AGENT
PRESS BARON
PRESS BOXES
PRESSGANGS
PRESSINGLY
PRESS-STUDS
PRESSURING
PRESSURIZE
PRESUMABLE
PRESUMABLY
PRESUMEDLY
PRESUPPOSE
PRETENDERS
PRETENDING
PRETENSION
PRETTIFIED
PRETTINESS
PREVAILING
PREVALENCE
PREVENIENT
PREVENTING
PREVENTION
PREVENTIVE
PREVIEWING
PREVIOUSLY
PREVISIONS
PREVOCALIC
PRICKLIEST
PRIEST-HOLE
PRIESTHOOD
PRIESTLIER

PRIGGISHLY
PRIMA DONNA
PRIMA FACIE
PRIMAQUINE
PRIME MOVER
PRIME RATES
PRIMITIVES
PRIMORDIAL
PRIMORDIUM
PRINCEDOMS
PRINCELING
PRINCESSES
PRINCIPALS
PRINCIPIUM
PRINCIPLED
PRINCIPLES
PRINTMAKER
PRIORITIES
PRIORITIZE
PRISMATOID
PRISMOIDAL
PRISON CAMP
PRISON GATE
PRISSINESS
PRIVATEERS
PRIVATIONS
PRIVATIZED
PRIVILEGED
PRIVILEGES
PRIVY PURSE
PRIZEFIGHT
PROCAMBIAL
PROCAMBIUM
PROCEDURAL
PROCEDURES
PROCEEDING
PROCESSING
PROCESSION
PROCESSORS
PROCLAIMED
PROCLIVITY
PROCONSULS
PROCREATED
PROCREATOR
PROCRYPTIC

PROCTOLOGY
PROCTORIAL
PROCUMBENT
PROCURATOR
PRODIGALLY
PRODIGIOUS
PRODUCIBLE
PRODUCTION
PRODUCTIVE
PROFESSING
PROFESSION
PROFESSORS
PROFFERING
PROFICIENT
PROFITABLE
PROFITABLY
PROFITEERS
PROFITLESS
PROFLIGACY
PROFLIGATE
PROFOUNDLY
PROFUNDITY
PROGENITOR
PROGLOTTIS
PROGNOSTIC
PROGRAMERS
PROGRAMING
PROGRAMMED
PROGRAMMER
PROGRAMMES
PROGRESSED
PROGRESSES
PROHIBITED
PROHIBITER
PROJECTILE
PROJECTING
PROJECTION
PROJECTIVE
PROJECTORS
PROKARYOTE
PROLAPSING
PROLOCUTOR
PROLONGING
PROMENADED
PROMENADER
PROMENADES
PROMETHIUM
PROMINENCE
PROMISSORY
PROMONTORY
PROMOTABLE

PROMOTIONS
PROMPTBOOK
PROMPTNESS
PROMULGATE
PRONEPHRIC
PRONEPHROS
PRONOMINAL
PRONOUNCED
PRONOUNCER
PRONUCLEAR
PRONUCLEUS
PRO-OESTRUS
PROPAGABLE
PROPAGANDA
PROPAGATED
PROPAGATOR
PROPELLANT
PROPELLENT
PROPELLERS
PROPELLING
PROPENSITY
PROPERNESS
PROPER NOUN
PROPERTIED
PROPERTIES
PROPHECIES
PROPHESIER
PROPHESIED
PROPHESIES
PROPIONATE
PROPITIATE
PROPITIOUS
PROPONENTS
PROPORTION
PROPOSABLE
PROPOSITUS
PROPOUNDED
PROPOUNDER
PROPRIETOR
PROPULSION
PROPULSIVE
PROPYLAEUM
PROROGUING
PROSCENIUM
PROSCRIBED
PROSECUTED
PROSECUTOR
PROSELYTES
PROSELYTIC

PROSPECTED
PROSPECTOR
PROSPECTUS
PROSPERING
PROSPERITY
PROSPEROUS
PROSTHESIS
PROSTHETIC
PROSTITUTE
PROSTOMIUM
PROSTRATED
PROTANOPIA
PROTANOPIC
PROTECTING
PROTECTION
PROTECTIVE
PROTECTORS
PROTECTORY
PROTEINASE
PRO TEMPORE
PROTESTANT
PROTESTERS
PROTHALLIC
PROTHALLUS
PROTOCTIST
PROTOHUMAN
PROTONEMAL
PROTOPATHY
PROTOPLASM
PROTOPLAST
PROTOSTELE
PROTOTYPAL
PROTOTYPES
PROTOXYLEM
PROTOZOANS
PROTRACTED
PROTRACTOR
PROTRUDENT
PROTRUDING
PROTRUSILE
PROTRUSION
PROTRUSIVE
PROVENANCE
PROVENCALE
PROVERBIAL
PROVIDENCE
PROVINCIAL
PROVISIONS
PROVITAMIN
PRUDENTIAL

PRURIENTLY
PSALMODIST
PSALTERIES
PSALTERIUM
PSEPHOLOGY
PSESPHITIC
PSEUDOCARP
PSEUDONYMS
PSILOCYBIN
PSITTACINE
PSITTACISM
PSYCHIATRY
PSYCHOLOGY
PSYCHOPATH
PSYCHOTICS
PTOLEMAIST
PUB-
CRAWLED
PUBERULENT
PUBESCENCE
PUBLIC
BARS
PUBLICISTS
PUBLICIZED
PUBLISHERS
PUBLISHING
PUERPERIUM
PUERTO
RICO
PUGILISTIC
PUGNACIOUS
PUISSANCES
PULLULATED
PULSATIONS
PULSIMETER
PULVERABLE
PULVERIZED
PULVERIZER
PUMMELLING
PUNCH
BALLS
PUNCHBOARD
PUNCH
BOWLS
PUNCH-
DRUNK
PUNCHINESS
PUNCH
LINES
PUNCTATION
PUNCTILIOS
PUNCTUALLY

PUNCTUATED
PUNCTUATOR
PUNCTURING
PUNISHABLE
PUNISHMENT
PUNITIVELY
PUPIPAROUS
PUPPETEERS
PURCHASERS
PURCHASING
PURGATIVES
PURITANISM
PURLOINING
PURPLENESS
PURPORTING
PURPOSEFUL
PURSUANCES
PURSUIVANT
PURVEYANCE
PUSH-
BUTTON
PUSHCHAIRS
PUT A STOP
TO
PUTREFYING
PUTRESCENT
PUTRESCINE
PUZZLEMENT
PUZZLINGLY
PYCNOMETER
PYOGENESIS
PYORRHOEAL
PYRACANTHA
PYRETHROID
PYRIDOXINE
PYRIMIDINE
PYROGALLIC
PYROGALLOL
PYROGRAPHY
PYROLUSITE
PYROMANCER
PYROMANIAC
PYROMANTIC
PYROMETRIC
PYROPHORIC
PYROSTATIC
PYROXENITE
PYRRHOTITE
PYTHAGORAS

Q

QARAGHANDY
QUADRANGLE
QUADRANTAL
QUADRATICS
QUADRATURE
QUADRICEPS
QUADRILLES
QUADRISECT
QUADRIVIAL
QUADRUPEDS
QUADRUPLED
QUADRUPLET
QUADRUPLEX
QUAINTNESS
QUALIFIERS
QUALIFYING
QUANDARIES
QUANTIFIED
QUANTIFIER
QUANTITIES
QUARANTINE
QUARRELING
QUARRELLED
QUARRELLER
QUARTERAGE
QUARTER
DAY
QUARTERING
QUARTERSAW
QUATERNARY
QUATERNION
QUATREFOIL
QUEASINESS
QUEENSLAND
QUENCHABLE
QUESTINGLY
QUESTIONED
QUESTIONER
QUEZON
CITY
QUICKENING
QUICKSANDS
QUICKSTEPS
QUID PRO
QUO
QUIESCENCE
QUIETENING
QUINTUPLET
QUIRKINESS
QUITTANCES

QUIZMASTER
QUONSET
HUT
QUOTATIONS

R

RABBINICAL
RABBITFISH
RABBITTING
RACECOURSE
RACEHORSES
RACETRACKS
RACHMANISM
RACIALISTS
RACKETEERS
RACK-
RENTER
RACONTEURS
RADARSCOPE
RADIATIONS
RADICALISM
RADIO
ALARM
RADIOGENIC
RADIOGRAMS
RADIOGRAPH
RADIOLYSIS
RADIOMETER
RADIOMETRY
RADIOPAQUE
RADIOPHONY
RADIOSCOPE
RADIOSCOPY
RADIOSONDE
RADIOTOXIC
RAFSANJANI
RAGAMUFFIN
RAGGEDNESS
RAILROADED
RAIN
CHECKS
RAIN
FOREST
RAIN
GAUGES
RAINMAKING
RAINSTORMS
RAISE A
DUST
RAJYA
SABHA
RAKISHNESS

RAMPAGEOUS
RAMSHACKLE
RANCH
HOUSE
RANCIDNESS
RANDOMNESS
RANSACKING
RANUNCULUS
RAPPORTEUR
RARE
EARTHS
RAREFIABLE
RATABILITY
RAT-A-TAT-
TAT
RATE-
CAPPED
RATIFIABLE
RATIONALES
RATIONALLY
RAT-
RUNNING
RATTLETRAP
RAUNCHIEST
RAVAGEMENT
RAVENOUSLY
RAVISHMENT
RAWALPINDI
RAWINSONDE
RAZZMATAZZ
REACTIONAL
REACTIVATE
REACTIVELY
REACTIVITY
READERSHIP
READJUSTED
READJUSTER
READY
MONEY
REAFFIRMED
REAFFOREST
REAL
ESTATE
REALIGNING
REALIZABLE
REALIZABLY
REALLOCATE
REANIMATED
REAPPEARED
REAPPRAISE
REARGUARDS
REARMAMENT

REARRANGED
REARRANGER
REASONABLE
REASONABLY
REASSEMBLE
REASSURING
REBELLIONS
REBELLIOUS
REBIRTHING
REBOUNDING
REBUILDING
REBUKINGLY
REBUTTABLE
RECALLABLE
RECAPTURED
RECEIVABLE
RECENTNESS
RECEPTACLE
RECEPTIONS
RECESSIONS
RECHARGING
RECHRISTEN
RECIDIVISM
RECIDIVIST
RECIPIENCE
RECIPIENTS
RECIPROCAL
RECITATION
RECITATIVE
RECKLESSLY
RECKONINGS
RECLAIMANT
RECLAIMING
RECLINABLE
RECOGNIZED
RECOGNIZEE
RECOGNIZER
RECOGNIZOR
RECOILLESS
RECOMMENCE
RECOMPENSE
RECONCILED
RECONCILER
RECONSIDER
RECORDABLE
RECORDINGS
RECOUNTING
RECOUPABLE
RECOUPMENT
RECOVERIES

RE-
   COVERING
RECREATING
RECREATION
RECRUDESCE
RECRUITING
RECTANGLES
RECTIFIERS
RECTIFYING
RECUMBENCE
RECUPERATE
RECURRENCE
RED
   ADMIRAL
RED-
   BLOODED
REDBREASTS
REDCURRANT
REDECORATE
REDEDICATE
REDEEMABLE
REDEEMABLY
REDELIVERY
REDEMPTION
REDEPLOYED
RED
   HERRING
RED
   INDIANS
REDIRECTED
REDISCOUNT
REDOUBLING
REDOUNDING
RED
   PEPPERS
REDRESSING
REDUCTIONS
REDUNDANCY
RE-
   EDUCATED
RE-
   ELECTING
RE-
   ELECTION
RE-
   ENFORCER
RE-
   ENTRANCE
RE-
   EXAMINER
RE-
   EXPORTER

REFEREEING
REFERENCER
REFERENCES
REFERENDUM
REFILLABLE
REFINEMENT
REFINERIES
REFINISHER
REFLECTING
REFLECTION
REFLECTIVE
REFLECTORS
REFLEXIVES
REFORESTED
REFRACTING
REFRACTION
REFRACTIVE
REFRACTORY
REFRAINING
REFRESHFUL
REFRESHING
REFRINGENT
REFUELLING
REFUGEEISM
REFULGENCE
REFUNDABLE
REFUTATION
REGAINABLE
REGALEMENT
REGARDABLE
REGARDLESS
REGELATION
REGENERACY
REGENERATE
REGENSBURG
REGENTSHIP
REGIMENTAL
REGIMENTED
REGIONALLY
REGISTERED
REGISTERER
REGISTRANT
REGISTRARS
REGISTRIES
REGRESSING
REGRESSION
REGRESSIVE
REGRETTING
REGROUPING
REGULARITY
REGULARIZE

REGULATING
REGULATION
REGULATIVE
REGULATORS
REGULATORY
REHEARSALS
REHEARSING
REIMBURSED
REIMBURSER
REINFORCED
REINSTATED
REINSTATOR
REINSURING
REISSUABLE
REITERATED
REJECTABLE
REJECTIONS
REJOINDERS
REJUVENATE
REKINDLING
RELATIONAL
RELATIVELY
RELATIVISM
RELATIVIST
RELATIVITY
RELAXATION
RELEGATING
RELEGATION
RELENTLESS
RELEVANTLY
RELIEF
   MAPS
RELIEF
   ROAD
RELIEVABLE
RELINQUISH
RELISHABLE
RELOCATING
RELOCATION
RELUCTANCE
REMAINDERS
REMANDMENT
REMARKABLE
REMARKABLY
REMARRYING
REMEDIABLE
REMEDIABLY
REMEDIALLY
REMEDILESS
REMEMBERED
REMEMBERER

REMINISCED
REMISSIBLE
REMISSIONS
REMISSNESS
REMITTABLE
REMITTANCE
REMITTENCE
REMODELING
REMODELLED
REMODELLER
REMONETIZE
REMORSEFUL
REMOTENESS
REMOULDING
REMOUNTING
REMOVAL
   VAN
REMUNERATE
RENDERABLE
RENDERINGS
RENDEZVOUS
RENDITIONS
RENEWABLES
RENOUNCING
RENOVATING
RENOVATION
RENOVATIVE
RENOWNEDLY
RENT
   STRIKE
REORGANIZE
REPAIRABLE
REPARATION
REPARATIVE
REPATRIATE
REPAYMENTS
REPEALABLE
REPEATABLE
REPEATEDLY
REPELLENCE
REPELLENTS
REPENTANCE
REPERTOIRE
REPETITION
REPETITIVE
REPHRASING
REPLICATED
REPORTABLE
REPORTEDLY
REPOSITION
REPOSITORY

REPRESSING
REPRESSION
REPRESSIVE
REPRIEVING
REPRIMANDS
REPRINTING
REPROACHED
REPROACHER
REPROACHES
REPROBATER
REPROBATES
REPRODUCED
REPRODUCER
REPROVABLE
REPTILIANS
REPUBLICAN
REPUDIABLE
REPUDIATED
REPUDIATOR
REPUGNANCE
REPULSIONS
REPURCHASE
REPUTATION
REQUESTING
REQUIESCAT
REQUIRABLE
REQUISITES
REQUITABLE
RESCHEDULE
RESCINDING
RESCISSION
RESCISSORY
RESEARCHED
RESEARCHER
RESEARCHES
RESEMBLANT
RESEMBLING
RESENTMENT
RESERVABLE
RESERVEDLY
RESERVISTS
RESERVOIRS
RESETTLING
RESHIPMENT
RESHUFFLED
RESHUFFLES
RESIDENCES
RESIGNEDLY
RESILEMENT
RESILIENCE
RESILIENCY

RESISTANCE
RESISTIBLY
RESISTLESS
RESOLUTELY
RESOLUTION
RESOLVABLE
RESONANCES
RESONANTLY
RESONATING
RESONATION
RESONATORS
RESORCINOL
RESORPTION
RESORPTIVE
RESOUNDING
RESPECTERS
RESPECTFUL
RESPECTING
RESPECTIVE
RESPIRABLE
RESPIRATOR
RESPONDENT
RESPONDING
RESPONSIVE
RESPONSORY
RES
  PUBLICA
RESTAURANT
RESTHARROW
RESTLESSLY
RESTOCKING
RESTORABLE
RESTRAINED
RESTRAINER
RESTRAINTS
RESTRICTED
RESUMPTION
RESUMPTIVE
RESUPINATE
RESURFACED
RESURGENCE
RETAINABLE
RETAINMENT
RETALIATED
RETALIATOR
RETHINKING
RETICENTLY
RETICULATE
RETIREMENT
RETOUCHING
RETRACTILE

RETRACTING
RETRACTION
RETRACTIVE
RETREADING
RETREATING
RETRENCHED
RETRIEVERS
RETRIEVING
RETROCHOIR
RETROGRADE
RETROGRESS
RETROSPECT
RETROVERSE
RETROVIRUS
RETURNABLE
REUNIONISM
REUNIONIST
REUNITABLE
REUTLINGEN
REVANCHISM
REVANCHIST
REVEALABLE
REVEALEDLY
REVEALMENT
REVEGETATE
REVELATION
REVENGEFUL
REVERENCED
REVERENCER
REVERENCES
REVERENTLY
REVERSIBLE
REVERTIBLE
REVETMENTS
REVIEWABLE
REVILEMENT
REVILINGLY
REVISIONAL
REVITALIZE
REVIVALISM
REVIVALIST
REVIVIFIED
REVIVINGLY
REVOCATION
REVOCATIVE
REVOKINGLY
REVOLUTION
REVOLVABLE
REVOLVABLY
REWARDABLE

REWARD
  CARD
RHAPSODIES
RHAPSODIST
RHAPSODIZE
RHEOLOGIST
RHEOMETRIC
RHEOSTATIC
RHEOTACTIC
RHEOTROPIC
RHETORICAL
RHEUMATICS
RHEUMATISM
RHEUMATOID
RHINESTONE
RHINOCEROS
RHINOSCOPY
RHIZOGENIC
RHIZOMORPH
RHIZOPODAN
RHOMBOIDAL
RHUMBATRON
RHYMESTERS
RHYTHMICAL
RIBBONFISH
RIBOFLAVIN
RICKETTSIA
RICOCHETED
RIDGEPOLES
RIDICULING
RIDICULOUS
RIEMANNIAN
RIFLE
  RANGE
RIFT
  VALLEY
RIGHTABOUT
RIGHT
  ANGLE
RIGHTFULLY
RIGHT OF
  WAY
RIGHTWARDS
RIGMAROLES
RIGORISTIC
RIGOROUSLY
RINDERPEST
RING
  BINDER
RING
  FINGER
RINGLEADER

RINGMASTER
RING-
  NECKED
RING-
  TAILED
RIPPLINGLY
RIP-
  ROARING
RISIBILITY
RISING
  DAMP
RITARDANDO
RITORNELLO
RIVER
  BASIN
ROADBLOCKS
ROADHOUSES
ROAD
  ROLLER
ROADRUNNER
ROAD-
  TESTED
ROADWORTHY
ROBUSTNESS
ROCK
  BOTTOM
ROCK
  GARDEN
ROCK
  PLANTS
ROCK
  SALMON
ROISTERERS
ROISTEROUS
ROLE
  MODELS
ROLE-
  PLAYED
ROLLED
  GOLD
ROLLICKING
ROLLING
  PIN
ROLY-
  POLIES
ROMAN
  BLIND
ROMANESQUE
ROMAN
  NOSES
ROOD
  SCREEN

ROOF
GARDEN
ROPE
LADDER
ROSANILINE
ROSEMALING
ROSE
WINDOW
ROSTELLATE
ROTARY
CLUB
ROTATIONAL
ROTISSERIE
ROTOVATORS
ROTTENNESS
ROTTWEILER
ROUGHENING
ROUGHHOUSE
ROUGH
HOUSE
ROUGHNECKS
ROUGH
PAPER
ROUGHRIDER
ROUGH
STUFF
ROUNDABOUT
ROUNDHEADS
ROUNDHOUSE
ROUND
ROBIN
ROUND-
TABLE
ROUND
TRIPS
ROUSEDNESS
ROUSSILLON
ROUSTABOUT
ROUTE
MARCH
ROWING
BOAT
ROYAL
FLUSH
ROYALISTIC
RUB' AL
KHALI
RUBBER
BAND
RUBBERNECK
RUBBER
TREE

RUBBISH
BIN
RUBBISHING
RUBBLEWORK
RUBESCENCE
RUBIACEOUS
RUBIGINOUS
RUBRICATOR
RUDDERHEAD
RUDDERLESS
RUDDERPOST
RUEFULNESS
RUFESCENCE
RUFFIANISM
RUGBY
UNION
RUGGEDIZED
RUGGEDNESS
RUMBLINGLY
RUMINATING
RUMINATION
RUMINATIVE
RUMPUS
ROOM
RUNNER
BEAN
RUN-OF-
PAPER
RUN
THROUGH
RUN-
THROUGH
RUPESTRIAN
RUPTURABLE
RURITANIAN
RUSHLIGHTS
RUSSOPHILE
RUSSOPHOBE
RUSTICATED
RUSTICATOR
RUSTLINGLY
RUTHENIOUS
RUTHERFORD
RUTHLESSLY

S

SABBATICAL
SABOTAGING
SABULOSITY
SACCHARASE
SACCHARATE
SACCHARIDE

SACCHARIFY
SACCHARINE
SACCHAROID
SACCHAROSE
SACERDOTAL
SACRAMENTO
SACRAMENTS
SACRED
COWS
SACREDNESS
SACRIFICED
SACRIFICER
SACRIFICES
SACRILEGES
SACRISTANS
SACRISTIES
SACROILIAC
SACROSANCT
SADDLEBACK
SADDLEBAGS
SADDLEBILL
SADDLERIES
SADDLE-
SORE
SADDLETREE
SAFARI
PARK
SAFEGUARDS
SAFE
HOUSES
SAFETY
BELT
SAFETY
LAMP
SAFETY
NETS
SAFETY
PINS
SAHARANPUR
SAILBOARDS
SAILOR
SUIT
SAILPLANES
SAINT-
CLOUD
SAINT
CROIX
SAINT-
DENIS
SAINT
JOHN'S
SAINT
KILDA

SAINT
KITTS
SAINT
LOUIS
SAINT-
LOUIS
SAINT
LUCIA
SAINT'S
DAYS
SALABILITY
SALAD
CREAM
SALAMANDER
SALBUTAMOL
SALESCLERK
SALESGIRLS
SALES
PITCH
SALES
SLIPS
SALES
TAXES
SALESWOMAN
SALESWOMEN
SALICORNIA
SALICYLATE
SALIFEROUS
SALIFIABLE
SALIMETRIC
SALIVATING
SALIVATION
SALLOWNESS
SALMANAZAR
SALMONELLA
SALMON
LEAP
SALOON
BARS
SALOPETTES
SALPINGIAN
SALTARELLO
SALTCELLAR
SALTIGRADE
SALT
SHAKER
SALUBRIOUS
SALUTARILY
SALUTATION
SALUTATORY
SALVERFORM
SALZGITTER

SAMARITANS
SAMARSKITE
SAMOTHRACE
SAN
ANTONIO
SANATORIUM
SANCTIFIED
SANCTIFIER
SANCTIMONY
SANCTIONED
SANCTIONER
SANCTITUDE
SANDALWOOD
SANDBAGGED
SANDBAGGER
SANDCASTLE
SAND
CASTLE
SANDERLING
SANDGROUSE
SAND
MARTIN
SANDPIPERS
SANDSTORMS
SANDWICHED
SANDWICHES
SANFORIZED
SANFORIZED
SANGUINARY
SANGUINELY
SANITARIAN
SANITARILY
SANITARIUM
SANITATION
SANITIZING
SANSKRITIC
SANTA
CLARA
SANTA
CLAUS
SANTA
MARIA
SANTA
MARTA
SAPIENTIAL
SAPONIFIER
SAPPANWOOD
SAPPHIRINE
SAPROGENIC
SAPROLITIC
SAPROPELIC
SAPROPHYTE

SAPROTROPH
SARCOPHAGI
SARMENTOSE
SARRACENIA
SASH
  WINDOW
SATELLITES
SATINWOODS
SATIRIZING
SATISFYING
SATURATING
SATURATION
SATURNALIA
SATYRIASIS
SAUERKRAUT
SAUNTERING
SAUSAGE
  DOG
SAVAGENESS
SAVAGERIES
SAXICOLOUS
SAXOPHONES
SAXOPHONIC
SCABRINESS
SCAFFOLDER
SCALEBOARD
SCALLOPING
SCALLYWAGS
SCALOPPINE
SCALPELLIC
SCAMPERING
SCANDALIZE
SCANDALOUS
SCANSORIAL
SCANTINESS
SCAPEGOATS
SCAPEGRACE
SCARABAEID
SCARABAEUS
SCARCEMENT
SCARCENESS
SCARCITIES
SCARECROWS
SCAREDY
  CAT
SCARIFYING
SCARLATINA
SCARPERING
SCATHINGLY
SCATTER-
  GUN
SCATTERING

SCATTINESS
SCAVENGERS
SCAVENGING
SCENICALLY
SCEPTICISM
SCHAERBEEK
SCHEDULING
SCHEMATISM
SCHEMATIZE
SCHEMINGLY
SCHERZANDO
SCHIPPERKE
SCHISMATIC
SCHIZOCARP
SCHIZOGONY
SCHLEPPING
SCHNITZELS
SCHOLASTIC
SCHOOLGIRL
SCHOOLMARM
SCHOOLMATE
SCHOOLWORK
SCHUMACHER
SCIENTIFIC
SCIENTISTS
SCILLONIAN
SCIOMANCER
SCIOMANTIC
SCLEROTIUM
SCLEROTOMY
SCOFFINGLY
SCOLDINGLY
SCOLLOPING
SCOREBOARD
SCORECARDS
SCORNFULLY
SCORNINGLY
SCORPAENID
SCORPIONIC
SCOTCH
  EGGS
SCOTCH
  MIST
SCOTCH
  SNAP
SCOTCH
  TAPE
SCOTTICISM
SCOUNDRELS
SCOWLINGLY
SCRABBLING
SCRAGGIEST

SCRAMBLING
SCRAPBOOKS
SCRAP
  HEAPS
SCRAP
  METAL
SCRAP
  PAPER
SCRAPPIEST
SCRATCHIER
SCRATCHILY
SCRATCHING
SCRATCH
  PAD
SCRATCHPAD
SCRAWNIEST
SCREECHING
SCREENABLE
SCREENINGS
SCREENPLAY
SCREEN
  TEST
SCREWBALLS
SCRIBBLERS
SCRIBBLING
SCRIMMAGED
SCRIMMAGER
SCRIMMAGES
SCRIPTURAL
SCROFULOUS
SCROLLWORK
SCROUNGERS
SCROUNGING
SCRUBBIEST
SCRUFFIEST
SCRUMMAGED
SCRUMMAGER
SCRUMMAGES
SCRUNCHING
SCRUPULOUS
SCRUTINEER
SCRUTINIES
SCRUTINIZE
SCULLERIES
SCULPTRESS
SCULPTURAL
SCULPTURED
SCULPTURES
SCUNTHORPE
SCUPPERING
SCURRILITY
SCURRILOUS

SCURVINESS
SCUTELLATE
SCYPHIFORM
SCYPHOZOAN
SEA
  ANEMONE
SEABORGIUM
SEA
  BREEZES
SEA
  CAPTAIN
SEA
  CHANGES
SEALED-
  BEAM
SEALING
  WAX
SEAMANLIKE
SEAMANSHIP
SEAMSTRESS
SEARCHABLE
SEA
  SERPENT
SEASONABLE
SEASONABLY
SEASONEDLY
SEASONINGS
SEA
  URCHINS
SEBIFEROUS
SEBORRHOEA
SECOND
  BEST
SECOND-
  HAND
SECONDMENT
SECOND-
  RATE
SECOND
  WIND
SECRETAIRE
SECRETIONS
SECTIONING
SECULARISM
SECULARIST
SECULARITY
SECULARIZE
SECUNDINES
SECUREMENT
SECURENESS
SECURITIES

SEDAN
  CHAIR
SEDATENESS
SEDUCINGLY
SEDUCTRESS
SEDULOUSLY
SEEMLINESS
SEERSUCKER
SEETHINGLY
SEE-
  THROUGH
SEGMENTARY
SEGMENTING
SEGREGABLE
SEGREGATED
SEGREGATOR
SEISMICITY
SEISMOLOGY
SELECTIONS
SELECTNESS
SELENOLOGY
SELF
  ACTING
SELF-
  ACTION
SELF-
  DENIAL
SELF-
  ESTEEM
SELF-
  FEEDER
SELFLESSLY
SELF-
  REGARD
SELF-
  SEEKER
SELF-
  STYLED
SELF-
  WILLED
SELL-BY
  DATE
SELLOTAPED
SEMAPHORES
SEMAPHORIC
SEMATOLOGY
SEMIANNUAL
SEMIBREVES
SEMICIRCLE
SEMICOLONS
SEMIFINALS
SEMINALITY

SEMINARIAL
SEMINARIAN
SEMINARIES
SEMIQUAVER
SEMIVOWELS
SEMIWEEKLY
SENATORIAL
SENEGALESE
SENEGAMBIA
SENESCENCE
SENSATIONS
SENSE
ORGAN
SENSIBILIA
SENSITIZED
SENSITIZER
SENSUALISM
SENSUALIST
SENSUALITY
SENSUOUSLY
SENTENCING
SENTENTIAL
SENTIMENTS
SEPARATELY
SEPARATING
SEPARATION
SEPARATISM
SEPARATIST
SEPARATIVE
SEPARATORS
SEPARATRIX
SEPTENNIAL
SEPTICALLY
SEPTICIDAL
SEPTIC
TANK
SEPTILLION
SEPULCHRAL
SEPULCHRES
SEQUACIOUS
SEQUENCING
SEQUENTIAL
SEQUESTRAL
SEQUESTRUM
SERBO-
CROAT
SERENADING
SERENENESS
SERIALIZED
SERIGRAPHY
SERIOCOMIC

SERMONICAL
SERMONIZED
SERMONIZER
SEROLOGIST
SERPENTINE
SERVICEMAN
SERVICEMEN
SERVIETTES
SERVOMOTOR
SETSQUARES
SETTING
OUT
SETTLEABLE
SETTLEMENT
SEVASTOPOL
SEVENTIETH
SEVERANCES
SEVERENESS
SEVERITIES
SEXAGENARY
SEXAGESIMA
SEXIVALENT
SEX
OBJECTS
SEXOLOGIST
SEXPARTITE
SEXTILLION
SEXTUPLETS
SEYCHELLES
SHABBINESS
SHADOWIEST
SHAGGED
OUT
SHAGGINESS
SHAKEDOWNS
SHALLOWEST
SHALLOWING
SHAMANISMS
SHAMANISTS
SHAMATEURS
SHAMEFACED
SHAMEFULLY
SHAMPOOING
SHANGHAIED
SHANTYTOWN
SHAPELIEST
SHARE
PRICE
SHARPENERS
SHARPENING
SHATTERING
SHEARWATER

SHEATHBILL
SHEATHINGS
SHEEPISHLY
SHEEP'S
EYES
SHEEPSHANK
SHEEPSHEAD
SHEEPSKINS
SHEET
MUSIC
SHEIKHDOMS
SHELF
LIVES
SHELLPROOF
SHELLSHOCK
SHELTERING
SHENANIGAN
SHEPHERDED
SHERARDIZE
SHERBROOKE
SHIBBOLETH
SHIFTINESS
SHIFTINGLY
SHIFT
STICK
SHILLELAGH
SHIMMERING
SHIPBOARDS
SHIPMASTER
SHIP-
RIGGED
SHIPWRECKS
SHIPWRIGHT
SHIRE
HORSE
SHIRTFRONT
SHIRTTAILS
SHISH
KEBAB
SHOALINESS
SHOCKINGLY
SHOCKPROOF
SHODDINESS
SHOEMAKING
SHOESHINES
SHOESTRING
SHOGUN
BOND
SHOOT A
LINE
SHOPAHOLIC
SHOPKEEPER

SHOPLIFTED
SHOPLIFTER
SHOPSOILED
SHOPWALKER
SHOPWORKER
SHORE
LEAVE
SHOREWARDS
SHORTBREAD
SHORTENING
SHORTFALLS
SHORT
LISTS
SHORT-
LIVED
SHORT-
RANGE
SHORT
STORY
SHOULDERED
SHOVELHEAD
SHOVELLING
SHOVELNOSE
SHOW
JUMPER
SHOWPIECES
SHOW
TRIALS
SHREVEPORT
SHREWDNESS
SHREWISHLY
SHREWSBURY
SHRIEVALTY
SHRILLNESS
SHRINKABLE
SHRINK-
WRAP
SHRIVELING
SHRIVELLED
SHROPSHIRE
SHROUD-
LAID
SHROVETIDE
SHUDDERING
SHUNT-
WOUND
SHUTTERING
SIALAGOGIC
SIALAGOGUE
SIAMESE
CAT
SIBILATION

SICKLEBILL
SICKLINESS
SICKNESSES
SICK
PARADE
SIDEBOARDS
SIDE
DISHES
SIDE
EFFECT
SIDE
ISSUES
SIDELIGHTS
SIDELINING
SIDE
ORDERS
SIDEROLITE
SIDEROSTAT
SIDESADDLE
SIDE
STREET
SIDESTROKE
SIDESWIPED
SIDESWIPER
SIDESWIPES
SIDETRACKS
SIDEWINDER
SIGHTSEERS
SIGNALIZED
SIGNALLING
SIGNATURES
SIGNIFYING
SIGNORINAS
SIGNPOSTED
SILENTNESS
SILHOUETTE
SILICULOSE
SILK
SCREEN
SILLY
BILLY
SILVERFISH
SILVERWARE
SILVERWEED
SIMFEROPOL
SIMILARITY
SIMILITUDE
SIMONIACAL
SIMPLE
LIFE
SIMPLENESS
SIMPLETONS

SIMPLICITY
SIMPLIFIED
SIMPLIFIER
SIMPLISTIC
SIMULACRUM
SIMULATING
SIMULATION
SIMULATIVE
SIMULATORS
SINCIPITAL
SINECURISM
SINECURIST
SINE QUA NON
SINEWINESS
SINFULNESS
SINGHALESE
SINGLE FILE
SINGLENESS
SINGLETONS
SINGULARLY
SINHAILIEN
SINISTROUS
SINN FEINER
SINOLOGIST
SINUSOIDAL
SISTERHOOD
SITOSTEROL
SITUATIONS
SIX-FOOTERS
SIX-SHOOTER
SIXTEENTHS
SIXTH FORMS
SIXTH SENSE
SKATEBOARD
SKEDADDLED
SKEPTICISM
SKETCHABLE
SKETCHBOOK
SKETCHIEST
SKETCHPADS
SKIMPINESS
SKIN DIVERS
SKIN DIVING

SKIN FLICKS
SKINFLINTS
SKIN GRAFTS
SKINNINESS
SKIPPERING
SKIRMISHED
SKIRMISHER
SKIRMISHES
SKITTERING
SKITTISHLY
SKYJACKERS
SKYJACKING
SKYLARKING
SKYROCKETS
SKYSCRAPER
SKYWRITING
SLACKENING
SLANDERERS
SLANDERING
SLANDEROUS
SLANGINESS
SLANTINGLY
SLASHINGLY
SLATTERNLY
SLAVE TRADE
SLAVOPHILE
SLEAZINESS
SLEEPINESS
SLEEPYHEAD
SLEEVELESS
SLENDERIZE
SLIDE RULES
SLIGHTNESS
SLINGSHOTS
SLINKINESS
SLINKINGLY
SLIPPINESS
SLIPPINGLY
SLIPSTREAM
SLITHERING
SLOBBERING
SLOPPINESS
SLOPWORKER
SLOTHFULLY
SLOUCH HATS
SLOW MOTION

SLOW-WITTED
SLUGGISHLY
SLUICEGATE
SLUMBERERS
SLUMBERING
SLUMBEROUS
SLUSH FUNDS
SLUSHINESS
SMALL HOURS
SMALL PRINT
SMALL-SCALE
SMALL-TIMER
SMARAGDITE
SMART ALECK
SMARTENING
SMARTINGLY
SMATTERING
SMEARINESS
SMEAR TESTS
SMELLINESS
SMIRKINGLY
SMOKEHOUSE
SMOKESTACK
SMOLDERING
SMOOTHABLE
SMOOTHBORE
SMOOTHNESS
SMOTHERING
SMOULDERED
SMUDGINESS
SMUTTINESS
SNAIL'S PACE
SNAKEMOUTH
SNAPDRAGON
SNAPPINESS
SNAPPINGLY
SNAPPISHLY
SNARE DRUMS
SNARLINGLY
SNAZZINESS
SNEAKINESS
SNEAKINGLY

SNEAK THIEF
SNEERINGLY
SNEEZEWORT
SNICKERING
SNIFFINGLY
SNIGGERING
SNIPPINESS
SNIVELLERS
SNIVELLING
SNOBBISHLY
SNOOKERING
SNOOTINESS
SNORKELLED
SNORTINGLY
SNOTTINESS
SNOWBALLED
SNOW-CAPPED
SNOWDRIFTS
SNOWFIELDS
SNOWFLAKES
SNOWMAKING
SNOWMOBILE
SNOWPLOUGH
SNOWSTORMS
SNUBBINGLY
SNUFFINESS
SNUFFINGLY
SOAP BUBBLE
SOAP OPERAS
SOBERINGLY
SOBRIQUETS
SOB STORIES
SOCIALISTS
SOCIALITES
SOCIALIZED
SOCIALIZER
SOCIALNESS
SOCIAL WORK
SOCIOMETRY
SOCIOPATHY
SODDENNESS
SOFT-BOILED
SOFT-FINNED

SOFT FRUITS
SOFT-HEADED
SOFT OPTION
SOFT PALATE
SOFT-SOAPED
SOFT-SPOKEN
SOJOURNERS
SOJOURNING
SOLAR CELLS
SOLAR PANEL
SOLAR YEARS
SOLDERABLE
SOLDIERING
SOLECISTIC
SOLEMNIZED
SOLEMNIZER
SOLEMNNESS
SOLENOIDAL
SOLFATARIC
SOLICITING
SOLICITORS
SOLICITOUS
SOLICITUDE
SOLIDARITY
SOLIDIFIED
SOLIDIFIER
SOLID-STATE
SOLITAIRES
SOLITARIES
SOLITARILY
SOLSTITIAL
SOLUBILITY
SOLUBILIZE
SOLVOLYSIS
SOMALILAND
SOMATOLOGY
SOMATOTYPE
SOMBRENESS
SOMERSAULT
SOMNOLENCE
SONGSTRESS
SONGWRITER

273

SONIC
  BOOMS
SONIFEROUS
SONOROUSLY
SONS-OF-
  GUNS
SOOTHINGLY
SOOTHSAYER
SOPHOMORES
SORDIDNESS
SORORICIDE
SORORITIES
SOUBRIQUET
SOULLESSLY
SOUNDPROOF
SOUNDTRACK
SOUP
  SPOONS
SOUR
  GRAPES
SOURPUSSES
SOUSAPHONE
SOUTHBOUND
SOUTH
  DOWNS
SOUTHERNER
SOUTH
  KOREA
SOUTHWARDS
SOU'WESTER
  S
SOVEREIGNS
SPACECRAFT
SPACE
  PROBE
SPACESHIPS
SPACESUITS
SPACEWOMAN
SPACIOUSLY
SPADICEOUS
SPALLATION
SPARE
  PARTS
SPARE
  TYRES
SPARK
  PLUGS
SPARSENESS
SPARTANISM
SPATCHCOCK
SPATIALITY
SPATTERING

SPEARHEADS
SPECIALISM
SPECIALIST
SPECIALITY
SPECIALIZE
SPECIATION
SPECIESISM
SPECIFYING
SPECIOSITY
SPECIOUSLY
SPECTACLES
SPECTATING
SPECTATORS
SPECULATED
SPECULATOR
SPEECH
  DAYS
SPEECHLESS
SPEEDBOATS
SPEEDINESS
SPEED
  LIMIT
SPEED
  TRAPS
SPELEOLOGY
SPELLBOUND
SPELUNKING
SPEND
  LIMIT
SPERMACETI
SPERMATIUM
SPERMICIDE
SPERM
  WHALE
SPERRYLITE
SPHALERITE
SPHENOIDAL
SPHERICITY
SPHEROIDAL
SPHERULITE
SPHINCTERS
SPICEBERRY
SPIDERWEBS
SPIDERWORT
SPINAL
  CORD
SPINDLIEST
SPIN-
  DRYING
SPINESCENT
SPINNAKERS
SPIRACULAR

SPIRALLING
SPIRITEDLY
SPIRITLESS
SPIRITUALS
SPIRITUOUS
SPIROGRAPH
SPIROMETER
SPIROMETRY
SPITEFULLY
SPLANCHNIC
SPLASHBACK
SPLASH
  BACK
SPLASHDOWN
SPLASHIEST
SPLATTERED
SPLEENWORT
SPLENDIDLY
SPLINTERED
SPLIT
  HAIRS
SPLIT
  LEVEL
SPLIT-
  LEVEL
SPLIT
  RINGS
SPLUTTERED
SPLUTTERER
SPOILSPORT
SPOKESHAVE
SPOLIATION
SPONGE
  BAGS
SPONGE
  CAKE
SPONGINESS
SPONSORIAL
SPONSORING
SPOOKINESS
SPOONERISM
SPORANGIAL
SPORANGIUM
SPOROPHORE
SPOROPHYLL
SPOROPHYTE
SPOROZOITE
SPORTINESS
SPORTINGLY
SPORTIVELY
SPORTS
  CARS

SPORTSWEAR
SPOT
  CHECKS
SPOTLESSLY
SPOTLIGHTS
SPOTTINESS
SPREADABLE
SPRINGBOKS
SPRINGHAAS
SPRINGHEAD
SPRINGIEST
SPRING
  ROLL
SPRINGTAIL
SPRING
  TIDE
SPRINGTIME
SPRINGWOOD
SPRINKLERS
SPRINKLING
SPRUCENESS
SPUMESCENT
SPUNKINESS
SPURIOUSLY
SPUTTERING
SPYGLASSES
SQUABBLING
SQUALIDITY
SQUALLIEST
SQUAMATION
SQUAMULOSE
SQUANDERED
SQUANDERER
SQUARE
  DEAL
SQUARE
  KNOT
SQUARE
  MEAL
SQUARENESS
SQUARE
  ROOT
SQUASHIEST
SQUEAKIEST
SQUEEZABLE
SQUEEZEBOX
SQUELCHIER
SQUELCHING
SQUETEAGUE
SQUIDGIEST
SQUIFFIEST
SQUISHIEST

STABILATOR
STABILIZED
STABILIZER
STABLE
  BOYS
STABLEFORD
STABLENESS
STAFF
  NURSE
STAG
  BEETLE
STAGECOACH
STAGECRAFT
STAGE
  DOORS
STAGEHANDS
STAGE
  NAMES
STAGGERING
STAGNANTLY
STAGNATING
STAGNATION
STAIRCASES
STAIRWELLS
STALACTITE
STALAGMITE
STALEMATED
STALEMATES
STALKINESS
STALWARTLY
STAMMERERS
STAMMERING
STAMPEDING
STANCHABLE
STANCHIONS
STANDPIPES
STANDPOINT
STANDSTILL
STARCHIEST
STARFISHES
STARFLOWER
STARGAZERS
STARGAZING
STARRINESS
STARRY-
  EYED
STARVATION
STARVELING
STATECRAFT
STATEMENTS
STATEROOMS
STATIONARY

STATIONERS
STATIONERY
STATIONING
STATISTICS
STATOBLAST
STATOSCOPE
STATUESQUE
STATUETTES
STATUS ZERO
STATUTABLE
STATUTE LAW
STAUNCHEST
STAUNCHING
STAUROLITE
STAVESACRE
STAY-AT-HOME
ST BERNARDS
STEADINESS
STEAKHOUSE
STEALTHIER
STEALTHILY
STEAMBOATS
STEAM-CHEST
STEAMINESS
STEAM IRONS
STEAMSHIPS
STEAMTIGHT
STEEL BANDS
STEELINESS
STEELWORKS
STEEPENING
STELLIFORM
STEM-WINDER
STENCILING
STENCILLED
STENCILLER
STENOGRAPH
STENOTYPIC
STENTORIAN
STEPFAMILY
STEPFATHER
STEPLADDER
STEPMOTHER
STEPPARENT

STEPSISTER
STEREOBATE
STEREOGRAM
STEREOPSIS
STEREOTOMY
STEREOTYPE
STEREOTYPY
STERICALLY
STERILIZED
STERILIZER
STERNWARDS
STERTOROUS
STEVEDORES
STEWARDESS
STICKINESS
STICK SHIFT
STICKTIGHT
STICKY ENDS
STIFFENERS
STIFFENING
STIFLINGLY
STIGMATISM
STIGMATIST
STIGMATIZE
STILLBIRTH
STILL LIFES
STIMULABLE
STIMULANTS
STIMULATED
STIMULATOR
STINGINESS
STINGINGLY
STINK-BOMBS
STINKINGLY
STINKSTONE
STIPELLATE
STIPULABLE
STIPULATED
STIPULATOR
STIR-FRYING
STIRRINGLY
STIRRUP CUP
STITCHWORT
STOCHASTIC
STOCKADING

STOCK CUBES
STOCKINESS
STOCKPILED
STOCKPILER
STOCKPILES
STOCKROOMS
STOCK-STILL
STOCKYARDS
STODGINESS
STOKEHOLDS
STOMACHING
STOMATITIC
STOMATITIS
STOMATOPOD
STOMODAEAL
STOMODAEUM
STONE-BLIND
STONE FRUIT
STONEHENGE
STONEMASON
STONY BROKE
STOOPINGLY
STOPPERING
STOREHOUSE
STOREROOMS
STORKSBILL
STORMBOUND
STORM CLOUD
STORMINESS
STORMPROOF
STORY LINES
STRABISMAL
STRABISMUS
STRADDLING
STRAGGLERS
STRAGGLIER
STRAGGLING
STRAIGHTEN
STRAIGHTER
STRAITENED
STRAITNESS
STRAMONIUM
STRANGLERS
STRANGLING
STRASBOURG

STRATAGEMS
STRATEGICS
STRATEGIES
STRATEGIST
STRATIFIED
STRATIFORM
STRATOCRAT
STRAWBERRY
STRAWBOARD
STRAW POLLS
STREAKIEST
STREAMLINE
STREET ARAB
STREETCARS
STREETWISE
STRELITZIA
STRENGTHEN
STRESS MARK
STRETCHERS
STRETCHIER
STRETCHING
STRIATIONS
STRICTNESS
STRICTURES
STRIDENTLY
STRIDULATE
STRIDULOUS
STRIGIFORM
STRIKINGLY
STRING BEAN
STRINGENCY
STRINGENDO
STRINGHALT
STRINGIEST
STRIPAGRAM
STRIP CLUBS
STRIPLINGS
STRIPTEASE
STROKE PLAY
STRONGHOLD
STRONGNESS
STRONG ROOM
STROPPIEST
STRUCTURAL
STRUCTURED

STRUCTURES
STRUGGLING
STRUTHIOUS
STRYCHNINE
STUBBINESS
STUBBORNER
STUBBORNLY
STUDIOUSLY
STUFFINESS
STULTIFIED
STULTIFIER
STUMPINESS
STUNNINGLY
STUPEFYING
STUPENDOUS
STUPIDNESS
STURDINESS
STUTTERERS
STUTTERING
STYLISTICS
STYLOGRAPH
STYLOLITIC
STYPTICITY
SUBACETATE
SUBACIDITY
SUBALTERNS
SUBAQUATIC
SUBAQUEOUS
SUBCALIBRE
SUBCLAVIAN
SUBCOMPACT
SUBCULTURE
SUBDIVIDED
SUBDIVIDER
SUBDUCTION
SUBEDITING
SUBEDITORS
SUBGENERIC
SUBGLACIAL
SUBHEADING
SUBJACENCY
SUBJECTIFY
SUBJECTING
SUBJECTION
SUBJECTIVE
SUBJOINING
SUBJUGABLE
SUBJUGATED
SUBJUGATOR
SUBKINGDOM
SUBLEASING

SUBLETTING	SUBTRACTER	SUMMERTIME	SUPPLIANTS	SUTHERLAND
SUBLIMABLE	SUBTRAHEND	SUMMERWOOD	SUPPLICANT	SUZERAINTY
SUBLIMATED	SUBTROPICS	SUMMINGS-	SUPPLICATE	SVERDLOVSK
SUBLIMATES	SUBTYPICAL	UP	SUPPORTERS	SWAGGERERS
SUBLIMINAL	SUBVENTION	SUMMONABLE	SUPPORTING	SWAGGERING
SUBLINGUAL	SUBVERSION	SUMMONSING	SUPPORTIVE	SWALLOWING
SUBMARINER	SUBVERSIVE	SUNBATHERS	SUPPOSABLE	SWANKINESS
SUBMARINES	SUBVERTING	SUNBATHING	SUPPOSEDLY	SWAN-
SUBMEDIANT	SUCCEEDING	SUNDAY	SUPPRESSED	UPPING
SUBMERGING	SUCCESSFUL	BEST	SUPPRESSOR	SWARTHIEST
SUBMERSION	SUCCESSION	SUNDERLAND	SUPPURATED	SWASHINGLY
SUBMISSION	SUCCESSIVE	SUNDOWNERS	SUPRARENAL	SWEARINGLY
SUBMISSIVE	SUCCESSORS	SUNFLOWERS	SURCHARGED	SWEARWORDS
SUBMITTING	SUCCINCTLY	SUNGLASSES	SURCHARGER	SWEATBANDS
SUBMONTANE	SUCCOURING	SUNLOUNGER	SURCHARGES	SWEAT
SUBOCEANIC	SUCCULENCE	SUN	SUREFOOTED	GLAND
SUBOPTIMAL	SUCCULENTS	LOUNGES	SURFACTANT	SWEATINESS
SUBORBITAL	SUCCUMBING	SUPERBNESS	SURFBOARDS	SWEATSHIRT
SUBORDINAL	SUCCUSSION	SUPERCARGO	SURFCASTER	SWEATSHOPS
SUBPOENAED	SUCCUSSIVE	SUPERCLASS	SURFEITING	SWEEPINGLY
SUBPROGRAM	SUCKERFISH	SUPERDUPER	SURGICALLY	SWEEPSTAKE
SUBREPTION	SUCKING	SUPER	SURINAMESE	SWEETBREAD
SUBROUTINE	PIG	DUPER	SURJECTION	SWEETBRIER
SUB-	SUDDENNESS	SUPERFLUID	SURJECTIVE	SWEETENERS
SAHARAN	SUFFERABLE	SUPERGIANT	SURMISABLE	SWEETENING
SUBSCRIBED	SUFFERANCE	SUPERGRASS	SURMISEDLY	SWEETHEART
SUBSCRIBER	SUFFERINGS	SUPERHUMAN	SURMOUNTED	SWEETMEATS
SUBSECTION	SUFFICIENT	SUPERLUNAR	SURMOUNTER	SWEET
SUBSEQUENT	SUFFOCATED	SUPERMODEL	SURPASSING	TOOTH
SUBSIDENCE	SUFFRAGISM	SUPERNOVAS	SURPLUSAGE	SWELTERING
SUBSIDIARY	SUFFRAGIST	SUPERORDER	SURPRISING	SWERVINGLY
SUBSIDIZED	SUGAR	SUPEROXIDE	SURREALISM	SWIMMINGLY
SUBSIDIZER	DADDY	SUPERPOWER	SURREALIST	SWINEHERDS
SUBSISTENT	SUGARINESS	SUPERSEDED	SURRENDERS	SWINGINGLY
SUBSISTING	SUGGESTING	SUPERSEDER	SURROGATES	SWING
SUBSPECIES	SUGGESTION	SUPERSONIC	SURROUNDED	SHIFT
SUBSTANCES	SUGGESTIVE	SUPERSTARS	SURVEYABLE	SWIRLINGLY
SUBSTATION	SUICIDALLY	SUPERTONIC	SURVIVABLE	SWISHINGLY
SUBSTITUTE	SULLENNESS	SUPERVENED	SUSCEPTIVE	SWISS
SUBSTRATUM	SULPHA	SUPERVISED	SUSPECTING	CHARD
SUBSUMABLE	DRUG	SUPERVISOR	SUSPENDERS	SWITCHABLE
SUBTANGENT	SULPHATION	SUPINENESS	SUSPENDING	SWITCHBACK
SUBTENANCY	SULPHONATE	SUPPLANTED	SUSPENSION	SWITCH
SUBTENANTS	SULPHURATE	SUPPLANTER	SUSPENSIVE	CARD
SUBTENDING	SULPHURIZE	SUPPLEJACK	SUSPENSOID	SWITCHED-
SUBTERFUGE	SULPHUROUS	SUPPLEMENT	SUSPENSORY	ON
SUBTILIZER	SULTANATES	SUPPLENESS	SUSPICIONS	SWITCHGEAR
SUBTITULAR	SULTRINESS	SUPPLETION	SUSPICIOUS	SWIVELLING
SUBTLENESS	SUMMARIZED	SUPPLETIVE	SUSTAINING	SWOONINGLY
SUBTLETIES	SUMMARIZER	SUPPLETORY	SUSTENANCE	SWORDCRAFT
SUBTRACTED	SUMMATIONS	SUPPLIABLE	SUSTENTION	SWORD
				DANCE

SWORDSTICK
SYCOPHANTS
SYLLABUSES
SYLLOGISMS
SYLLOGIZER
SYLPHIDINE
SYLVESTRAL
SYMBIONTIC
SYMBOLIZED
SYMMETRIZE
SYMPATHIES
SYMPATHIZE
SYMPHONIES
SYMPHONIST
SYMPHYSIAL
SYMPHYSTIC
SYMPOSIUMS
SYNAGOGUES
SYNCARPOUS
SYNCHRONIC
SYNCLASTIC
SYNCOPATED
SYNCOPATOR
SYNCRETISM
SYNCRETIST
SYNCRETIZE
SYNDICATED
SYNDICATES
SYNDICSHIP
SYNECDOCHE
SYNECOLOGY
SYNERGETIC
SYNOECIOUS
SYNONYMITY
SYNONYMIZE
SYNONYMOUS
SYNTACTICS
SYNTHESIST
SYNTHESIZE
SYNTHETISM
SYNTHETIST
SYPHILITIC
SYSTEMATIC
SYSTEMIZER

T
TABERNACLE
TABESCENCE
TABLECLOTH
TABLE
 D'HOTE

TABLELANDS
TABLE
 LINEN
TABLESPOON
TABULARIZE
TABULATING
TABULATION
TACHOGRAPH
TACHOMETER
TACHOMETRY
TACHYLYTIC
TACHYMETER
TACHYMETRY
TACITURNLY
TACTICALLY
TACTICIANS
TACTLESSLY
TAENIACIDE
TAENIAFUGE
TAGLIATELE
TAILBOARDS
TAILGATING
TAILLIGHTS
TAILORBIRD
TAILOR-
 MADE
TAILPIECES
TAJIKISTAN
TAKE IN
 HAND
TAKINGNESS
TALCAHUANO
TALEBEARER
TALISMANIC
TALKING-
 TOS
TAMABILITY
TAMAULIPAS
TAMBOURINE
TANANARIVE
TANGANYIKA
TANGENTIAL
TANGERINES
TANGLEMENT
TANTALIZED
TANTALIZER
TANTALUSES
TANTAMOUNT
TAP
 DANCERS
TAP
 DANCING

TAPERINGLY
TAPESTRIED
TAPESTRIES
TARANTELLA
TARANTULAS
TARDIGRADE
TARMACKING
TARNISHING
TARPAULINS
TASIMETRIC
TASK
 FORCES
TASKMASTER
TASTEFULLY
TATTERSALL
TATTLETALE
TATTLINGLY
TATTOOISTS
TAUNTINGLY
TAUROMACHY
TAUTOMERIC
TAUTONYMIC
TAWDRINESS
TAXABILITY
TAXATIONAL
TAXIDERMAL
TAXIMETERS
TAXONOMIST
TAX
 SHELTER
TEA
 CADDIES
TEAGARDENS
TEAM
 SPIRIT
TEA
 PARTIES
TEARJERKER
TEA
 SERVICE
TEA
 TROLLEY
TECHNETIUM
TECHNICIAN
TECHNIQUES
TECHNOCRAT
TECHNOLOGY
TECTRICIAL
TEDDY
 BEARS
TEENY
 WEENY

TELECASTER
TELEGNOSIS
TELEGRAPHS
TELEGRAPHY
TELEMETRIC
TELEPATHIC
TELEPHONED
TELEPHONER
TELEPHONES
TELESCOPED
TELESCOPES
TELESCOPIC
TELESCRIPT
TELEVISING
TELEVISION
TELEVISUAL
TELEWRITER
TELIOSPORE
TELLING-
 OFF
TELOPHASIC
TELPHERAGE
TEMPERABLE
TEMPERANCE
TEMPORIZED
TEMPORIZER
TEMPTATION
TEMPTINGLY
TENABILITY
TENDENCIES
TENDERABLE
TENDERFEET
TENDERFOOT
TENDERIZED
TENDERIZER
TENDERLOIN
TENDERNESS
TENDRILLAR
TENEMENTAL
TENGRI
 KHAN
TENNESSEAN
TENOTOMIST
TENSIMETER
TENTACULAR
TENTERHOOK
TERATOLOGY
TERENGGANU
TERMAGANCY
TERMAGANTS
TERMINABLE

TERMINALLY
TERMINATED
TERMINATOR
TERMINUSES
TERRACOTTA
TERRA
 FIRMA
TERRAMYCIN
TERREPLEIN
TERRE-
 VERTE
TERRIFYING
TERRORISTS
TERRORIZED
TERRORIZER
TERRYCLOTH
TESSELLATE
TESTACEOUS
TESTAMENTS
TESTICULAR
TESTIFYING
TEST
 PILOTS
TESTUDINAL
TETCHINESS
TETE-A-
 TETES
TETRABASIC
TETRABRACH
TETRACHORD
TETRAGONAL
TETRAPLOID
TETRAPODIC
TETRARCHIC
TETRASPORE
TETRASTICH
TETRATOMIC
TEWKESBURY
TEXTUALISM
TEXTUALIST
TEXTURALLY
THANKFULLY
THEATRICAL
THEME
 PARKS
THEME
 SONGS
THEMSELVES
THENARDITE
THEOCRATIC
THEODOLITE
THEOLOGIAN

THEOLOGIES
THEOLOGIZE
THEOPHOBIA
THEORETICS
THEORIZING
THEOSOPHIC
THERAPISTS
THEREAFTER
THEREUNDER
THERMALIZE
THERMIONIC
THERMISTOR
THERMOGRAM
THERMOPILE
THERMOSTAT
THEROPODAN
THESSALIAN
THETICALLY
THICKENERS
THICKENING
THIEVINGLY
THIEVISHLY
THIMBLEFUL
THIMEROSAL
THINK
  TANKS
THIOURACIL
THIRD
  PARTY
THIRD
  WORLD
THIRSTIEST
THIRTEENTH
THIRTIETHS
THIXOTROPY
THORIANITE
THORNINESS
THOROUGHLY
THOUGHTFUL
THOUGHT-
  OUT
THOUSANDTH
THRASH
  PUNK
THREADBARE
THREADWORM
THREATENED
THREATENER
THREEPENCE
THREE-
  PHASE

THREE-
  PIECE
THREESOMES
THRENODIES
THRESHOLDS
THRIFTIEST
THRIFTLESS
THROATIEST
THROATLASH
THROMBOGEN
THROMBOSES
THROMBOSIS
THROMBOTIC
THROTTLING
THROUGHOUT
THROUGHPUT
THROUGHWAY
THROWBACKS
THUMBNAILS
THUMBSCREW
THUMBSTALL
THUMBTACKS
THUMPINGLY
THUNDER
  BAY
THUNDERERS
THUNDERFLY
THUNDERING
THUNDEROUS
THURINGIAN
THWARTEDLY
TICKERTAPE
TICKING
  OFF
TICKLISHLY
TIDAL
  WAVES
TIEBREAKER
TIED
  HOUSES
TIEMANNITE
TIGHTENING
TIGHTROPES
TIGLIC
  ACID
TILIACEOUS
TILLANDSIA
TIMBERHEAD
TIMBERLINE
TIMBERWORK
TIMBERYARD
TIMEKEEPER

TIMELESSLY
TIME
  LIMITS
TIMELINESS
TIMEPIECES
TIMESAVING
TIME-
  SAVING
TIMESERVER
TIME
  SHEETS
TIME
  SIGNAL
TIME
  SWITCH
TIMETABLED
TIMETABLES
TIMEWORKER
TIMOROUSLY
TIMPANISTS
TINCTORIAL
TINGALINGS
TINGLINGLY
TIN
  OPENERS
TIRELESSLY
TIRESOMELY
TITANESQUE
TITILLATED
TITIVATING
TITIVATION
TITLE
  DEEDS
TITLE
  PAGES
TITLE
  ROLES
TITRATABLE
TITUBATION
T-
  JUNCTION
  S
TOADSTOOLS
TOBOGGANED
TOBOGGANER
TOCOPHEROL
TOILETRIES
TOILET
  ROLL
TOLERANTLY
TOLERATING
TOLERATION

TOLERATIVE
TOLLBOOTHS
TOLLUIDINE
TOLUIC
  ACID
TOMBSTONES
TOMFOOLERY
TOMOGRAPHY
TONALITIES
TONELESSLY
TONGUE-
  TIED
TONIC SOL-
  FA
TONIC
  WATER
TONOMETRIC
TOOL-
  MAKING
TOOTHACHES
TOOTHBRUSH
TOOTHCOMBS
TOOTHINESS
TOOTHPASTE
TOOTHPICKS
TOPAZOLITE
TOPGALLANT
TOP-
  HEAVILY
TOPICALITY
TOPOGRAPHY
TOPOLOGIST
TOPPING
  OUT
TOPSY-
  TURVY
TORBERNITE
TORCHLIGHT
TORMENTING
TORMENTORS
TORPEDOING
TORRENTIAL
TORTELLINI
TORT-
  FEASOR
TORTUOSITY
TORTUOUSLY
TORTUREDLY
TOTEMISTIC
TOTEM
  POLES
TOTIPOTENT

TOUCH-AND-
  GO
TOUCHDOWNS
TOUCHINESS
TOUCHINGLY
TOUCHLINES
TOUCHPAPER
TOUCHSTONE
TOUCH-
  TYPED
TOUGHENING
TOURMALINE
TOURNAMENT
TOURNIQUET
TOWER
  BLOCK
TOWN
  CLERKS
TOWN
  CRIERS
TOWN
  HOUSES
TOWNSCAPES
TOWNSVILLE
TOWNSWOMAN
TOXALBUMIN
TOXICOLOGY
TRABEATION
TRABECULAR
TRACHEIDAL
TRACHEITIS
TRACHYTOID
TRACK
  EVENT
TRACKLAYER
TRACKSUITS
TRACTILITY
TRACTIONAL
TRADEMARKS
TRADE
  NAMES
TRADE
  PRICE
TRADE
  ROUTE
TRADE
  UNION
TRADE
  WINDS
TRADITIONS
TRADUCIBLE

TRAFFIC JAM	TRASHINESS	TRIFLINGLY	TROMBONIST	TUBULARITY
TRAFFICKED	TRAUMATISM	TRIFOLIATE	TROOPSHIPS	TUBULATION
TRAFFICKER	TRAUMATIZE	TRIFURCATE	TROPAEOLIN	TUFFACEOUS
TRAGACANTH	TRAVAILING	TRIGEMINAL	TROPAEOLUM	TUGS-OF-LOVE
TRAGEDIANS	TRAVELLERS	TRIGGERING	TROPICALLY	TULARAEMIA
TRAGICALLY	TRAVELLING	TRIGLYPHIC	TROPICBIRD	TULARAEMIC
TRAGICOMIC	TRAVELOGUE	TRIGRAPHIC	TROPOLOGIC	TUMBLEDOWN
TRAILINGLY	TRAVELSICK	TRIHYDRATE	TROPOPAUSE	TUMBLEWEED
TRAITOROUS	TRAVERSING	TRILATERAL	TROPOPHYTE	TUMESCENCE
TRAJECTILE	TRAVERTINE	TRILINGUAL	TROTSKYISM	TUMULOSITY
TRAJECTION	TRAVESTIES	TRILITERAL	TROTSKYIST	TUMULTUOUS
TRAJECTORY	TREADMILLS	TRILLIONTH	TROTSKYITE	TUNELESSLY
TRAMONTANE	TREAD WATER	TRILOBITES	TROUBADOUR	TUNING FORK
TRAMPOLINE	TREASURERS	TRILOCULAR	TROUBLEDLY	TUNING PEGS
TRANCELIKE	TREASURIES	TRIMESTERS	TROUSSEAUS	TUNNELLING
TRANQUILLY	TREASURING	TRIMESTRAL	TROUSSEAUX	TUPPERWARE
TRANSACTED	TREATMENTS	TRIMONTHLY	TROWBRIDGE	TURBOPROPS
TRANSACTOR	TREBLE CLEF	TRIMORPHIC	TROY WEIGHT	TURBULENCE
TRANSCRIBE	TREEHOPPER	TRINOCULAR	TRUCK FARMS	TURGESCENT
TRANSCRIPT	TREMENDOUS	TRIOECIOUS	TRUCKLOADS	TURNABOUTS
TRANSDUCER	TRENCHANCY	TRIPARTITE	TRUCK STOPS	TURNAROUND
TRANSEPTAL	TRENCH COAT	TRIPHAMMER	TRUCULENCE	TURNBUCKLE
TRANSFEREE	TRENDINESS	TRIPHTHONG	TRUMP CARDS	TURNROUNDS
TRANSFEROR	TREPANNING	TRIPHYLITE	TRUMPETERS	TURNSTILES
TRANSFIXED	TREPHINING	TRIPINNATE	TRUMPETING	TURNTABLES
TRANSGRESS	TREPPANNER	TRIPLE JUMP	TRUNCATING	TURPENTINE
TRANSIENCE	TRESPASSED	TRIPLETAIL	TRUNCATION	TURQUOISES
TRANSIENCY	TRESPASSER	TRIPLICATE	TRUNCHEONS	TURTLEBACK
TRANSISTOR	TRESPASSES	TRIPLICITY	TRUNK CALLS	TURTLEDOVE
TRANSITION	TRIANGULAR	TRIPPINGLY	TRUNK ROADS	TURTLENECK
TRANSITIVE	TRIBRACHIC	TRIPTEROUS	TRUNK ROUTE	TUT-TUTTING
TRANSITORY	TRICHIASIS	TRIRADIATE	TRUSTFULLY	TWELVE-TONE
TRANSKEIAN	TRICHINIZE	TRISECTING	TRUST FUNDS	TWENTIETHS
TRANSLATED	TRICHINOUS	TRISKELION	TRUSTINESS	TWIN-BEDDED
TRANSLATOR	TRICHOCYST	TRISTICHIC	TRUTHFULLY	TWINFLOWER
TRANSLUNAR	TRICHOGYNE	TRITANOPIA	TRUTH-VALUE	TWINKLINGS
TRANSMUTED	TRICHOLOGY	TRITANOPIC	TRYINGNESS	TWISTINGLY
TRANSMUTER	TRICHOTOMY	TRITURABLE	TRYPTOPHAN	TWITTERING
TRANSPIRED	TRICHROISM	TRITURATOR	TRIVANDRUM	TYMPANITES
TRANSPLANT	TRICHROMAT	TRIUMPHANT	TUBERCULAR	TYMPANITIC
TRANSPOLAR	TRICKINESS	TRIUMPHING	TUBERCULIN	TYMPANITIS
TRANSPORTS	TRICKINGLY	TRIVALENCY	TUBEROSITY	TYPECASTER
TRANSPOSED	TRICKSTERS	TRIVANDRUM	TUB-THUMPER	TYPESCRIPT
TRANSPOSER	TRICOLOURS	TRIVIALITY		TYPESETTER
TRANSPUTER	TRICOSTATE	TRIVIALIZE		TYPE SETTER
TRANSUDATE	TRICROTISM	TROCHANTER		
TRANSVALUE	TRIDENTATE	TROGLODYTE		
TRANSVERSE	TRIDENTINE	TROLLEYBUS		
TRAPEZIUMS		TROLLEY BUS		
TRAPEZOIDS				

TYPEWRITER
TYPHLOLOGY
TYPHOGENIC
TYPING
    POOL
TYPOGRAPHY
TYPOLOGIST
TYRANNICAL
TYRANNIZED
TYRANNIZER
TYROCIDINE
TYROSINASE

U

UBIQUITOUS
ULCERATING
ULCERATION
ULCERATIVE
ULTIMATELY
ULTIMATUMS
ULTRAFICHE
ULTRAISTIC
ULTRASHORT
ULTRASONIC
ULTRASOUND
ULTRAVIRUS
UMBILICATE
UMBILIFORM
UMBRAGEOUS
UMPIRESHIP
UMPTEENTHS
UNABRIDGED
UNACCENTED
UNADJUSTED
UNAFFECTED
UN-
    AMERICAN
UNASSISTED
UNASSUMING
UNATTACHED
UNATTENDED
UNAVAILING
UNBALANCED
UNBEARABLE
UNBEARABLY
UNBEATABLE
UNBECOMING
UNBELIEVER
UNBENDABLE
UNBLINKING
UNBLUSHING

UNBOSOMING
UNBUCKLING
UNBUNDLING
UNBURDENED
UNCANNIEST
UNCARED-
    FOR
UNCARPETED
UNCIVILITY
UNCOMMONLY
UNCONFINED
UNCOUPLING
UNCOVERING
UNCREDITED
UNCRITICAL
UNCTUOSITY
UNCTUOUSLY
UNDECEIVED
UNDECEIVER
UNDEFEATED
UNDEFENDED
UNDENIABLE
UNDENIABLY
UNDERACTED
UNDERBELLY
UNDERBRUSH
UNDERCOATS
UNDERCOVER
UNDERCROFT
UNDERDRAIN
UNDERFLOOR
UNDERGLAZE
UNDERGOING
UNDERGROWN
UNDERLINED
UNDERLINGS
UNDERLYING
UNDERMINED
UNDERMINER
UNDERNAMED
UNDERNEATH
UNDERPANTS
UNDERPRICE
UNDERPROOF
UNDERQUOTE
UNDERRATED
UNDERSCORE
UNDERSEXED
UNDERSHIRT
UNDERSHOOT
UNDERSIZED

UNDERSKIRT
UNDERSLUNG
UNDERSPEND
UNDERSTAND
UNDERSTATE
UNDERSTOCK
UNDERSTOOD
UNDERSTUDY
UNDERTAKEN
UNDERTAKER
UNDERTONES
UNDERTRICK
UNDERTRUMP
UNDERVALUE
UNDERWATER
UNDERWIRED
UNDERWORLD
UNDERWRITE
UNDERWROTE
UNDETERRED
UNDIRECTED
UNDISPUTED
UNDRESSING
UNDULATING
UNDULATION
UNDULATORY
UNEARTHING
UNEASINESS
UNECONOMIC
UNEDIFYING
UNEDUCATED
UNEMPLOYED
UNENVIABLE
UNEQUALLED
UNERRINGLY
UNEVENNESS
UNEVENTFUL
UNEXAMPLED
UNEXPECTED
UNEXPLODED
UNFAIRNESS
UNFAITHFUL
UNFAMILIAR
UNFATHERED
UNFEMININE
UNFETTERED
UNFINISHED
UNFLAGGING
UNFORESEEN
UNFORGIVEN
UNFRIENDLY

UNFROCKING
UNFRUITFUL
UNGENEROUS
UNGRATEFUL
UNGRUDGING
UNGUENTARY
UNHALLOWED
UNHAMPERED
UNHANDSOME
UNHERALDED
UNHOLINESS
UNHOPED-
    FOR
UNHYGIENIC
UNICAMERAL
UNICOSTATE
UNICYCLIST
UNIFOLIATE
UNIFORMITY
UNILATERAL
UNILOCULAR
UNIMPOSING
UNIMPROVED
UNINFORMED
UNINSPIRED
UNINTENDED
UNIONISTIC
UNIONIZING
UNIQUENESS
UNISEPTATE
UNITARIANS
UNITEDNESS
UNIT
    TRUSTS
UNIVALENCY
UNIVERSITY
UNJUSTNESS
UNKINDNESS
UNKNOWABLE
UNLAWFULLY
UNLEARNING
UNLEASHING
UNLEAVENED
UNLETTERED
UNLICENSED
UNLOCKABLE
UNLOOSENED
UNMANNERED
UNMANNERLY
UNMEASURED
UNMEDIATED

UNMERCIFUL
UNMORALITY
UNNUMBERED
UNOCCUPIED
UNOFFICIAL
UNORIGINAL
UNORTHODOX
UNPATENTED
UNPLAYABLE
UNPLEASANT
UNPREPARED
UNPROMPTED
UNPROVIDED
UNPROVOKED
UNPUNCTUAL
UNPUNISHED
UNRAVELING
UNRAVELLED
UNRAVELLER
UNREACTIVE
UNREADABLE
UNREADABLY
UNRELIABLE
UNRELIEVED
UNREQUITED
UNRESERVED
UNRESOLVED
UNRIVALLED
UNRULINESS
UNSADDLING
UNSANITARY
UNSCHOOLED
UNSCRAMBLE
UNSCREENED
UNSCREWING
UNSCRIPTED
UNSEALABLE
UNSEASONED
UNSEEINGLY
UNSETTLING
UNSHAKABLE
UNSOCIABLE
UNSPEAKING
UNSPECIFIC
UNSTEADILY
UNSTINTING
UNSTOPPING
UNSTRAINED
UNSTRESSED
UNSTRIATED
UNSUITABLE

UNSURFACED
UNSWERVING
UNTANGLING
UNTHANKFUL
UNTHINKING
UNTIDINESS
UNTIRINGLY
UNTOWARDLY
UNTRUSTING
UNTRUTHFUL
UNWIELDILY
UNWINDABLE
UNWORKABLE
UNWORTHILY
UNYIELDING
UP-AND-
    UNDER
UPBRAIDING
UPBRINGING
UPHOLSTERY
UP IN THE
    AIR
UPLIFTMENT
UPON MY
    WORD
UPPER
    CLASS
UPPER
    CRUST
UPPER
    EGYPT
UPPER
    HOUSE
UPPER
    VOLTA
UPPISHNESS
UPROARIOUS
UPSETTABLE
UPSIDE
    DOWN
UPSTANDING
UP THE
    SPOUT
UP THE
    STAKE
UP THE
    STICK
UPWARDNESS
URAL-
    ALTAIC
URBANENESS
UREDOSORUS

UREDOSPORE
URETHRITIC
URETHRITIS
URINALYSIS
UROCHORDAL
UROGENITAL
UROSCOPIST
URTICARIAL
URTICATION
USEFULNESS
USHERETTES
USQUEBAUGH
USTULATION
USURPATION
USURPATIVE
USURPINGLY
UTILIZABLE
UTO-
    AZTECAN
UTOPIANISM
UTTERANCES
UXORICIDAL
UZBEKISTAN

V

VACANTNESS
VACATIONED
VACATIONER
VACCINATED
VACILLATED
VACILLATOR
VACUUM
    PUMP
VAGINISMUS
VAGOTROPIC
VAL-DE-
    MARNE
VALENTINES
VALIDATING
VALIDATION
VALIDATORY
VALLADOLID
VALLECULAR
VALPARAISO
VALUATIONS
VALVULITIS
VAMPIRE
    BAT
VANADINITE
VANDALIZED
VAN DER
    POST

VANISHMENT
VANQUISHED
VANQUISHER
VAPORIZING
VAPOURABLE
VARIATIONS
VARICELLAR
VARICOCELE
VARICOSITY
VARICOTOMY
VARIEDNESS
VARIEGATED
VARIFOCALS
ANGLO-
    SAXON
VARIOLITIC
VARIOMETER
VARITYPIST
VARNISHING
VASTNESSES
VAUDEVILLE
VAUNTINGLY
VEGETABLES
VEGETARIAN
VEGETATING
VEGETATION
VEGETATIVE
VEHEMENTLY
VELOCIPEDE
VELOCITIES
VELUTINOUS
VENATIONAL
VENDETTIST
VENERATING
VENERATION
VENEZUELAN
VENGEANCES
VENGEFULLY
VENOMOUSLY
VENOUSNESS
VENTILABLE
VENTILATED
VENTILATOR
VENTRICLES
VENTRICOSE
VERBALIZED
VERBALIZER
VERBAL
    NOUN
VERIFIABLE
VERKRAMPTE

VERMICELLI
VERMICIDAL
VERMICULAR
VERNACULAR
VERNISSAGE
VERSAILLES
VERTEBRATE
VERTICALLY
VERY
    LIGHTS
VESICATION
VESICULATE
VESPERTINE
VESTIBULAR
VESTIBULES
VESTMENTAL
VESTMENTED
VETERINARY
VIBRACULAR
VIBRACULUM
VIBRAPHONE
VIBRATIONS
VICEGERENT
VICEREINES
VICINITIES
VICOMTESSE
VICTIMIZED
VICTIMIZER
VICTIMLESS
VICTORIANA
VICTORIANS
VICTORIOUS
VICTUALING
VICTUALLED
VICTUALLER
VIDEODISCS
VIDEO
    NASTY
VIDEOPHILE
VIDEOPHONE
VIDEOTAPED
VIETNAMESE
VIEWFINDER
VIEWPOINTS
VIGILANTES
VIGILANTLY
VIGNETTING
VIGNETTIST
VIGOROUSLY
VIJAYAWADA
VILLAINOUS

VILLANELLA
VILLANELLE
VILLANOVAN
VINA DEL
    MAR
VINDICABLE
VINDICATED
VINDICATOR
VINDICTIVE
VINIFEROUS
VINYLIDENE
VIOLACEOUS
VIOLATIONS
VIOLINISTS
VIRAGINOUS
VIRESCENCE
VIROLOGIST
VIRTUALITY
VIRTUOSITY
VIRTUOUSLY
VIRULENTLY
VISCOMETER
VISCOMETRY
VISCOUNTCY
VISIBILITY
VISITATION
VISITORIAL
VISUAL
    AIDS
VISUALIZED
VISUALIZER
VITALISTIC
VITAL
    SIGNS
VITRESCENT
VITRIFYING
VITRIOLIZE
VITUPERATE
VIVIPARITY
VIVIPAROUS
VIVISECTOR
VOCABULARY
VOCAL
    CORDS
VOCATIONAL
VOCIFERANT
VOCIFERATE
VOCIFEROUS
VOETSTOETS
VOICE
    BOXES

VOICE-OVERS
VOICEPRINT
VOLAPUKIST
VOLATILITY
VOLATILIZE
VOL-AU-VENTS
VOLITIONAL
VOLLEYBALL
VOLT-AMPERE
VOLTE-FACES
VOLUBILITY
VOLUMETRIC
VOLUMINOUS
VOLUNTEERS
VOLUPTUARY
VOLUPTUOUS
VORARLBERG
VORTICELLA
VOTIVENESS
VOUCHSAFED
VULCANIZED
VULCANIZER
VULGARIZED
VULGARIZER
VULGARNESS
VULNERABLE
VULNERABLY
VULPECULAR

W
WADDLINGLY
WADING POOL
WAGE SLAVES
WAGGA WAGGA
WAGGLINGLY
WAGONS-LITS
WAINWRIGHT
WAISTBANDS
WAISTCOATS
WAISTLINES
WAITPERSON
WAKEY WAKEY
WALKABOUTS

WALK OF LIFE
WALLCHARTS
WALLFLOWER
WALLPAPERS
WALL STREET
WALL-TO-WALL
WANDERINGS
WANDERLUST
WANDSWORTH
WANTONNESS
WAREHOUSES
WARMING PAN
WARMONGERS
WARRANTIES
WARRANTING
WARRINGTON
WASHBASINS
WASHCLOTHS
WASHING DAY
WASHINGTON
WASHSTANDS
WASTEFULLY
WASTELANDS
WASTE PAPER
WATCHFULLY
WATCHMAKER
WATCH NIGHT
WATCHSTRAP
WATCHTOWER
WATCHWORDS
WATER BIRDS
WATERBORNE
WATER BUTTS
WATERCRAFT
WATERCRESS
WATERFALLS
WATERFOWLS
WATERFRONT
WATERHOLES
WATERINESS
WATER JUMPS

WATER LEVEL
WATER MAINS
WATERMARKS
WATERMELON
WATER METER
WATERMILLS
WATER PIPES
WATERPOWER
WATERPROOF
WATER RATES
WATERSCAPE
WATERSHEDS
WATER SKIER
WATERSPOUT
WATER TABLE
WATERTIGHT
WATER VOLES
WATERWHEEL
WATERWINGS
WATERWORKS
WATTLEBIRD
WAVELENGTH
WAVERINGLY
WAXED PAPER
WEAKLINESS
WEAK-MINDED
WEAKNESSES
WEAK-WILLED
WEALTHIEST
WEARYINGLY
WEATHERING
WEATHERMAN
WEATHERMEN
WEAVERBIRD
WEDNESDAYS
WEEDKILLER
WEEKENDERS
WEEKENDING
WEEKNIGHTS
WEIGHTLESS

WELL-ARGUED
WELL-CHOSEN
WELL-EARNED
WELL-HEELED
WELL I NEVER
WELLINGTON
WELL-JUDGED
WELL-SPOKEN
WELLSPRING
WELL-TURNED
WELL-WISHER
WELL-WORDED
WENTLETRAP
WEREWOLVES
WEST BENGAL
WESTERLIES
WESTERNERS
WESTERNISM
WESTERNIZE
WEST INDIAN
WEST INDIES
WESTPHALIA
WEST RIDING
WET BLANKET
WET-NURSING
WHARFINGER
WHATSOEVER
WHEELBASES
WHEELCHAIR
WHEELHOUSE
WHEELIE BIN
WHEEZINESS
WHEEZINGLY
WHENSOEVER
WHEREFORES
WHETSTONES

WHICKERING
WHIMPERING
WHIPLASHES
WHIP-ROUNDS
WHIPSTITCH
WHIRLABOUT
WHIRLIGIGS
WHIRLINGLY
WHIRLPOOLS
WHIRLWINDS
WHIRLYBIRD
WHISPERERS
WHISPERING
WHIST DRIVE
WHITEBOARD
WHITE DWARF
WHITE FLAGS
WHITE HOPES
WHITEHORSE
WHITE HORSE
WHITE HOUSE
WHITE MAGIC
WHITE METAL
WHITE PAPER
WHITE SAUCE
WHITESMITH
WHITE TRASH
WHITEWATER
WHITLEY BAY
WHITTLINGS
WHOLEFOODS
WHOLE NOTES
WHOLESALER
WHOREHOUSE
WICKEDNESS
WICKERWORK
WICKET GATE

WIDE-
SCREEN
WIDESPREAD
WIDOWS
MITE
WIFELINESS
WILDCATTED
WILDEBEEST
WILDERNESS
WILDFOWLER
WILFULNESS
WILLEMSTAD
WILLOWHERB
WILLY-
NILLY
WILMINGTON
WINCEYETTE
WINCHESTER
WINDBREAKS
WIND-
BROKEN
WINDEDNESS
WINDFLOWER
WINDGALLED
WIND
GAUGES
WINDJAMMER
WINDLASSES
WINDOWPANE
WINDOW-
SHOP
WINDOWSILL
WINDSCREEN
WINDSHIELD
WIND
SLEEVE
WINDSTORMS
WINDSUCKER
WIND-
SURFER

WIND
TUNNEL
WINEBIBBER
WINE
COOLER
WINEMAKING
WINTERFEED
WINTERTHUR
WINTERTIME
WINTRINESS
WIRE-
HAIRED
WIRELESSES
WIREWORKER
WISECRACKS
WISHY-
WASHY
WITCHCRAFT
WITCH-
HAZEL
WITCH-
HUNTS
WITHDRAWAL
WITHDRAWER
WITHHOLDER
WITNESS
BOX
WITNESSING
WITTENBERG
WITTICISMS
WOBBLINESS
WOEFULNESS
WOLFHOUNDS
WOLFRAMITE
WOLLONGONG
WOMANIZERS
WOMANIZING
WOMENSWEAR
WONDERLAND
WONDERMENT
WONDERWORK

WOODBLOCKS
WOODCARVER
WOODCUTTER
WOODENNESS
WOODLANDER
WOODPECKER
WOODWORKER
WOOKEY
HOLE
WOOLGROWER
WOOLLINESS
WORDLESSLY
WORKAHOLIC
WORKBASKET
WORK-
HARDEN
WORKHORSES
WORKING
DAY
WORKINGMAN
WORKPEOPLE
WORKPLACES
WORK-TO-
RULE
WORLD-
CLASS
WORLDLIEST
WORLD
POWER
WORLD-
WEARY
WORRYINGLY
WORRYWARTS
WORSHIPFUL
WORSHIPING
WORSHIPPED
WORSHIPPER
WORTHINESS
WORTHWHILE
WOUNDINGLY
WRAITHLIKE

WRATHFULLY
WRETCHEDLY
WRISTBANDS
WRISTWATCH
WRITHINGLY
WRONGDOERS
WRONGDOING
WRONGFULLY
WUNDERKIND

X

XANTHATION
XENOGAMOUS
XENOLITHIC
XENOPHOBIA
XENOPHOBIC
XEROGRAPHY
XEROPHYTIC
XIPHOSURAN
XOCHIMILCO
X-
RADIATIO
N
X-RAY
BINARY
XYLOGRAPHY
XYLOPHONES
XYLOPHONIC
XYLOTOMIST
XYLOTOMOUS

Y

YARBOROUGH
YARDSTICKS
YEASTINESS
YELLOWBARK
YELLOWBIRD
YELLOWCAKE
YELLOWLEGS
YELLOWTAIL
YELLOWWEED

YELLOWWOOD
YESTERDAYS
YESTERYEAR
YIELDINGLY
YLANG-
YLANG
YOGYAKARTA
YOSHKAR-
OLA
YOUNGBERRY
YOUNGSTERS
YOUNGSTOWN
YOURSELVES
YOUTHFULLY
YUGOSLAVIA

Z

ZAPOROZHYE
ZENER
DIODE
ZIGZAGGING
ZINCOGRAPH
ZOOGRAPHER
ZOOGRAPHIC
ZOOLATROUS
ZOOLOGICAL
ZOOLOGISTS
ZOOM
LENSES
ZOOMORPHIC
ZOOPHAGOUS
ZOOPHILISM
ZOOPHILOUS
ZOOPHOBOUS
ZOOPLASTIC
ZWITTERION
ZYGODACTYL
ZYGOMYCETE
ZYGOSPORIC
ZYMOLOGIST

A

ABANDONEDLY
ABANDONMENT
ABBEVILLIAN
ABBREVIATED
ABBREVIATOR
ABDICATIONS
ABERRATIONS
ABERYSTWYTH
ABIETIC ACID
ABIOGENESIS
ABIOGENETIC
ABLUTIONARY
ABNORMALITY
ABOLISHMENT
ABOMINATING
ABOMINATION
ABORIGINALS
ABORTIONIST
ABRACADABRA
ABRANCHIATE
ABRIDGMENTS
ABROGATIONS
ABSENTEEISM
ABSORBINGLY
ABSORPTANCE
ABSTENTIONS
ABSTENTIOUS
ABSTRACTING
ABSTRACTION
ABSTRACTIVE
ABSTRICTION
ABSURDITIES
ABUSIVENESS
ACADEMICALS
ACADEMICIAN
ACADEMICISM
ACARPELLOUS
ACATALECTIC
ACAULESCENT
ACCELERANDO
ACCELERATED
ACCELERATOR
ACCENTUATED
ACCEPTANCES
ACCEPTATION
ACCESSIONAL
ACCESSORIAL
ACCESSORIES
ACCESSORILY
ACCIPITRINE

ACCLAMATION
ACCLAMATORY
ACCLIMATIZE
ACCLIVITIES
ACCLIVITOUS
ACCOMMODATE
ACCOMPANIED
ACCOMPANIER
ACCOMPANIST
ACCOMPLICES
ACCORDANCES
ACCORDINGLY
ACCOUNTABLE
ACCOUNTANCY
ACCOUNTANTS
ACCULTURATE
ACCUMULABLE
ACCUMULATED
ACCUMULATOR
ACCUSATIONS
ACCUSATIVAL
ACCUSATIVES
ACCUSTOMING
ACETANILIDE
ACETYLATION
ACHIEVEMENT
ACHONDRITIC
ACHROMATISM
ACHROMATIZE
ACHROMATOUS
ACID-FORMING
ACIDIFIABLE
ACIDIMETRIC
ACIDOPHILIC
ACIDOPHILUS
ACIDULATION
ACINACIFORM
ACKNOWLEDGE
ACLINIC LINE
ACOUSTICIAN
ACQUAINTING
ACQUIESCENT
ACQUIESCING
ACQUIREMENT
ACQUISITION
ACQUISITIVE
ACQUITTANCE
ACRIFLAVINE
ACRIMONIOUS
ACROCARPOUS
ACROMEGALIC

ACTINICALLY
ACTINOMETER
ACTINOMETRY
ACTINOMYCIN
ACTUALITIES
ACUMINATION
ACUPRESSURE
ACUPUNCTURE
ADAM'S APPLES
ADAPTATIONS
ADIAPHORISM
ADIAPHORIST
ADIAPHOROUS
AD INFINITUM
ADIPOCEROUS
ADJOURNMENT
ADJUDICATED
ADJUDICATOR
ADJUSTMENTS
ADMIRATIONS
ADMONISHING
ADMONITIONS
ADOLESCENCE
ADOLESCENTS
ADOPTIONISM
ADOPTIONIST
ADULTERATED
ADULTERATOR
ADUMBRATING
ADUMBRATION
ADUMBRATIVE
ADVANCEMENT
ADVANCINGLY
ADVENTURERS
ADVENTURESS
ADVENTURISM
ADVENTURIST
ADVENTUROUS
ADVERBIALLY
ADVERSARIAL
ADVERSARIES
ADVERSATIVE
ADVERSITIES
ADVERTENTLY
ADVERTISERS
ADVERTISING
ADVERTORIAL
AEOLIAN HARP
AERODYNAMIC
AEROGRAMMES
AERONAUTICS

AEROSTATICS
AEROSTATION
AESTIVATION
AETIOLOGIST
AFFECTATION
AFFECTINGLY
AFFECTIONAL
AFFECTIVITY
AFFILIATING
AFFILIATION
AFFIRMATION
AFFIRMATIVE
AFFLICTIONS
AFFORESTING
AFFRANCHISE
AFFRICATIVE
AFGHANISTAN
AFICIONADOS
AFRO-ASIATIC
AFTERBIRTHS
AFTERBURNER
AFTEREFFECT
AFTERSHAVES
AFTERTASTES
AGAMOSPERMY
AGELESSNESS
AGGLOMERATE
AGGLUTINANT
AGGLUTINATE
AGGRADATION
AGGRANDIZER
AGGRAVATING
AGGRAVATION
AGGREGATING
AGGREGATION
AGGRIEVEDLY
AGNOSTICISM
AGONIZINGLY
AGONY COLUMN
AGORAPHOBIA
AGORAPHOBIC
AGRARIANISM
AGRICULTURE
AGROBIOLOGY
AGROLOGICAL
AGROSTOLOGY
AIDE-MEMOIRE
AIDES-DE-CAMP
AILUROPHILE
AILUROPHOBE
AIMLESSNESS

AIRCRAFTMAN	ALTOSTRATUS	ANALEMMATIC	ANORTHOSITE
AIRCRAFTMEN	ALUMINOSITY	ANALYSATION	ANTAGONISMS
AIRLESSNESS	ALVEOLATION	ANAMORPHISM	ANTAGONISTS
AIRSICKNESS	AMABOKOBOKO	ANAPHYLAXIS	ANTAGONIZED
AIR TERMINAL	AMALGAMATED	ANARCHISTIC	ANTALKALINE
AIX-LES-BAINS	AMARANTHINE	ANASTOMOSIS	ANTECEDENCE
ALARM CLOCKS	AMBASSADORS	ANASTOMOTIC	ANTECEDENTS
ALBATROSSES	AMBIGUGUITY	ANCIENTNESS	ANTECHAMBER
ALBUMINURIA	AMBIGUOUSLY	ANCILLARIES	ANTEPENDIUM
ALBUQUERQUE	AMBITIOUSLY	ANDROGENOUS	ANTEVERSION
ALCOHOL-FREE	AMBIVALENCE	ANDROGYNOUS	ANTHERIDIAL
ALDERMASTON	AMBLYGONITE	ANDROSPHINX	ANTHERIDIUM
ALDERPERSON	AMELIORATED	ANEMOGRAPHY	ANTHEROZOID
ALDOSTERONE	AMELIORATOR	ANEMOMETERS	ANTHOCYANIN
ALESSANDRIA	AMENABILITY	ANEMOMETRIC	ANTHOLOGIES
ALGEBRAICAL	AMENORRHOEA	ANESTHETICS	ANTHOLOGIST
ALGINIC ACID	AMERICANISM	ANESTHETIST	ANTHOLOGIZE
ALGOLAGNIST	AMERICANIZE	ANESTHETIZE	ANTHRACITIC
ALGORITHMIC	AMETHYSTINE	ANFRACTUOUS	ANTHRACNOSE
ALKALIMETER	AMICABILITY	ANGELICALLY	ANTIBIOTICS
ALKALIMETRY	AMINOPHENOL	ANGIOMATOUS	ANTICATHODE
ALKALIZABLE	AMINOPYRINE	ANGIOPLASTY	ANTICIPATED
ALL-AMERICAN	AMMONIATION	ANGLICANISM	ANTICIPATOR
ALLANTOIDAL	AMONTILLADO	ANGLICIZING	ANTICLASTIC
ALLEGATIONS	AMOROUSNESS	ANGLO-INDIAN	ANTICYCLONE
ALLEGIANCES	AMOR PATRIAE	ANGLOPHILES	ANTIFEBRILE
ALLEGORICAL	AMORPHOUSLY	ANGLOPHILIA	ANTIFOULING
ALLEVIATING	AMORTIZABLE	ANGLOPHOBES	ANTIMISSILE
ALLEVIATION	AMOUR-PROPRE	ANGLOPHOBIA	ANTIMYCOTIC
ALLEVIATIVE	AMPHETAMINE	ANGLO-SAXONS	ANTINEUTRON
ALLOCATIONS	AMPHIBIOTIC	ANIMALCULAR	ANTINUCLEAR
ALLOGRAPHIC	AMPHIBOLITE	ANIMOSITIES	ANTINUCLEON
ALLOMORPHIC	AMPHIBOLOGY	ANISEIKONIA	ANTIOXIDANT
ALLOPLASMIC	AMPHICHROIC	ANISEIKONIC	ANTIPATHIES
ALLOPURINOL	AMPHICTYONY	ANISODACTYL	ANTIPHONARY
ALL-POWERFUL	AMPHISBAENA	ANISOGAMOUS	ANTIPHRASIS
ALL-ROUNDERS	AMPHISTYLAR	ANISOMEROUS	ANTIPYRESIS
ALLUREMENTS	AMPHITRICHA	ANISOMETRIC	ANTIPYRETIC
ALMIGHTIEST	AMPLEXICAUL	ANISOTROPIC	ANTIQUARIAN
ALPHABETIZE	AMPLIFIABLE	ANNABERGITE	ANTIQUITIES
ALTARPIECES	AMPUTATIONS	ANNEXATIONS	ANTIRRHINUM
ALTERATIONS	AMYL NITRITE	ANNIHILABLE	ANTI-SEMITES
ALTERCATION	AMYLOPECTIN	ANNIHILATED	ANTI-SEMITIC
ALTERNATELY	ANACHRONISM	ANNIHILATOR	ANTISEPTICS
ALTERNATING	ANACOLUTHIA	ANNIVERSARY	ANTITUSSIVE
ALTERNATION	ANACOLUTHIC	ANNOTATIONS	ANTOFAGASTA
ALTERNATIVE	ANACOLUTHON	ANNUNCIATOR	ANTONOMASIA
ALTERNATORS	ANADIPLOSIS	ANOINTMENTS	ANXIOUSNESS
ALTITUDINAL	ANAEMICALLY	ANOMALISTIC	APATOSAURUS
ALTOCUMULUS	ANAESTHESIA	ANOMALOUSLY	APHETICALLY
ALTOGETHERS	ANAESTHETIC	ANONYMOUSLY	APHRODISIAC

APICULTURAL	AQUATICALLY	ASCETICALLY	ATOMIC PILES
APOCALYPSES	AQUICULTURE	ASKING PRICE	ATOMIZATION
APOCALYPTIC	ARABICA BEAN	ASPERGILLUS	ATRABILIOUS
APOCOPATION	ARALIACEOUS	ASPHYXIATED	ATROCIOUSLY
APOCYNTHION	ARAN ISLANDS	ASPHYXIATOR	ATTACHE CASE
APOLOGETICS	ARBITRAGEUR	ASPIDISTRAS	ATTACHMENTS
APOLOGIZING	ARBITRAMENT	ASPIRATIONS	ATTAINMENTS
APOMORPHINE	ARBITRARILY	ASSASSINATE	ATTEMPTABLE
APONEUROSIS	ARBITRATING	ASSEMBLAGES	ATTENDANCES
APONEUROTIC	ARBITRATION	ASSEMBLYMAN	ATTENTIVELY
APOPHYLLITE	ARBITRATORS	ASSEMBLYMEN	ATTENUATING
APOSIOPESIS	ARBORESCENT	ASSENTATION	ATTENUATION
APOSIOPETIC	ARCHAEOLOGY	ASSERTIVELY	ATTESTATION
A POSTERIORI	ARCHAEOZOIC	ASSESSMENTS	ATTITUDINAL
APOSTROPHES	ARCHAICALLY	ASSESSORIAL	ATTRACTABLE
APOTHEOSIZE	ARCHANGELIC	ASSEVERATED	ATTRACTIONS
APPALLINGLY	ARCHBISHOPS	ASSIDUOUSLY	ATTRIBUTING
APPARATCHIK	ARCHDEACONS	ASSIGNATION	ATTRIBUTION
APPARATUSES	ARCHDIOCESE	ASSIGNMENTS	ATTRIBUTIVE
APPARELLING	ARCHDUCHESS	ASSIMILABLE	ATTRITIONAL
APPARITIONS	ARCHEGONIUM	ASSIMILATED	AUCTIONEERS
APPEALINGLY	ARCHENEMIES	ASSOCIATING	AUDACIOUSLY
APPEARANCES	ARCHENTERIC	ASSOCIATION	AUDIOLOGIST
APPEASEMENT	ARCHENTERON	ASSOCIATIVE	AUDIOMETRIC
APPELLATION	ARCHIPELAGO	ASSORTATIVE	AUDIOTYPING
APPELLATIVE	ARDUOUSNESS	ASSORTMENTS	AUDIOTYPIST
APPERTAINED	ARENICOLOUS	ASSUAGEMENT	AUDIO-VISUAL
APPLICATION	ARGENTINEAN	ASSUMPTIONS	AUDITIONING
APPLICATIVE	ARGYLLSHIRE	ASSUREDNESS	AUDITORIUMS
APPLICATORY	ARISTOCRACY	ASSYRIOLOGY	AUGMENTABLE
APPOINTMENT	ARISTOCRATS	ASTATICALLY	AURIGNACIAN
APPORTIONED	ARMED FORCES	ASTERISKING	AUSCULTATOR
APPORTIONER	ARMIPOTENCE	ASTIGMATISM	AUSTERENESS
APPRECIABLE	ARMOURED CAR	ASTONISHING	AUSTERITIES
APPRECIABLY	ARMOUR PLATE	ASTRAPHOBIA	AUSTRALASIA
APPRECIATED	AROMATICITY	ASTRAPHOBIC	AUSTRALIANA
APPREHENDED	ARONOMASTIC	ASTRINGENCY	AUSTRALIANS
APPRENTICED	ARRAIGNMENT	ASTRINGENTS	AUSTRONESIA
APPRENTICES	ARRANGEMENT	ASTROBOTANY	AUTHORITIES
APPROACHING	ARRESTINGLY	ASTROLOGERS	AUTHORIZING
APPROBATION	ARTERIALIZE	ASTROMETRIC	AUTOCHANGER
APPROBATIVE	ARTHROMERIC	ASTRONAUTIC	AUTOCRACIES
APPROPRIATE	ARTHROSPORE	ASTRONOMERS	AUTOGENESIS
APPROVINGLY	ARTICULATED	ASTROSPHERE	AUTOGENETIC
APPROXIMATE	ARTICULATOR	ATELECTASIS	AUTOGRAPHED
APPURTENANT	ARTILLERIES	ATHEISTICAL	AUTOGRAPHIC
AQUACULTURE	ARTIODACTYL	ATHERMANOUS	AUTOKINETIC
AQUAEROBICS	ARTLESSNESS	ATHLETICISM	AUTOMOBILES
AQUAMARINES	ARYTENOIDAL	ATLANTICISM	AUTOPLASTIC
AQUAPLANING	ASCENSIONAL	ATMOSPHERES	AUTOTROPHIC
AQUARELLIST	ASCERTAINED	ATMOSPHERIC	AUXANOMETER

AUXILIARIES
AVOIRDUPOIS
AVUNCULARLY
AWESOMENESS
AWKWARDNESS
AXIOLOGICAL
AXONOMETRIC
AZERBAIJANI
AZOTOBACTER

B
BABY-MINDERS
BABY ON BOARD
BABY'S-BREATH
BABY-SITTERS
BABY-SITTING
BACCHANALIA
BACCIFEROUS
BACCIVOROUS
BACILLIFORM
BACKBENCHER
BACKBENCHES
BACKCOMBING
BACK COUNTRY
BACKGROUNDS
BACKHANDERS
BACK NUMBERS
BACKPACKERS
BACKPACKING
BACK PASSAGE
BACKPEDALED
BACKROOM BOY
BACKSLAPPER
BACKSLIDERS
BACKSLIDING
BACK STREET
BACKSTROKES
BACK TO FRONT
BACKTRACKED
BACTERAEMIA
BACTERICIDE
BADDERLOCKS
BAD-MOUTHING
BAGGAGE CARS
BAGGAGE ROOM
BAHIA BLANCA
BAKERS DOZEN
BAKER'S DOZEN
BALANCEABLE
BALEFULNESS
BALL BEARING

BALLBREAKER
BALLETOMANE
BALLOONISTS
BALLOT PAPER
BALUCHISTAN
BALUSTRADES
BAMBOOZLING
BANANA SKINS
BANDMASTERS
BANGLADESHI
BANK ACCOUNT
BANKER'S CARD
BANK HOLIDAY
BANKROLLING
BANKRUPTING
BANNOCKBURN
BANTERINGLY
BARBARITIES
BARBARIZING
BARBAROUSLY
BARBASTELLE
BARBITURATE
BARCOO RIVER
BAREFACEDLY
BARIUM MEALS
BARLEY SUGAR
BARLEY WATER
BAR MITZVAHS
BARNSTORMED
BARNSTORMER
BAROGRAPHIC
BARONETCIES
BAROTSELAND
BARQUENTINE
BARREL ORGAN
BARRICADING
BASHFULNESS
BASINGSTOKE
BASKERVILLE
BASS GUITARS
BASSOONISTS
BASTARDIZED
BASTINADOED
BASTINADOES
BASTNAESITE
BATHING SUIT
BATHOLITHIC
BATHOMETRIC
BATHYMETRIC
BATHYSPHERE
BATSMANSHIP

BATTLE CRIES
BATTLEFIELD
BATTLEMENTS
BATTLE ROYAL
BATTLESHIPS
BATTY RIDERS
BEACHCHAIRS
BEACHCOMBER
BEAN COUNTER
BEANSPROUTS
BEARISHNESS
BEAR'S-BREECH
BEASTLINESS
BEAUHARNAIS
BEAUTEOUSLY
BEAUTICIANS
BEAUTIFULLY
BEAUTIFYING
BEAUTY QUEEN
BEAUTY SLEEP
BEAUTY SPOTS
BEAVERBOARD
BECKENBAUER
BED AND BOARD
BEDEVILLING
BEDEVILMENT
BEFITTINGLY
BEFRIENDING
BEGUILEMENT
BEGUILINGLY
BEHAVIOURAL
BELABOURING
BELARUSSIAN
BELATEDNESS
BELEAGUERED
BELL-BOTTOMS
BELLICOSITY
BELLIGERENT
BELL-RINGING
BELLYACHING
BELLY BUTTON
BELLY DANCER
BELLY DANCES
BELLY LAUGHS
BENEDICTINE
BENEDICTION
BENEDICTORY
BENEFACTION
BENEFACTORS
BENEFICENCE
BENEFICIARY

BENEVOLENCE
BENIGHTEDLY
BEQUEATHING
BEREAVEMENT
BERGSCHRUND
BESMIRCHING
BESPATTERED
BEST-SELLERS
BEST-SELLING
BETA-BLOCKER
BETES-NOIRES
BETULACEOUS
BEWILDERING
BHUBANESWAR
BIAS BINDING
BIBLIOLATRY
BIBLIOMANCY
BIBLIOMANIA
BIBLIOPHILE
BIBLIOPHISM
BIBLIOTHECA
BICARBONATE
BICENTENARY
BICEPHALOUS
BICONCAVITY
BIEDERMEIER
BIFOLIOLATE
BIFURCATING
BIFURCATION
BIG BUSINESS
BIKER JACKET
BILATERALLY
BILIOUSNESS
BILLETS-DOUX
BILLIONAIRE
BILLOWINESS
BILLS OF FARE
BILLS OF SALE
BIMETALLISM
BIMOLECULAR
BIOCATALYST
BIOCENOLOGY
BIODYNAMICS
BIOENGINEER
BIOFEEDBACK
BIOGRAPHERS
BIOGRAPHIES
BIOPHYSICAL
BIPARTITION
BIQUADRATIC
BIQUARTERLY

BIRD-BRAINED	BLINDSTOREY	BOOTLEGGING	BRITTLENESS
BIRDS OF PREY	BLOCKBUSTER	BORDERLANDS	BRITTLE-STAR
BIRD-WATCHER	BLOCKHOUSES	BORDERLINES	BROADCASTER
BIROBIDZHAN	BLOOD COUNTS	BOTANICALLY	BROAD CHURCH
BIRTHPLACES	BLOOD GROUPS	BOTHERATION	BROAD GAUGES
BIRTHRIGHTS	BLOODHOUNDS	BOTTLE BANKS	BROADMINDED
BIRTHWEIGHT	BLOODLESSLY	BOTTLEBRUSH	BROADSHEETS
BISEXUALISM	BLOOD PLASMA	BOTTLE GREEN	BROADSWORDS
BISEXUALITY	BLOOD SPORTS	BOTTLENECKS	BROMINATION
BISYMMETRIC	BLOODSTAINS	BOUNDLESSLY	BRONCHIOLAR
BIT OF FLUFFS	BLOODSTREAM	BOUNTEOUSLY	BRONTOSAURI
BITTERSWEET	BLOODSUCKER	BOURGEOISIE	BRONX CHEERS
BITTER SWEET	BLOOD VESSEL	BOURNEMOUTH	BRONZE MEDAL
BIVOUACKING	BLOOMINGTON	BOWDLERIZED	BROOMSTICKS
BLACKAMOORS	BLOTCHINESS	BOYOMA FALLS	BROTHERHOOD
BLACKBALLED	BLUDGEONING	BOYSENBERRY	BROWBEATING
BLACKBOARDS	BLUEBERRIES	BRACE AND BIT	BROWNSTONES
BLACK COMEDY	BLUE-BLOODED	BRACHIATION	BRUCELLOSIS
BLACK FOREST	BLUEBOTTLES	BRACTEOLATE	BRUSQUENESS
BLACKGUARDS	BLUE CHEESES	BRADYCARDIA	BRUTALITIES
BLACK HUMOUR	BLUE-EYED BOY	BRADYCARDIC	BRUTALIZING
BLACKLEGGED	BLUE MURDERS	BRAGGADOCIO	BRUTISHNESS
BLACKLISTED	BLUNDERBUSS	BRAHMAPUTRA	BRYOLOGICAL
BLACKMAILED	BLURREDNESS	BRAIN DRAINS	BUCARAMANGA
BLACKMAILER	BOBSLEIGHED	BRAINLESSLY	BUCKET SEATS
BLACK MARIAS	BODHISATTVA	BRAINSTORMS	BUCKET SHOPS
BLACK MARKET	BODY-CENTRED	BRAINS TRUST	BUCKLER-FERN
BLACK MASSES	BODY POLITIC	BRAINTEASER	BUCOLICALLY
BLACK MUSLIM	BOGNOR REGIS	BRAINWASHED	BUDGERIGARS
BLACK PEPPER	BOILERMAKER	BRAINWASHER	BUENOS AIRES
BLACKSHIRTS	BOILERPLATE	BRANCHIOPOD	BUFFER STATE
BLACKSMITHS	BOILER SUITS	BRANDENBURG	BUFFER STOCK
BLACK WIDOWS	BOLLOCKS-UPS	BRANDISHING	BUFFER ZONES
BLADDERWORT	BOLL WEEVILS	BRATTISHING	BULBIFEROUS
BLAMELESSLY	BOMBARDIERS	BRAZZAVILLE	BULLDOG CLIP
BLAMEWORTHY	BOMBARDMENT	BREADBASKET	BULLETPROOF
BLANCMANGES	BONDHOLDERS	BREADBOARDS	BULLFIGHTER
BLANK CHEQUE	BONE MARROWS	BREADCRUMBS	BULLFINCHES
BLASPHEMERS	BONESHAKERS	BREADFRUITS	BULLISHNESS
BLASPHEMIES	BOOBY PRIZES	BREADTHWAYS	BULLSHITTED
BLASPHEMING	BOOKBINDERS	BREADWINNER	BULL TERRIER
BLASPHEMOUS	BOOKBINDERY	BREAKFASTED	BUMPTIOUSLY
BLASTOGENIC	BOOKBINDING	BREAK THE ICE	BUNDELKHAND
BLASTOMERIC	BOOKISHNESS	BREASTPLATE	BUPIVACAINE
BLASTOPORIC	BOOKKEEPERS	BREATHALYSE	BUREAUCRACY
BLENCHINGLY	BOOKKEEPING	BREATHINESS	BUREAUCRATS
BLEPHARITIC	BOOKMOBILES	BRECONSHIRE	BURGOMASTER
BLEPHATITIS	BOOKSELLERS	BREECHBLOCK	BURKINA-FASO
BLESSEDNESS	BOOMERANGED	BREMERHAVEN	BURLESQUING
BLIND ALLEYS	BOORISHNESS	BRIDGEBOARD	BURNISHABLE
BLINDFOLDED	BOOTLEGGERS	BRISTLETAIL	BUSHWHACKER

BUSINESS END
BUSINESSMAN
BUSINESSMEN
BUS STATIONS
BUTCHERBIRD
BUTTER BEANS
BUTTERFLIES
BUTTONHOLED
BUTTONHOLES
BUTTONMOULD
BUTTRESSING
BUTYRACEOUS
BY-ELECTIONS
BYELORUSSIA

C

CABINETWORK
CABORA BASSA
CACHE MEMORY
CACOGRAPHIC
CACOPHONOUS
CALCEOLARIA
CALCICOLOUS
CALCIFEROUS
CALCIFUGOUS
CALCINATION
CALCULATING
CALCULATION
CALCULATORS
CALEFACIENT
CALEFACTION
CALEFACTORY
CALIBRATING
CALIBRATION
CALIFORNIAN
CALIFORNIUM
CALLIGRAPHY
CALLIPYGIAN
CALLOUSNESS
CALORIMETER
CALORIMETRY
CALUMNIATED
CALVINISTIC
CALYPTROGEN
CAMARADERIE
CAMERA-READY
CAMOUFLAGED
CAMOUFLAGES
CAMPAIGNERS
CAMPAIGNING
CAMPANOLOGY

CAMPANULATE
CAMPGROUNDS
CAMPO GRANDE
CANALICULAR
CANALICULUS
CANDELABRUM
CANDIDACIES
CANDLEBERRY
CANDLELIGHT
CANDLEPOWER
CANDLESTICK
CANDLEWICKS
CANINE TEETH
CANINE TOOTH
CANNIBALISM
CANNIBALIZE
CANNONBALLS
CANTHARIDES
CANTILEVERS
CAPACIOUSLY
CAPACITANCE
CAPILLARIES
CAPILLARITY
CAPITALISTS
CAPITALIZED
CAPITAL LEVY
CAPITATIONS
CAPITULATED
CAPITULATOR
CAPRICCIOSO
CAPRICORNUS
CAPSULATION
CAPTIVATING
CAPTIVATION
CARABINIERE
CARAVANNING
CARBAMIDINE
CARBONATION
CARBONIZING
CARBON PAPER
CAR-BOOT SALE
CARBORUNDUM
CARBOXYLASE
CARBOXYLATE
CARBUNCULAR
CARBURETTOR
CARBYLAMINE
CARCASSONNE
CARCINOGENS
CARDINALATE
CARD INDEXES

CARDIOGRAPH
CARDPUNCHES
CARDUACEOUS
CAREFULNESS
CARESSINGLY
CARICATURED
CARICATURES
CARMINATIVE
CARNIVOROUS
CAROLINGIAN
CARPOGONIAL
CARPOGONIUM
CARPOLOGIST
CARRAGEENAN
CARRIAGEWAY
CARRIER BAGS
CARSICKNESS
CARTOGRAPHY
CARTOONISTS
CARTWHEELED
CARUNCULATE
CARVEL-BUILT
CARVING FORK
CASE HISTORY
CASE STUDIES
CASEWORKERS
CASSITERITE
CASTELLATED
CASTER SUGAR
CASTIGATING
CASTIGATION
CASTING VOTE
CASTLEREAGH
CASTOR SUGAR
CATACAUSTIC
CATACHRESIS
CATACLASTIC
CATACLYSMIC
CATADROMOUS
CATAFALQUES
CATALOGUING
CATAPLASTIC
CATAPULTING
CATASTROPHE
CAT BURGLARS
CATCHPHRASE
CATCHWEIGHT
CATECHISMAL
CATECHISTIC
CATECHIZING
CATEGORICAL

CATEGORIZED
CATERPILLAR
CATERWAULED
CATHETERIZE
CATHOLICISM
CATHOLICITY
CATHOLICIZE
CATTLE GRIDS
CAULIFLOWER
CAUSABILITY
CAUSATIVELY
CAUSTICALLY
CAUSTICNESS
CAUTERIZING
CAVACO SILVA
CAVALIERISM
CAVERNOUSLY
CAVITY WALLS
CAVO-RELIEVO
CEASELESSLY
CELEBRATING
CELEBRATION
CELEBRATIVE
CELEBRITIES
CEMENTATION
CEMENT MIXER
CENOSPECIES
CENTENARIAN
CENTENARIES
CENTENNIALS
CENTIMETRES
CENTRALIZED
CENTREBOARD
CENTRE-FOLDS
CENTREPIECE
CENTRIFUGAL
CENTRIFUGES
CENTRIPETAL
CENTROBARIC
CENTROMERIC
CENTROSOMIC
CEPHALALGIA
CERARGYRITE
CEREBRATION
CEREBROSIDE
CEREMONIALS
CEREMONIOUS
CEROGRAPHIC
CEROPLASTIC
CERTAINTIES
CERTIFIABLE

CERTIFICATE	CHEERLEADER	CHORDOPHONE	CITIZENSHIP
CETOLOGICAL	CHEERLESSLY	CHOREODRAMA	CITRONELLAL
CHAETOGNATH	CHEESECAKES	CHOREOGRAPH	CITY FATHERS
CHAFFINCHES	CHEESECLOTH	CHOROGRAPHY	CIVIL RIGHTS
CHAFING DISH	CHEF D'OEUVRE	CHRISMATORY	CIVVY STREET
CHAIN LETTER	CHELICERATE	CHRISTENDOM	CLAIRVOYANT
CHAIN-SMOKED	CHELIFEROUS	CHRISTENING	CLAMATORIAL
CHAIN-SMOKER	CHELYABINSK	CHRISTINGLE	CLANDESTINE
CHAIN STITCH	CHEMOSMOSIS	CHRISTMASES	CLARINETIST
CHAIN STORES	CHEMOSMOTIC	CHRISTOLOGY	CLASP KNIVES
CHAIRPERSON	CHEMOSPHERE	CHROMATINIC	CLASS ACTION
CHALCANLITE	CHEMOTACTIC	CHROMINANCE	CLASSICISTS
CHALCEDONIC	CHEMOTROPIC	CHROMOGENIC	CLASSIFYING
CHALKBOARDS	CHEQUE CARDS	CHROMONEMAL	CLAVICHORDS
CHALLENGERS	CHEREMKHOVO	CHROMOPHORE	CLAY PIGEONS
CHALLENGING	CHERISHABLE	CHROMOPLASM	CLEAN-LIMBED
CHAMBERLAIN	CHESHIRE CAT	CHROMOPLAST	CLEANLINESS
CHAMBERMAID	CHESSBOARDS	CHROMOSOMAL	CLEAN-SHAVEN
CHAMBER POTS	CHEVAL GLASS	CHROMOSOMES	CLEAN SWEEPS
CHAMELEONIC	CHIAROSCURO	CHRONICALLY	CLEAR-HEADED
CHAMPERTOUS	CHIASTOLITE	CHRONICLERS	CLEAR THE AIR
CHAMPIONING	CHICANERIES	CHRONICLING	CLEETHORPES
CHANCELLERY	CHICHIHAERH	CHRONOGRAPH	CLEFT PALATE
CHANCELLORS	CHICKENFEED	CHRONOMETER	CLEFT STICKS
CHANCROIDAL	CHICKEN FEED	CHRONOMETRY	CLEISTOGAMY
CHANDELIERS	CHIFFONIERS	CHRONOSCOPE	CLERGYWOMAN
CHANGELINGS	CHILDMINDER	CHRYSALISES	CLEVER DICKS
CHANGEOVERS	CHIMNEYPOTS	CHRYSAROBIN	CLIENT STATE
CHANNELLING	CHIMPANZEES	CHRYSOBERYL	CLIFFHANGER
CHANTERELLE	CHINCHILLAS	CHRYSOLITIC	CLIMACTERIC
CHANTICLEER	CHINESE LEAF	CHRYSOPRASE	CLIMATOLOGY
CHAOTICALLY	CHINOISERIE	CHURCHGOERS	CLINANDRIUM
CHAPERONAGE	CHIPPENDALE	CHURCHGOING	CLINOMETRIC
CHAPERONING	CHIROGRAPHY	CHURCHWOMAN	CLOCK TOWERS
CHARCUTERIE	CHIROPODIST	CHURCHYARDS	CLODHOPPERS
CHARGE CARDS	CHIROPTERAN	CICATRICIAL	CLOISTERING
CHARGE HANDS	CHITCHATTED	CICATRIZANT	CLOSED SHOPS
CHARGE NURSE	CHLAMYDEOUS	CINDERELLAS	CLOSEFISTED
CHARGE SHEET	CHLORINATED	CINEMASCOPE	CLOSE-HAULED
CHAR-GRILLED	CHLORINATOR	CIRCULARITY	CLOSE SEASON
CHARIOTEERS	CHLOROPHYLL	CIRCULARIZE	CLOSE SHAVES
CHARISMATIC	CHLOROPLAST	CIRCULAR SAW	CLOSING TIME
CHASTISABLE	CHLOROPRENE	CIRCULATING	CLOSTRIDIAL
CHATELAINES	CHLOROQUINE	CIRCULATION	CLOSTRIDIUM
CHATTANOOGA	CHOANOCYTAL	CIRCULATIVE	CLOTHESLINE
CHAUFFEURED	CHOCK-A-BLOCK	CIRCULATORY	CLOTHES PEGS
CHAULMOOGRA	CHOIRMASTER	CIRCUMCISED	CLOUDBURSTS
CHAUVINISTS	CHOIR SCHOOL	CIRCUMLUNAR	CLOUD-CAPPED
CHEAPSKATES	CHOKECHERRY	CIRCUMPOLAR	CLOYINGNESS
CHECKMATING	CHOLESTEROL	CIRCUMSPECT	CLUSTER BOMB
CHECKPOINTS	CHOLINERGIC	CIRENCESTER	COADUNATION

COADUNATIVE	COLLARBONES	COMMITMENTS	COMPOSITION
COAGULATING	COLLAR STUDS	COMMODITIES	COMPOSITORS
COAGULATION	COLLECTABLE	COMMON NOUNS	COMPOUNDING
COAGULATIVE	COLLECTANEA	COMMONPLACE	COMPRESSING
COALBUNKERS	COLLECTEDLY	COMMON ROOMS	COMPRESSION
COALESCENCE	COLLECTIONS	COMMON SENSE	COMPRESSIVE
COALITIONAL	COLLECTIVES	COMMOTIONAL	COMPRESSORS
COALSCUTTLE	COLLEMBOLAN	COMMUNALISM	COMPRISABLE
COARCTATION	COLLENCHYMA	COMMUNALIST	COMPROMISED
COASTGUARDS	COLLIGATION	COMMUNALITY	COMPROMISER
COAT HANGERS	COLLIGATIVE	COMMUNALIZE	COMPROMISES
COATS OF ARMS	COLLIMATION	COMMUNICANT	COMPTOMETER
COBBLESTONE	COLLOCATING	COMMUNICATE	COMPTROLLER
COCCIDIOSIS	COLLOCATION	COMMUNIONAL	COMPULSIONS
COCCIFEROUS	COLOGARITHM	COMMUNIQUES	COMPUNCTION
COCK-A-LEEKIE	COLONIALISM	COMMUNISTIC	COMPUTATION
COCKCHAFERS	COLONIALIST	COMMUNITIES	COMPUTERATE
COCKLESHELL	COLONIZABLE	COMMUTATION	COMPUTERIZE
COCKLE SHELL	COLONOSCOPY	COMMUTATIVE	COMRADESHIP
COCKROACHES	COLORATURAS	COMMUTATORS	CONCATENATE
CODICILLARY	COLORIMETER	COMPACT DISC	CONCAVITIES
COD-LIVER OIL	COLOUR-BLIND	COMPACTEDLY	CONCEALMENT
COEDUCATION	COLOURISTIC	COMPACTNESS	CONCEITEDLY
COEFFICIENT	COLTISHNESS	COMPANY TOWN	CONCEIVABLE
COELENTERIC	COLUMBARIUM	COMPARATIVE	CONCEIVABLY
COELENTERON	COMBATIVELY	COMPARISONS	CONCENTRATE
COERCIONARY	COMBINATION	COMPARTMENT	CONCEPTACLE
COERCIONIST	COMBINATIVE	COMPASSABLE	CONCEPTIONS
COESSENTIAL	COMBUSTIBLE	COMPATRIOTS	CONCERNEDLY
COEXISTENCE	COMESTIBLES	COMPELLABLE	CONCERTANTE
COEXTENSION	COME-UPPANCE	COMPENDIOUS	CONCERTEDLY
COEXTENSIVE	COMFORTABLE	COMPENDIUMS	CONCERTGOER
COFFEE BREAK	COMFORTABLY	COMPENSATED	CONCERTINAS
COFFEE HOUSE	COMFORTLESS	COMPENSATOR	CONCESSIBLE
COFFEE SHOPS	COMIC OPERAS	COMPETENTLY	CONCESSIONS
COFFEE TABLE	COMIC STRIPS	COMPETITION	CONCILIATED
COGITATIONS	COMMANDANTS	COMPETITIVE	CONCILIATOR
COGNITIVELY	COMMANDMENT	COMPETITORS	CONCLUSIONS
COGNITIVIST	COMME IL FAUT	COMPILATION	CONCOCTIONS
COGNIZANCES	COMMEMORATE	COMPLACENCE	CONCOMITANT
COGNOSCENTI	COMMENDABLE	COMPLACENCY	CONCORDANCE
COINCIDENCE	COMMENDABLY	COMPLAINANT	CONCUBINAGE
COINSURANCE	COMMENTATED	COMPLAINERS	CONCURRENCE
COLD-BLOODED	COMMENTATOR	COMPLAINING	CONDEMNABLE
COLD CHISELS	COMMERCIALS	COMPLAISANT	CONDENSABLE
COLD COMFORT	COMMINATION	COMPLEMENTS	CONDITIONAL
COLD-HEARTED	COMMINATORY	COMPLEXIONS	CONDITIONED
COLD STORAGE	COMMINUTION	COMPLIANTLY	CONDITIONER
COLEOPTERAN	COMMISERATE	COMPLICATED	CONDOLATORY
COLLABORATE	COMMISSIONS	COMPLIMENTS	CONDOLENCES
COLLAPSIBLE	COMMISSURAL	COMPORTMENT	CONDOMINIUM

CONDONATION	CONJUGATIVE	CONSTRUCTED	CONTROVERSY
CONDUCTANCE	CONJUNCTION	CONSTRUCTOR	CONTUMELIES
CONDUCTIBLE	CONJUNCTIVA	CONSULSHIPS	CONTUSIONED
CONDUCTRESS	CONJUNCTIVE	CONSULTANCY	CONURBATION
CONFABULATE	CONJUNCTURE	CONSULTANTS	CONVALESCED
CONFECTIONS	CONJURATION	CONSUMERISM	CONVENIENCE
CONFEDERACY	CONNECTIBLE	CONSUMMATED	CONVENTICLE
CONFEDERATE	CONNECTICUT	CONSUMMATOR	CONVENTIONS
CONFERENCES	CONNECTIONS	CONSUMPTION	CONVERGENCE
CONFERMENTS	CONNOISSEUR	CONSUMPTIVE	CONVERGENCY
CONFESSEDLY	CONNOTATION	CONTACT LENS	CONVERSABLE
CONFESSIONS	CONNOTATIVE	CONTAINMENT	CONVERSANCE
CONFIDENCES	CONSCIENCES	CONTAMINANT	CONVERSIONS
CONFIDENTLY	CONSCIOUSLY	CONTAMINATE	CONVERTIBLE
CONFIDINGLY	CONSCRIPTED	CONTEMNIBLE	CONVEXITIES
CONFINEMENT	CONSECRATED	CONTEMPLATE	CONVEYANCER
CONFISCABLE	CONSECRATOR	CONTENTEDLY	CONVEYANCES
CONFISCATED	CONSECUTION	CONTENTIONS	CONVICTABLE
CONFISCATOR	CONSECUTIVE	CONTENTIOUS	CONVICTIONS
CONFLATIONS	CONSENSUSES	CONTENTMENT	CONVINCIBLE
CONFLICTING	CONSENTIENT	CONTESTANTS	CONVIVIALLY
CONFLICTION	CONSEQUENCE	CONTEXTURAL	CONVOCATION
CONFLICTIVE	CONSERVABLE	CONTINENTAL	CONVOCATIVE
CONFLUENCES	CONSERVANCY	CONTINGENCE	CONVOLUTION
CONFORMABLE	CONSERVATOR	CONTINGENCY	CONVOLVULUS
CONFORMABLY	CONSIDERATE	CONTINGENTS	CONVULSIONS
CONFORMANCE	CONSIDERING	CONTINUALLY	COOKERY BOOK
CONFORMISTS	CONSIGNABLE	CONTINUANCE	COOK ISLANDS
CONFOUNDING	CONSIGNMENT	CONTINUATOR	COOPERATING
CONFRONTING	CONSISTENCY	CONTORTIONS	COOPERATION
CONFUSINGLY	CONSOLATION	CONTRACTILE	COOPERATIVE
CONFUTATION	CONSOLATORY	CONTRACTING	COOPERATORS
CONFUTATIVE	CONSOLIDATE	CONTRACTION	COOPER CREEK
CONGEALMENT	CONSONANCES	CONTRACTIVE	COORDINATED
CONGELATION	CONSONANTAL	CONTRACTORS	COORDINATES
CONGENIALLY	CONSORTIUMS	CONTRACTUAL	COORDINATOR
CONGESTIBLE	CONSPECIFIC	CONTRACTURE	COPARCENARY
CONGREGATED	CONSPICUOUS	CONTRAFLOWS	COPING STONE
CONGREGATOR	CONSPIRATOR	CONTRAPTION	COPLANARITY
CONGRESSMAN	CONSTANTINE	CONTRARIETY	COPPERPLATE
CONGRESSMEN	CONSTELLATE	CONTRASTING	COPPERSMITH
CONGRUENTLY	CONSTERNATE	CONTRASTIVE	COPROCESSOR
CONGRUITIES	CONSTIPATED	CONTRAVENED	COPROPHILIA
CONJECTURAL	CONSTITUENT	CONTRAVENER	COPYWRITERS
CONJECTURED	CONSTITUTED	CONTRAYERVA	CORACIIFORM
CONJECTURER	CONSTITUTER	CONTRETEMPS	CORDILLERAS
CONJECTURES	CONSTRAINED	CONTRIBUTED	CORMOPHYTIC
CONJOINEDLY	CONSTRAINER	CONTRIBUTOR	CORNERSTONE
CONJUGALITY	CONSTRAINTS	CONTRIVANCE	CORNFLOWERS
CONJUGATING	CONSTRICTED	CONTROLLERS	CORNICULATE
CONJUGATION	CONSTRICTOR	CONTROLLING	CORNUCOPIAS

COROLLARIES
CORONAGRAPH
CORONATIONS
CORONERSHIP
CORPORALITY
CORPORATELY
CORPORATION
CORPORATIVE
CORPOREALLY
CORPUSCULAR
CORRECTABLE
CORRECTIONS
CORRECTIVES
CORRECTNESS
CORRELATING
CORRELATION
CORRELATIVE
CORRIGENDUM
CORROBORATE
CORROSIVELY
CORRUGATION
CORRUPTIBLE
CORRUPTIONS
CORRUPTNESS
CORS ANGLAIS
CORTICATION
CORUSCATING
CORUSCATION
COSIGNATORY
COS LETTUCES
COSMETICIAN
COSMOGONIES
COSMOGONIST
COSMOLOGIST
COSMOPOLITE
COTERMINOUS
COTES-DU-NORD
COTONEASTER
COTTAGE LOAF
COTTON CANDY
COTTONTAILS
COTYLEDONAL
COUNCIL AREA
COUNCILLORS
COUNSELLING
COUNSELLORS
COUNTENANCE
COUNTERFEIT
COUNTERFOIL
COUNTERMAND
COUNTERMINE

COUNTERMOVE
COUNTERPANE
COUNTERPART
COUNTERPLOT
COUNTERSANK
COUNTERSIGN
COUNTERSINK
COUNTERSUNK
COUNTERTYPE
COUNTERVAIL
COUNTERWORD
COUNTERWORK
COUNTIFIED
COUNTRY CLUB
COUNTRY SEAT
COUNTRYSIDE
COUNTY COURT
COUNTY TOWNS
COUP DE GRACE
COURTEOUSLY
COURTHOUSES
COURTLINESS
COVENANTING
COVER CHARGE
COWCATCHERS
CRABBEDNESS
CRACKERJACK
CRANBERRIES
CRANIOMETER
CRANIOMETRY
CRANKSHAFTS
CRASH COURSE
CRASH-DIVING
CRASH HELMET
CRASH-LANDED
CRAZY PAVING
CREAM CHEESE
CREDENTIALS
CREDIBILITY
CREDIT CARDS
CREDIT NOTES
CREDULOUSLY
CREMATORIUM
CRENELLATED
CRENULATION
CREOPHAGOUS
CREPITATION
CREPUSCULAR
CRESTFALLEN
CRIMINALITY
CRIMINOLOGY

CRINKLEROOT
CRINKLINESS
CRITICIZING
CROCIDOLITE
CROCODILIAN
CROOKEDNESS
CROP-DUSTING
CROSSBREEDS
CROSS-GARNET
CROSS-LEGGED
CROSSPIECES
CROSS-STITCH
CROWDEDNESS
CROWN COLONY
CROWN COURTS
CROWNED HEAD
CROWN JEWELS
CROWN PRINCE
CRUCIFEROUS
CRUCIFIXION
CRUNCHINESS
CRUSTACEANS
CRUSTACEOUS
CRYOBIOLOGY
CRYOHYDRATE
CRYOSURGERY
CRYOTHERAPY
CRYPTICALLY
CRYPTOGAMIC
CRYPTOGENIC
CRYPTOGRAPH
CRYPTOZOITE
CRYSTAL BALL
CRYSTALLINE
CRYSTALLITE
CRYSTALLIZE
CRYSTALLOID
CRYSTAL SETS
CTENOPHORAN
CUCKOO CLOCK
CULMIFEROUS
CULMINATION
CULPABILITY
CULTIVATING
CULTIVATION
CULTIVATORS
CUMMERBUNDS
CUNNILINGUS
CUPELLATION
CUPRIFEROUS
CUPRONICKEL

CURATORSHIP
CURIOSITIES
CURIOUSNESS
CURMUDGEONS
CURRICULUMS
CURRY POWDER
CURTAILMENT
CURTAIN CALL
CURVILINEAR
CUSPIDATION
CUSTARD PIES
CUSTOMARILY
CUSTOM-BUILT
CUSTOMIZING
CUT-AND-DRIED
CUTTING EDGE
CYANIDATION
CYANOHYDRIN
CYBERNATION
CYBERNETICS
CYBERPHOBIA
CYCADACEOUS
CYCLOALKANE
CYCLOHEXANE
CYCLOPLEGIA
CYCLOSPORIN
CYCLOSTYLED
CYCLOTHYMIA
CYCLOTHYMIC
CYLINDRICAL
CYPERACEOUS
CYPRINODONT
CYPRIPEDIUM
CYSTICERCUS
CYSTOCARPIC
CYSTOSCOPIC
CYTOGENESIS
CYTOKINESIS
CYTOLOGICAL
CYTOLOGISTS
CYTOPLASMIC
CZESTOCHOWA

D

DACTYLOLOGY
DAGGERBOARD
DAIL EIREANN
DAIRY CATTLE
DAIRY FARMER
DAISY WHEELS
DAMAN AND DIU

DAMNABILITY
DAMP COURSES
DANGER MONEY
DANGEROUSLY
DAPPLE-GREYS
DARDANELLES
DAREDEVILRY
DAR ES SALAAM
DATABLENESS
DAUNTLESSLY
DAWSON CREEK
DAYDREAMERS
DAYDREAMING
DEACCESSION
DEACTIVATOR
DEAD LETTERS
DEAD MARCHES
DEAD RINGERS
DEAD SOLDIER
DEAF-AND-DUMB
DEALERSHIPS
DEAMINATION
DEATH DUTIES
DEATHLESSLY
DEATHLINESS
DEATH RATTLE
DEATH'S-HEADS
DEATH SQUADS
DEATTRIBUTE
DEBARKATION
DEBASEDNESS
DEBASEMENTS
DEBILITATED
DEBOUCHMENT
DEBRIDEMENT
DECALCIFIER
DECALESCENT
DECANEDIOIC
DECAPITATED
DECAPITATOR
DECARBONIZE
DECEITFULLY
DECELERATED
DECELERATOR
DECEPTIVELY
DECEREBRATE
DECILLIONTH
DECIMALIZED
DECIPHERING
DECKLE-EDGED
DECLAMATION

DECLAMATORY
DECLARATION
DECLARATIVE
DECLARATORY
DECLENSIONS
DECLINATION
DECLINATORY
DECLIVITIES
DECLIVITOUS
DECOLLATION
DECOLLETAGE
DECOLONIZED
DECOMPOSING
DECORATIONS
DECORTICATE
DECREPITATE
DECREPITUDE
DECRESCENCE
DECRETALIST
DECUSSATION
DEDICATEDLY
DEDICATIONS
DEDUCTIVELY
DEEP FREEZES
DEERSTALKER
DE-ESCALATED
DEFALCATION
DEFECTIVELY
DEFENCELESS
DEFENSIVELY
DEFERENTIAL
DEFICIENTLY
DEFINIENDUM
DEFINITIONS
DEFLECTIONS
DEFLORATION
DEFLOWERING
DEFOLIATING
DEFOLIATION
DEFORCEMENT
DEFORESTING
DEFORMATION
DEFORMITIES
DEFRAUDMENT
DEGENERATED
DEGENERATES
DEGLUTINATE
DEGLUTITION
DEGRADATION
DEHUMANIZED
DEHYDRATING

DEHYDRATION
DEICTICALLY
DEIFICATION
DELECTATION
DELEGATIONS
DELETERIOUS
DELIBERATED
DELIBERATOR
DELICIOUSLY
DELINEATING
DELINEATION
DELINEATIVE
DELINQUENCY
DELINQUENTS
DELIRIOUSLY
DELITESCENT
DELIVERABLE
DELIVERANCE
DELIVERYMAN
DELIVERYMEN
DELPHINIUMS
DEMAGNETIZE
DEMAGOGUERY
DEMARCATING
DEMARCATION
DEMOCRACIES
DEMOCRATIZE
DEMODULATOR
DEMOGRAPHER
DEMOGRAPHIC
DEMOLISHING
DEMOLITIONS
DEMONETIZED
DEMONICALLY
DEMONOLATER
DEMONOLATRY
DEMONSTRATE
DEMORALIZER
DEMOTIVATED
DEMOUNTABLE
DEMULSIFIER
DEMUTUALIZE
DEMYSTIFIED
DENIGRATING
DENIGRATION
DENITRATION
DENOMINABLE
DENOMINATED
DENOMINATOR
DENOTATIONS
DENOUEMENTS

DENSIMETRIC
DENTAL FLOSS
DENTAL PLATE
DENTICULATE
DENTILABIAL
DENUMERABLE
DENUNCIATOR
DEODORIZING
DEOXYGENATE
DEOXYRIBOSE
DEPARTMENTS
DEPLORINGLY
DEPLUMATION
DEPOLARIZER
DEPOPULATED
DEPORTATION
DEPOSITIONS
DEPRAVATION
DEPRAVITIES
DEPRECATING
DEPRECATION
DEPRECATIVE
DEPRECATORY
DEPRECIABLE
DEPRECIATED
DEPRECIATOR
DEPREDATION
DEPRESSIBLE
DEPRESSIONS
DEPRIVATION
DEPUTATIONS
DERAILMENTS
DERANGEMENT
DERECOGNIZE
DEREGULATED
DERELICTION
DERIVATIONS
DERIVATIVES
DERMATOLOGY
DESALINATED
DESCENDABLE
DESCENDANTS
DESCENDIBLE
DESCRIBABLE
DESCRIPTION
DESCRIPTIVE
DESECRATING
DESECRATION
DESEGREGATE
DESENSITIZE
DESERVINGLY

DESEXUALIZE	DIACRITICAL	DIMENSIONAL	DISBELIEVED
DESICCATING	DIADELPHOUS	DIMERCAPROL	DISBELIEVER
DESICCATION	DIAGNOSABLE	DIMIDIATION	DISBURSABLE
DESICCATIVE	DIAGNOSTICS	DIMINISHING	DISCERNIBLE
DESIDERATUM	DIALECTICAL	DIMINUENDOS	DISCERNIBLY
DESIGNATING	DIALOGISTIC	DIMINUTIONS	DISCERNMENT
DESIGNATION	DIALYSATION	DIMINUTIVES	DISCHARGING
DESIGNATIVE	DIAMAGNETIC	DINING ROOMS	DISC HARROWS
DESPATCHING	DIAMONDBACK	DINING TABLE	DISCIPLINAL
DESPERADOES	DIAPHORESIS	DINNER BELLS	DISCIPLINED
DESPERATELY	DIAPHORETIC	DINNER TABLE	DISCIPLINER
DESPERATION	DIAPOPHYSIS	DINOSAURIAN	DISCIPLINES
DESPOILMENT	DIARTHROSIS	DIOPTOMETER	DISC JOCKEYS
DESPONDENCY	DIASTROPHIC	DIOPTOMETRY	DISCLAIMERS
DESPUMATION	DIATESSARON	DIPHOSPHATE	DISCLAIMING
DESSERT WINE	DIATOMICITY	DIPHTHEROID	DISCLOSURES
DESTABILIZE	DIATONICISM	DIPHTHONGAL	DISCOGRAPHY
DESTINATION	DICEPHALISM	DIPHYCERCAL	DISCOLOURED
DESTITUTION	DICEPHALOUS	DIPLOCOCCAL	DISCOMFITED
DESTROYABLE	DICHOGAMOUS	DIPLOCOCCUS	DISCOMFITER
DESTRUCTION	DICHOTOMIES	DIPLOMATIST	DISCOMFORTS
DESTRUCTIVE	DICHOTOMIST	DIPROTODONT	DISCOMMODED
DESULTORILY	DICHOTOMIZE	DIPSOMANIAC	DISCOMPOSED
DETACHMENTS	DICHOTOMOUS	DIPSWITCHES	DISCONTINUE
DETERIORATE	DICHROMATIC	DIRECT DEBIT	DISCORDANCE
DETERMINANT	DICHROSCOPE	DIRECTIONAL	DISCOTHEQUE
DETERMINATE	DICOTYLEDON	DIRECTORATE	DISCOUNTING
DETERMINERS	DICTAPHONES	DIRECTORIAL	DISCOURAGED
DETERMINING	DICTATIONAL	DIRECTORIES	DISCOURAGER
DETERMINISM	DICTATORIAL	DIRECT TAXES	DISCOURSING
DETERMINIST	DIDACTICISM	DIRT FARMERS	DISCOURTESY
DETESTATION	DIE-CASTINGS	DIRTY OLD MAN	DISCOVERERS
DETONATIONS	DIFFERENCES	DIRTY OLD MEN	DISCOVERIES
DETRAINMENT	DIFFERENTIA	DIRTY TRICKS	DISCOVERING
DETRIBALIZE	DIFFERENTLY	DISABLEMENT	DISCREDITED
DETRIMENTAL	DIFFIDENTLY	DISACCREDIT	DISCREPANCY
DEUTERANOPE	DIFFRACTING	DISACCUSTOM	DISCUSSIBLE
DEUTEROGAMY	DIFFRACTION	DISAFFECTED	DISCUSSIONS
DEUTSCHMARK	DIFFRACTIVE	DISAFFOREST	DISEMBARKED
DEVALUATION	DIFFUSENESS	DISAGREEING	DISEMBODIED
DEVASTATING	DIFFUSIVITY	DISALLOWING	DISENCUMBER
DEVASTATION	DIGESTIONAL	DISAPPEARED	DISENGAGING
DEVASTATIVE	DIGITIGRADE	DISAPPROVAL	DISENTANGLE
DEVELOPABLE	DIGNITARIES	DISAPPROVED	DISENTHRALL
DEVELOPMENT	DIGRESSIONS	DISAPPROVER	DISFIGURING
DEVIOUSNESS	DIHYBRIDISM	DISARMAMENT	DISFORESTED
DEVITALIZED	DILAPIDATED	DISARRANGED	DISGRACEFUL
DEVOLVEMENT	DILAPIDATOR	DISASSEMBLE	DISGRUNTLED
DEVOTEDNESS	DILATOMETER	DISASSEMBLY	DISGUISABLE
DEVOURINGLY	DILATOMETRY	DISAVOWEDLY	DISGUSTEDLY
DEXTEROUSLY	DILETTANTES	DISBANDMENT	DISHEVELLED

DISHONESTLY	DISSEMINATE	DIVERSIFORM	DOUBLE-SPACE
DISHONOURED	DISSEMINULE	DIVERSIONAL	DOUBLESPEAK
DISHONOURER	DISSENSIONS	DIVERTINGLY	DOUBLE TAKES
DISHWASHERS	DISSENTIENT	DIVESTITURE	DOUBLETHINK
DISILLUSION	DISSENTIOUS	DIVINATIONS	DOUROUCOULI
DISILLUSIVE	DISSEPIMENT	DIVINE RIGHT	DOVETAILING
DISINCLINED	DISSIMILATE	DIVING BELLS	DOWN-AND-OUTS
DISINFECTED	DISSIMULATE	DIVINGBOARD	DOWNGRADING
DISINFECTOR	DISSIPATING	DIVISIONISM	DOWNHEARTED
DISINTEREST	DISSIPATION	DIVISIONIST	DOWNLOADING
DISINTERRED	DISSIPATIVE	DIVORCEABLE	DOWNPATRICK
DISJOINABLE	DISSOCIABLE	DIVORCEMENT	DOWN PAYMENT
DISJUNCTION	DISSOCIATED	DOCTRINAIRE	DOWNPLAYING
DISJUNCTIVE	DISSOLUTELY	DOCUMENTARY	DOWN-TO-EARTH
DISJUNCTURE	DISSOLUTION	DOCUMENTING	DOWNTRODDEN
DISLOCATING	DISSOLUTIVE	DODDERINGLY	DOXOLOGICAL
DISLOCATION	DISSOLVABLE	DODECAGONAL	DRAGONFLIES
DISLODGMENT	DISSONANCES	DODECAPHONY	DRAMATIZING
DISMANTLING	DISSUADABLE	DOGBERRYISM	DRAMATURGIC
DISMASTMENT	DISSYLLABIC	DOG BISCUITS	DRASTICALLY
DISMEMBERED	DISSYLLABLE	DOGCATCHERS	DRAUGHTSMAN
DISMEMBERER	DISSYMMETRY	DOLABRIFORM	DRAUGHTSMEN
DISMISSIBLE	DISTASTEFUL	DOLEFULNESS	DRAWBRIDGES
DISMOUNTING	DISTEMPERED	DOLL'S HOUSES	DRAWING PINS
DISOBEDIENT	DISTENSIBLE	DOLORIMETRY	DRAWING ROOM
DISOBLIGING	DISTILLABLE	DOMESTICATE	DRAWSTRINGS
DISORDERING	DISTINCTION	DOMESTICITY	DREADNOUGHT
DISORGANIZE	DISTINCTIVE	DOMICILIARY	DREAMLESSLY
DISPARAGING	DISTINGUISH	DOMICILIATE	DREAM TICKET
DISPARATELY	DISTORTIONS	DOMINEERING	DREAM WORLDS
DISPARITIES	DISTRACTING	DOORKEEPERS	DRESS CIRCLE
DISPATCH BOX	DISTRACTION	DOORKNOCKER	DRESSMAKERS
DISPATCHING	DISTRACTIVE	DOORSTOPPER	DRESSMAKING
DISPENSABLE	DISTRAINING	DORMITORIES	DRILLMASTER
DISPIRITING	DISTRESSFUL	DOTTED LINES	DROMEDARIES
DISPLEASING	DISTRESSING	DOUBLE AGENT	DRUNKENNESS
DISPLEASURE	DISTRIBUTED	DOUBLE BINDS	DRY CLEANERS
DISPOSITION	DISTRIBUTOR	DOUBLE-BLIND	DRY-CLEANING
DISPROVABLE	DISTRUSTFUL	DOUBLE BLUFF	DSCONTINUER
DISPUTATION	DISTRUSTING	DOUBLE-CHECK	DUAL-PURPOSE
DISQUIETING	DISTURBANCE	DOUBLE CHINS	DUBIOUSNESS
DISQUIETUDE	DISULPHURIC	DOUBLE CREAM	DUDE RANCHES
DISREGARDED	DITHYRAMBIC	DOUBLE-CROSS	DUFFEL COATS
DISREGARDER	DITTOGRAPHY	DOUBLE DATED	DUMBFOUNDED
DISRELISHED	DIVARICATOR	DOUBLE DATES	DUMBFOUNDER
DISROBEMENT	DIVE-BOMBERS	DOUBLE-DUTCH	DUMBWAITERS
DISRUPTIONS	DIVE-BOMBING	DOUBLE-EDGED	DUNDERHEADS
DISSECTIBLE	DIVERGENCES	DOUBLE-FACED	DUNE BUGGIES
DISSECTIONS	DIVERGENTLY	DOUBLE FAULT	DUNFERMLINE
DISSEMBLERS	DIVERSIFIED	DOUBLE-GLAZE	DUPLEX HOUSE
DISSEMBLING	DIVERSIFIER	DOUBLE-QUICK	DUPLICATING

DUPLICATION
DUPLICATIVE
DUPLICATORS
DUST JACKETS
DUTCH TREATS
DUTCH UNCLES
DUTIABILITY
DUTIFULNESS
DYNAMICALLY
DYNAMOMETER
DYNAMOMETRY
DYSFUNCTION
DYSFUNCTION

E

EAGER BEAVER
EARNESTNESS
EARTHENWARE
EARTH-GRAZER
EARTHLINESS
EARTHQUAKES
EAR TRUMPETS
EASEFULNESS
EAST ANGLIAN
EASTERN CAPE
EASTERNMOST
EAST GERMANY
EAST LOTHIAN
EATING APPLE
EBULLIENTLY
ECCLESIARCH
ECCRINOLOGY
ECHCHYMOSED
ECHOPRACTIC
ECLECTICISM
ECOFRIENDLY
ECONOMETRIC
ECONOMIZING
ECOSPECIFIC
ECTOBLASTIC
ECTOGENESIS
ECTOMORPHIC
ECTOPLASMIC
ECTOSARCOUS
EDAPHICALLY
EDIFICATION
EDIFICATORY
EDITORIALLY
EDUCABILITY
EDUCATIONAL
EFFECTIVELY

EFFECTUALLY
EFFECTUATED
EFFERVESCED
EFFICACIOUS
EFFICIENTLY
EGALITARIAN
EGOCENTRISM
EGOMANIACAL
EGOTISTICAL
EGREGIOUSLY
EIDETICALLY
EIFFEL TOWER
EIGHTEENTHS
EINSTEINIAN
EINSTEINIUM
EISTEDDFODS
EJACULATING
EJACULATION
EJACULATIVE
EJACULATORY
EJECTOR SEAT
ELABORATELY
ELABORATING
ELABORATION
ELABORATIVE
ELASTICALLY
ELASTIC BAND
ELASTOMERIC
ELASTOPLAST
ELBOW GREASE
ELDERFLOWER
ELECTIONEER
ELECTORATES
ELECTORSHIP
ELECTRIC EYE
ELECTRICIAN
ELECTRICITY
ELECTRIFIED
ELECTRIFIER
ELECTROCUTE
ELECTROFORM
ELECTROLYSE
ELECTROLYTE
ELECTRONICS
ELECTROTYPE
ELEGIACALLY
ELEPHANTINE
ELEPHANTOID
ELICITATION
ELIGIBILITY
ELIMINATING

ELIMINATION
ELIMINATIVE
ELIZABETHAN
ELLIPSOIDAL
ELLIPTICITY
ELONGATIONS
ELUCIDATING
ELUCIDATION
ELUCIDATIVE
ELUCIDATORY
ELUSIVENESS
ELUTRIATION
EMANATIONAL
EMANCIPATED
EMANCIPATOR
EMASCULATED
EMASCULATOR
EMBANKMENTS
EMBARKATION
EMBARRASSED
EMBELLISHED
EMBELLISHER
EMBITTERING
EMBLAZONING
EMBLEMATIZE
EMBOLDENING
EMBOLECTOMY
EMBRACEABLE
EMBRACEMENT
EMBROCATION
EMBROIDERED
EMBROIDERER
EMBROILMENT
EMBRYECTOMY
EMBRYOGENIC
EMENDATIONS
EMERGENCIES
EMIGRATIONS
EMMENAGOGIC
EMMENAGOGUE
EMOTIONALLY
EMOTIONLESS
EMOTIVENESS
EMPANELLING
EMPANELMENT
EMPERORSHIP
EMPHASIZING
EMPIRICALLY
EMPLACEMENT
EMPLOYMENTS
EMPOWERMENT

EMPTY-HANDED
EMPTY-HEADED
EMULOUSNESS
EMULSIFYING
EMULSIONING
ENARTHROSIS
ENCAMPMENTS
ENCAPSULATE
ENCEPHALOMA
ENCEPHALOUS
ENCHAINMENT
ENCHANTMENT
ENCHANTRESS
ENCHONDROMA
ENCOMIASTIC
ENCOMPASSED
ENCOUNTERED
ENCOUNTERER
ENCOURAGING
ENCROACHING
ENCUMBERING
ENCUMBRANCE
ENCYCLICALS
ENDANGERING
ENDEARINGLY
ENDEARMENTS
ENDEAVOURED
ENDEAVOURER
ENDEMICALLY
ENDLESSNESS
ENDOBLASTIC
ENDOCARDIAL
ENDOCARDIUM
ENDOCENTRIC
ENDOCRANIUM
ENDOCRINOUS
ENDODONTICS
ENDODONTIST
ENDOMETRIAL
ENDOMETRIUM
ENDOMORPHIC
ENDONEURIUM
ENDOPLASMIC
ENDORSEMENT
ENDOSCOPIST
ENDOSPERMIC
ENDOSPOROUS
ENDOTHECIAL
ENDOTHECIUM
ENDOTHELIAL
ENDOTHELIUM

ENDOTHERMIC
END PRODUCTS
ENFORCEABLE
ENFORCEMENT
ENFRANCHISE
ENGAGEMENTS
ENGENDERING
ENGINEERING
ENGLISH HORN
ENGORGEMENT
ENGRAILMENT
ENGROSSEDLY
ENGROSSMENT
ENHANCEMENT
ENLARGEABLE
ENLARGEMENT
ENLIGHTENED
ENLIGHTENER
ENLISTED MAN
ENLISTED MEN
ENLISTMENTS
ENLIVENMENT
ENNEAHEDRAL
ENNEAHEDRON
ENNISKILLEN
ENNOBLEMENT
ENNOBLINGLY
ENRAPTURING
ENSHROUDING
ENSLAVEMENT
ENSNAREMENT
ENTABLATURE
ENTABLEMENT
ENTEROSTOMY
ENTEROVIRUS
ENTERPRISER
ENTERPRISES
ENTERTAINED
ENTERTAINER
ENTHRALLING
ENTHRALMENT
ENTHUSIASMS
ENTHUSIASTS
ENTICEMENTS
ENTITLEMENT
ENTOBLASTIC
ENTOMBMENTS
ENTOMOPHILY
ENTRAINMENT
ENTREATMENT
ENTRENCHING

ENTRUSTMENT
ENTWINEMENT
ENUCLEATION
ENUMERATING
ENUMERATION
ENUMERATIVE
ENUNCIATING
ENUNCIATION
ENUNCIATIVE
ENVELOPMENT
ENVIOUSNESS
ENVIRONMENT
ENZYMOLYSIS
ENZYMOLYTIC
EPHEMERALLY
EPIDERMISES
EPIDIASCOPE
EPIGASTRIUM
EPIGENESIST
EPIGRAPHIST
EPIPHYTOTIC
EPITHALAMIC
EPITHELIOMA
EPITOMIZING
EPOCH-MAKING
EQUIANGULAR
EQUIDISTANT
EQUILATERAL
EQUILIBRANT
EQUILIBRATE
EQUILIBRIST
EQUILIBRIUM
EQUINOCTIAL
EQUIPOLLENT
EQUIVALENCE
EQUIVALENCY
EQUIVALENTS
EQUIVOCALLY
EQUIVOCATED
ERADICATING
ERADICATION
ERADICATIVE
ERADICATORS
ERASTIANISM
ERGATOCRACY
EROSIVENESS
EROTOMANIAC
ERRATICALLY
ERRONEOUSLY
ERUBESCENCE
ERUCTATIONS

ERYSIPELOID
ERYTHEMATIC
ERYTHRISMAL
ERYTHROCYTE
ESCAPEMENTS
ESCAPE WHEEL
ESCARPMENTS
ESCHATOLOGY
ESCUTCHEONS
ESEMPLASTIC
ESOPHAGUSES
ESOTERICISM
ESSENTIALLY
ESTABLISHED
ESTABLISHER
ESTATE AGENT
ESTREMADURA
ETHANEDIOIC
ETHEREALITY
ETHEREALIZE
ETHICALNESS
ETHNOBOTANY
ETHNOGENIST
ETHNOGRAPHY
ETHNOLOGIST
ETIOLOGICAL
ETYMOLOGIES
ETYMOLOGIST
EUCHARISTIC
EUCHROMATIC
EUCHROMATIN
EUDIOMETRIC
EUGENICALLY
EUPHEMISTIC
EURHYTHMICS
EUROCENTRIC
EUROCHEQUES
EURODOLLARS
EUROPEANISM
EUROPEANIZE
EURO-SCEPTIC
EURYTHERMAL
EVACUATIONS
EVAGINATION
EVALUATIONS
EVANESCENCE
EVANGELICAL
EVANGELISTS
EVANGELIZED
EVANGELIZER
EVAPORATING

EVAPORATION
EVAPORATIVE
EVASIVENESS
EVENING STAR
EVENTUALITY
EVENTUATION
EVERLASTING
EVISCERATED
EVISCERATOR
EXACERBATED
EXAGGERATED
EXAGGERATOR
EXALTEDNESS
EXAMINATION
EXAMINATION
FXASPERATED
EXASPERATER
EXCAVATIONS
EXCEEDINGLY
EXCELLENTLY
EXCEPTIONAL
EXCERPTIBLE
EXCERPTTION
EXCESSIVELY
EXCITEDNESS
EXCITEMENTS
EXCLAMATION
EXCLAMATORY
EXCLUSIVELY
EXCOGITATOR
EXCORIATING
EXCORIATION
EXCREMENTAL
EXCRESCENCE
EXCRESCENCY
EXCULPATING
EXCULPATION
EXCULPATORY
EX-DIRECTORY
EXECRATIONS
EXECUTIONER
EXECUTORIAL
EXEMPLARILY
EXEMPLIFIED
EXEMPLIFIER
EXERCISABLE
EXFOLIATION
EXFOLIATIVE
EXHAUSTIBLE
EXHIBITIONS
EXHILARATED

EXHILARATOR
EXHORTATION
EXHORTATIVE
EXHUMATIONS
EXISTENTIAL
EXONERATING
EXONERATION
EXONERATIVE
EXORABILITY
EXORBITANCE
EXOSKELETAL
EXOSKELETON
EXOTERICISM
EXPANSIVELY
EXPATIATING
EXPATIATION
EXPATRIATED
EXPATRIATES
EXPECTANTLY
EXPECTATION
EXPECTATIVE
EXPECTORANT
EXPECTORATE
EXPEDIENTLY
EXPEDITIONS
EXPEDITIOUS
EXPENDITURE
EXPENSIVELY
EXPERIENCED
EXPERIENCES
EXPERIMENTS
EXPLAINABLE
EXPLANATION
EXPLANATORY
EXPLICATING
EXPLICATION
EXPLICATIVE
EXPLOITABLE
EXPLORATION
EXPLORATORY
EXPLOSIVELY
EXPONENTIAL
EXPORTATION
EXPOSEDNESS
EXPOSITIONS
EX POST FACTO
EXPOSTULATE
EXPRESSIBLE
EXPRESSIONS
EXPRESSWAYS
EXPROPRIATE

EXPURGATING
EXPURGATION
EXPURGATORY
EXQUISITELY
EXSICCATION
EXSICCATIVE
EXSTIPULATE
EXTEMPORIZE
EXTENSIONAL
EXTENSIVELY
EXTENUATING
EXTENUATION
EXTENUATORY
EXTERIORIZE
EXTERMINATE
EXTERNALISM
EXTERNALIST
EXTERNALITY
EXTERNALIZE
EXTIRPATING
EXTIRPATION
EXTIRPATIVE
EXTOLLINGLY
EXTRACTABLE
EXTRACTIONS
EXTRADITING
EXTRADITION
EXTRAPOLATE
EXTRAVAGANT
EXTRAVAGATE
EXTRAVASATE
EXTREMENESS
EXTREMITIES
EXTRICATING
EXTRICATION
EXTROVERTED
EXUBERANTLY
EYE-CATCHING

F

FABRICATING
FABRICATION
FABRICATIVE
FACE-CENTRED
FACETIOUSLY
FACILITATED
FACILITATOR
FACT-FINDING
FACTORIZING
FACTORY FARM
FACTS OF LIFE

FACTUALNESS
FACULTATIVE
FAIRGROUNDS
FAIR-WEATHER
FAIRY LIGHTS
FAITH HEALER
FAITHLESSLY
FALCONIFORM
FALLIBILITY
FALLING STAR
FALSE ALARMS
FALSE BOTTOM
FALSE STARTS
FALSIFIABLE
FALSTAFFIAN
FALTERINGLY
FAMILIARITY
FAMILIARIZE
FAMILY NAMES
FAMILY TREES
FANATICALLY
FANTASIZING
FARCICALITY
FARINACEOUS
FARNBOROUGH
FARRAGINOUS
FAR-REACHING
FARTHERMOST
FARTHINGALE
FASCINATING
FASCINATION
FASCINATIVE
FASHIONABLE
FAST-BREEDER
FAST-FORWARD
FATEFULNESS
FATHER-IN-LAW
FATHERLANDS
FATUOUSNESS
FAULT-FINDER
FAULTLESSLY
FAVOURINGLY
FAVOURITISM
FAWNINGNESS
FEARFULNESS
FEASIBILITY
FEATHER BEDS
FEATHER BOAS
FEATHEREDGE
FEATURE FILM
FEATURELESS

FECUNDATION
FECUNDATORY
FEDERALISTS
FEDERATIONS
FELDSPATHIC
FELICITATED
FELICITATOR
FELLOWSHIPS
FELT-TIP PENS
FEMME FATALE
FENESTRATED
FERMENTABLE
FEROCIOUSLY
FERRICYANIC
FERRIFEROUS
FERRIS WHEEL
FERROCYANIC
FERRUGINOUS
FERTILIZERS
FERTILIZING
FERULACEOUS
FERVENTNESS
FESTINATION
FESTSCHRIFT
FETISHISTIC
FEUDALISTIC
FIBRE OPTICS
FIBROMATOUS
FIBROUSNESS
FICTIONALLY
FIDGETINGLY
FIELD-EFFECT
FIELD EVENTS
FIELD HOCKEY
FIELD-HOLLER
FIELD-TESTED
FIELDWORKER
FIFTH COLUMN
FIFTH-DEGREE
FIGURED BASS
FIGUREHEADS
FILAMENTARY
FILIBUSTERS
FILL THE BILL
FILMOGRAPHY
FILMSETTING
FILTHY LUCRE
FILTRATABLE
FIMBRIATION
FINANCIALLY
FIN DE SIECLE

FINE-GRAINED	FLEET STREET	FOOT FAULTED	FORMULATION
FINES HERBES	FLESHLINESS	FOOT-LAMBERT	FORMULISTIC
FINGERBOARD	FLESH WOUNDS	FOOT-POUNDAL	FORNICATING
FINGER BOWLS	FLETCHERISM	FOOTSLOGGED	FORNICATION
FINGERNAILS	FLEURS-DE-LIS	FOPPISHNESS	FORSWEARING
FINGERPLATE	FLEXIBILITY	FORAMINIFER	FORTHCOMING
FINGERPRINT	FLICK KNIVES	FORASMUCH AS	FORTIFIABLE
FINGERSTALL	FLIGHT DECKS	FORBEARANCE	FORTNIGHTLY
FIRE BRIGADE	FLIGHTINESS	FORBIDDANCE	FORTUNATELY
FIRECRACKER	FLIGHT PATHS	FOREBODINGS	FORT WILLIAM
FIRE ENGINES	FLINCHINGLY	FORECASTERS	FORWARDNESS
FIRE ESCAPES	FLIRTATIONS	FORECASTING	FOSSILIZING
FIRE FIGHTER	FLIRTATIOUS	FORECLOSING	FOSTERINGLY
FIRE HYDRANT	FLOATATIONS	FORECLOSURE	FOUL-MOUTHED
FIRELIGHTER	FLOCCULENCE	FOREFATHERS	FOUNDATIONS
FIREPROOFED	FLOODLIGHTS	FOREFINGERS	FOUNTAIN PEN
FIRE-RAISERS	FLOORBOARDS	FOREGROUNDS	FOURDRINIER
FIRE-RAISING	FLOOR CLOTHS	FOREMANSHIP	FOUR-POSTERS
FIRE STATION	FLOORWALKER	FOREQUARTER	FOURTEENTHS
FIRING SQUAD	FLOPPY DISKS	FORERUNNERS	FOX TERRIERS
FIRMAMENTAL	FLORESCENCE	FORESEEABLE	FRACTIONARY
FIRST COUSIN	FLORILEGIUM	FORESHORTEN	FRACTIONATE
FIRST-DEGREE	FLOUNDERING	FORESIGHTED	FRACTIONIZE
FIRST-FOOTER	FLOURISHING	FORESTALLED	FRACTIOUSLY
FIRST NATION	FLOWCHARTED	FORESTALLER	FRACTURABLE
FIRST NIGHTS	FLOWER GIRLS	FORESTATION	FRAGMENTARY
FIRST PERSON	FLOWERINESS	FORETELLING	FRAGMENTING
FIRST STRIKE	FLUCTUATING	FORETHOUGHT	FRAME OF MIND
FIRST-STRING	FLUCTUATION	FORE-TOPMAST	FRANCHISING
FISHEYE LENS	FLUID OUNCES	FORE-TOPSAIL	FRANCISCANS
FISH-EYE LENS	FLUORESCEIN	FOR EVERMORE	FRANCOPHILE
FISH FARMING	FLUORESCENT	FOREWARNING	FRANCOPHOBE
FISH FINGERS	FLUORIDATED	FORFEITABLE	FRANCOPHONE
FISHMONGERS	FLUOROMETER	FORGATHERED	FRANKFURTER
FISSIONABLE	FLUOROMETRY	FORGETFULLY	FRANKLINITE
FISSIPAROUS	FLUOROSCOPE	FORGET-ME-NOT	FRANTICALLY
FLABBERGAST	FLUOROSCOPY	FORGETTABLE	FRATERNALLY
FLAGELLANTS	FLYCATCHERS	FORGIVENESS	FRATERNIZED
FLAGELLATED	FLYING BOATS	FORGIVINGLY	FRATERNIZER
FLAMBOYANCE	FLYING FOXES	FORJUDGMENT	FRATRICIDAL
FLANNELETTE	FLYING SQUAD	FORLORN HOPE	FRATRICIDES
FLANNELLING	FLYING START	FORLORNNESS	FRAUDULENCE
FLASHLIGHTS	FLYSWATTERS	FORMALISTIC	FREDERICTON
FLASH POINTS	FOCAL LENGTH	FORMALITIES	FREDRIKSTAD
FLAT-CHESTED	FOLK DANCERS	FORMALIZING	FREEBOOTERS
FLATTERABLE	FOLLICULATE	FORMATIONAL	FREE-FLOATER
FLAUNTINGLY	FOMENTATION	FORMATIVELY	FREE-FOR-ALLS
FLAVOURINGS	FOOLISHNESS	FORMICATION	FREE-HEARTED
FLAVOURLESS	FOOL'S ERRAND	FORMULAICLY	FREEHOLDERS
FLAVOURSOME	FOOTBALLERS	FORMULARIZE	FREELANCING
FLEA MARKETS	FOOTBRIDGES	FORMULATING	FREELOADERS

FREELOADING
FREEMASONIC
FREEMASONRY
FREE PARDONS
FREE-SWIMMER
FREETHINKER
FREEWHEELED
FREEZE-DRIED
FRENCH BEANS
FRENCH BREAD
FRENCH DOORS
FRENCH FRIES
FRENCH HORNS
FRENCH LEAVE
FRENCH TOAST
FRENCHWOMAN
FREQUENCIES
FREQUENTING
FRETFULNESS
FREUDIANISM
FRIENDLIEST
FRIENDSHIPS
FRIGHTENING
FRIGHTFULLY
FRINGILLINE
FRIVOLITIES
FRIVOLOUSLY
FROGMARCHED
FRONDESCENT
FRONTOLYSIS
FRONT-RUNNER
FROSTBITTEN
FRUCTIFYING
FRUGIVOROUS
FRUITLESSLY
FRUIT SALADS
FRUSTRATING
FRUSTRATION
FRUTESCENCE
FULGURATING
FULGURATION
FULL-BLOODED
FULL-FLEDGED
FULL-MOUTHED
FULMINATING
FULMINATION
FULMINATORY
FULSOMENESS
FUNAMBULIST
FUN AND GAMES
FUNCTIONARY

FUNCTIONING
FUNDAMENTAL
FUNDHOLDING
FUNGIBILITY
FUNGISTATIC
FURALDEHYDE
FURIOUSNESS
FURNISHINGS
FURTHERANCE
FURTHERMORE
FURTHERMOST
FURTIVENESS

G
GAFF-TOPSAIL
GAINFULNESS
GALLANTNESS
GALLANTRIES
GALL BLADDER
GALLINACEAN
GALLIVANTED
GALLUP POLLS
GALVANIZING
GAMEKEEPERS
GAMEKEEPING
GAMETANGIAL
GAMETANGIUM
GAMETOGENIC
GAMETOPHORE
GAMETOPHYTE
GAMOGENESIS
GAMOGENETIC
GANG-BANGING
GARAGE SALES
GARBAGE CANS
GARDEN PARTY
GARNISHMENT
GARRISONING
GARRULOUSLY
GASEOUSNESS
GAS STATIONS
GASTRECTOMY
GASTRONOMES
GASTRONOMIC
GASTROPODAN
GASTROSCOPE
GASTROSCOPY
GASTROSTOMY
GASTROTRICH
GAS TURBINES
GATECRASHED

GATECRASHER
GATEKEEPERS
GEANTICLINE
GEGENSCHEIN
GELATINIZER
GEMMIPAROUS
GEMMULATION
GEMOLOGICAL
GENDARMERIE
GENEALOGIES
GENEALOGIST
GENE LIBRARY
GENERALIZED
GENERALIZER
GENERALNESS
GENERALSHIP
GENERATIONS
GENERATION X
GENERICALLY
GENETICALLY
GENETIC CODE
GENETICISTS
GENTEELNESS
GENTIANELLA
GENTLEMANLY
GENTLEWOMAN
GENTLEWOMEN
GENTRIFYING
GENUFLECTED
GENUFLECTOR
GENUINENESS
GEOCHEMICAL
GEODYNAMICS
GEOGRAPHERS
GEOGRAPHIES
GEOMAGNETIC
GEOPHYSICAL
GEOPOLITICS
GEOSTRATEGY
GEOSTROPHIC
GEOSYNCLINE
GEOTECTONIC
GERATOLOGIC
GERMANENESS
GERMINATING
GERMINATION
GERM WARFARE
GERONTOLOGY
GERRYMANDER
GESTATIONAL
GESTICULATE

GET CRACKING
GET-TOGETHER
GHASTLINESS
GHOSTBUSTER
GHOSTLINESS
GHOSTWRITER
GIANT KILLER
GIANT PANDAS
GIBBERELLIN
GIBBOUSNESS
GIFT-WRAPPED
GIGANTESQUE
GILA MONSTER
GILLYFLOWER
GINGER BEERS
GINGERBREAD
GINGER GROUP
GIRL FRIDAYS
GIRLFRIENDS
GIRLISHNESS
GIVE-AND-TAKE
GLADIOLUSES
GLAMORIZING
GLAMOROUSLY
GLARINGNESS
GLASSBLOWER
GLASSCUTTER
GLASSHOUSES
GLASS-MAKING
GLASS-WORKER
GLASTONBURY
GLAUCONITIC
GLEEFULNESS
GLOBEFLOWER
GLOBIGERINA
GLOCHIDIATE
GLOMERATION
GLOMERULATE
GLORIFIABLE
GLOSSECTOMY
GLOSSOLALIA
GLOTTAL STOP
GLOVE PUPPET
GLOWERINGLY
GLUE-SNIFFER
GLUTATHIONE
GLYPHOGRAPH
GNATCATCHER
GOALKEEPERS
GOALKEEPING
GO BALLISTIC

GODCHILDREN
GODDAUGHTER
GODFORSAKEN
GODLESSNESS
GOLD-BEATING
GOLD DIGGERS
GOLD-DIGGING
GOLDEN EAGLE
GOLDEN SYRUP
GOLDFINCHES
GOLF COURSES
GONIOMETRIC
GONOCOCCOID
GONORRHOEAL
GOOD EVENING
GOOD LOOKERS
GOOD-LOOKING
GOOD MORNING
GOOD-NATURED
GOOD OFFICES
GORDIAN KNOT
GORMANDIZED
GORMANDIZER
GOSSIPINGLY
GO TO THE DOGS
GOURMANDISE
GOURMANDISM
GOVERNESSES
GOVERNMENTS
GRACELESSLY
GRADABILITY
GRADATIONAL
GRADE SCHOOL
GRADUALNESS
GRADUATIONS
GRAECO-ROMAN
GRAMMARIANS
GRAMMATICAL
GRAMOPHONES
GRANDADDIES
GRAND BAHAMA
GRAND CANARY
GRANDE-TERRE
GRANDFATHER
GRANDIOSITY
GRAND JURIES
GRAND MASTER
GRANDMOTHER
GRAND OPERAS
GRANDPARENT
GRAND PIANOS

GRAND RAPIDS
GRANDSTANDS
GRANGEMOUTH
GRANGERIZER
GRANITEWARE
GRANIVOROUS
GRANNY KNOTS
GRANOLITHIC
GRANOPHYRIC
GRANULARITY
GRANULATION
GRANULATIVE
GRANULOCYTE
GRAPEFRUITS
GRAPHICALLY
GRAPHOLOGIC
GRAPHOMOTOR
GRASSHOPPER
GRASS WIDOWS
GRAVESTONES
GRAVIMETRIC
GRAVITATING
GRAVITATION
GRAVITATIVE
GREASEPAINT
GREASY SPOON
GREAT CIRCLE
GREAT-NEPHEW
GREENBOTTLE
GREENGROCER
GREENHOUSES
GREENLANDER
GREENOCKITE
GREEN PAPERS
GREEN PEPPER
GRETNA GREEN
GRIDDLECAKE
GRIMACINGLY
GRINDELWALD
GRINDSTONES
GRISTLINESS
GRIZZLY BEAR
GROTESQUELY
GROTESQUERY
GROUCHINESS
GROUND CREWS
GROUND FLOOR
GROUND GLASS
GROUNDLINGS
GROUND PLANS
GROUND RENTS

GROUND RULES
GROUNDSHEET
GROUNDSPEED
GROUND STAFF
GROUNDSWELL
GROUPUSCULE
GRUELLINGLY
GRUMBLINGLY
GUADALAJARA
GUADALCANAL
GUARDEDNESS
GUARDHOUSES
GUELDER-ROSE
GUESSTIMATE
GUESTHOUSES
GUEST WORKER
GUILELESSLY
GUILLOTINED
GUILLOTINER
GUILLOTINES
GUILTLESSLY
GULLIBILITY
GUN CARRIAGE
GUNSMITHING
GURGITATION
GUTLESSNESS
GUTTA-PERCHA
GUTTER PRESS
GUTTERSNIPE
GUTTURALIZE
GYNAECOLOGY
GYPSIFEROUS
GYROCOMPASS
GYROSCOPICS
GYROSTATICS

H

HABERDASHER
HABILITATOR
HABITATIONS
HABITUATING
HABITUATION
HABITUDINAL
HADROSAURUS
HAEMACHROME
HAEMATOCELE
HAEMATOCRIT
HAEMATOLOGY
HAEMATOZOON
HAEMOCHROME
HAEMOCYANIN

HAEMOGLOBIN
HAEMOPHILIA
HAEMOPHILIC
HAEMOPTYSIS
HAEMORRHAGE
HAEMOSTASIA
HAEMOSTASIS
HAEMOSTATIC
HAGGADISTIC
HAGGARDNESS
HAGGISHNESS
HAGIOGRAPHA
HAGIOGRAPHY
HAGIOLOGIST
HAGIOSCOPIC
HAIRBREADTH
HAIRBRUSHES
HAIRDRESSER
HAIRPIN BEND
HAIR-RAISING
HAIRSPRINGS
HAIRSTYLIST
HAIR TRIGGER
HAIRWEAVING
HALBERSTADT
HALCYON DAYS
HALF-BROTHER
HALF-CENTURY
HALF-HEARTED
HALF-HOLIDAY
HALFPENNIES
HALF-SISTERS
HALF VOLLEYS
HALLMARKING
HALLUCINATE
HALOPHYTISM
HALTEMPRICE
HALTERNECKS
HALTINGNESS
HAMILTONIAN
HAMMERSMITH
HAMMERSTEIN
HAMMOCK-LIKE
HANDBREADTH
HANDCUFFING
HANDFASTING
HANDICAPPED
HANDICAPPER
HANDICRAFTS
HAND IN GLOVE
HAND LUGGAGE

HANDMAIDENS
HAND-ME-DOWNS
HANDWRITING
HANDWRITTEN
HANG GLIDING
HAPHAZARDLY
HAPLESSNESS
HAPLOGRAPHY
HAPPY EVENTS
HAPPY MEDIUM
HARASSINGLY
HARBOURLESS
HARD-AND-FAST
HARDECANUTE
HARD-HEARTED
HARD-HITTING
HARDICANUTE
HARD PALATES
HARD-PRESSED
HARDWEARING
HARDY ANNUAL
HAREBRAINED
HARMFULNESS
HARMONISTIC
HARMONIZING
HARNESSLESS
HARNESS-LIKE
HARPOON-LIKE
HARPSICHORD
HARRIS TWEED
HARROWINGLY
HARTEBEESTS
HARUM SCARUM
HARUM-SCARUM
HARVEST HOME
HARVESTLESS
HARVEST MOON
HATCHET JOBS
HATCHET-LIKE
HATEFULNESS
HAUGHTINESS
HAUSTELLATE
HAUTES-ALPES
HAUTE-SAVOIE
HAUTE-VIENNE
HAWKISHNESS
HAZARDOUSLY
HEADDRESSES
HEADHUNTERS
HEADHUNTING
HEADMASTERS

HEALTH FOODS
HEALTHFULLY
HEALTHINESS
HEARING AIDS
HEART ATTACK
HEARTBROKEN
HEARTHSTONE
HEARTLESSLY
HEARTSOMELY
HEARTTHROBS
HEAT SHIELDS
HEAVENWARDS
HEAVY-HANDED
HEAVYWEIGHT
HEBDOMADARY
HEBEPHRENIA
HEBEPHRENIC
HEBRAICALLY
HECKELPHONE
HECTOGRAPHY
HEDGEHOPPER
HEEDFULNESS
HEGELIANISM
HEIGHTENING
HEINOUSNESS
HELICHRYSUM
HELICOGRAPH
HELICOPTERS
HELIOCHROME
HELIOGRAPHS
HELIOGRAPHY
HELIOLITHIC
HELIOMETRIC
HELIOSTATIC
HELIOTACTIC
HELIOTROPES
HELIOTROPIC
HELIOTROPIN
HELLEBORINE
HELLENISTIC
HELLISHNESS
HELMINTHOID
HELPFULNESS
HELPING HAND
HELSINGBORG
HEMERALOPIA
HEMERALOPIC
HEMIANOPSIA
HEMIELYTRAL
HEMIELYTRON

HEMIHYDRATE
HEMIMORPHIC
HEMIPTEROUS
HEMISPHERES
HEMISPHERIC
HEMITERPENE
HEMITROPISM
HEMOPHILIAC
HEMORRHAGES
HEMORRHOIDS
HEMSTITCHER
HEPPLEWHITE
HEPTAHEDRAL
HEPTAHEDRON
HEPTAMEROUS
HEPTANGULAR
HEPTAVALENT
HERBIVOROUS
HERCEGOVINA
HERCULANEUM
HEREDITABLE
HEREDITABLY
HEREINAFTER
HERETICALLY
HERMENEUTIC
HERMOUPOLIS
HERO WORSHIP
HERPESVIRUS
HERPETOLOGY
HERRINGBONE
HERZEGOVINA
HESITATIONS
HESPERIDIAN
HESPERIDIUM
HESYCHASTIC
HETAERISTIC
HETEROCLITE
HETEROECISM
HETEROGRAFT
HETEROLYSIS
HETEROLYTIC
HETEROPHONY
HETEROPHYTE
HETEROPOLAR
HETEROSPORY
HETEROSTYLY
HETEROTAXIS
HETEROTOPIA
HETEROTOPIC
HETEROTYPIC
HEXADECIMAL

HEXAGONALLY
HEXAHYDRATE
HEXASTICHIC
HEXASTICHON
HEXATEUCHAL
HIBERNATING
HIBERNATION
HIBERNICISM
HIDE-AND-SEEK
HIDEOUSNESS
HIERARCHIES
HIERARCHISM
HIEROCRATIC
HIEROGLYPHS
HIEROLOGIST
HIGH COMMAND
HIGHFALUTIN
HIGH JUMPERS
HIGHLANDERS
HIGHLIGHTED
HIGHLIGHTER
HIGH-PITCHED
HIGH-POWERED
HIGH PRIESTS
HIGH PROFILE
HIGH-RANKING
HIGH SCHOOLS
HIGH SHERIFF
HIGH-TENSION
HIGH TREASON
HIGHWAY CODE
HIGH WYCOMBE
HILARIOUSLY
HILLBILLIES
HINDERINGLY
HINDQUARTER
HINSHELWOOD
HIPPEASTRUM
HIPPOCAMPAL
HIPPOCAMPUS
HIPPOCRATES
HIPPOCRATIC
HIPPOPOTAMI
HIPPO REGIUS
HIRSUTENESS
HISPANICISM
HISPANICIST
HISPANICIZE
HISTAMINASE
HISTIOCYTIC
HISTOLOGIST

HISTORIATED	HONEYMOONED	HULLABALOOS	ICOSAHEDRON
HISTORICISM	HONEYMOONER	HUMAN RIGHTS	IDENTICALLY
HISTORICIST	HONEYSUCKER	HUMDRUMNESS	IDENTIFYING
HISTORICITY	HONEYSUCKLE	HUMIDIFIERS	IDEOLOGICAL
HISTRIONICS	HONORARIUMS	HUMIDIFYING	IDIOBLASTIC
HITCHHIKERS	HONOURS LIST	HUMILIATING	IDIOGRAPHIC
HITCHHIKING	HOODWINKING	HUMILIATION	IDIOMORPHIC
HOBBLEDEHOY	HOOLIGANISM	HUMILIATIVE	IDIOTICALLY
HOBBYHORSES	HOPEFULNESS	HUMILIATORY	IDOLATRIZER
HOGGISHNESS	HOPLOLOGIST	HUMMINGBIRD	IDOLIZATION
HOLKAR STATE	HORIZONLESS	HUNCHBACKED	IDYLLICALLY
HOLLANDAISE	HORIZONTALS	HUNGER MARCH	IGNIS FATUUS
HOLOBLASTIC	HORNBLENDIC	HUNNISHNESS	IGNOMINIOUS
HOLOCAUSTAL	HORNET'S NEST	HURRIEDNESS	IGNORAMUSES
HOLOGRAPHIC	HORNSWOGGLE	HURTFULNESS	ILE-DE-FRANCE
HOLOHEDRISM	HORROR FILMS	HUSBANDLESS	ILL-ASSORTED
HOLOMORPHIC	HORS D'OEUVRE	HYACINTHINE	ILL-FAVOURED
HOLOTHURIAN	HORSE DOCTOR	HYDNOCARPIC	ILLIBERALLY
HOMECOMINGS	HORSELAUGHS	HYDRARGYRIC	ILLIMITABLE
HOMEOPATHIC	HORSE OPERAS	HYDRARGYRUM	ILL-MANNERED
HOMEOSTASIS	HORSERADISH	HYDROCARBON	ILLOGICALLY
HOMEOSTATIC	HORTATORILY	HYDROCYANIC	ILL-TEMPERED
HOMERICALLY	HOSPITALITY	HYDROGENATE	ILL-TREATING
HOMESTEADER	HOSPITALIZE	HYDROGENIZE	ILLUMINANCE
HOME STRETCH	HOSPITALLER	HYDROGENOUS	ILLUMINATED
HOMICIDALLY	HOSTILITIES	HYDROGRAPHY	ILLUMINATOR
HOMOCENTRIC	HOT-CROSS BUN	HYDROLOGIST	ILLUSIONARY
HOMOEOPATHS	HOTHEADEDLY	HYDROLYSATE	ILLUSIONISM
HOMOEOPATHY	HOT POTATOES	HYDROMANCER	ILLUSIONIST
HOMOEROTISM	HOT-TEMPERED	HYDROMANTIC	ILLUSTRATED
HOMOGENEITY	HOURGLASSES	HYDROMEDUSA	ILLUSTRATOR
HOMOGENEOUS	HOUSE ARREST	HYDROMETEOR	ILLUSTRIOUS
HOMOGENIZED	HOUSEBROKEN	HYDROPHOBIA	ILLUVIATION
HOMOGENIZER	HOUSEFATHER	HYDROPONICS	I'M A DUTCHMAN
HOMOGRAPHIC	HOUSEHOLDER	HYPERACTIVE	IMAGINARILY
HOMOIOUSIAN	HOUSEKEEPER	HYPERMARKET	IMAGINATION
HOMOLOGICAL	HOUSE LIGHTS	HYPHENATING	IMAGINATIVE
HOMOLOGIZER	HOUSEMASTER	HYPHENATION	IMBRICATION
HOMOMORPHIC	HOUSEMOTHER	HYPNOTIZING	IMITABILITY
HOMOPHONOUS	HOUSEPARENT	HYPODERMICS	IMITATIONAL
HOMOPHYLLIC	HOUSEPLANTS	HYPOSTATIZE	IMITATIVELY
HOMOPLASTIC	HOUSEWIFELY	HYPOTHERMIA	IMMEDIATELY
HOMOPTEROUS	HOUSEWIFERY		IMMEDICABLE
HOMO SAPIENS	HOUSEWORKER	**I**	IMMIGRATING
HOMOSEXUALS	HOVERCRAFTS	ICEBREAKERS	IMMIGRATION
HOMOSPOROUS	HOW DO YOU DOS	ICHNOGRAPHY	IMMOBILIZED
HOMOTHALLIC	HSIN-HAI-LIEN	ICHTHYOLOGY	IMMOBILIZER
HOMOTHERMAL	HUCKLEBERRY	ICONOCLASTS	IMMORTALITY
HOMOZYGOSIS	HUCKSTERISM	ICONOGRAPHY	IMMORTALIZE
HOMOZYGOTIC	HUDIBRASTIC	ICONOLOGIST	IMMUNOASSAY
HONEYCOMBED	HUGUENOTISM	ICOSAHEDRAL	IMMUNOGENIC

IMMUNOLOGIC	IMPRECATION	INCOME TAXES	INDIVIDUATE
IMPANELLING	IMPRECATORY	INCOMMODING	INDIVISIBLE
IMPARTATION	IMPRECISION	INCOMPETENT	INDIVISIBLY
IMPARTIALLY	IMPREGNABLE	INCOMPLIANT	INDOCHINESE
IMPASSIONED	IMPREGNABLY	IN CONDITION	INDO-HITTITE
IMPASSIVELY	IMPREGNATED	INCONGRUITY	INDO-IRANIAN
IMPASSIVITY	IMPREGNATOR	INCONGRUOUS	INDOMITABLE
IMPASTATION	IMPRESARIOS	INCONSONANT	INDOMITABLY
IMPATIENTLY	IMPRESSIBLE	INCONSTANCY	INDO-PACIFIC
IMPEACHABLE	IMPRESSIONS	INCONTINENT	INDORSEMENT
IMPEACHMENT	IMPRESSMENT	INCORPORATE	INDUBITABLE
IMPECUNIOUS	IMPRIMATURS	INCORPOREAL	INDUBITABLY
IMPEDIMENTA	IMPRISONING	INCORRECTLY	INDUCEMENTS
IMPEDIMENTS	IMPROPRIATE	INCREASABLE	INDUCTILITY
IMPENITENCE	IMPROPRIETY	INCREASEDLY	INDUCTIONAL
IMPERATIVES	IMPROVEMENT	INCREDULITY	INDUCTIVELY
IMPERFECTLY	IMPROVIDENT	INCREDULOUS	INDULGENCES
IMPERFORATE	IMPROVINGLY	INCREMENTAL	INDULGENTLY
IMPERIALISM	IMPROVISING	INCRIMINATE	INDULGINGLY
IMPERIALIST	IMPRUDENTLY	INCULCATING	INDUPLICATE
IMPERILLING	IMPUGNATION	INCULCATION	INDUSTRIOUS
IMPERIOUSLY	IMPUISSANCE	INCULPATING	INEBRIATING
IMPERMANENT	IMPULSIVELY	INCULPATION	INEBRIATION
IMPERMEABLE	IMPUTATIONS	INCUNABULAR	INEDIBILITY
IMPERSONATE	INADVERTENT	INCURIOSITY	INEFFECTIVE
IMPERTINENT	INADVISABLE	INCURVATION	INEFFECTUAL
IMPETRATION	INALIENABLE	INCURVATURE	INEFFICIENT
IMPETRATIVE	INALTERABLE	INDECIDUOUS	INELEGANTLY
IMPETUOSITY	INATTENTION	INDEFINABLE	INELOQUENCE
IMPETUOUSLY	INATTENTIVE	INDEFINABLY	INELUCTABLE
IMPINGEMENT	INAUGURATED	INDEHISCENT	INELUCTABLY
IMPIOUSNESS	INAUGURATOR	INDEMNIFIED	INEQUITABLE
IMPLAUSIBLE	INAUTHENTIC	INDEMNIFIER	INEQUITABLY
IMPLAUSIBLY	INCALESCENT	INDEMNITIES	INERTIA REEL
IMPLEADABLE	INCANTATION	INDENTATION	INESCAPABLE
IMPLEMENTAL	INCAPSULATE	INDENTURING	INESCAPABLY
IMPLEMENTED	INCARCERATE	INDEPENDENT	INESSENTIAL
IMPLEMENTER	INCARDINATE	INDEX FINGER	INESTIMABLE
IMPLICATING	INCARNATING	INDIA RUBBER	INESTIMABLY
IMPLICATION	INCARNATION	INDICATABLE	INEXACTNESS
IMPLICATIVE	INCERTITUDE	INDICATIONS	INEXCUSABLE
IMPLORATION	INCESSANTLY	INDICATIVES	INEXCUSABLY
IMPLORATORY	INCIDENTALS	INDICTMENTS	INEXISTENCE
IMPLORINGLY	INCINERATED	INDIFFERENT	INEXPEDIENT
IMPORTANTLY	INCINERATOR	INDIGESTION	INEXPENSIVE
IMPORTATION	INCIPIENTLY	INDIGESTIVE	INFANTICIDE
IMPORTUNATE	INCLINATION	INDIGNANTLY	INFANTILISM
IMPORTUNING	INCLUSIVELY	INDIGNATION	INFANTILITY
IMPORTUNITY	INCOERCIBLE	INDIGNITIES	INFANTRYMAN
IMPOSITIONS	INCOGNIZANT	INDIRECTION	INFANTRYMEN
IMPRACTICAL	INCOHERENCE	INDIVIDUALS	INFATUATION

INFERENTIAL	INJUNCTIONS	INSOUCIANCE	INTERCOSTAL
INFERIORITY	INJURIOUSLY	INSPECTABLE	INTERCOURSE
INFERNALITY	IN-LINE SKATE	INSPECTIONS	INTERDENTAL
INFERTILITY	INNER CITIES	INSPECTORAL	INTERDICTOR
INFESTATION	INNERVATION	INSPIRATION	INTERESTING
INFILTRATED	INNOCUOUSLY	INSPIRATIVE	INTERFACING
INFILTRATOR	INNOVATIONS	INSPIRATORY	INTERFERING
INFINITIVAL	INNS OF COURT	INSPIRINGLY	INTERFUSION
INFINITIVES	INNUMERABLE	INSTABILITY	INTERJECTED
INFIRMARIES	INNUTRITION	INSTALMENTS	INTERJECTOR
INFIRMITIES	INOBSERVANT	INSTATEMENT	INTERLACING
INFLAMINGLY	INOCULATING	INSTIGATING	INTERLARDED
INFLAMMABLE	INOCULATION	INSTIGATION	INTERLINEAR
INFLECTIONS	INOCULATIVE	INSTIGATIVE	INTERLINGUA
INFLICTIONS	INOFFENSIVE	INSTIGATORS	INTERLINING
INFLUENCING	INOFFICIOUS	INSTINCTIVE	INTERLINKED
INFLUENTIAL	INOPERATIVE	INSTITUTING	INTERLOCKED
INFOMERCIAL	INOPPORTUNE	INSTITUTION	INTERLOCKER
INFORMALITY	IN PERPETUUM	INSTITUTIVE	INTERLOPERS
INFORMATION	INQUILINISM	INSTRUCTING	INTERMEZZOS
INFORMATIVE	INQUILINOUS	INSTRUCTION	INTERMINGLE
INFORMINGLY	INQUIRINGLY	INSTRUCTIVE	INTERMITTOR
INFRACOSTAL	INQUISITION	INSTRUCTORS	INTERNALITY
INFRACTIONS	INQUISITIVE	INSTRUMENTS	INTERNALIZE
INFRANGIBLE	INQUISITORS	INSUFFLATOR	INTERNECINE
INFREQUENCY	IN-RESIDENCE	INSUPERABLE	INTERNEURON
INFURIATING	INSALUBRITY	INSUPERABLY	INTERNMENTS
INFURIATION	INSCRIBABLE	INTAGLIATED	INTERNSHIPS
INFUSIONISM	INSCRIPTION	INTEGRATING	INTERNUNCIO
INFUSIONIST	INSCRIPTIVE	INTEGRATION	INTERPOLATE
INGENIOUSLY	INSCRUTABLE	INTEGRATIVE	INTERPOSING
INGENUOUSLY	INSCRUTABLY	INTEGUMENTS	INTERPRETED
INGRAINEDLY	INSECTARIUM	INTELLIGENT	INTERPRETER
INGRATIATED	INSECTICIDE	INTEMPERATE	INTERRACIAL
INGRATITUDE	INSECTIVORE	INTENSIFIED	INTERRADIAL
INGREDIENTS	INSEMINATED	INTENSIFIER	INTERREGNAL
INGURGITATE	INSEMINATOR	INTENSIONAL	INTERREGNUM
INHABITABLE	INSENSITIVE	INTENSIVELY	INTERRELATE
INHABITANCY	INSENTIENCE	INTENTIONAL	INTERROBANG
INHABITANTS	INSEPARABLE	INTERACTING	INTERROGATE
INHALATIONS	INSEPARABLY	INTERACTION	INTERRUPTED
INHERITABLE	INSERTIONAL	INTERACTIVE	INTERRUPTER
INHERITANCE	INSESSORIAL	INTERATOMIC	INTERSECTED
INHIBITABLE	INSIDE TRACK	INTERBEDDED	INTERSEXUAL
INHIBITEDLY	INSIDIOUSLY	INTERCALARY	INTERSPERSE
INHIBITIONS	INSINCERELY	INTERCALATE	INTERSTICES
INITIALLING	INSINCERITY	INTERCEDING	INTERTRIBAL
INITIATIONS	INSINUATING	INTERCEPTED	INTERTWINED
INITIATIVES	INSINUATION	INTERCEPTOR	INTERVENING
INITIATRESS	INSINUATIVE	INTERCESSOR	INTERVIEWED
INJUDICIOUS	INSISTENTLY	INTERCHANGE	INTERVIEWEE

INTERVIEWER	INVITATIONS	ITHYPHALLIC	KINDREDNESS
INTERWEAVER	INVOCATIONS	ITINERARIES	KINETICALLY
INTIMATIONS	INVOLUCRATE	ITINERATION	KINETOPLAST
INTIMIDATED	INVOLUNTARY	IVORY TOWERS	KINGFISHERS
INTIMIDATOR	INVOLVEMENT		KISS OF DEATH
INTOLERABLE	IONOSPHERIC	**J**	KITCHENETTE
INTOLERABLY	IPECACUANHA		KITCHENWARE
INTOLERANCE	IRIDESCENCE	JACKHAMMERS	KITTENISHLY
INTONATIONS	IRISH COFFEE	JACK-KNIFING	KLEPTOMANIA
INTOXICABLE	IRON CURTAIN	JACKRABBITS	KNEECAPPING
INTOXICANTS	IRONMONGERS	JACTITATION	KNICK-KNACKS
INTOXICATED	IRONMONGERY	JAM SESSIONS	KNIGHTHOODS
INTOXICATOR	IRON RATIONS	JANISSARIES	KNUCKLEBONE
INTRA-ATOMIC	IRRADIATING	JAWBREAKERS	KOOKABURRAS
INTRACOSTAL	IRRADIATION	JAYAWARDENE	KRASNOYARSK
INTRACTABLE	IRRADIATIVE	JEHOSHAPHAT	KRISTIANSEN
INTRACTABLY	IRRECUSABLE	JELLYFISHES	KRUGERRANDS
INTRADERMAL	IRREDENTISM	JEOPARDIZED	KRUGERSDORP
INTRAVENOUS	IRREDENTIST	JETTISONING	KUALA LUMPUR
INTRENCHING	IRREDUCIBLE	JOHORE BAHRU	KUMARATUNGE
INTREPIDITY	IRREDUCIBLY	JOIE DE VIVRE	KWANGCHOWAN
INTRICACIES	IRREFUTABLE	JOURNALISIS	KWASHIORKOR
INTRICATELY	IRREFUTABLY	JOURNALIZER	KYANIZATION
INTRODUCING	IRREGULARLY	JOYLESSNESS	KYMOGRAPHIC
INTROVERTED	IRRELEVANCE	JUDAIZATION	
INTRUDINGLY	IRRELIGIOUS	JUDGMENT DAY	**L**
INTRUSIONAL	IRREMOVABLE	JUDICATURES	
INTUITIONAL	IRREPARABLE	JUDICIOUSLY	LABIODENTAL
INTUITIVELY	IRREPARABLY	JUGGERNAUTS	LABORIOUSLY
INTUITIVISM	IRRESOLUBLE	JUGULAR VEIN	LABOR UNIONS
INTUITIVIST	IRRETENTIVE	JUMBLE SALES	LABOURINGLY
INTUMESCENT	IRREVERENCE	JUSTICESHIP	LABOUR PARTY
INUNDATIONS	IRREVOCABLE	JUSTICIABLE	LABRADORITE
INVAGINABLE	IRREVOCABLY	JUSTIFIABLE	LACCOLITHIC
INVALIDATED	IRRITATIONS	JUSTIFIABLY	LACERATIONS
INVALIDATOR	ISAAC NEWTON	JUVENESCENT	LACERTILIAN
INVENTIONAL	ISOCHRONIZE	JUXTAPOSING	LACINIATION
INVENTIVELY	ISODIAPHERE		LACONICALLY
INVENTORIAL	ISOELECTRIC	**K**	LACQUERWARE
INVENTORIES	ISOGEOTHERM		LACRIMATION
INVERTEBRAL	ISOLABILITY	KALASHNIKOV	LACRIMATORY
INVESTIGATE	ISOLECITHAL	KALININGRAD	LACTALBUMIN
INVESTITIVE	ISOMAGNETIC	KANCHIPURAM	LACTATIONAL
INVESTITURE	ISOMETRICAL	KARLOVY VARY	LACTESCENCE
INVESTMENTS	ISOMETROPIA	KERB CRAWLER	LACTIFEROUS
INVIABILITY	ISOMORPHISM	KETTLEDRUMS	LADY-KILLERS
INVIDIOUSLY	ISORHYTHMIC	KEYBOARDERS	LAEVOGYRATE
INVIGILATED	ISOTONICITY	KEYBOARDING	LAGOMORPHIC
INVIGILATOR	ITACOLUMITE	KEYPUNCHERS	LAICIZATION
INVIGORATED	ITALICIZING	KIDNEY BEANS	LAKE DWELLER
INVIGORATOR	ITEMIZATION	KILIMANJARO	LAKE SUCCESS
		KILLER WHALE	LAMELLATION
		KIND-HEARTED	

LAMELLICORN	LEGATIONARY	LIGHT-FOOTED	LO AND BEHOLD
LAMELLIFORM	LEGERDEMAIN	LIGHT-HEADED	LOATHSOMELY
LAMELLOSITY	LEGIONARIES	LIGHTHOUSES	LOBSTERPOTS
LAMENTATION	LEGIONNAIRE	LIGHTWEIGHT	LOCAL COLOUR
LAMENTINGLY	LEGISLATING	LIKABLENESS	LOCALIZABLE
LAMINAR FLOW	LEGISLATION	LILLIPUTIAN	LOCAL OPTION
LAMMERGEIER	LEGISLATIVE	LILY-LIVERED	LOCKER ROOMS
LAMPROPHYRE	LEGISLATORS	LIMITATIONS	LOCK KEEPERS
LANARKSHIRE	LEGISLATURE	LIMITLESSLY	LOCOMOTIVES
LANCASTRIAN	LEGITIMIZED	LIMNOLOGIST	LOCUM TENENS
LANCINATION	LEMON SQUASH	LIMP-WRISTED	LOGARITHMIC
LANDHOLDING	LENGTHENING	LINDISFARNE	LOGGERHEADS
LANDING GEAR	LENGTHINESS	LINEAMENTAL	LOGISTICIAN
LANDING NETS	LENTIGINOUS	LINE DANCING	LOGOGRAPHER
LANDLUBBERS	LEPIDOSIREN	LINE DRAWING	LOGOGRIPHIC
LANDSCAPING	LEPRECHAUNS	LINEN BASKET	LOGOMACHIST
LANDSCAPIST	LEPROSARIUM	LINE OF SIGHT	LOGOPAEDICS
LANGUISHING	LEPTORRHINE	LINE PRINTER	LOITERINGLY
LAPAROSCOPY	LESE-MAJESTY	LINERTRAINS	LOLLIPOP MAN
LAPIS LAZULI	LET OFF STEAM	LINGERINGLY	LOLLIPOP MEN
LARGE-MINDED	LETTER BOMBS	LINGUISTICS	LONDONDERRY
LARKISHNESS	LETTERBOXES	LION-HEARTED	LONG JUMPERS
LARYNGOLOGY	LETTERHEADS	LIONIZATION	LONGSIGHTED
LARYNGOTOMY	LETTERPRESS	LIPOPROTEIN	LONGWEARING
LATITUDINAL	LEUCOCRATIC	LIPOSUCTION	LOOSE CANNON
LAUDABILITY	LEUCODERMAL	LIQUEFIABLE	LOOSE CHANGE
LAUGHING GAS	LEUCORRHOEA	LIQUESCENCE	LOOSESTRIFE
LAUNDERETTE	LEUCOTOMIES	LIQUIDAMBAR	LOPHOBRANCH
LAURUSTINUS	LEVEL-HEADED	LIQUIDATING	LORD PROVOST
LAW-BREAKERS	LIABILITIES	LIQUIDATION	LORD'S PRAYER
LAWBREAKING	LIANYUNGANG	LIQUIDATORS	LOSS LEADERS
LAWLESSNESS	LIBELLOUSLY	LIQUIDIZERS	LOTUS-EATERS
LAWN PARTIES	LIBERAL ARTS	LIQUIDIZING	LOUDHAILERS
LAY BROTHERS	LIBERALIZED	LISTERIOSIS	LOUDMOUTHED
LEADING LADY	LIBERALIZER	LITERALNESS	LOUDSPEAKER
LEAF-CLIMBER	LIBERALNESS	LITERATURES	LOUNGE SUITS
LEAPFROGGED	LIBERATRESS	LITHOGRAPHS	LOUTISHNESS
LEARNEDNESS	LIBERTARIAN	LITHOGRAPHY	LOVE AFFAIRS
LEASEHOLDER	LIBERTICIDE	LITHOLOGIST	LOW COMEDIES
LEATHERBACK	LIBERTINISM	LITHOMETEOR	LOWER SAXONY
LEATHERETTE	LIBRATIONAL	LITHOPHYTIC	LOW-PRESSURE
LEATHERHEAD	LIBRETTISTS	LITHOSPHERE	LOW PROFILES
LEATHERWOOD	LICENTIATES	LITHOTOMIST	LOW-SPIRITED
LEAVENWORTH	LICKSPITTLE	LITTERATEUR	LOXODROMICS
LEAVE TAKING	LIE DETECTOR	LITTERLOUTS	LOYALTY CARD
LECHEROUSLY	LIEUTENANCY	LITTLE WOMAN	LUBRICATING
LECITHINASE	LIEUTENANTS	LITURGISTIC	LUBRICATION
LECTURESHIP	LIFE JACKETS	LIVABLENESS	LUBRICATIVE
LEFT-HANDERS	LIFE OF RILEY	LIVELIHOODS	LUBRICATORS
LEFT-WINGERS	LIFE STORIES	LIVING ROOMS	LUCRATIVELY
LEGAL TENDER	LIGAMENTOUS	LLOYD WEBBER	LUCUBRATION

LUDICROUSLY	MAGNIFICENT	MANIFESTOES	MASS-PRODUCE
LUDWIGSBURG	MAHARASHTRA	MANIPULATED	MASTER CARDS
LUGGAGE RACK	MAIDENHEADS	MANIPULATOR	MASTERCLASS
LUGGAGE VANS	MAIDEN NAMES	MANNERISTIC	MASTERFULLY
LUMBERINGLY	MAIDSERVANT	MANNISHNESS	MASTERMINDS
LUMBERJACKS	MAILING LIST	MANOEUVRING	MASTERPIECE
LUMBER-ROOMS	MAIN CLAUSES	MANOR HOUSES	MASTERWORKS
LUMBERYARDS	MAINSPRINGS	MANSERVANTS	MASTICATING
LUMBRICALIS	MAINTAINING	MANTELPIECE	MASTICATION
LUMINESCENT	MAINTENANCE	MANTELSHELF	MASTICATORY
LUNAR MONTHS	MAIN-TOPMAST	MANTOUX TEST	MASTOIDITIS
LUSTFULNESS	MAINTOPSAIL	MANUFACTORY	MASTROIANNI
LUTHERANISM	MAISONETTES	MANUFACTURE	MASTURBATED
LUXULIANITE	MAKE-BELIEVE	MANUSCRIPTS	MATCHLESSLY
LUXURIANTLY	MAKES A POINT	MARASCHINOS	MATCHMAKERS
LUXURIATING	MAKHACHKALA	MARCESCENCE	MATCHMAKING
LUXURIATION	MALADJUSTED	MARCHIONESS	MATCH POINTS
LUXURIOUSLY	MALADROITLY	MAR DEL PLATA	MATCHSTICKS
LYMPHANGIAL	MALAPROPIAN	MARE CLAUSUM	MATERIALISM
LYMPHOBLAST	MALAPROPISM	MARE LIBERUM	MATERIALIST
LYMPHOCYTIC	MALCONTENTS	MARGINALITY	MATERIALITY
LYTHRACEOUS	MALEDICTION	MARGINATION	MATERIALIZE
	MALEDICTIVE	MARICULTURE	MATERNALISM
M	MALEFACTION	MARINE CORPS	MATHEMATICS
	MALEFACTORS	MARIONETTES	MATINEE IDOL
MACADAMIZER	MALEFICENCE	MARKETPLACE	MATRIARCHAL
MACHICOLATE	MALEVOLENCE	MARKET PRICE	MATRICULANT
MACHINATION	MALFEASANCE	MARKET TOWNS	MATRICULATE
MACHINE CODE	MALFUNCTION	MARKOV CHAIN	MATRILINEAL
MACHINEGUNS	MALICIOUSLY	MARLBOROUGH	MATRIMONIAL
MACHINE TOOL	MALIGNANTLY	MARQUESSATE	MAUDLINNESS
MACROBIOTIC	MALINGERERS	MARQUISETTE	MAUNDY MONEY
MACROCOSMIC	MALINGERING	MARRAM GRASS	MAURITANIAN
MACROGAMETE	MALOCCLUDED	MARROWBONES	MAWKISHNESS
MACROPHAGIC	MALONIC ACID	MARSHALLING	MAYONNAISES
MACROSCOPIC	MALPOSITION	MARSHMALLOW	MEADOWSWEET
MADDENINGLY	MALPRACTICE	MARTENSITIC	MEANDERINGS
MADEIRA CAKE	MALTED MILKS	MARTIAL ARTS	MEANINGLESS
MADRIGALIAN	MALTREATING	MARTINETISH	MEASURELESS
MADRIGALIST	MAMMALOGIST	MARTINETISM	MEASUREMENT
MAGDALENIAN	MAMMIFEROUS	MARTYROLOGY	MECHANICIAN
MAGGOTINESS	MAMMOGRAPHY	MASCULINIST	MECHANISTIC
MAGHERAFELT	MAMMONISTIC	MASCULINITY	MECHANIZING
MAGIC BULLET	MANAGEMENTS	MASKING TAPE	MECKLENBURG
MAGISTERIAL	MANDATORILY	MASOCHISTIC	MEDIASTINAL
MAGISTRALLY	MANDOLINIST	MASONICALLY	MEDIASTINUM
MAGISTRATES	MANEUVERING	MASQUERADED	MEDICAMENTS
MAGLEMOSIAN	MANHANDLING	MASQUERADER	MEDICATIONS
MAGNANIMITY	MANICHAEISM	MASQUERADES	MEDICINALLY
MAGNANIMOUS	MANICURISTS	MASSACHUSET	MEDICINE MAN
MAGNETIZING	MANIFESTING	MASSIVENESS	MEDICINE MEN
MAGNIFIABLE			

MEDIEVALISM	MERRYMAKERS	MICROMETERS	MISALLIANCE
MEDIEVALIST	MERRYMAKING	MICROMETRIC	MISANTHROPE
MEDITATIONS	MESALLIANCE	MICROPHONES	MISANTHROPY
MEERSCHAUMS	MESENCHYMAL	MICROPHONIC	MISAPPLYING
MEGACEPHALY	MESMERIZING	MICROPHYTIC	MISBEGOTTEN
MEGALOBLAST	MESOBENTHOS	MICROREADER	MISBEHAVING
MEGALOMANIA	MESOCEPHALY	MICROSCOPES	MISCARRIAGE
MEGALOPOLIS	MESOGASTRIC	MICROSCOPIC	MISCARRYING
MEIOTICALLY	MESOMORPHIC	MICROSECOND	MISCELLANEA
MELANCHOLIA	MESONEPHRIC	MICROSPORIC	MISCHIEVOUS
MELANCHOLIC	MESONEPHROS	MICROTOMIST	MISCIBILITY
MELIORATION	MESOPHYLLIC	MIDDLEBROWS	MISCONCEIVE
MELIORATIVE	MESOPOTAMIA	MIDDLE CLASS	MISCONSTRUE
MELLIFEROUS	MESOSPHERIC	MIDDLE NAMES	MISCOUNTING
MELLIFLUOUS	MESOTHELIAL	MIDDLE-SIZED	MISCREATION
MELODICALLY	MESOTHELIUM	MIDNIGHT SUN	MISDESCRIBE
MELODIOUSLY	MESOTHORIUM	MIGRATIONAL	MISDIRECTED
MELTABILITY	METABOLISMS	MILITARISTS	MISE-EN-SCENE
MELTING POTS	METACENTRIC	MILITARIZED	MISERLINESS
MEMBERSHIPS	METAGENESIS	MILLEFLEURS	MISFEASANCE
MEMORABILIA	METAGENETIC	MILLENARIAN	MISFORTUNES
MEMORANDUMS	METALLOCENE	MILLILITRES	MISGOVERNOR
MEMORIALIST	METALLOIDAL	MILLIMETRES	MISGUIDANCE
MEMORIALIZE	METALLURGIC	MILLIMICRON	MISGUIDEDLY
MEMORIZABLE	METALWORKER	MILLIONAIRE	MISHANDLING
MENAQUINONE	METAMORPHIC	MILLISECOND	MISINFORMED
MENDELEVIUM	METANEPHROS	MIMEOGRAPHS	MISJUDGMENT
MENDEL'S LAWS	METAPHYSICS	MIMETICALLY	MISMANAGING
MENORRHAGIA	METAPLASMIC	MIMOSACEOUS	MISMATCHING
MENORRHAGIC	METASTASIZE	MINAS GERAIS	MISOGYNISTS
MENSTRUATED	METATHERIAN	MIND-BENDING	MISONEISTIC
MENSURATION	METATHESIZE	MIND-BLOWING	MISPRINTING
MENSURATIVE	METEMPIRICS	MINDFULNESS	MISREMEMBER
MENTALISTIC	METEOROLOGY	MIND READERS	MISREPORTED
MENTALITIES	METHODOLOGY	MIND READING	MISSING LINK
MENTAL NOTES	METHYLAMINE	MINERALIZER	MISSISSAUGA
MENTHACEOUS	METHYLATION	MINERAL OILS	MISSISSIPPI
MENTHOLATED	METONYMICAL	MINESWEEPER	MISSPELLING
MENTIONABLE	METRICATION	MINIATURIST	MISSPENDING
MEPROBAMATE	METRICIZING	MINIATURIZE	MISTRUSTFUL
MERCENARIES	METROLOGIST	MINIMUM WAGE	MISTRUSTING
MERCENARILY	MICHIGANDER	MINISTERIAL	MITHRIDATIC
MERCHANDISE	MICHIGANITE	MINISTERING	MITOTICALLY
MERCHANTMAN	MICKEY MOUSE	MINISTERIUM	MIXED GRILLS
MERCHANTMEN	MICROCOCCUS	MINISTRANTS	MOBILE HOMES
MERCILESSLY	MICROCOSMIC	MINNEAPOLIS	MOBILE PHONE
MERCURATION	MICROFICHES	MINOR PLANET	MOBILIZABLE
MERCURIALLY	MICROFILMED	MINUTE STEAK	MOCKINGBIRD
MERITOCRACY	MICROGAMETE	MIRACLE PLAY	MODERNISTIC
MERITORIOUS	MICROGRAPHY	MIRROR IMAGE	MODERNIZING
MEROBLASTIC	MICROGROOVE	MIRTHLESSLY	MODULATIONS

MOHAMMEDANS
MOISTURIZED
MOISTURIZER
MOLESTATION
MOLLIFIABLE
MOLLYCODDLE
MOLYBDENITE
MOLYBDENOUS
MOMENTARILY
MONARCHICAL
MONARCHISTS
MONASTERIAL
MONASTERIES
MONASTICISM
MONETARISTS
MONEYLENDER
MONEYMAKERS
MONEYMAKING
MONEY ORDERS
MONEY SUPPLY
MONITORSHIP
MONOCHASIAL
MONOCHASIUM
MONOCHROMAT
MONOCHROMIC
MONOCLINISM
MONOCLINOUS
MONOCULTURE
MONOGENESIS
MONOGENETIC
MONOGRAMMED
MONOGRAPHER
MONOGRAPHIC
MONOHYDRATE
MONOHYDROXY
MONOLATROUS
MONOLINGUAL
MONOMANIACS
MONOMORPHIC
MONONUCLEAR
MONOPHAGOUS
MONOPHTHONG
MONOPOLISTS
MONOPOLIZED
MONOPOLIZER
MONOSTICHIC
MONOSTROPHE
MONOSTYLOUS
MONOTERPENE
MONOTHEISTS
MONOVALENCE

MONSEIGNEUR
MONSTRANCES
MONSTROSITY
MONSTROUSLY
MONS VENERIS
MONTENEGRAN
MONTPELLIER
MOONLIGHTER
MORAVIANISM
MORIBUNDITY
MORNING COAT
MORNING STAR
MORONICALLY
MORPHOLOGIC
MORRIS DANCE
MORTALITIES
MORTARBOARD
MORTISE LOCK
MOSQUITO NET
MOTHERBOARD
MOTHER-IN-LAW
MOTHER'S BOYS
MOTHER'S RUIN
MOTHERS-TO-BE
MOTHPROOFED
MOTORCYCLES
MOTOR LODGES
MOUNTAINEER
MOUNTAINOUS
MOUNTAINTOP
MOUNTBATTEN
MOUNTEBANKS
MOUTHORGANS
MOUTHPIECES
MOUTHWASHES
MOXIBUSTION
MUCOPROTEIN
MUCRONATION
MUDDLEDNESS
MUDSLINGING
MUHAMMADANS
MULTANGULAR
MULTINOMIAL
MULTIPARITY
MULTIPAROUS
MULTIPLEXER
MULTIPLYING
MULTIRACIAL
MULTISCREEN
MULTISTOREY
MULTIVALENT

MUMS THE WORD
MUNDANENESS
MUNICIPALLY
MUNIFICENCE
MURDERESSES
MURDEROUSLY
MURMURINGLY
MUSCLE-BOUND
MUSCOVY DUCK
MUSCULARITY
MUSCULATURE
MUSEUM PIECE
MUSHROOMING
MUSICALNESS
MUSIC CENTRE
MUSKELLUNGE
MUSTACHIOED
MUTAGENESIS
MUTILATIONS
MUTTERINGLY
MUTTONCHOPS
MUTUAL FUNDS
MYCOLOGICAL
MYCOPROTEIN
MYCORRHIZAL
MYELOMATOID
MYOCARDITIS
MYRIAPODOUS
MYRMECOLOGY
MYSTERY PLAY
MYSTERY TOUR
MYSTIFIEDLY
MYTHOLOGIES
MYTHOLOGIST
MYTHOLOGIZE
MYTHOMANIAC
MYTHOPOEISM
MYTHOPOEIST
MYXOMATOSIS

N
NAILBRUSHES
NAIL VARNISH
NAKHICHEVAN
NAMEDROPPED
NAMEDROPPER
NAPHTHALENE
NAPKIN RINGS
NARAYANGANJ
NARCISSISTS
NARCISSUSES

NARCOLEPTIC
NARRATOLOGY
NARROW BOATS
NARROW GAUGE
NASOFRONTAL
NASOGASTRIC
NASOPHARYNX
NASTURTIUMS
NATIONALISM
NATIONALIST
NATIONALITY
NATIONALIZE
NATION STATE
NATURALISTS
NATURALIZED
NATURALNESS
NATUROPATHS
NATUROPATHY
NAUGHTINESS
NEANDERTHAL
NEAR EASTERN
NEARSIGHTED
NECESSARIES
NECESSARILY
NECESSITATE
NECESSITIES
NECESSITOUS
NECKERCHIEF
NECROBIOSIS
NECROBIOTIC
NECROLOGIST
NECROMANCER
NECROMANTIC
NECROPHILIA
NECROPHILIC
NECROPHOBIA
NECROPHOBIC
NEEDFULNESS
NEEDLEPOINT
NEEDLEWOMAN
NEEDLEWOMEN
NE'ER-DO-WELLS
NEFARIOUSLY
NEGLIGENTLY
NEGOTIATING
NEGOTIATION
NEGOTIATORS
NEIGHBOURLY
NEOCOLONIAL
NEOLOGISTIC
NEPHELINITE

NEPHOLOGIST	NITTY-GRITTY	NOTABLENESS	OBSCENITIES
NEPHRECTOMY	NIZHNI TAGIL	NOTHINGNESS	OBSCURATION
NE PLUS ULTRA	NOBEL PRIZES	NOTHING TO IT	OBSCURITIES
NERVE CENTRE	NOCICEPTIVE	NOTICE BOARD	OBSERVANCES
NERVELESSLY	NOCTILUCENT	NOTOCHORDAL	OBSERVATION
NERVOUSNESS	NOCTURNALLY	NOTORIOUSLY	OBSERVATORY
NETHERLANDS	NOISELESSLY	NOTOTHERIUM	OBSESSIONAL
NEUROFIBRIL	NOISOMENESS	NOURISHMENT	OBSOLESCENT
NEUROLOGIST	NOMADICALLY	NOVOSIBIRSK	OBSTINATELY
NEUROMATOUS	NO-MAN'S-LANDS	NOXIOUSNESS	OBSTIPATION
NEUROPATHIC	NOMENCLATOR	NUCLEAR-FREE	OBSTRUCTING
NEUROPTERAN	NOMINATIONS	NUCLEIC ACID	OBSTRUCTION
NEUROTICISM	NOMINATIVES	NUCLEOPLASM	OBSTRUCTIVE
NEUROTOMIST	NOMOGRAPHER	NUEVO LAREDO	OBTRUSIVELY
NEUTRALIZED	NOMOGRAPHIC	NULL AND VOID	OBVIOUSNESS
NEUTRALIZER	NOMOLOGICAL	NULLIFIDIAN	OCCASIONING
NEUTRON BOMB	NOMS DE PLUME	NULLIPAROUS	OCCIDENTALS
NEVER-NEVERS	NONCHALANCE	NUMBERPLATE	OCCULTATION
NEVER SAY DIE	NONCREATIVE	NUMERATIONS	OCCUPATIONS
NEW PLYMOUTH	NONDESCRIPT	NUMERICALLY	OCCURRENCES
NEWPORT NEWS	NONENTITIES	NUMISMATICS	OCHLOCRATIC
NEW POTATOES	NONETHELESS	NUMISMATIST	OCHLOPHOBIA
NEWSCASTERS	NONEXISTENT	NUNCUPATIVE	OCTAHEDRITE
NEWSLETTERS	NONFEASANCE	NURSING HOME	OCTILLIONTH
NEWSREADERS	NONHARMONIC	NUTCRACKERS	ODDS AND ENDS
NEWSVENDORS	NONILLIONTH	NUTRITIONAL	ODONTOBLAST
NEW YEAR'S DAY	NONINVASIVE	NYCTINASTIC	ODONTOGRAPH
NEW YEAR'S EVE	NONIRRITANT	NYCTITROPIC	ODONTOPHORE
NICENE CREED	NONMETALLIC	NYCTOPHOBIA	ODORIFEROUS
NICKELODEON	NONOPERABLE	NYCTOPHOBIC	ODOROUSNESS
NICTITATION	NONPARTISAN	NYMPHOLEPSY	OENOLOGICAL
NIETZSCHEAN	NONPLUSSING	NYMPHOMANIA	OESOPHAGEAL
NIGHTINGALE	NONRESIDENT		OESTROGENIC
NIGHTLIGHTS	NONSENSICAL	**O**	OFFENSIVELY
NIGHTMARISH	NON SEQUITUR	OARSMANSHIP	OFFERTORIES
NIGHT-PORTER	NONSTANDARD	OBFUSCATING	OFFHANDEDLY
NIGHT SCHOOL	NONSTARTERS	OBFUSCATION	OFFICE BLOCK
NIGHTSHADES	NONVERBALLY	OBITER DICTA	OFFICIALDOM
NIGHT SHIFTS	NONVIOLENCE	OBJECTIVELY	OFFICIALESE
NIGHTSHIRTS	NORMALIZING	OBJECTIVISM	OFFICIATING
NIGHTSTICKS	NORTHAMPTON	OBJECTIVIST	OFFICIATION
NIGRESCENCE	NORTH DAKOTA	OBJECTIVITY	OFFICIOUSLY
NINCOMPOOPS	NORTHEASTER	OBJET TROUVE	OFF-LICENCES
NINETEENTHS	NORTHERNERS	OBJURGATION	OIL PAINTING
NINETY-NINES	NORTH ISLAND	OBJURGATORY	OIL-SEED RAPE
NISHINOMIYA	NORTHUMBRIA	OBLIGATIONS	OLD-WOMANISH
NITRIFIABLE	NORTHWESTER	OBLIQUITOUS	OLEOGRAPHIC
NITROGENIZE	NOSOGRAPHER	OBLITERATED	OLIGARCHIES
NITROGENOUS	NOSOGRAPHIC	OBLITERATOR	OLIGOCHAETE
NITROMETRIC	NOSOLOGICAL	OBLIVIOUSLY	OLIGOTROPHY
NITROSAMINE	NOSY PARKERS	OBNOXIOUSLY	OLIVE BRANCH

OMINOUSNESS
OMMATOPHORE
OMNIFARIOUS
OMNIPOTENCE
OMNIPRESENT
OMNISCIENCE
ONAGRACEOUS
ONCOLOGICAL
ONE-MAN BANDS
ONEROUSNESS
ONTOLOGICAL
OPALESCENCE
OPEN-AND-SHUT
OPENHEARTED
OPENING TIME
OPEN LETTERS
OPEN-MOUTHED
OPEN SEASONS
OPEN SECRETS
OPEN SESAMES
OPEN VERDICT
OPERABILITY
OPERATIONAL
OPHIOLOGIST
OPHTHALMIAC
OPINIONATED
OPINION POLL
OPPORTUNELY
OPPORTUNISM
OPPORTUNIST
OPPORTUNITY
OPPOSITIONS
OPPROBRIOUS
OPTICAL DISC
OPTOMETRIST
ORANGUTANGS
ORCHESTRATE
ORDER-DRIVEN
ORDERLINESS
ORDER PAPERS
ORDINATIONS
ORGANICALLY
ORIEL WINDOW
ORIENTALISM
ORIENTALIST
ORIENTALIZE
ORIENTATING
ORIENTATION
ORIGINALITY
ORIGINAL SIN
ORIGINATING

ORIGINATION
ORIGINATORS
ORNAMENTING
ORNITHOLOGY
ORNITHOPTER
ORTHOCENTRE
ORTHODONTIC
ORTHOGRAPHY
ORTHOPAEDIC
ORTHOPTERAN
ORTHOSCOPIC
ORTHOSTICHY
ORTHOTROPIC
OSCILLATING
OSCILLATION
OSCILLATORS
OSCILLATORY
OSCILLOGRAM
OSMOTICALLY
OSTENTATION
OSTEOCLASIS
OSTEOLOGIST
OSTEOPATHIC
OSTEOPHYTIC
OSTEOPLASTY
OSTRACIZING
OSTRACODERM
OSTRACODOUS
OUAGADOUGOU
OUIJA BOARDS
OUTBALANCED
OUTBUILDING
OUTCLASSING
OUTDISTANCE
OUTERCOURSE
OUTFIELDERS
OUTFIGHTING
OUTFLANKING
OUT-HERODING
OUTNUMBERED
OUT OF BOUNDS
OUT OF POCKET
OUT-OF-THE-WAY
OUTPATIENTS
OUTPOINTING
OUTPOURINGS
OUTRIVALING
OUTRIVALLED
OUTSMARTING
OUT SOURCING
OUTSPOKENLY

OUTSTANDING
OUTSTRIPPED
OUTWEIGHING
OVERACHIEVE
OVERANXIOUS
OVERARCHING
OVERBALANCE
OVERBEARING
OVERBIDDING
OVERBOOKING
OVERCHARGED
OVERCHARGES
OVERCLOUDED
OVERCROPPED
OVERCROWDED
OVERDEVELOP
OVERDRAUGHT
OVERDRAWING
OVERDRESSED
OVEREXPOSED
OVERFLOWING
OVERGARMENT
OVERHAULING
OVERHEARING
OVERINDULGE
OVERLAPPING
OVERLOADING
OVERLOOKING
OVERMANNING
OVERPLAYING
OVERPOWERED
OVERPRODUCE
OVERPROTECT
OVERREACHED
OVERREACTED
OVERRUNNING
OVERSELLING
OVERSTAFFED
OVERSTATING
OVERSTAYING
OVERSTEPPED
OVERSTOCKED
OVERSTUFFED
OVERTOPPING
OVERTURNING
OVERWEENING
OVERWHELMED
OVERWORKING
OVERWROUGHT
OVIPOSITION
OWNER-DRIVER

OXFORDSHIRE
OXIDATIONAL
OXIDIMETRIC
OXIDIZATION
OXYCEPHALIC
OXYGENATING
OXYGENATION
OXYGEN MASKS
OXYGEN TENTS
OXYHYDROGEN
OXYSULPHIDE
OZONIFEROUS
OZONIZATION
OZONOSPHERE

P

PACE BOWLERS
PACIFICALLY
PACKAGE DEAL
PACKAGE TOUR
PACK ANIMALS
PACKING CASE
PAEDIATRICS
PAEDOLOGIST
PAINFULNESS
PAINKILLERS
PAINSTAKING
PALAEARCTIC
PALATINATES
PALEOGRAPHY
PALEOLITHIC
PALESTINIAN
PALIMPSESTS
PALINDROMES
PALINDROMIC
PALLBEARERS
PALLIATIVES
PALM SPRINGS
PALPABILITY
PALPITATING
PALPITATION
PAMPAS GRASS
PAMPHLETEER
PAN-AMERICAN
PANCAKE ROLL
PANCHEN LAMA
PANDEMONIAC
PANDEMONIUM
PANDORA'S BOX
PANEGYRICAL
PANHANDLERS

PANHANDLING
PANHELLENIC
PANIC ATTACK
PANJANDRUMS
PANTELLERIA
PANTHEISTIC
PANTOGRAPHS
PANTOGRAPHY
PANTOMIMIST
PAPER CHASES
PAPER-CUTTER
PAPERHANGER
PAPER KNIVES
PAPER TIGERS
PAPERWEIGHT
PAPIER-MACHE
PAPYRACEOUS
PARABLASTIC
PARACETAMOL
PARACHUTING
PARACHUTIST
PARADOXICAL
PARAGENESIS
PARAGENETIC
PARAGLIDING
PARAGRAPHIA
PARAGRAPHIC
PARALDEHYDE
PARALEIPSIS
PARALLACTIC
PARALLELING
PARALLELISM
PARALLELIST
PARALLELLED
PARALYMPICS
PARAMEDICAL
PARAMORPHIC
PARAMOUNTCY
PARAPHRASED
PARAPHRASES
PARAPLASTIC
PARAPLEGICS
PARASAILING
PARATHYROID
PARATROOPER
PARATYPHOID
PARENTHESES
PARENTHESIS
PARENTHETIC
PARESTHESIA
PARESTHETIC

PARI-MUTUELS
PARIPINNATE
PARISH CLERK
PARISHIONER
PARKING LOTS
PARK KEEPERS
PARLIAMENTS
PARLOUR GAME
PAROCHIALLY
PARONOMASIA
PARSON'S NOSE
PART COMPANY
PARTIALNESS
PARTICIPANT
PARTICIPATE
PARTICIPIAL
PARTICIPLES
PARTICULARS
PARTICULATE
PARTING SHOT
PARTITIONED
PARTITIONER
PARTITIVELY
PARTNERSHIP
PARTURIENCY
PARTURITION
PARTY PIECES
PARTY POOPER
PAS-DE-CALAIS
PASQUINADER
PASSIBILITY
PASSIONLESS
PASSION PLAY
PASSIONTIDE
PASSIVENESS
PASTEBOARDS
PASTEURIZED
PASTEURIZER
PAST MASTERS
PAST PERFECT
PASTURELAND
PATCH POCKET
PATELLIFORM
PATERNALISM
PATERNALIST
PATERNOSTER
PATHFINDERS
PATHFINDING
PATHOLOGIST
PATISSERIES
PATRIARCHAL

PATRILINEAL
PATRIMONIAL
PATROL WAGON
PATRONIZING
PATRON SAINT
PATRONYMICS
PAUNCHINESS
PAVING STONE
PAWNBROKERS
PAWNBROKING
PAY ENVELOPE
PAY STATIONS
PEACH MELBAS
PEACOCK BLUE
PEARL DIVERS
PEARLY GATES
PEASHOOTERS
PECCABILITY
PECCADILLOS
PECTINATION
PECTIZATION
PECULATIONS
PECULIARITY
PECUNIARILY
PEDESTRIANS
PEDICULOSIS
PEDICURISTS
PEDOLOGICAL
PEDUNCULATE
PEEPING TOMS
PEEVISHNESS
PELARGONIUM
PELLUCIDITY
PELOPONNESE
PENALTY AREA
PENDULOUSLY
PENETRALIAN
PENETRATING
PENETRATION
PENETRATIVE
PENICILLATE
PENICILLIUM
PENITENTIAL
PENNYWEIGHT
PENNYWORTHS
PENOLOGICAL
PENSIONABLE
PENSIVENESS
PENTADACTYL
PENTAHEDRON
PENTAMEROUS

PENTAMETERS
PENTANGULAR
PENTATHLONS
PENTAVALENT
PENTECOSTAL
PENTLANDITE
PENULTIMATE
PENURIOUSLY
PEOPLE MOVER
PEPPERCORNS
PEPPER MILLS
PEPPERMINTS
PEPTIC ULCER
PEPTIZATION
PERAMBULATE
PERCEIVABLE
PERCENTAGES
PERCEPTIBLE
PERCEPTIBLY
PERCHLORATE
PERCHLORIDE
PERCIPIENCE
PERCOLATING
PERCOLATION
PERCOLATIVE
PERCOLATORS
PEREGRINATE
PERENNIALLY
PERFECTIBLE
PERFORATING
PERFORATION
PERFORATIVE
PERFORMABLE
PERFORMANCE
PERFUNCTORY
PERICARDIUM
PERICARPIAL
PERICLASTIC
PERICRANIAL
PERICRANIUM
PERIDOTITIC
PERIGORDIAN
PERIHELIONS
PERIMORPHIC
PERINEURIUM
PERIODICALS
PERIODICITY
PERIODONTAL
PERIODONTIC
PERIOD PIECE
PERIOSTITIC

PERIOSTITIS	PERTINENTLY	PHOTOCOPIED	PILLOWCASES
PERIPATETIC	PERTURBABLE	PHOTOCOPIER	PILLOW FIGHT
PERIPETEIAN	PERTURBABLY	PHOTOCOPIES	PILOCARPINE
PERIPHERALS	PERVASIVELY	PHOTO FINISH	PILOT LIGHTS
PERIPHERIES	PERVERSIONS	PHOTOGRAPHS	PINA COLADAS
PERIPHRASES	PERVERTEDLY	PHOTOGRAPHY	PINCUSHIONS
PERIPHRASIS	PERVERTIBLE	PHOTOMETRIC	PINEAL GLAND
PERISHABLES	PESSIMISTIC	PHOTONASTIC	PINE MARTENS
PERISHINGLY	PESTERINGLY	PHOTO-OFFSET	PINNATISECT
PERISPERMAL	PESTIFEROUS	PHOTOPERIOD	PINOCYTOSIS
PERISTALSIS	PESTILENCES	PHOTOPHOBIA	PINPOINTING
PERISTALTIC	PETITIONARY	PHOTOPHOBIC	PIPE CLEANER
PERITHECIUM	PETITIONERS	PHOTOSETTER	PIPE OF PEACE
PERITONEUMS	PETITIONING	PHOTOSPHERE	PIPERACEOUS
PERITONITIC	PETRODOLLAR	PHOTOSTATIC	PIPISTRELLE
PERITONITIS	PETROGRAPHY	PHOTOTACTIC	PIRATICALLY
PERIWINKLES	PETROLOGIST	PHOTOTROPIC	PIROUETTING
PERLOCUTION	PETTIFOGGER	PHRASAL VERB	PISCATORIAL
PERMANENTLY	PETTISHNESS	PHRASEBOOKS	PISCIVOROUS
PERMISSIBLE	PHAGOMANIAC	PHRASEOGRAM	PISTON RINGS
PERMISSIBLY	PHAGOPHOBIA	PHRASEOLOGY	PITCHBLENDE
PERMUTATION	PHAGOPHOBIC	PHTHIRIASIS	PITCHFORKED
PERORATIONS	PHALANSTERY	PHYCOLOGIST	PITCHOMETER
PERPETRATED	PHANEROZOIC	PHYCOMYCETE	PITEOUSNESS
PERPETRATOR	PHARMACISTS	PHYLLOCLADE	PITH HELMETS
PERPETUALLY	PHARYNGITIS	PHYLLOTAXIS	PITIFULNESS
PERPETUATED	PHELLOGENIC	PHYLOTACTIC	PITUITARIES
PERPLEXEDLY	PHENETIDINE	PHYSIATRICS	PLACABILITY
PERQUISITES	PHENOLOGIST	PHYSICALISM	PLAGIARISMS
PERSECUTING	PHILANDERER	PHYSICALIST	PLAGIARISTS
PERSECUTION	PHILATELIST	PHYSIOGNOMY	PLAGIARIZED
PERSECUTIVE	PHILHELLENE	PHYTOGRAPHY	PLAGIARIZER
PERSECUTORS	PHILIPPINES	PICKPOCKETS	PLAGIOCLASE
PERSEVERANT	PHILISTINES	PICKWICKIAN	PLAINSPOKEN
PERSEVERING	PHILOLOGIST	PICTORIALLY	PLAINTIVELY
PERSIAN CATS	PHILOSOPHER	PICTURE BOOK	PLANETARIUM
PERSISTENCE	PHLEBOTOMIC	PICTURE CARD	PLANETOIDAL
PERSNICKETY	PHONETICIAN	PICTURESQUE	PLANIMETRIC
PERSONALISM	PHONOGRAMIC	PIECE OF CAKE	PLANISPHERE
PERSONALIST	PHONOGRAPHS	PIECE OF WORK	PLANO-CONVEX
PERSONALITY	PHONOGRAPHY	PIEDMONTITE	PLANOGAMETE
PERSONALIZE	PHONOLOGIST	PIEDS-A-TERRE	PLANOGRAPHY
PERSONATION	PHONOMETRIC	PIEZOMETRIC	PLANOMETRIC
PERSONATIVE	PHONOTYPIST	PIGEONHOLED	PLANTAGENET
PERSONIFIED	PHOSPHATASE	PIGEONHOLES	PLANTATIONS
PERSPECTIVE	PHOSPHATIZE	PIGGISHNESS	PLANTIGRADE
PERSPICUITY	PHOSPHORATE	PIGHEADEDLY	PLASMAGENIC
PERSPICUOUS	PHOSPHORISM	PIGSTICKING	PLASMODESMA
PERSUADABLE	PHOSPHORITE	PILE DRIVERS	PLASMOLYSIS
PERSUASIONS	PHOSPHOROUS	PILGRIMAGES	PLASMOLYTIC
PERTINACITY	PHOTOACTIVE	PILLAR BOXES	PLASTER CAST

PLASTICALLY	POINSETTIAS	PONTIFICATE	PRACTICABLY
PLASTIC ARTS	POINTEDNESS	POOH-POOHING	PRACTICALLY
PLASTICIZER	POINTE-NOIRE	POPULARIZED	PRAEDIALITY
PLASTOMETER	POINTILLISM	POPULARIZER	PRAESIDIUMS
PLASTOMETRY	POINTILLIST	POPULATIONS	PRAGMATISTS
PLATELAYERS	POINTLESSLY	PORK BARRELS	PRAIRIE DOGS
PLATINOTYPE	POINT OF VIEW	PORNOGRAPHY	PRATTLINGLY
PLATS DU JOUR	POISONOUSLY	PORPHYRITIC	PRAYER WHEEL
PLATYRRHINE	POLARIMETER	PORTABILITY	PREARRANGED
PLAYER PIANO	POLARIMETRY	PORTERHOUSE	PREARRANGER
PLAYFELLOWS	POLARISCOPE	PORTMANTEAU	PRECAMBRIAN
PLAYFULNESS	POLARIZABLE	PORT MORESBY	PRECAUTIONS
PLAYGROUNDS	POLEMICALLY	PORTO ALEGRE	PRECAUTIOUS
PLAYING CARD	POLE VAULTED	PORT OF CALLS	PRECESSIONS
PLAY ON WORDS	POLE VAULTER	PORT OF ENTRY	PRECIPITANT
PLAYSCHOOLS	POLICE STATE	PORT OF SPAIN	PRECIPITATE
PLAYWRIGHTS	POLICEWOMAN	PORTRAITIST	PRECIPITOUS
PLAYWRITING	POLICEWOMEN	PORTRAITURE	PRECISENESS
PLEASANTEST	POLITICALLY	PORTRAYABLE	PRECLINICAL
PLEASURABLE	POLITICIANS	POSITIONING	PRECLUDABLE
PLEASURABLY	POLITICIZED	POSITIVISTS	PRECONCEIVE
PLEASUREFUL	POLITICKING	POSITRONIUM	PRECONTRACT
PLEBEIANISM	POLLEN COUNT	POSSESSIONS	PRECRITICAL
PLEBISCITES	POLLINATING	POSSESSIVES	PREDATORILY
PLECTOGNATH	POLLINATION	POSSIBILITY	PREDECEASED
PLEISTOCENE	POLTERGEIST	POSTAL ORDER	PREDECESSOR
PLENTEOUSLY	POLYANDROUS	POSTERITIES	PREDESTINED
PLENTIFULLY	POLYCHASIUM	POSTER PAINT	PREDICAMENT
PLEOCHROISM	POLYGAMISTS	POSTGLACIAL	PREDICATING
PLEOMORPHIC	POLYGENESIS	POSTMARKING	PREDICATION
PLICATENESS	POLYGENETIC	POSTMASTERS	PREDICATIVE
PLOUGHSHARE	POLYGLOTISM	POSTMORTEMS	PREDICATORY
PLOUGHSTAFF	POLYGRAPHIC	POSTNUPTIAL	PREDICTABLE
PLUG-AND-PLAY	POLYHYDROXY	POST OFFICES	PREDICTABLY
PLUM PUDDING	POLYNUCLEAR	POSTPONABLE	PREDICTIONS
PLUNDERABLE	POLYPEPTIDE	POSTSCRIPTS	PREDIGESTED
PLURALISTIC	POLYPHONOUS	POSTULATING	PREDISPOSAL
PLURALITIES	POLYPLOIDAL	POSTULATION	PREDISPOSED
PLUTOCRATIC	POLYSTYRENE	POTATO CHIPS	PREDOMINANT
PLUVIOMETER	POLYTECHNIC	POTATO CRISP	PREDOMINATE
PLUVIOMETRY	POLYTHEISTS	POTENTIALLY	PRE-EMINENCE
PNEUMECTOMY	POLYTROPHIC	POTTING SHED	PRE-EXISTENT
PNEUMOGRAPH	POLYVALENCY	POVERTY TRAP	PRE-EXISTING
POCKETBOOKS	POLYZOARIUM	POWDER PUFFS	PREFATORILY
POCKETKNIFE	POMEGRANATE	POWDER ROOMS	PREFECTURAL
POCKET KNIFE	POMICULTURE	POWER BROKER	PREFECTURES
POCKET MONEY	POMOLOGICAL	POWERHOUSES	PREFERENCES
POCOCURANTE	POMPOUSNESS	POWERLESSLY	PREFIGURING
POCTOSCOPIC	PONDEROUSLY	POWER PLANTS	PREGNANCIES
PODIATRISTS	PONDICHERRY	POWER POINTS	PREHISTORIC
PODOPHYLLIN	PONTIFICALS	PRACTICABLE	PRE-IGNITION

PREJUDGMENT	PRETTY PENNY	PROFANENESS	PROPER NOUNS
PREJUDICIAL	PREVALENTLY	PROFANITIES	PROPHESYING
PREJUDICING	PREVARICATE	PROFESSEDLY	PROPHYLAXES
PRELIMINARY	PREVENTABLE	PROFESSIONS	PROPHYLAXIS
PRELITERACY	PREVENTABLY	PROFICIENCY	PROPINQUITY
PRELITERATE	PREVENTIVES	PROFITEERED	PROPITIABLE
PREMATURELY	PRICKLINESS	PROFITEROLE	PROPITIATED
PREMEDITATE	PRICKLY HEAT	PROFLIGATES	PROPITIATOR
PREMIERSHIP	PRICKLY PEAR	PROFUSENESS	PROPORTIONS
PREMIUM BOND	PRIESTCRAFT	PROGENITIVE	PROPOSITION
PREMONITION	PRIESTLIEST	PROGENITORS	PROPOUNDING
PREMONITORY	PRIMA DONNAS	PROGNATHISM	PROPRANOLOL
PREMUNITION	PRIMATOLOGY	PROGNATHOUS	PROPRIETARY
PREOCCUPIED	PRIME MOVERS	PROGRAMMERS	PROPRIETIES
PREORDAINED	PRIME NUMBER	PROGRAMMING	PROPRIETORS
PREPARATION	PRIMIPARITY	PROGRESSING	PROROGATION
PREPARATIVE	PRIMIPAROUS	PROGRESSION	PROSAICALLY
PREPARATORY	PRIMITIVELY	PROGRESSIVE	PROSAICNESS
PREPOSITION	PRIMITIVISM	PROHIBITING	PROS AND CONS
PREPOSITIVE	PRIMITIVIST	PROHIBITION	PROSCENIUMS
PREP SCHOOLS	PRINCIPALLY	PROHIBITIVE	PROSCRIBING
PRERECORDED	PRINTING INK	PROHIBITORY	PROSECUTING
PREROGATIVE	PRIORITIZED	PROJECTILES	PROSECUTION
PRESBYTERAL	PRISON CAMPS	PROJECTIONS	PROSECUTORS
PRESCRIBING	PRIVATIZING	PROKOPYEVSK	PROSELYTISM
PRESENTABLE	PRIZEFIGHTS	PROLATENESS	PROSELYTIZE
PRESENTABLY	PROBABILISM	PROLEGOMENA	PROSENCHYMA
PRESENT ARMS	PROBABILIST	PROLETARIAN	PROSPECTING
PRESENTIENT	PROBABILITY	PROLETARIAT	PROSPECTIVE
PRESENTMENT	PROBATIONAL	PROLIFERATE	PROSPECTORS
PRESERVABLE	PROBATIONER	PROLIFEROUS	PROSTATITIS
PRESS AGENCY	PROBLEMATIC	PROLONGMENT	PROSTHETICS
PRESS AGENTS	PROBOSCIDES	PROMENADING	PROSTITUTED
PRESS BARONS	PROBOSCISES	PROMINENCES	PROSTITUTES
PRESSGANGED	PROCEEDINGS	PROMINENTLY	PROSTITUTOR
PRESSURIZED	PROCEPHALIC	PROMISCUITY	PROSTRATING
PRESSURIZER	PROCESSIONS	PROMISCUOUS	PROSTRATION
PRESTIGIOUS	PROCHRONISM	PROMISINGLY	PROTAGONISM
PRESTISSIMO	PROCLAIMING	PROMOTIONAL	PROTAGONIST
PRESTONPANS	PROCONSULAR	PROMPTITUDE	PROTANDROUS
PRESTRESSED	PROCREATING	PROMULGATED	PROTECTIONS
PRESUMINGLY	PROCREATION	PROMULGATOR	PROTECTORAL
PRESUMPTION	PROCRUSTEAN	PROMYCELIUM	PROTECTRESS
PRESUMPTIVE	PROCTOSCOPE	PRONOUNCING	PROTEOLYSIS
PRESUPPOSED	PROCTOSCOPY	PROOFREADER	PROTEOLYTIC
PRETENDEDLY	PROCURATION	PROOF SPIRIT	PROTEROZOIC
PRETENSIONS	PROCUREMENT	PROPAGATING	PROTESTANTS
PRETENTIOUS	PRODIGALITY	PROPAGATION	PROTHROMBIN
PRETERITION	PRODUCTIONS	PROPAGATIVE	PROTOGYNOUS
PRETERITIVE	PROFANATION	PROPAGATORS	PROTOLITHIC
PRETTIFYING	PROFANATORY	PROPELLANTS	PROTOPATHIC

PROTOSTELIC	PULAU PINANG	QUADRENNIUM	RABBIT PUNCH
PROTRACTILE	PULCHRITUDE	QUADRILLION	RABELAISIAN
PROTRACTING	PULL STRINGS	QUADRUPEDAL	RACECOURSES
PROTRACTION	PULLULATING	QUADRUPLETS	RACE MEETING
PROTRACTIVE	PULLULATION	QUADRUPLING	RACQUETBALL
PROTRACTORS	PULSATILITY	QUALIFIABLE	RADIATIONAL
PROTRUDABLE	PULVERIZING	QUALITATIVE	RADICALNESS
PROTRUSIONS	PULVERULENT	QUANGOCRACY	RADIOACTIVE
PROTUBERANT	PUMPKINSEED	QUANTIFIERS	RADIO ALARMS
PROVABILITY	PUNCHED CARD	QUANTIFYING	RADIO BEACON
PROVIDENCES	PUNCTILIOUS	QUANTUM LEAP	RADIOCARBON
PROVIDENTLY	PUNCTUALITY	QUARANTINED	RADIOGRAPHY
PROVINCIALS	PUNCTUATING	QUARRELLING	RADIOLARIAN
PROVISIONAL	PUNCTUATION	QUARRELSOME	RADIOLOGIST
PROVISIONED	PUNCTURABLE	QUARTER DAYS	RADIOLUCENT
PROVISIONER	PUNISHINGLY	QUARTERDECK	RADIOMETRIC
PROVISORILY	PUNISHMENTS	QUARTER-HOUR	RADIOPACITY
PROVOCATION	PUNTA ARENAS	QUARTERLIES	RADIOPHONIC
PROVOCATIVE	PURCHASABLE	QUARTER NOTE	RADIOSCOPIC
PROVOKINGLY	PURCHASE TAX	QUAVERINGLY	RADIOTHERMY
PROXIMATELY	PUREBLOODED	QUEENLINESS	RAFFISHNESS
PROXIMATION	PURGATORIAL	QUEEN MOTHER	RAGAMUFFINS
PRUDENTNESS	PURIFICATOR	QUEEN'S BENCH	RAILROADING
PRUDISHNESS	PURITANICAL	QUERULOUSLY	RAIN FORESTS
PRUSSIC ACID	PURPLE HEART	QUESTIONARY	RAISON D'ETRE
PSEUDOMORPH	PURPOSELESS	QUESTIONERS	RALLENTANDO
PSILOMELANE	PUSHINGNESS	QUESTIONING	RAMAN EFFECT
PSITTACOSIS	PUSSYFOOTED	QUESTION TAG	RAMBOUILLET
PSYCHEDELIA	PUSSY WILLOW	QUEUE-JUMPED	RANCH HOUSES
PSYCHEDELIC	PUSTULATION	QUEUE-JUMPER	RANCOROUSLY
PSYCHIATRIC	PUTREFIABLE	QUIBBLINGLY	RANGE FINDER
PSYCHICALLY	PUTRESCENCE	QUICK-CHANGE	RANK AND FILE
PSYCHOBILLY	PYCNOMETRIC	QUICK-FREEZE	RAPACIOUSLY
PSYCHODRAMA	PYELOGRAPHY	QUICKSILVER	RAPSCALLION
PSYCHOGENIC	PYLORECTOMY	QUICK-WITTED	RAPTUROUSLY
PSYCHOGRAPH	PYRANOMETER	QUID PRO QUOS	RAREFACTION
PSYCHOMETRY	PYRARGYRITE	QUIESCENTLY	RASPBERRIES
PSYCHOMOTOR	PYROCLASTIC	QUINCUNCIAL	RASTAFARIAN
PSYCHOPATHS	PYROGALLATE	QUINDECAGON	RATE-CAPPING
PSYCHOPATHY	PYROGRAPHER	QUINTANA ROO	RATIOCINATE
PTERIDOLOGY	PYROGRAPHIC	QUINTILLION	RATIONALISM
PTERODACTYL	PYROMANIACS	QUINTUPLETS	RATIONALIST
PTOCHOCRACY	PYROTECHNIC	QUIVERINGLY	RATIONALITY
PUB-CRAWLING	PYRRHULOXIA	QUIZMASTERS	RATIONALIZE
PUBLICATION	PYRROLIDINE	QUIZZICALLY	RATTLESNAKE
PUBLIC HOUSE	PYTHAGOREAN	QUONSET HUTS	RATTLETRAPS
PUBLICIZING	PYTHONESQUE	QUOTABILITY	RAUCOUSNESS
PUBLIC WORKS		QUOTE-DRIVEN	RAUNCHINESS
PUBLISHABLE	**Q**		RAVEN-HAIRED
PUCKISHNESS	QUADRANGLES		RAVISHINGLY
PUERTO RICAN	QUADRENNIAL	**R**	REACH-ME-DOWN
		RABBIT HUTCH	

REACTIONARY	RECONDITION	REFRESHMENT	REMONSTRANT
REACTIONISM	RECONNOITRE	REFRIGERANT	REMONSTRATE
REACTIVATED	RECONSTRUCT	REFRIGERATE	REMORSELESS
READABILITY	RECOVERABLE	REFRINGENCY	REMOVAL VANS
READDRESSED	RECREATIONS	REFURBISHED	REMUNERABLE
READERSHIPS	RECREMENTAL	REFUTATIONS	REMUNERATED
READJUSTING	RECRIMINATE	REGENERABLE	REMUNERATOR
READ-THROUGH	RECRUITABLE	REGENERATED	RENAISSANCE
READY-TO-WEAR	RECRUITMENT	REGIMENTALS	RENEGOTIATE
READY-WITTED	RECTANGULAR	REGIMENTING	RENOVATIONS
REAFFIRMING	RECTIFIABLE	REGIONALISM	RENTABILITY
REALIGNMENT	RECTILINEAR	REGIONALIST	RENT STRIKES
REALIZATION	RECUPERATED	REGISTERING	REORGANIZED
REALPOLITIK	RECUPERATOR	REGISTRABLE	REORGANIZER
REANIMATING	RECURRENCES	REGRETFULLY	REPARATIONS
REANIMATION	RECURRENTLY	REGRETTABLE	REPARTITION
REAPPEARING	RECURRINGLY	REGRETTABLY	REPATRIATED
REAPPORTION	REDACTIONAL	REGULARIZED	REPELLINGLY
REAPPRAISAL	RED ADMIRALS	REGULATIONS	REPENTANTLY
REAPPRAISED	RED CRESCENT	REGURGITANT	REPERTOIRES
REAR ADMIRAL	REDCURRANTS	REGURGITATE	REPERTORIAL
REARRANGING	REDECORATED	REIFICATION	REPERTORIES
REASSURANCE	REDEPLOYING	REIMBURSING	REPETITIONS
REASSUREDLY	REDEVELOPED	REINCARNATE	REPETITIOUS
REBARBATIVE	REDEVELOPER	REINFORCING	REPLACEABLE
RECALESCENT	RED HERRINGS	REINSTATING	REPLACEMENT
RECANTATION	REDIFFUSION	REINSURANCE	REPLENISHED
RECAPTURING	REDIRECTING	REINTRODUCE	REPLENISHER
RECEIVABLES	REDIRECTION	REITERATING	REPLETENESS
RECEPTACLES	REDOUBTABLE	REITERATION	REPLEVIABLE
RECEPTIVELY	REDOUBTABLY	REITERATIVE	REPLICATING
RECEPTIVITY	REDRESSABLE	REJUVENATED	REPLICATION
RECESSIONAL	REDUCTIONAL	REJUVENATOR	REPLICATIVE
RECIDIVISTS	REDUNDANTLY	RELATEDNESS	REPOSSESSED
RECIPROCATE	REDUPLICATE	RELAXATIONS	REPOSSESSOR
RECIPROCITY	RE-EDUCATING	RELIABILITY	REPREHENDED
RECITATIONS	RE-EDUCATION	RELIEF ROADS	REPREHENDER
RECITATIVES	RE-ELECTIONS	RELIGIONISM	REPRESENTED
RECLAIMABLE	REFECTORIES	RELIGIOSITY	REPRESSIBLE
RECLAMATION	REFERENDUMS	RELIGIOUSLY	REPRESSIONS
RECLINATION	REFERENTIAL	RELIQUARIES	REPRIEVABLE
RECOGNITION	REFINEMENTS	RELISHINGLY	REPRIMANDED
RECOGNIZING	REFLECTANCE	RELUCTANTLY	REPRIMANDER
RECOILINGLY	REFLECTIONS	RELUCTIVITY	REPROACHFUL
RECOLLECTED	REFORESTING	REMAINDERED	REPROACHING
RECOMBINANT	REFORMATION	REMEMBERING	REPROBATION
RECOMMENDED	REFORMATIVE	REMEMBRANCE	REPROBATIVE
RECOMMENDER	REFORMATORY	REMINISCENT	REPROCESSED
RECOMPENSED	REFRACTABLE	REMINISCING	REPRODUCERS
RECOMPENSER	REFRAINMENT	REMITTANCES	REPRODUCING
RECONCILING	REFRANGIBLE	REMODELLING	REPROGRAPHY

REPROVINGLY
REPUBLICANS
REPUBLISHER
REPUDIATING
REPUDIATION
REPUDIATIVE
REPUDIATORY
REPULSIVELY
REPUTATIONS
REQUEST STOP
REQUIREMENT
REQUISITION
REQUITEMENT
RERADIATION
RESCHEDULED
RESCINDABLE
RESCINDMENT
RESCISSIBLE
RESEARCHERS
RESEARCHING
RESECTIONAL
RESEMBLANCE
RESENTFULLY
RESERVATION
RESHUFFLING
RESIDENTIAL
RESIGNATION
RESILIENTLY
RESISTANCES
RESISTENCIA
RESISTINGLY
RESISTIVITY
RESOLUTIONS
RESOURCEFUL
RESPECTABLE
RESPECTABLY
RESPIRATION
RESPIRATORS
RESPIRATORY
RESPLENDENT
RESPONDENCE
RESPONDENTS
RESPONSIBLE
RESPONSIBLY
RESPONSIONS
RESTATEMENT
RESTAURANTS
RESTFULNESS
RESTITUTION
RESTITUTIVE
RESTIVENESS

RESTORATION
RESTORATIVE
RESTRAINING
RESTRICTING
RESTRICTION
RESTRICTIVE
RESTRUCTURE
RESURFACING
RESURRECTED
RESUSCITATE
RETALIATING
RETALIATION
RETALIATIVE
RETALIATORY
RETARDATION
RETARDATIVE
RETARDINGLY
RETENTIVELY
RETENTIVITY
RETICULATED
RETINACULAR
RETINACULUM
RETINOSCOPY
RETIREMENTS
RETOUCHABLE
RETRACEABLE
RETRACEMENT
RETRACTABLE
RETRACTIONS
RETRENCHING
RETRIBUTION
RETRIBUTIVE
RETRIEVABLE
RETRIEVABLY
RETROACTION
RETROACTIVE
RETROLENTAL
RETRO-ROCKET
RETROVERTED
REUPHOLSTER
REUSABILITY
REVALUATION
REVEALINGLY
REVELATIONS
REVENGINGLY
REVERBERANT
REVERBERATE
REVERENCING
REVERENTIAL
REVERSIONER
REVISIONISM

REVISIONIST
REVITALIZED
REVIVALISTS
REVIVIFYING
REVOCATIONS
REVOLTINGLY
REVOLUTIONS
REVOLVINGLY
RHABDOMANCY
RHABDOMYOMA
RHAMNACEOUS
RHAPSODIZED
RHEOLOGICAL
RHEOTROPISM
RHETORICIAN
RHEUMATICKY
RHINESTONES
RHINOLOGIST
RHINOPLASTY
RHINOSCOPIC
RHIZOMATOUS
RHIZOPODOUS
RHIZOSPHERE
RHODE ISLAND
RHOTACISTIC
RHYTHMICITY
RICE PADDIES
RICKETINESS
RICKETTSIAL
RICOCHETING
RICOCHETTED
RIFLE RANGES
RIFT VALLEYS
RIGHT-ANGLED
RIGHT ANGLES
RIGHTEOUSLY
RIGHT-HANDED
RIGHT-HANDER
RIGHT-MINDED
RIGHTS ISSUE
RIGHTS OF WAY
RIGHT-WINGER
RIGOR MORTIS
RING BINDERS
RING FINGERS
RINGLEADERS
RINGMASTERS
RINSABILITY
RIOTOUSNESS
RITUALISTIC
RIVER BASINS

ROADHOLDING
ROAD MANAGER
ROAD PRICING
ROAD ROLLERS
ROAD TESTING
ROCK-AND-ROLL
ROCK GARDENS
ROCKHAMPTON
RODENTICIDE
RODOMONTADE
ROENTGEN RAY
ROGUISHNESS
ROLE PLAYING
ROLLERBLADE
ROLLERBLADE
ROLLER BLIND
ROLLER SKATE
ROLLER TOWEL
ROLLICKINGS
ROLLICKSOME
ROLLING MILL
ROLLING PINS
ROLLTOP DESK
ROMAN CANDLE
ROMANTICISM
ROMANTICIST
ROMANTICIZE
ROOD SCREENS
ROOF GARDENS
ROOM SERVICE
ROPE LADDERS
ROSE WINDOWS
ROTARIANISM
ROTISSERIES
ROTOGRAVURE
ROTTENSTONE
ROTUNDITIES
ROUGHCASTER
ROUGH-SPOKEN
ROUNDABOUTS
ROUNDEDNESS
ROUND ROBINS
ROUSTABOUTS
ROWING BOATS
ROYAL TENNIS
RUBBER BANDS
RUBBER PLANT
RUBBER STAMP
RUBBER TREES
RUBBISH BINS
RUBEFACIENT

RUBEFACTION	SAGITTARIUS	SANGUINEOUS	SCHIZOPHYTE
RUBICUNDITY	SAILING BOAT	SANITARIUMS	SCHLESINGER
RUBRICATION	SAILOR SUITS	SAN MARINESE	SCHOLARSHIP
RUDESHEIMER	SAINT ALBANS	SAN SALVADOR	SCHOLIASTIC
RUDIMENTARY	SAINT-BRIEUC	SANSEVIERIA	SCHOOLCHILD
RUGBY LEAGUE	SAINT GALLEN	SANSKRITIST	SCHOOLHOUSE
RULE OF THUMB	SAINT HELENA	SAPONACEOUS	SCHOOLMARMS
RUMBUSTIOUS	SAINT HELENS	SAPOTACEOUS	SCHOOLMATES
RUMINATIONS	SAINT HELIER	SAPROPHYTIC	SCHWEINFURT
RUMMAGE SALE	SAINTLINESS	SARCOMATOID	SCIENCE PARK
RUMPUS ROOMS	SAINT MARTIN	SARCOPHAGUS	SCIENTISTIC
RUNNER BEANS	SAINT MORITZ	SARDONICISM	SCIENTOLOGY
RUNNING JUMP	SAINT THOMAS	SARGASSO SEA	SCINTILLATE
RUNNING MATE	SALACIOUSLY	SARTORIALLY	SCIRRHOSITY
RUN-THROUGHS	SALAMANDERS	SASH WINDOWS	SCLERODERMA
RUNTISHNESS	SALEABILITY	SATANICALLY	SCLEROMETER
RUSSOPHOBIA	SALESCLERKS	SATELLITIUM	SCLEROTIOID
RUSSOPHOBIC	SALESPEOPLE	SATIABILITY	SCOPOLAMINE
RUSTICATING	SALESPERSON	SATIRICALLY	SCOREBOARDS
RUSTICATION	SALICACEOUS	SATISFIABLE	SCORIACEOUS
RUSTPROOFED	SALIENTNESS	SATURNALIAS	SCORPAENOID
RUTTISHNESS	SALINOMETER	SAUDI ARABIA	SCOTCH BROTH
	SALINOMETRY	SAURISCHIAN	SCOTCH MISTS
S	SALMONBERRY	SAUROPODOUS	SCOTCH TAPED
SAARBRUCKEN	SALMON TROUT	SAUSAGE DOGS	SCOTOMATOUS
SABBATARIAN	SALPINGITIC	SAUSAGE ROLL	SCOURGINGLY
SABBATICALS	SALPINGITIS	SAVABLENESS	SCOUTMASTER
SACCULATION	SALTATORIAL	SAVING GRACE	SCRAGGINESS
SACRAMENTAL	SALTCELLARS	SAVINGS BANK	SCRAPPINESS
SACRIFICIAL	SALT SHAKERS	SAVOIR-FAIRE	SCRATCHCARD
SACRIFICING	SALUTATIONS	SAVOURINGLY	SCRATCHIEST
SACRILEGIST	SALVABILITY	SAXOPHONIST	SCRATCHINGS
SACROILIACS	SALVADORIAN	SCAFFOLDING	SCRATCHPADS
SADDENINGLY	SALVAGEABLE	SCALARIFORM	SCRAWNINESS
SADDLECLOTH	SALVATIONAL	SCAMMONIATE	SCREAMINGLY
SAFARI PARKS	SAL VOLATILE	SCANDALIZED	SCREENPLAYS
SAFEBREAKER	SAMURAI BOND	SCANDALIZER	SCREENSAVER
SAFE-CONDUCT	SAN ANTONIAN	SCANDINAVIA	SCREEN TESTS
SAFE-DEPOSIT	SANATORIUMS	SCARABAEOID	SCREWDRIVER
SAFEGUARDED	SANCTIFYING	SCARBOROUGH	SCRIMMAGING
SAFEKEEPING	SANCTIONING	SCAREDY CATS	SCRIMPINESS
SAFETY BELTS	SANCTUARIES	SCAREMONGER	SCRIPTORIUM
SAFETY CATCH	SANDBAGGING	SCARLATINAL	SCRUBBINESS
SAFETY-FIRST	SANDBLASTED	SCATOLOGIST	SCRUMHALVES
SAFETY GLASS	SANDBLASTER	SCATTERABLE	SCRUMMAGING
SAFETY LAMPS	SAND-CASTING	SCENOGRAPHY	SCRUMPTIOUS
SAFETY MATCH	SANDCASTLES	SCEPTICALLY	SCRUTINEERS
SAFETY RAZOR	SANDPAPERED	SCHEMATIZED	SCRUTINIZED
SAFETY VALVE	SANDWICHING	SCHISMATICS	SCRUTINIZER
SAGACIOUSLY	SAN FERNANDO	SCHISTOSITY	SCUBA DIVING
SAGITTARIAN	SANGUINARIA	SCHISTOSOME	SCULPTURING

SCYPHISTOMA	SELF-IMPOSED	SEPTICAEMIC	SHIFTLESSLY
SEA ANEMONES	SELF-INDUCED	SEPTIC TANKS	SHIFT STICKS
SEA CAPTAINS	SELFISHNESS	SEPTIFRAGAL	SHIMONOSEKI
SEARCHINGLY	SELF-LOADING	SEPTIVALENT	SHIP BISCUIT
SEARCHLIGHT	SELF-LOCKING	SEQUESTERED	SHIPBUILDER
SEARCH PARTY	SELF-PITYING	SEQUESTRANT	SHIPWRECKED
SEASICKNESS	SELF-RELIANT	SEQUESTRATE	SHIPWRIGHTS
SEBORRHOEAL	SELF-RESPECT	SERENDIPITY	SHIRE HORSES
SECESSIONAL	SELF-SEALING	SERIALIZING	SHIRTFRONTS
SECONDARILY	SELF-SEEKERS	SERICULTURE	SHIRTSLEEVE
SECOND CLASS	SELF-SEEKING	SERIES-WOUND	SHISH KEBABS
SECOND-CLASS	SELF-SERVICE	SERIOUSNESS	SHIVERINGLY
SECOND-GUESS	SELF-STARTER	SERMONIZING	SHOCKHEADED
SECOND HANDS	SELF-WINDING	SERPIGINOUS	SHOCK TROOPS
SECONDMENTS	SELL-BY DATES	SERRULATION	SHOESTRINGS
SECOND-RATER	SELLOTAPING	SERTULARIAN	SHOPKEEPERS
SECOND SIGHT	SELL-THROUGH	SERVICEABLE	SHOPLIFTERS
SECRET AGENT	SEMANTICIST	SERVICEABLY	SHOPLIFTING
SECRETARIAL	SEMASIOLOGY	SERVICE FLAT	SHOP STEWARD
SECRETARIAT	SEMIAQUATIC	SERVICE ROAD	SHOPWALKERS
SECRETARIES	SEMIARIDITY	SERVOMOTORS	SHORT CHANGE
SECRETIVELY	SEMICIRCLES	SESQUIOXIDE	SHORT-CHANGE
SECULARIZED	SEMIDIURNAL	SETTLEMENTS	SHORTCOMING
SECULARIZER	SEMIFLUIDIC	SEVENTEENTH	SHORT CORNER
SEDAN CHAIRS	SEMIMONTHLY	SEVENTIETHS	SHORTHANDED
SEDENTARILY	SEMIOTICIAN	SEXAGESIMAL	SHORT-HANDED
SEDIMENTARY	SEMIPALMATE	SEXLESSNESS	SHORT-LISTED
SEDIMENTOUS	SEMIQUAVERS	SEXOLOGISTS	SHORT SHRIFT
SEDITIONARY	SEMISKILLED	SEXTODECIMO	SHORT-SPOKEN
SEDITIOUSLY	SEMITONALLY	SHADOW-BOXED	SHORT-WINDED
SEDUCTIVELY	SEMITRAILER	SHADOWGRAPH	SHOULDERING
SEGREGATING	SEMITROPICS	SHADOWINESS	SHOWERPROOF
SEGREGATION	SEMIVOCALIC	SHALLOWNESS	SHOW JUMPERS
SEGREGATIVE	SEMPERVIVUM	SHAMANISTIC	SHOW JUMPING
SEIGNIORAGE	SEMPITERNAL	SHAMELESSLY	SHOWMANSHIP
SEISMICALLY	SENSATIONAL	SHANGHAIING	SHOW OF HANDS
SEISMOGRAPH	SENSELESSLY	SHANKS'S PONY	SHOWSTOPPER
SEISMOLOGIC	SENSE ORGANS	SHANTYTOWNS	SHRINKINGLY
SEISMOSCOPE	SENSIBILITY	SHAPELESSLY	SHRIVELLING
SELAGINELLA	SENSITIVELY	SHAPELINESS	SHRUBBERIES
SELECTIVELY	SENSITIVITY	SHAREHOLDER	SHRUBBINESS
SELECTIVITY	SENSITIZING	SHARPBENDER	SHUFFLE PLAY
SELENOGRAPH	SENSUALISTS	SHARP-WITTED	SHUTTLECOCK
SELF-ASSURED	SENSUALNESS	SHAVING FOAM	SIAMESE CATS
SELF-CENTRED	SENTENTIOUS	SHEATH KNIFE	SIAMESE TWIN
SELF-COMMAND	SENTIMENTAL	SHEET ANCHOR	SICKENINGLY
SELF-CONCEPT	SENTRY BOXES	SHELLACKING	SIDE EFFECTS
SELF-CONTROL	SEPARATIONS	SHENANIGANS	SIDESADDLES
SELF-DEFENCE	SEPARATISTS	SHEPHERDESS	SIDESLIPPED
SELF-DENYING	SEPTAVALENT	SHEPHERDING	SIDESTEPPED
SELF-EVIDENT	SEPTICAEMIA	SHIBBOLETHS	SIDESTEPPER

SIDE STREETS	SINO-TIBETAN	SLOUCHINESS	SOLILOQUIZE
SIDESWIPING	SINUOSITIES	SLOUCHINGLY	SOLIPSISTIC
SIDETRACKED	SINUOUSNESS	SLOWCOACHES	SOLMIZATION
SIDE-WHEELER	SISTERHOODS	SLUMGULLION	SOLUBLENESS
SIENKIEWICZ	SISTER-IN-LAW	SMALL CHANGE	SOLVABILITY
SIERRA LEONE	SITTING BULL	SMALLHOLDER	SOMATICALLY
SIERRA MADRE	SITTING DUCK	SMALL-MINDED	SOMATOLOGIC
SIGHTLINESS	SITTING ROOM	SMALL SCREEN	SOMATOPLASM
SIGHT-READER	SITUATIONAL	SMALL-TIMERS	SOMERSAULTS
SIGHTSCREEN	SIX-SHOOTERS	SMART ALECKS	SOMNOLENTLY
SIGHTSEEING	SIXTH-FORMER	SMART ALECKY	SONGFULNESS
SIGNAL BOXES	SIZABLENESS	SMARTY-PANTS	SON-OF-A-BITCH
SIGNALIZING	SKATEBOARDS	SMATTERINGS	SOOTHSAYERS
SIGNATORIES	SKEDADDLING	SMILINGNESS	SOPHISTRIES
SIGNIFIABLE	SKELETONIZE	SMITHEREENS	SORORICIDAL
SIGNIFICANT	SKELETON KEY	SMITHSONITE	SORROWFULLY
SIGNPOSTING	SKEPTICALLY	SMOKESCREEN	SOTTISHNESS
SILHOUETTED	SKETCHINESS	SMOKESTACKS	SOUBRIQUETS
SILHOUETTES	SKILFULNESS	SMOOTH-FACED	SOUGHT-AFTER
SILICON CHIP	SKIMMED MILK	SMORGASBORD	SOUL BROTHER
SILLIMANITE	SKIRMISHERS	SMOULDERING	SOULFULNESS
SILLY SEASON	SKIRMISHING	SNAPDRAGONS	SOUNDLESSLY
SILVER BIRCH	SKULDUGGERY	SNIPERSCOPE	SOUNDTRACKS
SILVERINESS	SKYJACKINGS	SNORKELLING	SOUP KITCHEN
SILVER MEDAL	SKYROCKETED	SNOWBALLING	SOUSAPHONES
SILVER PAPER	SKYSCRAPERS	SNOWMOBILES	SOUTH AFRICA
SILVER PLATE	SLAUGHTERED	SNOWPLOUGHS	SOUTHAMPTON
SILVERPOINT	SLAUGHTERER	SOAP BUBBLES	SOUTH DAKOTA
SILVERSMITH	SLAVE DRIVER	SOCIABILITY	SOUTHEASTER
SIMMERINGLY	SLAVE LABOUR	SOCIALISTIC	SOUTHERNERS
SIMPERINGLY	SLAVISHNESS	SOCIALIZING	SOUTH ISLAND
SIMPLIFYING	SLEEPING BAG	SOCIOLOGIST	SOUTHWESTER
SIMPLON PASS	SLEEPING CAR	SOCIOMETRIC	SOVEREIGNTY
SIMULACRUMS	SLEEPLESSLY	SOCIOPATHIC	SOVIETISTIC
SIMULATIONS	SLEEPWALKED	SOFTHEARTED	SPACE HEATER
SINE QUA NONS	SLEEPWALKER	SOFT LANDING	SPACE PROBES
SINFONIETTA	SLEEPYHEADS	SOFT OPTIONS	SPARINGNESS
SINGAPOREAN	SLENDERIZED	SOFT PALATES	SPARROWHAWK
SINGLE-BLIND	SLENDERNESS	SOFT-PEDALED	SPASTICALLY
SINGLE-CROSS	SLEUTHHOUND	SOFT-SOAPING	SPATHACEOUS
SINGLE-PHASE	SLICED BREAD	SOFT TOUCHES	SPEAKEASIES
SINGLE-SPACE	SLICE OF LIFE	SOLANACEOUS	SPEAKERSHIP
SINGLE-TRACK	SLICKENSIDE	SOLARIMETER	SPEARHEADED
SINGULARITY	SLIDE-ACTION	SOLAR PANELS	SPECIALISMS
SINGULARIZE	SLIDING DOOR	SOLAR PLEXUS	SPECIALISTS
SINISTRORSE	SLIGHTINGLY	SOLAR SYSTEM	SPECIALIZED
SINKING FUND	SLIPPED DISC	SOLEMNITIES	SPECIALNESS
SINLESSNESS	SLIPSTREAMS	SOLEMNIZING	SPECIFIABLE
SINN FEINISM	SLOOP-RIGGED	SOLIDIFYING	SPECIFICITY
SINOLOGICAL	SLOPINGNESS	SOLILOQUIES	SPECTACULAR
SINOLOGISTS	SLOT MACHINE	SOLILOQUIST	SPECTRALITY

SPECULATING	SPONGE CAKES	STALEMATING	STEREOGRAPH
SPECULATION	SPONSORSHIP	STALLHOLDER	STEREOMETRY
SPECULATIVE	SPONTANEITY	STANDARDIZE	STEREOSCOPE
SPECULATORS	SPONTANEOUS	STANDOFFISH	STEREOSCOPY
SPEECHIFIED	SPOONERISMS	STANDPOINTS	STEREOTAXIS
SPEECHIFIER	SPOROGENOUS	STANLEY POOL	STEREOTYPED
SPEED LIMITS	SPOROGONIAL	STARA ZAGORA	STEREOTYPER
SPEEDOMETER	SPOROGONIUM	STAR CHAMBER	STEREOTYPES
SPELLBINDER	SPOROPHYTIC	STARCHINESS	STEREOTYPIC
SPENDTHRIFT	SPORTSWOMAN	STAR-CROSSED	STERILIZERS
SPERMATHECA	SPORULATION	STAR-STUDDED	STERILIZING
SPERMATOZOA	SPOT CHECKED	STARTER HOME	STERLITAMAK
SPERMICIDES	SPOTTED DICK	STARTLINGLY	STERNUTATOR
SPERMOPHILE	SPREAD-EAGLE	STARVELINGS	STETHOSCOPE
SPERM WHALES	SPREADSHEET	STATELINESS	STETHOSCOPY
SPESSARTITE	SPRINGBOARD	STATELY HOME	STEWARDSHIP
SPHEROMETER	SPRING-CLEAN	STATESWOMAN	STICHICALLY
SPHERULITIC	SPRINGFIELD	STATISTICAL	STICHOMETRY
SPHINCTERAL	SPRINGINESS	STATOLITHIC	STICKHANDLE
SPHINGOSINE	SPRING ONION	STATUTE BOOK	STICK INSECT
SPHRAGISTIC	SPRING ROLLS	STATUTORILY	STICKLEBACK
SPINA BIFIDA	SPRING TIDES	STAUNCHABLE	STICK SHIFTS
SPINAL CORDS	SPRINKLINGS	STAUNCHNESS	STIFF-NECKED
SPINELESSLY	SPUMESCENCE	STAUROLITIC	STIGMATICAL
SPINESCENCE	SQUANDERERS	STAUROSCOPE	STIGMATIZED
SPINIFEROUS	SQUANDERING	STAY-AT-HOMES	STIGMATIZER
SPINSTERISH	SQUARE DANCE	STEADFASTLY	STILLBIRTHS
SPINY-FINNED	SQUARE KNOTS	STEALTHIEST	STILTEDNESS
SPIRACULATE	SQUARE MEALS	STEAM-BOILER	STIMULATING
SPIRIFEROUS	SQUARE ROOTS	STEAM-ENGINE	STIMULATION
SPIRIT LEVEL	SQUASHINESS	STEAMROLLER	STIMULATIVE
SPIRITUALLY	SQUEAMISHLY	STEAM SHOVEL	STIPENDIARY
SPIRKETTING	SQUELCHIEST	STEAROPTENE	STIPULATING
SPIROCHAETE	SQUIGGLIEST	STEATOLYSIS	STIPULATION
SPIROMETRIC	SQUIREARCHY	STEATOPYGIA	STIPULATORY
SPITSTICKER	SQUIRMINGLY	STEATOPYGIC	STIRRUP CUPS
SPLASHBOARD	STABILIZERS	STEELWORKER	STIRRUP PUMP
SPLASHDOWNS	STABILIZING	STEEPLEJACK	STOCKBROKER
SPLASH GUARD	STADIOMETER	STEERAGEWAY	STOCKHOLDER
SPLASHINESS	STAFF NURSES	STELLARATOR	STOCKJOBBER
SPLATTERING	STAGE FRIGHT	STENCILLING	STOCK MARKET
SPLAYFOOTED	STAGE-MANAGE	STENOGRAPHY	STOCKPILING
SPLENDOROUS	STAGESTRUCK	STENOHALINE	STOCKTAKING
SPLENECTOMY	STAGGERBUSH	STENOPHAGUS	STOICALNESS
SPLENETICAL	STAGING POST	STENOTROPIC	STOMACHACHE
SPLINTERING	STAG PARTIES	STENOTYPIST	STOMACHICAL
SPLIT SECOND	STAKEHOLDER	STEPBROTHER	STOMACH PUMP
SPLUTTERING	STALACTITES	STEPHANOTIS	STOMATOLOGY
SPOILSPORTS	STALACTITIC	STEPLADDERS	STONECUTTER
SPOKESWOMAN	STALAGMITES	STEPPARENTS	STONE FRUITS
SPONDYLITIS	STALAGMITIC	STEPSISTERS	STONE-GROUND

STONEMASONS	STROBOSCOPE	SUBMERSIBLE	SUFFICIENCY
STONE'S THROW	STRONGBOXES	SUBMISSIONS	SUFFOCATING
STONEWALLED	STRONGHOLDS	SUBMITTABLE	SUFFOCATION
STONEWALLER	STRONG POINT	SUBMULTIPLE	SUFFOCATIVE
STONEWORKER	STRONG ROOMS	SUBORDINARY	SUFFRAGETTE
STOOLPIGEON	STRUCTURING	SUBORDINATE	SUFFUMIGATE
STOPWATCHES	STRUCTURIST	SUBORNATION	SUGGESTIBLE
STOREHOUSES	STRUTTINGLY	SUBORNATIVE	SUGGESTIONS
STOREKEEPER	STUBBORNEST	SUBPOENAING	SUITABILITY
STORE KEEPER	STUDENTSHIP	SUBREGIONAL	SULPHA DRUGS
STORM CLOUDS	STUDIEDNESS	SUBROGATION	SULPHUREOUS
STORYTELLER	STUDIO COUCH	SUBROUTINES	SUMMARINESS
STOURBRIDGE	STULTIFYING	SUBSCAPULAR	SUMMARIZING
STRAGGLIEST	STUMBLINGLY	SUBSCRIBERS	SUMMATIONAL
STRAIGHTEST	STUNTEDNESS	SUBSCRIBING	SUMMERHOUSE
STRAIGHT-OUT	STUPIDITIES	SUBSECTIONS	SUMMERINESS
STRAIGHTWAY	STYLISHNESS	SUBSEQUENCE	SUMPTUOUSLY
STRAININGLY	STYLIZATION	SUBSERVIENT	SUNDRENCHED
STRAITLACED	STYLOGRAPHY	SUBSIDENCES	SUNLESSNESS
STRANGENESS	STYLOPODIUM	SUBSIDIZERS	SUNNY-SIDE UP
STRANGULATE	STYLOSTIXIS	SUBSIDIZING	SUPERABOUND
STRAPHANGER	SUBASSEMBLY	SUBSISTENCE	SUPERCHARGE
STRATEGISTS	SUBAUDITION	SUBSPECIFIC	SUPERFAMILY
STRATHCLYDE	SUBAXILLARY	SUBSTANDARD	SUPERFETATE
STRATIFYING	SUBBASEMENT	SUBSTANTIAL	SUPERFICIAL
STRATOCRACY	SUBCHLORIDE	SUBSTANTIVE	SUPERFLUITY
STRATOPAUSE	SUBCOMPACTS	SUBSTATIONS	SUPERFLUOUS
STRAWFLOWER	SUBCONTRACT	SUBSTITUENT	SUPERIMPOSE
STRAWWEIGHT	SUBCONTRARY	SUBSTITUTED	SUPERINDUCE
STREAKINESS	SUBCORTICAL	SUBSTITUTES	SUPERINTEND
STREAMLINED	SUBCULTURAL	SUBSTRATIVE	SUPERIORITY
STREETLIGHT	SUBCULTURES	SUBSUMPTION	SUPERJACENT
STREET VALUE	SUBDELIRIUM	SUBSUMPTIVE	SUPERLATIVE
STRENUOSITY	SUBDIACONAL	SUBTERFUGES	SUPERLUNARY
STRENUOUSLY	SUBDIVIDING	SUBTRACTING	SUPERMARKET
STRESS MARKS	SUBDIVISION	SUBTRACTION	SUPERNATANT
STRETCHABLE	SUBDOMINANT	SUBTRACTIVE	SUPERNORMAL
STRETCHIEST	SUBDUEDNESS	SUBTROPICAL	SUPERSCRIBE
STRETCHMARK	SUBHEADINGS	SUBURBANITE	SUPERSCRIPT
STRIDULATED	SUBIRRIGATE	SUBVENTIONS	SUPERSEDEAS
STRIDULATOR	SUBJECTABLE	SUBVERSIVES	SUPERSEDING
STRIKEBOUND	SUBJUGATING	SUCCEDANEUM	SUPERSEDURE
STRING BEANS	SUBJUGATION	SUCCEEDABLE	SUPERSONICS
STRINGBOARD	SUBJUNCTION	SUCCESSIONS	SUPERSTRUCT
STRINGENTLY	SUBJUNCTIVE	SUCCESSORAL	SUPERTANKER
STRINGINESS	SUBLIMATING	SUCCOURABLE	SUPERVENING
STRINGPIECE	SUBLIMATION	SUCH AND SUCH	SUPERVISING
STRIP MINING	SUBLITTORAL	SUCKING PIGS	SUPERVISION
STRIP-SEARCH	SUBLUXATION	SUCTION PUMP	SUPERVISORS
STRIPTEASES	SUBMARGINAL	SUDETENLAND	SUPERVISORY
STROBE LIGHT	SUBMARINERS	SUFFERINGLY	SUPPLANTING

SUPPLEMENTS
SUPPLICANTS
SUPPLICATED
SUPPORTABLE
SUPPOSITION
SUPPOSITIVE
SUPPOSITORY
SUPPRESSANT
SUPPRESSING
SUPPRESSION
SUPPRESSIVE
SUPPRESSORS
SUPPURATING
SUPPURATION
SUPPURATIVE
SUPREMACIST
SUPREMATISM
SUPREMATIST
SUPREMENESS
SURBASEMENT
SURCHARGING
SURFCASTING
SURGEONFISH
SURMOUNTING
SURPASSABLE
SURPRISEDLY
SURREALISTS
SURREBUTTAL
SURREBUTTER
SURRENDERED
SURRENDERER
SURROGATION
SURROUNDING
SURVEILLANT
SURVIVAL KIT
SUSCEPTANCE
SUSCEPTIBLE
SUSPENDIBLE
SUSPENSEFUL
SUSPENSIONS
SUSPICIONAL
SUSTAINABLE
SUSTAINEDLY
SUSTAINMENT
SUSURRATION
SWALLOWABLE
SWALLOW DIVE
SWALLOWTAIL
SWALLOWWORT
SWARTHINESS
SWEAT GLANDS

SWEATSHIRTS
SWEEPSTAKES
SWEETBREADS
SWEETHEARTS
SWEET PEPPER
SWEET POTATO
SWEET-TALKED
SWINDLINGLY
SWINISHNESS
SWISS CHARDS
SWISS CHEESE
SWITCHBACKS
SWITCHBLADE
SWITCHBOARD
SWITZERLAND
SWOLLEN HEAD
SWOLLENNESS
SWORD DANCER
SWORD DANCES
SWORDFISHES
SYCOPHANTIC
SYLLABOGRAM
SYLLOGISTIC
SYMBOLISTIC
SYMBOLIZING
SYMBOLOGIST
SYMMETRICAL
SYMPATHETIC
SYMPATHIZED
SYMPATHIZER
SYMPETALOUS
SYMPHONIOUS
SYMPTOMATIC
SYNAGOGICAL
SYNCHROMESH
SYNCHRONISM
SYNCHRONIZE
SYNCHRONOUS
SYNCHROTRON
SYNCOPATING
SYNCOPATION
SYNDESMOSIS
SYNDESMOTIC
SYNDICALISM
SYNDICALIST
SYNDICATING
SYNDICATION
SYNECDOCHIC
SYNECOLOGIC
SYNKARYONIC
SYNTHESIZED

SYNTHESIZER
SYNTHETICAL
SYPHILITICS
SYPHILOLOGY
SYSSARCOSIS
SYSSARCOTIC
SYSTEMATICS
SYSTEMATISM
SYSTEMATIST
SYSTEMATIZE
SZOMBATHELY

T

TABERNACLES
TABLECLOTHS
TABLESPOONS
TABLE TENNIS
TABULATIONS
TACHEOMETER
TACHOGRAPHS
TACHOMETERS
TACHOMETRIC
TACHYCARDIA
TACHYMETRIC
TACITURNITY
TACTFULNESS
TAGLIATELLE
TAKE AGAINST
TAKE-HOME PAY
TALEBEARERS
TALENT SCOUT
TALKABILITY
TALKING BOOK
TALLAHASSEE
TALL STORIES
TAMABLENESS
TAMBOURINES
TANGIBILITY
TANTALIZING
TAPE MACHINE
TAPE MEASURE
TARANTELLAS
TARNISHABLE
TARRADIDDLE
TARTAR SAUCE
TASKMASTERS
TASTELESSLY
TAUTOLOGIES
TAUTOLOGIZE
TAUTOMERISM
TAXIDERMIST

TAX SHELTERS
TEARFULNESS
TEARJERKERS
TEA SERVICES
TEA TROLLEYS
TECHNICALLY
TECHNICIANS
TECHNICOLOR
TECHNOCRACY
TECHNOCRATS
TECHNOPHILE
TECHNOPHOBE
TEDIOUSNESS
TEENYBOPPER
TEETOTALISM
TEETOTALLER
TEGUCIGALPA
TELEBANKING
TELECOMMUTE
TELECOTTAGE
TELEGNOSTIC
TELEGRAPHED
TELEGRAPHER
TELEGRAPHIC
TELEKINESIS
TELEKINETIC
TELEOLOGISM
TELEOLOGIST
TELEPATHIST
TELEPHONING
TELEPHONIST
TELEPRINTER
TELESCOPING
TELESELLING
TELEVISIONS
TELEWORKING
TELLING-OFFS
TELUKBETUNG
TEMERARIOUS
TEMPERAMENT
TEMPERATURE
TEMPESTUOUS
TEMPORALITY
TEMPORARILY
TEMPORIZING
TEMPTATIONS
TEMPTRESSES
TENACIOUSLY
TENDENTIOUS
TENDERFOOTS
TENDERIZING

TENEBROSITY	THEOCENTRIC	THREADINESS	TOMBOYISHLY
TENNIS ELBOW	THEODOLITES	THREATENING	TONSILLITIS
TENORRHAPHY	THEODOLITIC	THREEPENCES	TOOTH POWDER
TENSIBILITY	THEODORAKIS	THRIFTINESS	TOPDRESSING
TENSIOMETER	THEOLOGIANS	THRILLINGLY	TOPOGRAPHER
TENTATIVELY	THEOLOGICAL	THROATINESS	TOPOGRAPHIC
TENTERHOOKS	THEOLOGIZER	THROBBINGLY	TORCHBEARER
TENUOUSNESS	THEOPHOBIAC	THROMBOCYTE	TORMENTEDLY
TEPEFACTION	THEOREMATIC	THROUGHPUTS	TORONTONIAN
TERATOGENIC	THEORETICAL	THROUGHWAYS	TORSIBILITY
TERATOLOGIC	THEOSOPHISM	THUMBSCREWS	TORTICOLLAR
TEREBIC ACID	THEOSOPHIST	THUNDERBIRD	TORTICOLLIS
TERMINATING	THERAPEUTIC	THUNDERBOLT	TORTURESOME
TERMINATION	THEREABOUTS	THUNDERCLAP	TORTURINGLY
TERMINATIVE	THEREMINIST	THYROIDITIS	TORTUROUSLY
TERMINATORY	THERETOFORE	THYROTROPIN	TOTALIZATOR
TERMINOLOGY	THERIOMORPH	THYRSANURAN	TOTEMICALLY
TERRESTRIAL	THERMIONICS	TICKINGS OFF	TOTIPALMATE
TERRICOLOUS	THERMOCLINE	TICK-TACK-TOE	TOTIPOTENCY
TERRIGENOUS	THERMOGRAPH	TIDDLYWINKS	TOUCHPAPERS
TERRITORIAL	THERMOLYSIS	TIEBREAKERS	TOUCHSTONES
TERRITORIES	THERMOLYTIC	TIED COTTAGE	TOUCH-TYPING
TERRORISTIC	THERMOMETER	TIGHTFISTED	TOUCH-TYPIST
TERRORIZING	THERMOMETRY	TIGHT-LIPPED	TOUCHY-FEELY
TERTIUM QUID	THERMOSCOPE	TIME CAPSULE	TOUR DE FORCE
TESSELLATED	THERMOSTATS	TIMEKEEPERS	TOURMALINIC
TESTABILITY	THERMOTAXIC	TIMESERVERS	TOURNAMENTS
TESTAMENTAL	THERMOTAXIS	TIMESERVING	TOURNIQUETS
TESTICULATE	THESAURUSES	TIME-SHARING	TOUT LE MONDE
TESTIMONIAL	THICKHEADED	TIME SIGNALS	TOWER BLOCKS
TESTIMONIES	THICKNESSES	TIMETABLING	TOWN PLANNER
TEST MATCHES	THICK-WITTED	TINDERBOXES	TOWNSPEOPLE
TETANICALLY	THIGMOTAXIS	TIN PAN ALLEY	TOXICOGENIC
TETRADYMITE	THIMBLEFULS	TIN-PAN ALLEY	TOXOPHILITE
TETRAHEDRAL	THIMBLEWEED	TIRUNELVELI	TOXOPLASMIC
TETRAHEDRON	THINGAMAJIG	TITANICALLY	TRACHEOTOMY
TETRAMERISM	THIN-SKINNED	TITILLATING	TRACK EVENTS
TETRAMEROUS	THIOCYANATE	TITILLATION	TRACKLAYERS
TETRAPLEGIA	THIOPENTONE	TITILLATIVE	TRACK RECORD
TETRARCHATE	THIRD DEGREE	TITLEHOLDER	TRACKSUITED
TETRASPORIC	THIRD-DEGREE	TITTERINGLY	TRADE PRICES
TETRAVALENT	THIRD PERSON	TOASTMASTER	TRADE ROUTES
THALIDOMIDE	THIRSTINESS	TOAST MASTER	TRADES UNION
THALLOPHYTE	THIRTEENTHS	TOBACCONIST	TRADESWOMAN
THANKLESSLY	THISTLEDOWN	TOBOGGANING	TRADE UNIONS
THAUMATROPE	THIXOTROPIC	TOFFEE APPLE	TRADING POST
THEATREGOER	THORACOTOMY	TOFFEE-NOSED	TRADITIONAL
THEATRICALS	THOROUGHPIN	TOILET PAPER	TRADUCEMENT
THEIRSELVES	THOUGHTLESS	TOILET ROLLS	TRADUCINGLY
THENCEFORTH	THOUSANDTHS	TOILET WATER	TRAFFICATOR
THEOBROMINE	THRASH METAL	TOLBUTAMIDE	TRAFFIC JAMS

TRAFFICKERS	TRANSPORTER	TRINIDADIAN	TUNEFULNESS
TRAFFICKING	TRANSPOSING	TRIPALMITIN	TUNING FORKS
TRAGEDIENNE	TRANSPUTERS	TRIPLICATES	TURBINATION
TRAGICOMEDY	TRANSSEXUAL	TRIQUETROUS	TURBOCHARGE
TRAILBLAZER	TRANSURANIC	TRISTICHOUS	TURBULENTLY
TRAINBEARER	TRANSVAALER	TRISULPHIDE	TURGESCENCE
TRAMPOLINER	TRANSVALUER	TRITURATION	TURKISH BATH
TRAMPOLINES	TRANSVERSAL	TRIUMVIRATE	TURNAROUNDS
TRANQUILITY	TRAPSHOOTER	TRIVIALIZED	TURRICULATE
TRANSACTING	TRAUMATIZED	TROCHOPHORE	TURTLEDOVES
TRANSACTION	TRAVEL AGENT	TROCORNERED	TURTLENECKS
TRANSALPINE	TRAVELOGUES	TROGLODYTES	TUTTI FRUTTI
TRANSCEIVER	TRAVERSABLE	TROGLODYTIC	TWELVEMONTH
TRANSCENDED	TREACHERIES	TROJAN HORSE	TWITCHINGLY
TRANSCRIBED	TREACHEROUS	TROMBONISTS	TYNE AND WEAR
TRANSCRIBER	TREACLINESS	TROMPE L'OEIL	TYPECASTING
TRANSCRIPTS	TREASONABLE	TROPHICALLY	TYPESCRIPTS
TRANSECTION	TREASONABLY	TROPHOBLAST	TYPESETTERS
TRANSFERASE	TREASURABLE	TROPHOZOITE	TYPE SETTING
TRANSFERRED	TREBLE CLEFS	TROPICALITY	TYPEWRITERS
TRANSFERRIN	TRELLISWORK	TROPICALIZE	TYPEWRITING
TRANSFIGURE	TREMBLINGLY	TROPISMATIC	TYPEWRITTEN
TRANSFINITE	TREMULOUSLY	TROPOPHYTIC	TYPICALNESS
TRANSFIXING	TRENCHANTLY	TROPOSPHERE	TYPING POOLS
TRANSFIXION	TRENCH COATS	TROTSKYISTS	TYPOGRAPHER
TRANSFORMED	TRENCHERMAN	TROUBADOURS	TYPOGRAPHIC
TRANSFORMER	TRENCHERMEN	TROUBLESOME	TYPOLOGICAL
TRANSFUSION	TRENDSETTER	TROUBLE SPOT	TYRANNICIDE
TRANSFUSIVE	TREPIDATION	TROUBLINGLY	TYRANNIZING
TRANSHUMANT	TRESPASSING	TRUCULENTLY	TYROTHRICIN
TRANSISTORS	TRESTLETREE	TRUEHEARTED	TZETZE FLIES
TRANSITABLE	TRESTLEWORK	TRUK ISLANDS	
TRANSITIONS	TRIABLENESS	TRUMPETWEED	**U**
TRANSITIVES	TRIANGULATE	TRUNK ROUTES	ULOTRICHOUS
TRANS-JORDAN	TRIBULATION	TRUSTEESHIP	ULTRAFILTER
TRANSLATING	TRIBUTARIES	TRUSTWORTHY	ULTRAMARINE
TRANSLATION	TRIBUTARILY	TRYPANOSOME	ULTRAMODERN
TRANSLATORS	TRICERATOPS	TRYPSINOGEN	ULTRASONICS
TRANSLOCATE	TRICHINOSIS	TSELINOGRAD	ULTRAVIOLET
TRANSLUCENT	TRICHLORIDE	TSETSE FLIES	ULVERIZABLE
TRANSMITTAL	TRICHOMONAD	TUBERCULATE	UMBELLULATE
TRANSMITTED	TRICHOTOMIC	TUBERCULOUS	UNACCOUNTED
TRANSMITTER	TRICKLE-DOWN	TUB-THUMPERS	UNADVISEDLY
TRANSMUTING	TRICKLINGLY	TUB-THUMPING	UNALTERABLE
TRANSPADANE	TRICKSINESS	TUDORBETHAN	UNAMBIGUOUS
TRANSPARENT	TRICUSPIDAL	TUMBLE-DRIED	UNAMBITIOUS
TRANSPIERCE	TRIGGERFISH	TUMBLE DRIER	UNANIMOUSLY
TRANSPIRING	TRILLIONTHS	TUMBLE DRYER	UNANNOUNCED
TRANSPLANTS	TRIMETROGON	TUMBLE-DRYER	UNAVAILABLE
TRANSPONDER	TRIMORPHISM	TUMEFACIENT	UNAVOIDABLE
TRANSPORTED	TRINCOMALEE	TUMEFACTION	UNAWARENESS

UNBALANCING
UNBALLASTED
UNBELIEVERS
UNBLEMISHED
UNBREAKABLE
UNBURDENING
UNCALLED-FOR
UNCATCHABLE
UNCERTAINLY
UNCERTAINTY
UNCHARTERED
UNCHASTENED
UNCHRISTIAN
UNCIVILIZED
UNCLEANNESS
UNCOMMITTED
UNCONCERNED
UNCONCLUDED
UNCONFIDENT
UNCONNECTED
UNCONSCIOUS
UNCONSULTED
UNCONTESTED
UNCONTRIVED
UNCONVERTED
UNCONVINCED
UNCORRECTED
UNCOUNTABLE
UNCOUTHNESS
UNCRUSHABLE
UNDECEIVING
UNDECIDABLE
UNDECIDEDLY
UNDEMANDING
UNDERACTING
UNDERBIDDER
UNDERCHARGE
UNDEREXPOSE
UNDERGROUND
UNDERGROWTH
UNDERLETTER
UNDERLINING
UNDERMANNED
UNDERMINING
UNDERPASSES
UNDERPAYING
UNDERPINNED
UNDERPLAYED
UNDERRATING
UNDERSCORED
UNDERSELLER

UNDERSHIRTS
UNDERSIGNED
UNDERSTAIRS
UNDERSTATED
UNDERTAKERS
UNDERTAKING
UNDERTHRUST
UNDERVALUED
UNDERVALUER
UNDERWEIGHT
UNDERWRITER
UNDESIGNING
UNDESIRABLE
UNDESIRABLY
UNDEVELOPED
UNDISCLOSED
UNDISCUSSED
UNDISTORTED
UNDOUBTEDLY
UNDREAMED-OF
UNDRINKABLE
UNDULATIONS
UNEQUALNESS
UNEQUIVOCAL
UNESSENTIAL
UNEXPLAINED
UNEXPRESSED
UNFAILINGLY
UNFALTERING
UNFLAPPABLE
UNFLAPPABLY
UNFLINCHING
UNFORTUNATE
UNFULFILLED
UNGODLINESS
UNGUICULATE
UNGULIGRADE
UNHAPPINESS
UNHEALTHILY
UNICELLULAR
UNIFICATION
UNIFORMNESS
UNINHABITED
UNINHIBITED
UNINITIATED
UNINSPIRING
UNINSULATED
UNIPERSONAL
UNIPOLARITY
UNIVERSALLY
UNJUSTIFIED

UNKEMPTNESS
UNKNOWINGLY
UNKNOWNNESS
UNLOOKED-FOR
UNLOOSENING
UNLUCKINESS
UNMANLINESS
UNMITIGATED
UNNATURALLY
UNNECESSARY
UNOBTRUSIVE
UNORGANIZED
UNPALATABLE
UNPATRIOTIC
UNPERTURBED
UNPOLITICAL
UNPRACTICAL
UNPRACTISED
UNPRINTABLE
UNPROCESSED
UNPROFESSED
UNPROMISING
UNPUBLISHED
UNQUALIFIED
UNRAVELLING
UNRAVELMENT
UNREALISTIC
UNREASONING
UNREFLECTED
UNREHEARSED
UNRELENTING
UNREMITTING
UNRIGHTEOUS
UNSATISFIED
UNSATURATED
UNSAVOURILY
UNSCHEDULED
UNSCRAMBLED
UNSCRAMBLER
UNSCRATCHED
UNSHAKEABLE
UNSOCIALIST
UNSPARINGLY
UNSPEAKABLE
UNSPEAKABLY
UNSPECIFIED
UNSPONSORED
UNSTOPPABLE
UNSURPASSED
UNSURPRISED
UNSUSPECTED

UNTERWALDEN
UNTHEORIZED
UNTHINKABLE
UNTOUCHABLE
UNTRAVELLED
UNUTTERABLE
UNUTTERABLY
UNVARNISHED
UNWARRANTED
UNWATCHABLE
UNWHOLESOME
UNWILLINGLY
UNWITNESSED
UNWITTINGLY
UP-AND-COMING
UPHOLSTERED
UPHOLSTERER
UPRIGHTNESS
UPS AND DOWNS
UPSTRETCHED
URANOGRAPHY
URINIFEROUS
UROCHORDATE
URTICACEOUS
USELESSNESS
UTILITARIAN
UTILITY ROOM
UTILIZATION
UTRICULITIS

V

VACATIONERS
VACATIONING
VACCINATING
VACCINATION
VACILLATING
VACILLATION
VACUOLATION
VACUOUSNESS
VACUUM FLASK
VACUUM PUMPS
VAGABONDAGE
VAGABONDISM
VAGINECTOMY
VAGRANTNESS
VALEDICTION
VALEDICTORY
VALIDATIONS
VALLE D'AOSTA
VALUATIONAL
VAMPIRE BATS

VANDALISTIC
VANDALIZING
VANISHINGLY
VANQUISHING
VAPORESCENT
VAPORIMETER
VAPORIZABLE
VAPOUR TRAIL
VARGAS LLOSA
VARIABILITY
VARIATIONAL
VARICELLATE
VARICELLOID
VARIEGATION
VARIOLATION
VARIOUSNESS
VASCULARITY
VASCULARIZE
VASECTOMIES
VASODILATOR
VASOPRESSIN
VATICAN CITY
VEGETARIANS
VELOCIPEDES
VENDIBILITY
VENEREOLOGY
VENESECTION
VENTILATING
VENTILATION
VENTILATIVE
VENTILATORS
VENTILATORY
VENTRICULAR
VENTRICULUS
VENTURESOME
VERACIOUSLY
VERATRIDINE
VERBALIZING
VERBAL NOUNS
VEREENIGING
VERISIMILAR
VERMICULATE
VERMICULITE
VERMINATION
VERMIVOROUS
VERNACULARS
VERRUCOSITY
VERSATILITY
VERSICOLOUR
VERTEBRATES
VERTICALITY
330

VERTIGINOUS
VESTIGIALLY
VETERANS DAY
VEXATIOUSLY
VEXILLOLOGY
VIBRACULOID
VIBRAPHONES
VIBRATILITY
VIBRATINGLY
VIBRATIONAL
VICARIOUSLY
VICEGERENCY
VICEROYALTY
VICEROYSHIP
VICHYSSOISE
VICIOUSNESS
VICISSITUDE
VICTIMIZING
VICTUALLING
VIDEOPHONIC
VIDEOTAPING
VIEWFINDERS
VINAIGRETTE
VINDICATING
VINDICATION
VINDICATORY
VINEDRESSER
VINEGARROON
VINEYARDIST
VINICULTURE
VINIFICATOR
VIOLABILITY
VIOLONCELLO
VIRGIN BIRTH
VIRIDESCENT
VIROLOGICAL
VISCOMETRIC
VISCOUNTESS
VISCOUSNESS
VISIBLENESS
VISIONARIES
VISITATIONS
VISUALIZING
VITICULTURE
VITRESCENCE
VITRIFIABLE
VITUPERATOR
VIVACIOUSLY
VIVISECTION
VLAARDINGEN
VLADIKAVKAZ

VLADIVOSTOK
VOCIFERANCE
VOCIFERATED
VOCIFERATOR
VOLCANICITY
VOLCANOLOGY
VOLTAMMETER
VOLUNTARIES
VOLUNTARILY
VOLUNTARISM
VOLUNTARIST
VOLUNTEERED
VOODOOISTIC
VOORTREKKER
VORACIOUSLY
VORTIGINOUS
VOUCHSAFING
VOYEURISTIC
VULCANIZING
VULGARITIES
VULGARIZING
VULGAR LATIN

W
WADING POOLS
WAGGISHNESS
WAINSCOTING
WAINSCOTTED
WAITING GAME
WAITING LIST
WAITING ROOM
WAITRESSING
WAKEFULNESS
WALKS OF LIFE
WALLFLOWERS
WALLPAPERED
WANDERINGLY
WANNE-EICKEL
WARM-BLOODED
WARM-HEARTED
WARMING PANS
WAR OF NERVES
WARRANTABLE
WASHABILITY
WASH DRAWING
WASHERWOMAN
WASHERWOMEN
WASHING DAYS
WASPISHNESS
WATCHKEEPER
WATCHMAKERS

WATCHMAKING
WATCHSTRAPS
WATCHTOWERS
WATER CANNON
WATER CLOSET
WATERCOLOUR
WATERCOURSE
WATERED-DOWN
WATERFRONTS
WATERING CAN
WATER LEVELS
WATER LILIES
WATERLOGGED
WATER MEADOW
WATERMELONS
WATERPROOFS
WATER SKIERS
WATER SKIING
WATERSPOUTS
WATER SUPPLY
WATER TABLES
WATER VAPOUR
WATERWHEELS
WATHAWURUNG
WAVELENGTHS
WAYWARDNESS
WEALTHINESS
WEARABILITY
WEAR AND TEAR
WEATHERCOCK
WEATHER SHIP
WEATHER VANE
WEATHER-WISE
WEDDING RING
WEIGHBRIDGE
WEIGHTINESS
WELCOMENESS
WELDABILITY
WELL-ADAPTED
WELL-ADVISED
WELL AND GOOD
WELLBEHAVED
WELL-DEFINED
WELL-ENDOWED
WELL-FOUNDED
WELL-GROOMED
WELLINGTONS
WELL-MEANING
WELL-ROUNDED
WELLSPRINGS
WELL-WISHERS

WELL-WISHING
WELWITSCHIA
WENSLEYDALE
WESLEYANISM
WEST COUNTRY
WESTERNIZED
WESTERNMOST
WEST GERMANY
WEST LOTHIAN
WESTMINSTER
WESTPHALIAN
WET BLANKETS
WETTABILITY
WHEEDLINGLY
WHEELBARROW
WHEELCHAIRS
WHEELHOUSES
WHEELWRIGHT
WHEREABOUTS
WHERESOEVER
WHEREWITHAL
WHIFFLETREE
WHIMSICALLY
WHIPPING BOY
WHIRLYBIRDS
WHIST DRIVES
WHITEBOARDS
WHITE-COLLAR
WHITE DWARFS
WHITE HORSES
WHITE KNIGHT
WHITE METALS
WHITE PAPERS
WHITE PEPPER
WHITE RUSSIA
WHITE-SLAVER
WHITE SPIRIT
WHITETHROAT
WHITEWASHED
WHITEWASHER
WHITEWASHES
WHITSUNTIDE
WHOLE NUMBER
WHOLESALERS

WHOREHOUSES
WICKET GATES
WILDEBEESTS
WILDFOWLING
WILLINGNESS
WINDCHEATER
WINDFALL TAX
WINDJAMMERS
WINDOW BOXES
WINDOWPANES
WINDOW SHADE
WINDOWSILLS
WINDSCREENS
WINDSHIELDS
WIND-SUCKING
WIND-SURFERS
WIND-SURFING
WIND TUNNELS
WIND TURBINE
WINEBIBBING
WINNINGNESS
WINNING POST
WINNIPEGGER
WINSOMENESS
WINTERGREEN
WIRE NETTING
WIRE-TAPPING
WISDOM TEETH
WISDOM TOOTH
WISECRACKED
WISECRACKER
WISHFULNESS
WISTFULNESS
WITCHDOCTOR
WITCH-HUNTER
WITHDRAWALS
WITHDRAWING
WITHHOLDING
WITHOUT FAIL
WITHSTANDER
WITLESSNESS
WITNESSABLE
WIZARD PRANG
WOBBLE BOARD

WOLFISHNESS
WOLF WHISTLE
WOMANLINESS
WONDERFULLY
WONDERINGLY
WONDERLANDS
WOOD ALCOHOL
WOODCARVING
WOODCUTTERS
WOODCUTTING
WOODEN SPOON
WOODPECKERS
WOODTURNING
WOODWORKING
WOOLGROWING
WORD-PERFECT
WORKABILITY
WORKAHOLICS
WORKAHOLISM
WORKBASKETS
WORKBENCHES
WORKING DAYS
WORKING WEEK
WORKMANLIKE
WORKMANSHIP
WORKSTATION
WORLD-BEATER
WORLDLINESS
WORLDLY-WISE
WORLD POWERS
WORLD SERIES
WORSHIPABLE
WORSHIPPERS
WORSHIPPING
WORTHLESSLY
WRIGGLINGLY
WRITING DESK
WRONGDOINGS
WRONGHEADED
WROUGHT IRON

X

XANTHOPHYLL
X CHROMOSOME

XENOGENESIS
XENOGENETIC
XENOGLOSSIA
XENOMORPHIC
XEROGRAPHER
XEROGRAPHIC
XEROMORPHIC
XEROPHILOUS
XEROPHYTISM
XYLOCARPOUS
XYLOGRAPHER
XYLOGRAPHIC
XYLOPHAGOUS
XYLOPHONIST

Y

YACHTSWOMAN
Y CHROMOSOME
YELLOW FEVER
YELLOWKNIFE
YELLOW PAGES
YELLOWSTONE
YEVTUSHENKO
YOUTH HOSTEL
YTTRIFEROUS
YUGOSLAVIAN
YUWAALARAAY

Z

ZANTHOXYLUM
ZEALOUSNESS
ZESTFULNESS
ZHANGJIAKOU
ZINCIFEROUS
ZINCOGRAPHY
ZOOCHEMICAL
ZOOMORPHISM
ZOOPLANKTON
ZOOTECHNICS
ZYGOMORPHIC
ZYGOTICALLY
ZYMOGENESIS
ZYMOTICALLY

A

ABBREVIATING	ACHILLES' HEEL	AFRO-AMERICAN	AMALGAMATION
ABBREVIATION	ACHILL ISLAND	AFTERBURNING	AMATEURISHLY
ABELIAN GROUP	ACHLAMYDEOUS	AFTEREFFECTS	AMBASSADRESS
ABOLITIONARY	ACHLORHYDRIA	AFTER THE FACT	AMBIDEXTROUS
ABOLITIONISM	ACKNOWLEDGED	AFTERTHOUGHT	AMBITENDENCY
ABOLITIONIST	ACKNOWLEDGER	AGAMOGENESIS	AMBIVALENTLY
ABOMINATIONS	ACOUSTICALLY	AGAMOGENETIC	AMELIORATING
ABORTIONISTS	ACQUAINTANCE	AGARICACEOUS	AMELIORATION
ABORTION PILL	ACQUIESCENCE	AGE OF CONSENT	AMELIORATIVE
ABRACADABRAS	ACQUISITIONS	AGGLOMERATED	AMERICANISMS
ABSENT MINDED	ACROSTICALLY	AGGLUTINABLE	AMERICANIZED
ABSENT-MINDED	ACTINOMETRIC	AGGLUTINOGEN	AMERICANIZER
ABSOLUTENESS	ACTINOMYCETE	AGGRAVATIONS	AMITOTICALLY
ABSOLUTE ZERO	ADAPTABILITY	AGGREGATIONS	AMORTIZATION
ABSORPTIVITY	ADDERS TONGUE	AGGRESSIVELY	AMORTIZEMENT
ABSTEMIOUSLY	ADDITIONALLY	AGONY COLUMNS	AMPHETAMINES
ABSTRACTEDLY	ADHESIVENESS	AGORAPHOBICS	AMPHIBRACHIC
ABSTRACTIONS	ADJECTIVALLY	AGRICULTURAL	AMPHICOELOUS
ABSTRACT NOUN	ADJOURNMENTS	AGROFORESTRY	AMPHICTYONIC
ABSTRUSENESS	ADJUDICATING	AILUROPHILIA	AMPHIDIPLOID
ACADEMICALLY	ADJUDICATION	AILUROPHOBIA	AMPHISBAENIC
ACADEMICIANS	ADJUDICATORS	AIR COMMODORE	AMPHITHEATRE
ACANTHACEOUS	ADMINISTERED	AIR-CONDITION	AMPHITHECIUM
ACCELERATING	ADMINISTRATE	AIRHOSTESSES	AMPHITROPOUS
ACCELERATION	ADSCITITIOUS	AIR TERMINALS	AMPULLACEOUS
ACCELERATIVE	ADULTERATING	ALCOHOLICITY	AMYGDALOIDAL
ACCELERATORS	ADULTERATION	ALHAMBRESQUE	ANACHRONISMS
ACCENTUATING	ADUMBRATIONS	ALICE SPRINGS	ANAESTHETICS
ACCENTUATION	ADVANTAGEOUS	ALIENABILITY	ANAESTHETIST
ACCESS COURSE	ADVENTITIOUS	ALIMENTATION	ANAESTHETIZE
ACCIACCATURA	ADVISABILITY	ALIMENTATIVE	ANAGOGICALLY
ACCIDENTALLY	AERIFICATION	ALKALIMETRIC	ANAGRAMMATIC
ACCLAMATIONS	AERODONETICS	ALL-IMPORTANT	ANALPHABETIC
ACCLIMATIZED	AERODYNAMICS	ALL-INCLUSIVE	ANALYTICALLY
ACCLIMATIZER	AEROEMBOLISM	ALLITERATION	ANAMORPHOSIS
ACCOMMODATED	AEROMECHANIC	ALLITERATIVE	ANAPHRODISIA
ACCOMPANISTS	AERONAUTICAL	ALLOMORPHISM	ANAPHYLACTIC
ACCOMPANYING	AERONEUROSIS	ALLUSIVENESS	ANARCHICALLY
ACCOMPLISHED	AESTHETICIAN	ALMIGHTINESS	ANASTIGMATIC
ACCOMPLISHER	AESTHETICISM	ALPHABETICAL	ANATHEMATIZE
ACCORDIONIST	AETHEREALITY	ALPHABETIZER	ANATOMICALLY
ACCOUPLEMENT	AETIOLOGICAL	ALPHA-BLOCKER	ANCHORPERSON
ACCOUTREMENT	AFFECTATIONS	ALPHANUMERIC	ANCIEN REGIME
ACCUMULATING	AFFECTEDNESS	ALSTROEMERIA	ANDROSTERONE
ACCUMULATION	AFFECTIONATE	ALTERABILITY	ANEMOGRAPHIC
ACCUMULATIVE	AFFILIATIONS	ALTERCATIONS	ANEMOPHILOUS
ACCUMULATORS	AFFINITY CARD	ALTERNATIONS	ANESTHETISTS
ACCUSATORIAL	AFFIRMATIONS	ALTERNATIVES	ANESTHETIZED
ACETALDEHYDE	AFFIRMATIVES ·	ALTHORP HOUSE	ANGLO-INDIANS
ACHIEVEMENTS	AFORETHOUGHT	ALTIMETRICAL	ANGLOPHILIAC
	AFRIKANERDOM	AMALGAMATING	ANGUILLIFORM

ANGULARITIES
ANIMADVERTED
ANIMAL RIGHTS
ANIMATRONICS
ANNEXATIONAL
ANNIHILATING
ANNIHILATION
ANNIHILATIVE
ANNOUNCEMENT
ANNUNCIATION
ANNUNCIATIVE
ANTAGONISTIC
ANTAGONIZING
ANTANANARIVO
ANTECHAMBERS
ANTEDILUVIAN
ANTEMERIDIAN
ANTE MERIDIEM
ANTHOLOGICAL
ANTHOLOGISTS
ANTHROPOIDAL
ANTHROPOLOGY
ANTI-AIR-CRAFT
ANTICATALYST
ANTICIPATING
ANTICIPATION
ANTICIPATIVE
ANTICIPATORY
ANTICLERICAL
ANTICLIMAXES
ANTICYCLONES
ANTICYCLONIC
ANTIHALATION
ANTIMACASSAR
ANTIMAGNETIC
ANTINEUTRINO
ANTIPARALLEL
ANTIPARTICLE
ANTIPATHETIC
ANTIPERIODIC
ANTIQUARIANS
ANTIRACHITIC
ANTI-SEMITISM
ANTITHETICAL
ANTONOMASTIC
ANURADHAPURA
AORISTICALLY
APAGOGICALLY
APERIODICITY
APHRODISIACS
APICULTURIST

APLANOSPHERE
APOCHROMATIC
APOCYNACEOUS
APOGEOTROPIC
APOSTROPHIZE
APOTHECARIES
APPALACHIANS
APPARATCHIKS
APPARENTNESS
APPASSIONATO
APPEASEMENTS
APPELLATIONS
APPENDECTOMY
APPENDICITIS
APPENDICULAR
APPERCEPTION
APPERCEPTIVE
APPERTAINING
APPETIZINGLY
APPLAUDINGLY
APPLICATIONS
APPOGGIATURA
APPOINIMENIS
APPORTIONING
APPRAISINGLY
APPRECIATING
APPRECIATION
APPRECIATIVE
APPREHENDING
APPREHENSION
APPREHENSIVE
APPRENTICING
APPROACHABLE
APPROPRIABLE
APPROPRIATED
APPROXIMATED
APPURTENANCE
A PRETTY PENNY
APRON STRINGS
AQUICULTURAL
ARBITRAGEURS
ARBORESCENCE
ARBORIZATION
ARCHDEACONRY
ARCHDIOCESAN
ARCHDIOCESES
ARCHEOLOGIES
ARCHESPORIAL
ARCHETYPICAL
ARCHIPELAGIC
ARCHIPELAGOS

ARCHITECTURE
ARCHOPLASMIC
ARCTIC CIRCLE
ARGILLACEOUS
ARISTOCRATIC
ARMOURED CARS
ARMOUR-PLATED
AROMATHERAPY
AROMATICALLY
ARRAIGNMENTS
ARRANGEMENTS
ARSENOPYRITE
ARTESIAN WELL
ARTHROPODOUS
ARTHROSPORIC
ARTICULATELY
ARTICULATING
ARTICULATION
ARTICULATORY
ARTIFICIALLY
ARTILLERYMAN
ARTISTICALLY
ASCENSION DAY
ASCERTAINING
ASCOMYCETOUS
ASH WEDNESDAY
ASKING PRICES
ASPHYXIATING
ASPHYXIATION
ASSASSINATED
ASSEMBLY LINE
ASSEVERATING
ASSEVERATION
ASSIBILATION
ASSIGNATIONS
ASSIMILATING
ASSIMILATION
ASSIMILATIVE
ASSOCIATIONS
ASTONISHMENT
ASTOUNDINGLY
ASTRINGENTLY
ASTROBIOLOGY
ASTROCOMPASS
ASTROGEOLOGY
ASTROLOGICAL
ASTRONAUTICS
ASTRONOMICAL
ASTROPHYSICS
ASYMPTOMATIC
ASYNCHRONISM

ASYNCHRONOUS
ATHEROMATOUS
ATHLETE'S FOOT
ATHLETICALLY
ATHWARTSHIPS
ATLANTIC CITY
ATMOSPHERICS
ATOMIC ENERGY
ATTACHE CASES
ATTENBOROUGH
ATTESTATIONS
ATTESTED MILK
ATTITUDINIZE
ATTRACTIVELY
ATTRIBUTABLE
AUDIOLOGICAL
AUDIOMETRIST
AUGMENTATION
AUGMENTATIVE
AULD LANG SYNE
AUSCULTATION
AUSPICIOUSLY
AUSTRALASIAN
AUSTRONESIAN
AUTHENTICATE
AUTHENTICITY
AUTISTICALLY
AUTOANTIBODY
AUTOEXPOSURE
AUTOGRAPHING
AUTOHYPNOSIS
AUTOHYPNOTIC
AUTOMOBILIST
AUTONOMOUSLY
AUTOROTATION
AUTOXIDATION
AVAILABILITY
AVANT GARDISM
AVARICIOUSLY
AVICULTURIST
AVITAMINOSIS
AVOGADRO'S LAW
AWE-INSPIRING
AZATHIOPRINE

B

BABY CARRIAGE
BACCHANALIAN
BACKBENCHERS
BACKBREAKING
BACKHANDEDLY

BACK OF BEYOND	BEACH BUGGIES	BILL OF HEALTH	BLOCKBUSTERS
BACK PASSAGES	BEACHCOMBERS	BILL OF LADING	BLOCK LETTERS
BACKPEDALING	BEACONSFIELD	BILL OF RIGHTS	BLOEMFONTEIN
BACKPEDALLED	BEAT A RETREAT	BIOCATALYTIC	BLOOD BROTHER
BACKROOM BOYS	BEATIFICALLY	BIOCHEMISTRY	BLOODLETTING
BACKSLAPPERS	BEAUTY QUEENS	BIODIVERSITY	BLOODSTAINED
BACKSLAPPING	BECHUANALAND	BIOECOLOGIST	BLOODSTREAMS
BACKTRACKING	BEDAZZLEMENT	BIOFLAVONOID	BLOODSUCKERS
BACKWARDNESS	BEDFORDSHIRE	BIOGEOGRAPHY	BLOODTHIRSTY
BACKWOODSMAN	BEGGARLINESS	BIOGRAPHICAL	BLOOD VESSELS
BACKWOODSMEN	BEGRUDGINGLY	BIOLOGICALLY	BLOODY-MINDED
BACTERICIDAL	BEHAVIOURISM	BIOMECHANICS	BLUE-EYED BOYS
BACTERIOLOGY	BEHAVIOURIST	BIONOMICALLY	BLUESTOCKING
BAGGAGE ROOMS	BELEAGUERING	BIOPHYSICIST	BLUNDERINGLY
BAKING POWDER	BELGIAN CONGO	BIOSYNTHESIS	BLUSTERINGLY
BALANCED DIET	BELITTLEMENT	BIOSYNTHETIC	BOARDING CARD
BALANCE SHEET	BELITTLINGLY	BIPROPELLANT	BOASTFULNESS
BALCONY SCENE	BELLETRISTIC	BIRDS-EYE VIEW	BOBSLEIGHING
BALL BEARINGS	BELLIGERENCE	BIRD'S-EYE	BODY LANGUAGE
BALLOTTEMENT	BELLIGERENCY	VIEW	BODY SNATCHER
BALNEOLOGIST	BELLIGERENTS	BIRD-WATCHERS	BODY STOCKING
BALTIC STATES	BELLY BUTTONS	BIREFRINGENT	BOILING POINT
BANDARANAIKE	BELLY DANCERS	BIRTH CONTROL	BOISTEROUSLY
BANDERILLERO	BELLY-LANDING	BISMUTHINITE	BOLSTERINGLY
BANDJARMASIN	BELOW THE BELT	BLABBERMOUTH	BOMBACACEOUS
BANK ACCOUNTS	BENEDICTINES	BLACK AND BLUE	BOMBARDMENTS
BANKER'S CARDS	BENEDICTIONS	BLACKBALLING	BOOBY-TRAPPED
BANKER'S ORDER	BENEFACTIONS	BLACKBERRIES	BOOK-LEARNING
BANK HOLIDAYS	BENEFACTRESS	BLACK COUNTRY	BOOMERANGING
BANKRUPTCIES	BENEFICENTLY	BLACKCURRANT	BOROSILICATE
BANTAMWEIGHT	BENEFICIALLY	BLACK ECONOMY	BOTTOM DRAWER
BARBARIANISM	BENEVOLENTLY	BLACK ENGLISH	BOUGAINVILLE
BARBARICALLY	BENZALDEHYDE	BLACKGUARDLY	BOUNCY CASTLE
BARBITURATES	BENZOPHENONE	BLACK-HEARTED	BOWDLERIZING
BARLEY SUGARS	BENZOQUINONE	BLACKLEGGING	BOWLING ALLEY
BARNSTORMERS	BEREAVEMENTS	BLACKLISTING	BOWLING GREEN
BARNSTORMING	BERWICKSHIRE	BLACKMAILERS	BRACHYLOGOUS
BARORECEPTOR	BESPECTACLED	BLACKMAILING	BRACKISHNESS
BARQUISIMETO	BEVERLY HILLS	BLACK MUSLIMS	BRAINS TRUSTS
BARRANQUILLA	BEWILDERMENT	BLACK PUDDING	BRAIN SURGEON
BARREL ORGANS	BEWITCHINGLY	BLADDERWRACK	BRAINTEASERS
BASIDIOSPORE	BIAURICULATE	BLAENAU GWENT	BRAINWASHING
BASTARDIZING	BIBLIOGRAPHY	BLAMEFULNESS	BREADWINNERS
BASTINADOING	BIBLIOMANIAC	BLANK CHEQUES	BREAKFASTING
BATAN ISLANDS	BIBLIOPHILES	BLARNEY STONE	BREASTSTROKE
BATCH PROCESS	BICOLLATERAL	BLAST FURNACE	BREATHALYSER
BATHING SUITS	BIELSKO-BIALA	BLASTODERMIC	BREATHALYZER
BATHYSPHERES	BIFLAGELLATE	BLASTOSPHERE	BREATHTAKING
BATTERING RAM	BIFURCATIONS	BLINDFOLDING	BREECHLOADER
BATTLEFIELDS	BILHARZIASIS	BLISSFULNESS	BREWERS YEAST
BATTLE ROYALS	BILINGUALISM	BLISTERINGLY	BRILLIANTINE

BRINKMANSHIP
BRISTLE-GRASS
BROADCASTERS
BROADCASTING
BRONCHOSCOPE
BRONCHOSCOPY
BRONCOBUSTER
BRONTOSAURUS
BRONZE MEDALS
BROTHERHOODS
BROTHER-IN-LAW
BROWNIE POINT
BUENAVENTURA
BUFFER STATES
BUFFER STOCKS
BULLDOG CLIPS
BULLET-HEADED
BULLFIGHTERS
BULLFIGHTING
BULLHEADEDLY
BULLSHITTING
BULL TERRIERS
BUNSEN BURNER
BUREAUCRATIC
BURGLAR ALARM
BURSERACEOUS
BUSINESSLIKE
BUSINESS SUIT
BUTTERSCOTCH
BUTTONHOLING
BUYER'S MARKET
BYELORUSSIAN

C

CABBAGE WHITE
CABIN CRUISER
CABINET-MAKER
CABLE RAILWAY
CACHINNATION
CAENOGENESIS
CAENOGENETIC
CALAMITOUSLY
CALCULATIONS
CALENDAR YEAR
CALIBRATIONS
CALISTHENICS
CALLIGRAPHER
CALLIGRAPHIC
CALLISTHENIC
CALL OF NATURE
CALORIMETRIC

CALUMNIATING
CALUMNIATION
CAMELOPARDUS
CAMI-KNICKERS
CAMOUFLAGING
CAMP FOLLOWER
CANALIZATION
CANCELLATION
CANDELABRUMS
CANDLESTICKS
CANDY-STRIPED
CANNIBALIZED
CANNON FODDER
CANONIZATION
CANTABRIGIAN
CANTANKEROUS
CAPABILITIES
CAPACITATION
CAPARISONNED
CAPE COLOURED
CAPE PROVINCE
CAPERCAILLIE
CAPILLACEOUS
CAPITAL GAINS
CAPITALIZING
CAPITULATING
CAPITULATION
CAPRICIOUSLY
CAPTIOUSNESS
CARAVANSERAI
CARBOHYDRATE
CARBONACEOUS
CARBON COPIES
CARBON DATING
CARBON PAPERS
CARBURETTORS
CARCINOGENIC
CARD-CARRYING
CARDIOGRAPHY
CARDIOLOGIST
CARDIOMEGALY
CARELESSNESS
CARIBBEAN SEA
CARICATURING
CARICATURIST
CARILLONNEUR
CARPETBAGGER
CARPET KNIGHT
CARPOLOGICAL
CARPOPHAGOUS
CARRIAGEWAYS

CARTE BLANCHE
CARTOGRAPHER
CARTOGRAPHIC
CARTWHEELING
CARVING FORKS
CARVING KNIFE
CASH AND CARRY
CASH REGISTER
CASTELLATION
CASTING VOTES
CATACHRESTIC
CATADIOPTRIC
CATASTROPHES
CATASTROPHIC
CATCHPHRASES
CATECHETICAL
CATEGORIZING
CATERPILLARS
CATERWAULING
CATS WHISKERS
CAULIFLOWERS
CAUSE CELEBRE
CAUTIOUSNESS
CAVEAT EMPTOR
CELEBRATIONS
CEMENT MIXERS
CENSORIOUSLY
CENTENARIANS
CENTRALIZING
CENTRAL KAROO
CENTREPIECES
CENTROCLINAL
CENTROSPHERE
CENTUPLICATE
CEPHALOMETER
CEPHALOMETRY
CEPHALOPODAN
CEPHALOPODIC
CEREMONIALLY
CEROGRAPHIST
CERRO DE PASCO
CERTIFICATED
CERTIFICATES
CHAIN LETTERS
CHAIN-SMOKERS
CHAIN-SMOKING
CHAIRMANSHIP
CHAIRPERSONS
CHAISE LONGUE
CHALCOGRAPHY
CHALCOPYRITE

CHAMBERLAINS
CHAMBERMAIDS
CHAMBER MUSIC
CHAMPIONSHIP
CHANGCHIAKOW
CHANGELESSLY
CHANGE OF LIFE
CHANGING ROOM
CHAPLAINCIES
CHAPTERHOUSE
CHARACTERFUL
CHARACTERIZE
CHARGE NURSES
CHARGE SHEETS
CHARLATANISM
CHARNEL HOUSE
CHASTISEMENT
CHASTITY BELT
CHATTERBOXES
CHAUFFEURING
CHAUVINISTIC
CHECKERBERRY
CHECKERBLOOM
CHEERFULNESS
CHEERLEADERS
CHEESEBURGER
CHEESEPARING
CHEESE-PARING
CHEFS D'OEUVRE
CHEMOSPHERIC
CHEMOTHERAPY
CHEMOTROPISM
CHEQUERBOARD
CHERUBICALLY
CHESHIRE CATS
CHESTERFIELD
CHIAROSCUROS
CHIEF JUSTICE
CHIEF OF STAFF
CHILDBEARING
CHILD BENEFIT
CHILDISHNESS
CHILDMINDERS
CHILDMINDING
CHILD PRODIGY
CHILPANCINGO
CHIMNEYPIECE
CHIMNEYSTACK
CHIMNEYSWEEP
CHIROGRAPHER
CHIROGRAPHIC

CHIROPODISTS
CHIROPRACTIC
CHIROPRACTOR
CHITCHATTING
CHITTERLINGS
CHIVALROUSLY
CHLORAMBUCIL
CHLORENCHYMA
CHLORINATING
CHLORINATION
CHLOROFORMED
CHLOROHYDRIN
CHLOROPICRIN
CHOCOLATE BOX
CHOIRMASTERS
CHOIR SCHOOLS
CHOLERICALLY
CHONDRIOSOME
CHOREOGRAPHS
CHOREOGRAPHY
CHOROGRAPHER
CHOROGRAPHIC
CHRISTCHURCH
CHRISTENINGS
CHRISTIAN ERA
CHRISTIANITY
CHRISTIANIZE
CHRISTMAS BOX
CHRISTMAS EVE
CHRIST'S-THORN
CHROMATICISM
CHROMATICITY
CHROMATOGRAM
CHROME YELLOW
CHROMOPHORIC
CHROMOSPHERE
CHRONOGRAPHS
CHRONOLOGIES
CHRONOLOGIST
CHRONOMETERS
CHRONOMETRIC
CHRONOSCOPIC
CHURCHWARDEN
CHURLISHNESS
CHURRASCARIA
CHYMOTRYPSIN
CINCHONIDINE
CINEMATHEQUE
CIRCUITOUSLY
CIRCULARIZED
CIRCULARIZER

CIRCULAR SAWS
CIRCUMCISING
CIRCUMCISION
CIRCUMFLUOUS
CIRCUMFUSION
CIRCUMNUTATE
CIRCUMSCRIBE
CIRCUMSTANCE
CIRCUMVENTED
CIRCUMVENTER
CIRROCUMULUS
CIRROSTRATUS
CITIZENS' BAND
CITRICULTURE
CIVIL DEFENCE
CIVILIZATION
CIVIL LIBERTY
CIVIL SERVANT
CIVIL SERVICE
CLAIRVOYANCE
CLAIRVOYANTS
CLANGOROUSLY
CLANNISHNESS
CLAPPERBOARD
CLARINETTIST
CLASS ACTIONS
CLASSICALITY
CLASSICISTIC
CLASSIFIABLE
CLASSIFIED AD
CLAUDICATION
CLEAR-SIGHTED
CLEFT PALATES
CLERESTORIED
CLERESTORIES
CLERK OF WORKS
CLIENT STATES
CLIFFHANGERS
CLIFFHANGING
CLIMACTERICS
CLIMATICALLY
CLIMATOLOGIC
CLIMBING IRON
CLINKER-BUILT
CLIQUISHNESS
CLODDISHNESS
CLOSE-CROPPED
CLOSED SEASON
CLOSE-GRAINED
CLOSE SEASONS
CLOSING PRICE

CLOSING TIMES
CLOTHESHORSE
CLOTHESLINES
CLOTHES-PRESS
CLOTTED CREAM
CLOVE HITCHES
CLOVERLEAVES
CLOWNISHNESS
CLUB SANDWICH
CLUSTER BOMBS
COACERVATION
COACHBUILDER
COACH STATION
COALITIONIST
COALSCUTTLES
COBBLESTONES
COCKFIGHTING
COCKLESHELLS
COCONUT SHIES
COCOS ISLANDS
CODEPENDENCY
CODIFICATION
COEFFICIENTS
COELENTERATE
COENESTHESIA
COENESTHESIS
COENESTHETIC
COERCIVENESS
COFFEE BREAKS
COFFEE HOUSES
COFFEE KLATCH
COFFEE TABLES
COHABITATION
COHESIVENESS
COINCIDENCES
COINCIDENTAL
COLD SHOULDER
COLEOPTEROUS
COLLABORATED
COLLABORATOR
COLLECTIVELY
COLLECTIVISM
COLLECTIVIST
COLLECTIVITY
COLLECTIVIZE
COLLECTORATE
COLLOCATIONS
COLLOIDALITY
COLLOQUIALLY
COLLYWOBBLES
COLONIALISTS

COLONIZATION
COLORIMETRIC
COLOURLESSLY
COLOUR SCHEME
COLUMNIATION
COMBINATIONS
COMBUSTIBLES
COME A CROPPER
COME-UPPANCES
COMFORTINGLY
COMMANDEERED
COMMANDMENTS
COMMEMORATED
COMMEMORATOR
COMMENCEMENT
COMMENDATION
COMMENDATORY
COMMENSALISM
COMMENSURATE
COMMENTARIAL
COMMENTARIES
COMMENTATING
COMMENTATORS
COMMERCIALLY
COMMISERATED
COMMISERATOR
COMMISSARIAL
COMMISSARIAT
COMMISSARIES
COMMISSIONAL
COMMISSIONED
COMMISSIONER
COMMITTEEMAN
COMMITTEEMEN
COMMODIOUSLY
COMMON MARKET
COMMONPLACES
COMMONWEALTH
COMMUNICABLE
COMMUNICABLY
COMMUNICANTS
COMMUNICATED
COMMUNICATOR
COMMUNIONIST
COMMUTATIONS
COMPACT DISCS
COMPANIONATE
COMPANIONWAY
COMPARTMENTS
COMPASS POINT
COMPATRIOTIC

COMPELLINGLY	CONCURRENCES	CONNOISSEURS	CONSUMMATIVE
COMPENSATING	CONCURRENTLY	CONNOTATIONS	CONSUMPTIONS
COMPENSATION	CONDEMNATION	CONNUBIALITY	CONSUMPTIVES
COMPENSATIVE	CONDEMNATORY	CONQUISTADOR	CONTAGIOUSLY
COMPENSATORY	CONDENSATION	CONSCIONABLE	CONTAINERIZE
COMPETITIONS	CONDESCENDED	CONSCRIPTING	CONTAMINANTS
COMPILATIONS	CONDITIONERS	CONSCRIPTION	CONTAMINATED
COMPLACENTLY	CONDITIONING	CONSECRATING	CONTAMINATOR
COMPLAINANTS	CONDOMINIUMS	CONSECRATION	CONTEMPLATED
COMPLAISANCE	CONDUCTIVITY	CONSECRATORY	CONTEMPLATOR
COMPLEMENTED	CONDUPLICATE	CONSENTIENCE	CONTEMPORARY
COMPLETENESS	CONFABULATED	CONSEQUENCES	CONTEMPORIZE
COMPLEXITIES	CONFABULATOR	CONSEQUENTLY	CONTEMPTIBLE
COMPLICATING	CONFECTIONER	CONSERVATION	CONTEMPTIBLY
COMPLICATION	CONFEDERATED	CONSERVATISM	CONTEMPTUOUS
COMPLIMENTED	CONFEDERATES	CONSERVATIVE	CONTENTIONAL
COMPONENTIAL	CONFERENTIAL	CONSERVATORY	CONTERMINOUS
COMPOSITIONS	CONFESSIONAL	CONSIDERABLE	CONTESTATION
COMPOS MENTIS	CONFIDENTIAL	CONSIDERABLY	CONTEXTUALLY
COMPREHENDED	CONFINEMENTS	CONSIGNATION	CONTIGUOUSLY
COMPRESSIBLE	CONFIRMATION	CONSIGNMENTS	CONTINENTALS
COMPROMISING	CONFIRMATORY	CONSISTENTLY	CONTINGENTLY
COMPTROLLERS	CONFISCATING	CONSISTORIAL	CONTINUALITY
COMPULSIVELY	CONFISCATION	CONSOCIATION	CONTINUATION
COMPULSORILY	CONFISCATORY	CONSOLATIONS	CONTINUATIVE
COMPUNCTIOUS	CONFORMATION	CONSOLIDATED	CONTINUINGLY
COMPUTATIONS	CONFOUNDEDLY	CONSOLIDATOR	CONTINUOUSLY
COMPUTERIZED	CONFRATERNAL	CONSPECTUSES	CONTORTIONAL
CONCATENATED	CONFUCIANISM	CONSPIRACIES	CONTRABASSES
CONCELEBRATE	CONFUCIANIST	CONSPIRATORS	CONTRACTIBLE
CONCENTRATED	CONFUTATIONS	CONSTABULARY	CONTRACTIONS
CONCENTRATES	CONGENIALITY	CONSTIPATION	CONTRADICTED
CONCENTRATOR	CONGENITALLY	CONSTITUENCY	CONTRADICTER
CONCEPTIONAL	CONGLOBATION	CONSTITUENTS	CONTRAPTIONS
CONCEPTUALLY	CONGLOMERATE	CONSTITUTING	CONTRAPUNTAL
CONCERTGOERS	CONGLUTINANT	CONSTITUTION	CONTRARINESS
CONCERT GRAND	CONGLUTINATE	CONSTITUTIVE	CONTRARIWISE
CONCERTINAED	CONGRATULATE	CONSTRAINING	CONTRAVENING
CONCERT PITCH	CONGREGATING	CONSTRICTING	CONTRIBUTING
CONCHIFEROUS	CONGREGATION	CONSTRICTION	CONTRIBUTION
CONCHOLOGIST	CONGREGATIVE	CONSTRICTIVE	CONTRIBUTIVE
CONCILIATING	CONIDIOPHORE	CONSTRICTORS	CONTRIBUTORS
CONCILIATION	CONJECTURING	CONSTRUCTING	CONTRIBUTORY
CONCILIATORS	CONJUGATIONS	CONSTRUCTION	CONTRIVANCES
CONCILIATORY	CONJUNCTIONS	CONSTRUCTIVE	CONTROLLABLE
CONCLUSIVELY	CONJUNCTIVAL	CONSTRUCTORS	CONTROVERTER
CONCOMITANCE	CONJUNCTIVES	CONSULTATION	CONTUMACIOUS
CONCOMITANTS	CONJUNCTURAL	CONSULTATIVE	CONTUMELIOUS
CONCORDANCES	CONJUNCTURES	CONSUMMATELY	CONURBATIONS
CONCRESCENCE	CONNECTIONAL	CONSUMMATING	CONVALESCENT
CONCUPISCENT	CONNING TOWER	CONSUMMATION	CONVALESCING

CONVECTIONAL
CONVENIENCES
CONVENIENTLY
CONVENTICLES
CONVENTIONAL
CONVERGENCES
CONVERSATION
CONVERSIONAL
CONVERTIBLES
CONVEYANCING
CONVEYER BELT
CONVINCINGLY
CONVIVIALITY
CONVOCATIONS
CONVOLUTEDLY
CONVOLUTIONS
CONVULSIVELY
COOKERY BOOKS
COOKING APPLE
COOPERATIVES
COORDINATELY
COORDINATING
COORDINATION
COPOLYMERIZE
COPROPHAGOUS
COPROPHILOUS
COPTIC CHURCH
COQUETTISHLY
CORDUROY ROAD
CORESPONDENT
CORNERSTONES
CORN EXCHANGE
CORNISH PASTY
COROLLACEOUS
CORPORALSHIP
CORPORATIONS
CORPOREALITY
CORRECTITUDE
CORRECTIVELY
CORRELATIONS
CORRELATIVES
CORRESPONDED
CORROBORATED
CORROBORATOR
CORRUGATIONS
COSMETICALLY
COSMETICIANS
COSMOLOGICAL
COSMOPOLITAN
COSTERMONGER
COST OF LIVING

COST THE EARTH
COTYLEDONARY
COTYLEDONOUS
COUNTENANCED
COUNTENANCES
COUNTERACTED
COUNTERBLAST
COUNTERCHECK
COUNTERCLAIM
COUNTERFOILS
COUNTERPANES
COUNTERPARTS
COUNTERPARTY
COUNTERPOINT
COUNTERPOISE
COUNTERPROOF
COUNTERPUNCH
COUNTERSHAFT
COUNTERSIGNS
COUNTERTENOR
COUNTRY CLUBS
COUNTRY DANCE
COUNTRY SEATS
COUNTY COURTS
COUPS DE GRACE
COURAGEOUSLY
COURT MARTIAL
COURT-MARTIAL
COVENT GARDEN
COVER CHARGES
COVERED WAGON
COVETOUSNESS
COWARDLINESS
CRACKBRAINED
CRANIOLOGIST
CRANIOMETRIC
CRASH BARRIER
CRASH HELMETS
CRASH LANDING
CREEPY-CRAWLY
CREMATIONISM
CREMATIONIST
CREMATORIUMS
CRENELLATION
CRISSCROSSED
CRISSCROSSES
CROP-SPRAYING
CROSSBENCHER
CROSS BENCHER
CROSSBENCHES
CROSSCHECKED

CROSS-COUNTRY
CROSSCURRENT
CROSS-DRESSER
CROSS-EXAMINE
CROSS-GRAINED
CROSSPATCHES
CROSS-SECTION
CROWNED HEADS
CROWN PRINCES
CRUSH BARRIER
CRYOPLANKTON
CRYPTANALYST
CRYPTOGRAPHY
CRYPTOLOGIST
CRYSTAL BALLS
CRYSTAL CLEAR
CRYSTAL GAZER
CRYSTALLITIC
CRYSTALLIZED
CUCKOO CLOCKS
CUMULATIVELY
CUMULONIMBUS
CUPBOARD LOVE
CURARIZATION
CURATORSHIPS
CURMUDGEONLY
CURTAILMENTS
CURTAIN CALLS
CURVACEOUSLY
CUT AND THRUST
CUTTLEFISHES
CYCLOPENTANE
CYCLOSTOMATE
CYCLOSTYLING
CYSTICERCOID
CYTOCHEMICAL
CYTOGENETICS
CYTOSKELETON
CYTOTAXONOMY
CZECHOSLOVAK

D

DACTYLICALLY
DAEMONICALLY
DAIRY FARMERS
DANGER SIGNAL
DANISH PASTRY
DARBY AND JOAN
DAY NURSERIES
DEACTIVATION
DEAF-MUTENESS

DEATH FUTURES
DEATH RATTLES
DEATH WARRANT
DEBARKATIONS
DEBAUCHERIES
DEBILITATING
DEBILITATION
DEBILITATIVE
DEBT OF HONOUR
DECALCOMANIA
DECALESCENCE
DECAPITATING
DECAPITATION
DECARBONIZER
DECASYLLABIC
DECASYLLABLE
DECELERATING
DECELERATION
DECENTRALIST
DECENTRALIZE
DECIMALIZING
DECIPHERABLE
DECIPHERMENT
DECISION TREE
DECISIVENESS
DECLAMATIONS
DECLARATIONS
DECLASSIFIED
DECLENSIONAL
DECLINATIONS
DECLINOMETER
DECOLLETAGES
DECOLONIZING
DECOLORATION
DECOMMISSION
DECOMPOSABLE
DECOMPRESSED
DECONGESTANT
DECONTROLLED
DECORATIVELY
DECORTICATOR
DEDUCIBILITY
DEERSTALKERS
DE-ESCALATING
DE-ESCALATION
DEFAMATORILY
DEFICIENCIES
DEFINITENESS
DEFINITIONAL
DEFINITIVELY
DEFLAGRATION

DEFLATIONARY
DEFLATIONIST
DEFLOCCULATE
DEFORMATIONS
DEFORMEDNESS
DEFRAUDATION
DEGENERATING
DEGENERATION
DEGENERATIVE
DEGRADATIONS
DEHUMANIZING
DEHUMIDIFIER
DEJECTEDNESS
DELAMINATION
DELIBERATELY
DELIBERATING
DELIBERATION
DELIBERATIVE
DELICATESSEN
DELIGHTFULLY
DELIMITATION
DELIMITATIVE
DELIQUESCENT
DELITESCENCE
DELTIOLOGIST
DEMAGNETIZED
DEMAGNETIZER
DEMENTEDNESS
DEMILITARIZE
DEMIMONDAINE
DEMOCRATIZED
DEMODULATION
DEMOGRAPHERS
DEMOGRAPHICS
DEMOLISHMENT
DEMONETIZING
DEMONIACALLY
DEMONOLOGIST
DEMONOPOLIZE
DEMONSTRABLE
DEMONSTRABLY
DEMONSTRATED
DEMONSTRATOR
DEMOTIVATING
DEMOTIVATION
DEMYSTIFYING
DENATURALIZE
DENATURATION
DENBIGHSHIRE
DENDROLOGIST
DENG XIAOPING

DENICOTINIZE
DENOMINATING
DENOMINATION
DENOMINATIVE
DENOMINATORS
DENOUNCEMENT
DENSITOMETER
DENSITOMETRY
DENTAL PLATES
DENTILINGUAL
DENUNCIATION
DENUNCIATORY
DEONTOLOGIST
DEPARTMENTAL
DEPENDENCIES
DEPILATORIES
DEPOLITICIZE
DEPOPULATING
DEPOPULATION
DEPORTATIONS
DEPOSITORIES
DEPRAVEDNESS
DFPRECIATING
DEPRECIATION
DEPRECIATORY
DEPREDATIONS
DEPRESSINGLY
DEPRIVATIONS
DERACINATION
DERANGEMENTS
DEREGULATING
DFRFGULATION
DERELICTIONS
DERESTRICTED
DERISIVENESS
DERIVATIONAL
DERIVATIVELY
DERMATOPHYTE
DEROGATORILY
DESALINATING
DESALINATION
DESCRIPTIONS
DESEGREGATED
DESENSITIZED
DESENSITIZER
DESERVEDNESS
DESIDERATION
DESIDERATIVE
DESIGNATIONS
DESIRABILITY
DESPAIRINGLY

DESPOLIATION
DESPONDENTLY
DESPOTICALLY
DESQUAMATION
DESSERTSPOON
DESSERT WINES
DESTABILIZED
DESTINATIONS
DESTRUCTIBLE
DESULPHURIZE
DETERIORATED
DETERMINABLE
DETERMINANTS
DETHRONEMENT
DETOXICATION
DETRUNCATION
DETUMESCENCE
DEUTERANOPIA
DEUTERANOPIC
DEUTOPLASMIC
DEUTSCHE MARK
DEUTSCHMARKS
DEVALUATIONS
DEVELOPMENTS
DEVIATIONISM
DEVIATIONIST
DEVILISHNESS
DEVIL-MAY-CARE
DEVITALIZING
DEXTROGYRATE
DIABOLICALLY
DIAGEOTROPIC
DIAGRAMMATIC
DIALECTICIAN
DIALECTOLOGY
DIALLING CODE
DIALLING TONE
DIALYTICALLY
DIAMAGNETISM
DIAPOPHYSIAL
DIARTHRODIAL
DIASTROPHISM
DIATHERMANCY
DIATOMACEOUS
DIATONICALLY
DIAZOMETHANE
DIBRANCHIATE
DICARBOXYLIC
DICHROMATISM
DICHROSCOPIC
DICTATORSHIP

DICTIONARIES
DIDACTICALLY
DIENCEPHALIC
DIENCEPHALON
DIESEL ENGINE
DIETETICALLY
DIFFERENTIAL
DIFFICULTIES
DIGITAL VIDEO
DIGITIZATION
DIGRESSIONAL
DILAPIDATION
DILATABILITY
DILATATIONAL
DILATOMETRIC
DILATORINESS
DILETTANTISH
DILETTANTISM
DILLYDALLIED
DIMINISHABLE
DIMINISHMENT
DINING TABLES
DINNER JACKET
DIOPTRICALLY
DIPHTHERITIC
DIPHTHONGIZE
DIPLOBLASTIC
DIPLOCARDIAC
DIPLOMATISTS
DIPROPELLANT
DIPSOMANIACS
DIRECT DEBITS
DIRECT OBJECT
DIRECTORATES
DIRECTORSHIP
DIRECT SPEECH
DIRIGIBILITY
DISABILITIES
DISABLEMENTS
DISACCHARIDE
DISADVANTAGE
DISAFFECTION
DISAFFILIATE
DISAGGREGATE
DISAGREEABLE
DISAGREEABLY
DISAGREEMENT
DISALLOWABLE
DISALLOWANCE
DISAMBIGUATE
DISANNULMENT

DISAPPEARING	DISESTABLISH	DISSEMINATED	DOMESTICABLE
DISAPPOINTED	DISFORESTING	DISSEMINATOR	DOMESTICALLY
DISAPPOINTER	DISFRANCHISE	DISSENTIENCE	DOMESTICATED
DISAPPROVING	DISGORGEMENT	DISSERTATION	DOMESTICATOR
DISARRANGING	DISGUSTINGLY	DISSEVERANCE	DOMINO EFFECT
DISASSEMBLER	DISHEVELMENT	DISSIMILARLY	DONKEY JACKET
DISASSOCIATE	DISHONOURING	DISSIMULATED	DONKEYS YEARS
DISASTROUSLY	DISINCENTIVE	DISSIMULATOR	DONKEY'S YEARS
DISBELIEVERS	DISINFECTANT	DISSOCIATING	DOORKNOCKERS
DISBELIEVING	DISINFECTING	DISSOCIATION	DOORSTEPPING
DISBURSEMENT	DISINFECTION	DISSOCIATIVE	DOORSTOPPERS
DISCIPLESHIP	DISINFLATION	DISSOLUTIONS	DORSIVENTRAL
DISCIPLINARY	DISINGENUOUS	DISSYMMETRIC	DORSOVENTRAL
DISCIPLINING	DISINHERITED	DISTEMPERING	DOUBLE-ACTING
DISCLAMATION	DISINTEGRATE	DISTILLATION	DOUBLE AGENTS
DISCOGRAPHER	DISINTERMENT	DISTILLATORY	DOUBLE BASSES
DISCOLOURING	DISINTERRING	DISTILLERIES	DOUBLE-BEDDED
DISCOMFITING	DISJOINTEDLY	DISTINCTIONS	DOUBLE BLUFFS
DISCOMFITURE	DISLOCATIONS	DISTINCTNESS	DOUBLE DAGGER
DISCOMMODING	DISLODGEMENT	DISTORTIONAL	DOUBLE-DATING
DISCOMMODITY	DISLOYALTIES	DISTRACTEDLY	DOUBLE DEALER
DISCOMPOSING	DISMEMBERING	DISTRACTIBLE	DOUBLE-DEALER
DISCOMPOSURE	DISMOUNTABLE	DISTRACTIONS	DOUBLE-DECKER
DISCONCERTED	DISOBEDIENCE	DISTRAINABLE	DOUBLE-DOTTED
DISCONNECTED	DISOPERATION	DISTRAINMENT	DOUBLE FAULTS
DISCONNECTER	DISORGANIZED	DISTRIBUTARY	DOUBLE-GLAZED
DISCONSOLATE	DISORGANIZER	DISTRIBUTING	DOUBLE-HEADER
DISCONTENTED	DISORIENTATE	DISTRIBUTION	DOUBLE-PARKED
DISCONTINUED	DISPENSARIES	DISTRIBUTIVE	DOUBLE-TALKED
DISCORDANTLY	DISPENSATION	DISTRIBUTORS	DOUBLE-TONGUE
DISCOTHEQUES	DISPENSATORY	DISTURBANCES	DOUGHNUTTING
DISCOUNTABLE	DISPIRITEDLY	DITTOGRAPHIC	DOWN PAYMENTS
DISCOURAGING	DISPLACEABLE	DIURETICALLY	DOWNSHIFTING
DISCOURTEOUS	DISPLACEMENT	DIVARICATION	DOWN SHIFTING
DISCOVERABLE	DISPOSITIONS	DIVERSIFYING	DRACONIANISM
DISCOVERTURE	DISPOSSESSED	DIVERSIONARY	DRACONICALLY
DISCREDITING	DISPOSSESSOR ·	DIVERTICULAR	DRAG ONES FEET
DISCREETNESS	DISPUTATIONS	DIVERTICULUM	DRAMATICALLY
DISCRETENESS	DISPUTATIOUS	DIVERTIMENTO	DRAMATIZABLE
DISCRIMINANT	DISQUALIFIED	DIVINGBOARDS	DRAUGHTBOARD
DISCRIMINATE	DISQUALIFIER	DIVINIZATION	DRAWING BOARD
DISCURSIVELY	DISQUIETEDLY	DIVISIBILITY	DRAWING ROOMS
DISCUSSIONAL	DISQUISITION	DIVISIVENESS	DREADFULNESS
DISDAINFULLY	DISREGARDFUL	DOCTRINALITY	DREADNOUGHTS
DISEMBARKING	DISREGARDING	DOCTRINARIAN	DRESS CIRCLES
DISEMBARRASS	DISRELISHING	DODECAHEDRAL	DRESSING DOWN
DISEMBOWELED	DISREPUTABLE	DODECAHEDRON	DRESSING-DOWN
DISENCHANTED	DISREPUTABLY	DODECAPHONIC	DRESSING GOWN
DISENCHANTER	DISRUPTIVELY	DOGMATICALLY	DRESSING ROOM
DISENDOWMENT	DISSATISFIED	DO-IT-YOURSELF	DRY BATTERIES
DISENTANGLED	DISSEMBLANCE	DOMESDAY BOOK	DUCKING STOOL

DUMBFOUNDING
DUMORTIERITE
DUTCH AUCTION
DUTCH COURAGE
DUTY-FREE SHOP
DWARFISHNESS
DYNAMOMETRIC
DYSTELEOLOGY

E

EAGER BEAVERS
EARSPLITTING
EARTHSHAKING
EAST AYRSHIRE
EAST BERLINER
EASTER CACTUS
EASTER ISLAND
EASTER-LEDGES
EAST FLANDERS
EAST GERMANIC
EAST KILBRIDE
EASY ON THE
EYE
EAT HUMBLE PIE
EATING APPLES
EAT ONES WORDS
EAU DE COLOGNE
EAVESDROPPED
EAVESDROPPER
EBULLIOSCOPY
ECCENTRICITY
ECCLESIASTIC
ECCLESIOLOGY
ECHINOCOCCUS
ECHINODERMAL
ECHOLOCATION
ECLECTICALLY
ECLIPTICALLY
ECOLOGICALLY
ECONOMETRICS
ECONOMICALLY
ECOTERRORIST
ECOTYPICALLY
ECSTATICALLY
ECTOPARASITE
ECUMENICALLY
EDACIOUSNESS
EDITORIALIST
EDITORIALIZE
EDULCORATION
EFFECTUALITY

EFFECTUATING
EFFECTUATION
EFFEMINATELY
EFFERVESCENT
EFFERVESCING
EFFLORESCENT
EFFORTLESSLY
EFFUSIOMETER
EFFUSIVENESS
EGOISTICALLY
EGYPTOLOGIST
EISTEDDFODIC
EJACULATIONS
EJECTOR SEATS
ELABORATIONS
ELASMOBRANCH
ELASTICATION
ELASTIC BANDS
ELECTRICALLY
ELECTRIC EYES
ELECTRICIANS
ELECTRIFYING
ELECTROCUTED
ELECTROGRAPH
ELECTROLYSER
ELECTROLYSIS
ELECTROLYTES
ELECTROLYTIC
ELECTROMETER
ELECTROMETRY
ELECTRONVOLT
ELECTROPHONE
ELECTROPLATE
ELECTROSCOPE
ELECTROSHOCK
ELECTROTONIC
ELECTROTONUS
ELECTROTYPER
ELEEMOSYNARY
ELEPHANT'S-EAR
ELEVENTH HOUR
ELIZABETHANS
ELLIPTICALLY
ELOCUTIONARY
ELOCUTIONIST
ELOQUENTNESS
ELYSEE PALACE
EMANCIPATING
EMANCIPATION
EMANCIPATIVE
EMANCIPATORY

EMARGINATION
EMASCULATING
EMASCULATION
EMASCULATIVE
EMBARKATIONS
EMBARRASSING
EMBELLISHING
EMBEZZLEMENT
EMBITTERMENT
EMBLAZONMENT
EMBRANCHMENT
EMBROCATIONS
EMBROIDERIES
EMBROIDERING
EMBRYOLOGIST
EMIGRATIONAL
EMOTIONALISM
EMOTIONALIST
EMOTIONALITY
EMOTIONALIZE
EMPATHICALLY
EMPHATICALLY
EMPLACEMENTS
EMULSIFIABLE
ENANTIOMORPH
ENARTHRODIAL
ENCEPHALITIC
ENCEPHALITIS
ENCHANTMENTS
ENCIPHERMENT
ENCIRCLEMENT
ENCLITICALLY
ENCOMPASSING
ENCOUNTERING
ENCROACHMENT
ENCRUSTATION
ENCUMBRANCER
ENCUMBRANCES
ENCYCLOPEDIA
ENCYCLOPEDIC
ENDAMAGEMENT
ENDANGERMENT
ENDEAVOURING
ENDOCARDITIC
ENDOCARDITIS
ENDOMORPHISM
ENDOPARASITE
ENDORSEMENTS
ENDOSKELETAL
ENDOSKELETON
ENDOTHELIOID

ENDOTHELIOMA
ENDOTHERMISM
ENDURABILITY
ENERGETICIST
ENFEEBLEMENT
ENFRANCHISED
ENFRANCHISER
ENGAGINGNESS
ENGENDERMENT
ENGINE DRIVER
ENGLISH HORNS
ENGLISHWOMAN
ENGRAFTATION
ENGROSSINGLY
ENHANCEMENTS
ENLARGEMENTS
ENLIGHTENING
ENLIVENINGLY
ENORMOUSNESS
ENSHRINEMENT
ENSILABILITY
ENTANGLEMENT
ENTEROKINASE
ENTERPRISING
ENTERTAINERS
ENTERTAINING
ENTHRONEMENT
ENTHUSIASTIC
ENTHYMEMATIC
ENTICINGNESS
ENTOMOLOGIST
ENTOMOLOGIZE
ENTRANCEMENT
ENTRANCINGLY
ENTREATINGLY
ENTRENCHMENT
ENTREPRENEUR
ENUMERATIONS
ENVIABLENESS
ENVIRONMENTS
ENVISAGEMENT
ENZOOTICALLY
ENZYMOLOGIST
EOSINOPHILIC
EPENCEPHALIC
EPENCEPHALON
EPHEMERALITY
EPICUREANISM
EPICYCLOIDAL
EPIDEMIOLOGY
EPIGLOTTIDES

EPIGLOTTISES	EUPHORICALLY	EXOPHTHALMOS	EXTORTIONIST
EPIGRAMMATIC	EUSTATICALLY	EXORBITANTLY	EXTRADITABLE
EPIMORPHOSIS	EVANGELISTIC	EXOTERICALLY	EXTRADITIONS
EPISCOPALIAN	EVANGELIZING	EXPANSIONARY	EXTRAMARITAL
EPISCOPALISM	EVAPORIMETER	EXPANSIONISM	EXTRAMUNDANE
EPISODICALLY	EVENING DRESS	EXPANSIONIST	EXTRANEOUSLY
EPISTEMOLOGY	EVEN-TEMPERED	EXPATRIATING	EXTRANUCLEAR
EPITHALAMIUM	EVENTFULNESS	EXPATRIATION	EXTRAPOLATED
EQUALITARIAN	EVERY MAN JACK	EXPECTATIONS	EXTRAPOLATOR
EQUALIZATION	EVISCERATING	EXPECTORATED	EXTRASENSORY
EQUATABILITY	EVISCERATION	EXPECTORATOR	EXTRAUTERINE
EQUESTRIENNE	EVOLUTIONARY	EXPEDIENTIAL	EXTRAVAGANCE
EQUIDISTANCE	EVOLUTIONISM	EXPERIENCING	EXTRAVAGANZA
EQUILIBRATOR	EVOLUTIONIST	EXPERIENTIAL	EXTROVERSION
EQUIPOLLENCE	EXACERBATING	EXPERIMENTAL	EXTROVERSIVE
EQUIVALENTLY	EXACERBATION	EXPERIMENTED	EYEWITNESSES
EQUIVOCALITY	EXACTINGNESS	EXPERIMENTER	
EQUIVOCATING	EXAGGERATING	EXPERT SYSTEM	**F**
EQUIVOCATION	EXAGGERATION	EXPLANATIONS	
EQUIVOCATORY	EXAGGERATIVE	EXPLANTATION	FABRICATIONS
ERGASTOPLASM	EXAMINATIONS	EXPLICITNESS	FABULOUSNESS
ERYTHROBLAST	EXASPERATING	EXPLOITATION	FACELESSNESS
ERYTHROCYTIC	EXASPERATION	EXPLOITATIVE	FACILITATING
ERYTHROMYCIN	EXCELLENCIES	EXPLORATIONS	FACILITATION
ESCAPE CLAUSE	EXCHANGEABLE	EXPOSITIONAL	FACILITATIVE
ESCAPOLOGIST	EXCHANGE RATE	EXPOSITORILY	FACTIONALISM
ESCUTCHEONED	EXCITABILITY	EXPOSTULATED	FACTIONALIST
ESOTERICALLY	EXCLAMATIONS	EXPOSTULATOR	FACTIOUSNESS
ESSENTIALISM	EXCLUSIONARY	EXPRESSIONAL	FACTORY FARMS
ESSENTIALIST	EXCOGITATION	EXPRESSIVELY	FACTUALISTIC
ESSENTIALITY	EXCOGITATIVE	EXPRESSIVITY	FAINT-HEARTED
ESTABLISHING	EXCORIATIONS	EXPROPRIABLE	FAIT ACCOMPLI
ESTATE AGENCY	EXCRESCENCES	EXPROPRIATED	FAITHFULNESS
ESTATE AGENTS	EXCRUCIATING	EXPROPRIATOR	FAITH HEALERS
ESTHETICALLY	EXCRUCIATION	EXPURGATIONS	FAITH HEALING
ESTRANGEMENT	EXCURSIONIST	EXSANGUINITY	FALLACIOUSLY
ETERNITY RING	EXECUTIONERS	EX-SERVICEMAN	FALLING STARS
ETERNIZATION	EXECUTORSHIP	EX-SERVICEMEN	FALSE BOTTOMS
ETHERIZATION	EXEGETICALLY	EXTEMPORIZED	FAMILIARIZED
ETHNOCENTRIC	EXEMPLIFYING	EXTEMPORIZER	FAMILIARIZER
ETHNOGRAPHER	EXENTERATION	EXTENDEDNESS	FAMILIARNESS
ETHNOGRAPHIC	EXHAUSTIVELY	EXTENSOMETER	FAMILY CIRCLE
ETHNOLOGICAL	EXHIBITIONER	EXTERMINABLE	FAMILY DOCTOR
ETHNOLOGISTS	EXHILARATING	EXTERMINATED	FANCIFULNESS
ETHOXYETHANE	EXHILARATION	EXTERMINATOR	FARADIZATION
ETHYL ALCOHOL	EXHILARATIVE	EXTERNALIZED	FARSIGHTEDLY
ETYMOLOGICAL	EXHORTATIONS	EXTEROCEPTOR	FASCINATEDLY
ETYMOLOGISTS	EXIGUOUSNESS	EXTINGUISHED	FASTIDIOUSLY
EUCALYPTUSES	EXOBIOLOGIST	EXTINGUISHER	FATHER FIGURE
EUHEMERISTIC	EXOPEPTIDASE	EXTORTIONARY	FATHERLINESS
EUPHONICALLY	EXOPHTHALMIC	EXTORTIONATE	FATHERS-IN-LAW
			FATIGABILITY

FAULT-FINDING
FAUTE DE MIEUX
FEARLESSNESS
FEARSOMENESS
FEATHERBRAIN
FEATURE FILMS
FEBRIFACIENT
FECKLESSNESS
FEDERALISTIC
FEEBLEMINDED
FEEL THE PINCH
FELDSPATHOSE
FELICITATING
FELICITATION
FELICITOUSLY
FEMINIZATION
FENESTRATION
FENNELFLOWER
FERLINGHETTI
FERMENTATION
FERMENTATIVE
FERRICYANIDE
FERRIS WHEELS
FERROCYANIDE
FERROSILICON
FERTILIZABLE
FEVERISHNESS
FIBRILLATION
FIBRILLIFORM
FIBRINOGENIC
FIBRINOLYSIN
FIBRINOLYSIS
FIBRINOLYTIC
FIBROBLASTIC
FICTIONALIZE
FICTITIOUSLY
FIDDLE-FADDLE
FIDDLESTICKS
FIELD GLASSES
FIELD MARSHAL
FIELD-TESTING
FIELDWORKERS
FIENDISHNESS
FIFTH COLUMNS
FIGURATIVELY
FIGURE-GROUND
FIGURE SKATER
FILIBUSTERED
FILIBUSTERER
FILM PREMIERE
FILTER-TIPPED

FINALIZATION
FINGERBOARDS
FINGERPLATES
FINGERPRINTS
FINGERSTALLS
FIRE BRIGADES
FIRECRACKERS
FIRE FIGHTERS
FIRE FIGHTING
FIRE HYDRANTS
FIRELIGHTERS
FIREPROOFING
FIRE STATIONS
FIRING SQUADS
FIRST COUSINS
FIRST-FOOTING
FIRST-NIGHTER
FIRST OFFENCE
FIRST REFUSAL
FISH AND CHIPS
FISH HATCHERY
FISSIPALMATE
FISSIROSTRAL
FLAGELLATING
FLAGELLATION
FLAGELLIFORM
FLAMBOYANTLY
FLAME-THROWER
FLAMMABILITY
FLATTERINGLY
FLAVOPROTEIN
FLEET ADMIRAL
FLICKERINGLY
FLITTERMOUSE
FLOATABILITY
FLOCCULATION
FLOORWALKERS
FLORICULTURE
FLOWCHARTING
FLUCTUATIONS
FLUIDEXTRACT
FLUIDIZATION
FLUORESCENCE
FLUORIDATING
FLUORIDATION
FLUORINATION
FLUOROCARBON
FLUOROMETRIC
FLUOROSCOPIC
FLUTTERINGLY
FLUVIOMARINE

FLYING DOCTOR
FLYING PICKET
FLYING SAUCER
FLYING SQUADS
FOCALIZATION
FOLKLORISTIC
FOOL'S-PARSLEY
FOOT-AND-MOUTH
FOOT FAULTING
FOOTSLOGGING
FORBEARINGLY
FORBIDDINGLY
FORCE-FEEDING
FORCEFULNESS
FORCIBLENESS
FORE-AND-AFTER
FORECLOSABLE
FORECLOSURES
FOREGONENESS
FOREKNOWABLE
FORENSICALLY
FOREORDAINED
FORESHADOWED
FORESHADOWER
FORESTALLING
FORESTALMENT
FORESTAYSAIL
FORETRIANGLE
FORGATHERING
FORGET-ME-NOTS
FORMALDEHYDE
FORMLESSNESS
FORMULARIZER
FORMULATIONS
FORT-DE-FRANCE
FORTUITOUSLY
FOSSILIZABLE
FOUNDATIONAL
FOUNTAINHEAD
FOUNTAIN PENS
FOURIERISTIC
FOURTH-DEGREE
FOURTH ESTATE
FOURTH OF JULY
FRACTIONALLY
FRACTIONATOR
FRAMES OF MIND
FRANCHE-COMTE
FRANCO GERMAN
FRANGIBILITY
FRANKFURTERS

FRANKINCENSE
FRATERNALISM
FRATERNITIES
FRATERNIZING
FRAUDULENTLY
FREAKISHNESS
FREE CHURCHES
FREE-FLOATING
FREESTANDING
FREE-SWIMMING
FREETHINKERS
FREETHINKING
FREEWHEELING
FREEZE-DRYING
FREIGHTLINER
FRENCH KISSES
FRENCH LOAVES
FRENCH POLISH
FRENETICALLY
FREQUENTABLE
FREUDIAN SLIP
FRIENDLINESS
FRIGHTENABLE
FROGMARCHING
FRONDESCENCE
FRONTBENCHER
FRONTBENCHES
FRONTIERSMAN
FRONTIERSMEN
FRONTISPIECE
FRONT-RUNNERS
FRUCTIFEROUS
FRUITFULNESS
FRUIT MACHINE
FRUMPISHNESS
FRUSTRATIONS
FUDDY-DUDDIES
FULLER'S EARTH
FULLY-FLEDGED
FULMINATIONS
FUNCTIONALLY
FUNDAMENTALS
FURFURACEOUS
FURUNCULOSIS
FUTILITARIAN
FUTUROLOGIST

G

GALACTAGOGUE
GALACTOMETER
GALACTOMETRY

GALL BLADDERS
GALLINACEOUS
GALLIVANTING
GALVANICALLY
GALVANOMETER
GALVANOMETRY
GALVANOSCOPE
GALVANOSCOPY
GAMESMANSHIP
GAMETOPHORIC
GAMETOPHYTIC
GAMOPETALOUS
GAMOPHYLLOUS
GAMOSEPALOUS
GARBAGE TRUCK
GARDEN CITIES
GASIFICATION
GASTIGHTNESS
GASTRONOMIST
GASTROPODOUS
GASTROSCOPIC
GASTRULATION
GATECRASHERS
GATECRASHING
GAVANIZATION
GEANTICLINAL
GENDER-BENDER
GENEALOGICAL
GENEALOGISTS
GENERALITIES
GENERALIZING
GENERAL STAFF
GENEROSITIES
GENEROUSNESS
GENICULATION
GENOTYPICITY
GENUFLECTING
GENUFLECTION
GEOCHEMISTRY
GEOGRAPHICAL
GEOLOGICALLY
GEOMAGNETISM
GEOMECHANICS
GEOPHYSICIST
GEOPOLITICAL
GEOSYNCLINAL
GERANIACEOUS
GERIATRICIAN
GERMANOPHILE
GERMANOPHOBE
GERONTOCRACY

GESTICULATED
GESTICULATOR
GET ONES CARDS
GET-TOGETHERS
GHOULISHNESS
GIANT KILLERS
GIBRALTARIAN
GIFT-WRAPPING
GIGANTICALLY
GIGANTICNESS
GINGER GROUPS
GINGERLINESS
GLABROUSNESS
GLACIOLOGIST
GLADIATORIAL
GLASSBLOWERS
GLASS-BLOWING
GLASS CEILING
GLASSCUTTERS
GLAUCOMATOUS
GLIMMERINGLY
GLISTENINGLY
GLITTERINGLY
GLOBETROTTER
GLOCKENSPIEL
GLORIOUSNESS
GLOSSOGRAPHY
GLOTTAL STOPS
GLOVE PUPPETS
GLUCOGENESIS
GLUCOGENETIC
GLUE-SNIFFERS
GLUE-SNIFFING
GLUTTONOUSLY
GLYCOGENESIS
GLYCOGENETIC
GLYCOPROTEIN
GLYPHOGRAPHY
GLYPTOGRAPHY
GNOMONICALLY
GNOTOBIOTICS
GOBBLEDEGOOK
GOBBLEDYGOOK
GOLDEN EAGLES
GOLDEN FLEECE
GOLDFISH BOWL
GOLD STANDARD
GONADOTROPIN
GOOD-HUMOURED
GOODY-GOODIES
GOOSEBERRIES

GOOSE PIMPLES
GOOSESTEPPED
GO OVER THE
TOP
GORGEOUSNESS
GORMANDIZING
GOSSIPMONGER
GOVERNMENTAL
GOVERNORSHIP
GRACEFULNESS
GRACIOUSNESS
GRADE SCHOOLS
GRADUALISTIC
GRALLATORIAL
GRAMMATOLOGY
GRAM-NEGATIVE
GRAM-POSITIVE
GRANDFATHERS
GRAND MASTERS
GRANDMOTHERS
GRANDPARENTS
GRANODIORITE
GRANULOCYTIC
GRAPHOLOGIST
GRASSHOPPERS
GRATEFULNESS
GRATIFYINGLY
GRATUITOUSLY
GREASY SPOONS
GREAT BRITAIN
GREAT CIRCLES
GREAT RED SPOT
GREEN FINGERS
GREENGROCERS
GREENGROCERY
GREEN PEPPERS
GREGARIOUSLY
GRIEVOUSNESS
GRIZZLY BEARS
GROSSULARITE
GROUND FLOORS
GROUNDLESSLY
GROUNDSHEETS
GROUND STAFFS
GROUND STROKE
GROUNDSWELLS
GROUP CAPTAIN
GROUP THERAPY
GROVELLINGLY
GROWING PAINS
GRUESOMENESS

GUADALQUIVIR
GUARANTEEING
GUARDIANSHIP
GUERRILLAISM
GUESSTIMATES
GUEST WORKERS
GUILLOTINING
GUINEA-BISSAU
GUN CARRIAGES
GUTTERSNIPES
GUTTURALNESS
GYNAECOCRACY
GYROMAGNETIC

H

HABEAS CORPUS
HABERDASHERS
HABERDASHERY
HABILITATION
HABITABILITY
HABITATIONAL
HABITUALNESS
HACKING COUGH
HAEMATEMESIS
HAEMATOBLAST
HAEMATOCRYAL
HAEMATOGENIC
HAEMATOLOGIC
HAEMATOLYSIS
HAEMATOXYLIC
HAEMATOXYLIN
HAEMATOXYLON
HAEMOPHILIAC
HAEMOPOIESIS
HAEMOPOIETIC
HAEMORRHAGIC
HAEMORRHOIDS
HAGIOGRAPHER
HAGIOGRAPHIC
HAGIOLATROUS
HAIRDRESSERS
HAIRDRESSING
HAIRPIN BENDS
HAIR-RESTORER
HAIR'S BREADTH
HAIRSPLITTER
HAIR TRIGGERS
HALF-BROTHERS
HALF-HOLIDAYS
HALF MEASURES
HALF-TIMBERED

HALFWAY HOUSE	HEARTRENDING	HERITABILITY	HIGH-PRESSURE
HALF-WITTEDLY	HEARTSTRINGS	HERMANNSTADT	HIGH PROFILES
HALLOWEDNESS	HEART TO HEART	HERMENEUTICS	HIGH SHERIFFS
HALLSTATTIAN	HEART-TO-HEART	HERMENEUTIST	HIGH-SOUNDING
HALLUCINATED	HEARTWARMING	HERMETICALLY	HIGH-SPIRITED
HALLUCINATOR	HEATHENISHLY	HERMITICALLY	HINAYANISTIC
HALLUCINOGEN	HEAVENLINESS	HERMOTENSILE	HINDQUARTERS
HALLUCINOSIS	HEAVYHEARTED	HEROD ANTIPAS	HIPPOCRENIAN
HALOGENATION	HEAVY PETTING	HEROICALNESS	HIPPOPOTAMUS
HAMBLETONIAN	HEAVYWEIGHTS	HERPES ZOSTER	HIRE PURCHASE
HAMMARSKJOLD	HEBDOMADALLY	HERPETOLOGIC	HISTOGENESIS
HAMMERHEADED	HEBETUDINOUS	HERRINGBONES	HISTOGENETIC
HAMPEREDNESS	HEBRAIZATION	HERSTMONCEUX	HISTOLOGICAL
HAMSTRINGING	HECTOCOTYLUS	HESITATINGLY	HISTORICALLY
HANDICAPPING	HECTOGRAPHIC	HETEROCERCAL	HIT A BAD
HANDKERCHIEF	HEDGEHOPPING	HETEROCYCLIC	PATCH
HAND OVER FIST	HEDGE SPARROW	HETERODACTYL	HOBBLEDEHOYS
HANDSOMENESS	HEEDLESSNESS	HETEROECIOUS	HOBSON-JOBSON
HAPPENSTANCE	HEILONGJIANG	HETEROGAMETE	HOHENZOLLERN
HAPPY-GO-LUCKY	HEILUNGKIANG	HETEROGAMOUS	HOLIDAYMAKER
HAPPY MEDIUMS	HEIR APPARENT	HETEROGENOUS	HOLISTICALLY
HAPTOTROPISM	HELICOIDALLY	HETEROGONOUS	HOLOPHRASTIC
HARD CURRENCY	HELIOCENTRIC	HETEROGRAPHY	HOLOPLANKTON
HARD FEELINGS	HELIOCHROMIC	HETEROGYNOUS	HOLY OF HOLIES
HARD SHOULDER	HELIOGABALUS	HETEROLOGOUS	HOME COUNTIES
HARE COURSING	HELIOGRAPHER	HETEROMEROUS	HOME FROM HOME
HARLEQUINADE	HELIOGRAPHIC	HETERONOMOUS	HOMELESSNESS
HARLEY STREET	HELIOGRAVURE	HETERONYMOUS	HOMEOMORPHIC
HARMLESSNESS	HELIOLATROUS	HETEROOUSIAN	HOMEOPATHIST
HARMONICALLY	HELIOTHERAPY	HETEROPHYLLY	HOMESICKNESS
HARMONIOUSLY	HELIOTROPISM	HETEROPLASTY	HOMING PIGEON
HARMONIZABLE	HELLENICALLY	HETEROSEXISM	HOMOCHROMOUS
HARPSICHORDS	HELLGRAMMITE	HETEROSEXUAL	HOMOGENIZING
HARQUEBUSIER	HELPING HANDS	HETEROTACTIC	HOMOGONOUSLY
HARTHACANUTE	HELPLESSNESS	HETEROZYGOTE	HOMOLOGATION
HARVEST HOMES	HEMICHORDATE	HETEROZYGOUS	HOMOMORPHISM
HARVEST MOONS	HEMIHYDRATED	HEXACOSANOIC	HOMOPOLARITY
HATCHET-FACED	HEMIMORPHISM	HEXAGRAMMOID	HOMOTAXIALLY
HAUTE COUTURE	HEMIMORPHITE	HEXAHYDRATED	HOMOTHALLISM
HAUTE CUISINE	HEMIPARASITE	HIBERNACULUM	HOMOZYGOUSLY
HAUTE-GARONNE	HEMISPHEROID	HIBERNIANISM	HONEYMOONERS
HAUTS-DE-SEINE	HEMOPHILIACS	HIDDEN AGENDA	HONEYMOONING
HAZARD LIGHTS	HENDECAGONAL	HIERARCHICAL	HONEYSUCKLED
HEADQUARTERS	HENOTHEISTIC	HIERATICALLY	HONEYSUCKLES
HEADSHRINKER	HERALDICALLY	HIEROGLYPHIC	HOPELESSNESS
HEADSTRONGLY	HERBACEOUSLY	HIEROPHANTIC	HORIZONTALLY
HEART ATTACKS	HERD INSTINCT	HIGH FIDELITY	HORNET'S NESTS
HEARTBREAKER	HERE AND THERE	HIGH-HANDEDLY	HORN OF PLENTY
HEART DISEASE	HEREDITAMENT	HIGHLIGHTING	HORRENDOUSLY
HEARTENINGLY	HEREDITARILY	HIGHLY-STRUNG	HORRIBLENESS
HEART FAILURE	HEREINBEFORE	HIGH-MINDEDLY	HORRIFICALLY

HORRIFYINGLY	HYDROCHLORIC	ILL-TREATMENT	IMPOLITENESS
HORS DE COMBAT	HYDRODYNAMIC	ILLUMINATING	IMPONDERABLE
HORS D'OEUVRES	HYDROFLUORIC	ILLUMINATION	IMPORTAIIONS
HORSEMANSHIP	HYDROGENATOR	ILLUMINATIVE	IMPOVERISHED
HORSE TRADING	HYDROGEN BOMB	ILLUSIONISTS	IMPOVERISHER
HORSE-TRADING	HYDROGEOLOGY	ILLUSORINESS	IMPRECATIONS
HORSEWHIPPED	HYDROGRAPHER	ILLUSTRATING	IMPREGNATING
HORSEWHIPPER	HYDROGRAPHIC	ILLUSTRATION	IMPREGNATION
HORTICULTURE	HYDROKINETIC	ILLUSTRATIVE	IMPRESSIONAL
HORTUS SICCUS	HYDROLYSABLE	ILLUSTRATORS	IMPRESSIVELY
HOSPITALIZED	HYDROMEDUSAN	IMAGINATIONS	IMPRISONMENT
HOT-CROSS BUNS	HYDROTHERAPY	IMBECILITIES	IMPROPRIATOR
HOT-GOSPELLER	HYGIENICALLY	IMMACULATELY	IMPROVEMENTS
HOUSE ARRESTS	HYPERCORRECT	IMMEASURABLE	IMPROVIDENCE
HOUSEBREAKER	HYPERMARKETS	IMMEASURABLY	IMPUTABILITY
HOUSEFATHERS	HYPNOTHERAPY	IMMEMORIABLE	INACCESSIBLE
HOUSEHOLDERS	HYPNOTICALLY	IMMERSIONISM	INACCESSIBLY
HOUSE HUSBAND	HYPOCHONDRIA	IMMERSIONIST	INACCURACIES
HOUSEKEEPERS	HYPOCRITICAL	IMMETHODICAL	INACCURATELY
HOUSEKEEPING	HYPOTHETICAL	IMMOBILIZING	INACTIVATION
HOUSEMASTERS	HYSTERECTOMY	IMMODERATELY	INADEQUACIES
HOUSEMOTHERS	HYSTERICALLY	IMMODERATION	INADEQUATELY
HOUSE OF CARDS		IMMORALITIES	INADMISSIBLE
HOUSE OF LORDS	**I**	IMMORTALIZED	INADMISSIBLY
HOUSEPARENTS		IMMORTALIZER	INADVERTENCE
HOUSE PARTIES	ICE-CREAM SODA	IMMOVABILITY	INAPPLICABLE
HOUSE SPARROW	ICHNEUMON FLY	IMMUNE SYSTEM	INAPPLICABLY
HOUSE-TO-HOUSE	ICHNOGRAPHIC	IMMUNIZATION	INARTICULATE
HOUSE-TRAINED	ICHNOLOGICAL	IMMUNOLOGIST	IN ATTENDANCE
HOUSEWARMING	ICHTHYOLOGIC	IMMUTABILITY	INAUDIBILITY
HOUSEY HOUSEY	ICHTHYOPHAGY	IMPARTIALITY	INAUGURATING
HOUSEY-HOUSEY	ICONOCLASTIC	IMPEDIMENTAL	INAUGURATION
HUBBLE-BUBBLE	ICONOGRAPHER	IMPENETRABLE	INAUSPICIOUS
HUDDERSFIELD	ICONOGRAPHIC	IMPENITENTLY	INCALCULABLE
HUGGER-MUGGER	ICONOLATROUS	IMPERATIVELY	INCALCULABLY
HUMANITARIAN	ICONOLOGICAL	IMPERCEPTION	INCALESCENCE
HUMANIZATION	IDEALIZATION	IMPERCEPTIVE	INCANDESCENT
HUMILIATIONS	IDENTIFIABLE	IMPERFECTION	INCANTATIONS
HUMMINGBIRDS	IDENTITY CARD	IMPERFECTIVE	INCAPABILITY
HUMOROUSNESS	IDEOLOOGICAL	IMPERIALISTS	INCAPACITATE
HUMPTY DUMPTY	IDIOMORPHISM	IMPERISHABLE	INCARCERATED
HUNGER STRIKE	IDIOSYNCRASY	IMPERMANENCE	INCARCERATOR
HURDY-GURDIES	IDOLATROUSLY	IMPERSONALLY	INCARNATIONS
HURSTMONCEUX	IGNITABILITY	IMPERSONATED	INCAUTIOUSLY
HUSEIN IBN-ALI	ILLEGAL ENTRY	IMPERSONATOR	INCENDIARISM
HYALOPLASMIC	ILLEGALITIES	IMPERTINENCE	INCESTUOUSLY
HYBRIDIZABLE	ILLEGIBILITY	IMPETIGINOUS	INCIDENTALLY
HYDNOCARPATE	ILLEGITIMACY	IMPLANTATION	INCINERATING
HYDRASTININE	ILLEGITIMATE	IMPLEMENTING	INCINERATION
HYDROCARBONS	ILLIBERALITY	IMPLICATIONS	INCINERATORS
HYDROCEPHALY	ILLITERATELY	IMPLICITNESS	INCISIVENESS
	ILLOGICALITY		

INCIVILITIES	INDELIBILITY	INEXTIRPABLE	INSECTICIDAL
INCLINATIONS	INDELICATELY	INEXTRICABLE	INSECTICIDES
INCLINOMETER	INDEMNIFYING	INEXTRICABLY	INSECTIVORES
INCOGNIZANCE	INDENTATIONS	INFANTICIDAL	INSEMINATING
INCOHERENTLY	INDEPENDENCE	INFANTICIDES	INSEMINATION
INCOMMODIOUS	INDEPENDENCY	INFANT SCHOOL	IN SHORT ORDER
INCOMMUTABLE	INDEPENDENTS	INFATUATEDLY	INSINUATIONS
INCOMPARABLE	INDEX FINGERS	INFATUATIONS	INSOLUBILITY
INCOMPARABLY	INDEX FUTURES	INFECTIOUSLY	INSPECTINGLY
INCOMPATIBLE	INDIANAPOLIS	INFELICITOUS	INSPECTIONAL
INCOMPATIBLY	INDIAN SUMMER	INFESTATIONS	INSPECTORATE
INCOMPETENCE	INDICATIVELY	INFIBULATION	INSPIRATIONS
INCOMPETENTS	INDIFFERENCE	INFIDELITIES	INSPIRITMENT
INCOMPLETELY	INDIGENOUSLY	INFILTRATING	INSTALLATION
INCOMPLIANCE	INDIGESTIBLE	INFILTRATION	INSTILLATION
INCOMPUTABLE	INDIGESTIBLY	INFILTRATIVE	INSTITUTIONS
INCONCLUSIVE	INDIRECTNESS	INFILTRATORS	INSTRUCTIBLE
INCONFORMITY	INDISCIPLINE	INFLAMMATION	INSTRUCTIONS
INCONSEQUENT	INDISCREETLY	INFLAMMATORY	INSTRUMENTAL
INCONSISTENT	INDISCRETION	INFLATIONARY	INSUFFERABLE
INCONSOLABLE	INDISPUTABLE	INFLATIONISM	INSUFFERABLY
INCONSOLABLY	INDISPUTABLY	INFLATIONIST	INSUFFICIENT
INCONSONANCE	INDISSOLUBLE	INFLECTIONAL	INSUFFLATION
INCONSUMABLE	INDISSOLUBLY	INFLORESCENT	INSURABILITY
INCONTINENCE	INDISTINCTLY	INFOTAINMENT	INSURGENCIES
INCONVENIENT	INDIVIDUALLY	INFREQUENTLY	INSURRECTION
INCOORDINATE	INDIVIDUATOR	INFRINGEMENT	INTELLECTION
INCORPORABLE	INDOCTRINATE	INFUNDIBULAR	INTELLECTIVE
INCORPORATED	INDO-EUROPEAN	INFUNDIBULUM	INTELLECTUAL
INCORPORATOR	INDOLEACETIC	INFUSIBILITY	INTELLIGENCE
INCORPOREITY	INDOMETHACIN	INGLORIOUSLY	INTELLIGIBLE
INCORRIGIBLE	INDRE-ET-LOIRE	INGRATIATING	INTELLIGIBLY
INCORRIGIBLY	INDUSTRIALLY	INGRATIATION	INTEMPERANCE
INCRASSATION	INEFFABILITY	INHABITATION	INTENSIFIERS
INCREASINGLY	INEFFACEABLE	INHARMONIOUS	INTENSIFYING
INCRETIONARY	INEFFICIENCY	INHERITANCES	INTERACTIONS
INCRIMINATED	INELASTICITY	INHOSPITABLE	INTERCEPTING
INCRIMINATOR	INEQUALITIES	INHOSPITABLY	INTERCEPTION
INCRUSTATION	INERADICABLE	INHUMANITIES	INTERCEPTIVE
INCUBATIONAL	INERADICABLY	INIMICALNESS	INTERCEPTORS
INCUMBENCIES	INERTIA REELS	INIQUITOUSLY	INTERCESSION
INCURABILITY	INESCUTCHEON	INNOVATIONAL	INTERCESSORY
INDEBTEDNESS	INESSENTIALS	INNUTRITIOUS	INTERCHANGED
INDECISIVELY	INEXACTITUDE	INOBSERVANCE	INTERCHANGES
INDECLINABLE	INEXPEDIENCE	INOCULATIONS	INTERCONNECT
INDECOROUSLY	INEXPERIENCE	INORDINATELY	INTERCURRENT
INDEFEASIBLE	INEXPERTNESS	INOSCULATION	INTERDICTION
INDEFENSIBLE	INEXPLICABLE	INQUISITIONS	INTERDICTIVE
INDEFENSIBLY	INEXPLICABLY	INSALIVATION	INTERESTEDLY
INDEFINITELY	INEXPRESSIVE	INSALUBRIOUS	INTERFERENCE
INDEHISCENCE	INEXTENSIBLE	INSCRIPTIONS	INTERFERTILE

INTERFLUVIAL
INTERGLACIAL
INTERJECTING
INTERJECTION
INTERJECTORY
INTERLACEDLY
INTERLAMINAR
INTERLARDING
INTERLINKING
INTERLOCKING
INTERLOCUTOR
INTERMARRIED
INTERMEDIACY
INTERMEDIARY
INTERMEDIATE
INTERMINABLE
INTERMINABLY
INTERMINGLED
INTERMISSION
INTERMISSIVE
INTERMITTENT
INTERMIXABLE
INTERMIXTURE
INTERNALIZED
INTERNUNCIAL
INTEROCEPTOR
INTERPELLANT
INTERPELLATE
INTERPLEADER
INTERPOLATED
INTERPOLATER
INTERPOSABLE
INTERPRETERS
INTERPRETING
INTERPRETIVE
INTERREGNUMS
INTERROGATED
INTERROGATOR
INTERRUPTING
INTERRUPTION
INTERRUPTIVE
INTERSECTING
INTERSECTION
INTERSPATIAL
INTERSPERSED
INTERSTADIAL
INTERSTELLAR
INTERSTITIAL
INTERTEXTURE
INTERTWINING
INTERVENTION

INTERVIEWEES
INTERVIEWERS
INTERVIEWING
INTERVOCALIC
INTERWEAVING
IN THE LONG
  RUN
INTIMIDATING
INTIMIDATION
INTOLERANTLY
INTONATIONAL
INTOXICATING
INTOXICATION
INTOXICATIVE
INTRACARDIAC
INTRACRANIAL
INTRANSIGENT
INTRANSITIVE
INTRANUCLEAR
INTRAPRENEUR
INTRAUTERINE
INTRIGUINGLY
INTRODUCIBLE
INTRODUCTION
INTRODUCTORY
INTROJECTION
INTROJECTIVE
INTROVERSION
INTROVERSIVE
INTUITIONISM
INTUITIONIST
INTUMESCENCE
INTUSSUSCEPT
INVAGINATION
INVALIDATING
INVALIDATION
INVERCARGILL
INVERTEBRACY
INVERTEBRATE
INVERTED SNOB
INVESTIGABLE
INVESTIGATED
INVESTIGATOR
INVESTITURES
INVIGILATING
INVIGILATION
INVIGILATORS
INVIGORATING
INVIGORATION
INVIGORATIVE
INVISIBILITY

INVITATIONAL
INVOCATIONAL
INVOLUCELATE
INVOLUTIONAL
INVULNERABLE
INVULNERABLY
INVULTUATION
IRASCIBILITY
IRISH COFFEES
IRONING BOARD
IRRADIATIONS
IRRATIONALLY
IRREDEEMABLE
IRREDEEMABLY
IRREFRAGABLE
IRREGULARITY
IRRELEVANCES
IRRELEVANTLY
IRRELIEVABLE
IRREMEDIABLE
IRREMEDIABLY
IRREMISSIBLE
IRRESISTIBLE
IRRESISTIBLY
IRRESOLUTELY
IRRESOLUTION
IRRESOLVABLE
IRRESPECTIVE
IRRESPIRABLE
IRRESPONSIVE
IRREVERENTLY
IRREVERSIBLE
IRREVERSIBLY
IRRIGATIONAL
IRRITABILITY
ISOCHROMATIC
ISODIAMETRIC
ISOLATIONISM
ISOLATIONIST
ISOTOPICALLY
ITALIANESQUE

J
JACK-IN-THE-
  BOX
JACK O LANTERN
JACK-O'-
  LANTERN
JACK ROBINSON
JACKSONVILLE
JACOBS LADDER

JE NE SAIS
  QUOI
JEOPARDIZING
JET-PROPELLED
JIGSAW PUZZLE
JOHANNESBURG
JOURNALISTIC
JUDICATORIAL
JUGULAR VEINS
JUNIOR SCHOOL
JURISCONSULT
JURISDICTION
JURISDICTIVE
JURISPRUDENT
JUSTIFYINGLY
JUVENESCENCE

K
KALEIDOSCOPE
KARYOKINESIS
KARYOKINETIC
KARYOPLASMIC
KEEP ONES HEAD
KEEP THE PEACE
KERATOGENOUS
KERATOPLASTY
KERB CRAWLERS
KERB CRAWLING
KEYNESIANISM
KEY SIGNATURE
KILLER WHALES
KILOWATT-HOUR
KINAESTHESIA
KINAESTHETIC
KINDERGARTEN
KING'S COUNSEL
KING'S ENGLISH
KINROSS-SHIRE
KITCHENETTES
KLEPTOMANIAC
KLIPSPRINGER
KNACKER'S YARD
KNEE BREECHES
KNIGHT ERRANT
KNIGHT-ERRANT
KNOX-JOHNSTON
KOMI REPUBLIC
KOTA KINABALU
KREMLINOLOGY
KRISTIANSTAD
KYRGYZ STEPPE

L

LABORATORIES
LABOUR MARKET
LABOUR OF LOVE
LABOURSAVING
LABYRINTHINE
LACERABILITY
LACHRYMOSITY
LACTOPROTEIN
LADY'S FINGERS
LADY'S-SLIPPER
LAISSEZ-FAIRE
LAKE DISTRICT
LAMENTATIONS
LANDED GENTRY
LANDING CRAFT
LANDING FIELD
LANDING STAGE
LANDING STRIP
LANDLUBBERLY
LANGUISHMENT
LANGUOROUSLY
LANTERN-JAWED
LANTERNSLIDE
LAPIS LAZULIS
LARYNGOSCOPE
LARYNGOSCOPY
LASCIVIOUSLY
LASER PRINTER
LAST JUDGMENT
LATEENRIGGED
LATICIFEROUS
LATINIZATION
LAUNDERETTES
LAUNDRYWOMAN
LAUREATESHIP
LEADING LIGHT
LEAPFROGGING
LEASEHOLDERS
LEATHERINESS
LEAVE TAKINGS
LECTURESHIPS
LEGALIZATION
LEGIONNAIRES
LEGISLATRESS
LEGISLATURES
LEGITIMATELY
LEGITIMATION
LEGITIMATIZE
LEGITIMISTIC
LEGITIMIZING

LENTICELLATE
LEOPARD'S-BANE
LEPIDOPTERAN
LEPIDOPTERON
LETTER OPENER
LEUCOCYTOSIS
LEUCOCYTOTIC
LEUCOPOIESIS
LEUCOPOIETIC
LEUCORRHOEAL
LEVALLOISIAN
LEXICOGRAPHY
LEXICOLOGIST
LIBERALISTIC
LIBERALITIES
LIBERALIZING
LIBERAL PARTY
LIBERTARIANS
LIBERTICIDAL
LIBIDINOUSLY
LICENSE PLATE
LICENTIATION
LICENTIOUSLY
LICHTENSTEIN
LIE DETECTORS
LIFELESSNESS
LIGHT BRIGADE
LIGHT-HEARTED
LIGHTWEIGHTS
LIMNOLOGICAL
LINCOLNSHIRE
LINE DRAWINGS
LINE-ENGRAVER
LINEN BASKETS
LINE PRINTERS
LINE PRINTING
LINGUA FRANCA
LIQUEFACIENT
LIQUEFACTION
LIQUEFACTIVE
LIRIODENDRON
LISTLESSNESS
LITERALISTIC
LITERARINESS
LITERATENESS
LITHOGRAPHED
LITHOGRAPHER
LITHOGRAPHIC
LITTERATEURS
LITTLE FINGER

LITTLE PEOPLE
LITURGICALLY
LIVERPUDLIAN
LIVER SAUSAGE
LIVERY STABLE
LIVING FOSSIL
LOCAL DERBIES
LOCALIZATION
LOCAL OPTIONS
LOCI CLASSICI
LOCKSMITHERY
LOCKSTITCHES
LODGING HOUSE
LOGANBERRIES
LOGANIACEOUS
LOGISTICALLY
LOLLAPALOOZA
LOMENTACEOUS
LONELY HEARTS
LONESOMENESS
LONG-DISTANCE
LONG DIVISION
LONG DRAWN OUT
LONG-DRAWN-OUT
LONGITUDINAL
LONGSHOREMAN
LONGSHOREMEN
LONG-STANDING
LONG VACATION
LONGWINDEDLY
LOOKING GLASS
LOOSE-JOINTED
LOOSE-TONGUED
LOPHOPHORATE
LOQUACIOUSLY
LOSS ADJUSTER
LOST PROPERTY
LOT-ET-GARONNE
LOUDSPEAKERS
LOUGHBOROUGH
LOVECHILDREN
LOWER AUSTRIA
LOWER CLASSES
LOW-WATER MARK
LUDWIGSHAFEN
LUGGAGE RACKS
LUGUBRIOUSLY
LUMBERJACKET
LUMINESCENCE
LUNCHEONETTE
LUSCIOUSNESS

LYMPHANGITIC
LYMPHANGITIS
LYMPHOMATOID
LYSERGIC ACID

M

MACCLESFIELD
MACHINATIONS
MACHINE CODES
MACHINE TOOLS
MACKINTOSHES
MACROCLIMATE
MACROCYTOSIS
MACROGRAPHIC
MACRONUCLEUS
MACROPHYSICS
MACROPTEROUS
MADEMOISELLE
MAGIC LANTERN
MAGISTRACIES
MAGISTRATURE
MAGNETICALLY
MAGNETIC HEAD
MAGNETIC POLE
MAGNETIC TAPE
MAGNETIZABLE
MAGNETOGRAPH
MAGNETOMETER
MAGNETOMETRY
MAGNIFICENCE
MAGNILOQUENT
MAGNITOGORSK
MAGNUM OPUSES
MAIDENLINESS
MAIDEN SPEECH
MAIDEN VOYAGE
MAID OF HONOUR
MAIDSERVANTS
MAILING LISTS
MAINE-ET-LOIRE
MAINTAINABLE
MAITRE D'HOTEL
MAJESTICALLY
MAJOR GENERAL
MAKE ENDS MEET
MALACOLOGIST
MALAPROPISMS
MALEDICTIONS
MALEFACTRESS
MALEVOLENTLY
MALFEASANCES

MALFORMATION	MASS-PRODUCED	MENAGE A TROIS	METHODICALLY
MALFUNCTIONS	MASS-PRODUCER	MENDACIOUSLY	METHOTREXATE
MALIGNANCIES	MASTECTOMIES	MEN OF LETTERS	METICULOUSLY
MALIMPRINTED	MASTER-AT-ARMS	MENSTRUATING	METONIC CYCLE
MALLEABILITY	MASTERLINESS	MENSTRUATION	METROLOGICAL
MALNOURISHED	MASTER OF ARTS	MEPHITICALLY	METROPOLISES
MALNUTRITION	MASTERMINDED	MERCANTILISM	METROPOLITAN
MALOCCLUSION	MASTERPIECES	MERCANTILIST	METRORRHAGIA
MALPRACTICES	MASTERSTROKE	MERCHANDISED	MEZZO-RELIEVO
MALTESE CROSS	MASTIGOPHORE	MERCHANDISER	MEZZO-SOPRANO
MALTREATMENT	MASTURBATING	MERCHANTABLE	MICROANALYST
MAMMALOGICAL	MASTURBATION	MERCHANT BANK	MICROBALANCE
MAN ABOUT TOWN	MATABELELAND	MERCHANT NAVY	MICROBIOLOGY
MAN-ABOUT-TOWN	MATERIALISTS	MERCIFULNESS	MICROCEPHALY
MANAGERESSES	MATERIALIZED	MERCURIALIZE	MICROCIRCUIT
MANAGERIALLY	MATERIALIZER	MERCY KILLING	MICROCLIMATE
MANDARIN DUCK	MATHEMATICAL	MERETRICIOUS	MICROFILMING
MANEUVERABLE	MATINEE IDOLS	MERISTEMATIC	MICROGRAPHER
MANGEL-WURZEL	MATRIARCHIES	MEROPLANKTON	MICROGRAPHIC
MANIFESTABLE	MATRICLINOUS	MERRY-GO-ROUND	MICROGRAVITY
MANIPULATING	MATRICULATED	MESENTERITIS	MICROHABITAT
MANIPULATION	MATRICULATOR	MESENTERONIC	MICRONUCLEUS
MANIPULATIVE	MATRONLINESS	MESMERICALLY	MICROPHYSICS
MANIPULATORY	MATTER-OF-FACT	MESOCEPHALIC	MICROSCOPIST
MANNERLINESS	MATURATIONAL	MESOGASTRIUM	MICROSECONDS
MANOEUVRABLE	MAXIMIZATION	MESOGNATHISM	MICROSEISMIC
MAN OF LETTERS	MEALY-MOUTHED	MESOGNATHOUS	MICROSTOMOUS
MANSION HOUSE	MEAN BUSINESS	MESOMORPHISM	MIDDLE COURSE
MANSLAUGHTER	MEANDERINGLY	MESOMORPHOUS	MIDDLE FINGER
MANTELPIECES	MEANINGFULLY	MESOPOTAMIAN	MIDDLE SCHOOL
MANUFACTURAL	MEASUREMENTS	MESOTHORACIC	MIDDLEWEIGHT
MANUFACTURED	MECAMYLAMINE	MESSAGE STICK	MID GLAMORGAN
MANUFACTURER	MECHANICALLY	METAGALACTIC	MIDSUMMER DAY
MARCASITICAL	MEDALLIONIST	METAGNATHISM	MIDWESTERNER
MARIE GALANTE	MEDICAMENTAL	METAGNATHOUS	MIFEPRISTONE
MARITIME ALPS	MEDICINE BALL	METALANGUAGE	MIGHT AND MAIN
MARKET FORCES	MEDIOCRITIES	METALLICALLY	MILFORD HAVEN
MARKET GARDEN	MEDITATINGLY	METALLURGIST	MILITARISTIC
MARKETPLACES	MEDITATIVELY	METALWORKERS	MILITARIZING
MARKET PRICES	MEETINGHOUSE	METALWORKING	MILLEFEUILLE
MARKSMANSHIP	MEGACEPHALIC	METAMORPHISM	MILLENARIANS
MARLINESPIKE	MEGALOCARDIA	METAMORPHOSE	MILLIONAIRES
MARRIAGEABLE	MEGALOMANIAC	METAPHORICAL	MILTON KEYNES
MARSEILLAISE	MELANCHOLIAC	METAPHRASTIC	MIMEOGRAPHED
MARSHALL PLAN	MELANCHOLILY	METAPHYSICAL	MIND-BOGGLING
MARSHMALLOWS	MELODRAMATIC	METASOMATISM	MINDLESSNESS
MARSUPIALIAN	MELTING POINT	METATHORACIC	MINE DETECTOR
MARVELLOUSLY	MEMORABILITY	METEMPIRICAL	MINERALOGIST
MASQUERADERS	MEMORIALIZER	METEORICALLY	MINERAL WATER
MASQUERADING	MEMORIZATION	METEOROGRAPH	MINESWEEPERS
MASSOTHERAPY	MEN-ABOUT-TOWN	METHACRYLATE	MINESWEEPING

MINIATURISTS
MINICOMPUTER
MINIFICATION
MINIMIZATION
MINIMUM WAGES
MINISTRATION
MINISTRATIVE
MINOR PLANETS
MINUTE STEAKS
MIRACLE PLAYS
MIRROR IMAGES
MIRTHFULNESS
MISADVENTURE
MISALIGNMENT
MISALLIANCES
MISANTHROPES
MISANTHROPIC
MISAPPREHEND
MISBEHAVIOUR
MISCALCULATE
MISCARRIAGES
MISCEGENETIC
MISCELLANIES
MISCELLANIST
MISCONCEIVED
MISCONCEIVER
MISCONDUCTED
MISCONSTRUED
MISDEMEANANT
MISDEMEANOUR
MISDIRECTING
MISDIRECTION
MISE-EN-SCENES
MISINFORMANT
MISINFORMING
MISINTERPRET
MISJUDGEMENT
MISJUDGMENTS
MISLEADINGLY
MISPLACEMENT
MISPRONOUNCE
MISQUOTATION
MISREPORTING
MISREPRESENT
MISSING LINKS
MISSIONARIES
MISSPELLINGS
MISSTATEMENT
MISTREATMENT
MITHRIDATISM
MIXED-ABILITY

MIXED DOUBLES
MIXED ECONOMY
MIXED FARMING
MNEMONICALLY
MOBILIZATION
MOCKINGBIRDS
MODERATENESS
MODIFICATION
MODIFICATORY
MODULABILITY
MODUS VIVENDI
MOHAVE DESERT
MOISTURIZING
MOLLIFYINGLY
MOLLYCODDLED
MONADELPHOUS
MONARCHISTIC
MONASTICALLY
MONETIZATION
MONEYCHANGER
MONEY-GRUBBER
MONEYLENDERS
MONFYLENDING
MONEY SPINNER
MONEY-SPINNER
MONISTICALLY
MONKEY-PUZZLE
MONKEY WRENCH
MONOCHLORIDE
MONOCHROMIST
MONODRAMATIC
MONOFILAMENT
MONOGAMISTIC
MONOGAMOUSLY
MONOMANIACAL
MONOMETALLIC
MONOMETRICAL
MONOMORPHISM
MONOPETALOUS
MONOPHTHONGS
MONOPHYLETIC
MONOPHYLLOUS
MONOPOLISTIC
MONOPOLIZING
MONOSEPALOUS
MONOSPERMOUS
MONOSTROPHIC
MONOSYLLABIC
MONOSYLLABLE
MONOTHEISTIC
MONOTONOUSLY

MONOTRICHOUS
MONTPARNASSE
MONUMENTALLY
MOONLIGHTERS
MOONLIGHTING
MORALITY PLAY
MORALIZATION
MORALIZINGLY
MORBIFICALLY
MORNING COATS
MORNING DRESS
MORNING GLORY
MORPHALLAXIS
MORPHOLOGIES
MORPHOLOGIST
MORRIS DANCER
MORRIS DANCES
MORTARBOARDS
MORTGAGEABLE
MORTIFYINGLY
MORTISE LOCKS
MOSQUITO NETS
MOTHERFUCKER
MOTHERLINESS
MOTHER NATURE
MOTHERS-IN-LAW
MOTHER TONGUE
MOTHPROOFING
MOTIONLESSLY
MOTIVATIONAL
MOTORCYCLIST
MOTORIZATION
MOTOR SCOOTER
MOULDABILITY
MOUNTAINEERS
MOUNTAIN LION
MOUNTAINSIDE
MOUNTAINTOPS
MOURNFULNESS
MOUTHBROODER
MOUTH-TO-MOUTH
MOVABLE FEAST
MUCILAGINOUS
MUCOPURULENT
MUDDLE-HEADED
MULLIGATAWNY
MULTICHANNEL
MULTIFACETED
MULTIFARIOUS
MULTIFOLIATE
MULTIFORMITY

MULTIGRAVIDA
MULTILAMINAR
MULTILATERAL
MULTILINGUAL
MULTINUCLEAR
MULTIPARTITE
MULTIPLIABLE
MULTIPLICAND
MULTIPLICATE
MULTIPLICITY
MULTIPURPOSE
MULTITASKING
MULTIVALENCY
MULTIVARIATE
MUNICIPALITY
MUNICIPALIZE
MUNIFICENTLY
MUSEUM PIECES
MUSICAL BOXES
MUSIC CENTRES
MUSICIANSHIP
MUSICOLOGIST
MYRMECOPHILE
MYSTERIOUSLY
MYSTERY PLAYS
MYSTERY TOURS
MYSTIFYINGLY
MYTHOLOGICAL
MYTHOLOGISTS
MYTHOLOGIZER
MYXOMYCETOUS

N

NAIL SCISSORS
NAMBY-PAMBIES
NAMEDROPPERS
NAMEDROPPING
NANOPLANKTON
NANSEN BOTTLE
NARCISSISTIC
NARCOTICALLY
NARRAGANSETT
NARROW GAUGES
NARROW-MINDED
NARROW SQUEAK
NASALIZATION
NATIONAL DEBT
NATIONAL HUNT
NATIONALISTS
NATIONALIZED
NATIONAL PARK

NATION STATES
NATIVITY PLAY
NATURALISTIC
NATURALIZING
NATUROPATHIC
NAUSEATINGLY
NAUSEOUSNESS
NAUTICAL MILE
NAVIGABILITY
NAVIGATIONAL
NEANDERTHALS
NEBULIZATION
NEBULOUSNESS
NECESSITATED
NECKERCHIEFS
NECROLOGICAL
NECROMANCERS
NECROPHILIAC
NECROPHILISM
NECROPOLISES
NEEDLESSNESS
NEGATIVENESS
NEGATIVE POLE
NEGATIVE SIGN
NEGATIVISTIC
NEGLECTFULLY
NEGOTIATIONS
NEIGHBOURING
NEMATOCYSTIC
NEOANTHROPIC
NEOCLASSICAL
NEOLOGICALLY
NEOTERICALLY
NEPHELOMETER
NEPHOLOGICAL
NERVE CENTRES
NERVE-RACKING
NETHERLANDER
NETTLE RASHES
NEURASTHENIA
NEURASTHENIC
NEUROANATOMY
NEUROBIOLOGY
NEUROLOGICAL
NEUROLOGISTS
NEUROPTEROUS
NEUROSCIENCE
NEUROSURGEON
NEUROSURGERY
NEUROTICALLY
NEUROTOMICAL

NEUTRALIZING
NEUTRON BOMBS
NEVERTHELESS
NEW BRUNSWICK
NEW CALEDONIA
NEWFOUNDLAND
NEW HAMPSHIRE
NEWS AGENCIES
NEWSPAPERMAN
NEW TESTAMENT
NEWTOWNABBEY
NEW ZEALANDER
NIAGARA FALLS
NICOTINAMIDE
NIDIFICATION
NIETZSCHEISM
NIGHTDRESSES
NIGHTINGALES
NIMBOSTRATUS
NITROBENZENE
NITROMETHANE
NO-CLAIM BONUS
NOCTAMBULISM
NOCTAMBULIST
NOCTILUCENCE
NOCTURNALITY
NOLENS VOLENS
NOMENCLATURE
NOMINALISTIC
NONADDICTIVE
NONAGENARIAN
NONALCOHOLIC
NONALIGNMENT
NONCHALANTLY
NONCOMBATANT
NONCOMMITTAL
NONCONDUCTOR
NONCORRODING
NONE SO PRETTY
NONESSENTIAL
NONEXISTENCE
NONEXPLOSIVE
NONFICTIONAL
NONFLAMMABLE
NONIDENTICAL
NONIDIOMATIC
NONMALIGNANT
NONOPERATIVE
NONPOISONOUS
NONPOLITICAL
NONRESIDENCE

NON RESIDENCE
NONRESIDENTS
NONRESISTANT
NONSCHEDULED
NONSECTARIAN
NON SEQUITURS
NONSTRATEGIC
NONTECHNICAL
NONVIOLENTLY
NORTH AMERICA
NORTH BRABANT
NORTHEASTERN
NORTHEASTERS
NORTHERNMOST
NORTH HOLLAND
NORTHUMBRIAN
NORTHWESTERN
NOTEWORTHILY
NOTICE BOARDS
NOTIFICATION
NOURISHINGLY
NOUVEAU RICHE
NOVOKUZNETSK
NUBIAN DESERT
NUCLEOPHILIC
NUMBERPLATES
NUMEROUSNESS
NUMINOUSNESS
NUMISMATISTS
NURSERY RHYME
NURSING HOMES
NUSA TENGGARA
NUTRITIONIST
NUTRITIOUSLY
NUTS AND BOLTS
NYCTITROPISM
NYMPHOLEPTIC
NYMPHOMANIAC

O

OBERAMMERGAU
OBITER DICTUM
OBJECT LESSON
OBLANCEOLATE
OBLATE SPHERE
OBLIGATIONAL
OBLIGATORILY
OBLITERATING
OBLITERATION
OBLITERATIVE
OBSCURANTISM

OBSCURANTIST
OBSEQUIOUSLY
OBSERVATIONS
OBSOLESCENCE
OBSOLETENESS
OBSTETRICIAN
OBSTREPEROUS
OBSTRUCTIONS
OCCASIONALLY
OCCUPATIONAL
OCEANOGRAPHY
OCTOGENARIAN
OCTOSYLLABIC
OCTOSYLLABLE
ODONTOGRAPHY
ODONTOLOGIST
ODONTOPHORAL
OESOPHAGUSES
OFFICE BLOCKS
OFFICEHOLDER
OFF ONES HANDS
OFF-THE-RECORD
OIL PAINTINGS
OKLAHOMA CITY
OLD-FASHIONED
OLD MANS BEARD
OLD PRETENDER
OLD SCHOOL TIE
OLD TESTAMENT
OLD WIVES'
      TALE
OLEORESINOUS
OLIGOTROPHIC
OLYMPIC GAMES
OMNIPRESENCE
ONEIROCRITIC
ONE-SIDEDNESS
ONE-TRACK MIND
ONE-UPMANSHIP
ONOMASIOLOGY
ONOMATOPOEIA
ONOMATOPOEIC
ON THE RAMPAGE
ONYCHOPHORAN
OOPHORECTOMY
OPEN-HANDEDLY
OPENING TIMES
OPEN-MINDEDLY
OPEN QUESTION
OPEN SANDWICH
OPEN VERDICTS

OPERA GLASSES	OSTEOBLASTIC	**P**	PARALLEL BARS
OPERATICALLY	OSTEOCLASTIC	PACIFICATION	PARALLELISMS
OPHIOLOGICAL	OSTEOLOGICAL	PACKAGE DEALS	PARALLELLING
OPHTHALMITIS	OSTEOMALACIA	PACKAGE TOURS	PARALOGISTIC
OPINION POLLS	OSTEOPLASTIC	PACKING CASES	PARALYSATION
OPPORTUNISTS	OSTRACIZABLE	PADDLING POOL	PARAMAGNETIC
OPPOSABILITY	OTHERWORLDLY	PAEDOGENESIS	PARAMILITARY
OPPOSITENESS	OUTBALANCING	PAEDOGENETIC	PARAMORPHISM
OPPOSITIONAL	OUTBUILDINGS	PAEDOLOGICAL	PARAPHRASING
OPPRESSINGLY	OUTDISTANCED	PAGANIZATION	PARAPHRASTIC
OPPRESSIVELY	OUTGENERALED	PAINTBRUSHES	PARASITICIDE
OPSONIZATION	OUTLANDISHLY	PALAEOBOTANY	PARASITOLOGY
OPTIMIZATION	OUTMANOEUVRE	PALAEOGRAPHY	PARATHYROIDS
ORANGE ROUGHY	OUTNUMBERING	PALAEOLITHIC	PARATROOPERS
ORATORICALLY	OUTRAGEOUSLY	PALATABILITY	PARENTHESIZE
ORBICULARITY	OUTRIVALLING	PALATIALNESS	PARISH CLERKS
ORCHESTRA PIT	OUTSTRETCHED	PALAZZO PANTS	PARISHIONERS
ORCHESTRATED	OUTSTRIPPING	PALEOGRAPHER	PARISYLLABIC
ORCHIDACEOUS	OVERBALANCED	PALEONTOLOGY	PARKING LIGHT
ORDINARINESS	OVERBURDENED	PALETTE KNIFE	PARKING METER
ORGAN GRINDER	OVERCAPACITY	PALINGENESIS	PARLOUR GAMES
ORGANICISTIC	OVERCAUTIOUS	PALINGENETIC	PAROCHIALISM
ORGANIZATION	OVERCHARGING	PALPIIATIONS	PARSIMONIOUS
URGANOGRAPHY	OVERCLOUDING	PALYNOLOGIST	PARSON'S NOSES
ORGANOLEPTIC	OVERCRITICAL	PAMPHLETEERS	PART EXCHANGE
ORGANOLOGIST	OVERCROPPING	PANCAKE ROLLS	PARTHIAN SHOT
ORIEL WINDOWS	OVERCROWDING	PANCHROMATIC	PARTIALITIES
ORIENTALISTS	OVERDRESSING	PANDANACEOUS	PARTICIPANTS
ORIENTATIONS	OVEREMPHATIC	PANDEMONIUMS	PARTICIPATED
ORIENTEERING	OVERESTIMATE	PANHELLENISM	PARTICIPATOR
ORNAMENTALLY	OVEREXPOSING	PANHELLENIST	PARTICULARLY
OROGENICALLY	OVERGENEROUS	PANOPTICALLY	PARTING SHOTS
OROLOGICALLY	OVERINDULGED	PANTECHNICON	PARTISANSHIP
ORTHOCEPHALY	OVERMASTERED	PANTISOCRACY	PARTITIONING
ORTHODONTICS	OVERPOPULATE	PANTOGRAPHER	PARTNERSHIPS
ORTHOGENESIS	OVERPOWERING	PANTOGRAPHIC	PART OF SPEECH
ORTHOGENETIC	OVERREACHING	PAPERHANGERS	PARTY POOPERS
ORTHOGRAPHER	OVERREACTING	PAPERHANGING	PASQUEFLOWER
ORTHOGRAPHIC	OVERREACTION	PAPERWEIGHTS	PASSE PARTOUT
ORTHOMORPHIC	OVERSHADOWED	PAPULIFEROUS	PASSE-PARTOUT
ORTHOPAEDICS	OVERSHOOTING	PARABOLOIDAL	PASSIONATELY
ORTHOPAEDIST	OVERSIMPLIFY	PARACHRONISM	PASSION PLAYS
ORTHOPTEROUS	OVERSLEEPING	PARACHUTISTS	PASTEURIZING
ORTHORHOMBIC	OVERSTEPPING	PARADE GROUND	PAST PERFECTS
ORTHOTROPISM	OVERSTOCKING	PARADIGMATIC	PATCH POCKETS
ORTHOTROPOUS	OVERTHROWING	PARADISE LOST	PATERNALISTS
OSCILLATIONS	OVERWHELMING	PARADISIACAL	PATERNOSTERS
OSCILLOGRAPH	OWNER-DRIVERS	PARAESTHESIA	PATHETICALLY
OSCILLOSCOPE	OXYACETYLENE	PARAESTHETIC	PATHOGENESIS
OSSIFICATION	OXYGENIZABLE	PARAHYDROGEN	PATHOGENETIC
OSTENTATIOUS		PARALANGUAGE	PATHOLOGICAL

PATHOLOGISTS	PERINEURITIC	PETROLOGISTS	PHOTOCURRENT
PATRIARCHATE	PERINEURITIS	PETROZAVODSK	PHOTODYNAMIC
PATRIARCHIES	PERIODICALLY	PETTIFOGGING	PHOTOENGRAVE
PATRICLINOUS	PERIODONTICS	PETTY LARCENY	PHOTOGEOLOGY
PATROL WAGONS	PERIOD PIECES	PETTY OFFICER	PHOTOGRAPHED
PATRON SAINTS	PERIONYCHIUM	PHAGOCYTOSIS	PHOTOGRAPHER
PAVING STONES	PERIPHERALLY	PHANEROGAMIC	PHOTOGRAPHIC
PAY ENVELOPES	PERIPHRASTIC	PHANEROPHYTE	PHOTOGRAVURE
PEACEFULNESS	PERITRICHOUS	PHARMACOLOGY	PHOTOKINESIS
PEAK DISTRICT	PERMACULTURE	PHARYNGOLOGY	PHOTOKINETIC
PEANUT BUTTER	PERMANENT WAY	PHARYNGOTOMY	PHOTOMETRIST
PEARL HARBOUR	PERMANGANATE	PHELLODERMAL	PHOTOMONTAGE
PEASE PUDDING	PERMEABILITY	PHENANTHRENE	PHOTONEUTRON
PECCADILLOES	PERMISSIVELY	PHENOLOGICAL	PHOTONUCLEAR
PECKING ORDER	PERMITTIVITY	PHENOMENALLY	PHOTOPHILOUS
PEDANTICALLY	PERMUTATIONS	PHI BETA KAPPA	PHOTOPOLYMER
PEDIATRICIAN	PERNICIOUSLY	PHILADELPHIA	PHOTOREALISM
PEEBLESSHIRE	PERPETRATING	PHILADELPHUS	PHOTOSPHERIC
PEJORATIVELY	PERPETRATION	PHILANDERERS	PHOTOSTATTED
PENALIZATION	PERPETRATORS	PHILANDERING	PHOTOTHERAPY
PENALTY AREAS	PERPETUATING	PHILANTHROPY	PHOTOTHERMIC
PENDENTE LITE	PERPETUATION	PHILATELISTS	PHOTOTROPISM
PENITENTIARY	PERPETUITIES	PHILHARMONIC	PHRASAL VERBS
PENNSYLVANIA	PERPLEXITIES	PHILISTINISM	PHRASEOGRAPH
PENNULTIMATE	PERSECUTIONS	PHILODENDRON	PHRENOLOGIST
PENNY PINCHER	PERSEVERANCE	PHILOLOGICAL	PHYCOLOGICAL
PENNY WHISTLE	PERSISTENTLY	PHILOLOGISTS	PHYLETICALLY
PENTARCHICAL	PERSONA GRATA	PHILOSOPHERS	PHYSICALNESS
PEPTIC ULCERS	PERSONALIZED	PHILOSOPHIES	PHYSIOCRATIC
PERADVENTURE	PERSONIFYING	PHILOSOPHIZE	PHYSIOGNOMIC
PERAMBULATED	PERSPECTIVES	PHLEBOTOMIST	PHYSIOGRAPHY
PERAMBULATOR	PERSPICACITY	PHONEMICALLY	PHYSIOLOGIES
PERCEPTIONAL	PERSPIRATION	PHONE-TAPPING	PHYSIOLOGIST
PERCEPTIVELY	PERSPIRATORY	PHONETICALLY	PHYSOSTOMOUS
PERCEPTIVITY	PERSPIRINGLY	PHONETICIANS	PHYTOGENESIS
PERCOLATIONS	PERSUASIVELY	PHONOGRAPHER	PHYTOGENETIC
PERCUTANEOUS	PERTINACIOUS	PHONOLOGICAL	PHYTOHORMONE
PEREGRINATOR	PERTURBATION	PHONOLOGISTS	PHYTOPHAGOUS
PEREMPTORILY	PERTURBINGLY	PHONOTACTICS	PICCANINNIES
PERFECT PITCH	PERVERSENESS	PHOSPHATURIA	PICKERELWEED
PERFIDIOUSLY	PERVERSITIES	PHOSPHATURIC	PICTURE BOOKS
PERFOLIATION	PERVIOUSNESS	PHOSPHOLIPID	PICTURE CARDS
PERFORATIONS	PESTILENTIAL	PHOSPHORESCE	PIECE OF EIGHT
PERFORMANCES	PETALIFEROUS	PHOSPHORITIC	PIECES OF WORK
PERFORMATIVE	PETERBOROUGH	PHOTOACTINIC	PIGEONHOLING
PERICARDITIC	PETIT LARCENY	PHOTOCATHODE	PIGMENTATION
PERICARDITIS	PETRIFACTION	PHOTOCHEMIST	PILOT OFFICER
PERICYNTHION	PETRODOLLARS	PHOTOCHROMIC	PINEAL GLANDS
PERILOUSNESS	PETROGRAPHER	PHOTOCOMPOSE	PINK ELEPHANT
PERIMORPHISM	PETROGRAPHIC	PHOTOCOPIERS	PIPE CLEANERS
PERINEPHRIUM	PETROLOGICAL	PHOTOCOPYING	PIPES OF PEACE

PISCICULTURE
PITCHFORKING
PITIABLENESS
PITILESSNESS
PITTER-PATTER
PLACENTATION
PLACE SETTING
PLAGIARISTIC
PLAGIARIZING
PLAGIOCLIMAX
PLAIN-CLOTHES
PLAIN SAILING
PLANETARIUMS
PLANETESIMAL
PLANISPHERIC
PLANO-CONCAVE
PLANOGRAPHIC
PLASTERBOARD
PLASTER CASTS
PLASTOMETRIC
PLATONICALLY
PLAUSIBILITY
PLAYER PIANOS
PLAYING CARDS
PLAYING FIELD
PLAYS ON WORDS
PLEASANTNESS
PLEASANTRIES
PLEASINGNESS
PLEIOTROPISM
PLEOMORPHISM
PLIMSOLL LINE
PLODDINGNESS
PLOUGHSHARES
PLUMBIFEROUS
PLUM PUDDINGS
PLUTOCRACIES
PLUVIOMETRIC
PNEUMOCOCCUS
PNEUMOTHORAX
POET LAUREATE
POINTILLISTS
POINT OF ORDER
POINTS OF VIEW
POINT-TO-POINT
POLARIMETRIC
POLARIZATION
POLAROGRAPHY
POLE POSITION
POLE VAULTERS
POLE VAULTING

POLICE STATES
POLICYHOLDER
POLITICIZING
POLLEN COUNTS
POLLING BOOTH
POLTERGEISTS
POLYANTHUSES
POLYCENTRISM
POLYCHAETOUS
POLYCYTHEMIA
POLYEMBRYONY
POLYETHYLENE
POLYISOPRENE
POLYMORPHISM
POLYMORPHOUS
POLYPETALOUS
POLYPHYLETIC
POLYPHYODONT
POLYRHYTHMIC
POLYSEPALOUS
POLYSULPHIDE
POLYSYLLABIC
POLYSYLLABLE
POLYSYNDETON
POLYTECHNICS
POLYTHEISTIC
POLYTONALIST
POLYTONALITY
POLYURETHANE
POMEGRANATES
PONS ASINORUM
PONTA DELGADA
PONTIFICATED
PONTIFICATES
PONY-TREKKING
POOR RELATION
POOR-SPIRITED
POPOCATEPETL
POPULAR FRONT
POPULARIZING
POPULOUSNESS
PORNOGRAPHER
PORNOGRAPHIC
PORPHYROPSIN
PORT ADELAIDE
PORT-AU-PRINCE
PORTCULLISES
PORTE-COCHERE
PORTENTOUSLY
PORTERHOUSES
PORT HARCOURT

PORTMANTEAUS
PORTMANTEAUX
PORTS OF ENTRY
POSITIVENESS
POSITIVE POLE
POSITIVISTIC
POSSESSIVELY
POSTAGE STAMP
POSTAL ORDERS
POSTDILUVIAL
POSTDILUVIAN
POSTDOCTORAL
POSTER COLOUR
POSTER PAINTS
POSTGRADUATE
POSTHUMOUSLY
POSTMERIDIAN
POST MERIDIEM
POSTPONEMENT
POSTPOSITION
POSTPOSITIVE
POSTPRANDIAL
POTATO BEETLE
POTATO CRISPS
POTENTIALITY
POTTER'S WHEEL
POTTING SHEDS
POTTY-TRAINED
POVERTY TRAPS
POWER BROKERS
POWERFULNESS
POWER-SHARING
POWER STATION
PRACTICALITY
PRACTITIONER
PRAGMATISTIC
PRAISEWORTHY
PRASEODYMIUM
PRAYER WHEELS
PREAMPLIFIER
PREARRANGING
PREBENDARIES
PRECARIOUSLY
PRECEDENTIAL
PRECENTORIAL
PRECEPTORATE
PRECEPTORIAL
PRECESSIONAL
PRECIOUSNESS
PRECIPITANCE
PRECIPITATED

PRECIPITATES
PRECIPITATOR
PRECISIANISM
PRECISIONISM
PRECISIONIST
PRECLASSICAL
PRECOCIOUSLY
PRECOGNITION
PRECOGNITIVE
PRECONCEIVED
PRECONDITION
PRECONSCIOUS
PREDECEASING
PREDECESSORS
PREDESTINATE
PREDESTINING
PREDETERMINE
PREDICAMENTS
PREDICTIVELY
PREDIGESTING
PREDIGESTION
PREDILECTION
PREDISPOSING
PREDOMINANCE
PREDOMINATED
PREDOMINATOR
PRE-ECLAMPSIA
PRE-EMINENTLY
PRE-EMPTIVELY
PRE-EXISTENCE
PREFABRICATE
PREFECTORIAL
PREFERENTIAL
PREFORMATION
PREGNABILITY
PREJUDGEMENT
PREJUDGMENTS
PREMARITALLY
PREMAXILLARY
PREMEDITATED
PREMEDITATOR
PREMENSTRUAL
PREMIERSHIPS
PREMIUM BONDS
PREMONITIONS
PREOCCUPYING
PREORDAINING
PREPARATIONS
PREPAREDNESS
PREPONDERANT
PREPONDERATE

PREPOSITIONS
PREPOSSESSED
PREPOSTEROUS
PRERECORDING
PREREQUISITE
PREROGATIVES
PRESBYTERATE
PRESBYTERIAL
PRESBYTERIAN
PRESBYTERIES
PRESCRIPTION
PRESCRIPTIVE
PRESENTATION
PRESENTATIVE
PRESENTIMENT
PRESERVATION
PRESERVATIVE
PRESIDENCIES
PRESIDENTIAL
PRESS CUTTING
PRESS GALLERY
PRESSGANGING
PRESSINGNESS
PRESS RELEASE
PRESSURIZING
PRESUMPTIONS
PRESUMPTUOUS
PRESUPPOSING
PRETTY-PRETTY
PREVAILINGLY
PREVARICATED
PREVARICATOR
PREVENTIVELY
PREVIOUSNESS
PRICKLY PEARS
PRIDE OF PLACE
PRIESTLINESS
PRIEST-RIDDEN
PRIGGISHNESS
PRIME NUMBERS
PRIMOGENITOR
PRIMORDIALLY
PRIMULACEOUS
PRIMUM MOBILE
PRINCELINESS
PRINCE REGENT
PRINCE RUPERT
PRINCIPAL BOY
PRINCIPALITY
PRINTABILITY
PRIORITIZING

PRISMATOIDAL
PRIVATE PARTS
PRIVY COUNCIL
PRIZEFIGHTER
PROBATIONARY
PROBATIONERS
PROBLEMATIZE
PROBOSCIDEAN
PROCATHEDRAL
PROCESSIONAL
PROCLAMATION
PROCLIVITIES
PROCONSULATE
PROCTOLOGIST
PRODIGIOUSLY
PRODUCTIONAL
PRODUCTIVELY
PRODUCTIVITY
PROFANATIONS
PROFESSIONAL
PROFESSORIAL
PROFICIENTLY
PROFITEERING
PROFITLESSLY
PROFIT MARGIN
PROFOUNDNESS
PROFUNDITIES
PROGESTERONE
PROGRAMMABLE
PROGRAMMATIC
PROGRESSIONS
PROGRESSIVES
PROHIBITIONS
PROJECTIONAL
PROLEGOMENAL
PROLEGOMENON
PROLETARIANS
PROLIFERATED
PROLIFICALLY
PROLIFICNESS
PROLONGATION
PROMISED LAND
PROMONTORIES
PROMULGATING
PROMULGATION
PROMULGATORS
PRONOMINALLY
PRONOUNCEDLY
PROOFREADERS
PROOFREADING
PROPAEDEUTIC

PROPAGANDISM
PROPAGANDIST
PROPAGANDIZE
PROPENSITIES
PROPHESIABLE
PROPHYLACTIC
PROPITIATING
PROPITIATION
PROPITIATIVE
PROPITIATORY
PROPITIOUSLY
PROPORTIONAL
PROPORTIONED
PROPOSITIONS
PROROGATIONS
PROSCRIPTION
PROSCRIPTIVE
PROSECUTABLE
PROSECUTIONS
PROSELYTIZED
PROSELYTIZER
PROSOPOPOEIA
PROSPECTUSES
PROSPEROUSLY
PROSTITUTING
PROSTITUTION
PROSTRATIONS
PROTACTINIUM
PROTAGONISTS
PROTECTIVELY
PROTECTORATE
PROTESTATION
PROTESTINGLY
PROTHALAMION
PROTHONOTARY
PROTOHISTORY
PROTOMORPHIC
PROTOPLASMIC
PROTOPLASTIC
PROTOSEMITIC
PROTOTHERIAN
PROTOTROPHIC
PROTOZOOLOGY
PROTRACTEDLY
PROTUBERANCE
PROVERBIALLY
PROVIDENTIAL
PROVINCETOWN
PROVINCIALLY
PROVISIONING
PROVOCATIONS

PRUDENTIALLY
PRUSSIAN BLUE
PSEPHOLOGIST
PSEUDONYMITY
PSEUDONYMOUS
PSEUDOPODIUM
PSYCHIATRIST
PSYCHOACTIVE
PSYCHOBABBLE
PSYCHOGNOSIS
PSYCHOGRAPHY
PSYCHOLOGIES
PSYCHOLOGISM
PSYCHOLOGIST
PSYCHOLOGIZE
PSYCHOMETRIC
PSYCHOPATHIC
PSYCHOSEXUAL
PSYCHOSOCIAL
PSYCHROMETER
PTERIDOPHYTE
PTERIDOSPERM
PTERODACTYLS
PUBLICATIONS
PUBLIC HOUSES
PUBLIC SCHOOL
PUBLIC SECTOR
PUBLIC SPIRIT
PUGNACIOUSLY
PULL A FAST
  ONE
PULVERULENCE
PUMPERNICKEL
PUNCHED CARDS
PUNITIVENESS
PURIFICATION
PURIFICATORY
PURISTICALLY
PURPLE HEARTS
PURPOSE-BUILT
PURPOSEFULLY
PURSE STRINGS
PUSSYFOOTING
PUSSY WILLOWS
PUT INTO WORDS
PUT ONES OAR
  IN
PUTREFACTION
PUTREFACTIVE
PYELOGRAPHIC
PYRIDOXAMINE

PYROCATECHOL
PYROCHEMICAL
PYROELECTRIC
PYROGNOSTICS
PYROLIGNEOUS
PYROMANIACAL
PYROMORPHITE
PYROPHYLLITE
PYROSULPHATE
PYROTECHNICS

Q

QUADRAGESIMA
QUADRANGULAR
QUADRAPHONIC
QUADRILLIONS
QUADRINOMIAL
QUADRIPLEGIA
QUADRIPLEGIC
QUADRIVALENT
QUADRUMANOUS
QUALIFYINGLY
QUANTIFIABLE
QUANTITATIVE
QUANTIZATION
QUANTUM LEAPS
QUAQUAVERSAL
QUARANTINING
QUARTER-BOUND
QUARTERFINAL
QUARTERLIGHT
QUARTER NOTES
QUARTER PLATE
QUARTERSTAFF
QUEEN CONSORT
QUEEN MOTHERS
QUELQUE CHOSE
QUESTIONABLE
QUESTIONABLY
QUESTION MARK
QUESTION TAGS
QUESTION TIME
QUEUE-JUMPERS
QUEUE-JUMPING
QUINDECAPLET
QUINQUENNIAL
QUINQUENNIUM
QUINTESSENCE
QUIXOTICALLY
QUIZZICALITY

R .
RABBIT WARREN
RABBLE-ROUSER
RACE MEETINGS
RACEMIZATION
RADICALISTIC
RADIO BEACONS
RADIOBIOLOGY
RADIOCHEMIST
RADIOELEMENT
RADIOGRAPHER
RADIOGRAPHIC
RADIOISOTOPE
RADIOLOGICAL
RADIOLOGISTS
RADIONUCLIDE
RADIOTHERAPY
RAISE THE ROOF
RAISON D'ETRES
RALLENTANDOS
RAMBUNCTIOUS
RAMENTACEOUS
RAMIFICATION
RANGE FINDERS
RANKINE SCALE
RAPHAELESQUE
RAPSCALLIONS
RASTAFARIANS
RATIFICATION
RATIOCINATOR
RATIONALISTS
RATIONALIZED
RATIONALIZER
RATTLESNAKES
RAVENOUSNESS
RAYLEIGH DISC
RAZZLE-DAZZLE
REACH-ME-DOWNS
REACTIVATING
REACTIVATION
REACTIVENESS
READDRESSING
READJUSTABLE
READJUSTMENT
REAFFIRMANCE
REAFFORESTED
REALIGNMENTS
REALIZATIONS
REALLOCATION
REAL PROPERTY
REAPPEARANCE

REAPPRAISALS
REAPPRAISING
REAR ADMIRALS
REASSURANCES
REASSURINGLY
REAUMUR SCALE
REBELLIOUSLY
RECALCITRANT
RECALESCENCE
RECANTATIONS
RECAPITALIZE
RECAPITULATE
RECEIVERSHIP
RECEPTIONIST
RECESSIONALS
RECIDIVISTIC
RECIPROCALLY
RECIPROCATED
RECIPROCATOR
RECKLESSNESS
RECOGNITIONS
RECOGNIZABLE
RECOGNIZABLY
RECOGNIZANCE
RECOLLECTING
RECOLLECTION
RECOLLECTIVE
RECOMMENDING
RECOMMISSION
RECOMMITMENT
RECOMPENSING
RECONCILABLE
RECONCILABLY
RECONNOITRED
RECONNOITRER
RECONSECRATE
RECONSIDERED
RECONSTITUTE
RECONVERSION
RECORD PLAYER
RECREATIONAL
RECRIMINATED
RECRIMINATOR
RECUPERATING
RECUPERATION
RECUPERATIVE
RED BLOOD CELL
REDECORATING
REDEMANDABLE
REDEMPTIONAL
REDEPLOYMENT

REDEVELOPING
REDINTEGRATE
REDISTRIBUTE
RED-LETTER DAY
REDUCIBILITY
REDUNDANCIES
REDUPLICATED
REEFER JACKET
RE-EMPLOYMENT
RE-EXAMINABLE
REFLATIONARY
REFLECTINGLY
REFLECTIONAL
REFLECTIVITY
REFORMATIONS
REFRACTIONAL
REFRACTORILY
REFRESHINGLY
REFRESHMENTS
REFRIGERANTS
REFRIGERATED
REFRIGERATOR
REFURBISHING
REFUTABILITY
REGENERATING
REGENERATION
REGENERATIVE
REGISTRATION
REGULARIZING
REGURGITATED
REHABILITATE
REIMBURSABLE
REIMPOSITION
REIMPRESSION
REINCARNATED
REINVESTMENT
REITERATIONS
REJECTIONIST
REJUVENATING
REJUVENATION
RELATIONSHIP
RELATIVISTIC
RELENTLESSLY
RELINQUISHED
RELINQUISHER
REMAINDERING
REMAINDERMAN
REMEMBRANCER
REMEMBRANCES
REMINISCENCE
REMONSTRANCE

357

REMONSTRATED
REMONSTRATOR
REMORSEFULLY
REMOVABILITY
REMUNERATING
REMUNERATION
REMUNERATIVE
RENAISSANCES
RENEGOTIABLE
RENEWABILITY
RENFREWSHIRE
RENOUNCEMENT
RENUNCIATION
RENUNCIATIVE
REORGANIZING
REPARABILITY
REPATRIATING
REPATRIATION
REPERCUSSION
REPERCUSSIVE
REPLACEMENTS
REPLENISHING
REPLICATIONS
REPOSITORIES
REPOSSESSING
REPOSSESSION
REPREHENDING
REPREHENSION
REPREHENSIVE
REPREHENSORY
REPRESENTING
REPRESSIVELY
REPRIMANDING
REPROACHABLE
REPROACHABLY
REPROCESSING
REPRODUCIBLE
REPRODUCTION
REPRODUCTIVE
REPROGRAPHIC
REPUTABILITY
REQUEST STOPS
REQUIREMENTS
REQUISITIONS
RESCHEDULING
RESEARCHABLY
RESEMBLANCES
RESERVATIONS
RESERVEDNESS
RESETTLEMENT
RESIDENTIARY

RESIDENTSHIP
RESIGNATIONS
RESIGNEDNESS
RESINIFEROUS
RESINOUSNESS
RESOLUBILITY
RESOLUTENESS
RESOLUTIONER
RESOLVEDNESS
RESOUNDINGLY
RESOURCELESS
RESPECTFULLY
RESPECTIVELY
RESPLENDENCE
RESPONSIVELY
RESPONSORIAL
RESTATEMENTS
RESTAURATEUR
RESTLESSNESS
RESTORATIONS
RESTORATIVES
RESTRAINABLE
RESTRAINEDLY
RESTRICTEDLY
RESTRICTIONS
RESTRUCTURED
RESUPINATION
RESURRECTING
RESURRECTION
RESUSCITABLE
RESUSCITATED
RESUSCITATOR
RETICULATION
RETINOSCOPIC
RETRACTILITY
RETRENCHABLE
RETRENCHMENT
RETROCESSION
RETROCESSIVE
RETROFLEXION
RETROGRESSED
RETRO-ROCKETS
RETROVERSION
REUNIONISTIC
REVALUATIONS
REVEGETATION
REVELATIONAL
REVERBERATED
REVERBERATOR
REVERENDSHIP
REVERENTNESS

REVERSIONARY
REVISABILITY
REVISIONISTS
REVITALIZING
REVIVABILITY
REVIVALISTIC
REVOCABILITY
REVOKABILITY
REVULSIONARY
RHAPSODISTIC
RHAPSODIZING
RHESUS FACTOR
RHETORICALLY
RHETORICIANS
RHINOCEROSES
RHINOCEROTIC
RHINOLOGICAL
RHINOPLASTIC
RHIZOCARPOUS
RHODODENDRON
RHOMBOHEDRAL
RHOMBOHEDRON
RHYMING SLANG
RHYTHMICALLY
RHYTHM METHOD
RIBONUCLEASE
RICHTER SCALE
RICOCHETTING
RIDICULOUSLY
RIGHTFULNESS
RIGHT-HANDERS
RIGHT-HAND MAN
RIGHT-HAND MEN
RIGHTS ISSUES
RIGHT-WINGERS
RIGOROUSNESS
RING-STREAKED
RIO DE JANEIRO
ROAD MANAGERS
ROBBEN ISLAND
ROCKING CHAIR
ROCKING HORSE
ROCKUMENTARY
ROLLER BLINDS
ROLLER SKATED
ROLLER SKATER
ROLLER-SKATER
ROLLER SKATES
ROLLER TOWELS
ROLLICKINGLY
ROLLING MILLS

ROLLING STOCK
ROLLING STONE
ROLL OF HONOUR
ROLLTOP DESKS
ROMAN CANDLES
ROMAN NUMERAL
ROMANTICALLY
ROMANTICISTS
ROMANTICIZED
ROOMING HOUSE
ROOTLESSNESS
ROSE-COLOURED
ROSTROPOVICH
ROTARY TILLER
ROUGH DIAMOND
ROUND BRACKET
ROUND THE BEND
ROUTE MARCHES
ROYAL FLUSHES
ROYAL SOCIETY
RUBBER BRIDGE
RUBBER DINGHY
RUBBERNECKED
RUBBER PLANTS
RUBBER STAMPS
RULES OF THUMB
RUMINATINGLY
RUMINATIVELY
RUMMAGE SALES
RUMOURMONGER
RUNNING JUMPS
RUNNING MATES
RUN OF THE
  MILL
RUN-OF-THE-
  MILL
RURALIZATION
RUSTPROOFING
RUTHLESSNESS

S

SABBATARIANS
SACCHARINITY
SACRILEGIOUS
SADISTICALLY
SAFE AS HOUSES
SAFEBREAKERS
SAFEGUARDING
SAFETY ISLAND
SAFETY RAZORS
SAFETY VALVES

SAILING BOATS
SAINT ANDREWS
SAINT AUSTELL
SAINT-ETIENNE
SAINT LAURENT
SAINT LEONARD
SAINT-NAZAIRE
SAINT-QUENTIN
SAINT VINCENT
SALAMANDRINE
SALESMANSHIP
SALES PITCHES
SALIFICATION
SALINOMETRIC
SALMON LADDER
SALMON TROUTS
SALPIGLOSSIS
SALT LAKE CITY
SALUTARINESS
SALUTATORILY
SALVATIONISM
SALVATIONIST
SAMARITANISM
SAMOA ISLANDS
SANCTIFIABLE
SANCTIONABLE
SANDBLASTING
SAND BLASTING
SANDPAPERING
SAN FRANCISCO
SANGUINARILY
SANGUINENESS
SANGUINOLENT
SANITARINESS
SAN PEDRO SULA
SAN SEBASTIAN
SANTALACEOUS
SANTO DOMINGO
SAONE-ET-LOIRE
SAPINDACEOUS
SAPONIFIABLE
SAPROPHAGOUS
SARCOMATOSIS
SARDONICALLY
SARSAPARILLA
SASKATCHEWAN
SATIRIZATION
SATISFACTION
SATISFACTORY
SATISFYINGLY
SATURABILITY

SAUDI ARABIAN
SAUSAGE ROLLS
SAVING GRACES
SAVINGS BANKS
SAXONY-ANHALT
SAXOPHONISTS
SCALABLENESS
SCANDALIZING
SCANDALOUSLY
SCANDINAVIAN
SCAREMONGERS
SCARIFICATOR
SCARLET FEVER
SCARLET WOMAN
SCARLET WOMEN
SCATOLOGICAL
SCATTERBRAIN
SCENESHIFTER
SCENOGRAPHER
SCENOGRAPHIC
SCHAFFHAUSEN
SCHEMATIZING
SCHIZOMYCETE
SCHIZOPHYTIC
SCHIZOTHYMIA
SCHIZOTHYMIC
SCHOLARSHIPS
SCHOLASTICAL
SCHOOLFELLOW
SCHOOLHOUSES
SCHOOL-LEAVER
SCHOOLMASTER
SCHORLACEOUS
SCIENCE PARKS
SCINTILLATED
SCINTILLATOR
SCLERENCHYMA
SCLEROMETRIC
SCOLOPENDRID
SCORNFULNESS
SCOTCH TAPING
SCOTCH WHISKY
SCOTLAND YARD
SCOUTMASTERS
SCRATCHINESS
SCRATCH PAPER
SCREWDRIVERS
SCRIMSHANDER
SCRIPTWRITER
SCROBICULATE
SCRUPULOUSLY

SCRUTINIZING
SCURRILOUSLY
SCUTELLATION
SEAMSTRESSES
SEARCH ENGINE
SEARCHLIGHTS
SEASONALNESS
SEASON TICKET
SEATON VALLEY
SECESSIONISM
SECESSIONIST
SECLUDEDNESS
SECOND COMING
SECOND COUSIN
SECOND-DEGREE
SECOND NATURE
SECOND PERSON
SECOND-STRING
SECRET AGENTS
SECRETARIATS
SECRETIONARY
SECRET POLICE
SECTARIANISM
SECTIONALISM
SECTIONALIST
SECTIONALIZE
SECULARISTIC
SECULARIZING
SECURITY RISK
SEDULOUSNESS
SEGMENTATION
SEINE-ET-MARNE
SEISMOGRAPHS
SEISMOGRAPHY
SEISMOLOGIST
SEISMOSCOPIC
SELENOGRAPHY
SELENOLOGIST
SELF-ABSORBED
SELF-ANALYSIS
SELF-ASSEMBLY
SELF-CATERING
SELF-COLOURED
SELF-DESTRUCT
SELF-EDUCATED
SELF-EFFACING
SELF-EMPLOYED
SELF-INTEREST
SELFLESSNESS
SELF PORTRAIT
SELF-PORTRAIT

SELF-RELIANCE
SELF-REPROACH
SELF-STARTERS
SELKIRKSHIRE
SELLING PLATE
SELLING POINT
SEMANTICALLY
SEMICIRCULAR
SEMIDETACHED
SEMIDIAMETER
SEMIFINALIST
SEMIFLUIDITY
SEMINIFEROUS
SEMIOTICIANS
SEMIPALMATED
SEMIPRECIOUS
SEMITROPICAL
SEMIVITREOUS
SEMPITERNITY
SENARMONTITE
SENSIBLENESS
SENSITOMETER
SENSITOMETRY
SENSORIMOTOR
SENSUOUSNESS
SEPARABILITY
SEPARATENESS
SEPARATISTIC
SEPTILATERAL
SEPTILLIONTH
SEPTUAGESIMA
SEPTUPLICATE
SEQUENTIALLY
SEQUESTRABLE
SEQUESTRATED
SEQUESTRATOR
SERIAL NUMBER
SERICULTURAL
SERINGAPATAM
SERONEGATIVE
SEROPOSITIVE
SERVICEBERRY
SERVICE FLATS
SERVICE ROADS
SESQUIALTERA
SET BY THE
  EARS
SEVENTEENTHS
SEVENTY-EIGHT
SEVERANCE PAY
SEXAGENARIAN

359

SEXCENTENARY	SHREWISHNESS	SKITTISHNESS	SODA FOUNTAIN
SEXTILLIONTH	SHUDDERINGLY	SKYROCKETING	SOFT LANDINGS
SEXTUPLICATE	SHUFFLEBOARD	SLANDEROUSLY	SOFT-PEDALING
SHADOW-BOXING	SHUTTLECOCKS	SLAUGHTERING	SOFT-PEDALLED
SHAHJAHANPUR	SIAMESE TWINS	SLAUGHTEROUS	SOLARIZATION
SHAMATEURISM	SICK HEADACHE	SLAVE DRIVERS	SOLAR SYSTEMS
SHAMEFACEDLY	SIDEROSTATIC	SLAVONICALLY	SOLICITATION
SHAMEFULNESS	SIDESLIPPING	SLEDGEHAMMER	SOLICITOUSLY
SHARECROPPER	SIDESTEPPING	SLEEPING BAGS	SOLIDIFIABLE
SHAREHOLDERS	SIDETRACKING	SLEEPING CARS	SOLIFLUCTION
SHARPSHOOTER	SIDE-WHEELERS	SLEEPING PILL	SOLILOQUIZED
SHARP-SIGHTED	SIDE WHISKERS	SLEEPWALKERS	SOLITARINESS
SHARP-TONGUED	SIDI-BEL-ABBES	SLEEPWALKING	SOLITUDINOUS
SHATTERINGLY	SIERRA NEVADA	SLENDERIZING	SOLVENT ABUSE
SHATTERPROOF	SIGHT-READERS	SLIDING DOORS	SOMATOLOGIST
SHAVING CREAM	SIGHT-READING	SLIDING SCALE	SOMATOPLEURE
SHEATH KNIVES	SIGNIFICANCE	SLIPPERINESS	SOMERSAULTED
SHEEPISHNESS	SIGN LANGUAGE	SLIPPINGNESS	SOMNAMBULANT
SHEEPSHEARER	SILHOUETTING	SLIPSTREAMED	SOMNAMBULATE
SHEET ANCHORS	SILICIFEROUS	SLOANE RANGER	SOMNAMBULISM
SHELLACKINGS	SILICON CHIPS	SLOTHFULNESS	SOMNAMBULIST
SHELLSHOCKED	SILIQUACEOUS	SLOT MACHINES	SON ET LUMIERE
SHEPHERD'S PIE	SILVERFISHES	SLOVENLINESS	SONG AND DANCE
SHETLAND PONY	SILVER LINING	SLUGGARDNESS	SONOROUSNESS
SHIFTINGNESS	SILVER MEDALS	SLUGGISHNESS	SOOTHINGNESS
SHIJIAZHUANG	SILVERSMITHS	SLUMBERINGLY	SOPHISTICATE
SHILLY-SHALLY	SILVICULTURE	SLUTTISHNESS	SOPORIFEROUS
SHIMMERINGLY	SIMILARITIES	SMALL FORTUNE	SOUL BROTHERS
SHIPBUILDERS	SIMPLE-MINDED	SMALLHOLDERS	SOULLESSNESS
SHIPBUILDING	SIMULTANEITY	SMALLHOLDING	SOUND BARRIER
SHIPWRECKING	SIMULTANEOUS	SMASH-AND-GRAB	SOUND EFFECTS
SHIRTSLEEVES	SINANTHROPUS	SMILACACEOUS	SOUNDPROOFED
SHIRTWAISTER	SINGLE-ACTING	SMOKESCREENS	SOUP KITCHENS
SHOCKABILITY	SINGLE-ACTION	SMOOTH-SPOKEN	SOUSAPHONIST
SHOCKINGNESS	SINGLE-DECKER	SMORGASBORDS	SOUTH AMERICA
SHOCKING PINK	SINGLE-HANDED	SNAGGLETOOTH	SOUTHEASTERN
SHOOTING STAR	SINGLE-MINDED	SNAKE CHARMER	SOUTHERNMOST
SHOP STEWARDS	SINGULARNESS	SNAP FASTENER	SOUTHERNWOOD
SHORT-CHANGED	SINISTERNESS	SNAPPISHNESS	SOUTH HOLLAND
SHORT-CHANGER	SINISTRORSAL	SNEAKINGNESS	SOUTH OSSETIA
SHORT CIRCUIT	SINKING FUNDS	SNEAK PREVIEW	SOUTH SHIELDS
SHORTCOMINGS	SIPHONOPHORE	SNEAK THIEVES	SOUTHWESTERN
SHORT-LISTING	SIPHONOSTELE	SNICKERINGLY	SPACE CAPSULE
SHORTSIGHTED	SISTERLINESS	SNIGGERINGLY	SPACE HEATERS
SHORT STORIES	SISTERS-IN-LAW	SNOBBISHNESS	SPACE SHUTTLE
SHORT-WAISTED	SITTING DUCKS	SNOOPERSCOPE	SPACE STATION
SHOT IN THE	SITTING ROOMS	SOCIALIZABLE	SPACIOUSNESS
ARM	SITUATIONISM	SOCIAL WORKER	SPEAKING TUBE
SHOW BUSINESS	SKELETON KEYS	SOCIOLOGICAL	SPEARHEADING
SHOWSTOPPERS	SKELMERSDALE	SOCIOLOGISTS	SPECIALISTIC
SHOWSTOPPING	SKIPPING-ROPE	SOCIOMETRIST	SPECIALITIES

SPECIALIZING	SPORTFULNESS	STATION HOUSE	STOCKBREEDER
SPECIFICALLY	SPORTIVENESS	STATION WAGON	STOCKBROKERS
SPECIOUSNESS	SPORTSPERSON	STATISTICIAN	STOCKHOLDERS
SPECTACULARS	SPOT-CHECKING	STAYING POWER	STOCK-IN-TRADE
SPECTROGRAPH	SPOTLESSNESS	STEAK TARTARE	STOCKJOBBERS
SPECTROMETER	SPOTLIGHTING	STEAL THE SHOW	STOCKJOBBERY
SPECTROMETRY	SPOTTED DICKS	STEALTHINESS	STOCK MARKETS
SPECTROSCOPE	SPREAD-EAGLED	STEAMROLLERS	STOICHIOLOGY
SPECTROSCOPY	SPREADSHEETS	STEAM SHOVELS	STOKE-ON-TRENT
SPECULATIONS	SPRINGBOARDS	STEATOPYGOUS	STOMACHACHES
SPEECHIFYING	SPRING ONIONS	STEATORRHOEA	STOMACH PUMPS
SPEECHLESSLY	SPURIOUSNESS	STEEPLECHASE	STONECUTTING
SPEEDOMETERS	SQUAMOUSNESS	STEEPLEJACKS	STONEMASONRY
SPEEDWRITING	SQUARE DANCES	STELLIFEROUS	STONEWALLERS
SPELEOLOGIST	SQUARE-RIGGED	STENOGRAPHER	STONEWALLING
SPELLBINDERS	SQUARE-RIGGER	STENOGRAPHIC	STONY-HEARTED
SPELLBINDING	SQUEAKY-CLEAN	STENOTHERMAL	STOOLPIGEONS
SPELLCHECKER	SQUEEZEBOXES	STEPBROTHERS	STOREKEEPERS
SPENDTHRIFTS	SQUELCHINGLY	STEPCHILDREN	STOREKEEPING
SPERMATHECAL	SQUIRRELFISH	STEPDAUGHTER	STORM TROOPER
SPERMATOCYTE	STADDLESTONE	STEREOCHROME	STORMY PETREL
SPERMATOZOAL	STAFF OFFICER	STEREOCHROMY	STORYTELLERS
SPERMATOZOID	STAGECOACHES	STEREOGRAPHY	STORYTELLING
SPERMATOZOON	STAGE-MANAGED	STEREOISOMER	STOUTHEARTED
SPERMOGONIUM	STAGE MANAGER	STEREOMETRIC	STOVEPIPE HAT
SPHRAGISTICS	STAGE WHISPER	STEREOPHONIC	STRADIVARIUS
SPHYGMOGRAPH	STAGGERINGLY	STEREOPTICON	STRAGGLINGLY
SPICK AND SPAN	STAGING POSTS	STEREOSCOPIC	STRAIGHTAWAY
SPICK-AND-SPAN	STAINABILITY	STEREOTACTIC	STRAIGHTEDGE
SPIEGELEISEN	STAINED GLASS	STEREOTROPIC	STRAIGHTENED
SPINSTERHOOD	STAKEHOLDERS	STEREOTYPING	STRAIGHTENER
SPIRITEDNESS	STALACTIFORM	STEREOVISION	STRAIGHTNESS
SPIRIT LEVELS	STALLHOLDERS	STERILIZABLE	STRAINEDNESS
SPIRITUALISM	STALWARTNESS	STERNUTATION	STRAITJACKET
SPIRITUALIST	STAMMERINGLY	STERNUTATIVE	STRANGLEHOLD
SPIRITUALITY	STANDARDIZED	STERNUTATORY	STRANGULATED
SPIRITUALIZE	STANDARDIZER	STERNWHEELER	STRAPHANGERS
SPIRITUOSITY	STANDARD LAMP	STERTOROUSLY	STRAPHANGING
SPIROGRAPHIC	STANDARD TIME	STETHOSCOPES	STRATICULATE
SPITEFULNESS	STANDING ROOM	STETHOSCOPIC	STRATIGRAPHY
SPLASH GUARDS	STANDOFF HALF	STICHOMETRIC	STRATOCRATIC
SPLATTERPUNK	STAND-OFF HALF	STICK INSECTS	STRATOSPHERE
SPLENDIDNESS	STANLEY KNIFE	STICKLEBACKS	STRAWBERRIES
SPLENOMEGALY	STANNIFEROUS	STICKY WICKET	STREAMLINING
SPLIT SECONDS	STAR CHAMBERS	STIGMASTEROL	STREETS AHEAD
SPOKESPEOPLE	STAR-SPANGLED	STIGMATIZING	STREET VALUES
SPOKESPERSON	STARTING GATE	STILBOESTROL	STREETWALKER
SPONGIOBLAST	STATELY HOMES	STILETTO HEEL	STRENGTHENED
SPOON-FEEDING	STATEN ISLAND	STINKINGNESS	STRENGTHENER
SPORADICALLY	STATIONARILY	STIPULATIONS	STREPTOCOCCI
SPOROGENESIS	STATION BREAK	STIRRUP PUMPS	STREPTOMYCIN

STRETCHINESS
STRETCHMARKS
STRIDULATING
STRIDULATION
STRIDULATORY
STRIKINGNESS
STRIP CARTOON
STRIP MININGS
STROBE LIGHTS
STROBILATION
STROBOSCOPES
STROBOSCOPIC
STROMATOLITE
STRONG-MINDED
STRONG POINTS
STRONG-WILLED
STRONTIANITE
STROPHANTHIN
STROPHANTHUS
STRUCTURALLY
STRUGGLINGLY
STRYCHNINISM
STUBBORNNESS
STUDDINGSAIL
STUDIOUSNESS
STUFFED SHIRT
STUPEFACIENT
STUPEFACTION
STUPEFYINGLY
STUPENDOUSLY
STUTTERINGLY
STYLOGRAPHIC
STYRACACEOUS
SUBALTERNATE
SUBANTARCTIC
SUBAURICULAR
SUBCELESTIAL
SUBCLIMACTIC
SUBCOMMITTEE
SUBCONSCIOUS
SUBCONTINENT
SUBCUTANEOUS
SUBDEACONATE
SUBDIACONATE
SUBDIVISIONS
SUBERIZATION
SUBINFEUDATE
SUBJECTIVELY
SUBJECTIVISM
SUBJECTIVIST
SUBJECTIVITY

SUBJUNCTIVES
SUBMAXILLARY
SUBMERSIBLES
SUBMISSIVELY
SUBMITTINGLY
SUBNORMALITY
SUBORDINATED
SUBORDINATES
SUBPRINCIPAL
SUBSCRIPTION
SUBSCRIPTIVE
SUBSEQUENTLY
SUBSERVIENCE
SUBSIDIARIES
SUBSIDIARILY
SUBSIDIARITY
SUBSIDIZABLE
SUBSISTINGLY
SUBSTANTIATE
SUBSTANTIVAL
SUBSTANTIVES
SUBSTITUTING
SUBSTITUTION
SUBSTITUTIVE
SUBSTRUCTURE
SUBTEMPERATE
SUBTERRANEAN
SUBTRACTIONS
SUBURBANITES
SUBVERSIVELY
SUCCEDANEOUS
SUCCEEDINGLY
SUCCESSFULLY
SUCCESSIONAL
SUCCESSIVELY
SUCCINCTNESS
SUCTION PUMPS
SUDORIFEROUS
SUFFRAGETTES
SUFFRUTICOSE
SUGAR DADDIES
SUGGESTINGLY
SUGGESTIVELY
SUITABLENESS
SULPHONAMIDE
SULPHURATION
SUMMARIZABLE
SUMMERHOUSES
SUMMER SCHOOL
SUNDAY SCHOOL
SUPERABILITY

SUPERANNUATE
SUPERCHARGED
SUPERCHARGER
SUPERCILIARY
SUPERCILIOUS
SUPEREMINENT
SUPERFICIARY
SUPERGLACIAL
SUPERGRASSES
SUPERIMPOSED
SUPERLATIVES
SUPERMARKETS
SUPERNATURAL
SUPERPOSABLE
SUPERSEDABLE
SUPERSESSION
SUPERSTITION
SUPERSTRATUM
SUPERTANKERS
SUPERVENIENT
SUPPLEMENTAL
SUPPLEMENTED
SUPPLEMENTER
SUPPLETORILY
SUPPLICATING
SUPPLICATION
SUPPLICATORY
SUPPOSITIONS
SUPPOSITIOUS
SUPPRESSIBLE
SUPRAGLOTTAL
SUPRALIMINAL
SUPRAORBITAL
SUPRAPROTEST
SUPREMACISTS
SUPREME BEING
SUPREME COURT
SUREFOOTEDLY
SURFACE-TO-AIR
SURMOUNTABLE
SURPASSINGLY
SURPRISINGLY
SURREALISTIC
SURREJOINDER
SURRENDERING
SURROUNDEDLY
SURROUNDINGS
SURVEILLANCE
SURVEYORSHIP
SURVIVAL KITS
SUSCEPTIVITY

SUSPICIOUSLY
SUSTAININGLY
SWAGGERINGLY
SWALLOW DIVES
SWASHBUCKLER
SWEEPINGNESS
SWEET-AND-SOUR
SWEET PEPPERS
SWEET POTATOS
SWEET-TALKING
SWELTERINGLY
SWIMMING BATH
SWIMMING POOL
SWING THE LEAD
SWITCHBLADES
SWITCHBOARDS
SWIZZLE STICK
SWORD DANCERS
SYLLABICALLY
SYMBOLICALLY
SYMBOLOGICAL
SYMMETALLISM
SYMPATHIZERS
SYMPATHIZING
SYNAESTHESIA
SYNAESTHETIC
SYNAPTICALLY
SYNARTHROSIS
SYNCHROFLASH
SYNCHRONIZED
SYNCHRONIZER
SYNCHROSCOPE
SYNCLINORIUM
SYNDACTYLISM
SYNDETICALLY
SYNDICALISTS
SYNDIOTACTIC
SYNODIC MONTH
SYNONYMOUSLY
SYNOPTICALLY
SYNTHESIZERS
SYNTHESIZING
SYNTONICALLY
SYSTEMATIZED
SYSTEMATIZER
SYSTEMICALLY

T

TABERNACULAR
TABLE MANNERS
TABLE-TURNING

TACHEOMETRIC	TERATOLOGIST	THERMOSTABLE	TONSILLOTOMY
TACHYCARDIAC	TERCENTENARY	THERMOSTATIC	TOOTHBRUSHES
TACTLESSNESS	TEREBINTHINE	THERMOTROPIC	TOPDRESSINGS
TADZHIKISTAN	TERGIVERSATE	THEURGICALLY	TOP-HEAVINESS
TALCUM POWDER	TERMINATIONS	THICK-SKINNED	TOPOGRAPHERS
TALENT SCOUTS	TERRIBLENESS	THIEVISHNESS	TORMENTINGLY
TALKING POINT	TERRIFICALLY	THIGMOTACTIC	TORREFACTION
TAMBOURINIST	TERRIFYINGLY	THIGMOTROPIC	TORTUOUSNESS
TANGENTIALLY	TERRITORIALS	THINGAMAJIGS	TOTALITARIAN
TAPE MEASURES	TESSELLATION	THIOSINAMINE	TOTALIZATORS
TAPE RECORDER	TESTAMENTARY	THIOSULPHATE	TOURIST CLASS
TAPE STREAMER	TESTIMONIALS	THIRD PARTIES	TOUT ENSEMBLE
TARAMASALATA	TESTOSTERONE	THOROUGHBRED	TOWER HAMLETS
TARDENOISIAN	TEST-TUBE BABY	THOROUGHFARE	TOWER OF BABEL
TARTARIC ACID	TETANIZATION	THOROUGHNESS	TOWN PLANNERS
TASTEFULNESS	TETRACHORDAL	THOUGHTFULLY	TOWN PLANNING
TAUROMACHIAN	TETRACYCLINE	THREE QUARTER	TOXICOLOGIST
TAUTOLOGICAL	TETRAHEDRITE	THREE-QUARTER	TOXOPHILITIC
TAX COLLECTOR	TETRAPTEROUS	THREE-WHEELER	TRACEABILITY
TAXIDERMISTS	TETRASTICHIC	THROMBOCYTIC	TRACE ELEMENT
TECHNICALITY	TETRAVALENCY	THUNDERBOLTS	TRACHEOPHYTE
TECHNOBABBLE	TEUTONICALLY	THUNDERCLAPS	TRACHEOSTOMY
TECHNOGRAPHY	THALAMICALLY	THUNDERCLOUD	TRACHOMATOUS
TECHNOLOGIES	THALASSAEMIA	THUNDERFLASH	TRACING PAPER
TECHNOLOGIST	THALLOPHYTIC	THUNDERINGLY	TRACK RECORDS
TECTONICALLY	THANKFULNESS	THUNDEROUSLY	TRACTABILITY
TEENYBOPPERS	THANKSGIVING	THUNDERSTONE	TRACUCIANIST
TEETER-TOTTER	THAUMATOLOGY	THUNDERSTORM	TRADESCANTIA
TEETOTALLERS	THEANTHROPIC	THUNDER STORM	TRADESPEOPLE
TELAESTHESIA	THEATREGOERS	TICKLISHNESS	TRADING POSTS
TELAESTHETIC	THEATRICALLY	TIED COTTAGES	TRADING STAMP
TELAUTOGRAPH	THE HERMITAGE	TIME CAPSULES	TRADITIONIST
TELEGRAPHERS	THEISTICALLY	TIME EXPOSURE	TRADUCIANISM
TELEGRAPHESE	THEMATICALLY	TIME HONOURED	TRAFFICATORS
TELEGRAPHING	THEOCENTRISM	TIME-HONOURED	TRAFFIC LIGHT
TELEMEDICINE	THEOPHYLLINE	TIMELESSNESS	TRAGEDIENNES
TELEOLOGICAL	THEORETICIAN	TIME SWITCHES	TRAILBLAZING
TELEOLOGISTS	THEORIZATION	TIMOROUSNESS	TRAILER HOUSE
TELEPHONE BOX	THERAPEUTICS	TIRELESSNESS	TRAINBEARERS
TELEPHONISTS	THE REAL THING	TIRESOMENESS	TRAIN SPOTTER
TELEPRINTERS	THEREINAFTER	TITANIFEROUS	TRAINSPOTTER
TELEPROMPTER	THERMOCOUPLE	TITLEHOLDERS	TRAITOROUSLY
TELESHOPPING	THERMOGENOUS	TITTLE-TATTLE	TRAJECTORIES
TELEUTOSPORE	THERMOGRAPHY	TOASTING FORK	TRAMPISHNESS
TELEVISIONAL	THERMOLABILE	TOASTMASTERS	TRANQUILLITY
TELGENICALLY	THERMOMETERS	TOBACCONISTS	TRANQUILLIZE
TELLUROMETER	THERMOMETRIC	TOFFEE APPLES	TRANSACTIONS
TEMPERAMENTS	THERMOSCOPIC	TOGETHERNESS	TRANSCENDENT
TEMPERATURES	THERMOS FLASK	TOMFOOLERIES	TRANSCENDING
TENANT FARMER	THERMOSIPHON	TONE LANGUAGE	TRANSCRIBING
TEN-GALLON HAT	THERMOSPHERE	TONELESSNESS	TRANSCURRENT

TRANSDUCTION
TRANSFERABLE
TRANSFERENCE
TRANSFERRING
TRANSFIGURED
TRANSFORMERS
TRANSFORMING
TRANSFORMISM
TRANSFORMIST
TRANSFUSIBLE
TRANSFUSIONS
TRANSGRESSED
TRANSGRESSOR
TRANSHUMANCE
TRANSITIONAL
TRANSITORILY
TRANSLATABLE
TRANSLATIONS
TRANSLUCENCE
TRANSLUCENCY
TRANSMIGRANT
TRANSMIGRATE
TRANSMISSION
TRANSMISSIVE
TRANSMITTERS
TRANSMITTING
TRANSMOGRIFY
TRANSMUNDANE
TRANSMUTABLE
TRANSOCEANIC
TRANSPARENCY
TRANSPIRABLE
TRANSPLANTED
TRANSPLANTER
TRANSPONDERS
TRANSPORTERS
TRANSPORTING
TRANSPORTIVE
TRANSPOSABLE
TRANSUDATORY
TRANSVAALIAN
TRANSVERSELY
TRANSVESTISM
TRANSVESTITE
TRANSYLVANIA
TRAPSHOOTING
TRAUMATIZING
TRAVEL AGENCY
TRAVEL AGENTS
TREBLE CHANCE
TREELESSNESS

TREMENDOUSLY
TRENDSETTERS
TRENDSETTING
TREPHINATION
TRIBESPEOPLE
TRIBULATIONS
TRICHINIASIS
TRICHOCYSTIC
TRICHOGYNIAL
TRICHOLOGIST
TRICHOPTERAN
TRICHROMATIC
TRICK OR TREAT
TRIFURCATION
TRIGGER HAPPY
TRIGGER-HAPPY
TRIGLYCERIDE
TRIGONOMETRY
TRILINGUALLY
TRIMOLECULAR
TRIPARTITION
TRIPHTHONGAL
TRIPLE-TONGUE
TRIPLICATION
TRIPOLITANIA
TRIUMPHANTLY
TRIUMVIRATES
TRIVIALITIES
TRIVIALIZING
TROCHAICALLY
TROCHOIDALLY
TROJAN HORSES
TROLLEYBUSES
TROMBIDIASIS
TROOP CARRIER
TROPHALLAXIS
TROPOPHILOUS
TROUBLEMAKER
TROUBLE SPOTS
TROUSER PRESS
TRUSTABILITY
TRUSTEESHIPS
TRUSTFULNESS
TRUTHFULNESS
TRYPANOSOMAL
TRYPARSAMIDE
TUBERCULOSIS
TUMBLE-DRYERS
TUMBLE-DRYING
TUMULTUOUSLY
TUNELESSNESS

TUNNEL VISION
TURBELLARIAN
TURBIDIMETER
TURBOCHARGED
TURBOCHARGER
TURKISH BATHS
TURKMENISTAN
TURNING POINT
TUVA REPUBLIC
TU-WHIT TU-
  WHOO
TWILIGHT ZONE
TWISTABILITY
TWO-FACEDNESS
TWO-WAY MIRROR
TYPIFICATION
TYPOGRAPHERS
TYRANNICALLY
TYRANNICIDAL

U

UBIQUITOUSLY
UGLIFICATION
UGLY CUSTOMER
UGLY DUCKLING
ULTRAMONTANE
ULTRAMUNDANE
UMBILICATION
UNACCEPTABLE
UNACCUSTOMED
UNACQUAINTED
UNAFFECTEDLY
UNAFFORDABLE
UNAGGRESSIVE
UNANSWERABLE
UNAPOLOGETIC
UNAPPEALABLE
UNASSAILABLE
UNASSOCIATED
UNASSUMINGLY
UNATTAINABLE
UNATTRACTIVE
UNATTRIBUTED
UNBELIEVABLE
UNBELIEVABLY
UNBIASEDNESS
UNCELEBRATED
UNCHALLENGED
UNCHARITABLE
UNCHARITABLY
UNCHASTENESS

UNCINARIASIS
UNCLASSIFIED
UNCOMMERCIAL
UNCOMMONNESS
UNCONFORMITY
UNCONSENTING
UNCONSIDERED
UNCONVINCING
UNCOVENANTED
UNCRITICALLY
UNCTUOUSNESS
UNDECEIVABLE
UNDEMOCRATIC
UNDERACHIEVE
UNDERBELLIES
UNDERCHARGED
UNDERCLOTHES
UNDERCURRENT
UNDERCUTTING
UNDERDEVELOP
UNDERDRAWING
UNDERDRESSED
UNDEREXPOSED
UNDERGARMENT
UNDERGROUNDS
UNDERNOURISH
UNDERPAYMENT
UNDERPINNING
UNDERPLAYING
UNDERSCORING
UNDERSELLING
UNDERSHERIFF
UNDERSTAFFED
UNDERSTATING
UNDERSTUDIED
UNDERSTUDIES
UNDERSURFACE
UNDERTAKINGS
UNDERTRAINED
UNDERUTILIZE
UNDERVALUING
UNDERWRITERS
UNDERWRITING
UNDERWRITTEN
UNDESIRABLES
UNDETERMINED
UNDISCHARGED
UNECONOMICAL
UNEMPLOYABLE
UNEMPLOYMENT
UNEVENTFULLY

UNEXPRESSIVE
UNEXPURGATED
UNFAITHFULLY
UNFATHOMABLE
UNFATHOMABLY
UNFAVOURABLE
UNFAVOURABLY
UNFLAGGINGLY
UNFLATTERING
UNFORGIVABLE
UNFORTUNATES
UNFREQUENTED
UNGAINLINESS
UNGOVERNABLE
UNGRATEFULLY
UNHESITATING
UNHYPHENATED
UNIDENTIFIED
UNIFOLIOLATE
UNILATERALLY
UNIMAGINABLE
UNIMPRESSIVE
UNINFLUENCED
UNINTERESTED
UNIONIZATION
UNISEXUALITY
UNITARIANISM
UNIVERSALISM
UNIVERSALIST
UNIVERSALITY
UNIVERSALIZE
UNIVERSITIES
UNKINDLINESS
UNLAWFULNESS
UNLIKELIHOOD
UNLIKELINESS
UNMANAGEABLE
UNMEASURABLE
UNMISTAKABLE
UNMISTAKABLY
UNMODERNIZED
UNOFFICIALLY
UNPARALLELED
UNPERFORATED
UNPLEASANTLY
UNPOPULARITY
UNPREJUDICED
UNPRINCIPLED
UNPRODUCTIVE
UNPROFITABLE
UNPUBLICIZED

UNQUESTIONED
UNREASONABLE
UNREASONABLY
UNRECKONABLE
UNRECOGNIZED
UNREFLECTIVE
UNREGENERACY
UNREGENERATE
UNRESERVEDLY
UNRESPONSIVE
UNRESTRAINED
UNRESTRICTED
UNSANCTIONED
UNSATURATION
UNSCIENTIFIC
UNSCRAMBLING
UNSCRUPULOUS
UNSEARCHABLE
UNSEASONABLE
UNSEASONABLY
UNSEEMLINESS
UNSEGREGATED
UNSETTLEMENT
UNSTEADINESS
UNSTRATIFIED
UNSTRUCTURED
UNSUCCESSFUL
UNSUPPORTIVE
UNSUSPECTING
UNTENABILITY
UNTHINKINGLY
UNTIMELINESS
UNTOUCHABLES
UNTOWARDNESS
UNTRAMMELLED
UNWIELDINESS
UNWORTHINESS
UNWRITTEN LAW
UPHOLSTERERS
UPHOLSTERING
UPPER AUSTRIA
UPRIGHT PIANO
UPROARIOUSLY
UP-TO-DATENESS
URANOGRAPHER
URANOGRAPHIC
URBANIZATION
URETHROSCOPE
URETHROSCOPY
URINOGENITAL
USER FRIENDLY

USER-FRIENDLY
USUFRUCTUARY
USURIOUSNESS
UTILITY ROOMS
UTTAR PRADESH
UXORIOUSNESS

V

VACCINATIONS
VACILLATIONS
VACUUM FLASKS
VACUUM-PACKED
VAINGLORIOUS
VALEDICTIONS
VALENCIENNES
VALORIZATION
VALUABLENESS
VANQUISHABLE
VANQUISHMENT
VANTAGEPOINT
VANTAGE POINT
VAPORESCENCE
VAPORIZATION
VAPOROUSNESS
VAPOUR TRAILS
VARICOLOURED
VASODILATION
VAUDEVILLIAN
VAUDEVILLIST
VEGETATIONAL
VELARIZATION
VELOCIRAPTOR
VENERABILITY
VENERATIONAL
VENGEFULNESS
VENIPUNCTURE
VENTRICOSITY
VERBENACEOUS
VERIDICALITY
VERIFICATION
VERIFICATIVE
VERTEBRATION
VERTICILLATE
VESICULATION
VESTAL VIRGIN
VIBRAPHONIST
VICE-CHAIRMAN
VICISSITUDES
VICTORIANISM
VICTORIA PLUM
VICTORIOUSLY

VIDEO NASTIES
VIGOROUSNESS
VILIFICATION
VILLAGE GREEN
VILLAHERMOSA
VILLEURBANNE
VINDICTIVELY
VINICULTURAL
VIN ORDINAIRE
VIOLONCELLOS
VIRGIN'S-BOWER
VIRIDESCENCE
VIRTUOUSNESS
VISCEROMOTOR
VISCOUNTCIES
VISITATIONAL
VISITATORIAL
VISITING CARD
VISITORS' BOOK
VITALIZATION
VITICULTURAL
VITICULTURER
VITREOUSNESS
VITUPERATION
VITUPERATIVE
VIVIFICATION
VIVISECTIONS
VIXENISHNESS
VOCABULARIES
VOCALIZATION
VOCIFERATING
VOCIFERATION
VOCIFEROUSLY
VOIDABLENESS
VOLCANICALLY
VOLTA REDONDA
VOLUMINOSITY
VOLUMINOUSLY
VOLUNTARYISM
VOLUNTARYIST
VOLUNTEERING
VOLUNTEERISM
VOLUPTUARIES
VOLUPTUOUSLY
VOMITURITION
VOTE OF THANKS
VOWELIZATION
VULCANIZABLE

W

WAGES COUNCIL

WAITING LISTS
WAITING ROOMS
WALKIE-TALKIE
WALKING STICK
WALLCOVERING
WALL PAINTING
WALLPAPERING
WANKEL ENGINE
WAREHOUSEMAN
WARMONGERING
WARS OF NERVES
WARWICKSHIRE
WASH DRAWINGS
WASTEFULNESS
WASTE PRODUCT
WATCHFULNESS
WATER BISCUIT
WATER BUFFALO
WATER CANNONS
WATER CLOSETS
WATERCOLOURS
WATERCOURSES
WATERING CANS
WATERING HOLE
WATERMANSHIP
WATER MEADOWS
WATERPROOFED
WATTENSCHEID
WAYS AND MEANS
WEATHERBOARD
WEATHER-BOUND
WEATHERCOCKS
WEATHERGLASS
WEATHERPROOF
WEATHER SHIPS
WEATHER VANES
WEDDING RINGS
WEIGHBRIDGES
WEIGHTLESSLY
WEIGHT LIFTER
WELFARE STATE
WELL-ADJUSTED

WELL-ASSORTED
WELL-ATTENDED
WELL BALANCED
WELL-BALANCED
WELL-DESERVED
WELL DISPOSED
WELL-DISPOSED
WELL-EDUCATED
WELL-EQUIPPED
WELL-FAVOURED
WELL-GROUNDED
WELL-INFORMED
WELL-MANNERED
WELL-PROVIDED
WELL-RECEIVED
WELL-SITUATED
WELL-TEMPERED
WELSH RAREBIT
WELTERWEIGHT
WENSLEYDALES
WEST BROMWICH
WESTERLINESS
WESTERN ISLES
WESTERNIZING
WESTERN SAMOA
WEST FLANDERS
WEST MIDLANDS
WEST VIRGINIA
WETTING AGENT
WHEELBARROWS
WHEELWRIGHTS
WHENCESOEVER
WHEREWITHALS
WHIGGISHNESS
WHIMPERINGLY
WHIMSICALITY
WHIPPING BOYS
WHIPPOORWILL
WHITE KNIGHTS
WHITE-LIVERED
WHITE SLAVERY
WHITEWASHING

WHITE WEDDING
WHOLE-HEARTED
WHOLE NUMBERS
WHORTLEBERRY
WICKET KEEPER
WIDE RECEIVER
WIFE SWAPPING
WIGTOWNSHIRE
WILDERNESSES
WILLIAMSBURG
WILL-O'-THE-
   WISP
WINDCHEATERS
WINDING SHEET
WINDOW SHADES
WIND TURBINES
WINEGLASSFUL
WINGLESSNESS
WINSTON-SALEM
WINTERBOURNE
WINTER SPORTS
WISCONSINITE
WISECRACKING
WITCHDOCTORS
WITCH-HUNTING
WITCHING HOUR
WITHDRAWABLE
WITHEREDNESS
WITH OPEN ARMS
WITH PLEASURE
WITHSTANDING
WITNESS BOXES
WOLF WHISTLES
WOLLASTONITE
WOMANISHNESS
WONDER-WORKER
WONDROUSNESS
WOODENHEADED
WOOLGATHERER
WOOLLY-HEADED
WORDLESSNESS
WORD OF HONOUR
WORKER-PRIEST

WORKING CLASS
WORKING ORDER
WORKING PARTY
WORKING WEEKS
WORKINGWOMAN
WORKSTATIONS
WORLD-BEATERS
WORLD-BEATING
WORLDSHAKING
WORLD WIDE WEB
WORMS EYE VIEW
WRATHFULNESS
WRETCHEDNESS
WRISTWATCHES
WRITER'S CRAMP
WRITING DESKS
WRITING PAPER
WRONGFULNESS

X

X CHROMOSOMES
XERODERMATIC
XIPHISTERNUM

Y

Y CHROMOSOMES
YELLOWHAMMER
YIELDINGNESS
YINDJIBARNDI
YOUTHFULNESS
YOUTH HOSTELS

Z

ZINCOGRAPHER
ZINCOGRAPHIC
ZOOCHEMISTRY
ZOOGEOGRAPHY
ZOOSPERMATIC
ZOOTOMICALLY
ZWITTERIONIC
ZYGAPOPHYSIS
ZYGOMORPHISM

A

ABBREVIATIONS
ABERDEENSHIRE
ABNORMALITIES
ABOLITIONISTS
ABORTIFACIENT
ABSORBABILITY
ACCELEROMETER
ACCENTUATIONS
ACCEPTABILITY
ACCESSIBILITY
ACCESSORINESS
ACCIDENT-PRONE
ACCLIMATIZING
ACCOMMODATING
ACCOMMODATION
ACCOMMODATIVE
ACCOMPANIMENT
ACCOMPLISHING
ACCOUTREMENTS
ACCREDITATION
ACCULTURATION
ACCUMULATIONS
ACETIFICATION
ACETYLCHOLINE
ACHILLES'
  HEELS
ACIDIFICATION
ACKNOWLEDGING
ACOTYLEDONOUS
ACQUAINTANCES
ACQUIESCENTLY
ACQUIRED TASTE
ACQUISITIVELY
ACRIMONIOUSLY
ACROBATICALLY
ACRYLONITRILE
ACTINOMORPHIC
ACTINOMYCOSIS
ACTINOMYCOTIC
ACTINOTHERAPY
ACTINOURANIUM
ACTUALIZATION
ADDITIONALITY
ADDRESSOGRAPH
ADENOIDECTOMY
ADIAPHORISTIC
ADMEASUREMENT
ADMINISTERING
ADMINISTRATOR
ADMISSIBILITY

ADMONISHINGLY
ADNYAMATHANHA
ADSORBABILITY
ADVANCED LEVEL
ADVENTURESSES
ADVENTUROUSLY
ADVERTISEMENT
AEROMECHANICS
AESTHETICALLY
AFFENPINSCHER
AFFIRMATIVELY
AFFORESTATION
AFTERTHOUGHTS
AGGIORNAMENTO
AGGLOMERATING
AGGLOMERATION
AGGLOMERATIVE
AGGLUTINATION
AGGLUTINATIVE
AGGRAVATINGLY
AGREEABLENESS
AGRICULTURIST
AGROBIOLOGIST
AIR COMMODORES
AIRCRAFTWOMAN
AIRWORTHINESS
AIX-EN-
  PROVENCE
ALBURY-WODONGA
ALCOHOLICALLY
ALCOHOLOMETER
ALDUS MANUTIUS
ALGEBRAICALLY
ALLEGORICALLY
ALLOCHTHONOUS
ALPHA AND
  OMEGA
ALTAI REPUBLIC
ALTERNATIVELY
ALUMINIFEROUS
ALUMINOTHERMY
AMALGAMATIONS
AMBASSADORIAL
AMBIDEXTERITY
AMBIGUGUITIES
AMBIGUOUSNESS
AMBITIOUSNESS
AMERICANIZING
AMERICAN SAMOA
AMNIOCENTESIS
AMORPHOUSNESS

AMPHIBLASTULA
AMPHIPROSTYLE
AMPHITHEATRES
AMPHITRICHOUS
AMPLIFICATION
AMUSEMENT PARK
ANACHRONISTIC
ANAEROBICALLY
ANAESTHETISTS
ANAESTHETIZED
ANAGRAMMATISM
ANAGRAMMATIST
ANAGRAMMATIZE
ANAL RETENTIVE
ANAPHORICALLY
ANAPHRODISIAC
ANATHEMATIZED
ANATOMIZATION
ANCHORPERSONS
ANDHRA PRADESH
ANEMOMETRICAL
ANESTHETIZING
ANFRACTUOSITY
ANGIOSPERMOUS
ANGLICIZATION
ANGLO-AMERICAN
ANGLO-CATHOLIC
ANIMADVERSION
ANIMADVERTING
ANIMALIZATION
ANISOMETROPIA
ANNEXATIONISM
ANNEXATIONIST
ANNIVERSARIES
ANNOUNCEMENTS
ANSWERABILITY
ANTAGONIZABLE
ANTHRAQUINONE
ANTHROPOMETRY
ANTHROPOPATHY
ANTHROPOPHAGI
ANTHROPOSOPHY
ANTI-APARTHEID
ANTIBACTERIAL
ANTICLIMACTIC
ANTICLINORIUM
ANTICLOCKWISE
ANTI-COMMUNIST
ANTIGENICALLY
ANTIHISTAMINE
ANTILOGARITHM

ANTIMACASSARS
ANTIMONARCHIC
ANTINOMICALLY
ANTIPERSONNEL
ANTIPRAGMATIC
ANTIPSYCHOTIC
ANTISPASMODIC
ANTISUBMARINE
APATHETICALLY
APERIODICALLY
APHELIOTROPIC
APLANATICALLY
APOCHROMATISM
APODICTICALLY
APOGEOTROPISM
APOSTROPHIZED
APPLE PIE
  ORDER
APPLICABILITY
APPORTIONABLE
APPORTIONMENT
APPRECIATIONS
APPREHENSIBLE
APPREHENSIONS
APPROPRIATELY
APPROPRIATING
APPROPRIATION
APPROXIMATELY
APPROXIMATING
APPROXIMATION
APPURTENANCES
AQUICULTURIST
ARABIAN DESERT
ARABIC NUMERAL
ARACHNOPHOBIA
ARBITRARINESS
ARBORICULTURE
ARCHAEOLOGIST
ARCHBISHOPRIC
ARCHIDIACONAL
ARCHIMANDRITE
ARCHIPELAGOES
ARCHITECTONIC
ARCHITECTURAL
ARGENTIFEROUS
ARGILLIFEROUS
ARGUMENTATION
ARGUMENTATIVE
ARGYLL AND
  BUTE
ARISTOCRACIES

ARITHMETICIAN
AROMATIZATION
ARRIERE-PENSEE
ARTERIOVENOUS
ARTESIAN WELLS
ARTICULATIONS
ARTIFICIALITY
ARTS AND
    CRAFTS
ARUNDINACEOUS
ASCERTAINABLE
ASCERTAINMENT
ASCHAFFENBURG
ASPERGILLOSIS
ASSASSINATING
ASSASSINATION
ASSAULT COURSE
ASSEMBLY LINES
ASSERTIVENESS
ASSET-STRIPPER
ASSEVERATIONS
ASSIDUOUSNESS
ASSIGNABILITY
ASSYRIOLOGIST
ASTHENOSPHERE
ASTHMATICALLY
ASTIGMATISTIC
ASTONISHINGLY
ASTRODYNAMICS
ASTROPHYSICAL
ASYNDETICALLY
ATACAMA DESERT
ATAVISTICALLY
ATHEISTICALLY
ATOMISTICALLY
ATROCIOUSNESS
ATTAINABILITY
ATTENTIVENESS
AT THE SAME
    TIME
ATTITUDINIZER
ATTRIBUTIVELY
AUBERVILLIERS
AUDACIOUSNESS
AUGMENTATIONS
AUNG SAN SUU
    KYI
AUSTRALASIANS
AUSTRO-ASIATIC
AUTECOLOGICAL
AUTHENTICALLY

AUTHENTICATED
AUTHENTICATOR
AUTHORITARIAN
AUTHORITATIVE
AUTHORIZATION
AUTOBIOGRAPHY
AUTOCATALYSIS
AUTOCHTHONISM
AUTOCHTHONOUS
AUTOMATICALLY
AUTOMATIC DOOR
AUTONOMICALLY
AUTOSTABILITY
AUXILIARY VERB
AXIOMATICALLY

B

BABY CARRIAGES
BACCALAUREATE
BACK FORMATION
BACKPEDALLING
BACKWARDATION
BACTERIOLYSIS
BACTERIOLYTIC
BACTERIOPHAGE
BALANCED DIETS
BALANCE SHEETS
BALKANIZATION
BALLISTICALLY
BALL LIGHTNING
BALNEOLOGICAL
BALSAMIFEROUS
BAMBOOZLEMENT
BANDSPREADING
BANKER'S
    ORDERS
BANTAMWEIGHTS
BARBAROUSNESS
BARBOUR JACKET
BAREFACEDNESS
BASIDIOMYCETE
BASOTHO-QWAQWA
BATTERING RAMS
BATTLE CRUISER
BATTLE-SCARRED
BEAST OF
    BURDEN
BEATIFICATION
BEAUFORT SCALE
BEAUTY PARLOUR
BEHAVIOURALLY

BEHAVIOURISTS
BELISHA BEACON
BELLES-LETTRES
BELLY-LANDINGS
BELO HORIZONTE
BENEFICIARIES
BENEFIT IN
    KIND
BERCHTESGADEN
BEWILDERINGLY
BIBLIOGRAPHER
BIBLIOGRAPHIC
BICENTENARIES
BIDIRECTIONAL
BIG BANG
    THEORY
BIGHEADEDNESS
BIGNONIACEOUS
BILLS OF
    HEALTH
BILLS OF
    LADING
BILLS OF
    RIGHTS
BIODEGRADABLE
BIOECOLOGICAL
BIOENERGETICS
BIOMETRICALLY
BIOSTATICALLY
BIOTECHNOLOGY
BIRD OF
    PASSAGE
BIRD'S-EYE
    VIEWS
BIREFRINGENCE
BLABBERMOUTHS
BLACK AND
    WHITE
BLACKBERRYING
BLACK COMEDIES
BLACKCURRANTS
BLACKGUARDISM
BLACK MOUNTAIN
BLACK PUDDINGS
BLAMELESSNESS
BLANDISHMENTS
BLANTYRE-LIMBE
BLASPHEMOUSLY
BLAST FURNACES
BLASTOGENESIS
BLIND MAN'S
    BUFF

BLOOD BROTHERS
BLOODCURDLING
BLOODLESSNESS
BLOOD PRESSURE
BLOOD RELATION
BLOTTING PAPER
BLUE MOUNTAINS
BLUE-PENCILLED
BLUESTOCKINGS
BLUNDERBUSSES
BOARDING CARDS
BOARDINGHOUSE
BOBO-DIOULASSO
BODY SNATCHERS
BODY STOCKINGS
BOILING POINTS
BOMBASTICALLY
BOOBY TRAPPING
BOON COMPANION
BORAGINACEOUS
BORDERS REGION
BOTTLE-FEEDING
BOTTOM DRAWERS
BOUGAINVILLEA
BOUILLABAISSE
BOUNDLESSNESS
BOUNTEOUSNESS
BOUNTIFULNESS
BOUSTROPHEDON
BOWLING ALLEYS
BOWLING GREENS
BRACHYCEPHALY
BRACHYPTEROUS
BRAINLESSNESS
BRAINSTORMING
BRASSICACEOUS
BRASS KNUCKLES
BROADMINDEDLY
BROKEN-HEARTED
BROMELIACEOUS
BRONCHIAL TUBE
BRONCHOSCOPIC
BROTHERLINESS
BROTHERS-IN-
    LAW
BROWNIE GUIDES
BROWNIE POINTS
BRUTALIZATION
BUBONIC PLAGUE
BUDGET DEFICIT
BUILDING BLOCK

BULLETIN BOARD
BUMPTIOUSNESS
BUNGEE JUMPING
BUNSEN BURNERS
BURDEN OF
  PROOF
BUREAUCRACIES
BUREAUCRATISM
BURGLAR ALARMS
BURNT OFFERING
BURY ST
  EDMUNDS
BUSH CARPENTER
BUSH TELEGRAPH
BUSINESS CLASS
BUSINESS SUITS
BUSINESSWOMAN
BUTCHER'S-
  BROOM
BUTTERFINGERS
BUTTER-FINGERS
BUTYRALDEHYDE

C

CABIN CRUISERS
CABINET-MAKERS
CABLE RAILWAYS
CAICOS ISLANDS
CALCARIFEROUS
CALCIFICATION
CALCULABILITY
CALENDAR MONTH
CALENDAR YEARS
CALLIGRAPHIST
CALLISTHENICS
CALORIFICALLY
CAMBRIDGE BLUE
CAMPANOLOGIST
CAMP FOLLOWERS
CAMPYLOBACTER
CANARY ISLANDS
CANCELLATIONS
CANNIBALISTIC
CANNIBALIZING
CANONIZATION
CAPACIOUSNESS
CAPARISONNING
CAPE COLOUREDS
CAPITAL LEVIES
CAPITULATIONS
CAPRIFICATION

CARAVANSERAIS
CARBOHYDRATES
CARBON DIOXIDE
CARBONIFEROUS
CARBONIZATION
CARBURIZATION
CARCINOMATOID
CARDIGANSHIRE
CARDINAL POINT
CARDIOGRAPHER
CARDIOGRAPHIC
CARDIOLOGICAL
CARICATURISTS
CARNIFICATION
CARPETBAGGERS
CARPET SWEEPER
CARRICKFERGUS
CARRIER PIGEON
CARTILAGINOUS
CARTOGRAPHERS
CARVING KNIVES
CASE HISTORIES
CASH DISPENSER
CASH REGISTERS
CASSEGRAINIAN
CASUISTICALLY
CATASTROPHISM
CATASTROPHIST
CATCHMENT AREA
CATECHIZATION
CATECHOLAMINE
CATEGORICALLY
CATER-CORNERED
CATHARTICALLY
CAT-O'-NINE-
  TAILS
CAUTERIZATION
CAYENNE PEPPER
CAYMAN ISLANDS
CELLULAR RADIO
CENTRAL REGION
CENTRE FORWARD
CEPHALIZATION
CEPHALOMETRIC
CEPHALOTHORAX
CEREBRAL PALSY
CEREBROSPINAL
CEREMONIALISM
CEREMONIALIST
CEREMONIOUSLY
CERTIFICATION

CERTIFICATORY
CERTIFIED MAIL
CERTIFIED MILK
CHAFING DISHES
CHAIN REACTION
CHAIN STITCHES
CHAIRMANSHIPS
CHAISE LONGUES
CHALCOGRAPHER
CHALCOGRAPHIC
CHALLENGEABLE
CHAMPIONSHIPS
CHANCELLERIES
CHANDERNAGORE
CHANDRASEKHAR
CHANGEABILITY
CHANGE OF
  HEART
CHANGE RINGING
CHANGING ROOMS
CHANNEL TUNNEL
CHANTRY CHAPEL
CHARACTERIZED
CHARACTERLESS
CHARGEABILITY
CHARGE ACCOUNT
CHARLOTTETOWN
CHARNEL HOUSES
CHARTER MEMBER
CHASTISEMENTS
CHASTITY BELTS
CHATEAUBRIAND
CHEERLESSNESS
CHEMISORPTION
CHEMORECEPTOR
CHESTERFIELDS
CHEVAL GLASSES
CHIAROSCURISM
CHIAROSCURIST
CHIEF JUSTICES
CHIEFS OF
  STAFF
CHIEFTAINSHIP
CHILDLESSNESS
CHIMNEYBREAST
CHIMNEY CORNER
CHIMNEYPIECES
CHIMNEYSTACKS
CHIMNEYSWEEPS
CHIROPRACTORS
CHLAMYDOSPORE

CHLOROBENZENE
CHLOROFORMING
CHLOROMYCETIN
CHLOROPLASTIC
CHONDRIOSOMAL
CHONDROMATOUS
CHOREOGRAPHED
CHOREOGRAPHER
CHOREOGRAPHIC
CHRISTIANIZER
CHRISTIAN NAME
CHRISTMAS CAKE
CHRISTMAS CARD
CHRISTMASTIDE
CHRISTMASTIME
CHRISTMAS TREE
CHRISTOLOGIST
CHROMATICALLY
CHROMATICNESS
CHROMATOLYSIS
CHROMATOPHORE
CHROMOPLASMIC
CHROMOPROTEIN
CHROMOSPHERIC
CHRONOBIOLOGY
CHRONOGRAPHER
CHRONOGRAPHIC
CHRONOLOGICAL
CHRYSANTHEMUM
CHURCHWARDENS
CICATRIZATION
CINEMATICALLY
CINEMATOGRAPH
CIRCULARIZING
CIRCUMAMBIENT
CIRCUMCISIONS
CIRCUMFERENCE
CIRCUMFLEXION
CIRCUMSCRIBED
CIRCUMSPECTLY
CIRCUMSTANCES
CIRCUMVALLATE
CIRCUMVENTING
CIRCUMVENTION
CIUDAD GUAYANA
CIVIL ENGINEER
CIVILIZATIONS
CIVIL SERVANTS
CLAIRAUDIENCE
CLANDESTINELY
CLAPPERBOARDS

CLARIFICATION	COMMENDATIONS	CONCATENATION	CONGRESSIONAL
CLARINETTISTS	COMMENSURABLE	CONCAVO-CONVEX	CONGRESSWOMAN
CLASSIFIED ADS	COMMERCIALISM	CONCENTRATING	CONJUGATIONAL
CLASSLESSNESS	COMMERCIALIST	CONCENTRATION	CONJUNCTIONAL
CLASS STRUGGLE	COMMERCIALITY	CONCENTRATIVE	CONNECTING ROD
CLAUSTROPHOBE	COMMERCIALIZE	CONCENTRICITY	CONNING TOWERS
CLAVICHORDIST	COMMISERATING	CONCEPTUALISM	CONNOTATATIVE
CLEARANCE SALE	COMMISERATION	CONCEPTUALIST	CONQUISTADORS
CLEAR-HEADEDLY	COMMISERATIVE	CONCEPTUALIZE	CONSANGUINITY
CLEARINGHOUSE	COMMISSARIATS	CONCERT GRANDS	CONSCIENTIOUS
CLEISTOGAMOUS	COMMISSIONERS	CONCERTINAING	CONSCIOUSNESS
CLERKS OF	COMMISSIONING	CONCESSIONARY	CONSECUTIVELY
WORKS	COMMUNALISTIC	CONCHOLOGICAL	CONSEQUENTIAL
CLIMACTERICAL	COMMUNAUTAIRE	CONCHOLOGISTS	CONSERVANCIES
CLIMATOLOGIST	COMMUNICATING	CONCOMITANTLY	CONSERVATIVES
CLIMBING FRAME	COMMUNICATION	CONCRETE MIXER	CONSERVATOIRE
CLIMBING IRONS	COMMUNICATIVE	CONCRETIONARY	CONSIDERATELY
CLOSED-CIRCUIT	COMMUNICATORY	CONCUPISCENCE	CONSIDERATION
CLOSED SEASONS	COMMUNITARIAN	CONDEMNATIONS	CONSISTENCIES
CLOSING PRICES	COMMUNITY HOME	CONDEMNED CELL	CONSOLIDATING
CLOTHES HANGER	COMMUNIZATION	CONDENSED MILK	CONSOLIDATION
CLOTHESHORSES	COMPANIONABLE	CONDESCENDING	CONSPICUOUSLY
CLUSTER-BOMBED	COMPANIONABLY	CONDESCENSION	CONSPIRATRESS
COACHBUILDERS	COMPANIONSHIP	CONDITIONALLY	CONSTELLATION
COACH STATIONS	COMPANIONWAYS	CONDUCIVENESS	CONSTELLATORY
COBELLIGERENT	COMPARABILITY	CONDUCTOR RAIL	CONSTERNATION
COCAINIZATION	COMPARATIVELY	CONDYLOMATOUS	CONSTITUTIONS
COCKER SPANIEL	COMPARTMENTAL	CONFABULATING	CONSTRAINEDLY
COCKTAIL STICK	COMPASSIONATE	CONFABULATION	CONSTRICTIONS
CODECLINATION	COMPASS POINTS	CONFABULATORY	CONSTRUCTIBLE
CODIFICATIONS	COMPATIBILITY	CONFECTIONARY	CONSTRUCTIONS
COEDUCATIONAL	COMPATRIOTISM	CONFECTIONERS	CONSULTANCIES
COLD-BLOODEDLY	COMPENDIOUSLY	CONFECTIONERY	CONSULTATIONS
COLD-HEARTEDLY	COMPETITIVELY	CONFEDERACIES	CONSUMMATIONS
COLLABORATING	COMPLAININGLY	CONFEDERATING	CONTACT LENSES
COLLABORATION	COMPLAISANTLY	CONFEDERATION	CONTAINERIZED
COLLABORATIVE	COMPLEMENTARY	CONFESSIONALS	CONTAMINATING
COLLABORATORS	COMPLEMENTING	CONFESSIONARY	CONTAMINATION
COLLATERALIZE	COMPLICATEDLY	CONFIGURATION	CONTAMINATORS
COLLETIVISTIC	COMPLICATIONS	CONFIRMATIONS	CONTEMPLATING
COLLOQUIALISM	COMPLIMENTARY	CONFISCATIONS	CONTEMPLATION
COLOUR SCHEMES	COMPLIMENTING	CONFLAGRATION	CONTEMPLATIVE
COMBAT FATIGUE	COMPOSITIONAL	CONFLAGRATIVE	CONTENTIOUSLY
COMBINING FORM	COMPREHENDING	CONFORMATIONS	CONTEXTUALISM
COMMANDEERING	COMPREHENSION	CONFRATERNITY	CONTEXTUALIZE
COMMANDERSHIP	COMPREHENSIVE	CONFRONTATION	CONTINGENCIES
COMMAND MODULE	COMPRESSIONAL	CONGLOMERATES	CONTINUATIONS
COMMEMORATING	COMPUTABILITY	CONGLOMERATIC	CONTORTIONIST
COMMEMORATION	COMPUTATIONAL	CONGRATULATED	CONTRABANDIST
COMMEMORATIVE	COMPUTERIZING	CONGRATULATOR	CONTRABASSIST
COMMENCEMENTS	CONCATENATING	CONGREGATIONS	CONTRABASSOON

CONTRACEPTION
CONTRACEPTIVE
CONTRACTILITY
CONTRACTIONAL
CONTRACTUALLY
CONTRADICTING
CONTRADICTION
CONTRADICTIVE
CONTRADICTORY
CONTRAPUNTIST
CONTRAVENTION
CONTRIBUTIONS
CONTROVERSIAL
CONTROVERSIES
CONVALESCENCE
CONVALESCENTS
CONVERSATIONS
CONVERSAZIONE
CONVERTIPLANE
CONVEXO-CONVEX
CONVEYER BELTS
CONVOCATIONAL
CONVOLVULUSES
COOKING APPLES
COOPERATIVELY
CORDUROY ROADS
CORELIGIONIST
CO-RESPONDENCY
CO-RESPONDENTS
CORN EXCHANGES
CORPS DE
  BALLET
CORPUS CHRISTI
CORRESPONDENT
CORRESPONDING
CORRIGIBILITY
CORROBORATING
CORROBORATION
CORROBORATIVE
CORROBORATORS
CORRODIBILITY
CORROSIVENESS
CORRUPTIONIST
COSIGNATORIES
COSMOPOLITANS
COSMOPOLITISM
COST-EFFECTIVE
COSTERMONGERS
COTERMINOUSLY
COTTAGE CHEESE
COTTAGE LOAVES

COTTON-PICKING
COUNTENANCING
COUNTERACTING
COUNTERACTION
COUNTERACTIVE
COUNTERATTACK
COUNTERBLASTS
COUNTERCHARGE
COUNTERCLAIMS
COUNTERFEITED
COUNTERFEITER
COUNTERMANDED
COUNTERPOINTS
COUNTERPOISED
COUNTERPOISES
COUNTERSIGNED
COUNTERTENORS
COUNTERWEIGHT
COUNTINGHOUSE
COUNTRY COUSIN
COUNTRY DANCES
COUNTY BOROUGH
COUNTY COUNCIL
COURT CIRCULAR
COURTEOUSNESS
COURT MARTIALS
COURTS-MARTIAL
COVERED WAGONS
CRAFTSMANSHIP
CRANIOLOGICAL
CRASH BARRIERS
CRASH LANDINGS
CRASSULACEOUS
CREAM OF
  TARTAR
CREDIT ACCOUNT
CREDIT SQUEEZE
CREME DE
  MENTHE
CRIMINOLOGIST
CRISSCROSSING
CROSSBENCHERS
CROSSBREEDING
CROSSCHECKING
CROSSCURRENTS
CROSS-DRESSERS
CROSS-DRESSING
CROSS-EXAMINED
CROSS-EXAMINER
CROSS-HATCHING
CROSS-PURPOSES

CROSS-QUESTION
CROSS-REFERRED
CROSS-SECTIONS
CROSS-STITCHES
CROWN COLONIES
CROWN IMPERIAL
CROWN PRINCESS
CRUISE MISSILE
CRUISERWEIGHT
CRUSH BARRIERS
CRYOBIOLOGIST
CRYPTANALYSIS
CRYPTANALYTIC
CRYPTOCLASTIC
CRYPTOGRAPHER
CRYPTOGRAPHIC
CRYPTOZOOLOGY
CRYSTAL GAZERS
CRYSTAL GAZING
CRYSTALLINITY
CRYSTALLIZING
CUMULOSTRATUS
CURTAIN RAISER
CUSTODIANSHIP
CUT ONES
  LOSSES
CYANOBACTERIA
CYBERNETICIST
CYLINDRICALLY
CYTOCHEMISTRY
CYTOTAXONOMIC
CZECH REPUBLIC

D

DADAISTICALLY
DADDY LONGLEGS
DAGUERREOTYPE
DAGUERREOTYPY
DAMAGEABILITY
DAMNIFICATION
DANDIFICATION
DARK CONTINENT
DASTARDLINESS
DAUGHTER-IN-
  LAW
DEAD-CAT
  BOUNCE
DEAD RECKONING
DEATH WARRANTS
DEBTS OF
  HONOUR

DECAPITATIONS
DECEITFULNESS
DECENTRALIZED
DECEPTIVENESS
DECEREBRATION
DECK PASSENGER
DECLAMATORILY
DECLARATORILY
DECLASSIFYING
DECOMPOSITION
DECOMPRESSING
DECOMPRESSION
DECOMPRESSIVE
DECONGESTANTS
DECONTAMINANT
DECONTAMINATE
DECONTROLLING
DECORTICATION
DECREPITATION
DEDUCTIBILITY
DEFECTIVENESS
DEFENSIBILITY
DEFENSIVENESS
DEFERENTIALLY
DEFIBRILLATOR
DEFORESTATION
DEGLUTINATION
DEHYDROGENASE
DEHYDROGENATE
DEHYDROGENIZE
DELETERIOUSLY
DELIBERATIONS
DELICATESSENS
DELICIOUSNESS
DELINQUENCIES
DELIQUESCENCE
DELIRIOUSNESS
DEMAGNETIZING
DEMAGOGICALLY
DEMERARA SUGAR
DEMERITORIOUS
DEMILITARIZED
DEMOCRATIZING
DEMOLITIONIST
DEMONOLOGICAL
DEMONSTRATING
DEMONSTRATION
DEMONSTRATIVE
DEMONSTRATORS
DENATIONALIZE
DENDRITICALLY

DENDROLOGICAL	DIAMETRICALLY	DISCONTINUING	DISPUTABILITY
DENOMINATIONS	DIAPHRAGMATIC	DISCONTINUITY	DISQUALIFYING
DENSITOMETRIC	DIATHERMANOUS	DISCONTINUOUS	DISQUISITIONS
DENTAL SURGEON	DIATONIC SCALE	DISCOUNT STORE	DISRESPECTFUL
DENTICULATION	DIAZOTIZATION	DISCOURTESIES	DISSATISFYING
DENUNCIATIONS	DICHLAMIDEOUS	DISCREDITABLE	DISSEMINATING
DEODORIZATION	DICTATORIALLY	DISCREDITABLY	DISSEMINATION
DEONTOLOGICAL	DICTATORSHIPS	DISCREPANCIES	DISSEMINATIVE
DEOXIDIZATION	DIEFFENBACHIA	DISCRETIONARY	DISSEPIMENTAL
DEOXYGENATION	DIESEL ENGINES	DISCRIMINATED	DISSERTATIONS
DEPENDABILITY	DIFFERENTIALS	DISCRIMINATOR	DISSIMILARITY
DEPERSONALIZE	DIFFERENTIATE	DISEMBODIMENT	DISSIMILATION
DEPRECATINGLY	DIFFUSIBILITY	DISEMBOWELING	DISSIMILATIVE
DEPRECATORILY	DIGESTIBILITY	DISEMBOWELLED	DISSIMILATORY
DEPRESSOMOTOR	DIGITAL CAMERA	DISENABLEMENT	DISSIMILITUDE
DERMATOLOGIST	DILAPIDATIONS	DISENGAGEMENT	DISSIMULATING
DERMATOPHYTIC	DILLYDALLYING	DISENTAILMENT	DISSIMULATION
DERMATOPLASTY	DIMENSIONLESS	DISENTANGLING	DISSIMULATIVE
DESCRIPTIVELY	DIM-WITTEDNESS	DISFIGUREMENT	DISSOLUBILITY
DESCRIPTIVISM	DINNER JACKETS	DISFRANCHISED	DISSOLUTENESS
DESEGREGATING	DINNER SERVICE	DISGRACEFULLY	DISTASTEFULLY
DESEGREGATION	DIPHENYLAMINE	DISHARMONIOUS	DISTILLATIONS
DESENSITIZING	DIPSOMANIACAL	DISHONOURABLE	DISTINCTIVELY
DESPICABILITY	DIRECT CURRENT	DISHONOURABLY	DISTINGUISHED
DESSERTSPOONS	DIRECT OBJECTS	DISILLUSIONED	DISTINGUISHER
DESTABILIZING	DIRECTORSHIPS	DISINCENTIVES	DISTRESSINGLY
DESTRUCTIVELY	DISADVANTAGED	DISINFECTANTS	DISTRIBUTABLE
DESULTORINESS	DISADVANTAGES	DISINHERITING	DISTRIBUTIONS
DETACHABILITY	DISAFFECTEDLY	DISINTEGRABLE	DISTRUSTFULLY
DETERIORATING	DISAFFILIATED	DISINTEGRATED	DITRANSITIVES
DETERIORATION	DISAFFIRMANCE	DISINTEGRATOR	DIVERSIFIABLE
DETERIORATIVE	DISAFFORESTED	DISINTERESTED	DIVISIONALIZE
DETERMINATION	DISAGREEMENTS	DISINTERMENTS	DIVISION LOBBY
DETERMINATIVE	DISAPPEARANCE	DISINVESTMENT	DOCTRINAIRISM
DETERMINISTIC	DISAPPOINTING	DISMANTLEMENT	DOCUMENTARIES
DETESTABILITY	DISARTICULATE	DISMEMBERMENT	DOCUMENTARILY
DETRIMENTALLY	DISASSOCIATED	DISOBEDIENTLY	DOCUMENTARIST
DEUTEROGAMIST	DISBURDENMENT	DISOBLIGINGLY	DOCUMENTATION
DEVASTATINGLY	DISBURSEMENTS	DISORIENTATED	DODECAPHONISM
DEVELOPMENTAL	DISCHARGEABLE	DISPARAGEMENT	DODECAPHONIST
DEVIATIONISTS	DISCIPLINABLE	DISPARAGINGLY	DOGMATIZATION
DEVOLUTIONARY	DISCOLORATION	DISPASSIONATE	DOG'S
DEVOTIONALITY	DISCOMMODIOUS	DISPATCH BOXES	BREAKFAST
DEXTEROUSNESS	DISCOMPOSEDLY	DISPENSATIONS	DOLLARIZATION
DEXTROGLUCOSE	DISCONCERTING	DISPLACEMENTS	DOME OF THE
DIAGEOTROPISM	DISCONCERTION	DISPOSABILITY	ROCK
DIAGNOSTICIAN	DISCONFORMITY	DISPOSITIONAL	DOMESTICATING
DIALECTICIANS	DISCONNECTING	DISPOSSESSING	DOMESTICATION
DIALLING CODES	DISCONNECTION	DISPOSSESSION	DOMESTICATIVE
DIALLING TONES	DISCONNECTIVE	DISPOSSESSORY	DOMESTICITIES
DIALYSABILITY	DISCONTENTING	DISPROPORTION	DONKEY JACKETS

DOSIMETRICIAN
DOTHEBOYS HALL
DOUBLE-CHECKED
DOUBLE-CROSSED
DOUBLE-CROSSER
DOUBLE-CROSSES
DOUBLE-DEALERS
DOUBLE-DEALING
DOUBLE-DECKERS
DOUBLE FEATURE
DOUBLE FIGURES
DOUBLE-GLAZING
DOUBLE-JOINTED
DOUBLE OR
  QUITS
DOUBLE-PARKING
DOUBLE-TALKING
DOWNHEARTEDLY
DOWNING STREET
DOWN'S
  SYNDROME
DRAINING BOARD
DRAMATIC IRONY
DRAMATIZATION
DRAWING BOARDS
DRESSING GOWNS
DRESSING ROOMS
DRESSING TABLE
DRINKING WATER
DRUM MAJORETTE
DRYOPITHECINE
DUALISTICALLY
DUCKING STOOLS
DUCTLESS GLAND
DUMFRIESSHIRE
DUPLICABILITY
DUQUE DE
  CAXIAS
DUTCH AUCTIONS
DWELLING HOUSE
DYED-IN-THE-
  WOOL
DYSFUNCTIONAL
DYSMENORRHOEA

E

EAST-NORTHEAST
EAST-SOUTHEAST
EAVESDROPPERS
EAVESDROPPING
ECCENTRICALLY

ECCLESIASTICS
ECCLESIOLATER
ECCLESIOLATRY
ECONOMIZATION
ECTOPARASITIC
ECUMENICALISM
EDITORIALIZER
EDUCATED GUESS
EFFECTIVENESS
EFFERVESCENCE
EFFERVESCIBLE
EFFICACIOUSLY
EFFLORESCENCE
EGOCENTRICITY
EGOTISTICALLY
EGREGIOUSNESS
EGYPTOLOGICAL
EIGHTEEN HOLES
ELABORATENESS
ELECTIONEERER
ELECTRIC CHAIR
ELECTRIC FENCE
ELECTRIC SHOCK
ELECTRIFIABLE
ELECTROCUTING
ELECTROCUTION
ELECTROGRAPHY
ELECTROMAGNET
ELECTROMERISM
ELECTROMETRIC
ELECTROMOTIVE
ELECTROPHILIC
ELECTROPHONIC
ELECTROPHORUS
ELECTROPLATER
ELECTROSCOPIC
ELECTROSTATIC
ELECTROVALENT
ELEPHANTIASIC
ELEPHANTIASIS
ELEPHANT'S-
  FOOT
ELLESMERE PORT
EMBARRASSMENT
EMBELLISHMENT
EMBRYOLOGICAL
EMBRYONICALLY
EMILIA-ROMAGNA
EMINENCE GRISE
EMOTIONLESSLY
EMPHYSEMATOUS

EMPIRE-BUILDER
EMPIRICALNESS
EMPLOYABILITY
EMULSION PAINT
ENCAPSULATION
ENCAUSTICALLY
ENCEPHALOGRAM
ENCHANTRESSES
ENCOMPASSMENT
ENCOURAGEMENT
ENCOURAGINGLY
ENCROACHINGLY
ENCROACHMENTS
ENCULTURATION
ENCULTURATIVE
ENCUMBERINGLY
ENCYCLOPEDIAS
ENCYCLOPEDISM
ENCYCLOPEDIST
ENDOCRINOLOGY
ENDODONTOLOGY
ENDOLYMPHATIC
ENDOMETRIOSIS
ENDOPARASITIC
ENDOPEPTIDASE
ENERGETICALLY
ENFRANCHISING
ENGINE DRIVERS
ENIGMATICALLY
ENLIGHTENMENT
ENROLLED NURSE
ENTANGLEMENTS
ENTERTAINMENT
ENTHRALLINGLY
ENTHRONEMENTS
ENTOMOLOGICAL
ENTOMOLOGISTS
ENTOMOPHAGOUS
ENTOMOPHILOUS
ENTOMOSTRACAN
ENTREPRENEURS
ENUNCIABILITY
ENVIRONMENTAL
ENZYMOLOGICAL
EPIGRAMMATISM
EPIGRAMMATIST
EPIGRAMMATIZE
EPILEPTICALLY
EPIPHENOMENAL
EPIPHENOMENON
EPIPHYTICALLY

EPISCOPALIANS
EPITOMIZATION
EPIZOOTICALLY
EQUESTRIANISM
EQUILIBRATION
EQUILIBRISTIC
EQUIMOLECULAR
EQUIPONDERANT
EQUIPONDERATE
EQUIPOTENTIAL
EQUITABLENESS
EQUIVOCATIONS
ERGONOMICALLY
ERRONEOUSNESS
ERYSIPELATOUS
ESCAPOLOGISTS
ESCHATOLOGIST
ESPIRITO SANTO
ESPRIT DE
  CORPS
ESTABLISHMENT
ESTIMABLENESS
ESTRANGEMENTS
ETHNOCENTRISM
ETHNOGRAPHERS
ETHOLOGICALLY
ETIOLOGICALLY
EUROCOMMUNISM
EUSPORANGIATE
EVAPORABILITY
EVENTUALITIES
EVERLASTINGLY
EVERY WHICH
  WAY
EVOCATIVENESS
EXAGGERATEDLY
EXAGGERATIONS
EXAMINATIONAL
EXANTHEMATOUS
EXASPERATEDLY
EXCEPTIONABLE
EXCEPTIONALLY
EXCESSIVENESS
EXCHANGE RATES
EXCLAMATIONAL
EXCLAMATORILY
EXCLUDABILITY
EXCLUSIVENESS
EXCOMMUNICATE
EXCURSIVENESS
EXCUSABLENESS

EXECRABLENESS
EXEMPLARINESS
EXEMPLIFIABLE
EXEMPLI GRATIA
EXHIBITIONISM
EXHIBITIONIST
EXPANSIBILITY
EXPANSIONISTS
EXPANSIVENESS
EXPECTORATING
EXPECTORATION
EXPEDITIONARY
EXPEDITIOUSLY
EXPENDABILITY
EXPENSIVENESS
EXPERIMENTING
EXPERT SYSTEMS
EXPLANATORIES
EXPLANATORILY
EXPLOSIVENESS
EXPONENTIALLY
EXPORTABILITY
EXPOSTULATING
EXPOSTULATION
EXPOSTULATORY
EXPRESSIONISM
EXPRESSIONIST
EXPROPRIATING
EXPROPRIATION
EXPROPRIATORS
EXQUISITENESS
EXTEMPORARILY
EXTEMPORIZING
EXTENDIBILITY
EXTENSIBILITY
EXTENSIVENESS
EXTENUATINGLY
EXTERMINATING
EXTERMINATION
EXTERMINATIVE
EXTERMINATORS
EXTERNALIZING
EXTEROCEPTIVE
EXTERRITORIAL
EXTINGUISHANT
EXTINGUISHERS
EXTINGUISHING
EXTORTIONABLE
EXTORTIONISTS
EXTRACELLULAR
EXTRAGALACTIC

EXTRAJUDICIAL
EXTRAORDINARY
EXTRAPOLATING
EXTRAPOLATION
EXTRAPOLATIVE
EXTRAPOSITION
EXTRAVAGANCES
EXTRAVAGANTLY
EXTRAVAGANZAS
EXTRAVAGATION
EXTRAVASATION
EXTRAVASCULAR
EXTRINSICALLY
EYEBROW PENCIL
EYE-CATCHINGLY

F

FACETIOUSNESS
FACTORABILITY
FACTORIZATION
FAITHLESSNESS
FALLOPIAN TUBE
FALSIFICATION
FAMILIARITIES
FAMILIARIZING
FAMILY DOCTORS
FAMILY SUPPORT
FANTASTICALLY
FASCICULATION
FASCINATINGLY
FASCISTICALLY
FATHEADEDNESS
FATHER FIGURES
FAULTLESSNESS
FEATHERBEDDED
FEATHERSTITCH
FEATHER-VEINED
FEATHERWEIGHT
FEATURE-LENGTH
FEEDING BOTTLE
FELICITATIONS
FELLOW FEELING
FELONIOUSNESS
FEMMES FATALES
FEROCIOUSNESS
FERRIMAGNETIC
FERROCHROMIUM
FERROCONCRETE
FERROELECTRIC
FERROMAGNETIC
FERTILIZATION

FEUDALIZATION
FEUILLETONISM
FEUILLETONIST
FIBROVASCULAR
FICTIONALIZED
FIELD MARSHALS
FIELD OF
  VISION
FIGHTER-BOMBER
FIGURED BASSES
FIGURE OF
  EIGHT
FIGURE SKATERS
FIGURE-SKATING
FILIBUSTERING
FILING CABINET
FILM PREMIERES
FILTERABILITY
FINANCIAL YEAR
FINE-TOOTH
  COMB
FINGERPRINTED
FIRST MINISTER
FIRST OFFENDER
FISH-EYE
  LENSES
FISSION-FUSION
FLABBERGASTED
FLAGELLANTISM
FLAME-THROWERS
FLAVOPURPURIN
FLEET ADMIRALS
FLESH AND
  BLOOD
FLIGHT CAPITAL
FLIRTATIOUSLY
FLOATING-POINT
FLOATING VOTER
FLOODLIGHTING
FLORIANOPOLIS
FLORICULTURAL
FLORISTICALLY
FLOURISHINGLY
FLYING COLOURS
FLYING DOCTORS
FLYING OFFICER
FLYING PICKETS
FLYING SAUCERS
FOLLOW-THROUGH
FONTAINEBLEAU
FOOD POISONING
FOOD PROCESSOR

FOOLHARDINESS
FOOL'S
  PARADISE
FOOTBALL POOLS
FORAMINIFERAL
FORBIDDEN CITY
FOREIGN OFFICE
FOREJUDGEMENT
FOREKNOWINGLY
FOREKNOWLEDGE
FORENSICALITY
FOREORDAINING
FORESHADOWING
FORESHORTENED
FOREWARNINGLY
FORGETFULNESS
FORGIVINGNESS
FORKLIFT TRUCK
FORMALIZATION
FORMATIVENESS
FORMIDABILITY
FORTIFICATION
FORTITUDINOUS
FORTUNE HUNTER
FORTUNE-TELLER
FOSSILIFEROUS
FOSSILIZATION
FOUNDATIONARY
FRACTIONATION
FRACTIOUSNESS
FRACTOCUMULUS
FRACTOSTRATUS
FRAGMENTATION
FRANCHISEMENT
FREDERIKSBERG
FREEZING POINT
FREIGHTLINERS
FRENCH WINDOWS
FREQUENTATION
FREQUENTATIVE
FREUDIAN SLIPS
FRIDGE-FREEZER
FRIGHTENINGLY
FRIGHTFULNESS
FRINGE BENEFIT
FRIVOLOUSNESS
FRONTBENCHERS
FRONTISPIECES
FRONTOGENESIS
FRUITLESSNESS
FRUIT MACHINES

FRUMENTACEOUS
FULL-FASHIONED
FUNCTIONALISM
FUNCTIONALIST
FUNCTIONARIES
FUNDAMENTALLY
FUNNY BUSINESS
FUTURE PERFECT

G

GALLICIZATION
GALLOWS HUMOUR
GALVANOMETRIC
GALVANOSCOPIC
GALVANOTROPIC
GAMBREL-ROOFED
GAMETOGENESIS
GAMMA GLOBULIN
GARBAGE TRUCKS
GARDEN PARTIES
GARRULOUSNESS
GASTROSCOPIST
GEIGER COUNTER
GELANDESPRUNG
GELSENKIRCHEN
GENDER-BENDERS
GENERALISSIMO
GENERAL STRIKE
GENERATION GAP
GENTIANACEOUS
GENUFLECTIONS
GEOCHRONOLOGY
GEODYNAMICIST
GEOMETRICALLY
GEOMORPHOLOGY
GEOPOLITICIAN
GEOSTATIONARY
GEOTACTICALLY
GEOTROPICALLY
GERIATRICIANS
GERMANIZATION
GERMAN MEASLES
GERMANOPHILIA
GERMANOPHOBIA
GERONTOCRATIC
GERONTOLOGIST
GERRYMANDERED
GESTICULATING
GESTICULATION
GESTICULATIVE
GHETTO BLASTER

GLACIOLOGICAL
GLAMORIZATION
GLAMOROUSNESS
GLOBETROTTERS
GLOBETROTTING
GLOBULIFEROUS
GLOCKENSPIELS
GLORIFICATION
GLOSSOGRAPHER
GLUTINOUSNESS
GLYPHOGRAPHER
GLYPHOGRAPHIC
GLYPTOGRAPHER
GLYPTOGRAPHIC
GO-AS-YOU-
  PLEASE
GOING STRAIGHT
GOLDEN HAMSTER
GOLDEN JUBILEE
GOLDEN WEDDING
GOLDFISH BOWLS
GOOD AFTERNOON
GOOD-NATUREDLY
GOOD SAMARITAN
GOOSESTEPPING
GOVERNABILITY
GRACELESSNESS
GRADE CROSSING
GRAMINIVOROUS
GRAMMAR SCHOOL
GRAMMATICALLY
GRAM-MOLECULAR
GRANDCHILDREN
GRANDDAUGHTER
GRANDILOQUENT
GRANULOMATOUS
GRAPHEMICALLY
GRAPHICALNESS
GRAPHIC DESIGN
GRAPHOLOGISTS
GRAPPLING IRON
GRATIFICATION
GRAVEYARD SLOT
GRAVITATIONAL
GREAT YARMOUTH
GREEN-FINGERED
GROTESQUENESS
GROUND STROKES
GROUP CAPTAINS
GROUP PRACTICE
GUARDIAN ANGEL

GUATEMALA CITY
GUBERNATORIAL
GUIDED MISSILE
GUILELESSNESS
GUILTLESSNESS
GUNPOWDER PLOT
GYMNOSPERMISM
GYMNOSPERMOUS
GYNAECOCRATIC
GYNAECOLOGIST
GYNANDROMORPH

H

HACKING COUGHS
HAEMATOGENOUS
HAEMATOLOGIST
HAEMODIALYSIS
HAEMOPHILIOID
HAEMORRHOIDAL
HAGIOGRAPHIES
HAILE SELASSIE
HAIR-RESTORERS
HAIR SPLITTING
HALE AND
  HEARTY
HALF-HEARTEDLY
HALFWAY HOUSES
HALICARNASSUS
HALLUCINATING
HALLUCINATION
HALLUCINATORY
HAMILCAR BARCA
HANDBRAKE TURN
HANDKERCHIEFS
HANG SENG
  INDEX
HAPHAZARDNESS
HARD-HEARTEDLY
HARD-LUCK
  STORY
HARD OF
  HEARING
HARD SHOULDERS
HARMONIZATION
HARUN AL-
  RASHID
HAVE NO TIME
  FOR
HAZARDOUSNESS
HEADSHRINKERS
HEALTHFULNESS
HEALTH VISITOR

HEARTBREAKING
HEARTBROKENLY
HEART DISEASES
HEARTLESSNESS
HEARTSICKNESS
HEARTSOMENESS
HEART-TO-
  HEARTS
HEATH ROBINSON
HEAVY HYDROGEN
HEAVY INDUSTRY
HEDGE SPARROWS
HEEBIE-JEEBIES
HEIRS APPARENT
HELLENIZATION
HELMINTHIASIS
HELMINTHOLOGY
HELTER SKELTER
HELTER-SKELTER
HEMICELLULOSE
HENDECAHEDRON
HEPTADECANOIC
HEPTAMETRICAL
HERBIVOROUSLY
HEREDITAMENTS
HEREFORDSHIRE
HERMAPHRODITE
HERNIORRHAPHY
HEROIC COUPLET
HERPES SIMPLEX
HERPETOLOGIST
HERTFORDSHIRE
HETEROGENEITY
HETEROGENEOUS
HETEROGENESIS
HETEROGENETIC
HETEROGRAPHIC
HETEROMORPHIC
HETEROPLASTIC
HETEROPTEROUS
HETEROSEXUALS
HETEROSPOROUS
HETEROSTYLOUS
HETEROTHALLIC
HETEROTROPHIC
HETEROZYGOSIS
HEURISTICALLY
HIERACOSPHINX
HIEROGLYPHICS
HIEROGLYPHIST

HIGH-AND-
 MIGHTY
HIGH CHURCHMAN
HIGHER-RATE
 TAX
HIGH EXPLOSIVE
HIGHLAND FLING
HIGH-PRESSURED
HIGH-WATER
 MARK
HILARIOUSNESS
HILDEBRANDIAN
HILDEBRANDINE
HISTOCHEMICAL
HOBSON'S
 CHOICE
HO CHI MINH
 CITY
HOIDENISHNESS
HOLE-AND-
 CORNER
HOLIDAYMAKERS
HOLIDAYMAKING
HOLY COMMUNION
HOME ECONOMICS
HOMEOMORPHISM
HOMILETICALLY
HOMOCHROMATIC
HOMOEROTICISM
HOMOGENEOUSLY
HOMOIOTHERMIC
HOMOLOGICALLY
HOMOLOGRAPHIC
HOMOOUSIANISM
HOMOSEXUALITY
HONEYDEW MELON
HONORIFICALLY
HORNS OF
 PLENTY
HORRIFICATION
HORRIPILATION
HORSE CHESTNUT
HORSEWHIPPING
HORTICULTURAL
HOSPITALIZING
HOT-GOSPELLERS
HOT-GOSPELLING
HOT-HEADEDNESS
HOUSEBREAKERS
HOUSEBREAKING
HOUSEHOLD NAME
HOUSE HUSBANDS

HOUSEMISTRESS
HOUSES OF
 CARDS
HOUSE SPARROWS
HOUSEWARMINGS
HOYDENISHNESS
HUCKLEBERRIES
HUMANITARIANS
HUMILIATINGLY
HUNDREDWEIGHT
HUNGER MARCHER
HUNGER MARCHES
HUNGER STRIKER
HUNGER STRIKES
HUNTING GROUND
HURRICANE LAMP
HYALURONIDASE
HYBRIDIZATION
HYDRAULICALLY
HYDROCEPHALIC
HYDROCEPHALUS
HYDROCHLORIDE
HYDRODYNAMICS
HYDROELECTRIC
HYDROGENATION
HYDROGEN BOMBS
HYDROKINETICS
HYDROLYSATION
HYPERCRITICAL
HYPOCHONDRIAC

I

IATROGENICITY
ICE-CREAM
 SODAS
ICHTHYOLOGIST
ICONOMATICISM
IDEALIZATIONS
IDENTICAL TWIN
IDENTITY CARDS
IDEOLOGICALLY
IDIOMATICALLY
IDIOSYNCRATIC
IGNOMINIOUSLY
ILL-CONSIDERED
ILLE-ET-
 VILAINE
ILLOCUTIONARY
ILLUMINATIONS
ILLUSIONISTIC
ILLUSTRATIONS

ILLUSTRIOUSLY
IMAGINATIVELY
IMAGISTICALLY
IMITATIVENESS
IMMATERIALISM
IMMATERIALIST
IMMATERIALITY
IMMATERIALIZE
IMMIGRATIONAL
IMMISCIBILITY
IMMORTALIZING
IMMUNIZATIONS
IMMUNOGENETIC
IMMUNOTHERAPY
IMPALPABILITY
IMPARIPINNATE
IMPARTIBILITY
IMPASSABILITY
IMPASSIONEDLY
IMPASSIVENESS
IMPECCABILITY
IMPECUNIOUSLY
IMPERCEPTIBLE
IMPERCEPTIBLY
IMPERFECTIONS
IMPERFORATION
IMPERIALISTIC
IMPERIOUSNESS
IMPERMISSIBLE
IMPERSONALITY
IMPERSONALIZE
IMPERSONATING
IMPERSONATION
IMPERSONATORS
IMPERTINENTLY
IMPERTURBABLE
IMPERTURBABLY
IMPETUOUSNESS
IMPLACABILITY
IMPONDERABLES
IMPORTUNATELY
IMPOSSIBILITY
IMPOVERISHING
IMPRACTICABLE
IMPRACTICABLY
IMPRACTICALLY
IMPRESSIONISM
IMPRESSIONIST
IMPROBABILITY
IMPROPRIATION
IMPROPRIETIES

IMPROVABILITY
IMPROVIDENTLY
IMPROVISATION
IMPULSIVENESS
INADVERTENTLY
INAPPROPRIATE
INATTENTIVELY
INAUGURATIONS
INCANDESCENCE
INCANTATIONAL
INCAPACITATED
INCAPSULATION
INCARCERATING
INCARCERATION
INCARDINATION
INCLINATIONAL
INCOMBUSTIBLE
INCOME SUPPORT
INCOMMUNICADO
INCOMPETENTLY
INCONCEIVABLE
INCONCEIVABLY
INCONDENSABLE
INCONGRUITIES
INCONGRUOUSLY
INCONSEQUENCE
INCONSIDERATE
INCONSISTENCY
INCONSPICUOUS
INCONSTANCIES
INCONTESTABLE
INCONTESTABLY
INCONVENIENCE
INCONVERTIBLE
INCONVINCIBLE
INCORPORATING
INCORPORATION
INCORPORATIVE
INCORPOREALLY
INCORRECTNESS
INCORRUPTIBLE
INCORRUPTIBLY
INCREDIBILITY
INCREDULOUSLY
INCREMENTALLY
INCRIMINATING
INCRIMINATION
INCRIMINATORY
INCRUSTATIONS
INCULPABILITY
INDEFATIGABLE

INDEFATIGABLY	INFLECTEDNESS	INSUPPORTABLE	INTERPOLATION
INDENTURESHIP	INFLEXIBILITY	INSURRECTIONS	INTERPOLATIVE
INDEPENDENTLY	INFLORESCENCE	INSUSCEPTIBLE	INTERPOSINGLY
INDESCRIBABLE	INFLUENCEABLE	INTANGIBILITY	INTERPOSITION
INDESCRIBABLY	INFLUENTIALLY	INTEGRABILITY	INTERPRETABLE
INDETERMINACY	INFORMATIONAL	INTEGUMENTARY	INTERRACIALLY
INDETERMINATE	INFORMATIVELY	INTELLECTUALS	INTERRELATION
INDETERMINISM	INFRINGEMENTS	INTELLIGENTLY	INTERROGATING
INDETERMINIST	INFURIATINGLY	INTEMPERATELY	INTERROGATION
INDIAN SUMMERS	INGENUOUSNESS	INTENTIONALLY	INTERROGATIVE
INDIFFERENTLY	INGRAINEDNESS	INTERACTIONAL	INTERROGATORS
INDISCERNIBLE	INGURGITATION	INTERACTIVELY	INTERROGATORY
INDISCRETIONS	INHOSPITALITY	INTERACTIVITY	INTERRUPTIBLE
INDISPENSABLE	INIMITABILITY	INTERBREEDING	INTERRUPTIONS
INDISPENSABLY	INJUDICIOUSLY	INTERCALARILY	INTERSECTIONS
INDISPOSITION	INLAND REVENUE	INTERCALATION	INTERSPERSING
INDISTINCTIVE	INNER MONGOLIA	INTERCALATIVE	INTERSPERSION
INDIVIDUALISM	INNOCUOUSNESS	INTERCELLULAR	INTERSTRATIFY
INDIVIDUALIST	INNOVATIONIST	INTERCEPTIONS	INTERTROPICAL
INDIVIDUALITY	INOCULABILITY	INTERCESSIONS	INTERVENTIONS
INDIVIDUALIZE	INOFFENSIVELY	INTERCHANGING	INTRACELLULAR
INDIVIDUATION	INOPERABILITY	INTERCLAVICLE	INTRAMUSCULAR
INDOCTRINATED	INOPPORTUNELY	INTERCOLUMNAR	INTRANSIGENCE
INDOCTRINATOR	INORGANICALLY	INTERCURRENCE	INTRAPERSONAL
INDOLEBUTYRIC	INQUISITIONAL	INTEREST GROUP	INTRATELLURIC
INDUPLICATION	INQUISITIVELY	INTERESTINGLY	INTRAVASATION
INDUSTRIALISM	INQUISITORIAL	INTERFACIALLY	INTRAVENOUSLY
INDUSTRIALIST	INSATIABILITY	INTERFERINGLY	INTRINSICALLY
INDUSTRIALIZE	INSCRIPTIONAL	INTERGALACTIC	INTRODUCTIONS
INDUSTRIOUSLY	INSECTIVOROUS	INTERGRADIENT	INTROGRESSION
INEDUCABILITY	INSENSIBILITY	INTERJECTIONS	INTROSPECTION
INEFFECTIVELY	INSENSITIVELY	INTERLACEMENT	INTROSPECTIVE
INEFFECTUALLY	INSENSITIVITY	INTERLAMINATE	INTUITIVENESS
INEFFICACIOUS	INSIDIOUSNESS	INTERLOCUTION	INVARIABILITY
INEFFICIENTLY	INSIGNIFICANT	INTERLOCUTORS	INVENTIVENESS
INELIGIBILITY	INSOLVABILITY	INTERLOCUTORY	INVENTORIABLE
INEVITABILITY	INSPECTORATES	INTERLUNATION	INVERTEBRATES
INEXHAUSTIBLE	INSPECTORSHIP	INTERMARRIAGE	INVERTED COMMA
INEXHAUSTIBLY	INSPIRATIONAL	INTERMARRYING	INVERTED SNOBS
INEXORABILITY	INSPIRITINGLY	INTERMEDIATOR	INVERTIBILITY
INEXPENSIVELY	INSTABILITIES	INTERMINGLING	INVESTIGATING
INEXPERIENCED	INSTALLATIONS	INTERMISSIONS	INVESTIGATION
INEXPRESSIBLE	INSTANTANEOUS	INTERMITTENCE	INVESTIGATIVE
INEXPRESSIBLY	INSTIGATINGLY	INTERNALIZING	INVESTIGATORS
INFALLIBILITY	INSTINCTIVELY	INTERNATIONAL	INVIDIOUSNESS
INFANT PRODIGY	INSTITUTIONAL	INTEROCEPTIVE	INVINCIBILITY
INFECTIVENESS	INSTRUCTIONAL	INTEROPERABLE	INVIOLABILITY
INFERENTIALLY	INSTRUCTIVELY	INTEROSCULATE	INVOLUNTARILY
INFILTRATIONS	INSUBORDINATE	INTERPELLATOR	IONIAN ISLANDS
INFINITESIMAL	INSUBSTANTIAL	INTERPERSONAL	IRONING BOARDS
INFLAMMATIONS	INSUFFICIENCY	INTERPOLATING	IRRATIONALITY

IRRECLAIMABLE
IRRECOVERABLE
IRRECOVERABLY
IRREFRANGIBLE
IRRELIGIONIST
IRREPLACEABLE
IRREPLEVIABLE
IRREPRESSIBLE
IRREPRESSIBLY
IRRESPONSIBLE
IRRESPONSIBLY
IRRETRIEVABLE
IRRETRIEVABLY
ISOAGGLUTININ
ISODIMORPHISM
ISODIMORPHOUS
ISOELECTRONIC
ISOGEOTHERMAL
ISOLATIONISTS
ISOMERIZATION
ISOSPONDYLOUS
ITALICIZATION

J

JACK-O'-
  LANTERNS
JARGONIZATION
JEFFERSON CITY
JELLIFICATION
JET PROPULSION
JIGGERY-POKERY
JIGSAW PUZZLES
JOBS COMFORTER
JOB'S
  COMFORTER
JOLLIFICATION
JUDICIOUSNESS
JUGLANDACEOUS
JUNIOR SCHOOLS
JURISPRUDENCE
JUSTICIARSHIP
JUSTIFICATION
JUSTIFICATORY
JUXTAPOSITION

K

KALEIDOSCOPES
KALEIDOSCOPIC
KANGAROO COURT
KANGCHENJUNGA

KARL-MARX-
  STADT
KERATOPLASTIC
KETTLEDRUMMER
KEY SIGNATURES
KIDDERMINSTER
KIDNEY MACHINE
KINDERGARTENS
KIND-HEARTEDLY
KINEMATICALLY
KINETIC ENERGY
KINETONUCLEUS
KING'S
  COUNSELS
KING'S
  EVIDENCE
KIRKCUDBRIGHT
KITCHEN GARDEN
KITTY-CORNERED
KLEPTOMANIACS
KNAVE OF
  HEARTS
KNIGHTS-ERRANT
KNOWLEDGEABLE
KNOWLEDGEABLY
KNUCKLE-DUSTER
KWANGSI-CHUANG

L

LABIALIZATION
LABORIOUSNESS
LABOURS OF
  LOVE
LACKADAISICAL
LACTOBACILLUS
LADY BOUNTIFUL
LADY-IN-
  WAITING
LAEVOROTATION
LAEVOROTATORY
LAMELLIBRANCH
LANCE CORPORAL
LANDING FIELDS
LANDING STAGES
LANDING STRIPS
LANDOWNERSHIP
LANTERNSLIDES
LAPAROSCOPIES
LARYNGOLOGIST
LARYNGOSCOPIC
LASER PRINTERS
LATCHKEY CHILD

LATEROVERSION
LATIN AMERICAN
LAUGHINGSTOCK
LAUNDRY BASKET
LEADING LADIES
LEADING LIGHTS
LEAMINGTON SPA
LEATHERJACKET
LECHEROUSNESS
LEGISLATORIAL
LEISHMANIASIS
LEISURELINESS
LEPIDOPTERIST
LEPIDOPTEROUS
LEPTOCEPHALUS
LEPTOPHYLLOUS
LETHARGICALLY
LETTER OPENERS
LETTER PERFECT
LETTER-PERFECT
LETTERPRESSES
LEVEL CROSSING
LEXICOGRAPHER
LEXICOGRAPHIC
LEXICOLOGICAL
LIBRARIANSHIP
LICENSE PLATES
LICENSING LAWS
LIEBFRAUMILCH
LIECHTENSTEIN
LIFE PRESERVER
LIGHT AIRCRAFT
LIGHT-FINGERED
LIGHT-HEADEDLY
LIGNIFICATION
LIMITLESSNESS
LINE-ENGRAVING
LINGUA FRANCAS
LIPARI ISLANDS
LITHOGRAPHING
LITIGIOUSNESS
LITTLE FINGERS
LIVERY COMPANY
LIVERY STABLES
LIVING FOSSILS
LOATHSOMENESS
LODGING HOUSES
LOGOGRAMMATIC
LONDON BRIGADE
LONG HOT
  SUMMER

LONGSUFFERING
LONG VACATIONS
LONS-LE-
  SAUNIER
LOSS ADJUSTERS
LOTHIAN REGION
LOWER EAST
  SIDE
LOW-PASS
  FILTER
LOW-WATER
  MARKS
LUBRICATIONAL
LUDICROUSNESS
LUNATIC FRINGE
LUNCHEONETTES
LYMPHADENITIS
LYMPHATICALLY
LYMPHOBLASTIC
LYMPHOCYTOSIS
LYMPHOCYTOTIC
LYMPHOPOIESIS
LYMPHOPOIETIC

M

MACARONICALLY
MACHIAVELLIAN
MACHICOLATION
MACHINABILITY
MACHINEGUNNED
MACRENCEPHALY
MACROCLIMATIC
MACROECONOMIC
MACROMOLECULE
MACRONUTRIENT
MADE-TO-
  MEASURE
MADHYA PRADESH
MADRIGALESQUE
MAGIC LANTERNS
MAGISTERIALLY
MAGNANIMOUSLY
MAGNETIC FIELD
MAGNETIC HEADS
MAGNETIC NORTH
MAGNETIC POLES
MAGNETIC TAPES
MAGNETIZATION
MAGNETOMETRIC
MAGNETOMOTIVE
MAGNETOSPHERE
MAGNIFICATION

MAGNIFICENTLY	MATERNALISTIC	METALLIZATION	MILLIONAIRESS
MAGNILOQUENCE	MATHEMATICIAN	METALLOGRAPHY	MIMEOGRAPHING
MAGNITUDINOUS	MATRICULATING	METALLURGICAL	MINE DETECTORS
MAGNOLIACEOUS	MATRICULATION	METALLURGISTS	MINERALOGICAL
MAIDS OF HONOUR	MATRILOCALITY	METAMERICALLY	MINERALOGISTS
MAJOR GENERALS	MATURE STUDENT	METAMORPHOSED	MINERAL WATERS
MALACOLOGICAL	MAXILLIPEDARY	METAMORPHOSES	MINICOMPUTERS
MALACOSTRACAN	MEALS ON WHEELS	METAMORPHOSIS	MINISTERIALLY
MALADJUSTMENT	MEANINGLESSLY	METAPHOSPHATE	MIRABILE DICTU
MALADMINISTER	MEASURABILITY	METAPHYSICIAN	MIRROR WRITING
MALADROITNESS	MECHANIZATION	METASTABILITY	MIRTHLESSNESS
MALFORMATIONS	MEDIATIZATION	METEMPIRICIST	MISADVENTURES
MALFUNCTIONED	MEDIATORIALLY	METENCEPHALIC	MISCALCULATED
MALICIOUSNESS	MEDIEVALISTIC	METENCEPHALON	MISCEGENATION
MALIMPRINTING	MEDITERRANEAN	METEOROLOGIST	MISCELLANEOUS
MALTHUSIANISM	MEETINGHOUSES	METHODIZATION	MISCHIEVOUSLY
MANAGEABILITY	MEGACEPHALOUS	METHODOLOGIES	MISCONCEIVING
MANDARIN DUCKS	MEGALOBLASTIC	METHODOLOGIST	MISCONCEPTION
MANGEL-WURZELS	MEGALOMANIACS	METHYL ALCOHOL	MISCONDUCTING
MANIFESTATION	MEGALOPOLITAN	METRONIDAZOLE	MISCONSTRUING
MANIPULATABLE	MELODIOUSNESS	METROPOLITANS	MISDEMEANOURS
MANIPULATIONS	MELODRAMATISI	MEZZO-SOPRANOS	MISERABLENESS
MANTELSHELVES	MELTING POINTS	MICROANALYSIS	MISGOVERNMENT
MANUFACTURERS	MELTON MOWBRAY	MICROANALYTIC	MISJUDGEMENTS
MANUFACTURING	MENINGOCOCCUS	MICROCEPHALIC	MISMANAGEMENT
MANY-SIDEDNESS	MENSTRUATIONS	MICROCHEMICAL	MISPROPORTION
MARAGING STEEL	MENSURATIONAL	MICROCLIMATIC	MISQUOTATIONS
MARCHIONESSES	MENTAL ILLNESS	MICROCOMPUTER	MISSISSIPPIAN
MARKETABILITY	MERCENARINESS	MICRODETECTOR	MISSTATEMENTS
MARKET GARDENS	MERCERIZATION	MICRONUTRIENT	MISTRUSTFULLY
MARRIAGE LINES	MERCHANDISING	MICROORGANISM	MISTRUSTINGLY
MARRONS GLACES	MERCHANT BANKS	MICROPARASITE	MISUNDERSTAND
MARTYRIZATION	MERCILESSNESS	MICROPHYSICAL	MISUNDERSTOOD
MARTYROLOGIST	MERCURIALNESS	MICROTONALITY	MITOCHONDRIAL
MASSACHUSETTS	MERCUROCHROME	MIDDLEBROWISM	MITOCHONDRION
MASSIF CENTRAL	MERCY KILLINGS	MIDDLE EASTERN	MIXED BLESSING
MASS-PRODUCING	MERITOCRACIES	MIDDLE ENGLAND	MIXED METAPHOR
MASTERFULNESS	MERITORIOUSLY	MIDDLE FINGERS	MOBILE LIBRARY
MASTERMINDING	MERRY-GO-ROUNDS	MIDDLE PASSAGE	MOBILIZATIONS
MASTERS-AT-ARMS	MERTHYR TYDFIL	MIDDLESBROUGH	MODERNIZATION
MASTERS OF ARTS	MESENCEPHALIC	MIDDLE SCHOOLS	MODIFIABILITY
MASTERSTROKES	MESENCEPHALON	MIDDLEWEIGHTS	MODIFICATIONS
MASTIGOPHORAN	MESMERIZATION	MIDDLE WESTERN	MODUS OPERANDI
MASTOIDECTOMY	MESSIANICALLY	MID-LIFE CRISES	MOHAMMEDANISM
MATCHLESSNESS	METABOLICALLY	MID-LIFE CRISIS	MOLLIFICATION
MATERFAMILIAS	METABOLIZABLE	MIDWAY ISLANDS	MOLLYCODDLING
MATERIALISTIC	METACHROMATIC	MILK CHOCOLATE	MOMENT OF TRUTH
MATERIALIZING	METALANGUAGES	MILLENNIALIST	MONEYCHANGERS
	METALLIFEROUS	MILLENNIUM BUG	MONEY-GRUBBERS
			MONEY-GRUBBING

MONEY-SPINNERS
MONKEY-PUZZLES
MONMOUTHSHIRE
MONOCHROMATIC
MONOCOTYLEDON
MONOGRAMMATIC
MONOMETALLISM
MONOMETALLIST
MONOMOLECULAR
MONONUCLEOSIS
MONOPHTHONGAL
MONOPSONISTIC
MONOSYLLABISM
MONOSYLLABLES
MONOTREMATOUS
MONSTROSITIES
MONS VENERISES
MONUMENTALITY
MOONLIGHT FLIT
MORALITY PLAYS
MORAL MAJORITY
MORNING PRAYER
MORPHEMICALLY
MORPHOGENESIS
MORPHOGENETIC
MORPHOLOGICAL
MORPHOPHONEME
MORRISDANCERS
MORTIFICATION
MOTHER COUNTRY
MOTHER-OF-
  PEARL
MOTHER TONGUES
MOTION PICTURE
MOTORCYCLISTS
MOTOR SCOOTERS
MOUNTAIN LIONS
MOUNTAINSIDES
MOUNTEBANKERY
MOUTH WATERING
MOUTH-WATERING
MOVABLE FEASTS
MOVING PICTURE
MUHAMMADANISM
MULTICELLULAR
MULTICOLOURED
MULTINATIONAL
MULTIPLE STORE
MULTITUDINOUS
MULTIVIBRATOR
MUMMIFICATION

MURDEROUSNESS
MUSICAL CHAIRS
MUSICOLOGICAL
MYCOBACTERIUM
MYRMECOLOGIST
MYSTIFICATION
MYTHICIZATION

N

NARCOANALYSIS
NARCOTIZATION
NARROW SQUEAKS
NATIONAL DEBTS
NATIONALISTIC
NATIONALITIES
NATIONALIZING
NATIONAL PARKS
NATIONAL TRUST
NATIVITY PLAYS
NATURAL NUMBER
NAUTICAL MILES
NEARSIGHTEDLY
NECESSARY EVIL
NECESSITARIAN
NECESSITATING
NECESSITATION
NECESSITATIVE
NECESSITOUSLY
NECKERCHIEVES
NECROPHILIACS
NEFARIOUSNESS
NEGATIVE POLES
NEGLIGIBILITY
NEGOTIABILITY
NEGRI SEMBILAN
NEIGHBOURHOOD
NEMATHELMINTH
NEOCLASSICISM
NEOCLASSICIST
NEOPLASTICISM
NERVELESSNESS
NERVOUS SYSTEM
NEUROFIBRILAR
NEUROMUSCULAR
NEUROSURGICAL
NEUROVASCULAR
NEW PROVIDENCE
NEW SOUTH
  WALES
NEW TECHNOLOGY
NICKELIFEROUS

NIGGARDLINESS
NIGHTCLUBBING
NIGHTMARISHLY
NIGHT WATCHMAN
NITRIFICATION
NITROBACTERIA
NITROGLYCERIN
NITROPARAFFIN
NO-CLAIMS
  BONUS
NO HOLDS
  BARRED
NOISELESSNESS
NOLI-ME-
  TANGERE
NOLLE PROSEQUI
NOMENCLATURES
NOMOGRAPHICAL
NOMOLOGICALLY
NONAGENARIANS
NONAGGRESSION
NONAPPEARANCE
NONATTENDANCE
NONCOMBATANTS
NONCOMPLIANCE
NONCONCURRENT
NONCONDUCTORS
NONCONFORMISM
NONCONFORMIST
NONCONFORMITY
NONCONTAGIOUS
NONCOOPERATOR
NONFUNCTIONAL
NONINDUSTRIAL
NONINFECTIOUS
NONPRODUCTIVE
NONRETURNABLE
NONSENSICALLY
NO OIL
  PAINTING
NORADRENALINE
NORFOLK ISLAND
NORFOLK JACKET
NORMALIZATION
NORTHALLERTON
NORTH AYRSHIRE
NORTH CAROLINA
NORTHEASTERLY
NORTHEASTWARD
NORTH OSSETIAN
NORTH SOMERSET
NORTH TYNESIDE

NORTHWESTERLY
NORTHWESTWARD
NOSOLOGICALLY
NOSTALGICALLY
NOTICEABILITY
NOTIFICATIONS
NOTORIOUSNESS
NUCLEAR ENERGY
NUCLEAR FAMILY
NUCLEAR WINTER
NUCLEONICALLY
NUCLEOPLASMIC
NUCLEOPROTEIN
NUISANCE VALUE
NULLIFICATION
NUMEROLOGICAL
NUMISMATOLOGY
NURSERY RHYMES
NURSERY SCHOOL
NYMPHAEACEOUS
NYMPHOMANIACS

O

OBJECTIONABLE
OBJECTIONABLY
OBJECTIVENESS
OBJECTIVISTIC
OBJECT LESSONS
OBLATE SPHERES
OBLIVIOUSNESS
OBNOXIOUSNESS
OBSERVATIONAL
OBSERVATORIES
OBSESSIVENESS
OBSTETRICALLY
OBSTETRICIANS
OBSTRUCTIONAL
OBSTRUCTIVELY
OBTAINABILITY
OBTRUSIVENESS
OCCASIONALISM
OCCIDENTALISM
OCCIDENTALIST
OCCIDENTALIZE
OCCLUSIVENESS
OCEANOGRAPHER
OCEANOGRAPHIC
OCTOGENARIANS
ODONTOBLASTIC
ODONTOGLOSSUM
ODONTOGRAPHIC

ODONTOLOGICAL
OFFENSIVENESS
OFFHANDEDNESS
OFFICEHOLDERS
OFFICIOUSNESS
OLD AGE
  PENSION
OLD-BOY
  NETWORK
OLD SCHOOL
  TIES
OLD WIVES'
  TALES
OLIGOPOLISTIC
OLIVE BRANCHES
OMMATOPHOROUS
ONE-NIGHT
  STAND
ONE-TRACK
  MINDS
ON THE
  PREMISES
ONTOGENICALLY
ONTOLOGICALLY
OPENHEARTEDLY
OPEN THE DOOR
  TO
OPERATIONALLY
OPERATIVENESS
OPHTHALMOLOGY
OPISTHOBRANCH
OPPORTUNENESS
OPPORTUNISTIC
OPPORTUNITIES
OPPOSITIONIST
OPPROBRIOUSLY
ORANGE BLOSSOM
ORCHESTRA PITS
ORCHESTRATING
ORCHESTRATION
ORDINARY LEVEL
ORDZHONIKIDZE
ORGAN GRINDERS
ORGANIZATIONS
ORGANOGENESIS
ORGANOGENETIC
ORGANOGRAPHIC
ORGANOLOGICAL
ORGANOTHERAPY
ORIENTALISTIC
ORIENTATIONAL
ORNAMENTATION

ORNITHISCHIAN
ORNITHOLOGIST
ORTHOCEPHALIC
ORTHOEPICALLY
ORTHOGNATHISM
ORTHOGNATHOUS
ORTHOHYDROGEN
ORTHOSTICHOUS
OSCILLOGRAPHY
OSTENSIBILITY
OSTEOMALACIAL
OSTEOMYELITIS
OTHER-DIRECTED
OUTBOARD MOTOR
OUTDISTANCING
OUTGENERALING
OUTGENERALLED
OUTMANOEUVRED
OUTSPOKENNESS
OUTSTANDINGLY
OVERABUNDANCE
OVERAMBITIOUS
OVERBALANCING
OVERBEARINGLY
OVERBURDENING
OVERCONFIDENT
OVERCRITICIZE
OVERCULTIVATE
OVERDEVELOPED
OVERELABORATE
OVEREMPHASIZE
OVERESTIMATED
OVERESTIMATES
OVERINDULGING
OVERMASTERING
OVERPOPULATED
OVERREACTIONS
OVERSHADOWING
OVERSTATEMENT
OVERSUBSCRIBE
OVERWEENINGLY
OVOVIVIPAROUS
OWNER-OCCUPIED
OWNER-OCCUPIER
OYSTERCATCHER

P

PADDLE STEAMER
PADDLING POOLS
PAEDIATRICIAN
PAINSTAKINGLY

PAINTBALL GAME
PALAEOECOLOGY
PALAEOGRAPHIC
PALAEONTOLOGY
PALAEOZOOLOGY
PALEOGRAPHERS
PALETTE KNIVES
PALYNOLOGICAL
PANCHROMATISM
PANDORA'S
  BOXES
PANIC DISORDER
PANIC STATIONS
PANIC-STRICKEN
PANORAMICALLY
PANSOPHICALLY
PANTECHNICONS
PAPAVERACEOUS
PAPILLOMATOUS
PARABOLICALLY
PARADE GROUNDS
PARADOXICALLY
PARAGOGICALLY
PARALLELOGRAM
PARALYTICALLY
PARAMAGNETISM
PARANOIACALLY
PARAPHERNALIA
PARASITICALLY
PARASITICIDAL
PARASYNTHESIS
PARASYNTHETON
PARENT COMPANY
PARENTHETICAL
PAR EXCELLENCE
PARKING GARAGE
PARKING LIGHTS
PARKING METERS
PARKINSON'S
  LAW
PARLIAMENTARY
PARROT-FASHION
PART EXCHANGES
PARTHENOCARPY
PARTICIPATING
PARTICIPATION
PARTICIPIALLY
PARTI-COLOURED
PARTICULARISM
PARTICULARIST
PARTICULARITY

PARTICULARIZE
PARTS OF
  SPEECH
PASSEMENTERIE
PASSIONFLOWER
PASSIONLESSLY
PASSIVIZATION
PATENT LEATHER
PATERFAMILIAS
PATERNALISTIC
PATHOGNOMONIC
PATRIOTICALLY
PATRISTICALLY
PATRONIZINGLY
PAY-AND-
  DISPLAY
PEACEABLENESS
PEACE DIVIDEND
PEACE OFFERING
PECKING ORDERS
PECTORAL CROSS
PECULIARITIES
PEDAGOGICALLY
PEDESTRIANIZE
PEDIATRICIANS
PEDUNCULATION
PELOPONNESIAN
PELTIER EFFECT
PEMBROKESHIRE
PENALTY CORNER
PENEPLANATION
PENETRABILITY
PENETRATINGLY
PENETRATIVELY
PENICILLATION
PENITENTIALLY
PENNILESSNESS
PENNSYLVANIAN
PENNY-DREADFUL
PENNY FARTHING
PENNY-FARTHING
PENNY-PINCHERS
PENNY-PINCHING
PENNY WHISTLES
PENTANOIC ACID
PEOPLE CARRIER
PEPPER-AND-
  SALT
PEPTONIZATION
PERAMBULATING
PERAMBULATION

PERAMBULATORS
PERAMBULATORY
PERCUSSION CAP
PERCUSSIONIST
PEREGRINATION
PERFECTIONISM
PERFECTIONIST
PERFUNCTORILY
PERICARPOIDAL
PERICHONDRIUM
PERIODIC TABLE
PERIOPERATIVE
PERISHABILITY
PERISSODACTYL
PERMANENT WAVE
PERMANENT WAYS
PERMUTATIONAL
PERPENDICULAR
PERSEVERATION
PERSONALISTIC
PERSONALITIES
PERSONALIZING
PERSONIFIABLE
PERSPECTIVISM
PERSPICACIOUS
PERVASIVENESS
PERVERTEDNESS
PETROCHEMICAL
PETROL STATION
PETROPAVLOVSK
PETTY OFFICERS
PHALLOCENTRIC
PHARMACEUTICS
PHARMACOGNOSY
PHARMACOPOEIA
PHARYNGOSCOPE
PHARYNGOSCOPY
PHELLOGENETIC
PHENCYCLIDINE
PHENOMENALISM
PHENOMENALIST
PHENOMENOLOGY
PHENOTHIAZINE
PHENYLALANINE
PHI BETA
KAPPAS
PHILANTHROPIC
PHILHELLENISM
PHILOSOPHICAL
PHILOSOPHIZED
PHILOSOPHIZER

PHI-PHENOMENON
PHOSPHORYLASE
PHOTOCHEMICAL
PHOTOCOMPOSER
PHOTODYNAMICS
PHOTOELECTRIC
PHOTOELECTRON
PHOTOEMISSION
PHOTOEMISSIVE
PHOTOENGRAVER
PHOTO FINISHES
PHOTOGRAPHERS
PHOTOGRAPHING
PHOTOPERIODIC
PHOTORECEPTOR
PHOTOSTATTING
PHRASEOGRAPHY
PHRASEOLOGIST
PHRENOLOGICAL
PHYCOMYCETOUS
PHYLLOQUINONE
PHYSICALISTIC
PHYSICAL JERKS
PHYSIOGNOMIES
PHYSIOGNOMIST
PHYSIOGRAPHER
PHYSIOGRAPHIC
PHYSIOLOGICAL
PHYSIOLOGISTS
PHYSIOTHERAPY
PHYSOCLISTOUS
PHYSOSTIGMINE
PHYTOPLANKTON
PICTURESQUELY
PICTURE WINDOW
PIECES OF
EIGHT
PIEZOELECTRIC
PIGEON-CHESTED
PIGHEADEDNESS
PILOT OFFICERS
PINK ELEPHANTS
PINKING SHEARS
PISCICULTURAL
PITCHED BATTLE
PLACE SETTINGS
PLAGIOTROPISM
PLAINTIVENESS
PLASTIC BULLET
PLATINIFEROUS
PLATINIRIDIUM

PLATINIZATION
PLATINUM-BLOND
PLATITUDINIZE
PLATITUDINOUS
PLATYHELMINTH
PLAYING FIELDS
PLENTEOUSNESS
PLENTIFULNESS
PLIMSOLL LINES
PLOUGHMANSHIP
PLURALIZATION
PNEUMATICALLY
PNEUMATOLYSIS
PNEUMATOMETER
PNEUMATOMETRY
PNEUMATOPHORE
PNEUMOGASTRIC
PNEUMONECTOMY
POETIC JUSTICE
POETIC LICENCE
POETS LAUREATE
POINTLESSNESS
POINTS OF
ORDER
POINT-TO-
POINTS
POISONOUSNESS
POLE POSITIONS
POLICE OFFICER
POLICE STATION
POLIOMYELITIS
POLLING BOOTHS
POLLINIFEROUS
POLYADELPHOUS
POLYCHROMATIC
POLYCOTYLEDON
POLYDACTYLOUS
POLYEMBRYONIC
POLYGALACEOUS
POLYGONACEOUS
POLYPHOSPHATE
POLYPROPYLENE
POLYPROTODONT
POLYSYLLABLES
POLYSYLLOGISM
POLYSYNTHESIS
PONDERABILITY
PONDEROUSNESS
PONTIFICATING
POOR RELATIONS
PORCELLANEOUS

PORNOGRAPHERS
PORT ELIZABETH
POSITIVE POLES
POSSIBILITIES
POSTAGE STAMPS
POSTCLASSICAL
POSTER COLOURS
POSTE RESTANTE
POSTGRADUATES
POSTMAN'S
KNOCK
POST OFFICE
BOX
POSTOPERATIVE
POSTPONEMENTS
POTATO BEETLES
POTENTIOMETER
POTTER'S
WHEELS
POTTY-TRAINING
POWERLESSNESS
POWER POLITICS
POWER STATIONS
POWER STEERING
PRACTICAL JOKE
PRACTITIONERS
PRAGMATICALLY
PRAYER MEETING
PRAYING MANTIS
PREADAPTATION
PREADOLESCENT
PRECAUTIONARY
PRECEPTORSHIP
PRECIOUS METAL
PRECIOUS STONE
PRECIPITATELY
PRECIPITATING
PRECIPITATION
PRECIPITATIVE
PRECIPITOUSLY
PRECONCEPTION
PRECONDITIONS
PRECONIZATION
PREDATORINESS
PREDETERMINED
PREDETERMINER
PREDICABILITY
PREDICATIVELY
PREDILECTIONS
PREDOMINANTLY
PREDOMINATING

PREDOMINATION
PREFABRICATED
PREFABRICATOR
PREFERABILITY
PREFIGURATION
PREFIGURATIVE
PREFIGUREMENT
PREJUDGEMENTS
PRELIMINARIES
PRELIMINARILY
PREMATURENESS
PREMEDICATION
PREMEDITATION
PREMEDITATIVE
PREOCCUPATION
PREORDINATION
PREPARATORILY
PREPONDERANCE
PREPONDERATED
PREPOSITIONAL
PREPOSSESSING
PREPOSSESSION
PRE-RAPHAELITE
PREREQUISITES
PRESBYTERIANS
PRESCRIPTIBLE
PRESCRIPTIONS
PRESENTATIONS
PRESENTIMENTS
PRESERVATIVES
PRESS AGENCIES
PRESS CUTTINGS
PRESS RELEASES
PRESSURE GROUP
PRESSURE POINT
PRESUMPTIVE_Y
PRETENTIOUSLY
PRETERNATURAL
PREVARICATING
PREVARICATION
PREVARICATORS
PRICELESSNESS
PRIMARY COLOUR
PRIMARY SCHOOL
PRIMARY STRESS
PRIME MERIDIAN
PRIME MINISTER
PRIMITIVENESS
PRIMITIVISTIC
PRIMOGENITURE
PRINCE CONSORT

PRINCIPAL BOYS
PRINTED MATTER
PRINTING PRESS
PRISONER OF
    WAR
PRISON VISITOR
PRIVATE MEMBER
PRIVATE SCHOOL
PRIVATE SECTOR
PRIVATIZATION
PRIZEFIGHTERS
PRIZEFIGHTING
PROBABILISTIC
PROBABILITIES
PROCESS-SERVER
PROCLAMATIONS
PROCONSULATES
PROCRASTINATE
PROCTOLOGICAL
PRODUCIBILITY
PROFESSIONALS
PROFESSORIATE
PROFESSORSHIP
PROFITABILITY
PROFIT MARGINS
PROFIT SHARING
PROGNOSTICATE
PROGRESSIONAL
PROGRESSIVELY
PROGRESSIVISM
PROGRESSIVIST
PROHIBITIVELY
PROJECTIONIST
PROLEPTICALLY
PROLIFERATING
PROLIFERATION
PROLIFERATIVE
PROLONGATIONS
PROMENADE DECK
PROMINENTNESS
PROMISCUOUSLY
PROMISED LANDS
PROMISINGNESS
PROMOTIVENESS
PRONOMINALIZE
PRONOUNCEABLE
PRONOUNCEMENT
PRONUNCIATION
PROPAGABILITY
PROPAGANDISTS
PROPAGANDIZED

PROPAGATIONAL
PROPAROXYTONE
PROPHETICALLY
PROPHYLACTICS
PROPITIATIOUS
PROPORTIONATE
PROPORTIONING
PROPOSITIONAL
PROPOSITIONED
PROPRIETARILY
PROPRIETORIAL
PROPRIOCEPTOR
PROSCRIPTIONS
PROSELYTIZERS
PROSELYTIZING
PROSOPOPOEIAL
PROSTAGLANDIN
PROSTATECTOMY
PROTECTIONISM
PROTECTIONIST
PROTECTORATES
PROTEINACEOUS
PROTESTANTISM
PROTESTATIONS
PROTHETICALLY
PROTOCHORDATE
PROTOHISTORIC
PROTOLANGUAGE
PROTUBERANCES
PROTUBERANTLY
PROVINCIALISM
PROVINCIALITY
PROVING GROUND
PROVISIONALLY
PROVOCATIVELY
PROXIMATENESS
PSEPHOLOGICAL
PSEPHOLOGISTS
PSEUDOMORPHIC
PSYCHIATRISTS
PSYCHOANALYSE
PSYCHOANALYST
PSYCHOANALYZE
PSYCHOBIOLOGY
PSYCHODYNAMIC
PSYCHOGENESIS
PSYCHOGENETIC
PSYCHOGNOSTIC
PSYCHOGRAPHIC
PSYCHOHISTORY
PSYCHOKINESIS

PSYCHOKINETIC
PSYCHOLOGICAL
PSYCHOLOGISTS
PSYCHOMETRICS
PSYCHOPHYSICS
PSYCHOSOMATIC
PSYCHOSURGERY
PSYCHOTHERAPY
PSYCHOTICALLY
PSYCHROPHILIC
PTERIDOLOGIST
PTERIDOPHYTIC
PUBLIC COMPANY
PUBLIC SCHOOLS
PULVERIZATION
PUNCTILIOUSLY
PUNISHABILITY
PURITANICALLY
PURPLE PASSAGE
PURPOSELESSLY
PURPOSIVENESS
PUSILLANIMITY
PUSILLANIMOUS
PUT OUT OF
    SIGHT
PYRHELIOMETER
PYROPHOSPHATE

Q

QUADRICIPITAL
QUADRILATERAL
QUADRILLIONTH
QUADRIPARTITE
QUADRISECTION
QUADRIVALENCY
QUADRUPLICATE
QUADRUPLICITY
QUALIFICATION
QUALIFICATORY
QUALITATIVELY
QUANTUM THEORY
QUARTERFINALS
QUARTERMASTER
QUARTERSTAFFS
QUARTERSTAVES
QUARTZIFEROUS
QUEENS CONSORT
QUEEN'S
    COUNSEL
QUEEN'S
    ENGLISH

QUERULOUSNESS
QUESTIONINGLY
QUESTION MARKS
QUESTIONNAIRE
QUICK-TEMPERED
QUINDECENNIAL
QUINQUAGESIMA
QUINQUEVALENT
QUINTILLIONTH
QUINTUPLICATE
QUODLIBETICAL
QUOTATION MARK

R
RABBIT HUTCHES
RABBIT PUNCHES
RABBIT WARRENS
RABBLE-ROUSING
RACK-AND-
 PINION
RADIOACTIVATE
RADIOACTIVITY
RADIOCHEMICAL
RADIOGRAPHERS
RADIOISOTOPIC
RADIOTELEGRAM
RADIOTELETYPE
RAG-AND-BONE
 MAN
RAINBOW NATION
RAMIFICATIONS
RANCOROUSNESS
RANDOMIZATION
RAPPROCHEMENT
RAPTUROUSNESS
RAREFACTIONAL
RATEABLE VALUE
RATIOCINATION
RATIONALISTIC
RATIONALIZING
RATUSHINSKAYA
REACTIONARIES
READJUSTMENTS
READ-WRITE
 HEAD
REAFFIRMATION
REAFFORESTING
REALISTICALLY
REAPPOINTMENT
REARRANGEMENT
RECALCITRANCE

RECAPITULATED
RECEPTIONISTS
RECEPTION ROOM
RECESSIVENESS
RECIPROCALITY
RECIPROCATING
RECIPROCATION
RECIPROCATIVE
RECOGNITIONAL
RECOLLECTIONS
RECOMBINATION
RECOMMENDABLE
RECOMPENSABLE
RECOMPOSITION
RECONCILEMENT
RECONCILINGLY
RECONDITENESS
RECONDITIONED
RECONDITIONER
RECONNOITRING
RECONSIDERING
RECONSTITUENT
RECONSTITUTED
RECONSTRUCTED
RECONSTRUCTOR
RECORD-CHANGER
RECORD LIBRARY
RECORD PLAYERS
RECRIMINATING
RECRIMINATION
RECRIMINATIVE
RECRIMINATORY
RECRUDESCENCE
RECRYSTALLIZE
RECTIFICATION
RED BLOOD
 CELLS
REDEEMABILITY
REDEVELOPMENT
REDISTRIBUTED
RED-LETTER
 DAYS
REDUPLICATING
REDUPLICATION
REDUPLICATIVE
REEFER JACKETS
RE-ENFORCEMENT
RE-EXAMINATION
RE-EXPORTATION
REFERENCE BOOK
REFLEXIVENESS

REFORESTATION
REFORMATIONAL
REFORMATORIES
REFRACTOMETER
REFRACTOMETRY
REFRIGERATING
REFRIGERATION
REFRIGERATIVE
REFRIGERATORS
REFURBISHMENT
REGARDFULNESS
REGIMENTATION
REGISTRARSHIP
REGISTRATIONS
REGRETFULNESS
REGURGITATING
REGURGITATION
REHABILITATED
REIGN OF
 TERROR
REIMBURSEMENT
REIMPORTATION
REINCARNATING
REINCARNATION
REINFORCEMENT
REINSTATEMENT
REJUVENESCENT
RELATIONSHIPS
RELIGIOUSNESS
RELINQUISHING
REMINISCENCES
REMISSIBILITY
REMONSTRANCES
REMONSTRATING
REMONSTRATION
REMONSTRATIVE
REMORSELESSLY
REMOTE CONTROL
RENATIONALIZE
RENEGOTIATION
RENSSELAERITE
RENUNCIATIONS
REPEATABILITY
REPELLINGNESS
REPERCUSSIONS
REPLENISHMENT
REPOSEFULNESS
REPREHENDABLE
REPREHENSIBLE
REPREHENSIBLY
REPRESENTABLE

REPROACHFULLY
REPROACHINGLY
REPRODUCTIONS
REPROGRAPHICS
REPUBLICANISM
REPUBLICANIZE
REPUBLICATION
REPUBLISHABLE
REPULSIVENESS
REQUISITIONED
REQUISITIONER
RESENTFULNESS
RESISTIBILITY
RESISTIVENESS
RESOLVABILITY
RESOURCEFULLY
RESPIRABILITY
RESPIRATIONAL
RESPLENDENTLY
RESTAURANT CAR
RESTAURATEURS
RESTRAININGLY
RESTRICTIVELY
RESTRUCTURING
RESURRECTIONS
RESUSCITATING
RESUSCITATION
RESUSCITATIVE
RETAINABILITY
RETENTIVENESS
RETICULATIONS
RETINOSCOPIST
RETROACTIVELY
RETROACTIVITY
RETROGRESSING
RETROGRESSION
RETROGRESSIVE
RETROSPECTION
RETROSPECTIVE
RETURNABILITY
REUNIFICATION
REUTILIZATION
REVEALABILITY
REVELATIONIST
REVERBERATING
REVERBERATION
REVERBERATIVE
REVERBERATORY
REVERENTIALLY
REVERSIBILITY
REVOLUTIONARY

REVOLUTIONIST
REVOLUTIONIZE
RHABDOMANTIST
RHAPSODICALLY
RHIZOCEPHALAN
RHIZOMORPHOUS
RHODOCHROSITE
RHODODENDRONS
RIBEIRAO PRETO
RIGHTEOUSNESS
RIGHT TRIANGLE
ROAD ALLOWANCE
ROCK-AND-
   ROLLER
ROCKING CHAIRS
ROCKING HORSES
ROGUES'
   GALLERY
ROLLER COASTER
ROLLER-SKATERS
ROLLER SKATING
ROLLING STONES
ROLL OF
   HONOURS
ROLL-ON ROLL-
   OFF
ROMAN CATHOLIC
ROMAN NUMERALS
ROMANTICIZING
ROOMING HOUSES
RORSCHACH TEST
ROTARY TILLERS
ROTTEN BOROUGH
ROUGH AND
   READY
ROUGH-AND-
   READY
ROUGH DIAMONDS
ROUND BRACKETS
ROUND-THE-
   CLOCK
ROXBURGHSHIRE
ROYAL HIGHNESS
RUBBERNECKING
RUBBER-STAMPED
RUMOURMONGERS
RUTHERFORDIUM
RYUKYU ISLANDS

S

SABRE-RATTLING
SACCHARIMETER

SACCHAROMETER
SACRIFICEABLE
SACRIFICIALLY
SACRIFICINGLY
SACROSANCTITY
SADOMASOCHISM
SADOMASOCHIST
SAFETY CATCHES
SAFETY CURTAIN
SAFETY ISLANDS
SAFETY MATCHES
SAGACIOUSNESS
SAINT LAWRENCE
SAKHA REPUBLIC
SALACIOUSNESS
SALAD DRESSING
SALPINGECTOMY
SALVATION ARMY
SALVATIONISTS
SAM BROWNE
   BELT
SAN BERNARDINO
SANCTIMONIOUS
SAND-BLINDNESS
SANDWICH BOARD
SAN FRANCISCAN
SANGUINOLENCY
SANITARY TOWEL
SAN LUIS
   POTOSI
SANTA CATARINA
SAPROGENICITY
SARCASTICALLY
SARCOPHAGUSES
SATANICALNESS
SATIRICALNESS
SATISFACTIONS
SATURNINENESS
SCANDALMONGER
SCARIFICATION
SCATTERBRAINS
SCENESHIFTERS
SCEPTICALNESS
SCHEMATICALLY
SCHIZOCARPOUS
SCHIZOGENESIS
SCHIZOGENETIC
SCHIZOMYCETIC
SCHIZOPHRENIA
SCHIZOPHRENIC
SCHOLARLINESS

SCHOLASTICATE
SCHOLASTICISM
SCHOOLFELLOWS
SCHOOL-LEAVERS
SCHOOLMARMISH
SCHOOLMASTERS
SCHOOLTEACHER
SCIENTOLOGIST
SCILLY ISLANDS
SCINTILLATING
SCINTILLATION
SCLEROPROTEIN
SCOLOPENDRINE
SCORCHED EARTH
SCORIFICATION
SCRIPTWRITERS
SCRIPTWRITING
SCULPTURESQUE
SEANAD EIREANN
SEA OF
   TROUBLES
SEARCH PARTIES
SEARCH WARRANT
SEASON TICKETS
SEAWORTHINESS
SECESSIONISTS
SECLUSIVENESS
SECONDARINESS
SECOND COUSINS
SECOND-GUESSED
SECOND THOUGHT
SECRETARYSHIP
SECRETIVENESS
SECRET SERVICE
SECURITY RISKS
SEDENTARINESS
SEDIMENTARILY
SEDIMENTATION
SEDIMENTOLOGY
SEDITIOUSNESS
SEDUCTIVENESS
SEGREGATIONAL
SEINE-MARITIME
SEISMOGRAPHER
SEISMOGRAPHIC
SEISMOLOGISTS
SELECTIVENESS
SELENOGRAPHER
SELENOGRAPHIC
SELF-ABASEMENT
SELF-ADDRESSED

SELF-ANNEALING
SELF-APPOINTED
SELF-ASSERTION
SELF-ASSERTIVE
SELF-ASSURANCE
SELF-CONFESSED
SELF-CONFIDENT
SELF-CONSCIOUS
SELF-CONTAINED
SELF-DECEPTION
SELF-DECEPTIVE
SELF-DEFEATING
SELF-EVIDENTLY
SELF-IMPORTANT
SELF-INDUCTION
SELF-INDUCTIVE
SELF-INDULGENT
SELF-INFLICTED
SELF-KNOWLEDGE
SELF-PITYINGLY
SELF-POSSESSED
SELF PROPELLED
SELF-RESTRAINT
SELF-RIGHTEOUS
SELF-SACRIFICE
SELF-SATISFIED
SELLER'S
   MARKET
SELLING-PLATER
SELLING POINTS
SEMASIOLOGIST
SEMIAUTOMATIC
SEMICONDUCTOR
SEMICONSCIOUS
SEMIDETACHEDS
SEMIFINALISTS
SEMIPALATINSK
SEMIPARASITIC
SEMIPERMEABLE
SEMIPORCELAIN
SEMPER FIDELIS
SEMPER PARATUS
SENIOR CITIZEN
SENSATIONALLY
SENSELESSNESS
SENSITIVENESS
SENSITIZATION
SENTENTIOUSLY
SENTIMENTALLY
SEQUENTIALITY
SEQUESTRATING

SEQUESTRATION
SERBO-CROATIAN
SERGEANT MAJOR
SERIALIZATION
SERIAL NUMBERS
SERICULTURIST
SERJEANT AT
LAW
SERVICE CHARGE
SEVENTH HEAVEN
SEVEN-YEAR
ITCH
SEWING MACHINE
SEXAGENARIANS
SEXPLOITATION
SHAKESPEAREAN
SHAMELESSNESS
SHAPELESSNESS
SHARP PRACTICE
SHARPSHOOTERS
SHEEPSHEARING
SHEPHERDESSES
SHIFTLESSNESS
SHIP'S
CHANDLER
SHIRTWAISTERS
SHOCK ABSORBER
SHOOTING MATCH
SHOOTING STARS
SHOOTING STICK
SHOP ASSISTANT
SHORT-CHANGING
SHORT CIRCUITS
SHORT-TEMPERED
SHOULDER BLADE
SHOULDER STRAP
SHROVE TUESDAY
SICK HEADACHES
SIDESPLITTING
SIERRA LEONEAN
SIGHTLESSNESS
SIGMOIDOSCOPE
SIGMOIDOSCOPY
SIGNATURE TUNE
SIGNIFICANTLY
SIGNIFICATION
SIGNIFICATIVE
SILENT PARTNER
SILVER BIRCHES
SILVER JUBILEE
SILVER-TONGUED

SILVER WEDDING
SILVICULTURAL
SIMPLE MACHINE
SINGLE-DECKERS
SINGULARITIES
SIPHONOSTELIC
SIT ON THE
FENCE
SITTING PRETTY
SITTING TARGET
SIXTEENTH NOTE
SKEET SHOOTING
SKIRTING BOARD
SLAP AND
TICKLE
SLEDGEHAMMERS
SLEEPING PILLS
SLEEP LEARNING
SLEEPLESSNESS
SLEIGHT OF
HAND
SLIDING SCALES
SLIPSTREAMING
SMALL FORTUNES
SMALLHOLDINGS
SMELLING SALTS
SMOOTH-TONGUED
SNAKE CHARMERS
SNAP FASTENERS
SNEAK PREVIEWS
SNOW BLINDNESS
SOCIAL CHAPTER
SOCIAL CLIMBER
SOCIALIZATION
SOCIAL SCIENCE
SOCIAL SERVICE
SOCIAL WORKERS
SOCIOECONOMIC
SOCIOLINGUIST
SODA FOUNTAINS
SOFT-PEDALLING
SOLAR CONSTANT
SOLDERING IRON
SOLDIERLINESS
SOLEMNIZATION
SOLICITATIONS
SOLICITORSHIP
SOLILOQUIZING
SOLVAY PROCESS
SOMATOPLASTIC
SOMATOPLEURAL

SOMERSAULTING
SOMNAMBULANCE
SOMNAMBULATOR
SOMNAMBULISTS
SONS-OF-
BITCHES
SOPHISTICALLY
SOPHISTICATED
SOPHISTICATES
SOPHISTICATOR
SOPORIFICALLY
SORROWFULNESS
SOUL-SEARCHING
SOUNDING BOARD
SOUNDLESSNESS
SOUNDPROOFING
SOUTH CAROLINA
SOUTHEAST ASIA
SOUTHEASTERLY
SOUTHEASTWARD
SOUTHEND-ON-
SEA
SOUTHERLINESS
SOUTHERN OCEAN
SOUTH TYNESIDE
SOUTHWESTERLY
SOUTHWESTWARD
SOVIETIZATION
SPACE INVADERS
SPACE SHUTTLES
SPACE STATIONS
SPASMODICALLY
SPEAKING TUBES
SPECIAL BRANCH
SPECIAL SCHOOL
SPECIFICATION
SPECIFICATIVE
SPECTACULARLY
SPECTROGRAPHY
SPECTROMETRIC
SPECTROSCOPES
SPECTROSCOPIC
SPECULATIVELY
SPEECH THERAPY
SPELEOLOGICAL
SPELEOLOGISTS
SPENDING MONEY
SPERMATICALLY
SPERMATOPHORE
SPERMATOPHYTE
SPHERICALNESS

SPHEROIDICITY
SPHINGOMYELIN
SPHYGMOGRAPHY
SPINE-CHILLING
SPINELESSNESS
SPINNING JENNY
SPINNING WHEEL
SPIRITUALISTS
SPIRITUALIZER
SPIT AND
POLISH
SPITTING IMAGE
SPLAYFOOTEDLY
SPLENDIFEROUS
SPLINTER GROUP
SPONTANEOUSLY
SPORTSMANLIKE
SPORTSMANSHIP
SPREAD BETTING
SPREAD-EAGLING
SPRIGHTLINESS
SPRING CHICKEN
SPRING-CLEANED
SQUANDERINGLY
SQUARE-BASHING
SQUARE BRACKET
SQUEAMISHNESS
SQUIREARCHIES
STABILIZATION
STAFF OFFICERS
STAFFORDSHIRE
STAFF SERGEANT
STAGE MANAGERS
STAGE-MANAGING
STAGE WHISPERS
STALKING-HORSE
STAMINIFEROUS
STANDARDIZING
STANDARD LAMPS
STANDING ORDER
STANDOFFISHLY
STAPHYLOCOCCI
STARCH-REDUCED
STARTING BLOCK
STARTING GATES
STARTING PRICE
STATELESSNESS
STATE-OF-THE-
ART
STATESMANLIKE
STATESMANSHIP

STATION BREAKS
STATION HOUSES
STATIONMASTER
STATION WAGONS
STATISTICALLY
STATISTICIANS
STEADFASTNESS
STEAMROLLERED
STEEPLECHASER
STEEPLECHASES
STEERING WHEEL
STENOGRAPHERS
STENOPETALOUS
STENOPHYLLOUS
STEPPING-STONE
STERCORACEOUS
STEREOGRAPHIC
STEREOSCOPIST
STEREOTROPISM
STEREOTYPICAL
STERILIZATION
STICKING POINT
STICK IN THE
    MUD
STICK-IN-THE-
    MUD
STIFF UPPER
    LIP
STILETTO HEELS
STIMULATINGLY
STIPENDIARIES
STIRLINGSHIRE
STOCKBREEDERS
STOCKBREEDING
STOCK EXCHANGE
STOICHIOMETRY
STOLONIFEROUS
STOMATOPLASTY
STOP AT
    NOTHING
STORM TROOPERS
STORMY PETRELS
STOVEPIPE HATS
STRAIGHTEDGES
STRAIGHTENING
STRAIGHT-FACED
STRAIGHT FIGHT
STRAIGHT RAZOR
STRAITJACKETS
STRANGLEHOLDS
STRANGULATING
STRANGULATION

STRATEGICALLY
STRATIGRAPHER
STRATIGRAPHIC
STRATOCUMULUS
STRATOSPHERIC
STRAW-COLOURED
STREETWALKERS
STRENGTHENING
STRENUOUSNESS
STREPTOCARPUS
STREPTOCOCCAL
STREPTOCOCCUS
STREPTOKINASE
STRIKEBREAKER
STRIP CARTOONS
STRIP LIGHTING
STROBILACEOUS
STROMATOLITIC
STRUCTURALISM
STRUCTURALIST
STUDENTS'
    UNION
STUDIO COUCHES
STUFFED SHIRTS
STYLISTICALLY
SUBCOMMITTEES
SUBCONTINENTS
SUBCONTRACTED
SUBCONTRACTOR
SUBDIVISIONAL
SUBEQUATORIAL
SUBIRRIGATION
SUBJECT MATTER
SUBLIEUTENANT
SUBMACHINE GUN
SUBORDINATING
SUBORDINATION
SUBORDINATIVE
SUBPOPULATION
SUBREPTITIOUS
SUBSCRIPTIONS
SUBSERVIENTLY
SUBSIDIZATION
SUBSTANTIALLY
SUBSTANTIATED
SUBSTANTIATOR
SUBSTANTIVELY
SUBSTANTIVIZE
SUBSTITUTABLE
SUBSTITUTIONS
SUBSTRUCTURAL

SUBSTRUCTURES
SUBTILIZATION
SUBVENTIONARY
SUFFICIENCIES
SUFFOCATINGLY
SUFFRAGANSHIP
SUFFRAGETTISM
SUFFUMIGATION
SULPHADIAZINE
SULPHURIC ACID
SUMMARIZATION
SUMMER SCHOOLS
SUMPTUOUSNESS
SUNDAY SCHOOLS
SUPERABUNDANT
SUPERADDITION
SUPERANNUATED
SUPERCALENDER
SUPERCHARGERS
SUPERCHARGING
SUPERCOLUMNAR
SUPERCRITICAL
SUPEREMINENCE
SUPERFETATION
SUPERFICIALLY
SUPERFLUIDITY
SUPERFLUOUSLY
SUPERHUMANITY
SUPERIMPOSING
SUPERINTENDED
SUPERLATIVELY
SUPERNATATION
SUPERNUMERARY
SUPERORDINATE
SUPERPHYSICAL
SUPERPOSITION
SUPERSENSIBLE
SUPERSTITIONS
SUPERSTITIOUS
SUPERVENIENCE
SUPPLANTATION
SUPPLEMENTARY
SUPPLEMENTING
SUPPLICATIONS
SUPPLY TEACHER
SUPPOSITIONAL
SUPPOSITORIES
SUPRANATIONAL
SURFACE-ACTIVE
SURREPTITIOUS
SURROGATESHIP

SURVIVABILITY
SUSTENTACULAR
SWASHBUCKLING
SWEET NOTHINGS
SWIMMING BATHS
SWIMMING POOLS
SWIZZLE STICKS
SWOLLEN HEADED
SWORDSMANSHIP
SYBARITICALLY
SYLLABOGRAPHY
SYLLEPTICALLY
SYLLOGISTICAL
SYLLOGIZATION
SYMBOLIZATION
SYMMETRICALLY
SYMPATHECTOMY
SYMPATHOLYTIC
SYMPATRICALLY
SYMPHONICALLY
SYMPHYSICALLY
SYNARTHRODIAL
SYNCHRONISTIC
SYNCHRONIZING
SYNDICALISTIC
SYNTACTICALLY
SYNTHETICALLY
SYPHILOLOGIST
SYRINGOMYELIA
SYRINGOMYELIC
SYSTEMATIZING
SYSTEMATOLOGY
SYSTEMIZATION
SYZYGETICALLY

T

TACHISTOSCOPE
TACHYPHYLAXIS
TAKE A BACK
    SEAT
TAKE THE
    PLEDGE
TALKATIVENESS
TALKING POINTS
TANGENTIALITY
TANTALIZATION
TANTALIZINGLY
TAPE RECORDERS
TAR AND
    FEATHER

TARN-ET-
GARONNE
TARTARIZATION
TASTELESSNESS
TATAR REPUBLIC
TAX-DEDUCTIBLE
TAXONOMICALLY
TAYSIDE REGION
TEAR A STRIP
OFF
TECHNOLOGICAL
TECHNOLOGISTS
TEETER-TOTTERS
TELAUTOGRAPHY
TELECOMMUTING
TELEGRAPH POLE
TELEMARKETING
TELENCEPHALIC
TELENCEPHALON
TELEPHOTO LENS
TELEPROMPTERS
TELEUTOSPORIC
TELEVISIONARY
TEMPERABILITY
TEMPERAMENTAL
TEMPERATENESS
TEMPESTUOUSLY
TEMPORARINESS
TEMPORIZATION
TEMPORIZINGLY
TENACIOUSNESS
TENANT FARMERS
TENDENTIOUSLY
TENDERHEARTED
TENDERIZATION
TEN-GALLON
HATS
TENPIN BOWLING
TENTATIVENESS
TERGIVERSATOR
TERMINABILITY
TERMINATIONAL
TERMINOLOGIES
TERMINOLOGIST
TERPSICHOREAN
TERRACED HOUSE
TERRESTRIALLY
TERRORIZATION
TESTIFICATION
TETARTOHEDRAL
TETRABASICITY

TETRACHLORIDE
TETRADYNAMOUS
TETRASTICHOUS
TETRASYLLABIC
TETRASYLLABLE
THALASSOCRACY
THANKLESSNESS
THANKSGIVINGS
THEANTHROPISM
THEANTHROPIST
THEATRICALITY
THE CUT OF A
CARD
THE GONDOLIERS
THE LIONS
SHARE
THE MAGIC
FLUTE
THENCEFORWARD
THEOLOGICALLY
THEORETICALLY
THERIOMORPHIC
THERMOCHEMIST
THERMODYNAMIC
THERMOGENESIS
THERMOGRAPHER
THERMOGRAPHIC
THERMONUCLEAR
THERMOPLASTIC
THERMOSETTING
THERMOS FLASKS
THERMOSTATICS
THERMOTHERAPY
THERMOTROPISM
THETFORD MINES
THIGMOTROPISM
THORACOPLASTY
THOROUGHBREDS
THOROUGHFARES
THOROUGHGOING
THOROUGHPACED
THOUGHTLESSLY
THOUGHT POLICE
THREATENINGLY
THREE-CORNERED
THREE-DAY
EVENT
THREE LINE
WHIP
THREE-LINE
WHIP
THREMMATOLOGY

THUNDERCLOUDS
THUNDERSHOWER
THUNDERSTORMS
THUNDERSTRUCK
THYROIDECTOMY
TIME AFTER
TIME
TIME-AND-
MOTION
TIME-CONSUMING
TIME EXPOSURES
TIME SIGNATURE
TINTINNABULAR
TINTINNABULUM
TITILLATINGLY
TITTLE-TATTLED
TITTLE-TATTLER
TOAD-IN-THE-
HOLE
TOASTING FORKS
TOILET-TRAINED
TOLERABLENESS
TOLERATIONISM
TOLERATIONIST
TONE LANGUAGES
TONGUE TWISTER
TONSILLECTOMY
TOOTHSOMENESS
TOPOGRAPHICAL
TOPOLOGICALLY
TORRE DEL
GRECO
TORTOISESHELL
TOTIPALMATION
TOXICOLOGICAL
TOXICOLOGISTS
TOXOPLASMOSIS
TRACE ELEMENTS
TRACHEOTOMIST
TRADE UNIONISM
TRADE UNIONIST
TRADING ESTATE
TRADING STAMPS
TRADITIONALLY
TRAFFIC CIRCLE
TRAFFIC ISLAND
TRAFFIC LIGHTS
TRAFFIC WARDEN
TRAGICOMEDIES
TRAILER HOUSES
TRANQUILLIZED
TRANQUILLIZER

TRANSACTINIDE
TRANSACTIONAL
TRANSATLANTIC
TRANSCAUCASIA
TRANSCENDENCE
TRANSCENDENCY
TRANSCRIBABLE
TRANSCRIPTION
TRANSFIGURING
TRANSFORMABLE
TRANSGRESSING
TRANSGRESSION
TRANSGRESSIVE
TRANSGRESSORS
TRANSISTORIZE
TRANSLATIONAL
TRANSLATORIAL
TRANSLITERATE
TRANSLOCATION
TRANSMIGRATOR
TRANSMISSIBLE
TRANSMISSIONS
TRANSMITTANCE
TRANSMITTANCY
TRANSMUTATION
TRANSPARENTLY
TRANSPIRATION
TRANSPIRATORY
TRANSPLANTING
TRANSPORTABLE
TRANSPORT CAFE
TRANSPORTEDLY
TRANSPOSITION
TRANSSHIPMENT
TRANSVESTITES
TRANSYLVANIAN
TRAPEZOHEDRAL
TRAPEZOHEDRON
TRAUMATICALLY
TREACHEROUSLY
TREASURERSHIP
TREASURE TROVE
TREASURE-TROVE
TREASURY NOTES
TREMULOUSNESS
TREPONEMATOUS
TRIANGULARITY
TRIANGULATION
TRIATOMICALLY
TRIBOELECTRIC
TRICENTENNIAL

TRICHOLOGISTS
TRICHOMONADAL
TRICHROMATISM
TRIGONOMETRIC
TRILATERATION
TRILINGUALISM
TRIMETHADIONE
TRIPLOBLASTIC
TRIPOLITANIAN
TRISACCHARIDE
TROOP CARRIERS
TROPHALLACTIC
TROPHOBLASTIC
TROUBLEMAKERS
TRUCIAL STATES
TRUSTWORTHILY
TRUTH-FUNCTION
TUBERCULATION
TUBUAI ISLANDS
TUBULIFLOROUS
TURBOCHARGERS
TURBOCHARGING
TURBO-ELECTRIC
TURING MACHINE
TURNING CIRCLE
TURNING POINTS
TWO-WAY
  MIRRORS
TYPOGRAPHICAL
TYRANNIZINGLY
TYRANNOSAURUS
TYRANNOUSNESS

U

UGLY DUCKLINGS
ULTRANATIONAL
UMBELLIFEROUS
UMBILICAL CORD
UNACCOMPANIED
UNACCOUNTABLE
UNACCOUNTABLY
UNADULTERATED
UNADVENTUROUS
UNADVISEDNESS
UNASHAMEDNESS
UNBELIEVINGLY
UNBENDINGNESS
UNBLESSEDNESS
UNCEASINGNESS
UNCEREMONIOUS
UNCERTAINNESS

UNCHALLENGING
UNCHARISMATIC
UNCIRCUMCISED
UNCLEANLINESS
UNCOMFORTABLE
UNCOMFORTABLY
UNCOMPENSATED
UNCOMPETITIVE
UNCOMPLAINING
UNCOMPLICATED
UNCONCERNEDLY
UNCONDITIONAL
UNCONDITIONED
UNCONFORMABLE
UNCONSCIOUSLY
UNCONSTRAINED
UNCONSUMMATED
UNCONTENTIOUS
UNCOORDINATED
UNCROWNED KING
UNDECIDEDNESS
UNDERACHIEVED
UNDERACHIEVER
UNDERBREEDING
UNDERCARRIAGE
UNDERCHARGING
UNDERCURRENTS
UNDERDRAINAGE
UNDEREDUCATED
UNDEREMPLOYED
UNDERESTIMATE
UNDEREXPOSING
UNDEREXPOSURE
UNDERGARMENTS
UNDERGRADUATE
UNDERHANDEDLY
UNDER MILK
  WOOD
UNDERMININGLY
UNDERPAINTING
UNDERPINNINGS
UNDERSTANDING
UNDERSTRENGTH
UNDERSTUDYING
UNDISCIPLINED
UNDISTRIBUTED
UNEARTHLINESS
UNEMBARRASSED
UNENFORCEABLE
UNENLIGHTENED
UNEQUIVOCALLY

UNEXCEPTIONAL
UNEXPERIENCED
UNFALTERINGLY
UNFAMILIARITY
UNFASHIONABLE
UNFEELINGNESS
UNFLINCHINGLY
UNFORESEEABLE
UNFORGETTABLE
UNFORGETTABLY
UNFORTUNATELY
UNFOUNDEDNESS
UNGUARDEDNESS
UNHEALTHINESS
UNICAMERALISM
UNICAMERALIST
UNILATERALISM
UNILLUSTRATED
UNIMPEACHABLE
UNIMPEACHABLY
UNINHABITABLE
UNINHIBITEDLY
UNINTELLIGENT
UNINTENTIONAL
UNINTERRUPTED
UNITED KINGDOM
UNITED NATIONS
UNIVERSALNESS
UNIVERSAL TIME
UNMENTIONABLE
UNMUSICALNESS
UNNATURALNESS
UNNECESSARILY
UNOBTRUSIVELY
UNPATRONIZING
UNPRECEDENTED
UNPREDICTABLE
UNPRESSURIZED
UNPRETENTIOUS
UNQUALIFIABLE
UNQUESTIONING
UNREADABILITY
UNRELENTINGLY
UNRELIABILITY
UNREMITTINGLY
UNREPRESENTED
UNRUFFLEDNESS
UNSAVOURINESS
UNSELFISHNESS
UNSERVICEABLE
UNSIGHTLINESS

UNSOCIABILITY
UNSUBSTANTIAL
UNSUITABILITY
UNSUSTAINABLE
UNTHREATENING
UNTRADITIONAL
UNTRANSFORMED
UNWARRANTABLE
UNWILLINGNESS
UNWRITTEN LAWS
UPRIGHT PIANOS
UP TO THE
  MINUTE
UP-TO-THE-
  MINUTE
URETHROSCOPIC
UTI POSSIDETIS
UTTERABLENESS

V

VACILLATINGLY
VACUUM CLEANER
VALUE-ADDED
  TAX
VALUE JUDGMENT
VALUELESSNESS
VANTAGE POINTS
VAPOURABILITY
VAPOURISHNESS
VARICOSE VEINS
VARIOLIZATION
VASOINHIBITOR
VAULTING HORSE
VEGETARIANISM
VENEREOLOGIST
VENETIAN BLIND
VENTRILOQUIAL
VENTRILOQUISM
VENTRILOQUIST
VENTRILOQUIZE
VERACIOUSNESS
VERBALIZATION
VERBIFICATION
VERITABLENESS
VERMICULATION
VERMINOUSNESS
VERNACULARISM
VERNALIZATION
VERSIFICATION
VESTAL VIRGINS
VESTMANAEYJAR

VEXATIOUSNESS
VEXED QUESTION
VEXILLOLOGIST
VICARIOUSNESS
VICE PRESIDENT
VICIOUS CIRCLE
VICTIMIZATION
VICTORIA CROSS
VICTORIA PLUMS
VILIFICATION
VINDICABILITY
VINICULTURIST
VIOLONCELLIST
VIRGINIA BEACH
VIRGIN ISLANDS
VISCOUNTESSES
VISIONARINESS
VISITING CARDS
VISITORS'
   BOOKS
VISUALIZATION
VITRIFICATION
VITRIOLICALLY
VIVACIOUSNESS
VIVISECTIONAL
VOCIFERATIONS
VOICELESSNESS
VOLATILIZABLE
VOLCANIZATION
VOLCANOLOGIST
VOLUNTARINESS
VOLUNTARISTIC
VOTE OF
   CENSURE
VOTES OF
   THANKS
VOUCHSAFEMENT

VRAISEMBLANCE
VULCANIZATION
VULGARIZATION
VULNERABILITY

W

WALKIE-TALKIES
WALKING PAPERS
WALKING STICKS
WALL PAINTINGS
WALTHAM FOREST
WARM-HEARTEDLY
WASHINGTONIAN
WASTE PRODUCTS
WATCH THE
   CLOCK
WATER BISCUITS
WATER BUFFALOS
WATERING HOLES
WATERING PLACE
WATERPROOFING
WATER SOFTENER
WATER SUPPLIES
WATTLE AND
   DAUB
WEARISOMENESS
WEATHER-BEATEN
WEATHERBOARDS
WEIGHT LIFTERS
WEIGHT LIFTING
WELFARE STATES
WELL-APPOINTED
WELL-CONNECTED
WELL-DEVELOPED
WELL-PRESERVED
WELL-QUALIFIED
WELL-SUPPORTED

WELL-THOUGHT-
   OF
WELSH RAREBITS
WELTERWEIGHTS
WEST BERKSHIRE
WESTERN SAHARA
WEST GLAMORGAN
WEST-NORTHWEST
WEST-SOUTHWEST
WEST YORKSHIRE
WETTING AGENTS
WHEELER DEALER
WHEELER-DEALER
WHIMSICALNESS
WHIPPOORWILLS
WHITE ELEPHANT
WHITE WEDDINGS
WHOLESOMENESS
WHOOPING COUGH
WICKET KEEPERS
WIDE-AWAKENESS
WILDCAT STRIKE
WILHELMSHAVEN
WILL-O'-THE-
   WISPS
WILLOW PATTERN
WINDING SHEETS
WINDOW-DRESSER
WINDOW-SHOPPED
WINDOW-SHOPPER
WING COMMANDER
WITHDRAWNNESS
WITHERINGNESS
WITWATERSRAND
WOLVERHAMPTON
WOMEN'S
   STUDIES

WONDERFULNESS
WONDER-WORKING
WOODCRAFTSMAN
WOOLGATHERING
WORD BLINDNESS
WORD PROCESSOR
WORK-HARDENING
WORSHIPPINGLY
WORTHLESSNESS
WRONGHEADEDLY

X

XANTHOCHROISM
XEROPHTHALMIA
XEROPHTHALMIC
XINJIANG UYGUR

Y

YACHTSMANSHIP
YEOMAN SERVICE
YOUNG MARRIEDS

Z

ZEBRA CROSSING
ZEUGMATICALLY
ZIGZAGGEDNESS
ZINJANTHROPUS
ZOOGEOGRAPHER
ZOOGEOGRAPHIC
ZOOSPORANGIAL
ZOOSPORANGIUM
ZYGAPOPHYSEAL
ZYGODACTYLISM
ZYGODACTYLOUS

A

ABOVE-MENTIONED
ABSENT-MINDEDLY
ABSORBEFACIENT
ABSTEMIOUSNESS
ABSTRACTEDNESS
ABSTRACTIONISM
ACCLIMATIZABLE
ACCOMMODATIONS
ACCOMPANIMENTS
ACCOMPLISHABLE
ACCOMPLISHMENT
ACCOUNTABILITY
ACCUMULATIVELY
ACHONDROPLASIA
ACHROMATICALLY
ACKNOWLEDGMENT
ACQUIRED TASTES
ACROSS THE BOARD
ACROSS-THE-BOARD
ACTION STATIONS
ADENOCARCINOMA
ADMINISTRATION
ADMINISTRATIVE
ADMINISTRATORS
ADMINISTRATRIX
ADULT EDUCATION
ADVANCED LEVELS
ADVANTAGEOUSLY
AEROBALLISTICS
AEROMECHANICAL
AFFECTIONATELY
AFOREMENTIONED
AGGLOMERATIONS
AGGRANDIZEMENT
AGGRESSIVENESS
AGRICULTURISTS
AGROBIOLOGICAL
AGUASCALIENTES
AIR-CONDITIONED
AIR VICE-MARSHAL
ALCOHOLIZATION

ALLEGORIZATION
ALL-IN WRESTLING
ALLITERATIVELY
ALLOPATHICALLY
ALLOPATRICALLY
ALLOTROPICALLY
ALL OVER THE SHOP
ALPES MARITIMES
ALPHABETICALLY
ALSACE-LORRAINE
ALTRUISTICALLY
AMARANTHACEOUS
AMATEURISHNESS
AMBASSADORSHIP
AMBASSADRESSES
AMBIDEXTROUSLY
AMERICAN INDIAN
AMMONIFICATION
AMPHIARTHROSIS
AMPHIBOLOGICAL
AMPHIPROSTYLAR
AMUSEMENT PARKS
ANACARDIACEOUS
ANAESTHETIZING
ANAMNESTICALLY
ANAMORPHOSCOPE
ANATHEMATIZING
ANCIENT MARINER
ANDORRA LA VELLA
ANGINA PECTORIS
ANGLO-AMERICANS
ANGLO-CATHOLICS
ANIMADVERSIONS
ANISODACTYLOUS
ANTAGONIZATION
ANTHROPOLOGIST
ANTHROPOMETRIC
ANTHROPOPATHIC
ANTHROPOSOPHIC
ANTICHLORISTIC
ANTICIPATORILY

ANTIDEPRESSANT
ANTIHISTAMINES
ANTILOGARITHMS
ANTIMONARCHIST
ANTIPERSPIRANT
ANTIPHLOGISTIC
ANTIPRAGMATISM
ANTIQUATEDNESS
ANTIREPUBLICAN
ANTISEPTICALLY
ANTITHETICALLY
APARTMENT HOUSE
APOLOGETICALLY
APOPLECTICALLY
APOSTROPHIZING
APPENDECTOMIES
APPENDICECTOMY
APPLES AND PEARS
APPORTIONMENTS
APPRECIATIVELY
APPREHENSIVELY
APPRENTICESHIP
APPROPRIATIONS
APPROVED SCHOOL
APPROXIMATIONS
ARABIC NUMERALS
ARCHAEOLOGICAL
ARCHAEOLOGISTS
ARCHBISHOPRICS
ARCHETYPICALLY
ARCHIDIACONATE
ARCHIEPISCOPAL
ARCHIMANDRITES
ARCHITECTONICS
ARITHMETICALLY
ARITHMETICIANS
ARRONDISSEMENT
ARTICULATENESS
ARTIODACTYLOUS
AS CLEAR AS A BELL
AS DRUNK AS A LORD
AS SAFE AS HOUSES
ASSASSINATIONS
ASSAULT COURSES

ASSET-STRIPPING
ASSOCIATIONISM
AS THE CASE MAY BE
ASTIGMATICALLY
ASTROLOGICALLY
ASTRONAVIGATOR
ASTRONOMICALLY
ASTROPHYSICIST
ASYMMETRICALLY
ASYMPTOTICALLY
AT DAGGERS DRAWN
ATTRACTIVENESS
AUF WIEDERSEHEN
AUSPICIOUSNESS
AUTHENTICATING
AUTHENTICATION
AUTHENTICITIES
AUTHORITARIANS
AUTHORIZATIONS
AUTOBIOGRAPHER
AUTOBIOGRAPHIC
AUTOCRATICALLY
AUTOIONIZATION
AUTOMATIC PILOT
AUTOPHYTICALLY
AUTORADIOGRAPH
AUTOSUGGESTION
AUTOSUGGESTIVE
AUXILIARY VERBS
AWE-INSPIRINGLY

B

BACCALAUREATES
BACHELOR OF ARTS
BACK FORMATIONS
BACKHANDEDNESS
BACK-SEAT DRIVER
BACTERIOLOGIST
BACTERIOPHAGIC
BACTERIOSTASIS
BACTERIOSTATIC

BALANCE OF
 POWER
BALANCE OF
 TRADE
BALSAMINACEOUS
BANANA
 REPUBLIC
BANNER
 HEADLINE
BAROMETRICALLY
BASIDIOSPOROUS
BASTARDIZATION
BATCH
 PROCESSED
BATHING
 MACHINE
BATTLE
 CRUISERS
BE-ALL AND
 END-ALL
BEASTS OF
 BURDEN
BEATIFICATIONS
BEAUTIFICATION
BEAUTY
 PARLOURS
BEHIND THE
 TIMES
BELISHA
 BEACONS
BERBERIDACEOUS
BERKSHIRE
 DOWNS
BESIDE THE
 POINT
BEST BEFORE
 DATE
BIBLIOGRAPHERS
BIBLIOGRAPHIES
BIG GAME
 HUNTING
BIOCLIMATOLOGY
BIODEGRADABLES
BIOENGINEERING
BIOGENETICALLY
BIOGRAPHICALLY
BIOLUMINESCENT
BIPARTISANSHIP
BIRD OF
 PARADISE
BIRDS OF
 PASSAGE
BITUMINIZATION

BLACK
 MARKETEER
BLANK
 CARTRIDGE
BLOCK AND
 TACKLE
BLOOD
 POISONING
BLOOD
 PRESSURES
BLOOD
 RELATIONS
BLOOD
 SACRIFICE
BLOODTHIRSTILY
BLUE-
 PENCILLING
BOARDINGHOUSES
BOARDING
 SCHOOL
BOIS DE
 BOULOGNE
BOISTEROUSNESS
BOLOMETRICALLY
BOON
 COMPANIONS
BOUCHES-DU-
 RHONE
BOUGAINVILLEAS
BOUILLABAISSES
BOULEVERSEMENT
BOWDLERIZATION
BRACHYCEPHALIC
BRACHYDACTYLIA
BRACHYDACTYLIC
BREAD-AND-
 BUTTER
BREAKFAST
 TABLE
BREATHLESSNESS
BREMSSTRAHLUNG
BRIGHT AND
 EARLY
BRONCHIAL
 TUBES
BRONCHIECTASIS
BRONCHOSCOPIST
BRUSSELS
 SPROUT
BUILDING
 BLOCKS
BULLETIN
 BOARDS

BULLHEADEDNESS
BUREAU DE
 CHANGE
BURNT
 OFFERINGS
BUSMAN'S
 HOLIDAY

C

CADAVEROUSNESS
CALAMINE
 LOTION
CALENDAR
 MONTHS
CALLIGRAPHISTS
CAMPANOLOGISTS
CAMPANULACEOUS
CANTANKEROUSLY
CAPITALIZATION
CAPITAL
 LETTERS
CAPPARIDACEOUS
CAPRICIOUSNESS
CARBON
 MONOXIDE
CARCINOMATOSIS
CARDINAL
 POINTS
CARDIOVASCULAR
CARPET
 SWEEPERS
CARRIER
 PIGEONS
CARRYING
 CHARGE
CARTOGRAPHICAL
CARTRIDGE
 PAPER
CASEMENT
 WINDOW
CASH AND
 CARRIES
CASH
 DISPENSERS
CATCHMENT
 AREAS
CATECHETICALLY
CATEGORIZATION
CATHEDRAL
 CLOSE
CATHERINE
 WHEEL

CATHODE RAY
 TUBE
CAUGHT
 UNAWARES
CAUSES
 CELEBRES
CENSORIOUSNESS
CENTRAL
 HEATING
CENTRALIZATION
CENTRE
 FORWARDS
CENTRIFUGATION
CERCOPITHECOID
CHAIN
 REACTIONS
CHAISES
 LONGUES
CHANGEABLENESS
CHANTRY
 CHAPELS
CHARACTER
 ACTOR
CHARACTERISTIC
CHARACTERIZING
CHARGE
 ACCOUNTS
CHARITABLENESS
CHARLATANISTIC
CHARTER
 MEMBERS
CHECHENO-
 INGUSH
CHEMOSYNTHESIS
CHEMOSYNTHETIC
CHEMOTHERAPIST
CHEST OF
 DRAWERS
CHICKENHEARTED
CHIEF
 CONSTABLE
CHIEF
 EXECUTIVE
CHIEF
 INSPECTOR
CHIEFTAINSHIPS
CHILD
 PRODIGIES
CHIMNEYBREASTS
CHIMNEY
 CORNERS
CHINCHERINCHEE

CHINESE
LANTERN
CHINLESS
WONDER
CHLOROPHYLLOID
CHLOROPHYLLOUS
CHLOROTHIAZIDE
CHLORPROMAZINE
CHLORPROPAMIDE
CHOLINESTERASE
CHOREOGRAPHERS
CHOREOGRAPHING
CHRISTIAN
NAMES
CHRISTMAS
BOXES
CHRISTMAS
CAKES
CHRISTMAS
CARDS
CHRISTMAS
TREES
CHRISTOLOGICAL
CHROMATOGRAPHY
CHROMATOPHORIC
CHRYSANTHEMUMS
CIGARETTE
PAPER
CINCHONIZATION
CINEMATOGRAPHY
CIRCUIT
BREAKER
CIRCULAR
LETTER
CIRCUMAMBIENCE
CIRCUMAMBULATE
CIRCUMFERENCES
CIRCUMLOCUTION
CIRCUMLOCUTORY
CIRCUMNAVIGATE
CIRCUMNUTATION
CIRCUMSCISSILE
CIRCUMSCRIBING
CIRCUMSPECTION
CIRCUMSTANTIAL
CIRCUMVOLUTION
CIRCUMVOLUTORY
CIVIL
ENGINEERS
CLARIFICATIONS
CLASS-
CONSCIOUS

CLASSIFICATION
CLASSIFICATORY
CLAUSTROPHOBIA
CLAUSTROPHOBIC
CLEARANCE
SALES
CLEARINGHOUSES
CLEAR-
SIGHTEDLY
CLIMBING
FRAMES
CLOAK-AND-
DAGGER
CLOTHES
HANGERS
CLUB
SANDWICHES
CLUSTER
BOMBING
COCK-A-DOODLE-
DOO
COCKER
SPANIELS
COCKTAIL
LOUNGE
COCKTAIL
STICKS
COESSENTIALITY
COFFEE
KLATCHES
COINCIDENTALLY
COLD
SHOULDERED
COLLAPSIBILITY
COLLECTIVE
FARM
COLLECTIVE
NOUN
COLLECTOR'S
ITEM
COLLOQUIALISMS
COLORADO
BEETLE
COLOURFASTNESS
COLOURLESSNESS
COMBINING
FORMS
COMBUSTIBILITY
COMFORTABLY
OFF
COMFORT
STATION

COMMAND
MODULES
COMMENSURATION
COMMERCIALIZED
COMMISERATIONS
COMMISSIONAIRE
COMMITTEE
STAGE
COMMON
FRACTION
COMMON-OR-
GARDEN
COMMUNICATIONS
COMMUNITY
CHEST
COMMUNITY
HOMES
COMPLEMENTIZER
COMPREHENSIBLE
COMPREHENSIBLY
COMPREHENSIONS
COMPREHENSIVES
COMPULSIVENESS
CONCATENATIONS
CONCAVO-
CONCAVE
CONCELEBRATIÓN
CONCENTRATIONS
CONCEPTUALIZED
CONCESSIONAIRE
CONCRETE
JUNGLE
CONCRETE
MIXERS
CONCRETE
POETRY
CONCRETIZATION
CONDEMNED
CELLS
CONDENSABILITY
CONDITIONALITY
CONDUCTOR
RAILS
CONDUPLICATION
CONFABULATIONS
CONFEDERATIONS
CONFIDENTIALLY
CONFIGURATIONS
CONFLAGRATIONS
CONFORMABILITY
CONFRONTATIONS
CONGLOMERATION

CONGLUTINATIVE
CONGRATULATING
CONGRATULATION
CONGRATULATORY
CONGREGATIONAL
CONJUNCTIVITIS
CONNECTING
RODS
CONQUISTADORES
CONRAIL,
CONRAIL
CONSANGUINEOUS
CONSCRIPTIONAL
CONSERVATIONAL
CONSERVATIVELY
CONSERVATOIRES
CONSERVATORIES
CONSIDERATIONS
CONSOLIDATIONS
CONSPIRATORIAL
CONSTABULARIES
CONSTANTINOPLE
CONSTELLATIONS
CONSTITUENCIES
CONSTITUTIONAL
CONSTRUCTIONAL
CONSTRUCTIVELY
CONSTRUCTIVISM
CONSTRUCTIVIST
CONSUETUDINARY
CONTAGIOUSNESS
CONTAINERIZING
CONTEMPORARIES
CONTEMPORARILY
CONTEMPTUOUSLY
CONTINENTALISM
CONTINENTALIST
CONTINENTALITY
CONTORTIONISTS
CONTRACEPTIVES
CONTRACT
BRIDGE
CONTRADICTIONS
CONTRAINDICANT
CONTRAINDICATE
CONTRAPOSITION
CONTRAPUNTALLY
CONTRAVENTIONS
CONTRIBUTORIAL
CONTROVERTIBLE
CONTUMACIOUSLY

CONTUMELIOUSLY
CONVENTIONALLY
CONVERSATIONAL
CONVERSAZIOONI
CONVERTIBILITY
CONVEXO-
  CONCAVE
COPPER-
  BOTTOMED
CORELIGIONISTS
CORNISH
  PASTIES
CORPORATION
  TAX
CORRESPONDENCE
CORRESPONDENTS
CORRUPTIBILITY
CORTICOSTEROID
CORTICOSTERONE
CORTICOTROPHIN
COUNTERACTIONS
COUNTERATTACKS
COUNTERBALANCE
COUNTERFEITERS
COUNTERFEITING
COUNTERMANDING
COUNTERMEASURE
COUNTERMENSURE
COUNTERPOISING
COUNTERSHADING
COUNTERSIGNING
COUNTERSINKING
COUNTERVAILING
COUNTINGHOUSES
COUNTRY
  COUSINS
COUNTY
  COUNCILS
COURAGEOUSNESS
COURT-
  MARTIALED
COURT OF
  INQUIRY
COVERING
  LETTER
CRADLE
  SNATCHER
CRAMP ONES
  STYLE
CREDIBILITY
  GAP
CREDITABLENESS
394

CREDIT
  ACCOUNTS
CREDIT
  SQUEEZES
CREEPY-
  CRAWLIES
CRIMINAL
  RECORD
CRIMINOLOGICAL
CRIMINOLOGISTS
CROCODILE
  TEARS
CROSS-
  COUNTRIES
CROSS-
  EXAMINERS
CROSS-
  EXAMINING
CROSS-
  FERTILIZE
CROSS-
  POLLINATE
CROSS
  REFERENCE
CROSS-
  REFERENCE
CROSS-
  REFERRING
CROSS-
  SECTIONAL
CROWN AND
  ANCHOR
CRUISE
  MISSILES
CRYPTAESTHESIA
CRYPTOGRAPHERS
CSECHOSLOVAKIA
CUCURBITACEOUS
CURRENT
  ACCOUNT
CURRICULA
  VITAE
CURRUGATED
  IRON
CURTAIN
  RAISERS
CURVILINEARITY
CYANOCOBALAMIN
CYBERNETICALLY
CYTOTAXONOMIST

D

DAGUERREOTYPER

DAGUERREOTYPES
DANISH
  PASTRIES
DATA
  PROCESSING
DAUGHTERLINESS
DAUGHTERS-IN-
  LAW
DAY OF
  RECKONING
DEAD MANS
  HANDLE
DEAD TO THE
  WORLD
DECEIVABLENESS
DECENTRALIZING
DECIMALIZATION
DECLASSIFIABLE
DECLENSIONALLY
DECLINE AND
  FALL
DECOLONIZATION
DECOLORIZATION
DECONTAMINATED
DECONTAMINATOR
DEFENESTRATION
DEFLOCCULATION
DEGENERATENESS
DEHUMANIZATION
DELECTABLENESS
DELIBERATENESS
DELIGHTFULNESS
DELOCALIZATION
DEMILITARIZING
DEMISEMIQUAVER
DEMOBILIZATION
DEMOCRATICALLY
DEMONETIZATION
DEMONSTRATIONS
DEMORALIZATION
DENATIONALIZED
DENOMINATIONAL
DENTAL
  SURGEONS
DEPLORABLENESS
DEPOLARIZATION
DEPOSIT
  ACCOUNT
DERMATOLOGICAL
DERMATOLOGISTS
DERMATOPLASTIC
DEROGATORINESS

DESTRUCTIONIST
DETERMINEDNESS
DEVIL'S
  ADVOCATE
DEVITALIZATION
DEXTROROTATION
DEXTROROTATORY
DIABOLICALNESS
DIAGNOSTICALLY
DIALECTOLOGIST
DIAMOND
  JUBILEE
DIAMOND
  WEDDING
DIAPHANOUSNESS
DIAPHOTOTROPIC
DICHROMATICISM
DICOTYLEDONOUS
DIELECTRICALLY
DIESEL-
  ELECTRIC
DIEU ET MON
  DROIT
DIFFERENTIABLE
DIFFERENTIATED
DIFFERENTIATOR
DIFFRACTOMETER
DIGITALIZATION
DIG ONES HEELS
  IN
DIMENHYDRINATE
DIMENSIONALITY
DINITROBENZENE
DINNER
  SERVICES
DINOFLAGELLATE
DIPLOMATICALLY
DIPLOSTEMONOUS
DIRECTIONALITY
DIRECT
  TAXATION
DISAFFILIATING
DISAFFILIATION
DISAFFORESTING
DISAPPEARANCES
DISAPPOINTEDLY
DISAPPOINTMENT
DISAPPROBATION
DISAPPROVINGLY
DISARRANGEMENT
DISARTICULATOR
DISASSOCIATING

DISASSOCIATION
DISBELIEVINGLY
DISCIPLINARIAN
DISCOLORATIONS
DISCOMPOSINGLY
DISCONNECTEDLY
DISCONNECTIONS
DISCONSOLATELY
DISCONSOLATION
DISCONTENTEDLY
DISCONTENTMENT
DISCONTINUANCE
DISCOUNTENANCE
DISCOUNT
  STORES
DISCOURAGEMENT
DISCOURAGINGLY
DISCOURTEOUSLY
DISCRIMINATING
DISCRIMINATION
DISCRIMINATORY
DISCURSIVENESS
DISEMBARKATION
DISEMBOGUEMENT
DISEMBOWELLING
DISEMBOWELMENT
DISENCHANTMENT
DISENFRANCHISE
DISENTHRALMENT
DISEQUILIBRIUM
DISESTABLISHED
DISFEATUREMENT
DISFIGUREMENTS
DISFORESTATION
DISFRANCHISING
DISGRUNTLEMENT
DISHEARTENMENT
DISILLUSIONING
DISINCLINATION
DISINFESTATION
DISINGENUOUSLY
DISINHERITANCE
DISINTEGRATING
DISINTEGRATION
DISINTEGRATIVE
DISJOINTEDNESS
DISORDERLINESS
DISORIENTATING
DISORIENTATION
DISPARAGEMENTS
DISPENSABILITY

DISPENSATIONAL
DISPUTATIOUSLY
DISQUALIFIABLE
DISQUIETEDNESS
DISRESPECTABLE
DISSERTATIONAL
DISSERVICEABLE
DISSIMULATIONS
DISSOCIABILITY
DISSOLVABILITY
DISSUASIVENESS
DISTENSIBILITY
DISTINGUISHING
DISTRIBUTIONAL
DISTRIBUTIVELY
DIURETICALNESS
DIVERTICULITIS
DIVERTICULOSIS
DIVERTISSEMENT
DNEPROPETROVSK
DOG IN THE
  MANGER
DO-IT-
  YOURSELFER
DOMESTIC
  ANIMAL
DOUBLE
  BREASTED
DOUBLE-
  BREASTED
DOUBLE-
  CHECKING
DOUBLE-
  CROSSERS
DOUBLE-
  CROSSING
DOUBLE
  ENTENDRE
DOUBLE
  FEATURES
DOUBTING
  THOMAS
DOWN IN THE
  DUMPS
DRAINING
  BOARDS
DRAMATIZATIONS
DRESSING
  TABLES
DRESS
  REHEARSAL
DRIVING
  LICENCE

DROP IN THE
  OCEAN
DRUM
  MAJORETTES
DUCKS AND
  DRAKES
DUCTLESS
  GLANDS
DWELLING
  HOUSES
DYER'S-
  GREENWEED
DYNAMOELECTRIC
DYSMENORRHOEAL

E

ECCENTRICITIES
ECCLESIASTICAL
ECCLESIOLOGIST
ECONOMETRICIAN
EDITIO
  PRINCEPS
EDUCATIONALIST
EFFERVESCENTLY
EFFERVESCINGLY
EFFORTLESSNESS
EGALITARIANISM
EGOCENTRICALLY
ELDER
  STATESMAN
ELDER
  STATESMEN
ELECTIONEERING
ELECTRA
  COMPLEX
ELECTROCHEMIST
ELECTROCUTIONS
ELECTRODEPOSIT
ELECTRODYNAMIC
ELECTROGRAPHIC
ELECTROKINETIC
ELECTRONICALLY
ELECTRONIC
  MAIL
ELECTROSTATICS
ELECTROSURGERY
ELECTROTHERMAL
ELECTROVALENCY
ELEMENTARINESS
ELLIPTICALNESS
EMBARRASSINGLY
EMBARRASSMENTS

EMBELLISHMENTS
EMBLEMATICALLY
EMOTIONALISTIC
EMPHATICALNESS
EMULSIFICATION
EMULSION
  PAINTS
ENANTIOMORPHIC
ENCAPSULATIONS
ENCEPHALOGRAPH
ENCOURAGEMENTS
ENDOCRINE
  GLAND
ENDOCRINOLOGIC
ENDOPHYTICALLY
ENDOSMOTICALLY
ENFANT
  TERRIBLE
ENFORCEABILITY
ENGAGEMENT
  RING
ENHARMONICALLY
ENLIGHTENINGLY
ENROLLED
  NURSES
ENTEROGASTRONE
ENTERPRISINGLY
ENTERTAININGLY
ENTERTAINMENTS
ENTOMOSTRACOUS
EPEXEGETICALLY
EPICONTINENTAL
EPIDEMIOLOGIST
EPIGENETICALLY
EPIGRAPHICALLY
EPISTEMOLOGIST
EQUIPONDERANCE
EQUIVOCATINGLY
ERYTHROBLASTIC
ERYTHROPOIESIS
ERYTHROPOIETIC
ESCAPE
  VELOCITY
ESCHATOLOGICAL
ESTABLISHMENTS
ESTATE
  AGENCIES
ESTERIFICATION
ETERNALIZATION
ETHERIFICATION
ETHNOCENTRISMS
ETHNOLOGICALLY

ETYMOLOGICALLY
EULOGISTICALLY
EUPHONICALNESS
EUPHORBIACEOUS
EUPHUISTICALLY
EUSTACHIAN
  TUBE
EUTROPHICATION
EVANGELICALISM
EVANGELIZATION
EVAPORATED
  MILK
EVEN-
  HANDEDNESS
EVENING
  DRESSES
EVIL-
  MINDEDNESS
EVOLUTIONISTIC
EXACERBATINGLY
EXAGGERATINGLY
EXASPERATINGLY
EXCEPTIONALITY
EXCLAUSTRATION
EXCOMMUNICABLE
EXCOMMUNICATED
EXCOMMUNICATOR
EXCRUCIATINGLY
EXHAUSTIBILITY
EXHAUSTIVENESS
EXHIBITIONISTS
EXHILARATINGLY
EXISTENTIALISM
EXISTENTIALIST
EXOTHERMICALLY
EXPANSIONISTIC
EXPENSE
  ACCOUNT
EXPERIMENTALLY
EXPOSTULATIONS
EXPRESSIONISTS
EXPRESSIONLESS
EXPRESSIVENESS
EXPROPRIATIONS
EXTEMPORANEOUS
EXTENDED
  FAMILY
EXTENSIONALITY
EXTINGUISHABLE
EXTINGUISHMENT
EXTORTIONATELY
EXTRACANONICAL

EXTRACTABILITY
EXTRANEOUSNESS
EXTRAVEHICULAR
EYEBROW
  PENCILS

F

FACTITIOUSNESS
FACTORY
  FARMING
FAINT-
  HEARTEDLY
FAIR-
  MINDEDNESS
FAIRY
  GODMOTHER
FAITS
  ACCOMPLIS
FALLACIOUSNESS
FALLOPIAN
  TUBES
FALSE
  PRETENCES
FALSIFICATIONS
FAMILY
  PLANNING
FARSIGHTEDNESS
FASTIDIOUSNESS
FATALISTICALLY
FATHERS AND
  SONS
FAVOURABLENESS
FEATHERBEDDING
FEATHERBRAINED
FEATHERWEIGHTS
FEDERALIZATION
FEEDING
  BOTTLES
FEEL THE
  DRAUGHT
FELICITOUSNESS
FEMININE
  ENDING
FEMME DE
  CHAMBRE
FERMENTABILITY
FERRIMAGNETISM
FERROMAGNESIAN
FERROMAGNETISM
FERROMANGANESE
FICTIONALIZING
FICTITIOUSNESS
FIDEICOMMISSUM

FIELDS OF
  VISION
FIELD
  TELEGRAPH
FIFTH
  COLUMNIST
FIGHTING
  CHANCE
FIGURATIVENESS
FIGURE OF
  SPEECH
FIGURES OF
  EIGHT
FILING
  CABINETS
FILLING
  STATION
FINANCIAL
  YEARS
FINE-TOOTH
  COMBS
FINGER
  PAINTING
FINGERPRINTING
FINSTERAARHORN
FIRST
  OFFENDERS
FISSIONABILITY
FLABBERGASTING
FLIGHT-
  RECORDER
FLIGHT
  SERGEANT
FLOATING
  VOTERS
FLOG A DEAD
  HORSE
FLORICULTURIST
FLOWER-OF-AN-
  HOUR
FLYING
  BUTTRESS
FLYING
  DUTCHMAN
FLYING
  OFFICERS
FOLLOW MY
  LEADER
FOLLOW-MY-
  LEADER
FOLLOW-
  THROUGHS
FOOD
  PROCESSORS

FORBIDDEN
  FRUIT
FORBIDDINGNESS
FOREIGN
  AFFAIRS
FOREORDAINMENT
FORESHORTENING
FORETHOUGHTFUL
FORE-
  TOPGALLANT
FORKLIFT
  TRUCKS
FORTHRIGHTNESS
FORTIFICATIONS
FORTUITOUSNESS
FORTUNE
  HUNTERS
FORTUNE-
  TELLERS
FORWARD-
  LOOKING
FOUNDING
  FATHER
FOUR-LETTER
  WORD
FRATERNIZATION
FREE
  ENTERPRISE
FREEZING
  POINTS
FRENCH
  DRESSING
FRENCH
  POLISHED
FRIDGE-
  FREEZERS
FRIENDLESSNESS
FRINGE
  BENEFITS
FROZEN
  SHOULDER
FRUCTIFICATION
FULLY-
  FASHIONED
FUNCTIONALISTS
FUNDAMENTALISM
FUNDAMENTALIST
FUNDAMENTALITY
FUNERAL
  PARLOUR
FURFURALDEHYDE
FUTURISTICALLY

G

GALACTOPOIESIS
GALACTOPOIETIC
GALVANOTROPISM
GASTROVASCULAR
GAVE UP THE GHOST
GEIGER COUNTERS
GELATINIZATION
GENEALOGICALLY
GENERALISSIMOS
GENERALIZATION
GENERAL STRIKES
GENTRIFICATION
GEOCENTRICALLY
GEOGRAPHICALLY
GERMAN SHEPHERD
GERONTOLOGICAL
GERRYMANDERING
GESTICULATIONS
GET ONES OWN BACK
GHETTO BLASTERS
GLANDULAR FEVER
GLOBE ARTICHOKE
GLOBETROTTINGS
GLORIFICATIONS
GLORY-OF-THE-SNOW
GLOSSY MAGAZINE
GLUCOCORTICORD
GOLDEN JUBILEES
GOLDEN WEDDINGS
GOLD-OF-PLEASURE
GOOD-FOR-NOTHING
GOOD-HUMOUREDLY
GOOD SAMARITANS
GRACE-AND-FAVOUR

GRADE CROSSINGS
GRAMMAR SCHOOLS
GRAMMATICALITY
GRAMMATOLOGIST
GRANDDAUGHTERS
GRANDILOQUENCE
GRANGERIZATION
GRAPHITIZATION
GRAPPLING IRONS
GRASP THE NETTLE
GRATIFICATIONS
GRATUITOUSNESS
GREGARIOUSNESS
GREGORIAN CHANT
GROUNDLESSNESS
GROUP PRACTICES
GUARDIAN ANGELS
GUIDED MISSILES
GUY FAWKES NIGHT
GYNAECOLOGICAL
GYNAECOLOGISTS
GYROSTABILIZER

H

HABERDASHERIES
HAEMACYTOMETER
HAEMAGGLUTININ
HAEMATOBLASTIC
HAEMATOGENESIS
HAEMATOPOIESIS
HAEMATOPOIETIC
HAEMATOTHERMAL
HAEMOCYTOMETER
HALFPENNYWORTH
HALFWITTEDNESS
HALICARNASSIAN
HALLUCINATIONS
HALLUCINOGENIC
HANDICRAFTSMAN
HANDSOME SALARY
HANGING GARDENS

HAPAX LEGOMENON
HARD CURRENCIES
HARD-HEADEDNESS
HARMONIOUSNESS
HARPSICHORDIST
HEAD LIKE A SIEVE
HEADMASTERSHIP
HEADSTRONGNESS
HEARTRENDINGLY
HEARTWARMINGLY
HEATHENISHNESS
HEBRAISTICALLY
HEGIRA CALENDAR
HELL FOR LEATHER
HELTER-SKELTERS
HEMEL HEMPSTEAD
HEMISPHEROIDAL
HENRIETTA MARIA
HEREDITABILITY
HEREDITARINESS
HERMAPHRODITES
HERMAPHRODITIC
HERMAPHRODITUS
HEROIC COUPLETS
HERO WORSHIPPED
HERPES LABIALIS
HETEROCHROMOUS
HETEROGONOUSLY
HETEROLECITHAL
HETEROMORPHISM
HETERONOMOUSLY
HETERONYMOUSLY
HETEROPHYLLOUS
HETEROPOLARITY
HETEROSEXUALLY
HIERARCHICALLY
HIGH COMMISSION
HIGH COURT JUDGE

HIGH EXPLOSIVES
HIGH-HANDEDNESS
HIGHLAND FLINGS
HIGH-MINDEDNESS
HIGH-PRESSURING
HIGH-PRINCIPLED
HIGH SPEED TRAIN
HIGH TECHNOLOGY
HIGH WATER MARKS
HIPPOPOTAMUSES
HISTOCHEMISTRY
HISTOLOGICALLY
HISTOLYTICALLY
HISTOPATHOLOGY
HISTOPLASMOSIS
HISTORICALNESS
HISTORIOGRAPHY
HISTRIONICALLY
HOEK VAN HOLLAND
HOLDING COMPANY
HOLD NO BRIEF FOR
HOLIER-THAN-THOU
HOMOCHROMATISM
HOMOGENIZATION
HOMOIOUSIANISM
HOMOPHONICALLY
HONEYDEW MELONS
HONOURABLENESS
HORATIUS COCLES
HORIZONTALNESS
HORRENDOUSNESS
HORROR-STRICKEN
HORSE CHESTNUTS
HORSE LATITUDES
HORTICULTURIST

HOSPITABLENESS
HOT WATER
  BOTTLE
HOT-WATER
  BOTTLE
HOUSEHOLD
  NAMES
HOUSEMAID'S
  KNEE
HOUSE OF
  COMMONS
HOUSING
  PROJECT
HUMIDIFICATION
HUMOURLESSNESS
HUNGER
  MARCHERS
HUNGER
  STRIKERS
HUNTING
  GROUNDS
HURRICANE
  LAMPS
HYDROCELLULOSE
HYDROCORTISONE
HYDROGENOLYSIS
HYDROLOGICALLY
HYDROMAGNETICS
HYDROMECHANICS
HYPERBOLICALLY
HYPERSENSITIVE
HYPOCHONDRIACS
HYPOCRITICALLY
HYPODERMICALLY
HYPOTHETICALLY
HYSTERECTOMIES

I

ICEBERG
  LETTUCE
ICHNEUMON
  FLIES
ICHTHYOPHAGOUS
IDEALISTICALLY
IDENTICAL
  TWINS
IDENTIFICATION
IDEOLOOGICALLY
IDIOSYNCRASIES
ILLEGALIZATION
ILLEGITIMATELY
ILLIMITABILITY

ILLUSTRATIONAL
ILLUSTRATIVELY
IMMETHODICALLY
IMMOBILIZATION
IMMUNOGENETICS
IMMUNOGLOBULIN
IMMUNOREACTION
IMPARISYLLABIC
IMPEACHABILITY
IMPERCEPTIVITY
IMPERMEABILITY
IMPERSONATIONS
IMPERTURBATION
IMPLAUSIBILITY
IMPLEMENTATION
IMPOLITENESSES
IMPRACTICALITY
IMPREGNABILITY
IMPRESSIONABLE
IMPRESSIONABLY
IMPRESSIONALLY
IMPRESSIONISTS
IMPRESSIVENESS
IMPROVISATIONS
INADVISABILITY
INALIENABILITY
INALTERABILITY
INAPPRECIATIVE
INAPPREHENSIVE
INAPPROACHABLE
INARTICULATELY
INARTISTICALLY
INAUSPICIOUSLY
INCANDESCENTLY
INCAPACITATING
INCAPACITATION
INCAUTIOUSNESS
INCESTUOUSNESS
INCOMMENSURATE
INCOMMODIOUSLY
INCOMMUNICABLE
INCOMPLETENESS
INCOMPRESSIBLE
INCONCLUSIVELY
INCONSIDERABLE
INCONSISTENTLY
INCONVENIENCED
INCONVENIENCES
INCONVENIENTLY
INCOORDINATION
INDECIPHERABLE

INDECIPHERABLY
INDECOROUSNESS
INDEFINITENESS
INDESTRUCTIBLE
INDESTRUCTIBLY
INDETERMINABLE
INDETERMINABLY
INDIAN
  ELEPHANT
INDIFFERENTISM
INDIFFERENTIST
INDIGENOUSNESS
INDIRECT
  OBJECT
INDIRECT
  SPEECH
INDISCRIMINATE
INDISPOSITIONS
INDISTINCTNESS
INDIVIDUALISTS
INDIVIDUALIZED
INDIVIDUALIZER
INDIVISIBILITY
INDOCTRINATING
INDOCTRINATION
INDOMITABILITY
INDUBITABILITY
INDUSTRIALISTS
INDUSTRIALIZED
INEFFECTUALITY
INELUCTABILITY
INERTIA
  SELLING
INESSENTIALITY
INESTIMABILITY
INEXCUSABILITY
INFECTIOUSNESS
INFLAMMABILITY
INFLAMMATORILY
INFRALAPSARIAN
INFRANGIBILITY
INFRASTRUCTURE
INGRATIATINGLY
INHABITABILITY
INHARMONIOUSLY
INHERITABILITY
INITIALIZATION
IN LOCO
  PARENTIS
INNUMERABILITY
INQUISITIONIST
INSANITARINESS

INSCRUTABILITY
INSEPARABILITY
INSIDER
  DEALING
INSIGNIFICANCE
INSTITUTIONARY
INSTRUCTORSHIP
INSUFFICIENTLY
INSUPERABILITY
INSUPPRESSIBLE
INSURMOUNTABLE
INSURRECTIONAL
INTEGRATIONIST
INTELLECTUALLY
INTELLIGENTSIA
INTENTIONALITY
INTERCESSIONAL
INTERCOMMUNION
INTERDEPENDENT
INTEREST
  GROUPS
INTERFERENTIAL
INTERFEROMETER
INTERFEROMETRY
INTERFERTILITY
INTERGRADATION
INTERJECTIONAL
INTERLOCUTRESS
INTERMEDIARIES
INTERMIGRATION
INTERMITTENTLY
INTERMITTINGLY
INTERMOLECULAR
INTERNAL
  MARKET
INTERNATIONALE
INTERNATIONALS
INTERPELLATION
INTERPENETRANT
INTERPENETRATE
INTERPLANETARY
INTERPOLATIONS
INTERPOSITIONS
INTERPRETATION
INTERPRETATIVE
INTERRELATIONS
INTERROGATIONS
INTERROGATIVES
INTERSECTIONAL
INTERSEXUALITY
INTERSPERSEDLY

INTERTWININGLY
INTERVENTIONAL
INTOLERABILITY
INTO THE
BARGAIN
INTOXICATINGLY
INTRACTABILITY
INTRACUTANEOUS
INTRAMOLECULAR
INTRANSIGENTLY
INTRANSITIVELY
INTRODUCTORILY
INVERTED
COMMAS
INVESTIGATIONS
INVIGORATINGLY
IODOMETRICALLY
IRRECONCILABLE
IRRECONCILABLY
IRREDUCIBILITY
IRREFUTABILITY
IRREGULARITIES
IRREMOVABILITY
IRREPARABILITY
IRREPROACHABLE
IRREPROACHABLY
IRRESOLUBILITY
IRREVOCABILITY
ISOPIESTICALLY

J

JACK-IN-THE-
BOXES
JOB'S
COMFORTERS
JOLLIFICATIONS
JOURNALIZATION
JURISDICTIONAL
JUSTICIABILITY
JUSTIFIABILITY

K

KAISERSLAUTERN
KAMENSK-
URALSKI
KANGAROO
COURTS
KEEP ONES CHIN
UP
KEEP ONES HAND
IN
KERATINIZATION

KEYHOLE
SURGURY
KIDNEY
MACHINES
KINDERGARTENER
KITCHEN
GARDENS
KNICKERBOCKERS
KNIGHT-
ERRANTRY
KNOCK ON THE
HEAD
KNUCKLE-
DUSTERS
KOSOVO-
METOHIJA

L

LABOUR
EXCHANGE
LAMELLIROSTRAL
LANCE
CORPORALS
LAND ON ONES
FEET
LARGE
INTESTINE
LARGER THAN
LIFE
LARYNGOLOGICAL
LARYNGOSCOPIST
LASCIVIOUSNESS
LATITUDINARIAN
LAUGHINGSTOCKS
LAUNDRY
BASKETS
LAW OF THE
JUNGLE
LEADING
ARTICLE
LEADING
STRINGS
LEAVE OF
ABSENCE
LEFT-
HANDEDNESS
LEFT IN THE
LURCH
LEGALISTICALLY
LEGERDEMAINIST
LEGION OF
HONOUR
LEGITIMIZATION

LENDING
LIBRARY
LETS CALL IT A
DAY
LETTER OF
CREDIT
LEVEL
CROSSINGS
LEXICOGRAPHERS
LIBERALIZATION
LIBERAL
STUDIES
LIBERTARIANISM
LIBIDINOUSNESS
LICENTIATESHIP
LICENTIOUSNESS
LIFE
EXPECTANCY
LIFE
PRESERVERS
LIGHT
AIRCRAFTS
LIGNOCELLULOSF
LIKE
MINDEDNESS
LINE ONES
POCKET
LINGUISTICALLY
LISTEN TO
REASON
LITHOLOGICALLY
LITTLE BY
LITTLE
LITTLE GREEN
MEN
LOCAL
AUTHORITY
LOCUS
CLASSICUS
LONGITUDINALLY
LONG-
SUFFERANCE
LONGWINDEDNESS
LOOKING
GLASSES
LOVING
KINDNESS
LOXODROMICALLY
LUGUBRIOUSNESS

M

MACADAMIZATION
MACHINEGUNNING

MACROECONOMICS
MACROEVOLUTION
MACROMOLECULAR
MAGNETIC
FIELDS
MAGNIFICATIONS
MAHALLA EL
KUBRA
MAKE
ALLOWANCES
MAKE THE
RUNNING
MAKE UP ONES
MIND
MALACOPHYLLOUS
MALACOSTRACOUS
MALE
CHAUVINIST
MALFUNCTIONING
MALPIGHIACEOUS
MALTESE
CROSSES
MANIFESTATIONS
MAN IN THE
STREET
MANIPULABILITY
MANNERLESSNESS
MANOMETRICALLY
MANUFACTURABLE
MARCHING
ORDERS
MARKET
GARDENER
MARKET
RESEARCH
MARTYROLOGICAL
MASON-DIXON
LINE
MASSAGE
PARLOUR
MASSOTHERAPIST
MASS
PRODUCTION
MATERNITY
LEAVE
MATHEMATICALLY
MATHEMATICIANS
MATTER OF
COURSE
MATTER-OF-
FACTLY
MATURE
STUDENTS

MAUNDY
  THURSDAY
MEANINGFULNESS
MECHANOTHERAPY
MEDDLESOMENESS
MEDITATIVENESS
MEGALOCEPHALIC
MEGALOMANIACAL
MEGAPHONICALLY
MEGASPOROPHYLL
MELANCHOLINESS
MENDACIOUSNESS
MENTAL
  HOSPITAL
MEPHISTOPHELES
MERCAPTOPURINE
MERCHANT
  NAVIES
MERETRICIOUSLY
MESDEMOISELLES
METACHROMATISM
METALLOGRAPHER
METALLOGRAPHIC
METAMORPHOSING
METAPHORICALLY
METAPHYSICALLY
METAPSYCHOLOGY
METASTATICALLY
METEMPSYCHOSIS
METEOROGRAPHIC
METEOROLOGICAL
METEOROLOGISTS
METHAEMOGLOBIN
METHODICALNESS
METHODOLOGICAL
METICULOUSNESS
MICROBAROGRAPH
MICROBIOLOGIST
MICROCEPHALOUS
MICROCHEMISTRY
MICROCIRCUITRY
MICROCOMPUTERS
MICROECONOMICS
MICROMETEORITE
MICROORGANISMS
MICROPARASITIC
MICROPROCESSOR
MICROPYROMETER
MICROSTOMATOUS
MICROSTRUCTURE
MIDDLE-
  DISTANCE

MIGHT-HAVE-
  BEENS
MILITARIZATION
MILITARY
  POLICE
MILLENARIANISM
MINERALIZATION
MISAPPLICATION
MISAPPREHENDED
MISAPPROPRIATE
MISCALCULATING
MISCALCULATION
MISCONCEPTIONS
MISINFORMATION
MISINTERPRETED
MISINTERPRETER
MISREPRESENTED
MISREPRESENTER
MIXED
  ECONOMIES
MIXED
  METAPHORS
MOCK-
  HEROICALLY
MOCK TURTLE
  SOUP
MODERNIZATIONS
MOMENTS OF
  TRUTH
MONGRELIZATION
MONKEY
  BUSINESS
MONKEY
  WRENCHES
MONOCARPELLARY
MONOCHROMATISM
MONOLITHICALLY
MONOPOLIZATION
MONOPROPELLANT
MONOSACCHARIDE
MOONLIGHT
  FLITS
MORALISTICALLY
MORGANATICALLY
MORNING
  GLORIES
MORPHOPHONEMIC
MOTHER
  SUPERIOR
MOTIONLESSNESS
MOTION
  PICTURES

MOTIVELESSNESS
MOUNTAINEERING
MOVING
  PAVEMENT
MOVING
  PICTURES
MUCOMEMBRANOUS
MUCOUS
  MEMBRANE
MULTIFACTORIAL
MULTIFARIOUSLY
MULTILATERALLY
MULTINATIONALS
MULTIPLE
  STORES
MULTIPLICATION
MULTIPLICATIVE
MUNICIPALITIES
MUSTARD
  PLASTER
MYELENCEPHALIC
MYELENCEPHALON
MYOCARDIOGRAPH
MYOGRAPHICALLY
MYRMECOLOGICAL
MYRMECOPHAGOUS
MYRMECOPHILOUS
MYSTAGOGICALLY
MYSTERIOUSNESS

N

NANSEN
  PASSPORT
NARCOSYNTHESIS
NARRATIVE
  VERSE
NASOPHARYNGEAL
NASTY BIT OF
  WORK
NATIONAL
  ANTHEM
NATIVE
  AMERICAN
NATURAL
  HISTORY
NATURALIZATION
NATURAL
  SCIENCE
NEANDERTHAL
  MAN
NEBUCHADNEZZAR
NEGLECTFULNESS

NEIGHBOURHOODS
NEOCOLONIALISM
NEOCOLONIALIST
NERVOUS
  SYSTEMS
NEUROPATHOLOGY
NEUTRALIZATION
NEWFOUNDLANDER
NEWS
  CONFERENCE
NEWSWORTHINESS
NIGHT
  BLINDNESS
NIGHT
  WATCHMANS
NIL
  DESPERANDUM
NINE DAYS'
  WONDER
NITROCELLULOSE
NITROGLYCERINE
NOBLESSE
  OBLIGE
NO-CLAIM
  BONUSES
NOLO
  CONTENDERE
NONATTRIBUTIVE
NONCOMMITTALLY
NONCONFORMISTS
NONCOOPERATION
NONCOOPERATIVE
NONDISJUNCTION
NONEQUIVALENCE
NONINFLAMMABLE
NONPROGRESSIVE
NON
  PROSEQUITUR
NONRESIDENTIAL
NONRESTRICTIVE
NONSTIMULATING
NORFOLK
  JACKETS
NORTHERN
  LIGHTS
NORTH-
  NORTHEAST
NORTH-
  NORTHWEST
NORTHUMBERLAND
NOTEWORTHINESS
NOUVEAUX
  RICHES

NO-WIN
SITUATION
NUCLEAR
REACTOR
NUCLEAR
WINTERS
NURSERY
SCHOOLS
NUTRITIOUSNESS
NYCTAGINACEOUS
NYMPHOMANIACAL

O

OBSEQUIOUSNESS
OBSERVABLENESS
OBSTREPEROUSLY
OBSTRUCTIONISM
OBSTRUCTIONIST
OCCUPATIONALLY
OCEAN
GRAYHOUND
OCEANOGRAPHERS
OEDIPUS
COMPLEX
OLD MAN OF THE
SEA
OLD PEOPLE'S
HOME
OLD TIME
DANCING
OLIGARCHICALLY
OLIGOPSONISTIC
ONE-ARMED
BANDIT
ONEIROCRITICAL
ONE-NIGHT
STANDS
ON ONES BEAM
ENDS
ON THE OTHER
HAND
ON THE
THRESHOLD
OPEN-
HANDEDNESS
OPEN-
MINDEDNESS
OPEN
SANDWICHES
OPEN
UNIVERSITY
OPERATING
TABLE

OPERATIONALISM
OPHTHALMOSCOPE
OPHTHALMOSCOPY
OPPOSITE
NUMBER
OPPRESSIVENESS
OPTIMISTICALLY
ORCHESTRATIONS
ORDINARY
LEVELS
ORDINARY
SEAMAN
ORDNANCE
SURVEY
ORGANIZATIONAL
ORGANIZED
CRIME
ORGANOGRAPHIST
ORGANOMETALLIC
ORNITHOLOGICAL
ORNITHOLOGISTS
OROBANCHACEOUS
OROGRAPHICALLY
ORTHOCHROMATIC
ORTHODOX
CHURCH
ORTHOGENICALLY
ORTHOGRAPHICAL
ORTHOPHOSPHATE
OSCILLOGRAPHIC
OSMOMETRICALLY
OSTENTATIOUSLY
OSTEOARTHRITIC
OSTEOARTHRITIS
OSTEOLOGICALLY
OTOLARYNGOLOGY
OUTBOARD
MOTORS
OUTGENERALLING
OUTLANDISHNESS
OUTMANOEUVRING
OUTRAGEOUSNESS
OVERCAPITALIZE
OVERCOMPENSATE
OVERDEVELOPING
OVERENTHUSIASM
OVERESTIMATING
OVERESTIMATION
OVERINDULGENCE
OVERPOPULATION
OVERPOWERINGLY
OVERPRODUCTION

OVERPROTECTION
OVERSIMPLIFIED
OVERSTATEMENTS
OVERSUBSCRIBED
OVER-THE-
COUNTER
OVERWHELMINGLY
OWNER-
OCCUPIERS
OXYHAEMOGLOBIN
OYSTERCATCHERS

P

PACHYDERMATOUS
PACKAGE
HOLIDAY
PADDLE
STEAMERS
PAEDIATRICIANS
PAEDOMORPHOSIS
PAGANISTICALLY
PALAEANTHROPIC
PALAEETHNOLOGY
PALAEOBOTANIST
PALATALIZATION
PALEONTOLOGIST
PAN-
AMERICANISM
PANCAKE
LANDING
PANGENETICALLY
PANHELLENISTIC
PAPILLOMATOSIS
PARABOLIZATION
PARALLELEPIPED
PARALLELOGRAMS
PARAPHERNALIAS
PARAPSYCHOLOGY
PARASITOLOGIST
PARATACTICALLY
PARENCHYMATOUS
PARKING
GARAGES
PARSIMONIOUSLY
PARTHENOCARPIC
PARTICULARIZED
PARTICULARIZER
PARTURIFACIENT
PASSENGER
TRAIN
PASSING THE
BUCK

PASSIONATENESS
PASSIONFLOWERS
PASSIVE
SMOKING
PASTEURIZATION
PAST
PARTICIPLE
PATE DE FOIE
GRAS
PATENT
MEDICINE
PATHOLOGICALLY
PAVEMENT
ARTIST
PEACE
OFFERINGS
PENITENTIARIES
PENNY
DREADFULS
PENNY-
FARTHINGS
PENNY-
HALFPENNY
PEPPERCORN
RENT
PERAMBULATIONS
PERCEIVABILITY
PERCEPTIBILITY
PERCUSSION
CAPS
PERCUSSIONISTS
PEREGRINATIONS
PEREMPTORINESS
PERFECT
BINDING
PERFECTIBILITY
PERFECTIONISTS
PERFIDIOUSNESS
PERIMETRICALLY
PERISCOPICALLY
PERLOCUTIONARY
PERMANENT
WAVES
PERMISSIBILITY
PERMISSIVENESS
PERNICIOUSNESS
PERNICKETINESS
PEROXIDE
BLONDE
PERPENDICULARS
PERSONABLENESS
PERSONAL
COLUMN

PERSONAL
  ESTATE
PERSONAL
  STEREO
PERSON-TO-
  PERSON
PERSUADABILITY
PERSUASIVENESS
PERTINACIOUSLY
PETIT
  BOURGEOIS
PETIT
  LARCENIST
PETROCHEMICALS
PETROCHEMISTRY
PETROLEUM
  JELLY
PETROL
  STATIONS
PETTY
  BOURGEOIS
PETTY
  LARCENIES
PHANTASMAGORIA
PHANTASMAGORIC
PHARMACEUTICAL
PHARMACOLOGIST
PHARMACOPOEIAL
PHARMACOPOEIAS
PHARMACOPOEIST
PHARYNGOLOGIST
PHARYNGOSCOPIC
PHENOBARBITONE
PHENOTYPICALLY
PHILANTHROPIST
PHILATELICALLY
PHILOLOGICALLY
PHILOSOPHIZING
PHLEGMATICALLY
PHONOLOGICALLY
PHOSPHOPROTEIN
PHOSPHORESCENT
PHOSPHOROSCOPE
PHOTOCHEMISTRY
PHOTOCONDUCTOR
PHOTOENGRAVING
PHOTOGENICALLY
PHOTOGRAMMETRY
PHOTOPERIODISM
PHOTOSENSITIVE
PHOTOSENSITIZE
PHOTOSYNTHESIS

PHOTOSYNTHETIC
PHOTOTYPICALLY
PHRASEOGRAPHIC
PHRASEOLOGICAL
PHTHALOCYANINE
PHYTOGEOGRAPHY
PHYTOPATHOLOGY
PHYTOSOCIOLOGY
PICTURE
  WINDOWS
PIEZOCHEMISTRY
PILGRIM
  FATHERS
PINCER
  MOVEMENT
PINNATIPARTITE
PINS AND
  NEEDLES
PISCICULTURIST
PITCH-
  BLACKNESS
PITCHED
  BATTLES
PLAIN
  CHOCOLATE
PLANCK
  CONSTANT
PLASTER OF
  PARIS
PLASTIC
  BULLETS
PLASTICIZATION
PLASTIC
  SURGEON
PLASTIC
  SURGERY
PLATINOCYANIDE
PLATINUM
  BLONDE
PLATITUDINIZER
PLEA
  BARGAINING
PLEONASTICALLY
PLETHYSMOGRAPH
PLUMBER'S
  FRIEND
PNEUMATIC
  DRILL
PNEUMOBACILLUS
PNEUMOCONIOSIS
PNEUMODYNAMICS
POIKILOTHERMAL
POLEMONIACEOUS

POLICE
  OFFICERS
POLICE
  STATIONS
POLITICIZATION
POLLING
  STATION
POLYCARPELLARY
POLYCHROMATISM
POLYMERIZATION
POLYNUCLEOTIDE
POLYPHONICALLY
POLYSACCHARIDE
POLYSYNTHESISM
PONTOON
  BRIDGES
POOR-
  SPIRITEDLY
POPULARIZATION
PORPHYROGENITE
PORTENTOUSNESS
PORTULACACEOUS
POSSESSIVENESS
POSTMILLENNIAL
POSTPOSITIONAL
POTENTIALITIES
PRACTICABILITY
PRACTICALITIES
PRACTICAL
  JOKER
PRACTICAL
  JOKES
PRAISEWORTHILY
PRAYER
  MEETINGS
PREADOLESCENCE
PREARRANGEMENT
PRECARIOUSNESS
PRECIOUS
  METALS
PRECIOUS
  STONES
PRECIPITATIONS
PRECOCIOUSNESS
PRECONCEPTIONS
PREDACIOUSNESS
PREDESTINARIAN
PREDESTINATION
PREDETERMINATE
PREDETERMINERS
PREDETERMINING
PREDICTABILITY

PREDISPOSITION
PREFABRICATING
PREFABRICATION
PREFERENTIALLY
PREFIGURATIONS
PREMEDITATEDLY
PREOCCUPATIONS
PREORDINATIONS
PREPONDERANTLY
PREPONDERATING
PREPONDERATION
PREPOSSESSIONS
PREPOSTEROUSLY
PRE-
  RAPHAELITES
PRESCRIPTIVELY
PRESCRIPTIVISM
PRESCRIPTIVIST
PRESENCE OF
  MIND
PRESENTATIONAL
PRESENT
  PERFECT
PRESERVABILITY
PRESIDENT
  ELECT
PRESIDENT-
  ELECT
PRESS
  GALLERIES
PRESSURE
  COOKER
PRESSURE
  GROUPS
PRESSURE
  POINTS
PRESSURIZATION
PRESUMPTUOUSLY
PRESUPPOSITION
PREVARICATIONS
PREVENTIVENESS
PRIMA
  BALLERINA
PRIMARY
  COLOURS
PRIMARY
  SCHOOLS
PRIME
  MINISTERS
PRINCE
  CHARMING
PRINCES
  CONSORT

PRINCIPALITIES
PRINCIPAL
  PARTS
PRINTED
  CIRCUIT
PRISONERS OF
  WAR
PRISON
  VISITORS
PRIVATE
  MEMBERS
PRIVATE
  SCHOOLS.
PRIVATE
  SOLDIER
PRO BONO
  PUBLICO
PROCRASTINATED
PROCRASTINATOR
PROCRYPTICALLY
PRODIGIOUSNESS
PRODUCTION
  LINE
PRODUCTIVENESS
PROFESSIONALLY
PROFESSORIALLY
PROFESSORSHIPS
PROGESTATIONAL
PROGNOSTICATED
PROGNOSTICATOR
PROGRAMME
  MUSIC
PROHIBITIONARY
PROHIBITIONISM
PROHIBITIONIST
PROJECTIONISTS
PROLETARIANISM
PROLIFERATIONS
PROMENADE
  DECKS
PRONOUNCEMENTS
PRONUNCIATIONS
PROPAEDEUTICAL
PROPAGANDIZING
PROPER
  FRACTION
PROPITIOUSNESS
PROPORTIONALLY
PROPORTIONMENT
PROPOSITIONING
PROPRIETORALLY
PROPRIOCEPTIVE

PROSENCEPHALON
PROSPEROUSNESS
PROSTHETICALLY
PROSTHODONTICS
PROSTHODONTIST
PROTECTIONISTS
PROTECTIVENESS
PROTHONOTARIAL
PROTOZOOLOGIST
PROTRACTEDNESS
PROTRUSIVENESS
PROVENTRICULAR
PROVENTRICULUS
PROVIDENTIALLY
PROVINCIALISMS
PROVING
  GROUNDS
PSEUDOMORPHISM
PSYCHOANALYSED
PSYCHOANALYSIS
PSYCHOANALYSTS
PSYCHOANALYTIC
PSYCHOANALYZER
PSYCHOCHEMICAL
PSYCHODRAMATIC
PSYCHODYNAMICS
PSYCHOLINGUIST
PSYCHOLOGISTIC
PSYCHONEUROSIS
PSYCHONEUROTIC
PSYCHOPHYSICAL
PSYCHOSOMATICS
PSYCHOSURGICAL
PSYCHOTECHNICS
PTERIDOLOGICAL
PUBLIC
  NUISANCE
PUBLIC
  SPIRITED
PUBLIC-
  SPIRITED
PUGILISTICALLY
PUGNACIOUSNESS
PURCHASABILITY
PURPLE
  PASSAGES
PURPOSEFULNESS
PURSE
  STRINGSES
PUT THE SCREWS
  ON
PYELONEPHRITIS

PYRAMID
  SELLING
PYRHELIOMETRIC
PYROMETALLURGY
PYROMETRICALLY
PYROPHOTOMETER
PYROPHOTOMETRY
PYROTECHNICSES
PYRRHIC
  VICTORY

Q

QUADRAGENARIAN
QUADRILATERALS
QUALIFICATIONS
QUANTIFICATION
QUANTITATIVELY
QUARTERMASTERS
QUEEN'S
  COUNSELS
QUEEN'S
  EVIDENCE
QUESTION
  MASTER
QUESTIONNAIRES
QUICK ON THE
  DRAW
QUINQUEFOLIATE
QUINQUEPARTITE
QUINQUEVALENCY
QUINTESSENTIAL
QUOTATION
  MARKS

R

RADIOBIOLOGIST
RADIOCHEMISTRY
RADIO
  FREQUENCY
RADIOSENSITIVE
RADIOTELEGRAPH
RADIOTELEMETRY
RADIOTELEPHONE
RADIOTELEPHONY
RADIO
  TELESCOPE
RADIOTHERAPIST
RAILWAY
  STATION
RAMBUNCTIOUSLY
RAMPAGEOUSNESS
RANUNCULACEOUS

RAPPROCHEMENTS
RASTAFARIANISM
RATEABLE
  VALUES
RATE OF
  EXCHANGE
READY FOR
  ACTION
REAFFIRMATIONS
REAL-TIME
  SYSTEM
REARRANGEMENTS
REAR VIEW
  MIRROR
REASONABLENESS
REBELLIOUSNESS
RECAPITULATING
RECAPITULATION
RECAPITULATIVE
RECEPTION
  ROOMS
RECKLINGHAUSEN
RECOMMENCEMENT
RECOMMENDATION
RECOMMENDATORY
RECONCILIATION
RECONCILIATORY
RECONDITIONING
RECONNAISSANCE
RECONSTITUTING
RECONSTITUTION
RECONSTRUCTING
RECONSTRUCTION
RECONSTRUCTIVE
RECORD-
  BREAKING
RECOVERABILITY
RECREATION
  ROOM
RECRIMINATIONS
RECRUDESCENCES
RECTANGULARITY
RECTIFICATIONS
REDEVELOPMENTS
REDINTEGRATION
REDINTEGRATIVE
REDISTRIBUTING
REDISTRIBUTION
REFERENCE
  BOOKS
REFLECTIVENESS
REFRACTIVENESS

REFRACTOMETRIC
REFRACTORINESS
REFRANGIBILITY
REGARDLESSNESS
REGISTERED
    POST
REGISTER
    OFFICE
REGISTRATIONAL
REGISTRY
    OFFICE
REGRESSIVENESS
REGULARIZATION
REHABILITATING
REHABILITATION
REHABILITATIVE
REIGNS OF
    TERROR
REIMBURSEMENTS
REINCARNATIONS
REINFORCEMENTS
REINSTALLATION
REINSTATEMENTS
REINTRODUCTION
REJUVENESCENCE
RELATIVE
    CLAUSE
RELENTLESSNESS
RELINQUISHMENT
REMARKABLENESS
REMEMBRANCE
    DAY
REMONETIZATION
REMORSEFULNESS
REMUNERABILITY
REMUNERATIVELY
REORGANIZATION
REPETITIVENESS
REPLACEABILITY
REPORTED
    SPEECH
REPRESENTATION
REPRESENTATIVE
REPRESSIVENESS
REPRIMANDINGLY
REQUISITIONARY
REQUISITIONING
RESPECTABILITY
RESPECTFULNESS
RESPONSIBILITY
RESPONSIVENESS

RESTAURANT
    CARS
RESTRICTEDNESS
RESTRICTIONIST
RESURRECTIONAL
RETRACTABILITY
RETRIEVABILITY
RETROGRADATION
RETROGRADATORY
RETRO-
    OPERATIVE
RETROSPECTIVES
REVERBERATIONS
REVEREND
    MOTHER
REVISED
    VERSION
REVITALIZATION
REVIVIFICATION
REVOLUTIONIZED
REVOLUTIONIZER
RHEUMATIC
    FEVER
RHINENCEPHALIC
RHINENCEPHALON
RHIZOCEPHALOUS
RHYTHM AND
    BLUES
RICINOLEIC
    ACID
RIDICULOUSNESS
RIGHT
    TRIANGLES
RIO GRANDE DO
    SUL
ROADWORTHINESS
ROARING
    FORTIES
ROCKET-
    LAUNCHER
ROCKY
    MOUNTAINS
ROENTGENOPAQUE
ROLLER
    COASTERS
ROMAINE
    LETTUCE
ROMAN
    CATHOLICS
RORSCHACH
    TESTS
ROTTEN
    BOROUGHS

ROUGH-AND-
    TUMBLE
RUBBER
    DINGHIES
RUBBER-
    STAMPING
RUBBING
    ALCOHOL
RUDIMENTARILLY
RUNNING
    REPAIRS
RUN THE
    GAUNTLET
RUSH ONES
    FENCES

S

SACRAMENTALISM
SACRAMENTALIST
SACRAMENTALITY
SACRAMENTARIAN
SACRILEGIOUSLY
SADOMASOCHISTS
SAFE-DEPOSIT
    BOX
SAFETY
    CURTAINS
SALAD
    DRESSINGS
SALUBRIOUSNESS
SANCTIFICATION
SANDWICH
    BOARDS
SANDWICH
    COURSE
SANGUINARINESS
SANITARY
    TOWELS
SANTIAGO DE
    CUBA
SAPONIFICATION
SATELLITE
    STATE
SATISFACTIONAL
SATISFACTORILY
SAVE ONES
    BREATH
SAVINGS
    ACCOUNT
SAWN-OFF
    SHOTGUN
SAXIFRAGACEOUS
SCANDALIZATION

SCANDALMONGERS
SCANDALOUSNESS
SCATTERBRAINED
SCHEMATIZATION
SCHISMATICALLY
SCHIZOMYCETOUS
SCHIZOPHRENICS
SCHIZOPHYCEOUS
SCHOOLCHILDREN
SCHOOLMISTRESS
SCHOOLTEACHERS
SCIENCE
    FICTION
SCIENTIFICALLY
SCINTILLOMETER
SCOTCH
    WHISKIES
SCREEN
    PRINTING
SCRUBBING
    BRUSH
SCRUPULOUSNESS
SCRUTINIZINGLY
SCURRILOUSNESS
SEARCH
    WARRANTS
SEASONABLENESS
SECOND-
    GUESSING
SECOND
    THOUGHTS
SECULARIZATION
SEGREGATIONIST
SELF-
    ABNEGATION
SELF-
    ABSORPTION
SELF-
    ANALYTICAL
SELF-
    CONFIDENCE
SELF-
    CONTROLLED
SELF-
    DESTRUCTED
SELF-
    DISCIPLINE
SELF-
    EFFACEMENT
SELF-
    EMPLOYMENT
SELF-
    GOVERNMENT

SELF-IMPORTANCE
SELF-INDUCTANCE
SELF-INDULGENCE
SELF-INFLICTION
SELF-INTERESTED
SELF-JUSTIFYING
SELF-POSSESSION
SELF-PROTECTION
SELF-RESPECTFUL
SELF-RESPECTING
SELF-SUFFICIENT
SELF-SUPPORTING
SEMAPHORICALLY
SEMASIOLOGICAL
SEMICENTENNIAL
SEMICONDUCTION
SEMICONDUCTORS
SEMIELLIPTICAL
SEMIPARASITISM
SENIOR CITIZENS
SENSATIONALISM
SENSATIONALIST
SENTIMENTALISM
SENTIMENTALIST
SENTIMENTALITY
SENTIMENTALIZE
SEPARATE TABLES
SEPARATIVENESS
SEPTUAGENARIAN
SEQUESTRATIONS
SERGEANT-AT-ARMS
SERGEANT MAJORS
SERIALIZATIONS
SERIOCOMICALLY
SERJEANT-AT-ARMS
SERVICEABILITY

SERVICE CHARGES
SERVICE STATION
SERVOMECHANISM
SESQUIPEDALIAN
SEWING MACHINES
SHAGGY-DOG STORY
SHAMEFACEDNESS
SHEET LIGHTNING
SHEPHERD'S-PURSE
SHERARDIZATION
SHETLAND PONIES
SHIHCHIACHUANG
SHILLY-SHALLIED
SHILLYSHALLIER
SHIP'S CHANDLERS
SHOCK ABSORBERS
SHOCK TREATMENT
SHOOTING STICKS
SHOP ASSISTANTS
SHOPPING CENTRE
SHORT-CIRCUITED
SHORTSIGHTEDLY
SHOTGUN WEDDING
SHOULDER BLADES
SHOULDER STRAPS
SIDEWALK ARTIST
SIGMOIDOSCOPIC
SIGNATURE TUNES
SIGNIFICATIONS
SILENT PARTNERS
SILICIFICATION

SILVER JUBILEES
SILVER WEDDINGS
SILVICULTURIST
SIMAROUBACEOUS
SIMPLE FRACTURE
SIMPLE INTEREST
SIMPLE MACHINES
SIMPLIFICATION
SIMPLIFICATIVE
SIMPLISTICALLY
SIMULTANEOUSLY
SINGLE-BREASTED
SINGLE-MINDEDLY
SINKIANG-UIGHUR
SINKING FEELING
SIPHONOPHOROUS
SITTING TARGETS
SIXTEENTH NOTES
SKATE ON THIN ICE
SKIRTING BOARDS
SLANDEROUSNESS
SLAP ON THE WRIST
SLATTERNLINESS
SLAUGHTERHOUSE
SLIPSHODDINESS
SLOTTED SPATULA
SLUGGARDLINESS
SLUMBEROUSNESS
SMALL INTESTINE
SOCIAL CLIMBERS
SOCIAL SCIENCES
SOCIAL SECURITY
SOCIAL SERVICES

SOCIOLOGICALLY
SOCIOPOLITICAL
SODIUM CHLORIDE
SOLDERING IRONS
SOLICITOUSNESS
SOLIDIFICATION
SOMNAMBULATION
SOMNAMBULISTIC
SOPHISTICATION
SOUL-DESTROYING
SOUNDING BOARDS
SOUTHEASTWARDS
SOUTHERN LIGHTS
SOUTH-SOUTHEAST
SOUTH-SOUTHWEST
SOUTHWESTWARDS
SPATIOTEMPORAL
SPEAKERS CORNER
SPECIALIZATION
SPECIAL LICENCE
SPECIAL SCHOOLS
SPECIFICATIONS
SPECTROGRAPHIC
SPECTROSCOPIST
SPEECHLESSNESS
SPERMATOGONIAL
SPERMATOGONIUM
SPERMATOPHORAL
SPERMATOPHYTIC
SPERMATORRHOEA
SPERMIOGENESIS
SPERMIOGENETIC
SPHEROIDICALLY
SPHYGMOGRAPHIC
SPINNING WHEELS
SPINTHARISCOPE
SPIRITLESSNESS
SPIRITUALISTIC
SPIROCHAETOSIS
SPIRONOLACTONE

SPITTING
IMAGES
SPLINTER
GROUPS
SPONGIOBLASTIC
SPORADICALNESS
SPRECHSTIMMUNG
SPRING
CHICKENS
SPRING-
CLEANING
SQUADRON
LEADER
SQUARE
BRACKETS
STAFF
SERGEANTS
STAGE
DIRECTION
STAMPING
GROUND
STANDARD-
BEARER
STANDING
ORDERS
STANDOFF
HALVES
ST ANDREWS
CROSS
STAPHYLOCOCCAL
STAPHYLOCOCCUS
STAPHYLOPLASTY
STARTING
BLOCKS
STARTING
PISTOL
STARTING
PRICES
START
SOMETHING
STATE'S
EVIDENCE
STATIONARINESS
STATIONMASTERS
STATUESQUENESS
STEAMROLLERING
STEAMTIGHTNESS
STEERING
WHEELS
STEPPING-
STONES
STERCORICOLOUS
STERCULIACEOUS

STEREOMETRICAL
STEREOSPECIFIC
STERTOROUSNESS
STICKING
POINTS
STIGMATIZATION
STINGING
NETTLE
STIPPLING
BRUSH
STIR ONES
STUMPS
STOCHASTICALLY
STOCKBROKERAGE
STOCK
EXCHANGES
STOCKING-
FILLER
STOICHIOMETRIC
STOLEN
PROPERTY
STOPS AT
NOTHING
STORE
DETECTIVE
STORM IN A
TEACUP
STRAIGHT
FIGHTS
STRAIGHTJACKET
STRAIGHT
JACKET
STRATICULATION
STRATIFICATION
STRAWBERRY
MARK
STREET-
CREDIBLE
STREPTOTHRICIN
STRETCHABILITY
STRETCHER
PARTY
STRIDULOUSNESS
STRIKEBREAKERS
STRIKEBREAKING
STRONG
LANGUAGE
STRONG-
MINDEDLY
STUDENTS'
UNIONS
STULTIFICATION

STUMBLING
BLOCK
STUPENDOUSNESS
SUBALTERNATION
SUBCONSCIOUSLY
SUBCONTINENTAL
SUBCONTRACTING
SUBCONTRACTORS
SUBCUTANEOUSLY
SUBINFEUDATION
SUBINFEUDATORY
SUBJECTABILITY
SUBJECTIVISTIC
SUBJECT-
RAISING
SUBLIEUTENANCY
SUBLIEUTENANTS
SUBMACHINE
GUNS
SUBMERSIBILITY
SUBMICROSCOPIC
SUBMISSIVENESS
SUBSIDIARINESS
SUBSTANTIALISM
SUBSTANTIALIST
SUBSTANTIALITY
SUBSTANTIATING
SUBSTANTIATION
SUBSTANTIATIVE
SUBTERRESTRIAL
SUBVERSIVENESS
SUCCESSFULNESS
SUCCESSIVENESS
SUGGESTIBILITY
SUGGESTIVENESS
SULPHANILAMIDE
SULPHATHIAZOLE
SULPHISOXAZOLE
SULPHONMETHANE
SULPHURIZATION
SULPHUROUSNESS
SUPERABUNDANCE
SUPERANNUATION
SUPERCILIOUSLY
SUPERCONDUCTOR
SUPERELEVATION
SUPERFICIALITY
SUPERINCUMBENT
SUPERINDUCTION
SUPERINTENDENT
SUPERINTENDING

SUPERNATURALLY
SUPERNORMALITY
SUPERPHOSPHATE
SUPERSATURATED
SUPERSCRIPTION
SUPERSONICALLY
SUPERSTRUCTURE
SUPPLY
TEACHERS
SUPPORTABILITY
SUPPORTING
PART
SUPRAMOLECULAR
SUPRASEGMENTAL
SUREFOOTEDNESS
SURGICAL
SPIRIT
SURPASSINGNESS
SURPRISINGNESS
SUSCEPTIBILITY
SUSPENDIBILITY
SUSPENSIVENESS
SUSPICIOUSNESS
SWIMMING
TRUNKS
SWORD-
SWALLOWER
SYMBIONTICALLY
SYMBOLICALNESS
SYMMETRIZATION
SYMPATHIZINGLY
SYMPTOMATOLOGY
SYNCHRONICALLY
SYNCRETIZATION
SYNERGETICALLY
SYNONYMOUSNESS
SYNTHESIZATION
SYNTHETIZATION
SYPHILITICALLY
SYSTEMATICALLY
SYSTEMS
ANALYST

T
TACHISTOSCOPIC
TAKE IN GOOD
PART
TALK OF THE
DEVIL
TARTAN
TROUSERS
TAUTOLOGICALLY

TECHNICALITIES
TELANGIECTASIS
TELANGIECTATIC
TELAUTOGRAPHIC
TELEGRAPH
POLES
TELEMETRICALLY
TELEOLOGICALLY
TELEPATHICALLY
TELEPHONE
BOXES
TELESCOPICALLY
TELETYPESETTER
TERCENTENARIES
TERGIVERSATION
TERGIVERSATORY
TERMINOLOGICAL
TERRACED
HOUSES
TERRITORIALISM
TERRITORIALIST
TERRITORIALITY
TERRITORIALIZE
TERROR-
STRICKEN
TEST-TUBE
BABIES
TETRAETHYL
LEAD
THAUMATROPICAL
THE
AMBASSADORS
THE FOUR
SEASONS
THE LIFE OF
RILEY
THEOCENTRICITY
THEOCRATICALLY
THEOLOGIZATION
THEOSOPHICALLY
THERIANTHROPIC
THERMAESTHESIA
THERMOCHEMICAL
THERMODYNAMICS
THERMOELECTRIC
THERMOELECTRON
THERMOJUNCTION
THERMOMAGNETIC
THERMOPLASTICS
THIOCYANIC
ACID
THOUGHTFULNESS

THREE-DAY
EVENTS
THREE-
HALFPENCE
THREE-LINE
WHIPS
THREE-POINT
TURN
THRIFTLESSNESS
THROMBOPLASTIC
THROMBOPLASTIN
THYMELAEACEOUS
THYROTOXICOSIS
TICKLED TO
DEATH
TIERRA DEL
FUEGO
TIME
IMMEMORIAL
TIME
SIGNATURES
TITTLE-
TATTLING
TOAD OF TOAD
HALL
TOILET
TRAINING
TO-ING AND
FRO-ING
TONGUE
TWISTERS
TORTOISESHELLS
TRACTION
ENGINE
TRADE
UNIONISTS
TRADING
ESTATES
TRADITIONALISM
TRADITIONALIST
TRADUCIANISTIC
TRAFFIC
CALMING
TRAFFIC
CIRCLES
TRAFFIC
ISLANDS
TRAFFIC
WARDENS
TRAGICOMICALLY
TRAITOROUSNESS
TRANQUILLIZERS
TRANQUILLIZING

TRANSCAUCASIAN
TRANSCENDENTAL
TRANSCENDENTLY
TRANSCENDINGLY
TRANSCRIPTIONS
TRANSFERENTIAL
TRANSFORMATION
TRANSFORMATIVE
TRANSGRESSIBLE
TRANSGRESSIONS
TRANSISTORIZED
TRANSITIONALLY
TRANSITIVENESS
TRANSITORINESS
TRANS-
JORDANIAN
TRANSLITERATED
TRANSLITERATOR
TRANSMIGRATION
TRANSMIGRATIVE
TRANSMIGRATORY
TRANSMISSIVITY
TRANSMOGRIFIED
TRANSMUTATIONS
TRANSPARENCIES
TRANSPLANTABLE
TRANSPORTATION
TRANSPORT
CAFES
TRANSPOSITIONS
TRANSVALUATION
TRANSVERSENESS
TRAUMATIZATION
TRAVEL
AGENCIES
TRAVELLERS
TALE
TRAVELSICKNESS
TREAD THE
BOARDS
TREASURE
ISLAND
TREASURE
TROVES
TREMENDOUSNESS
TRICHINIZATION
TRICHOMONIASIS
TRICHOTOMOUSLY
TRICK OR
TREATED
TRIDIMENSIONAL
TRINITROCRESOL

TRINITROPHENOL
TRISOCTAHEDRAL
TRISOCTAHEDRON
TRISTAN DA
CUNHA
TRIVIALIZATION
TROPIC OF
CANCER
TROUBLESHOOTER
TROUSER
PRESSES
TUMULTUOUSNESS
TUNBRIDGE
WELLS
TURBOGENERATOR
TURF
ACCOUNTANT
TURKISH
DELIGHT
TURN A DEAF
EAR TO
TURNING
CIRCLES
TWO-
DIMENSIONAL
TYRANNICALNESS

U

UBIQUITOUSNESS
ULTIMOGENITURE
ULTRAMODERNISM
ULTRAMODERNIST
ULTRAMONTANISM
ULTRAMONTANIST
ULTRASONICALLY
ULTRASTRUCTURE
UMBILICAL
CORDS
UNACCOMMODATED
UNACCOMPLISHED
UNACCOUNTED
FOR
UNACCOUNTED-
FOR
UNAPPRECIATIVE
UNAPPROACHABLE
UNAPPROPRIATED
UNAVOIDABILITY
UNBEARABLENESS
UNBECOMINGNESS
UNCOMPROMISING
UNCONSCIONABLE

UNCONSCIONABLY
UNCONTAMINATED
UNCONTROLLABLE
UNCONVENTIONAL
UNCONVINCINGLY
UNCORROBORATED
UNDERACHIEVERS
UNDERACHIEVING
UNDERCARRIAGES
UNDERESTIMATED
UNDERESTIMATES
UNDERGRADUATES
UNDERMENTIONED
UNDERNOURISHED
UNDERSECRETARY
UNDERSTANDABLE
UNDERSTANDABLY
UNDERSTANDINGS
UNDERSTATEMENT
UNDERVALUATION
UNDESIRABILITY
UNECONOMICALLY
UNENTHUSIASTIC
UNEVENTFULNESS
UNEXPECTEDNESS
UNFAITHFULNESS
UNFLAPPABILITY
UNFRIENDLINESS
UNFRUITFULNESS
UNGRATEFULNESS
UNHANDSOMENESS
UNHOLY
  ALLIANCE
UNICELLULARITY
UNIDENTIFIABLE
UNIDIRECTIONAL
UNIFORMITARIAN
UNINCORPORATED
UNINTELLIGENCE
UNINTELLIGIBLE
UNIPERSONALITY
UNIVERSALISTIC
UNIVERSAL
  JOINT
UNKNOWABLENESS
UNMENTIONABLES
UNPLEASANTNESS
UNPRACTICALITY
UNPREMEDITATED
UNPREPAREDNESS
UNPROFESSIONAL

408

UNQUESTIONABLE
UNQUESTIONABLY
UNRECOGNIZABLE
UNRESERVEDNESS
UNRESTRAINEDLY
UNSATISFACTORY
UNSCRUPULOUSLY
UNTHANKFULNESS
UNTHINKABILITY
UNTOUCHABILITY
UPSIDE-
  DOWNNESS
UPSTANDINGNESS
UPWARDLY-
  MOBILE
UST-
  KAMENOGORSK
UTILITARIANISM

V

VACUUM
  CLEANERS
VALERIANACEOUS
VALETUDINARIAN
VALUE
  JUDGMENTS
VASOINHIBITORY
VAULTING
  HORSES
VEGETABLE
  KNIFE
VEGETATIVENESS
VENDING
  MACHINE
VENETIAN
  BLINDS
VENTRILOQUISTS
VENTURE
  CAPITAL
VERISIMILITUDE
VERTICILLASTER
VERTICILLATION
VESPERTILIONID
VESTED
  INTEREST
VEXED
  QUESTIONS
VICE-
  CHANCELLOR
VICE-
  PRESIDENCY
VICIOUS
  CIRCLES

VICTORIOUSNESS
VIEW ON THE
  STOUR
VILLAINOUSNESS
VINDICTIVENESS
VISHAKHAPATNAM
VITRIFIABILITY
VITRIOLIZATION
VITUPERATIVELY
VIVISECTIONIST
VOCIFEROUSNESS
VOLATILIZATION
VOLCANOLOGICAL
VOLUMETRICALLY
VOLUMINOUSNESS
VOLUPTUOUSNESS
VOROSHILOVGRAD
VOTES OF
  CENSURE
VULGAR
  FRACTION
VULGARIZATIONS
VULVOVAGINITIS

W

WARRANTABILITY
WARRANT
  OFFICER
WASHING
  MACHINE
WATERCOLOURIST
WATERING
  PLACES
WATERPROOFNESS
WATER-
  REPELLENT
WATER-
  RESISTANT
WATER
  SOFTENERS
WATERTIGHTNESS
WEAK-
  MINDEDNESS
WEATHERABILITY
WEATHERPROOFED
WEATHER
  STATION
WEIGHTLESSNESS
WE LIVE AND
  LEARN
WELL-
  ACCUSTOMED

WELL-
  ACQUAINTED
WELL-
  DOCUMENTED
WESTERNIZATION
WET ONES
  WHISTLE
WHEELER-
  DEALERS
WHEELER-
  DEALING
WHIMSICALITIES
WHIPPERSNAPPER
WHITE BLOOD
  CELL
WHITE
  ELEPHANTS
WHOLE-
  HEARTEDLY
WHORTLEBERRIES
WILDCAT
  STRIKES
WILD GOOSE
  CHASE
WILD-GOOSE
  CHASE
WILLIAM AND
  MARY
WIND
  INSTRUMENT
WINDOW
  DRESSING
WINDOW-
  SHOPPERS
WINDOW
  SHOPPING
WINDOW-
  SHOPPING
WIND-
  POLLINATED
WING
  COMMANDERS
WOMEN'S
  MOVEMENT
WORCESTER
  SAUCE
WORD
  PROCESSING
WORD
  PROCESSORS
WORKING
  PARTIES
WORLD-
  WEARINESS

WORMWOOD
  SCRUBS
WORSHIPFULNESS
WORTHWHILENESS

X
XANTHOPHYLLOUS
XEROPHYTICALLY

Y
YOUTH
  HOSTELLER

Z
ZEBRA
  CROSSINGS
ZINGIBERACEOUS

A

A BUNDLE OF NERVES
ACANTHOCEPHALAN
ACCLIMATIZATION
ACCOMMODATINGLY
ACCOMPLISHMENTS
ACHONDROPLASTIC
ACHROMATIZATION
ACIDIMETRICALLY
ACKNOWLEDGEABLE
ACKNOWLEDGMENTS
ACOUSTIC COUPLER
ACQUISITIVENESS
ADMINISTRATIONS
A DROP IN THE OCEAN
AERODYNAMICALLY
AFFRANCHISEMENT
AGAINST THE GRAIN
AGGLUTINABILITY
AGRANULOCYTOSIS
AIR CHIEF MARSHAL
AIR-CONDITIONING
AIRCRAFT CARRIER
AIR VICE-MARSHALS
ALGORITHMICALLY
ALIMENTARY CANAL
ALIVE AND KICKING
ALPHABETIZATION
ALUMINOSILICATE
AMARYLLIDACEOUS
AMBASSADORSHIPS
AMERICAN INDIANS
AMERICANIZATION
A MONTH OF SUNDAYS
AMUSEMENT ARCADE
ANABOLIC STEROID
ANARCHISTICALLY
ANCYLOSTOMIASIS
ANIMAL HUSBANDRY
ANIMATED CARTOON
ANOMALISTICALLY
ANTARCTIC CIRCLE
ANTEPENULTIMATE
ANTHROPOCENTRIC
ANTHROPOGENESIS
ANTHROPOGENETIC
ANTHROPOLOGICAL
ANTHROPOLOGISTS
ANTHROPOMETRIST
ANTHROPOMORPHIC
ANTICHOLINERGIC

ANTICLERICALISM
ANTI-IMPERIALISM
ANTI-IMPERIALIST
ANTILOGARITHMIC
ANTINATIONALIST
ANTIPERISTALSIS
ANTIPERSPIRANTS
APARTMENT HOUSES
APOCALYPTICALLY
APPRENTICESHIPS
APPROACHABILITY
APPROPRIATENESS
APPROVED SCHOOLS
ARCHIEPISCOPATE
ARCHITECTURALLY
ARGUMENTATIVELY
ARTERIALIZATION
ASCLEPIADACEOUS
ASSIMILATIONIST
ASSOCIATE DEGREE
ASTRONAUTICALLY
ASTRONAVIGATION
ASTROPHYSICISTS
ATHEROSCLEROSIS
ATHEROSCLEROTIC
ATMOSPHERICALLY
AT THE DROP OF A
HAT
ATTORNEY GENERAL
AUDIOMETRICALLY
AUTHORITATIVELY
AUTOBIOGRAPHIES
AUTOCORRELATION
AUTOGRAPHICALLY
AUTOMATIC PILOTS
AUTORADIOGRAPHY
AUTOTRANSFORMER
AVERSION THERAPY

B

BACHELOR'S DEGREE
BACK-SEAT DRIVERS
BACTERIOLOGICAL
BACTERIOLOGISTS
BACTERIOPHAGOUS
BALLROOM DANCING
BANANA REPUBLICS
BANNER HEADLINES
BANQUETING HOUSE
BASIDIOMYCETOUS
BATCH PROCESSING

BATHING MACHINES
BATHOMETRICALLY
BATHYMETRICALLY
BEATEN AT THE POST
BED AND BREAKFAST
BENEFIT OF CLERGY
BIBLIOGRAPHICAL
BIBLIOPHILISTIC
BINOCULAR VISION
BIOASTRONAUTICS
BIOGEOGRAPHICAL
BIOLUMINESCENCE
BIOTECHNOLOGIST
BIRDS OF A FEATHER
BIRDS OF PARADISE
BISYMMETRICALLY
BLACK MARKETEERS
BLACKWATER FEVER
BLAMEWORTHINESS
BLANK CARTRIDGES
BLOCK AND TACKLES
BLOOD-AND-THUNDER
BOARDING SCHOOLS
BONDED WAREHOUSE
BOW STREET RUNNER
BRAKE HORSE POWER
BREAKING THE NEWS
BRING AND BUY SALE
BROADMINDEDNESS
BROKEN-HEARTEDLY
BRUSSELS SPROUTS
BUBBLE AND SQUEAK
BUILDING SOCIETY
BUREAU DE CHANGES
BUSMAN'S HOLIDAYS
BUTTERFLY STROKE

C

CABLE TELEVISION
CANNIBALIZATION
CAPRIFOLIACEOUS
CARDIOPULMONARY
CARPOMETACARPUS
CARRYING CHARGES
CASEMENT WINDOWS
CATEGORIZATIONS
CATHERINE WHEELS
CATHETERIZATION
CATHODE RAY TUBES
CATHOLICIZATION
CENTRE OF GRAVITY

CEPHALOCHORDATE
CEPHALOTHORACIC
CEREBROVASCULAR
CEREMONIOUSNESS
CHAPTER AND VERSE
CHARACTERISTICS
CHARENT-MARITIME
CHARGE D'AFFAIRES
CHECKING ACCOUNT
CHEMICAL WARFARE
CHEMOTACTICALLY
CHEMOTROPICALLY
CHENOPODIACEOUS
CHESTS OF DRAWERS
CHIEF CONSTABLES
CHIEF INSPECTORS
CHINESE CHEQUERS
CHINESE LANTERNS
CHINLESS WONDERS
CHLORAMPHENICOL
CHOLECALCIFEROL
CHOLECYSTECTOMY
CHONDRIFICATION
CHROMATOGRAPHER
CHROMATOGRAPHIC
CHROMATOPHOROUS
CHRONOGRAMMATIC
CHRONOLOGICALLY
CHUCK-WILL'S-WIDOW
CHURCH OF ENGLAND
CIGARETTE HOLDER
CIGARETTE PAPERS
CINEMATOGRAPHER
CINEMATOGRAPHIC
CIRCUIT BREAKERS
CIRCULARIZATION
CIRCUMAMBULATOR
CIRCUMFERENTIAL
CIRCUMLOCUTIONS
CIRCUMNAVIGABLE
CIRCUMNAVIGATED
CIRCUMNAVIGATOR
CIRCUMSCRIPTION
CIRCUMSTANTIATE
CIRCUMVALLATION
CLANDESTINENESS
CLASSIFICATIONS
CLAUSTROPHOBICS
CLEAR-HEADEDNESS
CLERMONT-FERRAND
CLOUD CUCKOO LAND

CLOUD-CUCKOO-LAND
COCK-A-DOODLE-DOOS
COCKNEYFICATION
COCKTAIL LOUNGES
COFFEE-TABLE BOOK
COLD-BLOODEDNESS
COLD-HEARTEDNESS
COLD-SHOULDERING
COLLECTIVE FARMS
COLLECTIVE NOUNS
COLLECTOR'S ITEMS
COLLISION COURSE
COLORADO BEETLES
COLOUR BLINDNESS
COMBINATION LOCK
COMEDY OF MANNERS
COME INTO ONES OWN
COMFORT STATIONS
COMITY OF NATIONS
COMMERCIALISTIC
COMMERCIALIZING
COMMISSIONAIRES
COMMITTEE STAGES
COMMODIFICATION
COMMON FRACTIONS
COMMUNALIZATION
COMMUNICABILITY
COMMUNITY CENTRE
COMMUNITY CHESTS
COMPASSIONATELY
COMPETITIVENESS
COMPLICATEDNESS
COMPREHENSIVELY
COMPRESSIBILITY
COMPUTERIZATION
CONCEPTUALISTIC
CONCEPTUALIZING
CONCESSIONAIRES
CONCRETE JUNGLES
CONFECTIONERIES
CONFIDENCE TRICK
CONFIDENTIALITY
CONFIGURATIONAL
CONFRATERNITIES
CONGLOMERATIONS
CONGRATULATIONS
CONSCIENCE MONEY
CONSCIENTIOUSLY
CONSCRIPTIONIST
CONSENTING ADULT
CONSERVATIONISM

CONSERVATIONIST
CONSIDERATENESS
CONSPICUOUSNESS
CONSTITUTIONALS
CONSUMER DURABLE
CONTEMPORANEITY
CONTEMPORANEOUS
CONTEMPTIBILITY
CONTENTIOUSNESS
CONTORTIONISTIC
CONTRACTIBILITY
CONTRAINDICATED
CONTROVERSIALLY
CONVENIENCE FOOD
CONVENTIONALISM
CONVENTIONALIST
CONVENTIONALITY
CONVENTIONALIZE
CONVOLVULACEOUS
CORRELATIVENESS
CORRESPONDINGLY
COSMOPOLITANISM
COST-EFFECTIVELY
COTTAGE HOSPITAL
COTTAGE INDUSTRY
COUNTERATTACKED
COUNTERATTACKER
COUNTERBALANCED
COUNTERBALANCES
COUNTERCLAIMANT
COUNTERIRRITANT
COUNTER IRRITANT
COUNTERMEASURES
COUNTERPROPOSAL
COURT-MARTIALING
COURT-MARTIALLED
COURTS OF INQUIRY
COVERING LETTERS
CREASE RESISTANT
CREATIVE WRITING
CREDIBILITY GAPS
CRICKET PAVILION
CRIMINAL CLASSES
CROSS-FERTILIZED
CROSSOPTERYGION
CROSS-QUESTIONED
CROSS-QUESTIONER
CROSS-REFERENCES
CROSSWORD EDITORS
CROWN PRINCESSES
CRYSTALLIZATION

CRYSTALLOGRAPHY
CUCKOO IN THE NEST
CURRENT ACCOUNTS
CURRICULUM VITAE
CUT AND COME AGAIN
CYTOMEGALOVIRUS

D

DAYLIGHT ROBBERY
DAYS OF RECKONING
DECALCIFICATION
DECARBONIZATION
DECARBOXYLATION
DECIPHERABILITY
DECOMPOSABILITY
DECONTAMINATING
DECONTAMINATION
DECONTAMINATIVE
DECONTEXTUALIZE
DEFINITE ARTICLE
DEHYDROGENATION
DELIRIUM TREMENS
DELIVER THE GOODS
DEMAGNETIZATION
DEMOCRATIZATION
DEMONSTRABILITY
DEMONSTRATIONAL
DEMONSTRATIVELY
DEMULSIFICATION
DEMYSTIFICATION
DENATIONALIZING
DENITRIFICATION
DEPARTMENTALISM
DEPARTMENTALIZE
DEPARTMENT STORE
DEPARTURE LOUNGE
DEPENDENT CLAUSE
DEPOSIT ACCOUNTS
DERMATOGLYPHICS
DERMATOPHYTOSIS
DESCRIPTIVENESS
DESENSITIZATION
DESEXUALIZATION
DESTABILIZATION
DESTRUCTIBILITY
DESTRUCTIVENESS
DETRIBALIZATION
DEVELOPMENT AREA
DEVIL'S ADVOCATES
DEVITRIFICATION
DIALECTOLOGICAL

DIAMAGNETICALLY
DIAMOND JUBILEES
DIAMOND WEDDINGS
DIAPHOTOTROPISM
DICHOTOMIZATION
DIESEL-HYDRAULIC
DIFFERENTIATING
DIFFERENTIATION
DIGITAL COMPUTER
DIRECTION FINDER
DISADVANTAGEOUS
DISAPPOINTINGLY
DISAPPOINTMENTS
DISARTICULATION
DISCIPLINARIANS
DISCONCERTINGLY
DISCONTINUATION
DISCONTINUITIES
DISCONTINUOUSLY
DISCOUNTENANCED
DISCOURAGEMENTS
DISCRETIONARILY
DISENCUMBERMENT
DISENTANGLEMENT
DISESTABLISHING
DISHEARTENINGLY
DISHEARTENMENTS
DISILLUSIONMENT
DISINCLINATIONS
DISINFLATIONARY
DISINTERESTEDLY
DISORDERLY HOUSE
DISORGANIZATION
DISPASSIONATELY
DISREPUTABILITY
DISRESPECTFULLY
DISSATISFACTION
DISSATISFACTORY
DISSERTATIONIST
DISSIMILARITIES
DISTASTEFULNESS
DISTINCTIVENESS
DISTINGUISHABLE
DISTRACTIBILITY
DISTRUSTFULNESS
DITHYRAMBICALLY
DIVERSIFICATION
DIVISION LOBBIES
DO-IT-YOURSELFERS
DOLICHOCEPHALIC
DOMESTIC ANIMALS

DOMESTIC SCIENCE
DOMESTIC SERVICE
DORSIVENTRALITY
DOUBLE-BARRELLED
DOUBLE ENTENDRES
DOUBLE STANDARDS
DOUBLE WHITE LINE
DRAUGHTSMANSHIP
DRESSING STATION
DRESS REHEARSALS
DRIVE-BY SHOOTING
DRIVING LICENCES
DRUIDICAL CIRCLE
DUAL CARRIAGEWAY
DUAL CITIZENSHIP
DUTCH ELM DISEASE

E

EARTHSHATTERING
EAT ONES HEART OUT
ECCLESIASTICISM
ECCLESIOLOGICAL
EDUCATED GUESSES
EDUCATIONALISTS
ELECTRIC BLANKET
ELECTRIFICATION
ELECTROACOUSTIC
ELECTROANALYSIS
ELECTROANALYTIC
ELECTROCHEMICAL
ELECTRODIALYSIS
ELECTRODYNAMICS
ELECTROKINETICS
ELECTROLYSATION
ELECTROMAGNETIC
ELECTRONEGATIVE
ELECTROPHORESIS
ELECTROPHORETIC
ELECTROPOSITIVE
ELECTROSURGICAL
ELEVATED RAILWAY
EMANCIPATIONIST
EMINENCES GRISES
ENANTIOMORPHISM
ENCEPHALOGRAPHY
ENCHONDROMATOUS
ENCOMIASTICALLY
ENDOCRINE GLANDS
ENDOCRINOLOGIST
ENDOTHERMICALLY
ENDOWMENT POLICY

ENFRANCHISEMENT
ENGAGEMENT RINGS
ENTENTE CORDIALE
ENTREPRENEURIAL
ENVIRONMENTALLY
EPIDEMIOLOGICAL
EPISCOPALIANISM
EPISTEMOLOGICAL
EPITHELIOMATOUS
EQUALITARIANISM
ETERNAL TRIANGLE
ETHEREALIZATION
ETHNIC CLEANSING
ETHNOCENTRICITY
EUCHARISTICALLY
EUDIOMETRICALLY
EUPHEMISTICALLY
EUROPEANIZATION
EUSTACHIAN TUBES
EVERLASTINGNESS
EXCEPTIONALNESS
EXCHANGEABILITY
EXCLAMATION MARK
EXCOMMUNICATING
EXCOMMUNICATION
EXCOMMUNICATIVE
EXEMPLIFICATION
EXEMPLIFICATIVE
EXHIBITIONISTIC
EXPEDITIOUSNESS
EXPENSE ACCOUNTS
EXPERIMENTALISM
EXPERIMENTALIST
EXPERIMENTATION
EXPOSTULATINGLY
EXPRESSIONISTIC
EXTEMPORARINESS
EXTEMPORIZATION
EXTERIORIZATION
EXTERNALIZATION
EXTRACURRICULAR
EXTRALINGUISTIC
EXTRAORDINARILY

F

FAIRY GODMOTHERS
FAMILIARIZATION
FAMILY ALLOWANCE
FASHIONABLENESS
FATHER CHRISTMAS
FEATURELESSNESS

FELLOW TRAVELLER
FEUILLETONISTIC
FIDEICOMMISSARY
FIFTH COLUMNISTS
FIGURES OF SPEECH
FILLING STATIONS
FINISHING SCHOOL
FIRST LIEUTENANT
FLIBBERTIGIBBET
FLIGHT SERGEANTS
FLIRTATIOUSNESS
FOLDING ONES ARMS
FOOT-POUND-SECOND
FOREIGN EXCHANGE
FORESIGHTEDNESS
FORKED LIGHTNING
FORMULARIZATION
FOUNDATION STONE
FOUNDING FATHERS
FOUR-DIMENSIONAL
FOUR-LETTER WORDS
FOURTH DIMENSION
FRACTIONIZATION
FRAGMENTARINESS
FRANKFURT AM MAIN
FREE ASSOCIATION
FRENCH POLISHING
FRIENDLY SOCIETY
FROM STEM TO STERN
FULL-BLOODEDNESS
FUNDAMENTALISTS
FUNERAL DIRECTOR
FUNERAL PARLOURS
FUTILITARIANISM

G

GAME SET AND MATCH
GASTROENTERITIC
GASTROENTERITIS
GASTRONOMICALLY
GENERAL DELIVERY
GENERAL ELECTION
GENERALIZATIONS
GENERAL PRACTICE
GENTLEMAN-AT-ARMS
GENTLEMAN FARMER
GENTLEMANLINESS
GENTLEMEN-AT-ARMS
GERMAN SHEPHERDS
GET ONES SKATES ON
GIVE ONESELF AWAY

GIVE THE GAME AWAY
GLOBE ARTICHOKES
GLOSSY MAGAZINES
GLOUCESTERSHIRE
GLUCONEOGENESIS
GNOTOBIOTICALLY
GOLDEN HANDSHAKE
GOLDEN RETRIEVER
GOOD-FOR-NOTHINGS
GOOD-NATUREDNESS
GO OFF THE DEEP END
GORNO-BADAKHSHAN
GOVERNOR-GENERAL
GRAPHIC DESIGNER
GREGORIAN CHANTS
GUTTURALIZATION
GYNANDROMORPHIC

H

HACKNEY CARRIAGE
HAEMAGGLUTINATE
HAEMOFLAGELLATE
HAEMOGLOBINURIA
HALF-HEARTEDNESS
HALL OF RESIDENCE
HALLUCINATIONAL
HAMAMELIDACEOUS
HAMMER AND SICKLE
HARD-HEARTEDNESS
HARD LUCK STORIES
HARMONISTICALLY
HARVEST FESTIVAL
HAVE A BONE TO PICK
HEARTBREAK HOUSE
HEARTBREAKINGLY
HEARTBROKENNESS
HEAVY-HANDEDNESS
HEIR PRESUMPTIVE
HELIOCENTRICITY
HELIOMETRICALLY
HELIOTROPICALLY
HELLENISTICALLY
HELMINTHOLOGIST
HENDECASYLLABIC
HENDECASYLLABLE
HERBIVOROUSNESS
HEREDITARIANISM
HERMAPHRODITISM
HERMENEUTICALLY
HERO-WORSHIPPING
HETEROCHROMATIC

HETEROCHROMATIN
HETEROGENEOUSLY
HETEROSEXUALITY
HEXACHLOROPHENE
HEXYLRESORCINOL
HIGH COMMISSIONS
HIGHER EDUCATION
HIMACHAL PRADESH
HIPPOCRATIC OATH
HISPANICIZATION
HISTORIC PRESENT
HISTORIOGRAPHER
HISTORIOGRAPHIC
HOLOBLASTICALLY
HOLOGRAPHICALLY
HOLY ROMAN EMPIRE
HOMEOPATHICALLY
HOMOCENTRICALLY
HOMOGENEOUSNESS
HOMOPLASTICALLY
HOPE AGAINST HOPE
HORTICULTURALLY
HOSPITALIZATION
HOT-WATER BOTTLES
HOUSEHOLDERSHIP
HOUSEHOLD TROOPS
HOUSEWIFELINESS
HOUSING PROJECTS
HUMANITARIANISM
HUMANITARIANIST
HUNTINGDONSHIRE
HYDROBROMIC ACID
HYDROGENIZATION
HYDROMECHANICAL
HYDROMETALLURGY
HYPERCRITICALLY

I

ICEBERG LETTUCES
IDIOMORPHICALLY
IMMEASURABILITY
IMMERSION HEATER
IMMORTALIZATION
IMMUNOCHEMISTRY
IMMUNOGENICALLY
IMMUNOLOGICALLY
IMPECUNIOUSNESS
IMPENETRABILITY
IMPERISHABILITY
IMPONDERABILITY
IMPRESCRIPTIBLE

IMPRESSIONISTIC
IMPROBABILITIES
IMPROVISATIONAL
INACCESSIBILITY
INADMISSIBILITY
INAPPLICABILITY
INAPPROPRIATELY
INATTENTIVENESS
IN BLACK AND WHITE
INCALCULABILITY
INCIDENTAL MUSIC
INCOMMENSURABLE
INCOMMUNICATIVE
INCOMMUTABILITY
INCOMPARABILITY
INCOMPATIBILITY
INCOMPREHENSION
INCOMPREHENSIVE
INCOMPUTABILITY
INCONGRUOUSNESS
INCONSEQUENTIAL
INCONSIDERATELY
INCONSIDERATION
INCONSISTENCIES
INCONSOLABILITY
INCONSPICUOUSLY
INCONVENIENCING
INCORRIGIBILITY
INCREDULOUSNESS
INDECENT ASSAULT
INDEFEASIBILITY
INDEFENSIBILITY
INDEMNIFICATION
INDETERMINISTIC
INDIAN ROPE-TRICK
INDIGESTIBILITY
INDIRECT OBJECTS
INDISCRETIONARY
INDISPUTABILITY
INDISSOLUBILITY
INDIVIDUALISTIC
INDIVIDUALIZING
INDUSTRIALIZING
INDUSTRIOUSNESS
INEFFACEABILITY
INEFFECTIVENESS
INEXPENSIVENESS
INEXPLICABILITY
INEXTENSIBILITY
INEXTRICABILITY
INFANT PRODIGIES

INFINITESIMALLY
INFRASTRUCTURES
INFUNDIBULIFORM
INJUDICIOUSNESS
INOFFENSIVENESS
INOPPORTUNENESS
INQUISITIVENESS
INQUISITORIALLY
INSENSIBILITIES
INSIGNIFICANTLY
INSTALLMENT PLAN
INSTANTANEOUSLY
INSTRUMENTALISM
INSTRUMENTALIST
INSTRUMENTALITY
INSTRUMENTATION
INSUBORDINATELY
INSUBORDINATION
INSURANCE POLICY
INSURRECTIONARY
INSURRECTIONISM
INSURRECTIONIST
INTELLECTUALISE
INTELLECTUALISM
INTELLECTUALIST
INTELLECTUALITY
INTELLECTUALIZE
INTELLIGIBILITY
INTENSIFICATION
INTERCHANGEABLE
INTERCHANGEABLY
INTERCLAVICULAR
INTERCOLLEGIATE
INTERCONNECTION
INTERDEPENDENCE
INTERFEROMETRIC
INTERLAMINATION
INTERLOCUTORILY
INTERNALIZATION
INTERNAL REVENUE
INTERNATIONALES
INTERNATIONALLY
INTEROSCULATION
INTERPENETRABLE
INTERPRETATIONS
INTERROGATINGLY
INTERROGATIONAL
INTERROGATIVELY
INTERROGATORIES
INTERROGATORILY
INTERSCHOLASTIC

INTERVENTIONISM
INTERVENTIONIST
IN THE LAST RESORT
INTRANSIGENTIST
INTROSPECTIONAL
INTROSPECTIVELY
INTUSSUSCEPTION
INTUSSUSCEPTIVE
INVESTIGATIONAL
INVOLUNTARINESS
INVOLUNTATARILY
INVULNERABILITY
IRREDEEMABILITY
IRREFRAGABILITY
IRREMISSIBILITY
IRRESISTIBILITY
IRRESOLVABILITY
IRREVERSIBILITY

J

JACK-OF-ALL-TRADES
JAPANESE LANTERN
JEHOVAH'S WITNESS
JUMPING-OFF PLACE
JURISPRUDENTIAL
JUXTAPOSITIONAL

K

KABARDINO-BALKAR
KEEPS ONES HAND IN
KIND-HEARTEDNESS

L

LABOUR EXCHANGES
LABOUR INTENSIVE
LABOUR-INTENSIVE
LABYRINTHICALLY
LACKADAISICALLY
LADIES-IN-WAITING
LAISSEZ-FAIREISM
LARGE INTESTINES
LATERAL THINKING
LAUGHING JACKASS
LEADING ARTICLES
LEADING QUESTION
LET ONES HAIR DOWN
LETTERS OF CREDIT
LEVEL-HEADEDNESS
LIGHT-HEADEDNESS
LIGHT MACHINE GUN
LIGHTNING STRIKE

LIKE THE CLAPPERS
LILY OF THE VALLEY
LIVERY COMPANIES
LOCAL GOVERNMENT
LOGARITHMICALLY
LOIRE-ATLANTIQUE
LOPHOBRANCHIATE
LOURENCO MARQUES

M

MACHINE-READABLE
MACROCOSMICALLY
MACROSCOPICALLY
MACROSPORANGIUM
MAD AS A MARCH HARE
MAGNANIMOUSNESS
MAGNETOCHEMICAL
MAGNETOELECTRIC
MAGNETO ELECTRIC
MAGNIFYING GLASS
MALACOPTERYGIAN
MALASSIMILATION
MALE CHAUVINISTS
MALPRACTITIONER
MANIC-DEPRESSIVE
MANIFESTATIONAL
MANNERISTICALLY
MANOEUVRABILITY
MARKET GARDENERS
MARKET GARDENING
MARRIAGEABILITY
MARSHALLING YARD
MARXISM-LENINISM
MARXIST-LENINIST
MASSAGE PARLOURS
MASTER CRAFTSMAN
MASTER OF SCIENCE
MATERIALIZATION
MEANINGLESSNESS
MECHANISTICALLY
MEGALOCEPHALOUS
MELANCHOLICALLY
MELLIFLUOUSNESS
MEMORIALIZATION
MENDING ONES WAYS
MENISPERMACEOUS
MENSTRUAL PERIOD
MENTAL DEFECTIVE
MENTAL HOSPITALS
MENTALISTICALLY
MEPHISTOPHELEAN

MEROBLASTICALLY
METACINNABARITE
METAGENETICALLY
METALINGUISTICS
METALLURGICALLY
METAMATHEMATICS
METHODISTICALLY
METROPOLITANISM
MICROBIOLOGICAL
MICROBIOLOGISTS
MICROELECTRONIC
MICROPHOTOGRAPH
MICROPROCESSORS
MICROSCOPICALLY
MICROSPORANGIUM
MICROSPOROPHYLL
MIDDLE OF NOWHERE
MIDDLE-OF-THE-ROAD
MINIATURIZATION
MISAPPLICATIONS
MISAPPREHENDING
MISAPPREHENSION
MISAPPREHENSIVE
MISAPPROPRIATED
MISCALCULATIONS
MISCELLANEOUSLY
MISCHIEVOUSNESS
MISCONSTRUCTION
MISINTERPRETING
MISREPRESENTING
MISTRUSTFULNESS
MOBILE LIBRARIES
MODERNISTICALLY
MOLOTOV COCKTAIL
MONCHEN-GLADBACH
MONEY FOR OLD ROPE
MONOGRAPHICALLY
MONOUNSATURATED
MONTE CARLO RALLY
MONTMORILLONITE
MOOG SYNTHESIZER
MOONLIGHT SONATA
MORNING SICKNESS
MORPHOLOGICALLY
MORPHOPHONEMICS
MOTHER COUNTRIES
MOTHER SUPERIORS
MOVING STAIRCASE
MULTITUDINOUSLY
MUSCULOSKELETAL
MUSTARD AND CRESS

MUSTARD PLASTERS
MUTATIS MUTANDIS
MYTHOLOGIZATION

N

NAGORNO-KARABAKH
NATIONAL ANTHEMS
NATIONAL GALLERY
NATIONALIZATION
NATIONAL SERVICE
NATURAL SCIENCES
NEARSIGHTEDNESS
NEEDLE AND THREAD
NEGATIVE-RAISING
NEIGHBOURLINESS
NEOARSPHENAMINE
NEOLOGISTICALLY
NEUROHYPOPHYSIS
NEUROPATHICALLY
NEUROPHYSIOLOGY
NEUROPSYCHIATRY
NEUROPSYCHOLOGY
NEUROSURGICALLY
NEWS CONFERENCES
NIGHTMARISHNESS
NINE DAYS' WONDERS
NITROCHLOROFORM
NITROGENIZATION
NOMOGRAPHICALLY
NON COMPOS MENTIS
NONCONTRIBUTING
NONCONTRIBUTORY
NONINTERVENTION
NON INTERVENTION
NONINTOXICATING
NONPRODUCTIVITY
NON-PROFIT-MAKING
NONSENSICALNESS
NONSTANDARDIZED
NORTH COUNTRYMAN
NOTWITHSTANDING
NOUVELLE CUISINE
NO-WIN SITUATIONS
NUCLEAR FAMILIES
NUCLEAR REACTORS
NUCLEOSYNTHESIS
NUMBER-CRUNCHING

O

OBJECTIFICATION
OBSERVATION POST

OBSTRUCTIONISTS
OBSTRUCTIVENESS
OESTROGENICALLY
OLD AGE PENSIONER
OLD PEOPLE'S HOMES
OLIGOSACCHARIDE
OMNIDIRECTIONAL
ONCE IN A BLUE MOON
ONE-ARMED BANDITS
ONES HEART BLEEDS
ON THE BACK BURNER
OPEN-AND-SHUT CASE
OPENHEARTEDNESS
OPERATING SYSTEM
OPHTHALMOLOGIST
OPHTHALMOSCOPIC
OPINIONATEDNESS
OPISTHOGNATHISM
OPISTHOGNATHOUS
OPPOSITE NUMBERS
OPTICAL ILLUSION
OPTOELECTRONICS
ORIENTALIZATION
ORNITHORHYNCHUS
ORTHOCHROMATISM
ORTHOPSYCHIATRY
OSTEOPATHICALLY
OUT OF THE PICTURE
OVERCAPITALIZED
OVERCOMPENSATED
OVERDEVELOPMENT
OVERSIMPLIFYING
OXYTETRACYCLINE

P

PAINSTAKINGNESS
PALAEOBOTANICAL
PALAEOGRAPHICAL
PALAEONTOGRAPHY
PALAEONTOLOGIST
PALAEOZOOLOGIST
PALEONTOLOGISTS
PANCAKE LANDINGS
PANTHEISTICALLY
PARAGENETICALLY
PARAGRAPHICALLY
PARALLACTICALLY
PARASITOLOGICAL
PARASYMPATHETIC
PARENT COMPANIES
PARENTHETICALLY

PARLIAMENTARIAN
PARTHENOGENESIS
PARTHENOGENETIC
PARTICULARISTIC
PARTICULARITIES
PARTICULARIZING
PASSIFLORACEOUS
PASSIONLESSNESS
PAST PARTICIPLES
PATENT MEDICINES
PATHETIC FALLACY
PAVEMENT ARTISTS
PAYING IN ADVANCE
PELICAN CROSSING
PENTATONIC SCALE
PENTOTHAL SODIUM
PEPPERCORN RENTS
PEREGRINE FALCON
PERFUNCTORINESS
PERIODONTICALLY
PERIPATETICALLY
PERISTALTICALLY
PEROXIDE BLONDES
PERPENDICULARLY
PERPETUAL MOTION
PERSONAL COLUMNS
PERSONALITY CULT
PERSONALIZATION
PERSONAL PRONOUN
PERSONAL STEREOS
PERSONA NON GRATA
PERSONIFICATION
PERSPICACIOUSLY
PERSPICUOUSNESS
PESSIMISTICALLY
PHANTASMAGORIAS
PHARMACODYNAMIC
PHARMACOGNOSIST
PHARMACOGNOSTIC
PHARMACOLOGICAL
PHARMACOLOGISTS
PHARYNGOLOGICAL
PHENOLPHTHALEIN
PHENYLKETONURIA
PHILANTHROPISTS
PHILOSOPHICALLY
PHLEBOSCLEROSIS
PHOSPHATIZATION
PHOSPHOCREATINE
PHOSPHORESCENCE
PHOTOCONDUCTION

PHOTODEGRADABLE
PHOTOELASTICITY
PHOTOGRAMMETRIC
PHOTOJOURNALISM
PHOTOJOURNALIST
PHOTOLITHOGRAPH
PHOTOMECHANICAL
PHOTOMETRICALLY
PHOTOMICROGRAPH
PHOTOMULTIPLIER
PHOTOSENSITIZED
PHOTOTELEGRAPHY
PHOTOTOPOGRAPHY
PHOTOTRANSISTOR
PHOTOTYPESETTER
PHOTOTYPOGRAPHY
PHOTOZINCOGRAPH
PHYSICOCHEMICAL
PHYSIOTHERAPIST
PHYTOGEOGRAPHER
PHYTOPLANKTONIC
PICTURE-POSTCARD
PICTURESQUENESS
PIEZOMETRICALLY
PINCER MOVEMENTS
PITHECANTHROPUS
PLASMOLYTICALLY
PLASTIC SURGEONS
PLATINUM BLONDES
PLATYHELMINTHIC
PLEASURABLENESS
PLENIPOTENTIARY
PLEUROPNEUMONIA
PLIGHT ONES TROTH
PLOUGHMAN'S LUNCH
PLUMBAGINACEOUS
PLUMBER'S FRIENDS
PLUTOCRATICALLY
PNEUMATIC DRILLS
POIKILOTHERMISM
POISON-PEN LETTER
POLICE CONSTABLE
POLITICAL ASYLUM
POLLING STATIONS
POLYGENETICALLY
POLYGRAPHICALLY
POLYUNSATURATED
PORTMANTEAU WORD
POST OFFICE BOXES
POVERTY-STRICKEN
POWER OF ATTORNEY

PRAYING MANTISES
PREACHIFICATION
PRECANCELLATION
PRECIPITOUSNESS
PREDISPOSITIONS
PREFERENTIALITY
PREHISTORICALLY
PREPOSITIONALLY
PRESBYTERIANISM
PRESCRIPTIVISTS
PRESENCE CHAMBER
PRESENTABLENESS
PRESENTATIONISM
PRESENTATIONIST
PRESS CONFERENCE
PRESSURE COOKERS
PRESTIDIGITATOR
PRESTIGIOUSNESS
PRESUMPTIVENESS
PRESUPPOSITIONS
PRETENTIOUSNESS
PRETERNATURALLY
PRIMA BALLERINAS
PRIMARY STRESSES
PRINCE CHARMINGS
PRINTED CIRCUITS
PRINTING PRESSES
PRIVATE PROPERTY
PRIVATE SOLDIERS
PRIVY COUNCILLOR
PROBLEMATICALLY
PROCRASTINATING
PROCRASTINATION
PRODUCTION LINES
PROFESSIONALISM
PROFESSIONALIST
PROGENITIVENESS
PROGNOSTICATING
PROGNOSTICATION
PROGNOSTICATIVE
PROGNOSTICATORS
PROGRESSIVENESS
PROHIBITIONISTS
PROHIBITIVENESS
PROLETARIANNESS
PROMISCUOUSNESS
PROPER FRACTIONS
PROPORTIONALITY
PROPORTIONATELY
PROPYLENE GLYCOL
PROSELYTIZATION

PROSENCHYMATOUS
PROTOZOOLOGICAL
PROVOCATIVENESS
PSEPHOLOGICALLY
PSEUDOMUTUALITY
PSYCHEDELICALLY
PSYCHIATRICALLY
PSYCHOACOUSTICS
PSYCHOANALYSING
PSYCHOBIOLOGIST
PSYCHOGENICALLY
PSYCHOLOGICALLY
PSYCHOMETRICIAN
PSYCHOPATHOLOGY
PSYCHOSEXUALITY
PSYCHOTECHNICAL
PSYCHOTHERAPIST
PSYCHOTOMIMETIC
PTOLEMAIC SYSTEM
PUBLIC COMPANIES
PUBLIC NUISANCES
PUBLIC OWNERSHIP
PUBLIC RELATIONS
PULCHRITUDINOUS
PUNCTILIOUSNESS
PUNCTUATION MARK
PURITANICALNESS
PURPOSELESSNESS
PUSILLANIMOUSLY
PUT ONES FOOT DOWN
PUT OUT MORE FLAGS
PYROELECTRICITY

Q

QUADRUPLICATION
QUARRELSOMENESS
QUARTER SESSIONS
QUATERCENTENARY
QUEEN'S EVIDENCES
QUESTION MASTERS
QUICK-WITTEDNESS
QUINQUAGENARIAN
QUINTUPLICATION
QUODLIBETICALLY

R

RADIOACTIVATION
RADIOBIOLOGICAL
RADIOLOCATIONAL
RADIOMICROMETER
RADIOPHONICALLY

417

RADIOSCOPICALLY
RADIOTELEGRAPHY
RADIOTELEPHONIC
RADIO TELESCOPES
RADIOTHERAPISTS
RAILWAY STATIONS
RASTAFARIANISMS
RATE OF EXCHANGES
RATIONALIZATION
REAFFORESTATION
REAL-ESTATE AGENT
REARGUARD ACTION
RECAPITULATIONS
RECOGNIZABILITY
RECOMMENDATIONS
RECONCILABILITY
RECONNAISSANCES
RECONSIDERATION
RECONSTRUCTIBLE
RECONSTRUCTIONS
RECORD LIBRARIES
RECREATION ROOMS
REDOUBTABLENESS
REFRESHER COURSE
REGISTERED NURSE
REGISTER OFFICES
REGISTRY OFFICES
REGIUS PROFESSOR
REINDUSTRIALIZE
RELATIVE CLAUSES
RELATIVE PRONOUN
REMORSELESSNESS
REPETITIOUSNESS
REPRESENTATIONS
REPRESENTATIVES
REPROACHFULNESS
REPRODUCIBILITY
RESOURCEFULNESS
RESPECTABLENESS
RESPONSIBLENESS
RESTRICTIVENESS
RESURRECTIONARY
RESURRECTIONISM
RESURRECTIONIST
RESURRECTION MEN
RETROGRESSIVELY
RETROSPECTIVELY
REVEREND MOTHERS
REVOLUTIONARIES
REVOLUTIONARILY
REVOLUTIONIZING

RHOMBENCEPHALON
RIBONUCLEIC ACID
RIGHT-HANDEDNESS
RIGHT-MINDEDNESS
RITUALISTICALLY
ROBIN GOODFELLOW
ROGUES' GALLERIES
ROMANTICIZATION
ROUGH-AND-TUMBLES
ROUND-SHOULDERED
ROYAL HIGHNESSES
RUMBUSTIOUSNESS
RUSSIAN ROULETTE

S

SADOMASOCHISTIC
SALES RESISTANCE
SANCTIMONIOUSLY
SANDWICH COURSES
SAPROPHYTICALLY
SARRACENIACEOUS
SATURATION POINT
SAVINGS ACCOUNTS
SAWN-OFF SHOTGUNS
SCARBOROUGH FAIR
SCHISTOSOMIASIS
SCHOOL OF THOUGHT
SCINTILLATINGLY
SCLERODERMATOUS
SCRUMPTIOUSNESS
SEA ISLAND COTTON
SECONDARY MODERN
SECONDARY STRESS
SECOND CHILDHOOD
SECOND IN COMMAND
SECOND-IN-COMMAND
SECURITY COUNCIL
SEINE-SAINT-DENIS
SELECT COMMITTEE
SELF-CENTREDNESS
SELF-CONFIDENTLY
SELF-CONSCIOUSLY
SELF-DESTRUCTING
SELF-DESTRUCTION
SELF-DISCIPLINED
SELF-EXAMINATION
SELF-EXPLANATORY
SELF-IMPORTANTLY
SELF-IMPROVEMENT
SELF-INDULGENTLY
SELF-LIQUIDATING

SELF-POLLINATION
SELF-POSSESSEDLY
SELF-REPROACHFUL
SELF-RIGHTEOUSLY
SELF-SACRIFICING
SELF-SUFFICIENCY
SENSATIONALISTS
SENSE OF OCCASION
SENTENTIOUSNESS
SENTIMENTALISTS
SENTIMENTALIZED
SEPTUAGENARIANS
SERGEANTS-AT-ARMS
SERVICE STATIONS
SERVOMECHANICAL
SERVOMECHANISMS
SESQUICARBONATE
SHARP-WITTEDNESS
SHILLY SHALLYING
SHILLY-SHALLYING
SHOOTING GALLERY
SHOOTING MATCHES
SHOPPING CENTRES
SHORT-CIRCUITING
SHORT-HANDEDNESS
SHORTHAND TYPIST
SHOTGUN WEDDINGS
SHOWING ONES HAND
SHRINKING VIOLET
SHRINK RESISTANT
SICKNESS BENEFIT
SIDEWALK ARTISTS
SIESMOLOGICALLY
SIMPLE FRACTURES
SIMPLICIDENTATE
SIMPLIFICATIONS
SINGULARIZATION
SINISTRODEXTRAL
SITUATION COMEDY
SITUATION ETHICS
SLAUGHTERHOUSES
SLEEPING PARTNER
SLOTTED SPATULAS
SLOUGH OF DESPOND
SLOW ON THE UPTAKE
SMALL INTESTINES
SMALL-MINDEDNESS
SMELLS OF THE LAMP
SOCIAL DEMOCRATS
SOCIALISTICALLY
SOCIOLINGUISTIC

SOFT FURNISHINGS
SOFTHEARTEDNESS
SOLEMNIFICATION
SOUNDED THE ALARM
SOW DRAGONS TEETH
SPANISH-AMERICAN
SPANISH OMELETTE
SPECIALIZATIONS
SPECIAL LICENCES
SPECIAL PLEADING
SPECIFIC GRAVITY
SPECULATIVENESS
SPEECHIFICATION
SPEECH THERAPIST
SPERMATOGENESIS
SPERMATOGENETIC
SPINNING JENNIES
SPLIT INFINITIVE
SPONTANEOUSNESS
SPUR-OF-THE-MOMENT
SQUADRON LEADERS
SQUARE THE CIRCLE
STAGE DIRECTIONS
STAMPING GROUNDS
STANDARD-BEARERS
STANDARDIZATION
STANDOFFISHNESS
STAND ONES GROUND
STAPHYLOPLASTIC
STAPHYLORRHAPHY
STAR-OF-BETHLEHEM
STARS AND STRIPES
STARVATION WAGES
STATE DEPARTMENT
STEREOCHEMISTRY
STEREOISOMERISM
STEREOISOMETRIC
STICKING PLASTER
STINGING NETTLES
STOCKBROKER BELT
STOCKING-FILLERS
STOICHIOLOGICAL
STORE DETECTIVES
STRAIGHTFORWARD
STRAIGHTJACKETS
STRATIFICATIONS
STRAWBERRY MARKS
STRETCHER-BEARER
STUMBLING BLOCKS
SUBORDINATENESS
SUBSISTENCE CROP

SUBSPECIFICALLY
SUBSTANTIVENESS
SUGGESTIBLENESS
SULPHUREOUSNESS
SUNRISE INDUSTRY
SUPERADDITIONAL
SUPERCONDUCTION
SUPERCONDUCTIVE
SUPERCONDUCTORS
SUPERFLUOUSNESS
SUPERIMPOSITION
SUPERINCUMBENCE
SUPERINDUCEMENT
SUPERINTENDENCE
SUPERINTENDENCY
SUPERINTENDENTS
SUPERLATIVENESS
SUPERNATURALISM
SUPERNATURALIST
SUPERNUMERARIES
SUPERSTITIOUSLY
SUPERSTRUCTURAL
SUPERSTRUCTURES
SUPPLEMENTARILY
SUPPLEMENTATION
SUPPLY AND DEMAND
SUPPORTING PARTS
SURREPTITIOUSLY
SUSCEPTIBLENESS
SWIMMING COSTUME
SWIM WITH THE TIDE
SWORD OF DAMOCLES
SYCOPHANTICALLY
SYLLABIFICATION
SYMBOL-FORMATION
SYMBOLISTICALLY
SYMMETRICALNESS
SYMPATHETICALLY
SYMPATHOMIMETIC
SYMPTOMATICALLY
SYNCHRONIZATION
SYNCHRONOUSNESS
SYNECDOCHICALLY
SYNECOLOGICALLY
SYNOPTIC GOSPELS
SYSTEMATIZATION
SYSTEMS ANALYSTS

T

TACHOMETRICALLY
TACHYMETRICALLY

TAKEN FOR GRANTED
TAKE TO ONES HEELS
TARSOMETATARSAL
TARSOMETATARSUS
TECHNOLOGICALLY
TECHNOSTRUCTURE
TELEGRAPHICALLY
TELEPHONE NUMBER
TELEPHOTOGRAPHY
TELEPHOTO LENSES
TELESTEREOSCOPE
TELETYPESETTING
TEMPERAMENTALLY
TEMPESTUOUSNESS
TEN COMMANDMENTS
TENDENTIOUSNESS
TENDERHEARTEDLY
TERMINOLOOGICAL
TERRITORIAL ARMY
TETRABRANCHIATE
THALASSOTHERAPY
THATS MORE LIKF IT
THE BACK OF BEYOND
THE COAST IS CLEAR
THEOREMATICALLY
THE POWERS THAT BE
THERAPEUTICALLY
THERIANTHROPISM
THERMIONIC VALVE
THERMOBAROGRAPH
THERMOCHEMISTRY
THERMOSTABILITY
THICKHEADEDNESS
THICK-WITTEDNESS
THOUGHTLESSNESS
THREE-LEGGED RACE
THREE-POINT TURNS
THROMBOEMBOLISM
THYROCALCITONIN
TIGHTFISTEDNESS
TIGHTROPE WALKER
TIMES IMMEMORIAL
TOOK SOME BEATING
TOPOGRAPHICALLY
TOTALITARIANISM
TO THE MANNER BORN
TOWER OF STRENGTH
TRACTION ENGINES
TRADITIONALISTS
TRAINING COLLEGE
TRANSCRIPTIONAL

TRANSFERABILITY
TRANSFIGURATION
TRANSFIGUREMENT
TRANSFORMATIONS
TRANSGRESSINGLY
TRANSILLUMINATE
TRANSISTORIZING
TRANSLATABILITY
TRANSLITERATING
TRANSLITERATION
TRANSMOGRIFYING
TRANSMUTATIONAL
TRANSPARENTNESS
TRANSPLANTATION
TRANSPOSABILITY
TRANSPOSITIONAL
TRANSUBSTANTIAL
TREACHEROUSNESS
TREASONABLENESS
TRIBROMOETHANOL
TRICHLOROETHANE
TRICK OR TREATING
TRINITROBENZENE
TRINITROTOLUENE
TROPICALIZATION
TROUBLESHOOTERS
TROUBLESOMENESS
TRUSTWORTHINESS
TRYPANOSOMIASIS
TURF ACCOUNTANTS
TYPOGRAPHICALLY
TYRANNOSAURUSES

U

ULTRACENTRIFUGE
ULTRAFILTRATION
ULTRAMICROMETER
ULTRAMICROSCOPE
ULTRAMICROSCOPY
ULTRASTRUCTURAL
UNBELIEVABILITY
UNCEREMONIOUSLY
UNCHALLENGEABLE
UNCOMMUNICATIVE
UNCOMPLIMENTARY
UNCONCERNEDNESS
UNCONDITIONALLY
UNCONNECTEDNESS

UNCONSCIOUSNESS
UNDEMONSTRATIVE
UNDERCAPITALIZE
UNDEREMPLOYMENT
UNDERESTIMATING
UNDERESTIMATION
UNDERHANDEDNESS
UNDERPRIVILEGED
UNDERPRODUCTION
UNDERSTATEMENTS
UNDER-THE-COUNTER
UNDISTINGUISHED
UNEMPLOYABILITY
UNEQUIVOCALNESS
UNEXCEPTIONABLE
UNEXCEPTIONABLY
UNFLINCHINGNESS
UNFORTUNATENESS
UNHOLY ALLIANCES
UNINTERRUPTEDLY
UNIVERSAL JOINTS
UNKNOWN QUANTITY
UNOBTRUSIVENESS
UNPARLIAMENTARY
UNPRECEDENTEDLY
UNPREMEDITATION
UNPRETENTIOUSLY
UNPROFITABILITY
UNPRONOUNCEABLE
UNSOPHISTICATED
UNWHOLESOMENESS

V

VALETUDINARIANS
VALUE-ADDED TAXES
VASCULARIZATION
VASOCONSTRICTOR
VEGETABLE KNIVES
VEGETABLE MARROW
VENDING MACHINES
VENEREAL DISEASE
VENTRILOQUISTIC
VENTURESOMENESS
VERTIGINOUSNESS
VESPERTILIONINE
VESTED INTERESTS
VICE-CHANCELLORS
VICISSITUDINARY

VICTORIA CROSSES
VIDEOCONFERENCE
VIRGINIA CREEPER
VITAL STATISTICS
VIVISECTIONISTS
VOYEURISTICALLY
VULGAR FRACTIONS

W

WALRUS MOUSTACHE
WARM-BLOODEDNESS
WARM-HEARTEDNESS
WAR OF JENKINS EAR
WARRANT OFFICERS
WASHING MACHINES
WEATHERBOARDING
WEATHER BOARDING
WEATHER FORECAST
WEATHERPROOFING
WEATHER STATIONS
WELL-CONSTRUCTED
WELL-ESTABLISHED
WELL-INTENTIONED
WHIPPERSNAPPERS
WHISTLE-STOP TOUR
WHITE BLOOD CELLS
WHITED SEPULCHRE
WHITE MANS BURDEN
WILD-GOOSE CHASES
WIND INSTRUMENTS
WIND-POLLINATION
WINDSCREEN WIPER
WISHFUL THINKING
WRONGHEADEDNESS

X

XENOMORPHICALLY
XEROGRAPHICALLY

Y

YOURS FAITHFULLY
YOUTH HOSTELLERS
YOUTH HOSTELLING

Z

ZYGOPHYLLACEOUS

Words that contain letter Q not followed by U

Anqing City in China

Aqaba Port in Jordan, on the Gulf of Aqaba

Aqmola Former name of Astana, capital of Kazakhstan

Basotho-Qwaqwa Former Bantu Homeland in South Africa

Chongqing City in China

Dimashq Arabic name for Damascus, capital of Syria

faqir Muslim or Hindu holy man

inqilab Urdu word for revolution

Iqbal Sir Mohammed Iqbal, Indian Muslim poet, philosopher, and political leader

Iraq Country in the Middle East

Iraqi **1** Inhabitant of Iraq **2** Relating to Iraq

Jiang Qing Chinese communist politician, widow of Mao Tse-Tung

Lailat-ul-Qadr Annual night of prayer and study for Muslims

Masqat Arabic name for Muscat, capital of Oman

mbaqanga Style of Black popular music in South Africa

Qabis Arabic name for Gabés, port in Tunisia

Qabis bin Said Sultan of Oman

Qaddafi Moamar al-Qaddafi, leader of Libya

Qaddish Jewish prayer, especially for the dead

qadi Muslim judge

Qairwan Holy city in Tunisia

QANTAS Australian national airline (Queensland and Northern Territory Aerial Services)

qat Type of bush found in Ethiopia

Qatar Country in Arabia

Qattara Depression Depression in the Sahara

qawwali Muslim religious song

Qeshm Iranian island

Qian Long Chinese emperor

qibla The direction of Mecca

Qingdao Port in China

Qinghai Province of China

qintar Albanian coin

Qiqihar City in China

Qishm Iranian island

Qom Holy city in Iran

qoph Hebrew letter Q

qorma Indian dish of meat and vegetables

Qu Qiu Bai Chinese communist leader and writer

Qwaqwa Former Bantu Homeland in South Africa

qwerty Standard layout of English typewriter/computer keyboard

Sercq French name for Sark in the Channel Islands

Si-ma Qian Ancient Chinese historian

Zaqaziq City in Egypt

Zarqa City in Jordan

Words that start with letter X

xanthate Salt or ester of xanthic acid

xanthein Yellow pigment found in flowers

xanthene Crystalline compound used in dyes

xanthic Relating to xanthic acid

xanthin Orange-yellow pigment found in plants

xanthine Crystalline compound found in urine

Xanthippe The wife of Socrates; any nagging or quarrelsome woman

xanthism Abnormal yellowness of skin, fur, etc.

xanthochroid Relating to races having light hair and pale skin

xanthochroism Excessive yellowness in goldfish, etc.

xanthoma Yellow-brown patch or nodule on the skin

xanthophyll Yellow pigment found in plants

xanthous Relating to races having light hair and pale skin

Xanthus The chief city of ancient Lycia in Asia Minor

Xavier St Francis Xavier, Spanish Jesuit missionary

xebec Small three-masted ship

xenia 1 Gift or offering **2** Influence of pollen upon the developed fruit

Xenocrates Greek philosopher

xenocryst Crystal of different origin found in igneous rock

xenogamy Cross-fertilization

xenogeneic Derived from an individual of a different species

xenogenesis Production of offspring unlike either parent

xenoglossia Ability to speak a language one has never learned

xenograft Graft of tissue from an individual of a different species

xenolith Rock fragment of different origin found in igneous rock

xenomorphic (Of a mineral) having a different form from the surrounding rock

xenon Gaseous chemical element

Xenophanes Greek philosopher and poet

xenophile Person who likes foreign people or things

xenophobe Person who dislikes foreign people or things

xenophobia Fear or hatred of foreign people and things

Xenophon Greek general and historian

xeranthemum Several Mediterranean plants, especially the immortelle

xerarch (Of plant successions) originating in a dry habitat

Xeres Former name of Jerez in Spain

xeric (Of plants) growing in dry conditions

xeroderma Abonormal dryness of the skin

xerography Photocopying process

xeromorphic (Of plants) having protection against excessive water loss

xerophilous Adapted to a dry habitat

xerophthalmia Dryness in the eye

xerophyte Plant that is adapted to dry conditions

xerosere Plant succession originating in a dry habitat

xerosis Abnormal dryness of skin or other tissues

xerostomia Abnormal dryness of the mouth

Xerox Tradename for a photocopying process

Xhosa Bantu people and language of South Africa

xi Greek letter X

Xia Gui Chinese landscape painter

Xi An City in China

Xiang River in China

Ximenes Ximenes de Cisneros, Spanish cardinal and statesman

Xingú River in Brazil

Xining City in China

Xinjiang Uygur Administrative division of China

xiphisternum The lowest part of the breast bone

xiphoid (Of bodily parts) sword-shaped

xiphosuran Horseshoe crab

Xizang Chinese name for Tibet

Xmas Christmas

xoanon Carved image of a god

Xochimilco Town and lake in Mexico

x-ray Electromagnetic radiation of very short wavelength, used in medical diagnosis etc.

Xuthus Son of Hellen in Greek mythology

Xuzhou City in China

xylan Yellow carbohydrate found in wood and straw

xylem Plant tissue that conducts water and nutrients

xylene Liquid hydrocarbon used as a solvent.

xylidine Xylene derivative used in dyes.

xylocarp Fruit with a hard woody shell

xylogenous (Of insects etc.) living in or on wood

xylograph Engraved wooden block or print made from one

xylography Art of printing from wooden blocks

xyloid Relating to or like wood

xylophagous (Of insects etc.) feeding on wood

xylophone Tuned wooden percussion instrument

xylorimba Large xylophone

xylose Sugar found in wood and straw, used in food for diabetics

xylotomous (Of insects etc.) boring into wood

xylotomy Preparation of wood sections for microscope examination

xylyl Derived from xylene

xyst 1 (In ancient Greece) covered portico used for athletics 2 (In ancient Rome) treelined garden walk

xyster Surgical file for scraping bone